BURT FRANKLIN: BIBLIOGRAPHY & REFERENCE SERIES 410
American Classics in History and Social Science 154

BIBLIOTHECA AMERICANA

VOLUME I

HISTORICAL NUGGETS

BIBLIOTHECA AMERICANA OR A
DESCRIPTIVE ACCOUNT OF MY
COLLECTION OF RARE
BOOKS RELATING
TO AMERICA

HENRY STEVENS GMB FSA

I will buy with you, sell with you.
Shakespeare.

BURT FRANKLIN
NEW YORK

Published by LENOX HILL Pub. & Dist. Co. (Burt Franklin)
235 East 44th St., New York, N.Y. 10017
Originally Published: 1862
Reprinted: 1971
Printed in the U.S.A.

S.B.N.: 8337-34075
Library of Congress Card Catalog No.: 77-154649
Burt Franklin: Bibliography and Reference Series 410
American Classics in History and Social Science 154

DILIGENT BIBLIOSCOPER.

I F with your pleasing occupation of looking for books, you possess the love of reading them, you may some-where have met with the quaint old comparison, that, as geography and chronology are the eye and the ear, so Bibliography is both the hands of History; and, as these two poor hands are the slaves of the eye and the ear, so Bibliography without distinction or re-ward, ministers to the wants of History. He who catalogues beetles or star-fish, in a language that never lived, is by common consent a savant, and may walk, with his brows above his temples, unrebuked in the paths of science, while he who diligently ransacks the remotest nooks, clears away literary rubbish, sorts, calendars, and elaborately describes the dry and isolated materials of history; arranges, indexes, describes, and catalogues books and manu-scripts, must content himself with the unappreciated airs of the bibliographer, mindful of the fate of the bad speller, whose blunders are open to censure, while his merits are without praise. The highest incentive, then, that actuates the maker of catalogues is the fear of disgrace for a bad one, while he knows that a good one will bring him no applause.

The day may come, however, when the varied

knowledge, the patience, the perseverance, and the industry of the true bibliographer will take their true rank, and he be rewarded according to his aim and his labours. Nay, it must be so, or we shall soon be papered up and smothered in print. Were the sheets of *The Times* spread out like maps and piled one upon another, we might behold every Saturday a pyramid of world-wide intelligence overtopping the London Monument. Just face this then my indifferent reader, and imagine for a moment what comes and has come from all the teaming and steaming presses of the world during this and the last two centuries ! Knowledge is booked, and therefore bibliography has become a necessity. Catalogues are multiplying, and a demand for better ones is increasing. Even now a catalogue of catalogues is required, so that the writer upon any given topic may readily ascertain what has been written upon it, and thus avoid going over ground already sufficiently explored. Many a good historian, less tough than a Gibbon or a Robertson, in amassing his materials has broken down before he has taken up his pen, so that one may now fairly consider his work half written when he knows what and where are his materials.

The BIBLIOGRAPHY of AMERICA is the subject I had the youthful presumption, twenty years ago, to choose. There is not, perhaps, in the whole range of modern history, a more gigantic theme for the future historian than the story of the discovery, conquest, planting, and development of the New World. From the embarcation of Columbus at Palos in 1492, to the abolition of slavery in the District of Columbia in 1862, is a period worthy the genius of a master-mind, nay, of many master-minds, for so numerous, scattered, and crude are the materials, that it will require the energies of many collaborators to work up the innumerable minor topics before the master historian can with advantage digest and combine them into one harmonious whole.

The impulse which the valuable and well-known BIBLIOTHECAS of Mr. Warden, M. Ternaux-Compans (not to mention the previous excellent works of Leon Pinelo, Barcia, Eguira, White Kennet, Alcedo, Homar, Berestein de Souza and others) and more especially of my late and lamented friend Mr. O. Rich, gave to the collection of books relating to America, shows how highly such works are appreciated. More recently, however, the indefatigable researches of many collectors, both public and private, in Europe as well as in America, combined with the unprecedented high prices of books and manuscripts of this class, have been the means of bringing to light so many works hitherto uncatalogued and undescribed, that a larger, a more comprehensive, and a more accurate Bibliotheca is now much needed. Following therefore my own inclination, but at first little dreaming of the amount of labour undertaken, I many years since volunteered to devote my humble energies to the bibliography of the American Continent. In other words, my aim was and still is, according to the best of my powers to afford (as far as one poor painstaking life can do it) to the future historians of my country and continent, a ' BIBLIOGRAPHIA AMERICANA ; or, a Bibliographical Account of the Sources of American History from the earliest period to the present time.'

PLAN OF THE WORK.

1. A BRIEF biography will, whenever practicable, precede the list of each author's works.

2. The work will contain a descriptive list of all historical books relating to America (North and South, and the West India Islands) and of all such

books printed therein, from the earliest period to the present time, which may be found in the principal public and private libraries of Europe and America, or which are described in other works; together with notices of many of the more important unpublished manuscripts.

3. The descriptions will be made, as far as possible, from an examination of the books themselves. If any be taken from other sources of information they will be distinguished by some peculiar mark.

4. The titles including the imprint or colophon will, in all cases, be given in full, word for word, and letter for letter, together with a translation into English of all titles in other languages.

5. The *collation* of each book will be given; that is, such a description as will indicate a perfect copy.

6. The market value of the books, with the prices at which they have been sold at public or private sales, wi l, whenever possible, be given.

7. Different editions and various translations of the principal works will be diligently compared with each other, and their variations and relative merits pointed out, especially of such works as the Collections of Voyages and Travels by Grynæus, Ramusio, Leon d'Afrique, Hakluyt, Colyn, De Bry, Hulsius, Purchas, Hartgerts, Thevenot and others; the corresponding parts of which will be compared, not only with each other, but with the editions of the works from which they were translated, abridged, or reprinted.

8. Bibliographical notes will be appended when deemed necessary, containing abstracts of the contents of the works where the titles fail to give a proper idea of them; anecdotes of authors, printers, engravers, etc.; important items of historical and geographical information; notices of peculiarities of copies, as large paper, MS. notes, vellum, cancelled leaves, etc.; the number of copies printed; sup-

pressed editions; together with the comparative rarity and intrinsic value of the works.

9. The notes upon the books printed in America will comprise a full history of the origin and progress of printing in North and South America from the year 1543 to the present time.

10. Under the title of every work will be designated one or more libraries in which it may be found.

11. The titles will be arranged alphabetically, under the names of the authors, or the leading word of the title, with cross references from other names or words when deemed necessary.

12. The work will contain a full Introductory Memoir upon the Materials of early American History, together with an account of the principal collections of them which have been made in Europe and America.

13. Three indexes to the contents of the work will be given, viz. (1) A chronological index, in which the titles briefly given, will be arranged according to the years in which the works were printed; (2) An index of the subjects treated in the books; (3) A general alphabetical index of the persons and subjects mentioned in the notes and introductory memoirs.

14. Facsimile woodcuts, maps, and other early pictorial illustrations will be given when deemed essential.

15. The work will be printed in the form, style, and fashion best suited to such a production, and most approved at the day of its completion; and may we continue in health and vigour till then.

Now, in all these years of research and catalogue-making, I have advanced sufficiently far in the BIB-LIOGRAPHIA AMERICANA, to feel that my love of accuracy has been so far taken out of me as to compel me to admit that it is perfectly impossible to prepare the

copy with sufficient accuracy to print from at a time
and place when and where the rare books described
cannot be referred to. It has therefore been found
necessary to make this preliminary issue of the more
difficult parts of the work by throwing into type the
titles of each work in full, correcting the proofs from
the books themselves as they pass through my hands,
or are found in the library of the British Museum or
elsewhere. By this means I shall not only record
the materials for the *Bibliographia* as I meet with
them, but, what is of the greatest importance to me
and to the work, I shall be enabled to receive the
kind co-operation of librarians and bibliographers in
the examination and collation of rare books in libraries remote from each other.

The materials thus collected it is proposed to re-ar-
range and elaborate according to the plan detailed
above. Brief collations of each book will be given,
with occasional notes, illustrations, etc.; but desiring
to interfere as little as possible with the Bibliographia Americana, nothing will be printed in this which
can as well be printed, for the first time, in the larger
work. Although no expense or pains will be spared
to secure accuracy in this preliminary issue, yet, as
it is but a mere stepping-stone to a larger and better
work, I deem it expedient to print but very few copies, and shall think myself fortunate if they fall into
the hands of collectors and librarians interested in the
subject, who will kindly point out to me such inac-
curacies and variations as they may from time to
time detect in comparing my titles with their own.
Lest this comparatively private and very imperfect
edition may hereafter be mistaken for, and confounded
with, the Bibliographia Americana, I have pur-
posely given it a name more forcible, perhaps, than
elegant, 'Historical Nuggets.' The name is, however, to me a matter of no sort of consequence,
provided it answers the purpose for which it is in-

tended, viz. to assist in reducing my observations and collections, and securing accuracy for the larger work.

These two volumes contain about 3000 titles alphabetically arranged according to the names of the authors, or generally the first words of the titles, not articles. This rule however has not been very strictly kept. The books catalogued are not a selection of works of this class, but are just such as I happened to have on hand for sale in 1857, when these volumes were printed. I therefore added the prices, printing not a title unless I had the book for sale. Since the last of the sheets was printed off, many of the lots have been sold, and of many I still possess duplicates. Most of the books were priced ten years ago, and consequently the prices given are not now in all cases to be relied upon. Those books still on hand are for sale, together with several thousand others not yet described.

Considerable progress has been made with a second alphabet of about 4500 titles, all differing from those given in these first two volumes, which when printed will form volumes 3, 4, and 5 of this stepping-stone series to be completed in ten volumes. Volume 6 will probably contain the collations of the great collections of voyages, as De Bry, Hulsius, Romusio, Hakluyt, Purchas, etc. It is proposed to fill volumes 7, 8 and 9 with the titles of such books as may pass through my hands in the meantime, together with the titles which I find in the library of the British Museum and elsewhere, of books which do not occur for sale. These latter ones will of course be given without prices. Volume 10 and last will contain an index of the whole, and such preliminary notes and queries as may be required for promoting investigations not finished.

It may not be out of place here to mention that I have printed, and they will be published simultaneously with these two volumes, a catalogue of all the American books, maps etc. in the library of the British Museum to the beginning of 1857, including the books of British and Spanish America and the West Indies. This catalogue will be kept up and re-issued from time to time, with additions, notes, biographies, etc. according to the plan detailed in the preface of the first Volume. It is intended to keep the Bibliographia Americana and the Catalogue of American Books in the British Museum as distinct as possible, so as not to cover the same ground more than once. When complete, the two works will be only different series of the same, both together forming a history of American literature, and an account of the literature of American history.

Hoping, diligent Reader, that we may all survive the publications of these long-projected works,

I am, Yours patiently,

HENRY STEVENS.

4, Trafalgar Square, w. c.
  London, July 4, 1862.

BIBLIOTHECA AMERICANA.

ABBEVILLE (Claude d'). Histoire/ de la Mission/ des Peres Capvcins/ en l' Isle de Maragnan et/ terres circonuoifines/ ov/ est traicte des sin⸗/gularitez admirables & des/ Meurs merueilleufes des Indiens/ habitans de ce pais Auec les mifiues/ et aduis qui ont este enuoyez de nouue^au./ Par/ le R. P. Claude dAbbeuille/ Predicateur Capucin./ Prædicabitur Euangelium/ Regni In vniuerfo orbe Mat. 24/ Auec priuilege du Roy./ A Paris/ De l'Imprimerie de François/ Hvby, ruë S^t. Iacques à la Bible d'or,/ et en fa boutique au Palais en la galle⸗/rie des Prifonniers. 1614./ *Engraved title-page, and 7 prel. leaves including* 'Table des Chapitres.' 395 *folied leaves and* 'Table des choses,' 35 *unnumbered pages. Large and splendid copy, in Bedford's best calf extra, gilt edges. Fine copper-plate Portraits.* 8vo. (3l. 13s. 6d. No. 1)

ABBOT (Hull). The Duty of God's People to pray for the Peace of Jerufalem : and efpecially for the Prefervation and Continuance of their own Privileges both Civil and Religious, when in Danger at Home or from Abroad. A Sermon on Ocafion of the Rebellion in Sctoland Rais'd in Favour of a Popifh Pretender ; With Defign to overthrow our prefent Happy Eftablifhment, And to Introduce Popery and Arbitrary Power into Our Nations, From which, by a Series of Wonders, in the good Providence of God, they have been often delivered, Preached at Charleftown in New-England, Jan. 12. 1745, 6. By Hull Abbot, A. M. A Paftor of the

B

Church there. *Boston*, Printed and Sold by Rogers & Fowle in Queen-ſtreet. 1746. *Title and pp. 5 to 26. 8vo.* (4s. 6d. 2)

ABINGDON (Earl of). Thoughts on the Letter of Edmund Burke, Esq; to the Sheriffs of Bristol, on the Affairs of America. By the Earl of Abingdon [Willoughby Bertie]. *Oxford*, W. Jackson, [1777] 68 *pp. Half morocco, 8vo.* (2s. 6d. 3)

ABINGDON (Earl of). Thoughts on the Letter of Edmund Burke, Esq; to the Sheriffs of Bristol, on the Affairs of America. By the Earl of Abingdon. The Fourth Edition. *Oxford.* W. Jackson. [1777]. 68 *pp. half mor. 8vo.* (3s. 6d. 4)

ABINGDON (Earl of). Thoughts on the Letter of Edmund Burke, Eſq; to the Sheriffs of Bristol, on the Affairs of America. By the Earl of Abingdon. The Sixth Edition. *Oxford*, W. Jackson: [1777]. *Title; '* Dedication,' *pp. iii to xci; text* 60 *pp. half mor.* (7s. 6d. 5)

The long ' Dedication to the Collective Body of the People of England,' in which the author enlarges upon his theme, and replies to the several answers to his previous editions, appears for the first time in this sixth edition.

ABINGDON (Earl of). Second Thoughts: or, Observations upon Lord Abingdon's Thoughts on the Letter of Edmund Burke, Esq. to the Sheriffs of Bristol. By the author of the Answer to Mr. Burke's Letter. The second edition. *London:* T. Cadell, m. dcc. lxxvii. *Half-title, title, and* 74 *pp. 8vo.* (3s. 6d. 6)

ABRIDGEMENT (An) of the Laws In Force and Uſe in Her Majeſty's Plantations (Viz.) Of Virginia, Jamaica, Barbadoes, Maryland, New-England, New-York, Carolina, &c. Digeſted under proper Heads in the Method of Mr. Wingate, and Mr. Waſhington's Abridgements. *London,/* John Nicholſon, R. Parker, and R. Smith, 1704. *Title and Preface, 2 leaves; text* 284 *pp ;* ' Maryland,' 71 *pp ;* ' New-England,' 100 *pp;* ' Appendix,' *pp.* 285 *to* 304. *Fine copy calf. 8vo.* (10s. 6d. 7)

ABSTRACT (An) of the Charter granted to the Society for the Propagation of the Gospel in Foreign Parts; with a short Account of what hath been, and what is designed to be done by it. [*London*, 1702.] 3 *pp. Folio.* (3s. 6d. 8)

ABSTRACT (AN) of the Proceedings of the Corporation, for the Relief of the Widows and Children
of Clergymen, in the Communion of the Church of
England in America. *Philadelphia,* James Humphreys, junior. M, DCC, LXXIII. *52 pp. half morocco.
8vo.* (7s. 6d. 9)

ACCOUNT (AN) of the Conduct of the War in the
Middle Colonies. Extracted from a late Author.
London: Printed in the Year M DCC LXXX. *55 pp.
half mor. 12mo.* (4s. 6d. 10)

ACCOUNT (AN) of the Donations for the Relief of
the Sufferers by Fire, at Bridge Town in the Iſland
of Barbadoes, In May and December 1766, and of
the Application of the Same. S. Goadby, *London,*
[1769]. *Title, and Advertisement; 2 leaves;* ' A List
of the Donations,' *etc.* 40 *pp.* 'Contra.' 1 *page: half
mor. 4to.* (5s. 6d. 11)

ACCOUNT (AN) of the European Settlements in
America. In Six Parts. I. A ſhort History of the
Diſcovery of that Part of the World. II. The
Manners and Cuſtoms of the original Inhabitants.
III. Of the Spaniſh Settlements. IV. Of the Por-
tugueſe. V. Of the French, Dutch, and Daniſh.
VI. Of the Engliſh. Each Part contains An accurate Deſcription of the Settlements in it, their
Extent, Climate, Produ¢tions, Trade, Genius and
Diſpoſition of their Inhabitants: the Intereſts of
the ſeveral Powers of Europe with reſpe¢t to
thoſe Settlements; and their Political and Com-
mercial Views with regard to each other. In two
Volumes. *London:* Printed for R. and J. Dodsley in Pall-Mall. MDCCLVII. *Vol. I. 5 prel. leaves
and text pp.* 3 *to* 312. *Map of* ' South America,'
1747; II. *Title, half-title and text pp.* 3 *to* 300,
' *Contents'* 10 *leaves. map of* ' North America,' 1747,
First Edition. 8vo. (7s. 6d. 12)

ACCOUNT (AN) of the European Settlements in
America, *etc.* In two Volumes. The Second
Edition, with Improvements. *London:* R. and J.
Dodsley. MDCCLVIII. *Vol. I.* 5 *prel. leaves, text pp.*
3 *to* 324. '*Contents'* 5 *leaves;* II. 7 *prel. leaves, text
pp.* 3 *to* 308. *Maps as in* 1st *edition. 8vo.* (6s. 13)

ACCOUNT (AN) of the European Settlements in
America, *etc.* In two Volumes. The Fourth Edi-

tion, with Improvements. *Dublin:* Printed for Peter Wilson, in Dame-ftreet M,DCC,LXII. *Vol. I.* 8 *prel. leaves and text* 319 *pp.* II. 5 *prel. leaves & 301 pp. No maps.* 12mo. (7s. 6d. 14)

ACCOUNT (An) of the European Settlements in America, *etc.* In two Volumes. The Fourth Edition, with Improvements. *London:* J. Dodsley, MDCCLXV. *Vol. I.* 11 *prel. leaves and text pp.* 3 *to* 324. II. 7 *prel. leaves and text pp.* 308. *No Maps.* 8*vo.* (6s. 15)

ACCOUNT (An) of the European Settlements in America, *etc.* In two Volumes. The Fifth Edition, with Improvements. *London:* J. Dodsley, MDCCLXX. *Vol. I.* 11 *prel. leaves and pp.* 3 *to* 324. II. 7 *prel. leaves, and pp.* 3 *to* 308. *Maps as in first edition but with date* 1747 *omitted.* 8*vo.* (7s. 6d. 16)

ACCOUNT (An) of the European Settlements in America, *etc.* In two Volumes. The Sixth Edition, with Improvements. *London:* J. Dodsley, MDCCLXXVII. *Vol. I.* 11 *prel. leaves & pp.* 3 *to* 324. II. 7 *prel. leaves and pp.* 3 *to* 308. *Maps as in the* 5*th edition.* 8*vo.* (7s. 6d. 17)

ACCOUNT (An) of the Loss of his Majesty's Ship Deal Castle, commanded by Capt. James Hawkins, off the Island of Port Rico, during the Hurricane in the West-Indies, in the year 1780. *London:* J. Murray, M DCC LXXXVII. 3 *prel. leaves & 48 pp. half mor.* 8*vo.* (4s. 6d. 18)

ACCOUNT (An) of the Massachusetts Society for promoting Christian Knowledge. Published by order of the Society. *Cambridge,* William Hilliard, 1806. *Title and pp.* 4 *to* 34. 12*mo.* (2s. 6d. 19)

ACCOUNT (An) of the Massachusetts Society for promoting Christian Knowledge. Printed by order of the Society for the use of the Members. *Andover,* Flagg and Gould. 1815. 83 *pp.* 'Destitute of the Stated Ministry.' 1 *sheet.* 12*mo.* (2s. 6d. 20)

ACCOUNT (An) of the Propagation of the Gospel in Foreign Parts. What the Society eftablifh'd in England by Royal Charter hath done fince their Incorporation, June the 16th 1701. in Her Majesty's Plantations, Colonies, and Factories: As

alſo what they Deſign to do upon further Encouragement from their own Members and other well-
diſpoſed Chriſtians, either by Annual Subſcriptions,
preſent Benefactions, or future Legacies. *London*,
Joseph Downing, 1704. 4 *pp. folio.* (7s. 6d. 21)

ACCOUNT (An) of the Society for Propagating the
Gospel In Foreign Parts, Eſtabliſhed by the Royal
Charter of King William III. With their Proceedings and Succeſs, and Hopes of continual Progreſs
under the Happy Reign of Her Moſt Excellent
Majeſty Queen Anne. *London*, Joseph Downing,
1706. *Frontispiece; title; & 97 pp. half calf,*
4to. (5s. 22)

ACCOUNT (An) of the Spanish Settlements in
America. In four Parts. I. An account of the diſcovery of America by the celebrated Chriſtopher
Columbus; with a deſcription of the Spaniſh inſu-
lar colonies in the Weſt Indies. II. Their ſettlements on the continent of North America. III.
Their ſettlements in Peru, Chili, Paraguay, and Rio
de La Plata. IV. Their ſettlements in Terra Firma.
Of the different countries in South America ſtill
poſſeſſed by the Indians, &c. With a deſcription of
the Canary iſlands. Each Part contains An accurate deſcription of the ſettlements in it, their ſituation, extent, climate, ſoil, produce, former and preſent condition, trading commodities, manufactures,
the genius, diſpoſition, and number of their inhabitants, their government, both civil and eccleſiaſtic,
together with a conciſe account of their chief cities,
ports, bays, rivers, lakes, mountains, minerals, fortifications, &c.; with a very particular account of
the trade carried on betwixt them and Old Spain.
To which is annexed, A ſuccinct account of the
climate, produce, trade, manufactures, &c. of Old
Spain. Illuſtrated with a Map of America. *Edinburgh:* Printed by A. Donaldson and J. Reid.
MDCCLXII. *xvi and* 512 *pp. Copper-plate map* 16¾ *by*
13½ *inches.* 8vo. (7s. 6d. 23)

The value of this volume is greatly enhanced by the addition at
the end, from page 472 to 512, of the Official " Accounts of the
ſiege and ſurrender of the Havannah " in 1762, conſiſting of a
Journal of the Siege, the Articles of Capitulation, the Dis-
patches, &c.

ACORES. A Report of the Trvth of/ the fight about
the Iles of/ Açores, this laſt Sommer./ Betvvixt

the/ Reuenge, one of her Maiefties/ Shippes,/ And
an Armada of the King/ of Spaine./ *London* Printed
for william Ponfonbie :/ 1591. 1 *Title and* 13 *unnumbered leaves. sign A. to D. in fours. Morocco by
Bedford.* 4*to.* (4*l.* 14*s.* 6*d.* 24)

ACOSTA (Joseph de). De Natvra/ Novi Orbis/
Libri dvo,/ et/ de Promvlgatione/ Evangelii, apvd/
Barbaros,/ sive/ de Procvranda/ Indorvm salvte/
Libri sex./ Avtore Iosepho Acosta/ presbytero fo-
cietatis Iesv./ *Salmanticæ./* Apud Guillelmum
Foquel./ M.D.LXXXIX./ 8 *prel. leaves and* 640 *pp.
First edition, vellum,* 8*vo.* (2*l.* 2*s.* 25)

ACOSTA (Joseph de). Iosephi/ Acosta,/ Societatis/
Iesv,/ de Natvra Novi Orbis/ Libri dvo./ Et/ de
Promvlgatione/ Evangelii apvd/ Barbaros,/ fiue,/ de
Procvranda Indorvm/ falute, Libri fex./ Coloniae
Agrippinae,/ In officina Birckmannica, Sumpti-/bus
Arnoldi Mylij./ cIɔ. Iɔ. xcvi./ 8 *prel. leaves and*
581 *pp.* 8*vo.* (1*l.* 11*s.* 6*d.* 26)

ACOSTA (Joseph de). Historia/ Natvral/ y/ Moral
de las/ Indias,/ en qve se tratan las cosas/ notables
del cielo, y elementos, metales, plantas, y ani-/
males dellas : y los ritos; y ceremonias, leyes y/
gouierno, y guerras de los Indios./ Compuefta por
el Padre Iofeph de Acofta Religiofo/ de la Compañia de Iefus./ Dirigida a la Serenissima/ Infanta Doña Ifabella Clara Eugenia de Auftria./
Con Privilegio./ Impreffo en *Seuilla* en cafa de
Iuan de Leon./ Año de 1590./ *Title, reverse blank ;
followed by one leaf beginning* 'Yo Christoval de
Leon,' 1 *p. errata* 1 *p; Text, pp.* 3 *to* 535, *with*
'*Tabla*' 18 *leaves.* 4*to.* (1*l.* 11*s.* 6*d.* 27)

ACOSTA (Joseph de). Historia/ Natvrale, e Morale/
delle Indie ;/ scritta/ dal R. P. Gioseffo di Acosta/
della Compagnia del Giesù ;/ Nellaquale fi trattano
le cofe notabili del Cielo, & de gli/ Elementi, Me-
talli, Piante, & Animali di quelle :/ i fuo i riti, & ce-
remonie : Leggi, & gouerni,/ & guerre de gli Indi-
ani./ Nouamente tradotta della lingua Spagnuola
nella Italiana/ da Gio. Paolo Galvcci Salodiano/
Academico Veneto./ Con Privilegii./ In *Venetia,/*
Preffo Bernardo Bafa. All' infegna del Sole./
M.D.xcvi./ 24 *prelim. leaves, and text in italics,
folioed* 1-173. 4*to.* (1*l.* 11*s.* 6*d.* 28)

ACOSTA (Joseph de). The/ Natvrall/ and Morall
Hiftorie of the/ Eaft and Weft/ Indies./ Intreating
of the remarkeable things of Heaven, of the/ Elements, Mettalls, Plants and Beafts which are pro-/
per to that Country : Together with the Manners,/
Ceremonies, Lawes, Governements, and Warres of/
the Indians./ Written in Spanifh by the R. F. Iofeph Acofta, and/ tranflated into Englifh by E. G./
London/ Printed by Val : Sims for Edward Blount
and William/ Afpley. 1604./ *4 prel. leaves, viz. 1st
blank, 2d title, 3d and 4th Dedication and To the
Reader. Text 590 pages, followed by seven leaves of
Table and Errata. Fine copy, 4to.*   (2l. 2s. 29)

ACOSTA (Joseph de). Historia/ Natvral/y/ Moral
de las/ Indias,/ en qve se tratan las cosas/ notables
del cielo, y elementos, mentales, plantas, y anima-/
les dellas : y los ritos, y ceremonias, leyes, y gouier-/
no, y guerras de los Indios./ Compuefta por el
Padre Iofeph de Acofta Religiofo/ de la Compañia de Iefus./ Dirigida a la Serenissima/ Infanta
Doña Ifabela Clara Eugenia de Auftria./ Año
1608./ Con Licencia./ Impreffo en *Madrid* en cafa
de Alonfo Martin./ *Title, reverse blank;* 'Tassa'1 *p;*
'Erratas' 1 *p; Licencias, pp.* 5-6 ; *Dedication* ' A la
Serenissima Infanta,' *pp.* 7-9 ; 'Proemio,' *pp.* 10-
12 ; *Text pp.* 13-535. 'Tabla,' 21 *leaves. Fine copy.
Calf. 4to.*   (1l. 11s. 6d. 30)

ACUNA (Christoval de). Nvevo/ De scubrimi-
ento/ del gran Rio de las/ Amazonas./ Por el Padre
Christoval/ de Acuña, Religiofo de la Compañia de/
Iefus, y Calificador de la Suprema General Inquificion./ Al qval fue, y se hizo por Orden/ de fu
Mageftad, el año de 1639./ Por la Provincia de
Qvito/ en los Reynos del Perù./ Al Excelentissimo Señor Conde/ Duque de Olïuares./ Con Licencia ; En *Madrid*, en la Imprenta de Reyno,/ año de
1641./ *6 prel. leaves, viz. Title;* 'Al Excelentissimo,'
etc ; 3 pages; 'Al Lector,' 1 *page ; Certificates 2
leaves;* Clavsvla, *etc.* 1 *leaf ; Text 46 folioed leaves.
Fine large, and clean copy in morocco by Bedford.
4to.*   (10l. 10s. 31)

ACUNA (Christoval de) Voyages/ and/ Disco-
veries/ in/ South=America./ The Firft up the River
of Amazons to/ Quito in Peru, and back again to

Brazil,/ perform'd at the Command of the King/ of Spain./ By Christopher d'Acvgna./ The Second up the River of Plata, and/ thence by Land to the Mines of Potoſi./ By Monſ. Acarete./ The Third from Cayenne into Guiana, in ſearch/ of the Lake of Parima, reputed the richeſt/ Place in the World./ By M. Grillet and Bechamel./ Done into Engliſh from the Originals, being the on-/ly Accounts of thoſe Parts hitherto extant./ The whole illuſtrated with Notes and Maps./ *London,*/ Printed for S. Buckley at the Dolphin over againſt/ St. Dunſtan's Church in Fleetſtreet, 1698./ *On the reverse of the Title,* 'Advertisement'; 'Introduction,' *pp. iii-viii; Map,* 'The Course of the River of Amazons'; *text,* 190 *pp; Title,* ' An Account of a Voyage up the River de la Plata, *etc.* By Monſ. Acarete du Biſcay. 1698.' 'A Map of the Provinces Paraguay' *etc.* Text, 79 *pp; Title,* 'A Journal of the Travels of John Grillet, and Francis Bechamel into Gviana,' *etc.* 1698. 'A Letter,' 1 *leaf; and text* 68 *pp. calf.* 8vo. (1*l.* 1*s.* 32)

ADAIR (JAMES) The History of the American Indians; particularly thoſe Nations adjoining to the Miſſiſippi, East and West Florida, Georgia, South and North Carolina and Virginia: Containing an Account of their Origin, Language, Manners, Religious and Civil Customs, Laws, Form of Government, Punishments, Conduct in War and Domestic Life, their Habits, Diet, Agriculture, Manufactures, Diseases and Method of Cure, and other Particulars, ſufficient to render it a complete Indian System. With Observations on former Historians, the Conduct of our Colony Governors, Superintendents, Missionaries, &c. Also an Appendix, containing a Deſcription of the Floridas, and the Miſſiſippi Lands, with their Productions—The Benefits of coloniſing Georgiana, and civilizing the Indians—And the way to make all the Colonies more valuable to the Mother Country. With a new Map of the Country referred to in the History. By James Adair, Eſquire, A Trader with the Indians, and Reſident in their Country for Forty Years. *London:* Edward and Charles Dilly, MDCCLXXV. 6 *prel. leaves, viz. Half-title, title;* 'Dedication,' 2 *leaves;* 'Preface,' 1 *leaf;* 'Contents,'

1 *leaf: text* 448 *pp.* & *Appendix, ending on page* 464.
With Map of American Indian Nations 13 *by* 9½
inches. Calf, 4to.   (1*l.* 1*s.* 33)

ADAMS (Amos). A Concise, Historical View of
the Difficulties, Hardships, and Perils Which attended the Planting and progreſſive Improvements of New-England. With A particular Account of its long and Deſtructive Wars, Expen-
sive Expeditions, &c. By Amos Adams, A.M.
Paſtor of the Firſt Church of Roxbury. Boston printed. *London* reprinted for Edward and
Charles Dilly, MDCCLXX. *Title and* 68 *pp. half mor.*
8*vo.*   (10*s.* 6*d.* 34)

ADAMS (John). Autograph Letter to Commodore
John Paul Jones, dated from Grosvenor Square,
London, Jan. 21, 1786, promising " to support
Dr. Bancroft's application to the Danish Minister,
etc. 1 *page: a good specimen.* 4*to.*   (1*l.* 1*s.* 35)

ADAMS (John). A Defence of the Conſtitutions
of Government of the United States of America. By
John Adams, LL. D. And a Member of the Aca-
demy of Arts and Sciences at Boſton. *Philadelphia:*
Printed for Hall and Sellers : J. Crukshank ; and
Young and M'Culloch. M. DCC. LXXXVII. *xx pp.*
prel. & *Text pp.* 3 *to* 390. *Very fine copy in calf.*
First Edition. 12*mo.*   (15*s.* 36)

ADAMS (John). A Defence of the Constitutions
of Government of the United States of America,
against the Attack of M. Turgot in his Letter to Dr.
Price, dated the twenty-second day of March, 1778.
By John Adams, LL. D. and a Member of the
Academy of Arts and Sciences at Boston. In
Three Volumes. A new Edition. *London: J.* Stockdale, 1794. *Vol. I.* 22 *prel. leaves, viz. Half-title,*
Portrait, title, Life, Preface and Contents; Text 392
pp. II. Half-title, title and 451 *pp. III. Half-*
title, title, and 528 *pp.; Index* 18 *leaves. Fine copy,*
half calf, 8*vo.*   (16*s.* 6*d.* 37)

ADAMS (John). Political Sketches inscribed to
his Excellency John Adams, Minister Plenipotentiary from the United States to the Court of Great
Britain. By a Citizen of the United States. *Lon-*
don: C. Dilly. MDCCLXXXVII. 3 *prelim. leaves and*
96 *pages. Half morocco.* 8*vo.*   (7*s.* 6*d.* 38)

ADAMS (John Quincy). An Oration, pronounced
July 4th, 1793, at the request of the Inhabitants
of the Town of Boston, in Commemoration of the
Anniversary of American Independence. By John
Quincy Adams. *Boston :* Edes and Son, 1793. 2
prel. leaves and 16 *pp. half mor.* 8*vo.* (3*s.* 6*d.* 39)

ADAMS (Samuel). An Oration delivered at the
State-House, in Philadelphia, to a very numerous
Audience; on Thursday the 1ſt of August, 1776.
By Samuel Adams, Member of the * * * * * * *
* * * * * * * the General Congress of the * * * * * *
* * * * * * of America. Philadelphia printed;
London, Re-printed for J. Johnson, M. DCC. LXXVI.
Half-title, title and 42 *pp. hf. mor.* 8*vo.* (4*s.* 6*d.* 40)

ADAMS (William). God's Eye/ on the/ Contrite
/or a/ Discourse/ shewing/ That True Poverty and
Contrition of ſpirit and Trembling at God's Word
is the Infallible and only way for the Obtaining
and Retaining/ of Divine Acceptation./ As it was
made in the Audience of the General Aſſembly of
the/ Maſſachuſetts Colony at Boston in New-England ;/ May 27. 1685. being the Day of Election
there./ By Mr. William Adams./ *Boston* in New-
England,/ Printed by Richard Pierce for Samuel
Sewall 1685./ *Title, reverse blank, and* 41 *pp. Fine
copy in morocco by Bedford.* 4*to.* (3*l.* 3*s.* 41)

ADDISON (Henry). Autograph Manuscript Memorial of Capt Henry Addison of the 100th Regiment to Sir George Yonge Secretary at War, praying to be exchanged into the 52 Regiment. 2 *pages*
4*to.* (5*s.* 42)

The Memorialist states that his father and uncle, captains in the
52d Regiment, both fell at the battle of Bunker Hill, and that
his brother, a Lieut. in the same Regiment, was killed at the
battle of Long Island.

ADDITIONAL Papers concerning the Province of
Quebeck: Being an Appendix to the Book entitled,
" An Account of the Proceedings of the Britiſh and
other Proteſtant Inhabitants of the Province of
Quebeck in North America, sn order to obtain a
Houſe of Aſſembly in that Province." *London :*
W. White, M. DCC. LXXVI. 510 *pages. Boards uncut.*
8*vo.* (10*s.* 6*d.* 43)

ADDRESS (An) from the Brethren's Society for the
furtherance of the Gospel among the Heathen, to

the Members of the Congregations and Societies of the Brethren, And to all those Friends who wifh Succefs to the Missions of the Church of the Brethren. [*London,* 1781]. 16 *and* 4 *pp. Half mor. 8vo.* (4s. 6d. 44)

This tract relates chiefly to the great Storm and Hurricane at Jamaica and Barbadoes in 1780.

ADDRESS (An) from the Clergy of New-York and New-Jersey, to the Episcopalians in Virginia; Occasioned by some late Transactions in that Colony relative to an American Episcopate. [By Dr. Myles Cooper.] *New-York:* Hugh Gaine, 1771. *Title and* 58 *pp. half mor. 8vo.* (10s. 6d. 45)

ADDRESS from the Committee appointed at Mrs. Vandewater's On the 13th Day of September, 1784. To the People of the State of New-York. *New-York:* Printed by Shepard Kollock, oppofite the Coffee-House. M,DCC,LXXXIV. 16 *pp.* ¡*Signed '* Melanĉton Smith, Peter Ricker, Jonathan Lawrence, Anthony Rutgers, Peter T. Curtenius, Thomas Tucker, Daniel Shaw, Adam Gilchrift, jun. John Wiley.' *8vo.* (10s. 6d. 46)

ADDRESS (The) of the People of Great-Britain to the Inhabitants of America. *London:* T. Cadell, M DCC LXXV. *Title & 60 pp. half mor. 8vo.* (4s. 6d. 47)

ADDRESS (An) to a Provincial Bashaw. O Shame! where is thy Blufh? By a Son of Liberty. Printed in (the Tyrannic Adminiftration of St. Francifco) [*Gov. Francis Bernard.*] 1769. [*Boston*] 8 *pp. half mor.* 4to. (12s. 6d. 48)

This Address consists of 27 four-line stanzas against Sir Francis Bernard, Governor of Massachusetts. The following being the last stanza, will serve as a specimen of the versification.
Yet trufr me B ——— not the Heartwrung Tear,
Shall fuatch thy Name from obloquy below,
Nor fore Repentance, which abfolves thee there,
Shall footh the Vengeance of a mortal Foe.

ADDRESS (An) to Protestant Dissenters of all Denominations, on the Approaching Election of Members of Parliament, with refpeĉt to the State of Public Liberty in General, and of American affairs in Particular. *London:* Joseph Johnson, 1774. 16 *pp. half mor. 8vo.* (4s. 6d. 49)

ADDRESS (An) to the Inhabitants of Pennsylvania, by those Freemen, of the City of Philadelphia, who are now confined in the Mason's Lodge, by virtue

of a general warrant. Signed in Council by the
Vice President of the Council of Pennsylvania.
Philadelphia: Robert Bell, M DCC LXXVII. *2 prel.
leaves and 52 pp. half mor. 8vo.*   (6s. 50)

ADDRESS (An) to the Inhabitants of the Britiſh
Settlements in America, upon Slave-Keeping. The
Second Edition. To which are added, Observations on a Pamphlet, entitled, " Slavery not forbidden by Scripture; or, A Defence of the Weſt-
India Planters." By a Pennsylvanian. *Philadelphia:* John Dunlap. M. DCC. LXXIII. *Title and
28 pages, followed by an* 'Advertisement,' *1 leaf,
and a second title:* A Vindication of the Address,
To the Inhabitants of the British Settlements, on
the Slavery of the Negroes in America, in Anſwer
to a Pamphlet entitled, " Slavery not Forbidden
by Scripture; Or a Defence of the West India
Planters from the Aspersions thrown out againſt
them by the Author of the Address." By a Pennsylvanian. *Philadelphia:* M, DCC, LXXIII. *54 pages.
Half mor. 8vo.*   (7s. 6d. 51)

ADDRESS (An) to the Roman Catholics of the
United States of America. By a Catholic Clergy-
man. Aunapolis: Printed by Frederick Green.
And *Worcester:* Reprinted by J. Tymbs, at the
Cross. MDCCLXXXV. *Title and Preface, 2 leaves;
text, 120 pp. 8vo.*   (5s. 6d. 52)

AFRICA. A Short Account Of that Part of Africa,
Inhabited by the Negroes. With Reſpect to the
Fertility of the Country; the good Diſpoſition of
many of the Natives, and the Manner by which
the Slave Trade is carried on. Extracted from
divers Authors, in order to ſhew the Iniquity of
that Trade, and the Falſity of the Arguments
uſually advanced in its Vindication. With Quotations from the Writings of ſeveral Perſons of
Note, viz. George Wallis, Francis Hutcheson, and
James Foster, and a large Extract from a Pamphlet, lately publiſhed in London, on the Subjeсt of
the Slave Trade. The Second Edition, with large
Additions and Amendments. *Philadelphia:* Printed
by W. Dunlap, in the Year MDCCLXII. *Title and
pp. 3-80. half mor. 8vo.*   (5s. 6d. 53)

AFRICAN TRADE (The), the great Pillar and

Support of the Britiſh Plantation Trade in America: Shewing that our Loſs, by being beat out of all the Foreign Markets for Sugar and Indigo by the French, has been owing to the Negleƈt of our African Trade; which only, can ſupply our Colonies with Negroes, for the making of Sugars, and all other Plantation Produce: That the Support and Security of the Negroe-Trade depends wholly on the due and effeƈtual Support of the Royal African Company of England, which has hitherto preſerved this invaluable Trade to theſe Kingdoms: That the Difficulties and Diſcouragements which the said Company labours under, threaten the abſolute Loſs of the Negroe Trade to this Nation; and consequently the total Ruin of all the Britiſh Plantations in America: And alſo, What the Royal African Company have a natural Right to hope for this Seſſion of Parliament from their Country, in order to enable them to ſupport and maintain the Britiſh Intereſt, Rights and Privileges in Africa againſt the French, and all other Rivals in the ſame moſt valuable Trade. In a Letter to the Right Honourable * * * * * * * * * * * * *London*: J. Robinson, 1745. *Title and 44 pp. half morocco.* 4to. (7s. 6d. 54)

AITKEN (ROBERT). Aitken's general American Register, and the Gentleman's and Tradesman's complete Annual Account Book, and Calendar, For the Pocket or Desk; For the Year of our Lord, 1773. *Philadelphia:* Printed by Joseph Crukshank, For R. Aitken, Bookseller, opposite the London-coffee-house, Front-Street. 2 *prel. leaves, and text* A *to* M *in fours &* N *in five leaves. followed by a second title* ' Aitken's General American Register, for the Year of our Lord 1773.' *etc.* *Title and 64 pp.* 8vo. (10s. 6d. 55)

This volume is interesting from the fact of its being the first attempt of this kind in the American Colonies.

ALBAREZ DE TOLEDO, (FR. DOMINGO). Copia de la Espantosa Carta, Escrita por el/ P- Fr. Domingo Albarez de Toledo, Procurador General de Corte, del/ Orden de N. P. S. Franciſco, embiada deſde la Ciudad de Lima, al/ Reverendiſſimo P. Commiſſario General en Eſtecharque, que ſu fecha es/ de 29. de Oƈtubre de 1687. años, dandole cu-

enta de los laſtimoſos eſtragos/ y deſgracias que
han ſucedido en dicha Ciudad./ [Colophon] Con
licencia: En *Barcelona*, en caſa Vicente Surià,/
à la calle de la Paja, Año 1688./ Vendeſe el Flos
Sanctorum del Padre Ribadeneyra,/ aumentado
con los Santos nuevos, en la/ miſma Imprenta./
4 *pages. 4to.*   (*2l. 2s.* 56)

ALCAFARADO (FRANCISCO). An/ Historical/ Re-
lation/ Of the Firſt/ Discovery/ of the/ Isle/ of/
Madera./ Written Originally in Portugueze by
Don Franciſ-/co Alcafarado (gentleman of the Bed-
Chamber/ to the Infant Don Henry younger/ Son
of John the firſt King of/ Portugal;)/ Who was one
of the Firſt Diſcoverers, thence tranſla-/ted into
French, and now made Engliſh./ *London,*/ Printed
for William Cademan at the ſign of the/ of the
Popes-Head at the Entrance into the/ New Ex-
change in the Strand. 1675./ *Title and 37 pp.
Calf by Bedford. 4to.*   (*1l. 11s. 6d.* 57)

ALCEDO (ANTONIO DE). The Geographical and
Historical Dictionary of America and the West
Indies. Containing an entire Translation of the
Spanish Work of Colonel Don Antonio de Alcedo,
Captain of the Royal Spanish Guards, and Member
of the Royal Academy of History : with Large Ad-
ditions and Compilations from Modern Voyages
and Travels, and from Original and Authentic In-
formation. By G. A. Thompson, Esq. In Five
Volumes. *London*, 1812. *Vol. I.* 10 *prel. leaves,*
1*st blank ; and Text,* 574 *pp. ; II. Title & 597 pp.
III. Title & 512 pp. ; IV.* 1814, *Title and 636 pp.
V.* 1815, 20 *prel. leaves,* 1*st blank ; Text 462 pp.*
' Errata' *to the 5 Vols.* 1 *leaf ;* ' General Appendix'
105 *pp. Half calf. 4to.*   (*1l. 11s. 6d.* 58)

ALEXANDER (SIR WILLIAM). The/ Mapp and/
Description of/ New-England ;/ Together with/ A
Diſcourſe of Plantation, and/ Colonies :/ Also,/ A
Relation of the nature of the Climate,/ and how it
agrees with our owne Country/ England./ How
neere it lyes to New-found-Land, Virginia,/ Noua
Francia, Canada, and other Parts of/ the West-
Indies./ Written by/ Sʳ. William Alexander,
Knight./ *London,*/ Printed for Nathaniel Bvtter./
An. Dom. 1630./ *Title ; and text in* 47 *pp. With*

copper plate map of New England, etc. 13½ *by* 10 *inches.*
Fine copy, in green mor. 4*to.* (21*l.* 59)

ALEXO DE ORRIO (FRANCISCO XAVIER). Solu-
cion/ del gran problema/ acerca de la poblacion/ de
las Americas,/ en que fobre el fundamento de los
Libros/ Santos fe defcubre facil camino á la tranf-
migracion de/ los Hombres del uno al otro Continente; y como pudieron/ pafar al Nuevo Mundo, no
folamente las Beftias de fervicio,/ fino tambien las
Fieras, y nocivas./ Y con esta ocasion se satisface/
plenamente al délirio de los Pre-Adamitas, apoyado
con/ efta dificil objecion hafta ahora no bien defa-
tada./ Por el P. Francisco Xavier Alexo/ de Orrio,
de la Sagrada Compañia de Jesus./ Sacala a luz/
Don Francisco Carmona, Godoy,/ y Bucareli, Cor-
regidor, Juez de Minas de la Ciudad de/ Nueftra
Señora de los Zacatecas : Quien la dedica/ a el M.
Il^{tre}. Sr. Coronèl de los Reales Exercitos/ Don
Pedro Montesinos de Lara,/ Gobernado, que hà
fido de la Puebla de los Angeles,/ y actual Capitàn
General, Gobernador del Nuevo Reyno/ de la Ga-
licia, y Prefidente de la Real Audiencia, que/ refide en la Ciudad de Guadalaxara./ En *Mexico :*
En la Imprenta Real del Superior Gobierno, y del/
Nuevo Rezado, de los Herederos de Doña Maria
de Ribera ;/ Calle de San Bernardo. Año de 1763./
22 *prel. leaves and* 72 *pp. vellum,* 4*to.* (3*l.* 3*s.* 60)

ALLEN (ETHAN). Reason the only Oracle of Man,
or a Compenduous Syftem of Natural Religion.
Alternately Adorned with Confutations of a variety of Doctrines incompatible to it; Deduced
from the moft exalted Ideas which we are able to
form of the Divine and Human Characters, and
from the Univerfe in General. By Ethan Allan,
Efq; *Bennington :* State of Vermont; Printed by
Haswell and Russell. M,DCC,LXXXIV. 477 *pp. Fine*
copy, in the original binding. (2*l.* 2*s.* 61)

ALLEN (ETHAN). A Narrative of Col. Ethan Allen's Captivity, From the time of his being taken
by the Britifh, near Montreal, on the 25th of September, 1775, to the time of his Exchange, on
the 6th of May, 1778. Containing his Voyages
and Travels, With the moft remarkable Occurrences
respecting himfelf, and many other Continental

Prifoners of different ranks and characters, which
fell under his obfervation in the courfe of the fame;
particularly the deftruction of the Prifoners at
New-York, by General Sir William Howe, in the
Years 1776, and 1777. Interfperfed with fome
Political Obfervations./ Written by himfelf, and
now Publifhed for the Information of the Curious,
in all Nations. *Newbury:* Printed by John My-
call, for Nathaniel Coverly of Boston and Sold at
his Shop between Seven-ftar Lane and the Sign of
the Lamb. 1780. 80 *pp. uncut 8vo.* (*2l. 2s.* 62)

ALLEN (Ethan). A Narrative of Col. Ethan Allen's Captivity, From the time of his being taken
by the British, near Montreal, on the 25th day of
September, in the year 1775, to the time of his exchange, on the 6th day of May, 1778. Containing
his Voyages and Travels, With the most remarkable occurrences respecting himself, and many
other continental Prisoners, of different ranks and
characters, which fell under his observation in the
course of the same; particularly the destruction of
the prisoners at New-York, by General Sir William Howe, in the years 1776 and 1777; interspersed
with some Political Observations. Written by himself, and now published for the information of the
curious in all Nations. To which are now added
a considerable number of explanatory and occasional notes together with an index of reference to
the most remarkable occurrences in the narrative.
Walpole, N. H. Published by Thomas & Thomas.
From the Press of Charter & Haile. 1807. 158 *pp.*
'Subscribers' Names' 1 *page. half calf.*
12*mo.* (*1l. 11s. 6d.* 63)

ALLEN (Ethan). A Narrative of the Captivity
of Col. Ethan Allen, From the time of his being
taking by the British, near Montreal, on the 25th
day of September, in the year 1775, to the time of
his exchange, on the 6th day of May, 1778. Containing his Voyages and Travels, With the most
remarkable occurrences respecting himself, and
many other continental Prisoners, of different
ranks and characters, which fell under his observation in the course of the same; particularly the
destruction of the prisoners at New-York, by General Sir William Howe, in the years 1776 and

1777; interspersed with some Political Observations. Written by himself. *Albany*: Pratt & Clark.
1814. *144 pp. small 8vo.*   (15s. 6d. 64)

ALLEN (IRA). The Natural and Political History
of the State of Vermont, one of the United States
of America. To which is added, an Appendix,
containing answers to sundry queries, addressed
to the Author. By ·Ira Allen, Esquire, Major-
General of the Militia in the State of Vermont.
London: J. W. Myers, 1798. *vii and 300 pp.*
Large copper-plate map of Vermont. Boards, uncut.
8vo.   (16s. 65)

ALLEN (IRA). The Same, *wanting the map, boards*
uncut.   (7s. 6d. 66)

ALLEN (JAMES). New-Englands/ choiceſt Bleſſ-
ing/ And the Mercy moſt to be deſired by/ all that
wiſh well to this People./ Cleared in a/ Sermon/
Preached before the/ Covrt of Election/ At Boſton
on May 28./ 1679./ By James Allen,/ Teacher
to the firſt gathered Church therein./ *Boston*,/
Printed by John Foſter, 1679./ *2 prel. leaves; viz.*
Title in a type metal border, reverse blank, 'To the
Reader.' 2 pp. Text 14 pp. followed by a blank leaf.
Fine copy in morocco by Bedford. 4to. (4l. 4s. 67)

ALLEN (JAMES). Neglect of Supporting/ and/
Maintaining the Pure/ Worship of God,/ By the
Profeſſing People of God : is a God-provoking
and/ Land-Waiting Sin./ And Repentance with
Reformation of it, the only way to/ their Out-
ward Felicity :/ Or,/ The Cauſe of New-Englands
Scarcity : And right way to its/ Plenty./ As it
was Diſcovered and Applied in a Sermon Preached
at Roxbury,/ on a Faſt-Day : July 26, 1687./ By
James Allen, Teacher to the firſt Gathered Church
in Boſton./ *Boston:*/ Printed for Job How, and
John Allen : And are to be Sold/ at Mr. Samuel
Greens by the South Meeting/ House, 1687./ *2 prel.*
leaves; viz. Title, reverse blank; 'To the Christian
Reader.' 2 pp. Text 16 pp. Morocco by Bedford.
4to.   (4l. 4s. 68)

ALLEN (ROBERT). An Essay on the Nature and
Methods of carrying on a Trade to the South-Sea.
By Robert Allen, Who Reſided ſome Years in the

Kingdom of Peru. *London:* John Baker, 1712. *Title; Dedication, etc.* 1 *leaf; Text* 37 *pp. half morocco.* 8*vo.*   (7*s.* 6*d.*   69)

ALLEN (Timothy). Salvation for all Men, Put out of all Dispute. By Timothy Allen, A.M. & V.D.M. Granville, Maſſachuſetts. *Hartford:* Printed by Nathaniel Patten, a few Rods North of the Court-Houſe. [1782.] *Title;* ' Escapes of the Press,' 1 *leaf inserted;* ' Epistle' *to the Reader. pp. iii-viii; and Text, pp.* 9-56. 8*vo.*   (5*s.* 6*d.*   70)

ALLEN (William). An/ American/ Biographical and Historical/ Dictionary,/ containing an account of the/ Lives, Characters, and Writings/ of the/ most eminent Persons in North America from its first Settlement,/ and a summary of the/ History of the several Colonies/ and of the/ United States./ By William Allen, D. D., President of Bowdoin College;/ Fellow of the Amer. Acad. of Arts and Sciences; and Member of the Amer. Antiq./ Soc., and of the Hist. Soc. of Maine, N. Hampshire, and N. York./   Second Edition./   *Boston:/* Published by William Hyde & Co./ MDCCXXXII. *viii and* 800 *pp. Calf extra by Bedford. Roy.* 8*vo.*   (1*l.* 1*s.*   71)

ALLEN (William). The American Crisis: A Letter, addressed by permission to The Earl Gower, Lord Preſident of the Council, &c. &c. &c. On the preſent alarming Disturbances in the Colonies. Wherein Various important Points, relative to Plantation Affairs, are brought into Diſcuſſion; as well as ſeveral Perſons adverted to of the moſt diſtinguiſhed Charaĉters. And an Idea is offered towards a complete Plan of reſtoring the Dependence of America upon Great Britain to a State of Perfeĉtion. By William Allen, Eſq; *London:* T. Cadell, M DCC LXXIV. *iv and* 72 *pp. Half morocco.* 8*vo.*   (10*s.* 6*d.*   72)

ALLIES (The) and the Late Miniſtry Defended againſt France, and the Preſent Friends of France. In Anſwer to a Pamphlet, entitled, The Conduĉt of the Allies. [*In four parts*]. Part I. Shewing the Neceſſity of England's entering into the Grand Alliance; and that by it we are oblig'd to inſiſt on the Reſtitution of Spain and the Indies to the Houſe of Auſtria. With a particular Vindication of the

Eight Article from the grofs Corruptions, with which the Author of the Conduct has falfify'd the two Claufes of it that relate to England and the Weft-Indies. The Third Edition, Corrected. London, Egbert Sanger, 1711. *Part I,* 48 *pp. Part II,* 2 *prel. leaves &* 71 *pp. Part III,* 2 *prel. leaves &* 74 *pp. & Part IV,* 2 *prel. leaves and* 84 *pp. Half mor.* 8*vo.* (6*s.* 6*d.* 73)

ALLIN (John). An/ Exact Relation/ of/ The moft Execrable, Attempts/ of/ John Allin,/ Committed on the Perfon of/ His Excellency/ Francis Lord Willovghby/ of Parham, Captain General of the Continent of/ Guiana, and of all the Caribby-Iflands,/ and our Lord Proprietor./ *Loudon,/* Printed for Richard Lowndes, at the white Lion in S. Pauls/ Churchyard near the little North door. 1665./ *Title &* 12 *pages, followed by one leaf having on the reverse the Licence to print. Fine copy, uncut, half mor.* 4*to.* (1*l.* 11*s.* 6*d.* 74)

This Account of John Allin was drawn up by William Byam.

ALLIN (John) and SHEPARD (Thomas). A/ Defence/ of the/ Anfwer made unto the Nine Queftions/ or Pofitions fent from New-England,/ Against the/ Reply thereto/ by That Reverend fervant of Christ,/ Mr. John Ball;/ Entituled,/ A Tryall of the New Church-way in/ New-England and in Old./ Wherein, befide a more full opening of fundry particulars/ concerning Liturgies, Power of the Keys, matter of/ the vifible Church, &c. is more largely handled, that/ controverfie concerning the Catholick vifible/ Church; tending to cleare up the/ Old-way of Chrift in New-/England Churches./ By Iohn Allin, Paftor of Dedham, [and] Tho. Shepard of Cambridge in New-England/. *London,* Printed by R. Cotes for Andrew Crooke, and are to be fold at the Green/ Dragon in Pauls Church yard. 1648./ 16 *prel. leaves; viz. Title,* 'Preface' *pp.* 1-25. 'Advertisements,' *pp.* 26-30; *and text, pp.* 31-211. 4*to.* (1*l.* 1*s.* 75)

ALZATE RAMIREZ (Joseph Antonio de). Gazette de Literatura de Mexico. From N° 1 of Vol. I, 15 January 1788 to N° 44 of Vol. III, 22 Oct. 1795. *Mexico.* 1788-1795. *Wanting three or four numbers only.* 4*to.* (5*l.* 5*s.* 76)

AMERICA. Dife figur anzaigt vns das volck vnd
infel die gefunden ift durch den chriftenlichen künig
zů Portigal oder von feinen vnderthonen. Die leüt
find alfo nacket hübfch. braun wolgeftalt von leib.
ir heübter./ halfz. arm. fcham. fufz. frawen vnd
mann ain wenig mit federn bedeckt. Auch haben
die mann in iren angeftichten vnd bruft vid edel
geftain. Es hat auch nyemantz nichts funder find
alle ding gemain./ Vnnd die mann habendt weyber
welche in gefallen. es fey mütter. fchwefter oder
freüudt. darjnn haben fy kain vnderfchayd. Sy
ftreyten auch mit einander. Sy effen auch ainander
felbs die erfchlagen/ werden. vnd hencken das
felbig fleifch in den rauch. Sy werden alt hundert
vnd füntzig iar. Vnd haben kain regiment./ [*Trans.*]
(This figure reprefents to us the people and ifland
which have been difcovered by the Chriftian King
of Portugal or by his fubjeƈts. The people are thus
naked, handfome, brown, well fhaped in body;
their heads, necks, arms, private parts, feet of men
and women are a little covered with feathers. The
men alfo have many precious ftones in their faces
and breafts. No one alfo has any thing, but all
things are in common. And the men have as wives
thofe who pleafe them, be they mothers, fifters, or
friends, therein make they no diftinƈtion. They
alfo fight with each other. They alfo eat each
other, even thofe who are flain, and hang the flefh
of them in the fmoke. They become a hundred
and fifty years old. And have no government.)
[1500?] *Folio.* (12*l.* 12*s.* 77)

The above text in German, occupies four lines beneath an old
   block leaf, nine by thirteen inches square, representing the manners and customs of the natives of the Northern and Eastern
   coast of South America as first found by the Portuguese at the end
   of the 15th or beginning of the 16th century. It is without date,
   but was probably printed at Augsburg, or Nuremberg, between
   the years 1497 and 1504. It is believed to be unique. A facsimile
   of this earliest known xylographic leaf respecting America is
   given in Stevens's American Bibliographer, Part I.

AMERICA. Geographifche vnd/ Hiftorifche Befchreibung der vber=/aufz groffer Landtfchafft America: welche auch/ Weft India, vnd jhrer gröffe hal-
ben die New Welt genennet wirt./ Gar artig, vnd
nach der kunft in XX. Mappen oder Land=/taf-
feln verfaffet, vnd jetzt newlich in Kupffer ge=/
ftochen, vnd an tag gegeben./ Dabey auff dem
Rücken ieder Mappen gefunden/ wirdt, die Gef-
talt, Art vnd vornembfte Gelegenheit ders Landt=

ſchafft: Nemblich, wie der Himmel vnd Lufft da-
ſelbſt geſtalt, ober Kalt oder/ Warm, Geſund oder
Vngeſund ſey: was dariñ fur Völcker vnd Leut
ſeind,/ wie dieſelb bekleydet, vnd wa von ſie gele-
ben: was im Land wächſet: was fur/ Thier wilde
vnnd zame, auch Vögel darinn zu finden: darnach
was/ Wildnuſz, Berge, Wäſſer, Seen, Bergwercken,
Goldgru=/ben, Edelgeſteine, vnd anders dariñ iſt,/
vnd gefunden wirdt./ Zu mehrem verſtand vnd
erklärung gemelter Landſchafft Ameri=/ca, iſt hie-
bey gefügt Ein ſchön vnd nützlicher Tractat von
der Natur, Art vnd/ Eygenſchafft der Newer Welt,
dariñ viel nützliche ding, derſelben Newen Welt
betref=/ſend gehandelt werden, welche den alten
Philoſophis Ariſtoteli, Lactantio, vnd audern/ gar
vnbekandt geweſen, ja von jhnen geläugnet ſind:
derer jrrige meynungen entdeckt/ werden, vnd das
widerſpiell klärlich dargethan wirt: Nemblich,
daſz die Zona Torrida/ (Brennende Reuier) nicht
vbermäſſig, ſonder mittelmäſſig Warm/ ſey, vnd
die Menſchen darinn gantz komlich/ leben mögen.
Erſtlich durch einen Hochgelehrten vnd deſz Lan-
des Wolerfahrnen Mann,/ in Lateiniſcher Spraach
gar herrlich beſchrieben. Nun aber durch ein
Liebhaber/ der Hiſtorien vnd Landbeſchreibungen
dem gemeinen Teutſchen/ Mann zu gutem, gar trew-
lich vbergeſetzt,/ vnd ins Teutſch bracht./ Ge-
drückt zu Cölln,/ Bey Johann Chriſtoffel, auff S.
Marcellenſtraſz./ Jm jahr M. D. XCVIII./ *2 prelim.*
leaves and 51 *pp. followed by* 20 *copper-plate maps,*
on guards, having 2 *pp. of text on the reverse of each.*
Calf extra by Bedford.   *Folio.*   (2l. 12s. 6d. 78)

AMERICA:/ or/ An exact Deſcription/ of the/
West-Indies:/ More eſpecially of thoſe/ Provinces
which are under/ the Dominion of the/ King of
Spain./ Faithfully repreſented by N. N Gent./
London, printed by Ric. Hodgkinſonne for Edw.
Dod,/ and are to be ſold at the Gun in Ivy-lane.
1655./ 7 *prel. leaves; viz. Title, dedication, the*
Publiſher's Advertiſement, and the Contents; text
484 *pp.* 'Errata' 1 *p;* 'Book printed,' 1 *p. Map*
wanting. 16*mo.*   (1l. 1s. 79.)

AMERICA Vindicated from the High Charge of
Ingratitude and Rebellion: with a Plan of Legis-
lation, Proposed to the Consideration of Both

Houses, For Eftablifhing a Permanent and Solid
Foundation, For a juft conftitutional Union, Be-
tween Great Britain and her Colonies. By a
Friend to Both Countries. *Devizes*, T. Burrough;
M. DCC. LXXIV. *Title and* 48 *pp. half morocco,*
8vo. (6s. 6d. 80)

AMERICAN (The) and Britifh Chronicle of War
and Politics; being an Accurate and Comprehen-
sive Register of the most memorable Occurrences
in the last ten Years of his Majesty's Reign: in
which will be found above Eighteen Hundred
Interefting Events, During the late War between
Great Britain and America, France, Spain, and
Holland; From May 10, 1773, to July 16, 1783.
The Whole carefully collected from Authentic
Records, and correctly arranged in Chronological
Order. Multum in Parvo. This compendium, or
Political Syftem of Foreign and Domestic Affairs,
is a faithful Diary of Civil and Military Tranf-
actions, extracted from Government Difpatches
and Official Papers, Votes of the Houfe of Com-
mons and Lords, Refolutions of Congrefs, Acts
of Council, Royal Proclamations, Edicts, &c.
Provincial Confiderations, Debates, Petitions,
Addreffes, Meetings, and Determinations. Every
Engagement by Sea and Land, Military Operations, Civil Eftablifhments, Changes in Adminiftration, Political Struggles, and Principal
Appointments; Treaties of Alliance, Commerce,
and Peace; Conftitutional and Financial Reform;
Land and Marine Force of the Belligerent Powers;
Public Revenue, Debt, and Expenditure, &c.
&c. &c. To the Recapitulation of Public Occurrences during the late War in America and
in Europe, is added a general Table of Prior
Events; Britifh Governors in America at the
Commencement of Hoftilities; Members of the
firft Congrefs; Conftitution and Form of Government of the feveral States, and Population in
each; Ships of War taken, loft, or deftroyed;
Roads in America; and a copious Abridgement
of the Treaties of Peace. *London*: Printed for
the Author, [1783]. *Title and Dedication, 2*
leaves; sign. A to O in fours & P in 2 leaves.
8vo. (10s. 6d. 81)
The Dedication is dated 1783 and signed E. I. S.

AMERICAN ANECDOTES: Original and Select. By an American. *Boston:* Putnam and Hunt. MDCCCXXX. *Two Volumes.* Vol. I. 300 *pp.* Vol. II. 300 *pp. Uncut 8vo.* (10s. 6d. 82)

AMERICAN CRISIS (THE). Number II. By the Author of Common Sense [Thomas Paine.] *Philadelphia:* Printed and Sold by Styner and Cist, in Second-ſtreet, ſix doors above Arch-ſtreet. [1777]. *Title, and pp.* 10-56. *half mor. 8vo.* (4s. 6d. 83)

AMERICAN INDEPENDENCE the Interest and Glory of Great Britain ; or, Arguments to prove, that not only in Taxation, but in Trade, Manufac-tures, and Government, the Colonies are entitled to an entire Independency on the British Legislature; and that it can only be by a formal Declaration of theſe Rights, and forming thereupon a friendly League with them, that the true and laſting Wel-fare of both Countries can be promoted. In a Series of Letters to the Legislature. To which are added copious Notes; containing Reflections on the Boston and Quebec Acts; and a full Juſti-fication of the People of Boſton, for deſtroying the Britiſh-taxed Tea ; ſubmitted to the Judgment, not of thoſe who have none but borrowed Party-opi-nions, but of the Candid and Honeſt. [By Major John Cartwright]. London: Printed for the Au-thor, by H. S. Woodfall. M. DCC. LXXIV. *xvi, iv and* 72 *pp. half mor. 8vo.* (7s. 6d. 84)

AMERICAN INDEPENDENCE the Interest and Glory of Great Britain; Containing Arguments which prove, that not only in Taxation, but in Trade, Manufactures, and Government, the Colonies are entitled to an entire Independency on the British Legislature; and that it can only be by a formal Declaration of theſe Rights, and forming thereupon a friendly League with them, that the true and laſting Welfare of both Countries can be promoted. In a Series of Letters to the Legislature. *Phila-delphia*, Robert Bell, MDCCLXXVI. *xxiv pp. prel. and Text, pp.* 25 *to* 127. *half mor. 8vo.* (7s. 6d. 85)

AMERICAN/ (THE)/ Military Pocket Atlas ;/ being an approved/ Collection of Correct Maps,/ both general and particular,/ of/ The British

Colonies,/ Eſpecially thoſe which now are, or probably may be,/ The Theatre of War;/ Taken principally from the actual Surveys and judicious Obſer-/vations of Engineers De Brahm and Romans ; Cook,/ Jackson, and Collet; Maj. Holland, and other Officers,/ employed in/ His Majesty's Fleet and Armies./ *London :/* Printed for R. Sawyer and J. Bennett, Map and Print-/Sellers, No. 53, Fleet-Street./ [1776] *Title, Dedication, pp. v-vi*; 'Advertisement,' *pp. vii-viii and* 'List of the Maps'. *in all 4 leaves.* 6 *large folding and coloured Maps.* 8vo. (10s. 6d. 86)

> The following is a list of the 6 maps :
> 1. North America.
> 2. The Weſt Indies.
> 3. The Northern Colonies.
> 4. The Middle Colonies.
> 5. The Southern Colonies.
> 6. Lake Champlain.

AMERICAN (The) Military Pocket Atlas ;/ being/ An approved Collection of Correct Maps,/ both general and particular,/ of/ the British Colonies;/ Eſpecially thoſe which now are, or probably may be/ The Theatre of War :/ Taken principally from the actual Surveys and judicious Obſer-/vations of Engineers De Brahm and Romans ; Cook,/ Jackson, and Collet; Maj. Holland, and other Officers,/ employed in/ His Majeſty's Fleets and Armies./ *London/* Printed for R. Sayer and J. Bennet, Map and Print-Sellers/ (No. 53) Fleet-Street./ [1776] *Title, Dedication, pp. v-vi*; 'Advertisement,' *pp. vii-viii, and* 'List of the Maps.' *in all 4 leaves,* 6 *large folding coloured Maps.* 8vo. (10s. 6d. 87)

> The Maps in this edition are the same as in the preceding.

AMERICAN QUERIST (The): Or, Some Questions Proposed relative to The Present Disputes between Great Britain, and her American Colonies. By a North-American. The Tenth Edition. *New-York*: Printed by James Rivington, 1774. ☞ This Pamphlet, on the 8th Day of September laſt, was, in full Conclave of the Sons of Liberty in New-York, committed to the Flames by the Hands of their Common Executioner ; as it contains ſome Queries they cannot, and others they will not anſwer ! *Half-title, title, and* 31 *pp.* 8vo. (10s. 6d. 88)

AMERICAN QUERIST (The): or some Ques-

tions proposed relative to the present Disputes between Great Britain and her American Colonies.
By a North-American. *Boston :* Re-printed by
Mills and Hicks, and Sold at their Printing-Office
in School-ftreet, 1774. *32 pp. half morocco.*
8vo.   (*7s. 6d.*   89)

AMERICAN QUERIST (The): or, Some
Questions Proposed relative to the present Dis-
putes between Great Britain, and her American
Colonies. By a North-American. Printed in
North-America, in 1774. *London :* T. Caddel,
M.DCC.LXXV. *Half-title, title, and text pp. 5-55.
half mor. 8vo.*   (*5s. 6d.*   90)

AMERICAN REVIEW (The) of History and
Politics, and General Repository of Literature and
State Papers. *Philadelphia,* Printed for Farrand
and Nicholas. 1811. *4 Volumes. I. 9 prel. leaves
and Text 408 pp.* 'Appendix.' *112 pp.* 'Statement.'
1 leaf. 'An Estimate.' *1 leaf.* 'Chronological,
Account' *1 leaf. II. Title and contents 2 leaves;
Text 358 pp.* 'Appendix.' *203 pp. III. 1812. Title
and contents 2 leaves; Text 159 pp.* 'Appendix,'
116 pp; 4 leaves; Text pp. 161-332; 'Appendix;'
*pp. 117-175. IV. Title and contents 2 leaves; Text
192 pp;* 'Appendix' *44 pp; 2 leaves; Text pp.
193-375;* 'Appendix' *pp. 45-103. Calf extra.*
8vo.   (*1l. 1s.*   91)

AMERICAN SONGSTER (The): being a select
collection of the most celebrated American, Englifh, Scotch and Irifh Songs. *New-York:* Printed
for Samuel Campbell, No. 44, Hanover-Square,
and Thomas Allen, No. 16, Queen-Street.
M,DCC,LXXXVIII. *xii & 204 pp. calf, 8vo.* (*1l. 1s.*   92)

AMERICAN TRAVELLER (The): or Observations on the Present State, Culture and Commerce of
the British Colonies in America, And the further
Improvements of which they are capable; with
An Acconnt of the Exports, Imports and Returns
of each Colony refpectively,—and of the Numbers
of Britifh Ships and Seamen, Merchants, Traders
and Manufacturers employed by all collectively :
Together with The Amount of the Revenue
arifing to Great-Britain therefrom. In a Series
of Letters, written originally to the Right Hon-

ourable the Earl of * * * * * * * * * * By an Old
and Experienced Trader.   *London:* E. and C.
Dilly, MDCCLXIX. *Frontispiece, Title, dedication,*
Advertisement, and Contents, 5 leaves. 'A Map of
North and South America' *etc.* 28 *by* 21 *inches.*
Text 122 *pp. half mor.* 4*to.*   (10*s.* 6*d.* 93)

AMERICAN'S GUIDE (THE): Comprising the
Declaration of Independence; The Articles of
Confederation; The Constitution of the United
States, and the Constitutions of the several States
composing the Union. viz. Maine, Massachusetts,
New Hampshire, Vermont, Rhode Island, Con-
necticut, New York, New Jersey, Pennsylvania,
Delaware, Maryland, Virginia, North Carolina,
South Carolina, Georgia, Kentucky, Tennessee,
Ohio, Indiana, Louisiana, Mississipi, Illinois,
Alabama, Missouri.   *Philadelphia:* Hogan and
Thompson. 380 *pp. calf.* 12*mo.*   (4*s.* 6*d.* 94)

AMERICANS againſt Liberty: Or an Essay on the
Nature and Principles of True Freedom, Shewing
that the Designs and Conduct of the Americans
tend only to Tyranny and Slavery.   *London:*
J. Mathews, M DCC LXXV.   64 *pp. half morocco,*
8*vo.*   (5*s.* 6*d.* 95)

AMERICANS ROUSED (THE), in a Cure for the
Spleen.   Or Amusement for a Winter's Evening;
Being the Subſtance of a Converſation on the
Times, over A Friendly Tankard and Pipe.   Be-
tween Sharp, A Country Parſon. Bumper, A
Country Juſtice. Fillpot, An Inn-keeper. Grave-
airs, A Deacon.   Trim, A Barber. Brim, A Qua-
ker. Puff, A late Repreſentative. Taken in Short-
Hand, by Sir Roger de Coverley.   New-England,
Printed; *New-York,* Re-printed, by James Riving-
ton. [1774] 32 *pp.* 8*vo.*   (15*s.* 96)

ÀMES (FISHER). Works of Fisher Ames. Compiled
by a number of his friends.   To which are prefixed,
Notices of his Life and Character.   *Boston:* 1809.
20 *prel. leaves. viz. half-title, portrait, title;* '*Pre-*
face.' '*Contents.*' *and* '*Notices.*' *Text,* 519 *pp. half-*
calf. 8*vo.*   (7*s.* 6*d.* 97)

AMHERST (JEFFREY.)   Autograph Letter to Sir
William Johnson, dated New York, 11th Dec.
1761, transmitting copies of papers from Govenor

Colden, with a request to take some effectual
method for recovering the unhappy Captives
amongst a Tribe of the Delaware Indians, *etc.*
One page. A fine Specimen. Folio. (10s. 6d. 98)

ANALYSE de la Carte Générale de l'Océan At-
lantique ou Occidental, Dreffée au Dépôt des
Cartes, Plans and Journaux de la Marine, et
Publiée par Ordre du Roi, Pour le fervice des
Vaiffeaux de Sa Majefté, Sous le Miniftère de M.
le Maréchal de Castries, Miniftre & Secrétaire d'
Etat ayant le départment de lar Marine & des
Colonies, en 1786. A *Paris*, de l'Imprimerie
Royale. M.DCCLXXXVI. *Title, and 42 pp. half mor.*
4to. (7s. 6d. 99)

ANATOMY (An) of Independency, or A Briefe
Commentary, and Moderate Difcourfe upon The
Apologeticall Narration of Mr. Thomas Goodwin,
and Mr. Philip Nye, &c. By Argument, laying
naked the dangers of their Pofitions, and From
Experience, difcovering their fpirits and wayes.
Publifhed by Authority. *London* Printed for
Robert Boftock, dwelling in Pauls Church-yard,
at the fign of the Kings head, 1644. *Title and*
preface 2 leaves; Text 52 pp. half morocco.
4to. (7s. 6d. 100)

ANBUREY (Thomas). Travels through the Interior Parts of America. In a Series of Letters.
By an Officer. *London :* William Lane, MDCC-
LXXXIX. *2 Volumes. I. Half-title, Title and 14*
other prel. leaves; Text 467 pp. II. Title, and Text
558 pp. Copper-plate map 16 by 14 inches and 7
plates with a lift thereof. Calf. 8vo. (16s. 6d. 101)

ANDERSON (James). The Interest of Great
Britain with regard to her American Colonies, con-
sidered. To which is added an Appendix, con-
taining the outlines of a plan for a General Paci-
fication. By James Anderson, M.A. Author of
Observations on the Means of Exciting a spirit of
National Industry, &c. *London:* T. Cadell.
M. DCC. LXXXII. *vii & 136 pp; Appendix, 36 pp.*
Half mor. 8vo. (6s. 6d. 102)

ANDERSON (Rufus). Memoir of Catharine
Brown, a Christian Indian of the Cherokee Nation.
By Rufus Anderson, A.M. Assistant Secretary of

the American Board of Commissioners for Foreign
Missions. *York*: W. Alexander and Son, 1827.
202 pp. With Frontispiece. Uncut. 12mo. (3s. 6d. 103)

ANDERSON (WILLIAM WEMYSS). A Description
and History of the Island of Jamaica, comprising
an Account of its Soil, Climate, and Productions,
shewing its Value and Importance as an Agricultural Country, and a desirable place of residence
for certain Classes of Settlers. Reprinted (it is
believed for the first time,) from the great Work,
" An Account of America, or the New World," by
John Ogilby, Esq., Master of the Revels in Ireland; first published in the year 1671, with preliminary chapter and notes, to connect the Work
with our own times ; By William Wemyss
Anderson, Esq., (With a Map of the Island.)
Jamaica and the other West India Islands are
destined to be the true and final homes of the civi-
lized Coloured Races. *Kingston,* Jamaica: George
Henderson, 1851. *46 pp. Errata 9 lines, on a slip.
Half mor. Map. 8vo.*   (4s. 6d. 104)

ANDRE (JOHN). The Cow Chace: an Heroick Poem,
in Three Cantos. Written at New York, 1780, By
the late Major André, With Explanatory Notes,
by the Editor. *London:* John Fielding, 1781. *32
pp. half mor. 4to.*   (15s. 105)

The following is the last stanza of this mock-heroic poem, to
which subsequent events gave a melancholy interest probably
little dreamed of by the writer.
            And now I've clos'd my epic ſtrain,
               I tremble as I ſhow it,
            Leſt this ſame warrior-drover, Wayne,
               Should ever catch the poet.

ANECDOTES Secrètes sur la Révolution du 18
Fructidor ; et Nouveaux Mémoires des Déportés
à la Guiane, écrits par eux-mêmes : contenant des
Lettres du Général Murinais, de Barthélemy, de
Tronçon du Coudray, de Laffond Ladebat, de De
La Rue, &c.—Relation des Evénemens qui suivi-
rent à la Guiane l'Evasion de Pichegru, Ramel,
&c.—Tableau des Prisons de Rochefort, par
Richer-Sérisy.—Narration de la Captivité et de
l'Evasion de Sir Sidney Smith de la Prison du
Temple.—Mémoire de Barbé Marbois, &c. &c.
Faisant suite au Journal du Général Ramel.
Seconde Edition, revué, corrigée et augmentée.
A *Paris*, Chez. Giguet et Co. Imprimeurs-Li-

braires; et se trouves a Londres, J. Wright, 1799.
Title and Table, 2 leaves; Text 215 *pp. half mo.*
8vo. (5s. 106)

ANGLERIUS. *See* MARTYR, Peter.

ANSON (GEORGE, *Lord*). An Authentic Journal
Of the late Expedition Under the Command of
Commodore Anson. Containing A Regular and
Exact Account of the whole Proceedings and feve-
ral Tranfactions thereof: Particularly at Madeira,
St. Catharine's, St. Julian's, St. Juan Fernandez;
their Manner of Living here upon Sea-Lions, Sea-
Dogs, &c. the taking of Payta; their cruizing on
the Coaft of Acapulco, Chequatan Bay, Tenian,
one of the Ladrone Iflands, and Macao; the tak-
ing of the rich Spanifh Galleon, called the Nueftro,
Signora de Cabodongo, from Acapulco bound to
Manila, commanded by Don Geronimo Montero,
a Portuguefe; their going to Canton in China, &c.
To which is added, A Narrative of the extraordinary Hardfhips fuffered by the Adventures in this
Voyage. By John Philips, Midfhipman of the Centurion. *London:* J. Robinson, 1744. *Title and
Preface, 2 leaves; Text, pp.* 5 to 516. *Half calf.
8vo.* (15s. 107)

ANSON (GEORGE, *Lord*). A voyage round the
world, in the Years M DCC XL, I, II, III, IV. By George
Anson, Esq; Commander in Chief of a Squadron
of His Majesty's Ships, sent upon an Expedition
to the South-Seas. Compiled from Papers and
other Materials of the Right Honourable George
Lord Anson, and published under his Direction.
By Richard Walter, M.A. Chaplain of His Majesty's Ship the Centurion, in that Expedition.
The Second Edition. With Charts of the Southern
Part of South America, of Part of the Pacific Ocean,
and of the Track of the Centurion round the World.
London: John and Paul Knapton, M DCC XLVIII. 12
prel. leaves & 548 *pp.* 3 *Charts, calf. 8vo.* (7s. 6d. 108)

ANSON (GEORGE, *Lord*). Voyage round the World,
In the Years MDCCXL, I, II, III, IV. By George Anson, Esq; *etc.* The Third Edition. *London:* John
and Paul Knapton, MDCCXLVIII. 12 *prel. leaves &*
548 *pp.* 3 *Charts, calf. 8vo.* (7s. 6d. 109)

ANSON (GEORGE, *Lord*). A Voyage round the

world, in the years M DCC XL, I, II, III, IV. By George
Anson, Esq; Now Lord Anson, *etc.* The Sixth
Edition. *London :* M DCC XLIX. 12 *prel. leaves,* 548
pp. 3 *charts, calf, 8vo.* (7s. 6d. 110)

ANSON (GEORGE, Lord). A Voyage round the
World, In the Year MDCCXL, I, II, III, IV. By George
Anson, Efq; Commander in Chief of a Squadron
of His Majefty's Ships, fent upon an Expedition to
the South - Seas. Compiled From Papers and other
Materials of the Right Honourable George Lord
Anson, and publifhed under his Direction. By
Richard Walter, M.A. Chaplain of his Majefty's
Ship the Centurion, in that Expedition. The Se-
venth Edition. Illuftrated with Charts, Views, &c.
Dublin : Printed for G. and A. Ewing, at the Angel
and Bible in Dame Street. MDCCXLVIII. 9 *prel.*
leaves & 350 pp. 8 copper-plate charts and plates, with a
list thereof. Calf. 8vo. (10s. 6d. 111)

ANSON (GEORGE, Lord). Des Herrn Admirals,
Lord Anfons Reife um die Welt, welche er als Ober-
befehlshaber über ein Gefchwader von Sr. Grofz-
britannifchen Majeftät Kriegsfchiffen, die zu einer
Unternehmung in die Südfee ausgefchickt worden,
in den Jahren 1740, 41, 42, 43, 44, verrichtet hat,
aus deffen Auffätzen und Urkunden zufammenge-
tragen und unter feiner eigenen Auffcht an das
Licht geftellet von M. Richard Waltern, Capellan
auf Sr. Majeftät Schiffe, dem Centurion in diefem
Kriegszuge, aus dem Englifchen in das Deutfche
überfetzt. Nebft vielen Kupfertafeln und Land-
karten. Mit Konigl. Pohlnifcher und Churfürftl.
Sächfifcher allergnädigfter Freyheit. *Leipzig* und
Göttingen, Verlegts Abraham Vanderhoeck. 1749.
xliv. prel. pp. Text 382 *pp.* ' Erklärung,' 'Register,' *and list of the* 34 *copper-plates and maps.* 14
leaves. Calf. 4*to.* (10s. 6d. 112)

ANSON (GEORGE, Lord). An Affecting Narrative
Of the Unfortunate Voyage and Catastrophe Of his
Majefty's Ship Wager, One of Commodore Anson's
Squadron in the South Sea Expedition. Contain-
ing A full Account of its being caft away on a de-
folate Ifland, and of the ftrange Proceedings of the
Officers and private Men, after that unhappy Event :
More efpecially, of thofe important Incidents, the
Shooting of Mr. Henry Cofins, and the imprifoning

of Capt. C — p for that Action. The Whole compiled from authentic Journals, and tranfmitted, by Letter, to a Merchant in London, from a Perfon who was an Eye-Witnefs of all the Affair : Exhibiting a compleat View of the Perils and terrible Difafters which the Crew underwent ; the wonderful Adventure of near an hundred of them, in their Boat, along the vaft fouthern Coaft of Patagonia, and thro' the Streights of Magellan, for above a thoufand Leagues, during which the greateft Part of them perifh'd by Cold and Famine ; the Arrival of thofe few that furviv'd in the miferableft Condition at Rio Grand ; their hofpitable Reception and Entertainment at that Place ; their Paffage from thence to Rio Janeiro, next to Lifbon, and finally to England. Intermix'd with feveral entertaining Paffages and Remarks. Printed for John Norwood, and fold by the Bookfellers of *London*, Briftol, and Liverpool, MDCCLI. *Title, and* 160 *pp. calf.* 8*vo.* (12*s.* 6*d.* 113)

ANSON (GEORGE, *Lord*). The History of Commodore Anson's Voyage round the World, at the Commencement of the late Spanish War. Performed in three Years and nine Months, viz. from September 1740 to June 1744. By a Midshipman on Board the Centurion. *London :* M. Cooper. MDCCLXVII. *Title & Contents,* 2 *leaves; Text,* 192 *pp. Copperplate portrait of Anson.* 8*vo.* (12*s.* 6*d.* 114)

ANSON (GEORGE, *Lord*). A voyage round the world, in the years MDCCXL, I, II, III, IV. By George Anson, Esq ; *etc.* The Fourteenth Edition. *London :* MDCCLXIX. 12 *prel. leaves,* 536 *pp.* 3 *charts, large paper, calf,* 8*vo.* (10*s.* 6*d.* 115)

ANSWER (THE) of the Assembly of Divines by Authority of Parliament Now fitting at Westminster. Unto the Reafons given in to this Assembly by the Diffenting Brethren, Of their not bringing in a Model of their Way. And fince Published in Print, under the Title of *A Copy of a Remonftrance.* Which Answer was humbly prefented to the Right Honorable the Houfe of Peers Affembled in Parliament. *London,* John Field for Ralph Smith, 1645. 2 *prel. leaves : Text pp.* 3 *to* 24. *Half mor.* 4*to.* (5*s.* 116)

ANSWER (THE) of The Friend in the Weſt, to a
Letter from A Gentleman in the Eaſt, entitled, The
preſent State of the Colony of Connecticut conſidered.   N.B. This Answer happened to fall into the
Hands of a Gentleman, who thought it beſt that
it ſhould be communicated to the Publick.   *New-
Haven :* Printed and Sold by James Parker, at the
Poſt-office, near the Hay-Market, 1755.   *Title and
pp. 3-18. half mor. 4to.*   (10s. 6d.   117)

ANSWER (AN) to a Pamphlet call'd, The Conduct
of the Ministry Impartially Examined. In which is
proved, That neither Imbecillity nor Ignorance in
the M——r have been the Causes of the preſent
unhappy Situation of this Nation. By the Author
of the Four Letters to the People of England.
London : M. Cooper. MDCCLVI.   100 *pp. half mor.
8vo.*   (4s. 6d.   118)

ANSWER to an Introduction to the Observations
made by the Judges of the Court of Common Pleas,
for the District of Quebec, upon the oral and written
testimony adduced upon the Investigation, into the
past administration of justice, ordered in consequence of an address of the legislative Council.
With Remarks on the laws and government of
the Province of Quebec. *London :* 1790. *Half-
title, title and* 107 *pp. half mor. 8vo.* (4s. 6d.   119)

ANSWER (AN) to the Declaration of the American
Congreſs. *London :* T. Cadell. MDCCLXXVI.   132
pp. half mor.   8vo.   (4s. 6d.   120)

ANSWER (AN) to the Declaration of the American
Congress. The Fourth Edition. *London :* T.Cadell.
MDCCLXXVI. 132 *pp. half mor. 8vo.* (4s. 6d.   121)

ANSWER (AN) to the Declaration of the American
Congress. The Fifth Edition. *London :* T.Cadell.
MDCCLXXVI. 132 *pp. half mor. 8vo.* (4s. 6d.   122)

ANSWER (AN) to the Reasons against an African
Company Humbly Submitted to the Conſideration
of the Patriots of Great-Britain, in this Preſent
Parleament Aſſembled. *London,* Printed in the
Year, 1711. 31 *pp. half mor. 8vo.* (4s. 6d.   123)

ANTEQUERA Y CASTRO (JOSEPH DE). Coleccion
General de Documentos, que contiene los sucesos
tocantes á la segunda época de las conmociones de

los Regulares de la Compañía en el Paraguay, y
señaladamente la persecucion, que hicieron a Don
Josef de Antequera y Castro. Vá añadido en esta
edicion el Informe de Don Mathias Angles y Gor-
tari. Tomo Tercero. *Madrid :* M. DCC. LXIX. *xiv
prel. pages ; Text*, 239, 374, 64 *pp. and 2 ſequent
leaves, vellum.* 4*to.* (15*s.* 124)

ANTICIPATION : Containing the Subſtance of His
M - - - - - - - - y's Moſt Gracious Speech to both
H - - - - - s of P - - - - l - - - - - t, on the Opening of the approaching Session, Together With a
full and authentic Account of the Debate which will
take place in the H - - - - e of C - - - - - - s, on
the Motion for the Address, and the Amendment.
With Notes. (First publiſhed three Days before the
Opening of the Seſſion.) The Third Edition, corrected [By Richard Tickell]. *London :* T. Becket,
1778. 4 *prel. leaves and text*, 74 *pp.* (5*s.* 6*d.* 125)

ANTICIPATION continued. Containing the subſtance of The Speech Intended to be delivered from
The T - - - - - - - - - e to both H - - - - - - s of
P - - r - - - m - - - t, On the Opening of the enſuing
Session. To which is added, A Sketch of the Debate which will take Place in the H — e of L — ds
on the Motion for an Address and Amendment.
London : Printed for the Editor ; MDCCLXXIX. 57
pp. 8*vo.* (4*s.* 6*d.* 126)

ANTICIPATION : (For the Year MDCCLXXIX.)
Containing the Subſtance of His M——y's Moſt
Gracious Speech to both H - - - - e of P - - - - l - -
- - - t, on the Opening of the approaching Session.
Together With a full and authentic Account of the
Debate which will take place in the H - - e of
C - - - s on the Motion for the Address, and the
Amendment. With Notes. (First publiſhed Five
Days before the Opening of the Seſſion.) The Se-
cond Edition. *London :* S. Bladon. MDCCLXXIX.
viii and 51 *pp.* 8*vo.* (4*s.* 6*d.* 127)

APIANUS (PETRUS). Cosmographia/ Petri Apiani,
per Gemmam Fri-/sivm apvd Lovanienses Medicvm
et Mathe/maticvm insignem, iam demvm ab omni-
bvs vindi-/cata mendis, ac nonnullis quoque locis
aucta, & annotationi-/bus marginalibus illuſtrata.
Additis eiuſdem argumen-/ti libellis ipſius Gemmæ

D

Frifij./ *Coloniae Agrippinae,*/ Apud Hæredes Arnoldi Birckmanni. cIↃ IↃ LXXIV. *2 prelim. and* 58 *folioed leaves, with revolving diagrams, and with woodcuts.* 4*to.* (10s. 6d. 128)

APOLLONIUS (LEVINIUS). Levini Apol-/lonii, Gandobrv-/gani, Mittelbvrgensis,/ de Peruuiæ, Regionis, inter Noui Orbis prouincias/ celeberrimæ, inuentione: & rebus in/ eadem geftis,/ Libri V./ Ad Iacobvm Clarovtivm Mal-/deghemmae ac Pitte-/miae Dominvm./ Breuis, exactáque Noui Orbis, & Peruuiæ/ regionis chorographia./ *Antverpiae,*/ Apud Ioannem Bellerum fub/ Aquila aurea./ M. D. LXVI./ *8 prelim. leaves; Text folioed 9 to 236, followed by index, errata, and colophon,* ' Antverpiae,/ Typis Amati Ta-/vernerii.'/ *8 leaves. Woodcut map. First Edition. Fine copy in morocco,* 8*vo.* (3l. 13s. 6d. 129)

APOLLONIUS (LEVINIUS). Another copy, 1567. *Map.* 8*vo.* (2l. 2s. 130)

<small>This copy is the same as the preceding, except that the date on the title-page is 1567 instead of 1566.</small>

APOLLONIUS (LEVINIUS). Another copy, 1567 *stained. Map wanting.* 8*vo.* (8s. 6d. 131)

APOLOGY (AN)/ for the/ Builder ;/ or a/ Discourse/ shewing the/ Caufe and Effects/ of the/ Increafe of Building./ *London,* Printed in the Year,/ MDCLXXXIX./ *Title, and 37 pp. half morocco.* 4*to.* (1l. 1s. 132)

<small>Among the several references to America in this quaint little book the following extract is not the least curious : " Now the reafon of this was, the People of England were a little before that time under the fame miftake, as they are generally now, and cried out againft the Builders, that the City would grow ǀtoo big ; and therefore in the 38 of Queen Elizabeth, they made a Law to prohibit Buildings in the City of London; which though it was but a probationary Act, to continue only to the next Seffions of Parliament (which was but a fhort time) yet its effects were long ; For it frighted the Builders, and obftructed the growth of the City ; and none built for thirty years after, all King James His Reign, without his Majefties Licenfe; But for want of Houfes the increafe of the People went into other parts of the world; For within this fpace of time were thofe great Plantations of New-England, Virginia, Mariland, and Burmudas began ; and that this want of Houfes was the occafion, is plain ; For they could not build in the Country, becaufe of the Law againft Cottages. For people may get children and fo increafe, that had not four Acres of ground to Build on." *Page* 28.</small>

APPEAL (AN) to the candour and justice of the people of England, in behalf of the West India Merchants and Planters, founded on plain facts and incontrovertible arguments. *London:* J. Debrett, 1792. *xvi, & 118 pp. half mor. 8vo.* (4*s.* 6*d.* 133)

APPEAL (An) to the Justice and Interests of the People of Great Britain, in the present disputes with America. By an old Member of Parliament. *London:* J. Almon. MDCCLXXIV. *Half-title, title and 63 pp. half mor. 8vo.* (5*s.* 6*d.* 134)

APPEAL (An) to the Justice and Interests of the People of Great Britain, in the present disputes with America. By an old Member of Parliament. The Fourth Edition, Corrected. London Printed: Reprinted at *Newcastle upon Tyne,* MDCCLXXVI. *72 pp. half mor. 8vo.* (5*s.* 6*d.* 135)

APPEAL (An) to the Public; stating and considering the Objections to the Quebec Bill. *London:* T. Payne, MDCCLXXIV. *58 pp. and 1 leaf of errata. half mor. 8vo.* (5*s.* 6*d.* 136)

APPEAL (An) to the Senfe of the People, on the Prefent Pofture of Affairs. Wherein the Nature of the late Treaties are inquired into, and the Conduct of the M---i---y with Regard to M--n--ca, A--r--ca, &c. is confidered; With Some Remarks upon the Light in which thefe, and other Publick Affairs have been lately reprefented. *London:* David Hookham, MDCCLVI. *Title and 54 pp. half mor. 8vo.* (7*s.* 6*d.* 137)

APPEAL (An) to the Unprejudiced, Concerning the prefent Discontents Occafioned by the late Convention with Spain. *London:* T. Cooper, 1739. *32 pp. half mor. 8vo.* (4*s.* 6*d.* 138)

APPENDIX (An) to the Memoirs of the Duke de Ripperda: containing Some Papers on the Balance of Europe; The Present State of Spain; and The Consequences of a War in the Weft Indies. *London:* John Stagg, and Daniel Browne, M.DCC.XL. *Title, and text pp.* 356-390. *8vo.* (2*s.* 6*d.* 139)

APPENDIX (An) to the Prefent State of the Nation. Containing a Reply to the Observations on that Pamphlet. *London:* J. Almon, MDCCLXIX. *Title, and text pp.* 5-68. *half mor. 8vo.* (4*s.* 6*d.* 140)

APPLETON (Jesse). Autograph Letter to Rev. Joseph Lothrop DD of West Springfield, dated at

Hampton, N.H. 11 April 1797, giving an Account
of his ordination on the 22d Feb. 1797: *etc. etc.*
3 pages. 4to.   (5*s.*   141)

Dr. Appleton was for twelve years the President of Bowdoin College, the author of very many printed Sermons, Addresses and
Lectures, and was one of the most distinguished of the Clergy
of New England. He was born in 1772 and died in 1819.

APPLETON (NATHANIEL).   Autograph Letter.
dated at Cambridge May 14, 1760. *one page.*
4to.   (5*s.*   142)

Dr. Nathaniel Appleton was for about 67 years the pastor of the
Church at Cambridge, Maſſachuſetts, where he died in 1784 at
the age of 91. He was a distinguished Theologian and a writer
of eminence.

APPLICATION (AN) of ſome General Political
Rules, to the present state of Great-Britain, Ireland
and America. In a letter to the Right Honourable
Earl Temple. *London:* J. Almon, 1766. *86pp. half
mor. 8vo.*   (4*s.* 6*d.* 143)

APTHORP (EAST). The Character and Example
of a Christian Woman. A Discourse at Christ-
Church, Cambridge, on the death of Mrs. Anne
Wheelwright. By East Apthorp, M.A. Mis-
sionary at Cambridge. *Boston:* Green and Russell.
M DCC LXIV. *32 pp. half mor. 4to.* (4*s.* 6*d.* 144)

ARANGO (JOSE DE). Nadie se asuste por la segunda y ultima esplicacion mia sobre la Independencia de la isla de Cuba. *Text pp.* 4-42, [1820]
half mor. 8vo.   (4*s.* 6*d.* 145)

ARCHDALE (JOHN). A New/ Description/ of that/
Fertile and Pleaſant Province/ of Carolina :/ With
a/ Brief Account/ of its/ Diſcovery, Settling,/ and
the/ Government/ Thereof to this Time./ With
ſeveral Remarkable Paſſages of Divine/ Providence
during my Time./ By John Archdale: Late/
Governour of the ſame/. *London:/* Printed for
John Wyat, at the Roſe in St. Paul's/ Church-Yard.
1707./ *Half-title, title,* To the Courteous Readers,
3 pp. Text *32 pages. Fine copy in half morocco.*
4to.   (2*l.* 12*s.* 6*d.* 146)

ARDAS. Doctrina Christiana ; Y/ explicacion de
ſus Miſterios, en nueſ-/tro idioma Español, y en
len-/gua Arda./ Consagranse, y Dedicanla a la/
Concepcion Puriſsima de Maria Santiſsima/ Señora
nueſtra los primeros Miſio-/neros de aquel Reyno./

Año 1658./ En *Madrid*, por Domingo Garcia Mor-
ràs./ *Title, with 19 lines on the reverse : Text 13
folioed leaves in double columns. Signatures A in 8,
B in 4 and C in 2 leaves. sm. 8vo.* (10*l*. 10*s*. 147)

The *Ardas* are a barbarous tribe of Indians dwelling between the
rivers Naſſo and Marañon in the Province of Quijos, in Quito
This, as far as I can learn, is not only the sole book published in
the Arda Language, but is the only copy known at present.

ARENAS (PEDRO DE). Vocabvlario/ Manual/ de
las Lengvas/ Caſtellana, y Mexicana./ En qve se
contienen las/ palabras, preguntas, y reſpueſtas
mas comunes,/ y ordinarias que ſe ſuelen ofrecer
en el/ trato, y comunicacion entre/ Eſpañoles, è
Indios./ Enmendado en eſta vltima impreſſion./
Compueſto por Pe-/dro de Arenas./ Impreſſo con
licencia, y Aprobacion./ En *Mexico*./ En la Imprenta de la Vivda de/ Bernardo Calderon. Año de
M.DC.LXXXIII./ *On the reverse of the title* ' ¶ Con
licencia' *etc.* ' Prologo,' 2 *pp*. ' Tabla,' 4 *pp. Text*
117 *pp*. ' Tabla' 3 *pp. Fine copy in red morocco by
Bedford. 12mo.* (7*l*. 7*s*. 148)

ARGENSOLA (BARTOLOMEO LEONARDO). Histoire/
de la/ Conquète/ des Isles/ Moluques/ par les Espagnols,/ par les Portugais,/ & par les Hollandois./
Traduite de l'Eſpagnol d'Argensola,/ et/ Enrichie
des Figures & Cartes Géographiques,/ pour l'intelligence de cet Ouvrage./ *A Amsterdam*,/ Chez
Jaques Desbordes./ M. D. CCVI. 3 *Volumes. Tome I.
7 prel. leaves, and 405 pp. Tome II. 2 prel. leaves and
402 pp. and Table, 15 unnumbered leaves. Tome III.
3 prel. leaves, 388 pp. and Table, 10 unnumbered
leaves. Maps and Plates in each volume, old calf.
12mo.* (15*s*. 149)

ARGUMENT (AN) in Defence of the Exclusive
Right claimed by the Colonies to tax themselves,
With a Review of the Laws of England relative to
Representation and Taxation. To which is added,
An Account of the Rise of the Colonies ; and the
Manner in which the rights of the ſubjeƈts within
the realm were communicated to thoſe that went to
America, with the exerciſe of thoſe rights from their
firſt ſettlement to the present time. *London :*
Printed for the Author, M DCC LXXIV. *Title, Con-
tents, pp. v-vii. and Text 163 pp. half morocco.
8vo.* (7*s*. 6*d*. 150)

ARMITAGE (John). The History of Brazil, from
the period of the Arrival of the Braganza family in
1808, to the Abdication of Don Pedro the first in
1831. Compiled from State Documents and other
Original Sources. Forming a continuation to
Southey's History of that Country. By John Armitage, Esq. In two Volumes. *London:* Smith,
Elder and Co., 1836. *Vol. I. 9 prel. leaves, viz. half-
title, portrait, title; dedication ; Preface ; Contents.
Text* 371. *pp. II. 5 prel. leaves, viz. half-title, portrait, title, Contents. Text* 141 *pp.* 'Notes,' *pp.* 144-
155. 'Appendix' *pp.* 157-297. *Cloth, uncut.*
8vo.   (7s. 6d.   151)

ARNOLD (Benedict, *Traitor*). Autograph Letter,
dated at Fort Edward, June 24th 1776, to Lt Col.
Gansevoort, commanding at Fort George, desiring
him to assist in getting forward certain goods for
the use of the Army. 1 *page. small* 4*to.* (1*l.* 1*s.* 152)

ARNOLD (Benedict, *Traitor*). Autograph Letter
to General Washington, dated at Head Quarters
Robinson House, Augt. 20th 1780 ; Sends by Express a copy of Col. Wills' Letter just received,
containing information of importance, *etc.*   One
page, Folio.   (1*l.* 11*s.* 6*d.*   153)

> With this Letter is an oval copperplate portrait of General Arnold
> engraved by B. Reading, drawn from the Life by Du Simetier
> in Philadelphia, Published May 10th 1783 by Wm Richardson
> No 174 Strand [London]. This letter was written only a month
> before he bolted.

ARROYO Y DAZA (Diego de). Relacion de/ las
Vitorias qve Don Diego Arroyo y Daza,/ Gouernador y Capitan General de la Prouincia de Cu-
ma-/nà, tuuo en la grã ſalina de Arraya a 30. de
Nouiembre del/ año paſſado de 622. y a treze de
Enero deſte año, contra/ ciento y quatro nauios de
Olandeſes./ [*Colophon*] Con licencia en *Madrid,*
por la viuda de Alonſo Martin./ [1623]. 4 *large
pages, closely printed, half mor. Folio.* (1*l.* 1*s.* 154)

ARTHUR (John). The Genealogy of Jesus Christ,
According to St. Matthew and St. Luke; Exa-
mined, Illustrate dand Vindicated. Wherein, The
Differences between the Accounts of the two Evan-
geliſts are explained, and the ſeeming Inconſiſten-
cies reconciled. By John Arthur, Gent. *New-
York:* Printed and Sold by James Parker, and
Company, at the New-Printing-Office, in Beaver-

ftreet. 1762. *Title, reverse blank, and text pp.* 3-16.
half mor. 8vo. (1*l.* 1*s.* 155)

ARTHUS (GOTARD). Historia/ Indiae/ Orientalis,/
ex variis Avctoriɀ/bvs collecta, et ivxta/ Seriem To-
pographicam Regno-/rum, Prouinciarum & Infula-
rum, per Africæ,/ Afiæque littora, ad extremos
vſque Ia-/ponios deducta,/ Qva Regionvm et In-
svlarvm/ ſitus & commoditas ; Regum & populorum mores &/ habitus; Religionum & fuperſtitio-
num abſurda varie-/tas ; Luſitanorum item Hiſpano-
rum & Batauorum res/ geſtæ atque Commercia varia, cum rebus admira-/tione & memoratu digniſsi-
mis alijs, iucun-/da breuitate percenſentur atq;/
deſcribuntur./ Avtore/ M. Gotardo Arthvs/ Dan-
tiſcano./ *Coloniae Agrippinae,*/ Svmptibvs VVil-
helmi/ Lutzenkirch./ Anno M. DC. VIII./ 10 *prelim.*
leaves (8th blank) and 616 *pp. Small* 8vo. (18*s.* 156)

ARTICLES Exhibited againſt Lord Archibald Hamilton, Late Governour of Jamaica. With Sundry
Depoſitions and Proofs relating to the ſame. *Lon-*
don, Printed in the Year M. DCC. XVII. *Half-title,*
title, pp. v to viii and 1 *to* 32. 8vo. (7*s.* 6*d.* 157)

ARTICLES of Agreement, for carrying on an Expedition, by Hudſon's Straights, for the Discovery of
a North-Weſt Paſſage to the Weſtern and Southern
Ocean of America. Dated March 30, 1745. *Dub-*
lin : Printed in the Year MDCCXLVI. 16 *pp. half*
mor. 8vo. (10*s.* 6*d.* 158)

ASH (ST. GEORGE, *Bishop of Clogher*). A Sermon
Preach'd before the Incorporated Society for the
Propagation of the Gospel in Foreign Parts; at
their Anniversary Meeting in the Pariſh-Church
of St. Mary-le-Bow; on Friday the 18th of February, 1714. By the Right Reverend Father in
God, St. George, Lord Biſhop of Clogher in Ireland. *London :* J. Dowing, 1715. *Title and pp.* 3-
62. *half mor.* 8vo. (3*s.* 6*d.* 159)

ASHER (ADOLPH). Bibliographical Essay on the
collection of Voyages and Travels, edited and published by Levinus Hulsius and his successors at Nuremberg and Francfort from anno 1598 to 1660. By
A. Asher. *London* and *Berlin.* A. Asher, 1839.
3 *prel. leaves and* 118 *pp. bds.* 4to. (1*l.* 1*s.* 160)

ASHLEY (JOHN). Memoirs and Considerations concerning the Trade and Revenues of the Britifh Colonies in America. With Proposals for rendering thofe Colonies more Beneficial to Great Britain. By John Ashley, Esq; *London:* C. Corbett, 1740. *vi & 154 pp. half mor. 8vo.* (7s. 6d. 161)

ASHLEY (JOHN). The Second Part of Memoirs and Considerations Concerning the Trade and Revenues of the Britifh Colonies in America; Tending to fhew How the Trade and Interest of thofe Colonies are interwoven with the Interest of Great Britain, and that the Traffick, Wealth and Strength of the whole Britifh Empire may thereby be greatly increafed. By John Ashley, Efq; Late Deputy-Surveyor and Auditor-General of all his Majefty's Revenues arifing in Barbados, and the Windward Caribbee Iflands in America, and a Member of his Majefty's Council in the faid Ifland of Barbados. *London:* H. Kent, MDCCXLIII. *6 prel. leaves and 127 pp. old calf, 8vo.* (10s. 6d. 162)

ASHTON'S (PHILIP) Memorial: Or, An Authentick Account of The Strange Adventures and Signal Deliverances of Mr. Philip Afhton; Who, After he had made his Efcape from the Pirates, liv'd alone on a defolate Ifland for about 16 months, &c. With a fhort Account of Mr. Nicholas Merritt, who was taken at the fame time. To which is added, A Sermon on Dan. iii. 17. By John Barnard, V. D. M. *London:* Printed for Richard Ford, and Samuel Chandler, both in the Poultry. 1726. *4 prel. leaves and 148 pp. old calf, 12mo.* (1l. 1s. 163)

Philip Afhton was a native of Marble Head in Massachusetts, and on the 15th of June, 1722, with Nicholas Merritt, his kinsman, was taken prisoner by the Pirate Low, at Port Rossaway, Cape Sable, and carried into the West Indies, Central America, &c. He returned after long wanderings and many hardships to New England, and landed at Salem on the first of May, 1725. Mr. Barnard, the Minister of Marble Head, preached a sermon upon the joyful occasion of his return to his native town. The book is full of incident, and little known to the Book collectors of New England.

ASPINWALL (THOMAS). Catalogue of Books relating to America, in the collection of Colonel Aspinwall, Consul of the United States of America at London. [*Paris* 1832?] *2 prel. leaves; and 66 pp. 8vo.* (7s. 6d. 164)

ASSIENTO, y Capitvla-/çion que por mandado de fu Mageftad fe/ ha tomado con diuerfas perfonas in-

teref-/ſadas en el comercio de las Indias, ſobre la/
cobrança, y adminiſtracion del derecho/ del aueria
por tres años, que comiençan/ a correr deſde principio deſte/ de 1618./ *30 leaves, wanting the last leaf.*
Half mor. Folio. (10s. 6d. 165)

ASSIENTO y/ Capitvlacion, qve/ los ſeñores Preſidente, y del Conſejo/ Real de las Indias tomaron cõ
Adriano de Legaſo, por/ ſi y en nombre del Prior y
Conſules de la Vniuerſidad/ de los cargadores a las
Indias de la ciudad de Seuilla, y/ demas perſonas
intereſſadas en el comercio dellas, ſo-/bre la cobrança
y adminiſtraciõ del derecho de la Aue-/ria, y deſpacho de las armada y flotas de las Indias, por/ tiempo de ſeis años, que començaràn acorrer deſ-/de
principio del venidero de 1628. y ſe/ cumpliràn en
fin del/ de 633./ En *Madrid*, Por luan Gonçalez./
Año de m. dc. xxvii./ *44 leaves, half morocco.*
Folio. (12s. 6d. 166)

ASSIENTO y/ Capitvlacion, qve/ los ſeñores Preſidente, y del Conſe-/jo Real de las Indias tomaron
con el Prior, y Conſu-/les, y Comercio de Seuilla,
ſobre la cobrança, y ad-/miniſtracion del derecho de
la Aueria, y deſpacho de/ las Armadas, y Flotas de
las Indias, por tiempo de/ tres años, que comiençan
a correr deſde prin-/cipio deſte de mil y ſeiſcientos,/
y quarenta./ En *Madrid*, Por Andres de Parra./
Año de m. dc. xxxx./ *Title and 50 leaves, half mor.*
Folio. (12s. 6d. 167)

ASSIENTO. [*Begins*] En/ el Nom=/bre de/ Dios,/
Amen./ Sepan/ qvan-/tos esta/ carta vierẽ/ como
nos Crhis-/toval de Barnvevo Boni-/faz, y lvan de
Vergara Gaviria,/ *etc.* [Asiento del Aueria de prior
y Consules año de 1618]. *27 leaves, half morocco.*
Folio. (12s. 6d. 168)

ASSIENTO CONTRACT (The) Consider'd as also,
The Advantages and Decay of the Trade of Jamaica and the Plantations. With the Causes and
Consequences thereof. In ſeveral Letters to a
Member of Parliament. *London,* Ferd. Burleigh.
1714. *Title; Preface, 4 leaves; & text, 50 pp. half*
mor. 8vo. (5s. 6d. 169)

ASSOCIATION, (The) &c. of the Delegates of the
Colonies, at the Grand Congress, held at Philadel-

phia, Sept. 1, 1774, Versified, and adapted to Music, calculated for Grave and Gay Dispositions; with a short Introduction. By Bob Jingle, Eſq; Poet Laureat to the Congress, Printed in the Year M,DCC,LXXIV. [*Philadelphia*]. *22 pp. half morocco, 8vo.* (12s. 6d. 170)

ATKINS (JOHN). A Voyage to Guinea, Braſil, and the Weſt-Indies; In His Majeſty's Ships, the Swallow and Weymouth. Deſcribing the ſeveral Iſlands and Settlements, viz. Madeira, the Canaries, Cape de Verd, Sierraleon, Seſthos, Cape Apollonia, Cabo Corſo, and others on the Guinea Coaſt; Barbadoes, Jamaica, &c. in the Weſt-Indies. The Colour, Diet, Languages, Habits, Manners, Customs, and Religions of the reſpeɛtive Natives and Inhabitants. With Remarks on the Gold, Ivory, and Slave-Trade; and on the Winds, Tides and Currents of the ſeveral Coaſts. By John Atkins, Surgeon in the Royal Navy. *London:* Cæsar Ward and Richard Chandler. M.DCC.XXXV. *Title, xxv pp. Text pp.* 1-2, *and* 19-254. '*An Abstract*' *etc. pp.* 255-265. '*Errata.*' *7 lines. Calf, 8vo.* (7s. 6d. 171)

ATKINSON (REV. W. CHRISTOPHER). A Historical and Statistical Account of New Brunswick, B.N.A. With Advice to Emigrants. By the Rev. W. Christopher Atkinson, A.M. Pastor of the Presbyterian Church, Mascreen, St. George's. Third Edition, greatly improved and corrected. Edinburgh: Printed by Anderson & Bryce. MDCCCXLIV. *8 prel. leaves; viz. title;* '*Contents*' *pp. iii-v.* '*Preface*' *pp. vii-xvi; and text pp.* 14-284, *with map.* 'Sketch of the River St. John.' *Calf, 12mo.* (3s. 6d. 172)

ATLAS GEOGRAPHUS: or, a compleat Syſtem of Geography, (Ancient and Modern) for America. Containing What is of moſt Use in Bleau, Varenius, Cellarius, Cluverius, Luyts, Baudrand, Sanſon, the Royal Commentaries of Peru, &c. With the Discoveries and Improvements of the beſt Spaniſh, Dutch, French and Engliſh Authors and Travellers, Ancient and Modern, to this Time; with about 30 new Maps, Cuts, Sanſon's Tables, &c. as may be ſeen in the Catalogues thereof annex'd to the Index. The Maps done by Herman Moll, Geographer, in which are all the lateſt Obſervations.

Europe is two Volumes, Asia the Third, Africa the
Fourth, and this the Fifth. Vol. V. To which is
added, A Catalogue of the Maps, Cuts, and San-
fon's Tables in all the five Volumes, and a Defcription
of Bofnia by Omiffion left out in Europe. In the
Savoy: Eliz. Nutt. MDCCXVII. *Title;* 'Preface,'
1 *leaf; text* 798 *pp.* 'Index,' *pp.* 799-807. ' An
Account of the Plates, Maps, and Tables,' 2 *leaves.*
Maps; Calf, 4to. (7s. 6d. 173)

ATWATER (CALEB). The Writings of Caleb Atwater. *Columbus.* Published by the Author. Printed by Scott and Wright. 1833. 408 *pp. Cloth.*
8vo. (5s. 174)

AUCHINCLOSS (J. *D.D.*). The Sophistry of both
the first and second part of Mr Paine's Age of
Reason; or a Rational Vindication of the Holy
Scriptures as a positive Revelation from God.
With The Causes of Deism. In Four Sermons.
By J. Auchincloss, D.D. Dissenting Minister,
Stockport. *Edinburgh:* Mudie and Son, 1796.
Title and Dedication 2 *leaves. Text, pp.* 5-96, *uncut.*
8vo. (3s. 6d. 175)

AUTEROCHE (CHAPPE D'). A Voyage to California, to observe the Transit of Venus. By Mons.
Chappe d'Auteroche. With an historical description of the Author's Route through Mexico, and
the Natural History of that Province. Also, a
Voyage to Newfoundland and Sallee, to make experiments on Mr. Le Roy's Time Keepers. By
Monsieur De Cassini. *London:* Edward and Charles
Dilly. MDCCLXXVIII. *Half-title, title,* 'Advertisement,' *and* 'Contents,' 4 *leaves. Text* 215 *pp. Plan
of the City of Mexico* 10 *by* 7½ *inches, Old calf.*
8vo. (8s. 6d. 176)

AUTHENTIC (AN) Journal of the Siege of the
Havana. By an Officer. To which is prefixed, A
Plan of the Siege of the Havana, Shewing the Landing, Encampments, Approaches, and Batteries of
the Englifh Army. With the Attacks and Stations
of the Fleet. *London:* T. Jefferys. MDCCLXII. *Half-
title, title* & *pages* 5-44; *Copper-plate Plan* 14½ *by* 8½
inches. 8vo. (10s. 6d. 177)

AUTHENTIC (AN) Narrative of Facts relating to
the Exchange of Prisoners taken at the Cedars; sup-

ported by the Testimonies and Depositions of His
Majesty's Officers, with Several Original Letters
and Papers. Together with Remarks upon the
Report and Resolves of the American Congress on
that Subject. *London:* T. Cadell, MDCCLXXVII.
Title and 50 *pp. half mor.* 8vo.　　(10s. 6d. 178)

AUTHENTIC Papers from America: Submitted to
the dispassionate consideration of the Public. *London:* T. Becket, 1775. *Title and 33 pp. half morocco,*
8vo.　　　　　　　　　　　　　　(7s. 6d. 179)

AVITY (SIEUR D'). Les/ Estats, Empires,/ et Prin-
cipavtez/ dv Monde,/ Representez par la/ Description des Paÿs,/ mœurs des habitans,/ Richesses des
Prouinces,/ les forces, le gouuernement/ la Religion,
et les Princes/ qui ont gouuerné/ chacun Estat./
Auec L'origine de toutes les/ Religions, et de tous
les/ Cheualiers et ordres/ Militaires./ Par le S^r.
D. T. V. Y. gentilhome/ ordᵉ. de la Chambre du
Roÿ./ A Paris. M.D.C.XIX. 10 *prel. leaves; Text* 1467
pp. followed by ' Privilege,' old calf, 4to. (15s. 180)
The History of the New World in this volume occupies 67 pages;
viz. from page 255 to 322.

AZARA (FELIX DE). Apuntamientos para la Historia Natural de los Quadrúpedos del Paragüay y
Rio de La Plata, escritos por Don Felix de Azara.
Tomo Primero. *Madrid:* MDCCCII. En la Imprenta
de la Viuda de Ibarra. Con Licencia. *Half-title.
Title, and 8 other prel. leaves: Text* 318 *pp.* ' Erratas.' 1 *page. Uncut,* 4to.　　　　　(6s. 181)

AZARA (FELIX DE). Voyages dans L'Amérique Méridionale, par Don Félix de Azara, Commissaire
et Commandant des Limites Espagnoles dans le Paraguay depuis 1781 jusqu'en 1801 ; Contenant la description géographique, politique et civile du Paraguay et de la rivière de La Plata ; l'histoire de la
découverte et de la conquête de ces contrées ; des
détails nombreux sur leur histoire naturelle, et sur
les peuples sauvages qui les habitent ; le récit des
moyens employés par les Jésuites pour assujétir et
civiliser les indigènes, etc. Publiés d'après les
Manuscrits de l'Auteur, avec une notice sur sa vie
et ses écrits, par C. A. Walckenaer; enriches de
notes par G. Cuvier, Secrétaire Perpétuel de la
Classe des Sciences Physiques de l'Institut, etc.
Suivis de l'histoire naturelle des Oiseaux du Para-

guay et de La Plata, par le même auteur, traduite,
d'après l'original espagnol, et augmentée d'un
grand nombre de notes, par M. Sonnini; accom=
pagnés d'un Atlas de vingt-cinq Planches.   Tome
Premier.   *Paris*, Dentu, Imprimeur-Libraire, Rue
du Pont-de-Lodi, n° 3. 1809. 4 *Volumes*. *I. Half-
title, Title & pp. v to lx prel. Text 389 pp. II. Half-
title, Title, and Text 362 pp. III. Half-title, Title,
and Avis, 3 leaves; & Text 479 pp. IV. Half-title,
Title, and Text 380 pp. 8vo.*   (1*l.* 1*s.* 182)

BACKUS (Isaac). A/ Fish caught in his own Net./ An/ Examination/ of Nine Sermons, from Matt. 16. 18./ Published last Year, by Mr. Joseph Fish of Stonington ;/ Wherein/ He labours to prove, that those called Standing Churches/ in New-England are built upon the Rock, and upon/ the same Principles with the first Fathers of this/ Country: And that Separates and Baptists are joining/ with the Gates of Hell against them./ In Answer to which ;/ Many of his Mistakes are corrected; The Constitution/ of those Churches opened; the Testimonies of Prophets/ and Apostles, and also of many of those Fathers are/ produced, which as plainly condemn his plan, as any/ Separate or Baptist can do./ By Isaac Backus./ Pastor of a Church of Christ in Middleborough./ *Boston*: Printed by Edes and Gill, in/ Queen-Street, MDCCLXVIII./ 130 *pp.* 'Errata.' 1 *page.* 8*vo.* (7*s.* 6*d.* 183)

BACKUS (Isaac.) A History of New-England, With particular Reference to the Denomination of Christians called Baptists. Containing The first principles and settlements of the Country; The rise and increase of the Baptist Churches therein; The intrusion of Arbitrary Power under the cloak of Religion; The Christian Testimonies of the Baptists and others against the same, with their Sufferings under it, from the Beginning to the present Time. Collected from most authentic Records and Writings, both Ancient and Modern. By Isaac Backus, Pastor of the first Baptist Church in Midleborough. Vol. I. *Boston:* Printed by Edward Draper, at his Printing-Office in Newbury-Street, and sold by Phillip Freeman, in Union-Street. 1777.

Title & Preface, 4 leaves ; Text 544 pp. 'Appendix'
15 pp. Errata 1 p. half calf, 8vo. (15s. 184)

BACKUS (ISAAC). Policy, as well as Honesty, for-
bids the use of Secular Force in Religious Affairs.
Massachusetts-State. *Boston :* Printed by Draper
and Folsom, and Sold by Phillip Freeman, in
Union-Street. M,DCC,LXXIX. *26 pp. Index to 'our*
Baptist History,' *2 leaves.* (15s. 185)

At the end of this tract is the Index to the Author's History of
New-England, under the following heading, " Not having time
and Room therefor, when our Baptiſt Hiſtory was finiſhed, a
brief Index to it is inſerted here."

BACON (THOMAS). Two Sermons, preached to a
Congregation of Black Slaves, at the Parish Church
of S. P. in the Province of Maryland. By an American Pastor [Thomas Bacon]. *London :* John
Oliver, M. DCC.XLIX. *79 pp. half morocco.*
12mo. (4s. 6d. 186)

BACON (THOMAS). Four Sermons, upon the Great
and Indiſpenſible Duty of all Christian Masters
and Mistresses to bring up their Negro Slaves in the
Knowledge and Fear of God. Preached at the
Pariſh Church of St. Peter in Talbot County, in the
Province of Maryland. By the Rev. Thomas Ba-
con, Rector of the ſaid Pariſh. *London :* J. Oliver.
M. DCC. L. *142 pp. half mor. 12mo.* (7s. 6d. 187)

BAILEY (JOHN). Man's chief End/ To Glorifie
God,/or/ Some Brief/ Sermon-Notes/ On 1 Cor.
10. 31./ By the Reverend Mr. John Bailey,/
Sometime Preacher and Priſoner of Chriſt/ at Li-
merick in Ireland,/ And now Paſtor to the Church
of Chriſt/ in Watertown in New=England. /*Boston,*
Printed by Samuel Green, and are/ to be Sold by
Richard Wilkins Book-/Seller near the Town-
Houſe./ Anno. 1689./ *4 prel. leaves ; viz. Title re-*
verse blank, 'To the Reader.' *6 pp. Signed* 'J. M.'
Text 160 pp. 'To my Loving and Dearly Beloved/
Chriſtian Friends, in and about/ Lymerick./ *40*
pp. dated 'May 8, 1684.' *signed* 'John Baily.'
'Poſtſcript.' *3 pp. signed* 'John Baily.' *Blue mo-*
rocco. Small 8vo. (2l. 2s. 188)

BAILLIE (HUGH). A Letter to Dr. Shebear : containing a Refutation of his Arguments concerning
the Boston and Quebec Acts of Parliament : and his
Aspersions upon the Memory of King William,

and the Protestant Dissenters. By Hugh Baillie,
L.L.D. Late Judge of the Court of Admiralty in
Ireland. *London:* J. Donaldson. MDCCLXXV.
Title and 54 pp. half mor. 8vo. (6s. 6d. 189)

BAILY (FRANCIS). Journal of a Tour in Unsettled
Parts of North America in 1796 & 1797. By the
late Francis Baily, F.R.S., President of the Royal
Astronomical Society. With a Memoir of the Author. *London:* Baily Brothers, MDCCCLVI. *xii. and*
439 *pp. 8vo.* (7s. 6d. 190)

BAIN (WILLIAM). Memorial of Capt Wm Bain, of
the 67th Regiment of Foot, to Sir George Yonge,
dated Granada 15 Feb. 1791, praying to be per-
mitted to have the command of a company of In-
valids. *2 pages Folio.* (5s. 191)

The Memorialist served as Ensign and Lieutenant in the 71st Regiment from the beginning of the American Revolution to Dec.
1780. He was wounded before Charleston, and was present at
the siege of Savannah.

BAKER (DANIEL). Yet one/ Warning/ More, To
Thee O/ England, *etc. London,* Printed for Robert
Wilfon, 1660. *Title & 37 pp. 4to.* (5s. 192)

BAKER (JAMES). The Life of Sir Thomas Bernard,
Baronet. By the Rev. James Baker, His Nephew
and Executor. *London:* John Murray, 1819. *xiii*
pp. & Text 190 pp. With Portrait of Sir Thomas Ber-
nard. Morocco, extra gilt, 8vo. (10s. 6d. 193)

BALL (JOHN). An/ Answer/ to two/ Treatises/ Of
Mr. Iohn Can,/ the Leader of the Englifh Brown-
ifts in Amfterdam./ The former called,/ A Necef-
fitie of Separation from the Church of England,/
proved by the Nonconformifts Principles./ The
other,/ A Stay againft Straying: Wherein in oppofition to/ M. Iohn Robinfon, he undertakes to prove
the unlaw-/fulneffe of hearing the Minifters of the/
Church of England./ Very feafonable for the prefent times./ By the late learned, laborious and
faithfull fervant of Jefus Chrift,/ John Ball./ *Lon-*
don,/ Printed by R. B. and are to be fold by John
Burroughes, at his Shop at/ the figne of the Golden
Dragon neere the Inner Temple gate,/ in Fleet-
street. 1642/. *Title, the reverse blank;* 'To/ the
Chriftian Reader;' *4 leaves;* 'An Advertisement to
the Reader.' *1 leaf, the reverse blank;* 'The Answers to the Epistles.' *4 leaves; Text,* 144 *pp.*

E

'Chap. II.' 92 *pp.* 'Table,' 2 *pp*; 'Errata,' 1 *page,*
4*to.*   (1*l.* 1*s.* 194)

BANCROFT (AARON). Life of George Washington, Commander in Chief of the American Army
through the Revolutionary War, and the First President of the United States. By Aaron Bancroft,
A. A. S. Pastor of a Congregational Church in
Worcester. *London,* John Stockdale, 1808. *Title;
Preface & Contents xii pp ; text* 560 *pp. Boards, uncut.*
8*vo.*   (6*s.* 6*d.* 195)

BANCROFT (AARON). Letters and Remarks, occasioned by a Sermon, delivered, by the Rev. Aaron
Bancroft, A.M. November 30, MDCCXCIV, in Opposition to the Doctrine of Election. *Worcester,*
L. Worcester. MDCCXCV. 30 *pp.* 8*vo.* (1*s.* 6*d.* 196)

BANCROFT (EDWARD). An Essay on the Natural
History of Guiana, In South America. Containing
A Defcription of many Curious Productions in the
Animal and Vegetable Systems of that Country.
Together with an Account of The Religion, Manners, and Customs of feveral Tribes of its Indian
Inhabitants. Interfperfed with A Variety of Literary and Medical Observations. In Several Letters
from A Gentleman of the Medical Faculty, During his Refidence in that Country. *London,* T.
Becket and P. A. De Hondt, MDCCLXIX. *Frontispiece, Title, Dedication, and Advertisement.* 5 *leaves;
text* 402 *pp.* 'Contents.' 1 *leaf.* 8*vo.* (7*s.* 6*d.* 197)

BARBADOES. Acts and Statutes/ Of the Ifland
of/ Barbados./ Made and Enaĉted fince the Re-
ducement of/ the fame, unto the Authority of the/
Common-wealth of England./ And/ Set forth the
feventh day of September, in the/ year of our Lord
God, 1652. By the Ho-/nourable Governour of the
faid Ifland,/ the Worfhipfull the Council, and/
Gentlemen of the Affembly./ Together with the
Charter of the faid Ifland,/ or Articles made on the
Surrender, and/ Rendition of the fame./ Publifhed
for the publick good./ *London,* Printed by Will.
Bentley, and are to be/ fould by him at the India
Bridge. [1654]. *Title; Dedication,* and *Table,* 8
leaves; Text, 176 *pp.* small 8*vo.*   (1*s.* 1*s.* 198)

BARBADOES. A Representation of the Miferable
State of Barbadoes, Under the Arbitary and Cor-

rupt Adminiſtration of his Excellency, Robert
Lowther, Eſq; the preſent Governor. Humbly
offer'd to the Conſideration of His Moſt Sacred
Majesty, and the Right Honourable the Lords of
His Majeſty's moſt Honourable Privy-Council.
With A Preface, containing Remarks on an Ad-
dress, printed in the Poſtman, and in the Whitehall
Evening-Poſt of May 14. 1719. *London:* Bernard
Lintot. [1719]. *Half-title, title, and 44 pp. half
mor. 8vo.* (10s. 6d. 199)

BARBADOES. A Detection of the State and Situation of the Preſent Sugar Planters, of Barbadoes
and the Leward Islands; With an Anſwer to this
Query, Why does not England, or her Sugar Iſlands, or both, make and ſettle more Sugar Colonies
in the Weſt-Indies? Written in the Month of December 1731, by an Inhabitant of one of His Majesty's Leward Caribbee Iſlands; and humbly
Dedicated to the Right Honourable Sir Robert
Walpole. *London:* J. Wilford, 1732. *Half-title,
title, viii & 99 pp. half mor. 8vo.* (7s. 6d. 200)

BARBADOES. A Supplement to the Detection of
the State and Situation of the Sugar Planters of
Barbadoes and the Leeward-Iſlands: Shewing,
among other New Matters, That the ſureſt Way for
England to command the Sugar-Market Abroad, is
to contraćt rather than inlarge her Sugar Colonies.
In a Letter from an Inhabitant of One of His Majesty's Leeward Caribbee Iſlands, to a Member of
the House of Commons in England. To which is
added, a Letter from a Traveller in the Caribbees
to his Friend in London. *London:* J. Wilford,
1733. *Half-title, title, and 84 pp. Half morocco,
8vo.* (7s. 6d. 201)

BARBADOES. Memoirs of the First Settlement
Of the Iſland of Barbados, and other the Carribbee
Iſlands, with the Succeſſion of the Governors and
Commanders in Chief of Barbados to the Year
1742. Extraćted from Ancient Records, Papers
and Accounts taken from Mr. William Arnold,
Mr. Samuel Bulkly, and Mr. John Summers, ſome
of the Firſt Settlers, the laſt of whom was alive in
1688, aged 82. Alſo ſome Remarks on the Laws
and Conſtitution of Barbados. *London:* E. Owen,

M.DCC.XLIII. *Title; the Publisher to the Reader, and
Introduction, 3 leaves; text* 84 *pp.* ' An Appendix.'
15 *pp. small 8vo.*   (10s. 6d. 202)

BARBADOES PACKET (THE); Containing Several Original Papers: giving an Account of the
Moſt Material Tranſactions that have lately happened in a certain Part of the Weſt-Indies. In a
Letter from a Gentleman of the ſaid Iſland to his
Friend in London. *London:* S. Popping. 1720. 6
prel. leaves and 68 *pp. 8vo.*   (7s. 6d. 203)

BARBE-MARBOIS (Mr). Histoire de Louisiane
et de la cession de cette Colonie par la France aux
Etats-Unis de l'Amérique Septentrionale: précédée
d'un discours sur la Constitution et le Gouvernement
des Etats-Unis. Par M. Barbé-Marbois, avec une
Carte relative a l'étendue des pays cédés. *Paris,*
Firmin Didot. 1829. 3 *prel. leaves and* 485 *pp. Map
at page* 109. *half calf. 8vo.*   (8s. 6d. 204)

BARCLAY (ROBERT). The Anarchy of the Ranters,
And other Libertines; the Hierarchy of the Ro-
manists, and other Pretended Churches, equally
refuſed and refuted, in a two-fold Apology for the
Church and People of God, called in Deriſion,
Quakers. Wherein They are vindicated from thoſe
that accuſe them of Diſorder and Confuſion on the
one Hand, and from ſuch as calumniate them with
Tyranny and Impoſition on the other; ſhewing,
that as the true and pure Principles of the Goſpel
are reſtored by their Teſtimony; ſo is alſo the antient Apoſtolick Order of the Church of Chriſt re-
eſtabliſhed among them, and ſettled upon its right
Baſis and Foundation. By Robert Barclay. *Philadelphia:* Re-printed, and Sold by B. Franklin,
and D. Hall, 1757. *viii and* 112 *pp: followed by:*
' An Epistle to the National Meeting of Friends,
in Dublin, Concerning good Order and Discipline
in the Church.' Written by Joseph Pike. *Philadelphia:* Re-printed, and Sold by B. Franklin, and
D. Hall, 1757. 23 *pp. Fine copy, original binding.*
8vo.   (1l. 11s. 6d. 205)

BARHAM (HENRY). Hortus Americanus: contain-
ing an account of the Trees, Shrubs, and other
Vegetable Produćtions, of South-America and the
Weſt-India Iſlands, and particularly of the Island

of Jamaica ; Interfperfed with many curious and
ufeful Observations, refpecting their Uses in Medicine, Diet, and Mechanics. By the late Dr. Henry
Barham. To which are added, a Linnæan Index,
&c. &c. &c. *Kingston*, Jamaica : Alexander Aikman, MDCCXCIV. *Title, Dedication, and* Preface, 4
leaves ; *Text* 212 *pp.* ' Linnæan Index,' 7 *leaves* ;
' Index of Diseases, Remedies,' &c. 11 *leaves* ;
8vo. (15*s.* 6*d.* 206)

BARING (ALEXANDER). An Inquiry into the
Causes and Consequences of the Orders in Council ; and an Examination of the Conduct of Great
Britain towards the Neutral Commerce of America. By Alexander Baring, Esq. M.P. *London :*
J. M. Richardson and J. Ridgeway. 1808. *iv and*
179 *pp.* 8*vo.* (2*s.* 6*d.* 207)

BARING (ALEXANDER). An Inquiry into the Causes
and Consequences of the Orders in Council ; and
an Examination of the Conduct of Great Britain
towards the Neutral Commerce of America. By
Alexander Baring, Esq. M.P. Second Edition.
London : J. M. Richardson, 1808. *Title, and Introduction,* 2 *leaves* ; *text,* 179 *pp.* 8*vo.* (2*s.* 6*d.* 208)

BARLÆUS (CASPAR). Brafilianifche/ Gefchichte,/
Bey Achtjähriger in felbigen Landen/ geführeter
Regierung/ Seiner Fürftlichen Gnaden/ Herrn/ Johann Moritz,/ Fürftens zu Naffau ꝛc./ Erftlich in
Laftein durch Casparem/ Barlæum befchrieben,/
Vnd jetzo in Teutfche Sprach vbergefetzt./ [Vig-
nette] Cum Grat. & Privil. Sac. Cæfar. Majeft./
Cleve, Gedruckt bey Tobias Silberling,/ Im Jahr
1659./ 15 *prel. leaves, viz. Engraved title, title, Portrait and Arms of Count Muriːz, Dedication in* 10
leaves, and 1 *blank leaf. Text* 848 *pp. with* 10 *leaves
of Register :* 8 *Maps and plates at pages* 111, 213,
352, 418, 422 (2) *and* 569 (2). 8*vo.* (1*l.* 1*s.* 209)

BARLÆUS (CASPAR). Casparis Barlæi,/ Rervm
per Octennivm/ in/ Brasilia/ Et alibi geftarum,/ Sub
Præfectura Illuftriffimi Comitis/ I. Mauritii/ Nas-
saviæ &c. Comitis,/ Historia./ Editio fecunda./
Cui accefferunt/ Gulielmi Pisonis Medici/ Amftelæ-
damensis/ Tractatvs/ 1. De Aeribus, aquis & locis
in Brafilia./ 2. De Arundine faccharifera. 3. De
Melle filveftri. 4. De Radice altili Mandihoca./

Cum Grat. & Privil. Sac. Cæfar. Majeſt./ *Clivis,* ex Officinâ Tobiæ Silberling./ M. DC. LX./ *8 prelim. leaves, including the engraved title, portrait, and arms; text 664 pp; index 11 leaves; maps or plates at pp. 1. 2. 58. 121. 242. 248 (2). 342. 8vo.* (18s. 210)

BARLOW (E.). An Exact Survey of the Tide. Ex-·plicating its Production and Propagation, Variety and Anomaly, in all Parts of the World; Eſpecially near the Coaſts of Great Britain and Ireland. With a Preliminary Treatise concerning the Origin of Springs, Generation of Rain, and Produ¢tion of Wind. The Second Edition, with Curious Maps. By E. Barlow, Gent. *London :* John Hooke, 1722. *8 prel. leaves ; text 122 pp. followed by a second title and 212 pp; 12 copperplate maps, 8vo.* (10s. 6d. 211)

BARLOW (JOEL). Letters from Paris, to the Citizens of the United States of America, on the System of Policy hitherto pursued by their Government relative to their Commercial Intercourse with England and France, &c. By Joel Barlow. *London*, James Ridgway, and A. Wilson. 1800. 116 *pp. 8vo.* (2s. 6d. 212)

BARLOW (JOEL). The Columbiad. a Poem. With the last corrections of the Author. By Joel Barlow. *Paris :* F. Schoell, 1813. *Title ; Preface, pp. v-xx.* ' Introduction,' *pp. xxi-ɹl. half-title ; Text 448 pp. 4 Plates. fine copy on Large Paper, calf. 8vo.* (12s. 6d. 213)

BARLOW (JOEL). Autograph Letter to Samuel Miles Hopkins Esq. of New-York, dated at Paris 2 Jan. 1801. *1 page, 4to.* (5s. 214)

BARNARD (HANNAH). A Narrative of the Proceedings in America, of the Society called Quakers, in the Case of Hannah Barnard. With a brief review of the previous Transactions in Great Britain and Ireland: intended as a Sequel to an Appeal to the Society of Friends. *London :* 1804. *xvi & 145 pp. Errata, 1 page, 8vo.* (2s. 6d. 215)

BARNUM (NATHAN). Autograph Memorial and Statement of the Services of Ensign Nathan Barnum, of the 2d Battalion of De Lancey's Brigade of Provincial Forces, addressed to Sir George

Yonge, Secretary at War, praying for promotion.
6 pages, Folio.   (10s. 6d. 216)

Ensign Barnum entered the King's service in General Lyman's and
Col. Wightman's Connecticut Regiments, and was engaged
through the Old French War from 1757 to the Peace of 1763.
In the Revolution he joined the Tories and was employed " in
confidential and dangerous services " by Governor Tryon. He
made dangerous excursions into the country and enlisted above
200 men for the King's service. He was afterwards captured,
put in irons, charged with treason against the State of Connecticut, but by means of his wounds, and by inoculating for the
small pox, he managed to put off the day of this trial, which he
apprehended would prove fatal, until he found an opportunity
to escape.

BARRERE (Pierre). Nouvelle Relation de la
France Equinoxiale, contenant La Defcription des
Côtes de la Guiane; de l'Isle de Cayenne; le
Commerce de cette Colonie; les divers changemens
arrivés dans ce Pays; & les Mœurs & Coûtumes
des différens Peuples Sauvages qui l'habitent.
Avec Des Figures deffinées fur les lieux. Par
Pierre Barrere, Correfpondant de l'Académie
Royale des Sciences de Paris, Doƈteur & Profeffeur
en Médecine dans l'Univerfité de Perpignan;
Médecin de l' Hôpital Militaire de la même Ville,
ci-devant Médecin-Botanifte du Roi dans l'Isle de
Cayenne. *Paris,* Piget, m.dcc.xliii. *Half-title,
title, & Advertisement, 4 leaves; Text 240 pp.*
'Table' *pp.* 241-250. ' L'Approbation,' *1 leaf. 19
small Maps & Plates, calf, small 8vo.* (7s. 6d. 217)

BARRETO (Nicolas). Contestacion al Manifiesto
que ha dado el Escmo. Sr. D. Francisco de Arango
sobre la Junta proyectada en la Habana en Julio
del·año de 1808. *Habana:* 1821. *31 pp. and one
leaf of erratas, half mor. 8vo.*   (3s. 6d. 218)

BARRETO (El Conde de Casa). Contestacion
que dá el Conde de Casa Barreto, al papel del
Escmo. Señor D. Francisco de Arango; contray-
endose en parte a los publicados por el Señor D.
Jose del mismo appellido. *Habana:* 1821. *18
pp. half mor. 8vo.*   (3s. 6d. 219)

BARRINGTON (Daines). Miscellanies by the Honourable Daines Barrington. *London,* J. Nichols.
mdcclxxxi. *Title;* ' Contents,' *pp. iii, iv;* ' Possibility of Approaching the North Pole,' *etc.* 1 *leaf;*
' Preface,' *pp. iii-viii. and text 558 pp. 2 Portraits
& Maps, with the rare portrait of Sir Watkin Williams
Wynn inserted. 4to.*   (15s. 220)

BARRINGTON (DAINES). The Possibility of
Approaching the North Pole asserted by The Hon.
D. Barrington. A New Edition. With an Appendix, containing papers on the same subject, and
on a North West Passage. By Colonel Beaufoy,
F.R.S. Illustrated with a Map of the North Pole,
according to the latest discoveries. *London,* T.
and J. Allman, 1818. *xxiv pp. and 258 pp. Map,
boards, 8vo.* (6s. 6d. 221)

BARTOLOZZI (FRANCESCO). Ricerche Istorico-
Critiche circa alle scoperte d'Amerigo Vespucci
con l'Aggiunta di una Relazione del Medesimo
Fiu ora inedita compilate da Francesco Bartolozzi.
Firenze MDCCLXXXIX. Gætana Cambiagi. 180
pp. 'Indice' 181-182. *pp.* 'Errori Correzioni' 1
page. (10s. 6d. 222)

BARTRAM (JOHN). Observations on the Inhabitants, Climate, Soil, Rivers, Productions, Animals,
and other matters worthy of Notice. Made by Mr.
John Bartram, in his Travels from Pensilvania to
Onondago, Oswego and the Lake Ontario, in Canada. To which is annex'd, a curious Account of
the Cataracts at Niagara. By Mr. Peter Kalm,
A Swedish Gentleman who travelled there. *London :* J. Whiston and B. White, 1751. *Title,* 94
pp. and map, half mor. 8vo. (7s. 6d. 223)

BARTRAM (WILLIAM). Travels through North
and South Carolina, Georgia, East and West
Florida, the Cherokee Country, the Extensive
Territories of the Muscogulges or Creek Confederacy, and the Country of the Choctaws.
Containing an Account of the soil and natural productions of those Regions; together with observations on the manners of the Indians. Embellished with Copper-plates. By William Bartram.
Dublin : For J. Moore, W. Jones, R. M'Allister,
and J. Rice. 1793. *12 prel. leaves; viz. title,
contents, and introduction; Text 520 pp.* 'Index'
*11 pages; Directions to the Binder, 8 lines. With
Frontispiece Portrait of* 'Mico Chlucco,' *Map and
7 Plates. calf, 8vo.* (8s. 6d. 224)

BARTRAM (WILLIAM). Travels through North
and South Carolina, Georgia, East and West
Florida, the Cherokee Country, the Extensive

Territories of the Muscogulges or Creek Confederacy, and the Country of the Choctaws. Containing an Account of the Soil and Natural
Productions of those Regions ; together with
observations on the manners of the Indians. Embellished with Copper-plates. By William Bartram. The Second Edition in London. Philadelphia : printed by James and Johnson. 1791.
London : J. Johnson, 1794. *12 prel. leaves, viz.*
title, contents, and introduction. Text 520 pp. ' In-
dex.' 3 leaves ; ' Directions to the Binder.' 1 page.
With Frontispiece Portrait of 'Mico Chlucco,' *Map,*
and 7 Plates. calf, 8vo.   (8s. 6d.   225)

BATEMAN (Richard).   Autograph Memorial to
Sir George Yonge, Secretary at War, Dec. 21,
1790, asking for the rank of Captain, by Purchase or otherwise. *2 pages, Folio.*   (5s.   226)

The Memorialist went to America in 1776 as Ensign in the 20th
Regiment; served in the Campaign under Gen. Carlton, and in
1777 under Gen. Burgoyne, with whom he surrendered.

BATES (Joshua).   A Sermon delivered before the
Society for Propagating the Gospel among the
Indians and others in North America, at their
Anniversary, Nov. 4, 1813. By Joshua Bates,
A.M. Pastor of the First Church in Dedham.
Boston : 1813. 44 *pp.* 8vo.   (2s. 6d.   227)

BATTEL (Andries).   De gedenkwaardige Voyagie
van Andries Battel van Leigh in Eſſex, na Bra-
silien, *etc.* A°. 1589. Met ſchoone Kopere Platen.
Te *Leyden,* Pieter Vander Aa, 1706./   *Title, 46 pp.*
with Register, 5 pp. 3 maps, &c. at pp. 1, 23, & 37.
Half mor. 12mo.   (7s. 6d.   228)

BEACH (John).   A Calm and Diſpaſſionate Vin-
dication of the Professors of the Church of
England, against the abuſive Miſrepreſentations
and falacious Argumentations of Mr. Noah Hobart, in his late Address to them.   Humbly offered
to the Conſideration of the good People of New-
England, With a Preface by Dr. Johnson, and an
Appendix containing Mr. Wetmore's and Mr.
Caner's Vindication of their own Cauſe and
Characters from the Aſperſions of the ſame Author.
By John Beach, A.M. Miniſter of the firſt Church
of Christ in Reading.   *Boston :* Printed and Sold
by J. Draper in Newbury-ſtreet, 1749.   *Title,*

58   *Bibliotheca Americana.*

reverse blank; 'Preface,' *viii pp.*; *text* 75 *pp. half
calf. 4to.*   (10s. 6d.   229)

BEATTY (CHARLES). The Journal of a Two Months
    Tour; With a view of Promoting Religion among
    the Frontier Inhabitants of Pennsylvania, and of
    Introducing Christianity among the Indians to the
    Westward of the Alegh-geny Mountains.   To
    which are added, Remarks on the Language and
    Customs of fome particular Tribes among the In-
    dians, with a brief Account of the various Attempts
    that have been made to civilize and convert them,
    from the firft Settlement of New England to this
    Day; By Charles Beatty, A. M. *London:* William
    Davenhill, M DCC LXVIII. 110 *pp. half morocco,
    8vo.*   (7s. 6d.   230)

BELCHER (JONATHAN, *Governor of Maſsachusetts,
    New Jersey and New Hampshire*).   Autograph
    Letter to Mr. Secretary Waldron, dated at Boston,
    Oct. 19, 1741. *2 pages, 4to.*   (7s. 6d.   231)

BELCHER (JONATHAN, *Governor*). Autograph
    Letter to Godfrey Mallbone, Esq.   Newport,
    Rhode Island, dated at Milton, Dec. 6th, 1743,
    with another letter on the same sheet dated at
    Milton Jan. 16, 174¾. *3 pages, 4to.* (7s. 6d.   232)

BELCHER (JOSEPH). The Life of Faith, Exempli-
    fied and Recommended, in a Letter found in the
    Study of the Reverend Mr. Joseph Belcher, late
    of Dedham in New-England, fince his Deceafe.
    An Anfwer to this Question, How to live in this
    World, fo as to live in Heaven? To which is
    added, A few Verses by the late Reverend Mr.
    Killinghall, upon reading of it. *London:* J.
    Oswald. MDCCXLI. 8 *pp. 8vo.*   (4s. 6d.   233)

BELENA (EUSEBIO BENTURA).   Recopilacion
    sumaria de todos los Autos acordados de la Real
    Audencia y Sala del Crimen de esta Nueva Epaña,
    y providencias de su superior Gobierno; de varias
    Reales Cédulas y Ordenes que despues de publi-
    cada la Recopilacion de Indias han podido recogerse
    asi dè las dirigidas á la misma Audenica ó Go-
    bierno, como de algunas otras que por sus notables
    decisiones convendrá no ignorar: Por el Doctor
    Don Eusebio Bentura Beleña, del Consejo de S.
    M. Oydor de la misma Real Audencia, Consultor

del Santo Oficio de la Inquisicion, Juez Protector
de la Villa y Santuario de Nrà. Srà. de Guadalupe,
Asesor de la Renta de Correos, del Juzgado
General de Naturales, y del Real Tribunal del
Importante Cuerpo de Mineria. Tomo Primero.
Con Licencia: Impresa en *México* por Don Felipe
de Zúñiga y Ontiveros, calle del Espéritu Santo,
año de 1787. 2 vol. *Vellum. Folio.* (1*l.* 1*s.* 234)

BELKNAP (JEREMY). American Biography: or,
An Historical Account of those Persons who have
been distinguished in America, as Adventurers,
Statesmen, Philosophers, Divines, Warriors, and
other remarkable Characters. Comprehending a
Recital of the Events connected with their Lives
and Actions. By Jeremy Belknap, D.D. Published according to Act of Congress. *Boston*, Isaiah
Thomas, MDCCXCIV. *Two volumes. I.* 416 *pp; II.*
1798, 476 *pp. Tree calf extra by Robert Reviere,*
8*vo.* (1*l.* 11*s.* 6*d.* 235)

BELKNAP (JEREMY). Autograph Letter to
John Pickering Esq; dated Boston, April 26,
1793, pressing for an early decision of his suit
with Charles Clapham. 1 *page,* 4*to.* (5*s.* 236.)

BELKNAP (JEREMY.) Autograph Letter to Rev.
David McClure, dated at Boston, Dec. 26, 1796.
1 *page,* 4*to.* (5*s.* 237)

BELLAMY (JOSEPH). Letters and Dialogues be-
tween Theron, Paulinus, and Aspasio. Upon
the Nature of Love to God, Faith in Christ, and
Assurance of a Title to eternal Life. With some
Remarks on The Sentiments of the Rev. Messrs.
Hervey and Marshall, on these Subjects. Pub-
lished at the Request of many. By Joseph Bellamy,
A.M. of Bethlem in New England. *London:*
Edward Dilly, MDCCLXI. 240 *pp* 12*mo.* (3*s.* 6*d.* 238)

BELLAMY (JOSEPH). Autograph Letter to Rev.
Levi Hart, dated at Spingfield, Jan. 13, 1786.
1 *page,* 4*to.* (5*s.* 239)

BELLEISLE. An Impartial Narrative of the Reduction of Belleisle. Containing a Detail of the
Military Operations, and every interesting Anec-
dote, since the first landing of our Forces on the

Ifland, to the Surrender of the Citadel of Palais. In a Series of Letters, Written by an Officer, employed on the Expedition. *London: J. Burd.* 1761. *Half-title, title,* 48 *pp. half mor. 8vo.* (6s. 6d. 240)

BELNEAVIS (ARCHIBALD). Manuscript Statement of the Military Services of Lieut. Belneavis, asking promotion. *2 pages, Folio.* (5s. 241)

In 1776 the Memorialist enlisted for America and was in the principal engagements in the Southern Department: He served at the capture and subsequent defence of Savannah, and was at the capture of Charlestown. He afterwards served with Lord Cornwallis, and participated in his glorious termination of the War at York Town.

BELTRAMI (J. C.). A Pilgrimage in Europe and America, leading to the Discovery of the Sources of the Mississippi and Bloody River; with a description of the whole course of the former, and of the Ohio. By J. C. Beltrami, Esq. Formerly Judge of a Royal Court in the Ex-Kingdom of Italy. In two Volumes. *London :* Hunt and Clarke, 1828. *Volume* I. *lxxvi and* 472 *pp.* II. *Title and* 545 *pp.* ' Errata ;' 7 *lines with 4 sequent leaves. With Portrait,* 2 *Plans, Map, and three Plates. Boards, uncut,* 8vo. (10s. 6d. 242)

BENEZET (ANTHONY). A caution and warning to Great Britain and Her Colonies, in A Short Representation of the calamitous state of the enslaved Negroes in the British Dominions. Collected from various Authors, and submitted to the Serious Consideration of all, more efpecially of those in Power. By Ant. Benezet. *Philadelphia:* Henry Miller, M DCC LXVI. 35 *pp. and* ' Extract of a Sermon,' 4 *pp. half mor. 8vo.* (6s. 243)

BENEZET (ANTHONY). The Plainnefs and Innocent Simplicity of the Christian Religion. With its falutary Effects, compared to the corrupting Nature and dreadful Effects of War. With Some Account of the blefling which attends on a Spirit influenced by divine Love, producing Peace and Good-Will to Men. Collected by Anthony Benezet. *Philadelphia :* Printed by Joseph Crukshank, in Market-Street, between Second and Third-Streets. M DCC LXXXII. 48 *pp.* A Letter from Elizabeth Webb to A. W. Boehm, with his Answer, M,DCC,LXXXI. 44 *pp.* Short Observations on Slavery; 12 *pp.* Notes on the Slave Trade, &c. 8 *pp.* Re-

marks on the Nature and bad Effects of Spirituous
Liquors, 12 *pp.* Benezet's Short Account of the
people called Quakers. Second edition. 36 *pp.*
Serious Reflections, &c. 4 *pp. half mor. 8vo.* (6s. 244)

BENEZET (ANTOINE). Observations sur l'Origine,
les Principes, et L'Etablissement en Amerique,
De la Societé Connue fous la Denomination de
Quakers ou Trembleurs: Extraites de divers
Auteurs. Redigées, principalement, en faveur des
Etrangers. Par Antoine Benezet. Imprimé à
Philadelphie : Et r'imprimé à *Londres* per Jacques
Phillips, en George-Yard, Lombard-Street. MDCC
LXXXIII. *Title, and* 48 *pp. uncut,* 12*mo.* (5s. 245)

BENZONI (GIROLAMO). La Historia del/ Mondo
Nvovo/ di M. Girolamo Benzoni/ Milanese./ La
qval tratta dell' Isole,/ & Mari nuouamente
ritrouati, & delle nuoue/ Città da lui proprio
vedute, per acqua/ & per terra in quattordeci
anni./ Con Privilegio della Illuftrifsima Signoria/
di Venetia, Per anni XX. [*Colophon*] In *Venetia,*/
appresso Francesco Rampazetto./ M D LXV. *Title,
reverse blank ; dedication,* 2 *leaves ;* 'Tavola ;'
1 *leaf ; Text* 175 *folioed leaves ; Imperfect ; wanting
folios* 171-4. *First Edition.* 8*vo.* (2*l.* 2*s.* 246)

BENZONI (GIROLAMO). La Historia del/ Mondo
Nvovo/ di M. Girolamo Benzoni/ Milanese./ La
qval tratta delle/ Ifole, & mari nuouamente ritrouati, et delle/ nuoue Città da lui proprio vedute,/
per acqua, & per terra in/ quattordeci anni./ Nuouamente riftampata, et illuftrata con la giunta d'
alcune/ cofe notabile dell' Ifole di Canaria./ Con
Privilegio./ In *Venetia,* Ad inftantia di Pietro, &
Francefco/ Tini, fratelli. M.D.LXXII./ *Second Edition.*
4 *prel. leaves ; Text in* 179 *leaves, followed by a colophon leaf. Fine copy,* 8*vo.* (3*l.* 13*s.* 6*d.* 247)

BENZONI (GIROLAMO). Novae Novi/ Orbis His-
toriæ/ Jd est,/ Rerum ab Hifpanis in India Occidentali ha-/ctenus geftarum, & acerbo illorum/ in
eas gentes dominatu,/ Libri Tres, Vrbani Calve-
tonis/ opera induaftriàque ex Italicis Hieronymi
Benzo-/nis Mediolanenfis, qui eas terras XIIII.
anno-/rum peregrinatione obijt, commentarijs de-
fcripti,/ Latini facti, ac perpetuis notis, argumentis
et locu-/pleti memorabilium rerum accessione,

illuſtrati./ His ab eodem adiunẟta eſt,/ De Gallorum
in Floridam expeditione, & inſigni Hispanorum/
in eos ſæuitiæ exemplo, Breuis Hiſtoria./ Apvd
Evſtathivm Vignon./ M.D.LXXVIII./ *Title, reverse
blank;* ' Epistola.' 5 *leaves;* ' Præfatio,' 8 *leaves;*
' Epigrammata,' 1 *leaf;* ' Primi Libri Svmma.'
1 *leaf; Text* 480 *pp.* ' Index,' 6 *leaves; Errata,*
1 *page.* 8*vo.*   (1*l.* 1*s.* 248)

BENZONI (GIROLAMO). Novae Novi/ Orbis Historiæ,/ Jd eſt,/ Rerum ab Hiſpanis in India Occidentali ha-/ẟtenus geſtarum, & acerbo illorum/ in
eas gentes dominatu,/ Libri Tres,/ Vrbani Calve-
tonis/ opera induſtriáque ex Italicis Hieronymi/
Benzonis Mediolanêſis, qui eas terras XIIII./
annorum peregrinatione obijt, commentariis/ de-
ſcripti, Latini faẟti, ac perpetuis notis, ar-/gumentis
& locupleti memorabilium rerum/ acceſſione illuſtrati./ His ab eodem adiunẟta eſt,/ De Gallorum
in Floridam expeditione, & inſigni/ Hispanorum
in eos ſæuitiæ exemplo,/ breuis Hiſtoria./ Apud
Hæredes Euſtathij Vignon./ Anno M.DC./ *Title,
reverse blank;* ' Epistola.' 5 *leaves;* ' Præfatio,'
8 *leaves;* ' Epigrammata,' 1 *leaf;* 'Primi Libri
Svmma,' 1 *leaf; Text* 480 *pp.* ' Index,' 6 *leaves.
Fine Copy.* 8*vo.*   (1*l.* 1*s.* 249)

BENZONI (GIROLAMO). Histoire/ Novvelle/ dv
Novveav/ Monde,/ Contenant en ſomme ce que les
Heſpa-/ gnols ont fait iuſqu' à preſent aux Indes/
Occidentales, & le rude traitement/ qu'ils ſont à ces
poures peuples-la./ Extraite de l' Italien de M.
Hieroſme Benzoni Melanois, que ha/ voyagé XIIII.
ans en ces pays-la: & enrichie de/ pluſieurs Diſ-
cours & choſes digne de memoire./ Par M. Vrbain
Chavveton./ Enſemble,/ Vne petite Hiſtoire d' vn
Maſſacre commis par les He-/ ſpagnols ſur quelques
François en la Floride./ Auec vn Indice des choſes
les plus remarquables./ [*Geneve*] Par Evstace
Vignon./ M.D.LXXIX./ 12 *prelim. leaves; Text* 726
pp. Floride, 104 *pp; Indice* 7 *leaves.* 8*vo.* (1*l.* 1*s.* 250)

BENZONI (GIROLAMO). De Hiſtorie/ van de/ Nieuwe
werelt/ Te weten, de/ Beſchrijvinghe van Weſt-
Indien./ Waer in verhaelt wert, van de Eylanden
eñ Zeen/ nieuwlicx ghevonden, ende van den nieu-
wen/ Steden die hy daer zelfs ghezien heeft, ende/
'tghene daer is ghebeurt te water ende/ te lande, in

veertien jaren tijds/ die hy aldaer ghe=/ weeft is./
Door Ieronimus Benzonius van/ Milanen./ Wt
het Italiaens over-ghezet in Nederduyt/ door Karel
vander Mander Schilder./ Tot *Haerlem*, by Paf-
chier van Wef=/bus, Boecverkooper inden beflagen
Bybel./ Anno 1610./ 10 *prel. leaves (wanting the
fifth and sixth*), 404 *pp. boards. 8vo.* (18s. 251)

BENZONI. Der/ Newenn/ Weldt vnd In=/diani-
fchenKönigreichs, newe vnnd/ wahrhaffte'History,
etc. Bafel, Sebaftian Henricpetri. m. d. lxxix./ 4
prel. lvs. and ccxix pp. vellum, folio. (1l. 11s. 6d. 252)

BENZONI, MARTYR, APOLLONIUS. Der/
Newenn/ Weldt vnd In=/dianifchen Nidergängi-
fchenKönig=/reichs, Newe vnd Wahrhaffte Hiftory
etc. Auch Liebhabern der Hiftorien, aufz dem Latein in das/ Teutfch gebracht,/ Durch,/ Nicolaum
Höniger von Königshofen/ an der Tauber./ Getruckt
zu *Bafel.* Sebaftian Henricpetri. M. D. Lxxxij. 10
prel. leaves and text of Benzoni *ccxliij pp. followed by
the* ' Ander Theil,' *or* Peter Martyr, 12 *prelim. leaves
and text pp. ccxlv-dcij with the colophon leaf.* ' Dritte
Theil' *or* Apollonius, 6 *prel. leaves & text ccccvi. pp.
with a colophon leaf. Folio.* (2l. 12s. 6d. 253)

BERISTAIN DE SOUZA (José Mariano). Biblioteca Hispano-Americana Septentrional ó Catá-
logo y Noticia de los Literatos, que ó nacidos, ó edu-
cados, ó florecientes en la America Septentrional
Española, han dado a luz algun escrito, ó lo han
dexado preparado para la prensa. La escrebia, el
Doctor D. Jose Mariano Beristain de Souza, del
claustro de las Universidades de Valencia y Valladolid, Caballero de la Orden Española de Carlos III.
y Comendador de la Real Americana de Isabel la
Católica, y Dean de la Metropolitana de Mexico.
En *México:* Calle de Santo Domingo y Esquina de
Tacuba Año de 1816. 3 *volumes. Vol. I.* 14 *prel.
leaves and* 540 *pp. Vol. II. (in addition to the above
title)* Y la publica Don José Rafael Enriquez Tre-
spalacios Beristain, Sobrino del Autor. Officina de
D. Alexandro Valdés, 1819. 2 *prel. leaves and*
525 *pp. Vol. III.* 1821. 2 *prel. leaves, and* 365 *pp.*
3 *vols. bound in* 2, *in blue morocco by Bedford.
Large 4to.* (Priceless. 254)

This most valuable work is based upon the unfinished work of
Eguiara, one volume only of which, containing the letters A, B, C,

was published in Mexico, in 1755, under the title, *Bibliotheca
Mexicana.* This work, however, is greatly enlarged, and contains
the whole alphabet. It is alphabetically arranged under the names
of the authors, a biography of each author preceding the list of his
works both printed and manuscript. The author, Dr. Beristain
de Souza, was born in Puebla de los Angelos in Mexico, on the
22nd of May, 1756, and died at the age of sixty-eight, before the
first volume had passed through the press.

BERKEL (ADRIAN VAN). Adrian van Berkel's Befchreibung feiner Reifen nach Rio de Berbice und
Surinam. Aus dem Holländifchen überfetzt. *Mem-
mingen*, bey Andreas Seyler. 1789. 8 *prel. leaves,
and pp. 5 to 278, calf, 8vo.*   (3s. 6d. 255)

BERNARD (FRANCIS). Letters to the Ministry
from Governor Bernard, General Gage, and Commodore Hood. And also Memorials to the Lords
of the Treafury, from the Commiffioners of the
Cuftoms: With Sundry Letters and Papers annexed to the faid Memorials. *Boston :* Edes and
Gill. 1769. 108 *pp. half mor. 8 vo.*   (7s. 6d. 256)

BERNARD (Francis). Select Letters on the Trade
and Government of America; and the Principles
of Law and Polity, applied to the American Colonies. Written by Governor Bernard, at Boston,
In the Years 1763, 4, 5, 6, 7, and 8. Now firft publifhed : To which are added The Petition of the
Affembly of Maffachufet's Bay againft the Governor, his Anfwer thereto, and the Order of the
King in Council thereon. *London,* T. Payne.
MDCCLXXIV. *Title, vii, and* 130 *pp. Half mor.
8vo.*   (5s. 6d. 257)

BERNARD (FRANCIS). Select Letters on the Trade
and Government of America; and the Principles
of Law and Polity, applied to the American Colonies. Written by Governor Bernard, at Boston,
In the years 1763, 4, 5, 6, 7, and 8. Now firft
publifhed : To which are added The Petition of
the Affembly of Maffachufet's Bay againft the Governor, his Anfwer thereto, and the Order of the
King in Council thereon. The Second Edition.
London, T. Payne. 1774. *Half-title ; title, vii, &
130 pp. Half mor. 8vo.*   (5s. 6d. 258)

BEROA (JACOBUS DE). Litteræ Annvæ/ Provinciæ/
Paraqvariæ/ Societatis Iesv/ Ad admodùm R. P.
Mvtivm/ Vitellescvm ejufdem Socie-/tatis Prepo-
fitum Generalem/ Miffæ à R. P. Jacobo de Beroa

Para-/quariæ Præpofito Provinciæ./ Ex Hifpanico autographo Latinè/ redditæ à P. Francifco de Hamal/ Belgà Societatis ejufdem. / *Insvlis*/ Typis Tossani Le Clercq./ Anno M. DC. XLII./ *Title & 3 prel. leaves. Text 347 pp. followed by 1 page of Errata. Polished calf by Bedford, 8vo.* (1*l*. 1*s*. 259)

BERRIMAN (WILLIAM) A Sermon Preach'd before the Honourable Trustees for Eftablifhing the Colony of Georgia in America, and the Affociates of the late Reverend Dr. Bray; at their Anniversary Meeting, March 15, 1738-9. In the Parifh Church of St. Bridget, alias St. Bride, in Fleet-ftreet, London. By William Berriman, D.D. Rector of St. Andrew's Underfhaft, and Fellow of Eton College. Publifhed at the Defire of the Truftees and Affociates. *London.* John Carter, M.DCC.XXXIX. *24 pp. 4to.* (5*s*. 260.)

BERTONIO (LUDOVICO). Libro/ de la Vida y/ Milagros de Nvestro Señor/ Iefu Chrifto en dos Lenguas, Aymara, y Romance,/ traducido de el que recopilo el Licenciado Alon/ fo de Villegas, quitadas, y añadidas algunas/ cofas, y acomodado ala capacidad/ de los Indios./ Por el Padre Lvdovico Bertonio Ita-/liano dela Compañia de Iefus enla Prouincia de el Piru natural/ de Rocca Contrada dela Marca de Ancona./ Dedicado al Illvstrissimo y Reve-/rendifsimo Señor don Alonfo de Peralta primer Arço-/bifpo de los Charcas./ ¶ Impreffo enla Cafa de la Compañia de Iefus de Iuli Pueblo enla/ Prouincia de Chucuyto por Francifco del Canto. 1612./ Efta taffado efta libro a Real cada pliego en papel./ [*Colophon.*] Impreffo en el Pueblo de Iuli, de/ la Prouincia de Chucuyto, con la/ emprêta de Francifco del Canto./ Año M. DC. XII. *8 prel. leaves and 660 pp. with 3 (?) fequent leaves. Imperfect, wants 23 leaves, viz. all before page 9, (A 5,) also pp. 11 to 22, 29, 30, 659-60, and the sequent leaves. 4to.* (1*l*. 1*s*. 261)

BESOLDUS (CHRISTOPHORUS). Difcur-fus Politic-us/ de/ Incrementis/ Imperiorum, eorum-/que am-plitudine/ procurandà./ Cvi inserta est/ Differtatio fingularis, De No-/vo Orbe./ Auctore,/ Christophoro Besoldo, JCto./ *Argentorati,*/ Impenfis Hæredum Lazari Zetzneri./ Anno M DC XXIII. *65 pp. Half morocco. 4to.* (15*s*. 262)

BETAGH (WILLIAM). A Voyage round the World. Being an Account of a Remarkable Enterprize, begun In the Year 1719, chiefly to cruife on the Spaniards in the great South Ocean. Relating the True hiftorical Facts of that whole Affair: Teftifyd by many imployed therein; and confirmd by Authorities from the Owners. By William Betagh, Captain of Marines in that Expedition. *London:* T.Combes, J.Lacy, and J.Clarke, MDCCXXVIII. 8 *prel. leaves; viz. title, dedication, and contents; Text* 342 *pp.* ' Memorandum,' 2 *leaves. Map,* ' The World in Planisphere.' *8vo.* (7s. 6d. 263)

[BEVERLEY (ROBERT.)] The History and Prefent State of Virginia, In Four Parts. I. The History of the Firft Settlement of Virginia, and the Government thereof, to the prefent Time. II. The Natural Productions and Conveniences of the Country, fuited to Trade and Improvement. III. The Native Indians, their Religion, Laws, and Cuftoms, in War and Peace. IV. The prefent State of the Country, as to the Polity of the Government, and the Improvements of the Land. By a Native and Inhabitant of the Place. *London:* Printed for R. Parker, at the Vnicorn, under the Piazza's of the Royal-Exchange. MDCCV. 7 *prelim. leaves, including the frontifpiece, title, dedication, and preface; Table and errata,* 20 *pp; Text, Book* I, 104 *pp; Book* II, 40 *pp; Book* III, 64 *pp; and Book* IV, 83 *pp. followed by a folding fheet containing the* Census *of* 1703. *With* 14 *copper-plates reduced from De Bry's Part I. Calf,* 8vo. (1l. 1s. 264)

[BEVERLEY (ROBERT).] The History of Virginia, In Four Parts. I. The History of the Firft Settlement of Virginia, and the Government thereof, to the Year 1706. II. The natural Productions and Conveniences of the Country, fuited to Trade and Improvement. III. The Native Indians, their Religion, Laws, and Cuftoms, in War and Peace. IV. The Prefent State of the Country, as to the Polity of the Government, and the Improvements of the Land, the 10th of June 1720. By a Native and Inhabitant of the Place. The Second Edition revis'd and enlarg'd by the Author. *London:* Printed for B. and S. Tooke in Fleetftreet; F. Fayram and J. Clarke at the Royal-Exchange, and T.

Bickerton in Pater-Nofter Row, 1722. *Frontispiece, title and preface, 5 leaves; Text, 284 pp : Table, 12 leaves : 14 copper-plates. Calf, 8vo.* (*1l. 1s.* 265)

[BEVERLEY (ROBERT).] Histoire de la Virginie, contenant I. L'Hiftoire du premier Etabliffement dans la Virginie, & de fon Gouvernement jufques à préfent. II. Les productions naturelles & les commoditez du Païs, avant que es Anglois y negociaffent, & l'amélioraffent. III. La Religion, les Loix, & les Coutumes des Indiens Naturels, tant dans la Guerre, que dans la Paix. IV. L'Etat préfent du Païs, tant à l'égard de la Police, que de l'Amelioration du Païs. Par un Auteur natif & habitant du Païs. Traduite de l'Anglois. Enrichie de Figures. A *Amsterdam,* Chez Thomas Lombrail, M DCC VII. 4 *prel. leaves, including the engraved and printed titles; Text,* 433 *pp; Tables,* 8 *leaves;* 14 *copper plates, reduced from De Bry, at pages* 214, 229, 230, 232, 234, 238, 239, 244, 249, 270, 296, 304, *and* 315. *Calf.* (12s. 6d. 266)

BIBLE. Ne Raowenna Teyoninhokarawen Shakonadonire ne rondaddegenfhon ne rondadhawakfhon Rodinonghtsyoni Tsiniyoderighwagennoni ne Raorighwadogenghte ne ne Sanctus John. Address to the Six Nations ; recommending the Gospel of Saint-John. By Teyoninhokarawen, The Tranflator. —— London. *London :* Printed by Phillips & Fardon, George Yard, Lombard Street. 1805. 8 *prel. leaves; text* 125 *leaves; errata, &c.* 2 *pages. Calf extra by Bedford.* 12mo. (10s. 6d. 267)

BIBLE. The Gospel according to St. John. Translated into the Chippeway Tongue by John Jones, and Revised and corrected by Peter Jones, Indian Teachers. *London.* Printed for the British and Foreign Bible Society, Instituted MDCCCIV. 1831. Menwahjemoowin kahezhebeegaid owh St. John. Ahneshenahba anwaid keezhe ahnekahnootahbeung owh Thayendanegen, kiya owh Kahkewaquonaby, ahneshenahba kekenooahmahga-wenenewug. *London.* 1831. *Calf.* 12mo. (7s. 6d. 268)

BIBLIOTHECA AMERICANA ; or, a Chronological Catalogue of the most curious and interesting Books, Pamphlets, State Papers, &c. Upon the subject of North and South America, from the ear-

liest period to the present, in Print and Manuscript;
for which research has been made in the British
Museum, and the most celebrated Public and Private Libraries, Reviews, Catalogues, &c. With an
introductory discourse on the present state of Literature in those Countries. [By the Rev. Mr. Ho-
mer ?]   *London :* J. Debrett, MDCCLXXXIX. *2 prel.
leaves and* 271 *pp. Boards, uncut. 4to.*   (15s.   269)

BIBLIOTHEQUE Américaine ou Catalogue des
ouvrages relatifs a l'Amérique qui ont paru depuis
sa decouverte jusqu'a l'an 1700. Par. H. Ternaux.
Paris. M.DCCC.XXXVII. *viii. &* 191 *pp. Paper, uncut.*
8vo.   (12s. 6d.   270)

BIBLIOTHECA AMERICO-SEPTENTRIONA-
LIS : being a Choice Collection of Books in Various
Languages, Relating to the History, Climate, Geography, Produce, Population, Agriculture, Commerce, Arts, Sciences, etc. of North America, from
its first discovery to its present existing Government; among which are many valuable Articles
and rare together with all the important official
Documents published from time to time by the
Authority of Congress. [Paris]. 1820. 147 *pp.*
8vo.   (7s. 6d.   271)
<small>This is Mr. Warden's First Collection, now in the library of
Harvard College.</small>

BIBLIOTHECA AMERICANA, being a Choice
Collection of Books relating to North and South
America and the West Indies, including Voyages
to the Southern Hemisphere, Maps, Engravings
and Medals. *Paris,* 1831. *Half-title, title, and* 140
pp. Half calf, 8vo.   (7s. 6d.   272)
<small>This is the Catalogue of the Second Collection of the late Mr. War-
den of Paris.</small>

BIBLIOTHECA AMERICANA, being a Choice
Collection of Books relating to North and South
America and the West-Indies, including Voyages to
the Southern Hemisphere, Maps, Engravings and
Medals. *Paris,* 1840. *Half-title, title, and Index* 3
leaves ; text 124 *pp. 8vo.*   (7s. 6d.   273)
<small>Mr. Warden's Third Collection, now in the New York State Li-
brary at Albany.</small>

BIBLIOTHECA Inlustris. ac Praehonorabilis Domini Edvardi Vicecomitis de Kingsborough in Co-
mitatu Córcagiensi apud Hibernos. Catalogue of
the Rare and Valuable Library of the late Rt. Hon.

Edward Lord Viscount Kingsborough, comprising
His Collection of Printed Books and Manuscripts
in various languages of Europe and Asia, Drawings of Mexican Antiquities, etc. And the Chinese
Books which formerly belonged to the Jesuits' College at Pekin : which will be sold by Auction, (By
order of the Administrator,) by Charles Sharpe,
at his Literary Sale Room, Anglesea-Street, On
Tuesday, 12th July, 1842, and following days,
commencing each Day at One o'clock. *Dublin :*
cɪɔ ɪɔ cccxlɪI. *Title, preface, and contents, 4 leaves ;
Text,* 110 *pp.* 8*vo.* (7*s.* 6*d.* 274)

BIBLIOTHECÆ AMERICANÆ PRIMORDIA.
An Attempt Towards laying the Foundation of an
American Library, In several Books, Papers and
Writings, Humbly given to the Society for Pro-
pagation of the Gospel in Foreign Parts, For the
Perpetual Use and Benefit of their Members, their
Missionaries, Friends, Correspondents, and Others
concern'd in the Good Design of Planting and Pro-
moting Christianity within Her Majesties Colonies
and Plantations in the West-Indies. By a Member
of the said Society [*Dr. White Kennett*] *London :*
J. Churchill, 1713. *Title ; Advertisement signed by
Robert Watts, and dated Nov.* 1, 1714, *2 leaves.
Dedication, signed by White Kennett, and dated
Octob.* 20, 1713, *xvi pp ; Text, pp.* 3—275. *Index*
C ccc *to* M mmmmm *in twos. Fine copy, uncut, and
in boards.* 4*to.* (2*l.* 2*s.* 275)

BILL (A) for repealing several Subsidies and an
Impost now Payable on Tobacco of the British
Plantations, and for granting an Inland Duty in
lieu thereof. *London :* W. Webb, mdccxxxiii. 39
pp. Half mor. 8*vo.* (4*s.* 6*d.* 276)

BINGLEY (William). An/ Epistle of Love/ and
Tender Advice,/ to/ Friends and Brethren/ in/
America,/ Or elsewhere ;/ To live in the Truth,
that they may shew/ forth the Virtue and Effects
of it in a/ Holy Life./ By your Friend and Brother
in the Truth, who Travels/ for Sion's Prosperity,/
William Bingley./ [*London*] Printed by Andrew
Sowle: And sold at the three-Keys in/ Nags-Head-
Court in Grace-Church-Street, 1689./ 14 *pp.*
4*to.* (12*s.* 6*d.* 277)

BIRBECK (Morris). Notes on a Journey in America, from the Coast of Virginia to the Territory of Illinois. With proposals for the establishment of a Colony of English. By Morris Birbeck, Author of notes on a Tour in France. *Philadelphia:* Caleb Richardson, 1817. *Title, and pp.* 3—181. 'Postscript,' *pp.* 183—189. 12*mo.*   (3*s.* 6*d.* 278)

BIRBECK (Morris). Notes on a Journey in America, from the Coast of Virginia to the Territory of Illinois. The Fourth Edition. *London:* 1818. 156 *pp. Map. Boards uncut,* 8*vo.*   (3*s.* 6*d.* 279)

BISHOPE (George). New England Judged,/ Not by Man's, but the Spirit of the Lord :/ And/ the Summe fealed up of New-England's/ Persecutions./ Being/ A Brief Relation of the Sufferings of the People called Quakers in/ thofe Parts of America, from the beginning of the Fifth/ Moneth 1656. (the time of their firft Arrival at Boston from/ England) to the later end of the Tenth Moneth, 1660./ Wherein/ The Cruel Whippings and Scourgings, Bonds and Imprifonments, Beat-/ings and Chainings, Starvings and Huntings, Fines and Confif-/cati-/on of Eftates, Burning in the Hand and Cutting of Ears, Orders of/ Sale for Bond-men, and Bond-women, Banifhment upon pain of/ Death, and Putting to Death of thofe People, are shortly touched ;/ With a Relation of the Manner, and Some of the Other moft Ma-/terial Proceedings ; and a Judgement thereupon./ In Anfwer/ to a Certain Printed Paper, Intituled, A Declaration/ of the General Court of the Maffachufets holden at Bofton, the/ 18. October, 1658. Apologizing for the fame./ By George Bishope./ *London,* Printed for Robert Wilfon, in Martins Le Grand, 1661./ 176 *pp.* (97 *to* 104 *erroneously numbered.*) *Fine copy.* 4*to.*   (3*l.* 3*s.* 280)

BISHOPE (George). An/ Appendex/ to the Book, Entituled,/ New England Judged :/ being/ Certain Writings, (never yet Printed)/ of thofe Perfons which were there/ Executed./ Together/ with a short Relation, of the Tryal,/ Sentence, and Execution,/ of William Leddra./ Written by. Them in the time of their Imprifonment, in the/ Bloody Town of Boston./ *London,*/ Printed for Robert Wilfon, at the fign of the Black-fpread-/Eagle and

Windmil, in Martins Le Grand,/ 1661./ *Title and pp.* 177 *to* 208 *(pp.* 199-208, *being erroneously numbered* 191-198). 4*to.*   (2*l.* 12*s.* 6*d.* 281)

BISHOPE (GEORGE). New England/ Judged./ The Second Part./ Being,/ A Relation of the cruel and bloody Sufferings of the People called/ Quakers, in the Jurifdiction chiefly of the Maſſa-/chuſets; Beginning with the Sufferings of William Ledra,/ whom they murthered, and hung upon a Tree at Boſton, the/ 14th of the firſt month, 166⁹. barely for being ſuch a one as/ is called a Quaker, and coming within their Jurifdiction;/ And ending with the Sufferings of Edward Wharton, the 3d/ month, 1665. And the remarkable Judgements of God/ in the Death of John Endicot Gouernour, John Norton,/ High Prieſt, and Humphrey Adderton, Major General./ By George Bishope./ *London,* Printed in the Year, 1667./ 147 *pp. Errata,* 9 *lines on a slip.* 4*to.*   (3*l.* 13*s.* 6*d.* 282)

BISHOPE (GEORGE). New-England Judged,/ by the/ Spirit of the Lord./ In Two Parts./ Firſt, Containing a Brief Relation of the Sufferings/ of the People call'd Quakers in New-England, from the/ Time of their firſt Arrival there, in the Year 1656, to/ the Year 1660. Wherein their Mercileſs Whippings,/ Chainings, Finings, Impriſonings, Starvings, Burning in/ the Hand, Cutting off Ears, and Putting to Death, with/ divers other Cruelties, inflicted upon the Bodies of In-/nocent Men and Women, only for Conſcience-ſake, are/ briefly deſcribed. In Answer to the Declaration of their/ Perſecutors Apologizing for the ſame, MDCLIX./ Second Part, Being a farther Relation of the Cruel and/ Bloody Sufferings of the People call'd Quakers in New-/England, Continued from anno 1660, to anno 1665. Be-/ginning with the Sufferings of William Leddra, whom/ they put to Death./ Formerly Publiſhed by George Biſhop, and now/ ſomewhat Abreviated./ With an Appendix,/ Containing the Writings of ſeveral of the Sufferers ; with/ ſome Notes, ſhewing the Accompliſhment of their Pro-/phecies ; and a Poſtſcript of the Judgments of God, that/ have befallen divers of their Perſecutors./ Also,/ An Anſwer to Cotton Mather's Abuſes of the ſaid People,/ in his late

History of New-England, Printed anno 1702./ The whole being at this time Publiſhed in the ſaid Peoples/ Vindication, as a Reply to all his Slanderous Calumnies./ *London,* Printed and Sold by T. Sowle, in White- / Hart-Court in Gracious Street, 1703. / *1st Title;* To the Unprejudiced Reader, *6 pp. signed by Joseph Grove; 2d Title,* ' New-England Judged/ Not by Man's, but the Spirit of the Lord :'/ *etc. Text,* 498 *pp. followed by Whiting's* ' Truth and Innocency Defended,' *212 pp. Index and Errata, 6 leaves. Fine copy, old calf, 8vo.* (1*l.* 5*s.* 283)

BISSELIUS (JOHANNES). Joannis Bisselii,/ è Societate Jesu,/ Argonauticon Ame-/ricanorum,/ sive,/ Historiæ Pericu-/lorum/ Petri de Vi-/ctoria, ac So-/ciorum eius,/ Libri xv./ *Monachii,*/ Formis Lucæ Straubii,/ Sumptibus Iohannis VVagneri./ Bibliopolæ./ Anno Christi M.DC.XLVII./ *13 pret. leaves, including the engraved frontispiece and map of America. Text,* 471 *pp; Auctorum, pp.* 472-477 *; followed by 3 pages and Index, 6 leaves. Fine copy in old red morocco. small 12mo.* (1*l.* 11*s.* 6*d.* 284)

BLAKE'S Remarks on Com. Johnstone's Account of his engagement with a French Squadron, under the command of Monſ. de Suffrein, on April 16, 1781, in Port Praya Road, in the Island of St. Jago. A new Edition. To this Edition is prefixed a Letter from Blake to the Commodore, and a Plan of the Harbour, &c. *London.* J. Debrett. M DCC LXXXII. *Title & 38 pp. with Plan of Praya Bay. Half morocco. 8vo.* (7*s.* 6*d.* 285)

BLAND (RICHARD). An Enquiry into the Rights of the British Colonies; intended as an Anſwer to " The Regulations lately made concerning the Colonies, and the Taxes impoſed upon them conſidered." In a letter addreſſed to the author of that Pamphlet. By Richard Bland, of Virginia. [*Colophon*] *Williamsburg,* Printed by Alexander Purdie, and Co. *London,* Re-printed for J. Almon, oppoſite Burlington-Houſe, Piccadilly. MDCCLXIX. *pp.* 5 *to* 19. *Half mor. 8vo.* (7*s.* 6*d.* 286)

BLIGH (WILLIAM). A Voyage to the South Sea, undertaken by command of his Majesty, for the purpose of conveying the Bread-Fruit Tree to the West

Indies, in his Majesty's Ship the Bounty, com-
manded by Lieutenant William Bligh. Including
an account of the Mutiny on board the said Ship,
and the subsequent Voyage of Part of the Crew,
in the Ship's Boat, From Tofoa, one of the Friendly
Islands, To Timor, a Dutch Settlement in the East
Indies. The whole Illustrated with Charts, &c.
Published by permission of the Lords Commis-
sioners of the Admiralty. *London :* George Nicol,
M.DCC.XCII. *5 prel. leaves ; viz. Title, Advertisement,
Contents, and a List of the 8 plates. Text 264 pp.
Large paper, boards, uncut, 4to.* (10s. 6d. 287)

BLOME (RICHARD). A/ Description/ of the Island
of/ Jamaica ;/ With the other Isles and Territories/
in America, to which the/ English are Related,
viz./ Barbadoes, St. Christophers, Nievis, or Mevis, Antego, St. Vincent. Dominica, Montferrat,
Anguilla. Barbada,/ Bermudes,/ Carolina,/ Virginia,/ Maryland,/ New-York,/ New-England,/
New-Found-/Land./ Published by Richard Blome./
Together/ With the Present State of/ Algiers./
London,/ Printed by J. B. for Dorman Newman,
at the/ Kings-Arms in the Poultrey. 1678./ *3 prel.
leaves and 88 pp. followed by separate title, and 17 pp.
and two leaves. Portrait of De Ruyter and four
maps, all engraved on copper. viz. America at p. 1 ;
Barbadoes at p. 28 ; Carolina at p. 56 ; and Virginia
at p. 63. 8vo.* (1l. 1s. 288)

BLOME (RICHARD). L'Amerique/ Angloise,/ ou/
Description/ des/ Isles et Terres/ du Roi d'Angleterre,/ dans/ L'Amerique./ Avec de nouvelles Cartes
de cha-/que Isle & Terres./ Traduit de l'Anglois./ A *Amsterdam,*/ Chez Abraham Wolfgang,/
prés la Bourse./ M.DC.LXXXVIII. *Title and Advertissement, 2 leaves ; text 331 pp. Table 1 page. 5 Maps.
12mo.* (10s. 6d. 289)

BLUNDEVILE (THOMAS). M. BLVNDEVILE/ His/
Exercises,/ Contayning eight Treatises, the Titles
where-/of are set downe in the next Printed Page :
which Treati-/ses are very necessary to be read
and learned of all yong Gentlemen/ that haue not
beene exercised in such Disciplines, and yet are/
desirous to haue knowledge as well in Cosmographie, Astrono-/mie, and Geographie, as also in

the Art of Navigation,/ in which Art, it is im-
poffible to profit/ without the helpe of thefe, or
fuch/ like Inftructions./ To the furtherance of
which Art of Navigation, the fayd/ Mafter Blvn-
devile fpecially wrote the faid Treatifes,/ and
of meere good will doth dedicate the fame to/ all
young Gentlemen of this/ Realme./ The fixth
Edition corrected and augmented./ *London,/*
Printed by William Stansby, and are to be fold by
Richard,/ Meighen, at his fhop vnder Saint Clements Church without/ Temple Barre. 1622./ 7 *prel.*
leaves and 799 *pages. Black letter. Fine copy, in old*
calf, 4*to.* (1*l.* 1*s.* 290)

This is a work indispensable to the student of Geography, map and
globe making, so far as they relate to America. There are folding sheets inserted at pp. 80, 690, 695, 785, and 798.

BOCANEGRA (Juan Perez). Ritval/ Formvla-
rio, e/ Institvcion de Cvras, para/ Administrar a
los Natvrales de/ efte Reyno, los fantos Sacramentos del Baptifmo, Con-/firmacion, Eucariftia, y
Viatico, Penitencia, Extre-/mavncion, y Matrimonio, con aduertencias/ muy neceffarias./ Por el
Bachiller Ivan Perez Bo-/canegra, Presbitero,
en la lengua Quechua general : examinador en/
ella, y en la Aymara, en efte Obifpado. Benefi-
ciado propieta-/rio del pueblo de fan Pedro de An-
tahuaylla/ la chica./ Al Insigne Señor Licenciado Fran-/cifco Calderon de Robles y Peñafiel, Arce-
diano de la Ca-/tedral de la Ciudad del Cuzco, Prouifor, y/ Vicario General del./ Con Licencia/
Impresso en *Lima :* por Geronymo/ de Contreras,
Iunto al Conuento de fanto Domingo/ Año de
1631./ 16 *prel. leaves ; Text* 720 *pp ; Table* 4 *leaves.*
Fine large copy. 4*to.* (8*l.* 8*s.* 291)
In the Spanish and Quechuan languages.

BONNET (Stede). The Tryals of Major Stede Bon-
net, and other Pirates, viz. Robert Tucker, Edward
Robinfon, Neal Paterfon, William Scot, Job Bay-
ley, John-William Smith, Thomas Carman, John
Thomas, William Morrifon, William Livers alias
Evis, Samuel Booth, William Hewet, John Levit,
William Eddy alias Nedy, Alexander Annand,
George Rofs, George Dunkin, John Ridge, Mat-
thew King, Daniel Perry, Henry Virgin, James
Robbins, James Mullet alias Millet, Thomas Price,
John Lopez, Zachariah Long, James Wilfon, John

Brierly, and Robert Boyd. Who were all condemn'd for Piracy. As also the Tryals of Thomas
Nichols, Rowland Sharp, Jonathan Clarke, and
Thomas Gerrat, for Piracy, who were Acquitted.
At the Admiralty Seffions held at Charles-Town, in
the Province of South Carolina, on Tuefday the
28th of October, 1718. and by feveral Adjournments continued to Wednefday the 12th of November, following. To which is Prefix'd, An Account
of the Taking of the said Major Bonnet, and the
reft of the Pirates. *London:* Printed for Benj.
Cowse, at the Rofe and Crown in St. Paul's Church-
Yard. M.DCC.XIX. *Title and 'Prefatory Account'*
vi pp. Text, 50 *pp. Map of Carolina, facing Title.*
Folio. (1*l.* 11*s.* 6*d.* 292)

BONNYCASTLE (Richard Henry). Spanish
America; or a Descriptive, Historical, and Geographical Account of the Dominions of Spain in the
Western Hemisphere, Continental and Insular;
illustrated by a Map of Spanish North America,
and the West-India Islands; a Map of Spanish
South America, and an Engraving, representing the
Comparative Altitudes of the Mountains in those
Regions. By R. H. Bonnycastle, Captain in the
Corps of Royal Engineers. In two Volumes. *Lon-*
don; Longman, 1818. *Volume* I. 32 *pp. prel. Text*
336 *pp.* II. *vi and* 359 *pp. With Maps of North*
and South America and Plate of the Altitudes of the
Mountains; boards. 8vo. (8*s.* 6*d.* 293)

BOOK (A) of the/ Continuation of Forreign Paf-
fages./ That is,/ Of the Peace made between this
Common-wealth,/ and that of the united Provinces
of the Netherlands,/ with all the Articles of that
Peace. Apr. 5. 1654./ And the/ Articles of Peace,
Friendfhip and Entercourse agreed/ between England and Sweden, in a Treaty at Vpsall./ May 9,
1544./ As alfo/ The fubftance of the Articles of the
Treaty of Peace/ betwixt England and France.
Given at White Hall/ the 20 of Novemb: 1655./
From Generall Blakes Fleet,/ The Turks in Argier
do confent to deliver up all the/ Englifh flaves, and
defire a firme Peace for ever :/ And in Tunnis Road
we battered their Caftle of/ Porta-ferina, and fet on
fire their fleet in the Har-/bour. April 9. 1655./
Moreover,/ An attempt on the Ifland of Jamaica,
and taking the Town of St. Jago de la viga,/ beating

the Enemy from their Forts and Ordnance, being a
body of 3000 men, and/ fo took poffeffion of the
Ifland, May 10. 1655.· With a full Defcription
thereof./ With a true Narrative of the late Succeffe which it hath pleafed God to give/ to fome part
of the Fleet of this Common-wealth, the Speaker,
the Bridg-/water, the Plimouth Frigots, againft the
King of Spains Weft India Fleet :/ the value of what
is taken and pofeffed by the calculation of the Spa-
niards/ about nine millions of pieces of eight, and
350 prifoners and all this with-/out che loffe of one
veffell of the Englifh, 1656./ *London :* Printed by
M. S. for Thomas Jenner at the South entrance of
the Royal Exchange. 1657./ *Title, and* 61 *pp. Illustrated with* 8 *copper-plate Engravings in the text.*
4to.   (2*l.* 2*s.*   294)

BORDONE (BENEDETTO). Isolario/ di Benedetto
Bordone/ Nel qual fi ragiona di tutte l' Ifole del
mon-/do, con li lor nomi antichi & moderni,/ hiftorie, fauole, & modi del loro vi/uere, & in qual
parte del ma/re ftanno, & in qual pa/rallelo & clima/
giaciono./ Con la gionta del Monte del Oro/ nouamente retrouato./ Con il Breve del Papa/ Et
gratia & priuelegio della Illuftriffi/ma Signoria di Venetia co-/me in quelli appare./ M D XXXIIII./
[*Colophon*] Impreffe in *Vinegia* per Nicolo d'Ari-
ftotile, detto Zoppino, nel mefe/ di Giugno, del.
M.D.XXXIIII./ 10 *prel. and* 74 *folioed leaves. Fine
copy. Vellum. Folio.*   (1*l.* 11*s.* 6*d.*   295)

BORLAND (JOHN LINDALL). Autograph Memorial and Letter to Sir George Yonge, Secretary at
War, praying that he may be allowed to purchase
any independent company that may yet remain to
be sold. 1 *page, folio.*   (5*s.*   296)

Lieut. Borland was a native of Boston, and on the breaking out
of the war joined the Tories and served in the Campaigns of
1775, 1776, 1777, 1778. By Purchase he obtained the rank of
Lieut.

BOSMAN (WILLIAM). A New and Accurate Description of the Coast of Guinea, Divided into the
Gold, the Slave, and the Ivory Coasts. Containing A Geographical, Political and Natural Hiftory
of the Kingdoms and Countries : With a Particular Account of the Rife, Progrefs and Prefent Condition of all the European Settlements upon that
Coaft ; and the Juft Measures for Improving the

feveral Branches of the Guinea Trade. Illuftrated
with several Cutts. Written Originally in Dutch
by William Bofman, Chief Factor for the Dutch
at the Caftle of St. George d'Elmina. And now
faithfully done into English. To which is prefix'd,
an Exact Map of the whole Coaft of Guinea, that
was not in the Original. *London:* J. Knapton,
1705. *4 prel. leaves and 493 pp. Copper-plate Map
and 7 Plates. 8vo.* (*7s. 6d.* 297)

BOSMAN (William). A New and Accurate Description of the Coaft of Guinea, *etc.* The Second
Edition. *London:* J. Knapton, MDCCXXI. *4 prel.
leaves and 456 pp. Index* 16 *pp. Map & 7 Plates
the same as in the first Edition. 8vo.* (*7s. 6d.* 298)

BOSSU (Mr). Travels through that part of North
America formerly called Louisiana. By Mr. Bossu, Captain in the French Marines. Translated
from the French, by John Reinhold Forster, F.A.S.
Illustrated with Notes relative chiefly to Natural
History. To which is added by the Translator a
Systematic Catalogue of all the known Plants of
English North-America, or, a Flora Americæ Septentrionalis. Together with An Abstract of the
most useful and necessary Articles contained in
Peter Loefling's Travels through Spain and Cumana in South America. Referred to the Pages
of the original Swedish Edition. Vol. I. *London:*
T. Davies, MDCCLXXI. *2 Volumes.* I. *4 prel. leaves;
viz. half-title, title, dedication, and preface; text,*
407 *pp.* II. *Half-title, title; and 432 pp. calf.
8vo.* (*7s. 6d.* 299)

BOSTON. An Appeal to the World; or a Vindication
of the Town of Boston, from Many falfe and mali-
cious Afperfions contain'd in certain Letters and
Memorials, written by Governor Bernard, General
Gage, Commodore Hood, the Commiffioners of
the American Board of Cuftoms, and others, and
by them refpectively tranfmitted to the Britifh
Miniftry. Published by order of the Town.
Printed and Sold by Edes and Gill, in Queen Street,
Boston, 1769. *37 pp. Half mor. 8vo.* (*10s. 6d.* 300)

BOSTON. A Short Narrative of the horrid Maffacre
in Boston, perpetrated in the Evening of the Fifth
Day of March, 1770. By Soldiers of the xxixth

Regiment; which with the xivth Regiment were then Quartered there: With some Observations on the state of things prior to that Catastrophe. Printed by Order of the Town of Boston, And Sold by Edes and Gill in Queen-Street, And T. & J. Fleet, in Cornhill, 1770. *38 pp. and* 'Appendix' *83 pp. (pages 79 and 80 being duplicated). Half mor. 8vo.*   (10s. 6d. 301)

BOSTON. A Short Narrative of the horrid Maffacre in Boston, perpetrated in the Evening of the Fifth Day of March, 1770. By Soldiers of the xxixth Regiment; which with the xivth Regiment were then Quartered there: With some Observations on the state of things prior to that Catastrophe. Printed by Order of the Town of *Boston*, and Sold by Edes and Gill, in Queen-Street, And T. & J. Fleet, in Cornhill, 1770. *48 pp. and* 'Appendix,' *88 pp. Half mor. 8vo.*   (12s. 6d. 302)

When a part of the copies of this Narrative had been sent to England, a restraint was laid upon the publishing of the remaining copies by a vote in Town Meeting, lest it might be thought to give an undue bias to the minds of the Jury. This delay of a few days gave the committee time to add a few more facts. Accordingly the first paragraph of page 37 was rewritten, and pages 39 to 48 added to the Narrative. The pagination of the Index was corrected, and pages 85 to 88 added at the end of the Appendix.

BOSTON. A Short Narrative of the Horrid Maffacre in Boston, perpetrated in the evening of the Fifth Day of March 1770. By Soldiers of the xxixth Regiment, and with the xivth Regiment were then quartered there: with some Observations on the State of Things prior to the Catastrophe. To which is added, an Appendix, containing The feveral Depofitions referred to in the preceding Narrative; and alfo other Depofitions relative to the Subject of it. Boston, printed, Reprinted for W. Bingley, *London*, MDCCLXX. *83 pp. With folding Plate, 8vo.*   (7s. 6d. 304)

BOSTON. Additional Observations to A Short Narrative of the Horrid Massacre in Boston, perpetrated in the Evening of the 5th of March 1770. Printed by Order of the Town of *Bofton*. M DCC LXX. *12 pp. Half mor. 8vo.*   (7s. 6d. 305)

BOSTON. A fair Account of the late Unhappy Disturbance at Boston in New England; extracted from the Depositions that have been made concerning it by Persons of all Parties. With an

Appendix, containing Some Affidavits and other Evidences relating to this Affair, not mentioned in the Narrative of it that has been publifhed at Boston. *London*, B. White. M DCC LXX. *Half-title; title; pp.* 5-28; ' Appendix' 31 *pp. Half mor.* 8*vo.* (*7s. 6d.* 306)

BOSTON. The Votes and Proceedings of the Free-holders and other Inhabitants of the Town of Boston, In Town Meeting affembled, According to Law. [Publifhed by Order of the Town.] To which is prefixed, as Introductory, An attefted Copy of a Vote of the Town at a preceeding Meeting. *Boston:* Printed by Edes and Gill, in Queen Street, And T. and J. Fleet, in Cornhill. [1773]. *iv & 43 pp. Half mor.* 8*vo.* (*10s. 6d.* 307)

BOSTON. The Votes and Proceedings of the Free-holders and other Inhabitants of the Town of Boston, in Town Meeting affembled, according to Law. [Publifhed by Order of the Town.] To which is prefixed, as Introductory, An attefted Copy of a Vote of the Town at a preceding Meeting. The whole containing a particular Enumeration of thofe Grievances that have given Rife to the prefent alarming Difcontents in America. Boston, Printed: *London*, reprinted; J. Wilkie. M DCC LXXIII. *Half-title ; title, viii. prel. & 43 pp. Half morocco.* 8*vo.* (*7s. 6d.* 308)

BOSTON. Plan of the Town of Boston with the Attack on Bunkers-Hill in the Peninsula of Charles-town, the 17th of June 1775. *London*, Printed for R. Sayer, & J. Bennett. No. 53 Fleet Street, as the Act directs. 2d Septr. 1775. *A copperplate plan coloured*, 12 *by* 5½ *inches.* (*7s. 6d.* 309)

BOSTON. Description/ of the/ Town and Harbour of Boston,/ Communicated to the Publifher, by a Gentleman from America./ [*at End*] Given (gratis) with M. Armstrong's Plan of the Country, Thirty Miles round Boston. *A broadside.* *Folio.* (*4s. 6d.* 310)

BOSWORTH (BENJAMIN). Signs of Apoftacy/ Lamented. [A Poem. *Signed*] Benjamin Bofworth,/ of New England./ In the 81ft Year of my Age, 1693./ 2 *leaves paged* 1-4. (*5s. 6d.* 311)

BOTELLO DE MORAES Y VASCONCELOS
(Francisco). El Nuevo Mundo./ Poemma heroyco/
de D. Francisco Botello/ de Moraes y Vasconcelos;/
con las Alegorias de Don Pedro de/ Caftro, Cavallero Andaluz./ Dedicalo sv Avtor/ a la/ Catholica
Magestad/ de/ Philippo Qvinto,/ Avgvsto, piadoso,
feliz Rey de las/ Eſpañas, y Indias./ Por mano
del Ilvstriſsimo Señor/ D. Manvel de Toledo/
General de Batalla en los exercitos/ de ſu Magestad,
&c./ Con licencia: *Barcelona,/* en la Imprenta de/
Ivan Pablo Marti, por/ Francisco Barnola Impreſſor, Año 1701./ Vendeſe en ſu miſma Caſa, en la
Plaça de San Iayme, y à ſu coſta. 16 *prel. leaves,*
and 476 *pp. Vellum,* 4*to.*　　　　(1*l.* 1*s.* 312)

BOTERO (Giovanni). Le/ Relationi/ Vniversali/
di Giovanni Botero/ Benese,/ Divise en Qvattro
Parti./ Nella Prima Parte ſi contiene la deſcrittione dell' Europa, dell' Aſia,/ e dell' Africa; & i
coſtumi, ricchezze, negotij, & induſtria di cia-/
ſcuna natione. Et ſi tratta del Continente del Mondo
Nuouo./ *etc.* In *Venetia*, Nicolò Polo. M.D.XCVII./
16 *prel. and* 240, *and* 80 *pp. with* 4 *maps. Second*
Part, 1598, 10 *prel. leaves and* 152 *pp. Third*
Part, 1597, 183 *pp. and* 9 *pp. of Table. Fourth*
Part, 1597, 8 *prel. leaves,* 79 *pp.* 4*to.* (12*s.* 313)

BOTURINI BENADUCI (Lorenzo). Idea de una
Nueva Historia General de la America Septentrional. Fundada sobre Material Copioso de Figuras,
Symbolos, Caractères, y Geroglificos, Cantares, y
Manuſcritos de Autores Indios, ultimamente deſ-
cubiertos. Dedicala al Rey N.ᵗʳᵒ Señor en su
Real, y Supremo Consejo de las Indias el Cavallero Lorenzo Boturini Benaduci, Señor de la Torre,
y de Hono. Con Licencia. En *Madrid:* En la
Imprenta de Juan de Zuñiga. Año M. D. CC. XLVI.
22 *prel. leaves, including the engraved frontispiece and*
portrait; Text 167 *pp. followed by* 4 *leaves and* 96
pp. Vellum. 4*to.*　　　　(1*l.* 11*s.* 6*d.* 314)

BOUDINOT (Elias). Autograph Letter to Samuel
Bayard Esq. Princeton, dated at Burlington, 12th
Jan. 1806, respecting the death of Mr. Bayard's
father, *etc.* 2 *pp.* 4*to.*　　　　(5*s.* 315)

BOUGAINVILLE (Louis de). The History of a
Voyage to the Malouine (or Falkland) Iſlands,

Made in 1763 and 1764, Under the Command of M. de Bougainville, in order to form a Settlement there; and of Two Voyages to the Streights of Magellan, with An Account of the Patagonians: Tranflated from Dom Pernety's Hiftorical Journal written in French. Illustrated with Copper Plates. *London:* T. Jefferys, MDCCLXXI. *Title, and Advertisement, 2 leaves;* 'Preface' *xvii pp; Text 294 pp. With 16 Copper Plates, uncut.* 4*to.* (8*s.* 6*d.* 316)

BOUGAINVILLE (LOUIS DE). A Voyage round the World. Performed by Order of His Most Christian Majesty, In the years 1766, 1767, 1768, and 1769. By Lewis de Bougainville, Colonel of Foot, and Commodore of the Expedition in the Frigate La Boudeufe, and the Store-fhip L'Etoile. Tranflated from the French by John Reinhold Forster, F.A.S. *Dublin:* MDCCLXXII. *xxxii and* 480 *pp. Map and plate.* 8*vo.* (7*s.* 6*d.* 317)
At the end of the volume is a Vocabulary of the language of Taiti Island.

BOUQUET (HENRY). An Historical Account of the Expedition against the Ohio Indians, in the Year 1764. Under the Command of Henry Bouquet, Esq; Colonel of Foot, and now Brigadier General in America. Including His Tranfactions with the Indians, relative to the delivery of their prifoners, and the preliminaries of Peace. With an Introductory Account Of the Preceding Campaign, and Battle at Bushy-Run. To which are annexed Military Papers, containing Reflections on the War with the Savages; a method of forming frontier fettlements; fome account of the Indian country, with a lift of nations, fighting men, towns, diftances and different routs. The whole illustrated with a Map and Copper-Plates. Published from authentic Documents, by a Lover of his Country. *Philadelphia:* Printed and sold by William Bradford, at the London Coffee-House, the corner of Market and Front-ftreets. M.DCC.LXV. *Title;* 'Introduction,' *xiii pp; text* 71 *pp. With copper Plate Map; and* 2 *Plates.* 4*to.* (1*l.* 11*s.* 6*d.* 318)

BOUQUET (HENRY). An/ Hiftorical Account/ of the/ Expedition/ against the/ Ohio Indians,/ In the Year M DCC LXIV,/ under the Command of/ Henry Bouquet, Efq./ Colonel of foot, and now Brigadier

General/ in America. Including his Tranſactions
with the Indians, Relative to the Delivery of the/
Priſoners, and the Preliminaries of Peace./ With
an Introductory Account of the Preced-/ing Campaign, and Battle at Buſhy-Run./ To which are
annexed/ Military Papers,/ Containing/ Reflections on the War with the Savages; a/ Method of
forming Frontier Settlements; ſome/ Account of
the Indian Country; with a Liſt of/ Nations,
Fighting Men, Towns, Diſtances, and/ different
Routes./ Published, from authentic Documents,
by a/ Lover of his Country./ *Dublin.*/ Printed for
John Milliken, at (No 10,)/ in Skinner-Row,
M DCC LXIX. xx *and* 99 *pp. Polished calf by Bedford,* 12mo.   (15s. 319)

BOUQUET (HENRY). Relation Historique de L'Ex-
pédition, contre Les Indiens de l'Ohio en MDCCLXIV.
Commandée par le Chevalier Henry Bouquet, Colonel d'Infanterie, & enſuite Brigadier-Général en
Amérique; contenant ſes Tranſactions avec les Indiens, relativement à la délivrance des Priſonniers
& aux Préliminaries de la Paix; avec un Récit in-
troductoire de la Campagne précédente de l'an 1763,
& de la Bataille de Buſhy-Run. On y a joint des
Mémoires Militaires contenant des Reflexions ſur
la guerre avec les Sauvages : une Methode de former des établiſſemens ſur la Frontiere : quelques détails concernant la contrée des Indiens : avec une
liſte de nations, combattans, villes, diſtances, & di-
verſes routes. Le tout enrichi de Cartes & Tailles-
douces. Traduit de l'Anglois, Par C. G. F. Du-
mas. A *Amsterdam,* Chez Marc - Michel Rey,
M.DCC.LXIX. *Half-title & title 2 leaves;* ' Preface,'
pp. vi-xvi. ' Introduction,' 26 *pp. Text pp* 27-147.
' Avis au Relieur' 1 *page.* ' Table,' 5 *leaves. With*
6 *maps and plates, calf.* 8vo.   (15s. 320)
This French Edition contains some biographical notices of Bouquet
not to be found in any of the Editions in English.

BOWLES (WILLIAM AUGUSTUS). Authentic Me-
moirs of William Augustus Bowles, Esquire, Am-
bassador From the United Nations of Creeks and
Cherokees, to the Court of London. *London :* R.
Faulder, M.DCC.XCI. *Title,* ' To the Public.' *vi pp.
Text* 79 *pp.* 12mo.   (5s. 321)

BOYLE (RICHARD). Manuscript Memorial addressed to Sir George Yonge, Secretary at War, received Jan. 1788, applying to be brought into the Army in active service. 1 *page. Folio.* (5s. 322)

The memorialist went to America in 1777 as a Volunteer, and soon after raised a company and joined Gen. Delancy's Battalion of Provincials. He afterwards served in Georgia and South Carolina. In Oct. 1780 he was taken prisoner and confined until May 1781, " suffering every hardship and ignominious treatment that could be inflicted by an exasperated and deluded enemy." He was then released, and joined Cornwallis, and with that noble Earl had the honour of participating in the closing scenes of the American Revolution at York-Town.

BOYLSTON (ZABDIEL). An/ Hiftorical Account/ of the/ Small-Pox/ inoculated/ in/ New England,/ Upon all Sorts of Perfons, Whites, Blacks, and of all Ages and Conftitutions./ With fome Account of the Nature of the/ Infeétion in the Natural and Inoculated/ Way, and their different Effeéts on Human/ Bodies./ With fome fhort Directions to the Un-/experienced in this Method of Praétice./ Humbly dedicated to her Royal Highness the Princess of Wales,/ By Zabdiel Boylfton, F.R.S./ The Second Edition, Correéted./ *London :*/ Printed for S. Chandler, at the Crofs-Keys in the Poultry./ M.DCC.XXVI./ Re-Printed at *Boston* in N. E. for S. Gerrish in/ Cornhil, and T. Hancock at the Bible and Three Crowns/ in Annftreet. M.DCC.XXX./ 8 *prel. leaves; viz; half-title, title, dedication, and Preface. Text* 53 *pp. 8vo.* (15s. 323)

BRACKENRIDGE (HENRY M.). Views of Louisiana; together with a Journal of a Voyage up the Missouri River, in 1811. By H. M. Brackenridge, Esq. *Pittsburgh*, Cramer, Spear and Eichbaum, 1814. *Title;* 'To the Reader' *pp.* 3-7, *and text, pp.* 9-268. 'Appendix' *pp.* 269-302. 'Contents' *pp.* 303-304. *8vo.* (5s. 6d. 324)

BRACKENRIDGE (HENRY M.). Voyage to South America, performed by Order of the American Government, in the years 1817 and 1818, in the Frigate Congress. By H. M. Brackenridge, Esq. Secretary to the Mission. In two Volumes. *Baltimore:* Published by the Author. 1819. *Colored Map of South America; title and contents* 2 *leaves;* ' Preface' *pp. v-xv; text pp.* 17-351 ' Errata' 1 *page. II. Title and contents* 2 *leaves; text pp.* 5-381. *Calf. 8vo.* (10s. 6d. 325)

BRACKENRIDGE (HENRY M.). Voyage to South

America, performed by order of the American Government in the years 1817 and 1818, in the Frigate Congress. By H. M. Brackenridge, Esq. Secretary to the Mission. In two volumes. *London:* John Miller, 1820. *Vol. I. Half-title, title, dedication.* ' Preface,' *pp. vii-xviii.* ' Contents ' 1 *leaf. Text,* 331 *pp.* ' Appendix.' 40 *pp. II. Title, and contents; 2 leaves; Text,* 317 *pp. 8vo.* (8s. 6d. 326)

BRADBURY (John). Travels in the Interior of America, in the Years 1809, 1810, and 1811; including a description of Upper Louisiana, together with the States of Ohio, Kentucky, Indiana, and Tennessee, with the Illinois and Western Territories, and containing Remarks and Observations useful to persons emigrating to those Countries. By John Bradbury, F.L.S. London, Corresponding Member of the Liverpool Philosophical Society, and Honorary Member of the Literary and Philosophical Societies, New York, United States, America. *Liverpool:* Smith and Galway, 1817. *Title and dedication; 2 leaves;* ' Preface' *pp. v-viii.* ' Contents.' *ix-xii; and text, pp.* 9-209. ' Appendix' *pp.* 211-364. ' Errata' *on a slip,* 13 *lines. Boards. 8vo.* (4s. 6d. 327)

BRADBURY (Thomas). The Necessity Of Contending for Revealed Religion: with a Sermon on the Fifth of November, 1719. By Thomas Bradbury. To which is Prefix'd, A Letter from the Reverend Cotton Mather D.D. on the late Diſputes about the Ever-Bleſſed Trinity. *London,* H. Woodfall, M.DCC.XX. *xxiv and* 88 *pp. 8vo.* (3s. 6d. 328)

BRADFORD (Alexander W.). American Antiquities and Researches into the Origin and History of the Red Race. By Alexander W. Bradford. *New-York:* Drayton and Saxton, Boston: Saxton and Pierce. 1841. 435 *pp. cloth. 8vo.* (5s. 329)

BRADSTREET (Mrs. Anne). Several/ Poems/ Compiled with great variety of Wit and/ Learning, full of Delight;/ Wherein eſpecially is contained a compleat/ Diſcourſe, and Deſcription of/ The Four Elements,/ Constitutions,/ Ages of Man,/ Seasons of the Year./ Together with an exaċt Epitome of/ the three firſt Monarchyes/ Viz. The Assyrian,/ Persian,/ Grecian./ And beginning of

the Romane Common-wealth/ to the end of their
laft King :/ With diverfe other pleafant & ferious
Poems,/ By a Gentlewoman in New-England./
The fecond Edition, Corrected by the Author,/
and enlarged by an Addition of feveral other/
Poems found amongft her Papers/ after her Death./
Boston, Printed by John Fofter, 1678./ 7 *prel.
leaves and 256 pp. wanting the last leaf. Poor copy.
Small 8vo.* (15s. 330)

BRADSTREET (MRS. ANNE). Several/ Poems/
compiled with great Variety of Wit and Learn-/
ing, full of Delight;/ Wherein efpecially is con-
tained, a compleat Difcourfe and/ Defcription of/
The Four Elements,/ Constitutions,/ Ages of Man,/
Seasons of the Year./ Together with an exact
Epitome of the three firft/ Monarchies, viz. the/
Assyrian, Persian, Grecian, and Roman Common/
Wealth, from its begin-/ning, to the End of their/
last king.' With divers other pleafant and ferious
Poems./ By a Gentlewoman in New-England./
The Third Edition, corrected by the Author,/ and
enlarged by an Addition of feveral other/ Poems
found amongft her Papers after her/ Death./ Re-
printed from the fecond Edition, in the Year/
M. DCC. LVIII./ *xiii and* 234 *pp. Poor copy, wanting
the last leaf. Small 8vo.* (10s. 6d. 331)

BRADSTREET (LIEUTENANT COLONEL). An Impartial Account of Lieut. Col. Bradstreet's Expedition to Fort Frontenac. To which are added, A
few Reflections on the Conduct of that Enterprize,
and the Advantages refulting from its Succefs. By
a Volunteer on the Expedition. *London:* T. Wil-
cox, W. Owen, M. Cooper, and Mr. Cooke.
M.DCC.LIX. 2 *prel. lvs. and* 60 *pp.* 8vo. (10s. 6d. 332)

BRAGG (BENJAMIN). A Voyage to the North Pole,
by Benjamin Bragg, Accompanied by his Friend
Captain Slapperwhack; with An Account of the
Dangers and Accidents they experienced in the
Frozen Seas of the Polar Circle. Also the manner
of their wintering on the Island of Spitzberg, and
Discovery of the Polar Continent. Embellished with
an elegant Plate and Map. *London:* G. Walker,
1817. *Half-title, frontispiece, title, Preface, contents
5 leaves. Text* 211 *pp. With Map of the Polar Circle.*
12mo. (4s. 6d. 333)

BRAINARD (John).   Autograph Letter to Mrs.
Wm. Smith, Widow,Wethersfield, dated at Bridge-
town N. J. 21st Jan. 1772, respecting missionary
affairs among the Indians of New Jersey.   *2 pp.*
4to.   (*5s. 334*)

This Rev. John Brainard was brother of the celebrated Missionary,
David Brainard, and succeeded him in his Missionary Station
in New Jersey.

BRANDON (Lorenço).   ✠ Señor./ Medios para/
V. Mageftad ahorrar lo mucho que gafta/ cada año
en las Armadas del Reyno de/ Portugal, y Eftado
de la India, con mas/ fruto y cõmodidad, para po-
der/ venir la plata del Pirù con/ menos cofta y ri-
efgo./ [*Ending*] ¶ Suplico a V. M. fea feruido de
mandar confultar en/ razon de todo lo que pare-
ciere, &c.   *Madrid* 23. de Diziem/bre 1622.   D.
Lorenço Brandon.   *Title and 6 folioed leaves.*
Folio.   (*1l. 11s. 6d. 335*)

BRAZIL. De Zeeufche/ Verre-ky-/ker./ Ghedrucht
tot *Vliffingen* in't Groene Wout,/ Daermen foo
veel vande Capers hout, 1649./ *8 leaves, not
folioed. Half mor. 4to.*   (*10s. 6d. 336*)

BRASYLS/ Schuyt-Praetjen,/ Ghehouden tuffchen
een Officier,/ een Domine, en een Coopman, noo-
pende den/ Staet van Brafyl: Mede hoe de Officieren
en Sol-/daten tegenwoordich aldaer ghetraĉteert
werden,/ en hoe men placht te leven ten tyde doen
de Por-/togyfen noch onder het onverdraeghlijck
Iock/der Hollanderen faten./Dit door een onpar-
tydich toe-hoorder ghean=/noteert./ Ghedruckt
inde Weft-Indifche Kamer by Maerten,/Daer het
gelt foo luftich klinckt alffer zijn Aep-ftaertem/
Anno 1649./ (Brazilian Barge-Gossip, between an Officer, a
Clergyman, and a Merchant, relative to the State of Brazil; also
how the Officers and Soldiers are treated there at present, and how
one used to live at the time when the Portuguese were yet under
the insupportable yoke of the Hollanders noted down by an impartial listener.   Printed in the West India Chamber, at Martin's
where money sounds as jolly as ape's tails.   Anno 1649.)
12 leaves. Half mor. 4to.   (*15s. 337*)

BRAVO DE RIVERO Y ZAVALA (Diego Mi-
guel). Meritos,/ y servicios/ de D. Diego Miguel/
Bravo de Rivero [*the name in a Vignette.*] *Lima,*
1793. *24 pp. Half mor. Folio.* (*10s. 6d. 338*)

BRAY (Thomas). The/ Necessity/ of an early/ Religion /being a/ Sermon/ Preach'd the 5th of May
Before The/ Honourable/ Assembly of/ Maryland/

By Thomas Bray D.D./ *Annapolis,* Printed By
Order of the/ Assembly By Tho: Reading, For
Evan Jones book-/feller, Anno Domini 1700./ *On
the reverse of title, thanks to Dr. Bray ; text 20 pp:
half mor.* 4to. (1*l.* 1*s.* 339)

BRICKELL (John). The Natural History of North-
Carolina. With an Account of the Trade, Manners,
and Cuftoms of the Christian and Indian Inhabit-
ants. Illuftrated with Copper-Plates, wherein are
curioufly Engraved the Map of the Country, feve-
ral ftrange Beafts, Birds, Fifhes, Snakes, Infects,
Trees, and Plants, &c. By John Brickell, M.D.
Dublin : Printed by James Carson, in Coghill's-
Court, Dame-ftreet, oppofite to the Caftle-Market.
For the Author, 1737. *viii pp. prel.* ' A Map of
North Carolina.' *9 by 7 inches ; and Text 408 pp.
With 2 Plates; 8vo.* (10*s.* 6*d.* 340)

BRIEF (A) Account of the Proceedings of the Committee, appointed in the year 1795 by the Yearly
Meeting of Friends of Pennsylvania, New-Jersey,
&c. for promoting the Improvement and gradual
Civilization of the Indian Natives. Philadelphia
printed : *London* reprinted, Phillips & Fardon,
1806. *50 pp. followed by* A Brief Account of the
proceedings of the Committee, appointed by the
Yearly Meeting of Friends, held in Baltimore, for
promoting the Improvement and Civilization of
the Indian Natives. Baltimore printed : *London;*
reprinted, Phillips and Fardon, 1806. *43 pp. Half
mor. 12mo.* (4*s.* 6*d.* 341)

BRIEF (A) and perfect/ Journal/ of/ The late Proceedings and/ Succeffe of the Englifh Army in the/
West-Indies,/ Continued until June the 24ᵗʰ.1655./
Together with/ Some Quæres inferted and anfwered./ Publifhed for fatisfaction of all fuch who
defire truly/ to be informed in thefe particulars./
By I. S. an Eye-witneffe./ *London,* Printed 1655./
27 pp. Half mor. uncut, 4to. (1*l.* 11*s.* 6*d.* 342)

BRIEF/ (A) Discourse/ Concerning the/ Lawfulnefs
of Worfhipping God/ by the/ Common-Prayer./
Being in/ Anfwer/ To a Book, Entituled,/ A Brief
Difcourfe concerning the Vnlawfulnefs of the/
Common - Prayer Worfhip./ Lately Printed in
New-England, and Re-printed/ in London./ In

which, the Chief Things Objected againft/ the Liturgy, are confider'd./ The Second Edition Corrected./ London:/ Printed for Ri. Chiswell, at the Rose and Crown in/ St. Paul's Church-Yard, MDCXCIV./ *Title & preface, 2 leaves; text 36 pp. calf by Bedford. 4to.* (1l. 11s. 6d. 343)

BRIEF (A)/ Narrative/ and Deduction of the feveral Remark-/able Cafes of Sir William Courten, and Sir Paul/ Pyndar, Knights; and William Courten late of London/ Efquire, Deceafed: Their Heirs, Executors, Admi-/niftrators and Affigns, together with their Surviving/ Partners and Adventurers with them to the Eaft-In-/dies, China and Japan, and divers other parts of Afia,/ Europe, Africa and America: Faithfully reprefented/ to both Houfes of Parliament./ Reduced under four Principal Heads, viz./ I. The Difcovery and Plantation of Barbadoes./ II. Their Vndertakings, and Expeditions to the Eaft-/India, China and Japan./ III. The Denyal of Justice upon their civil Actions/ depending in Holland . and Zealand./ IV. Their Loanes and Supplyes for the Service of the/ Crown, upon the Collection of Fines and Compofiti-/ons out of the Popifh Recufants Eftates, &c./ Recollected out of the Original Writings and Records,/ for publick Satisfaction./ *London,* Printed in the Year 1679. *2 prel. leaves, 12 pp; and pp.* 115—118, *headed* " *Fraud and Oppreffion Detected and Arraigned.*" *Half morocco. Folio.* (1l. 1s. 344)

BRIEF Remarks on the Defence of the Halifax Libel, on the British-American-Colonies. *Boston:* Printed and Sold by Edes and Gill, M, DCC, LXV. *40 pp. Half mor. 8vo.* (10s. 6d. 345)

BRIEFE über Portugal, nebft einem Anhang über Brafilien. Aus dem Französifchen. Mit Anmerkungen herausgegeben von Matthias Chrift. Sprengel, Profeffor der Gefchichte in Halle. Leipzig, in der Weygandfchen Buchha. 1782. *Title,* ' Vorrede' *5 leaves; text* 290 *pp.* 12*mo.* (4s. 6d. 346)

BRISSOT DE WARVILLE (SIEUR J. P.). New Travels in the United States of America. Performed in 1788. By J. P. Brissot de Warville. Translated from the French. *London:* J. S. Jordan, MDCCXCII. *Half-title, title, 2 leaves;* 'Preface of the Translator,' *viii. pp.* 'Preface of the Author,' *pp. ix-xliii. Text pp.* 45-483. 'Contents and Errata,' *2 leaves;* 'A Comparative Table,' *etc. To face p.* 359.' *8vo.* (5s. 6d. 347)

BRISSOT DE WARVILLE (SIEUR J. P.). New Travels in the United States of America, performed in M.DCC.LXXXVIII. Containing the lateſt and moſt accurate Obſervations on the Charaĉter, Genius, and preſent State of the People and Government of that Country—Their Agriculture, Commerce, Manufaĉtures, and Finances—Quality and Price of Lands, and Progress of the Settlements on the Ohio and the Miſſiſſippi—Political and Moral Charaĉter of the Quakers, and a Vindication of that excellent Seĉt from the Miſrepreſentations of other Travellers—State of the Blacks—Progreſs of the Laws for their Emancipation, and for the final Deſtruĉtion of Slavery on that Continent—Accurate Accounts of the Climate, Longevity—Comparative Tables of the Probabilities of Life betwen America and Europe, &c. &c. By J. P. Brissot de Warville. Second Edition, Corrected. *London:* J. S. Jordan, M DCC XCIV. *2 Volumes. 1. Title;* 'Contents,' *etc. pp. iii-vi.* 'Preface of the Translator,' *pp. vii-xii.* 'The Author's Preface Revised,' *28 pp. Text pp.* 29-416. *With* 'A Comparative Table,' *etc. To face p.* 308.' II. *First title* 'New Travels in the United States,' *etc. Second title* 'The Commerce of America with Europe; particularly with France and Great Britain; comparatively stated, and explained. Shewing the importance of the American Revolution to the Interests of France, and pointing out the actual situation of the United States of North America, in regard to Trade, Manufactures, and Population. By J. P. Brissot de Warville, and Etienne Claviere. Translated from the last French Edition, revised by Brissot, and called the Second Volume of his View of America. With the life of Brissot, and an Appendix by the Translator. *London:* J. S. Jordan, MDCCXCIV. *pp. iii-lxiv. Text* 348 *pp. With portrait of* '*J. P. Brissot.' 8vo.* (10s. 6d. 348)

BROCKWELL (CHARLES). Brotherly Love Re-

commended in a Sermon Preached before the
Ancient and Honourable Society of Free and
Accepted Masons, in Christ-Church, Boston, on
Wednefday, the 27th of December, 1749. By
Charles Brockwell, A.M. His Majefty's Chaplain
in Boston. Publifhed at the request of the Society.
Boston ; in New-England: Printed by John Dra-
per, in Newbury Street. M,DCC,L. *2 prel. leaves
and pp.* 7-21 *8vo.* (4s. 6d. 349)

BROMLEY (THOMAS.) The Way to the Sabbath
of Rest. Or the Soul's Progrefs in the Work of the
New-Birth. With Two difcourfes of the Author
never before Printed viz. The Journeys of the
Children of Ifrael, as in their Names and hiftorical
Paffages, they comprife the great and gradual
Work of Regeneration: And A Treatife of Extraordinary divine Difpenfations, under the Jewifh
and Gofpel Adminiftrations. By Mr. Thomas
Bromley. To which are added A Difcourfe on
Miftakes concerning Religion, Enthufiafm, Experiences, &c. By Thomas Hartley Rector of
Winwick. London Printed. *Germantown,* Reprinted and fold by Chriftopher Sower, Alfo fold
by Solomon Fuffell and Jonathan Zane in Philadelphia. 1759. *viii and* 280 *pp.* ' A Discourse,' by
Thomas Hartley, *etc.* 168 *pp. 8vo.* (10s. 6d. 350)

BROMLEY (WALTER). Two Addresses on the
Deplorable State of the Indians *;* one delivered at
the Free-Masons' Hall, Aug, 3, 1813, the other
at the Royal Acadian School, March 8, 1814, at
Halifax in Nova-Scotia. By Walter Bromley,
Late Paymaster of the 23d Regiment, Welch
Fufiliers. *London:* Published (for the benefit of
the Indians) by T. Hamilton, 1815. 71 *pp.*
12*mo.* (4s. 6d. 351)

BROOKSOP (JONE). An/ Invitation of Love/
unto the/ Seed of God,/ Throughout the World./
With/ a Word/ To the Wise in Heart./ And a
Lamentation/ For New-England./ Given forth
from the movings of the Spirit of the/ Lord, by
one who is known to the World by the/ Name of/
Jone Brooksop./ *London,* Printed for Robert Wilfon. [1662.] *Title, and pp.* 3-15. 4*to.* (17s. 6d. 352)

BROUGHAM (HENRY). The Speech of Henry

Brougham, Esq. Before the House of Commons, Friday, April 1, 1808, in support of the Petitions from London, Liverpool and Manchester, against the Orders in Council. Taken in short-hand by Mr. A. Fraser. *London:* J. Ridgway, 1808. *ix and* 84 *pp.* 8*vo.* (2*s.* 6*d.* 353)

BROWN (Moses). From the Meeting for Sufferings for New-England, to the feveral Quarterly and Monthly-Meetings belonging to the Yearly-Meeting. [Colophon] *Providence:* Printed by John Carter. [1782.] 19 *pp.* 4*to.* (8*s.* 6*d.* 354)

BROWNE (Patrick). The Civil and Natural History of Jamaica. In Three Parts. Containing, I. An accurate Defcription of that Ifland, its Situation and Soil; with a brief Account of its former and prefent State, Government, Revenues, Produce, and Trade. II. A Hiftory of the natural Productions, including the various Sorts of native Foffils; perfect and imperfect Vegetables; Quadrupedes, Birds, Fifhes, Reptiles and Infects; with their Properties and Ufes in Mechanics, Diet, and Phyfic. III. An Account of the Nature of Climates in general, and their different Effects upon the human Body; with a Detail of the Difeafes arifing from this Source, particularly within the Tropics. In Three Dissertations. The Whole illuftrated with Fifty Copper-Plates: In which the moft curious Productions are reprefented of the natural Size, and delineated immediately from the Objects. By Patrick Browne, M.D. *London :* Printed for the Author; MDCCLVI. 7 *prel. leaves; viz. half-title, title, Dedication, list of Subscribers, Catalogue of Authors, and Preface. Text* 490 *pp.* 'Index.' *pp.* 491-503. *Map of Jamaica; Chart of the Harbours of Port Royal and Kingston;* 49 *numbered copper-plates. Folio.* (15*s.* 355)

BROWNE (Patrick). The Civil and Natural History of Jamaica. Containing I. An accurate Defcription of that Ifland, its Situation, and Soil; with a brief Account of its former and prefent State, Government, Revenue, Produce, and Trade. II. An Hiftory of the Natural Productions, including the various Sorts of native Foffils; Perfect and Imperfect Vegetables; Quadrupeds, Birds,

Fifhes, Reptiles, and Infects; with their Properties and Ufes in Mechanics, Diet, and Phyfic.
By Patrick Browne, M.D. Illustrated with Forty-
nine Copper Plates; in which the most curious
productions are represented of their natural sizes,
and delineated immediately from the objects, By
George Dionysius Ehret. There are now added
Complete Linnæan Indexes, and a large and
accurate Map of the Island./ *London./* B. White
and Son, m,dcc,lxxxix. 7 *prel. leaves; viz. half-
title, title, dedication, list of Subscribers, catalogue of
Authors, & ' Preface.'　Text;* 490 *pp.* 'Index,'
pp. 491-503. ' Four Additional Indexes.' 23 *leaves.
Map of Jamaica,* 1774, *and* 49 *numbered copper-
plates. Folio.*　　　　　　　　　(17s. 6d.　356)

This edition is the same as the preceding with the exception of
a few leaves being reprinted with some alterations, the substi-
tution of a new and improved map of Jamaica, the omission
of the Chart of the Harbours of Port Royal and Kingston, and
the addition of the four Indexes.

BRUCE (Lewis.)　The Happinefs of Man the
Glory of God.　A Sermon Preached before the
Honourable Truftees For Eftablifhing the Colony
of Georgia in America, and the Associates of the
late Rev. Dr. Bray; at their Anniversary Meet-
ing, March 15, 1743, in the Parifh Church of
St. Margaret, Weftminfter. By Lewis Bruce,
A.M. Preacher of his Majefty's Chapel, Somerfet-
Houfe.　*London:* Daniel Browne, mdccxliv.
Title, and 53 *pp.* 4to.　　　　　(5s. 6d.　357)

BRYAN (Hugh).　Living Christianity delineated,
in the Diaries and Letters of two Eminently pious
Persons lately deceafed; viz. Mr. Hugh Bryan,
and Mrs. Mary Hutson, Both of South-
Carolina.　With a Preface by the Reverend Mr.
John Conder, and the Reverend Mr. Thomas
Gibbons.　*London,* J. Buckland, mdcclx. *xi and*
171 *pp.* 12*mo.*　　　　　　　　(4s. 6d.　358)

BUCANIERS of America, *see* Esquemeling.

BUCHANAN (James).　Sketches of the History,
Manners, and Customs of the North American
Indians. By James Buchanan, Esq. His Majefty's
Consul for the State of New York.　*London:*
Black, Young, and Young, mdcccxxiv. *xi and*
371 *pp. with Map of North America.* 8*vo.* (4s. 6d. 359)

BUDD (Thomas). Good Order Establifhed/ in/ Pennfilvania & New-Jerfey/ in/ America,/ Being a true Account of the Country ;/ With its Produce and Commodities there made./ And the great Improvements that may be made by/ means of Public Store=houses for Hemp, Flax, and/ Linnen=Cloth; alfo the Advantages of a Publick=/School, the Profits of a Publick=Bank, and the Proba-/bility of its arifing, if thofe directions here laid down are/ followed. With the advantages of publick Granaries./ Likewife, feveral other things needful to be underftood by/ thofe that are or do intend to be concerned in planting in/ the faid Countries./ All which is laid down very plain, in this fmall Treatife; it/ being eafie to be underftood by any ordinary Capacity. To/ which the Reader is referred for his further fatisfaction./ By Thomas Budd./ [*London*] Pri::ted in the Year 1685./ *40 pp. Calf extra by Bedford.* (6l. 16s. 6d. 360)

BUDGET (The). Inscribed to the Man, who thinks himself Minister. *London:* J. Almon, MDCCLXIV. *Title, and pp.* 3-23. *4to.* (2s. 6d. 361)

BUELL (Samuel). An Account of the late Success of the Gospel, in the Province of New-York, North-America: Contained in Letters from the Rev. Meffrs. Buell, Hazard, and Prime. *Coventry:* T. Luckman, M,DCC,LXV. 16 *pp. 8vo.* (7s. 6d. 362)

BUELL (Samuel). A Sermon, delivered at the Ordination of the Reverend Aaron Woolworth, A. M. To the Paftoral Charge of the Church in Bridge-Hampton, on Long-Island, Auguft 30, 1787. By Samuel Buell, A.M. Paftor of the Church at East-Hampton, Long-Island. *Elizabeth-Town*, (New Jerfey) Printed by Shepard Kollock, on Golden-Hill, M, DCC, LXXXVIII. 46 *pp. Half morocco. 8vo.* (4s. 6d. 363)

BUELL (Samuel). Autograph Letter to his Brother, dated at Portsmouth, May 31st, 1742. 1 *page.* (5s. 364)

BUELL (Samuel). Autograph Letter to The Rev. Ephraim Woodbridge, V.D.M. New-London, respecting Rev. Mr. Hopkins. 1 *page 4to.* (7s. 6d. 365)

Mr. Buell was a remarkable man, one of the most eminent and successful preachers of his day. He was born at Coventry, Con-

necticut, in 1716, graduated at Yale College in 1741, was the
intimate friend of Brainard and Edwards, and in 1746 was in-
stalled as the Pastor of the Church at East Hampton on Long
Island, where he died in 1798, full of years and Christian virtues.

BUENOS AYRES. Real Cedula de Ereccion del
Consulado de Buenos=Ayres, expedida en Aranjuez
a xxx de Enero de m dcc xciv. *Madrid* m dcc xciv.
En la Oficina de Don Benito Cano. *Title and
36 pages. Half mor. Folio.* (7s. 6d. 366)

BUENOS AYRES. An authentic and interesting
Description of the City of Buenos Ayres, and the
adjacent Country; situate on the River Plate, on
the East side of South America, shewing the
Manners, Customs, Produce, and Commerce, of
that most important and valuable Country; includ-
ing an Account of the Capture of Buenos Ayres,
July 2, 1806. Illustrated with a Map of South
America. *London:* John Fairburn, [1806] 60 *pp.
Map. Half mor. 12mo.* (3s. 6d. 367)

BUENOS AYRES. A Five Years' Residence in
Buenos Ayres, during the years 1820 to 1825:
containing remarks on the Country and Inhabitants; and a visit to Colonia del Sacramento. By
an Englishman. With an Appendix, containing
Rules and Police of the Port of Buenos Ayres,
Navigation of the River Plate, &c. &c. *London*
G. Herbert, 1825. *viii and 176 pp. boards, uncut.
8vo.* (4s. 6d. 368)

After the title is a leaf inserted, dated Buenos Ayres, Feb. 1826,
by the author, apoligizing for his book, 'written solely for the
author's friends in England,' and asking that it may be viewed
with lenity.

BUENOS AYRES. Ultimatum of Mr. Aimé
Roger, Consul of France, Addressed to the
Government of Buenos Ayres, charged with the
Foreign Affairs of the Argentine Confederation,
its Answer and relative Documents. *Buenos
Ayres.* State Printing Office. 1838. 189 *pp. In
French and English. 4to.* (7s. 6d. 369)

BUENOS AYRES. Oficio del Consul encargado
interinamente del Consulado General de Francia
en Buenos-Aires, al Sr. Ministro de Relaciones
Exteriores de la Confederacion Argentina,
Reclaimando a nombre del derecho de gentes,
para que los Franceses, que publica y notoria-
mente se hallan establecidos en la Republica con

los mismos goces y libertades civiles que los
ciudadanos Argentinos, no sean considerados como
domiciliarios del lugar en donde estan establecidos.
Contestacion del Sr. Ministro, y otros Documentos
relativos al mismo asunto. *Buenos-Aires.* Imprenta del Estado. 1838. *Title and* 114 *pp.*
4*to.* (7*s.* 6*d.* 370)

BUENOS AYRES. Official Note from the Consul charged ad Interim of the General Consulate of
France in Buenos Ayres, to the Minister for
Foreign Affairs to the Argentine Confederation,
Reclaiming on the authority of international law,
that the French, who notoriously and publicly
have established themselves in the Republic with
the same enjoyments and civil liberties as the
Argentine Citizens, be not considered as domiciled
in the Place in which they have established themselves. The Answer from the Minister and other
Documents upon the same subject. *Buenos-Aires.*
State Printing Office. 1838. 229 *pp. In French
and English.* 4*to.* (7*s.* 6*d.* 371)

BUENOS AYRES. Supplemento a la Correspondencia Oficial con el Consul encargado interinamente del Consulado General de Francia en
Buenos-Aires. *Buenos-Aires.* Imprenta del Estado.
1838. *Title and pp.* 69-114. 4*to.* (5*s.* 372)

BUENOS AYRES. Ultimatum del Sr. Consul de
Francia Mr. Aimé Roger, dirigido al Gobierno de
Buenos-Aires, encargado de las relaciones exteriores de la Confederacion Argentina, con la
correspondiente contestacion y Documentos que
le son Relativos. *Buenos-Aires.* Imprenta del
Estado. 1838. 97 *pp.* 4*to.* (7*s.* 6*d.* 373)

BULKELEY (Peter.) The Gofpel-Covenant;/ or/
the Covenant/ of Grace Opened./ Wherein are
explained ;/ 1. The differences betwixt the Covenant of grace and Covenant/ of workes./ 2. The
different adminiftration of the Covenant before and/
fince Chrift./ 3. The benefits and blefsings of it./
4. The Condition./ 5. The properties of it./
Preached in Concord in Nevv-England/ by Peter
Bulkeley, fometimes fellow/ of Saint Johns Colledge in Cambridge./ Publifhed according to
Order./ *London*, Printed by M. S. for Benjamin

Allen, and are to be fold/ at the Crowne in Popes-head Alley. 1646./ 8 *prel. leaves; viz. title, dedication,* 'To the Reader.' 'To the Reader.' 'To the Church;' *Text,* 383 *pp.* 'The Table,' 4 *leaves,* 4*to.* (15*s.* 374)

BULKELEY (PETER). The Gofpel-Covenant;/ or/ the Covenant/ of Grace opened. / Wherein are explained;/ 1. The differences betwixt the Covenant of grace and Covenant/ of workes./ 2. The different adminiftration of the Covenant before and fince/ Chrift./ 3. The benefits and bleffings of it./ 4. The Condition./ 5. The properties of it. / Preached in Concord in New-England/ by Peter Bulkeley, fometimes fellow/ of Saint Johns Colledge in Cambridge./ The fecond Edition, much enlarged, and correĉted by the Author./ And the chiefe heads of Things (which was omitted in the former)/ diftinguifhed into Chapters./ *London,/* Printed by Matthew Simmons, dwelling in Alderfgate-ftreet/ next doore to the Golden Lyon. 1651./ 7 *prel. leaves and Text in* 432 *pp*; *Table* 5 *leaves.* 4*to.* (15*s.* 375)

BULKLEY (CHARLES). The Signs of the Times, Illuftrated and Improved. In a Sermon preached at the Evening-Lecture in the Old-Jewry, on Sunday, October 21, 1759. On Occasion of the Surrender of Quebec to His Majesty's Forces, September 18, 1759. By Charles Bulkley. *London:* M DCC LIX. 30 *pp. and one leaf.* 8*vo.* (5*s.* 376)

BULLOCK (W. *F. L. S.*). Six Months' Residence and Travels in Mexico ; containing Remarks on the Present State of New Spain, its Natural Productions, State of Society, Manufactures, Trade, Agriculture, and Antiquities, &c. With Plates and Maps. By W. Bullock, F.L.S. Proprietor of the late London Museum. *London:* John Murray, 1824. *xii and* 523 *pp.* 'Index,' *pp.* 525-530. 'List of Plates,' *pp.* 531-2. *With* 17 *Plates. cloth,* 8*vo.* (5*s.* 377)

BULLOCK (WILLIAM). Virginia/ Impartially examined, and left/ to publick view, to be confidered by all Iudi-/cious and honeft men./ Under which Title, is compre-/hended the Degrees from 34 to 39, wherein/ lyes the rich and healthfull Countries of Roanock,/ the new Plantations of

Virginia/ and Mary-land./ Looke not upon this Booke, as/ thofe that are fet out by private men, for private/ ends; for being read you'l find, the publick/ good is the Authors only aime./ For this Piece is no other then the Adventures/ of Planters faithfull Steward, difpofing the Ad-/venture for the beft advantage, advifing/ people of all degrees, from the higheft/ Mafter, to the meaneft Servant,/ how fuddenly to raife their fortunes./ Perufe the Table, and you fhall finde the way plainely lay'd downe./ By William Bvl-lock, Gent./ 19 April, 1649. Imprimatur, Hen: Whaley./ *London:* Printed by John Hammond, and are to be fold at his houfe/ over-againft S. Andrews Church in Holborne. 1649./ *6 prel. leaves; viz. Title, reverse blank*, 'To the Right Honourable, the Earle of Arundel and Surrey, and the Lord Baltamore.' 1 *page.* 'To the Gover-novr and Councell of Virginia, Health and Profperity.' 1 *page.* 'To his much efteemed Friends M. Samuel Vaffell,' *etc.* 1 *page.* 'To his much honored Friends, the Knights and Gentle-men that importuned this Worke. To the Reader,' *etc. 3 pp.* 'The Table' 4 *pp: Text* 66 *pp. Fine large copy with rough leaves: Morocco by Bed-ford.* 4*to.*   (10*l.* 10*s.* 378)

BUONAPARTE in the West Indies; or the His-tory of Toussaint Louverture, the African Hero. The Fourth Edition. *Dublin:* Printed by Holmes & Charles, No. 49 Mary-Street. 1804. 48 *pp. uncut, 8vo.*   (3*s.* 6*d.* 379)

BURDER (GEORGE). The Welch Indians; or, a Collection of Papers, respecting a people whose Ancestors emigrated from Wales to America, in the year 1170, with Prince Madoc, (three hun-dred years before the first Voyage of Columbus), And who are faid now to inhabit a beautiful Country on the Weft Side of the Mississippi. Dedicated to the Missionary Society by George Burder. *London:* T. Chapman, [1797.] 35 *pp.* 8*vo.*   (4*s.* 6*d.* 380)

BURGOYNE (LT. GEN. JOHN). A Letter from Lieut. Gen. Burgoyne to his Constituents, upon his late Resignation ; with the Correspondences between the Secretaries of War and him, relative

H

to his return to America. The Fourth Edition.
London : J. Almon, MDCCLXXIX. *Title, and 37 pp.*
half mor. 8vo.   (5s. 6d.   381.)

BURGOYNE (Lt. Gen. John). A Letter from
Lieut. Gen. Burgoyne to his Constituents upon
his late Resignation; with the Correspondences
between the Secretaries of War and him, relative
to his return to America. The Fifth Edition.
London : J. Almon, MDCCLXXIX. *Title, and 37 pp.*
half mor. 8vo.   (6s.   382.)

BURGOYNE (Lt. Gen. John). A Letter from
Lieut. Gen. Burgoyne to his Constituents, upon
his late resignation; with the correspondences between the Secretaries of War and him, relative to
his return to America. The Sixth Edition. *Lon-*
don : J. Almon. MDCCLXXIX. *Title, and 37 pp.*
Half mor. 8vo.   (6s.   383)

BURGOYNE (Lt. Gen. John). A Reply to Lieutenant General Burgoyne's Letter to his Constituents. *London :* J. Wilkie, MDCCLXXIX. *Half-title,*
title, and 46 pp. 8vo.   (6s.   384)

BURGOYNE (Lt. Gen. John). A Reply to Lieutenant General Burgoyne's Letter to his Constituents. The Second Edition. *London :* J. Wilkie,
MDCCLXXIX. *Half-title, title, and 46 pp. Half mor.*
8vo.   (5s.   385)

BURGOYNE (Lt. Gen. John). A Letter to
Lieut. Gen. Burgoyne, on his Letter to his
Constituents. *London :* T. Becket, 1779. *Title,*
and 35 pp. half mor. 8vo.   (6s.   386)

BURGOYNE (Lt. Gen. John). The Substance of
General Burgoyne's Speeches, on Mr. Vyner's
Motion, on the 26th of May; and upon Mr. Hart-
ley's Motion, on the 28th of May, 1778. With an
Appendix, containing General Waſhington's Letter
to General Burgoyne, &c. *London :* J. Almon.
MDCCLXXVIII. *Half-title, title, and 48 pp. Half mor.*
8vo.   (6s.   387)

BURGOYNE (John). The same. The Second
Edition. *London :* J. Almon, MDCCLXXVIII. *Half-*
title, title, and 48 pp. 8vo.   (6s.   388)

BURGOYNE (Lt. Gen. John) . The same. The
Third Edition. J. Almon. MDCCLXXVIII. *Half-title,*
title, and 48 pp. Half mor. 8vo.   (6s.   389)

BURGOYNE (Lt. Gen. John). A Brief Examination of the Plan and Conduct of the Northern
Expedition in America, in 1777. And of the Surrender of the Army under the Command of Lieutenant-General Burgoyne. *London:* T. Hookham,
M DCC LXXIX. *52 pp. Half mor. 8vo.* (*7s. 6d.* 390)

BURGOYNE (Lt. Gen. John). Essay on Modern
Martyrs: With a Letter to General Burgoyne.
London : Paynes. M DCC LXXX. *Half-title, title,
and 52 pp. Half mor. 8vo.* (*7s. 6d.* 391)

BURGOYNE (Lt. Gen. John). A State of the
Expedition from Canada, as laid before the House
of Commons, by Lieutenant-General Burgoyne,
and verified by Evidence; with a Collection of
Authentic Documents, and an addition of many
circumstances which were prevented from appearing before the House by the Prorogation of Parliament. Written and collected by Himself. *London:* J. Almon. MDCCLXXX. *viii prel. pp ; Text,
140 pp ; Appendix, lxii pp ; Advertisement,* 1 *page.
6 maps and plans. Boards, uncut, 4to.* (*18s.* 392)

BURGOYNE (Lt. Gen. John). A State of the
Expedition from Canada, as laid before the House
of Commons, by Lieutenant-General Burgoyne,
and verified by Evidence ; with a Collection of
Authentic Documents, and an Addition of many
Circumstances which were prevented from appear-
ing before the House by the Prorogation of Par-
liament. Written and Collected by Himself, and
Dedicated to the Officers of the Army he com-
manded. The Second Edition. *London:* J.
Almon, MDCCLXXX. *Title; Dedication, pp. iii-vi;
'* Introduction,*' pp. vii-ix. '* Advertisement,' 1 *leaf,
Text* 191 *pp.* '* Appendix,' cix pp.* 6 *Maps and
Plans. 8vo.* (*15s.* 393)

BURKE (Edmund). Speech of Edmund Burke,
Esq. on moving his Resolutions for Conciliation
with the Colonies, March 22, 1775. The Second
Edition. *London :* J. Dodsley. MDCCLXXV. *Half-
title, title and* 107 *pp. Half mor. 8vo.* (*2s. 6d.* 394)

BURKE (Edmund). A Letter from Edmund Burke,
Eſq ; One of the Repreſentatives in Parliament for
the City of Bristol, to John Farr and John Harris,
Eſqrs. Sheriffs of that City, on the Affairs of Ame-

rica. *London :* J. Dodsley. M DCC LXXVII. *75 pp.*
Half mor. 8vo. (2s. 6d. 395)

BURKE (EDMUND). A Letter from Edmund Burke,
Esq; One of the Reprefentatives in Parliament for
the City of Bristol, to John Farr and John Harris,
Efqrs. Sheriffs of that City, on the Affairs of Ame-
rica. The Third Edition. *London :* J. Dodsley,
MDCCLXXVII. *75 pp. 8vo.* (2s. 6d. 396)

BURKE (EDMUND). A Letter from Edmund Burke,
Efq ; one of the Representatives in Parliament for
the city of Bristol, to John Farr and John Harris,
Efqrs. Sheriffs of that city, on the affairs of Ame-
rica. The Fourth edition. *London :* J. Dodsley.
M. DCC. LXXVII. *79 pp.* 8vo. (2s. 6d. 397)

BURKE (EDMUND). Speech of Edmund Burke,
Esq. on American Taxation, April 19, 1774. The
Second Edition. *London :* J. Dodsley, MDCCLXXV.
96 pp. Half mor. 8vo. (2s. 6d. 398)

BURKE (EDMUND). A Speech of Edmund Burke,
Esq. At the Guildhall, in Bristol, Previous to the
late Election in that City, upon certain points relative to his Parliamentary Conduct. *London :* J.
Dodsley, M.DCC.LXXX. *Half-title, title, and 68 pp.*
8vo. (2s. 6d. 399)

BURKE (EDMUND). A Speech of Edmund Burke,
Esq. at the Guildhall, in Bristol, Previous to the
late Election in that City, upon certain points relative to his Parliamentary Conduct. The Second
Edition. *London :* J. Dodsley, M.DCC.LXXX. *Half-*
title, title, and 68 pp. 8vo. (2s. 6d. 400)

BURKE (EDMUND). An Answer to the Printed
Speech of Edmund Burke, Efq ; Spoken in the
Houfe of Commons, April 19, 1774. In which
His Knowledge in Polity, Legiflature, Humankind,
Hiftory, Commerce and Finance, is candidly ex-
amined ; his Arguments are fairly refuted; the
Conduct of Adminiftration is fully defended; and
his Oratoric Talents are clearly expofed to view.
Addressed to the People. *London :* T. Evans.
M. DCC. LXXV. *iv and 222 pp. Half morocco.*
8vo. (5s. 6d. 401)

BURKE (EDMUND). An Answer to the letter of
Edmund Burke, Esq. one of the Representatives

of the City of Bristol, to the Sheriffs of that City. *London :* T. Cadell. M. DCC. LXXVII. *Half-title, title, and* 60 *pp. Half mor.* 8*vo.*   (3*s.* 6*d.* 402)

BURKE (EDMUND). An Answer to the Letter from Edmund Burke, Esq. one of the Representatives of the city of Bristol, to the Sheriffs of that city. The Second Edition. *London :* T. Cadell. M. DCC. LXXVII. *2 prel. leaves and* 60 *pp.* 8*vo.*   (2*s.* 6*d.* 403)

BURKE (EDMUND). A Letter to Edmund Burke, Efq ; Controverting the Principles of American Government, Laid down in his lately publifhed Speech on American Taxation, Delivered in the House of Commons, on the 19th of April, 1774. *London :* Printed for the Author, by H. S. Woodfall. M. DCC. LXXV. 30*pp. Half mor.*8*vo.* (3*s.* 404)

BURKE (EDMUND). *See* ACCOUNT of the European Settlements in America. Nº 12 to 17.

BURKE (WILLIAM). South American Independence : or, the Emancipation of South America, the Glory and Interest of England. By William Burke, Author of the History of the Campaign of 1805, &c. *London :* J. Ridgway, 1807. *Title, preface, and advertisement,* 4 *leaves; text ;* 82 *pp. Unbound.* 8*vo.*   (4*s.* 6*d.* 405)

BURNABY (ANDREW). Travels through the Middle Settlements in North-America, in the Years 1759 and 1760. With Observations upon the State of the Colonies. By the Rev. Andrew Burnaby, A. M. Vicar of Greenwich. *London,* T. Payne. MDCCLXXV. *viii and* 106 *pp. and one leaf of Errata. Half calf,* 4*to.*   (6*s.* 406)

BURNABY (ANDREW). Travels through the Middle Settlements in North-America. In the Years 1759 and 1760. With Observations upon the State of the Colonies. By the Rev. Andrew Burnaby, A.M. Vicar of Greenwich. The Second Edition. *London,* T. Payne, MDCCLXXV. *Title ;* Introduction, *pp. v-xvi.* ' Map of Philadelphia'; *text* 198 *pp.* ' Erratum' 1 *page. calf.* 8*vo.*   (7*s.* 6*d.* 407)

BURNET (WILLIAM). Original Manuscript Proclamation bearing the Autograph Signature of Governor Burnet, adjourning the General Assembly of New York from the 25th to the 26th of August 1725. 1 *page, folio.* (7s. 6d. 408)

BURNEY (James). A Memoir on the Geography of the North-Eastern Part of Asia, and on the question whether Asia and America are contiguous, or are separated by the Sea. By Captain James Burney, F.R.S. From the Philosophical Transactions. *London:* William Bulmer and Co. 1818. *Title, and* 15 pp. *4to.* (2s. 6d. 409)

BURNEY (James). A Memoir of the Voyage of d'Entrecasteaux, in search of La Pérouse. By James Burney, Esq. Of the Royal Navy, and F.R.S. *London,/* Luke Hansard and Sons, 1820. 21 pp. *8vo.* (2s. 6d. 410)

BURROUGHS (Cornelius). Rich/ Newes/ from/ Jamaica :/ Of/ Great Spoyl made by the Englifh,/ upon the Enemy, both/ by/ Land, & Sea./ Being the Subftance Of a/ Letter/ from/ Cornelivs Bvrrovghs,/ Steward Generall, Dated/ from/ Point-Cagway./ *London,* Printed by M. Simmons, 1689./ *Title and* 4 pp. *4to.* (15s. 411)

The ' Rich Newes' of this rare little tract is chiefly on the title page.

BURTON (Dr. D.). Letter, partly Autograph to Sir William Johnson, dated at Westminster, Feb. 5th 1767, intimating that the Society for Propagating the Gospel in foreign Parts approve of Sir William's " Plan of an Establishment of Mifsionaries and Catechists under them for the Indians," and will appoint Missionaries as soon as suitable persons can be found; also for the Church at Schenectady: *etc.* 4 pp. *4to.* (10s. 412)

BURTON (Robert). The Englifh/ Empire/ in/ America :/ Or a Profpeét of His Majefties Dominions/ in the Weft-Indies. Namely,/

Newfoundland	Carolina	Antego
New-England	Bermuda's	Mevis, Or
New-York	Barbuda	Nevis
Penfylvania	Anguilla	S. Chriftophers
New-Jerfey	Montferrat	Barbadoes
Maryland	Dominica	Jamaica
Virginia	St. Vincent	

With an account of the Difcovery, Scituation,/ Produét, and other Excellencies of thefe Countries./ To which is prefixed a Relation of the firft Dif-

covery/ of the New World called America, by the
Spaniards./ And of the Remarkable Voyages of
feveral Englifh-/men to divers places therein./
Illuftrated with Maps and Pictures./ By R. B.
Author of England's Monarchs, &c. Admirable/
Curiofities in England, &c. Hiftorical Remarks
of Lon-/don, &c. The late Wars in England,
&c. And, the/ Hiftory of Scotland and Ireland./
London, Printed for Nath. Crouch at the Bell in/
the Poultrey near Cheapfide. 1685./ *2 prel. leaves,
and 209 pp. Copper-plate map facing the title, and
another at p.21. 2 copper-plates representing ' Strange
Creatures ' at pp. 165 and 180. Poor copy, in old
calf. 12mo.* (5s. 413)

BURTON (Robert). The/ Englifh Heroe:/ or,/ Sir
Francis Drake Revived./ Being a full Account of
the Dangerous Voyages,/ Admirable Adventures,
Notable Difcoveries,/ and Magnanimous Atchieve-
ments of that/ Valiant and Renowned Commander.
As,/ I. His Voyage in 1572. to Nombre de Dios in/
the Weft-Indies, where they faw a Pile of Bars of
Silver/ near feventy foot long, ten foot broad,
and 12 foot high./ II. His incompaffing the whole
World in 1577./ which he performed in Two years
and Ten months,/ gaining a vaft quantity of Gold
and Silver./ III. His Voyage into America in
1585. and/ taking the Towns of St. Jago, St. Domingo, Carthagena,/ and St. Auguftine./ IV. His
laft Voyage into thofe Countreys in/ 1595. with the
manner of his Death and Burial./ Recommended
as an Excellent Example to all/ Heroick and Active
Spirits in thefe days to endeavour/ to benefit their
Prince and Countrey, and Immortalize / their
Names by the like worthy Undertakings./ Revifed, Corrected, very much Inlarged, reduced
into Chap-/ters with Contents, and beautified with
Pictures./ By R. B./ Licenfed and Entred according to Order,/ March 30.1687./ *London,* Printed
for Nath. Crouch at the Bell in/ the Poultrey near
Cheapfide. 1687./ *Portrait of Drake; title; 'To the
Reader.' 1 leaf; text 206 pp. 12mo.* (15s. 414)

BURTON (Robert). The Englifh/ Empire/ in/
America:/ Or a Profpect of their Majefties Domi-/
nions in the Weft-Indies. Namely,/
Newfoundland | Carolina | Antego

New England	Bermuda's	Mevis, Or
New-York	Berbuda	Nevis
Penſylvania	Anguilla	S. Chriſtophers
New-Jerſey	Montſerrat	Barbadoes
Maryland	Dominica	Jamaica.
Virginia	St. Vincent	

With an Account of the Diſcovery, Sci-/tuation,
Product, and other Excellencies and/ Rarities of
theſe Countries./ To which is prefixed a Relation
of the firſt Diſco-/very of the New World, called
America, by/ the Spaniards. And of the Remarkable Voyages/ of ſeveral Engliſhmen to divers places
therein./ Illuſtrated with Maps and Pictures./
By R. B./ The Third Edition./ *London,* Printed
for Nath. Crouch at the Bell/ in the Poultry near
Cheapſide. 1698./ *Title and 176 pp. Map fronting
the title, and one at p. 21 ; woodcuts on pp. 157 and
166. Half russia, 12mo.*   (10s. 6d.   415)

BUSHEL (John). A true and perfect/ Narrative/
of/ The late dreadful fire which happened/ at
Bridge-Town, in the Barbadoes, April 18. 1688./
As the ſame was communicated in two/ Letters
from Mr. John Buſhel, and Mr. Francis Bond,/
two Eminent Merchants there, to Mr. Edward
Buſhel/ Citizen and Merchant of London./ Containing the beginning, progreſs, and event of that/
dreadful fire; with the eſtimation of the/ loſs ac-
crewing thereby, as it was delivered/ to his Majeſty, by ſeveral Eminent/ Merchants concerned in
that/ Loſs./ Licenced According to Order./ *London./* Printed by Peter Lillicrap, Living in Clerk-
en-/well Cloſe./ [1668]. *Title and 6 pp. half morocco, 4to.*   (1l. 1s.   416)

BUSTAMANTE (Carlos Maria de). Cuadro His-
tórico de la Revolucion de la América Mexicana,
comenzada en quince de Septiembre de Mil Ocho-
cientos Diez, por el Ciudadano Miguel Hidalgo y
Costilla. Primera [y Secunda] Epoca. Dedicada
al Ciudadano General José María Morelos. Su
Autor, Carlos María De Bustamante. *México:*
1823. Imprenta de la Aguila. *2 Volumes. Primera Epoca, title and 31 letters separately paged, with
index of 7 leaves. Secunda Epoca, title and 35 letters
separately paged, with index in 6 leaves. Unbound.
4to.*   (1l. 1s.   417)

BYERS (JOHN). References to the Plan of the Island of St. Vincent, As furveyed from the Year 1765 to 1773; by John Byers, Chief Surveyor. *London:* S. Hooper, MDCCLXXVII. *Title;* 'Alphabetical Lift,' *etc.* 'General State and Disposition of Lands;' *etc. viii pp.* ' Lands fold &c.' 8 *pp.* *8vo.* (7*s.* 6*d.* 418)

BYRES (JOHN). References to the Plan of the Island of Dominica, As furveyed from the Year 1765 to 1773; by John Byres, Chief Surveyor. *London:* S. Hooper. MDCCLXXVII. 5 *prelim. leaves* and 30 *pp.* 8*vo.* (7*s.* 6*d.* 419)

BYFIELD (NATHANAEL). An/ Account/ of the/ Late Revolution/ in/ New-England./ Together with the/ Declaration/ of the/ Gentlemen, Merchants, and Inhabitants of Boston,/ and the Country adjacent. April 18. 1689./ Written by Mᴿ. Nathanael Byfield,/ a Merchant of Bristol in New-England, to his Friends/ in London./ Licensed, June 27. 1689. J. Frafer./ *London:*/ Printed for Ric. Chifwell, at the Rofe and Crown in/ St. Paul's Church-Yard. MDCLXXXIX./ 20 *pp. Half morocco.* 4*to.* (1*l.* 12*s.* 6*d.* 420)

BYFIELD (NATHANAEL). Another copy. *Very fine, uncut, vellum.* 4*to.* (2*l.* 2*s.* 420*)

BYRON (JOHN). The Narrative of the Honourable John Byron (Commodore in a Late Expedition round the World) Containing an Account of the great Distresses Suffered by Himself and His Companions on the Coast of Patagonia, From the Year 1740, till their Arrival in England, 1746. With a Description of St. Jago de Chili, and the Manners and Customs of the Inhabitants. Also a Relation of the Lofs of the Wager Man of War, One of Admiral Anson's Squadron. Written by Himself and now Firft Publifhed. *London:* S. Baker, G. Leigh and T. Davies. MDCCLXVIII. *Half title, title, viii and 257 pp. with copperplate Frontispiece. Half morocco.* 8*vo.* (7*s.* 6*d.* 421)

BYRON (JOHN). The Narrative of the Honourable John Byron, *etc.* Written by himself. The Second Edition. *London.* S. Baker and G. Leigh. MDCCLXVIII. *Frontispiece, title, viii and 257 pp. Half morocco.* 8*vo.* (7*s.* 6*d.* 422)

BYRON (Commodore). A Voyage round the World, in His Majesty's Ship the Dolphin, Commanded by the Honourable Commodore Byron. In which is contained, A faithful Account of the feveral Places, People, Plants, Animals, &c. feen on the Voyage : And, among other particulars, A minute and exact Defcription of the Streights of Magellan, and of the Gigantic People called Patagonians. Together with an accurate Account of Seven Islands lately difcovered in the South Seas. By an Officer on Board the faid Ship. *London :* J. Newberry. MDCCLXVII. *Title and Preface, 2 leaves; Text,* 186 *pp; copper plates at pp.* 45 *and* 130, *besides the frontispiece. Half mor.* 8vo. (5s. 6d. 423)

BYRON (Commodore). A Voyage round the World, in His Majesty's ship The Dolphin, *etc.* By an Officer on Board the faid Ship. The Second edition. *London :* J. Newbery. M DCC LXVII. 2 *prel. leaves :* 186 *pp. Frontispiece, and plates at p.* 45, 130. *Old calf,* 8vo. (4s. 6d. 424)

ABOT (Sebastian). A Memoir of Sebastian Cabot; with a Review of the History of Maritime Discovery. Illustrated by Documents from the Rolls, now first published. [By Richard Biddle, of Philadelphia.] *London:* Hurst, Chance, & Co. 1831. *viii & v prel. pp. and Text 333 pp. Boards, uncut. 8vo.* (6s. 425)

CALADO (Manoel). O/ Valeroso/ Lvcideno,/ e/ Trivmpho/ da/ Liberdade./ Primeira Parte./ Composta/ por o P. Mestre Frei Manoel Calado/ da Orden de S. Paulo primeiro Ermitão, da Congregação dos/ Eremitas da Serra d'Ofsa, natural de Villaniçofa./ Dedicada/ ao Serenissimo Senhor Dom Theodosio/ Principe do Reyno, & Monarchia de Portugal./ Em *Lisboa.*/ Com licença da Sancta Inquifição, Ordinario, & Mefa do Paço./ Por Paulo CraesbeecK, Impreffor, and liureiro das Ordẽs Militares./ Anno do Senhor de 1648./ *The reverse of the title blank ; Approvaçam, etc. and Licenças,* 1 *leaf; Text in double columns* 356 *pp. Vellum, folio.* (5*l.* 5*s.* 426)

CALADO (Manoel). O Valeroso/ Lvcideno,/ e/ Trivmpho/ da/ Liberdade./ Primeira Parte./ Composta/ Pelo Padre Mestre Fr. Manoel Calado,/ Da Orden de Sam Paulo primeyro Ermitam, da Congregaçam dos Eremitas/ da Serra d'Ofsa, natural de Villa-Viçofa ;/ Dedicada/ Ao Excelentifsimo Senhor/ D. Theodosio./ Principe deste Reyno, e Monarqvia/ de Portugal./ Em *Lisboa.*/ Com todas as licenças necefsarias./ Na Officina de Domingos Carneiro. An. 1668./ *The reverse of the title blank; Dedication,* 'Ao Serenissimo Senhor,' *etc.* 7 *pp;* 'Prologo ao Leitor,' 1 *p.* 'Em

Lovvor,' Sonetos, ' Aprovaçam,' ' Licença,' 'Prologo, Licenças,' *etc.* 3 *leaves; Text in double columns in* 356 *pp. Folio.* (5*l.* 5*s.* 427)

These two editions are identical, excepting the title pages and preliminary leaves.

CALANCHA (Antonio de la). [*Engraved title*] Chronica/ Moralizada del/ Orden de S. Avgvstin/ en el Peru, con fucesos ex=/emplares vistos en esta/ Monarchia/ Tomo primero/ Por el P.c. M.o. F. Antonio/ de la Calancha Doctor/ Graduado en la Vniuersidad de/ Lima y criollo de la ciuidad de la plata./ Dedicada a Nra, S.a, de/ gratia Virgen Maria/ Madre de Dios Patrona de la/ Religion de Nro. P.c. S. Avgvstin./ [*Printed title*] Coronica/ Moralizada/ del Orden de/ San Avgvstin en el/ Perv, con Svcesos/ egenplares en esta/ Monarqvia. Dedicada a Nvestra Señora/ de Gracia, fingular Patrona i Abogada de la/ dicha Orden./ Compvesta por el mvy reverendo/ Padre Maeftro Fray Antonio de la Calancha de la mifma/ Orden, i Difinidor actual./ Dividese este primer Tomo en qvatro/ libros; lleva tablas de Capitulos, i lugares de la fagrada/ Efcritura. Año 1638./ Con Licencia,/ En *Barcelona* : Por Pedro Lacavalleria, en la/ calle de la Libreria./ 15 *prelim. leaves, including the engraved and printed titles : Text* 922 *pp. followed by* 14 *leaves of Table. Plate at p.* 783. *Large Folio.* (3*l.* 13*s.* 6*d.* 428)

A Second and important volume of this work was printed at Lima in 1653, but was never published, owing probably to certain obnoxious passages contained in it. It is a smaller volume than the first, and is of very rare occurrence. This copy wants the title, and some of the marginal notes have been cut off, probably by the Inquisition. It has 6 preliminary leaves, without the title. Book I is folioed to 15, and paged thence to 268. Book II has one preliminary leaf, and breaks off abruptly with the 42nd page. Then comes Book V in 92 pages, followed by 2 leaves containing the Table of the whole volume. In this the Fifth Book is called the *third* in order. I have never seen another copy.

(10*l.* 10*s.* 429)

CALATAYUD Y BORDA (Cypriano Geronimo de). Oracion Funebre que en las solemnes Exequias de la R. M. Maria Antonia de San Joseph, Larrea, Arispe, de los Reyes: Quatro veces Ministra en el Monasterio de Trinitarias Descalzas de esta Ciudad de Lima: Dixo en la Iglesia del Referido Monasterio en xxx. de Octubre de m.dcc. lxxxii. El R. P. Pr. Fr. Cypriano Gerónimo de Calatayud y Borda: del orden de Nra. Sra. de la Merced: Dr. Teólogo, sóstituto que fue de la

Cátedra de Prima de Sto Tomas: Regente actual
de la de Nona de Teologìa en la Real Vniuersidad
de S. Marcos: Examinador Sinodal de este
Arzobispado, y Rector del Colegio, de S. Pedro
Nolasco. Y la dedica a la Señora Condesa de
San Isidro. En *Lima*: en la Imprenta de los
Huérfanos. Año de M.DCC.LXXXIII. *The first
half of the Volume* (58 *leaves*) *unpaged: the second
144 pp. vellum 4to.* (15s. 430)

CALDWELL (CHARLES). A Discourse on the
Genius and Character of the Rev. Horace Holley,
LL.D. Late President of Transylvania University,
by Charles Caldwell, M.D. Professor of the In-
stitutes of Medicine and Clinical Practice in said
University; with an Appendix, containing copious
Notes Biographical and Illustrative. *Boston:*
Hilliard, Gray, Little, and Wilkins. 1828. *viii
prel. pp. and 294 pp. With Portrait of Horace
Holley; and 2 plates. bds. uncut, 8vo.* (5s. 431)

CALEF (ROBERT). More/ Wonders/ of the/ In-
visible World :/ Or, The Wonders of the/ Invifible
World,/ Display'd in Five Parts./ Part I. An
Account of the Sufferings of Margaret Rule,
Written by/ the Reverend Mr. C. M./ P. II.
Several Letters to the Author, &c. And his Reply
relating/ to Witchcraft./ P. III. The Differences
between the Inhabitants of Salem Village, and/
Mr. Parris their Minifter, in New-England./
P. IV. Letters of a Gentleman uninterefted, En-
deavouring to prove/ the received Opinions about
Witchcraft to be Orthodox. With fhort/ Effays to
their Anfwers./ P. V. A fhort Hiftorical Account
of Matters of Fact in that Affair./ To which is
added, A Poftfcript relating to a Book intitled,
The Life of Sir William Phips./ Collected by
Robert Calef, Merchant, of Bofton in New-
England./ Licenfed and Entered according to
Order./ *London:*/ Printed for Nath. Hillar, at
the Princes-Arms, in Leaden-Hall-ftreet,/ over
againft St. Mary-Ax, and Jofeph Collyer, at the
Golden Bible,/ on London-Bridge. 1700./ *Title;
'The Epistle to the Reader,' 6 pp;* ² *Index, 3 pp.
Letter of Cotton Mather, 1 page. Text 156 pp.
Fine large copy with rough leaves, in calf extra by
Bedford. 4to.* (5l. 5s. 432)

CALLANDER (John). Terra Australis Cognita: or Voyages to the Terra Australis, or Southern Hemisphere, during the Sixteenth, Seventeenth and Eighteenth Centuries. Containing An Account of the Manners of the People, and the Productions of the Countries, hitherto found in the Southern Latitudes ; the Advantages that may result from further Difcoveries on this great Continent, and the Methods of Eftablifhing Colonies there, to the advantage of Great Britain. With a Preface by the Editor, in which fome geographical, nautical, and commercial Questions are difcuffed. Vol. I. *Edinburgh:* Hawes, Clark, and Collins, mdcclxvi. 3 *Volumes. I. Title;* 'To Charles Townshned, Esq.' 'To Sir Lawrence Dundas, Bart.' 2 *leaves.* 'Contents,' *pp. v-vi. List of Books* 2 *pp.* 'Preface.' *viii. pp.* 'A Map of the Straits of Magellan,' *etc. Text* 516 *pp.* II. 1768. *Title, Contents, & Preface,* 3 *leaves; Text pp.* 3-692. *Map.* III. *Title & Contents,* 2 *leaves; Text* 745 *pp. Map.* 8*vo.* (15*s.* 433)

CALLAVA (Jose). Manifesto scbre las tropellas y bejaciones que cometió el Gobernador Americano de Panzacola Ardres Jackson, contra la persona y representacion del Comisario de la España Coronel Don José Callava nombrado para la entrega de la Florida occidental á los Estados — Unidos de América. Hecho y publicado por el Mismo Callava. *Habana.—*1821. 70 *pp. half morocco.* 4*to.* (10*s.* 6*d.* 434)

CALLE (Juan Diez de la). Memorial Informatorio/ al/ Rey Nvestro Señor,/ en sv Real y Svpremo Conseio/ de las Indias, Camara, y Ivnta/ de Gverra./ En Manos del Señor Ivan Baptista/ Saenz Nauarrete, Cauallero de la Orden de Alcantara,/ de fu Confejo, fu Secretario en èl, y el de la/ Camara, y Iunta./ Contiene/ Lo qve sv Magestad Provee en/ fu Còfejo, y Iunta, y por las dos Secretarias de la Nueua/ Efpaña, y Pirù, Eclefiaftico, Secular, Salarios, Eftipen-/ dios y Prefidios, fu Gente, y Cofta, y de que Cajas, y/ Hazienda Real fe paga: valor de las Encomiendas/ de Indios, y otras cofas curiofas, y ne-/ceffarias./ Por/ Ivan Diez de la Calle./ Año de m.dc. xxxxv./ *Title, reverse blank;* 'Senor,' 4 *pp ;* ' In-

dice' & 'Nota' 2 *pp.* 'En efte año de 1645,' *etc.*
8 *pp*; 'Al Lector,' 2 *pp*; 'Confejo Real de las
Indias,' *etc.* 6 *pp*; *Second Title.* 'Memorial In-
formatorio,/ al Rey Nuestro Señor,/ *etc. reverse
blank ; Text* 'Memorial Ajvstado,' *etc. folios* 2 *to*
32. *Fine copy, in mor. by Bedford.* 4*to.* (6*l.* 6*s.* 435)

CALLE (JUAN DIEZ DE LA). Memorial,/ y
Noticias Sacras,/ y Reales del Imperio/ de/ las
Indias Occidentales,/ al/ mvy Catolico, Piadoso,
y/ Poderofo Señor Rey de las Efpañas, y Nueuo/
Mundo, D. Felipe IV. N. S./ En sv real y svpremo Consejo de/ las Indias, Camara, y lvnta de
Gverra :/ En Manos/ de Iuã Baptifta Saenz
Nauarrete, Cauallero de la Ordẽ Mi-/litar de
Alcantara, de fu Confejo, y fu Secretario en el,
y en/ el de la Camara, y Iunta : Confirmador de
los priuile-/gios Reales de Caftilla./ Compre-
hende/ lo Ecclefiaftico, Secular, Politico, y Militar que por fu Secretaria/ de la Nueua-Efpaña fe
prouee : Prefidios, gente, y coftas, valor de las/
Encomiendas de Indios, y otras cofas curiofas,
necef-/rias, y dignas de faberfe./ Efcriuiale por
el año de 1646. Iuan Diez de la Calle, Oficial/
Segundo de la miffma Secretaria./ 12 *prelim.
leaves ; viz. Half-title ; title ; Epistle,* 'Señor'
signed Iuan Diez de la Calle, 5 *pp. followed by* 1
blank page ; 'Cedvla en qve sv Mageftad hizo
merced à Iuan Diez de la Calle' 4 *pp ;* 'Indice, y
Compendio' 10 *pp; Text in* 183 *folioed leaves,
followed by* 'Erratas' 1 *page, reverse blank ;* 'Memorial breve' 8 *pp. and* 'Noticias importantes' 5
*leaves. Privately printed. Fine copy, original
Spanish binding.* 4*to.* (7*l.* 17*s.* 6*d.* 436)

On the reverse of folio 180 the author says : ' Efte imprefsion fe
ha hecho de pocos cuerpos, hafta acabar la obra, porque por aora
folo fe haze para fu Mageftad, fu Confejo, y Miniftros.'

CALLE (JUAN DIEZ DE LA). Another copy, *very
fine, in blue morocco by Bedford.* 4*to.* (10*l.* 10*s.* 437)

This is probably a later issue of the preceding, with several important additions, alterations, and corrections. Two of the preliminary leaves have been cancelled and reprinted with alterations, viz. the last leaf of the Epiftle Dedicatory and the first
leaf of the *Indice*. Two preliminary leaves are added, making
in this impression 14, viz. ' Profegue el Indice defte Memorial '
and ' Notas' 2 pages ; and ' Erratas' one page, reverse blank ;
Folios 10, 11, 22, 23, 33 and 35 of the text are reprinted, with considerable additions and some omissions. The Errata after folio
183 are cancelled, and placed here on the 14th preliminary leaf,
reprinted with corrections. This copy possesses all these reprints, as well as the cancelled leaves.

CALLENDER (John). An/ Historical Difcourfe/ on the/ Civil and Religious Affairs/ of the Colony of/ Rhode-Island/ and/ Providence Plantations/ in/ New-England/ in America./ From the firft Settlement 1638, to the End of/ firft Century./ By John Callender, A.M./ *Boston :/* Printed and Sold by S. Kneeland and T. Green/ in Queen-Street. MDCCXXXIX./ *Title; Dedication* 14 *pp ; Text* 120 *pp.* 'Advertifement' 1 *p. Calf extra by Bedford. 8vo.*   (1*l.* 11*s.* 6*d.*   438)

CAMPBELL (Duncan). Manuscript Memorial of Capt. Duncan Campbell of the 84th Regiment desiring to be put on full pay. Signed and presented by the Duke of Argyle.   2 *pages. Folio.*   (5*s.*   439)

The Memorialist was Ensign in the 42nd Regiment in 1756, and served in America till the peace of 1763; was at the battle of Ticonderoga, and at the capture of Martinique and Guadaloupe, and was twice severely wounded. In the War of Independence he raised a company of Loyalists at Boston, and on his way to New York to join the army was shipwrecked, and made prisoner by the Americans, and suffered accordingly.

CAMPBELL (P.) Travels in the Interior Inhabited Parts of North America. In the years 1791 and 1792. In which is given an account of the manners and customs of the Indians, and the present war between them and the Fœderal States, the mode of life and system of farming among the new settlers of both Canadas, New York, New England, New Brunswick, and Nova Scotia; interspersed with anecdotes of people, observations on the soil, natural productions, and political situation of these countries. Illustrated with Copper-Plates. By P. Campbell.   *Edinburgh :* John Guthrie. MDCCXCIII. *x and* 387 *pp.* ' Errata,' *and Directions to the Binder,* 1 *page ; with Portrait of the Author.* 2 *plates, and Table of Distances* 1 *leaf. boards. 8vo.*   (8*s.* 6*d.*   440)

CAMPE (J. H.) Pizarro: or, the Conquest of Peru; being a continuation of the Discovery of America. For the use of Children and Young Persons. Translated from the German of J. H. Campe, Author of the New Robinson Crusoe. With a Map. *Birmingham,* J. Belcher, 1800. *Title,* 'Errata.' 6 *lines ; text,* 243 *pp.* 'Map of South America.' *half calf.* 12*mo.*   (5*s.* 441)

CAMPE (J. H.) Columbus; or the Discovery of

America. As related to his Children, And designed for the Instruction of Youth. Translated from the German of J. H. Campe, (Author of the New Robinson Crusoe.) By Elizabeth Helme, author of the History of England, Scotland, Rome, &c. &c. A New Edition, With the Translator's last Corrections and Improvements. *London:* C. Cradock and W. Joy, 1811. *iv and 271 pp.* 12mo. (*3s. 6d.* 442)

CAMPILLO Y COSIO (JOSEPH DEL). Nuevo Sistema de Gobierno Ecónomico para la América: Con los males y daños que le causa el que hoy tiene, de los que participa copiosamente España; y remedios universales para que la primera tenga considerables ventajas, y la segunda mayores intereses: Por el Señor Don Joseph del Campillo y Cosio. *Madrid.* Benito Cano. MDCCLXXXIX. *Title, Prologo del Editor, and Tabla pp. 3-32; text, 297 pp. calf,* 12mo. (*7s. 6d.* 443)

CANADA. From Canada. An Address and Caution to the Public. [dated from] Montreal 9th October 1789, [*London.*] J. Stockdale, and J. F. and C. Rivington, [1789]. *A single sheet. 2 pp. half mor.* 4to. (*2s. 6d.* 444)
This Address is signed by Boucherville and 22 other Canadians.

CANADA. A Short Topographical Description of His Majesty's Province of Upper Canada, in North America. To which is annexed A Provincial Gazeteer. *London:* W. Faden, 1799. *2 prel. leaves and 164 pp.* 8vo. (*4s. 6d.* 445)
By the Advertisement on the back of the title it appears that the Notes and Gazetteer were drawn up by David William Smith at the desire of Gen. Simcoe.

CANDID and Impartial Considerations on the Nature of the Sugar Trade; the Comparative Importance of the British and French Islands in the West-Indies: With the Value and Consequence of St. Lucia and Granada, truly ſtated. Illuſtrated with Copper Plates. *London:* R. Baldwin, MDCCLXIII. *Half-title & title, 2 leaves. Text 228 pp. With three Copper-plates;* ' A Map of the Caribbee Islands.' 'The Harbour of Calivenie.' *and* ' A Plan of Fort Royal in the Iſland of Granada.' *half mor.* 8vo. (*7s. 6d.* 446)

CANDID (A) Examination of the Mutual Claims

I

of Great-Britain, and the Colonies: with a Plan
of Accommodation, on Constitutional Principles.
New-York: Printed by James Rivington, m,dcc,
lxxv.   *On the reverse of the title ' Errata' 22 lines;
text 62 pp. half mor. 8vo.*   (7s. 6d.   447)

CANDID (A) Examination of the mutual claims
of Great-Britain, and the Colonies: with a Plan of
Accommodation, on Conſtitutional Principles. By
the Author of Letters to a Nobleman on the Con-
duɛ́t of the American War. New-York: Printed
by James Rivington, early in mdcclxxv. And
now [*London*] Republiſhed by G. Wilkie, and R.
Faulder, mdcclxxx.   *Half-title, title, ' Advertisement,' pp. iii-vi. and text pp. 7-116. Half-mor.
8vo.*   (4s. 6d.   448)

CANDID Thoughts; or, an Enquiry into the Causes
of National Diſcontents and Misfortunes since
the Commencement of the present Reign. *London:* W. Nicoll, 1781.   73 *pp. half-morocco.
8vo.*   (4s. 6d.   449)

CANER (Henry).   The Piety of Founding
Churches for the Worſhip of God : Being A Dis-
course Upon Nehemiah ii. 20. Preach'd at King's-
Chapel in Boston, Auguſt 11, 1749.   Upon
Occaſion of laying the Firſt Stone for re-building
and enlargiug the ſaid Chapel. By Henry Caner,
A.M. Miniſter of ſaid Chapel. *Boston;* New-
England : Printed and Sold by J. Draper, in
Newbury-Street. 1749.   3 *prel. leaves and* 18 *pp.
8vo.*   (4s. 6d.   450)

CAREY (Mathew). Autograph Letter to William
Dunlop, Esq., of New-York, dated at Philadelphia, June 19, 1832. 1 *page. 4to.*   (5s. 451)

In this interesting letter Mr. Carey says of himself: " I have been
myself a sort of devotee to litᵉrary pursuits. I have laboured
hard for the public, and ' worked for nothing and found myself.'
I have been in the vineyard for 53 years—and never wrote a line
with a view to profit, although some very few of my productions
were slightly profitable. I have written as much as would fill
20 or 25 octavo volumes, such as they print in London. On the
single subject of Political Economy I have written about 2000
pages, two-thirds of which were given away gratuitously at my
own expense."

CARIBBEANA. Containing Letters and Disser-
tations, together with Poetical Essays, on various
Subjects and Occasions; chiefly wrote by ſeveral
Hands in the West-Indies, and ſome of them to
Gentlemen reſiding there. Now colleɛ́ted together

in Two Volumes. Wherein are alſo compriſed,
divers Papers relating to Trade, Government,
and Laws in general; but more eſpecially, to thoſe
of the Britiſh Sugar-Colonies, and of Barbados
in particular: As likewiſe the Characters of the
moſt eminent Men that have died, of late years,
in that Iſland. To which are added in an Appendix, Some Pieces never before Publiſhed. Vol. 1.
[& II.] *London:* T. Osborne and W. Smith,
M.DCC.XLI. 2 Vólumes. I. *Title;* 'Preface,'
pp. iii-x; and text 404 *pp.* 'Index' and 'Errata,'
5 *leaves.* II. *Title,* 'Preface' *xvi pp; and text* 358
pp. 'Index' and 'Errata,' 4 *leaves.* *half-calf.*
4to. (1*l.* 1*s.* 452)

CARLETTI (Francesco). Ragionamenti di Francesco Carletti Fiorentino sopra le Cose da lui
vedute ne' suoi Viaggi Si dell' Indie Occidentali,
e Orientali Come d' altri Paeſi. All' Illustriss.
Sig. Marchese Cosimo de Castiglione Gentiluo-
mo della Camera del Serenissimo Granduca di
Toscana. In *Firenze nel Garbo,* Nella Stamperìa
di Giuſeppe Manni 1701. Per il Carlieri all' In-
ſegna di S. Luigi. Con Licenza de' Superiori.
Half-title, title, 'Illustriss.' *etc. pp. v-xii;* 'Appro-
vazione' *pp. xiii-xiv.* 'Tavola' *pp. xv-lxxxviii.*
'Ragionamenti.' 1 *leaf; and text,* 395 *pp.* 'Scor-
rezioni' 1 *page. Fine copy, vellum. 8vo.* (1*l.* 1*s.* 453)

CAROCHI (Horacio). Compendio del Arte de la
Lengua Mexicana del P. Horacio Carochi de la
Compañia de Jesvs; Diſpueſto con brevedad, clarì-
dad, y propriedad, por el P. Ignacio de Paredes de
la miſma Compañia, y morador del Colegio deſ-
tinado ſolamente para Indios, de S. Gregorio de la
Compañia de Jesvs de Mexico: Y dividido en tres
partes: En la primera ſe trata de todo lo pertene-
ciente à Reglas del Arte, con toda ſu variedad, ex-
cepciones, y anomalias; en que nada ſe podrà de-
ſear, que no ſe halle: En la ſegunda ſe enſeña la formacion de unos vocablos, de otros. Y aſſi con ſola
una voz, que ſe ſepa, se podràn con facilidad deri-
var otras muchas: En la tercera ſe ponen los Ad-
verbios màs neceſſarios de la Lengua. Con todo lo
qual qualquiera à poco trabajo, y en breve tiempo
podrá con facilidad, propriedad, y expedicion hab-
lar e Idioma. Y el miſmo no menos afectuoſo, que
rendido, y reverente lo dedica, y conſagra al Glo-

riofiffimo Patriarcha San Ignacio de Loyola, Autor, y Fundador de la Compañia de Jesus. Con Las Licencias Necessarias, En *Mexico,* en la Imprenta de la Bibliotheca Mexicana, en frente de S. Auguftin. Año de 1759. 12 *prel.leaves*; Text 202 *pp. With copperplate Frontispiece representing S. Ignacio de Loyola. Vellum, 4to.* (*5l. 15s. 6d.* 454)

CAROLINA;/ or a/ Description/ Of the Present State of that/ Country,/ and/ The Natural Excellencies thereof, viz. The/ Healthfulness of the Air, Pleafantnefs of the Place,/ Advantage and Usefulnefs of those Rich Commo-/dities there plentifully abounding, which much/ encreafe an flourifh by the Induftry of the Plan-/ters that daily enlarge that Colony./ Publifhed by T. A. Gent./ Clerk on Board his Majefties Ship the Richmond, which was/ fent out in the Year 1680, with particular Inftructions to/ enquire into the State of that Country, by His Majefties/ Special Command, and Return'd this Prefent Year, 1682./ *London,*/ Printed for W. C. and to be Sold by Mrs. Grover in Pilican/ Court in Little Britain, 1682./ *Title;* 'To the Reader,' 2 *pp.* Text, 40 *pp. signed,* 'T. A.' *4to.* (*2l. 12s. 6d.* 455)

CAROLINA. The Two/ Charters/ Granted by/ King Charles IId./ To the/ Proprietors/ of/ Carolina./ With the Firft and Laft/ Fundamental Constitutions/ of that/Colony./ *London :*/ Printed, and are to be Sold by Richard Parker, at the/ Vnicorn, under the Piazza of the Royal Exchange./ [1705.] *Title and 60 pages, followed by* 'The Copy of an Act lately pafs'd in Carolina,' *etc.* 8 *pages. Fine copy, half-morocco uncut. 4to.* (*1l. 11s. 6d.* 456)

CAROLINA. The Humble Address Of the Right Honourable the Lords Spiritual and Temporal, In Parliament Affembled, presented to Her Majesty On Wednefday the Thirteenth Day of March, 1705. Relating to the Province of Carolina, And the Petition therein mentioned. With Her Majesties most gracious Answer thereunto. *London,* Printed by Charles Bill, and the Executrix of Thomas Newcomb, deceas'd; Printers to the Queens moft Excellent Majefty. 1705. 2 *leaves; half mor. folio.* (*15s.* 457)

CAROLINA. The/ Case/ of/ Proteſtant Diſſenters/ in/ Carolina,/ Shewing/ How a Law to prevent Occaſional/ Conformity There, has ended in the Total/ Subverſion of the Conſtitution in Church and/ State./ Recommended to the ſerious Con-ſideration of all that are true/ Friends to our preſent Eſtabliſhment./ *London,/* Printed in the Year M.DCC.VI./ *Title, and pp. 3-42 in long lines and '(Numb. 1-9)' 44 pp. in double columns; '(Numb. 10)' pp. 44-55 in long lines; '(Numb. 11-14)' pp. 56-67 in double columns. Fine copy, un-cut. Half-morocco. 4to.* (3*l.* 3*s.* 458)

The second part of this work consists of a collection of documents numbered from 1 to 14. viz.

1. The first Charter of Carolina, 24th March, 1675.
2. The fundamental Constitutions of Carolina, March 1, 1669.
3. A Copy of the fundamental Conſtitutions of Carolina: Agreed on April the 11th 1689.
4. The Preſent State of Affairs in Carolina. By John Ash.
5. The Repreſentation and Addreſs of ſeveral of the Members of this preſent Aſſembly returned for Colleton County, &c. to his Excellency John Granvill.
6. An Act for the more effectual Preſervation of the Govern-ment of this Province, by requiring all Perſons that ſhall hereafter be choſen Members of the Commons Houſe of Aſſembly, and fit in the ſame, to take the Oaths and ſub-scribe the Declaration appointed by this Act; and to con-form to the Religious Worſhip in this Province, according to the Church of England; and to receive the Sacrament of the Lord's Supper, according to the Rites and Uſage of the ſaid Church. 6th May 1704.
7. To His Excellency, John Lord Granville, Palatine, &c. of Carolina [Addreſs of the Diſſenters] May 10, 1704.
8. Letter of Mrs. Blake, widow of the late Governor, to the Lords Proprietors. 16th May, 1704.
9. The Petition of the Committee of the Pennſylvania Com-pany, and divers other Merchants trading to Carolina.
10. An Act for the Eſtabliſhment of Religious Worſhip in this Province according to the Church of England, *etc.* Nov. 4, 1704.
11, 12, 13, 14. Papers respecting the persecution of Rev. Ed-ward Marſton, Rector of the Church of St. Philip, in Charleston, South Carolina.

CAROLINA. Allerneuſte Beſchreibung der Provintz Carolina in Weſt-Indien. Samt einem Reiſe-Journal von mehr als Tauſend Meilen unter aller-hand Indianiſchen Nationen. Auch einer Accu-raten Land-Carte und andern Kupfer-Stichen. Aus dem Engliſchen überſetzet durch M. Viſcher. *Hamburg,* Gedruckt und verlegt, durch ſeel. Thomas von Wierings Erben, bey der Börſe, im güldnen A, B, C. Anno 1712. Sind auch zu Franckfurt und Leipzig, bey Zacharias Herteln zu bekommen. *8 prel. leaves, viz. Frontispiece, title, and preface; Text 368 pp; Half-morocco. Map and plate. 8vo.* (1*l.* 1*s.* 459)

CARTA,/ qve el P. Francisco/ Xavier Rector del Colegio/ Maximo de S. Pablo, y al prefente Pre-pofito/ Provincial de la Provincia del Perù./ Re-mitio a Los Padres Rectores de/ los Colegios, y Casas de la Compañia de Iesvs/ de la dicha Pro-vincia./ Dandoles vna breve noticia/ de la exem-plarissima vida, y dichofa muerte/ del Venerable P. Diego de Avendaño./ Año. 1689./ Con licencia en *Lima.* Por Iofehp de Contreras./ *3 prel. and 63 folioed leaves. 4to.* (1. 11s. 6d. 459)

CARTHAGENA. An Account of the Expedition to Carthagena, with Explanatory Notes and Obser-vations. *London :* M. Cooper Mdccxliii. *Half-title, Title, and* 58 *pp. half mor. 8vo.* (7s. 6d. 461)

CARTHAGENA. An Account of the Expedition to Carthagena, with Explanatory Notes and Obser-vations. The Second Edition. *London :* M. Cooper. Mdccxliii. *Half-title, title, and* 58 *pp. half mor.* 8vo. (7s. 6d. 462)

CARTHAGENA. An Account of the Expedition to Carthagena, with Explanatory Notes and Obser-vations. The Third Eidtion. *London :* M. Cooper, Mdccxliii. *Half-title, title, &* 58 *pp. half mor.* 8vo. (7s. 6d. 463)

CARTHAGENA. Authentic Papers Relating to the Expedition against Carthagena: being the Re-solutions of the Councils of War; both of Sea and Land-Officers Refpectively, at Sea and on Shore: Also the Resolutions of the General Council of War, compofed of both the Sea and Land-Officers, held on Board the Princefs Carolina, &c. With Copies of the Letters which paffed between Admiral Vernon and General Wentworth; and alfo between the Governor of Carthagena and the Admiral. *Lon-don :* L. Raymond, 1744. *Half-title, title, & text* 100 *pp. half mor. 8vo.* (7s. 6d. 464)

CARTHAGENA. A Journal of the Expedition to Carthagena, With Notes. In Answer to a late Pamphlet ; Entitled, An Account of the Expedi-tion to Carthagena. *London,* J. Roberts, m.dcc.xliv. *Half-title, title & Introduction, 3 leaves ; text pp.* 3-59. *half mor. 8vo.* (7s. 6d. 465)

This Pamphlet is attributed to General Wentworth, who com-manded the Land Forces.

CARTHAGENA. A Journal of the Expedition to Carthagena, With Notes. In Answer to a late Pamphlet; Entitled, An Account of the Expedition to Carthagena. The Second Edition. *London:* J. Roberts, M.DCC.XLIV. *Half-title, title, & introduction, 3 leaves; text pp.* 3-59. *8vo.* (*7s. 6d.* 466)

CARTHAGENA. Original Papers Relating to the Expedition to Carthagena. *London:* M. Cooper, MDCCXLIV. *Title and Preface, 2 leaves; text* 154 *pp. half mor. 8vo.* (*7s. 6d.* 467)

CARTHAGENA. Original Papers Relating to the Expedition to Carthagena. The Second Edition. *London:* M. Cooper, MDCCXLIV. *Title, & preface, 2 leaves; text* 154 *pp. half mor. 8vo.* (*7s. 6d.* 468)

CARTWRIGHT (GEORGE.) A Journal of Transactions and Events, during a Residence of nearly Sixteen Years on the Coast of Labrador; containing many interesting particulars, both of the Country and its Inhabitants, not hitherto known. Illustrated with proper Charts. By George Cartwright, Efq. In three Volumes. Vol. I. *Newark:* Printed and Sold by Allin and Ridge; 1792. *Title, and Explanation of the Frontispiece. 2 leaves.* 'Preface' *pp. iii-viii.* 'Glossary' *pp. ix-xvi, and text,* 287 *pp.* II. *Title;* 'Glossary' *pp. iii-x;* and text, 505 *pp.* III. *Title;* 'Glossary,' *pp. iii-x and text,* 248 *pp.* 'Labrador: a Poetical Epistle.' 15 *pp. With Portrait of Captain Cartwright. Map of* 'The Island of Newfoundland,' *etc.* By Lieut. Michael Lane. 1790. 23 *by* 28 *inches.* 'Chart of Part of the Coast of Labrador, *etc.* By Michael Lane. 1792.' 17 *by* 24 *inches; and a Chart of Mecklenburgh Harbour etc.* 1792. 18½ *by* 24 *inches, fine copy, 4to.* (*18s.* 469)

CARVER (JONATHAN). Travels through the Interior Parts of North-America, in the Years 1766, 1767, and 1768. By J. Carver, Esq. Captain of a Company of Provincial Troops during the late War with France. Illustrated with Copper Plates. *London:* For the Author. MDCCLXXVIII. *Title and dedication 2 leaves; contents 8 leaves;* 'Introduction,' *xvi pp. and text* 543 *pp.* 'Directions for placing the Plates,' *and* 'Errata' 1 *page. With* 'A Plan of Captain Carver's Travels,' 'A New Map of North

America,' *and* 4 *plates at pp.* 70, 228, 230, 296.
Large paper. 8vo.   (8s. 6d. 470)

CARVER (JONATHAN). Travels through the Interior Parts of North-America, in the Years 1766,
1767, and 1768. By J. Carver, Esq. Captain of a
Company of Provincial Troops during the late War
with France. Illustrated with Copper Plates. *Dublin:* S. Price, MDCCLXXIX. *Title and dedication* 2
leaves; *Contents* 8 *leaves*; 'A New Map of North
America.' 'Introduction.' *xiii. pp. and Text pp.* 15-
508. 2 *plates at p.* 50. *and p.* 279. *Fine copy, calf.*
8vo.   (10s. 6d. 471)

CARVER (JONATHAN). Travels through the Interior Parts of North America, in the Years 1766,
1767, and 1768. By J. Carver, Esq. Captain of a
Company of Provincial Troops during the late War
with France. Illustrated with Copper Plates, coloured. The Third Edition. To which is added
Some Account of the Author, and a copious Index.
London: C. Dilly, MDCCLXXXI. *Title, and Advertisement* 1 *page*; *signed* 'John Coakley Lettsom.'
'Some Account of Captain J. Carver.' 22 *pp*; *Dedication* to Sir Joseph Bankes, 1 *leaf*; 'Address' 2
leaves; 'Contents,' 8 *leaves*; 'Introduction' *xvi pp.*
Text pp. 17-543. *Directions for Placing the Maps and
Plates,* 1 *page*; 'Index.' 10 *leaves. Portrait of Capt.
Jonathan Carver,* 2 *maps and* 4 *plates coloured. Half-
calf.* 8vo.   (10s. 6d. 472)

CARVER (JONATHAN). Three Years Travels through
the Interior parts of North-America, for more than
Five Thousand Miles; containing an Account of
the great Lakes, and all the Lakes, Islands, and
Rivers, Cataracts, Mountains, Minerals, Soil and
Vegetable Productions of the North-West Regions
of that vast Continent; with a Description of the
Birds, Beasts, Reptiles, Insects, and Fishes peculiar to the Country. Together with a concise History of the Genius, Manners, and Customs of the
Indians inhabiting the lands that lie adjacent to
the heads and to the Westward of the great River
Mississippi; and an Appendix, describing the un-
cultivated parts of America that are the most proper
for forming Settlements. By Captain Jonathan
Carver, of the Provincial Troops in America. *Philadelphia:* Key & Simpson;—1796. *Title; dedica-*

tion pp. iii-iv; *Address, pp. v-vii*; *contents, pp. ix-xx.*
'Introduction,' *ix pp. Text pp.* 11-349. 'Appendix.' *pp.* 351-360. 'List of Subscribers.' *20 pp. calf.*
8vo. (10s. 6d. 473)

CARVER (Jonathan). A Treatise on the Culture
of the Tobacco Plant; with the Manner in which
it is usually Cured. Adapted to Northern Climates,
and designed for the use of the Landholders of
Great-Britain, and Ireland./ By Jonathan Carver,
Esq. Author of Travels through the interior Parts
of North-America. *Dublin*: Luke White. 1779.
5 prel. leaves; half-title, title, books printed, etc. contents, and dedication; text 52 pp. 8vo. (7s. 6d. 474)

CARVER (Mary). Mary Carver, Executrix of
John Carver, Esq; Jane, Frances, and Ann Thompson, Administratrices of Richard Thompson, Esq;
Theobald Taaffe, Esq; and his Wife, Adminstratrix of Samuel Lowe, Esq; John Cranch and his
Wife, and Hannah Turbill, Executrices of George
Turbill, Esq; - - - - - Appellants. David Polhill,
Esq; and others, on Behalf of themselves and
others, Proprietors of Shares in the Gold and Silver
Mines in Jamaica. - - - Respondents. The Appellants Case. To be heard at the Bar of the House
of Lords, on [*Monday*] the [*Second*] Day of [*February*] 1746. *3 pp. large folio.* (4s. 6d. 475)

CARVER (Mary). Mary Carver, and others,—
Appellants. David Polhill, Esq; and others, Respondents. William Wood, - - Appellant. David
Polhill, Esq; and others, Respondents. The Case
of the Respondents on Both these Appeals. To be
Heard at the Bar of the House of Peers the   day
of   1746. *Respecting gold & silver Mines in
Jamaica. 7 pp. large folio.* (4s. 6d. 476)

CASE (The) and Claim of the American Loyalists
Impartially stated and considered. Printed by
Order of their Agents. *London*: G. Wilkie,
MDCCLXXXIII. *Title, and 38 pp. 8vo.* (4s. 6d. 477)

CASE (A) decided in the Supreme Court of the
United States, in February, 1793. In which is
discussed the Question—"Whether a State be
liable to be sued by a private Citizen of another

State?" *Philadelphia:* Printed by T. Dobson, at the Stone-House, No. 41, South-Second-Street. M,DCC,XCIII. *Title and* 120 *pp. and* 1 *p. uncut. Half mor. 8vo.* (4s. 6d. 478)

CASE of Great Britain and America, addressed to the King, and both Houses of Parliament. The Second Edition. *London:* T. Becket and P. A. de Hondt, M.D.CCLXIX. *Title and* 1 *leaf; text* 43 *pp. half mor.* 8vo. (4s. 6d. 479)

CASE (THE) of the Importation of Bar-Iron, from our own Colonies of North America; Humbly recommended to the Confideration of the prefent Parliament, by the Iron Manufacturers of Great Britain. *London:* Thomas Tyre, MDCCLVI. 29 *pp. half mor.* 8vo. (7s. 6d. 480)

CASOS/ Notables, Svcedi-/dos en las Costas de la Civdad/ de Lima, en las Indias, y como el armada Olandefa procuraua/ coger el armadilla nueftra, que baxa con la plata de or-/dinario a Cartagena, y fe pafsò dexandolos/ burlados : defde el mes de Iunio defte/ año paffado de 1624./ [*Colophon.*] Con licencia, en *Madrid,* por Iuan Gonçalez. Año de 1625./ 4 *pp. Half mor. folio.* (1l. 11s. 6d. 481)

CASSETTE (LA) Verte de Monsieur de Sartine, trouvée chez Mademoiselle du Thé. (Cinquième Edition revue & corrigée fur celles de Leipfic & d'Amfterdam.) *A La Haye:* Veuve Whifkerfeld, M,DCC,LXXIX. *Half-title, title, and* 71 *pp.* 8vo. (4s. 6d. 482)

CASTANEDA (HERNAN LOPES DE). ¶ The firft Booke/ Of The Histo-/rie of the Difcouerie and Con-/queft of the Eaft Indias, enterprifed by/ Portingales, in their daungerous/ Nauigations, in the time of King/ Don Iohn, the fecond of that/ name./ VVhich Historie conteineth/ much varietie of matter, very profitable/ for all Nauigators, and not vnplea-/faunt to the Readers./ Set foorth in the Por-/tingale language, by Hernan/ Lopes de Caftaneda./ And Now Trans-/lated into Englifh, by/ N. L. Gentleman./ ¶ Imprinted at *London,* by/ Thomas Eaft./ 1582./ *Title, reverse blank;* ' The Epiftle Dedicatorie' 2 *pp. Signed* ' Nicholas Lichefield;' 'The Prologue,' 7 *pp. Signed* ' Hernan Lopes de Castaneda.' *Text* 164 *folioed leaves. On recto*

of folio 164 [*Colophon*] ⅌ Imprinted at London
by/ Thomas Eaſt, dwelling betweene/ Paules
Wharfe and Bay-/nards Castle./ 1582./ *Very fine
copy.* 4*to.* (5*l.* 5*s.* 483)

CASTELL (WILLIAM). A Short/ Discoverie/ Of
the Coaſts and Continent of/ America,/ From the
Equinoctiall Northward, and/ of the adjacent Isles./
By William Castell, Miniſter of the Goſpell at/
Courtenhall in Northamptonſhire./ Whereunto is
prefixed the Author's Petition to this pre-/ſent
Parliament, for the propagation of the Goſpell/ in
America; atteſted by many eminent Engliſh/ and
Scottiſh Divines./ And a late Ordinance of Par-
liament for that/ purpoſe, and for the better go-
vernment of the/ Engliſh Plantations there./ To-
gether with Sir Benjamin Rudyers speech/ in Par-
liament, 21. Jan. concerning America./ *London*,
Printed in the yeer 1644./ 6 *prel. leaves; viz.
Title*; Ornatissimis Viris. *and* Ad Lectorem. 1 *leaf*;
An Ordinance, *and* Sir B. Rudyers Speech, 4 *leaves*;
Text, 48 *pp.* 'The Second Book.' 54 *pp. Fine, large,
clean and uncut copy, in Bedford's best calf extra.*
4*to.* (5*l.* 15*s.* 6*d.* 484)

CASTELLANOS (IUAN DE). Primera Parte,/ de
las Elegias/ de Varones Illvs-/tres de Indias./ Com-
pueſtas por Juan de Caſtellanos Clerigo, Benefi-/
ciado de la Cuidad de Tunja en el nueuo/ Reyno
de Granada./ Con Privilegio./ En *Madrid,*/ En
casa de la viuda de Alonſo Gomez Impreſſor de/ ſu
Magestad. Año 1589./ 15 *prel. leaves, viz. title*;
' Yo Miguel de Ondarça,' 1 *page* ; ' Erratas' 1 *page*;
' El Rey,' 2 *pp* ; ' Mvy Poderoso Señor,' 5 *pp*;
' Señor,' 2 *pp* ; *a woodcut filling* 1 *page* ; ' Hiſpanum
regnum,' *etc.* 1 *page* ; ' Tabla' 5 *pp* ; *Epigramma,
etc.* 9 *pp. Woodcut portrait of Castellanos,* 1 *page* ;
Text, in double columns, pp. 11 *to* 382. *Fine tall
copy in vellum. Large* 8*vo.* (3*l.* 13*s.* 6*d.* 485)

CASTRES (CAILLE DE). De Wilde, ov/ Les Sauvages Caribes Insullairres D'Amerique & Histoire Nouvelle, Par M. Caillé de Castres cy deuant
Employé aus affairres d'vne compagnie Royalle
en Affrique et En Amerique. 1694. *An important, original, unpublished manuscript, of* 196 *pages.*
4*to.* (2*l.* 2*s.* 486)

CATALOGUE of Books, for Sale by E. and S.
Larkin, Nº. 47, Cornhill, Boston, confifting of the
most efteemed Authors, and arranged under the
following Heads, viz. Law, Divinity, Surgery,
Physic, Chemistry, Anatomy, History, Biography,
Voyages, Travels, Memoirs, Lives, Novels, Ro-
mances, Poetry, Dramatics, Miscellanies, Agriculture, Mathematics, Philosophy, Trade and
Commerce, Classical and School Books. *Boston:*
Printed for E. and S. Larkin. *92 pp. half mor.
12mo.*   (*3s. 6d.*   487)

CATALOGUE (A) of Books in various Branches
of Literature, and in the Oriental, Greek, Latin,
Saxon, French and English Languages : To be
sold on Thursday, May 27th [1802] at Samuel
Bradford's Auction-Room, in Boston. ☞ Sale to
begin at 9 o'clock in the Forenoon. To be viewed
for three days preceding the Sale. Printed by
Joshua Cushing, *Salem* [1802]. *Title and pp. 3-58,
and 1 p. of* ' Corrections.' *12 lines : half mor.
8vo.*   (*3s. 6d.*   488)

CATALOGUE of Books in the Library of Yale-
College, New - Haven, January, 1808. New-
Haven : Printed by Oliver Steele and Co.
MDCCCVIII. *Half-title, Title, and pp. 6-79. Half
mor. 8vo.*   (*3s. 6d.*   489)

CATALOGUE of the Books, Pamphlets, News-
papers, Maps, Charts, Manuscripts, &c. in the
Library of the Massachusetts Historical Society.
Boston: From the prefs of John Eliot, Jun. 1811.
*Title, Preface & Contents 4 leaves; Text 96 pp.
half mor. 8vo.*   (*3s. 6d.*   490)

CATALOGUE of the Library [of the Congress] of
the United States. To which is annexed, a
Copious Index, alphabetically arranged. *Washington,* Printed by Jonathan Elliot. 1815. *4 prel.
leaves, Text 170 pp. and* 'Index' *xxxii pp. Boards,
uncut. 4to.*   (*5s. 6d.*   491)

CATALOGUE of the Library of the American
Philosophical Society, held at Philadelphia for
promoting Useful Knowledge. Published by order
of the Society. *Philadelphia:* Joseph R. A. Sker-
rett. 1824. *xv preliminary, and 290 pp. half calf.
8vo.*   (*4s. 6d.*   492)

CATALOGUE of Books relating to America including a large number of rare Works Printed before 1700 amongst which a nearly complete collection of the Dutch Publications on New-Netherland from 1612 to 1820. On sale at the prices affixed by Fr. Muller, Heerengragt Amsterdam. [*Amsterdam* 1850]. *Title, and* 102 *pp. half calf, large paper, uncut.* 4*to.*   (5*s.*   493)

CATALOGUS Eorum exhibens Nomina qui in Collegio Novæ Cæsareæ Laurea alicujus Gradus, donati funt ab Anno 1748, ad Annum 1773. *Philad.* Typis Gul. & Tho. Bradford. *Single large broad sheet, folio.*   (2*s.* 6*d.*   494)

CATALOGUE (A) of Plants, growing Spontaneously within thirty Miles of the City of New-York. Published by the Lyceum of Natural History of New-York. *Albany:* Websters and Skinners, 1819. 4 *prel. leaves; Text pp.* 9-100. *and* 1 *leaf. signed* ' A. E.' [i. e. A. Eaton]. *half mor.* 8*vo.*   (4*s.* 6*d.*   495)

CATECHISM. Kurzer/ Catechismus/ Vor etliche/ Gemeinen Jesu/ Aus der/ Reformirten Religion/ In Pennsylvania,/ Die fich zum alten Berner Synodo halten :/ Herausgegeben von/ Johannes Bechteln,/ Diener des Worts Gottes./ *Philadelphia,/* Gedruckt bey Benjamin Franklin, 1742./ 42 *pp. Fine copy, unique. Bound in blue morocco, Roger Payne pattern.* 24*mo.*   (10*l.* 10*s.*   496)
On the reverse of the title is the following: viz.
Zu haben
In *Philadelphia* bey Stephan Bennezet.
In *Germantown* bey Bechteln.
Im *Falckner Schwamm* bey H. Antes.
In *Oley* bey Johannes Leimbach dem Aeltern.
In *Lancaster Town* bey Daniel Maquenet.
In *Schippach* bey G. Merckeln.
In *Socken* bey Jacob Bachmann.
In den *Forks* bey Eyseck.

CATHCART (John). A Letter to the Honourable Edward Vernon, Esq; Vice-Admiral of the Red, &c. from John Cathcart, Director of the Hospital in the late Expedition to the Weft-Indies, under the Command of the Honourable General Wentworth: concerning some Grofs Misrepresentations in a Pamphlet, lately Publifhed, and Intitled, Original Papers relating to the Expedition to the Ifland of Cuba. *London:* M. Cooper, M.D.CC.XLIV. *Title, and pp.* 3-55. *half-mor.* 8*vo.* (7*s.* 6*d.*   497)

CAUSES (The) of the present Distractions in America explained : in two Letters to a Merchant in London. By F——. B——. Printed in the Year 1774. [*Boston.*] *Title and* 16 *pp. half mor.* 8*vo.* (7*s.* 6*d.* 498)

CAVENDISH (Sir Henry.) Government of Canada. Debates of the House of Commons in the Year 1774, on the Bill for making more effectual Provision for the Government of the Province of Quebec. Drawn up from the Notes of the Right Honorable Sir Henry Cavendish, Bart., Member for Lostwithiel ; now first published by J. Wright, Editor of the Parliamentary History, etc. With a Map of Canada, copied from the second edition of Mitchell's Map of North America, referred to in the Debates. *London :* Ridgway. MDCCCXXXIX. 6 *prel. leaves ; viz. Title, preface, pp. iii-x.* ' Contents' *pp. xi & xii. Text* 296 *pp. Appendix pp.* 297-303. 2 *Maps. Cloth, uncut.* 8*vo.* (4*s.* 6*d.* 499)

CEPEDA (Fernando de). Relacion/ Vniversal Legitima,/ y verdadera del sitio en qve esta fvndada/ la muy noble, infigne, y muy leal Ciudad de Mexico, cabeça de las Provincias de toda/ la Nueva Efpaña. Lagunas, Rios, y Montes que la ciñen y rodean. Calçadas que las dibiden. Y Aze-/quias que la atrauiefan. Ynundaciones que a padecido defde fu Gentilidad. Remedios aplicados./ Defagues propueftos, y emprendidos. Origen y fabrica del de Gueguetoca, y eftado en que/ oy fe halla. Ympoficiones, derramas, y gaftos que fe an hecho. Forma con que fe à auc-/tuado defde el año de 1553. hafta el prefente de 1637./ Año de [3 *Vignettes*] 1637./ De orden,/ y mandato del/ Excellëtifsimo/ Señor D. Lope/ Diez de Armë-/dariz, Marques/ de Cadereita,/ del Confejo de/ Guerra de fu/ Mageftad, fu/ Mayordomo,/ Virrey, Gouer-/nador y Capitã/ General de la/ Nueua Efpaña,/ y Prefidente de/ la Real Audië-/cia que en efta/ Ciudad refide./ ¶ Difpuefta, y ordenada por el Licenciado Don Fernando de Cepeda Relator della. Y Don Fernando Alfonfo/ Carrillo Efcriuano Mayor del Cauildo./ Corregida, ajuftada, y concertada con el Licenciado Don Iuan de Albares Serrano del Confejo de fu/ Mageftad

Oydor mas antiguo de la dicha Real Audiencia./
¶ En *Mexico*, en la Imprenta de Francifco Salbago, Miniftro del S. Officio./ [*Colophon*] En la
Emprenta de Francifco Salbago, Mi-/niftro del
fancto Officio, en la calle de fan Francifco. m.dc.
xxxvii. *2 prelim. leaves. Text in 31, 42, 30,*¹ *and
title and 39 folioed leaves. Folio. (3l. 13s. 6d.* 500)

CERTAINE INDUCEMENTS/ To well minded/
People,/ Who are heere ftraitned in their Eftates
or otherwife: or/ fuch as are willing out of Noble
and Publique Prin-/ciples, to tranfport themfelves,
or fervants,/ or Agents for them into the Weft-/
Indies, for the propagating/ the Gofpell, and in-/
creafe of Trade./ [*London* 1644?] *12 leaves;
paged* 1-24. *4to.* (*2l. 2s.* 501)

CESPEDES (Andres Garcia de). Regimiento de
Navegacion/ mando hazer el Rei Nves/tro Señor,/
por Orden de sv Conseio/ Real de las Indias/ a
Andres Garcia de Ces/ pedes sv Cosmografo
Maior/ siendo Presidente enel dicho/ Consejo el
conde de Lemos./ [*Colophon*] En *Madrid*,/ En cafa
de Iuan de la Cuefta,/ Año m.dcvi. *Engraved
title and 4 prelim. leaves; text folioed* 1-184. *Copperplate Map at fol.* 126. *Vellum. Folio.* (*2l. 2s.* 502)

CHALKLEY (Thomas). A Collection of the
Works of Thomas Chalkley. In Two Parts.
Philadelphia: Printed by B. Franklin, and D.
Hall, Mdccxlix. *Title;* The Testimony *etc. pp.
v to xiii, signed by Israel Pemberton; The Contents,
1 page; Title to the first part,* 'A Journal,' *etc.
1 leaf; Text 326 pp. followed by one blank leaf. The
title to the Second Part Containing the Epistles, and
other writings; Text pp.* 329 *to* 590. *Fine copy in
Calf extra by Bedford.* 8vo. (*1l. 11s. 6d.* 503)

CHALKLEY (Thomas). A Collection of the
Works of Thomas Chalkley. In Two Volumes.
Vol. I. The Second Edition. *Philadelphia:*
Printed and Sold by James Chattin, in Church-
Alley. 1754. *Title; The Contents,* 1 p; *Books
sold by Chattin,* 1 p; *Title to the first part,* 'A Jour-
nal,' *etc.* 1 *leaf;* 'The Testimony,' *etc. pp. iii-viii,
signed by Israel Pemberton; Text,* 325 pp. *The
Title to the second volume* 'Containing Epistles
and other Writings:' 'Preface' *pp. iii-iv, signed*

T. C. Text, 244 *pp.* 2 *volumes in* 1. *old calf. small* 8vo.   (10s. 6d.   504)

CHALKLEY (Thomas). A Journal or Historical Account of the Life, Travels and Christian Experiences, of that Antient, Faithful Servant of Jesus Christ, Thomas Chalkley, Who departed this Life in the Island of Tortola, the fourth Day of the Ninth Month, 1741. The Second Edition. *London:* Luke Hinde, 1751. *ix and* 326 *pp. old calf.* 8vo.   (10s. 6d.   505)

CHALMERS (George). Political Annals of the Prefent United Colonies, from their Settlement to the Peace of 1763: Compiled chiefly from Records, and authorifed often by the Infertion of State-Papers. By George Chalmers, Efq. Book I. *London:* For the Author, by J. Bowen, m.dcc. lxxx. *Title; Preface,* 8 *pp; Text,* 695 *pp. Fine copy, boards, uncut.* 4to.   (2l. 2s.   506)

CHALMERS (George). [An Introduction to the History of the Revolt of the Colonies. *London:* Printed by Baker and Galabin. 1782.] *Without title or any preliminary leaves. The Text begins on Signature* B, *page* 1, *and ends on page* 496, *with* 'End of Vol. 1.' *Fine copy, uncut, gilt top, russia extra.* 8vo.   (5l. 5s.   507)

Many accounts are given respecting the suppression of this book. At all events it is certain that not many copies were preserved, probably not a dozen. Mr. Rich states, on the authority of notes in his copy, which came from the library of Gilbert Buchanan, that it was printed by Baker and Galabin, and that the book was corrected for the press by Gilbert Buchanan. This copy belonged to Mr. Tutet, who wrote on the fly leaf, soon after the printing of the work: " This Book was printed in the year 1782, for George Chalmers, Esq. the Author, who wrote an history of the Rise and Progress of the American Colonies, published in Quarto. Note, the Reader will think it extraordinary there is no title page, but after the book was printed the Author suppressed it:—whether owing to the separation of the Colonies, which happened just at the season for publication, viz. December, 1782, or the prior cause in April, antecedent the dismission of a tory Administration, is only known to the Author, who is a Scotchman.   E. Tutet, 1783."
" This was to have made two volumes, the first only was finished, but never published. A few copies only were preserved."
The book is divided into Reigns, extending from James I. to George I. This volume was reprinted in Boston in 1845, together with a second volume, for the first time printed from the original Manuscript in the autograph of Mr. Chalmers.

CHALMERS (George). Opinions on interesting subjects of Public Law and Commercial Policy; arising from American Independence. § 1. The queftion anfwered—Whether the Citizens of the

United States are confidered by the Law of England
as Aliens; what Privileges are they entitled to
within the Kingdom; what Rights can they claim
in the remaining Colonies of Britain. §2. The
Regulations for opening the American Trade
confidered; Faults found; and Amendments propofed. How the late Proclamations affect the
United States discuffed: Objections pointed out;
and Alterations fuggefted. § 3. How far the
Britifh Weft Indies were injured by the late Proclamation fully inveftigated; the Amount of their
Wants difcovered; Modes of Supply fhewn; And
the Policy of admitting the American Veffels into
their Ports amply argued. § 4. An Enquiry how
far a Commercial Treaty with the American States
is neceffary, or would be advantageous: What
the Laws of England have already provided on
this Subject; and the fundamental Laws of the
United States compared with them. By George
Chalmers, author of Political Annals of the Revolted Colonies, and of an Eftimate of the Comparative Strength of Britain. A New Edition,
Corrected. *London:* J. Debrett, 1785. *Title, and*
200 *pp. half mor. 8vo.* (16s. 6d. 508)

CHAMPION (J.). Reflections on the State of
Parties; on the National Debt, and the Neceffity
and Expediency of Suppreffing the American Rebellion. By J. Champion. The Second Edition.
London: W. Davis. M,DCC,XLVI. [*in error for* 1776.]
Title and contents 2 leaves; text 64 *pp. half morocco.*
8vo. (4s. 6d. 509)

CHAMPION (RICHARD). Considerations on the
present Situation of Great Britain and the United
States of America, with a view to their future
Commercial Connexions. Containing remarks
upon the Pamphlet publifhed by Lord Sheffield,
entitled, "Obfervations on the Commerce of the
American States;" and alfo on the Act of Navigation, fo far as it relates to thofe States. Interfperfed with fome Obfervations upon the State of
Canada, Nova Scotia, aud the Fifheries; and upon
the Connexion of the West Indies with America:
Together with various Accounts, neceffary to fhew
the State of the Trade and Shipping of both
Countries. The Second Edition, with great Ad-

ditions. To which is now first added, the Plan of an Act of Parliament for the Eſtabliſhment and Regulation of our Trade with the American States. Also, a Preface, Containing Remarks upon the Authorities on which Lord Sheffield has formed the principal Part of his Obſervations. By Richard Champion, Esq. Late Deputy Paymaster General of his Majesty's Forces. *London:* John Stockdale, MDCCLXXXIV. *xxxw prel. pp. and text, pp.* 3-274. 'Appendix.' *36 pp. 8vo.* (6s. 510)

CHAMPLAIN (SIEUR SAMUEL DE). Les/ Voyages/ de la/ Novvelle France/ Occidentale, dicte/ Canada,/ faits par le Sʳ de Champlain/ Xainctongeois, Capitaine pour le Roy en la Marine du/ Ponant, & toutes les Deſcouuertes qu'il a faites en/ ce pais depuis l'an 1603, iuſques en l'an 1629./ Où ſe voit comme ce pays a eſté premierement deſcouuert par les François,/ ſous l'authorité de nos Roys tres-Chreſtiens, iuſques au regne/ de ſa Majeſté à preſent regnante Lovis XIII./ Roy de France & de Nauarre./ Auec vn traitté des qualitez & conditions requiſes à vn bon & parfaict Nauigateur/ pour cognoiſtre la diuerſité des Eſtimes qui ſe font en la Nauigation ; Les/ Marques & enſeignements que la prouidence de Dieu à miſes dans les Mers /pour redreſſer les Mariniers en leur routte, ſans leſquelles ils tomberoient en/ de grands dangers, Et la maniere de bien dreſſer Cartes marines auec leurs/ Ports, Radés, Iſles, Sondes, & autre choſe neceſſaire à la Nauigation./ Enſemble vne Carte generalle de la deſcription dudit pays faicte en ſon Meridien ſelon/ la declinaiſon de la guide Aymant, & vn Catechiſme ou Inſtruction traduicte/ du François au langage des peuples Sauuages de quelque contrée, auec/ ce qui s'eſt paſſé en ladite Nouuelle France en l'année 1631./ A Monſeignevr le Cardinal Dvc De Richeliev./ A *Paris./* Chez Clavde Collet au Palais, en la Gallerie des Priſonniers,/ à l'Eſtoille d'Or./ M.DC.XXXII./ Auec Priuilege du Roy./ *16 prel. pp. Text* 308 *pp.* ' Seconde Partie ' 310 *pp; one blank leaf* '; ' Table povr cognoistre les Lievx remarqvables en ceste carte,' 8 *pp;* ' Traité de la Marine,' 54 *pp; one blank leaf;* ' Doctrine Chreſtienne,' *etc.* 20 *pp. Large copper-plate map, entitled,* ' Carte de la nouuelle france, aumentée depuis la/ derniere, ſervant a la nauigation faicte

en son vray/ Meridien, par le f^r de Champlain
Capitaine pour le Roy/ en la Marine ; lequel depuis l'an 1603 jufques l'année/ 1629 ; a defcouuert
plufieurs coftes, terres, lacs, rivieres,/ et Nations
de fauuages, par cy deuant inconnuës, comme/ il
fe voit en fes relations quil a faict Imprimer en
1632./ *Printed on 2 sheets, 35 by 21 inches. Fine
copy. Vellum. 4to.* (*7l. 7s.* 511)

<small>This copy contains the objectionable passage on page 27, which
caufen the two leaves Dij and Diij to be cancelled and reprinted.
We ufually find that the first paragraph on page 27 endes with
the wordes " telles defcouuertes," but in the original iſſue it
reads " telles defcouuertes ; ce que n'ont pas les grands hom|-
mes d'eſtat, qui fçauent mieux manier & conduire le| gouuerne-
ment & l'adminiſtration d'vn Royaume,| que celle de la naui-
gation, des expeditions d'outre-| mer, & des pays loingtains,
pour ne l'auoir iamais practiqué."</small>

CHAMPLAIN (Sieur Samuel de). [*Engraved Title*]
1619./ Les/ Voyages/ du Sr de Cha=/mplain Ca-
pita-/ine ordinaire/ pour le Roy/ en la nouuelle/
France es an=/nees. 1615,/ et 1618,/ dedies au/ Roy./
chez C. Collet, au/ Pallais a Paris./ Auec preui-
lege du Roy./ [*Printed Title*] Voyages/ et Des-
covvertvres/ faites en la Novvelle/ France, depuis l'année 1615. iufques/ à la fin de l'année
1618./ Par le Sieur de Champlain, Cappitai-/ne
ordinaire pour le Roy en la Mer du Ponant./ Où
font defcrits les mœurs, couftumes, habits/ façons
de guerroyer, chaffes, dances, feftins, &/ enterre-
ments de diuers peuples Sauuages, & de/ plufieurs
chofes remarquables qui luy font arri-/uées au dit
païs, auec vne defcription de la beau-/té, fertilité,
& temperature d'iceluy./ Seconde Edition./ A
Paris,/ Chez Clavde Collet, au Palais, en la/ gallerie des Prifonniers./ m.d.c.xxvii./ Avec Privilege dv Roy./ *8 prel. leaves ; viz. 2 Titles, Epistre
av Roy, Preface, and Privilege ; Text 158 folioed
leaves. With 2 folding copper plates, at folios 44 &
52, and three others in the text, on the reverse of folios
87, 99, and recto of 110. Fine Copy in Vellum.
8vo.* (*4l. 4s.* 512)

CHANDLER (T. B.) Autograph Letter ' To John
Tabor Kempe, Esq. His Majesty's Attorney General in New York,' dated at Elizabeth Town,
Sept. 30th, 1771, introducing a Client, *etc. One
page. 4to.* (*7s. 6d.* 513)

<small>The Rev. Dr. Chandler was the famous champion of Episcopacy
before the American War of Independence.</small>

CHANNING (WILLIAM ELLERY). Autograph
Letter to Rev. Mr. Willard, Deerfield, Massachusetts, dated Boston, Feby. 26, 1810. *2 pages.*
4to. (5s. 514)

CHAPPELL (EDWARD). Voyage of His Majesty's
Ship Rosamond to Newfoundland and the Southern Coast of Labrador of which Countries no Account has been published by any British Traveller
since the reign of Queen Elizabeth. By Lieut.
Edward Chappell, R. N. Author of a " Voyage to
Hudson's Bay." *London :* J. Mawman, 1818. *5
prel. leaves; viz. Title, dedication, list of engravings,
and contents.* ' Introduction,' *xix pp. Text,* 270
*pp. With Frontispiece, Map of Newfoundland co-
lored; and 2 plates at pp.* 25, 42. *Large Paper,
calf extra. 8vo.* (8s. 6d. 515)

CHARLES II. His/ Majefties Propriety/ and/ Do-
minion/ on the/ Brittifh Seas/ Asserted :/ Together
with a true Account/ of the Neatherlanders In-
fupportable/ Infolencies, and Injuries, they have
com-/mitted ; and the Ineftimable Benefits they/
have gained in their Fifhing on the Englifh Seas :/
As alfo their Prodigious and Horrid Cruelties/ in
the East and West-Indies and other Places./ To
which is added, an Exact Mapp, containing/ the
Ifles of Great Brittain, and Ireland, with the fe-/
veral Coaftings, and the Adjacent Parts of our
Neighbours : By/ an Experienced Hand./ *London,*
Printed by T. Mabb, for Andrew Kembel,/ near
St. Margarets-Hill in Southwark, and Edward/
Thomas, at the Adam and Eve in Little Brittain ;
and Robert/ Clavel, at the Staggs-Head in Ivy-
Lane, 1665./ *8 prel. leaves; dedication signed* ' R.
C.' *and Text,* 176 *pp. Portrait of Charles the II and
Copper plate Map of Great Britain and Ireland.
Half mor. 8vo.* (1l. 1s. 516)

CHARLESTOWN LIBRARY SOCIETY. The
Rules and By-Laws of the Charlestown Library
Society : and the Act of the Legislature of South-
Carolina, incorporating the said Society, with the
Royal Confirmation. The Fourth Edition. *Charles-
ton :* Printed for the Society by Nathan Childs
& Co. MDCCLXXXV. [*With MS. corrections.*] *26
pp. half mor. 4to.* (4s. 6d. 517)

CHARLEVOIX (P. DE). Histoire et Description Generale de la Nouvelle France, avec le Journal Historique d'un Voyage fait par ordre du Roi dans l'Amérique Septentrionnale. Par le P. De Charlevoix, de la Compagnie de Jesus. Tome Premier. A *Paris*, Rolin; M.DCC.XLIV. *3 volumes*. I. *Halftitle ; title ; dedication, 2 leaves ;* ' Advertissement.' *viii pp.* 'Histoire Abregée,' *pp. ix-xxvi. and text* 600 *pp.* ' Table' *pp.* 601-644. *With* 10 *Maps.* II. *Half-title ; title ;* ' Projet ;' *iv pp.* ' Fastes Chronologiques ;' *pp. v-xl.* ' Liste et examen des Auteurs ;' *pp. xli-lxj. Table* 1 *p. Permission, Approbation & Privilege ;* 1 *leaf ;* 'Table,' *xv pp. Fautes,* 1 *p ;* Text, 502 pp. 'Table' *pp.* 503-582. *With* 8 *maps.* ' Description des Plantes Principales de L'Amerique Septentrionnale.' 56 *pp. With* 22 *Plates. Vol. III. wanting. Fine Copy, in old calf.* 4*to.* (1*l.* 1*s.* 518)

CHARTERS (THE) of the British Colonies in America. *London:* J. Almon [1774]. *Title, and* 142 *pp. half mor.* 8*vo.* (4*s.* 6*d.* 519)

CHASTELLUX (M. LE MARQUIS DE). Des Ritters von Chaſtellüx Reiſebeobachtungen über America. *Hamburg,* bey der Nordiſchen typographiſchen litteräriſchen Geſellſchaft. 1785. *viii. and* 182 *pp. Small* 8*vo.* (5*s.* 6*d.* 520)

CHASTELLUX (M. LE MARQUIS DE). Voyages de M. le Marquis de Chastellux dans L'Amérique Septentrionale dans les années 1780, 1781 & 1782. Tome Premier. A *Paris,* chez Prault, Imprimeur du Roi, 1786. *2 Volumes.* I. 8 *prel. pp ; text* 390 *pp. With Map.* II. *Half-title, title, and text,* 338 *pp.* 'Table,' 339-362. ' Fautes a Corriger,' 1 *page ; and* ' Approbation,' 1 *page. With map and* 3 *plates. half calf.* 8*vo.* (8*s.* 6*d.* 521)

CHASTELLUX (MARQUIS DE). Travels in North-America, in the Years 1780, 1781, and 1782. By the Marquis de Chastellux, one of the Forty Members of the French Academy, and Major General in the French Army, serving under the Count de Rochambeau. Translated from the French by an English Gentleman, who resided in America at that period. With notes by the Translator. *London:* for G. G. J. and J. Robinson, MDCCLXXXVII.

2 Volumes. I, *xv and 462 pp.   With 2 Charts.* II.
' Second Edition.' *xii and* 432 *pp.   With 3 plates.*
8vo.   (8s. 6d.   522)

CHASTELLUX (M. le Marquis de).   Travels in
North-America, In the years 1780, 1781 and 1782.
By the Marquis de Chastellux, One of the Forty
Members of the French Academy, and Major General in the French Army, ferving under the Count
de Rochambeau.   Translated from the French by
an English Gentleman, who resided in America at
that period.   With notes by the Translator.   *Dublin:* Colles. m.dcc.lxxxvii.   *2 Volumes.* I. *xv. and*
462 *pp.   Map.* II. *xv. and* 430 *pp.   Map and 3
plates.*   (10s. 6d.   523)

CHASTELLUX (Marquis de).   Remarks on the
Travels of the Marquis de Chastellux in North
America. *London,* G. and T. Wilkie, mdcclxxxvii.
Title, and Advertisement, 2 leaves; and text 80 *pp.
half mor. 8vo.*   (6s. 6d.   524.)

CHATHAM'S (William Pitt, Earl of) Speech
On the 20th of January, 1775 [on the motion made
by his Lordship that "it may graciously please his
Majesty, that immediate orders may be despatched
to General Gage for removing his Majesty's forces
from the town of Boston," *etc.*] Taken by a Member.   *London,* T. Freeman, m.dcc.lxxv.   *Title,
and pp.* 5-18. *half mor.* 4*to.*   (5s. 6d.   525)

CHATHAM (William Pitt, Earl of).   Plan Offered
by the Earl of Chatham, to the House of Lords,
entitled, A Provisional Act, for fettling the Troubles
in America, and for afferting the Supreme Legiflative Authority and Superintending Power of
Great Britain over the Colonies.   Which was re-
jected, and not fuffered to lie upon the Table.
London: J. Almon, m.dcc.lxxv.   14 *pp. half mor.*
4*to.*   (6s.   526)

CHATHAM (William Pitt, Earl of).   A Faithful
Abstract of Lord Chatham's Last Speech in Parliament, on Tuesday, April the 7th, 1778, The Day
he was ftruck with the Illnefs which terminated
in his Death : Copied from Notes taken within the
Bar.   *London,* G. Kearsly, m,dcc,lxxviii.   *Title
and pp.* 5-15. *half mor.* 4*to.*   (6s.   527)

CHATHAM (WILLIAM PITT, EARL OF). Genuine
Abstracts from Two Speeches of the late Earl of
Chatham: and his Reply to the Earl of Suffolk.
With some Introductory Observations and Notes.
London: J. *Dodsley.* M.DCC.LXXIX. *viii & 58 pp.
half mor. 8vo.* (4s. 6d. 528)
These are Chatham's famous speeches upon American Affairs.

CHAUNCY (CHARLES). The out-pouring of the
Holy Ghost. A Sermon Preach'd in Boston, May
13. 1742. On a day of prayer obferved by the
firft Church there, to afk of God the effufion of his
Spirit. By Charles Chauncy, A.M. Paftor of faid
Church. *Boston:* Printed by T. Fleet, for D.
Henchman and S. Eliot in Cornhill. 1742. *Half-
title, title, & pp. 5-46. 8vo.* (4s. 6d. 529)

CHAUNCY (CHARLES). Marvellous Things done
by the right Hand and holy Arm of God in getting
him the Victory. A Sermon Preached the 18th of
July, 1745. Being a Day fet apart for Solemn
Thankfgiving to almighty God, For the Reduction
of Cape Breton by his Majefty's New-England
Forces, under the Command of the honourable
William Pepperrell, Efq; Lieutenant-General and
Commander in Chief, and covered by a Squadron
of his Majesty's Ships from Great Britain, com-
manded by Peter Warren, Esq; By Charles
Chauncy, D.D. Paftor of a Church in Boston.
Boston: Printed and fold by T. Fleet at the Heart
and Crown in Cornhill. 1745. *Title and pp. 5-23.
Uncut. 8vo.* (4s. 6d. 530)

CHAUNCY (CHARLES). The Counfel of two confederate Kings to fet the Son of Tabeal on the
Throne, reprefented as evil, in it's natural Tendency and moral Afpect. A Sermon Occafion'd
by the Prefent Rebellion in Favour of the Pretender. Preach'd in Boston, at the Thurfday-Lec-
ture, February 6th. 1745,6. By Charles Chauncy,
D.D. Paftor of the firft Church of Christ in faid
Town. *Boston:* Printed for D. Gookin, over
againft the Old South Meeting-Houfe. 1746. *Title
and pp. 5-43. 8vo.* (4s. 6d. 531)

CHAUNCY (CHARLES). The Validity of Presbyterian Ordination asserted and maintained. A
Discourse delivered at the Anniversary Dudleian-

Lecture, at Harvard-College in Cambridge New-
England, May 12. 1762. With an Appendix,
Giving a brief hiftorical account of the epiftles
afcribed to Ignatius; and exhibiting fome of the
many reafons, why they ought not to be depended
on as his uncorrupted works. By Charles
Chauncy, D.D. One of the Pastors of the First
Church in Boston. *Boston*, New-England: Printed
and Sold by Richard Draper, in Newbury-Street,
and Thomas Leverett in Cornhill. 1762. *Half-
title, Title, and Text, pp.* 5-118. *half morocco.*
8vo.   (4s. 6d.   532)

CHAUNCY (CHARLES). A Compleat view of
Episcopacy, As exhibited from the Fathers of the
Christian Church, until the Clofe of the Second
Century: Containing An Impartial Account of
them, of their Writings, and of what they fay
concerning Bishops and Presbyters; with observations, and remarks, Tending to fhew, that they
efteemed thefe one and the same Order of Ecclefiaftical Officers. In Answer To thofe who have
reprefented it as a Certain Fact, univerfally handed
down, even from the Apoftles Days, that governing
and ordaining Authority was exercifed by fuch
Bifhops only, as were of an Order Superior to
Prefbyters. By Charles Chauncy, D.D. Paftor of
the Firft Church of Christ in Boston. *Boston*:
Printed by Daniel Kneeland, in Queen-Street, for
Thomas Leverett, in Corn-hill. M,DCC,LXXI. *Title
& Preface x pp. Text* 474 *pp. General Contents* 3
pp. half calf. 8vo.   (10s. 6d.   533)

CHECKLEY (JOHN). The Religion of Jesus Christ
the only True Religion, or, A Short and Eafie
Method with the Deists, Wherein the Certainty
of the Chriftian Religion Is demonftrated by
Infallible Proof from Four Rules, which are Incompatible to any Impofture that ever yet has been,
or that can poffibly be. In a Letter to a Friend.
The Seventh Edition. *Boston*: Printed by T.
Fleet, and are to be Sold by John Checkley, at
the Sign of the Crown and Blue Gate over againft
the Weft End of the Town-Houfe. 1719. *Title,
reverse blank;* 'The Preface,' [By Checkley] *xii
pp; Text* 51 *pp;* 'The Epistle of St. Ignatius to
the Trallians.' 7 *pp. 8vo.*   (3l. 3s.   534)

This book is a reprint of Charles Leslie's ' Short and Easie Method with the Deists,' first published in London in 1699, but Mr. Checkley prefixed a preface of his own of 12 pages, not in the 8th Ed. (v. No 535). This edition does not contain Checkley's Discourse concerning Episcopacy. Thomas, vol. ii. p. 428, says, " Whether he [Checkley] was a regular bookseller or not, I am not prepared to say; I have seen no book printed for him in America."

[CHECKLEY (John)]. A Short and Eafie Method with the Deists. Wherein the Certainty of the Christian Religion Is demonftrated, by infallible Proof from Four Rules, which are Incompatible to any Impofture that ever yet has been, or that can poffibly be. In a Letter to a Friend. The Eighth Edition. *London:* Printed by J. Applebee, and Sold by John Checkley, at the Sign of the Crown and Blue-Gate, over againft the West-End of the Town-Houfe in Boston. 1723. 132 *pp.* 8*vo.* (3*l.* 3*s.* 535)

Considerable interest attaches to this very rare book, in consequence of the alarm that it raised in New England, and the litigation that ensued. It contains Leslie's 'Short and Easie Method with the Deists,' but with the preface described in the previous article omitted. But instead of this there is appended (pp. 41 to 127) A Discourse concerning Episcopacy [By John Checkley], wherein he endeavours to prove that Dissenters, not being Episcopally ordained, are no ministers, *etc.* and comments rather harshly upon the Church Courses of New England. This gave great offence, and Checkley was prosecuted in 1724 at the Inferior Court for publishing " a false and scandalous libel." He was convicted, but appealed to the Superior Court, where, after a long speech in his own defence, endeavouring to show that this *Book is not a Libel*, the jury found the following verdict:

" The Jury's Verdict."

John Checkley }
ad fect' }
Dom. Reg. }

The Jury find specially: viz. If the Book intituled, A Short and Easy Method with the Deists, containing in it a Discourse concerning Episcopacy (published, and many of them sold by the said Checkley) be a false and scandalous Libel; Then we find the faid Checkley guilty of all and every Part of the Indictment (excepting that supposed to traduce and draw into dispute the undoubted Right and Title of our Sovereign Lord King George, to the Kingdoms of Great Britain and Ireland, and the Territories thereto belonging)—But if the said Book, containing a Discourse concerning Episcopacy as aforesaid, be not a false and scandalous Libel; Then we find him not guilty.

Att' Samuel Tyley Clerc."

The Defendant then put in his ' Plea in Arrest of Judgment,' which is given in extenso in his Speech (see No 536), concluding, " But be that as it will, the Dissenters are affirm'd to be *no Ministers*, to be *Schismatics*, and excommunicate by the Canons of the Church of England, which are part of the Law of the Land; and therefore, to say the same things of them, I humbly hope shall not be deemed a Libel."

The Sentence of the Court.

Suffolk, ff. At a Court of Assise, &c. Nov. 27, 1724.

Checkley } The Court having maturely advised on this special
ad fect' } Verdict, are of Opinion that the said John Checkley
Dom. Reg. } is guilty of publishing and selling of a false and scandalous Libel. It's therefore considered by the Court, That

the said John Checkley shall pay a Fine of Fifty Pounds to the King, and enter into Recognizance in the Sum of One Hundred Pounds, wih two Sureties in the Sum of Fifty Pounds each, for his good Behaviour for Six Months, and also pay Costs of Prosecution, standing committed until this Sentence be performed.
                                        Att' Samuel Tyley, Clerc."

CHECKLEY (JOHN). The Speech of Mr. John Checkley upon his Tryal, At Bofton in New-England, for publishing The Short and Eafy Method with the Deifts: To which was added, A Difcourfe concerning Episcopacy; In Defence of Chriftianity, and the Church of England, againft the Deifts and the Diffenters. To which is added: The Jury's Verdict; His Plea in Arreft of Judgment; and the Sentence of Court. *London:* Printed for J. Wilford, behind the Chapter-Houfe in St. Paul's Church-Yard. 1730. *Title, and text pp.* 40. 8*vo.*   (3*l.* 3*s.* 536)

CHECKLEY (JOHN). A Discourse Shewing Who is a true Paftor of the Church of Christ. 16 *pp.* Errata 1 *p.*   (10*s.* 6*d.* 537)
This tract is without separate title-page or imprint, but was probably printed in London soon after Mr. Checkley's trial. In a note on page 11, he says, "¶ Those who have a Mind to see the Propositions in this small Tract prov'd beyond the Possibility of a Reply, are desir'd to read a Discourse concerning Episcopacy, which they may have at the Crown and Gate oppo-ite to the West End of the Town-House in Boston. Where likewise may be had Barclay's Perswasive, printed in London, by Jonah Bowyer, with other Books of a like Nature."

[CHECKLEY (JOHN).] A Specimen of a True Diffenting Catechism, upon Right True-Blue Diffenting Principles, with * learned Notes, by Way of Explanation. *Question.* Why don't the Diffenters in their Publick Worship make ufe of the Creeds? *Answer.* Why?—Becaufe *they* are not fet down *Word for Word* in the Bible. *Question.* Well,—But why don't the Diffenters in their Publick Worfhip make use of the Lord's-Prayer? *Answer.* Oh!——Becaufe *that* is fet down *Word for Word* in the Bible. 1 *page.* 8*vo.* (10*s.* 6*d.* 538)
          * They're fo perverfe and oppofite
            As if they worfhip'd God for fpite.

CHEW (SAMUEL). The/ Speech/ of/ Samuel Chew, Esq;/ Chief Juftice of the Government of New-/ Caftle, Kent, and Sussex upon/ Delaware:/ Delivered from the Bench to the/ Grand-Jury of the County of/ New-Castle, Nov. 21. 1741; and now pub-/lifhed at their Request./ *Philadelphia:*

Printed and fold by B. Franklin./ MD,CC,XLI./
16 *pp. Calf extra by Bedford. 8vo.* (1*l.* 1*s.* 539)

CHILD (JOSIAH). A New/ Discourse/ of/ Trade/
Wherein is Recommended feveral/ weighty Points
relating to Com-/panies of Merchants./ The Act
of Navigation./ Naturalization of Strangers./
And our Woolen Manufactures./ The/ Ballance
of Trade./ And the Nature of Plantations, and
their Confequen-/ces in Relation to the Kingdom,
are ferioufly/ Difcuffed./ Methods for the Employment and Maintenance of/ the Poor are Propofed./ The Reduction of Intereft of Money to
4*l.* per/ Centum, is Recommended./ And fome
Propofals for erecting a Court of Mer-/chants for
determining Controversies, relating to/ Maritime
Affairs, and for a Law for Transfer-/rance of Bills
of Debts, are humbly Offered./ By Sir Jofiah
Child./ *London :* Printed and Sold by T. Sowle,
next Door to/ the Meeting-House in White-Hart-
Court in Gracious-/ftreet, and at the Bible in
Leaden-hall-ftreet, near/ the Market, 1698./ *24
prel. leaves, viz. Title, preface, and contents; Text*
238 *pp. Fine copy, old calf. 8vo.* (1*l.* 1*s.* 540)

CHILD (JOHN). New-Englands/ Jonas/ Caft up
at /London :/ Or,/ A Relation of the Proceedings
of/ the Court at Bofton in New-England againft
di-/vers honeft and godly perfons, for Petitioning
for Go-/vernment in the Common-wealth, according to the Laws of/ England, and for admittance
of themfelves and children/ to the Sacraments in
their Churches; and in cafe/ that fhould not be
granted, for leave to/ have Minifters and Church-
govern-ment according to the beft/ Reformation of
En-/gland and Scotland./ Together with a Con-
futation of fome Reports/ of a fained Miracle upon
the forefaid Petition, being/ thrown overboard at
Sea; As alfo a brief Anfwer to fome/ paffages in
a late Book (entituled Hypocrifie unmasked)/ fet
out by Mr. Winflowe, concerning the Inde-/pen-
dent Churches holding communion/ with the
Reformed Churches./ By Major John Child./
London : Printed for T. R. and E. M. 1647./
Title within a narrow type metal border, reverse blank;
'The Preface,' *pp.* 1-2; *Text pages* 3-22; *pages* 15 *to*
22 *being falsely marked respectively,* 9, 8, 9, 12, 13,

12, 13; *and p. 22 without any pagination, in a much
smaller type than the rest of the book. Fine large
copy in morocco by Bedford. 4to.* (21*l.* 541)

CHIPMAN (NATHANIEL). Sketches of the Prin-
ciples of Government; by Nathaniel Chipman,
Judge of the Court of the United States, for the
District of Vermont. *Rutland:* From the Press
of J. Lyon: Printed for the Author: June, M,DCC,
XCIII. *Half-title, title, 2 leaves;* 'Preface' *pp. iii-iv.*
'Errata' *1 page;* 'Contents,' *pp. viii-xii; Text pp.*
13-292. *Calf. First Edition.* 12*mo.* (7*s.* 6*d.* 542)

CHIQUITOS. Erbauliche und angenehme Gefchich-
ten derer Chiqvitos, und anderer von denen Patribus
der Gefellfchafft J Éfu in Paraquaria neu=bekehrten.
Völcker; famt einem ausführlichen Bericht von
dem Amazonen-Strom, wie auch einigen Nachrichten von der Landfchaft Guiana, in der neuen
Welt. Alles aus dem Spanifch=und Franzöfifchen
in das Teutfche überfetzet, von einem aus erwehnter Gefellfchaft. *Vienn,* Paul Straub, 1729. 8 *prel.
leaves; viz. Frontispiece, Title, and Preface; Text,*
744 *pp.* 'Regifter,' 7 *leaves; calf.* 8*vo.* (1*l.* 1*s.* 543)

CHRIST, the Christian's Life: in a Sermon on John
XIV. 19. *Burlington,* Printed by Isaac Collins,
M,DCC,LXXIII. 29 *pp.* 8*vo.* (2*s.* 6*d.* 544)

CHRISTENDOMS/ Saga/ Hliodande um pad hvor-
nenn/ Chriften Tru kom pyrft a Ifland, at for=/lage
pess haloplega Herra,/ Olafs Tryggvason/ ar No-
regs Kongs./ Cum gratia & Privilegio Sacræ Regiæ/
Maieftatis Daniæ & Norvegiæ./ Prentud i Skal
hollti ap Hendrick Krufe,/ Anno. M.DC.LXXXVIII.
(The Saga (History) of the planting of the Christian faith for the first time in Iceland under King
Olaf Tryggvason.) 2 *prel. leaves: Text 26 pp. and*
1 *sequent leaf. Half mor. 4to.* (2*l.* 2*s.* 545)

CHRISTIAN FAITH/ (THE)/ Of the People of
God, called in Scorn,/ Quakers/ In Rhode-Ifland
(who are in Unity with all faithfull Brethren/ of the
fame Profeffion in all parts of the World)/ Vindi-
cated/ From the Calumnies of Chriftian Lodowick,
that formerly/ was of that Profeffion, but is lately
fallen there-from./ As alfo from the bafe Forgeries,
and wicked Slanders of/ Cotton Mather, called a

Minifter, at Bofton, who hath greatly/ commended
the faid Chriftian Lodowick, and approved his
falfe/ Charges againft us, and hath added thereunto many grofs,/ impudent and vile Calumnies
againft us and our Brethren, in his/ late Addrefs,
fo called, to fome in New-England, the which in/
due time may receive a more full anfwer, to difcover his Igno-/rance, Prejudice and Perverfion
againft our Friends in gene-/ral, and G. K. in particular, whom he hath moft unworthily/ abufed./
To which is added, fome Teftimonies of our An-
tient/ Friends to the true Chrift of God ; Collected
out of their print-/ed Books, for the further Convincing of our Oppofers, that it/ is (and hath been)
our conftant and firm Belief to expect Salva-/tion
by the Man Chrift Jefus that was outwardly cru-
cified without/ the Gates of Jerufalem./ Printed
and Sold by William Bradford at *Philadelphia* in
Pennfyl-/vania, in the Year 1692./ *On the reverse
of the title,* ' Our Sincere Chriftian Belief is plainly
afferted ' *etc. Text pp.* 3-16. *signed,* ' William Bradford.' *Half calf. 4to.* (4*l.* 14*s.* 6*d.* 546)

CHRONOLOGIE Septenaire/ de/ L'Histoire/ de la
Paix entre/ les Roys de France/ et d'Espagne./
Contenant les chofes plus memorables adue-/nuës
en France, Efpagne, Allemagne, Italie, An-/gle-
terre ; Efcoffe, Flandres, Hongrie, Pologne,/ Suece,
Tranffiluanie, & autres endroits de l'Eu-/rope :
auec le fuccez de plufieurs navigations/ faictes aux
Indes Orientales, Occidentales &/ Septentrionales,
depuis le commencement de/ l'an 1598. iufques
à la fin de l'an 1604./ Divisee en Sept Livres./
Derniere Edition./ A *Paris,* Par Iean Richer, ruë
S. Iean de Latran à l'Arbre/ verdoyant : Et en fa
boutique au Palais, fur le Perron/ Royal, vis à vis
de la gallerie des Prifonniers./ M.D.CIX./ Avec privilege dv Roy./ 5 *prel. leaves; viz. Engraved title,*
' 1607.' *Title,* 2 *Epistles, signed* ' P.V.P.C.' *and* 506
*folioed leaves : the Privilege on reverse of the last leaf.
Old mor. 8vo.* (15*s.* 547)

CHUMILLAS (Julian). Memorial/ Jvridico, y Legal,/ qve pone/ en las Reales Manos de V. Mage-
stad/ el/ Comissario General de Indias/ Fray Julian Chumillas, del Orden de nueftro/ Padre San
Francifco./ En que representa/ la jvsta Razon qve

le precisa;/ las legales que le afsiften, para que
en nada fe alte-/ren, ni vulneren las prerrogativas
de fu cargo, ni fu/ jurifdicion, y que fe le reintegre
en lo que fe pueda/ confiderar defpojado. Y los
motivos para que fe/ mande recoger vn decreto, que
à inftancia del Pa-/dre General de toda la Familia
Fray Marcos Zar-/çofa ha mandado expedir V. Magestad, contra las/ Conftituciones de la Religion,
y fu obfervancia,/ y la creacion, y origen de efte Oficio, y el/ Real Patronato de V. Mageftad./ [1690?]
70 *leaves signed at the end* ' Lic. D. Balthafar de
Azebedo.' *Half mor. Folio.* (15*s.* 548)

CHURCH (Thomas). The History of Philip's War,
commonly called the Great Indian War, of 1675
and 1676. Also, of the French and Indian Wars at
the Eastward, in 1689, 1690, 1692, 1696, and 1704.
By Thomas Church, Esq. With numerous Notes
to explain the situation of the places of battles, the
particular geography of the ravaged country, and
the lives of the principal persons engaged in those
Wars. Also an Appendix, Containing an account
of the treatment of the natives by the early voyagers,
the settlement of N. England by the forefathers,
the Pequot War, narratives of persons carried into
captivity, anecdotes of the Indians, and the most
important late Indian wars to the time of the Creek
War. By Samuel G. Drake. Second Edition with
Plates. *Exeter, N. H. Published by J. & B. Williams.* 1829. *360 pp. With Frontispiece. Calf.*
12mo. (10*s.* 6*d.* 549)

CICERO (Marcus Tullius). M. T. Cicero's/ Cato
Major,/ or his/ Discourse/ of/ Old-Age :/ With
Explanatory Notes./ *Philadelphia :/* Printed and
Sold by B. Franklin,/ MDCC XLIV./ *Title in black
and red, reverse blank :* ' The Printer to the Reader.'
' Corrigenda ' *and* ' Index to the Notes' *pp. iii to
viii. Text,* 159 *pages. Fine and perfectly clean copy
entirely uncut; bound in blue morocco by Bedford.*
4to. ·(5*l.* 5*s.* 550)

This Book Franklin always considered the *chef d'œuvre* of his
press. He brought many copies to England, and distributed
them with evident satisfaction.

CICERO (Marcus Tullius). *Another copy, on Large
and thick Paper. Unique in this state. Old calf.*
4to. (5*l.* 5*s.* 551)

CICERO (Marcus Tullius). *Another copy, on ordinary paper, old calf.* 4*to.*   (1*l.* 11*s.* 6*d.* 552)

CICERO (Marcus Tullius). M. T. Cicero's Cato Major, or Discourse on Old Age. Addressed to Titus Pomponius Atticus. With Explanatory Notes. By Benj. Franklin LL.D. Philadelphia: Printed by B. Franklin. *London :* Re-printed for Fielding and Walker. mdcclxxviii. *Portrait of Dr. Franklin. Title ;* ' Introduction' 1 *p. signed* ' B. Franklin.' ' Index.' 1 *p. and text* 163 *pp. half mor.* 8*vo.*   (7*s.* 6*d.* 553)

CIECA DE LEON (Pedro de). Parte Primera/ Dela chronica del Peru. Que tracta la demarca=/ cion de fus prouincias : la defcripcion dellas. Las/ fundaciones de las nueuas ciudades. Los ritos y/ coftumbres de los indios. Y otras cofas eftrañas/ dignas de fer fabidas. Fecha por Pedro đ Cieça/ de Leon vezino de Seuilla./ 1553/ ℂ Con priuil-legio Real./ [*Colophon*] ℂ Impreffa en Seuilla en cafa de Martin/ de montesdoca. Acabofe a quinze de/ Março de mill y quinientos y/ cinquenta y tres años./ 10 *prel. leaves, viz* 1. *Title in red and black within a border and underneath the Arms of Spain, reverse blank :* ' El principe.' 2 *pp* ; ' *Dedication* ' Al muy alto y muy poderofo feñor don Philippe '/ 2 *pp* ; ' ℂ Prohemio del Author :' 6 *pp :* ' ✥ Tabla đlos capitulos ' *etc.* 7 *pp :* ' ℂ Los Errores de la impreffiõ ' *signature of the author at the end, over the Colophon.* 1 *page. Text folioed* j *to* cxxxiiij, *with the Autograph. Fine large and clean copy. Folio.*   (10*l.* 10*s.* 554)

CIECA DE LEON (Pedro de). La Chronica/ del Perv, Nveva=/mente escrita ,por/ Pedro de Cieça de Leon,/ vezino de Se=/uilla./ En *Anvers*/ En cafa de Martin Nucio,/ m.d.liiii./ Con preuilegio Imperial./ *On the reverse of the Title is the privilege* ; ' Al Mvy Alto,' *etc.* 2 *leaves* ; ' Prohemio del Autor :' *etc.* 5 *leaves* ; *Text* 204 *folioed leaves* ; *Fine copy with many small wood-cuts.* 8*vo.*   (3*l.* 13*s.* 6*d.* 555)

CLAIBORNE (Nathaniel Herbert). Notes on the War in the South; with Biographical Sketches of the Lives of Montgomery, Jackson, Sevier, The late Gov. Claiborne, and others. By Nathaniel Herbert Claiborne, of Franklin County, Va. A

Member of the Executive of Virginia during the
late War: *Richmond:* Published by William Ramsay. 1819. 112 *pp. calf.* 12*mo.*   (6*s.* 6*d.* 556)

CLAIM (The) of the Colonies to an Exemption
from Internal Taxes imposed by Authority of Parliament, examined: In a letter from a Gentleman
in London, to his Friend in America. *London,* W.
Johnston, MDCCLXV. *Title, and* 46 *pp. Half mor.*
8*vo.*   (5*s.* 557)

CLAP (Thomas). A Brief History and Vindication
of the Doctrines Received and Established in the
Churches of New-England, with A Specimen of
the New Scheme of Religion beginning to prevail.
By Thomas Clap, A.M. Prefident of Yale-College,
in New-Haven. *New-Haven:* Printed and Sold
by James Parker at the Post-Office, 1755. 44 *pp.*
8*vo.*   (7*s.* 6*d.* 558)

CLAP (Thomas). [A Catalogue of The moſt
valuable Books in the Library of Yale-College.
Difpofed under proper Heads. *New-Haven* 1755.]
ii and 40 *pp. Index* 3 *pp. Wanting the Title, and
stained.* 8*vo.*   (4*s.* 6*d.* 559)

CLAP (Thomas). An Essay on The Nature and
Foundation of Moral Virtue and Obligation; being
A Short Introduction To the Study of Ethics; For
the Ufe of the Students of Yale-College. By
Thomas Clap, M. A. Prefident of Yale-College,
in New-Haven. *New-Haven:* Printed by B.
Mecom. MDCCLXV. *Title, ii and* 66 *pp. Contents
and Errata* 2 *pp.* 8*vo.*   (7*s.* 6*d.* 560)

CLAP (Thomas). The/ Annals/ or/ History/ of/
Yale-College,/ In New-Haven,/ In the Colony of
Connecticut,/ from/ The firſt Founding thereof, in
the Year 1700,/ to the Year 1766:/ With An Appendix,/ Containing the Prefent State of the College, the/ Method of Inftruction and Government,
with the/ Officers, Benefactors and Graduates./
By Thomas Clap, A.M./ President of the said
College./ *New-Haven:*/ Printed for John Hotch-
kiss and B. Mecom./ M,DCC,LXVI./ *Title und
preface* 2 *leaves. Text* 103 *pp.* 'Errata' 1 *page;*
'Catalogus' *pp.* 105-124. *half mor.* 8*vo.* (15*s.* 561)

CLARK (Samuel). A New Description of the
World. Or, a Compendious Treatife of the Em-

pires, Kingdoms, States, Provinces, Countries, Iflands, Cities and Towns of Europe, Afia, Africa and America: In their Situation, Product, Manufactures and Commodities, Geographical and Hiftorical. With An Account of the natures of the People, in their Habits, Cuftoms, Wars, Religions and Policy, &c. As also, Of the Rarities, Wonders and Curiofities, of Fifhes, Beafts, Birds, Rivers, Mountains, Plants, &c. With feveral remarkable Revolutions, and delightful Hiftories. By S. Clark. *London*, Henry Rhodes, 1708. 3 *prel. leaves and 218 pp. 12mo.* (7s. 6d. 562)

CLARKE (John). An Impartial and Authentic Narrative of the Battle Fought on the 17th of June, 1775, between His Britannic Majesty's Troops and the American Provincial Army, on Bunker's Hill, Near Charles Town, in New-England. With A True and Faithful Account of the Officers who were killed and wounded in that memorable Battle. To which are added, Some particular Remarks and Anecdotes which have not yet tranfpired. The whole being collected and written on the Spot. The Second Edition, With Extracts from Three Letters lately received from America; And all the Promotions in the Army and Marines, fince the faid Battle. By John Clarke, First Lieutenant of Marines. *London*: for the Author: by J. Millan, M.DCCLXXV. *Title and 36 pp. 8vo.* (1l. 1s. 563)

CLARKE (Samuel). A True, and Faithful/ Account/ of the/ Four Chiefest/ Plantations/ of the/ Englifh in America./ To wit,/ Of Virginia./ New-England./ Bermvdvs./ Barbados./ With the Temperature of the Air: The nature of the/ Soil: The Rivers, Mountains, Beafts, Fowls, Birds,/ Fifhes, Trees, Plants, Fruits, &c./ As also,/ Of the Natives of Virginia, and New-England, their/ Religion, Cuftoms, Fifhing, Huntings, &c./ Collected/ By Samuel Clarke, fometimes Paftor in Saint Bennet-Fink, London./ *London*,/ Printed for Robert Clavel, Thomas Paffenger, William Cadman, William/ Whitwood, Thomas Sawbridge, and William Birch. 1670. *Title; and text pp. 3-85.* *Folio.* (10s. 6d. 564)

CLARKE (William). Observations On the late

and prefent Conduct of the French, with Regard
to their Encroachments upon the Britifh Colonies
in North America. Together With Remarks on
the Importance of thefe Colonies to Great-Britain.
To which is added, wrote by another Hand ; Observations concerning the Increafe of Mankind,
Peopling of Countries, &c. *Boston :* Printed and
Sold by S. Kneeland, in Queen-Street. 1755.
4 *prel. leaves; iv and* 47 *pp.* 'Observations,' *etc.*
15 *pp. half mor. 8vo.*   (10s. 6d. 565)

CLAVIGERO (Francesco Saverio). The History
of Mexico. Collected from Spanish and Mexican
Historians, from Manuscripts, and Ancient Paint-
ings of the Indians. Illustrated by Charts, and
other Copper Plates. To which are added, Critical
Dissertations on the Land, the Animals, and Inhabitants of Mexico. By Abbé D. Francesco
Saverio Clavigero. Translated from the Original
Italian, by Charles Cullen, Efq. In Two Volumes.
Vol. 1. *London,* G. G. J. and J. Robinson, mdcc
lxxxvii. 2 *Volumes.* I. *Title, and dedication,* 2
leaves. ' Translator's Preface.' *pp. iii-iv.* ' Preface.'
pp. vii-xi. 'An Account,' *etc. pp. xiii-xxxii.* 'Contents.' 2 *leaves ; and text* 476 *pp. Map, and* 24
Numbered Plates. II. *Title and Contents,* 2 *leaves ;*
463 *pp. Map and* 1 *Plate. Fine copy, in old calf.*
4to.   (2l. 2s. 566)

CLAVIGERO (Francesco Saverio). The History
of Mexico. Collected from Spanish and Mexican
Historians, from Manuscripts and Ancient Paint-
ings of the Indians. Illustrated by Charts and
other Copper Plates. To which are added, Critical
Dissertations on the Land, the Animals, and
Inhabitants of Mexico. By Abbé D. Francesco
Saverio Clavigero. Translated from the original
Italian, by Charles Cullen, Esq. The Second
Edition. In Two Volumes. Vol. I. *London :* J.
Johnson, 1807. 2 *Volumes.* I. 18 *prel. leaves and*
476 *pp. Map and* 24 *numbered plates.* II. 2 *prel.
leaves and* 463 *pp.* 1 *plate.* 4to. (1l. 11s. 6d. 567)

CLINTON (George, *Governor of New-York*).
Original Autograph of a Speech to the Senate and
Assembly of the State of New-York, at the opening
of the Legislature, January 7, 1794, entirely in the

handwriting of the Governor and having his Signature, Geo. Clinton. *Eleven pages, well preserved.* *Folio.* (1*l.* 1*s.* 568)

CLINTON (SIR HENRY). Narrative of Lieutenant-General Sir Henry Clinton, K.B. relative to his Conduct during part of his Command of the King's Troops in North America; Particularly to that which respects the unfortunate Issue of the Campaign in 1781. With an Appendix, containing Copies and Extracts of those Parts of his Correspondence with Lord George Germain, Earl Cornwallis, Rear Admiral Graves, &c. Which are referred to therein. *London :* J. Debrett, 1783. *Half-title; title ; and text 49 pp.* 'Appendix,' *pp.* 51-115. 'Errata,' *7 lines on a slip of paper.* *8vo.* (6*s.* 6*d.* 569)

CLINTON (SIR HENRY). Narrative of Lieutenant-General Sir Henry Clinton, K.B. relative to his Conduct during part of his Command of the King's Troops in North-America; Particularly to that which respects the unfortunate Issue of the Campaign in 1781. With an Appendix, containing Copies and Extracts of those Parts of his Correspondence with Lord George Germain, Earl Cornwallis, Rear Admiral Graves, &c. Which are referred to therein. Third Edition. *London :* J. Debrett, 1783. *Half-title; Title, and text 49 pp.* 'Appendix,' *pp.* 51-115. 'Errata,' *7 lines on the reverse of p.* 115. *8vo.* (6*s.* 6*d.* 570)

CLINTON (SIR HENRY.) Observations on some parts of the Answer of Earl Cornwallis to Sir Henry Clinton's Narrative. By Lieutenant-General Sir Henry Clinton, K.B. To which is added an Appendix; containing Extracts of Letters and other Papers, to which reference is necessary. *London :* J. Debrett, M.DCC.LXXXIII. *Half-title, title, and text 35 pp.* 'Appendix,' *113 pp.* 'Return,' *etc.* 1 *page ; with,* 'A View of the Strength of the Two Armies,' *etc.* A *folded sheet.* *Half mor.* *8vo.* (6*s.* 6*d.* 571)

CLINTON (SIR HENRY). A Letter from Lieut. Gen. Sir Henry Clinton, K.B. to the Commissioners of Public Accounts, relative to Some Observations in their Seventh Report, which may be

judged to imply Cenfure on the late Commanders
in Chief of His Majesty's Army in North America.
London: J. Debrett, M,DCC,LXXXIV. *Title, with
Advertisement pasted on the back; text pp.* 3-31. *half
mor.* 8vo. (5s. 6d. 572)

COOL Thoughts on the Confequences to Great Britain of American Independence. On the Expence
of Great Britain in the Settlement and Defence of
the American Colonies. On the Value and Importance of the American Colonies and the West
Indies to the British Empire. *London:* J. Wilkie.
MDCCLXXX. *Half-title, title, and* 70 *pp. half mor.*
8vo. [*Misplaced, See N*° 709.] (4s. 6d. 573)

COBBET (THOMAS). A/ Practical Discourse/ of/
Prayer./ Wherein is handled,/ The Nature, the
Duty, the Quali-/fications of Prayer; the feveral
forts of/ Prayer; viz. Ejaculatory, Publick/ Private, and Secret Prayer./ With the Neceffity of,
and In-/gagements unto Prayer./ Together, with
fundry Cafes of/ Confcience about it./ By Thomas
Cobbet,/ Minifter of the Word at Lyn./ Imprimatur, Edm. Calamy./ *London,* Printed by T. M.
for Ralph Smith/ at the Bible in Cornhil: 1654./
Half-title, title, ' To the Reader.' 4 *leaves and* 1 *p.*
'The Heads of the Chapters,' *etc.* 1 *p. and* 1 *leaf.
and text* 551 *pp. calf.* 8vo. (15s. 574)

COBBET (THOMAS). A/ Practical Discourse/ of
Prayer./ Wherein is handled,/ The Nature, the
Duty, the Quali-/fications of Prayer; the feveral
forts of/ Prayer; viz. Ejaculatory, Publick,/ Private, and Secret Prayer./ With the Neceffity of,
and In-/gagements unto Prayer./ Together with
fundry Cafes of/ Confcience about it./ By Thomas
Cobbet,/ Minifter of the Word at Lyn,/ in New-
England./ Imprimatur, Edm. Calamy. *London,*
Printed by T. M. for Joseph Crauford/at the Phœ-
nix in Pauls Church yard. 1654. *Title,* ' To the
Reader.' 4 *leaves and* 1 *p.* 'The Heads of the Chapters,' *etc.* 1 *p. and* 1 *leaf; and text* 551 *pp. calf.*
8vo. (15s. 575)

COBBET (THOMAS). A/ Practical Discourse/ of/
Prayer./ Wherein is handled,/ The Nature, the
Duty, the Quali-/fications of Prayer; the feveral
forts of/ Prayer; viz. Ejaculatory, Publick,/ Pri-

vate, and Secret Prayer./ With the Neceſſity of, and Ingage-/ments unto Prayer./ Together, with ſundry Caſes of/ Conſcience about it./ By Thomas Cobbet, Miniſter of the/ Word at Lyn, in New-England./ Imprimatur, Edm. Calamy./ *London,*/ Printed by R. I. for Thomas Newberry at the three/ Lions in Cornhill, near the Exchange. 1657./ *Half-title, title,* 'To the Reader' 4 *leaves and* 1 *p.* 'The Heads of the Chapters,' *etc.* 1 *p. and* 1 *leaf; and text* 550 *pp. calf.* 8*vo.* (15*s.* 576)

COBBET (THOMAS). Civil Magiſtrates/ Power/ In matters of Religion Modeſtly/ Debated, Impartially Stated according to the/ Bounds and Grounds of Scripture, And Anſwer/ returned to thoſe Objections againſt the ſame/ which ſeem to have any weight in them./ Together with/ A Brief Anſwer to a certain Slanderous/ Pamphlet called/ Ill News from New-England; or, A Narrative/ of New-Englands Perſecution./ By John Clark of Road-Iſland, Phyſiciàn./ By Thomas Cobbet Teacher of the Church at Lynne/ in New-England./ This Treatiſe concerning the Chriſtian Magiſtrates Power, and the exerting thereof,/ in, and about matters of Religion, written with much zeal and judgement by Mr./ Cobbet of New-England, I doe allow to be printed, as being very profitable for theſe/ times./ Feb. 7ᵗʰ. 1652. Obadiah Sedgwick./ *London,* Printed by W. Wilson for Philemon Stephens at the Gilded Lion/ in Paul's Churchyard. 1653./ *Title, and dedication to Cromwell* 4 *leaves; table* 3 *pp.* 'Errata' *and Privilege* 1 *page; text* 108 *pp. half calf,* 4*to.* (1*l.* 11*s.* 6*d.* 577)

The second part of this rare book, containing the answer to Clark's Ill News, is wanting in this copy.

COCHRANE (CHARLES STUART). Journal of a Residence and Travels in Colombia, during the Years 1823 and 1824, by Capt. Charles Stuart Cochrane, of the Royal Navy. In Two Volumes. Vol. I. London: Henry Colburn, 1825. 2 *Volumes.* I. 8 *prel. leaves; and text* 524 *pp. Frontispiece and* 'Map of Colombia, by Sidney Hall.' II. *Title; contents pp. iii-viii; text* 498 *pp.* 'Appendix.' *pp.* 499-515. *Frontispiece, fine copy, boards, uncut.* 8*vo.* (8*s.* 6*d.* 578)

COCHRANE (LORD). [*Half-title*] Vindicacion del

Vice-Almirante a los Cargos que le hicieron ante
el Gobierno de Chile los Legados del General San
Martin. [*Title*] Manifiesto de las Acusaciones que
a nombre del General San Martin hicieron sus
Legados ante el Gobierno de Chile contra el Vice-
Almirante Lord-Cochrane y Vindicacion de este
dirigida al Mismo San Martin. *Lima :* 1823. Imprenta Administrada por J. Antonio Lopez. 3 *prel.
leaves and* 68 *pages* ; *errata* 1 *page* ; *closely cut.*
12mo. 　　　　　　　　　　　　　　(7s. 6d. 579)

COCKBURN (James). The Trial of Lieutenant
Colonel Cockburne, Late Governor of the Ifland of
St. Eustatius, for the Loss of the faid Island, Be-
fore a Court Martial held at the Horfe Guards, on
Monday, May 12th, 1783, and Nine fubfequent
Days; Taken In Short Hand, By E. Hodgson,
Short Hand Writer at the Old Bailey, and Pub-
lifhed by Authority. *London :* Faulder, [1783] 71
pp. Half mor. 4to. 　　　　　　　　　(7s. 6d. 580)

COCKBURN (James). Dedicated to the Army, and
more particularly to the late Garrison of St. Eustatius. An authenticated copy of the proceedings
on the Trial of Lieut. Col. Cockburn, (Of the
Thirty-fifth Regiment,) for the Lofs of the Island of
St. Eustatius. *London :* J. Debrett, M.DCC.LXXXIII.
Title and dedication signed 'William Rogerson,' 2
leaves ; and text 194 *pp. with* 'Return,' *etc. a folded
sheet, half mor.* 8vo. 　　　　　　　　(4s. 6d. 581)

COCKBURN (John). A/ Journey over Land,/
from the/ Gulf of Honduras/ to the/ Great South-
Sea./ Performed by/ John Cockburn, and Five
other/ Englifhmen, viz./ Thomas Rounce, Richard
Banifter,/ John Holland,/ Thomas Robinfon, and
John Ballman;/ who were taken by a Spanifh
Guard-Cofta, in the John/ and Jane, Edward Burt
Mafter, and fet on Shoar at/ a Place called Porto-
Cavalo, naked and wounded, as/ mentioned in feveral News-Papers of October, 1731./ Containing,/ Variety of extraordinary Diftreffes and Adventures, and fome/ New and Ufeful Difcoveries of
the Inland of thofe almoft un-/known Parts of America : As alfo, An exact Account of the/ Manners,
Cuftoms, and Behaviour of the feveral Indians in-/
habiting a Tract of Land of 2400 Miles; particu-

larly of their/ Difpofitions towards the Spaniards and Englifh./ To which is added, a curious Piece, written in the Reign of King James I./ and never before printed, intitled,/ A Brief Difcoverye of fome Things beft worth Noteinge/ in the Travels of Nicholas Withington,/ a Factor in the Eaft-Indiafe./ *London :/* C. Rivington, M,DCC,XXXV. *viii and* 349 *pp. Map.* 8vo.   (10s. 6d.   582)

COCKBURN (JOHN). The Unfortunate English-men; or, a faithful Narrative of the Distresses and Adventures of John Cockburn, Thomas Rounce, John Holland, Richard Banister, John Balmain, and Thomas Robinson, who were taken by a Spa-nish Guarda Costa, in the John and Ann, Capt. Burt, And set on Shore, naked and wounded, at Porto Cavallo; containing a Journey over Land, from the Gulph of Honduras to the Great South Sea; wherein are many new and useful Discoveries of the Interior of those unknown Regions of Ame-rica. Also, An Account of the Manners, Customs and Behaviour of the several Indian Nations, in-habiting an Extent of Country upwards of 2500 Miles; particularly Of their Disposition to the Spaniards and English. A new Edition, carefully corrected. *London:* A. Cleugh, 1810. *2 prel. leaves and* 116 *pp.* 8vo.   (5s.   583)

CODDINGTON (WILLIAM). A/ Demonstration/ of/ True Love/ unto/ You the Rulers of the Colony of the/ Maffachufets/ in / Nevv-England ;/ Shewing/ to you that are now in Authority the unjuft/ Paths that your Predeceffors walked in, and of the/ Lord's Dealings with them in his fevere Judgments, for/ perfecuting his Saints and Children./ Which may be a Warning unto you, that you walk not in/ the fame Steps, left you come under the fame Con-demnation./ Written by one who was once in Authority with them; but al-/ways teftified againft their perfecuting Spirit, who am call'd/ William Coddington of Road-Ifland./ Printed in the Year 1674./ [*London*] *Title reverse blank:* 'To the Reader' *pp.* 3-4, *signed* ' William Coddington.' *Text, pp.* 5-20. 4*to.*   (5*l.* 15s. 6d.   584)

COELLO (MANUEL). Carta del Capitan Don/ Ma-nuel Coello, Sargento Mayor de la/ gente de guer-

ra, que lleuò el Excelentifsimo/ Señor Conde de Lemos Virrey del Perù,/ para la pacificacion de las
Prouincias de/ Puno, efcrita à vn correfpondiente/
fuyo de la Ciudad de/ Cadiz./ [*Colophon*] En *Cadiz.* Por Iuan Lorenço Machado, Impreffor/ de la
Ciudad. Año 1670./ *4 folioed leaves uncut, half
mor. Folio.*   (1*l.* 1*s.* 585)

COFFIN (WILLIAM). Autograph Memorial to Sir
George Yonge, Secretary at War, dated at London, March 1, 1792, soliciting the appointment
of Captain Lieutenant in the Corps of Queen's
Rangers, Commanded by Colonel Simcoe. *2 pages.
large* 4*to.*   (5*s.* 586)

Lieut. Coffin was at the time of presenting the memorial on half
pay of the late Royal Regiment of New York, for services during
the War of Independence. Memorialist's Father left Boston as a
Loyalist in 1775, with a large family, and became a resident at
Quebec.

COGHLAN (MARGARET). Memoirs of Mrs. Coghlan, (Daughter of the late Major Moncrieffe,)
written by herself, and Dedicated to the Britifh
Nation; being interspersed with Anecdotes of the
late American and present War, with remarks
Moral and Political. In Two Volumes. *London:*
C. and G. Kearsley, MD.CC.XCIV. *Two Volumes.*
Vol. I. *3 prel. leaves, xx and* 152 *pp. Vol. II. Title
and* 172 *pp. Thick Paper; calf.* 12*mo.* (10*s.* 6*d.* 587)

COKE (REV. DR.) A Journal of the Rev. Dr.
Coke's Vifit to Jamaica, and of his Third Tour on
the Continent of America. *London :* Printed in the
Year M,DCC,LXXXIX. *Title and text,* 16 *pp.*
12*mo.*   (4*s.* 6*d.* 588)

COKE (REV. DR.) [No. III.] A Journal of the Rev.
Dr. Coke's Fourth Tour on the Continent of Amè-
rica. *London:* G. Paramore, 1792. 23 *pp. Uncut.*
12*mo.*   (2*s.* 6*d.* 589)

COKE (THOMAS). The Substance of a Sermon,
preached at Baltimore, in the State of Maryland,
before the General Conference of the Methodist
Episcopal Church, on the 27th of December, 1784,
at the Ordination of the Rev. Francis Asbury, to
the office of a Superintendent. By Thomas Coke,
L.L.D. Superintendent of the faid Church. Publifhed at the Defire of the Conference. *London:*
J. Paramore, 1785. *Title, and dedicalion 2 leaves;
text, pp.* 5-22. *half mor.* 12*mo.*   (2*s.* 6*d.* 590)

COLDEN (CADWALLADER). An Explication of the
First Causes of Action in Matter; and of the Cause
of Gravitation. By Cadwallader Colden. New-
York: Printed in the Year, MDCCXLV. And
London Reprinted: for J. Brindley, 1746. *Title;
dedication pp. iii-vii; and text 9-75 pp, calf by
Bedford, 8vo.* (12s. 6d. 591)

COLDEN (CADWALLADER). The History of the
Five Indian Nations of Canada, which are de-
pendent on the Province of New-York in America,
and are the Barrier between the English and
French in that Part of the World. With Accounts
of their Religion, Manners, Cuſtoms, Laws, and
Forms of Government; their ſeveral Battles and
Treaties with the European Nations; particular
Relations of their ſeveral Wars with the other
Indians; and a true Account of the preſent State
of our Trade with them. In which are ſhewn the
great Advantage of their Trade and Alliance to
the Britiſh Nation, and the Intrigues and Attempts
of the French to engage them from us; a Subject
nearly concerning all our American Plantations,
and highly meriting the Conſideration of the Britiſh Nation at this Juncture. By the Honourable
Cadwallader Colden, Esq; One of his Majeſty's
Counſel, and Surveyor-General of New York. To
which are added, Accounts of the ſeveral other
Nations of Indians in North-America, their Numbers, Strength, &c. and the Treaties which have
been lately made with them. A Work highly
entertaining to all, and particularly uſeful to the
Perſons who have any Trade or Concern in that
Part of the World. *London:* T. Osborne,
MDCCXLVII. *Title, dedication* to Gen. Oglethorpe,
pp. iii-ix. Preface, pp. xi-xiv. ' Vocabulary' *pp.
xv-xvi.* 'Contents' *2 leaves.* Introduction, *19 pp.
and text pp. 21-204* ' Papers,' *etc. 283 pp. Map;
vellum. 8vo.* (12s. 6d. 592)

COLDEN (CADWALLADER). The Conduct of Cad-
wallader Colden, Esq; Lieutenant Governor of
New-York; relating to the Judges' Commiſſions,
—Appeals to the King,—and the Stamp-Duty.
[*New-York.*] Printed in the Year MDCCLXVII.
*Half-title, title, 2 leaves; and text pp. 2-56. half
mor. 8vo.* (15s. 593)

COLDEN (CADWALLADER). The History of the
Five Indian Nations of Canada, which are the
Barrier between the English and French in that
Part of the World. With particular Accounts of
their Religion, Manners, Customs, Laws, and Government; their feveral Battles and Treaties with
the European Nations; their Wars with the other
Indians; and a true Account of the prefent State
of our Trade with them. In which are fhewn,
the great Advantage of their Trade and Alliance
to the Britifh Nation; and the Intrigues and
Attempts of the French to engage them from us;
a Subject nearly concerning all our American
Plantations, and highly meriting the Confideration
of the Britifh Nation. By the Honourable Cadwallader Colden, Esq; One of His Majefty's
Counfel, and Surveyor-General of New-York. To
which are added, Accounts of the feveral other
Nations of Indians in North-America, their Numbers, Strength, &c. and the Treaties which have
been lately made with them. The Second Edition.
London: John Whiston, MDCCL. *xvi pp; Contents*
4 pp. Text, Part I. 90 *pp; Part II. pp. iv and* 91-
204; *Papers &c.* 283 *pp. Map.* 8vo. (10s. 6d. 594)

COLECCION de los Decretos y Ordenes de las
Cortes de España, que se Reputan Vigentes en la
Republica de los Estados-Unidos Mexicanos.
Mexico: 1829. Mariano Arévalo. *Title; xvi and*
216 *pp. calf.* 4to.   (10s. 6d. 595)

COLECCION de las Leyes y Decretos expedidos
por el Congreso General de los Estados-Unidos
Mejicanos, en los Años de 1829 y 1830. Comprende tambien los reglamentos del gobierno para
la ejecucion de varias leyes y decretos; algunos
acuerdos de la cámara de diputados y del consejo
de gobierno sobre asuntos notables de interes
general; los decretos expedidos por el poder
ejecutivo en virtud de las facultades extraordinarias
que se le concedieron en 25 de agosto de 1829, y
la declaracion del congreso general sobre todas las
providencias dictadas en virtud de las mismas facultades. *Méjico.* Mariano Arevalo. 1831. *Half-*
title, Title; xx and 212 *pp. Calf.* 4to. (10s. 6d. 596)

COLECCION de Ordenes y Decretos de la Sober-

ana Junta Provisional Gubernativa, y Soberanos
Congresos Generales de la Nacion Mexicana.
Tomo I. Que comprende los de la Mencionada
Junta. [II. del Primero Constituyente. III. del
Segundo Constituyente. IV. del Primero y Segundo Constitucionales.] Segunda Edicion Corregida y aumentada por una Comision de la Camara
de Diputados. *México:* 1829. Mariano Arévalo,
4 *Volumes.* I. 2 *prel. leaves; xvi and* 150 *pp.* II.
3 *prel. leaves; xiv and* 220 *pp.* III. 3 *prel. leaves;
x and* 172 *pp.* IV. 3 *prel. leaves; viii and* 198 *pp.
calf,* 4to.   (2l. 2s. 597)

COLLECTION (A) of Devotional Tracts, viz. An
Extract of the Spirit of Prayer. By W. Law,
A.M. A Discourse of Miſtakes concerning Reli-
gion, &c. By Thomas Hartley, A.M. Chriſt's
Spirit, a Chriſtian Strength. By William Dell.
The Stumbling Stone. By Ditto. The Doctrine
of Baptism. By Ditto. The Trial of Spirits. By
Ditto. The Liberty of Flesh and Spirit diſtin-
guiſhed. By J. Rutty. Observations on En-
ſlaving, Importing, and Purchaſing of Negroes, &c.
The Uncertainty of a Death-bed Repentance. *Fine
Copy in Calf by Bedford.* 8vo. (2l. 2s. 6d. 598)

This Collection consists of six tracts, printed in 1759 and 1760;
four by Franklin at Philadelphia, and two by Christopher Sower
at Germantown.

COLLECTION (A) of interesting, authentic Papers,
relative to the Dispute between Great Britain and
America; shewing the Causes and Progress of
that Misunderstanding, from 1764 to 1775. *London:*
J. Almon, M.DCCLXXVII. *Title with Advertisement
on the reverse; Text pp.* 3-280; *Index* 3 *pp. Boards,
uncut.* 8vo. (10s. 6d. 599)

These Papers are in the Advertisement called *Prior Documents,*
and are " necessary to accompany" *Almon's Remembrancer.*

COLLECTION (A) of Memorials concerning Di-
vers deceased Ministers and others of the People
called Quakers, in Pennſylvania, New-Jerſey, and
Parts adjacent, from nearly the firſt Settlement
thereof to the Year 1787. With ſome of the laſt
Expreſſions and Exhortations of many of them.
Philadelphia: Printed by Joseph Crukshank, in
Market-Street, between Second and Third-Streets.
M.DCCLXXXVII. *viii and* 439 *pp. calf, clean copy.*
8vo.   (1l. 1s. 600)

COLLECTION (A) of Poems. By feveral Hands. *Boston:* Printed and fold by B. Green and Company, at their Printing-Houfe in Newbury-ftreet; and D. Gookin in Cornhil. 1744. *55 pp. Calf extra by Bedford. 8vo.* (1*l*. 1*s*. 601)

> " This precious po'm fhall fure be read,
> in ev'ry town, I tro:
> In ev'ry chimney corner faid,
> to Portfmouth, Bofton fro."
> *Specimen Brick, from p.* 31.

COLLECTION (A) of Speeches and Writings on the Commitment of the Lord-Mayor to the Tower, &c. Re-printed from the London Papers, and fold by John Holt, on Hunter's Quay, Rotten Row, *New-York,* MDCCLXXI. *Title,* ' A Short Account,' *etc. pp. iii-iv. Text pp.* 5-48. *Half-mor. 8vo.* (6*s*. 6*d*. 602)

COLLECTION (A) of State-Papers, Relative to the Firft Acknowledgment of the Sovereignty of the United States of America, And the Reception of their Minifter Plenipotentiary, by their High Mightineffes the States General of the United Netherlands. To which is prefixed, the Political Charaĉter of John Adams, Ambaffador Plenipotentiary from the States of North America, to their High Mightineffes the States General of the United Provinces of the Netherlands. By an American. Likewise, an Essay on Canon and Feudal Law, by John Adams, Esq; *London:* John Fielding, John Debrett, and John Sewell. 1782. *Half-title, title and* 100 *pp. half-morocco, uncut. 8vo.* (4*s*. 6*d*. 603)

COLLECTION (A) of Voyages Undertaken by the Dutch Eaft-India Company, for the Improvement of Trade and Navigation. Containing an Account of feveral Attempts to find out the North-Eaft Paffage, and their Difcoveries in the Eaft-Indies, and the South Seas. Together with an Historical Introduĉtion, giving an account of the Rife, Eftablifhment and Progrefs of that great Body. Translated into English, and Illuftrated with feveral Charts. *London,* W. Freeman. 1703. *Title and Introduction,* 16 *leaves; text* 336 *pp. With* 10 *Maps at p.* 3. 9. 20. 48. 98. 103. 131. 136. 179. 252. *Old calf. 8vo.* (15*s*. 604)

COLLIBER (SAMUEL). Columna Roftrata: or, a Critical Hiftory of the English Sea-Affairs:

Wherein all the Remarkable Actions of the English Nation at Sea are described, and the moſt conſiderable Events (eſpecially in the Account of the three Dutch Wars) are proved, either from Original Pieces, or from the Teſtimonies of the Beſt Foreign Hiſtorians. By Samuel Colliber. *London:* R. Robinson. 1727. *Title; preface, pp. iii-vi; and text, pp.* 7-312. ' Index.' *4 leaves. Fine copy, old calf. 8vo.* (10s. 6d. 605)

A large part of this volume relates to affairs in America.

COLLINS (JOHN). Salt/ and/ Fiſhery,/ A Diſcourſe thereof/ Inſiſting on the following Heads./ 1. The ſeveral ways of making Salt in England, and Foreign/ Parts./ 2. The Character and Qualities good and bad, of theſe ſeveral/ ſorts of Salt, Engliſh refin'd aſſerted to be much better than/ any Foreign./ 3. The Catching and Curing, or Salting of the moſt Eminent or/ Staple ſorts of Fiſh, for long or ſhort keeping./ 4. The Salting of Fleſh./ 5. The Cookery of Fiſh and Fleſh./ 6. Extraordinary Experiments in preſerving Butter, Fleſh, Fiſh,/ Fowl, Fruit, and Roots, freſh and ſweet for long keeping./ 7. The Caſe and Sufferings of the Saltworkers./ 8. Propoſals for their Relief, and for the advancement of the/ Fiſhery, the Wollen, Tin, and divers other Manufactures./ By John Collins, Accomptant/ to the Royal Fiſhery Company./ E Reg. Soc. Philomath./ *London,* Printed by A. Godbid, and J. Playford, and are to be Sold by Mr. Robert Horne at the Royal Exchange, Mr. John Kerſey, and Mr. Hen-/ry Faithorn, at the Roſe in St. Pauls Church-yard, Mr. William Bury, Globe-/maker, at the Globe near Charing-Croſs, 1682./ *4 prel. leaves; and 164 pp.* ' The Contents ' *and* ' Errata' *2 leaves. half calf, 4to.* (10s. 6d. 606)

COLMAN (BENJAMIN). Practical Diſcourſes upon the Parable of the Ten Virgins. Being a ſerious Call and Admonition to Watchfulneſs and Diligence in preparing for Death and Judgment. By Benjamin Colman, M.A. Late Preacher at Bath in Somerſetſhire. *London,* Thomas Parkhurst, 1707. *4 prel leaves, and* 423 *pp. 8vo.* (10s. 6d. 607)

COLMAN (BENJAMIN). The Governement and Improvement of Mirth According To the Laws of Christianity. In Three Sermons.

I. Of Civil & Natural ⎱ Mirth
II. Of Carnal & Vicious ⎰
III. Of Spiritual & Holy Joy.

More efpecially defigned for the Ufe, and Recommended to the Serious Perufal of Young People,
and in Particular the Young Gentleman of Bofton. By Benj. Colman. *Boston* in New-England:
Printed by B. Green, for Samuel Phillips at the
Brick Shop. 1707. *Title;* 'To the Reader.' *4 leaves;
text,* 178 *pp. Fine copy.* 12*mo.*   (15*s.* 608)

COLMAN (Benjamin). The Piety and Duty of
Rulers To Comfort and Encourage the Ministry of
Christ. As it was reprefented in a Sermon at the
Lecture in Bofton, before His Excellency and the
General Court, June 10th, 1708. By Benjamin
Colman, M.A. Paftor of a Church in Bofton. *Bos-
ton* in N. E. Printed by B. Green: Sold by Benj.
Eliot, at his Shop under the Town-houfe, at the
Head of King Street. 1708. *2 prel. leaves and* 31
pp. Small 8vo.   (10*s. 6d.* 609)

COLMAN (Benjamin). A Devout Contemplation
On the Meaning of Divine Providence, in the Early
Death Of Pious and Lovely Children. Preached
upon the Sudden and Lamented Death of Mrs.
Elizabeth Wainwright. Who Departed this Life,
April the 8th. 1714. Having juft compleated the
Fourteenth Year of Her Age. By Benjamin Col-
man, Paftor to a Church in Bofton. *Boston,*
Printed by John Allen, for Joanna Perry, at her
Shop on the North-side of the Town-House. 1714.
Title, vi and 28 *pp. Small 8vo.*   (10*s. 6d.* 610)

COLMAN (Benjamin). A Sermon Preach'd at the
Ordination of Mr. William Cooper, In Boston,
N.E. May 23. 1716. By Benjamin Colman. With
Mr. Coopers Confeffion of Faith, and his Anfwers
to the Queftions propofed to him upon that Occa-
fion. ☞ N.B. Some Paragraphs omitted in the
Preaching, are here inferted in their proper places.
Boston: Printed by B. Green, for Samuel Gerrifh
and Daniel Henchman, and Sold at their Shops
near the Town-House. 1716. *Title;* 'To the
Reader' *2 pp;* Text 40 *pp.* 'Mr Cooper's Confes-
sion of Faith.' *etc,* 24 *pp. small 8vo.* (10*s. 6d.* 611)

COLMAN (Benjamin). The faithful Ministers of

Christ mindful of their own Death. A Sermon Preached at the Lecture in Boston; Upon the Death of the Learned and Venerable Solomon Stoddard Late Paſtor of the Church of Christ in Northampton: Who departed this Life Febr. 11. 1729. Ætat 86. By Benjamin Colman. *Boston,* New-England: Printed for D. Henchman in Cornhil, John Phillips and T. Hancock, near the Town Dock. MDCCXXIX. *Title and dedication 2 leaves; text 25 pp.* 'Appendix.' *4 pages: half morocco.* 8vo. (10s. 6d. 612)

The Appendix contains a biographical notice of Solomon Stoddard.

COLMAN (BENJAMIN). Autograph Letter 'For the Reverend Mr. Williams, President of Yale College at New Haven,' dated at Boston, Febr. 18. 1730, announcing that Dr. Isaac Watts of London is sending a complete set of his Works to the College Library. Rejoices in Mr. Belcher's appointment as Governor, *etc. one page,* 4to (10s. 6d. 613)

On the reverse of this letter is the rough draft of Mr. Williams' reply in his hand writing.

COLMAN (BENJAMIN). Autograph Letter 'For the Reverend Mr. Williams, Pastor of a Church in Springfield, The part of it called Long Meadow, dated Boston, August 19, 1735. *2 closely written pages. An interesting letter.* 4to. (10s. 6d. 614)

COLMAN (BENJAMIN). Faithful Pastors Angels of the Churches. A Sermon Preached to the Bereaved Flock, March 4, 1739. On the Lord's-Day after the Funeral of the Reverend Mr. Peter Thacher of Boſton. Ætat. 62. And now printed at their Deſire. By Benjamin Colman, D.D. *Boston:* Printed by J. Draper, for D. Henchman and S. Eliot in Cornhill. 1739. *Title and 26 pp. Uncut.* 8vo. (10s. 6d. 615)

COLMAN (BENJAMIN). Practical Diſcourses on the Parable of the Ten Virgins. Being A ſerious Call and Admonition to Watchfulneſs and Diligence in preparing for Death and Judgment. By Benjamin Colman, D.D. Paſtor of the Church in Brattle-Street, Boſton. The Second Edition. *Boston,* N.E. Printed and Sold by Rogers and Fowle in Queen-Street next to the Priſon, and J. Edwards in Cornhill. MDCCXLVII. *Title, vi and 344 pp. Large paper. Uncut.* 8vo. (1l. 1s. 616)

COLUMBUS (CHRISTOPHER.) Epiſtola de inſulis noui/ter repertis Impreſſa pariſius In campo gaillardi./ [*Vignette*] [*Second leaf begins*] Epiſtola Chriſtofori Co/lom: cui etas nra multũ debet: de Inſulis indie ſupra Gangem/ nuper inuentis. Ad quas per quirēdas octauo antea menſe au/ ſpicijs ꝛ ere inuictiſſimi Fernandi Hispaniarum Regis miſſus/ fuerat: ad magnificũ dñz Raphaelem Sanxis: eiuſdē ſereniſſi/mi Regis Teſaurariũ miſſa: quã nobilis ac lratus vir Aliāder/ de Coſco ab Hiſpano ideomate in latinũ conuertit: tercio kl's/ Maij. M. CCCC. XCIIj. Pōtificatus Alexādri. vi. Anno primo :/ *Four leaves, black letter, thirty-nine lines on a full page.* [*Paris*, 1493.] *4to.* (10*l*. 10*s*. 617)

COLUMBUS (CHRISTOPHER.) ❡ Epistola de inſulis de/ nouo repertis. Impreſſa/ pariſius in cãpo gaillardi/ [*Second leaf begins as in the preceding title.*] [*Colophon*] Chriſtoforus Colom Oceane claſſis Prefectus./ *4 leaves of 39 lines on a full page.* [*Paris* 1493.] *4to.* (10*l*. 10*s*. 618)

This edition is in every respect the same as the preceding, with the exceptions, on the first leaf, of the change in the title and the omission of the wood-cut in the title-page; and on the last leaf, the addition of the Colophon. The wood-cut on the reverse of the title-page is the same in both editions.

COLUMBUS (CHRISTOPHER). Eyn ſchön hübſch leſen von etlichen inſzlen/ die do in kurtzen zyten funden ſynd durch dē/ künig von hiſpania. vnd ſagt võ groſzen wun/ derlichen dingen die in dē ſelbē inſzlen ſynd. [*Colophon*] Getruckt zu ſtraſzburg vff gruneck võ meiſter Bartlomeſz/ küſtler ym iar. M. CCCC. XCVij. vff ſant Jeronymus tag./ *7 leaves, with 30 lines in a full page. The wood-cut on the title-page is repeated on the last page. Mor. extra by Bedford. 4to.* (10*l*. 10*s*. 619)

This is a translation into German, with some changes and additions, of the celebrated Letter of Columbus, first printed in Latin in 1493.

COLUMBUS (CHRISTOPHER.) Memorial del hecho, cerca dela hoia dela qve llaman minuta del teſtamento de don Chriſtoual Colon, primero Almerãte de las Indias, de año de. 97. Que los pretenſores del eſtado de Veragua pretenden que tomò don Franciſco de Mendoça Almirante de Aragon marido dela Marqueſa de Guadaleſte, que es la que ha pretendido y pretende la ſuceſsion del dicho Eſtado. *25 leaves. Folio.* (15*s*. 620)

COLUMBUS (CHRISTOPHER.) The History of the
Voyages of Christopher Columbus, in order to
diſcover America and the West Indies. *London* :
R. Crowder, M.DCC.LXXII. 201 *pp. Calf.*
12*mo.* (4*s.* 6*d.* 621)

COLUMBUS (CHRISTOPHER.) Del/ Primo Sco-
pritore/ del Continente/ del Nuovo Mondo/ e dei
Piú Antichi Storici che ne scrissero/ Ragionamento/
che serve di supplemento alle due lettere su la/
scoperta del Nuovo Mondo publicate nel Libro/
intitolato della patria di Cristoforo Colombo/
Stampato in Firenze nell'Anno MDCCCVIII. /*Firenze*/
Presso Molini, Landi e Comp./ MDCCCIX. *Calf by*
Bedford. 8*vo.* (10*s.* 6*d.* 622)

COLUMBUS (CHRISTOPHER.) Lettera Rarissima
di Cristoforo Colombo Riprodotta e Illustrata dal
Cavaliere Ab. Morelli Bibliotec. Regio in Venezia.
Bassano nella Stamperia Remondiniana. M.DCCC.X.
Title ; 'Prefazione,' *pp. iii-xvi.* 'Copia,' *etc.* 1 *leaf* ;
text, pp. 5-66 ; *large paper, half calf.* 8*vo.* (7*s.* 6*d.* 623)

COLUMBUS (CHRISTOPHER.) Vita di Christoforo
Colombo scritta e corredata di nuove osservazioni
di note storico-critiche e di un'Appendice di documenti rari o inediti dal Cavaliere Luigi Bossi
Membro del C. R. Istituto delle Scienze ecc. della
R. Academia delle Belle Arti di Milano, e di altre
Società scientifiche e letterarie. Con Tavole incise
in Rame. *Milano*, 1818. Vincenzo Ferrario. 4
prel. leaves and 255 *pp. Portrait and Plate. Uncut.*
8*vo.* (10*s.* 6*d.* 624)

COLUMBUS (CHRISTOPHER.) Codice Diplomatico
Colombo-Americano ofsia Raccolta di Documenti
Originali e inediti, spettanti a Cristoforo Colombo
alla scoperta ed al Governo dell' America Pubbli-
cato per ordine degl' Ill.mi Decurioni della Città
di Genova. *Genova*, dalla Stamperia e Fonderia
Ponthenier. Novembre 1823. *lxxx and* 348 *pp.*
Portrait of Columbus and 4 *plates.* 4*to.* (15*s.* 625)

COLUMBUS (CHRISTOPHER). Memorials of Columbus ; or a Collection of Authentic Documents
of that Celebrated Navigator, now first published
from the original manuscripts, by order of the
Decurions of Genoa ; Preceded by a Memoir of

M

his Life and Discoveries. Translated from the
Spanish and Italian. *London:* 1823. *Half-title;
title; 2nd title; clix prel. pp. and 251 pp. Index
and list of plates 2 leaves. With 5 plates. Boards,
uncut. 8vo.* (8s. 6d. 626)

COLUMBUS (Diego). An Original Manuscript
Letter or Memorial of Diego Columbus, son of
the Discoverer of America, and the First Admiral
and Viceroy of the Indies, addressed to the Emperor Charles the Fifth, respecting the affairs and
benevolent plans of Las Casas, to whom he offers
aid under certain conditions towards colonizing
Tierra Firme. Signed in the Autograph of Columbus. 'El Almirante y Virrey de las Indias.' Not
dated, but evidently written in 1518. *5 pages
folio.* (15l. 15s. 627)

COLUMBUS (Fernando). Histoire/ Del S. D. Fernando Colombo ;/ Nelle quali s'ha particolare, &
vera relatione/ della vita, & de' fatti dell' Ammi-
raglio/ D.Christoforo Colombo,/suo padre:/ Et dello
scoprimento, ch'egli fece dell' Indie/ Occidentali,
dette Mondo Nvovo,/ hora poffedute dal Sereniss./
Re Catolico:/ Nuouamente di lingua Spagnuola
tradotte nell' Italiana/ dal S. Alfonso Vlloa./ Con
Privilegio./ In *Venetia*, MDLXXI./ Appreffo Francesco de' Francefchi Sanese./ *20 prel. leaves; viz.
Title the reverse blank.* 'Al Molto Mag^{co}. S^r./ Il
S. Baliano/ di Fornari,/ Jiofeppe Moleto.'/ *4 pp.*
'Tavola delle cose/ piv degne.'/ *24 pp.* 'Tavola
de' Capitoli.'/ *7 pp.* 'Errori corsi nel corso dell'
impreffione/ di questo volume./ *1 page;* 1 *blank
leaf, and Text* 247 *folioved leaves. Fine copy. Small
8vo.* (3l. 13s. 6d. 628)

COLYN (Michiel). Journalen/ vande/ Reysen/ op/
Oostindie./ [*Amsterdam*, 1617-1619.] *Preliminary
matter to the Collection 3 leaves, comprising the En-
graved general title reverse blank* ; *Michiel Colyn's
Dedication, dated the 28th of Feb.* 1619, 2 *pp. Voor-
Redan,* 1 *page. Oblong 4to.* (10l. 10s. 629)
The 10 Parts have the following separate titles.

PART I.

Oost-Indische ende Vvest-Indifche voyagien, | Namelijck, | De
waerachtighe befchrijvinghe vande drie feylagien, drie Jaren
achtermal- | kanderen deur de Hollandtfche ende Zeelandtfche
Schepen, by noorden | Noorvveghen, Mofcovien ende Tartarien
nae de Coninckrijcken, van | Catthay ende China ghedaen. |

De eerfte voyagie der Hollandtfche Schepen op de Landen van
Iava. | De tweede voyagie der Hollandtfcher Schepen op de
Eylanden van Amboina, Banda ende Molucken. | Ioris van
Speilberghens voyagie op't Eyl•ndt van Ceylon. | Pieter de
Marées befchrijvinghe vande Kuften van Guinea. | De Zee-
vaert van Meefter Thomas Candi en gaende rontom de Aerdt-
kloot. | Met de voyagie van Sir Françoys Draeck, ende Sir P.
Haukens naer VVeft-Indien. | Be chrijvinghe van het Gout-
rijcke Coninck-tijcke van Guiana, gelelezhen in America, by-
noorden de groote Riviere Orelliana. | Iournael vande voyagie
nae Rio de Plata, order't Admirael-fchap van Laurens Bicker. |
Wijtloopich verhael van't weder-varen der vijf Schepen die met
Capiteyn Sybold de VVaerdt de Magellaenfche Strate hebben
vevaren. | Olivier van Noordts voyagie om den Aerdt-kloot. I
Tot Amsterdam, | By Michael Colijn, Boeck-verkooper, op't
Water, in't Huyf-boeck, aen de Kooren-marckt. 1619. | 80
leaves.

PART II.

'TEER-TE BOECK. | Hiftorie van Indien, waer inne verhaelt is |
de avonturen die de Hollantfe Schepen bejegent zijn : Oock een
particulier verhael der Conditien, Re-| ligien, manieren en
huyf-houdinge der volckeren, die fy bezeylt hebben : Wat gelt,
specerye, Drogues en Coopmanfchappe | by haer gevonden
wort, met den prijs van dien : Daer by gevoecht de conterfeytfels
der inwoonderé, en met veel caertjens | verciert: Door alle
Zeevarende ende curieufe Lief hebbers, feer gheneuchlijck om
lefen. Door G. M. A. W. L. | [*Vignette*] Tot Amftelredat., By
Michiel Colijn, Boeckvercooper opt Water, int Huyfboeck,
Anno 1617. 83 *leaves.*

PART III.

HISTORIALE BESCHRIJVINGHE, | Inhoudende een waerachtich ver-
hael vande | reyfe ghedaen met acht Schepen van Amfterdam,
onder't beleydt van den Kloeck- | moedighen Admirael Iacob
Cornelifz. Neck, ende VVybrant van VVarvvijck Vice-Admirael,
van't | ghene haer op de felfde reyfe is bejeghent ende weder-
varen. | Midtfgaders hare handelinge in't koopen ende ver-
koopen, oock Hiftorifch verhael vande plaetfen die fy befeylt |
hebben inde Molucken, den handel, vvandel, krijchs-ruftinghe,
ende ghelegentheyt der plaetfen. | Hier is by-ghevoecht een
Vocabulaer in Duytfch, Malleys, ende Iavaens. | [*Vignette*]
t'Amfterdam, By Michiel Colijn, Boeck-verkooper, vvoonende
op't VVater, in't Huyfboeck. Anno 1519. | *Title and* 64 *leaves.*

PART IV.

t'HISTORIAEL JOURNAEL, van tghene ghepaffeert is | van weghen
drie Schepen, ghenaemt den Ram, Schaep ende het Lam,
ghevaren uyt | Zeelandt vander Stadt Camp-Vere naer d'Ooft-
Indien, onder t'beleyt van Ioris van | Speilberghen, Generael,
Anno 1601. den 5 Mey, tot in t'Eylant Celon, | vervatende veel
fchoone ghefchiedenilien, die by haer op defe reyfe ghefchiedt
zijn, | inden tijdt van twee Jaer, elif maenden, ueghenthien
daghen. | Defe Hiftorie is verciert met feventhien vvelghefnie-
den platen, daer in ghefigureert zijn Eylanden, Steden, Kuften, |
Havens, ghevechten op verfcheyden plaetfen, met meer ander
afbeeldinghen, als meede een heerlijcke befchryvinghe van |
ander landen, feer profijtelijck voor de Zeevarende man. Ghe-
corrigeert verbetert ende vermeerdert. | [*Vignette*] t'Amfter-
dam, | By Michiel Colijn Boeck-vercooper opt Water, int
Huyfboeck aende Cooren-Marct. 1617. | 42 *leaves.*

PART V.

BESCHRIJVINGHE ende Hiftorifche verhael, vant Gout | Koninck-
rijck van Guinea, anders de Gout-cufte de Mina genaemt,
leggende in het | deel van Africa, met haren gelooven, opinien,
handelinghen, manieren, talen, | ende hare ghelegentheyt van
Landen, Steden, hutten, huyfen ende Perfoonen. | Mitfgaders
oock een cort verhael van de paffagie die de fchepen derwaerts
nemen deur de Canarifche Eylanden, voorby Capo de Verde, |
langs de Cufte van Manigette, tot aen Capo de Trefpunctas,
voorts vande Revieren diemen verfoeet int verfeylen vande Gout-

cufte, tot | aende Capo° Lopo Gonfalves ,daermen flin affcheyt
neemt int t'Huyfwaert feylen, alles perfect eñ neerftich befch-
reven, door: P. D. M. | *[Vignette]* Tot Amftelredam, by Mi-
chiel Colijn, Wonende op't water int Huyf-boeck. Anno 1617. |
104 *leaves, plates in the text, except one large folding one.*

PART VI.

BESCHRYVINGE vande overtreffelijcke ende wydt- | vermaerde Zee-
vaerdt vanden Edelen Heer ende Meefter Thomas Candifch, met
drie | Schepen uytghevaren den 21. Julij, 1586. ende met een
Schip wederom ghekeert in Pley- | mouth den 9 September 1588.
Hebbende (door't cruycen vander Zee) ghefeylt 13000. | mylen.
Vertellende fyne vreemde wonderlijcke avonturen ende ghefchi-
edeniffen: De | outdockinghe der Landen by hem befeylt. Be-
fchreven door M. | Francois Prettie van Eye in Suffolck, die |
mede inde Voyagie was. | Hier noch by ghevoecht de Voyagie
van Siere François Draeck, en Siere Ian Haukens, Ridderen,
near Weft- | Indien, ghepretendeert Panama in te nemen met 6.
van des Coningins Majefteyts Schepen, ende 21. an- | dere, by
haer hebbende 2500. mannen. Anno 1595. Befchreven door
eenen die daer mede inde | Vlote gheweeft is. Van nieus Ge-
corrigeert ende verbeetert. | *[Vignette]* Tot Amfterdam by
Michiel Colijn, Boeckvercooper opt Water aende Oude Brugh, |
int Huyfboeck. Anno 1617. | *Title and* 39 *leaves.*

PART VII.

VVARACHTIGHE ende grondige befchryvinghe van | het groot en
Gout-rijck Coninginijck van Guiana, gelegen zijnde in America,
by Noorden de | groote Rivier Orelliana, vanden vijfden graet
by zuyden, totten vijfden graet by noorden de Middellinie, in |
welcke befchrijvinge de rechte gelegentheyt vande groote ende
rijcke Hooft-ftadt Manoa, Macureguarai, ende andere fteden
des felvigen Coning- | rijcx, ende van het groot Souten Meyr
Parime, (zijnde outrent 200. Spaenfche mijlen lang) verclaert
wort: Infghelijcx wat voor | rijcke Waren daer te lande ende
daer ontrent vallen: als namelijck groot overvloet van Gout,
coftelijck Ghe- | fteente, ghenaemt Piedras Hijadas, Peerlen,
Balfem olie, langhe Pejer, Gingber, Suycker, Wie- | roock,
verfcheyden Medicinale Wortelen, Droogheryen ende Gom-
men. | Item Zijde Cattoen ende Brafilie-hout. | Mitfgaders de
Befchrijvinghe vande omliggende rijcke Lantf-happen Emeria,
Arromaia, Amapaia, eñ Topago: in welt laetfte de Krijgsbrou-
wen | (Amazones ghenoemt) woonen: mette befchrijvinghe van
53. groote Rivieren, onder welcke Oronoque de voornaemfte
is, welcke fpruyt ontrent 500. duytfche mijlen te | lantwaert in,
niet verre van Quitio, een vermaerde hooftftadt in Peru. Alles
met groote neerfticheyt ontdeckt ende befchreven inden Jare
1595. ende | 1596. Door den E. Heere Walter Ralegh, Ridder
ende Capiteyn over de Guarde vande Majefteyt van Enghelandt,
ende den vermaerden Zeevaerder Capiteyn Laurens Keymis. |
[Vignette] Tot Amfterdam, By Michiel Colijn, Boeckvercooper
op t'Water, aende oude Brugge int Huyf-boeck, 1617. | *Title
and* 49 *leaves.*

PART VIII.

IOVRNAEL | Oft Daghelijcx-regifter van de Voyagie na Rio | de
Plata, ghedaen met het Schip ghenoemt de Silveren Werelt, het
welcke onder't Admi- | raelfchap van Laurens Bicker, ende het
bevel van Cornelis van Heemf-kerck als Commis die Cuften van
Guinea | verfocht hebbende, ende van den Admirael daer na
verftcken zijnde, alleen voorts feylende na Rio de Plata, daer in
de voorfz. Riviere | by de 60. mijlen oywaerts ghekomen we-
fende, tot Bonas Aeris den Commis (d' welcke op de valfche
aen-biedinghe van den | Gouverneur derfelver Plaetfen. om vry
te moghen handelen, aen Landt voer) met noch 8. ander Per-
foneu heeft | moeten achter laten, ende van daer wederom wech
varende, noch felven feer devrlijcken nae 't affterven | van by-
cans al het Volck, met die Kefte in de Bay Todos los Santes in der
Portuiifen handen | gevallen is, allen Zee-varende Luyden tot
eenen fpiegel ende Exempel befchreven | Door den Schipper
daer op ghewerft zijnde Hendrick Ottfen. | Zeer weerdich om

lefen, eñ aenmerckelijck om der Spaengiaerden gruwelijcke
wreedtheyt wille, die trouw, eer ende geloof fchandelijck mif-
bruycken. | om alle andere Natien ('tzy met gheweldt oft met
fchalckheyt) uyt de nieuwe VVerelt te fluyten, daer fy door
fulcken middel de verfte af werden fullen. | Nitimvr in Vetitvm
semper cvpimvsqve negata. | [*Vignette*] Tot Amftelredam by
Michiel Colijn, Boeck-vercooper, wondende op't Water by de
Oudebrugge in't Huyf-boeck, 1617. | *Title and 53 pages.*

HISTORISCH | Ende | VVijdtloopigh.verhael, van'tghene de vijf |
Schepen (die int Jaer 1698. tot Rotterdam toegherut zijn, om
door de Straet | Magellana haren handel te dryven) wedervaren
is, tot den 7. September 1599. op welcken | dagh Capiteyn Sebald
de VVeerdt, met twee fchepen door onweder vande Vlote ver-
ftekenis. Ende voort in | wat groot gevaer ende elende hy by
de vier maendendaer naer inde Strate ghelegen heeft, tot dat
hy | tenleften heel reddeloos fonder fchuyt oft boot, maer een
ancker behouden habbende, | door hooghdringende noodt
weder naer huys heeft moeten keeren. | Meeft befchreven door
M. Barent Ianfz. Chirurgijn. | [*Vignette*] Tot Amftelredam by
Michiel Colijn, Boeck-vercooper, wonende op't Water | by de
Oude-brugge aen de Cooren-marcktint Huyf-boeck. Anno 1617. |
Title and 73 pp.

BESCHRIJVINGE vande Voyagie om den geheelen | Werelt-Kloot,
ghedaen door Olivier van Noordt van Vtrecht, Generael over
vier Sche- | pen, te weten : Mauritius als Admirael, Hendriek
Frederick Vice-Admirael, de Eendracht, midtfgaders | de Hope,
op hebbende t'famen 148. Man, om te zeylen door de Strate
Magellanes, te handelen | langhs de Cuften van Cica, Chili ende
Peru, om den gantfchen Aerden-Cloot, ende door | de Moluc-
ques weder 'thuys te komen. Te zeyl gegaen van Rotterdam den
tweeden | Julij 1598. Ende den Generael met het Schip Mauri-
tius is alleen weder | ghekeert in Augufto, in't jaer onfes Heeren
1601. | Daer in dat vertelt vvordt fijne vvonderlijcke avonturen,
ende vreemdicheden hem bejegent, by hem | ghefien, ende de
hem wedervaren zijn. Met veel Copere Caerten ende Figueren
afghebeeldt, by hen | lieden nieulijcks gheteeckent ende mede
ghebracht. | [*Vignette*] t'Amsterdam, | By Michiel Colijn,
Boeckverkooper op't VVater, aen de Koorn-Marckt, in't Huyfboeck. Ao 1618. *Title and pp.* 3 *to* 131.

COMMENTARIUS de Republica in America Lusi-
tana, atque Hispana A Jesuitis inftituta, belloque ab
his cum Hifpaniæ, Lufitaniæque exercitibus gefto,
Ex iis quæ affervantur in fecretioribus conclavibus
legatorum, qui cum plena Regum poteftate negotia
huc pertinentia in America adminiftrabant, aliisque
inftrumentis certæ auctoritatis concinnatus. E Lu-
fitano in Latinum converfus. *Title, and* 77 *pp. small*
8vo.   (15s.   630)

COMMON SENSE; Addressed to the Inhabitants
of America; *etc. Philadelphia* Printed. And Sold
by W. & T. Bradford. [1776] *Half-title, title, and*
50 *pp. Half mor.* 8vo.   (6s.   631)

    The Introduction of this new Edition is dated, "Philadelphia, Feb-
ruary 14, 1776." This copy belonged to Ritson, and on the reverse
of the half-title are the following lines, in his own handwriting,
"On the King's illness, 1789 :—
      See the Vengeance of heaven ! America cries;
    George loses his senses; North loses his eyes:
    When they strove to enslave us, all Europe will find
    That the Tyrant was mad, and his Minister blind."

Inserted is a curious small oval portrait of Tom Paine, "Engraved
by James Godby, from an original Drawing done from the Life
in America, 1803." Above the portrait are these words, " Quin
said of Z .... that if he was not a Rascal, Nature did not write
a legible hand.—Quin was right; Z .... was a Rascal."

COMMON SENSE, addressed to the Inhabitants
of America, On the following interefting Subjects.
I. Of the Origin and Defign of Government in general, with concife Remarks on the Englifh Conftitution. II. Of Monarchy and Hereditary Succeffion. III. Thoughts on the prefent State of American Affairs. IV. Of the prefent Ability of America with fome mifcellaneous Reflections. Philadelphia Printed : *New-York*, Reprinted and Sold,
by John Anderson, the Corner of Beekman's-Slip.
[1776] *Title and Introduction 2 leaves; text 56 pp.
Half mor. 8vo.* (4s. 6d. 632)

COMMON SENSE; addressed to the Inhabitants
of America, On the following interefting subjects,
I. Of the Origin and Defign of Government in general, with concife Remarks on the Englifh Conftitution. II. Of Monarchy and Hereditary Succeffion. III. Thoughts on the prefent State of Ame-
rican·Affairs. IV. Of the prefent Ability of America, with some mifcellaneous Reflections. *Newport:* Printed and Sold by Solomon Southwick,
M,DCC,LXX,VI. *Title & Introduction 2 leaves; text
31 pp. half mor. 8vo.* (4s. 6d. 633)

COMMON SENSE: addressed to the Inhabitants
of America, on the following Interesting Subjects :
I. Of the Origin and Defign of Government in general; with concife Remarks on the Englifh Conftitution. II. Of Monarchy and Hereditary Succeffion. III. Thoughts on the prefent State of American Affairs. IV. Of the prefent ability of America ; with fome mifcellaneous Reflections. A New
Edition; with feveral Additions in the Body of the
Work. To which is added, an Appendix : together
with an Address to the People called Quakers.
Philadelphia, Printed : [To promote the traitorous
purpofes therein fet forth.] *Edinburgh,* reprinted :
To fhew the real fpirit and views of the Colonies,
or rather of their leaders in rebellion ; which cannot fail to roufe the indignation of every Briton,
without leaving them from henceforth a fingle advocate, who is not utterly loft to loyalty, to patriot-

iſm, and to Common Sense. Sold by Charles Elliot, Edinburgh; and William Anderson, Stirling.
M. DCC. LXXVI. *Title and Introduction 3 leaves;*
text pp. 99. 12*mo.* (*6s. 6d.* 634)

COMMON SENSE: In nine Conferences, between
a British Merchant and a candid Merchant of America, in their private capacities as friends; tracing
the ſeveral cauſes of the preſent conteſts between
the mother country and her American ſubjeċts; the
fallacy of their prepoſſeſſions; and the ingratitude
and danger of them; the reciprocal benefits of the
national friendship; and the moral obligations of
individuals which enforce it: with various anecdotes, and reasons drawn from faċts, tending to
conciliate all differences, and eſtabliſh a permanent
union for the common happineſs and glory of the
Britiſh empire. *London:* J. Dodsley, MDCCLXXV.
x and 117 *pp. Half morocco. Fine copy, uncut.*
4*to.* (*15s.* 635)

COMMUNICATIONS concerning the Agriculture
and Commerce of America: Containing Observa-
tions on the Commerce of Spain with her American
Colonies in time of War. Written by a Spanish
Gentleman in Philadelphia, this present year, 1800.
With sundry other papers concerning the Spanish
Interests. Edited in London by William Tatham.
London: J. Ridgway, 1800. *viii and* 120 *pp. Half*
mor. 8*vo.* (*4s. 6d.* 636)

COMPARATIVE (THE) Importance of our acquisitions from France in America, with Remarks on
a Pamphlet, intitled, An Examination of the Commercial Principles of the late Negociation in 1761.
London: J. Hinxman, MDCCLXII. *Title and an Ad-*
vertisement, 2 *leaves; text* 59 *pp. half morocco.*
8*vo.* (*5s.* 637)

COMPARISON (A) between the Britiſh Sugar Colonies and New-England, as they relate to the Interest of Great Britain. With Some Obſervations
on the State of the Case of New-England. To
which is added A Letter to a Member of Parliament. *London:* James Roberts. M.DCC.XXXII. 43
pp. Half mor. 8*vo.* (*15s.* 638)

COMPARISON (A) Between the Doċtrines taught
by the Clergy of the Church of England, And the

Doctrines taught by Whitefield, Seagrave, and Others; In which the true Notion of Preaching Chrift it ftated; the doctrinal Preaching of the Clergy of the Eftablifhed Church vindicated; and the Methodifts proved guilty of not Preaching the Gofpel of Chrift. To which is added, The Wifdom of fleeing from Perfecution, exemplified in the Conduct of the Rev. Mr. Whitefield at Charles-Town in South-Carolina. *London:* A. Smith, 1741. *2 prel. leaves and 28 pp. 8vo.* (*2s. 6d.* 639)

COMPLAINT (A) to the —— of —— against a Pamphlet intitled, a Speech intended to have been spoken on the bill for altering the Charters of the Colony of Massachuset's Bay. *London,* Benjamin White, MDCCLXXV. *Title; Advertisement pp. v-viii; text 40 pp. 8vo.* (*4s. 6d.* 640)

COMPLEAT/ (A)/ Collection/ of/ Papers./ In Twelve Parts :/ Relating to the Great Revolutions/ In England and Scotland,/ From the Time of the Seven Bifhops/ Petitioning K. James II. againft the/ Difpenfing Power, June 8. 1688. to/ the Coronation of King William/ and Queen Mary, April 11. 1689./ *London:* Printed by J. D. for R. Clavel at the Peacock, Henry/ Mortlock at the Phenix, and Jonathan Robinfon at/ the Golden Lion in St. Paul's Church-Yard, 1689./ *Title:* 'To the Reader. *2 pp;* 'The Contents' *of the 12 parts 4 pp; 1st Collection,* 3d Edition, 1689, *Title and 34 pp; 2nd Collection,* 3d Edition 1689, *Title and 34 pp; 3d Collection,* 1688, *Title and 38 pp; 4th Collection,* 1688, *Title and 34 pp; 5th Collection title & pp. 1 to 24, 1 to 8 and 33-54. 6th to 11th Collections each, Title and 34 pp; 12th Collection, Title & 40 pp. 4to.* (15s. 641)

The 10th Article of the 6th Collection contains 'A Narrative of the Miseries of New England, by reafon of an Arbitrary Government erected there.' pp. 29 to 34.

COMPLETE (A) and accurate Account of the Very Important Debate in the House of Commons, on Tuesday, July 9, 1782. In whicht he Caufe of Mr. Fox's Refignation, and the great Queftion of American Independence came under Confideration: Including the feveral Speeches and Replies of The Right Hon. Mr. Fox, The Right Hon. Ifaac Barré, Lord John Cavendiffh, General Conway, Mr. Burke, Sir William Wake, Mr. Coke, Mr. Frede-

rick Montague, The Hon. Mr. Townfend, Mr.
Martin, Lord Althorpe, Mr. Grenville, Mr. Au-
brey, The Hon. William Pitt, Mr. Lee, late Soli-
citor - General, Mr. Gafcoyne, fen. Commodore
Johnftone, and Sir Edward Deering. To which
are added, the Speeches of the Duke of Richmond
and of Lord Shelburne, in the House of Lords, the
following Day, on the fame Subject: With what
was thrown out in Reply by Mr. Burke, Lord John
Cavendifh, and Mr. Fox, afterwards, in the Houfe
of Commons. The Third Edition. *London:* J.
Stockdale, MDCCLXXXII. *Title, dedication, and an
advertisement, 3 leaves; text 57 pp.* 'Many of our
numerous Readers,' *etc. pp. 59-61. Half mor.*
8vo. (5s. 6d. 642)

COMPLETE (A) History of the Origin and Progress
of the late War, From its Commencement, to the
Exchange of the Ratifications of Peace, between
Great-Britain, France, and Spain; On the 10th of
February, 1763, and to the signing of the Treaty
at Hubertsberg, between the King of Prufsia, the
Emprefs-Queen, and the Elect, or of Saxony, On the
15th of the fame Month. In which, All the Battles,
Sieges, Sea-Engagements, and every other Tranfac-
tion worthy of public Attention, are faithfully re-
corded; with political and military Obfervations.
In Two Volumes. *London,* W. Nicol, MDCCLXIII.
Vol. I. Advertisement, Title, and Text in 358 pp. calf.
8vo. (10s. 6d. 643)

COMPRESSED (A) View of the Points to be Discussed, in Treating with the United States of America, A.D. 1814. With an Appendix and Two Maps.
London: J. M. Richardson, 1814. *2 prel. leaves; text
39 pp. Maps of* Passemaquoddy Bay *and* The Frontier of British North America. *8vo.* (6s. 6d. 644)

CONCESSIONS to America the Bane of Britain;
or the cause of the present distressed situation of
the British Colonial and Shipping Interests explained, and the proper Remedy suggested. *London:* W. J. and J. Richardson, 1807. *63 pp. half
mor. 8vo.* (4s. 6d. 645)

CONCILIATORY Address to the People of Great
Britain and of the Colonies, on the present important Crisis. *London:* J. Wilkie, MDCCLXXV. *Half
title, title, and 56 pp. half mor. 8vo.* (4s. 6d. 646)

CONCISE (A) Historical Account of all the British Colonies in North-America, comprehending their Rife, Progrefs, and Modern State; Particularly of the Massachusets-Bay, (The Seat of the prefent Civil War,) together with the other Provinces of New-England. To which is annexed, An accurate descriptive Table of the Several countries; Exhibiting, at One View, their refpective Boundaries, Dimensions, Longitudes, Latitudes, Divisions, or Counties, Chief Towns, Capes, Harbours, Bays, Rivers, Various Productions, Animals, &c. &c. Interspersed with Particulars relative to the different Soils and Climates, Capital Cities, &c. &c. *London,* J. Bew, 1775. *Title, Preface* 2 *pp.* ' Introduction,' 8 *pp. text pp.* 9-196. *With a large folding sheet containing* ' An Accurate descriptive Table.' *Half mor. 8vo.* (7s. 6d. 647)

CONCISE (A) Historical Account of all the British Colonies in North-America, comprehending their Rise, Progress, and Modern State; Particularly of the Mafsachusets-Bay, (The Seat of the prefent Civil War,) together with the Other Provinces of New-England. To which is annexed, An Accurate Descriptive Table of the several Countries; Exhibiting, at One View, Their refpective Boundries, Dimensions, Longitudes, Latitudes, Divifions, or Countries, Chief Towns, Capes, Harbours, Bays, Rivers, Various Productions, Animals, &c. &c. Interfperfed with Particulars relative to the different Soils and Climates, Capital Cities, &c. &c. *Dublin:* Caleb Jenkin, and John Beatty, MDCCLXXVI. *Title,* ' Preface,' *pp. iii-iv.* ' Introduction,' 8 *pp.* ' A Map of 100 Miles round Boston.' *Text, pp.* 9-228. *With a Table, folded sheet; calf,* 12*mo.* (8s. 6d. 648)

CONCISE (A) History of the Spanish America; containing a fuccinct Relation of the Difcovery and Settlement of its feveral Colonies: A circumftantial Detail of their refpective Situation, Extent, Commodities, Trade, &c. And a full and clear Account of the Commerce with Old Spain by the Galleons, Flota, &c. As alfo of the Contraband Trade with the Englifh, Dutch, French, Danes, and Portugueze. Together with an Appendix, in which is comprehended an exact Defcription of Paraguay. Collected chiefly from Spanifh Writers.

London: John Stagg, MDCCXLI. *Title and dedication 2 leaves;* ' Preface.' *pp. v-viii; table of contents 2 leaves; and text 336 pp. Fine copy in old calf.* 8vo.   (10s. 6d. 649)

CONDAMINE (M. DE LA). Relation abrégée d'un Voyage fait dans l'Intérieur de L'Amérique Méridionale, depuis la Côte de la Mer du Sud, jufqu'aux Côtes du Bréfil & de la Guyane, en defcendant La Riviere des Amazones, Par M. De La Condamine, de l'Académie des Sciences, Avec une Carte du Maragnon, ou de la Riviere des Amazones, levée par le même. Nouvelle Edition Augmentée de la Relation de l'Emeute populaire de Cuença au Pérou, Et d'une Lettre de M. Godin des Odonais, contenant la Relation du Voyage de Madame Godin, fon Epoufe, &c. A *Maestricht,* Chez Jean-Edme Dufour & Philippe Roux, M. DCC. LXXVIII. *Title;* ' Extrait,' *etc.* 1 *p.* ' Preface' *xvi pp; Text 379 pp. With Copper Plate of the* ' Ville de Cuença au Pérou,' *and* ' Carte du cours du Maragnon,' *etc. calf,* 8vo.   (10s. 6d. 650)

CONDUCT (THE) of a Noble Commander [*the Earl of Loudon*] in America, Impartially reviewed. With the genuine Caufes of the Difcontents at New-York and Halifax. And the true Occafion of the Delays in that important Expedition. Including A regular Account of all the proceedings and Incidents in the Order of Time wherein they happened. *London:* R. Baldwin, MDCCLVIII. *Title & 45 pp. half mor.* 8vo.   (6s. 6d. 651)

CONDUCT (THE) of a R. Hon. Gentleman in refigning the Seals of his Office juftified, by Facts, and upon the Principles of the British Constitution. By a Member of Parliament. The Second Edition. *London:* J. Newbery, MDCCLXI. *Title, and* 82 *pp.* 8vo.   (4s. 6d. 652)

CONDUCT (THE) of the Late Adminiftration Examined. With an Appendix, containing Original and Authentic Documents. *London:* J. Almon, MDCCLXVII. *Half-title and title,* 2 *leaves; text pp.* 5-160. *Appendix and Advertisement* 1 *leaf; text liv pp. half mor.* 8vo.   (6s. 6d. 653)

CONDUCT (THE) of the late Adminiftration Examined, Relative to the American Stamp-Act. With

an Appendix containing Original and Authentic
Documents. The Second Edition. *London :* J. Almon, MDCCLXVII. *Title; and pp.* 5-160. *Appendix
and Advertisement,* 1 *leaf ; text liv pp. half morocco.*
8vo.   (5s. 6d.   654)

CONDUCT (THE) of the Ministry Impartially Examined. In a Letter to the Merchants of London.
The Second Edition. *London :* S. Bladon. MDCCLVI.
Title, and text pp. 3-68. [*See No.* 118.] *Half mor.*
8vo.   (4s. 6d.   655)

CONFESSION/ (A)/ of/ Faith/ Owned and con-
fented unto bv the/ Elders and Meffengers/ of the
Churches/ Affembled at Bofton in New-England,/
May 12, 1680./ Being the fecond Seffion of that/
Synod./ *Boston ;/* Printed by John Fofter. 1680./
4 *prel. leaves ; viz.* 1. ' At a General Court held at/
Bofton, May 19./ 1680.'/ *signed* ' Edward Rawfon
Secr.' 2. *Title in a type metal border, the reverse
blank :* 3 & 4. ' A Preface.' *Text* 65 *pp. Title* ' A/
PLATFORM/ of/ Church- Difcipline/ Gathered out
of/ the Word of God,/ And Agreed upon by the/
Elders and Meffengers/ of the Churches Affembled
in the/ Synod./ At Cambridge in N. E./ To be
prefented to the Churches & General Court/ for
their Confideration and Acceptance in/ the Lord,
the 8th Moneth, Anno. 1649./ *Bofton :* Printed by
John Fofter. 1680./ 12 *prel. leaves ; viz. Title in a
type metal border, the reverse blank,* ' The Preface,'
21 *pp. Text* 64 *pp.* ' A Table,' *etc.* 3 *pp. Signatures
A to K in eights,* L *in three leaves running through
both parts. Old calf,* 16mo.   (2l. 12s. 6d. 656)

CONGRESS (THE) Canvassed : or An Examination
of the Conduct of the Delegates, at their Grand
Convention, Held in Philadelphia, Sept. 1, 1774.
Addressed, to the Merchants of New York. By
A. W. *Farmer,* Author of Free Thoughts, &c.
[New York] Printed in the Year M,DCCLXXIV.
28 *pp. Half mor.* 8vo.   (7s. 6d. 657)

CONGRESS (THE) Canvassed : or, an Examination
into the Conduct of the Delegates, at their Grand
Convention, held in Philadelphia, Sept. 1, 1774.
Addressed to the Merchants of New York. By
A. W. *Farmer,* Author of Free Thoughts, &c.
New York Printed. *London,* Reprinted for Rich-

ardson and Urquhart, 1775. *Half-title, title, and* 59 *pp. half mor.* 8*vo.* (5*s.* 6*d.* 658)

CONNECTICUT. A General History of Connecticut, from its Firſt Settlement under George Fenwick, Eſq. to its Lateſt Period of Amity with Great Britain; including a Description of the Country, And many curious and intereſting Anecdotes. To which is added, An Appendix, wherein new and the true Sources of the preſent Rebellion in America are pointed out; together with the particular Part taken by the People of Connecticut in its Promotion. By a Gentleman of the Province [Rev. Samuel Peters]. *London:* J. Bew, MDCCLXXXI. *Title;* 'Preface.' *pp. iii-x. and text* 366 *pp.* 'Appendix,' *pp.* 367-424. 'Index.' *pp.* 425-436. *Large Paper, calf,* 8*vo.* (15*s.* 659)

CONNECTICUT. Acts and Laws of the State of Connecticut, in America. *New-London:* Printed by Timothy Green, Printer to the Governor and Company of the State of Connecticut. MDCCLXXXIV. *Title;* 'Charter,' *etc. pp.* 3-8. 'Articles' *etc.* 6 *pp.* 'Catalogue' *etc.* 2 *pp. Text* 265 *pp. Old calf. Folio.* (1*l.* 10*s.* 660)

CONNECTICUT. The Code of 1650, being a compilation of the earliest Laws and Orders of the General Court of Connecticut: Also, the Constitutution, or Civil Compact, entered into and adopted by the Towns of Windsor, Hartford, and Whethersfield in 1638-9. To which is added some extracts from the Laws and Judicial Proceedings of New-Haven Colony commonly called Blue Laws. *Hartford,* Published by Silas Andrus. 1825. 119 *pp. including Frontispiece. Small* 8*vo.* (5*s.* 661)

CONNECTICUT (THE) Dissenters' Strong Box: No. I. Containing, The high-flying Churchman ſtript of his legal Robe, &c. By the rev. John Leland, Paſtor of the Baptiſt Church in Cheſhire, Maſs. The Diſſenter's Petition. Connecticut Eccleſiaſtical Laws. American Conſtitutions (Extracts from). Sixteen of which recogniſe the Rights of Conſcience—and Three the doctrine of Church and State. Some remarks. Compiled by a Dissenter. Printed by Charles Holt, *New-London.* 1802. 40 *pp. uncut.* 8*vo.* (8*s.* 6*d.* 662)

CONSEQUENCES (Not before adverted to) That
are likely to refult from the late Revolution of the
British Empire; with the probable Effects upon
the Territorial Possessions, the Commercial Inte-
rests, Naval Strength, Manufactures, Population,
Resources, Landed Interest, and Public Funds, of
Great Britain; and a Comparative Review of the
Strength, Resources, and Public Credit, of the late
Belligerent Powers, at the Conclusion of the Peace.
London. G. Wilkie, MDCCLXXXIII. *Title, and text;*
pp. 5-33. 8vo. (4s. 6d. 663)

CONSIDERATIONS Againſt Laying any New
Duty upon Sugar; wherein Is particularly ſhewn,
That a New Impoſition will be ruinous to the Sugar Colonies, inſufficient for the Purpoſes intended,
and greatly conducive to the Aggrandizement of
France. *London:* J. Roberts, MDCCXLIV. *Half-
title; title; iv and 30 pp. half morocco, fine copy.*
8vo. (4s. 6d. 664)

CONSIDERATIONS of the Propriety of imposing
Taxes in the British Colonies, For the Purpoſe of
raiſing a Revenue, by Act of Parliament. [By
Mr. Dulaney of Maryland] North-America:
Printed by a North-American. *New-York:* Reprinted by John Holt, in the Year 1765. *55 pp.*
8vo. (7s. 6d. 665)

CONSIDERATIONS On Behalf of the Colonists.
In a Letter to a Noble Lord. *London:* J. Almon,
MDCCLXV. *Title, and 52 pp. 8vo.* (4s. 6d. 666)

CONSIDERATIONS On Behalf of the Colonists.
In a Letter to a Noble Lord. The Second Edition.
London: J. Almon, MDCCLXV. *Title, and 52 pp.*
8vo. (4s. 6d. 667)

CONSIDERATIONS on certain Political Transactions of the Province of South Carolina: containing a View of the Colony Legislatures (Under
the Deſcription of That of Carolina in Particular).
With Observations, Shewing their Resemblance to
the British Model. *London:* T. Cadell, MDCCLXXIV.
Half-title, title, and 83 pp. Half morocco.
8vo. (7s. 6d. 668)

CONSIDERATIONS upon the American Enquiry.
[On the Parliamentary Examination into the pro-

ceedings of the army in America, under the Command of General Howe]. *London:* J. Wilkie, MDCCLXXIX. *Half-title, title, & 55 pp. half mor.* 8*vo.* (6*s.* 6*d.* 669)

CONSIDERATIONS on the American Trade, Before and Since the Establishment of the South-Sea Company. The Second Edition, with Additions. *London:* Roberts, MDCCXXXIX. *Title, and text, pp. 5-36. Half mor.* 8*vo.* (4*s.* 6*d.* 670)

CONSIDERATIONS on the Dependencies of Great Britain. With Observations on a Pamphlet intitled, *The Present State of the Nation. London:* J. Almon, MDCCLXIX. *Title, and Text pp. 5-92. Half mor.* 8*vo.* (4*s.* 6*d.* 671)

CONSIDERATIONS on the Expediency of admitting Representatives from the American Colonies into The Britiſh Houſe of Commons. *London:* B. White, M.DCC.LXX. *Title, and Text pp. 3-41. Half mor.* 8*vo.* (4*s.* 6*d.* 672)

CONSIDERATIONS on the Dispute Now depending before The Honourable House of Commons, between the Britiſh Southern, and Northern Plantations in America. In a Letter to——. *London:* J. Roberts, 1731. *Title, and 30 pp. Half mor.* 8*vo.* (10*s.* 6*d.* 673)

CONSIDERATIONS on the Importance of Canada, and the Bay and River of St. Lawrence; And of The American Fiſheries dependant on the Iſlands of Cape Breton, St. John's, Newfoundland, and the Seas adjacent. Address'd to The Right Hon. William Pitt. *London,* W. Owen, 1759. *Half-title, title, and dedication 4 leaves; text 23 pp. half mor.* 8*vo.* (7*s.* 6*d.* 674)

CONSIDERATIONS on the Imposition of 4½ per Cent. collected on Grenada, and the Southern Charibbee Islands, by Virtue of His Majesty's Letters Patent, Under Pretence of the Prerogative Royal, without grant of Parliament. *London:* J. Almon, 1774. *Title, and dedication 2 leaves; text; 40 pp. Half mor.* 8*vo.* (4*s.* 6*d.* 675)

CONSIDERATIONS on the Late Act for Prohibiting all Commercial Intercourse with the Rebellious Colonies: Or, the Weakness of America Exposed.

Edinburgh : Cha. Elliot. M,DCC,LXXVI.   19 *pp.*
8*vo.*   (4*s.* 6*d.*   676)

CONSIDERATIONS on the Measures Carrying
on with respect to the British Colonies in North
America. *London*, R. Baldwin [1774]. *Title and*
160 *pp.* 8*vo.*   (6*s.* 6*d.*   677)

CONSIDERATIONS on the Measures carrying on
with respect to the British Colonies in North America. The Second Edition. With Additions and
an Appendix Relative to the present State of Affairs on that Continent. *London:* R. Baldwin
[1774]. *Half-title, title, and text* 176 *pp.* ' Appendix,' 45 *pp. Half mor.* 8*vo.*   (6*s.* 6*d.*   678)

CONSIDERATIONS on the Nature and Extent of
the Legislative Authority of the British Parliament. *Philadelphia:* Printed and Sold, by William and Thomas Bradford, at the London Coffee-
House. M.DCC.LXXIV. *iv & 35 pp. half morocco.*
8*vo.*   (7*s.* 6*d.*   679)

CONSIDERATIONS on the present Crisis of Affairs, as it respects the West-India Colonies, And
the probable Effects of the French Decree for
Emancipating the Negroes, pointing out a Remedy
for preventing the Calamitous Consequences in the
British Islands. *London:* T. Gillet, J. Johnson,
1795. *Half-title, title, and* 76 *pp. Fine copy, uncut.*
8*vo.*   (3*s.* 6*d.*   680)

CONSIDERATIONS on the present Peace, as far
as it is relative to the Colonies, and the African
Trade. *London:* W. Bristow, MDCCLXIII. *Title,*
iv & 68 pp. half mor. 8*vo.*   (4*s.* 6*d.*   681)

CONSIDERATIONS on the Propriety of imposing
Taxes in the British Colonies, For the Purpoſe of
raiſing a Revenue, by Act of Parliament. The
Second Edition. *Annapolis:* Printed and Sold by
Jonas Green. 1765. *Title, and preface* 2 *leaves;*
text pp. 5-55. *half mor.* 4*to.*   (10*s.* 6*d.*   682)
By Mr. Dulaney, Chief Justice of Maryland.

CONSIDERATIONS on the Propriety of imposing
Taxes in the British Colonies, For the Purpoſe of
raiſing a Revenue, by Act of Parliament. North-
America: Printed by a North-American. *New-*
York: Re-printed by John Holt, in the Year 1765.

Title and Preface, 2 leaves: & text pp. 5-55. half
mor. 8vo. (*7s. 6d.* 683)

CONSIDERATIONS on the Propriety of imposing
Taxes on the Britifh Colonies, for the Purpofe of
raifing a Revenue, by Act of Parliament. North-
America Printed: *London,* Re-printed for J. Al-
mon, MDCCLXVI. *Half-title; title; Preface, 4 pages;*
Text 69 pp. 8vo. (*4s. 6d.* 684)

CONSIDERATIONS on the Propriety of imposing
Taxes in the Britifh Colonies, for the Purpofe of
raifing a Revenue, by Act of Parliament. The
Second Edition. North-America Printed: *Lon-*
don, Re-printed for J. Almon, MDCCLXVI. *Title*
and preface 3 leaves; and Text 81 pp. Half mor.
8vo. (*4s. 6d.* 685)

CONSIDERATIONS on the Provisional Treaty
with America, and the preliminary Articles of
Peace with France and Spain. *London:* T. Cadell,
M.DCC.LXXXIII. *Half-title, title, and 164 pp. half*
mor. 8vo. (*5s. 6d.* 686)

CONSIDERATIONS on the Provisional Treaty
with America, and the preliminary Articles of
Peace with France and Spain. The Second Edition Corrected. *London:* T. Cadell, M.DCC.LXXXIII.
Title, and 94 pp. half mor. 8vo (*4s. 6d.* 687)

CONSIDERATIONS on the Trade and Finances of
this Kingdom, and on the Measures of Administration, with Refpect to thofe great National Objects fince the conclusion of the Peace. The Second Edition. *London:* J. Wilkie, MDCCLXVI.
Title; and text pp. 3-119. Interesting MS. notes.
4to. (*10s. 6d.* 688)

CONSIDERATIONS on the Trade and Finances
of this Kingdom, and on the Measures of Administration, with Refpect to thofe great National
Objects fince the Conclusion of the Peace. The
Third Edition. *London.* J. Wilkie, MDCCLXIX.
239 pp. half mor. 8vo. (*4s. 6d.* 689)

CONSIDERATIONS Relating to the laying any
Additional Duty on Sugar From the British Plantations. Wherein is shewn, That fuch Duty will
be injurious to the Commerce and Navigation of
this Kingdom, ruinous to our Sugar Colonies, be-

neficial to thofe of *France*, and infufficient for the
Purpofes intended. *London :* John Clarke, 1747.
Title, and Text, pp. 5-31. *Half morocco.*
8vo.   (4s. 6d.   690)

CONSIDERATIONS sur l'Admission des Navires
Neutres aux Colonies Françoises de l'Amerique
En tems de guerre. 1779. *Title, and Avis,* 2
leaves; ' Advertisement,' *pp.* 5-8, *and text, pp.* 9-82.
calf, 12mo.   (10s. 6d.   691)

CONSIDERATIONS Upon the prefent State of
our Affairs, at Home and Abroad, in a Letter to a
Member of Parliament from a Friend in the Country. *London :* T. Cooper, MDCCXXXIX. *Title, and
pp.* 3-39. *8vo.*   (4s. 6d.   692)

CONSIDERATIONS Upon the prefent State of our
Affairs, at Home and Abroad. In a Letter to a
Member of Parliament from a Friend in the Coun-
try. The Second Edition. *London :* T. Cooper,
MDCCXXXIX. *Title, and* 67 *pp.* ' Postscript,' 2
pp. half mor. 8vo.   (4s. 6d.   693)

CONSIDERATIONS upon the Rights of the Colonists to the Privileges of Britifh Subjects, Introduc'd by a brief Review of the Rife and Progrefs
of Englifh Liberty, and concluded with fome Remarks upon our prefent Alarming Situation. *New-
York:* Printed and fold by John Holt, at the Exchange, 1766. *Title, and dedication,* 2 *leaves; text*
27 *pp. half mor. 8vo.*   (7s. 6d.   694)

CONSOLATORY Thoughts on American Independence; shewing the great Advantages that will
arife from it to the Manufactures, the Agriculture,
and commercial Intereft of Britain and Ireland.
Publifhed for the Benefit of the Orphan Hospital
at Edinburgh. By a Merchant. *Edinburgh :* James
Donaldson, 1782. *Half-title, title, and* 68 *pp. half
mor. 8vo.*   (4s. 6d.   695)

CONSTITVCIONES/ Synodales del/ Arçobispado
de los/ Reyes en el Perv./ Hechas y ordenades
por el Illustrissímo y Reve/ rendifsimo Señor Don
Bartholome Lobo Guerrero Arçobifpo de la dicha
Ciu-/dad de los Reyes, del Confejo de fu Mageftad./
Y pvblicadas en la Synodo Diocesana qve sv/ Se-
ñoria Illuftrifsima celebro en la dicha Ciudad en el

año del/ Señor de 1613./ En *Los Reyes.*/ [*Lima*]
Por Francisco del Canto./ Año de M.DC.XIIII. 6
*prelim. leaves; Text 94 folioed leaves, followed by ' In-
dice de los Titulos' in 6, and Errata one leaf. Vellum.
Folio.* (3*l.* 3*s.* 696)

CONSTITUTIONAL Law: Comprizing the Declaration of Independence; the Articles of Confederation; the Constitution of the United States;
and the Constitutions of the several States composing the Union, viz. New Hampshire, Massachusetts, Rhode Island, Connecticut, Vermont,
New York, New Jersey, Pennsylvania, Delaware,
Maryland, Virginia, North Carolina, South Carolina, Georgia, Louisiana, Kentucky, Ohio, Tennessee, Mississippi, Indiana, Illinois, Alabama,
Maine, *Washington:* Gales and Seaton. Dec. 1820.
2 prel. leaves; and Text in 409 pp. boards, uncut.
12*mo.* (6*s.* 6*d.* 697)

CONSTITUTIONAL (THE) Right of the Legislature of Great Britain, to Tax the British Colonies
in America, impartially stated. *London:* J. Ridley, M DCC LXVIII. *Title; Introduction xi pp. and
text 60 pp. Half mor. 8vo.* (4*s.* 6*d.* 698)

CONSTITUTIONS (THE) of the Sixteen States
which compose the Confederated Republic of
America, according to the latest Amendments.
To which are prefixed the Declaration of Independance; Articles of Confederation; and the Constitution of the United States, with all the Amendments. *Newburgh;* Printed by David Denniston,
for Self and H. Craig. 1800. *288 pp. Unbound.*
12*mo.* (5*s.* 699)

CONSTITUTIONS (THE) of the several Independent States of America; the Declaration of Independance; and the Articles of Confederation
between the said States. To which are now added,
the Declaration of Rights; the Non-Importation
Agreement; and the Petition of Congress to the
King delivered by Mr. Penn. With an Appendix,
containing the Treaties between His most Christian
Majesty and the United States of America; the
Provisional Treaty with America; and (never before published) an authentic copy of the Treaty
concluded between their High Mightinesses the

States-General, and the United States of America.
The whole arranged, with a Preface and Dedication, by the Rev. William Jackson. *London*: J.
Stockdale, 1783. *Portrait of Washington.* 18 *prel.*
leaves and 472 *pp. half calf.* 8*vo.* (7s. 6d. 700)

CONSTITUTIONS (The) of the several Independent States of America; The Declaration of Independence; The Articles of Confederation between
the said States; The Treaties between His Most
Christian Majesty and the United States of America.
With an Appendix, containing An Authentic Copy
of the Treaty concluded between their High Mightineffes the States-General and the United States of
America, and the Provisional Treaty. Published
by Order of Congress. Philadelphia Printed:
London, Reprinted, with an Advertisement by J.
L. De Lolme. J. Walker, J. Debrett, MDCCLXXXIII.
Portrait of Benjamin Franklin. Title, 'In Congress,' 1 *page.* 'The Editor's Advertisement,'
pp. v-viii; Text 168 *pp.* 'Appendix,' *pp.* 169-189.
'A List of the Presidents,' *etc.* 1 *leaf. Halfmor.*
8*vo.* (5s. 6d. 701)

CONSTITUTIONS (The) of the United States,
according to the Latest Amendments: To which
are prefixed, The Declaration of Independence;
and the Federal Constitution, with the amendments.
This Edition contains the late Conftitutions of Vermont, Delaware, Georgia, and Kentucky, with the
Regulations for the Government of the Territory
north-west of the River Ohio; alfo, the Amendments to the Conftitution of Maryland;—not in
any former Edition. *Philadelphia*: Printed for
Robert Campbell, 1800. *Title, and contents,* 2
leaves; 'Declaration,' *etc. v-xxiv. Text pp.* 5-272.
Calf. 12*mo.* (7s. 6d. 702)

CONTESTACION Rapida al Discurso Opinado
que Pronunció un M∴ con Motivo de la Plancha
que el G∴ Cons∴ Circuló a las ll∴ simb∴ del
rito esc∴ sobre el nuevo Juramento exigido y
demas de su contenido. *Habana*: 5821. [1821.]
Impresso en la oficina del G∴ Or. 15 *pp. half*
mor. 4*to.* (4s. 6d. 703)

CONTROVERSY (The) between Great Britain
and her Colonies Reviewed; the Several Pleas of

the Colonies. In Support of their Right to all the Liberties and Privileges of British Subjects, and to Exemption from the Legiflative Authority of Parliament, Stated and Considered; and the Nature of their Connection with, and Dependence on, Great-Britain, shown upon the Evidence of Historical Facts and Authentic Records. *Boston:* Printed by Mein and Fleeming, and fold at the London Book-Store King-Street. MDCCLXIX. *Title, and text pp. 3-100. half mor. 8vo.* (8s. 6d. 704)

CONWAY (GENERAL). The Speech of General Conway, Member of Parliament for Saint Edmondsbury, on moving in the House of Commons, (On the 5th of May, 1780) "That leave be given to bring in a Bill for Quieting the Troubles now Reigning in the British Colonies in America, and for enabling His Majesty to appoint Commissioners, with full Powers to treat, and conclude upon Terms of Conciliation with the faid Colonies." *London: T. Cadell.* M,DCC,LXXXI. *Half title, title, and 51 pp. half mor. 8vo.* (4s. 6d. 705)

COOKE (EDWARD). A Voyage to the South Sea, and Round the World, perform'd in the years 1708, 1709, 1710, and 1711, by the Ships Duke and Dutchefs of Briftol. Containing a Journal of all memorable Tranfactions during the faid Voyage; the Winds, Currents, and Variation of the Compafs; the taking of the Towns of Puna and Guayaquil, and feveral Prizes, one of which a rich Acapulco Ship. A Description of the American Coafts, from Tierra del Fuego in the South, to California in the North, (from the Coafting-Pilot, a Spanifh Manufcript.) Wherein an Account is given of Mr. Alexander Selkirk, his Manner of living and taming fome wild beafts during the four Years and four Months he liv'd upon the uninhabited Ifland of Juan Fernandes. Illuftrated with Cuts and Maps. In two Volumes. By Capt. Edward Cooke. *London:* B. Lintot and R. Gosling, MDCCXII. *2 Volumes. I. Title; dedication 2 leaves; contents 2 leaves; introduction 6 leaves; and text 432 pp. Index 5 leaves. With 18 plates at p. 23, 25, 84, 99, 108, 114, 119, 127, 147, 162, 163, 252, 300, 306, 312, 316, 322, 325. A Map of the World at p. 1, and Map of the River Amazons, at p. 248.* II.

Title, dedication and contents 4 *leaves; Introduction,
xxiv pp. Text* 328 *pp. Index* 4 *leaves.* 3 *Journal
Tables at p.* 3, 66, 92. 8vo.   (15s. 706)

COOK (JAMES). An Authentic Narrative of a
Voyage to the Pacific Ocean: Performed by Captain Cook, and Captain Clerke, In his Britannic
Majesty's Ships, The Resolution, and Discovery,
In the Years, 1776, 1777, 1778, 1779, and 1780.
Including, A faithful account of all their Diſcoveries
in this Laſt Voyage, the unfortunate Death of Captain Cook, at the Iſland of O-why-ee, and the return
of the Ships to England under Captain Gore. Also
A Large Introduction, Exhibiting, an Account of
the ſeveral Voyages round the Globe; with an abſtract of the principal expeditions to Hudson's Bay,
for the Diſcovery of a North-Weſt-Paſſage. By
an Officer on Board the Discovery. Volume the
First [& Volume the Second] *Philadelphia:* Printed
and Sold by Robert Bell, in Third-Street. Price
two thirds of a Dollar. M,DCC,LXXXIII. *Title and
pp.* 9-229. 2 *vol. in* 1. *Calf.* 8vo. (10s. 6d. 707)

COOK (JAMES). An Abridgement of Captain Cook's
last Voyage, Performed in the Years 1776, 1777,
1778, 1779, and 1780. For making Diſcoveries in
the Northern Hemiſphere, by Order of His Majeſty.
Extracted from the 4to Edition, in 3 Volumes.
Containing a Relation of all the intereſting Tranſactions, particularly thoſe relative to the unfortunate Death of Captain Cook; with his Life. By
Captain King. *London:* G. Kearsley, MD.CCL.XXXIV.
Frontispiece, xxiv and 441 *pp.* 12mo.   (6s. 708)

COOL (A) Reply to a Calm Address, Lately Publiſhed by Mr. John Weſley; By T. S. *London :*
J. Plummer, 1775. 33 *pp.* 12mo. (4s. 6d. 709)

COOL Thoughts, *etc. See* No. 573, *misplaced.*

COOLE/ (A) Conference/ Between the Scottiſh
Commiſſioners Cleared Reforma-/tion, and the
Holland Miniſters Apologeticall Nar-/ration,
brought together by a well-willer/ to both. 1644./
9 *leaves; paged* 1-18. *half mor.* 4to. (7s. 6d. 710)

COOPER. The Rev. Mr. Cooper and his calumnies
against Jamaica, particularly his late Pamphlet

in reply to Facts verified on Oath. By a West-Indian. *Jamaica*, 1825. 67 *pp.* 8*vo.* (3*s.* 6*d.* 711)

COOPER (Rev. Mr.). The History of North America. Containing, A Review of the Cuſtoms and Manners of the Original Inhabitants; The firſt Settlement of the British Colonies, their Rise and Progress, from The earlieſt Period to the Time of their becoming United, free and independent States. By the Rev. Mr. Cooper. Embelliſhed with Copper-Plate Cuts. *London:* E. Newbery, [1780? *date cut off*] 4 *prel. leaves and pp.* 13-184. *Frontispiece and plates at pp.* 60, 70, 82, 127, 180. 12*mo.* (4*s.* 6*d.* 712)

COOPER (Rev. Mr.). The History of South America. Containing the Discoveries of Columbus, the Conquest of Mexico and Peru, and the Other Tranſaćtions of the Spaniards in the New World. By the Rev. Mr. Cooper. Embelliſhed with Copper-plate Cuts. *London,* E. Newbery, 1780. 6 *prel. leaves and* 168 *pp. Frontispiece and plates at pp.* 48, 62, 105, 154, 166. 12*mo.* (4*s.* 6*d.* 713)

COOPER (Rev. Mr.). The History of North America. Containing, a Review of the Cuſtoms and Manners of the Original Inhabitants; The firſt Settlement of the British Colonies, their Rise and Progreſs, from The earlieſt Period to the Time of their becoming United, free and independent States. By the Rev. Mr. Cooper. Embelliſhed with Copper-Plate Cuts. *London:* E. Newbery, 1789. *Frontispiece, title, preface, and contents,* 5 *leaves; text,* 184 *pp. With* 5 *plates.* 12*mo.* (6*s.* 714)

COOPER (Rev. Mr.). The History of South America. Containing the Discoveries of Columbus, The Conquest of Mexico and Peru, and the Other Tranſaćtions of the Spaniards in the New World. By the Rev. Mr. Cooper. Embelliſhed with Copper-plate Cuts. *Bennington:* Printed by Anthony Haswell, For Thomas Spencer, Bookseller, Market-Street, Albany. [1793.] 6 *prel. leaves, and* 168 *pp. Copper plates,* 'A. Reed, ſculpt. 1793,' *at pp.* 48, 61, 105, 153, 166. 12*mo.* (10*s.* 6*d.* 715)

COOPER (Rev. Mr.). The History of North America. Containing a Review of the Cuſtoms and

Manners of the Original Inhabitants; The firſt
Settlement of the British Colonies, their Rise and
Progress, from The earlieſt Period to the Time of
their becoming United, free and independent States.
By the Rev. Mr. Cooper, Embelliſhed with Copper-
Plate Cuts. [Second American Edition.] *Lansing-
burgh.* Printed by Silveſte; Tiffany, for, and ſold
by Thomas Spencer, at his Book-Store, Albany.
MDCCXCV. *4 prel. leaves and 159 pp. Copper-plate
Frontispiece and plates at pp.* 44, 55, 66, 108, 156.
Calf. 12*mo.* (10*s.* 6*d.* 716)

COOPER (Thomas). Some Information respecting
America, collected by Thomas Cooper, late of
Manchester. *London:* J. Johnson, MDCCXCIV. *iv
prel. and* 240 *pp.* 'Errata,' 1 *page. With Map of
the Middle States of America,* 12¼ *by* 18¼ *inches;
half morocco.* 8*vo.* (5*s.* 717)

COOPER (Thomas). Some Information respecting
America, collected by Thomas Cooper, late of
Manchester. The Second Edition. *London:* J.
Johnson, MDCCXCV. *iv prel. and* 240 *pp. With
Map of the Middle States of America,* 12¼ *by* 18¼
inches. 8*vo.* (4*s.* 6*d.* 718)

COOPER (William). Three Discourses concerning the Reality, the Extremity, and the abſolute
Eternity of Hell Puniſhments. By William Cooper,
A. M. One of the Paſtors of the Church in Brattle-
Street, Boſton. Publiſh'd by Deſire of many of
the Hearers. *Boston,* Printed by S. Kneeland and
T. Green, for Joseph Edwards, at the Corner Shop
on the North-ſide of the Town-Houſe. MDCCXXXII.
Title, and 114 *pp. wanting pp.* 3-6: *followed by a
second title,* ' A Sermon Preached February 27th,
1731, 2,' *and* 26 *pp.* 12*mo.* (7*s.* 6*d.* 719)

COOPER (William). The Doctrine of Predeſti-
nation unto Life Explained and Vindicated: in
Four Sermons, Preached to the Church of Christ,
in Brattle-Street, Boſton, New-England; and publiſhed at their general Deſire. With Some additional Passages and Quotations. By William
Cooper, One of the Pastors of the ſaid Church.
With a Preface by the Senior Paſtors of Boston,
and a Recommendation by ſome Divines in London. Boston Printed: *London,* Re-printed for E.

and C. Dilly, Mdcclxv. *Title, iv, and 142 pp.*
Old calf. 12mo. (4s. 6d. 720)

COOPER (William). Autograph Letter dated at
Boston, March 1st, 1716, 7. *A neat specimen in one*
full page. 4to. (7s. 6d. 721)

COPPINGER (Jose). Manifesto, que hace el Coronel Español Don José Coppinger, demostrando
el injusto y violento proceder que se há observado
en San Augustin de Florida, despojandole De Orden
de la Autoridad gobernante, de los Archivos de su
Gobierno y otros papeles, despues de la Entrega
de la Provincia á los Estados Unidos de America.
Impresso en Filadelfia, por Juan F. Hurtel, No.
126, Calle Segunda, Sur. 1821. *Half-title, title,*
and text pp. 5-36. half mor. 8vo. (4s. 6d. 722)

COPYE,/ vande/ Refolutie van de Heeren/ Burge-
meefters ende Raden/ tot Amfterdam./ Op't ftuk
vande/ West-Indische/ Compagnie./ Genomen in
Augufti 1649. *8 leaves in Roman type. Half mor.*
4to. (7s. 6d. 723)

COPYEN. [Aen de Hoogh-Mogende Heeren Staten
Generael der Vereeneghde Nederlanden.] *relating*
to Brasil and the West India Company. 16 pp.
4to. (7s. 6d. 724)

COREAL (Francois). Voyages de François Co-
real aux Indes Occidentales, Contenant/ Ce qu'il
y a vù de plus remarquable pendant fon féjour depuis 1666, jufqu'en 1697. Traduits de l'Espagnol. Avec vne Relation de la Guiane de Walter
Raleigh, & le Voyage de Narborough à la Mer du
Sud par le Détroit de Magellan, &c. Nouvelle
Edition, Revûë, corrigée, & augmentée d'une nouvelle Découverte des Indes Meridionales & des
Terres Auftrales, enrichie de figures. *A Paris,*
Chez Andres Cailieau ; m dcc xxii. *Two Volumes.*
Vol. I. Title ; Text 438 pp ; Table 4 pp ; Privilege
2 pp : Map at p. 1 and plates at pp. 50, 157, 304,
324, 326, 352. Vol. II. Title & 406 pp ; table 2 pp ;
3 maps. Old Calf. 8vo. (8s. 6d. 725)

CORNELIUS (Elias). The Little Osage Captive,
an Authentic Narrative: To which are added some
interesting Letters Written by Indians. *York :*

W. Alexander & Son, 1824.   *Frontispiece, and* 182 *pp.* 12*mo.*   (2*s.* 6*d.*   726)

CORNWALLIS (EARL).   Examination of Lieutenant General The Earl Cornwallis before a Committee of the House of Commons, upon Sir William Howe's Papers.   *London:* J. Robson, MDCCLXXIX. 60 *pp. half mor.*   (6*s.* 6*d.*   727)

CORNWALLIS (EARL).   An Answer to that part of the Narrative of Lieutenant-General Sir Henry Clinton, K.B. Which relates to the Conduct of Lieutenant-General Earl Cornwallis, during the Campaign in North-America, in the year 1781. By Earl Cornwallis.   *London:* J. Debrett, M.DCC.LXXXIII. *Title; Introduction, xvi pp.* ' Contents,' 3 *leaves; and text* 260 *pp.* ' *Errata*' 8 *lines on a slip of paper. With* ' State of the Troops in Virginia, to face p. 236,' *a folding sheet. Half mor.* 8*vo.*   (6*s.* 6*d.*   728)

CORNWALLIS (EARL).   Autograph Letter to General Washington, dated Jan. 7, 1777, respecting money and stores sent with a flag of truce to the Hessians taken prisoners at Trenton, *etc.* 1 *page* 4*to.*   (1*l.* 1*s.*   729)

CORONADO (CARLOS VASQUEZ).   Por/ Don Car-/ los Vazquez Coronado, ve-/zino de Guatimala./ Con/ El Señor Fifcal./   Sobre los treynta y vn mil Toftones,/ en que fe le remato el Officio de Al-/guazil mayor de la Audiēcia de Gua-/timala, para don Antonio Vazquez/ Coronado fu hijo./ [1632]. 5 *leaves, half mor. Folio.*   (1*l.* 1*s.*   730)

CORREA (DIEGO).   El Ciudadano Don Diego Correa al Escmo. Sr. Capitan General Gefe Superior Politico &c. &c. &c.   Cuarta edicion.—Gratis. *Habana:* 1822. Impreso por Don Tiburcio Campe en la oficina Liberal. 13 *pp. half morocco.* 8*vo.*   (3*s.* 6*d.*   731)

CORREA (JUAN NUNEZ).   El Rey./   Lo qve Por mi mandado fe afsiē/ta, y concierta con Iuan Nu-/ñez/ Correa Portugues, vezino de la ciu/ dad de Lisboa, fobre la haberia que/ en las ciudades de Seuilla, y Cadiz, y/ otras partes, fe cobra de todo el oro, y plata, pie-/dras, perlas, y joyas, y otras cofas que vienen de las/ Indias: y de todas las

mercaderias que van a ellas, y/ a las Islas del mar
Oceano, y las q vienēdellas: y ſo-/bre el apreſto
y prouiſion de las armadas, que para/ ello ſe han
de poner en orden, y deſpachar por cuē/ ta de la
haberia./ [*Dated*] *Valladolid the 26th of September*
1603. 15 *leaves. Half mor. Folio.* (1*l.* 1*s.* 732)

CORRO (JUAN DEL). Forma de el nvevo/ beneficio
de metales de plata,/ por el Capitan de Iuan/ del
Corro./ [*Dated*] Potoſi, y Junio 24./ de 1676 años./
4 *leaves, half mor. Folio.* (1*l.* 1*s.* 733)

CORRY (JOHN). The Life of George Washington,
late President and Commander in Chief of the
Armies of the United States of America; interspersed with Biographical Anecdotes of the Most
Eminent Men who effected the American Revolution, Dedicated (by Permission) to the Right Honourable the Lord Mayor. By John Corry. *London*: 1800. 228 *pp. Index 3 pp. Portrait of Washington. 8vo.* (4*s.* 6*d.* 734)

CORRY (JOHN). The Life of George Washington,
late President and Commander-in-Chief of the
Armies of the United States of America; By John
Corry, Author of " A Satirical View of London,"
&c. A New Edition. Crosby & Co. [*London.*
1802.] 57 *pp. Index* 2 *pp. Portrait of General Washington. 12mo.* (7*s.* 6*d.* 735)

CORTES (HERNANDO). An Original unpublished
Manuscript Letter of the Conqueror of Mexico,
addressed to the Emperor Charles the Fifth, not
dated, but about 1530, signed by his title *El Marq*[s]
del Valle. 4 *pages. Folio.* (18*l.* 18*s.* 736)
This invaluable autograph and historical Manuscript has unfortu-
nately been injured by damp, and in sizing and strengthening it
the ink has run, so that the signature of the Conqueror is not
easy to be read, though there can be no doubt of the genuineness.

CORTES (HERNANDO). ⅍ De Insvlis Nv/ per
inventis Ferdinandi Cortesii/ ad Carolum V. Rom.
Imperatorum Narrationes, cum alio/ quodam Petri
Martyris ad Clementem VII. Pon-/tificem Max-
imum conſimilis argumenti/ libello. ¶ His accef-
ſerunt Epiſtolæ duæ, de feliciſſimo apud Indos/
Euangelij incremento, quas superioribus hiſce diebus qui-/dam fratres Mino. ab India in Hiſpaniam
tranſmiſerunt./ ¶ Item Epitome de inuentis nuper
Indiæ populis idolatris/ ad fidem Chriſti, atq; adeo

ad Ecclefiam Catholicam conuer-/tendis, Autore
R. P. F. Nicolao Herborn, regularis obfer-/uan-
tiæ, ordinis Minorum Generali Commiffario/ Cif-
montano./ ¶ Venduntur in pingui Gallina./ Anno
M.D.XXXII. [*Colophon*] ¶ Coloniæ, Impenfis ho-
nefti ciuis Ar-/noldi BircKman. Anno Domini/
M.D.XXXII. Menfe/ Septembri./ *4 prelim. leaves ;
8 leaves of P. Martyr ; Text 30 leaves in the 2nd,
and 33 leaves in the 3d Relation, with 7 seq. leaves.
Folio.*   (*2l. 2s.* 737)

CORTES (HERNANDO). Ferdinandi/ Cortesii./ Von
dem Newen Hifpanien, fo im/ Meer gegem Nider=
gang, Zwo gantz luftige vnnd/ fruchtreiche Hif=
torien, an den grofzmächtigiften vnüberwindt=/
lichiften Herren, Carolum. V. Römifchen/ Kaifer
&c. Künig in Hifpanien &c./ Die erft im M. D.
xx. jar zügefchriben, in wellicher grundt=/lich vnd
glaubwirdig erzelt wirdt, der Abendtländern, vnnd/
fonderlich der Hochberümpten ftatt Temixtitan
eroberung./ Die andere im 1524. jar, Wie Temix=
titan, fo abgefallen, wider erobert,/ Nachmals an=
dere herrliche Syg, fampt der erfindung des Meers
Svr,/ So man für das Indianifch Meer achtet./
Darzü auch von vilen andern Landfchafften Indiæ,/
So erfunden von dem 1536. bifz auf das 42. Jar./
Wellicher vilfältige frucht, nutz vnd luftparkait, in
ainer Sum̃,/ auff das kürtzeft, ainer yetwedern Hif=
torien volgendes/ Tittel begriffen vnd angezaigt
wirdt./ Erftlich in Hifpanifcher Sprach von Cór-
tefio felbft befchriben, Nachmals/ von Doctor Peter
Sauorghan aufz Friaul in Lateinifche fprach Tranf=
feriert,/ Entlich aber in Hochteütfche fprach, zü
ehren vnd aufz vnderthänigifter/ gehorfame, dem
Allerdurchleüchtigiften, Grofzmächtigiften Für=
ften/ vñ Herrn, Herrn Ferdinanden, Römifchen,
zü Hungern/ vnd Böhem &c. Künigen, Infantē
in Hifpanien, Ertzhertzo=/gen zü Ofterreich &c.
von Xyfto Betuleio vñ Andrea/ Diethero von Augf=
purg, baiden dafelbft/ gemainer Statt Lateinifchen/
Schulmaiftern./ Getruckt inn der Kaiferlichen
Statt *Augfpurg*, durch/ Philipp Vlhart, In der
Kirchgaflen, bey S. Vlrich,/ Anno Domini M. D. L./
Cum gratia & Priuilegio Ro: Regiæ/ Maieftatis
in Decennium. *6 prelim. leaves. Text in* xxxix *folioed leaves, followed by one blank and two not numbered leaves, and folios* i *to* lx. *Folio.* (*3l. 3s.* 738)

CORTES (HERNANDO). Historia/ de Nueva-España,/ escrita por su esclarecido Conquistador/ Hernan Cortes,/ aumentada/ con otros Documentos, y Notas./ Por el Ilustrissimo Señor/ Don Francisco Antonio/ Lorenzana,/ Arzobispo de Mexico./ [*Motto and Vignette*]/ Con las Licencias Necesarias/ En *México* en la Imprenta del Superior Gobierno, del Br. D. Joſeph Antonio de Hogal/ en la Calle de Tiburcio. Año de 1770./ 11 *prelim. leaves including the title, frontispiece, dedication, Prologue and erratas ; copper-plate map ;* 'Viage de Hernan Cortes,' *xvi pp; copper-plate* 'El Grande Templo de Mexico ;' *text* 400 *pp. Between pp.* 176 *and* 177 *is a title,* 'Cordillera de los Pueblos,' *etc. with* 31 *copper-plates, representing Mexican Hieroglyphics; Indices* 9 *leaves. Map of California in* 1541 *at page* 329. *Folio.* (3l. 13s. 6d. 739)

CORTES (HERNANDO). Correspondance de Fernand Cortès avec L'Empereur Charles-Quint, sur la Conquête du Mexique. Traduite par M. le Vicomte de Flavigny, Lieutenant-Colonel de Dragons, & Chevalier de l'ordre royal & militaire de Saint-Louis. En *Suisse*, 1779. *xvi and* 471 *pp. half calf.* 8*vo.* (7s. 6d. 740)

CORTES (HERNANDO). Correspondance de Fernand Cortès avec L'Empereur Charles-Quint, sur la Conquête du Mexique. Traduite par M. le Vicomte de Flavigny, Lieutenant-Colonel de Dragons, & Chevalier de l'Ordre Royal & Militaire de Saint-Louis. Prix broché 3 liv. A *Paris*, Chez Cellot & Jombert. *Half-title, title, Epitre, Avis, & Sommaires, xxvi pp. and* 508 *pp. of text, with* 2 *sequent leaves. Calf.* 12*mo.* (8s. 741)

CORTES (HERNANDO). Historia de Méjico, escrita por su esclarecido conquistador Hernan Cortés : aumentada con otros documentos y notas, por D. Francisco Antonio Lorenzana, Antiguo Arzobispo de Méjico. Revisada y adaptada à le ortografia Moderna, por D. Manuel Del Mar. *Neuva York.* Sres. White, Gallaher y White. 1828. *Title ;* 'Aviso' 1 *leaf ;* 'Noticia Historica,' *etc. pp.* 5-110 ; *blank leaf :* 'Prologo,' *vi pp ;* 'Gobierno Politico,' *pp.* 7-42 : 'Cartas' 1 *leaf ; text pp.* 45-614. *Lithograph frontispiece and* 3 *plates.* 8*vo.* (15s. 742)
This edition was printed in New York for the Mexican market, and the entire edition was probably exported.

CORTES (Hernando). The Despatches of Hernando Cortes, the Conqueror of Mexico, addressed to the Emperor Charles V. Written during the conquest, and containing a Narrative of its events. Now first translated into English from the original Spanish, with an Introduction and Notes, by George Folsom, one of the Secretaries of the New York Historical Society, Member of the American Antiquarian Society, of the Archaiological Society of Athens &c. &c. *New York:* London: 1843. *xii prel. pp; Introduction 36 pp: Text* 431 *pp. Large paper, boards, uncut.* 8vo.   (10s. 6d. 743)

CORTES (Hernando). *Another copy, ordinary paper, tree calf extra by Riviere.* 12mo. (10s. 6d. 744)

COSMOPOLITA (El). Prospecto, and N° 1, July 18 to N° 9, Sept. 21, 1822. *Prospecto in* 4 *pp. Nos* 1 *to* 8 *in* 8 *pp. each & No.* 9 *in* 16 *pp. Santiago de Chile.* 1822. 4to.   (10s. 6d. 745)

COSNARD (Captain). Manuscript Memorial of Captain Cosnard to Charles Townshend Esq. Secretary at War asking promotion. 1 *page, not dated,* 4to.   (5s. 746)

The Memorialist served twenty years as an officer in Flanders, Minorca, and North America. In the 45th Regiment he was at Louisbourg in 1758, and in 1759 was, under Wolfe, wounded at the taking of Quebec, and afterwards was appointed Town Major of that garrison.

COSTE (John Francis). Oratio Habita in capitolio Gulielmopolitano In Comitiis Universitatis Virginiæ, Die xii Junii m.dcc.lxxxii. Dùm favente Gallorum Ducum & Militum frequentiâ, Medicæ Cooptationis Laureâ donabatur Christianissimi Regis Excercitûs Archiater, Joannes-Franciscus Coste, Saluberrimarum Medicinæ Facultatum Parifienfis Alumnus, Valentinæ Doĉtor, Pennfylvanienfis Doĉtor Honorarius; Regiarum Medicinæ Societatum Londinenfis, Edimburg., Parif. Regii Lotharingorum Medicorum Collegii Honorarius ; è Regiis Scientiarum, Artium & Litterarum Academiis Nanceïanâ, Lugdunenfi, Divionenfi; ex Humanâ Societate Philadelphienfi ; Societatis Philofophicæ Americanæ Socius ; Arcis & Militaris Nofocomii Caleti, Navaliumque Regis Exercituum Medicus. *Lugduni Batavorum.* 1783. *Half-title, title, dedication to Washington,* 3 *leaves; text* 103 *pp. uncut, half mor.* 8vo.   (4s. 6d. 747)

COTTON (John). Gods/ Promise/ to his/ Plantation./ 2 Sam. 7. 10./ Moreover I will appoint a
place for my people Ifrael,/ and I will plant them,
that they may dwell in a/ place of their owne, and
move no more./ As it was delivered in a Sermon,/
By Iohn Cotton, B.D./ and Preacher of Gods/
word in Bofton./ *London*,/ Printed by William
Jones for John Bellamy, and/ are to be folde at the
three Golden Lyons by the/ Royall Exchange.
1630./ *Title reverse blank:* 'To the Christian
Reader:' 2 *leaves signed* 'I. H;' *Text* 20 *pp.*
4*to.*   (5*l.* 5*s.*   748)

COTTON (John). A/ Coppy/ of/ a Letter/ of M^r.
Cotton of/ Bofton, in New England, fent/ in anfwer of certaine Objections/ made againft their Dif-
cipline/ and Orders there, direct/ed to a Friend./
VVith the Queftions propounded to/ fuch as are
admitted to the Church-/fellowfhip, and the Cove-
nant/ it Selfe./ Printed in the yeare 1641./ [*London.*] *Title, and* 6 *pp.* 4*to.*   (18*s.*   749)

COTTON (John). The way of Life./ Or,/ Gods
VVay/ and Course,/ in bringing the Soule into,/
keeping it in, and carrying it on, in/ the wayes of
life and peace./ Laid downe in foure feverall Treatifes on foure/ Texts of Scripture./ viz. The pouring
out of the Spirit, on Zach. 12. 10, 11, &c./ Sins
deadly wound, on Acts 2. 37./ The Chriftians
Charge, on Prov. 4. 23./ The life of Faith, on Gal.
2. 19, 20./ By that learned and judicious Divine,
and faith-/ful Minifter of Iefus Chrift,/ John Cotton./ *London*,/ Printed by M. F. for L. Fawne,
and S. Gellibrand, at the Brafen/ Serpent in Pauls
Church-yard. 1641./ *Title;* 'To the Reader.' 3
leaves signed, 'William Morton,' *Text*, 481 *pp. old
calf.* 4*to.*   (1*l.* 1*s.*   750)

COTTON (John). The/ Churches Refurrection,/ or
the/ Opening of the/ Fift and fixt verfes of the 20th
Chap./ of the/ Revelation./ By that Learned and
Reverend,/ Iohn Cotton/ Teacher to the Church of
Boston in/ Nevv England, and there corrected/by
his own hand./ *London:* / Printed by R. O. &
G. D. for Henry Overton,/ and are to be fold at
his Shop in Popes-head-Alley,/ 1642./ 30 *pp. half
mor.* 4*to.*   (12*s.* 6*d.*   751)

COTTON (John). The/ Powring/ ovt of the/ Seven Vials :/ Or an/ Exposition, of the/ 16. Chapter of the Revelation, with/ an Application of it to our Times./ Wherein is revealed Gods powring out/ the full Vials of his fierce wrath./ 1. Upon the loweſt and baſeſt ſort of Catholicks./ 2. Their Worſhip and Religion./ 3. Their Prieſts and Miniſters./ 4. The Houſe of Auſtria, and Popes Supremacy./ 5. Epiſcopall Government./ 6. Their Euphrates, or the ſtreame of their ſupportments./ 7. Their groſſe Ignorance, and blind Superſtitions./ Very fit and neceſſary for this/ Preſent Age./ Preached in ſundry Sermons at Boſton in New-England :/ By the Learned and Reverend Iohn Cotton,/ BB. of Divinity, and Teacher to the Church there/ *London,*/ Printed for R. S. and are to be ſold at Henry Overtons ſhop/ in Popeshead Alley. 1642./ *Title ;* ' To the Chriſtian Reader.' 1 *leaf signed* ' I H.' *and text,* 35, 24, 24, 43, 16, 14, *and* 19 *pages. Calf. 4to.* (18s. 752)

COTTON (John). The/ Keyes/ Of the Kingdom of/ Heaven,/ and/ Power thereof,/ according to the/ VVord of God./ By/ That Learned and Judicious Divine./ Mr. Iohn Cotton, Teacher of the Church/ at Boſton in New England,/ Tending to reconcile ſome preſent differences about/ Diſcipline./ Publiſhed/ By/ Tho. Goodwin./ Philip Nye./ *London,*/ Printed by M. Simmons for Henry Overton, and are to be ſold at his/ Shop entring into Popeshead Alley, out of Lombard-ſtreet, 1644./ *Title ;* ' To the Reader.' 5 *leaves, signed* ' Tho: Goodwin. Philip Nye.' *text,* 59 *pp. Vellum. 4to.* (18s. 753)

COTTON (John). The/ Keyes/ Of the Kingdom of/ Heaven/ and/ Power thereof, according to the/ VVord of God./ By/ That Learned and judicious Divine,/ Mr. Iohn Cotton, Teacher of the Church/ at Boſton in New-England,/ Tending to reconcile ſome preſent differences about/ Diſcipline./ The ſecond time Imprinted./ Publiſhed/ By Tho. Goodwin./ Philip Nye./ *London* printed by M. Simmons for Henry Overton, and are to be/ ſold at his ſhop in Popes-head-Alley. 1644./ *Title ;* ' To the Reader.' 5 *leaves, signed Tho: Goodwin. Philip Nye./ Text,* 59 *pp. Vellum. 4to.* (18s. 754)

COTTON (John). The/ Way of the Churches/ of
Christ/ in New-England./ Or,/ the VVay of
Churches/ walking in Brotherly equalitie, or co-/
ordination, without Subjection of/ one Church to
another./ Meafured and examined by the/ Golden
Reed of the Sanctuary./ Containing a full Declaration of the Church-/way in all Particulars./ By
Mr. J. Cotton, Teacher of the/ Church at Bofton
in New-England./ Publifhed according to Order.
London,/ Printed by Matthew Simmons in Alderf-
gateftreet./ 1645./ *Title;* ' ¶ The Epistle to the
Reader,' 5 *pages, signed,* 'N. H. I. H.' *Text* 116
pp. and Table 2 *leaves. Vellum.* 4*to.* (1*l.* 1*s.* 755)

COTTON (John). The/ Way of the Churches/
of Christ/ in New-England./ Or/ the VVay of
Churches/ walking in Brotherly equalitie, or/ co-
ordination, without Subjection of/ one Church to
another./ Meafured and examined by the/ Golden
Reed of the Sanctuary./ Containing a full Declaration of the Church-/way in all Particulars./ By
Mr. J. Cotton, Teacher of the/ Church at Bofton
in New-England./ Publifhed according to Order./
London,/ Printed by Matthew Simmons in Alderf-
gate-ftreete./ 1645./ 4 *prel. leaves ; viz. Title reverse blank;* ' ℈ The Epiftle to the Reader,' *etc.
Signed* 'N. H. I. H.' 5 *pp: Text* 116 *pp.* 'An
Alphabeticall Table,' *etc.* 3 *pp.* (1*l.* 1*s.* 756)

COTTON (John). A/ Description/ of the/ Spirituall
Temple :/ or the/ Spouse/ Prepared for the/
Lambe,/ The Lord/ Jesus./ Written by Francis
Cornwell,/ a Minifter and Servant of Jefus, the/
Chrift, for the benefit of poore/ diftreffed confcences,
in/ City and Countrey,/ *London,*/ Printed by John
Dawfon. 1646./ 4 *prel. leaves, viz. Title, and* To
the Reader; *and Text* 48 *pp. Calf by Bedford. Small
8vo. (15*s.* 757)

Though the name of Francis Cornwell appears on the title, he
wrote nothing but the Epistle to the Reader, 5 pages.

COTTON (John). The/ Bloudy Tenent,/ Washed,/
And made white in the bloud of the/ Lambe: being
difcuffed and difcharged of/ bloud-guiltineffe by
juft Defence./ Wherein/ The great Queftions of
this prefent time are/ handled, viz. How farre Liberty of Confcience/ ought to be given to thofe that
truly feare God? And how farre/ reftrained to tur-

bulent and peftilent perfons, that not one-/ly raze
the foundation of Godlineffe, but difturb the Civill/
Peace where they live ? Alfo how farre the Magiftrate may pro-/ceed in the duties of the firft Table ?
And that all Magiftrates/ ought to ftudy the word
and will of God, that they may frame/ their Govern-
ment according to it./ Discussed./ As they are al-
ledged from divers Scriptures, out of/ the Old and
New Teftament. Wherein alfo the practife of/
Princes is debated, together with the Judgement of
An-/cient and late Writers of moft precious efteeme./
Whereunto is added a Reply to Mr. [Roger] Wil-
liams/ Anfwer, to Mr. Cottons Letter./ By John
Cotton Batchelor in Divinity, and/ Teacher of the
Church of Chrift at Bofton in New-England./ *Lon-
don,*/ Printed by Matthew Symmons for Hannah
Allen, at the Crowne in/ Popes-Head-Alley. 1647./
Title, and Text, 195 *pp.* 'A Reply to Mr. Williams,'
144 *pp. old calf.* 4*to.* (3*l.* 3*s.* 758)

COTTON (John). Severall/ Qvestions/ of/ Serious
and neceffary Confequence,/ Propounded by the/
Teaching Elders,/ Unto M. John Cotton of Bofton/
in New-England./ With/ His refpective Anfwer
to each Queftion./ *London,*/ Printed for Thomas
Banks, and are to bee fold in Black-/Friers on the
top of Bride-well Staires, and in Weft-/minfter
Hall, at the figne of the Seale. 1647./ *Title and* 10
pp. Fine large copy. 4*to.* (15*s.* 759)

COTTON (John). Severall/ Qvestions/ of/ Serious
and neceffary Confequence,/ Propounded by the/
Teaching Elders,/ Unto M. Iohn Cotton of Bofton/
in New-England./ With/ His refpective Anfwer
to each Queftion./ *London,*/ Printed for Thomas
Banks, and are to bee fold in Black-/Friers on the
top of Bride-well Staires, and in Weft-/minfter
Hall, at the figne of the Seale. 1647./ *Title, and*
10 *pp.* [*Duplicate of* Nº 759.] 4*to.* (15*s.* 760)

COTTON (John). Singing/ of/ Psalmes/ a Gospel-
Ordinance./ Or/ a Treatise,/ Wherein are handled
thefe foure Particulars./ 1. Touching the Duty it
felfe./ 2. Touching the Matter to be Sung./ 3.
Touching the Singers./ 4. Touching the Manner
of Singing./ By John Cotton, Teacher of the/
Church at Bofton in New-England./ *London ;*/

Printed by M. S. for Hannah Allen, at the Crowne/ in Popes-Head-Alley: and John Rothwell at the/ Sunne and Fountaine in Pauls- Church-yard./ 1647./ *Title, and* 72 *pp.* 4*to.* (2*l.* 12*s.* 6*d.* 761)

COTTON (John). Singing/ of/ Psalmes/ a Gospel-Ordinance./ Or/ a Treatise,/ wherein/ Are handled thefe Particulars: 1. Touching the Duty it felfe./ 2. Touching the Matter to be Sung./ 3. Touching the Singers./ 4. Touching the manner of Singing./ By John Cotton, Teacher of the/ Church at Bofton in New-England./*London*,/ Printed for J. R. at the Sunne and Fountaine in Pauls-/Church-yard: and H. A. at the Crowne in Popes-/Head Alley. 1650./ *Title, and* 72 *pp. half calf.* 4*to.* (2*l.* 12*s.* 6*d.* 762)

COTTON (John). Of the/ Holinesse/ of/ Church-Members./ By John Cotton, Teacher of/ the Church of Chrift in/ Bofton in/ New-England./ *London :*/ Printed by F. N. for Hanna Allen, and are to be fold at/ the Crown in Popes-head Alley. 1650./ *Title; Dedication,* 2 *pages, signed* 'John Cotton.' *Text* 95 *pp.* 4*to.* (15*s.* 763)

COTTON (John). An/ Abstract/ of/ Laws and Government./ Wherein as in a Mirrour may be feen/ the wisdom & perfection of the Government of/ Chrifts Kingdome./ Accomodable to any State or form of/ Government in the world, that is not Antichri-/ftian or Tyranicall./ Collected and digefted into the enfuing Method, by/ that Godly, Grave, and Judicious Divine, Mr. John/ Cotton, of Bofton in New-England, in his Life-time,/ and prefented to the generall Court of the Maffachufets./ And now publifhed after his death, by/ William Afpin-wall./ *London*,/ Printed by M. S. for Livewel Chapman, and are to be fold/ at the Crown in Popef-head Alley, 1655./ *Title;* 'To the Reader.' 3 *leaves, signed,* 'Will: Afpinwall.' *Text,* 35 *pp.* 'An Analyfis of Lawes and Government acco-/modated to New-England,' *with errata* 2 *pp. half mor.* 4*to.* (3*l.* 3*s.* 764)

COTTON (John). A Brief/ Exposition/ With Practical/ Observations/ Upon the whole Book of/ Canticles./ Never before Printed./ By that late Pious and Worthy Di-/vine Mr. John Cotton Paf-tor of/ Bofton in New England./ Publifhed by

Anthony Tuckney D.D. Mafter/ of Saint Johns
Colledge in Cambridge./ *London*, Printed by T.
R. & E. M. for Ralph Smith/ at the Signe of the
Bible in Cornhill, neere/ the Royall Exchange.
1655./ *Half-title, imprimatur, and title* 3 *leaves;*
'To the Reader,' 5 *leaves, signed* 'Anthony Tuck-
ney.' *Text,* 238 *pp.* 8*vo.* (12*s.* 6*d.* 765)

COTTON (JOHN). An/ Exposition/ upon/ The
Thirteenth Chapter/ of the/ Revelation./ By that
Reverend an Eminent fer-/vant of the Lord, M^r.
John Cotton, Teacher to/ the Church at Bofton in
New-England./ Taken from his mouth in Short-
writing, and fome/ part of it corrected by Himfelfe
soon after the Prea-/ching thereof, and all of it
fince viewed over by a/ friend to Him, and to the
Truth ; wherein fome mi-/ftakes were amended, but
nothing of the fence al-/tered./ *London*, Printed
by *M. S.* for Livewel Chapman, at the Crown/ in
Popes head Alley, 1655./ *Title; To the Reader,*
signed by Thomas Allen, 4 *pages;* Text, 262 *pp.*
followed by one blank leaf and 3 *leaves of Table and*
Errata. 4*to.* (15*s.* 766)

COTTON (JOHN). An/ Exposition/ upon/ The
Thirteenth Chapter/ of the/ Revelation./ By that
Reverend and an Eminent fervant of the Lord,/
Mr. John Cotton,/ Teacher to the Church at Bofton
in/ New-England./ Taken from his mouth in Short-
writing, and/ fome part of it Corrected by himfelf
foon after the/ Preaching thereof, and all of it fince
Viewed over/ by a friend to Him, and to the Truth :
wherein/ fome Miftakes were amended, but nothing
of the/ Senfe altered./ *London*, Printed for Tim.
Smart, at the Hand and Bible in/ The Old Bayly.
1656./ *Title; To the Reader* 4 *pp; The Analysis*
2 *pp. Errata* 2 *pp; Text* 262 *pp. followed by a*
blank leaf & 3 *leaves of Table.* 4*to.* (15*s.* 767)
This is the same edition as the preceding, except the new title and
the addition of the 2 leaves of Analyfis and Errata.

COTTON (JOHN). A Briefe/ Exposition/ With/
Practicall Obfervations/ upon/ The Whole Book/ of
Ecclesiastes./ By that late pious and worthy
Divine,/ Mr. John Cotton,/ Paftor of Bofton in
New-England./ Published,/ By Anthony Tuckney,
D.D./ Mafter of St. Johns Colledge in Cambridge./
The Second Impreffion, Corrected./ *London*,/

Printed by W. W. for Ralph Smith at the Bible/ in Cornhill. 1757./ *Title; Dedication 3 leaves, signed by Anthony Tuckney. Text 258 [for 260] pp. old calf. 8vo.* (15s. 768)

COTTON (JOHN). A/ Treatise/ of the/ Covenant/ of/ Grace,/ As it is difpenfed to the Elect Seed,/ effectually unto Salvation./ Being/ The fubftance of divers Sermons preached upon/ Act. 7. 8. by that eminently holy and judi-/cious man of God, Mr. John Cotton, Teacher/ of the Church at Bofton in N.E./ The fecond Edition, by a Copy far larger then the/ former; and Corrected alfo by the Authors own hand./ This Copy was fitted for the Prefs, by Mr. Tho./ Allen Minifter in Norwich./ *London,*/ Printed by Ja. Cottrel, for John Allen, at the/ Rifing-Sun in Pauls Church-yard./ 1659./ *12 pret. leaves; and Text, 250 pp. calf. 16mo.* (15s. 769)

COTTON (JOHN). A Treatise of the Covenant of Grace, As it is difpenfed to the Elect Seed, effectually unto Salvation. Being the fubftance of divers Sermons preached upon Act. 7. 8. by that eminently holy and judicious man of God, Mr. John Cotton, Teacher of the Church at Bofton in N.E. The Third Edition, Corrected, and very much enlarged, by the Author's own Hand. *London:* Printed for Peter Parker, in Popes-head-Alley, next Cornhill, 1671. *On the reverse of the Title,* 'To the Reader.' 'A Table of the Contents.' *7 leaves; & text 223 pp. 8vo.* (10s. 6d. 770)

COTTON (JOHN). Nafhauanittue Meninnunk/ wutch/ Mukkiesog,/ Wuffefemumun wutch Sog-/ kodtunganafh/ Naneefwe Testamentsash;/ Wutch/ Ukkefitchippooonganoo Ukketeahogkounooh./ Ne-gonáe wuffukhùmun ut Englifhmánne Unnon-/toowaonganit, nafhpe ne ánue, wunnegenùe/ Noh-tompeantog./ Noh afoowèfit/ John Cotton./ Kah yeuyeu qufhkinnúmun en Indiane Unnontoo-/waonganit wutch oonenehikqunàout Indiane/ Muk-kiesog,/ nafhpe/ Grindal Rawson./ Wunnaunche-mookáe Nohtompeantog ut kenugke/ Indianog./ *Cambridge:*/ Printeuoop nafhpe Samuel Green, kah/ Bartholomew Green. 1691./ *Title; and text pp. 3-13. Fine copy, in brown morroco extra by F. Bedford. 12mo.* (7l. 7s. 771)

COTTON (John). A leaf from a Manuscript Sermon of the Celebrated John Cotton, in his Autograph. 2 pp. *A fine specimen.* 4to. (2*l.* 2*s.* 772)

COTTON (John, *of Plymouth*). Autograph Letter to his Son addressed 'These For Mr. Rowland Cotton, Preacher of the Gospel, at Sandwich,' and dated at Plymouth, May 15, 1694. *2 pages, A fine specimen.* 4to. (1*l.* 1*s.* 773)

COTTON (John, *of Newtown*). Autograph note 'For the Revd. Mr. Prince in Boston, dated at Newtown, May 29, 1727, requesting of Mr. Prince the "favour as to correcting the press,—& making whatsoever corrections you think proper," *etc.* 1 *page.* 4to. (15*s.* 774)
This John Cotton was the son of Rowland Cotton and the grandson of John Cotton of Plymouth, and the great grandson of John Cotton of Boston.

COTTON (Rowland). Cain's Lamentations over Abel, in Six Books, containing: I. His Aftonifhment at Abel's Death—his melancholy Relation of the event to Adam and Eve, and his forrowful feparation from his parents when he became a fugitive Exile. II. His conviction and Penitence in his folitary Retirement, with Satan's appearing to him. III. The appearance of Abel unto him as a Meffenger from Heaven, and their Difcourfe. IV. His Reflections on Abel's Defcenfion and Afcenfion again to Heaven, and the Confolation it produced to his Soul. V. The appearance and Difcourfe of Adam with him from Heaven—Adam's departure—his fecond appearance to him as the Meffenger of glad Tidings—with Cain's melancholy reflections and doubts in the interval. VI. His patient waiting the will of God to depart from this fpot of Solitude, and earneft defire to fee his Mother before fhe goes to his Father and Brother—with the death of Eve in the prefence of Cain. The Third Edition. By Rowland Cotton. *New York:* Printed by Wayland and Davis, for the Author. 1795. 239 *pp.* 'A List of Subscribers Names. Philadelphia.' 9 *pp.* 12*mo.* (6*s.* 6*d.* 775)

COTTON (Seaborn). An Autograph order upon Lieutenant Brown of Haverhill requesting him to pay "the just sume of three pounds ten shillings in current New-England money as satisfaction

from mee for seven barrells of Cider," *etc.* Dated
Hampton, Dec. 18, 1678. On the same page is a
receipt signed by Samuel Dutton for thirty shillings
for the use of Seaborn Cotton. 1 *small page.*
4*to.* (1*l.* 1*s.* 776)

The Rev. Seaborn Cotton was born at sea in 1633, while his parents
were on their voyage to New England, and hence his unusual
name, which appears latinized in the Harvard College Triennial
Catalogue as " Marigena Cotton."

COURTOT (Francois). La Vie/ du Bien-Heureux
Pere/ Francois/ Solano/ Religieux de l'Ordre/ de
Saint Francois/ Patron du Perou,/ composée svr
les memoires/ prefentez au S. Siege pour fa Beatifi-
cation,/ Et le recit du Martyre d'onze Religieux
du/ mefme Ordre, qui fouffrirent la mort à Gor-
kom pour la defenfe de la Foy, l'an 1572./ Par le
R. P. Francois Covrtot/ Religieux du mefme Ordre,
Doƈteur en/ Thelogie de la Faculté de Paris, &c./
A *Paris,*/ Chez Estienne Michallet,/ ruë S. Jacques,
à l'Image S. Paul,/ proche la Fontaine S. Severin./
M.DCC.LXXVII./ Avec Privilege./ 10 *prel, leaves;
viz. Title, Epistre, Preface, & Approbations. Text* 158
pp. old calf. 12*mo.* (12*s.* 6*d.* 777)

COWDELL (Thomas D.). A Poetical Journal of a
Tour from British North America to England,
Wales & Ireland, interspersed with Reflections Na-
tural, Moral & Political. To which are subjoined,
Two Pieces of the Intended Jubilee. By Thomas
D. Cowdell. *Dublin :* Wilkinson & Courtney,
1809. 76 *pp. uncut.* 12*mo.* (4*s.* 6*d.* 778)

COXE (Daniel). A Description Of the English
Province of Carolana, By the Spaniards câll'd Florida, And by the French La Louisiane. As alfo of
the Great and Famous River Meschacebe or Missisipi, The Five vaft Navigable Lakes of Frefh
Water, and the Parts Adjacent. Together With
an Account of the Commodities of the Growth and
Produƈtion of the faid Province. And a Preface
containing fome Confiderations on the Confequences of the French making Settlements there.
By Daniel Coxe, Efq : *London;* Printed for B.
Cowse, at the Rofe and Crown in St. Paul's
Church-Yard. MDCCXXII. *Title,* 'The Preface.'
25 *leaves;* 'The Contents.' 1 *leaf.* 'Map of Carolana' *etc. 22 by 17 inches; and text* 122 *pp. calf.*
8*vo.* (15*s.* 779)

COXE (DANIEL). A Description Of the English
Province of Carolana, By the Spaniards call'd Florida, And by the French La Louisiane. As alfo of
the Great and Famous River Meschacebe or Missisipi, The Five vaft Navigable Lakes of Frefh
Water, and the Parts Adjacent. Together With
an Account of the Commodities of the Growth and
Produćtion of the faid Province. And a Preface
containing fome Confiderations on the Confequences of the French making a Settlement there.
By Daniel Coxe, Efq; *London :* Printed forEd-
ward Symon, againft the Royal Exchange in Cornhill. 1727. *Title,* ' The Preface.' 25 *leaves* ; ' The
Contents.' 1 *leaf ; and text* 122 *pp.* ' Map of Carolina.' *Calf by Bedford. 8vo.*   (15*s.*   780)

COXE (DANIEL). A Description of the Englifh
Province of Carolana. By the Spaniards call'd Florida, and by the French, La Louisiane. Viz. I. A
Defcription of the great and famous River Mefchacebe, or Miffifipi. II. A Defcription of the Countries, People, Rivers, Bays, Harbours and Iflands,
to the Eaft of Mefchacebe. III. A Defcription of
the Sea Coaft, the large Rivers ; their Heads and
Courfes, to the Weft of Mefchacebe. IV. A Defcription of the Five great Seas or Lakes of frefh
Water. V. A new and curious Difcovery of an
eafy Communication between the River Mefchacebe and the South-Sea, which feparates America
from China, by means of feveral large Rivers and
Lakes ; with a Defcription of the faid Sea, to the
Streights of Uries ; as alfo of a rich and confiderable Trade to be carry'd on from thence to Japan,
China and Tartary. VI. An Account of the ufeful
Animals, Vegetables, Metals, Minerals, and other
rich and valuable Commodities, which this Province naturally produces. VII. An Appendix, containing the original Charter, &c. With a large and
curious Preface, demonftrating the Right of the
English to that Country, and the unjuft Manner
of the French ufurping of it; their prodigious
Increafe there, &c. and the inevitable Danger
our other Colonies on the Continent will be expofed to, if not timely prevented ; interfperfed
with many ufeful Hints, in Regard to our Plantations in General. To which is added, A large

and accurate Map of Carolana, and of the River Meschacebe. By Daniel Coxe, Esq; [*London*] Printed for and fold by Olive Payne, at Horace's Head in Pope's-Head Alley, Cornhill, oppofite the Royal Exchange, 1741. *27 prel. leaves. Map. Text 122 pp. Half mor. 8vo.* (12s. 6d. 781)

These three editions are the same, except the title-pages.

COXE (RICHARD S.). Extent and Value of the Possessory Rights of the Hudson's Bay Company in Oregon, South of Forty-Ninth Degree. Printed by John Lovell, St. Nicholas Street, *Montreal.* [1849]. *Title, and* 51 *pp.* 8vo. (3s. 6d. 782)

COXE (TENCH). A View of the United States of America, in a Series of papers, written at various times between the years 1787 and 1794; by Tench Coxe, of Philadelphia, Commissioner of the Revenue. Interspersed with Authentic Documents: the whole tending to exhibit the progress and present state of Civil and Religious Liberty, Population, Agriculture, Exports, Fisheries, Navigation, Ship-Building, Manufactures, and general Improvement. Philadelphia, printed 1794. *London,* J. Johnson, 1795. *8 prel. leaves; viz. Title, prefatory note pp. iii-x; table, pp. xi-xiv. Book I. 1 leaf ; and text* 512 *pp. calf.* 8vo. (6s. 6d. 783)

COXE (WILLIAM). Account of the Russian Discoveries between Asia and America. To which are added, the Conquest of Siberia, and the History of the Transactions and Commerce between Russia and China. By William Coxe, A.M. F.R.S. F.S.A. Rector of Bemerton. The Fourth Edition, considerably enlarged. *London,* Cadell and Davies, 1803. *xxiv and* 500 *pp.* ' List of the principal Books' *etc.* 3 *pp.* 6 *Maps. calf.* 8vo. (5s. 6d. 784)

CRAWFORD (CHARLES). An Essay on the propagation of the Gospel; in which there are numerous facts and arguments adduced to prove that many of the Indians in America are descended from the Ten Tribes. The Second Edition. By Charles Crawford, Esq. *Philadelphia,* Printed and sold by James Humphreys. 1801. 154 *pp. Boards uncut.* 8vo. (4s. 6d. 785)

CRISIS (THE) of the Colonies considered; with

some Observations on the necessity of properly connecting their Commercial Interest with Great Britain and America. Addressed to the Duke of Richmond : With a Letter to Lord Penrhyn, late Chairman of the Committee of Planters : and West India Merchants. *London:* J. Bew, 1785, *Title; Dedication, pp. iii-v.* To Lord Penrhyn, *pp. vii-viii. Text* 38 *pp. signed* 'John Williams.' *Unbound.* 8vo. (5s. 6d. 786)

CRITICAL (A) Commentary on Archbifhop Secker's Letter to the Right Honourable Horatio Walpole, concerning Bishops in America. *London:* E. and C. Dilly, MDCCLXX. *Title, and text pp.* 3-93. ' Postscript.' *pp.* 95-111. 8vo. (5s. 787)

CRUSIUS (MARTIN). D. Solomoni/ Schvveigkero Sultzenfi, qui Con-/ftantinopoli in Aula Legati Imp. Rom. aliquot/ annos Ecclefiafta fuit : & in Aegypto, Palæfti-/na, Syria, peregrinatus eft :/ Gratulatio fcripta/ A/ Martino Crvsio./ Cum Defcriptione illius peregrinationis : & Græcorum/ Patriarcharum, aliorúmq ; qui nunc illis locis viuunt/ Chriftianorum commendationibus, fcriptisq ;/ alijs lectu dignif-fimis./ *Argentorati/* Excudebat Nicolaus Vvyriot. Anno/ M.D.LXXXII./ 18 *leaves. Calf extra by Bedford.* 4to. (1l. 1s. 788)

CUBA. Original Papers Relating to the Expedition to the Ifland of Cuba. *London:* M. Cooper, MDCCXLIV. *Half-title, title, and text, pp.* 5-219. *Half mor.* 8vo. (7s. 6d. 789)

CUBERO SEBASTIAN (PEDRO). Peregrinacion/ qve ha hecho de la/ Mayor Parte del/ Mundo/ Don Pedro Cvbero Sebastian,/ Predicador Apoftolico del Afsia, natural del Reyno/ de Aragon ; con las cofas mas fingulares que le han/ fucedido, y vifto, entre tan Barbaras Naciones, fu Re-/ligion, Ritos, Ceremonias, y otras cofas memorables, y/ curiofas, què ha podido inquirir ; con el viage/ por tierra, defde Efpaña, hafta las Indias/ Orientales./ Escrita/ por el mismo Don Pedro Cvbero/ Sebaftian./ Dedicado Al SS. Christo de las/ Injurias, fita en la Iglefia del Señor San Millan,/ anexo de S. Iufto, y Paftor defta Coronada Villa/ de Madrid./ Se-gvnda Impression./ En *Zaragoza,* Por Pafqual Bueno, Impreffor del Reyno/ de Aragon. Año de

1688./ 8 *prel. leaves, & 288 pages. Old calf.*
4to. (2*l.* 2*s.* 790)

CUDENA (Pedro). Befchreibung des Portugiefifchen Amerika vom Cudena. Ein Spanifches Manufcript in der Wolfenbüttelfchen Bibliothek, herausgegeben vom Herrn Hofrath Lesfing. Mit
Anmerkungen und Zufätzen begleitet von Chriftian
Leifte, Rektor der Herzoglichen grofzen Schule zu
Wolfenbüttel. *Braunschweig,* in der Buchhandlung
des Fürftl. Wayfenhaufes. 1780. 160 *pp. Paper.*
8vo. (3*s.* 6*d.* 791)

CUEVAS, AGUIRRE Y ESPINOSA (Joseph
Francisco de). Extracto/ de los autos de diligen-
cias,/ y reconocimientos de los Rios, Lagunas,/
Vertientes, y Desagues de la Capital/ Mexico, y
su Valle :/ De los Caminos para su comunicacion,/
y su comercio :/ De los Daños que se vieron : Remedios, que ce adbitraron :/ De los Puntos en particular decididos :/ De su Practica :/ y de otros y
mayor examen reservados,/ para con mejor acierto
resolverlos./ Todo por disposicion del Excmo.
Señor/ D. Juan Francisco/ de Huemez, y Horca-
sitas,/ del Consejo de su Magestad,/ Theniente
General de sus Reales Exercitos,/ Vi-Rey Gobernador y Capitan General de esta Nueva/ España,
y Presidente de su Real Audiencia./ Lo escribió
de su Mandato el Lic^do./ D. Joseph Francisco/ de
Cuevas, Aguirre, y Espinofa,/ Señor de las Cafas
de Aguirre, Sazia, Velaunza, y/ Suafola, Abogado
de la referida Real Audiencia :/ Colegial mayor
antiguo del Infigne Viejo Colegio/ Mayor de Santa
Maria de Todos Santos, Regidor/ perpetuo de la
Muy Noble, y Muy Leal Imperial/ Ciudad de Mexico, y fu Procurador General./ De Mandato el
Excmo. Sr. Vi-Rey :/ Imprefso en *Mexico* por la
Viuda de D. Joseph Bernardo de Hogal. Año de
1748./ *Title in red and black within a light border,
having a 'Soneto' on the reverse: Text* 71 *pages.
Fine copy. Folio.* (4*l.* 4*s.* 792)

At page 42 is a Map 14 by 16½ inches, engraved on copper by Antonio Morino of Mexico, entitled, " Mapa de las Aguas que por
el Circulo de 90 leguas uienen a la Laguna de Tescuco y de la
Estension que esta y lade Chalco tenian sacado del que en el Siglo
antecedente deligneo Dⁿ. Carlos de Siguenza." This book is of
the utmost topographical and historical importance.

CUNHA DE AZEREDO COUTINHO. (Joze

JOAQUIM DA). Ensaio Economico sobre o Comercio de Portugal e suas Colonias oferecido ao Serenisimo Princepe do Brazil noso Senhor e Publicado de ordem da Academia Real das Siencias pelo seu Socio Joze Joaquim da Cunha de Azeredo Coutinho. *Lisboa* na Oficina da Mesma Academia 1794. 6 *prel. leaves; Text* 153 *pp.* 4*to.* (8*s.* 6*d.* 793)

CUNHA DE AZEREDO COUTINHO (JOZE JO-AQUIM DA). A political Essay on the Commerce of Portugal and her Colonies, particularly of Brasil in South America. By J. J. da Cunha de Azeredo Coutinho Bishop of Fernambuco, and Fellow of the Royal Academy of Sciences of Lisbon. Translated from the Portuguese. *London:* G. G. and J. Robinson, 1801. 9 *prel. leaves: Text* 198 *pp.* [*wanting pp.* 1-6]. 'Errata' 2 *pp. boards, uncut.* 8*vo.* (3*s.* 6*d.* 794)

CURE (A) for the Spleen. Or Amusement for a Winter's Evening; Being the Subſtance of a Converſation on the Times, over a Friendly Tankard and Pipe. Between Sharp, — — — A Country Parſon. Bumper, — — — A Country Juſtice. Fillpot, — — — An Inn-keeper. Graveairs, — — — A Deacon. Trim, — — — A Barber. Brim, — — — A Quaker. Puff, — — — A late Repreſentative. Taken in ſhort Hand, by Sir Roger De Coverly. *America:* Printed and ſold in the Year MDCCLXXV. *Title, and text pp.* 3-32. *Fine copy, half morocco.* 8*vo.* (10*s.* 6*d.* 795)

The scene of this Conversation is laid near Boston, and the book is an amusing Exposition of the Grievances and Politics of the Colonies. On page 30 of this copy are four lines of the text with this manuscript note at the bottom of the page, " From this to the conclusion of the period is omitted in all the vendible impressions, as the printer was a woman and ashamed " [illegible].

CURRIE (WILLIAM). An Historical Account of the Climates and Diseases of the United States of America; and of the Remedies and methods of Treatment, which have been found most useful and efficacious, particularly in those Diseases which depend upon Climate and Situation. Collected principally from Personal Observation, and the communications of Physicians of Talents and experience, residing in the several States. By William Currie, Fellow of the College of Phyſicians of Philadelphia. *Philadelphia:* Printed by T. Dobson, at

the Stone-House, No. 41, South Second-Street.
M,DCC,XCII. *4 prel. leaves, and 409 pp. Index 5 pp.
Old calf. 8vo.* (10s. 6d. 796)

CURTIS (MARTIN). The Arte of Navi-/gation./
Firſt written in the Spaniſh tongue by/ that Excellent Mariner and Mathematici-/an of theſe times,
Martine/ Cvrtis./ From thence Tranſlated into
Engliſh by Richard Eden: And/ now newly Corrected and inlarged, with many neceſſa-/rie Tables,
Rules, and Inſtructions, for the more eaſie attai-/
ning to the knowledge of Nauigation:/ By John
Tapp./ *London:* Printed for Iohn Tapp, and are
to be ſold at his Shoppe at/ S. Magnus Corner.
1609./ *Title, reverse blank; Dedication to Sir William Wade signed by John Tapp, 4 pp; 'To the
Reader,' 1 page: 'How to uſe the next table' 1
page; 'A Table' 1 page: Kalendar 7 pp: Text in
black letter, 157 pp: 'Table of the Chapters' 4 pp.
4to.* (2l. 2s. 797)

CUSACK (GEORGE). The/ Grand Pyrate:/ Or, the/
Life and Death/ of/ Capt. George Cvsack/ The great
Sea-Robber./ With/ An Accompt of all his noto-
rious Robberies both at/ Sea and Land./ Together/
with his Tryal, Condemnation, and Execvtion./
Taken by an Impartial hand./ Licenſed Novemb.
19, 1675. Roger L'Estrange./ *London,/* Printed for
Jonathan Edwin at the Sign of the Three/ Roſes in
Ludgate-ſtreet. MDCLXXVI./ *31 pp. Fine copy in
half calf. 4to.* (1l. 1s. 798)

Cusack was much in New-England and Virginia.

 * * * * (M.) Abrégé Historique des Troubles de La Martinique. Par M. D *** * * * ***. Au *Fort Royal*, De l'imprimerie de J.-Fs. Bazille, imprimeur de la colonie. Et se trouve dans tous les quartiers de l'isle ; chez les directeurs de poste, & dans les autres isles, chez les marchands de nouveautés. 1791. *Title and Dedication 2 leaves; and Text 82 pp.* 8vo.   (7s. 6d.   799)

DALCHO (Frederick). An Historical Account of the Protestant Episcopal Church, in South-Carolina, from the first Settlement of the Province, to the War of the Revolution ; with notices of the present State of the Church in each Parish : and some account of the early Civil History of Carolina, never before published. To which are added, the Laws relating to Religious Worship ; the Journals and Rules of the Convention of South-Carolina ; the Constitution and Canons of the Protestant Episcopal Church, and the course of Ecclesiastical Studies : with An Index, and List of Subscribers. By Frederick Dalcho, M.D. Assistant Minister of St. Michael's Church, Charleston. *Charleston :* E. Thayer, 1820. *viii and 613 pp. Subscribers Names 3 pp. calf. 8vo.*   (14s.   800)

DAMPIER (William). A New Voyage round the World. Describing particularly, The Isthmus of America, several Coasts and Islands in the West Indies, the Isles of Cape Verde, the Passage by Terra del Fuego, the South Sea Coasts of Chili, Peru, and Mexico ; the Isle of Guam one of the Ladrones, Mindanas, and other Philippine and East India Islands near Cambodia, China, Formosa, Luconia, Celebes, &c. New Holland, Sumatra,

Nicobar Ifles; the Cape of Good Hope, and Santa
Hellena. Their Soils, Rivers, Harbours, Plants,
Fruits, Animals, and Inhabitants. Their Customs,
Religion, Government, Trade, &c. By William
Dampier. Illuftrated with Particular Maps and
Draughts. *London*, Printed for James Knapton,
at the Crown in St. Pauls Church-yard. MDCXCVII.
Title: Dedication 'To the Right Honourable Charles
Montague,' 2 *pp*; 'The Preface' 4 *pp*; 'The Con-
tents' 2 *pp*; 'The Author's Departure from Eng-
land' *vi pp*; *Text* 550 *pp*. 'Errata' 1 *page*: 'Books
fold by James Knapton' 3 *pages. Fine copy.*
8*vo.*   (10s. 6d.   801)

This is the *First Edition* of the First Volume. There are 5 copperplate Maps: viz.
   1. Map of the World, facing the Title.
   2. Isthmus of Darien, at page 1.
   3. Middle Part of America, at page 25.
   4. East Indies, at page 282.
   5. At page 384 is a plate in 4 compartments, belonging respec-
      tively to pages 384, 389, 390, and 421.

DAMPIER (WILLIAM). *The same.* The Second
Edition Corrected. *London*, Printed for James
Knapton, at the Crown in St. Pauls Church-yard.
MDCXCVII. 8*vo.*   (7s. 6d.   802)

This Second Edition of Vol. I. answers to the description of the
preceding, except that the errata having been corrected are
here omitted.

DAMPIER (WILLIAM). *The same.* The Third Edition Corrected. *London*, Printed for James Knapton, at the Crown in St. Paul's Church-yard.
MDCXCVIII. 8*vo.*   (7s. 6d.   803)

This Third Edition of Volume I answers to the description of the
preceding, though it has been reprinted throughout.

DAMPIER (WILLIAM). *The same.* The Fourth Edition Corrected. *London*, Printed for James Knapton, at the Crown in St. Pauls Church-yard.
MDCXCIX. 8*vo.*   (7s. 6d.   804)

This Fourth Edition of the First Volume has the same collation
as the preceding editions.

DAMPIER (WILLIAM). *The same.* The Fifth Edition Corrected. *London*: Printed for James Knapton, at the Crown in St. Pauls Churchyard. 1703.
8*vo.*   (7s. 6d.   805)

This Fifth Edition of the First Volume is reprinted page for page
with the preceding editions, and answers to their collation.

DAMPIER (WILLIAM). *The same.* The Sixth Edition Corrected. *London*: Printed for James Knap-

ton, at the Crown in St. Pauls Church-yard. 1717.
8*vo.*   (7*s.* 6*d.*   806)

This Sixth Edition of the First Volume is page for page with the
others, and the Maps are the same.

DAMPIER (WILLIAM). Voyages and Defcriptions.
Vol. II. In Three Parts, viz. 1. A Supplement of
the Voyage round the World, Defcribing the Countreys of Tonquin, Achin, Malacca, &c. their Product, Inhabitants, Manners, Trade, Policy, &c. 2.
Two Voyages to Campeachy; with a Defcription
of the Coafts, Product, Inhabitants, Logwood-Cut-
ting, Trade, &c. of Jucatan, Campeachy, New
Spain, &c.3 . A Difcourfe of Trade-Winds, Breezes,
Storms, Seafons of the Year, Tides and Currents of
the Torrid Zone throughout the World : With an
Account of Natal in Africk, its Product, Negro's
&c. By Captain William Dampier. Illustrated
with Particular Maps and Draughts. To which is
Added, A General Index to both Volumes. *Lon-
don,* Printed for James Knapton, at the Crown in
St. Pauls Church-yard. MDCXCIX. *Title: Dedication*
'To the Right Honourable Edward Earl of Or-
ford' 2 *pp* : 'The Preface' 3 *pp* : 'The Contents' 1
page : *Text, Vol. II. Part I,* 184 *pp* : *Part II,* 132 *pp* :
Part III, 2 *leaves and* 112 *pp* : *General Index and
Errata* 37 *leaves, and Catalogue of Books one leaf.
Fine copy in old calf.* 8*vo.*   (10*s.* 6*d.*   807)

This is the First Edition of the Second Volume. There are 4 copperplate maps : viz.—
    1. Streights of Malacca, Part I. page 1.
    2. Bay of Campeachy, Part II. page 1.
    3. Trade Winds in the Atlantic, Part III. page 1.
    4. Trade Winds in the South Sea, Part III. page 1.

DAMPIER (WILLIAM). *The same.* Vol. II. *etc.* The
Second Edition. London, MDCC. 8*vo.* (7*s.* 6*d.*   808)

This Second Edition of the Second Volume answers to the description of the first edition, though it has been reprinted throughout,
and the Errata corrected.

DAMPIER (WILLIAM). *The same.* Vol. II. *etc.* The
Third Edition. London, MDCCV. 8*vo.* (7*s.* 6*d.*   809)

With the same collation as the First and Second Editions.

DAMPIER (WILLIAM). A Voyage to New Hol-
land, &c. In the Year, 1699. Wherein are defcribed,
The Canary-Iflands, the Ifles of Mayo and St. Jago.
The Bay of All Saints, with the Forts and Town of
Bahia in Brafil. Cape Salvadore. The Winds on the
Brafilian Coaft. Abrohlo-Shoals. A Table of all

the Variations obferv'd in this Voyage. Occurrences near the Cape of Good Hope. The Courfe
to New Holland. Shark's Bay. The Ifles and
Coaft, &c. of New Holland. Their Inhabitants,
Manners, Cuftoms, Trade, &c. Their Harbours,
Soil, Beafts, Birds, Fifh, &c. Trees, Plants, Fruits,
&c. Illuftrated with feveral Maps and Draughts;
alfo divers Birds, Fifhes, and Plants, not found in
this part of the World, Curioufly Ingraven on
Copper-Plates. Vol. III. By Captain William
Dampier. *London:* Printed for James Knapton,
at the Crown in St. Paul's Church-yard, 1703.
Title; Dedication 'To the Right Honourable Thomas Earl of Pembroke,' 4 *pp:* 'The Preface' 12
pp: 'The Contents' 6 *pp: Text* 162 *pp:* 'The Index' 9 *pp:* 'Books printed for J. Knapton' 5 *pp:*
8*vo.*   (7*s.* 6*d.*   810)

This is the First Edition of the firft Part of the Third Volume.
The following is a list of the maps and plates : viz.—
  1. Map of the voyage to New Holland, facing the title.
  2. Canary Islands, page 4.
  3. Cape Verde Islands, page 14.
  4. Brazil, at page 48.
  5. Two Birds, at page 96.
  6. New Holland, at page 117.
  7. Four Birds, at page 123.
  8. Five Fishes, at page 141.
  9. Plants, in five plates, facing page 155.
  10. Fish, two plates, at page 162.

DAMPIER (William). *The same.* Vol. III. The
Second Edition. *London,* Printed by W. Botham;
for James Knapton, 1709. 8*vo.*   (7*s.* 6*d.*   811)

This Second Edition of the First Part of the Third Volume has the
same collation as the preceding. To it was added the same
year the Second Part, under the following title:

DAMPIER (William). A Continuation of a Voy-
age to New Holland, &c. In the Year 1699. Where-
in is defcribed, The Iflands Timor, Rotee and Ana-
bao. A Paffage between the Iflands Timor and
Anabao. Copang and Laphao Bays. The Iflands
Omba, Fetter, Bande, and Bird. A Defcription of
the Coaft of New-Guinea. The Iflands Pulo Sabu-
da, Cockle, King William's, Providence, Garret
Dennis, Ant. Cave's and St. John's. Alfo a new
Paffage between N. Guinea and Nova Britannia.
The Iflands Ceram, Bonao, Buoro, and feveral
Iflands before unknown. The Coaft of Java, and
Streights of Sunda. Author's arrival at Batavia,
Cape of Good Hope, St. Helens, I. Afcenfion, &c.
Their Inhabitants, Cuftoms, Trade, &c. Harbours,

Soil, Birds, Fiſh, &c. Trees, Plants, Fruits, &c.
Illuſtrated with Maps and Draughts : Alſo divers
Birds, Fiſhes, &c. not found in this part of the
World, Ingraven on Eighteen Copper-Plates. By
Captain William Dampier. *London,* Printed by
W. Botham ; for James Knapton, at the Crown in
St. Pauls Church Yard. 1709. *Title :* 'The Con-
tents' 8 *pp :* 'A Catalogue of the Maps and Cop-
per-Plates' 4 *pp :* 'Books Printed for J. Knapton,
2 *pp : Text* 198 *pp :* 'Index' 8 *pp :* 'Books Printed
for J. Knapton' 2 *pp. 8vo.*   (7s. 6d. 812)
This is the First Edition of the Second Part of the Third Volume.

DAMPIER (William). A Voyage round the
World. Containing an Account of Captain Dam-
pier's Expedition into the South Seas in the Ship
St. George, In the Years 1703 and 1704. *etc. See*
Funnell, Nº. 1179.   (10s. 6d. 813)

DAMPIER (William). Capt. Dampier's/ Vindi-
cation/ of his/ Voyage/ To the South-Seas in the
Ship St. George./ With ſome ſmall Obſervations
for the Preſent on Mr./ Funnell's Chimerical Relation of the Voyage Round/ the World ; and Detected in Little, until he ſhall be/ Examind more
at Large./ [*Colophon*] *London,* Printed and Sold
by *Mary Edwards,* againſt the Golden-Lion Tavern/
in Fetter-Lane. 2707 [1707]. 8 *pp. without a separate
title. Half calf. 4to.*   (1l. 1s. 814)

DAMPIER (William). See Wafer (Lionel).

DAMPIER (William.) A Collection of Voyages.
In Four Volumes. Containing I. Captain William
Dampier's Voyages round the World ; Deſcribing
particularly, the Coaſts and Iſlands in the Eaſt and
Weſt Indies. The South-Sea Coaſts of Chili, Peru
and Mexico. The Countries of Tonquin, Achin, and
Malacca. The Cape of Good Hope, New-Holland,
&c. II. The voyages of Lionel Wafer ; Giving an
Account of his being left on the Iſthmus of America,
amongſt the Indians, and of their Treatment of him ;
with a particular Deſcription of the Country, &c.
Alſo The natural History of thoſe Parts. By a Fellow of the Royal Society. And Davis's Expedition
to the Golden Mines. III. A Voyage round the
World : Containing an Account of Capt. Dampier's
Expedition into the South-Seas in the Ship St.

George. With his Various Adventures and En-
gagements, &c. together with a Voyage from the
Weſt Coast of Mexico to East-India. By W. Fun-
nell, Mate of Capt. Dampier. IV. Capt. Cowley's
Voyage round the Globe. V. Capt. Sharp's
Journey over the Iſthmus of Darien, and Expe-
dition into the South Seas. VI. Capt. Wood's
Voyage through the Streights of Magellan. VII.
Mr. Roberts's Adventures and Sufferings amongſt
the Corſairs of the Levant: His Deſcription of the
Archipelago Iſlands, &c. Illuſtrated with Maps
and Draughts: Alſo ſeveral Birds, Fiſhes, and
Plants, not found in this part of the World:
Curiouſly Engraven on Copper-Plates. *London:*
Printed for James and John Knapton, at the Crown
in St. Paul's Church-yard. MDCCXXIX. 4 *Volumes.*
8*vo.*   (2*s.* 12*s.* 6*d.* 815)

This is generally considered the best Edition of Dampier's Voyages, though it contains much that Dampier not only had no
hand in writing, but against which he protested. (See No. 814.)
The truth appears to be that he was at the mercy of his publisher,
Knapton, who used Dampier's saleable volumes as mules for
carrying off his unsaleable stock. Volumes I and II of this
edition are reprints of the earlier editions, page for page, and
with the same plates and maps, except that in the first volume,
the publisher has suppressed Dampier's Dedication to Charles
Mountague, President of the Royal Society, to make room for a
second title, " A New Voyage round the World," *etc.* " The
Seventh Edition Corrected," which here occupies A 2. Vol. III is
a reprint of Dampier's third volume, described above (No. 811-12),
but in a broader page, and paged continuously. It has eight
preliminary leaves, and the text is paged 1 to 260, including the
Index. The plates are the same as in the previous editions.
Beyond this Dampier had nothing to do with the work. The remaining half of this third volume consists of a reprint of Wafer's
Voyage, which is here called The Third Edition. It contains
title and pages 263 to 463, followed by 9 pages of Index. The
map and the three plates are the same as in the first and second
Editions, published also by Knapton in 1699 and 1704. Volume
IV contains Funnell's Voyage, exactly as described below, over
No. 1179, with a new title, thus working in bodily the remainder
of the edition of 1707, against which Dampier protested. To this
are added reprints of Cowley's, Sharp's, Wood's, and Roberts'
Voyages, filling 175 pp. and 6 pp. of Index, with 5 maps. In
some copies, however, Funnell's Voyage is reprinted with the
same maps and plates, but in a closer type, it being in 8 prel.
leaves, 208 pages of text, with 8 pages of Index.
With these facts in view, it seems to the writer that it is better to
have Dampier undefiled, and therefore the best editions of Dampier are his three volumes as originally published. Then let the
other works by Funnell, Wafer, Sharp, &c. stand on their own
merits, in their own editions, under their own names.

DAMPIER (WILLIAM). The Voyags and Adventures of Capt. William Dampier. Wherein are
Deſcribed the Inhabitants, Manners, Cuſtoms,
Trade, Harbours, Soil, Animals, Vegetables, &c.
of the principal Countries, Iſlands, &c. of Aſia,

Africa, and America. Vol. I.[II.] *London :* Printed
in the Year M,DCCC,LXXVI. *Two Volumes.* Vol. I.
Title ; 'Preface' 2 *pp ; Text pp.* 5-454. II. *Title ;
Text pp.* 3-396. *8vo.* (16s. 816)

> This edition contains only the three Volumes written by Dampier
> himself, and is without Maps or Plates. In the Preface the
> Editor says, "The first edition of Dampier's Voyages was pub-
> lished by himself, but not in the same order they were per-
> formed, which has a little perplexed the narrative ; the language
> is now partly become obsolete, which renders the perusal more
> difficult to common readers ; and the Edition is also now ex-
> tremely scarce. To remedy these inconveniences, the chronolo-
> gical order wherein the series of events happened is observed
> in this Edition ; all old phrases and expreſsions are modernized ;
> and to render this publication still more acceptable to naturalists
> and geographers ; where our author had only given the common
> country names of natural subjects, the present systematical
> names are added without altering his descriptions ; which have
> always been quoted as of the greatest authority by writers on
> Natural History, and the names of places are corrected according
> to the modern spelling of the latest geographers."

DAMPIER (WILLIAM). Nouveau/ Voyage/ au-
tour/ du Monde./ Où l'on décrit en particulier
l'Iſthme de l'Amé/rique, pluſieurs Côtes & Iſles
des Indes Oc-/cidentales, les Iſles du Cap Verd, le
paſſage/ par la Terre del Fuego, les Côtes Méri-
diona-/les du Chili, du Pérou, & du Méxique ;
l'Iſle/ de Guam, Mindanao, & des autres Philip-/
pines ; les Iſles Orientales qui ſont près de/ Cambodie, de la Chine, Formoſa, Luçon,/ Celebs, &c.
la Nouvelle Hollande, les Iſles/ de Sumatra, de
Nicobar, de Sainte Helene,/ & le Cap de Bonne-
Eſperance./ Où l'on traite des differens Terroirs
de tous ces Pays, de leurs Ports,/ des Plantes, des
Fruits, & des Animaux qu'on y trouve : De leurs/
Habitans, de leurs Coûtumes, de leur Religion, de
leur Gou-/vernement, de leur Négoce, &c./ Par
Guillaume Dampier./ Enrichi de Cartes & de
Figures./ Tome Premier./ A *Amsterdam./* Chez
la Veuve de Paul Marret, Marchand/ Libraire dans
le Beurs ſtraat à la Renommée./ M.DCC.XVII. *Five
Volumes. Vol. I. 7 prel. leaves including the engraved
title ; Text 408 pp. Table 12 leaves. Maps or plates
at pp.* 1, 6, 58, 119, 294, 345, (2), 370. *Vol. II.
engraved title and 2 prel. leaves ;* 396 *pp. and Table
5 leaves ; Maps or plates at pp.* 74, 75, 77, 79, 117,
273, 275 (2), 339. *Vol. III. 4 prel. leaves ;* 393 *pp.
and Table 10 pp. Maps or plates at pp.* 1, 3, 69, 218,
227 (2), 356, 361. *Vol. IV. 10 prel. leaves ;* 309
*pp. and 15 pp. of Table and errata. Maps or plates at
pp.* 1, 4, 15, 41, 85, 106, 110, 140, 141, 142, 143,

144, 145 (2) 149, 169, 221, 248, 286. *Vol. V.*
2 *prel. leaves; Text* 363 *pp. Table* 23 *pp. followed by*
1 *leaf containing the Privileges. Maps or plates at*
pp. 1, 10, 28, 51, 74, 76, 81, 84, 90, 95, 108, 123,
127, 135, 139, 166, 255, 305, 325. 12*mo.* (15*s.* 817)

DAMPIER (WILLIAM). Nouveau/ Voyage/ au-
tour/ du Monde/ Où l'on décrit en particulier l'Iftme
de l'Ameri-/que, plufieurs Côtes & Ifles des Indes
Occiden-/tales, les Ifles du Cap Verd, le paffage
par la/ Terre del Fuego, les Côtes Meridiolales de
Chi-/li, du Perou, & du Mexique; l' Ifle de Guam,/
Mindanao, & des autres Philippines; les Ifles/ Orientales qui font prés de Cambodie, de la/ Chine,
Formofa, Luçon, Celebes, &c. la Nou-/velle Hollande, les Ifles de Sumatra, de Nicobar,/ de fainte
Helene, & le Cap de Bonne Efperance./ Où l'on
traite des differens Terroirs de tout ces Païs, de/
leur Ports, des Plantes, des Fruits, & des Ani-
maux/ qu'on y trouve : De leur Habitans, de leurs
Coûtu-/mes, de leur Religion, de leur Gouverne-
ment, de leur/ Négoce, &c./ Par Guillaume Dampier./ Enrichi de Cartes & Figures./ A *Rouen,*/
Chez Jean - Baptiste Machuel, ruë Etoupee./
M.DCC.XXIII./ Avec Aprobation & Privilege du
Roi./ 5 *Volumes.* 12*mo.*   (15*s.* 818)

This edition is a reprint of the preceding, page for page. The
plates are the same, and from the same coppers. The collation
will also apply to this set.

DANA (JAMES). A Sermon preached before the
General Assembly of the State of Connecticut, at
Hartford on the Day of the Anniversary Election,
May 13, 1779. By James Dana, D.D. Pastor of
the first Church in Wallingford. *Hartford :* Printed
by Hudson and Goodwin. MDCCLXXIX. 46 *pp.*
' *Corrections.*' 1 *page. uncut.* 8*vo.*   (4*s.* 6*d.* 819)

DANFORTH (JOHN). The Blackness of Sins againft
Light. Or, Men offering Violence To their Knowledge, and Forcibly breaking thorow all the inter-
pofing Flames of it, to work Iniquity Confidered
in its Criminalness, & as no fmall Aggravation of
their vile Tranfgreffion. By John Danforth. *Boston*
in N.E. Printed and Sold by Timothy Green, in
Middle-Street. 1710. 2 *prel. leaves. Imperfect,*
wanting all after page 34. 12*mo.* (7*s.* 6*d.* 820)

D'ANVERS (CALEB.) Some Farther Remarks on

a late Pamphlet, intitled Observations on the
Conduct of Great-Britain; Particularly with Re-
lation to the Spanish Depredations and Letters of
Reprifal. In a Letter to the Craftsman. To which
is added, a Postscript, In Vindication of the Weft-
India Merchants, againft a late Charge of Theft
and Pyracy. By Caleb D'Anvers of Gray's-Inn,
Efq; *London:* Richard Francklin. MDCCXXIX.
Title and 38 *pp.* 8vo.   (6s. 821)

DARIEN. Act/ for a/ Company/ Trading to/ Africa
and the Indies./ June 26. 1695./ *Edinbvrgh,/*
Printed by the Heirs and Succeffors of Andrew
Anderfon, Printer to His moft/ Excellent Majefty,
Anno Dom. 1696./ 7 *pp. Folio.* (1*l.* 1*s.* 822)

DARIEN. An/ Act/ of the/ Parliament/ of/ Scot-
land/ For Erecting an/ Eaft-India Company/ in
that/ Kingdom./ *Edinbvrgh,/* Printed by the Heirs
and Succeffors of Andrew Anderfon, Printer to his
moft/ Excellent Majefty, 1695. And Re-printed at
London, for Sam. Manfhip at/ the Ship in Cornhill, and Hugh Newman at the Grafhopper in the
Poultrey./ [3 Oct. 1695.] *Title and* 8 *pp. Half-
calf. Folio.*   (1*l.* 1*s.* 823)

DARIEN. A/ Letter/ From a Member of the/ Parliament of Scotland,/ To his Friend at London,/
concerning Their Late Act/ For Eftablifhing a/
Company/ Of that Kingdom Tradeing to/ Africa
and the Indies./ *London,/* Printed, and are to be
Sold by John Whitlock near Stationers-/Hall, and
the Bookfellers of London and Weftminfter, 1695./
[13 *Dec.*] *Title and* 14 *pp. Signed* ' Philonax Verax.'
Folio.   (1*l.* 11*s.* 6*d.* 824)

DARIEN. A Perfect/ List/ Of the feveral Perfons
Residenters in/ Scotland,/ Who have Subfcribed as/
Adventurers in the Joynt-Stock/ of the/ Company
of Scotland/ Trading to Africa and the Indies./
Together/ With the refpective Sums which they
have feverally Subfcribed in the Books/ of the faid
Company, Amounting in the Whole to the Sum of
400000 lib./ Sterling./ *Edinbvrgh,/* Printed and
Sold by the Heirs and Succeffors of Andrew An-
derfon, Printer to the King's/ moft Excellent Ma-
jefty, Anno Dom. 1696./ *Title and* 14 *pp. of Names.
Folio.*   (2*l.* 2*s.* 825)

DARIEN. An Exact List of all the Men, Women, and Boys that Died on/ Board the Indian and African Company's Fleet, during their Voyage/ from Scotland to America, and since their Landing in Caledonia;/ Together with a particular account of their qualities, the several Days/ of their Deaths, and the respective Distempers or Accidents of which/ they Died./ [*Colophon*] *Edinburgh*, Printed by George Mosman, in the Year 1699./ *A broad sheet printed on one side. half mor. Folio.* (7s. 6d. 826)

DARIEN. A/ Just and Modest/ Vindication/ of the/ Scots Design,/ For the having Established a/ Colony at Darien./ With/ A Brief Display, how much it is/ their Interest, to apply themselves/ to Trade, and particularly to that/ which is Foreign./ [*London*?] Printed in the Year, 1699./ *15 prel. leaves, viz. Title, and* ' To the Reader.' *Text 214 pp. Half mor. 8vo.* (10s. 6d. 827)

DARIEN. A/ Defence/ of the/ Scots Settlement/ At Darien./ With/ An Answer to the Spanish /Memorial against it./ And/ Arguments to prove that it is the/ Interest of England to join with the/ Scots, and protect it./ To which is added,/ A Description of the/ Country, and a particular Account of/ the Scots Colony./ *Edinbvrgh*,/ Printed in the Year M.DC.XC.IX./ *On the reverse of the Title,* ' Errata.' *2 lines; Dedication 3 leaves, signed* ' Philo-Caledon.' *Text 86 pp. Half mor. 8vo.* (10s. 6d. 828)

DARIEN. A/ Defence/ of the/ Scots/ Abdicating/ Darien :/ Including An/ Answer/ to the/ Defence of the/ Scots Settlement there./ Authore Britanno sed Dunensi./ Printed in the Year, 1700./ *10 prel. leaves; viz. Title, and Dedication signed* ' Phil Scot.' *Text 168 pp. Fine copy, uncut. 8vo.* (15s. 829)

DARIEN. A/ Defence/ of the/ Scots/ Abdicating/ Darien :/ Including An/ Answer/ to the/ Defence of the/ Scot's Settlement there./ Authore Britanno sed Dunensi./ [*Edinburgh*,] Printed in the Year, 1700./ *6 prel. leaves; viz. Title, and Dedication signed* ' Phil. Scot.' *Text 50 pp. Half morocco. 12mo.* (10s. 6d. 830)

This Pamphlet was ordered to be burnt by the Parliament of Scotland. William III. 9th Session. See *Scotch Acts.*

DARIEN. The/ History/ of/ Caledonia :/ or, the/

Scots Colony/ in/ Darien/ In the Weſt Indies./
With an Account of the/ Manners of the Inhabitants,/ and Riches of the Country./ By a Gentleman lately Arriv'd./ *London :/* Printed, and Sold
by John Nutt, near/ Stationers-Hall. MDCXCIX./
54 pp. half mor. 8vo. (10s. 6d. 831)

DARIEN. A/ Full and Exaɛt/ Collection/ of/ All
the Conſiderable Addreſſes, Memorials,/ Petitions,
Anſwers, Proclamations, De-/clarations, Letters
and other Publick/ Papers, relating to the Company of/ Scotland Trading to Africa/ and the Indies, ſince the paſſing/ of the Aɛt of Parliament, by
which the ſaid/ Company was eſtabliſhed in June
1695, till/ November 1700./ Together with a ſhort
Preface (including/ the Aɛt it ſelf) as alſo a Table
of the/ whole Contents. Printed in the Year 1700./
*Title, and x prelim. pp; Text 144 pp. ' Contents' 6
pp. Half mor. 8vo.* (10s. 6d. 832)

DARIEN. The/ Original Papers/ and/ Letters,/
Relating to the/ Scots Company,/ Trading to/ Africa
and the Indies :/ From the Memorial given in/
againſt their taking Subſcripti-/ons at Hamburgh,
by Sir Paul/ Ricaut, His Majeſty's Reſident/ there,
to Their laſt Addreſs ſent/ up to His Majeſty in
December,/ 1699. Faithfully extracted from the
Companies Books./ Printed Anno 1700./ *56 pp.
half mor. 8vo.* (10s. 6d. 833)

DARIEN. A/ Supplement/ of/ Original Papers/
and/ Letters,/ relating to the Scots Company Trading to/ Africa and the Indies./ Anno Dom. 1700./
16 pp. half mor. 8vo. (10s. 6d. 834)

DARINEL DE TIREL. ☛ La Sphere/ des deux
mondes, compoſée en Fran-/çois, par Darinel paſ-
teur des Amadis./ Auec vn Epithalame, que le
meſme Autheur ha/ faiɛt, ſur les nopces & mariage
de Treſilluſtre,/ & Sereniſſime Prince, Don Philippe
Roy/ d'Angleterre, &c./ Commenté, gloſé, & en-
richy de pluſieurs fables Poeticques,/ Par. G. B.
D. B. C. C. de C./ N. L. Ovbli. Amys Leɛturs,
achetez ce liuret,/ Si vous aymez Cronicques & Hiſ-
toires,/ Car l'achetant y trouuerez au net,/ Bien
figurez pays & territoires./ En *Anvers*, Chez Ie.
Richart./ Auec Priuilege. 1555./ *4 prelim. and 58
folioed leaves, followed by a Colophon leaf. Signatures*

of text A to Piij. folio 58 *erroneously numbered* 57.
19 *woodcut maps. A folding Map. N iij. between
folios* 50 *and* 51. *Half calf.* 4to.   (3*l.* 3*s.* 835)

DARTMOUTH COLLEGE. A Candid Analytical
Review of the " Sketches of the History of Dartmouth College and Moor's Charity School, with a
particular Account of some late Remarkable Proceedings of the Board of Trustees, from the year
1779 to the year 1815. 32 *pp.* 8*vo.* (2*s.* 6*d.* 836)

DARTMOUTH COLLEGE. Sketches of the History of Dartmouth ·College and Moors' Charity
School, with a particular Account of some late Remarkable Proceedings of the Board of Trustees,
from the Year 1779 to the Year 1815. 88 *pp. uncut.*
8*vo.*   (3*s.* 6*d.* 837)

DARTMOUTH COLLEGE. A Vindication of the
Official Conduct of the Trustees of Dartmouth Col-
lege, in Answer to " Sketches of the History of
Dartmouth College," and " A Candid Analytical
Review of the Sketches," &c.   Published by the
Trustees. *Concord:* George Hough. 1815. 104
pp. uncut. 8*vo.*   (4*s.* 6*d.* 838)

[DAVENANT (Sir William).] The Cruelty of
the/ Spaniards/ in/ Peru./ Expreſt by Inſtrumen-
tall and/ Vocall Muſick, and by Art of/ Perſpec-
tive in Scenes, &c./ Repreſented daily at the Cock-
pit/ in Drury-Lane,/ at Three after noone/ punc-
tually./ *London,*/ Printed for Henry Herringman,
and are to be ſold at his Shop/ at the Anchor in the
Lower walk in the/ New Exchange. 1658./ 2 *prelim. leaves and* 27 *pp. in verse and prose. Half morocco.* 4*to.*   (10*s.* 6*d.* 839)

DAVENPORT (John). The/ Profession/ of the
Faith/ of that Reverend/ and worthy Divine Mr.
J. D. ſome-/times Preacher of Stevens Coleman-/
ſtreet. London./ Made publiquely before the Con-
grega-/tion at his Admiſſion into one of the Church-
eſ/ of God in New-England./ Containing twenty
ſeverall heads as it was drawn/ from his own Copy.
viz./ 1. Concerning the Scriptures./ 2. Concerning
the Godhead in the/ unity of eſſence, and Trinity of/
perſons./ 3. Concerning the Decrees of God./ 4.

Concerning Creation, and Provi-/dence./ 5. Concerning the fall of man and/ originall fin./ 6. Concerning mans Reftitution./ 7. Concerning the Perfon and natures/ in Chrift./ 8. Concerning the offices of Chrift./ 9. Concerning Chrifts propheticall/ office./ 10. Concerning the Priefthood of / Chrift./ 11. Concerning Chrifts kingly office./ 1. in general./ 12. Concerning his Kingdom. 2. In/ fpeciall./ 13. Concerning the Application of/ Redemption./ 14. Concerning a particular inftituted Church, and the Priviledges thereof./ 15. Concerning the manner of gather-/ing a Church./ 16. Concerning the Sacraments./ 17. Concerning the power of every Church./ 18. Concerning the Communion of/ Churches./ 19. Concerning Church Officers./ 20. Concerning giving every man his/ due./ *London* :/ Printed for John Handcock at the Bible in Burchin-Lane./ 1641./ 8 *pp. Half mor.* 4*to.* (1*l.* 1*s.* 840)

DAVENPORT (JOHN). The Power of/ Congregational Churches/ Afferted and Vindicated,/ In Anfwer to a/ Treatife/ of/ Mr. J. Paget,/ Intituled/ The Defence of Church-Government/ exercifed in Claffes and Synods./ By John Davenport, B. of D./ and Paftor to the Church in Newhaven/ in New-England./ *London,*/ Printed in the Year,/ 1672./ 5 *prelim. leaves; viz. Title, To the Reader. signed* ' M. N.' *and* ' Tertull. de præfcr. adv. Hæret. Cap. 21.' 2 *pp. Text* 179 *pp.* 16*mo.* (1*l.* 5*s.* 841)

DAVENPORT (JOHN). The/ Saints/ Anchor-Hold,/ in all/ Storms and Tempefts./ Preached in Sundry/ Sermons,/ And Publifhed for the Support/ and Comfort of Gods, People, in/ all Times of Tryal./ By John Davenport, B.D. fometime/ Minifter of Stephens Coleman-ftreet ;/ London ; and now Paf-tor of the Church/ of Chrift in New-Haven, in New-England./ *London.*/ Printed by W. L. for Geo. Hurlock, and/ are to be fold at his Shop at Magnus/ Church corner, in Thames-ftreet, 1661./ 4 *prel. leaves; viz. Title, Preface signed* ' William Hooke. Jofeph Caryl.' *and Errata* 1 *page. Text* 231 *pp.* 12*mo.* (1*l.* 10*s.* 842)

DAVENPORT (JOHN). The/ Saints/ Anchor-Hold,/ in all/ Storms and Tempefts./ Preached in Sundry/ Sermons ;/ And Publifhed for the Support and/

Comfort of God's People, in all/ Times of Tryal./
By J. D. *B.D.* fometimes Minifter of/ Stephens
Colemans-ftreet, London ; and Pa-/ftor of a Church
of Christ in New Haven/ in New-England./ *London*, Printed and Sold by Benj./ Harris, at the
Golden Boar's-Head, againft/ the Crofs-Keys-Inn,
in Grace church-ftreet,/ 1701./ *Title ; Preface 3 pp,
signed '* W.H. J.C.' *and 4 verses 1 page, signed '* B.
H.' *Text* 156 *pp.* 12*mo.*   (1*l.* 1*s.* 843)

DAVENPORT (JOHN). A small Manuscript consisting of nine lines in the autograph of John Davenport.   (2*l.* 2*s.* 844)

   John Davenport was the first Minister of New-Haven, and was
   one of the founders of that Colony. The authenticity of this
   fragment is vouched for in a note of Dr. Sprague of Albany,
   which is attached to it.

DAVENPORT (JOHN). Long and interesting Autograph Letter addressed to his son and daughter,
dated at Stamford, Connecticut, Jan. 8. 172½. 2 *pp.*
4*to.*   (15*s.* 845)

   This John was the Grandson of the first Davenport of New-Haven.
   He graduated at Harvard College, in 1687, and died in 1731, at
   the age of 61.

DAVENPORT (JAMES). Autograph Letter 'To
the Rev[d] M[r]. Steph. Williams att Longmeadow In
Springfield' dated at New Haven July 6th 1733.
1 *page* 4*to.*   (10*s.* 846)

   This James was the Son of John of Stamford, the Grandson of
   John, one of the founders of New-Haven Colony. He graduated
   at Yale College, in 1732, and in the time of Whitfield distinguished himself by his enthusiasm, or, as some have styled it,
   fanaticism.

DAVIDSON (GEORGE). The Case of the Caribbs
in St. Vincent's [*London*, 1787] 23 *pp. At page* 21,
Signed ' George Davidson.' 12*mo.* (5*s.* 6*d.* 847)

DAVIE (JOHN CONSTANSE). Letters from Paraguay : describing the Settlements of Monte Video
and Buenos Ayres ; the residences of Rioja Minor,
Nombre de Dios, St. Mary and St. John, &c. &c.
With the Manners, Customs, Religious Ceremonies, &c. of the Inhabitants. Written during a Residence of seventeen Months in that Country. By
John Constanse Davie, Esq. *London* : G. Robinson, 1805. *vii and* 293 *pp. boards.* 8*vo.*   (5*s.* 848)

DAVIES (JOHN). The/ History/ of the/ Caribby-
Iflands,/ viz./ Barbados, S[t] Christophers, S[t] Vin-

cents,/ Martinico, Dominico, Barbouthos,/ Mon-/
serrat, Mevis, Antego, &c. in all XXVIII./ In
Two Books./ The Firſt containing the Natural;
The/ Second, the Moral History of thoſe/ Iſlands./
Illuſtrated with ſeveral Pieces of Sculpture, re-
preſenting/ the moſt conſiderable Rarities therein
Deſcribed./ With a/ Caribbian-Vocabvlary./ Ren-
dered into Engliſh/ By John Davies of Kidwelly./
London,/ Printed by J. M. for Thomas Dring and
John Starkey, and/ are to be ſold at their Shops, at
the George in Fleet-ſtreet neer/ Clifford's-Inn, and
at the Mitre between Middle Temple-/Gate and
Temple-Bar. 1666./ 4 *prel. leaves ; viz. Title,
Dedication, and Preface. Text* 351 *pp.* ' A Carib-
bian Vocabulary.' 5 *leaves. Table* 3 *leaves. Old calf.
Folio.* (1*l.* 5*s.* 849)

DAVILA (GIL GONZALEZ). Teatro/ Eclesiastico/
de la Primitiva Iglesia/ de las Indias Occidentales,/
Vidas de svs Arzobispos,/ Obispos, y Cosas me-
morables/ de svs Sedes./ Al mvy Alto y mvy
Catolico/ y por esto mvy poderoso/ Señor Rey/
Don Filipe Qvarto/ de las Españas, y/ Nvevo
Mvndo./ Dedicasele sv Coronista/ Mayor de las
Indias, y de los Reynos de las/ dos Caſtillas/ el
Maestro Gil Gonzalez Davila./ Tomo Primero./
Con Privilegio/ En *Madrid,* por Diego Diaz de la
Carrera,/ Año M. DC. XLIX./ [Tomo Segvndo]
1655. *Two Volumes. Vol. 1.* 7 *prel. leaves and* 308
pp. with 4 *seq. leaves.* 16 *extra leaves are inserted as
titles etc. in the text. There is a Map engraved on
copper at p.* 105. *Vol. II.* 1655. 8 *prel. and* 119
folioed leaves. Folio. (1*l.* 11*s.* 6*d.* 850)

DAVILA (PEDRA ARIAS.) Carta del Rey/ Catholico a Pedra Arias Dauila Gouernador de Caſ/tilla
del oro, por la qual ſe conocera ſi pudo cortar la/
cabeça a ſu yerno el Adelantado Baſco Nunez de
Bal/boa, o a lomenos ſy como lo dize la Hiſtoria/
Pontifical deuiera otorgalle apelacion./ 3 *pp.
Folio.* (15*s.* 851)

DAY (JEREMIAH). The Divine Right of Infant
Baptism, Conciſely proved from the Holy Scriptures; and Objections answered. A Sermon, delivered by Jeremiah Day, A.M. Paſtor of the
Church of New-Preſton. (Publiſhed by Requeſt.)

Litchfield: Printed by Thomas Collier, in the South End of the Court-Houfe. 1790. 43 *pp.* 8*vo.* (4*s.* 6*d.* 852)

DAY (Thomas). Reflections upon the Present State of England, and the Independence of America. By Thomas Day, Efq; The Third Edition: with Additions. *London:* J. Stockdale, 1783, *Title and* 129 *pp.* 8*vo.* (4*s.* 6*d.* 853)

DEANE (John). A True Account of the Voyage of the Nottingham-Galley of London, John Deane Commander, from the River Thames to New-England, Near which Place fhe was caft away on Boon-Ifland, Dec. 11, 1710. by the Captain's Obftinacy, who endeavour'd to betray her to the French, or run her afhore; with an account of the Falfe-hoods in the Captain's Narrative. And a faithful Relation of the Extremities the Company was reduc'd to for Twenty-four Days on that defolate Rock, where they were forc'd to eat one of their Companions who died, but were at laft wonderfully deliver'd. The whole attefted upon Oath, by Chriftopher Langman, Mate; Nicholas Mellen, Boatfwain; and George White, Sailor in the faid Ship. *London:* S. Popping, 1711. 4 *prel. leaves; viz. Title and Preface; Text* 36 *pp. uncut, half mor. First Edition.* 8*vo.* (15*s.* 854)

DEANE (John). A Narrative of the Shipwreck of the Nottingham-Galley, &c. Publifh'd in 1711. Revis'd, and Reprinted with Additions in 1726, by John Deane, Commander. [London] 24 *pp. Thick paper. half mor.* 8*vo.* (10*s.* 6*d.* 855)

DEANE (John). A Narrative of the Shipwreck of the Nottingham Galley, In her Voyage from England to Bofton. With An Account of the Miraculous Efcape of the Captain and his Crew on a Rock, called Boone-Ifland; the Hard-fhips they endured there, and their happy Deliverance. By John Deane, then Commander of the faid Galley; But for many Years after His Majefty's Conful for the Ports of Flanders, refiding at Oftend. The Fifth Edition. [*London*] Printed in the Year M.DCC.LXII. 2 *prel. leaves, and Text in* 28 *pp.* 8*vo.* (7*s.* 6*d.* 856)

DEANE (Silas). An Address to the United States

of North America. To which is added, A Letter
to the Hon. Robert Morris, Efq. with Notes and
Obfervations. By Silas Deane, Esq. Late one of
the Commiffioners Plenipotentiary from the United
States, to the Court of Versailles. *London:* J.
Debrett, 1784. *Title and Advertisement 2 leaves ;
Text 95 pp. Half mor. 8vo.* (4s. 6d. 857)

DEANE (Silàs). Autograph Note to Jedediah
Elderkin, Esq. New-Haven, dated at Wethersfield,
17th Oct. 1763, appointing to be in New-Haven,
on the following Wednesday. 1 *page*, 4*to.* (5s. 858)

DE CASTRO (Henriquez). Don Henriquez/ De/
Castro./ Or, the Conquest/ of the Indies./ A/
Spaniſh Novel./ Translated out of Spaniſh, by a
Perſon/ of Honour./ *London,*/ Printed by R. E.
for R. Bentley/ and S. Magnes, in Ruffel-Street/
in Covent-Garden./ [1685.] 6 *prel. leaves ; viz.
License, Title, Advertisement, and Some Books printed.
Text 167 pp. calf.* 12*mo.* (8s. 6d. 859)

DECKER (Adolf). Diurnal vnd Hiſtoriſche/
Befchreybung der Naſsawiſchen/ Flotten So vnder
dem Admiral/ Jacob l' Heremite umb die/ gantze
welt gefahren iſt,/ Im 1623. 1624. 1625. vnd/ 1626.
Jahr./ Ordentlich in hochteútfch befchreiben/ was
ſich in dieſer raiſs von tag zü/tag zügetragen vnd
merckwürdiges/ vorgangen, vnd mit vnderfchie-
lichen,/ küpferſtücken gezieret/ Durch/ Adolf
Decker von Strasbürg./ Gedruckt zù *Strasbürg*
in verleſúng/ Eberhard Zetzners/ mdcxxix./ 6 *prel.
leaves including engraved and printed title pages ; Text
68 pp. Maps and plates at p.* 24, 28, 34, 45, 50, 52,
56, 60, *fine copy unbound.* 4*to.* (5l. 5s. 860)

DECLARATION and Testimony for the Doctrine
and Order of the Church of Christ, and against the
Errors of the Present Times. To which is prefixed,
a Narrative, concerning the Maintenance of the
Reformation-Testimony. By the Associate Pres-
bytery of Pennsylvania. The Second Edition.
Printed at Philadelphia in the year 1784. *Edinburgh:* Reprinted for A. Brown, 1786. 135 *pp.
Calf.* 12*mo.* (4s. 6d. 861)

DECLARATION (The) by the Representatives of
the United Colonies of North-America, now met
in General Congress at Philadelphia, Setting forth

the Caufes and Neceffity of taking up Arms. The
Letter of the Twelve United Colonies by their
Delegates in Congrefs to the Inhabitants of Great-
Britain, Their Humble Petition to his Majesty,
and their Address to the People of Ireland. Collected together for the Ufe of Serious Thinking
Men. By Lovers of Peace. *London:* Printed in
the year, MDCCLXXV. *32 pp. Half morocco.*
8vo. (4s. 6d. 862)

DECLARATION (A) of the Inhabitants of Barbados, respecting the demolition of the Methodist
Chapel. With an Appendix. *Barbados:* Printed
at the Barbadian Office. 1826. *20 pp. Uncut.*
8vo. (3s. 6d. 863)

DECLARATION/ (A)/ Of the Sad and Great/ Perfecution and Martyrdom/ Of the People of God,
called/ Quakers, in New-Enlgand,/ for the Worfhipping of God./ Wherof/ 22 have been Banifhed
upon pain of Death./ 03 have been Martyred./ 03
have had their Right-Ears cut./ 01 hath been
burned in the Hand with the letter H./ 31 Perfons
have received 650 Stripes./ 01 was beat while
his Body was like a jelly./ Several were beat with
Pitched Ropes./ Five Appeals made to England,
were denied/ by the Rulers of Bofton./ One thoufand forty four pounds worth of Goods hath/ been
taken from them (being poor men) for meeting/
together in the fear of the Lord, and for keeping
the/ Commands of Chrift./ One now lyeth in Iron-
fetters, condemned to dye./ Also,/ Some Considerations, prefented to the King, which is/ in
Anfwer to a Petition and Address, which was pre-
fented/ unto Him by the General Court at Bofton:
Subfcribed by/ J. Endicot, the chief Perfecutor
there; thinking thereby to/ cover themselves from
the Blood of the Innocent. [By Edward Burrough]/
London: Printed for Robert Wilfon, in Martins Le
Grand./ [1660] *32 pp. signed* ' E. B.' *Fine copy.*
4to. (2l. 2s. 864)

DEFENCE (A) of the Resolutions and Address of
the American Congress, in reply to Taxation no
Tyranny. By the Author of Regulus. To which
are added, General Remarks on the Leading Principles of that Work, As Publifhed in The London

Evening Post of the 2d and 4th of May ; and a
Short chain of Deductions from one clear Position
of Common Sense and Experience. *London:* J.
Williams, [1775.] *Title and Dedication, 2 leaves;
Text pp. 3 to 96. Half mor. 8vo.* (5s. 6d. 865)

DEFINITIVE (The) Treaty of Peace and Friendship, between His Britannick Majefty, the Moft
Chriftian King, and the King of Spain. Concluded
at Paris, the 10th Day of February, 1763. To
which, The King of Portugal acceded on the fame
Day. Publifhed by Authority. *London:* E. Owen
and T. Harrison, 1763. 48 *pp.* 4*to.* (4s. 6d. 866)

DELAFIELD (John). An Inquiry into the origin
of the Antiquities of America. By John Delafield Jr. With An Appendix, containing notes,
and " A View of the Caufes of the Superiority of
the Men of the Northern over those of the Southern
Hemisphere." By James Lakey, M.D. *Cincinnati:* N. G. Burgess & Co. 1839. 142 *pp. With*
10 *plates at pp.* 17, 30, 33, 36, 37, 38, 39, 43, 55,
61, *and large folding plate to face the Title. Blue
mor. gilt.* 4*to.* (1*l.* 10s. 867)

DELAPLAINE (Joseph). Delaplaine's Repository
of the Lives and Portraits of Distinguished
American Characters. *Philadelphia.* 1815. *En-
graved frontispiece & title, 2 leaves; Preface* 5 *pp;
Contents* 1 *leaf; Text* 106 *pp.* 4*to.* (7s. 6d. 868)
This is Volume I, Part I, containing 6 Portraits and Lives, viz.
Columbus, Vespitius, Benj. Rush, Fisher Ames, Alexander
Hamilton, and Washington.

DELAROCHE (Peter). The Gospel of Christ
preached to the Poor By Peter Delaroche, Miffionary. *Lunenburg.* [*Nova Scotia*] Printed: At
the Author's Expence, To be given and not to be
Sold.——Freely ye have received, freely give.
Jesus Christ, in Mat. 10. 8. MDCCLXXIII. 5 *prelim.
leaves; viz. Title, Dedication, and To the Reader.
Text* 99 *pp. Half mor.* 8*vo.* (7s. 6d. 869)

DELAVALL (John) and KEITH (George). The/
Herefie and Hatred/ Which was falfly Charged
upon the/ Innocent/ Juftly returned upon the/
Guilty./ Giving fome brief and impartial Account
of the moft ma-/terial Paffages of a late Difpute in
Writing, that hath/ paffed at Philadelphia betwixt/

John Delavall and George Keith,/ With fome in-
termixt Remarks and Obfervations on/ the whole./
Printed and Sold by William Bradford at *Philadelphia,*/ Anno Dom. 1693./ *22 pp.* ' The Printer's
Advertifement.' 1 *page Signed* ' W. B.' *Uncut
4to.*   (*3l. 13s. 6d.*   870)

DE-LA-WARRE [Thomas West] *Lord.* The/ Relation of/ the Right Honourable the Lord/ De-La-
Warre, Lord Gouernour/ and Captaine Generall of
the/ Colonie, planted in/ Virginia./ *London*/ ¶
Printed by William Hall, for/ William Welbie
dwelling in Pauls Church-/yeard at the Signe of
the Swan./ 1611./ *Title, and* 15 *unnumbered pages.
4to.*   (*5l. 15s. 6d.*   871)

DELBAS (Antonio Fernandez). Assiento qve se/
tomô con Antonio Fernandez Delbas, fo-/bre la
renta y prouifion general de efclauos/ negros para
las Indias, año de mil y feifcien/ tos y quinze.
[1615]. 20 *Folioed leaves. Half blue morocco.
Folio.*   (*12s. 6d.*   872

DELL (William). The Doctrine of Baptisms, Re-
duced from its Ancient and Modern Corruptions;
And reftored to its Primitive Soundness and In-
tegrity: According to the Word of Truth; the
Substance of Faith, and the Nature of Christ's King-
dom. By William Dell, Minifter of the Gofpel of
Gonvil and Caius College, in Cambridge. The
Fifth Edition. London Printed: *Philadelphia,*
Reprinted by B. Franklin and D. Hall, 1759. 43
pp. 8vo.   (*10s. 6d.*   873)

DENNIS (John). Liberty Afferted./ A/ Tragedy./
As it is Aſted at the/ New Theatre/ in/ Little Lincoln's Inn-Fields./ Written by Mr. Dennis./ London: Printed for George Strahan at the Golden
Ball, against the/ Royal Exchange, in Cornhill;
and Bernard Lintott at the/ Middle-Temple-Gate
in Fleetftreet. 1704./ *Price* 1s. 6d./ 7 *prelim. leaves
and* 64 *pp. Half mor. 4to.*   (*10s. 6d.*   874)
The Scene of this Tragedy lies at *Agnie* in Canada. The principal
Characters are Governor Frontenac (French) and General
Beaufort (English).

DENNIS (John). Liberty Afferted./ A/ Tragedy./
As it is Aſted at the/ New Theatre/ in/ Lincoln's-
Inn-Fields./ Written by Mr. Dennis./ *London:*/

Printed for George Strahan at the Golden Ball,
againſt the/ Royal Exchange, in Cornhill; and Bernard Lintott at the/ Middle-Temple-Gate in Fleet-
ſtreet. 1704./ *8 prel. leaves; viz. Half-title, title,
dedication, preface, prologue, epilogue, and dramatis
personæ. Text 68 pp. Fine copy in old Red morocco.*
4to. (1*l.* 1*s.* 875)

These two editions are identical as far as page 25, but from thence
to the end they differ, the preceding being in fewer pages and
with two or three more lines on a page.

DENNY (Joe). A Narrative of Facts relative to
the Tryal cf Joe Denny a Free Coloured Man, for
the Murder of John Stroud, a White-Man. At the
Grand Sessions in the Island of Barbadoes, held
December the 13th. 1796. And of a Conditional
Pardon granted to the said Joe Denny, by Our
Most Gracious Sovereign. *Barbadoes.* Printed at
the Office of Edw. Archer et Comp. 1797. *Title
and Contents, 2 leaves; Text in 45 pp. Unbound.*
4to. (10*s.* 6*d.* 876)

DENTON (Daniel). A/ Brief/ Deſcription/ of/
New-York:/ Formerly Called/ New-Netherlands./
With the Places thereunto Adjoyning./ Together
with the/ Manner of its Scituation, Fertility of the
Soyle,/ Healthfulneſs of the Climate, and the/
Commodities thence produced./ Also/ Some Directions and Advice to ſuch as ſhall go/ thither : An
Account of what Commodities they ſhall/ take
with them; The Profit and Pleaſure that/ may ac-
crew to them thereby./ Likewise/ A Brief Relation of the Cuſtoms of the/ Indians there./ By
Daniel Denton./ *London,/* [1670.] *Title, reverse
blank;* 'To the Reader' *2 pages; Text 21 pp. Morocco by Bedford. 4to.* (10*l.* 10*s.* 877)

DENYS (Mr.) Description/ Geographique/ et
Historique/ des Costes/ de l'Ameriqve/ Septentri-
onale./ Avec l'Hiſtoire naturelle de Païs./ Par
Monſieur Denys, Gouverneur Lieutenant/ General
pour le Roy, & proprietaire de toutes/ les Terres
& Iſles qui ſont depuis le Cap de/ Campſeaux, juſ-
ques au Caps des Roziers./ Tome I./ A *Paris,/* Chez
Loüis Billaine, au ſecond/ pillier de la grand'Salle
du Palais,/ à la Palme & au grand Ceſar./ M.DC.
LXXII./ Avec Privilege du Roy./ *Two Volumes.
Vol. I. 16 prelim. leaves; text 267 pp. Large Map.
Vol. II. wanting. Small 8vo.* (10*s.* 6*d.* 878)

DESBRISAY (Thomas). Autograph Memorial of
Lieut. Governor Desbrisay of the Island of St.
Johns addressed to Lord Barrington, Secretary at
War, dated May 24, 1775, offering his services to
raise at his own expense a Battalion of 500 men in
America or Europe, to serve in America, *etc.* 1
page. Folio.   (5s. 879)

DESCRIPTION des Terres Magellaniques et des
Pays adjacens. Traduit de l'Anglois par M. B**.
A *Geneve*, Chez François Dufart. Et à Paris, Hotel
Landier, No. 5. Rue Haute-Feuille, au coin de celle
Poupée. M.DCC.LXXXVII. *2 Volumes,* ' Partie I.' 3
prel. leaves ; viz. Half-title, Title, and Second Title ;
Text pp. 3-163. ' Partie II.' 3 *prel. leaves ; viz. Half-*
title, Title, and Second Title ; Text pp. 3-135. *calf.*
24mo.   (18s. 880)

DESCRIPTION (A) of a Great Sea-Storm,/ That
happened to fome Ships in the Gulph of Florida, in
September laft ; Drawn up by one of the/ Company,
and fent to his Friend at London. [*Colophon*] Licenfed, August the 5th. 1671. Roger L'Eftrange./
London, Printed by Thomas Milbourn, for Dorman
Newman, at the King's Armes in the Poultry,
1671./ *A broad sheet, in verse. Folio.* (18s. 881)

DESCRIPTION (A) of the Coast, Tides, and Currents, in Button's Bay, And in the Welcome: Being
The North-West Coaft of Hudfon's Bay, from
Churchill River, in 58° 56' North Latitude, to
Wager River or Strait, in 65° 24' taken from
Scrog's, Crow's, Napier's and Smith's Journals,
made in the Years 1722, 1737, 1740, 1742, 1743,
and 1744. Also, From the Difcoveries made in
1742, in the Voyage in the Furnace Bomb, and
Difcovery Pink, commanded by Captain Middleton
and Captain Moor ; Shewing from these Journals,
a Probability, that there is a Paffage from thence to
the Weftern Ocean of America. *Dublin:* Printed
in the Year M,DCC,XLVI. *27 pp. half morocco.*
8vo.   (10s. 6d. 882)

DESCRIPTION (A) of the English and French
Territories, in North America: being, An Explanation of a New Map of the Same. Shewing all
the Encroachments of the French, with their Forts.
and Usurpations on the English Settlements ; and

the Fortifications of the Latter. Done from the Neweſt Maps publiſhed in London. And compared with Dr. Mitchell's, F.R.S. and every Omiſſion carefully supplied from it. *Dublin:* J. Exshaw, MDCCLV. 28 *pp.* 8*vo.* (7*s.* 6*d.* 883)

DESCRIPTION/ (A)/ of the/ Four Parts/ of the/ World,/ viz./ Europe, Asia, Africa, and America./ Giving an Account/ Of their Dominions, Religions,/ Forms of Government, and Me-/tropolitan Cities./ Also,/ How America was Firſt Discovered/ by the Europeans, and what Purchaſes/ They have made therein./ Collected from the Writings of the beſt Hiſtorians./ *Edinburgh,*/ Re-printed in the Year, M.DC.XCV./ 23 *pp. Calf extra, red edges, by Bedford.* 8*vo.* (1*l.* 11*s.* 6*d.* 884)

DESCRIPTION (A) of the Windward Passage, and Gulf of Florida, with the Courſe of the Britiſh Trading-Ships to, and from the Island of Jamaica. Also An Account of the Trade-Winds, and of the variable Winds and Currents on the Coaſts there-abouts, at different Seaſons of the Year. Illuſ-trated with a Chart of the Coaſt of Florida, and of the Iſlands of Bahama, Cuba, Hiſpaniola, Jamaica, and the adjacent ſmaller Iſlands, Shoals, Rocks, and other remarkable Things in the Courſe of the Navigation in the Weſt-Indies. Whereby is de-monſtrated, The Precariouſneſs of thoſe Voyages to the Weſt-India Merchants, and the Impoſſibility of their Homeward-bound Ships keeping clear of the Spaniſh Guarda Coſta's : The Whole very ne-ceſſary for the Information of ſuch as never were in thoſe Parts of the World. To which are added, Some Proposals for the better ſecuring of the Bri-tiſh Trade and Navigation to and from the West-Indies. Note, At the End of this Treatiſe is a Ge-neral Index of the Names, with a Deſcription of the Scituations of all the Iſlands, &c. which are contained in the annexed Chart, diſtinguiſhed by numerical References to each other. Likewiſe an Alphabetical Catalogue of the ſame Names alone, with the like numerical References, the Uſes of which are mention'd at the End of the Whole. *London:* J. Applebee, 1739. 23 *pp. Index and Ca-talogue,* 5 *pp. With a Chart of the Bahama Islands.* 4*to.* (7*s.* 6*d.* 885)

DEVOTED LEGIONS (The) : A Poem. Addressed
to Lord George Germaine, and the Commanders of
the Forces againſt America. The Second Edition.
London : G. Kearsly, and J. Ridley, m,dcc,lxxvi.
Half-title, Title, and Argument, 4 *leaves ; Text* 14
pp. 4*to.*   (5*s.* 6*d.*   886)

DEVOTION (John). The Duty and Intereſt of a
People to ſanctify the Lord of Hoſts. A Sermon,
preached before the General Assembly of the State
of Connecticut, at Hartford, on the Day of the Anniversary Election, May 8th, 1777. By John Devotion, A.M. Paſtor of the third Church in Say-
brook. *Hartford :* Printed by Eben. Watson, near
the Great Bridge. m.dcc.lxxvii. 39 *pp. uncut.*
8*vo.*   (4*s.* 6*d.*   887)

DIAZ DEL CASTILLO (Bernal). Historia Verdadera de la Conquista de la Nueva España. Escrita Por el Capitan Bernal Diaz del Castillo, uno de
sus Conquistadores. En *Madrid* en la Imprenta de
Don Benito Cano Año de 1795. 4 *Volumes.* ' Tomo
I.' 4 *prel. leaves ; viz. Half-title, Title, & '* El Autor.'
Text 367 *pp.* ' Tomo II. 1796.' 382 *pp ; Erratas*
1 *page.* ' Tomo III. 1796.' 364 *pp ; Erratas* 1 *page.*
' Tomo IV. 1796.' 573 *pp. Old Spanish calf.*
16*mo.*   (2*l.* 2*s.*   888)

DIAZ DEL CASTILLO (Bernal). The True
History of the Conquest of Mexico, By Captain
Bernal Diaz del Castillo, One of the Conquerors.
Written in the year 1568. Tranſlated from the Ori-
ginal Spaniſh, by Maurice Keatinge Esq. *London,*
J. Wright, 1800. *viii. prel. pp. Text* 514 *pp.* ' *Notes
and Errata* ' 1 *page. Plan of Mexico. Boards uncut.*
4*to.*   (10*s.* 6*d.*   889)

DICKINSON (Jonathan). A Sermon Preached
at the opening of the Synod at Philadelphia, September 19, 1722. Wherein is conſidered the Character of the Man of God, and his Furniture for the
Exerciſe both of Doctrine and Diſcipline, with the
true boundaries of the Churches Power. By Jonathan Dickinſon, A.M. Miniſter of the Gospel at
Elizabeth-Town. *Boston :* Printed by T. Fleet, for
S. Gerriſh, at his Shop in Corn-Hill. 1723. *Half-
title, title, and* 24 *pp. Half brown morocco.*
8*vo.*   (8*s.* 6*d.*   890)

DICKINSON (JONATHAN). A Defence of Presbyterian Ordination. In Answer to a Pamphlet,
entituled, A Modest Proof, of the Order and Government settled by Chrift, in the Church. By Jonathan
Dickinfon, M.A. Minifter of the Gofpel at Elizabeth-Town, New-Jerfey. *Boston:* Printed for
Daniel Henchman, and fold at his Shop, over-
against the Brick Meet-ing Houfe. [1724] *Half-
title, title, Preface iii pp. and Text 44 pp. Closely cut.
8vo.* (10s. 6d. 891)

[DICKENSON (JONATHAN).] A Difplay of God's
fpecial Grace. In A familiar Dialogue between A
Minifter & a Gentleman of his Congregation,
About the Work of God, in the Conviction and
Converfion of Sinners, fo remarkably of late begun
and gofng on in thefe American Parts. Wherein
the Objections againft fome uncommon Appearances amongft us are diftinctly confider'd, Mistakes
rectify'd and the Work itfelf particularly prov'd to
be from the Holy Spirit. With An Addition, in a
fecond Conference, relating to fundry Antinomian
Principles, beginning to obtain in fome Places. [By
Jonathan Dickenson of N. Jersey.] To which is
prefixed an Attestation, by feveral Minifters of
Bofton. *Boston,* N.E. Printed by Rogers and
Fowle, for S. Eliot in Cornhill. 1742. *Title;*
'The Attestation.' *vi pp.* signed 'Benjamin Col-
man Joseph Sewall Thomas Prince John Webb
William Cooper Thomas Foxcroft Joshua Gee.'
Text 111 *pp. calf.* 12mo. (1l. 1s. 892)
This fine copy bears on the fly-leaf, in the hand writing of the do-
nor, "For the Rev. Dr. Watts, from Dr. Colman of N.E. 1742."

DICKINSON (JONATHAN). Familiar Letters To
a Gentleman, upon A Variety of feafonable and im-
portant Subjects in Religion. By Jonathan Dick-
inson, A.M. Minifter of the Gofpel at Elizabeth-
Town, New-Jerfey. *Boston:* Printed and Sold by
Rogers and Fowle in Queen-ftreet; next to the
Prifon: And by J. Blanchard at the Bible and
Crown in Dock-Square. 1745. *Title; Preface, 5 pp.
Contents* 1 *page. Text* 424 *pp. calf.* 8vo. (10s. 6d. 893)

DICKINSON (JONATHAN.) Familiar Letters upon
a Variety of Religious Subjects. viz. 1. The danger
of infidelity. 2. The evidences of Chriftianity.
3. The hiftory of our Saviour, collected from the

prophecies of the Old Teftament. 4. The certainty
of the facts reported in the gofpel. 5. The internal
evidences of Chriftianity. 6. Objections againft
the internal evidences anfwered. 7. God's fove-
reign grace vindicated, &c. 8. A true and falfe faith
diftinguifhed. 9. A legal and evangelical repentance diftinguifhed. 10. The characters in Rom. vii.
diftinctly illuftrated. 11. Moravian and Antinomian
juftification confidered. 12. Imputed righteoufnefs
explained and vindicated. 13. The new law of
grace examined and difproved. 14. Firft and
fecondary juftification, a groundlefs diftinction. 15.
Juftification by works, in James ii. confidered. 16.
Our obligations to good works diftinctly ftated 17.
The nature and neceffity of our union to Chrift.
18. Antinomian pleas for licentioufnefs confidered.
19. Directions for a clofe and comfortable walk
with God. By Jonathan Dickinson, A.M. Prefident of the College at New-Jersey. The Fourth
Edition. *Glasgow:* John Bryce, MDCCLXXV. *viii
and* 368 *pp.* 8*vo.*   (5s. 6d.   894)

DICKENSON (JONATHAN). God's Protecting
Providence, Man's Surest Help and Defence in
times of Greatest Difficulty and Most Imminent
Danger, Evidenced in the remarkable Deliverance
of Robert Barrow, with divers other Perfons from
the devouring Waves of the Sea, amongft which
they fuffered Shipwreck ; and alfo from the cruel
devouring Jaws of the inhuman Cannibals of
Florida. Faithfully related by one of the Perfons
concerned therein, Jonathan Dickenson. The
Seventh Edition. *London:* James Phillips, M,DCC,
XC. 136 *pp. signed* 'Jonathan Dickenson.' *half
calf.* 12*mo.*   (15s.   895)

DICKINSON (MOSES). An Answer to a Letter
From an aged Layman, to the Clergy of the Colony
of Connecticut. In which the Rights of the con-
fociated Churches are maintained ; the confociation
that appeared againft the Ordination of Mr. Dana
at Wallingford vindicated ; and the Minifters like
minded defended, againft the Infinuations, and
Reflections contained in that Letter. By an Aged
Minister. *New-Haven:* Printed by James Parker,
and Company, at the Post-Office. [1767?] 30 *pp.*
8*vo.*   (7s. 6d.   896)

DIEREVILLE. Relation du Voyage du Port Royal

de l'Acadie, ou de la Nouvelle France. Dans laquelle on voit un détail des divers mouvemens de la mer dans une traverſée de long cours; la Deſcription du Païs, les Occupations des François qui y ſont établis, les maniéres des differentes Nations Sauvages, leurs Superſtitions, & leurs chaſſes ; avec une diſſertation exaɡte ſur le Caſtor. Par Mr. Diere'ville. *A Amsterdam,* Chez Pierre Humbert M.DCCX. 10 *prel. leaves, consisting of engraved frontispiece, title, ‘ Epitre’ &* ‘ *Catalogue.’ Text* 236 *pp. with* 4 *sequent leaves. Calf by Clarke & Bedford.* 12*mo.* (1*l.* 11*s.* 6*d.* 897)

This is a fine copy, with the Autograph of Thomas Gray, the author of the Elegy in a Country Church-yard, on the title-page. Another copy without the Autograph, 12s.

DISCOURSE (A) Concerning the Currencies of the British Plantations in America. Eſpecially with regard to their Paper Money: more particularly In Relation to the Province of the Massachusetts-Bay, in New-England. *London:* T. Cooper. [1750 ?] 54 *pp. half mor.* 8*vo.* (10*s.* 6*d.* 898)

DISCOURSE (A) Concerning the Currencies of the British Plantations in America. Eſpecially with regard to their Paper Money. With a Postscript thereto. Boston: Printed MDCCXL. And *London:* Reprinted, MDCCLI. 62 *pp.* 8*vo.* (10*s.* 6*d.* 899)

DISCOURSE (A) on Trade; More particularly on Sugar and Tobacco: Shewing The True and Natural Means of their Support, and The Unreaſonablenefs of depending upon the Legislature for their Relief. *London:* J. Roberts, 1733. 24 *pp. Thick paper, half mor.* 8*vo.* (5*s.* 6*d.* 900)

DISCOVERY/ (A)/ of/ Fonseca/ In a Voyage to/ Surranam./ The Iſland ſo long ſought for in the/ Weſtern Ocean./ Inhabited by Women with the Account of their/ Habits, Cuſtoms and Religion./ And the Exaɡt Longitude and Latitude of the Place taken from/ the Mouth of a Perſon caſt away on the Place in an Hurricane/ with the Account of their being Caſt away./ Re-printed at *Dublin* Anno Domini. 1682./ 8 *pp. Signed* ‘ I. S.’ *Unbound.* 4*to.* (2*l.* 2*s.* 901)

DISSENTING GENTLEMAN'S (THE) Answer To the Reverend Mr. White's Three Letters ; in

which A Separation from the Eſtabliſhment is fully
juſtified ; The Charge of Schism is refuted and re-
torted ; and the Church of England and the Church
of Jesus Christ, are impartially compared, and
found to be Constitutions of a quite Different Nature. The Fourth Edition. *New York:* Printed
and sold by James Parker, at the New Printing-
Office, in Beaver-Street, 1748. *64 pp. At page 53
Signed ʻ A Dissenter.' half mor. 4to.* (15s. 902)

DISSERTATIONS, on the Grand Dispute between
Great-Britain and America. [*New York* 1774]
*Privately printed. Signed ʻ Amor Patriæ.' 10 pp.
Half mor. 8vo.* (4s. 6d. 903)

DISSERTATIONS, on the Grand Dispute between
Great-Britain and America. [*New York* 1774]
10 pp. Signed ʻ Amor Patriæ.' Privately printed.
[*Duplicate of No 903*] *8vo.* (4s. 6d. 904)

DIXON (GEORGE). A Voyage round the World ;
but more particularly to the North-West Coast of
America : Performed in 1785, 1786, 1787, and 1788,
in the King George and Queen Charlotte, Captains
Portlock and Dixon. Dedicated, by Permission,
to Sir Joseph Banks, Bart. By Captain George
Dixon. *London. G.* Goulding, 1789. *15 prel. leaves ;
viz. Title, Dedication, Introduction, Contents, Errata,
and Directions to the Binder ; Text 360 and ʻ Appendix No. II' 47 pp. 22 maps and plates. Calf.
4to.* (12s. 6d. 905)

DOBBS (ARTHUR). An Account Of the Countries
adjoining to Hudson's Bay, in the North-West Part
of America : Containing A Description of their
Lakes and Rivers, the Nature of the Soil and Climate, and their Methods of Commerce, &c. Shewing the Benefit to be made by ſettling Colonies, and
opening a Trade in theſe Parts ; whereby the French
will be deprived in a great Meaſure of their Traffick in Furs, and the Communication between Canada and Miffiſſippi be cut off. With An Abstract of Captain Middleton's Journal, and Observations upon his Behaviour during his Voyage, and
ſince his Return. To which are added. I. A Letter
from Bartholomew de Fonte, Vice-Admiral of Peru
and Mexico ; giving an Account of his Voyage
from Lima in Peru, to prevent or ſeize upon any

Ships that should attempt to find a North-Weſt Paſſage to the South Sea. II. An Abſtract of all the Diſcoveries which have been publiſh'd of the Iſlands and Countries in and adjoining to the Great Weſtern Ocean, between America, India, and China, &c. pointing out the Advantages that may be made, if a ſhort Paſſage ſhould be found thro' Hudſon's Streight to that Ocean. III. The Hudſon's Bay Company's Charter. IV. The Standard of Trade in thoſe Parts of America; with an Account of the Exports and Profits made annually by the Hudſon's Bay Company. V. Vocabularies of the Languages of ſeveral Indian Nations adjoining to Hudſon's Bay. The whole intended to ſhew the great Probability of a North-West Passage ſo long deſired; and which (if diſcovered) would be of the higheſt Advantage to theſe Kingdoms. By Arthur Dobbs, Esq; *London :* J. Robinson. MDCCXLIV. *Title*; *Dedication,* 2 *pp.* *Text* 211 *pp.* *With Map of North America by Joseph La France.* 4*to.* (10*s.* 6*d.* 906)

DOBBS (ARTHUR). Remarks upon Capt. Middleton's Defence: Wherein His Conduct during his late Voyage For diſcovering a Paſſage from Hudson's-Bay to the South-Sea is impartially Examin'd; His Neglects and Omissions in that Affair fully Prov'd; The Falsities and Evasions in his Defence Expos'd; The Errors of his Charts laid open, and His Accounts of Currents, Streights, and Rivers, Confuted; Whereby it will appear, with the higheſt Probability, That there is ſuch a Passage as he went in ſearch of. With An Appendix of Original Papers, and a Map of the In-land and Sea-Coaſt of North-America in and about Hudſon's Bay. By Arthur Dobbs, Esq; *London:* Jacob Robinson, MDCCXLIV. 6 *prel. leaves; viz. Half-title, Title, Dedication, and Preface; Text* 171 *pp. With Map of North America* 20 *by* 14 *inches,* by Joseph La France, a French Canadese Indian, who travelled thro those Countries and Lakes for 3 Years from 1739 to 1742. *Fine copy, half morocco.* 8*vo.* (10*s.* 6*d.* 907)

DOBBS (ARTHUR). A Reply to Capt. Middleton's Answer To the Remarks on his Vindication of his Conduct, In a late Voyage made by him in the Furnace Sloop, by Orders of the Lords Com-

miffioners of the Admiralty, to find out a Paffage
from the North-weft of Hudfon's Bay, to the
Weftern and Southern Ocean of America. Shewing
the Art and Evafions he makes ufe of to conceal
his Mif-conduct and Neglect in profecuting that
Difcovery: As alfo the falfe Currents, Tides,
Straits, and Rivers he has laid down in his Chart
and Journal to conceal the Difcovery; with Re-
marks upon fome extraordinary Affidavits he has
publifhed in his Favour. To which is added, A
Full Answer to a late Pamphlet publifhed by Capt.
Middleton, called Forgery Detected. By Arthur
Dobbs, Efq; *London:* J. Robinson, MDCCXLV.
Title, and 128 *pp.* 8*vo.*   (8*s.* 6*d.*   908)

DOBBS (ARTHUR). A Letter from a Ruffian Sea-
Officer, to a Perfon of Diftinction at the Court of
St. Petersburgh: Containing his Remarks upon
Mr. de l'Ifle's Chart and Memoir, relative to the
New Difcoveries Northward and Eastward from
Kamtfchatka. Together with Some Observations
on that Letter. By Arthur Dobbs, Efq; Governor
of North-Carolina. To which is added, Mr. de
l'Ile's Explanatory Memoir on his Chart Publifhed
at Paris, and now Tranflated from the Original
French. *London:* A. Linde. 1754. *Half-title,
title, and* 83 *pp. half mor.* 8*vo.*   (5*s.* 6*d.*   909)

DONNANT (D. F.). Statistical Account of the
United States of America. By D. F. Donnant,
Member of the Atheneum of Arts, &c. &c. at
Paris. Translated from the French, by William
Playfair: With an Addition on the Trade to
America, for the use of Commercial Men, by the
same. Illustrated by a divided Circle, representing
the Proportional Extent of the different States,
the Eastern Country, and the newly acquired
Territory of Louisiana, by a New Method, en-
graved and illuminated. *London:* Greeland and
Norris, 1805. 72 *pp. With a Divided Circle, colored.*
Half-mor. 8*vo.*   (4*s.* 6*d.*   910)

DOTY (JOHN). A Sermon preached at the opening
of Christ's Church at Sorel In the Province of
Canada, On Sunday the 25th of December 1785:
By The Reverend John Doty, a Prefbyter of the
Church of England; and Miffionary from the

incorporated Society for the Propagation of the
Gofpel in Foreign Parts. *Montreal;* Printed by
Fleury Mesplet. M.DCC.LXXXVI. 14 *pp. half mor.*
8*vo.* (4*s.* 6*d.* 911)

DOUGLASS (WILLIAM). A Summary, Hiftorical
and Political, Of the firſt Planting, progreſſive
Improvements, and preſent State of the Britiſh
Settlements in North-America. Containing I. Some
general Account of ancient and modern Colonies,
the granting and ſettling of the Britiſh Continent
and Weſt-India Iſland Colonies, with ſome tranſient
Remarks concerning the adjoining French and
Spaniſh Settlements, and other Remarks of various
Natures. II. The Hudſon's Bay Company's
Lodges, Fur and Skin Trade. III. Newfoundland
Harbours and Cod-Fiſhery. IV. The Province of
l'Accadie or Nova-Scotia; with the Viciſſitudes of
the Property and Juriſdiction thereof, and its pre-
ſent State. V. The ſeveral Grants of Sagadahock,
Province of Main, Maſſachuſetts-Bay, and New
Plymouth, united by a new Charter in the preſent
Province of Maſſachuſetts-Bay, commonly called
New-England. By William Douglass, M. D.
Boston, New-England: Printed and Sold by
Rogers and Fowle in Queen-Street. MD, CC, XLIX.
Two Volumes. Vol. I. 4 *prel. leaves and* 568 *pp.*
Vol. II. 1751. 2 *prel. leaves and* 416 *pp. Calf extra*
by Bedford. 8*vo.* (2*l.* 2*s.* 912)

DOUGLASS (WILLIAM). A Summary, Hiſtorical
and Political, of the Firſt Planting, Progreſſive
Improvements, and Preſent State of the Britiſh
Settlements in North-America. Containing I. Some
general Account of ancient and modern Colonies,
the granting and ſettling of the Britiſh Continent
and Weſt India Iſland Colonies, with ſome tranſient
Remarks concerning the adjoining French and
Spaniſh Settlements, and other Remarks of various
Natures. II. The Hudſon's-Bay Company's
Lodges, Furr and Skin Trade. III. Newfoundland Harbour and Cod-Fiſhery. IV. The Province
of L'Accadie or Nova-Scotia; with the Viciſſitudes
of the Property and Juriſdiction thereof, and its
preſent State. V. The ſeveral Grants of Sagadahock, Province of Main, Maſſachuſetts-Bay, and
New-Plymouth, united by a new Charter in the

preſent Province of Maſſachuſetts-Bay, commonly
called New-England. By William Douglass, M.D.
Vol. I. Boston, New-England, Printed: *London*,
re-printed for R. Baldwin in Pater-noſter-Row.
M.DCC.LV. *Vol. I. 5 prel. leaves and 568 pp; Map
of North America. Vol. II.* A Summary, Hiſtorical
and Political, of the Firſt Planting, Progreſſive
Improvements, and Preſent State of the Britiſh
Settlements in North America. Containing I. The
Hiſtory of the Provinces and Colonies of New-
Hampſhire, Rhode-Iſland, Connecticut, New-York,
New-Jerſies, Penſylvania, Maryland, and Virginia;
their ſeveral original Settlements and gradual
Improvements; their Boundaries, Produce and
Manufactures, Trade and Navigation, Laws and
Government. II. Their Natural Hiſtory, Religious
Sectaries, Paper Currencies, and other Miſcella-
nies. III. Several Medical Digreſſions, with a
curious Diſſertation on the Treatment of the Small-
Pox, and Inoculation. By William Douglass,
M.D. Vol. II. Boston, New-England, Printed:
London, re-printed for R. Baldwin in Pater-noſter-
Row. M.DCC.LV. *3 prel. leaves and 416 pp. Fine
copy in old calf. Two Volumes.* 8*vo.* (1*l.* 1*s.* 913)

DOUGLASS (WILLIAM). *Another Edition. London.*
Printed for R. and J. Dodsley, in Pall-Mall.
MDCCLX. *Two Volumes. The same collation as the
Edition of* 1755. 8*vo.* (1*l.* 1*s.* 914)

This is a reprint of the Edition of 1755, almost page for page.
There are a few alterations and corrections. At the heads of
each page are placed the Parts and Sections. Although at the
end of the *Contents* of Volume I. there is " Place the Map to
Face the Title of Vol. I." I have never yet met with a copy in the
original state bearing the Map.

DOWNING (*Sir* GEORGE). A/ Reply/ of/ Sir
George Downing/ Knight and Baronet,/ Envoy
Extraordinary from His Majeſty/ of Great-Britain,
&c./ To the/ Remarks/ of the/ Deputies of the
Eſtates-General,/ upon his/ Memorial/ Of De-
cember 20, 1644. Old Stile./ *London*, Printed
Anno Dom. 1665./ *Title and* 104 *pp. Uncut*,
4*to.* (10*s.* 6*d.* 915)

DOWNING (*Sir* GEORGE). A/ Discourse/ Written
by/ Sir George Downing,/ The King of Great
Britain's Envoy/ Extraordinary to the States of
the/ Vnited Provinces./ Vindicating his Royal

Matter from the/ Infolencies of a Scandalous Libel,
Printed/ under the Title of [An Extract out of the/
Regifter of the States General of the Vnited/ Pro-
vinces, upon the Memorial of Sir George/ Downing, Envoy, &c.] And delivered by/ the Agent
De Heyde for fuch, to feveral/ Publick Minifters./
Whereas no fuch Refolution was ever/ Communicated to the faid Envoy, nor any/ Anfwer returned
at all by their Lordships to/ the faid Memorial./
Whereunto is added a Relation of fome/ Former
and Later Proceedings of the/ Hollanders: By a
Meaner Hand./ *London*, Printed for Dorman
Newman,/ and John Luttone, at the Kings Arms
and/ Blew-Anchor in the Poultrey, 1672./ *Title,
and* 171 *pp. old calf.* 12*mo.* (10*s.* 6*d.* 916)

DOYLE (John). Autograph Memorial of Major
John Doyle of the 105th Regiment, addressed to
George III, soliciting promotion to the rank of
Lieut. Colonel. 1 *page, with a page of Testimonials.
Folio.* (10*s.* 917)

The Memorialist represents that he had been more than 20 years
an officer, and obtained all his commissions by purchase. He
gave £100 for his Lieutenancy in 1775, in order to be sent out to
Boston, and served in America from the commencement to the
end of the war. At the battle of Long Island, at Germantown,
in Virginia, in South Carolina, and elsewhere, he enumerates his
services. During the war he received the Public Thanks of the
Generals commanding upon *five* different occasions, and was
named *three* times in the Gazettes.

DRAKE (Daniel). An Anniversary Discourse,
on the State and Prospects of the Western Museum
Society: Delivered by Appointment, in the Chapel
of the Cincinnati College, June 10th, 1820, on the
opening of the Museum. By Daniel Drake, M.D.
Secretary of the Society ; Member of the American
Philosophical and Geological Societies; Counsellor
of the American Antiquarian Society, and Member
of the Philadelphia Academy of Natural Sciences.
Cincinnati, Ohio: Looker, Palmer and Reynolds.
1820. 36 *pp. small* 8*vo.* (4*s.* 6*d.* 918)

DRAKE (*Sir* Francis). A Svmmarie/ and Trve Dis-
covrse/ of Sir Frances Drakes/ VVeft Indian Voyage./ Wherein were taken, the Townes of/ Saint
Jago, Sancto Domingo, Cartagena &/ Saint Auguftine./ Imprinted at *London* by Richard Field,
dwelling/ in the Blacke-Friars by Ludgate./ 1589./
On the reverse of the Title an Advertisement; Dedi-

cation, 2 *pp. signed* ' Thomas Cates.' *Text* 52 *pp.*
Morocco by Bedford. 4to.   (5*l.* 15*s.* 6*d.* 919)

DRAKE (*Sir* FRANCIS). Le/ Voyage/ de l'Illvstre/
Seignevr et Che-/ualier Fraçois Drach, Admiral/
d'Angleterre, à l'entour du monde./ Augmentée
de la Seconde partie./ A Monfieur de S. Simon,
Seigneur &/ Baron de Courtomer./ A *Paris,*/ Chez
Iean Gesselin, ruë fainĉt Iacques,/ à la belle Image
& en fa boutique au Palais/ en la gallerie des prifonniers./ M.DC.XXVII./ Auec priuelege du Roy./
Title; Dedication 2 leaves signed 'F. de Lovvencovrt.' *Text* 230 *pp. Privilege dv Roy* 2 *pp. Calf
extra.* 8*vo*   (2*l.* 2*s.* 920)

DRAKE (*Sir* FRANCIS). The World/ Encompaffed/
by/ Sir Francis Drake,/ Being his next voyage to
that to Nombre/ de Dios formerly imprinted ;/
Carefully colleĉted out of the notes of Mafter/
Francis Fletcher Preacher in this im-/ployment,
and diuers others his followers in/ the fame :/ Offered now at laft to publique view, both for the
honour of/ the aĉtor, but efpecially for the stir-
ring vp of heroick fpirits,/ to benefit their Countrie and eternize their names/ by like noble attempts./   *London,* Printed for Nicholas Bovrnes/
and are to be fold at his fhop at the/ Royall Exchange. 1628./ *Title and Dedication,* 2 *leaves; Text*
108 *pp. Fine copy in morocco extra by F. Bedford.*
4to.   (4*l.* 14*s.* 6*d.* 921)

DRAKE (*Sir* FRANCIS). The/ World/ Encompassed/
By/ Sir Francis Drake./ Being/ His next Voyage
to that to Nombre de/ Dios, formerly imprinted ;/
Carefully colleĉted out of the Notes of Mafter/
Francis Fletcher, Preacher in this/ imployment,
and divers others his/ followers in the fame./ Offered now at laft to publike view, both for the honour of/ the Aĉtor, but efpecially for the ftirring up
of Heroick fpirits,/ to benefit their Country, and
eternize their names/ by like noble attempts./
London, Printed by E. P. for Nicholas Bourne,
and are to be fold at/ his Shop at the South Entrance of the/ Royall Exchange. 1635./ *Title and
Dedication* 2 *leaves; Text in* 90 *pp. Half morocco.*
4to.   (2*l.* 12*s.* 6*d.* 922)

DRAKE (*Sir* FRANCIS). Le/ Voyage/ Cvrievx,/

faict Avtovr/ du Monde, par François/ Drach,
Admiral d'Angle-/terre./ Augmentée de la Seconde partie./ A *Paris,*/Chez Antoine Robinot, en
la place/ Dauphine au Dauphin, & en fa boutique/
fur le Pont-Neuf./ m.dcc.xxxxi./ *Title; Dedication 3 leaves signed* ' F. de Lovvencovrt.' *Text* 230
pp. Calf extra by Bedford, 8*vo.* (2*l.* 2*s.* 923)

DRAKE (*Sir* Francis). The English Hero: *See*
Burton, No. 414.

DRAKE (*Sir* Francis). Sir Francis Drake Revived./ Who is or may be a Pattern to ftirre up
all/ Heroicke and active Spirits of thefe/ Times, to
benefit their Countrey and/ eternize their Names
by like Noble/ attempts./ Being a Summary and
true Reiation of foure/ severall Voyages made by
the faid/ Sir Francis Drake to the/ West-Indies./
Viz./ His dangerous adventuring for Gold and Silver with/ the gaining thereof. And the furprizing
of Nombre de dios by/ himfelfe and two and fifty
Men. His Encompaffing the World./ His Voyage
made with Christopher Carleill, Martin Frobufher,/
Francis Knollis, and others. Their taking the
Townes of Saint/ Jago, Sancto Domingo, Carthagena and Saint Auguftine./ His last Voyage (in
which he dyed) being accompanied/ with Sir John
Hawkins, Sir Thomas Baskerfield, Sir Nicholas
Clif-/ford, with others. His manner of Buriall./
Collected out of the Notes of the faid Sir Francis
Drake;/ Maftet Philip Nichols, Mafter Francis
Fletcher, Preach-/ers; and the Notes of divers
other Gentlemen (who/ went in the faid Voyages)
carefully compared together./ Printed at *London*
for Nicholas Bourne, dwelling at the/ South entrance of the royall Exchange, 1653./ 4 *prelim. leaves
including the engraved Portrait, title, and* 'To the
Reader;' *Text* 87 *pp. followed by a blank leaf. Second title:* — The/ World/ Encompassed/ by/ Sir
Francis Drake./ Offered now at laft to Publique
view, both/ for the honour of the Actor, but efpe-
cially/ for the ftirring up of heroicke Spirits, to be-
nefit/ their Countrey, and eternize their Names/ by
like noble attempts./ Collected out of the Notes of
Mafter Francis Fletcher/ Preacher in this imployment, and compared with/ divers others Notes that
went in the/ fame Voyage./ Printed at *London* for

Nicholas Bourne, dwelling at the/ South entrance
of the royall Exchange, 1652./ *Title and* 108 *pp.*
Followed by a third title :—A/ Summarie/ and/ True
Discourse/ of/ Sir Francis Drakes/ West-Indian
Voyage./ Accompanied with Chriftopher Carleill,/
Martin Frobufher, Francis Knollis, with/ many
other Captains and Gentlemen./ Wherein were
taken, the Townes of Saint/ Jago, Sanƈto Domingo,
Cartagena and/ Saint Auguftine./ Printed at *Lon-
don* for Nicholas Bourne, dwelling at the/ South
entrance of the royall Exchange, 1652./ 41 *pp.*
Followed by the Fourth title :—A Full/ Relation/ Of
another/ Voyage/ into the/ West Indies,/ made by/
Sir Francis Drake ;/ Accompanied with Sir John
Hawkins, Sir/ Thomas Baskerfield, Sir Nicholas
Clifford,/ and others./ Who fet forth from Pli-
mouth on the 28. of/ Auguft 1595./ Printed at
London for Nicholas Bourne, dwelling at/ the
South entrance of the Royall Exchange. 1652./
Title and pp. 45 *to* 60. *Fine copies in blue morocco
by Bedford.* 4to. (5*l.* 5*s.* 924)
These four tracts were published by Bourne in one volume.

DRAKE (*Sir* Francis). The/ Voyages & Travels/
Of that Renowned Captain,/ Sir Francis Drake,/
into the/ West-Indies,/ and/ Round about the
World :/ Giving a perfeƈt Relation of his ftrange
Adventures, and many wonderful Dif-/coveries, his
Fight with the Spaniard, and many barbarous Nations ; his/ taking St. Jago, St. Domingo, Carthagena, St. Au-/gusta, and many other Places in the
Golden Country of America,/ and other Parts of
the World : His Defcription of Monfters, and Mon-
ftrous Peo-/ple. With many other remarkable Paffages not before Extant : Contained in the/ Hiftory
of his Life and Death ; both pleafant and profitable
to the Reader./ Printed by C. B. for J. F. and
fold by E. Tracy, at the Three Bibles on/ London-
Bridge./ 24 *pp. beginning on the reverse of the title.*
half mor. 4*to.* (3*l.* 3*s.* 925)

DRAKE (*Sir* Francis). The Life And Dangerous
Voyages of Sir Francis Drak, With the Surprifing
of Nombre de Dios, and the manner of his gaining
large Quantities of Gold and Silver. And a large
Account of that Voyage, wherein he encompafled
the whole World. And the Voyage which he made

with Francis Knolls and others, with their taking
St. Jago, Sancto Domingo, Carthagena and St. Auguftin. With the laft Voyage in which he Died.
London : Printed by John Willis and Jos. Bodding-
ton, at the Angel and Bible in Tower-ftreet. *Woodcut Portrait of Drake, Title, and* 162 *pp. Old calf.*
12*mo.*   (16*s.* 926)

DRAKE (*Sir* FRANCIS). The Trumpet of Fame.
Written by H. R. And First Printed in 1595. The
Second Edition. *Kent:* Printed at the private Prefs
of Lee Priory; by John Warwick. 1818. *Title,*
[*Second Title*] The Trumpet of Fame: or Sir F.
Drake's and Sir J. Hawkins' Farewell: with an
encouragement to all Sailors and Soldiers, that are
minded to go, in this worthy enterprize. With the
Names of many Ships, and what they have done
against our foes. Written by H. R. Imprinted
at London by Thomas Creede, and are to be sold
by William Barley, at his Shop in Gratious Street.
1595. *Preface pp. iii-iv signed* ' T. Park.' *Text* 14
pp. Half mor. uncut. 12*mo.*   (10*s.* 6*d.* 927)

DRAKE (*Sir* FRANCIS). The Life of the Celebrated
Sir Francis Drake, the First Circumnavigator. Reprinted from the Biographia Britannica. Together
with the Historical and Genealogical Account of
Sir Francis Drake's Family, from Betham's Baron-
etage : And extracts from Nicholson's History of
Cumberland, containing an Account of the Richmond Family of Highhead Castle. Not Published.
London : Printed by J. Moyes, Took's Court, Chan-
cery Lane. 1828. 5 *prel. leaves and* 83 *pp. With
Portrait of Drake, Plate of a Chair and Verses,*
' Richmonds of Highhead Castle. Pedigree,' *at
page* 72. 4*to.*   (10*s.* 6*d.* 928)

DRAKE (SAMUEL GARDNER). Genealogical and
Biographical Account of the family of Drake in
America. With some notices of the Antiquities
connected with the early times of persons of the
name in England. [*Boston*] Printed at the private
press of George Coolidge, for Samuel Gardner
Drake, August, 1845 *Title and Dedication* 2 *leaves ;
Preface pp. iii-viii, signed* ' Sam¹. G. Drake.' *Text
pp.* 9-51. *Half morocco uncut. Privately printed.*
8*vo.*   (10*s.* 6*d.* 929)

DRAYTON (John). Letters written during a Tour through the Northern and Eastern States of America; By John Drayton. *Charleston:* South-Carolina, Printed by Harrison and Bowen. M,DCC,XCIV. *Title, iv pp. and pp.* 3-138. *Plates at pp.* 20, 79, 86. *8vo.* (5s. 6d. 929*)

DRESSERUS (Matthæus). Hiſtorien vnd Bericht,/ Von dem Newlicher/ Zeit erfundenen Königreich China,/ wie es nach vmbſienden, ſo zu einer rechtmeſsigen/ Beſchreibung gehören, darumb/ beſchaffen./ Item, Von dem auch new erfundenen/ Lande Virginia./ Jetzund auffs newe vberſehen, vnd mit einem Zuſatz ver=/mehret, Nemlich :/ Wie es vmb die Religion in Perſer vnd Moh=/ren land,/ vnter Prieſter Johan bewand ſey./ In Druck verfertiget, durch/ Matthævm Dresservm D./ der Sprachen vnd Hiſtorien Profeſſorn. Getruckt zu *Leipzig*, durch Frantz Schnelboltz./ Typis Haeredvm Beyeri./ Anno/ M.D.XCVIII./ *6 prelim. leaves; viz. Title, and* 'Vorrede.' *Text* 297 *pp.* [*Colophon dated*] 'M.D.XCVII.' *4to.* (2l. 2s. 930)

Pages 171 to 231 incluſive contain a tranſlation into German of Thomas Hariot's 'Briefe and True Report of the Newfound Land of Virginia,' firſt printed in Engliſh in 1588 in 4to.

DREWE (Edward). Dedicated to the British Army. Military Sketches. By Edward Drewe, late Major of the 35th Regiment of Foot. *Exeter:* B. Thorn and Son. MDCCLXXXIV. *Title, xxviii and* 128 *pp. 8vo.* (7s. 6d. 931)

On page 117 of this quaint book begins a Poem (ut vulgo) 'An Elegiac Epistle, addressed to a Friend, on my leaving Boston in 1775, for the cure of my Wounds, ſustained at Bunker's Hill.'

DUCHE (Jacob). Human Life a Pilgrimage: Or The Christian a Stranger and Sojourner upon Earth: A Sermon, Occasioned by the Death of the Hon. Richard Penn, Esq; One of the Proprietaries of the Province of Pennsylvania: Preached before the united Congregations of Christ-Church and St. Peter's, in theCity of Philadelphia, on Sunday, April XXI. 1771. By the Reverend Jacob Duché, M.A. *Philadelphia:* Printed by D. Hall, and W. Sellers. MDCCLXXI. *Title and Dedication iv pp. Text* 19 *pp. Uncut. 8vo.* (7s. 6d. 932)

DUCHE (Jacob). Discourses on Various Subjects, by Jacob Duché, M.A. Rector of Christ-Church and St. Peter's, in Philadelphia; and formerly of Clare - Hall, Cambridge. The Second Edition.

London : J. Phillips, M.DCC.LXXX. *Two Volumes.*
I. *xii pp. Contents and Subscribers Names 4 leaves;
Text 362 pp. With frontispiece and portrait.* II.
Title and Contents 4 leaves; Text 430 pp. With frontispiece. Tree calf extra, fine copy on Large Paper.
8vo. (14s. 933)

DU LAC (PERRIN). Voyage dans les Deux Louisianes, et chez les Nations Sauvages du Missouri,
par les Etats-Unis, l'Ohio et les Provinces qui le
bordent, en 1801, 1802 et 1803; Avec un aperçu
des Mœurs, des Usages, du Caractère et des Coutumes religieuses et civiles des Peuples de ces diverses Contrées. Par M. Perrin Du Lac. *A Paris,*
Capelle et Renand, 1805. *Title and Dedication 2
leaves. Preface 10 pp; Text 479 pp. With* ' Carte du
Missouri 1802 ' *and plate of the Mamoth at p. 253.
Tree calf. 8vo.* (6s. 6d. 934)

DUNHAM (JOSIAH). An Answer to the " Vindication of the Official Conduct of the Trustees of Dartmouth College," in Confirmation of the " Sketches :"
with remarks on the removal of President Wheelock. By Josiah Dunham. *Hanover :* David Watson, Jun. 1816. *94 pp. Errata 1 page. uncut.*
8vo. (2s. 6d. 935)

DUMMER (JEREMIAH). A Defence of the New-
England Charters. By Jer. Dummer. *London :*
Printed by W. Wilkins, and sold by J. Peele.
MDCCXXI. *First Edition. Title; Dedication 5 pp ;
Text 80 pp. Half morocco. 8vo.* (10s. 6d. 936)

DUMMER (JEREMIAH). A Defence of the New-
England Charters. By Jer. Dummer. *London :*
Printed for J. Almon, [1765.] *88 pp. Half mor.
8vo.* (5s. 6d. 937)

DUNLOP (CHARLES). Manuscript Memorial of
Lieut. Charles Dunlop addressed to Sir George
Yonge, Secretary at War, soliciting to be put on
active service. *1 page. 4to.* (5s. 938)

Lieut. Dunlop served six years in the Queen's Rangers under Col.
Simcoe, who " made a flattering mention" of him in his letter
published in the Gentleman's Magazine for Jan. 1787, respecting
the " Action fought at Spencers near Williamsburg in Virginia."
The Memorialist lost three brothers in the American War, " one
of them a Major intrusted by Lord Cornwallis with a separate
Command, in South Carolina, but had the misfortune to be
taken prisoner, and was five days afterwards murdered by the
Rebel Riflemen, in Cold Blood,—my Lord Cornwallis's situation was such at that time as to prevent much enquiry into so
villanous a transaction."

DUNTON (John). The Life and Errors of John
Dunton, Citizen of London; with the Lives and
Characters of more than a Thousand Contemporary
Divines, and other Persons of Literary Eminence.
To which are added, Dunton's Conversation in Ire-
land; Selections from his other genuine Works;
and a faithful Portrait of the Author. J. Nichols.
London, 1818. *Two Volumes.* I. *xxxii pp. and* 413
pp. II. *Title, and pp.* 414-776. *With Portrait of*
'John Dunton. 1817.' *half calf.* 8*vo.*   (15*s.* 939)

DUQUESNE (Marquis). The Marquis Duquefne
Vindicated; in a Letter to a Noble Lord; From the
Afperfions caft on his Conduct while Commander
of Fort Charles, at Port-Royal in Jamaica, under
His Grace the Duke of Portland. Which Afper-
fions were publifhed in a Letter, faid to be wrote
by a Gentleman of that Ifland, and addreffed to a
Member of Parliament. Dated February, 1725-6.
London: Printed in the Year M.DCC.XXVIII. 42 *pp.*
Thick paper, half mor. 8*vo.*   (7*s.* 6*d.* 940)

DURAN (Nicolas). Relation/ des Insignes Pro-
grez/ de la/ Religion Chrestienne,/ faits/ av Para-
qvai, Province/ de l'Amerique Meridionale, &/
dans les vaftes Regions de/ Guair & d'Vruaig./
Nouuellement découuertes par les Peres de la/
Compagnie de Iesvs, és années/ 1626. & 1627./
Enuoyée au R. P. Mvtio Vitelesci/ General de la
mefme Compagnie, par le/ R. P. Nicolas Dvran,
Prouincial/ en la Prouince de Paraquai./ Et traduite de Latin en François, par vn Pere/ de la
mefme Compagnie./ A *Paris.*/ Chez Sebastien
Cramoisy, Imprimeur/ ordinaire du Roy, ruë fainct
Iacques,/ aux Cicognes./ M.DC.XXXVIII./ Avec
Privilege de sa Maiesté./ 10 *prel. leaves; viz. Title,*
'Epistre,' *Signed* 'Iacqves de Machavd.' *and* 'Ad-
vertissement avx Lectevrs.' *Text* 162 *pp.* 'Appro-
bation' 1 *page. Vellum.* 8*vo.*   (1*l.* 1*s.* 941)

DVTCH (The) SVRVEY./ Wherein are related/
and truly difcourfed, the chiefeft loffes and/ ac-
quirements, which have paft betweene the Dutch/
and the Spaniards, in thefe laft four yeares Warres
of the/ Netherlands, with a comparative ballancing
and eftimation/ of that which the Spaniards haue
got in the Dutchies of Cleeve and/ Iuliers, with

that which they haue loſt vnto the/ Dutch and Per-
ſians, in Braſilia, Lima,/ and Ormus./ Whereunto
are annext the Mansfeldian/ motiues, directed vnto
all Colonels; Lieutenant-Co-/lonels, Sergeant Ma-
jors, priuate Captaines, inferiour Offi-/cers and
Souldiers, whoſe ſeruice is engag'd in this pre-/
ſent expedition, vnder the conduct and commaund
of the/ moſt illuſtrious Prince Erneſtvs,/ Earle of
Mansfield./ At *London*/ Printed by Edward Allde, for Nathaniel Bvtter./ 1625./ *Title; Dedication to Cromwell. 3 pp, signed '* W. C.' *To the
Reader 2 pp; Text* 36 *pp.* 4*to.* (1*l.* 1*s.* 942)

DU TERTRE (JEAN BAPTISTE). Histoire/ Generale,/ des Isles/ de S. Christophe,/ de la Gvade-
lovpe,/ de la Martiniqve,/ et avtres/ dans l'Ameriqve./ Où l'on verra l'eſtabliſſement des Colonies
Fran-/çoises, dans ces Iſles; leurs guerres Ciuiles
&/ Eſtrangeres, & tout ce qui ſe paſſe dans les/ voyages & retours des Indes./ Comme auſſi pluſieurs
belles particularitez des Antiſles de l'Amerique:/
Vne deſcription generale de l'Iſle de la Guadeloupe:
de tous ſes/ Mineraux, de ſes Pierreries, de ſes
Riuieres, Fontaines &/ Eſtangs : & de toutes ſes
Plantes./ De plus, la deſcription de tous les Ani-
maux de la Mer, de l'Air, & de la/ Terre : & vn
Traité fort ample des Mœurs des Sauuages du pays,
de l'Eſtat/ de la Colonie Françoise, & des Eſclaues,
tant Mores, que Sauuages./ Par le R. P. Iean Bap-
tiſte Dv Tertre, Religieux de l'Ordre des FF.
Preſ-/cheurs, du Nouitiat du Faux-bourg Sainct
Germain de Paris,/ Miſſionaire Apoſtolique dans
l'Amerique./ A *Paris*,/ Chez Iacqves Langlois,
Imprimeur Ordinaire du Roy,/ Au Mont de ſainte
Geneuiefve, vis à vis la Fontaine./ Et Emmanvel
Langlois, dans la grand' Salle du Palais,/ à la
Reyne de Paix./ M.DC.LIV./ Auec Priuilego du
Roy, & Approbation des Superieurs./ 8 *prelim.
leaves ; viz. Title, Epistre, Av Lectevr, Table, and Li-
centia ; Text* 488 *pp.* ' L'Impression de ce Livre '
6 *pp. Errata* 1 *page. Maps at pp.* 1, 27, *and* 68.
Old calf, 4*to.* (1*l.* 5*s.* 943)

DWIGHT (TIMOTHY). The Conquest of Canäan;
A Poem, in Eleven Books. By Timothy Dwight.
Hartford : Printed by Elisha Babcock. M,DCC,
LXXXV. 4 *prel. leaves; viz. Title, dedication, preface,*

and argument ; Text 304 *pp. First Edition. Calf.*
12*mo.*   (7s. 6d. 944)

DWIGHT (Timothy). A Statistical Account of the
Towns and Parishes in the State of Connecticut.
Published by the Connecticut Academy of Arts and
Sciences. Vol. I.—No. I. *New-Haven,* printed
and sold by Walter and Steele. 1811. *xi and* 83
pp. half mor. 8*vo.*   (4s. 6d. 945)

DWIGHT (Timothy). Autograph Letter to his
brother Theodore, dated at New Haven Sept. 3,
1799. 1 *page.* 4*to.*   (5s. 946)

ACHARD (LAURENCE). A moſt Compleat/ Compendium/ of/ Geography,/ General and Special ;/ Deſcribing all the/ Empires, Kingdoms, and Dominions,/ in the/ Whole World./ Shewing their/ Bounds, Situation, Dimenſions, Ancient and/ Modern Names, Hiſtory, Government, Religions,/ Languages, Commodities, Diviſions, Subdiviſions,/ Cities, Rivers, Mountains, Lakes, with their Arch-/ bishopricks, and Univerſities./ In a more Plain and Eaſie Method, more Compendious,/ and (perhaps) more Uſeful than any of this bigneſs./ To which are added,/ General Rules for making a large Geography./ Very neceſſary for the right Underſtanding of the Tran-/ſactions of theſe Times./ Collected according to the moſt late Diſcoveries, and/ agreeing with the choiceſt and neweſt Maps./ By Lavrence Eachard,/ of Chriſt's-College in Cambridge./ *London:* Printed for Thomas Salusbury at the Sign of/ the Temple, near Temple-Bar in Fleet-Street. 1691./ *9 prel. leaves; viz. Title, Dedication, Preface, Advertisement, and Verses; Signed* ' Anonymous.' *Text* 168 *pp.* ' Index' 17 *pp. With two small copper plate maps of* ' Europa—Asia' *facing the Title;* ' Africa—America,' *at page* 115, *calf.* 12mo. (7s. 6d. 947)

EASTMAN (TILTON). A Sermon, preached in Sharon, Vermont, March 12, 1806, at the Ordination of the Rev. Samuel Baſcom. By the Rev. Tilton Eastman, Pastor of the congregational Church in Randolph, Ver. *Hanover,* N. H. Printed by Moses Davis. 1806. 31 *pp.* 8*vo.* (2s. 6d. 948)

ECKLEY (JOSEPH). A Discourse before the Society for Propagating the Gospel among the Indians and

Others in North America, delivered Nov. 7, 1805.
By Joseph Eckley, D.D. Minister of the Old South
Church in Boston. *Boston:* Printed by E. Lincoln, Water Street. 1806. *36 pp. uncut.*
8vo.   (2s. 6d.   949)

EDEN (RICHARD). The/ Hiftory of Trauayle/ in
the/ VVeft and Eaft Indies, and other/ countreys
lying eyther way,/ towardes the fruitfull and ryche/
Moluccaes./ As/ Mofcouia, Perfia, Arabia, Syria,
Ægypte,/Ethiopia, Guinea, China in Cathayo, and/
Giapan : VVith a Difcourfe of/ the Northweft paf-/
fage./ In the hande of our Lorde be all the corners of/ the earth. Pfal. 94./ Gathered in parte,
and done into Englyfhe by/ Richarde Eden./ Newly fet in order, augmented, and finifhed/ by Richarde VVilles./ ¶ Imprinted at *London/* by Richarde Iugge./ 1577./ Cum Priuilegio./ 10 *prel.*
leaves; viz. *Title the reverse blank,* ' To the ryght
noble and excellent/ Lady, the Lady Brigit, Coun-
teffe of Bed-/forde, my finguler good Lady and/
Myftreffe.'/ *in roman type,* 10 *pp,* dated ' At London the 4. day. of Iuly. 1577.' *and Signed* ' Richarde
VVilles.' ' * R. VVilles Preface vnto the Reader,
wherein is/ fet downe a generall fumme as it were
of the/ whole worke.'/ 6 *pp. Black letter; half-
title,* ' Certayne Preambles here folowe, gea-/thered
by R. Eden, for the better vn-/derftanding of the
whole worke.' *the reverse blank; Text in Black Letter,* 466 *folioed leaves.* ' R. VVilles Speciall aduifes
to be obferued in readyng/ ouer this woorke.'/ 5
pp. ' The Table' 7 *pp. Fine large copy, but much
wormed. 4to.*   (4l. 14s. 6d.   950)

EDWARDS (BRIAN). Thoughts on the late Proceedings of Government, respecting the Trade of
the West India Islands with the United States of
America. The Second Edition, corrected and enlarged. To which is now firft added a Postscript,
addreffed To the Right Honorable Lord Sheffield.
By Brian Edwards, Esq. *London:* T. Cadell,
M.DCCLXXXIV. *iv prel. pp. and Text in* 91 *pp. half
mor. 8vo.*   (5s. 6d.   951)

EDWARDS (BRYAN). The History, Civil and
Commercial, of The Britifh Colonies in the Weft
Indies: In Two Volumes. By Bryan Edwards,

Esq. Of the Island of Jamaica; F.R.S. S.A. and Member of the American Philosophical Society at Philadelphia. The Second Edition, Illustrated with Maps. *London:* John Stockdale, M.DCC.XCIV. *2 Volumes.* Vol. I. *liv prel. pp ; and Text in* 494 *pp. with* 12 *Maps and Plates.* Vol. II. *Title and* 520 *pp. Errata* 1 *page. With* 4 *Copper plates. Calf.* 4*to.* (12*s.* 6*d.* 952)

EDWARDS (JONATHAN). A Faithful Narrative of the Surprizing Work of God in the Conversion of Many Hundred Souls in Northampton, and the Neighbouring Towns and Villages of New-Hampſhire in New-England. In a Letter to the Rev^d. Dr. Benjamin Colman of Boſton. Written by the Rev^d. Mr. Edwards, Miniſter of Northampton, on Nov. 6, 1736. And Publiſhed, With a Large Preface, By Dr. Watts and Dr. Guyse. *London:* John Oswald, M.DCC.XXXVII. *xvi and* 132 *pp. Calf.* 12*mo.* (7*s.* 6*d.* 953)

EDWARDS (JONATHAN). A Faithful Narrative of the Surprizing Work of God in the Conversion of Many Hundred Souls in Northampton, and the Neighbouring Towns and Villages of New-Hampſhire in New-England. In a Letter to the Rev^d. Dr. Benjamin Colman of Boſton. Written by the Reverend Mr. Edwards, Miniſter of Northampton, on Nov. 6. 1736. And publiſhed, With a Large Preface, by Dr. Watts and Dr. Guyse. The Second Edition. *London:* John Oswald, M.DCC.XXXVIII. *xvi and* 126 *pp.* 12*mo.* (7*s.* 6*d.* 954)

EDWARDS (JONATHAN). A Faithful Narrative of the Surpriſing Work of God in the Conversion of Many Hundred Souls in Northampton, and the Neighbouring Towns and Villages of New-Hampſhire in New-England. In a Letter to the Reverend Dr. Benjamin Colman of Boſton. Written by the Reverend Mr. Edwards, Miniſter of Northampton, on Nov. 6. 1736. And Publiſhed, With a Large Preface, by Dr. Watts and Dr. Guyse. *Edinburgh.* Thomas Lumisden and John Robertson, M.DCCXXXVIII. *xii prelim. pp. and Text in* 93 *pp.* 8*vo.* (12*s.* 6*d.* 955)

EDWARDS (JONATHAN). Some Thoughts Concerning the preſent Revival of Religion in New-

England, and The Way in which it ought to be
acknowledged and promoted; Humbly offer'd to
the Publick, in a Treatise on that Subject. In Five
Parts. Part I. Shewing that the Work that has
of late been going on in that Land, is a glorious
Work of God. Part II. Shewing the Obligations
that all are under, to acknowledge, rejoice in and
promote this Work; and the great Danger of the
contrary. Part III. Shewing, in many Inſtances,
wherein the Subjects, or zealous Promoters, of this
Work have been injuriouſly blamed. Part IV.
Shewing what Things are to be corrected or avoided
in promoting this Work, or in our Behaviour under
it. Part V. Shewing poſitively what ought to be
done to promote this Work. By Jonathan Edwards, A.M. Paſtor of the Church of Chriſt at
Northampton. Boston, Printed: *Edinburgh*, reprinted by T. Lumisden and J. Robertson, M.DCC.
XLIII. *iv and 221 pp. calf. 8vo.*   (*6s.* 956)

EDWARDS (JONATHAN). Thoughts Concerning
the Present Revival of Religion in New-England.
By Jonathan Edwards, A.M. Paſtor of the Church
of Chriſt at Northampton. Abridg'd by John
Wesley, A.M. Fellow of Lincoln-College, Oxford.
London: W. Strahan; and ſold by T. Tyre, *etc.*
MDCCXLV. *124 pp. 12mo.*   (*6s.* 957)

EDWARDS (JONATHAN). The Distinguishing
Marks of a Work of the Spirit of God. Extracted
from Mr. Edwards, Miniſter of Northampton in
New-England. By John Wesley, M.A. Late Fellow of Lincoln College, Oxon. The Second Edition. *London:* Henry Cocks; MDCCLV. *48 pp.*
12mo.   (*3s. 6d.* 958)

EDWARDS (JONATHAN). A Narrative of the late
Work of God At and Near Northampton in New-
England. Extracted from Mr. Edward's Letter
to Dr. Coleman. By John Wesley, M.A. Late
Fellow of Lincoln College, Oxon. The Second
Edition. *London:* Henry Cock; MDCCLV. *48 pp.*
12mo.   (*4s. 6d.* 959)

EDWARDS (JONATHAN). The/ Life/ of the/ Late
Reverend, Learned and Pious/ Mr. Jonathan Edwards,/ Some Time Minister of the Goſpel at Northampton,/ in New-England, and then Missionary

to the/ Indians at Stockbridge, and after that Pre-
sident/ of New-Jersey College./ Who departed
this Life at Princeton, March 22./ 1758. in the
55th. Year of his Age./ *Boston:*/ Printed and Sold
by S. Kneeland, oppofite/ the Probate Office, in
Queen Street./ M,DCC,LXV. 4 *prel. leaves; viz.
Title, Preface, and Contents; Text* 97 *pp. Calf extra
by Bedford. 8vo.* (12s. 6d. 960)

EDWARDS (JONATHAN). An Account of the Life
Of the late Reverend Mr David Brainerd, Minifter
of the Gofpel, Miffionary to the Indians, from the
Honourable Society in Scotland, for the Propagation of Chriftian Knowledge, and Paftor of a Church
of Chriftian Indians in New-Jerfey. Who died at
Northampton in New-England, October 9. 1747,
in the 30th Year of his Age. Chiefly taken from
his own Diary, and other private Writings, written
for his own Ufe; and now publifhed, by Jonathan
Edwards, A.M. Then Minifter of the Gofpel at
Northampton, afterwards Prefident of the College
of New-Jersey. To which is annexed, I. Mr.
Brainerd's Journal while among the Indians. II.
Mr. Pemberton's Sermon at his Ordination. With
an Appendix relative to the Indian Affairs. *Edinburgh:* John Gray and Gavin Alston. MDCCLXV.
xii prel. and 504 *pp. calf. 8vo.* (8s. 6d. 961)

EDWARDS (JONATHAN). A Faithful Narrative of
the Surprising Work of God, in the Conversion of
many Hundred Souls in Northampton, and the
Neighbouring Towns and Villages of New Hampshire, in New England; in a Letter to the Rev.
Dr. Colman, of Boston, written by the Rev. Mr.
Edwards, Minister of Northampton, on Nov. 6,
1737. And published, with a large Preface, By Dr.
Watts and Dr. Guyse. *London:* C. Whittingham
xii and 87 *pp.* 12mo. (3s. 6d. 962)

EDWARDS (JONATHAN). The Injustice and Impo-
licy of the Slave Trade, and of the Slavery of the
Africans: Illustrated in a Sermon Preached before
the Connecticut Society for the Promotion of Freedom, and for the Relief of Persons unlawfully
holden in Bondage, At their annual Meeting in
New-Haven, September 15, 1791. By Jonathan
Edwards, D.D. Pastor of a Church in New-Haven.

[*New London?*] Printed by Thomas and Samuel
Green, M,DCC,XCI. *Half-title, title, and pp.* 3-30.
Uncut, wanting the Appendix. 8vo. (2s. 6d. 963)

EDWARDS (THOMAS). A/ Letter/ to/ Mʳ. Tho.
Edwards/ The Dedication of the Letter/ To our
much fufpeċted friend, Mr. T. Edwards, Scavenger
Generall,/ throughout Great-Britaine, New-England, and the united Pro-/vinces, chiefly Amfterdam, and Munfter, and indeed by vertue of/ fome
faire pretences, Intermedler in all the ftates of
Chriftendome,/ principally there where any thing
of the Spirit of Chrift in the Saints/ appeares, trench-
ing upon the Honour, dignity, and preferment of
the/ Old man. The Grand Reformer, (alias Re-
ducer) of the free born/ Sons of God, into the
chaines of their old Babilonifh captivity, under/
the pretence of a Jus Divinum./ At his dwelling
in Club Court, between the Pope and the Prelate,
a/ little on this fide the Fagot in Smithfield, (or if
in his monethly Pil-grimage) in the Suburbs of
Canterbury, at the knowne houfe of Mi-/ftris Gan-
grena Triplex, where Confcience and he (but for
a time/ we hope) fhook hands and bad each other
farewell. Where he was/ lately difcovered by many
eye-witneffes : and where you may be fure/ at any
time to meet with him./ Publifhed by Authority./
London, Printed for Tho. Veere, and are to be fold
at his fhop/ at the upper-end of the Old Bayley,
near New-gate. 1647./ *Title and* 10 *pp. Fine copy.*
4to. (7s. 6d. 964)

EGEDE (HANS). Herrn Hans Egede, Missionärs
und Bifchofes in Grönland, Befchreibung und Na-
tur=Gefchichte von Grönland, übersetzet von D.
Joh. Ge. Krünitz. Mit Kupfern. *Berlin*, verlegts
Auguft Mylius, 1763. *xii pp. and* 237 *pp. Map at*
page 29. *and* 10 *plates at pages* 69. 85. 89. 98. 107.
125. 127. 137. 178. 179. *half calf.* 8vo. (4s. 6d. 965)

ELEUTHERIUS. The Scripture - Bifhop Vindicated. A Defence of the Dialogue between Præ-
laticus and Eleutherius, Upon the Scripture-Bishop,
or the Divine Right of Presbyterian Ordination and
Government: Againft The Exceptions of a Pamphlet, Intitled, The Scripture-Bifhop Examin'd. By
Eleutherius, V.D.M. In a Letter to a Friend.

Boston, New-England: Printed by S. Kneeland
& T. Green, for D. Henchman in Cornhill. 1733.
*Half-title, title, and 126 pp. followed by a Second
title,* 'Eusebius Inermatus. Juſt Remarks On a late
Book,' Intituled 'Eleutherius Enervatus,' *etc.* By
Phileluth Bangor, V. E. B. *etc. Title, and 158 pp.
Fine copy in the first binding. 8vo.* (10s. 6d. 966)

ELIOT (Andrew). The faithful Steward. A Sermon Delivered By Andrew Eliot, M.A. At his Ordination to the Pastoral Charge Of the New North
Church in Boston, in Conjunction with the Rev.
Mr. Webb. On April 14. 1742. *Boston:* Printed
by Tho. Fleet, for Samuel Eliot in Cornhill. 1742.
Title and pp. 5-35. *8vo.* (2s. 6d. 967)

ELIOT (Andrew). An inordinate Love of the
World inconſiſtent with the Love of God. A Sermon Preached at the Thurſday Lecture in Boston,
Auguſt 2. 1744. By Andrew Eliot, M.A. Paſtor
of a Church in Boston. *Boston,* Printed by Rogers
and Fowle, for S. Eliot in Cornhill. 1744. *Title
and pp.* 5-31. *8vo.* (2s. 6d. 968)

ELIOT (Andrew). A burning and ſhining Light
extinguiſhed. A Sermon Preached The Lord's-
Day after the Funeral Of the late Reverend Mr.
John Webb, Paſtor of the New-North Church in
Boston; Who died April 16. 1750. Ætat. 63. By
Andrew Eliot, A.M. Paſtor of the ſame Church.
Boston: Printed by Daniel Fowle, Joshua Winter
in Union Street oppoſite the King's Arms. [1750.]
Title and pp. 5-42. *8vo.* (2s. 6d. 969)

ELIOT (Andrew). An evil and adulterous Generation. A Sermon Preached on the Public Faſt,
April 19. 1753. By Andrew Eliot, M.A. Paſtor
of a Church in Boſton. *Boston:* Printed by S.
Kneeland, for J. Winter, over againſt the King's
Arms in Union-Street. 1753. *Title and 26 pp.
8vo.* (2s. 6d. 970)

ELIOT (Andrew). A Sermon Preached at the Ordination Of the Reverend Mr. Joſeph Roberts, To
the Paſtoral Care of a Church In Leiceſter. October
23d. 1754. By Andrew Eliot, A.M. Paſtor of a
Church in Boston. *Boston:* Printed by D. Fowle,
for J. Winter in Union-Street, oppoſite the King's-
Arms. [1754.] 41 *pp.* 8vo. (2s. 6d. 971)

ELIOT (Andrew). A Sermon Preached October 25th. 1759. Being a Day of Public Thanksgiving Appointed by Authority, For the Success Of the British Arms this Year; Especially In the Reduction of Quebec, The Capital of Canada. By Andrew Eliot, M.A. Pastor of the New-North Church in Boston. *Boston:* Printed by Daniel and John Kneeland, for J. Winter in Union-street, opposite to the Kings Arms, M,DCC,LIX. *Title and pp.* 5-43. 8vo. (2s. 6d. 972)

ELIOT (Andrew). A Sermon Preached before his Excellency Francis Bernard, Esq; Governor, The Honorable His Majesty's Council, and the honorable House of Representatives, Of the Province of the Massachusetts-Bay in New-England, May 29th 1765. Being the Anniversary for the Election of His Majesty's Council for the Province. By Andrew Eliot, A.M. Pastor of a Church in Boston. *Boston:* Printed by Green and Russell, Printers to the honorable House of Representatives. MDCCLXV. *Title and pp.* 5-59. 8vo. (2s. 6d. 973)

ELIOT (Andrew). A Sermon Preached September 17. 1766. At the Ordination of the Reverend Mr. Ebenezer Thayer, To the Pastoral Care of the First Church in Hampton. By Andrew Eliot, A.M. Pastor of a Church in Boston. *Boston:* N.E. Printed by Kneeland and Adams in Milk-Street for Thomas Leverett, in Cornhill. 1766. *35 pp.* 8vo. (2s. 6d. 974)

ELIOT (Andrew). A Discourse on Natural Religion Delivered in the Chapel of Harvard College in Cambridge, New-England, May 8. 1771. At the Lecture founded By the Hon. Paul Dudley, Esq; By Andrew Eliot, D.D. *Boston:* Printed by Daniel Kneeland, for Nicholas Bowes in Corn-hill. M,DCC,LXXI. *Title and pp. v-xlv.* 'A Lift' *etc.* 2 *pp.* 8vo. (2s. 6d. 975)

ELIOT (Andrew). A Sermon Preached at the Ordination of the Reverend Mr. Joseph Willard, to the Pastoral care of the first Church in Beverly, in conjunction with the Reverend Mr. Joseph Champney, November XXV. MDCCLXXII. By Andrew Eliot, D.D. Pastor of a Church in Boston. To which are annexed, The Charge, By the Rev. Dr.

Appleton, and the Right Hand of Fellowship, By the Rev. Mr. Holt. Publiſhed at the Deſire of the Church and Congregation in Beverley. *Boston*, New-England: Printed by Thomas and John Fleet, 1773. *Title and pp. 5-47. 8vo.* (2s. 6d. 976)

ELIOT (ANDREW). Christ's Promiſe to the penitent Thief. A Sermon Preached the Lord's-Day before the Execution of Levi Ames, Who ſuffered Death for Burglary, Oct. 21, 1773. Æt. 22. By Andrew Eliot, D.D. Paſtor of a Church in Boſton. N.B. This diſcourse was preached at the deſire of the Prisoner, who was preſent when it was delivered. *Boston:* Printed and Sold by John Boyle, next Door to the Three Doves in Marlborough-Street. 1773. *36 pp. 8vo.* (2s. 6d. 977)

ELIOT (ANDREW). A Sermon Preached at the Ordination of Andrew Eliot, A.M. To the Pastoral care of the First Church in Fairfield: June 22, 1774. By his Father, Andrew Eliot, D.D. Pastor of a Church in Boston. *Boston:* Printed by John Boyle in Marlborough-Street. MDCCLXXIV. *Title, Dedication, and pp. 7-46. 8vo.* (2s. 6d. 978)

ELIOT (JOHN). A Brief/ Narrative/ of the/ Progreſs of the Goſpel amongſt/ the Indians in New-England, in/ the Year 1670./ Given in/ By the Reverend Mr. John Elliot, Miniſter of the Goſpel there,/ In a Letter by him directed to/ the Right Worſhipfull the Com-/missioners under his Majeſties Great-Seal for Propagation of the/ Goſpel amongſt the poor blind Nat-/ives in thoſe United Colonies./ *London,/* Printed for John Allen, formerly living in Little-Britain at/ the Riſing-Sun, and now in Wentworth ſtreet near Bell-/Lane, 1671./ *11 pp. Calf extra, gilt edges by Bedford. 4to.* (5l. 5s. 979)

ELIOT (JOHN). Sampwutteahae/ Quinnuppekompauaenin./ Wahuwômook ogguſſemeſuog Sampwutteahae/ Wunnamptamwaenuog,/ Mache wuſſukhúmun ut English-Mane Unnontoowaonk naſhpe/ Ne muttae-wunnegenúe Wuttinneumoh Christ/ Noh aſooweſit/ Thomas Shephard/ Quinnuppenumun en Indiane Unnontoowaonganit naſhpe Ne Quttianatam wewuttinneumoh Christ/ Noh aſſooweſit/ John Eliot./ Kah nawhutche ut aiyeuongaſh

S

ogguffemefe outeheteânun/ Nafhpe/ Grindal Rawson./ *Cambridge.*/ Printed by Samuel Green, in
the Year, 1689./ *Title, and one leaf ; Text* 161 *pp.
Morocco extra gilt by Bedford.* 16mo. (7*l.* 7*s.* 980)

ELIOT (JOHN). A Biographical Dictionary, containing a brief account of the First Settlers, and
other Eminent Characters among the Magistrates,
Ministers, Literary and Worthy Men in New-England. By John Eliot, D.D. Corresponding Secretary of the Massachusetts Historical Society. *Boston.* 1809. *viii and* 511 *pp. Errata* 1 *page. Half
calf.* 8*vo.*   (10*s.* 6*d.* 981)

This volume is from the library of the late Robert Southey, it having been sent to the Poet laureate by Prof. Ticknor. On the fly-
leaf is a manuscript note,—" This book is worthy of the strictest
faith and credit. G. T."

ELISEO (PADRE). Aviendo Represen-/tado el
Conde de Monterey a fu Ma/gestad los agrauios
y moleftias, que los Indios/ de la Nueua Efpaña
recibian, por orden de los/ juezes que los repartian,
para feruicios perfona/les, fe le mandò que no fe
repartieffen, pero que/fe dieffe ordē como fe alqui-
laffen, y no eftuuief-/fen ociofos : con la qual los de
buen zelo queda-/ron contentos y fatisfechos. Y
porque los inte-/reffados refiftian, el Padre Elifeo
(Carmelita/ Defcalço) Confeffor del Conde, efcriuio
vn pa-/pel, perfuadiendole a executar punctual-
mente/ la orden de fu Mageftad, que es del tenor
fi-/guiente./ [1643]. 8 *folioed leaves. Fine copy.
Folio.*   (1*l.* 11*s.* 6*d.* 982)

ELIZABETH (QUEEN). The Life and Glorious
Reign/ of/ Queen Elizabeth :/ Containing/ Her
Great Victories by Land and Sea ;/ And her other
Succeffes againft the Enemies of the/ Proteftant Religion./ Likewise,/ An Account of Sir Francis
Drake's/ Voyage round the World./ Alfo, an Account of the Deftruction of the great Fleet,/ call'd
the Spanifh Armado./ With the Life and Death
of the Earl of Essex,/ Q, Elizabeth's Great Fa-
vourite./ *London :* Printed and Sold by J. Bradford, at the Bible in/ Fetter-Lane. 1708./ 16 *pp.*
8*vo.*   (10*s.* 6*d.* 983)

ELLIS (HENRY). A Voyage to Hudson's Bay, by
the Dobbs Galley and California, In the Years 1746
and 1747, For Difcovering a North West Passage ;

with An Accurate Survey of the Coaſt, and a ſhort
Natural Hiſtory of the Country. Together with A
fair View of the Faƈts and Arguments from which
the future finding of ſuch a Paſſage is rendered probable. By Henry Ellis, Gent. Agent for the Proprietors in the ſaid Expedition. To which is prefixed, An Historical Account of the Attempts
hitherto made for the finding a Paſſage that Way
to the East Indies. Illuſtrated with proper Cuts,
and a new and correƈt Chart of Hudſon's Bay with
the Countries adjacent. *London:* H. Whitridge,
M.DCC.XLVIII. *xxviii pp.* and 336 pp. *With New
Chart of North West Passage, and 9 Plates at pp.* 36.
39. 40. 131. 132. 134. 152. 232. 252. *Large Paper.
Old calf. 8vo.* (10s. 6d. 984)

ELLIS (HENRY). The Same. On ordinary Paper.
8vo. (7s. 6d. 985)

ELTON (ROMEO). Life of Roger Williams, the Ear-
liest Legislator and true Champion for a full and
Absolute Liberty of Conscience. By Romeo Elton,
D.D., F.R.P.S., Fellow of the Royal Society of
Northern Antiquaries, etc. etc. *London:* Albert
Cockshaw, [1852.] *viii and* 173 *pp. Cloth.*
12mo. (3s. 6d. 986)

ELLWOOD (THOMAS). An/ Epiſtle/ to/ Friends./
Briefly/ Commemorating the Gracious Dealings of
the/ Lord with them; and warning them to/ beware of that Spirit of/ Contention and Diviſion/
Which hath appeared of late in/ George Keith,/
And ſome few others that join with him, who/ have
made a Breach and Separation from/ Friends in
ſome Parts of America./ By Thomas Ellwood./
London, Printed by T. Sowle at the Crooked-Billet in Holy-/well-lane, Shoreditch, and near the
Meeting-Houſe in/ White-Hart-Court in Grace-
Church-Street. 1694./ *73 pp. Postscript and Errata pp.* 74-75. *Small* 8vo. (10s. 6d. 987)

ELLWOOD (THOMAS). A Further/ Discovery/ Of
that Spirit of/ Contention & Diviſion/ Which hath
appeared of late in/ George Keith, &c./ Being a
Reply to Two Late Printed/ Pieces of his, the one
Entituled, A Loving/ Epiſtle, &c. the other, A Sea-
ſonable Informa-/tion, &c. Wherein his Cavils are
Anſwered, his/ Falſhood is laid open, and the Guilt

and/ Blame of the Breach and Separation in Ame-/
rica; and of the Reproach he hath brought/ upon
Truth and Friends, by his late Printed/Books, are
fixed faster on him./ Written by way of Epistle,
and Recommended as a further/ Warning to all
Friends./ By Thomas Ellwood./ *London*, Printed
by T. Sowle at the Crooked-Billet in Holy-/well-
lane, Shoreditch, and neer the Meeting-House in/
White-hart-Court in Grace-Church-street. 1694./
128 pp. 8vo.   (10s. 6d. 988)

EMERSON (GEORGE B.). A Report on the Trees
and Shrubs growing naturally in the Forests of
Massachusetts. Published agreeably to an Order
of the Legislature, by the Commissioners of the
Zoological and Botanical Survey of the State.
Boston: Dutton and Wentworth, 1846. *xv pp;
and* 534 *pp. Explanation of the plates* 1 *page.
Index pp.* 538-547. *With* 17 *plates. Cloth.*
8vo.   (7s. 6d. 989)

EMIGRATION to America, candidly considered.
In a series of Letters from a Gentleman, resident
there, to his Friend, in England. [*London*]
Thomas Clio Rickman, 1798. *viii and 64 pp. uncut.*
8vo.   (3s. 6d. 990)

EMMONS (NATHANAEL). A Discourse, delivered
on the Annual Fast in Massachusetts, April 9,
1801. By Nathanael Emmons, D.D. Pastor of the
Church in Franklin. *Salem:* Reprinted by Joshua
Cushing. 1802. 36 *pp. uncut.* 8vo. (2s. 6d. 991)

ENGLISHMAN DECEIVED (THE); A Political
Piece: Wherein Some very important Secrets of
State are briefly recited, And offered to the Con-
fideration of the Public. London: Printed, *New-
York* reprinted by John Holt, at the Exchange,
M,DCC,LXVIII. *Title; Introduction, ii pp. Text* 40
pp. half mor. 8vo.   (5s. 6d. 992)

ENOS (ROGER). Autograph Letter to Col. Ebenezer
Walbridge, at Skeenesborough, dated at Castleton,
25 Sept. 1781. 1 *page.* 4to.   (5s. 6d. 993)

ENS (GASPAR). Indiae/ Occidentalis/ Historia :/
In qva prima re-/gionum istarum detectio, situs,/
incolarum mores, aliaque eò/ pertinentia, breuiter/
explicantur./ Ex variis Avtoribvs/ collecta,/ Opera

& ſtudio/ Gasparis Ens L./ *Coloniae*, Apud Gulielm. Lutzenkirchen/ Anno MDCXII./ 4 *prel. leaves; viz. Title with engraved Border, and Dedication; Text Signatures A* to *Z in eight, and A a in* 4 *leaves. Pagination very irregular. Last page* 370. *Calf by Bedford. Fine copy.* 8*vo.* (1*l.* 11*s.* 6*d.* 994)

ENSAYO sobre la Topografia de los Rios Plata, Parana, Paraguay, Vermejo y Pilcomayo, para servir de memoria a su Navegacion con un Mapa, calculado con arreglo a las Ultimas Observaciones. *Buenos Aires:* Impreso en la Imprenta de Hallet y Ca. 1831. 16 *pp. signed* 'Herman C. Dwerhagen.' 8*vo.* (4*s.* 6*d.* 995)

ENTERTAINMENT for a Winter's Evening: Being A Full and True Account Of a very ſtrange and wonderful Sight ſeen in Boſton on the twenty-ſeventh of December At Noon-Day. The Truth of which can be atteſted by a great Number of People, who actually ſaw the ſame With their own Eyes. By me, the Honble B. B. Eſq; *Boston:* Printed and Sold by G. Rogers, next to the Priſon in Queen-ſtreet. [1750.] *Title;* 'To the Reader,' *ii pp. Text in verse pp.* 5-15. 8*vo.* (10*s.* 6*d.* 996)

ENTICK (JOHN). The General History of the Late War: Containing it's Riſe, Progreſs, and Event, in Europe, Asia, Africa, and America. And exhibiting The State of the Belligerent Powers at the Commencement of the War; their Intereſts and Objects in its Continuation; and Remarks on the Measures, which led Great Britain to Victory and Conqueſt. Interspersed with The Characters of the able and diſintereſted Statesmen, to whoſe Wiſdom and Integrity, and of the Heroes, to whoſe Courage and Conduct, we are indebted for that Naval and Military Succeſs, which is not to be equalled in the Annals of this, or of any other Nation. And with Accurate Deſcriptions of the Seat of War, the Nature and Importance of our Conquests, and of the moſt remarkable Battles by Sea and Land. Illuſtrated with a Variety of Heads, Plans, Maps, and Charts, Deſigned and Engraved by the beſt Artiſts. By the Rev. John Entick, M.A. And other Gentlemen. The Third Edition, Corrected. *London.* Edward and Charles Dilly.

M.DCC.LXXV. *Five Volumes.* Vol. I. *2 prel. leaves and 495 pp. With* 8 *copper plates and maps.* II. 464 *pp.* 11 *copper plates and maps.* III. 480 *pp. with 9 portraits.* IV. 480 *pp. with* 10 *maps and portraits.* V. 470 *pp. with* 11 *portraits. Index 25 pp. with list of plates.* 8vo. (1*l.* 1*s.* 997)

EPISTLE (AN) From our Yearly-Meeting, Held at Philadelphia, for Pennsylvania and New-Jersey, by Adjournments, from the 24th Day of the 9th Month, to the 1ſt of the 10th Month, incluſive, 1774. [*Philadelphia*, 1774] 4 *pp.* ' Signed in and on behalf of the Yearly Meeting, by James Pemberton, Clerk.' *Folio.* (2*s.* 6*d.* 998)

EPISTLE (AN) of Caution and Advice concerning the Buying and Keeping of Slaves. *Philadelphia :* Printed and Sold by James Chattin, in Church-Alley. 1754. *Title, and* 8 *pp.* 16*mo.* (7*s.* 6*d.* 999)

EQUITY (THE) and Wisdom of Administration, in Measures That have unhappily occaſioned The American Revolt, Tried by the Sacred Oracles. *Edinburgh :* Printed in the Year MDCCLXXVI. 19 *pp. uncut.* 12*mo.* (5*s.* 1000)

ERCILLA y CUNIGA (ALONSO DE). Primera,/ Segvnda, y/ Tercera Par-/tes de la/ Aravcana,/ De don Alonſo de Ercilla y çuñiga,/ Cauallero de la orden de Santiago,/ Gentil hombre de la camara/ de la Mageſtad del/ Emperador./ Dirigidas al Rey/ don Felippe nueſtro Señor./ En *Anvers,*/ En caſa de *Pedro Bellero,* 1597./ Con Priuilegio Real. [*Colophon*] Antverpiae,/ Tipes Andree Bacxij Ty-/pographi iurati./ 1597./ *Part I.* 12 *prel. and* 146 *folioed leaves with* 8 *pp. of Table. Part II. Title ; one leaf & folios* 149 *to* 273. *Part III. Title and folios* 275 *to* 330. *Blue morocco by Bedford. Small* 12*mo.* (2*l.* 2*s.* 1001)

ESQUEMELING (JOHN). Bucaniers/ of/ America :/ Or, a true/ Account/ of the/ Moſt remarkable Aſſaults/ Committed of late years upon the Coaſts of/ The Weſt=Indies,/ By the Bucaniers of Jamaica and Tortuga,/ Both English and French./ Wherein are contained more eſpecially,/ The Unparallel'd Exploits of Sir Henry Morgan, our En-/gliſh Jamaican Hero, who ſack'd Puerto Velo, burnt Panama &c./ Written originally in Dutch, by

John Efquemeling, one of the/ Bucaniers, who was
present at thofe Tragedies; and thence/ tranflated
into Spanifh, by Alonfo de Bonne-maifon, Doctor
of/ Phyfick, and Practitioner at Amfterdam./ Now
faithfully rendred into Englifh./ *London :/* Printed
for William Crooke, at the Green Dragon, with-/
out Temple-bar. 1684./ 6 *prel. leaves; viz. Title,
and To the Reader. Text,* ' Part I.' 115 *pp. With
Copper Plate engraving on page* 24 ' Elisa, y Palas.'
Portrait of ' Bartolomew Portugues' *at page* 95 ;
and Portrait of ' Rock Brasiliano,' *at page* 102.
' Part II.' 151 *pp. With a Copper Plate of* 'The
Spanifh Armada deftroyed by Captaine Morgan.' *at
page* 135. ' Part III.' 124 *pp. With a Copper Plate,*
'A Map of the Countrey and City of Panama,' *at
page* 31. ' The Table.' 11 *pp.* 4*to.* (2*l.* 2*s.* 1002)

The following is from the London Gazette of June 8, 1685, and
probably refers to this first Edition.
" Weftminfter, June 1. There have been lately Printed and Pub-
lifhed two Books, one by Will. Crook, the other by Tho. Mal-
thus, both Intitled *The History of the Bucaniers:* both which
Books contained many Falfe, Scandalous and Malitious Reflec-
tions on the Life and Actions of Sir Henry Morgan of Jamaica
Kt. The faid Sir Henry Morgan hath by Judgment had in the
Kings-Bench-Court, recovered againft the faid Libel 200*l.* Dam-
ages. And on the humble Solicitation and Requeft of William
Crook, hath been pleafed to withdraw his Action againft the faid
Crook, and accept of his Submiffion and Acknowledgement in
Print."

ESQUEMELING (John). Bucaniers/ of/ America :/
Or, a True/ Account/ of the Moft Remarkable
Affaults/ Committed of late Years upon the Coafts
of/ The Weft=Indies,/ By the Bucaniers of Jamaica and Tortuga,/ Both English and French./
Wherein are contained more efpecially,/ The unparallel'd Exploits of Sir Henry Morgan, our
Englifh/ Jamaica Hero, who fack'd Puerto Velo,
burnt Panama, &c./ Written originally in Dutch
by John Efquemeling, one of the Bucaniers,/ who
was present at thofe Tragedies, and Tranflated into
Spanifh by/ Alonfo de Bonne-mafon, M.D. &c./
The Second Edition, Corrected, and Inlarged with
two/ Additional Relations, viz. the one of Captain
Cook, and the other of/ Captain Sharp./ Now
faithfully rendered into Englifh./ *London :* Printed
for William Crooke, at the Green Dra-/gon without Temple-bar. 1684./ 6 *prel. leaves; viz. Title,*
'An Advertisement, to the Reader, concerning this
Second Edition,' 2 *pp.* ' The Tranflator to the
Reader.' 7 *pp ; 1 blank page ; Text, Part I.* 55 *pp.*

*with portraits of Bartholomew Portugues at page 46,
and of Roche Brasiliano at page 49.   Part II. 80 pp.
with portraits of Francis Lolonois at page 1. and Sir
Henry Morgan at page 32, and 3 copper plates, viz.*
The Spanish Armada, The Cruelty of Lolonois *and*
The Town of Puerto del Principe taken and sackt.
*Part III. 84 pp. containing xii Chapters instead of
ten as in the first Edition, with Map of Panama, and*
The Battle before Panama; 'The Table,' 12 *pp.*
'The Preface to the Reader.' *of the Second Volume,*
13 *pp; with the Errata on the next page ; Text of
Part IV, 212 pp ; with Map of South America show-
ing Sharp's Voyage at page 1, and* 'Description of
Hilo' *at p.* 98, *with many small copper plate maps inserted in the text ;* 'The Table of the Second Volume'
17 *pp ;* 'Catalogue of Books,' 7 *pp. Old calf.*
4*to.*   (2*l.* 2*s.* 1003)

ESQUEMELING (John.)   The History of the
  Bucaniers of America; from their First Original
  down to this Time; Written in Several Languages;
  and now collected into one Volume.   Containing
  I. The Exploits and Adventures of Le Grand,
  Lolonois, Roche Brasiliano, Bat the Portuguese,
  Sir Henry Morgan, &c.   Written in Dutch by
  Jo. Esquemeling one of the Bucaniers, and thence
  Translated into Spanish.   II. The Dangerous
  Voyage and Bold Attempts of Capt. Barth. Sharp,
  Watlin, Sawkins, Coxon, and others, in the South
  Sea.   Written by Basil Ringrose, Gent. who was
  a Companion therein, and examin'd with the
  Original Journal.   III.   A Journal of a Voyage
  into the South Sea by the Freebooters of Ame-
  rica from 1684, to 1689.   Written in French by
  the Sieur Raveneau de Lussan: never before in
  English.   IV. A Relation of a Voyage of the
  Sieur de Montaubon, Capt. of the Freebooters in
  Guinea in the Year 1695, &c.   The whole newly
  Translated into English, and Illustrated with 25
  Copper Plates.   *London :* Printed for Tho. New-
  borough at the Golden Ball in St. Paul's Church
  Yard, John Nicholson at the King's Arms in Little
  Brittain, and Benj. Tooke at the Middle Temple
  Gate, Fleetstreet.   1699.   *Title and Preface 2
  leaves ; Text to end of the Third Part 180 pp. with
  Sharp's Map of South America at p. 1. Portraits of
  Bartholomew Portugues at p. 43, Rock Brasiliano at*

p. 47, *Francis Lolonois at p.* 52; *and of Sir Henry Morgan at p.* 79. *Copper plates, Cruelty of Lolonois at p.* 66; *Sacking of Puerto del Principe at p.* 86. *Text of the Second Volume, or Part IV.* 180 *pp. with Maps at pp.* 15, 17, 21, 22, 33, 128, 133, *and* 160, *besides several smaller ones inserted in the text.* Index 6 *leaves. Title* 'A Journal of a Voyage,' *etc. by Lussan, followed by* 1 *leaf; Text* 180 *pp; Voyage of De Montauban pp.* 181 *to* 204. *Fine copy in Old Calf.* 8*vo.* (1*l.* 11*s.* 6*d.* 1004)

ESQUEMELING (John.) The History of the Bucaniers of America: etc. [*the same as in the preceding.*] The Third Edition. *London:* Printed for Tho. Newborough, etc. 1704. *The collation and list of plates the same as in the Edition of* 1699. 8*vo.* (1*l.* 5*s.* 1005)

ESQUEMELING (John). The History of the Bucaniers of America: Being an Entertaining Narrative of the Exploits, Cruelties and Sufferings of the following noted Commanders, viz. Joseph Esquemeling, Pierre le Grand, Lolonois, Roche Brasiliano, Bat the Portuguefe, Capt. Sharp, Capt. Watling, Capt. Cook, &c. &c. Together with a curious Defcription of the Manners, Cuftoms, Drefs, and Ceremonies of the Indians inhabiting near Cape Gracias a Dios. Publifhed for the Improvement and Entertainment of the British Youth of both Sexes. *Glasgow:* James Knox, MDCCLXII. 132 *pp. including title: calf.* 12*mo.* (5*s.* 6*d.* 1006)

ESQUEMELING (John). The History of the Bucaniers of America. Containing I. The Exploits and Adventures of Le Grand, Lolonois, Roche Brasiliano, Bat the Portuguefe, Sir H. Morgan, &c. II. The dangerous Voyage and bold Attempts of Capt. Sharp, Watlin, Sawkins, Coxon, and others in the South Sea. III. A Journal of a Voyage into the South Sea by the Freebooters of America, from 1684 to 1689. IV. A Relation of a Voyage of the Sieur De Montauban, Captain of the Freebooters in Guinea, in the Year 1695. Exhibiting A particular Account and Defcription of Porto Bello, Chagre, Panama, Cuba, Havanna, and moft of the Spanifh Poffeffions on the Coafts of the

Weſt-Indies, and alſo all along the Coaſts of the South Sea; with the Manner in which they have been invaded, attempted, or taken by theſe Adventurers. The Whole written in ſeveral Languages by Persons preſent at the Tranſaᶜtions. In Two Volumes. The Fifth Edition. *London*: T. Evans, m.dcc.lxxi. *2 Volumes.* Vol. I. *Title and Preface 2 leaves; Text 360 pp.* Vol. II. *Title and 360 pp.* 'Index.' *12 pp. Fine copy in old Tree calf. 12mo.* (12s. 1007)

ESSAY (An) concerning Slavery, and the Danger Jamaica Is expos'd to from the Too great Number of Slaves, and the Too little Care that is taken to manage Them. And a Proposal to prevent the further Importation of Negroes into that Iſland. *London:* Charles Corbett, [1745?] *Title and Introduction 6 leaves; Text 67 pp. Half morocco. 8vo.* (4s. 6d. 1008)

ESSAY (An) in Vindication of the Continental Colonies of America, from a Cenſure of Mr Adam Smith, in his Theory of Moral Sentiments. With ſome Reflections on Slavery in general. By an American. *London:* Printed for the Author. mdcclxiv. *Half-title, viii and 46 pp. Half mor. 8vo.* (4s. 6d. 1009)

ESSAY (An) on the Constitutional Power of Great-Britain over the Colonies in America; with the Resolves of the Committee for the Province of Pennsylvania, and their Instructions To their Representatives in Assembly. *Philadelphia :* Printed and Sold, by William and Thomas Bradford, at the London Coffee-House. m.dcc.lxxiv. *vii and 127 pp.* 'Errata' *1 page. Fine copy; Half mor. 8vo.* (7s. 6d. 1010)

ESSAY (An) on the Legality of Impressing Seamen. *London:* T. Cadell, mdcclxxvii. *Title and 126 pp. 8vo.* (4s. 6d. 1011)

ESSAY (An) on the Merchandise of Slaves and Souls of Men; Revelations XVIII. 13. With an Application Thereof to the Church of Rome. By a Gentleman. Printed at Boston in New England : and Reprinted at *London*, for Joseph Downing, 1732. *6 prel. pp. Text 35 pp. (27 for 35) half mor. 8vo.* (4s. 6d. 1012)

ESSAY (An) On the Present State Of the Province
of Nova-Scotia, With fome Strictures on the Meafures purfued by Government from its firft Settlement by the Englifh in the Year 1749. [*Halifax*
1774] 24 *pp. Signed* ' A Member of Assembly.'
Half mor. 8vo. (5s. 1013)

ESSAY (An) on the Trade of the Northern Colonies
of Great Britain in North America. Printed at
Philadelphia. *London:* Reprinted for T. Becket
and P. A. De Hondt, MDCCLXIV. 2 *prelim. leaves
and* 38 *pp. Half mor. 8vo.* (5s. 6d. 1014)

ESTACIO DO AMARAL (Melchior). ꝭ Tratado, Das 30/ Batalhas, e Svcessos do/ Galeão
Sanctiago com os Olandefes na Ilha de/ Sancta
Elena. E da Náo Chagas com os Ynglefes/ antre
as Ilhas dos Açores : Ambas Capitainas da/ car-
reira da India. E da caufa, & defaftres, por-/que
em vinte annos fe perderão trinta &/ oito naos
della : com ontras/ coufas curiofas./ Efcripto por
Melchior Eftacio do Amaral./ Dirigido ao Excellentiffimo Principe Dom/ Theodofio Duque de Bragança./ ☞ Impreffo em *Lisboa:* Com licença
da Sancta Inqui-⌐⌐/fição : Por Antonio Aluarez.
Anno 1604./ *Title having on the reverse the Li-
cences; Dedication* ' A Dono Theodosio' 1 *page;*
' *Errata*' 1 *page; Text in* 65 *folioed leaves; followed
by a leaf with* 4 *woodcuts upon it. At folio* 23 *is a
copper plate map of the Island of St. Helena,* 14 *by*
10 *inches.* 4to. (15l. 15s. 1015)

ESTAING (Count d'). Autograph Letter in French
to Paul Jones, dated at Paris 27 May, 1785. *An
interesting Specimen.* 2 *pp.* 4to. (10s. 6d. 1016)

ESTRADA (Pedro de). Relacion/ Svmaria/ del
Anto parti-/cvlar de Fee, qve el/ Tribvnal del
Santo Officio de la/ Inquificion de los Reynos, y
Prouincias de la Nueua Efpaña,/ celebrò en la
muy noble, y muy leal Ciudad de Mexico a los/
diez y feis dias del mes de Abril, del año de mil y
feif-/cientos y quarenta y feis./ Siendo Inqvisidores
Apostolicos en el, los/ muy Illuftres Señores Doc-
tores Domingo Velez de Affas, y Argos, Don/
Francifco de Eftrada y, Efcouedo, Don Iuan Saenz
de Mañozca, y/ Licenciado Don Bernabe de la
Higuera, y Amarilla, y/ Fifcal el Señor Don An-

tonio de/ Gauiola./ Escribela/ El Doctor Don
Pedro de Estrada, y Escovedo,/ Racionero de la
Santa Iglefia Cathedral de Mexico, Abogado de/
prefos, y del Real Fifco del mefmo Tribunal./ Of-
recela/ Al Illvstrissimo, y Reverendissimo Señor,/
Don Iuan de Mañozca Arçobifpo de Mexico del
Confejo de fu Majef-/tad en el de la Santa, y Ge-
neral Inquificion, y Vifitador General/ de Tribunal
del Santo Officio de efta Nueua/ Efpaña./ Impreffo
en *Mexico*, Por Francifco Robledo, Impreffor del
Se-/creto del Santo 'Officio, Año de 1646./ *Title;*
Text, 26 folioed leaves. 4to.   (*2l. 2s.* 1017)

EVANS (JOHN). Memoirs of the Life and Writings
of the Rev. William Richards, LL.D. who Died
at Lynn, September 13, 1819, in the Sixty-ninth
year of his Age. With some Account of the Rev.
Roger Williams, Founder of the State of Rhode
Island, as well as First Assertor of complete Religious Liberty in the United States of America.
By John Evans, A.M. *Chiswick:* Charles Whittingham, 1819. *xxxii and 396 pp. With Portrait of*
William Richards; uncut, boards. 12mo. (5s. 1018)

EVANS (LEWIS). Geographical, Historical, Political, Philofophical and Mechanical Essays. The
First, Containing an Analysis Of a General Map of
the Middle British Colonies in America; And of
the Country of the Confederate Indians: A Description of the Face of the Country ; The Boundaries of the Confederates ; And the Maritime and
Inland Navigations of the feveral Rivers and Lakes
contained therein. By Lewis Evans. *Philadelphia:*
Printed by B. Franklin, and D. Hall. MDCCLV.
And fold by R. and J. Dodsley, in Pall-Mall, London. *iv and 32 pp. Map 27½ by 20½ inches. Half*
mor. 4to.   (*1l. 11s. 6d.* 1019)

EVANS (LEWIS). *The Same*. The Second Edition.
Philadelphia Printed by B. Franklin, and D. Hall.
MDCCLV. *4to.*   (*1l. 1s.* 1019*)

EVANS (LEWIS). Geographical, Hiftorical, Political, Philofophical and Mechanical Essays. The
First, Containing an Analysis Of a General Map
of the Middle British Colonies in America; And
of the Country of the Confederate Indians: A Description of the Face of the Country ; The Boun-

daries of the Confederates; And the Maritime and
Inland Navigations of the several Rivers and Lakes
contained therein. By Lewis Evans. The Second
Edition. *Philadelphia :* Printed by B. Franklin,
and D. Hall. MDCCLV. And sold by R. and J.
Dodsley, in Pall-Mall, London. *iv and 32 pp.
With the large map 27½ by 20½ inches. colored. Large
paper, half mor. Folio.* (2*l.* 12*s.* 6*d.* 1020)

This is a presentation copy from the Author to Dodsley the Publisher. On the back of the Map is the following Letter, in the
autograph of Mr. Evans. " To Mr. R. Dodsley, Bookseller in
Pall Mall, London. Sir, I am uncertain whether I shall be able
to transmit to New York, to overtake a ship to Hull, a Parcel of
these Maps, intended for you. Your most humble Servt.
    Philadelphia, July 30, 1755.   Lewis Evans.
" This comes under of favour of the Revᵈ. Mr. Phᵖ. Frances."

EVANS (LEWIS). Geographical, Historical, Political, Philosophical and Mechanical Essays. Number II. Containing, A Letter Representing, the Im-
propriety of sending Forces to Virginia : The Importance of taking Fort Frontenac; And that the
Preservation of Oswego was owing to General
Shirley's Proceeding thither. And containing Objections to those parts of Evans's General Map
and Analysis which relate to the French Title to
the Country, on the North-West Side of St. Laurence River, between Fort Frontenac and Montreal, &c. Published in the New-York Mercury,
No. 178, Jan. 5, 1756. With an Answer, To so
much thereof as concerns the Public ; And the several Articles set in a just Light. By Lewis Evans.
Philadelphia : Printed for the Author; and Sold
by him in Arch-Street : And at New-York by G.
Noel, Bookseller near Counts's Market. MDCCLVI.
38 *pp.* ' Postscript.' *pp.* 39-42. *Advertisement of
the Map of the Middle British Colonies* 1 *page.*
4*to.*   (1*l.* 11*s.* 6*d.* 1021)

EVANS (LEWIS). Geographical, Historical, Political, Philosophical and Mechanical Essays. Number II. Containing a Letter, Representing the Im-
propriety of sending Forces to Virginia : The Importance of taking Frontenac; And that the Preservation of Oswego was owing to General Shirley's proceeding thither. Containing Objections to
those Parts of Evans's General Map and Analysis,
which relate to the French Title to the Country, on
the North-West Side of St. Laurence River, be-

tween Fort Frontenac and Montreal, &c. Publifhed in the New-York Mercury, N° 178, Jan. 5,
1756. With an Answer To fo much thereof as concerns the Public: And the feveral Articles fet in a
juft Light: By Lewis Evans. *London:* R. and J.
Dodsley. MDCCLVI. *35 pp. 4to.* (1*l.* 5*s.* 1022)

EXAMINATION (An) of the British Doctrine
which subjects to Capture a Neutral Trade not
open in Time of Peace. The Second Edition. Containing A Letter from the Minister Plenipotentiary
of the United States, to Lord Mulgrave, late Secretary of State for Foreign Affairs. America,
Printed. *London,* reprinted for J. Johnson, 1806.
Title, and 200 pp.   (4*s.* 6*d.* 1023)

EXAMINATION (An) of the Rights of the Colonies, upon Principles of Law. By a Gentleman
at the Bar. *London:* R. Dymott, and J. Almon,
MDCCLXVI. *Title, and Text pp. 5-42. Half mor.*
8vo.   (5*s.* 6*d.* 1024)

EXPLANATION for the New Map of Nova Scotia
and Cape Britain, With the Adjacent Parts of New
England and Canada. *London:* T. Jefferys, MDCCLV.
22 pp. Errata on the reverse of Title 27 lines. Half
mor. 4to.   (18*s.* 1025)

EXTRACT, from the Journal of the proceedings, of
the honorable the American Continental Congrefs,
held at Philadelphia, September fifth 1774. Being
that part of their Addrefs to the Inhabitants of the
Province of Quebec, which enumerates, the glorious Rights of Englifhmen, and Englifh fubjeéts:
Among which are included, the Liberty of the
Press. The Committee, to whom the Addrefs to
the Inhabitants of Quebec was recommitted; reported a draught, which was read, and being debated by Paragraphs and amended, was approved,
and is as follows. To the Inhabitants of the Province of Quebec. Friends and Fellow-Subjeéts, *etc.*
6 pp ; followed by ' Additions to Plain Truth ; addressed to the Inhabitants of America,' *etc. Phila-*
delphia : Printed and Sold by R. Bell, in Third-
Street. MDCCLXXVI. *Title and pp. 97-136. Uncut.*
8vo.   (4*s.* 6*d.* 1026)

EXTRACT from the Minutes of Council, Containing
His Majefty's late regulations relating to the wafte

lands of the Crown, with His Excellency, the Governor General's order of reference refpecting the
fame, to a Committee of the whole Council, of the
Province of Lower-Canada, the faid Committee's
report thereon, and His Excellency's fpeech in reply. *Quebec:* Printed at the New-Printing Office.
Palace Street, 1798. *Title; Introduction iv pp.
Signed* ' William Berczy.' *Text* 45 *pp.* Extract of
the Minutes of Council, of the 20th September,
1798. On the Waste Lands of the Crown, Being a
Continuation, of the Extract, of the 11th of June
laft. *Quebec:* Printed at the New Printing-office,
Palace Street, 1798. *Title and pp.* 47-133. ' Errata' 1 *page. Both parts bound in one Volume, half
mor.* 8vo.   (10s. 6d.   1027)

EXTRACT of a Letter to a Gentleman in Maryland ;
Wherein is demonftrated the extreme wickednefs
of tolerating the Slave Trade, in order to favour
the illegalities of our Colonies, where the Two Firft
Foundations of Englifh Law, (Two Witneffes of
God) are supplanted by oppofite (and of courfe illegal) ordinances, which occafions a Civil Death of
the Englifh Conftitution, fo that thefe Two Witneffes may be faid to lie dead in all the Weft India
Iflands ! *London:* James Phillips, M.DCC.XCIII. 14
pp. Signed ' Granville Sharp.' *half morocco.*
12mo.   (4s. 6d.   1028)

EXTRACTS from the Records of the late Provincial
Congress, Held at Cambridge in the Months of
October, November and December, A.D. 1774.
Also Extracts from the Minutes of the Proceed-
ings of the Congress, Held at Cambridge, February
A.D. 1775. Publifhed by their Order. *Boston:*
Printed by Edes and Gill, in Queen-Street. M,DCC,
LXXV. 24 *pp. half mor.* 8vo.   (7s. 6d.   1029)

EXTRACTS from the Votes and Proceedings of the
American Continental Congress, held at Philadel-
phia, on the fifth of September, 1774. Containing,
The Bill of Rights, a Lift of Grievances, Occafional
Refolves, the Affociation, an Addrefs to the People
of Great-Britain, and a Memorial to the Inhabit-
ants of the Britifh American Colonies. Published
by Order of the Congress. Philadelphia Printed.
London: Reprinted for J. Almon, MDCCLXXIV.
Half-title, Title, and 82 *pp.* 8vo.   (4s. 6d.   1030)

EXTRACTS from the Votes and Proceedings Of the American Continental Congress, Held at Philadelphia on the 5th of September, 1774. Containing The Bill of Rights, a List of Grievances, Occasional Resolves, the Association, an Address to the People of Great-Britain, and a Memorial to the Inhabitants of the British American Colonies. Published by Order of the Congress. Philadelphia, Printed: *Boston*, Re-printed: And sold by John Boyle in Marlborough - Street, and Mills and Hicks in School-Street, and Cox and Berry in King Street. 1774. 43 *pp. Half mor. 8vo.* (5s. 6d. 1031)

I have another edition evidently from the same form as the above with the words ' and Cox and Berry in King Street,' omitted in the title, the double line at the top of p. 3 exchanged for an ornamental head-piece, and the addition of a Letter of the Congress ' To the Inhabitants of the Province of Quebec,' extending from p. 44 to 52. *Half mor. 8vo.* (7s. 6d.)

EXTRACT from the Votes of the House of Assembly of the Province of Nova-Scotia. Containing, An Address, Petition and Memorial, To the King's Most Excellent Majesty, The Lords Spiritual and Temporal and The Commons of Great-Britain, In Parliament, assembled. *Boston:* Printed and Sold at Draper's Printing Office, in Newbury Street. MDDCCLXXV. [1775]. 13 *pp. 8vo.* (7s. 6d. 1032)

EXTRACT of a Letter from the House of Representatives of the Massachusetts-Bay, to their Agent Dennys De Berdt, Esq; with some Remarks. *London:* J. and W. Oliver, MDCCLXX. 28 *pp. Half mor. 8vo.* (7s. 6d. 1033)

EYQUEM DU MARTINEAU (MATHURIN). Le/ Pilote/ de l'onde vive,/ ou/ le secret du Flux/ et Reflux de la Mer ;/ Contenant xxj Mouvemens ;/ et du Point Fixe./ D'un Voyage abregé des Indies, & de la/ Quadrature du Cercle, composez sur/ les Principes de la Nature; nouvelle-/ment découverts, & mis en lumiere./ Par Mathvrin Eyqvem,/ S^r, dv Martineav,/ Bourdelois./ Philosophie Naturelle./ A *Paris,* Chez Jean Dhoury, sur le Quay des Augustins,/ à l'Image Saint Jean./ Et chez l'Autheur, ruë neuve Saint Mederic, à l'Enseigne/ de la Ville de Calais./ M.DC.LXXVIII./ Avec Privilege dv Roy./ 8 *prel. leaves and* 221 *pp. Half calf.* 16mo. (10s. 6d. 1034)

ABRICIUS: Or, Letters to the People of Great Britain: on The Abſurdity and Miſchiefs of Defenſive Operations only in the American War; and on The Cauſes of the Failure in the Southern Operations. *London*: G. Wilkie, MDCCLXXXII. *Half-title, title, and* 111 *pp. Half mor. 8vo.* (5s. 6d. 1036)

FABRY (JOSEPH ANTONIO). Compendiosa Demostracion de los Creci̇dos adelantamientos que pudiera lograr la Real hacienda de Su Magestad mediante la rebaja evel precio del Azogue, que se conſume para el laborio de las Minas de eſte Reyno, ó del aumento tan conſiderable, que ſe avia de experimentar en el producto annual de fus Reales Rentas, en beneficio no menos grande, que univerſal de eſta Mineria, de ambos Comercios, y por conſiguiente de todo el comun de la Republica. Con una previa impugnacion a las Reflexiones del Contador D. Joſeph de Villa-Señor y Sanchez, ſobre el miſmo aſſumpto. Añadese un breve modo de reducir, ligar, y alear el Oro, y Plata à la ley de 22. quilates, ó de 11. dineros, de averiguar el valor de cada uno de eſtos metales, y los reſpectivos derechos, que deben pagar à S. M. en paſta, ó en eſpecies de moneda, de qualeſquiera cantidades propueſtas, y leyes averiguables por el enſaye, ſegun la diviſion de ſus respectivos Dinerales, muy comodo para el uſſo de las Reales Caſas de moneda, y Caxas de quintos, de los Mineros, Plateros, y de todos los que comercian en eſtos metales. Por Don Joseph Antonio Fabry, Guarda de Vista en las Fundiciones de S. M. en eſta su Real Caſa de Moneda, y Apoderado General para los negocios, y pretenſiones de Mineria de todos los principales

T

Reales de Minas de efte Reyno. Quien la confagra
à la R. M. de nueftro Catholico Monarcha el Señor
Don Philippo V. (que Dios guarde) Rey de Ef-
paña, y de las Indias. Impreffa en *Mexico* con
Licencia del Superior Gobierno Por la Viuda de
D. Jofeph Bernardo de Hogal. Año de 1743.
Title & 38 prelim. leaves; and Text 178 pp. *Vellum.*
4to.   (1*l.* 1*s.* 1037)

FACTION Detected, by the Evidence of Facts.
Containing An Impartial View of Parties at Home,
and Affairs Abroad. The Fourth Edition. *London* :
J. Roberts, M.DCC.XLIII. *Half-title, title, and pp.* 5-
175. *8vo.*   (4*s.* 6*d.* 1038)

FAGE (ROBERT). Cosmography / Or, / A Description /
of the / Whole World, / Reprefented (by a more exact and / certain Difcovery) in the Excellencies / of
its Situation, Commodities, / Inhabitants, and History : / Of / Their Particular and Diftinct / Governments, Religions, Arms, / and Degrees of Honour
ufed / amongft Them. / Enlarged with very many
and rare Additions. / Very delightful to be read
in fo fmall a Volum. / By Robert Fage Efquire. /
London, Printed by S. Griffin for John Overton
at / the White-Horfe in Little Brittain, next door /
to Little St. Bartholomews-Gate. 1667. / 3 *prel.*
leaves; *viz. Title and ' To the Reader.' Text pp.* 3-
166. *Calf. 8vo.*   (15*s.* 1039)
A great part of this book pertains to America, especially from
page 112 to 166.

FAIR (A) Representation of His Majefty's Right to
Nova-Scotia or Acadie. Briefly ftated from the
Memorials of the English Commiffaries ; with an
Answer to the Objections contained In the French
Memorials, and In a Treatise, Entitled, Difcuffion
Sommaire fur les anciennes Limites de l'Acadie.
London, Printed : and *Dublin :* Re-printed by
Richard James, M,DCCLVI. *Title and pp.* 3 *to* 48.
8vo.   (7*s.* 6*d.* 1040)

FAIRMAN (W. BLENNERHASSET). A Series of
Letters with Editorial Remarks on the Existing
Differences between England and America. Inscribed to the Earl of Darnley. By Captain Fairman, Aid-de-Camp and Military Secretary to the
late Governor and Commander in chief of Curacao,

and its Dependencies, &c. &c. &c. *London*: A. J. Valpy, 1813. *xi and* 68 *pp.* 8*vo.* (3*s.* 6*d.* 1041)

FALCONER (Richard). The Voyages, Dangerous Adventures And imminent Escapes of Captain Richard Falconer: Containing The Laws, Cuſtoms, and Manners of the Indians in America; his Shipwrecks; his Marrying an Indian Wife; his narrow Eſcape from the Iſland of Dominico, &c. Intermix'd with The Voyages and Adventures of Thomas Randal, of Cork, Pilot; with his Shipwreck in the Baltick, being the only Man that eſcap'd: His being taken by the Indians of Virginia, &c. Written by Himſelf, now alive. *London*, W. Chetwood, 1720. *Title, and Preface,* 2 *leaves; Text in* 136, *and* 180 *pp. With copper-plate frontispiece. Old calf.* 8*vo.* (10*s.* 6*d.* 1042)

FALCONER (Richard). The Voyages, dangerous Adventures, and imminent Escapes, of Capt. Richard Falconer. Containing The Laws, Cuſtoms, and Manners of the Indians in America; his Shipwrecks; his marrying an Indian Wife; his remarkable Eſcape from the Iſland of Dominico, &c. Intermixed with The Voyages and Adventures of Thomas Randal, of Cork, Pilot; with his Shipwreck in the Baltick, being the only Man that escaped; his being taken by the Indians of Virginia, &c. and an Account of his Death. The Fifth Edition Correƈted. To which is added, A Great Deliverance at Sea, by W. Johnſon, D.D. Chaplain to his Majeſty. *London*: G. Keith 1764. 222 *pp. Index* 4 *pp.* ' Narrative of a Great Deliverance at Sea.' *etc. vi and* 36 *pp. With a Copper Plate frontispiece. Calf.* 12*mo.* (7*s.* 6*d.* 1043)

FALCONER (Richard). The Voyages, dangerous Adventures, and imminent Escapes, of Capt. Richard Falconer, *etc.* The Sixth Edition, Correƈted, *etc. London*: G. Keith, 1769. 3 *prel. leaves; and* 276 *pp. Index.* 5 *pp.* ' Narrative of a Great Deliverance at Sea.' *etc. viii and* 46 *pp. Without the frontispiece. Calf.* 12*mo.* (7*s.* 6*d.* 1044)

FALCONER (Thomas). The Oregon Question; or, a Statement of the British Claims to the Oregon Territory, in Opposition to the Pretensions of the Government of The United States of America.

By Thomas Falconer, Esq., Barrister at Law of Lincoln's Inn, Member of the Royal Geographical Society, etc. *London:* Samuel Clarke, 1845. 46 *pp. Index* 1 *page.* 8vo. (2s. 6d. 1045)

FALCONER (THOMAS). The Oregon Question; *etc.* Second Edition. By Thomas Falconer, Esq. *etc. London:* Samuel Clarke, 1845. 50 *pp. Postscript* 4 *pp.* 8vo. (2s. 6d. 1046)

FALKNER (THOMAS). A Description of Patagonia, and the Adjoining Parts of South America : Containing an Account of the Soil, Produce, Animals, Vales, Mountains, Rivers, Lakes, &c. of thofe Countries ; the Religion, Government, Policy, Cuftoms, Drefs, Arms, and Language of the Indian Inhabitants ; and some Particulars relating to Falkland's Islands. By Thomas Falkner, Who refided near Forty Years in thofe Parts. Illustrated with A New Map of the Southern Parts of America, Engraved by Mr. Kitchin, Hydrographer to His Majesty. *Hereford:* C. Pugh. M.DCC.LXXIV. *Title and Advertisement* 2 *leaves; Contents, iv pp. Text* 144 *pp. With the Map in* 2 *Sheets.* 4to. (8s. 6d. 1047)

FALSE ALARM (THE) [By Dr. Samuel Johnson]. *London:* T. Cadell, MDCCLXX. 53 *pp. half mor.* 8vo. (3s. 6d. 1048)

FANCOURT (CHARLES ST. JOHN). The History of Yucatan from its Discovery to the Close of the Seventeenth Century. By Charles St. John Fancourt, Esq., recently H. M. Superintendent of the British Settlements in the Bay of Honduras. With a Map. *London:* John Murray, 1854. *xvi and* 340 *pp. With a Map of Yucatan. Cloth. uncut.* 8vo. (7s. 6d. 1049)

FARIA Y SOUSA (MANUEL DE). The Portugues Afia :/ Or, the/ History/ of the/ Difcovery and Conqueft/ of India/ by the/ Portugues ;/ Containing/ All their Difcoveries from the Coaft of/ Africk, to the fartheft Parts of China and/ Japan ; all their Battels by Sea and Land,/ Sieges and other Memorable Actions ; a/ Defcription of thofe Countries, and many/ Particulars of the Religion, Government/ and Cuftoms of the natives, &c./ In Three Tomes./ Written in Spanifh by Manuel de Faria y Soufa,/ of the Order of Chrift./ Tranflated into

Englifh by Cap. John Stevens./ *London*, Printed for *C. Brome*, at the Sign of/ the Gun, at the Weft-End of St. Paul's. 1695./ 3 *Volumes.* ' Tome the Firft.' 16 *prel. leaves and* 448 *pp.* ' Tome the Second.' 12 *prel. leaves and* 526 *pp.* ' Tome the Third.' 11 *prel. leaves and* 440 *pp. Fine copy in old calf.* 8vo.   (1*l.* 11*s.* 6*d.*   1050)

FARIBAULT (G. B.) Catalogue d'Ouvrages sur l'Histoire de l'Amérique, et en particulier sur celle du Canada, de la Louisiane, de l'Acadie, et autres lieux, Ci-devant connus sous le nom de Nouvelle-France; avec des Notes Bibliographiques, Critiques, et Littéraires. En Trois Parties. Rédigé par G. B. Faribault, Avocat. *Québec*: Des Presses de W. Cowan, No. 9. Rue de la Fabrique. 1837. 2 *prel. leaves and* 207 *pp: Calf.* 8vo.   (10*s.* 6*d.*   1051)

FARMER (The) Refuted: Or, A more impartial and comprehenfive View of the Dispute between Great-Britain and the Colonies, intended as a Further Vindication of the Congress : In Answer to a Letter from *A. W.* Farmer, intitled A View of the Controversy between Great-Britain and her Colonies : Including A Mode of determining the prefent Disputes finally and effectually, &c. *New-York*: Printed by James Rivington. 1775. *iv and* 78 *pp. Half mor.* 8vo.   (7*s.* 6*d.*   1052)

FARNHAM (Thomas J.) Travels in the Great Western Prairies, the Anahuac and Rocky Mountains, and in the Oregon Territory. By Thomas J. Farnham. In Two Volumes. *London*: Richard Bentley, 1843. 2 *Volumes.* Vol. I. *xxiii and* 297 *pp.* Vol. II. *viii and* 315 *pp. Boards, uncut.* 12mo.   (7*s.* 6*d.*   1053)

FARTHER (A) Examination and Explanation of the South-Sea Company's Scheme. Shewing, That it is not the Intereft of the South-Sea Company to offer the Annuitants fuch Terms as may induce them to come in; And that the Propofal of the Bank is more likely to be accepted by the Annuitants, and the Publick not disappointed. *London*: Printed, and Sold by J. Roberts, 1720. 39 *pp. half mor.* 8vo.   (4*s.* 6*d.*   1054)

FEARON (Henry Bradshaw). Sketches of America. A Narrative of a Journey of Five Thousand Miles through the Eastern and Western States of America; contained in eight reports addressed to the Thirty-nine English Families by whom the Author was deputed, in June 1817, to ascertain whether any, and what part of the United States would be suitable for their Residence. With remarks on Mr. Birkbeck's " Notes" and " Letters." By Henry Bradshaw Fearon. Second Edition. *London :* Longman, 1818. *Title, v-xi and 454 pp. Calf. 8vo.* (7s. 6d. 1055)

FEATHERSTONAUGH (William C.). 'Τα 'Αεθλααγγλαμερίκανα ἄρα δὴ Προγυμνας'ματα τῆς Φραγκίης νέης Πελαςγίκης.Μονόβιβλος. Gesta Anglo-Americana scilicet et Progymnasmata Novæ Franciæ Pelasgicæ. Liber Singularis. Μέτέγραφεν ἐκ περγαμήνων "Ιλερμος Π. ὁ Βραχὺς· 'Ελι θοκάφησεν ὁ Φεθερστονιος Τῇ 'Ειονίη πολει· Τῳδ "Ετει 'Αών' ἀπὸ θεογόνιας· 6 *prel. and* 114 *pp. Lithographed. 8vo.* (4s. 6d. 1056)

FEDERALIST : (The) a Collection of Essays, written in Favour of the New Constitution, as agreed upon by the Federal Convention, September 17, 1787. In Two Volumes. *New-York :* Printed and Sold by J. and A. M'Lean, No. 41, Hanover-Square. M,DCC,LXXXVIII. 2 *Volumes, in* 1. Vol. I. *vi and* 227 *pp.* Vol. II. *vi and* 384 *pp. Old calf.* 12*mo.* (7s. 6d. 1057)

FEDERALIST : (The) *etc. Another Copy,* on large and thick paper, bound in calf extra full gilt backs and sides. 12*mo.* (1l. 1s. 1058)

FEDERALIST, (The) on the New Constitution, written in the Year 1788, by Mr. Hamilton, Mr. Madison, and Mr. Jay, with an Appendix, containing the Letters of Pacificus and Helvidius, on the Proclamation of Neutrality of 1793; Also, the Original Articles of Confederation, and the Constitution of the United States, with the Amendments made thereto. A New Edition. The Numbers Written by Mr. Madison corrected by Himself.

City of Washington: Jacob Gideon, Jun. 1818.
671 *pp. Calf. 8vo.* (7s. 6d. 1059)

FIELD (JAMES). Manuscript Memorial of Ensign
James Field addressed to Sir George Yonge, Secretary at War, dated at 21 Oxenden Street, London,
Oct. 6, 1787, praying to be reinstated in full pay.
1 *page, folio.* (5s. 1060)

<small>The Memorialist's father " was deprived of his benefice as a Min-
ister, and obliged to retire from the State of Virginia, with a
large family, without any means of support, his whole property
being confiscated." He was then appointed chaplain by Sir Henry
Clinton in Lt. Col. De Lancy's corps; and his son, the Memorialist, was appointed Ensign in the Provincial Regiment of Orange
Rangers.</small>

FINLEY (SAMUEL). Autograph Letter to Ezra
Stiles, of Newport, Rhode Island, dated at Nassau
Hall, Dec. 4, 1765. 1 *page, a fine specimen.*
4to. (7s. 6d. 1061)

<small>Mr. Finley was President of New Jersey College, at Princeton, and
was the successor of Edwards.</small>

FISH (JOSEPH). The Church of Christ a firm and
durable Houſe. Shown in a Number of Sermons
On Matth. XVI. 18. Upon this rock I will build
my Church, and the gates of hell ſhall not prevail
againſt it. The Subſtance of which Was delivered
At Stonington, Anno Domini, 1765. By Joſeph
Fiſh, A.M. And Pastor of a Church there. *New-
London:* Printed and ſold by Timothy Green, 1767.
viii pp. Errata 1 *page, and Text* 196 *pp. Unbound.*
8vo. (7s. 6d. 1062)

FISH (JOSEPH). The Examiner Examined. Re-
marks On a Piece wrote by Mr. Iſaac Backus, of
Middleborough; printed in 1768. (Called, " An
Examination of Nine Sermons from Matth. 16. 18.
" publiſhed laſt Year, by Mr. Joseph Fish, of Stonington.") Wherein Thoſe Sermons are vindicated,
from the Exceptions taken againſt them by Mr.
Backus - - - Many of his Errors confuted, and his
Miſtakes correcked. By Joſeph Fiſh, A.M. Pastor
of a Church in Stonington, And Author of ſaid
Sermons. *New-London:* Printed and Sold by
Timothy Green, M.DCC.LXXI. 128 *pp. Unbound.*
8vo. (7s. 6d. 1063)

FLEEMING'S Register for New-England and Nova-
Scotia. With All the British Lists; And An Almanack for 1772, Being Leap year. Calculated for

the Meridian of Boston. *Boston :* Printed by John
Fleeming, and to be fold at his Shop in King-Street,
oppofite the South-Door of the Town-House [1772].
97 *for* 96 *pp.* 12*mo.*   (4s. 6d. 1064)

FLEET (T. *and* J.) A Pocket Almanack For the
Year of our Lord 1786. Being the Second after
Leap Year, and the Tenth of American Independ-
ence. Calculated for the Ufe of the Commonwealth
of Maffachufetts, in Latitude 42 deg. 25 min. North.
Longitude 71 deg. 4 min. Weft from the Royal
Obfervatory at Greenwich. *Boston :* Printed and
Sold by T. & J. Fleet, at the Bible and Heart in
Cornhill. [1786] 24 *pp.* ' The Massachusetts Re-
gister, [Printed and fold by T. & J. Fleet.]
[1786.]' 115 *pp.* 12*mo.*   (3s. 6d. 1065

FLEET'S Pocket Almanack For the Year of our
Lord 1792. Being Bissextile or Leap-Year, and
Sixteenth of American Independence. Calculated
chiefly for the Ufe of The Commonwealth of Massachusets, Boston, the Metropolis, being In Latitude 42 deg. 25 min. North. Longitude 71 deg.
4 min. Weft from the Royal Obfervatory at Greenwich. To which is annexed, the Maffachufetts
Regifter, &c. *Boston :* Printed and Sold by T. &
J. Fleet, at the Bible and Heart in Cornhill.
[1792.] 24 *pp.* ' Register for 1792.' 156 *pp.*
24*mo.*   (2s. 6d. 1066)

FLEET'S Pocket Almanack For the Year of our
Lord 1793. Being the First after Leap-Year, and
Sventeenth of American Independence Calculated
chiefly for the Use of The Commonwealth of Massachusetts, Boston, the Metropolis, being In Latitude 42 deg. 25 min. North Longitude 71 deg.
4 min. Weft from the Royal Observatory at Greenwich. To which is annexed, the Maffachufetts
Regifter, &c. *Boston :* Printed and Sold by T. &
J. Fleet, at the Bible and Heart in Cornhill.
[1793.] 20 *pp.* ' Register for 1793.' 144 *pp.*
24*mo.*   (2s. 6d. 1067)

FLEETS' Register, and Pocket Almanack For the
Year of our Lord 1800. Being the Fourth Year
fince the laft Leap Year, and the Twenty-fourth of
American Independence, which began July 4th,

1776. Calculated chiefly for the Ufe of the Commonwealth of Massachusetts, Boston, the Metropolis, being In Latitude 42 deg. 23 min. North, and 70 deg. 58,53. Weft Long. 348 Miles N.E. of Philadelphia. *Boston:* Printed and Sold by J. & T. Fleet, at the Bible and Heart in Cornhill. [1800] 20 *pp.* 'Register.' 172. *pp.* 24*mo.* (2*s.* 6*d.* 1068)

FLEETWOOD (WILLIAM). A Sermon Preached before the Society for the Propagation of the Gospel in Foreign Parts, At the Parifh-Church of St. Mary-le-Bow, On Friday the 16th of February, 17¹⁰/₁₁. Being the Day of their Anniverfary Meeting. By the Right Reverend Father in God, William Lord Bifhop of St. Afaph. *London,* J. Downing, MDCCXI. 32 *pp. Half mor.* 8*vo.* (3*s.* 6*d.* 1069)

FLETCHER (J.) American Patriotism Farther confronted with Reason, Scripture, and the Constitution: Being Observations on the Dangerous Politicks Taught by the Rev. Mr. Evans, M.A. And the Rev. Dr. Price. With a Scriptural Plea For the Revolted Colonies. By J. Fletcher, Vicar of Madeley, Salop. *Shrewsbury:* J. Eddowes: MDCCLXXVI. *viii and* 130 *pp. Half morocco.* 12*mo.* (5*s.* 6*d.* 1070)

FLINN (ANDREW). A Sermon occasioned by the Death of the Honble. Judge Wilds, delivered by desire of the Gentlemen of the Bar of Charleston, in the First Presbyterian Church in this City, On the 1st day of April, 1810. By the Rev. Andrew Flinn, A.M. Published by Particular Request. *Charleston:* Printed and Sold by J. Hoff, 1810. 23 *pp.* 8*vo.* (2*s.* 6*d.* 1071)

FLINT (TIMOTHY). A Condensed Geography and History of the Western States, or the Mississippi Valley. By Timothy Flint, Author of "Recolections of the last Ten Years in the Mississippi Valley." In Two Volumes. *Cincinnati:* E. H. Flint. 1828. 2 *Volumes.* Volume I. 592. *pp.* Volume II. 520 *pp. uncut.* 8*vo.* (16*s.* 1072)

FLORIDA. Verscheyde Scheeps-togten Na Florida, Door Pontius, Ribald, Laudonniere, Gourgues En Andere: Gedaan in het Jaar 1562. en vervolgens. Waar in veele zeldfame ontmoetingen zijn

voor-gevallen, van fware Nederlagen, Wreed-
heeden, Hongers-noo-den, Wraak-oeffeningen,
onderlinge Verdeeld-heeden, Muyteryen en won-
derbaarlijke Ont-koomingen, van eenige gevlugte
Franffen, uyt de handen der Spanjaards. Als
mede een nette en naauw-keurige Aanteekening,
van de geleegenheyd van dit Landfchap, de Gods-
dienft, Zeden, Gewoontens, Levens-manier, Oor-
logen, Dieren, Vogelen, Vrugten, Veld-gewaffen
en andere by fonderheeden. Door de Reyfigers
felfs opgeteekend, en door haar aan fijn Koning-
lijke Majefteyt van Vrankrijk, Karel de IX, per-
foonelijk verflag gedaan, en nu uyt die Taal alder-
eerft over-gefet. Met noodig Regifter en Konft-
Printen verrijkt. Te *Ieyden*, By Pieter Vander
Aa, Boekverkooper, 1706. Met Privilegie. *Title,
and* 171 *pp; Register* 18 *pp. and one page* ' *Berigt
voor den Boekbinder'*, [*showing the position of the
Plates.*]   *With Map, and 33 Plates copied from the
Second Part of De Bry's America.   Calf extra by
Bedford.   8vo.*   (12*s.* 6*d.*   1073)

FLURIEU (M. L. C. D.) Discoveries of the French
In 1768 and 1769 to the South-East of New-
Guinea, with the Subfequent Visits to the fame
Lands by English Navigators, who gave them new
Names. To which is prefixed, An Historical
Abridgement of the Voyages and Discoveries of
the Spaniards in the same Seas. By M. * * * ,
formerly a Captain in the French Navy. Trans-
lated from the French. *London* : John Stockdale,
M.DCC.XCI. *xxiv prel. pp; Text* 323 *pp. With Maps
and plates numbered i-xii.* 4*to.*   (8*s.* 6*d.*   1074)

FLYNT (J. C.). Autograph Letter To the Rev[d].
Mr. Prince in Boston dated 17th April, 1728.
1 *page*, 4*to.*   (5*s.*   1075)
Mr. Flynt was many years Professor in Harvard College.

FORBES (ALEXANDER). California: A History of
Upper and Lower California from their first
Discovery to the present time, comprising an
Account of the Climate, Soil, Natural Productions,
Agriculture, Commerce, &c. A full view of the
Missionary Establishments and Condition of the
Free and Domesticated Indians. With an Appen-
dix relating to Steam Navigation in the Pacific.
Illustrated with a New Map, Plans of the Har-

bours, and numerous engravings. By Alexander
Forbes, Esq. *London:* Smith Elder & Co. 1839.
xvi and 352 *pp. With* 10 *lithographed plates and a
map of California. Cloth, uncut.* 8*vo.* (7*s.* 6*d.* 1076)

FORM (A) of Prayer, Proper to be ufed In the
Churches throughout the Province of New-York,
On Friday the Twelfth of May, being the Day
appointed by Proclamation, for a General Faft
and Humiliation: To fupplicate the Pardon of our
Sins, and to implore the Divine Protection and
Bleffing on His Majefty's Sacred Perfon, His
illuftrious Family, His Kingdoms and Colonies,
His Fleets and Armies. *New-York:* Printed and
Sold by J. Parker and W. Weyman, in Beaver-
ftreet, MDCCLVIII. (Price 6*d.*) 12 *pp. half morocco.*
4*to.*   (10*s.* 6*d.* 1077)

FORM (A) of Prayer and Thanksgiving to Al-
mighty God; To be ufed In all Churches and
Chapels throughout that Part of Great Britain
called England, the Dominion of Wales, and the
Town of Berwick upon Tweed, on Thurfday the
Twenty ninth Day of November next, being the
Day appointed by Proclamation for a General
Thanksgiving to God; For vouchfafing fuch fignal
Succeffes to His Majefty's Arms, both by Sea and
Land, particularly by the Defeat of the French
Army in Canada, and the Taking of Quebec; and
for moft feafonably granting us at this Time an
uncommonly plentiful Harveft. By His Majefty's
Special Command. *London:* Thomas Bafkett, 1759.
15 *pp. Black letter. uncut.* 4*to.* (10*s.* 6*d.* 1078)

FORMA,/ y/ Modo Breve/ para tener a Punto/ de
guerra vna nao en ocafion de/ dar vifta al enemigo
en efta mar,/ fegun la inftruccion y orden,/ con que
Guarnecio/ el Galeon llamado S. Joseph Almi-/
ranta Real defte mar del Sur, al fe-/gundo dia que
falio del Puer-/to del Callao para el/ de Panama,/
A Conducir el Teso-/ro de fu Mageftad, y par-/ti-
culares/ El Almirante/ D. Ivan Zorrilla/ de la
Gandara,/ Año de 1672./ [*Lima*] Con licencia del
Real Gouierno./ Año de 1674./ [*End*] Fecha en
efta Almiranta Real San Iofeph en/ 13. de Iunio de
672./ 13 *leaves.* 4*to.*   (1*l.* 1*s.* 1079)

FOSTER (NICHOLAS). A Briefe/ Relation/ of the

late/ Horrid Rebellion/ Acted in the Island/ Barba-
das,/ In the West-Indies./ Wherein is contained,/
Their Inhumane Acts and/ Actions, in Fining and
Banishing the/ Well affected to the Parliament of/
England (both men and women) with-/out the
least cause given them so to doe :/ Dispossessing all
such as any way op-/posed these their mischievous
actions./ Acted by the Waldronds and their/ Abettors, Anno 1650./ Written at Sea by Nicholas
Foster./ *London*, Printed by I. G. for Richard
Lowndes on Ludgate-hill :/ and Robert Boydell in
the Bulwarke neere the Tower./ MDCL./ *Title,
Preface to the Reader, 2 leaves ; Text*, 112 *pp.*
16*mo.*   (1*l.* 1*s.*   1080)

FOWLER (MR.). A General Account of the Ca-
lamities occasioned by the late tremendous Hurri-
canes and Earthquakes in the West-India Islands,
Foreign as well as Domestic : With The Petitions
to, and Resolutions of, the House of Commons, in
Behalf of the Sufferers at Jamaica and Barbados :
Also a List of the Committee appointed to manage
the Subscriptions of the benevolent Public, towards
their further Relief.   Carefully collated from
Authentic Papers, By Mr. Fowler. *London* : J.
Stockdale, MDCCLXXXI. *Title, Contents, and* 86 *pp.
Advertisement* 1 *p. Half mor.* 8*vo.*   (5*s.* 6*d.*   1081)

FOWLER (JOHN). Journal of a Tour in the State
of New-York, in the year 1830 ; with Remarks on
Agriculture in those parts most eligible for settlers :
And return to England by the Western Islands, in
consequence of Shipwreck in the Robert Fulton.
By John Fowler.   *London* : Whittaker, 1831.
Title, and 333 *pp.* 12*mo.*   (4*s.* 6*d.*   1082)

FOX (GEORGE). To Friends in Barbadoes, Virginia,/
Maryland, New-England, and elf-/where. 3 *pp.
Dated* ' *London*, 29th of the 9th Month, 1666.'
Signed ' G. F.' 4to.   (10*s.* 6*d.*   1083)

FOX (GEORGE). An/ Epistle/ To all/ Professors/
in/ New-England, Germany, and other/ Parts of
the called/ Christian VVorld./ Also/ To the Jews
and Turks throughout the/ World./ That they
may see who are the true Worshippers of God,/
that he seeks, and in what he is worshipped./ An
Exhortation to them to read it over, that they may/

fee what they have all grieved, vext and quenched,
and what/ they have walked defpightfully, and re-
belled, and kickt,/ and ftopt their Ears, and clofed
their Eyes to; fo that they/ may all return again,
and turn within, and fee what they have/ profeft,
and not poffeft; fo that they may come to be the
true Pof-/feffors of the Truth, and true Worfhippers
in the Spirit of the/ True and Living God, who is
a Spirit, which is the perfect/ Worfhip, which
Chrift the Truth and perfect One fet up/ above
1600 Years fince./ George Fox./ [*London*]
Printed in the Year 1673./ 16 *pp. Unbound.*
4*to.*   (12*s.* 6*d.*   1084)

FOX (GEORGE). An/ Answer/ To feveral New/
Laws and Orders/ Made by the/ Rulers of Bofton/
in/ New-England./ The Tenth Day of the Eighth/
Moneth, 1677./ By G. F./ [*London*] Printed in
the year 1678. 7 *pp. Signed* 'G. F.' *Unbound.*
4*to.*   (1*l.* 1*s.*   1085)

FOX (GEORGE). Something in/ Answer/ to a/ Letter/
(Which I have feen) Of/ John Leverat Governour
of Bofton,/ to/ William Coddington Governour of
Rode-Ifland,/ Dated, 1677./ Wherein he men-
tiones my Name, and also/ wherein John Leverat
juftifies Roger Williams'/ Book of Lyes./ [*London*
1677?] 11 *pp. At pp.* 7 *and* 9, *Signed* ' G. F.'
4*to.*   (2*l.* 2*s.*   1086)

FOX (GEORGE). A/ Vision/ Concerning The/
Mifchievous Seperation/ among/ Friends/ in/ Old
England./ Printed and Sold by Will. Bradford at/
Philadelphia, 1692./ 7 *pp. uncut.* 4*to.* (2*l.* 2*s.* 1087)

FOX (GEORGE) and BURNYEAT (JOHN). New-
England-/Fire=Brand Quenched,/ Being an/ An-
swer/ unto a/ Slanderous Book, Entituled ; George
Fox/ Digged out of his Burrows, &c. Printed at
Bofton in the Year/ 1676. by Roger Williams of
Providence in New-England./ Which he Dedi-
cateth to the King, with Defires, That, if/ the
Moft-High pleafe, Old and New-England may Flourifh, when/ the Pope & Mahomet, Rome & Conftan-
tinople are in their Afhes./ Of a Dispute upon
XIV. of his Propofals held and debated/ betwixt
him, the faid Roger Williams, on the one part,
and/ John Stubs, William Edmundfon and John

Burnyeat on the other./ At Providence and Newport in Rode-Ifland, in the Year 1672./ In which
his Cavils are Refuted, & his Reflections Re-
proved./ In Two Parts./ As also,/ An Answer
to R. W.'s Apppendix, &c./ With a/ Post-Script
confuting his Blafphemous Affertions,/ viz. Of the
Blood of Chrift, that was Shed, its being Cor-
ruptible/ and Corrupted; and that Salvation was by
a Man, that was Cor-/ruptible, &c. Where-unto is
added a/ Catalogue of his Railery, Lies, Scorn &
Blafphemies: And/ His Temporizing Spirit made
manifeft. Alfo, The /Letters of W. Coddington of
Rode-Ifland, and R. Scot of/ Providence in New-
England concerning R. W. And Laftly, Some/
Testimonies of Antient & Modern Authors con-
cern-/ing the Light, Scriptures, Rvle & the Sovl
of Man./ By George Fox and John Burnyeat./
[*London.*] Printed in the Year MDCLXXIX./   14
prel. leaves; and 233 *pp.* ' The Second Part.' *Title*
and 256 *pp.* 4*to.*   (5*l.* 5*s.* 1088)

FOX'S MARTYRS. An Entire New Work. Fox's
Martyrs; or A New Book of the Sufferings of the
Faithful. *London,* J. Whitaker, M,DCC,LXXXIV.
Half-title, Title, and 70 *pp. Index* 1 *page. Uncut.*
8*vo.*   (4*s.* 6*d.* 1089)

FOXCROFT (Thomas). A Practical Difcourfe Relating to the Gospel-Ministry. Preach'd by Thomas Foxcroft, A. M. At His Ordination to the Office
of Paftor of a Church in Bofton, on Wednefday,
November 20. 1717. Publifhed and Enlarged at
the Urgent Requeft of a Gentleman of his Auditory. With a Preface by the Reverend Mr. Benjamin Wadfworth, Paftor of the faid Church. *Bos-*
ton : Printed for Nicholas Buttolph, at his Shop at
the lower end of Corn-Hill, 1718. *Title, iv, and* 65
pp. Errata facing title. Small 8*vo.* (10*s.* 6*d.* 1090)

FOXCROFT (Thomas). Eli the Priest dying Sud-
denly. A Sermon Preach'd at the Thurfday-Lec-
ture in Bofton, June 19. 1729. Upon Occafion of
the Sudden Death of the Reverend Mr. John Williams, who died June 12th, In the 65th Year of his
Age. And of the Reverend Mr. Thomas Blowers,
who died June 17th In the 52d Year of his Age.
By Thomas Foxcroft M.A. Paftor to the old Church

in Bofton. *Boston,* N. E. Printed for S. Gerrish in Cornhil. MDCCXXIX. *Title, Dedication* to Samuel Sewall, *ii pp; Text 36 pp.* ' Addenda.' *5 pp. half morocco. 8vo.* (8s. 6d. 1091)

FOXCROFT (THOMAS). The Pleas of Gofpel-Impenitents Examin'd & refuted. In Two Sermons At The Thurfday-Lecture/ In Bofton. On Febr. 5. & April 23. 1730. By Thomas Foxcroft, Paftor to the Old Church. Publifh'd by Defire of fome of the Hearers. *Boston :* Printed by S. Kneeland, and T. Green, for S. Gerrish, in Cornhil. 1730. *Halftitle, Title,* and 76 *pp. Very fine copy in the original binding.* 16mo. (2l. 12s. 6d. 1092)

On the fly-leaf is the presentation, in the handwriting of Dr. Foxcroft, " For the Revd. Ifaac Watts, D.D. In London." Underneath, in the handwriting of Dr. Watts, is " from the Author, 1731. A very good book." In the body of the book many passages are marked by Dr. Watts, and in feveral instances he has made notes, especially on page 51.

FOXCROFT (THOMAS). Autograph Letter [to Rev. Mr. Rogers of Exeter ?] dated at Boston Aug[t]. 15. 1750. 1 *page.* 4to. (5s. 1093)

FOXCROFT (THOMAS). Autograph Letter ' For The Rev[d] Mr. Daniel Rogers, Min[r]. of the Gospel In Exeter. pr fav[r] of Mr. Gilman' dated at Boston, Mar. 15. 1759. 1 *page, a very fine specimen.* 4to. (15s. 1094)

FOXKE (LUKE). North-VVest Fox,/ or,/ Fox from the North-west paffage./ Beginning/ VVith King Arthvr, Malga, Octhvr,/ the two Zeni's of Ifeland, Eftotiland, and Dorgia ;/ Following with briefe Abftracts of the Voyages of Cabot,/ Frobifher, Davis, Waymouth, Knight, Hudfon, Button, Gib-/ bons, Bylot, Baffin, Hawkridge: Together with the/ Courfes, Diftances, Latitudes, Longitudes, Variations,/ Depths of Seas, Sets of Tydes, Currents, Races,/ and over-Falls; vvith other Obfervations, Accidents/ and remarkable things, as our Miferies and/ fufferings./ M[r]. Iames Hall's three Voyages to Groynland, with a/ Topographicall defcription of the Countries, the Salvages/ lives and Treacheries, how our Men have beene flayne/ by them there, with the Commodities of all thofe/ parts; whereby the Merchant may have Trade, and/ the Mariner Imployment./ Demonftrated in a Polar Card, wherein are all the Maines, Seas,/ and Iflands, herein mentioned./ With the Author his owne Voyage, being the XVIth./ with the opinions and Collections of the moſt famous Ma-/thematicians, and Coſmographers; with a Probabilitie to/ prove the ſame by Marine Remonſtrations, compa-/red by the Ebbing and Flovving of the Sea, experimented/ vvith places of our ovvne Coaſt./ By Captaine Lvke Foxke of Kingſtone vpon Hull, Capt./ and Pylot for the Voyage, in his Majeſties Pinnace/ the Charles./ Printed by his Majeſties Command./ *London,/* Printed by B. Alsop and Tho. Favvcet, dwelling in Grubſtreet./ 1635./ *6 prel. leaves; viz. fly leaf with Sig A on the recto and a globe on the verso; title, Dedication to the King, 2 pp; Preface 6 pp. Text 272 pp. (pp. 169-172 repeated). Prel. leaves damaged; pages 169-172 bis, and all after p. 262, and the map wanting. Uncut. 4to.*   (2l. 2s. 1095)

FRANK (SEBASTIAN). Erſt theil dieſes Welt=/buchs, von Newen/ erfundnen Landt=/ſchafften./ Warhafftige Be=/ſchreibunge aller/ theil der Welt, dariun nicht allein etli=/che alte Landtſchafften, Königreich, Prouintzen, Inſulen, auch/ fürnehme Stedt vnd Märckte (ſo denn allen Weltbeſchreibern bekant ſeind) mit/ fleiſz beſchrieben werden, ſondern auch ſehr viel neuwe, ſo zu vnſern zeiten, zu Waſſer,/ durch vil ſorgliche vnd vormals vngebrauchte Schiffarten, erfunden ſeyn, welche im an=/dern, diſem nachfolgen=/den Buch von Schiffarten genant, auſz rechtem grundt der Coſmography vnd Geometry erfunden, augezeigt/ werden. Deſz=/gleichen auch etwas von New gefundenen Welten, vnd aller dariun gelegnen Völcker, jhrer Reli=/gion vnd Glaubens ſachen, jhren Regiment, Pollicey, Gewerb, handtierung vnd andern gebruchen/mehr, etc. auſz etlichen glaubwirdigen (fürnehmer Scribenten) Büchern, mit/ groſſer mühe vnd arbeyt, etc./ Durch Sebaſtian Franck von Wörd, zum erſten an tag/ geben, jetzt aber mit ſondern fleiſz auff ein neuwes vberſehen,/ vnd in ein wolgeformtes Handt=/buch vefaſſet. Anno. M.D.LXVII./ *6 prel. leaves; Text folioed* I *to* CCXLII: *Register,* 7 *leaves & one blank leaf. Followed by* Ander Theil dieſes Welt=/buchs von Schiff=/fahrten./ *etc.* Durch Ulrich Schridt von Straubingen. *Franckfurt.* 1567. *Title: Dedication* 4 *leaves; one blank leaf; Text fo-*

lioed 1 *to* 110, *and* 1 *to* 59. *Colophon* 1 *page: Fine
copy. Folio.* (5*l.* 5*s.* 1096)

[FRANKLIN (Benjamin).] A/ Dissertation/ on/
Liberty and Neceffity,/ Pleasure and Pain./ *Lon-
don :/* Printed in the Year MDCCXXV./ *32 pages.
Blue morocco by Bedford.* 8*vo.* (10*l.* 10*s.* 1097)

[FRANKLIN, Benjamin]. *The same, carefully reprinted by Whittingham in close imitation of the original, with the addition of a title and Preface by
Henry Stevens G. M. B. Only 25 copies printed.*
8*vo.* (1*l.* 1*s.* 1098)

FRANKLIN (Benjamin). Poor Richard, 1740./ An/
Almanack/ For the Year of Chrift/ 1740,/ Being
Leap Year./ And makes fince the Creation Years.
By the Account of the Eaftern Greeks . . 7248
By the Latin Church, when ⊙ ent. ♈ . . 6939
By the Computation of W. W. 5749
By the Roman Chronology 5689
By the Jewish Rabbies 5501
Wherein is contained,/ The Lunations, Eclipfes,
Judgment of/ the Weather, Spring Tides, Planets
Motions &/ mutual Afpects, Sun and Moon's Rif-
ing and Set-/ting, Length of Days, Time of High
Water,/ Fairs, Courts, and obfervable Days./
Fitted to the Latitude of Forty Degrees,/ and a
Meridian of Five Hours Weft from London,/ but
may without fenfible Error, ferve all the ad-/jacent
Places, even from Newfoundland to South-/Caro-
lina./ By Richard Saunders, Philom./ *Philadel-
phia :/* Printed and fold by B. Franklin, at the New/
Printing-Office near the Market./ *24 pp.*
12*mo.* (1*l.* 1*s.* 1099)
<small>This copy is stained, and the title and third leaf are torn, but no-
thing is gone; the upper half of the second leaf and the last
three leaves are wanting.</small>

FRANKLIN (Benjamin). *The Same,* Poor Richard, 1741. *etc.* 24 *pp.* 12*mo.* (2*l.* 2*s.* 1100)

FRANKLIN (Benjamin). *The Same,* Poor Rich-
ard, 1742, *etc.* 24 *pp. wanting the title and next leaf.*
12*mo.* (1*l.* 1*s.* ·1101)

FRANKLIN (Benjamin). *The Same,* Poor Richard, 1743. 24 *pp. wanting the last leaf; Good Copy.*
12*mo.* (1*l.* 1*s.* 1102)

FRANKLIN (Benjamin). Note, This Almanack us'd to contain but 24 Pages, and/ now has 36; yet the Price is very little advanc'd./ Poor Richard improved :/ Being an/ Almanack/ and Ephemeris/ of the/ Motions of the Sun and Moon ;/ the True/ Places and Aspects of the Planets ;/ the/ Rising and Setting of the Sun ;/ and the/ Riſing, Setting and Southing of the Moon,/ for the/ Bissextile Year, 1748./ Containing alſo,/ The Lunations, Conjunctions, Eclipſes, Judg-/ment of the Weather, Riſing and Setting of the/ Planets, Length of Days and Nights, Fairs, Courts,/ Roads, &c. Together with uſeful Tables, chro-/nological Obſervations, and entertaining Remarks./ Fitted to the Latitude of Forty Degrees, and a Meridian of near/ five Hours Weſt from London; but may, without ſenſible Error,/ ſerve all the Northern Colonies./ By Richard Saunders, Philom./ *Philadelphia :* Printed and Sold by B. Franklin./ *36 pp. Good sound copy, but wanting the last 2 leaves.* 12mo.   (2l. 12s. 6d. 1103)

This is the First Edition of Poor Richard Improved

FRANKLIN (Benjamin). *The Same,* Poor Richard improved : etc. For the Year of our Lord 1750. *Philadelphia :* Printed and Sold by B. Franklin, and D. Hall. *36 pp. 12mo.*   (2l. 2s. 1104)

FRANKLIN (Benjamin). *The Same,* Poor Richard improved : etc. For the Year of our Lord 1752: etc. *Philadelphia :* Printed and Sold by B. Franklin and D. Hall. *36 pp. 12mo.*   (2l. 2s. 1105)

FRANKLIN (Benjamin). *The Same,* Poor Richard improved : etc. For the Year of our Lord 1753: etc. *Philadelphia :* Printed and Sold by B. Franklin, and D. Hall. *36 pp. 12mo.*   (2l. 2s. 1106)

FRANKLIN (Benjamin). *The Same,* Poor Richard improved : etc. For the Year of our Lord 1754 : etc. *Philadelphia :* Printed and Sold by B. Franklin, and D. Hall. *36 pp : wanting only the last leaf.* 12mo.   (1l. 11s. 6d. 1107)

FRANKLIN (Benjamin). *The Same,* Poor Richard improved : etc. For the Year of our Lord 1756 : etc. *Philadelphia :* Printed and Sold by B. Franklin, and D. Hall. *36 pp : the 12th and the last leaf mutilated.* 12mo. (2*l.* 2*s.* 1108)

FRANKLIN (BENJAMIN). *The Same,* Poor Richard improved : *etc.* For the Year of our Lord 1757 : *etc. Philadelphia :* Printed and Sold by B. Franklin, and D. Hall. *36 pp. Wants the last 3 leaves.* 12mo. (1*l.* 11*s.* 6*d.* 1109)

FRANKLIN (BENJAMIN). *The Same,* Poor Richard improved : *etc.* For the Year of our Lord 1758 : *etc. Philadelphia :* Printed and Sold by B. Franklin and D. Hall. *36 pp. Fine and sound copy.* 12mo. (10*l.* 10*s.* 1110)

This is the most celebrated of all the Almanacs of the celebrated Poor Richard, and, as far as my experience goes, one of the rarest to be met with in a perfect state like the present copy. It is full of precious gems, but weighs, Troy weight, scarcely two sovereigns. I therefore mark it cheap enough at five times its weight in gold. In all the Almanacs previous to this from 1733, Franklin had dropped in to fill up the chinks between the remarkable days in the Calendar many proverbial sentences, designed to inculcate industry, frugality, and other virtues. In his Autobiography, written many years after, Franklin says, "These Proverbs, which contained the wisdom of many ages and nations, I assembled and formed into a connected discourse, prefixed to the Almanac of 1758, as the harangue of a wise old man to the people attending an auction. The bringing all these scattered counsels thus into a focus, enabled them to make greater impression. The piece being universally approved, was copied in all the newspapers of the American Continent; reprinted in Britain on a large sheet of paper, to be stuck up in houses. Two translations were made of it in France, and great numbers bought by the clergy and gentry to distribute gratis among their poor parishioners and tenants. In Pennsylvania, as it discouraged useless expense in foreign superfluities, some thought it had its share of influence in producing that growing plenty of money, which was observable for several years after its publication." Since Franklin wrote his autobiography, this summary has been many times reprinted, both in England and France, and in many languages, even in modern Greek by Didot; but such a chain of gems can never wear out or be lost, and therefore, at the risk of burying it, I insert it here in full, reprinted verbatim :—

COURTEOUS READER,

I HAVE heard that nothing gives an Author so great Pleasure, as to find his Works respectfully quoted by other learned Authors. This Pleasure I have seldom enjoyed ; for tho' I have been, if I may say it without Vanity, an *eminent Author* of Almanacks annually now a full Quarter of a Century, my Brother Authors in the same Way, for what Reason I know not, have ever been very sparing in their Applauses ; and no other Author has taken the least Notice of me, so that did not my Writings produce me some solid *Pudding,* the great Deficiency of *Praise* would have quite discouraged me.

I concluded at length, that the People were the best Judges of my Merit ; for they buy my Works ; and besides, in my Rambles, where I am not personally known, I have frequently heard one or other of my Adages repeated, with, *as Poor Richard says,* at the End on't ; this gave me some Satisfaction, as it showed not only that my Instructions were regarded, but discovered likewise some Respect for my Authority ; and I own, that to encourage the practice of remembering and repeating those wise Sentences, I have sometimes *quoted myself* with great Gravity.

Judge then how much I muſt have been gratified by an Incident I am going to relate to you. I ſtopt my Horſe lately where a great Number of People were collected at a Vendue of Merchant Goods. The Hour of Sale not being come, they were converſing on the Badneſs of the Times, and one of the Company call'd to a plain clean old Man, with white Locks, *Pray Father* Abra-ham, *whut think you of the Times? Won't these heavy Taxes quite ruin the Country? How shall we be ever able to pay them? What would you advise us to?*——Father *Abraham* ſtood up, and reply'd, If you'd have my Advice, I'll give it you in ſhort, for *a Word to the Wise is enough,* and *many Words won't fill a Bushel,* as *Poor Richard* says. They join'd in deſiring him to ſpeak his Mind, and gathering round him, he proceeded as follows;

" Friends, ſays he, and Neighbours, the Taxes are indeed very heavy, and if thoſe laid on by the Government were the only Ones we had to pay, we might more eaſily diſcharge them; but we have many others, and much more grievous to ſome of us. We are taxed twice as much by our *Idleness,* three times as much by our *Pride,* and four times as much by our *Folly,* and from theſe Taxes the Commiſſioners cannot eaſe or deliver us by allowing an Abatement. However let us hearken to good Advice, and ſome-thing may be done for us; *God helps them that help themselves,* as *Poor Richard* ſays, in his Almanack of 1733.

It would be thought a hard Government that ſhould tax its Peo-ple one tenth Part of their *Time,* to be employed in its Service. But *Idleness* taxes many of us much more, if we reckon all that is ſpent in abſolute *Sloth,* or doing of nothing, with that which is ſpent in idle Employments or Amuſements, that amount to nothing. *Sloth,* by bringing on Diſeaſes, abſolutely ſhortens Life. *Sloth, like Rust, consumes faster than Labour wears, while the used Key is always bright,* as *Poor Richard* ſays. But *dost thou love Life, then do not squander Time, for that's the Stuff Life is made of,* as *Poor Richard* ſays.—How much more than is neceſſary do we ſpend in Sleep! forgetting that *The sleeping Fox catches no Poultry,* and that *there will be sleeping enough in the Grave,* as *Poor Richard* ſays. If Time be of all Things the moſt precious, *wasting of Time* muſt be, as *Poor Richard* ſays, *the greatest Prodigality,* ſince, as he elſewhere tells us, *Lost Time is never found again;* and what we call *Time-enough, always proves little enough:* Let us then up and be doing, and doing to the Purpoſe; ſo by Diligence ſhall we do more with leſs Perplexity. *Sloth makes all Things difficult, but Industry all things easy,* as *Poor Richard* ſays; and *He that riseth late, must trot all Day, and shall scarce overtake his Business at Night.* While *Laziness travels so slowly, that Poverty soon overtakes him,* as we read in *Poor Richard,* who adds, *Drive thy Business, let not that drive thee;* and *Early to Bed, and early to rise, makes a Man healthy, wealthy and wise.* So what ſignifies *wishing* and *hoping* for better Times. We may make these Times better if we beſtir ourſelves. *Industry need not wish,* as *Poor Richard* ſays, and *He that lives upon Hope will die fasting. There are no Gains, without Pains;* then *Help Hands, for I have no Lands,* or if I have, they are ſmartly taxed. And as *Poor Richard* likewiſe obſerves, *He that hath a Trade hath an Estate,* and *He that hath a Calling hath an Office of Profit and Honour;* but then the *Trade* muſt be worked at, and the *Calling* well followed, or neither the *Estate,* nor the *Office,* will enable us to pay our Taxes.—If we are induſtrious we ſhall never ſtarve; for, as *Poor Richard* ſays, *At the work-ing Man's House* Hunger *looks in, but dares not enter.* Nor will the Bailiff or the Conſtable enter, for *Industry pays Debts, while Despair encreaseth them,* ſays *Poor Richard.*—What though you have found no Treaſure, nor has any rich Relation left you a Legacy, *Diligence is the mother of Good-luck,* as *Poor Richard* ſays, *and God gives all Things to Industry.* Then *plough deep, while Sluggards sleep, and you shall have Corn to sell and to keep,* ſays *Poor Dick.* Work while it is called To-day, for you know not how much you may be hindered To-Morrow, which makes *Poor Richard* ſay, *One To-day is worth two To-morrows;* and farther, *Have you somewhat to do To-morrow, do it to To-day.* If you were a Servant, would you not be afhamed that a good Mafter fhould catch you idle! Are you then your own Mafter, *be ashamed to catch yourself idle,* as *Poor Dick* fays. When there is fo much to be done for yourfelf, your Family, your Country, and your gracious King, he up by Peep of Day; *Let not the Sun look down and say, Inglorious here he lies.* Handle your Tools without Mittens; remember that *the Cat in Gloves catches no Mice,* as *Poor Richard* fays. 'Tis true there is much to be done, and perhaps you are weak handed, but ftick to it fteadily, and you will fee great Effects, for *constant Dropping wears away Stones,* and by *Diligence and Patience, the Mouse ate in two the Cable;* and *little Strokes fell great Oaks,* as *Poor Richard* fays in his Almanack, the Year I cannot juft now remember.

Methinks I hear fome of you fay, *Must a Man afford himself no Leisure?*—I will tell thee. My Friend, what *Poor Richard* fays, *Employ thy Time well if thou meanest to gain Leisure;* and, since thou art not sure of a Minute, throw not away an Hour. Leifure, is Time for doing fomething ufeful; this Leifure the diligent Man will obtain, but the lazy Man never; fo that, as *Poor Richard* fays, *a Life of Leisure and a Life of Laziness are two Things.* Do you imagine that Sloth will afford you more Comfort than Labour! No, for as *Poor Richard* fays, *Trouble springs from Idleness,* and grievous *Toil from needless Ease.* Many *without Labour,* would live by their WITS only, *but they break for want of stock.* Whereas Induftry gives Comfort, and Plenty and Refpect: *Fly Pleasures, and they'll follow you.* The diligent Spinner *has a large Shift;* and now *I have a Sheep and a Cow, every Body bids me Good morrow;* all which is well faid by *Poor Richard.*

But with our Induftry, we muft likewife be *steady, settled* and *careful,* and overfee our own Affairs *with our own Eyes,* and not truft too much to others; for, as *Poor Richard* fays,

> *I never saw an oft removed Tree,*
> *Nor yet an oft removed Family,*
> *That throve so well as those that settled be.*

And again, *Three Removes is as bad as a Fire;* and again, *Keep thy Shop, and thy Shop will keep thee;* and again, *If you would have your Business done, go; If not, send.* And again,

> *He that by the Plough would thrive,*
> *Himself must either hold or drive.*

And again, *The Eye of a Master will do more Work than both his Hands;* and again, *Want of Care does us more Damage than Want of Knowledge;* and again, *not to oversee Workmen, is to leave them your Purse open.* Trufting too much to others Care is the Ruin of many; for, as the *Almanack* fays, *In the Affairs of this World, Men are saved, not by Faith, but by the Want of it;* but a Man's own Care is profitable; for, faith *Poor Dick, Learning is to the Studious,* and *Riches to the Careful,* as well as *Power to the Bold,* and *Heaven to the Virtuous.* And farther, *If you would have a faithful Servant, and one that you like, serve yourself.* And again, he advifeth to Circumfpection and Care, even in the fmalleft Matters, becaufe fometimes *a little Neglect may breed great Mischief;* adding *For want of a Nail the Shoe was lost; for want of a Shoe the Horse was lost; and for want of a Horse the Rider was lost,* being overtaken and flain by the Enemy, all for want of Care about a Horfe-fhoe Nail.

So much for Induftry, my Friends, and Attention to one's own Bufinefs; but to thefe we muft add *Frugality,* if we would make our *Industry* more certainly fuccefsful. A Man may, if he knows not how to fave as he gets, *keep his Nose all his Life to the Grindstone,* and die not worth a *Groat* at laft. *A fat Kitchen makes a lean Will,* as *Poor Richard* fays; and,

> *Many Estates are spent in the Getting,*
> *Since Women for Tea forsook Spinning and Knitting,*
> *And Men for Punch forsook Hewing and Splitting.*

If you would be wealthy, fays he, in another Almanack, *think of Saving as well as of Getting:* The Indies *have not made* Spain *rich, because her* Outgoes *are greater than her* Incomes. Away then with your expenfive Follies, and you will not have fo much Caufe to complain of hard Times, heavy Taxes, and chargeable Families; for, as *Poor Dick* fays,

Women and Wine, Game and Deceit,
Make the Wealth small, and the Wants great.

And farther, *What maintains one Vice, would bring up two Children.* You may think perhaps, That a *little* Tea, or a *little* Punch now and then, Diet a *little* more coftly, Clothes a *little* finer, and a *little* Entertainment now and then, can be no *great* Matter; but remember what *Poor Richard* fays, *Many a* Little makes a *Mickle;* and farther, *Beware of* little *Expences; a small Leak will sink a great Ship;* and again, *Who Dainties love, shall Beggars prove;* and moreover, *Fools make Feasts, and wise Men eat them.*

Here you are all got together at this Vendue of *Fineries* and *Knicknacks.* You call them *Goods,* but if you do not take Care, they will prove *Evils* to fome of you. You expect they will be fold *cheap,* and perhaps they may for lefs than they coft; but if you have no Occafion for them, they must be *dear* to you. Remember what *Poor Richard* fays, *Buy what thou hast no Need of, and ere long thou shalt sell thy Necessaries.* And again, *At a great Pennyworth pause a while:* He means, that perhaps the Cheapnefs is *apparent* only, and not *real;* or the Bargain, by ftraitning thee in thy Bufinefs, may do thee more Harm than Good. For in another Place he fays, *Many have been ruined by buying good Pennyworths.* Again, *Poor Richard* fays, *'Tis foolish to lay out Money in a Purchase of Repentance;* and yet this Folly is practifed every Day at Vendues, for want of minding the Almanack. *Wise men,* as *Poor Dick* fays, *learn by others Harms, Fools scarcely by their own;* but, *Felix quem faciunt aliena Pericula cautum.* Many a one, for the Sake of Finery on the Back, have gone with a hungry Belly, and half ftarved their Families; *Silks and Sattins, Scarlet and Velvets,* as *Poor Richard* fays, *put out the Kitchen Fire.* Thefe are not the *Necessaries* of Life: they can fcarcely be called the *Conveniences,* and yet only becaufe they look pretty, how many *want to have* them. The *artificial* Wants of Mankind thus become more numerous than the *natural;* and, as *Poor Dick* fays, *For one* poor *Person, there are an hundred* indigent. By thefe, and other Extravagancies, the Genteel are reduced to Poverty, and forced to borrow of thofe whom they formerly defpifed, but who through *Industry* and *Frugality* have maintained their Standing; in which Cafe it appears plainly, that a *Ploughman on his Legs is higher than a Gentleman on his Knees,* as *Poor Richard* fays. Perhaps they have had a fmall Eftate left them, which they knew not the Getting of; they think *'tis Day, and will never be Night;* that a little to be fpent out of *so much,* is not worth minding; *(a Child and a Fool,* as *Poor Richard* fays, *imagine* Twenty Shillings *and Twenty Years can never be spent)* but, *always taking out of the Meal-tub, and never putting in, soon comes to the Bottom;* then, as *Poor Dick* fays, *When the Well's dry, they know the Worth of Water.* But this they might have known before, if they had taken his Advice; *If you would know the Value of Money, go and try to borrow some;* for he that goes a borrowing goes a sorrowing; and indeed fo does he that lends to fuch People, when he goes *to get it in* again.—*Poor Dick* farther advifes, and fays,

Fond Pride of Drefs, is sure a very Curse;
E'er Fancy you consult, consult your Purse.

And again, *Pride is as loud a Beggar as Want, and a great deal more saucy.* When you have bought one fine Thing you muft buy ten more, that your Appearance may be all of a Piece; but *Poor Dick* fays, *'Tis easier to fupprefs the first Desire, than to fatisfy all that follow it.* And 'tis as truly Folly for the Poor to ape the Rich, as for the Frog to fwell, in order to equal the Ox.

Great Estates may venture more.
But little Boats should keep near Shore.

'Tis however a Folly foon punifhed; for *Pride that dines on Vanity sups on Contempt,* as *Poor Richard* fays. And in another Place, *Pride breakfasted with Plenty, dined with Poverty, and supped with Infamy.* And after all, of what Ufe is this *Pride of Appearance*, for which fo much is rifked, fo much is fuffered! It cannot promote Health, or eafe Pain; it makes no Increafe of Merit in the Perfon, it creates Envy, it haftens Misfortune.

> *What is a Butterfly? At best*
> *He's but a Caterpillar drest.*
> *The gaudy Fop's his picture just,*

as *Poor Richard* fays.

But what Madnef- muft it be to *run in Debt* for thefe Superfluities! We are offered, by the Terms of this Vendue, *Six Months Credit;* and that perhaps has induced fome of us to attend it, becaufe we cannot fpare the ready Money, and hope now to be fine without it. But, ah, think what you do when you run in Debt; *You give to another Power over your Liberty.* If you cannot pay at the Time, you will be afhamed to fee your Creditor; you will be in Fear when you fpeak to him; you will make poor pitiful fneaking Excufes, and by Degrees come to lofe your Veracity, and fink into bafe downright lying; for, as *Poor Richard* fays, *The second Vice is Lying, the first is running in Debt.* And again, to the fame Purpofe, *Lying rides upon Debt's Back.* Whereas a freeborn *Englifhman* ought not to be afhamed or afraid to fee or fpeak to any Man living. But Poverty often deprives a Man of all Spirit and Virtue; *'Tis hard for an empty Bag to stand upright,* as *Poor Richard* truly fays. What would you think of that Prince, or that Government, who fhould iffue an Edict forbidding you to drefs like a Gentleman or a Gentlewoman, on Pain of Imprifonment or Servitude? Would you not fay, that you are free, have a Right to drefs as you pleafe, and that fuch an Edict would be a Breach of your Privileges, and fuch a Government tyrannical? And yet you are about to put yourfelf under that Tyranny when you run in Debt for fuch Drefs! Your Creditor has Authority at his Pleafure to deprive you of your Liberty, by confining you in Goal for Life, or to fell you for a Servant, if you fhould not be able to pay him! When you have got your Bargain, you may, perhaps, think little of Payment; but *Creditors, Poor Richard* tells us, *have better Memories than Debtors;* and in another Place fays, *Creditors are a fuperstitious Sect, great Observers of set Days and Times.* The Day comes round before you are aware, and the Demand is made before you are prepared to fatisfy it. Or if you bear your Debt in Mind, the Term which at firft feemed fo long, will, as it leffens, appear extreamly fhort. *Time* will feem to have added Wings to his Heels as well as Shoulders. *Those have a short Lent,* faith *Poor Richard. who owe Money to be paid at Easter.* Then fince, as he fays, *The Borrower is a Slave to the Lender, and the Debtor to the Creditor,* difdain the Chain, preferve your Freedom; and maintain your Independency: Be *industrious* and *free;* be *frugal* and *free.* At present, perhaps, you may think yourfelf in thriving Circumftances, and that you can bear a little Extravagance without Injury; but,

> *For Age and Want, save while you may;*
> *No Morning Sun lasts a whole Day,*

as *Poor Richard* fays.——Gain may be temporary and uncertain, but ever while you live, Expence is conftant and certain; and *'tis easier to build two Chimnies than to keep one in Fuel,* as *Poor Richard* fays. So rather go to Bed fupperlefs than rife in Debt.

Get what you can, and what you get hold;
'Tis the Stone that will turn all your Lead into Gold,

as *Poor Richard* fays. And when you have got the Philofopher's Stone, fure you will no longer complain of bad Times, or the Difficulty of paying Taxes.

This Doctrine, my Friends, is *Reason* and *Wisdom;* but after all, do not depend too much upon your own *Industry,* and *Frugality,* and *Prudence,* though excellent Things, for they may all be blafted without the Bleffing of Heaven; and therefore afk that Bleffing humbly, and be not uncharitable to thofe that at prefent feem to want it, but comfort and help them. Remember *Job* fuffered, and was afterwards profperous.

And now to conclude, *Experience keeps a dear School, but Fools will learn in no other, and scarce in that;* for it is true, *we may give Advice, but we cannot give Conduct,* as *Poor Richard* fays:

However, remember this, *They that won't be counselled, can't be helped,* as *Poor Richard* fays: and farther, That *if you will not hear Reason, she'll surely rap your Knuckles.*
Thus the old Gentleman ended his Harangue. The People heard it, and approved the Doctrine, and immediately practifed the contrary, juft as if it had been a common Sermon; for the Vendue opened, and they began to buy extravagantly, notwithftanding all his Cautions, and their own Fear of Taxes.—I found the good Man had thoroughly ftudied my Almanacks, and digefted all I had dropt on thofe Topicks during the Courfe of Five-and-twenty Years. The frequent Mention he made of me muft have tired any one elfe, but my Vanity was wonderfully delighted with it, though I was confcious that not a tenth Part of the Wifdom was my own which he afcribed to me, but rather the *Gleanings* I had made of the Senfe of all Ages and Nations. However, I refolved to be the better for the Echo of it; and though I had at firft determined to buy Stuff for a new Coat, I went away refolved to wear my old One a little longer. *Reader,* if thou wilt do the fame, thy Profit will be as great as mine.
      I am, as ever,
            Thine to serve thee,
July 7, 1757.   RICHARD SAUNDERS.

FRANKLIN (BENJAMIN). *The Same,* Poor Richard improved : *etc.* For the Year of our Lord 1759 : *etc. Philadelphia :* Printed and Sold by B. Franklin, and D. Hall. *36 pp. wanting the last 2 leaves.* 12*mo.* (1*l.* 1*s.* 1111)

FRANKLIN (BENJAMIN). *The Same,* Poor Richard improved : *etc.* For the Year of our Lord 1761 : *etc. Philadelphia :* Printed and Sold by B. Franklin, and D. Hall. 36 *pp. Fine copy.* 12*mo.* (2*l.* 2*s.* 1112)

FRANKLIN (BENJAMIN). *The Same,* Poor Richard improved : *etc.* For the Year of our Lord 1762 : *etc. Philadelphia :* Printed and Sold by B. Franklin, and D. Hall. 36 *pp.* 12*mo.* (2*l.* 2*s.* 1113)

FRANKLIN (BENJAMIN). *The Same,* Poor Richard improved : *etc.* For the Year of our Lord 1763 : *etc. Philadelphia :* Printed and Sold by B. Franklin, and D. Hall. 36 *pp.* 12*mo.* (2*l.* 2*s.* 1114)

FRANKLIN (BENJAMIN). *The Same,* Poor Richard improved : *etc.* For the Year 1764 : *etc. Philadelphia :* Printed and Sold by B. Franklin, and D. Hall. 32 *pp.* 12*mo.* (2*l.* 2*s.* 1115)

FRANKLIN (BENJAMIN). *The Same,* Poor Richard improved : *etc.* For the Year of our Lord 1765 : *etc. Philadelphia :* Printed and Sold by B. Franklin, and D. Hall. 36 *pp.* 12*mo.* (1*l.* 11*s.* 6*d.* 1116)

This is, I believe, the last almanac on which Franklin's name appears. It was continued as " Poor Richard improved," with the name of Richard Saunders, Philom. as author, by Hall and Sellers. I have those for the years 1767, 1768, 1775, 1780, 1781, 1782, 1783, 1784, 1790, 1792, and 1794. (10*s.* 6*d.* each. 1117)

FRANKLIN (Benjamin). A Pocket/ Almanack/ For the Year 1742./ Fitted for the Ufe of Penn-/ sylvania, and the neigh-/bouring Provinces./ By Richard Saunders, Phil./ *Philadelphia :*/ Printed by B. Franklin./ 16 *pp.* 32*mo.* (*2l. 2s.* 1118)

FRANKLIN (Benjamin). *The Same,* For the Year 1743. *etc. Philadelphia :*/ Printed by B. Franklin./ 16 *pp.* 32*mo.* (*2l. 2s.* 1119)

FRANKLIN (Benjamin). *The Same,* For the Year 1744. *etc.* With feveral ufeful Additions. *Philadelphia :*/ Printed and fold by B. Franklin./ 24 *pp.* 32*mo.* (*2l. 2s.* 1120)

FRANKLIN (Benjamin). *The Same,* For the Year 1745. *etc. Philadelphia :*/ Printed and fold by B. Franklin./ 24 *pp.* 32*mo.* (*2l. 2s.* 1121)

FRANKLIN (Benjamin). *The Same,* For the Year 1746. *etc. Philadelphia :*/ Printed and fold by B. Franklin./ 24 *pp.* 32*mo.* (*2l. 2s.* 1122)

FRANKLIN (Benjamin). *The Same,* For the Year 1747. *etc. Philadelphia :*/ Printed and fold by B. Franklin./ 24 *pp.* 32*mo.* (*2l. 2s.* 1123)

FRANKLIN (Benjamin). *The Same,* For the Year 1748. *etc. Philadelphia :*/ Printed and fold by B. Franklin./ 24 *pp.* 32*mo.* (*2l. 2s.* 1124)

FRANKLIN (Benjamin). *The Same,* For the Year 1749. *etc. Philadelphia :*/ Printed and fold by B. Franklin,/ and D. Hall. 24 *pp.* 32*mo.* (*2l. 2s.* 1125)

FRANKLIN (Benjamin). *The Same,* For the Year 1750. *etc. Philadelphia :*/ Printed and fold by B. Franklin/ and D. Hall. 24 *pp.* 32*mo.* (*2l. 2s.* 1126)

FRANKLIN (Benjamin). *The Same,* For the Year 1751. *etc. Philadelphia :*/ Printed and fold by B. Franklin,/ and D. Hall./ 24 *pp.* 32*mo.* (*2l. 2s.* 1127)

FRANKLIN (Benjamin). *The Same,* For the Year 1752. *etc. Philadelphia :*/ Printed and fold by B. Franklin,/ and D. Hall./ 24 *pp.* 32*mo.* (*2l. 2s.* 1128)

FRANKLIN (Benjamin). *The Same,* For the Year 1753. *etc. Philadelphia :*/ Printed and fold by B. Franklin,/ and D. Hall./

FRANKLIN (Benjamin). *The Same,* For the Year

1754. *etc. Philadelphia:/* Printed and fold by B. Franklin,/ and D. Hall. 24 *pp.* 32*mo.* (2*l.* 2*s.* 1129)

FRANKLIN (Benjamin). *The Same,* For the Year 1755. *etc. Philadelphia:/* Printed and fold by B. Franklin,/ and D. Hall./ 24 *pp.* 32*mo.* (2*l.* 2*s.* 1130)

FRANKLIN (Benjamin). *The Same,* For the Year 1756. *etc. Philadelphia:* Printed and fold by B. Franklin,/ and D. Hall./ 24 *pp.* 32*mo.* (2*l.* 2*s.* 1131)

FRANKLIN (Benjamin). *The Same,* For the Year 1757. *etc. Philadelphia:/* Printed and fold by B. Franklin,/ and D. Hall./ 24 *pp.* 32*mo.* (2*l.* 2*s.* 1132)

FRANKLIN (Benjamin). *The Same,* For the Year 1758. *etc. Philadelphia:/* Printed and fold by B. Franklin,/ and D. Hall. 24 *pp.* 32*mo.* (2*l.* 2*s.* 1133)

FRANKLIN (Benjamin). *The Same,* For the Year 1764. *etc. Philadelphia:/* Printed and fold by B. Franklin,/ and D. Hall. 24 *pp.* 32*mo.* (2*l.* 2*s.* 1134)

FRANKLIN (Benjamin). *The Same,* For the Year 1765. *etc. Philadelphia:/* Printed and fold by B. Franklin,/ and D. Hall./ 24 *pp.* 32*mo.* (2*l.* 2*s.* 1135)

FRANKLIN (Benjamin). *The Same,* For the Year 1766. *etc. Philadelphia:/* Printed and fold by B. Franklin/ and D. Hall./ 24 *pp.* 32*mo.* (2*l.* 2*s.* 1136)

FRANKLIN (Benjamin). An Answer to Mr. Franklin's Remarks, on a late Protest. *Philadelphia:* Printed and Sold by William Bradford, at his Book-Store, in Market ſtreet, adjoining the London Coffee-Houſe. M.DCC.LXIV. *22 pp. uncut.* 8*vo.*   (10*s.* 6*d.*   1137)

FRANKLIN (Benjamin). Experiments and Obſervations on Electricity, made at Philadelphia in America, by Benjamin Franklin, L.L.D. and F.R.S. To which are added, Letters and Papers on Philoſophical Subjects. The Whole correćted, methodized, improved, and now firſt collećted into one Volume, and Illuſtrated with Copper Plates. *London:* Printed for David Henry ; and fold by Francis Newbery, at the Corner of St. Paul's Churchyard. MDCCLXIX. *Fourth Edition. 4 prelim. leaves, 496 pp. and Index, 8 leaves. 7 Plates.* 4*to.*   (7*s.* 6*d.*   1138)

FRANKLIN (Benjamin). Œuvres de M. Franklin, Docteur ès Loix, Membre de l'Académie Royale des Sciences de Paris, des Sociétés Royales de
Londres & de Gottingue, des Sociétés Philofo-
phiques d'Edimbourg & de Rotterdam, Président
de la Société Philofophique de Philadelphie, & Ré-
fident à la Cour de la Grand Bretagne pour plufieurs Colonies Britanniques Américaines. Tra-
duites de L'Anglois sur la Quatrieme Edition.
Par M. Barbeu Dubourg. Avec des Additions
Nouvelles et des Figures en Taille douce. Tome
Premier. [& Tome Second.] A *Paris*, Chez Quillau l'aîné, Libraire, rue Chriftine, au Magafin Lit-
téraire. Esprit, Libraire de Mgr. le Duc de Chartres, au Palais Royal. Et l'Auteur, rue de la Buch-
erie, aux Ecoles de Medecine. M.DCC.LXXIII.
Avec Approbation & Permiffion du Roi. 2 *Volumes. Vol. I. Half-title, Portrait, Title, and xxiv
and* 338 *pp. with* 5 *Copper Plates. Vol. II. Half-
title, Title, and xv and* 320 *pp.* 7 *Copper Plates.*
4to.   (16s. 1139)

FRANKLIN (Benjamin). Interrogatoire de M^r
Franklin Deputé de Pensilvanie au Parlement de
la Grande Bretagne. Traduit de l'Anglois par
Ch . . . . D. H . . . . Maître de la langue Angloife
à Strasbourg. Prix 24 sols. [*Colophon.*] A *Strasbourg*, [*n. d.*] de l'Imprimerie de Simon Kürsner.
Avec Approbation. 35 *pp. half morocco ; fine copy.*
8vo.   (7s. 6d. 1140)

FRANKLIN (Benjamin). Experiments and Observations on Electricity, made at Philadelphia in
America, By Benjamin Franklin, L. L. D. and
F.R.S. Member of the Royal Academy of Sciences
at Paris, of the Royal Society at Gottingen, and of
the Batavian Society in Holland, and Prefident of
the Philofophical Society at Philadelphia. To
which are added Letters and Papers on Philosophical Subjects. The Whole corrected, methodized, improved, and now collected into one Volume,
and illuftrated with Copper Plates. The Fifth Edition. *London :* Printed for F. Newbery, at the
Corner of St. Paul's Church-Yard. M.DCC.LXXIV.
Half-title, vi and 514 *pp ; Index* 8 *leaves.* 7 *Plates.*
4to.   (10s. 6d. 1141)

FRANKLIN (Benjamin). Political, Mifcellaneous,

and Philofophical Pieces; Arranged under the fol-
lowing Heads, and Diftinguifhed by Initial Letters
in each Leaf: [G. P.] General Politics; [A. B. T.]
American Politics before the Troubles; [A. D. T.]
American Politics during the Troubles; [P. P.]
Provincial or Colony Politics; and [M. P.] Mifcellaneous and Philofophical Pieces; Written by
Benj. Franklin, LL.D. and F.R.S. Member of the
Royal Academy of Sciences at Paris, of the Royal
Society at Gottingen, and of the Batavian Society
in Holland; Prefident of the Philofophical Society
at Philadelphia;—late Agent in England for feveral of the American Colonies; and at prefent chofen
in America as Deputy to the General Congrefs for
the State of Penfylvania; Prefident of the Convention of the faid State, and Minifter Plenipotentiary
at the Court of Paris for the United States of America; Now firft collected, With Explanatory Plates,
Notes, And an Index to the Whole. *London:*
Printed for J. Johnson, N° 72, St. Paul's Church-
Yard. M DCC LXXIX. *xii and 574 pp. with Portrait,
3 plates, and Table of the Reformed Alphabet. Large
Paper. 4to.*   (10s. 6d.   1142)

FRANKLIN (Benjamin). Two Tracts: Information to those who would remove to America. And,
Remarks concerning the Savages of North America. By Benjamin Franklin. Third Edition. *London:* John Stockdale, MDCCLXXXIV. *39 pp. half
mor. 8vo.*   (3s. 6d.   1143)

FRANKLIN (Benjamin). Autograph Letter to
Commodore Paul Jones, dated at Philadelphia,
July 22, 1787. *1 page. A fine specimen.
4to.*   (2l. 2s.   1144)

FRANKLIN (Benjamin). Report of Dr. Benjamin Franklin, and other Commissioners, charged
by the King of France, with the examination of the
Animal Magnetism, as now practised at Paris.
Translated from the French. With an historical
Introduction. *London:* Printed for J. Johnson,
1785. *ix and 123 pp. 8vo.*   (5s. 6d.   1144*)

FRANKLIN (Benjamin). The Private Life of the
late Benjamin Franklin, LL.D. Late Minister Plenipotentiary from the United States of America to
France, &c. &c. &c. Originally written by Him-

self, and now Translated from the French. To
which are added, Some Account of his Public Life,
a variety of Anecdotes concerning him, by M.M.
Brissot, Condorcet, Rochefoucault, Le Roy, &c. &c.
And the Eulogium of M. Fauchet, Constitutional
Bishop of the Department of Calvados, and a Member
of the National Convention. *London: J. Parsons*, 1793. *xvi and 324 pp. 8vo.*   (*7s. 6d.* 1145)

FRANKLIN (BENJAMIN). Works of the late D.
Benjamin Franklin; consisting of his Life, written
by himself, together with Essays, Humourous,
Moral & Literary; chiefly in the manner of the
Spectator. The Second American Edition. Printed
by Samuel Campbell, Bookseller, No. 124, Pearl
Street, *New-York.* 1794. *Two Volumes.* Vol. I.
206 *pp.* Vol. II. 142 *pp. calf.* 12*mo.* (7s. 6d. 1146)

FRANKLIN (BENJAMIN). Information to those
who would remove to America. By Dr. Benjamin
Franklin. *London:* 1794. *23 pp. unbound.*
8*vo.*   (*3s. 6d.* 1147)

FRANKLIN (BENJAMIN). The Life of Dr. Benjamin
Franklin. Written by himself. Third American
Edition. *New-York:* Printed and fold by T.
and J. Swords. 1794. *214 pp. Portrait of Franklin.* 24*mo.*   (*5s. 6d.* 1148)

FRANKLIN (BENJAMIN). The Life of Benjamin
Franklin, L L D. [*Portrait engraved by Hopwood*]
Printed and Sold by George Nicholson, *Poughnill,*
near *Ludlow,* Sold in *London* by T. Conder, 30
Bucklersbury, Champante and Whitrow, 4 Jewry
Street, Aldgate, R. Bickerstaff, 210 Strand, and
by all other Booksellers. *Engraved title and 56 pp.
Small* 12*mo.*   (*5s. 6d.* 1149)

FRANKLIN (BENJAMIN). Works of the late Doctor
Benjamin Franklin: Consisting of his Life
Written by Himself, together with Efsays, Humorous,
Moral & Literary, Chiefly in the Manner
of the Spectator. In two Volumes. Vol. I. [*Portrait*] *London :* Printed for G. G. J. and J. Robinson,
Pater-nofter Row. *2 Volumes. Vol. I. Engraved
title and 4 prel. leaves. Text 317 pp. followed
by 1 leaf of errata. Vol. II. Engraved title, and
2 prel. leaves and Text 268 pp. 8vo.* (*7s. 6d.* 1150)

FRANKLIN (Benjamin). Works of the late Doctor Benjamin Franklin: Consisting of his Life written by himself, together with Eſsays, Humorous, Moral & Literary, Chiefly in the Manner of the Spectator. In two volumes. Third Edition. [*Portrait*] Vol. I. *London:* Printed for G. G. J. and J. Robinson, Pater-noſter Row. *2 Vols. Vol. I. Engraved title and 4 prel. leaves. Text* 317 *pp. Vol. II.* 3 *prel. leaves and* 290 *pp. Old calf.* 8vo.   (10s. 6d. 1151)

FRANKLIN (Benjamin). The Complete Works, in Philosophy, Politics, and Morals, of the late Dr. Benjamin Franklin, now first collected and arranged: with Memoirs of his early Life, written by Himself. In Three Volumes. Vol. I. *London:* Printed for J. Johnson. St. Paul's Church-yard; and Longman, Hurst, Rees and Orme, Paternoster-Row. 1806. 3 *Vols. Vol. I. Portrait, engraved title, title and* 5 *other prelim. leaves; Text* 440 *pp; Index* 18 *leaves;* 4 *plates; Vol. II.* 4 *prelim. leaves and* 468 *pp.* 8 *plates. Vol. III.* 4 *prelim. leaves and* 562 *pp.* 8vo.   (15s. 1152)

FRANKLIN (Benjamin). Works of the late Dr. Benjamin Franklin, consisting of his Life, written by himself; together with Essays, Humorous, Moral, and Literary. Vol. I. *Edinburgh:* Printed by D. Schaw & Son; and Sold by the Booksellers. 1809. 2 *Vols. Vol. I.* 4 *prelim. leaves and pp.* 5 *to* 203. *Vol. II.* 2 *prelim. leaves and* 186 *pp. Small* 12mo.   (5s. 6d. 1153)

FRANKLIN (Benjamin). Works of the late Dr. Benjamin Franklin; consisting of his Life written by Himself: Together with Essays, Humorous, Moral, and Literary. Vol. I. *Edinburgh:* Printed by D. Schaw and Son; And sold by the Booksellers. 1814. 2 *Vols. Vol. I.* 4 *prel. leaves and pp.* 5-203. *Vol II.* 2 *preliminary leaves and* 186 *pp. Small* 12mo.   (7s. 6d. 1154)

FRANKLIN (Benjamin). Memoirs of the Life and Writings of Benjamin Franklin, LL.D. F.R.S. &c. Minister Plenipotentiary from the United States of America, at the Court of France, and for the Treaty of Peace and Independence with Great Britain, &c. &c. Written by Himself to a late Period, and con-

tinued to the time of his Death, by his Grandson ;
William Temple Franklin. Now first published
from the original MSS. Comprising the Private
Correspondence and Public Negociations of Dr.
Franklin, and a selection from his Political, Philosophical, and Miscellaneous Works. *London:*
Printed for Henry Colburn, British and Foreign
Public Library, Conduit Street. 1818. 3 *Volumes.*
Vol. I. Portrait: x, 450 *and* Ixxxviii *pp. und* 1 *p.
of errata. Vol. II. Private Correspondence.* 13 *prel.
leaves and* 449 *pp.* 1 *Plate. Vol. III. Political, Philosophical, and Miscellaneous Writing.* 7 *prel. leaves
and* 570 *pp.* 8 *Plates.* 4*to.*   (1*l.* 5*s.* 1155)

FRANKLIN (BENJAMIN). Mémoires sur la vie et
les écrits de Benjamin Franklin, Docteur en droit,
Membre de la Société royale de Londres et de
l'Académie des Sciences de Paris ; Ministre pléni-
potentiaire des Etats-Unis d'Amérique, à la cour
de France, etc. etc. ; Publiés sur le manuscrit original rédigé par lui même en grande partie, et con-
tinué jusqu'a sa mort, Par William Temple Franklin, son petit-fils. Tome Premier, Avec une Portrait de B. Franklin. A *Paris,* Chez Treuttel et
Würtz, Libraires, rue de Bourbon, n° 17 ; Et à
Strasbourg, même Maison de Commerce. A Londres, Chez H. Colburne, 50 Conduit street, New-
Bond. 1818. 3 *Vols. Vol. I.* 10 *prel. leaves including collective title und portrait ; Text* 390 *pp. Vol.
II. Collective title, frontispiece & title, Text* 435 *pp.
Vol. III. Correspondence.* 16 *prel. leaves and* 410 *pp.*
8*vo.*   (12*s.* 6*d.* 1156)

FRANKLIN (BENJAMIN). Familiar Letters and
Miscellaneous Papers of Benjamin Franklin ; Now
for the first time published. Edited by Jared
Sparks, Author of "The Life of Gouvernour Mor-
ris," — "Memoirs of John Ledyard," &c. &c.
With Explanatory Notes. *London:* Jackson and
Walford, St. Paul's Church-Yard. 1833. *pp. xvi
and* 295. 12*mo.*   (5*s.* 1157)

FRANKLIN (BENJAMIN). Memoirs of the Life
and Writings of Benjamin Franklin, LL.D. F.R.S.
&c. Minister Plenipotentiary from the United
States of America at the Court of France, and for
the Treaty of Peace and Independence with Great

Britain, &c. &c. Written by Himself to a late period, and continued to the time of his Death by his Grandson, William Temple Franklin. Comprising the Private Correspondence and Public Negociations of Dr. Franklin; and his select Political, Philosophical, and Miscellaneous Works, Published from the Original MSS. New Edition. In Six Volumes. Vol. I. Life. *London:* Published for Henry Colburn, By R. Bently, New Burlington Street. 1833. 6 *Vols. Vol. I.* Life, *pp. xii and* 541 *with Portrait and 2 plates: Vol. II.* Life, *Title and 450 pp; Vol. III.* Correspondence, *xvi and 456 pp. Vol. IV.* Correspondence, *xii and 392 pp; Vol. V.* Posthumous and other writings, *xvi and 493 pp; Vol. VI.* Posthumous and other writings, *viii and* 523 *pp.* 8 *plates.* 8*vo.*   (1*l.* 11*s.* 6*d.* 1158)

FRANKLIN (Benjamin). The Works of Benjamin Franklin; containing several Political and Historical Tracts not included in any former edition, and many letters official and private not hitherto published; with Notes and a Life of the Author. By Jared Sparks. *Boston:* Hilliard Gray, and Company. 1840. 10 *Volumes. Large Paper.* 8*vo.*   (5*l.* 15*s.* 6*d.* 1159)

FRANKLIN (Benjamin). The Works of Dr. Benjamin Franklin; consisting of Essays, Humorous, Moral, and Literary. With His Life, written by Himself. *Chiswick:* C. Whittingham, 1824. *viii and 295 pp.* 16*mo.*   (5*s.* 1160)

FRANKLIN (William). Autograph Letter of William Franklin, Governour of New Jersey to Sir William Johnson, dated at Burlington, Aug. 1. 1769 respecting Political news from England, &c. *pp.* 4*to.*   (10*s.* 6*d.* 1161)
Governour William Franklin was a fun-child of Dr. Franklin.

FREE Thoughts, on The Proceedings of the Continental Congress, Held at Philadelphia Sept. 5, 1774: Wherein Their Errors are exhibited, their Reasonings Confuted, and The fatal Tendency of their Non-Importation, Non-Exportation, and Non-Consumption Measures, are laid open to the plainest Understandings; And the Only Means pointed out For Preserving and Securing Our Present Happy Constitution: In a Letter to the Far-

mers, and other Inhabitants of North America In
General, And to thofe of the Province of New-
York In Particular. By a Farmer. [Samuel Seabury, afterwards Bishop of Connecticut.] [*New
York.*] Printed in the Year M. DCC. LXXIV. 24 *pp.*
at page 23. *Signed* ' A. W. Farmer.' *Half mor.*
8vo.   (6s. 1162)

FREE Thoughts on the Proceedings of the Continental Congress, held at Philadelphia, Sept. 5,
1774: Wherein Their Errors are Exhibited, their
Reasonings confuted, and the Fatal Tendency of
their Non - Importation, Non - Exportation, and
Non-Consumption Measures, are laid open to the
plaineft Underftandings ; and the Only Means
pointed out for Preferving and Securing our prefent Happy Constitution : In a Letter to the Farmers, and other Inhabitants of North-America in
general, and to thofe of the Province of New-York
in particular. By a Farmer [S. Seabury] New-
York, Printed: *London* Reprinted for Richardson
and Urquhart, 1775. *Half-title, Title, and* 50 *pp.*
At page 48 *Signed* ' A. W. Farmer.' *Half mor.*
8vo.   (5s. 6d. 1163)

FREEDOM The firft of Bleffings. [*Colophon*] Sold
at the Heart and Crown in Cornhill, *Boston.* [1772 ?]
7 *pp. Half mor.* 4to.   (7s. 6d. 1164)

FRENCH Policy Defeated. Being, an Account of
all the hoftile Proceedings of the French, Againft
the Inhabitants of the British Colonies in North
America, For the laft Seven Years. Also, The vigo-
rous Meafures purfued both in England and America, to vindicate the Rights of the British Sub-
jeЄts, and the Honour of the Crown, from the Infults and Invafions of their perfidious Enemies.
With an Authentic Account of the Naval Engagement off Newfoundland, and the Taking of the
Forts in the Bay of Fundy. Embellifhed with Two
curious Maps, Defcribing all the Coafts, Bays,
Lakes, Rivers, Soundings, principal Towns and
Forts, confining on the British Plantations in America. *London* : M. Cooper, MDCCLV. *Title and* 114
pp. Two Maps. Half mor. 8vo. (10s. 6d. 1165)

FREZIER (MR.). Relation du Voyage de la Mer
du Sud aux Cotes du Chili, du Perou, et du Bre-

sil Fait pendant les années 1712, 1713 & 1714, Par
M. Frezier, Ingenieur Ordinaire du Roi. Ouvrage
enrichi de quantité de Planches en Taille-douce.
A *Amsterdam*, Chez Pierre Humbert, M.DCC.XVII.
2 Volumes. I. *Title, and prel. pp. v-xx; Text 294
pp. With Maps and plates numbered* I-XXII. II. *Title
& pp. 297-600. With Maps and plates numbered*
XXIII-XXXVII: *calf. 12mo.*   (8s. 6d. 1166)

FREZIER (MR.). A Voyage to the South Sea, And
along the Coasts of Chili and Peru, In the Years
1712, 1713, and 1714. Particularly describing The
Genius and Conſtitution of the Inhabitants, as well
Indians as Spaniards: Their Cuſtoms and Manners;
their Natural Hiſtory, Mines, Commodities, Traffick with Evrope, &c. By Monſieur Frezier, Engineer in Ordinary to the French King. Illuſtrated
with 37 Copper-Cutts of the Coaſts, Harbours, Cities, Plants and other Curioſities: Printed from the
Author's Original Plates inſerted in the Paris Edition. With a Postscript by Dr. Edmund Halley,
Savilian Profeſſor of Geometry in the Univerſity of
Oxford. And an Account of the Settlement, Commerce, and Riches of the Jeſuites in Paraguay.
London: Jonah Bowyer, MDCCXVII. *6 prel. leaves;
viz. Title, Preface, Letter, and Directions to the
Binder; Text 335 pp. Index 9 pp. With Maps and
plates numbered* I-XXXVII *and* 36. *Fine copy; Calf.
4to.*   (12s. 6d. 1167)

FREZIER (MR.). Relation du Voyage de la Mer
du Sud aux Côtes du Chily et du Perou, Fait pendant les années 1712, 1713, & 1714. Dediée à S.
A. R. Monſeigneur Le Duc D'Orleans, Regent du
Royaume. Avec une Réponse a la Preface Cri-
tique Du Livre intitulé, Journal des Obſervations
Phyſiques, Mathematiques & Botaniques du R. P.
Fevillée, contre la Relation du Voyage de la Mer
du Sud, & une Chronologie des Vicerois du Perou,
depuis ſon établiſſement jusqu'au tems de la Relation du Voyage de la Mer du Sud. Par M. Frezier, Ingenieur Ordinaire du Roy. Ouvrage enrichi de quantité de Planches en Taille-douce. A
Paris, Nyon, Didot, Quillau, M.DCC.XXXII. *Half-
title, and xiv prel. pp; Text 298 pp. Approbation &
Privilege 2 pp.* 'Réponse' *etc.* 63 pp. *Maps and
plates numbered* I *to* XXXVII *and* 36. *Fine copy;
Calf. 4to.*   (12s. 6d. 1168)

FRIENDLY (A) Address to All Reasonable Americans on The Subject of our Political Confusions: In which The necessary Consequences of Violently oppofing the King's Troops, And of a General Non-Importation are fairly stated. *America:* Printed for the Purchasers, 1774. *Imperfect, wanting all after page* 16. *8vo.* (*2s. 6d.* 1169)

FRIENDLY (A) Address to all Reasonable Americans, On the Subject of our Political Confusions: In which the Necessary Consequences of Violently oppofing the King's Troops, And of a General Non-Importation are fairly stated. New-York, Printed: *London*, Reprinted for Richardson and Urquhart, at the Royal-Exchange. 1774. *56 pp. Half mor. 8vo.* (*4s. 6d.* 1170)

FROBISHER (MARTIN). De/ Martini/ Forbisseri/ Angli Navigati-/one in Regiones Occi-/dentis et Septen-/trionis/ Narratio hiftorica,/ Ex Gallico fermone in La-/tinum tranflata/ per/ D. Joan. Tho. Freigivm./ Cum gratia & privilegio Imperiali./ cɔ. ɔ. xxc. [*Colophon*] *Noribergæ/* Imprimebatur, in officina Ca-/tharinæ Gerlachin, & Hære-/dum Iohannis Mon-/tani./ Anno/ cɔ ɔ xxc./ *44 leaves; Signatures A & F in sixes and B to E in eights. With a woodcut* ' Pictvra vel Delineatio hominum nvper ex Anglia advectorum, una cum eorum armis, tentoriis, & naviculis.' *8vo.* (*2l. 12s. 6d.* 1171)

FROGER (F). Relation d'un Voyage Fait en 1695. 1696. & 1697. Aux Cotes D'Afrique, Detroit de Magellan, Bresil, Cayenne et Isles Antilles, Par une Efcardre des Vaiffeaux du Roi, commandée par M. De Gennes. Faite par le Sieur Froger Ingenieur Volontaire fur le Vaiffeau le Faucon Anglois. Enrichie de grand nombre de Figures deffinées fur les lieux. A *Amsterdam*, Chez les Héritiers, d'Antoine Schelte. M.DC.XCIX. *Engraved title; title; Dedication* 4 *pp; Preface* 6 *pp; Text* 227 *pp. Maps or plates at pp.* 7, 11, 14, 16, 21, 32, 41, 43, 46, 57, 65, 73, 79, 87, 94, 101, 103, 104, 106, 119, 127, 130, 140 (2), 154, 162, 172, 218. 12*mo.* (*10s. 6d.* 1172)

FROGER (F.) A/ Relation/ of a/ Voyage/ Made in the Years 1695, 1696,/ 1697. on the Coafts of Africa,/ Streights of Magellan, Brafil Ca-/yenna,

and the Antilles, by a Squa-/dron of French Men
of War, under/ the Command of M. de Gennes./
By the Sieur Froger, Voluntier-Engineer/ on board
the Englifh Falcon./ Illuftrated with divers ftrange
Figures,/ drawn to the Life./ *London*,/ Printed for
M. Gillyflower in Weftminfter-/Hall; W. Freeman, M. Wotton in Fleet-/ftreet; J. Walthoe in
the Temple; and/ R. Parker in Cornhill. 1698./
*6 prel. leaves including the engraved frontispiece:
Text* 173 *pp. with* 3 *seq. pp.* 15 *copper plates and
maps at pp.* 10, 15, 32, 33, 35, 43, 49, 65(2), 66,
74, 77, 88, 99, & 120. 8*vo.*   (12*s.* 6*d.*   1173)

FROGER (F.) Relation d'un Voyage de la Mer
du Sud, Detroit de Magellan, Bresil, Cayenne et
les Isles Antilles. Où l'on voit les Obfervations
que l'Auteur a faites fur la Religion, Mœurs &
Coûtumes des Peuples qui y habitent, Et fur les
divers Animaux qui s'y trouvent, de même que des
Fruits & des Plantes qui y croiffent. Par Le Sr.
Froger. Enrichie de Figures deffinées fur les lieux,
& graveés fort proprement. A *Amsterdam.* Chez
L'Honoré et Chatelain. M.DCC.XV. *Title in red and
black;* 'Avertissement' 6 *pp;* *Text* 227 *pp: With
the* 28 *maps and plates from the same coppers as the
preceding.* 12*mo.*   (8*s.* 6*d.*   1174)

This edition is a reprint, almost page for page, of the edition of
1699; but the Dedication to Count Maurepas, and nearly all the
dates of the year, are omitted, so as to make the book read as if
the events narrated might have been recent.

FROST (John). Pictorial History of Mexico and
the Mexican War: Comprising an Account of the
Ancient Aztec Empire, the Conquest by Cortes,
Mexico under the Spaniards, the Mexican Revolution, the Republic, the Texan War, and the Recent War with the United States. By John Frost,
LL.D. Author of Pictorial history of the World,
Pictorial history of the United States, Book of the
Army, Book of the Navy, &c. &c. Embellished
with Five Hundred Engravings, from designs of
W. Croome and other distinguished Artists. *Philadelphia:* Thomas Cowperthwait and Co., 1849.
xii and 640 *pp. calf.* 8*vo.*   (6*s.* 6*d.*   1175)

FULL (A) and free Inquiry into the Merits of the
Peace; with some Strictures On the Spirit of Party.
London: T. Payne, MDCCLXV. *2 prelim. leaves and*
160 *pp. Half mor.; fine copy uncut.* 8*vo.* (6*s.*   1176)

FULTON (ROBERT). Torpedo War, and Submarine Explosions. By Robert Fulton, Fellow of the American Philosophical Society, and of the United States' Military and Philosophical Society. *New-York:* Printed by William Elliott, 114 Water-Street. 1810. 57 *pp.* ' Number and Nature of Ordnance for each of the Ships in the British Navy.' 1 *page.* ' Dimensions of Ships, Number of Men, and Draught of Water.' 1 *page.* ' Note on vessels of war of the United States.' 1 *page. With plates numbered* i-v; *half mor. Oblong* 4*to.* (18s. 6d. 1177)

FUNES (GREGORIO). Ensayo de la Historia Civil del Paraguay, Buenos-Ayres y Tucuman escrita por el Doctor D. Gregorio Funes, Dean de la Santa Iglesia Catedral de Cordova. Tomo Secundo [y Tercio]. *Buenos-Ayres:* Imprenta de M. J. Gandarillas y socios. (1816). 3 *volumes* [*vol.* 1 *wanting*]. ' Tomo Segundo.' *Half-title, title; and* 409 *pp.* ' Indice' 11 *pp.* ' Erratas' 1 *page.* ' Tomo Tercero. (1817).' 532 *pp.* ' Indice' 9 *pp.* ' Erratas' 1 *page. Uncut.* 8*vo.* (1*l.* 1*s.* 1178)

FUNNELL (WILLIAM). A Voyage round the World. Containing an Account of Captain Dampier's Expedition Into the South-Seas in the Ship St. George, in the Years 1703 and 1704. With his various Adventures, Engagements, &c. and a particular and exact Defcription of feveral Iflands in the Atlantick Ocean, the Brazilian Coaft, the Paffage round Cape Horn, and the Coafts of Chili, Peru, and Mexico. Together with the Author's Voyage from Amapalla on the Weft-Coaft of Mexico, to East-India. His paffing by Three Unknown Iflands, and thro' a New-difcover'd Streight near the Coaft of New Guinea; His Arrival at Amboyna: With a large Defcription of that and other Spice Iflands; as alfo of Batavia, the Cape of Good Hope, &c. Their Rivers, Harbours, Plants, Animals, Inhabitants, &c. With divers Maps, Draughts, Figures of Plants and Animals. By William Funnell, Mate to Captain Dampier. *London*, Printed by W. Botham for James Knapton, at the Crown in St. Paul's Churchyard. 1707. *Title ; Dedication* 'To the Honourable Jofiah Burchett' 6 *pp;* ' The Preface' 6 *pp;* ' The Contents'

10 *pp; Text* 300 *pp.* ' Index' 17 *pp. Fine copy, calf.* 8*vo.*   (10*s.* 6*d.*   1179)

First Edition, generally considered as the fourth volume of Dampier's Collection, though there is no indication of its having been
so intended at the time of publication. There is a map of the
world facing the title, and 14 other copper-plates at pages 6, 8,
9, 11, 12, 18, 40, 105, 120, 122, 131, 230, 254, and 266. *See* DAM-
PIER.

FURLONG (LAWRENCE). The American Pilot;
Containing the Courses and Distances between the
Principal Harbours, Capes and Headlands, from
Paſſamaquoddy through the Gulph of Florida, with
Directions for ſailing into the ſame, deſcribing the
Soundings, Bearings of the Light-Houſes and
Beacons from the Rocks, Shoals, Ledges, &c.
Together with the Courses and Distances From
Cape-Cod and Cape-Ann to George's-Bank,
through the South and Eaſt Channels, and the
ſetting of the Currents, with the Latitudes and
Longitudes of the principal Harbours on the Coast,
together with a Tide Table. By Capt. Lawrence
Furlong. Corrected and improved by the most
experienced Pilots in the United States—Also, Information to Masters of Veſſels, wherein the manner of tranſacting Buſineſs at the Cuſtom-Houses
is fully elucidated. Published according to Act of
Congress. Third Edition. *Newburyport* (Maſſa-
chusetts). Printed by Edmund M. Blunt, (Proprietor) 1800. 251 *pp. Calf.* 8*vo.*   (7*s.* 6*d.* 1180)

FURLONG (LAWRENCE). The American Coast
Pilot: Containing the Courses and Distances between the Principal Harbours, Capes, and Headlands, From Passamaquoddy, through the Gulph
of Florida; With Directions for sailing into the
same, describing the Soundings, Bearings, Shoals,
Ledges, &c. Together with the Courses and Distances From Cape Cod and Cape Ann to George's
Bank, through the South and East Channels, and
the setting of the Currents, with the Latitudes and
Longitudes of the principal Harbours on the Coast,
together with a Tide Table. By Capt. Lawrence
Furlong. Corrected and improved by the most experienced Pilots in the United States.—Also Information to Masters of Vessels, wherein the manner of transacting Business at the Custom Houses
is fully elucidated. Sixth Edition. *Newburyport*—
Edmund M. Blunt, Proprietor. June 1809. 389

pp. *With* 15 *Plans and Charts.* *Fine copy in old
calf.* 8vo.   (7s. 6d.   1181)

FURLONG (LAWRENCE). The American Coast
Pilot: Containing the Courses & Distances between the Principal Harbours, Capes & Headlands, From Passamaquoddy, through the Gulph
of Florida; With Directions for Sailing into the
same, describing the Sounding Bearings of the
Light-Houses and Beacons from the Rocks, Shoals,
Ledges, etc. Together with the Courses and Distances from Cape Cod and Cape Ann to George's
Bank, through the South and East Channels, and
the setting of the Currents: With the Latitudes
& Longitudes of the principal Harbours on the
Coast, together with a Tide Table. By Capt. Lawrence Furlong. Corrected and Improved by the
most Experienced Pilots in the United States.
Also, Information to Masters of Vessels, wherein
the manner of transacting Business at the Custom
Houses is fully elucidated. Seventh Edition. *New-
York*—Printed by Edmund M. Blunt, [June 1812]
311 *pp. Tables and Appendix* 63 *pp. With* 15 *Plans
and Charts.* 8vo.   (7s. 6d.   1182)

FURTHER (A) Examination of our Prefent American Meafures and of The Reafons and the Principles On which they are founded. By the Author
of Confiderations on the Meafures carrying on with
Refpect to the British Colonies in North-America. [Mathew Robinson.] *Bath:* R. Cruttwell,
MDCCLXXVI. *Title and* 256 *pp. Stitched and uncut.*
8vo.   (7s. 6d.   1183)

GAGE (Thomas). A full Survey/ of/ Sion and Babylon, /And/ A clear Vindication of the Parifh-Churches and Pa-/rochial-Minifters of Eng-land, from the uncharitable/ Cen-fure, the infamous Title, and the in-ju-/rious Nick-name of Babylonifh./ Or, A Scripture Difproof, and Syllogiftical Convic-tion of M. Charles/ Nichols, of Kent, his Errone-ous Affertions, Juftifying his/ Separated Congrega-tion for the true Houfe of God ;/ and branding all the Parochial Churches, and the/ Parifh Officiating Minifters in England, with/ the infamous Title of Babylonifh./ Delivered in three Sabbath-dayes Sermons, in the Parifh Church/ of Deal, in Kent, after a Publick Difpute in the fame/ Church with the faid Mr. Charles Nichols, upon/ the 20. day of October 1653./ By Thomas Gage, Preacher of the Word, to the Church within the/ Bounds and Li-mits of Deal in Kent./ *London*, Printed by W. Bentley, and are to be fold by Jofhuah/ Kirton, at the Kings Arms in St. Pauls Church-yard. 1654./ 9 *prel. leaves; Text 86 pp. half morocco; fine copy.* *4to.* (1*l*. 11*s*. 6*d*. 1184)

GAGE (Thomas). The Englifh-American his Tra-vail by Sea and Land :/ Or,/ A New Survey/ of the/ Weft-India's,/ Containing/ A Journall of Three thoufand and Three hundred/ Miles within the main Land of America./ Wherein is fet forth his Voyage from Spain to Sᵗ. Iohn de Vlhua ;/ and from thence to Xalappa, to Tlaxcalla, the City of Angeles, and/ forward to Mexico ; With the de-fcription of that great City,/ as it was in former times, and alfo at this prefent./ Likewife his Jour-ney from Mexico through the Provinces of Guax-

aca,/ Chiapa, Guatemala, Vera Paz, Truxillo, Comayagua; with his/ abode Twelve Years about
Guatemala, and efpecially in the/ Indian-towns of
Mixco, Pinola, Petapa, Amatitlan./ As alfo his
ftrange and wonderfull Converfion, and Calling
from thofe/ remote Parts to his Native Countrey./
With his return through the Province of Nicaragua, and Cofta Rica,/ to Nicoya, Panama, Portobelo, Cartagena, and Havana, with divers/ occurrents and dangers that did befal in the faid Journey./ Also,/ A New and exact Difcovery of the
Spanifh Navigation to/ thofe Parts; And of their
Dominions, Government, Religion, Forts,/ Caftles,
Ports, Havens, Commodities, fafhions, behaviour
of/ Spaniards, Priefts and Friers, Blackmores, Mulatto's Meftifo's,/ Indians; and of their Feafts and
Solemnities./ With a Grammar, or fome few Rudiments of the Indian Tongue,/ called, Poconchi,
or Pocoman./ By the true and painfull endevours
of Thomas Gage, now Preacher of/ the Word of
God at Acris in the County of Kent, Anno Dom.
1648./ *London*, Printed by R. Cotes, and are to
be fold by Humphrey Blunden at the/ Caftle in
Cornhill, and Thomas Williams at the Bible in
Little Britain, 1648./ *First Edition. 5 prel. leaves;
viz. Title, Dedication, and To the Reader, in verse,
Signed* 'Thomas Chaloner.' *Text* 220 *pp. The Contents* 12 *pp. Folio.*   (1*l.* 11*s.* 6*d.*   1185)
Presentation copy from the Author. " Ex dono Authoris. Tho:
Gage. Novemb 5to 1648."

GAGE (Thomas). A New Survey/ of the/ West-India's :/ Or,/ The Englifh American his Travail by
Sea and Land :/ Containing/ A Journal of Three
thoufand and Three hundred Miles within the main
Land of America./ Wherein is fet forth his Voyage from Spain to St. John de Vlhua ;/ and from
thence to Xalappa, to Tlaxcalla, the City of Angels,
and/ forward to Mexico ; With the defcription of
that great City,/ as it was in former times, and alfo
at this prefent./ Likewife, his Journey from Mexico, through the Provinces of Guaxaca,/ Chiapa,
Guatemala, Vera Paz, Truxillo, Comayagua ; with
his/ abode Twelve years about Guatemala, and
efpecially in the/ Indian-Towns of Mixco, Pinola,
Petapa, Amatitlan./ As alfo his ftrange and wonderfull Converfion and Calling from thofe/ remote

Parts, to his Native Countrey./ With his return through the Province of Nicaragua, and Cofta Rica, to/ Nicoya, Panama, Portobelo, Cartagena, and Havana, with divers/ Occurrents and Dangers that did befal in the faid Journey./ Alfo,/ A New and Exact Difcovery of the Spanifh Navigation/ to thofe Parts: And of their Dominions, Government, Re-ligion, Forts,/ Caftles, Ports, Havens, Commodities, Fafhions, Behaviour of/ Spaniards, Priefts and Friers, Blackmores, Mulatto's, Meftifo's,/ Indians; and of their Feafts and Solemnities./ With a Gram-mar, or fome few Rudiments of the Indian Tongue,/ called Poconchi, or Pocoman./ The Second Edi-tion enlarged by the Author, and beautified with Maps./ By the true and painful endevours of Thomas Gage, Preacher of the/ Word of God at Deal in the County of Kent./ *London,* Printed by E. Cotes, and fold by John Sweeting/ at the Angel in Popes-head-alley, M. DC. LV. *5 prel. leaves; viz. Title, Dedication, and To the Reader, Signed* 'Tho-mas Chaloner.' *Text* 220 pp. *The Contents* 12 pp. 4 *Copper-plate Maps, viz.* 1 'Americæ Defcrip.' *facing the title:* 2 'The Ylandes of the Weft Indies,' *at p.* 20: 3 'Hifpania Nova' *p.* 68; *and* 4 'Terra Firma' *at p.* 118. *Old calf. Folio.* (18s. 1186)

GAGE (THOMAS). A New Survey of the/ West-In-dies:/ Or,/ The Englifh American his Travel by Sea and Land:/ Containing/ A Journal of Three thou-fand and Three hundred Miles/ within the main Land of/ America:/ Wherein is fet forth/ His Voy-age from Spain to S. John de Vlhua; and thence/ to Xalappa, to Tlaxcalla, the City of Angels, and forward to/ Mexico: With the Defcription of that great City, as it/ was in former times, and alfo at this prefent./ Likewife/ His Journey from Mexi-co, through the Provinces of Gua-/xaca, Chiapa, Guatemala, Vera Paz, Truxillo, Comayagua,/ with his abode XII. years about Guatemala, efpeciall in/ the Indian Towns of Mixco, Pinola, Petapa, Ama-titlan./ As also/ His ftrange and wonderful Con-verfion and Calling from/ thofe remote Parts to his Native Countrey: With his Return/ through the Province of Nicaragua and Cofta Rica, to Nicoya,/ Panama, Porto bello, Cartegena and Havana, with divers Occur-/rents and Dangers that did befal in the faid Journey. Also/ A new and exact Difcovery

of the Spanifh Navigation/ to thofe Parts: And of
their Dominions, Government, Reli-/gion, Forts,
Castles, Ports, Havens, Commodities, Fa-/fhions,
Behavior of Spaniards, Priefts and Friers,/ Black-
moors, Mulatto's, Meftifo's, Indians ;/ and of their
Feafts and Solemnities./ With a Grammar, or fome
few Rudiments of/ the Indian Tongue, called Poconchi or Pocoman./ The third Edition enlarged
by the Author, with a new and accurate Map./ By
Thomas Gage./ *London :* Printed by A. Clark, and
are to be fold by/ John Martyn, Robert Horn and
Walter Kettilby. 1677./ 4 *prel. leaves ; viz. Title,
and To the Reader ; Text* 577 *pp. The Contents* 18
pp. 8*vo.* (12*s.* 6*d.* 1187)

GAGE (Thomas). A New Survey of the/ West-Indies./ Being/ a Journal of Three thoufand and Three
hundred Miles/ within the main Land of/ America :/ By Tho. Gage, the only Proteftant that was/
ever known to have travel'd thofe Parts./ Setting
forth/ His Voyage from Spain to S. John de Ul-
hua ; and thence/ to Xalapa, Tlaxcalla, the City of
Angels, and/ Mexico : With a Defcription of that
great/ City, as in former times, and at prefent./
Likewife/ His Journey thence through Guaxaca,
Chiapa, Guate-/mala, Vera Paz, &c. with his
abode xii. years about/ Guatemala, His wonderful
Converfion and Calling to/ his Native Country:
With his Return through Nica-/ragua and Cofta
Rica, to Nicoya, Panama, Porto bello,/ Cartagena,
and Havana./ With/ An Account of the Spanifh
Navigation thither; their/ Government, Caftles,
Ports, Commodities, Religion,/ Priefts and Friers,
Negro's, Mulatto's, Meftifo's, Indians ;/ and of their
Feafts and Solemnities./ With a Grammar, or fome
few Rudiments of/ the Indian Tongue, called Po-
conchi or Pocoman./ The fourth Edition enlarg'd
by the Author, with an accurate Map./ *London :*
Printed by M. Clark, for J. Nicolfon at/ the Kings
Arms in Little Britain and T. Newborough, at/
the Golden-Ball in S. Pauls Church-Yard. 1699./
Title, To the Reader 5 *pp. Text* 477 *pp. The Contents* 18 *pp. With a Map of Mexico. Old calf.*
8*vo.* (10*s.* 6*d.* 1188)

GAGE (Thomas). A Survey of the Spanifh-Weft-
Indies, *etc. London :* Printed for Thomas Horne,
at the South Entrance of the Royal Exchange.

1702. *Title, ' To the Reader,' 5 pp. Text 44 pp. The Contents 18 pp. Without the map. Half morocco. 8vo.* (14s. 6d. 1189)

GAGE (Thomas). The Traveller. Part I. Containing, A Journal of Three Thoufand Three Hundred Miles, through the Main Land of South-America. By Mr. Thomas Gage, an Englifhman ; and a Miffionary Friar in New-Spain, twelve Years. In which is fet forth, His Journey from St. John de Ulva to Mexico, with a Defcription of that great City as in former Times, and at prefent ; as alfo his Travels through many other Parts of New-Spain ; with an Account of their Government, Caftles, Ports and Commodities ; as alfo their ecclefiaftical State, in which the lafcivious Intrigues, and wicked Lives of the Jefuits and Friars in thofe Parts, and their grand Impofitions upon the poor ignorant Natives, are truly delineated. To which is added, The Policy, Manners, Behaviour, Arts and Sciences, religious Rites and Ceremonies, Feafts and Solemnities of the Native Indians. Concluding with The Wonderful Converfion of the Author to the Proteftant Religion ; his Efcape from the Spaniards, in South-America ; his Return to England, his Native Country ; and the Reception he met with there by his Relations, after an Abfence of four-and-twenty Years. To be publifhed Monthly in the New American Magazine. *Woodbridge,* in *New-Jersey : Printed and Sold by James Parker, 1758. 136 pp. 8vo.* (1l. 1s. 1190)

GAGE (Thomas). Nouvelle/ Relation,/ Contenant/ les Voyages de Thomas Gage/ dans la Nouvelle Efpagne, fes diverfes avan-/tures ; & fon retour par la Province de Ni-/caragua, jufques à la Havane./ Avec/ la Description de la Ville/ de Mexique telle qu'elle eftoit autrefois,/ & comme elle eft à prefent./ Ensemble vne Description/ exacte des Terres & Provinces que poffedent les E-/fpagnols en toute l'Amerique, de la forme de leur/ Gouvernement Ecclefiaftique & Politique, de leur/ Commerce, de leurs Mœurs, & de celles des Criol-/les, des Metifs, des Mulatres, des Indiens, &/ des Negres./ Tome I./ A *Amsterdam,*/ Chez Paul Marret, dans le Beurs-ftraat/ proche le Dam à la Renommée./ M. DC. LXXXXV. *Two Volumes. Vol. I. 12 prelim. leaves, including the engraved Title ; Text 200 and 178*

pp. 9 *Maps and Plates at pp.* 1, 54, 108, 114, 151,
152, 184, 1, 13. *Vol. 11.* 1694, 8 *prelim. leaves in-*
cluding the engraved Title (8*th blank*) *and* 318 *pp.*
7 *Maps and Plates at pp.* 1, 29, 126, 159, 291, 300,
and 305. *Calf. Small* 8*vo.*　　　(7*s.* 6*d.* 1191)

GAGE (Thomas).　Nouvelle/ Relation,/ Contenant/
les Voyages de Thomas Gage/ dans la Nouvelle
Efpagne, fes diverfes avan-/tures; & fon retour par
la Province de Ni-/caragua, jufques à la Havane./
Avec/ la Description de la Ville/ de Mexique telle
qu'elle eftoit autrefois,/ & comme elle eft à prefent./
Ensemble une Description/ exacte des Terres
& Provinces que poffedent les Efpagnols en/ toute
l'Amerique, de la forme de leur Gouvernement
Ecclefia-/ftique & Politique, de leur/Commerce, de
leurs Mœurs,&/de celles des Criolles,des Metifs,des
Mulatres des Indiens,/ and des Negres./　Tome I./
Troifiéme Edition Reveuë & Corrigée./　A *Am-*
sterdam,/ Chez Paul Marret, dans le Beurs-ftraat/
proche le Dam à la Renommée./　M.DC.XCIX. *Two*
Volumes. Vol. I. 12 *prel. leaves including the en-*
graved title; text 200 *and* 176 *pp.* 9 *maps and plates*
at pp. 1, 36, 108, 114, 152, 184, 191, 1, *and* 13.
Vol. 11. 8 *prel. leaves* (8*th blank*) *and* 318 *pp. with* 7
maps and plates at pp. 1, 29, 126, 159, 291, 300 &
305. *Calf. Small* 8*vo.*　　　(7*s.* 6*d.* 1192)

GAGE (Thomas).　Nouvelle Relation, contenant
les Voyages de Thomas Gage dans la Nouvelle
Efpagne, fes diverfes avantures, & fon retour par
la Province de Nicaragua, jufques à la Havane.
Avec la Description de la Ville de Mexique, telle
qu'elle étoit autrefois, & comme elle eft à prefent.
Ensemble une Description exacte des terres &
Provinces que poffedent les Espagnols en toute
l'Amerique, de la forme de leur Gouvernement
Ecclefiaftique & Politique, de leur Commerce, de
leurs Mœurs, & de celles des Criolles, des Metifs,
des Mulatres, des Indiens, & des Negres　Avec
Figures. Tome I. [& Tome II.] Quatriéme Edition revûë & corrigée [*vignette*].　A *Amsterdam*,
chez Paul Marret dans le Beurs-ftraat, proche le
Dam, à la Renommée. M.DCCXX. 2 *vols. Vol. I.*
Engraved half Title, Title, and 12 *prelim. leaves,*
Text 431 *pp. & maps or plates at pp.* 1, 43, 117, 123,
165, 167, 217 *and* 221. *Vol. II.　Engraved half*

*Title, Title, and 4 prelim. leaves, Text 360 pp. and maps
or plates at pp.* 10, 52, 145, 182, 236, 334, 340 *and*
342. *Calf. Small 8vo.* (10s. 6d. 1193)

GAGE (Thomas). Nouvelle/ Relation,/ Contenant/
les Voyages de Thomas Gage/ dans la nouvelle
Efpagne, fes diverfes avan-/tures, & fon retour
dans la Province de Ni-/caragua jufqu'à la
Havane./ Avec/ la Description de la Ville/ de
Mexique, telle qu'elle étoit autrefois, &/ comme elle
eft à prefent./ Ensemble vne Description/ exacte
des/Terres & Provinces que poffedent/ les Efpagnols
en toute l'Amérique, de la for-/me de leur Gouvernement Ecclefiaftique &/ Politique, de leur Commerce, de leurs Mœurs,/ & de celles des Creoles,
des Metifs,/ des Mu-/lâtres, des Indiens, & des
Négres./ Tome I. A *Amsterdam,*/ Chez Paul
Marret, Marchand Libraire/ dans le Beurs-ftraat./
M.DCC.XXI./ *Two Volumes. Vol. I.* 12 *prel. leaves,
inclusive of the Engraved and printed Titles; and
Text* 200 *and* 178 *pp.* 9 *Maps and Plates at pp.* 1,
36, 108, 114, 152, 184, 191; 1, 13. *Vol. II.* 6
*prel. leaves, including the engraved and printed Titles;
Text* 316 *pp.* 7 *Maps and Plates at pp.* 1, 29, 126,
159, 291, 300, 305. *Calf by Bedford. Small
8vo.* (18s. 1194)

GAGE (Thomas, *General*). Autograph Letter to
Governor Tryon of New York dated at Boston,
July 18, 1775. 2 *pages, entirely autograph, interest-
ing and important. Folio.* (1l. 10s. 1195)

GALLOWAY (Joseph). The Examination of
Joseph Galloway, Efq; Late Speaker of the House
of Assembly of Pennsylvania. Before the House
of Commons, in a Committee on the American
Papers. With explanatory Notes. *London:* J.
Wilkie. MDCCLXXIX. *Title and* 85 *pp. Half mor.
8vo.* (5s. 6d. 1196)

GALLOWAY (Joseph). The Examination of
Joseph Galloway, Efq; Late Speaker of the House
of Assembly of Pennsylvania. Before the House
of Commons, in a Committee on the American
Papers. With explanatory Notes. The Second
Edition. *London:* J. Wilkie. M DCC LXXX. *Title
and* 85 *pp. Half mor. 8vo.* (5s. 6d. 1197)

GALVANO (Antonio), The/ Discoveries/ of the

World from their/ firſt originall vnto the/ yeere of
our Lord/ 1555./ Briefly written in the Por-/tu-
gall tongue by Antonie/ Galvano, Gouernour of/
Ternate, the chiefe Iſland/ of the Malucos :/ Corrected, quoted, and now/ publiſhed in Engliſh by
Richard/ Hakluyt, ſometimes ſtudent/ of Chriſt-
church in/ Oxford./ *Londini,/* Impenſis G. Biſhop./ 1601./ *Title within a broad type metal border,
reverse blank; Dedication* ' To the Right/ Honorable,
Sir/ Robert Cecill,' *etc.* 5 *pp. in roman type, dated*
' 29. of October 1601.' *and Signed by* Richard Hakluyt; *next page blank;* Francis de Souſa Tauares
vnto the/ high and mightie Prince Don/ Iohn, *etc.*
4 *pp. Text in Black letter,* 97 *pp. Very fine copy in
blue morocco by Bedford.* 4*to.* (5*l.* 15*s.* 6*d.* 1198)

Hakluyt, in his Preface, says, " The worke, though ſmall in
bulke, containeth ſo much rare and profitable matter, as I know
not where to ſeeke the like, within ſo narrow and ſtreite a com-
paſſe." And again, " Now touching the tranſlation, it may
pleaſe you ſir, to be advertiſed that it was firſt done into our language by ſome honeſt and well affected merchant of our nation,
whoſe name by no meanes I could attaine vnto, and that as it
ſeemeth many yeeres ago. For it hath lien by me aboue theſe
twelue yeeres. In all which ſpace though I haue made much
inquirie, and ſent to Lifbon, where it ſeemeth it was printed,
yet to this day I could neuer obtain the originall copie; whereby
I might reforme the manifold errours of the tranſlator," &c.
The only copy of the original edition in Portuguese that I have
ever seen, or possessed, forms part of the wonderful collection
of John Carter Brown, Esq. of Providence, Rhode Island.

GALVANO (Antonio). Tratado dos Descobrimentos
Antigos, e Modernos, Feitos até a Era de 1550.
com os nomes particulares das peſſoas que os fizeraõ :
e em que tempos, e as ſuas alturas, e dos deſvairados
caminhos por onde a pimenta, e eſpeciaria veyo da
India ás noſſas partes: obra certo muy notavel, e
copioſa. Composto pelo famoso Antonio Galvaõ,
Offerecido ao Excellentissimo Senhor Dom Luiz
de Menezes, Quinto Conde da Ericeira, do Concelho
de Sua Mageſtade, Coronel, e Brigadeiro de Infan-
taria, Viſo Rey, e Capitaõ General, que foy dos
Eſtados da India, &c. *Lisboa* Occidental, Na
Officina Ferreiriana. M.DCC.XXXI. Com todas as
licenças neceſſarias. 8 *prel. leaves; and* 100 *pp.*
Folio. (2*l.* 12*s.* 6*d.* 1199)

GAMBIER (J.) A Narrative of Facts relative to
the Conduct of Vice-Admiral Gambier, during his
late Command in North America. Written by the
Admiral himself. *London:* M. Scott. MDCCLXXXII.
Half-title, title and 73 *pp. Signed* 'J. Gambier.'
Half-mor. 8*vo.* (10*s.* 6*d.* 1200)

GAONA (Joan de). ✛ Colloqvios de-❧/la paz,
y tranquilidad Chri/-ſtiana, en lengua/ Mexicana./
Con Licencia, y/ Priuilegio./ En *Mexico*, ē Cafa
d *Pedro Ocharte*./ M.D.LXXXII./ 15 *prel. leaves;*
Text 121 *folioed leaves. Calf extra by Bedford. Fine*
copy. 16*mo.* (6*l.* 16*s.* 6*d.* 1201)

GARAY (Jose de). An *Account of the Isthmus of*
Tehuantepec in the Republic of Mexico; with pro-
posals for Establishing a Communication between
the Atlantic and Pacific Oceans, based upon the
Surveys and Reports of a Scientific Commission,
Appointed by the Projector Don José de Garay.
London : J. D. Smith and Co., 1846. 128 *pp.*
With 2 Plans of Mexico. 8*vo.* (4*s.* 6*d.* 1202)

GARCIA (Gregorio). ✛ Origen de los Indios de
el Nuevo Mundo, e Indias Occidentales, averiguado
con discurſo de opiniones por el Padre Preſentado
Fr. Gregorio Garcia, de la Orden de Predicadores.
Tratanse en este Libro varias cosas, y puntos curioſos, tocantes à diverſas Ciencias, i Facultades,
con que ſe hace varia Hiſtoria, de mucho guſto para
el Ingenio, i Entendimiento de Hombres agudos, i
curioſos. Segunda Impresion. Enmendada, y añadida de algunas opiniones, ò coſas notables, en
maior prueba de lo que contiene, con Tres Tablas
mui puntuales de los Capitulos, de las Materias, y
Autores, que las tratan. Dirigido al Angelico
Doct. Sᵗᵒ. Tomas de Aquino. Con Privilegio Real.
En *Madrid* : En la Imprenta de Francisco Mra-
tinez Abad. Año de 1729. 16 *prel. leaves; and*
336 *pp. Tabla* 40 *leaves. Large paper, uncut.*
Folio. (1*l.* 11*s.* 6*d.* 1203)

GARCIA (Gregorio). *The same, on ordinary Paper.*
Folio. (15*s.* 1203*)

GARCILASSO DE LA VEGA (El Ynca). La
Florida/ del Ynca./ Historia del Adelanta-/do
Hernando de Soto, Gouernador y capi-/tan general del Reyno de la Florida, y de/ otros heroicos
caualleros Eſpañoles è/ Indios ; eſcrita por el Ynca
Garcilaſſo/ de la Vega, capitan de ſu Mageſtad,/
natural de la gran ciudad del Coz-/co, cabeça de
los Reynos y/ prouincias del Peru./ Dirigida al
ſereniſſimo Principe, Duque/ de Bragança, &c./
Con licencia de la ſanta Jnquiſicion./ En *Lisbona*./

Impreſſo por Pedro Crasbeeck./   Año 1605./ Con
priuilegio Real./   *9 prel. and* 351 *leaves.* 'Tabla.'
13 *pp.* 'Erratas.' 4 *pp.   Poor copy, much wormed.*
4*to.*   (15*s.*   1204)

GARCILASSO DE LA VEGA (El Ynca). Primera Parte de los/ Commentarios/ Reales,/ qve
Tratan del Ori-/gen de los Yncas, Reyes qve fve-/
ron del Perv, de ſv Idolatria, Leyes, y/ gouierno
en paz en guerra: de ſus vidas y con-/quiſtas, y de
todo lo que fue aquel Imperio y/ ſu Republica,
antes que los Eſpano-/les paſſaran a el./   Eſcritos
por el Ynca Garcilaſſo de la Vega, natural del
Cozco,/ y Capitan de ſu Mageſtad./ Dirigidos a la
Sereniſſima Prin-/ceſa Doña Catalina de Portugal,
Duqueza/ de Bragança, &c./   Con licencia de la
Sanĉta Inquiſicion, Ordinario, y Paço./   En *Lis-
boa :*/ En la officina de Pedro Crasbeeck./ Año de
M.DCIX./ [*Colophon, on the reverse of folio* 264] Con
Licencia de la Santa Inquiſicion./ En Lisbona./
Impreſſo en caſa de Pedro Crasbeeck./ Año de
MDCVIII./   11 *prel. and 264 folioed leaves. Copper
plate of the Arms of the Author on the Second leaf.
Old calf. Folio.*   (2*l.* 2*s.*   1205)

GARCILASSO DE LA VEGA (El Ynca). His-
toria/ General del/ Perv./ Trata el descvbrimiento
del ;/ y como lo ganaron los Eſpañoles. Las guerras
ciuiles/ que huuo entre Piçarros, y Almagros, ſobre
la partija/ de la tierra. Caſtigo y leuantamiẽto de
tiranos : y/ otros ſuceſſos particulares que en la/
Hiſto-/ria ſe contienen./ Escrita por El Ynca Garcilasso de la/ Vega, Capitan de ſu mageſtad, etc./
Dirigida a la Limpiſſima Virgen/ Maria Madre de
Dios, y Señora nueſtra./ Con Privilegio Real./
¶ En *Cordoua*, Por la Viuda de Andres Barrera,
y à ſu coſta. Año, M.DC.XVII./ 8 *prel. and Text in*
300 *folioed leaves;* 'Tabla,' 12 *pp. Vellum.
Folio.*   (1*l.* 11*s.* 6*d.* 1206)

This is the second volume or continuation of the preceding work.
The two volumes, though differing very much in size, should go
together.

GARCILASSO DE LA VEGA (El Ynca). [*Engraved Title*] Histoire/ des/ Gverres Civiles/ des
Espagnols/ dans les Indes :/ [*Printed Title*] His-
toire/ des Gverres Civiles/ des Espagnols/ dans les
Indes ;/ Cauſées par les Souſleumens des Picarres,

et des/ Almagres ; fuiuis de plufieurs Defolations,
à peine/ croyables ; Arriuées au Perv par l'Ambi-
tion, & par/ l'Auarice des Conquerans de ce grand
Empire./ Efcritte en Efpagnol par L'Ynca Gar-
cilasso/ de la Vega ;/ Et mife en François, Par. I.
Bavdoin./ *A Paris,*/ Chez Simeon Piget, Libraire
Iuré,/ ruë Saint Iacques, à la Prudence./ M.DC.
LVIII./ Avec Privilege dv Roy,/ 16 *prel. leaves ;
and* 631 *pp. Table* 17 *pp.* SVITTE/ des/ Gverres
Civiles/ des Espagnols/ dans le Perv ;/ Iufques à la
Mort tragique du Prince Tvpac Amarv,/ Heritier
de cét Empire ; Et à l'Eil funefte des Yncas/ les
plus proches de la Couronne./ Traduction de
l'Efpagnol de L'Ynca Garcilasso/ de la Vega ;/
Par. I. Bavdoin./ *A Paris,*/ Chez Simeon Piget,
Libraire Iuré,/ ruë Saint Iacques, à la Prudence./
M.DC.LVIII./ Avec Privilege dv Roy,/ *Title and*
555 *pp. Table* 20 *pp. Two Volumes. Calf extra.*
4*to.* (1*l.* 1*s.* 1207)

GARCILASSO DE LA VEGA (EL YNCA). The/
Royal/ Commentaries/ of/ Peru/ in/ Two Parts./
The First Part./ Treating of the Original of their
Incas or Kings: Of their Idola-/try : Of their
Laws and Government both in Peace and War :
Of the Reigns/ and Conquefts of the Incas : With
many other Particulars relating to their/ Empire
and Policies before fuch time as the Spaniards
invaded their Countries./ The Second Part./
Defcribing the manner by which that new World
was conquered/ by the Spaniards. Alfo the Civil
Wars between the Piçarrifts and Alma-/griens,
occafioned by Quarrels arifing about the Divifion
of that Land. Of/ the Rife and Fall of Rebels ;
and other Particulars contained in that Hiftory./
Illuftrated with Sculptures./ Written originally
in Spanifh,/ By the Inca Garcilasso de la Vega,/
And rendred into Englifh, by Sir Pavl Rycavt, Kt./
London,/ Printed by Miles Flefher, for Richard
Tonfon within Gray's-Inn-Gate/ next Gray's-Inn-
Lane, MDCLXXXVIII./ 4 *prel. leaves ; viz. Title, The
Translator to the Reader, and Epistle Dedicatory ;
Text* 1019 *pp. Index* 8 *pp. Portrait of Sir Paul
Rycaut, and* 10 *Copper plates at pp.* 13, 78, 193, 328,
402, 430, 450, 460, 474, 550. *Fine copy in old calf.*
Folio. (1*l.* 1*s.* 1208)

GARCILASSO DE LA VEGA (El Ynca). [*Engraved Title*] Histoire/ des/ Yncas/ Rois/ du/ Perou./ A'Amsterdam/ chez Gerard Kuyper/ [*Printed Title*] Histoire/ des/ Yncas,/ Rois du Perou ;/ Contenant leur origine, depuis le premier Ynca/ Manco Capac, leur Etabliſſement, leur Idolatrie,/ leurs Sacrifices, leurs Loix, leurs Conquêtes ;/ les merveilles du Temple du Soleil ; & tout/ l' Etat de ce grand Empire, avant que les/ Eſpagnols s'en rendiſſent maîtres./ Avec une Deſcription des Animaux, des Fruits,/ des Mineraux, des Plantes, &c./ Traduite de l'Eſpagnol de l'Ynca Garci-/ lasso de la Vega, par J. Baudoin./ A *Amsterdam,*/ Chez Gerard Kuyper./ MDCCIV./ *Two Volumes.* Tome Premier. 12 *prel. leaves ; and* 512 *pp. Copper Plate Map and 3 Plates at pp.* 28, 62, 63, *and* 308. Tome Second. 6 *prel. leaves ; and* 492 *pp. Table* 36 *pp. Old calf.* 12*mo.* (10*s.* 6*d.* 1209)

GARCILASSO DE LA VEGA (El Ynca). Histoire/ de la Conquéte/ de la/ Floride./ Ou/ Relation de ce qui s'eſt paſſé dans la décou-/verte de ce Pays par Ferdinand de Soto,/ Compoſée en Eſpagnol par l'Inca Garcilaſſo/ de la Vega, & traduite en François/ Par P. Richelet./ A *Paris.*/ Chez Geofroi Nyon Libraire Quai des/ Auguſtins. M.DCCIX./ Avec Approbation & Privilege du Roy./ *Title, and* 281 *pp.* Histoirf/ de la/ Floride,/ ou/ Relation/ de la Conquéte/ De ce Pays par Ferdinand/ de Soto./ Seconde Partie./ M.DCC.VII. *Title and* 249 *pp. Table* 10 *pp. Two Volumes. Unbound.* 12*mo.* (7*s.* 6*d.* 1210)

GARCILASSO DE LA VEGA (El Ynca). Hiſtoire/ de la Conquete/ de la/ Floride :/ ou/ Relation de ce qui s'eſt paſſé dans la Découverte/ de ce Pais/ par/ Ferdinand de Soto ;/ Compoſée en Eſpagnol/ par/ l'Inca Garcilasso de la Vega,/ & traduite en François/ Par Sr. Pierre Richelet./ Nouvelle Edition/ Diviseeen Deux Tomes :/ Corrigée & Augmentée,/ Avec tresbelles Cartes & Figures en taille douce & d'un/ Indice./ A *Leide,*/ Chez Pierre Vander Aa./ M DCC XXXI./ *Two Volumes.* Tome Premier. 13 *prel. leaves ; and* 290 *pp. Map of Florida at p.* 1, *and copper plates at pp.* 46, 121, 132, 231 *and* 261. Tome Second 582 *pp. Plates at pp.* 302, 309, 314, *and* 349. *Small* 8*vo.* (7*s.* 6*d.* 1211)

The date 1731 is sometimes found altered with a pen to 1735, in both volumes.

GARCILASSO DE LA VEGA (EL YNCA). Geschichte/ der/ Eroberung/ von/ Florida,/ Aus dem Spanifchen/ Les Ynca Garcilaffo de la Vega/ in die Franzöfifche, und aus diefer in die Teutfche Sprache/ überfetzet von/ Heinrich Ludewig Meier./ *Zelle, Franckfurt und Leipzig,* 1753./ In Verlag George Conrad Gfellius,/ Königl. privil. Buchhändler in Zelle./ 52 and 456 pp. 8vo. (7s. 6d. 1212)

GARDEN (ALEXANDER). Regeneration and the Testimony of the Spirit. Being the Subftance of Two Sermons Lately preached in the Parifh Church of St. Philip Charles-Town, in South-Carolina. Occafioned by fome erroneous Notions of certain Men who call themfelves Methodifts. By Alexander Garden, M.A. Rector of the faid Parifh. South-Carolina, *Charles-Town,* Printed by Peter Timothy, 1740. *Title, iii, and 33 pp. Unbound.* 8vo. (7s. 6d. 1213)

GARDINER (RICHARD). An Account of the Expedition to the West Indies, against Martinico, Guadelupe, and other the Leeward Islands; Subject to the French King, 1759. By Richard Gardiner, Efq; Captain of Marines on board His Majefty's Ship Rippon, on the Expedition. *London:* Zech. Stuart, 1759. *2 prel. leaves and 75 pp. Map of Guadeloupe; and Plan of the General Attack at page 24. 4to.* (10s. 6d. 1214)

GARDINER (RICHARD). An Account of the Expedition to the West Indies, against Martinico, With the Reduction of Guadelupe, And other the Leeward Islands; Subject to the French King, 1759. By Captain Gardiner of the King's Royal Mufqueteers, late Captain of Marines on Board his Majefty's Ship Rippon, employed on this Expedition. The Third Edition. *Birmingham,* John Baskerville, 1762. *Half-title, Title, Dedication, and 92 pp. With four copper plates. 4to.* (7s. 6d. 1215)

GARDINER (RICHARD). Relation de l'Expedition aux Indes Occidentales, contre la Martinique, Avec la Reduction de la Guadelupe, Et autres Isles fous Vent, Appartenant au Roi de France, en 1759. Par Monf. Gardiner Capitaine des Moufquetaires

Royaux de S. M. Autrefois Capitaine des Troupes
de Marine à bord le Rippon, Vaiſſeau de S. M. employé á cette Expedition. Troisieme Edition. A'
Birmingham, Jean Baskerville. 1762. *Half-title,
Title, Dedication, and* 91 *pp.* 4*to.* (7*s.* 6*d.* 1216)

GARDYNER (George). A/ Description/ Of the
New/ World./ Or,/ America Iſlands and Continent :/ and by what people thoſe Regions/ are now
inhabited./ And what places are there deſolate and/
without Inhabitants./ And the Bays, Rivers, Capes,
Forts, Cities and/ their Latitudes, the Seas of their
Coaſts:/ the Trade, Winds, the North-weſt Paſſage,/
and the Commerce of the Engliſh Nation, as/ they
were all in the Year 1649. Faithfully de-/ſcribed
for information of ſuch of his Coun-/trey as deſire
Intelligence of these perticulars./ By George Gardyner of Peck-/ham, in the County of Surrey Eſq./
London :/ Printed for Robert Leybourn, and are to
be ſold/ by Thomas Pirrepoint, at the Sun in S.
Pauls/ Churchyard, 1651./ 8 *prel. leaves; viz.* ' Al-
tvm. Sapere Noli' *with wood cut, the reverse blank ;
Title, the reverse blank ;* ' To the right honorable Sir
Henry Vane, junior.' 3 *pp.* ' Errata.' 1 *page ;* ' To
the Engliſh Nation.' 4 *pp.* ' The Contents of the
Book.' 4 *pp. ;* Text 187 *pp ; the reverse of the last page
blank:* ' November 18.1650./ Imprimatur/ Nathanael Brent.'/ 1 *page, the reverse blank. Morocco extra
by Bedford. Small* 8*vo.* (21*l.* 1217)

GARELLA (Napoleon). Projet d'un Canal de
Jonction de l'Océan Pacifique et de l'Ocean Atlan-
tique a Travers l'Isthme de Panama par Napoléon
Garella, Ingenieur en Chef au Corps Royal des
Mines. *Paris.* Carilian-Gœury et V^cr Dalmont,
1845. *viii and* 233 *pp. With Plans on a large sheet.*
8*vo.* (7*s.* 6*d.* 1218)

GASS (Patrick). A Journal of the Voyages and
Travels of a Corps of Discovery, under the command of Captain Lewis and Captain Clarke, of the
Army of the United States ;\ from the Mouth of the
River Missouri, through the Interior Parts of North
America, to the Pacific Ocean; during the years
1804, 1805, & 1806. Containing An Authentic Relation of the most interesting Transactions during
the Expedition: A Description of the Country:

And an Account of its Inhabitants, Soil, Climate,
Curiosities, and Vegetable and Animal Productions. By Patrick Gass. One of the Persons employed in the Expedition. Pittsburgh : Printed
for David M'Keehan. *London :* Re-Printed for
J. Rudd, 1808. *iv pp. prel ; and Text in 381 pp.
Uncut. 8vo.* (7s. 6d. 1219)

GASS (Patrick). Journal of the Voyages and Travels of a Corps of Discovery, under the command
of Capt. Lewis and Capt. Clarke of the Army of
the United States, from the mouth of the River
Missouri through the interior parts of North America to the Pacific Ocean, During the Years 1804,
1805, and 1806. Containing an authentic relation
of the most interesting transactions during the expedition ; a description of the country ; and an account of its inhabitants, soil, climate, curiosities,
and vegetable and animal productions. By Patrick
Gass, One of the persons employed in the expedition. With geographical and explanatory Notes.
Fourth Edition—with six Engravings. [Copy-right
secured according to Law.] Printed for Mathew
Carey, *Philadelphia.* 1812. *x pp. and Text,* 262 *pp.*
12mo. (5s. 6d. 1220)

GATFORD (Lionel). Publick/ Good/ Without Pri-
vate/ Interest :/ Or,/ A Compendious Remonſtrance
of the/ preſent ſad State and Condition of the Eng-
liſh/ Colonie in Virginia./ With/ A Modeſt Declaration of the ſeverall Cauſes/ (ſo far as by the Rules
of Right, Reaſon and Religious Obſer-/vation may
be Collected) why it hath not proſpered better
hitherto/ As also,/ A Submiſſive ſuggeſtion of the
moſt prudentiall probable wayes, and/ meanes, both
Divine and Civill (that the inexpert Remembrancer
could/ for the preſent recall to minde) for its hap-
pyer improvement/ and advancement for the future./ Humbly preſented to His Highneſs the Lord
Protectour,/ By a Perſon zealouſly devoted,/ To the
more effectual propagating of the Goſpel in that
Nation,/ and to the inlargement of the Honour and
Benefit, both of the ſaid/ Colonie, and this whole
Nation, from whence they/ have been tranſplanted./
London,/ Printed for Henry Marſh, and are to be
ſold at/ the Crown in S. Paul's Church-yard. 1657./
10 *prel. leaves ; viz. Title, The Epistle Dedicatory, &*

To the Candid Reader; Text 26 pp. Signed ' L. G.'
4to.   (5l. 15s. 6d.   1221)

GAULD (GEORGE). Observations on the Florida
Kays, Reef and Gulf; with Directions for sailing
along the Kays, From Jamaica by the Grand Cay-
man and the West End of Cuba : Also a Description, with sailing Instructions, of the Coast of
West-Florida, Between the Bay of Spiritu Santo
and Cape Sable. By George Gauld, To accompany
his Charts of those Coasts, surveyed and published
by Order of the Right Honourable the Lords Commissioners of Admiralty. To which have been
added, a Description of the East Coast of Florida,
between Cape Florida and Cape Canaveral; and
Instructions for Sailing from the Eastward within
the Florida Reef. Entered at Stationers Hall.
London. W. Faden, 1796. *28 pp. Half morocco.*
4to.   (7s. 6d.   1222)

GAY (EBENEZER). Autograph Letter addressed
' For the Revᵈ Mʳ Stephen Williams at Longmeadow Springfield ' dated at Hingham March 12.
174½. *1 page.* 4to.   (7s. 6d.   1223)

   Dr. Gay was born in 1696, graduated at Harvard College in 1714,
   and in 1718 was ordained as the successor of John Norton. He
   preached successfully for 68 years, and died in 1787 at the ripe
   age of 90. Dr. Chauncey pronounced him one of the greatest and
   most valuable men of the country.

GAZETA de Mexico, defde Enero de 1735, hafta fin
de Diciembre de 1736. [24 *Numbers*] Num. 86-109.
[*Colophon to each number*] Con Licencia, y Privilegio del Excᵐᵒ. Señor Virey. En Mexico, en la
Imprenta Real del Superior Gobierno, y del Nuevo
Rezado de Doña Maria de Ribera, en el Empedra-
dillo. *pp.* 682-873. *Calf.* 4to. (1l. 11s. 6d.   1224)

GEE (JOSHUA). The Trade and Navigation of Great-
Britain considered : Shewing That the furest Way
for a Nation to increafe in Riches, is to prevent the
Importation of fuch Foreign Commodities as may
be rais'd at Home. That this Kingdom is capable
of raifing within itfelf, and its Colonies, Materials
for employing all our Poor in thofe Manufactures,
which we now import from fuch of our Neighbours
who refufe the Admiffion of ours. Some Account
of the Commodities each Country we trade with
takes from us, and what we take from them; with

Obfervations on the Balance. The Second Edition. *London :* Sam. Buckley, 1730. 9 *prel. leaves and* 147 *pp. half mor.* 8*vo.* (4*s.* 6*d.* 1225)

GENERAL (The) Oppofition of the Colonies to the Payment of the Stamp Duty; and the Confequence of Enforcing Obedience by Military Meafures; Impartially confidered. Also A Plan for uniting them to this Kingdom, in fuch a manner as to make their Intereft infeparable from ours, for the future. In a Letter to a Member of Parliament. *London :* T. Payne, M. DCC. LXVI. 40 *pp. Large Paper.* 8*vo.* (10*s.* 6*d.* 1226)

GENGUINE LETTERS and Memoirs Relating to the Natural, Civil, and Commercial History Of the Islands of Cape Breton, and Saint John, From the firft fettlement there, to the taking of Louifburg by the Englifh, in 1758. In which, among many interefting particulars, the caufes and previous events of the prefent war are explained. By an impartial Frenchman [Th. Pichon]. Translated from the Author's original manufcript. *London,* J. Nourse, 1760. *xvi and* 400 *pp.* 8*vo.* (10*s.* 6*d.* 1227)

GENUINE (The) Principles of the Ancient Saxon, or English Constitution. Carefully collected from the beft Authorities; With fome Obfervations, on their peculiar fitnefs for the United Colonies in general, and Pennsylvania in particular. By Demophilus. *Philadelphia :* Printed and Sold, By Robert Bell, in Third Street. MDCCLXXVI. 46 *pp. Half mor.* 8*vo.* (7*s.* 6*d.* 1228)

GEOGRAPHICAL (A) and Hiftorical Description of the Principal Objects of the Prefent War in the Weft-Indies, viz. Cartagena, Puerto-Bello, La Vera Cruz, The Havana, and San Auguftin. Shewing their Situation, Strength, Trade &c. With An Account of the many Sieges they have Undergone to the prefent Time. The whole Compiled from the moft Authentic Memoirs, and Enlarged with many Curious Particulars not to be met with in former Authors. To which is prefix'd An Accurate Map of the Weft-Indies adapted to the Work. *London :* T. Gardner. 1741. 4 *prel. leaves ; and* 192 *pp. With the Map of the West Indies. Plan of Puerto*

Bello Harbour at page 85. *half morocco.*
8vo.　　　　　　　　　　(7s. 6d.　1229)

GEORGIA. An Account Shewing the Progress of
the Colony of Georgia in America from its Firſt
Eſtabliſhment. *London:* Printed in the Year M.DCC.
XLI. *Title and* 71 *pp. Fine large copy uncut, half
mor. Folio*　　　　　　　　(18s.　1230)

GEORGIA. A Impartial Enquiry into the State and
Utility of the Province of Georgia. *London:* W.
Meadows, MDCCXLI. *Half-title, title, and* 104 *pp.
Half mor.* 8vo.　　　　　　　(7s. 6d.　1231)

GEORGIA. A State of the Province of Georgia,
Atteſted upon Oath in the Court of Savannah, November 10, 1740. *London:* W. Meadows, MDCCXLII.
Half-title, title, and Text in 32 *pp. half morocco.*
8vo.　　　　　　　　　　(7s. 6d.　1232)

GEORGIA. A Brief Account of the Causes That
have retarded the Progress of the Colony of Georgia, in America; Atteſted upon Oath. Being A
proper Contrast to a State of the Province of Georgia. Atteſted upon Oath; And ſome other Miſrepreſentations on the ſame Subjeƈt. *London* Printed
in the Year M.DCC.XLIII. *Half-title, Title, and* 101
pp. Half mor. 8vo.　　　　　(7s. 6d.　1233)

GEORGIA. See SOUTH CAROLINA.

GERALDINUS (ALEXANDER). Itinerarivm/ ad/
Regiones svb Æqvinoctiali/ plaga conſtitvtas/
Alexandri Geraldini/ Epi. S. Dominici apud Indos
Occid^{es}./Ad/ Em^{um}. et R^{um}. Principem/ Franciscum
S. R. E. Card^{em}./ Barberinum/ Opus poſthumum./
[*Colophon*] *Romæ,*/ Typis Guilelmi Facciotti. M.DC.
XXXI./ Superiorum Permiſſu./ *Engraved Title,* 5
prel. leaves and 284 *pp. Index* 36 *pp. Vellum.
Small* 8vo.　　　　　　　　(2l. 2s.　1234)

GERRISH (MARTHA). The Happiness of a Holy
Life, Exemplified in the Sickness and Death Of the
Pious Mrs. Martha Gerrish, Of Boston in New-
England, Who died April the 14th, 1736. Ætat.
48. With A Colleƈtion of very Pathetick Letters
written by Her, during her Languiſhing Indiſpoſi-
tion, to her Children, Relations, and Friends, to
comfort them under all Afflictions; and defending
ſeveral Important Points of the Christian Religion,

in oppofition to fome late Deistical Writings. To
which is added, Her Funeral Sermon [By Nathaniel Appleton]. *London :* C. Rivington. m,dccxl.
Half-title, and xxii pp. Signed ' T. F.' [*Thomas Foxcroft*] *Text 207 pp. The bottom of C 4 is torn off.
Contents 5 pp. 12mo.* (10s. 6d. 1235)

GIBBONS (Thomas). Divine Conduct vindicated,
or the Operations of God fhown to be the Operations of Wifdom : In the Substance of Two Discourses, preached at Haberdashers-Hall, London,
March 29, 1761 ; Occafioned by the Decease of The
Rev. Mr. Samuel Davies, M.A. And Prefident of
the College of Naffau-Hall in New-Jerfey, February 4, 1761. By Thomas Gibbons, M.A. In which
are contained Some Memoirs of Mr. Davies, and
fome Extracts from his Letters. *London :* J. Buckland, 1761. *31 pp. 8vo.* (4s. 6d. 1236)

GIBSON (James). A Journal Of the Late Siege by
the Troops from North-America, against The
French at Cape Breton, the City of Louisbourg,
and the Territories thereunto belonging. Surrendered to the English, on the 17th of June, 1745,
after a Siege of Forty-eight Days. By James Gibson, Gentleman Voluntier at the above Siege. *London :* J. Newberry, mdccxlv. *Title and 49 pp.
Large Copper-plate map of Louisburg. Half mor.
8vo.* (15s. 1237)

GILBERT (Sir Humphrey). A Difcovrfe/ Of a
Difcouerie/ for a new Paf-/fage to Cataia./ VVritten by Sir Hvm-/frey Gilbert, Knight./ ❧ Imprinted at/ *London* by Hen-/ry Middleton, for/ Rich-
arde/ Ihones./ Anno Domini. 1576./ Aprilis. 12./
Title in a broad type metal border, the reverse blank ;
'George Gascoigne/ Efquire to the Reader.'/ 16
pp. in Italics ; ' ❧ A Prophetical So-/net of the
fame George Gafcoine,'/ *reverse blank,* 1 *page.* ¶
'A Letter of Sir/ Humfrey Gilbert, Knight, fent to/
his Brother, Sir Iohn Gilbert,' 6 *pp.* 'The Table'
2 *pp. in Black Letter. Text 29 leaves, commencing on
Sig B. ending on the reverse Sig. I. 1. in Black Letter.* 'Faultes efcaped in the/ printing./ 1 *page, on
the reverse a Wood-cut Globe and Colophon. Woodcut Map. Morocco extra by Francis Bedford.*
4to. (15l. 15s. 1238)

GILL (John). A Reply to a Defence of the Divine Right of Infant-Baptism, By Peter Clark, A.M. Minister at Salem, in a Letter to a Friend, At Boston in New-England. To which are added, Some Strictures on a late Treatise, called A Fair and Rational Vindication of the Right of Infants to the Ordinance of Baptism. Written by David Bostwick, A.M. late Minister of the Presbyterian Church in the City of New-York. By John Gill, D.D. *London.* G. Keith, MDCCLXV. *iv and* 112 *pp. Uncut. 8vo.*   (4s. 6d.   1239)

GILLESPIE (Alexander). Gleanings and Remarks: collected during many months of residence at Buenos Ayres, and within the Upper Country; with a prefatory account of the Expedition from England, until the Surrender of the Colony of the Cape of Good Hope, under the Joint Command of Sir D. Baird, G.C.B. K.C. and Sir Home Popham, K.C.B. By Major Alexander Gillespie, Now upon the Full-Pay retired List of the Royal Marines. Illustrated with a Map of South America, and a Chart of Rio de la Plata, with pilotage Directions. *Leeds:* B. Dewhirst 1818. 2 *prel. leaves; and* 242 *for* 342 *pp. Map of South-America. half calf. 8vo.*   (6s. 6d.   1240)

GILLIES (John). Memoirs of the Life of the Reverend George Whitefield, M.A. Late Chaplain to the Right Honorable The Countess of Huntingdon: In which Every Circumstance worthy of Notice, both in his private and public Character, is recorded. Faithfully selected from his Original Papers, Journals, and Letters. Illustrated by A Variety of interesting and entertaining Anecdotes, from the best Authorities. To which are added, A particular Account of his Death and Funeral; and Extracts from the Sermons, which were preached on that Occasion. Compiled By the Rev. John Gillies, D.D. *New-York:* Printed by Hodge and Shober, at the Newest Printing-Office, in Maiden-Lane. M.DCC.LXXIV. 312 *pp. Copper plate Portrait of Whitefield engraved by Elisha Gallaudet, New York,* 1774. 12mo.   (18s.   1241)

GILLIES (John). Memoirs of the Life of the Reverend George Whitefield, M.A. Late Chaplain to

the Right Honorable the Countess of Huntingdon:
In which Every Circumſtance worthy of Notice,
both in his private and public Charaĉter, is recorded. Faithfully ſeleĉted from his Original Papers, Journals and Letters. Illustrated by A Variety of intereſting and entertaining Anecdotes,
from the beſt Authorities. With A particular Account of his Death and Funeral; and Extraĉts from
the Sermons, which were preached on that Occaſion. Compiled By the Rev. John Gillies, D.D.
To which is now added, An Extract from Mr.
Whitefield's Tracts. *New-London*, (Conn.) Printed
by S. Green, for Cornelius Davis, N. York. 1798.
xii and 275 pp. 12mo. (15*s.* 1242)

GILLIES (John). Historical Collections relating
to Remarkable Periods of the Success of the Gospel, and Eminent Instruments employed in promoting it. In Two Volumes. Compiled by John
Gillies, One of the Ministers of Glasgow. In Mag-
nis Voluisse. *Glasgow*, Robert and Andrew Foulis
MDCCLIV. *2 Volumes.* Vol. I *x pp. 3 leaves and 464
pp.* Vol. II. *6 prel. leaves and 468 pp. 8vo.* Appen-
DIX to the Historical Collections, Relating to the
Succeſs of the Goſpel. By the Compiler of ſaid
Collections. *Glasgow:* John Orr, MDCCLXI. *2 prel.
leaves and 230 pp. 12mo.* (1*l.* 11*s.* 6*d.* 1243)

GIORGINI DA JESI (Giovanni). Il/ Mondo
Nvovo/ del Sig. Giovanni/ Giorgini da Ieſi,/ All
Inuittiſsimo Principe de Spagna, e ſue/ Sereniſsime
Sorelle./ Con gli argomenti in ottaua rima del Sig.
Gio. Pietro/ Colini, & in profa del Sig. Girolamo/
Ghiſilieri./ In *Ieſi*,/Appreſſo Pietro Farri, M.D.XCVI./
Con licenza a de' Superiori./ *Title in a type metal
border the reverse blank; Text in double columns fo-
lioed 2 to 153: with 5 sequent leaves; viz.* ' Discorso
Breve et Generale' *etc.* 4 *pp.* ' Al Sig. Giovanni
Giorgini,' *etc.* 1 *page.* ' Auertimento di M. Ago-
ſtino Campano a i Lettori.` 1 *page.* ' Erroti.' 3 *pp.
Wanting folio* 95. *Vellum. 4to.* (1*l.* 11*s.* 6*d.* 1244)

GLAREANUS (Henricus). Henrici/ Glareani,
Poetae Lav/reati, de Geogra=/phia Liber vnvs,/ ab
ipso Avthore/iam recognitvs./ *Basileae.*/ [*Colophon*]
Basileae. Anno/ M.D.XXVIII./ Excvdebat Ioannes
Fa=/ber Emmevs Ivliacensis./ *35 folioed leaves.*
4to. (10*s.* 6*d.* 1245)

GLAREANUS (Henricus). Henrici/ Glareani
Poetae Lav=/reati de Geogra=/phia Liber vnvs,/ ab
ipso Avthore/ recognitvs./ Apvd *Fribvrgvm Bris-*
gavdiae./ [*Colophon*] Apvd Fribvrgvm Brisgoi-
cvm./ Anno m.d.xxx./ Excvdebat Ioannes Fa=/ber
Emmevs Ivliacensis./ *35 folioed leaves; and* 1 *with*
woodcut on the reverse. 4to.   (7*s.* 6*d.*   1246)

GLAREANUS (Henricus). Henrici Gla/reani
Helvetii, Poetae Lav=/reati de Geographia Li=/ber
vnvs, ab ipso Av=/thore iam tertio/ recognitvs./
Apvd *Fribvrgvm Bris=/goiae,* An. m.d.xxxiii./ [*Co-*
lophon] Apvd Fribrvgvm Brisgoicvm/ Anno.
m.d.xxxiii./ Excvdebat Ioannes Faber/ Emmevs
Ivliacensis./ *35 folioed leaves; and one with wood-*
cut on the reverse. 4to.   (7*s.* 6*d.*   1247)

GLAREANUS (Henricus). Henrici/ Glareani
Helvetii,/ Poetae Lavreati de Geogra/phia Liber
unus, ab ipfo Authore iam no/uiffime recognitus./
Friburgi Brisgoiæ,/ Stephanus Grauius excudebat,/
Anno/ m.d.li./ *33 folioed leaves. Unbound.*
4to.   (7*s.* 6*d.*   1248)

GLAS (George). The History of the Discovery
and Conquest of the Canary Islands : Tranflated
from a Spanish Manuscript, lately found in the
Ifland of Palma. With an Enquiry into the Origin
of the Ancient Inhabitants. To which is added, A
Defcription of the Canary Islands, including The
Modern History of the Inhabitants, And an Account of their Manners, Customs, Trade, &c. By
George Glas. *London,* R. and J. Dodsley. mdcclxiv.
4 prel. leaves; viii and 368 pp. Map of the Canary
Islands at p. 1, *and two Charts at p.* 183. *half mor.*
4to.   (10*s.* 6*d.*   1249)

GLASCOTT (Cradock). The beft Method of putting
an End to the American War. Being the Substance of a Sermon Preached on the 13th of December, 1776 ; The Day of the General Faft, at
Tottenham-Court Chapel, (Erected by the Rev.
Mr. George Whitefield.) By the Rev. Cradock
Glascott, A.M. Chaplain to the Earl of Buchan,
and one of the Preachers in the Chapels of the
Countefs of Huntingdon. With an Address from
Henry Peckwell, A. M. And Chaplain to the Mar-
chionefs Dowager of Lothian, to his Fellow Sub-

jects on that Solemn Occasion. *London :* J. W. Pasham, 1776. 31 *pp.* 8*vo.* (3*s.* 6*d.* 1250)

GLASS/ (A)/ For the People of/ New-England,/ in which/ They may fee themfelves and Spirits, and/ if not too late, Repent and Turn from their/ Abo minable Ways and Curfed Contrivances :/ That fo the Lord God may turn away his Wrath,/ which he will bring upon them (if they Repent not) for/ their Blafphemies againft himself, and for all the Mur-/ders and Cruelties done to his tender People, ever fince/they ufurped Authority, to Banifh, Hang, Whip, and/ Cut Off Ears, and Spoil Goods of Dif-fenters from/ them in Religious Matters, while themselves difown/ Infallibility in thofe things./ By S. G./ [*London.*] Printed in the Year, 1676./ 43 *pp.* 4*to.* (4*l.* 4*s.* 1251)

GLOBUS MUNDI/ Declaratio fiue defcriptio mundi/ et totius orbis terrarum globulo rotundo comparati vt fpera foli/da. Qua cuiuis etiã mediocriter docto ad oculũ videre licet an-/tipodes effe, quoʀ pedes noftris oppofiti funt. Et qualiter in vna-/quaq; orbis parte homines vitam agere queunt falutarē, fole fin-/gula terræ loca illuftrantæ : que tamen terra in vacuo aere pendere/ videtur : folo dei nutu fuf-tētata, alijfq; permultis de quarta orbis/ terrarũ parte nuper ab Americo reperta./ [*Colophon*] Va-lete feliciter ex/ *Argentina* vltima Augufti, Anno poft natũ faluatorē. M.D.IX./ Joannes grüniger im-pri/mebat. Adelpho castigatore./ 14 *leaves, in Black letter. Signatures* A *and* B *in fours, and* C *in* 6 *leaves, ending with the* 10*th line on the recto of* Cvi. *Fine copy, unbound.* 4*to.* (10*l.* 10*s.* 1252)

On the title-page is a small wood-cut globe, in which the New World is laid down.

GLOVER (Mʀ). A Short Account Of the late Ap-plication to Parliament Made by the Merchants of London Upon the Neglect of their Trade : With The Substance of the Evidence Thereupon; As fum'd up by Mr. Glover. The Second Edition. *London :* T. Cooper, M.DCC.XLII. 61 *pp. Half mor.* 8*vo.* (4*s.* 6*d.* 1253)

GLOVER (Mʀ.) A Short Account of the late Ap-plication to Parliament made by the Merchants of London Upon the Neglect of their Trade : With

the Substance of the Evidence thereupon; As
Summed up by Mr. Glover. The Sixth Edition.
London: T. Cooper, 1742; and for J. Wilkie,
MDCCLXXIV. 71 *pp. Half mor. 8vo.* (4s. 6d. 1254)

GLOVER (MR.) The Substance of the Evidence
Delivered to a Committee of the Honourable House
of Commons by the Merchants and Traders of Lon-
don, Concerned in the Trade to Germany and Hol-
land, and of the Dealers in Foreign Linens, As
Summed up By Mr. Glover. To which is Annexed,
His Speech, Introductory to the Proposals Laid
before the Annuitants of Meff. Douglas, Heron and
Co. At the Kings'-Arms Tavern, Cornhill, on the
Ninth of February, 1774. *London:* J. Wilkie,
MDCCLXXIV. *Half-title, Title, and 72 pp. Unbound.*
8vo. (4s. 6d. 1255)

GLOVER (MR.) The Substance of the Evidence
on the Petition Prefented by the West-India Planters and Merchants to the Hon. House of Commons,
As it was introduc'd at the Bar, and fumm'd up
By Mr. Glover On Thursday the 16th of March,
1775. *London:* H. S. Woodfall [1775]. *Half-
title, title, and 47 pp. 8vo.* (4s. 6d. 1256)

GLOVER (MR.) The Evidence Delivered on the
Petition Prefented by the West-India Planters and
Merchants to the Hon. House of Commons, As it
was introduc'd at the Bar, and fumm'd up By Mr.
Glover. [*London* 1775.] *Title and 95 pp. Half
mor. 8vo.* (4s. 6d. 1257)

GLOVER (HABAKKUK.) An Essay, to difcover the
principal caufes/ of the Anger of God againft New-
England./ By Habakkuk Glover of Boston in
New England./ [*London* 1665] 8 *pp. Half mor.*
4to. (1l. 15s. 1258)

GODDARD (WILLIAM.) The Partnership: Or
the History of the Rise and Progress of the Pennsylvania Chronicle, &c. Wherein the Conduct of
Joseph Galloway, Efq ; Speaker of the Honourable
Houfe of Reprefentatives of the Province of Pennfylvania, Mr. Thomas Wharton, fen. and their
Man Benjamin Towne, my late Partners, with my
own, is properly delineated, and their Calumnies
againft me fully refuted. By William Goddard.

Philadelphia. Printed by William Goddard, in Arch-Street, between Front and Second Streets, M,DCC,LXX. 72 *pp. Calf. 8vo.* (*2l. 2s.* 1259)

GODWYN (Morgan). The/ Negro's & Indians/ Advocate,/ Suing for their Admiffion into the/ Church :/ Or/ A Perfuasive to the Inftruċting/ and Baptizing of the Negro's and/ Indians in our Plantations./ Shewing,/ That as the Compliance therewith can prejudice/ no Mans juft Intereft; So the wilful Negleċting/ and Oppofing of it, is no lefs than a manifeft/ Apoftacy from the Chriftian Faith./ To which is added, A brief Account of Religion in Virginia./ By Morgan Godwyn,/ Sometime St. of Ch. Ch. Oxon./ *London,* Printed for the Author, by J. D. and are/ to be Sold by moft Bookfellers. 1680./ 7 *prel. leaves and* 174 *pp. 8vo.* (*1l. 1s.* 1260)

GOLDEN/ (The)/ Fleece/ Diuided into three Parts, Vnder which are difcouered the Errours/ of Religion, the Vices and Decayes of the King-/dome, and laftly the wayes to get wealth, and to/ reftore Trading fo much com-/playned of./ Transported from/ Cambrioll Colchos, out of the Southermoft/ Part of the Iland, commonly called the/ Newfovndland,/ By Orpheus Iunior,/ For the generall and perpetuall Good of/ Great Britaine./ *London,*/ Printed for Francis Williams, and are to bee fold/ at his Shop at the figne of the Globe, ouer/ againft the Royall Exchange,/ 1626./ 14 *prel. leaves. viz.* 1, *Title, reverse blank;* 2, 'The Mvses and/ the Graces,' *etc.* 2 *pp*; 3, 'Mufsæ & Charites,' 1 *page, followed on the reverse by* ' To the indifferent Readers,' 3 *pp*; 5, 'To the vncharitable Readers,' 4 *pp*; 7, *Verses* 'In Commendation,' *etc.* 2 *pp*; 8 *to* 14, ' The Contents of the Chapters' *of the* 1st, 2d *and* 3d *parts. Copperplate map* 10½ *by* 7 *inches: Text* 1st *part,* 149 *pp*; 2d *part,* 105 *pp*; 3d *part* 96 *pp. Fine copy in morocco extra by F. Bedford.* 4*to.* (*10l. 10s.* 1261)

GOLDEN FLEECE. *Another copy, wanting the Map and unbound.* 4*to.* (*2l. 2s.* 1262)

GOLDING (William). Servants on/ Horse-Back :/ Or,/ A Free-People beftrided in their per-/fons, and Liberties, by worthleffe men :/ Being/ A Re-

z

prefentation of the dejected ftate/ of the Inhabitants
of Summer Iflands./ Containing/ Short Illuftra-
tions upon a Petition pre-/fented to the High Court
of Parliament/ for Redresse./ Publifhed by Will.
Golding Mafter of Arts, and/ Teacher to the Congregation in that Ifland/ [*London*] Printed in the
Yeare, 1648./ *Title, reverse blank,* 'The Epiftle,'
1 *page,* 'ΠΡΟΛΕΓΟΜΕΝΑ :' 1 *page, Text* 24 *pp.*
4*to.* (2*l.* 2*s.* 1263)

GOLDSON (WILLIAM). Observations on the
Passage between the Atlantic and Pacific Oceans,
in two Memoirs of the Straits of Anian, and the
Discoveries of De Fonte. Elucidated by a New
and Original Map. To which is prefixed an Historical Abridgement of Discoveries in the North
of America. By William Goldson. *Portsmouth:*
W. Mowbray, M,DCC,XCIII. *xii and* 162 *pp. Map.*
4*to.* (10*s.* 6*d.* 1264)

GOMARA (FRANCISCO LOPEZ DE). Historia/ delle
Nvove Indie/ Occidentali,/ con tvtti i discopri-
menti,/ & cofe notabili, auuenute dopo l'acquifto
di effe./ Compofta da Francesco Lopez di/ Gomara
in lingua Spagnuola,/ Tradotta nella Italiana da
Agostimo di Cravaliz./ In *Venetia,*/ Per Francefco
Lorenzini da Turino,/ MDLX. 10 *prel. leaves, and*
306 *folioed leaves, in Italic type. Vellum.*
Small 8*vo.* (2*l.* 2*s.* 1265)

GOMARA (FRANCISCO LOPEZ DE). Histoire/ Gene-
ralle/ des Indes Occiden-/tales et Terres Nevves,/
qui iufques à prefent ont/ efté defcouuertes./ Traduite en françois par M. Fumee Sieur/ de Marley
le Chaftel./ A *Paris,*/ Chez Michel Sonnius, rue
fainct Iacques/ à l'enfeigne de l'Efcu de Bafle./
M.D.LXXVII./ Avec Privilege dv Roy./ 6 *prel.*
and 355 *folioed leaves. Table* 29 *pp. Old calf.*
8*vo.* (2*l.* 2*s.* 1266)

GOMARA (FRANCISCO LOPEZ DE). The/ Pleafant
Hiftorie of/ the Conqueft of the/ Weft India, now
called/ new Spaine./ Atchieued by the moft woor-
thie Prince/ Hernando Cortes, Marqves of the
Valley of/ Huaxacac, moft delectable to reade./
Tranflated out of the Spanifh tongue, by/ T. N.
Anno 1578./ *London*/ Printed by Thomas Creede./
1596./ 6 *prel. leaves; viz. Title the reverse blank,*

'To the Right Honourable/ Sir Francis Wal-
fingham Knight, principall/ Secretary to the
Queenes moftt excellent Ma-/ieftie, and one of her
highneffe moft Ho-/nourable priuie Counfell.'/ 6
pp. Signed 'Thomas Nicholss.' *in roman type.*/ 'To
the Reader,' *2 pp.* '(T. N.)' *in black letter.*/
'Stephen Goffon in praife of the Translator.' 1 *page;*
'In Thomæ Nicholai occidentalem Indiam/ Stephen Goffon.'/ 1 *page; Text in black letter* 405 *pp.*
'A Table,' *etc.* 6 *pp; in roman type. Very fine, large
and clean copy.* (5*l.* 15*s.* 6*d.* 1267)

GONCALEZ DE CUETO (Damiano). Oratio
Fvne-/bris Habita a Magistro Da-/miano Goncalez
de Cveto, eorvm,/ qui ad Philofophiæ lauream
afcendunt exa-/minatore, & in Apollinea fcientia
denuo li-/centiando, in exequijs Religiofifsimi/
Patris Antonij Arias è Socie-/tate Iesu——/ (.⁎.)/
⅔⁘ Sacræ Theologiæ Interpre-/tis, & Congrega-
tionis Annuntiatæ primarij, ac vigilentifsimi Du-/
cis, quas eadem congregatio cohoneftauit, in Collegio Mexi-/cano eiufdem Societatis, decimo
Kalendas Iulij./ Anni 1603——/ ¶ *Mexici;*
Svperiorvm Permissv,/ Apud Henricum Martinez——/ *Title and 8 leaves, not paged or numbered.*
4*to.* (1*l.* 11*s.* 6*d.* 1268)

GONCALEZ DE NAGERA (Alonso). El Qvinto,
y Sexto Pvnto de la Relacion del Defengaño de la
guerra de Chile, facados de 14. de fu declaracion,
cuyos titulos han de ferlos que eftan pueftos al fin.
Por el Maeftre de Campo Alonfo Gonçalez de
Nagera. [*Madrid* 1647?] 16 *folioed leaves. Calf.*
4*to.* (1*l.* 11*s.* 6*d.* 1269)

GONZALES CARRANZA (Domingo). A Geographical Description of the Coafts, Harbours, and
Sea Ports of the Spanifh Weft-Indies; particularly
of Porto Bello, Cartagena, and the Ifland of Cuba.
With Obfervations of the Currents, and the Variations of the Compass in the Bay of Mexico, and the
North Sea of America. Translated from A curious
and authentic Manuscript, written in Spanifh by
Domingo Gonzales Carranza, his Catholick Majefty's principal Pilot of the Flota in New Spain,
Anno 1718. To which is added, An Appendix,
containing Capt. Parker's own Account of his

taking the town of Porto Bello, in the Year 1601. With An Index, and a New and Correct Chart of the Whole; as also Plans of the Havannah, Porto-Bello, Cartagena, and La Vera Cruz. *London:* Caleb Smith. M.DCC.XL. *xii and* 124 *pp. Index* 8 *pp. With Map of the West Indies at page* 1, *and* 4 *Plans at pp.* 23, 52, 93, 119. *Half morocco.* 8*vo.* (7*s.* 6*d.* 1270)

GOODWIN (JOHN) Moro-Mastix:/ Mr Iohn Goodwin/ whipt with his own Rod./ Or/ The diſ-ſecting of the ſixteenth Section of/ his book truly nam'd by himſelf/ Hagio-Mastix :/ So far as it falſly and frivolouſly mentions a/ late diſputation in Chriſt-Church Pariſh, concer-/ning the lawful-neſs of paying Tythes./ By a diligent observer of the ſaid Diſputation./ *London,*/ Printed for Tho. Underhill, and are to be ſold at his ſhop/ at the ſign of the Bible in great Woodſtreet. 1647./ 15 *pp.* 4*to.* (10*s.* 6*d.* 1271)

GOODWIN (THOMAS). An/ Apologeticall Narra-tion,/ hvmbly svbmitted/ to the/ Honourable Houses/ of/ Parliament./ By/ Tho : Goodwin,/ Philip Nye,/ William Bridge,/ Jer: Burroughes,/ Sidrach Simpſon./ *London,*/ Printed for Robert Dawlman./ M.DC.XLIII. 2 *prel. leaves and* 31 *pp. half mor.* 4*to.* (7*s.* 6*d.* 1272)

GOODWIN (THOMAS). A Copy of a/ Remonſtrance/ lately delivered/ in to the/ Assembly./ By/

Thomas Goodwin. ⎫ William Bridge./
Ierem: Burroughs. ⎬ Philip Nie./ Sidrach Simſon./
William Greenhill. ⎭ and William Carter./

Declaring the Grounds and Rea-/ſons of their de-clining to bring in to the Aſ-/ſembly, their Modell of Church-/Government./ *London:*/ Printed in the Yeer, 1645./ 8 *pp.* 4*to.* (7*s.* 6*d.* 1273)

GORDON (WILLIAM). Autograph Letter ' For Mrs. Smith, Wethersfield, by favour of Mr. John Child,' dated at Roxbury near Boston, May 30. 1772. 1 *page.* 4*to.* (1*l.* 1*s.* 1274)

There is, probably in the autograph of Mrs. Smith, a copy of a reply to this letter, written in shorthand or cypher, filling nearly a page, clearly written.

GORDON (William). A Discourse Preached December 15th 1774. Being the day recommended By the Provincial Congrefs; And Afterwards at the Boston Lecture. By William Gordon. Pastor of the Third Church in Roxbury, *Boston*: Printed for, and Sold by Thomas Leverett, in Corn-Hill. 1775. *32 pp. and 1 Seq. page. Half mor. 8vo.* (4s. 6d. 1275)

GORDON (William). Remarks upon a Discourse Preached December 15th 1774. Being the Day recommended by the Provincial Congress: And afterwards at the Boston Lecture. By William Gordon, Paftor of the third Church in Roxbury. In a Letter from a Gentleman in the Country to his Friend in Bofton. [*Boston*,] Printed in the Year MDCCLXXV. *11 pp. Half mor. 8vo.* (7s. 6d. 1276)

GORDON (William). Autograph Letter addressed 'For Mrs. Smith at Ezekiel Williams's Esq. Weathersfield with haste & care, containing matters of importance,' dated at 'J. P. Mar 9, 76.' *1 page 4to.* (1l. 1s. 1277)

The following is the whole of this important letter:—

My dear Madm. J. P. Mar. 9, 76.

I have an opportunity of conveying the following important intelligence which I therefore gladly embrace. Yesterday afternoon came out a flag of truce with a letter to Gen. Washington signed by the four select men remaining in Boston, acquainting that the inhabitants observing that Gen. How was preparing to embark his troops, were apprehensive that he would burn the town when he had evacuated it, & therefore several of the most respectable waited upon Col. Robinson, & he upon Gen. How who directed him to inform the gentlemen, that he should not destroy the town unless he was interrupted in his embarkation by those that were without. The letter requested that the inhabitants might have their fears dissipated by assurances that no such interruption would be given. The General's answer I know not. But there is reason to apprehend, that while How is preparing to push off immediately, he intends if he can catch the opportunity to attack us in one quarter or other before he goes. Lord Percy embarked with three thousand troops on the tuesday with a design of attacking our posts upon Dorchester hills on the wednesday morning at five; but God would not suffer, & blew with his winds in a manner scarce ever rememberd here, & thereby disconcerted their whole plan. Yours in great haste

William Gordon.

GORDON (William.) The Doctrine of Final Univerfal Salvation Examined and Shewn to be Unscriptural: in Anfwer to a Pamphlet entitled Salvation for all Men Illustrated and Vindicated as a Scripture Doctrine. By William Gordon, Paftor of the third Church in Roxbury. *Boston*: Printed and Sold by T. and J. Fleet, at the Bible

and Heart in Cornhill. 1783. *Title; Preface ii pp;*
Text 96 pp. Uncut. 8vo. (7s. 6d. 1278)
On the title-page is :—" For the Revd Dr John Erskine, from the
Author."

GORDON (WILLIAM). The History of the Rise,
Progress, and Establishment, of the Independence
of the United States of America: including an
Account of the late War; and of the Thirteen
Colonies, from their origin to that period. By
William Gordon, D.D. In Four Volumes. *Lon-*
don: Printed for the Author; MDCCLXXXVIII. *4*
Volumes. Vol. I. 13 *prel. leaves and* 504 *pp.* 'Plate
I. The United States of America.' Vol. II. 4 *prel.*
leaves and 584 *pp.* 'Plate II. Boston with its En-
virons.' ' Plate III. New York Island.' ' Plate IV.
The Jerseys.' ' Plate V. New Hampshire, Vermont.'
Vol. III. 4 *prel. leaves and* 499 *pp.* 'Plate VI. The
Carolina's with part of Georgia.' ' Plate VII. A
Sketch of the Operations before Charlestown.'
Vol IV. 4 *prel. leaves and* 445 *pp. Index* 34 *pp.*
' Plate VIII. The Part of Virginia which was the
Seat of Action.' ' Plate IX. York Town and Glou-
cester Point.' *8vo.* (1*l.* 1*s.* 1279)

GORDON (WILLIAM). The History of the Rise,
Progress, and Establishment, of the Independence
of the United States of America: Including an
Account of the late War; and of the Thirteen
Colonies, from their Origin to that Period. By
William Gordon, D.D. In Three Volumes. *New-*
York: Printed by Hodge, Allen, and Campbell;
and Sold at their respective Book-Stores. M.DCC.
LXXXIX. *Three Volumes.* Vol. I. 6 *prel. leaves and*
pp. 25-443. *With Map.* Vol. II. 5 *prel. leaves*
and pp. 25-474. *With Map.* Vol. III. 18 *prel. leaves*
and pp. 17-446. *Calf. 8vo.* (1*l.* 11*s.* 6*d.* 1280)

GORGES (FERDINANDO). America/ Painted to the
Life./ The true/ History/ of/ The Spaniards Proceedings in the Conquests of the/ Indians, and of
their Civil Wars among them-/felves, from Columbus his firft Difcovery,/ to thefe later Times./ As
also,/ Of the Original Undertakings of the Advancement of/ Plantations into thofe parts;/ With
a perfect Relation of our Englifh Difcoveries,
fhewing/ their Beginning, Progrefs and Continuance, from the Year/ 1628. to 1658. Declaring the

forms of their Govern-/ment, Policies, Religions,
Maners, Cuftoms, Military Difci-/pline, Wars with
the Indians, the Commodities of their/ Countries,
a Defcription of their Towns and Havens,/ the
Increafe of their Trading, with the Names of/ their
Governors and Magiftrates./ More efpecially, an
abfolute Narrative of the North/ parts of America,
and of the Difcoveries and/ Plantations of our
Englifh in/ Virginia, New-England, and Berba-
does./ Publifht by Ferdinando Gorges, Efq;/
A Work now at laft expofed for the publick good, to
ftir up the Heroick and/ Active Spirits of thefe
times, to benefit their Countrey, and Eternize/ their
Names by fuch Honorable Attempts./ For the
Readers clearer underftanding of the Countreys,
they are lively/ defcribed in a compleat and exqui-
fite Map./ *London*, Printed for Nath. Brook at the
Angel in Cornhil. 1659./ *Title ;* ' To/ The Judicious
Reader,' 4 *pp. Text,* 'A description of New Eng-
land' 51 *pp. Portrait and Map. Part II.* A / Briefe
Narration/ of the/ Originall Undertakings/ of the/
Advancement/ of/ Plantations/ Into the parts of/
America./ Efpecially,/ Shewing the begining, pro-
grefs/ and continuance of that of/ New-England./
Written by the right Worfhipfull, Sir Ferdinando
Gorges/ Knight and Governour of the Fort and
Ifland of/ Plymouth in Devonfhire./ *London :*/
Printed by E. Brudenell, for Nath. Brook at the/
Angell in Corn-hill. 1658./ *Title and* 57 *pp.*
Part III. America/ Painted to the Life./ A/ True
Hiftory of the Originall undertakings of the ad-
vancement/ of Plantations into thofe parts, with a
perfect relation of/ our English Difcoveries, fhewing their beginning, progrefs, and/ continuance,
form the Year, 1628. to 1658. declaring the forms
of / their Government, Policies, Religions, Manners, Cuftomes, Military Difcipline, Warres with
the Indians, the Commodities of their/ Countries,
a Defcription of their Townes, and Havens, the in-
creafe/ of their trading with the names of their
Governours and Magiftrates./ More/ Efpecially
an abfolute Narrative of the North parts of
America, and/ of the difcoveries and plantations of
our Englifh in/ New-England./ Written by Sir
Ferdinando Gorges Knight/ and Governour of the
Fort and Ifland of Plimouth in/ Devonshire, one

of the firſt and chiefeſt pro-/moters of thoſe Plantations./ Publiſht ſince his deceaſe, by his Grandchild Ferdinando Gorges Eſquire,/ who hath much
enlarged it and added ſeverall accurate Deſcripti-/
ons of his owne./ A work now at laſt expoſed
for the publick good, to ſtir up the heroick and
active ſpirits/ of theſe times, to benefit their Country, and Eternize their names,/ by ſuch honourable
attempts./ For the Readers clearer underſtanding
of the Country's they are lively deſcribed in a/
compleat, and exquiſite Map./ *London:* Printed
by E. Brudenell, for Nathaniel Brook dwelling at/
the Angel in Corn-hill. 1658./ *Title;* 'To the
Reader,' 1 *leaf*; *Text*, 'Wonder-working Providence,' 236 *pp*. *Part IV*. America/ Painted to
the Life./ The/ History/ of the/ Spaniards Proceedings in America, their Con-/queſts of the
Indians, and of their/ Civil Wars among themſelves./ From/ Columbus his firſt Diſcovery, to
theſe/ later Times./ By/ Ferdinando Gorges,
Esq ;/ *London*, Printed by T. J. for Nath. Brook
at the Angel/ in Cornhil. 1659./ *Title*, 'The
Preface,' 2 *pp*. *Text*, 'A true Relation,' 52 *pp*.
'The General Table' *of the Four Parts, and* 'Books
lately printed' 10 *leaves*. 4to. (5*l*. 5*s*. 1281)
This copy wants the engraved Portrait of *America*, and the first
two leaves of table at the end.

GRAHAM (John Andrew). A Descriptive Sketch
of the Present State of Vermont. One of the United
States of America. By J. A. Graham, L.L.D. Late
Lieutenant-Colonel in the Service of the above
State. *London*. Printed and sold for the Author,
by Henry Fry. 1797. *viii and* 187 *pp*. *Portrait of
the Author*. *Uncut*. 8*vo*. (10*s*. 6*d*. 1282)

GRAHAM (Maria). Journal of a Residence in
Chile, during the year 1822. And a Voyage from
Chile to Brazil in 1823. By Maria Graham. *Lon-
don:* Longman, 1824. 4 *prel. leaves and* 512 *pp*.
With 14 *Mezzotint plates. Uncut.* 4*to*. (7*s*. 6*d*. 1283)

GRAHAME (James). The History of the Rise and
Progress of the United States of North America,
till the British Revolution in 1688. By James
Grahame, Esq. In Two Volumes. *London:* Long-
man, 1827. *Two Volumes*. Vol. I. *xvi and* 531 *pp*.
Vol. II. *viii and* 528 *pp*. *calf*. 8*vo*. (10*s*. 6*d*. 1284)

GRAHAME (James). The History of the United States of North America, from the Plantation of the British Colonies till their Revolt and Declaration of Independence. By James Grahame, Esq. In Four Volumes. *London:* Smith, Elder and Co., 1836. *Four Volumes.* Vol. I. *xxiii and* 451 *pp.* Vol. II. *viii and* 448 *pp.* Vol. III. *viii and* 436 *pp.* Vol. IV. *vii and* 462 *pp. Uncut.* 8*vo.* (1*l.* 5*s.* 1285)

GRANADOS Y GALVEZ (Joseph Joaquin). Tardes/ Americanas :/ Gobierno Gentil y Catolico :/ Breve y particular Noticia/ de toda la Historia Indiana :/ Sucesos, casos notables, y cosas ignoradas, desde la/ entrada de la Gran Nacion Tulteca á esta tierra/ de Anahuac,/ hasta los presentes tiempos./ Trabajadas/ por un Indio, y un Español./ Sacalas a Luz/ El M. R. P. Fr. Joseph Joaquin Granados/ y Galvez, Predicador General de Jure, ex-Defini-/dor de la Provincia de Michoacan, y Guardian que fue/ de los Conventos de Xiquilpan, Valladolid, Rio-/verde, y Custodio de todas sus Misiones,/ y las dedica/ Al Excmô Sr. D. Joseph de Galvez,/ Caballero de la Real distinguida Orden de Car-/los III., del Consejo de Estado, Gobernador del/ Supremo de las Indias, y Secretario del Des-/pacho universal de ellas./ *Mexico:* En la nueva Imprenta Matritense de D. Felipe/ de Zúñiga y Ontiveros, calle de la Palma, año de 1778/. *36 prelim. leaves and text,* 540 *pp.* 3 *copperplates at pp.* 8, 56 *and* 57. 4*to.* (4*l.* 14*s.* 1286)

GRANT (Andrew). History of Brazil, comprising a Geographical account of that Country, together with a Narrative of the most remarkable events which have occurred there since its discovery; A Description of the Manners, Customs, Religion, &c. of the Natives and Colonists; Interspersed with Remarks on the Nature of its Soil, Climate, Productions, and Foreign and Internal Commerce. To which are subjoined cautions to New Settlers for the preservation of health. By Andrew Grant, M.D. *London:* Henry Colburn, 1809. 4 *prel. leaves, and* 304 *pp.* 8*vo.* (5*s.* 1287)

GRASSI (Giovanni). Notizie Sullo Stato Presente della Republica Degli Stati-Uniti dell' America Settentrionale Del P. Giovanni Grassi della Com-

pagnia di Gesù.   Terza Edizione Accrescinta di
recenti Memoire dello stesso Autore.   *Torino* Tipo-
grafia Chirio e Mina 1822.   140 *pp.*   Lettre de M.
Laval, ci-devant Ministre a Condé-Sur-Noireau.
24 *pp.*   *Map & 'Tavola' folded sheet*.   *Calf.*
8*vo.*   (5s. 6d.   1288)

GREAT BRITAIN.   Etat Militaire de la Grande
Bretagne pour l'Année MDCCLXXIV.   Quinzieme
Edition Corrigée & Augmentée de l'Etat Major.
A *Paris.* Quai des Augustins, Avec Approbation
& Privilege du Roi.   [1774].   *Engraved Title and*
76 *pp.*   16*mo.*   (4s. 6d.   1289)

GREAT BRITAIN'S Right to Tax her Colonies.
Placed in the clearest Light, by a Swiss.   *London* :
Printed by J. Delegal, MDCCLXXIV.   *Half-title and*
55 *pp ; Signed* ' Free Swiss.'   *Half morocco.*
8*vo.*   (4s. 6d.   1290)

GREAT PLOT/ (A)/ Discovered,/ or/ The notorious
and wicked Defign/ upon the River of Thames,
put/ in execution on Monday laft,/ With a Hu-and-
Cry after the Condemned Pri-/foners that made
their efcape upon their re-/moving from Newgate
to be tranfported for/ Jamaica ; And the manner
how they made their/ efcape, and got afhore in Effex, the killing of/ the Steer-man, the purfuing of
them by Soul-/diers, and the Names and Number
of thofe fince/ re-taken, which are now to be executed upon/ feveral Gibbets./ Likewife the appre-
hending of the wicked Vil-/lains ill-affected to his
Gracious Majefty, and/ his Royal Highneffe the
Duke of York./   *London*, Printed for G. Horton,
1661./   7 *pp.* 4*to.*   (1*l.* 1s.   1291)

GRECE (CHARLES F.).   Facts and Observations respecting Canada, and the United States of America : Affording a Comparative View of the Induce-
ments to Emigration presented in those Countries.
To which is added An Appendix of Practical Instructions to Emigrant Settlers in the British Colonies.   By Charles F. Grece, Member of the Montreal and Quebec Agricultural Societes; and Author of Essays on Husbandry, addressed to the Canadian Farmers.   *London* : J. Harding, 1819.   *xv*
and 172 *pp. uncut.* 8*vo.*   (4s. 6d.   1292)

GREENE (Nathaniel). Autograph Letter to Col. Ephraim Bowen, dated at Coventry Sept. 29. 1778. 1 *page.* 4*to.* (10*s.* 6*d.* 1293)

GREENWOOD (Isaac). A Philofophical Difcourfe concerning the Mutability and Changes of the Material World; Read to the Students of Havard-College, April 7. 1731. Upon the News of the Death of Thomas Hollis, Efq ; of London, The moft bountiful Benefactor to that Society. By Isaac Greenwood, A.M. Hollisian Profeffor of Philofophy and the Mathematicks. Made Public, At the Defire of the Reverend the President and Fellows of that Society. *Boston* in New-England : Printed for S. Gerrifh, at the lower End of Cornhil. mdccxxxi. 2 *prel. leaves and* 24 *pp.* 8*vo.* (4*s.* 6*d.* 1294)

GREGG (Josiah). Commerce of the Prairies : Or the Journal of a Santa Fé Trader, during Eight Expeditions across the Great Western Prairies, and a residence of nearly nine years in Northern Mexico. Illustrated with Maps and Engravings. By Josiah Gregg. In Two Volumes. *New York:* Henry G. Langley, *London :* Wiley and Putnam, m.dcccxliv. 2 *Volumes.* Vol. I. 320 *pp. Map of the Indian Territory, at p.* 17. 3 *plates at pp.* 1. 102. 182. Vol. II. 318 *pp. Map of the Interior of Northern Mexico at p.* 9. 3 *plates pp.* 1. 38. 230. 12*mo.* (8*s.* 6*d.* 1295)

GREGOIRE (Henry). A Defence of Bartholomew Las-Casas, Bishop of Chiapa. By Henry Gregoire, ex Bishop of Blois, Senator of France, and Member of the National Institute. To which are added, the Ruins of Port Royal in 1801, by the same Author. Translated from the French, by H. R. Yorke, Esq. With a Short Sketch of his Writings, &c. By the Translator. *London :* H. D. Symonds, 1802. 125 *pp.* 12*mo.* (7*s.* 6*d.* 1296)

GRENADA. A Brief Enquiry into the Causes of, and Conduct pursued by, the Colonial Government, for quelling the Insurrection in Grenada; From its Commencement on the Night of the 2d of March, to the Arrival of General Nichols, on the 14th of April, 1795. In a Letter from a Grenada Planter to a Merchant in London. *London:* R. Faulder, 1796. *Half-title, title, and* 125 *pp.* ' Ap-

pendix' 20 *pp.* 'Observations' *etc. pp.* 127-204.
Errata 1 *p. Map. Half calf.* 8*vo.* (5*s.* 6*d.* 1297)

GRENVILLE (George). The Regulations Lately
Made concerning the Colonies, and the Taxes Im-
pofed upon Them, confidered. By the late Right
Hon. George Grenville. The Third Edition. *London :* J. Wilkie, 1775. 114 *pp. Half morocco.*
8*vo.* (5*s.* 6*d.* 1298)

GRIEVANCES (The) of the American Colonies
Candidly Examined. Printed by Authority, at
Providence, in Rhode-Ifland. *London:* Reprinted
for J. Almon, MDCCLXVI. 47 *pp. Half morocco.*
8*vo.* (5*s.* 6*d.* 1299)

GROANS/ (The)/ of the/ Plantations :/ Or/ A True
Account/ of their/ Grievous and Extreme Suffer-
ings/ By the Heavy/ Impositions upon/ Sugar,/
And other Hardships./ Relating more particularly
to the/ Island of Barbados./ *London,/* Printed by
M. Clark in the Year MDCLXXXIX./ *Title and* 35
pp. Calf extra by Bedford. 4*to.* (1*l.* 5*s.* 1300)

GRYNÆUS (Simon). *See* Novus Orbis.

GUARD (Theodore de la). *See* Ward, Nathaniel.

GUERREIRO (Fernam). Relaçam Annal/ das
Covsas/ qve Fezeram/ os Padres da Companhia/ de
Iesvs nas Partes da India/ Oriental, & no Brafil,
Angola, Cabo Verde, Guine, nos annos/ de feis-
centos & dous & feiscentos & tres, & do pro-/ceffo
da conuerfam, & chriftandade daquellas par-/tes,
tirada das cartas dos mefmos padres/ que de là vie-
ram./ Pelo padre Fernam Guerreiro da mefma/
Companhia, natural de Almodouuar/ de Portugal./
Vay diuidido em quatro liuros. O primeiro de
Iapã/ O II. da China & Maluco. O III. da India./
O IIII. do Brafil, Angola, & Guiné/ Em *Lisboa :*
Per Iorge Rodrigues im-/prefsor de liuros./ Anno
M.D.CV./ *Title, reverse blank ;* ' Aprouaçam.' *et* Li-
semças.' 1 *page ;* ' Ao Lector.' 2 *pp ;* ' Errata,' 2 *pp ;*
Text ' Livro Primeero.' *Signatures A—N in fours*
O in two. ' Livro Segvndo,' *Signatures A—Nnn*
in fours. Vellum. 4*to.* (1*l.* 11*s.* 6*d.* 1301)

GUMILLA (Joseph). El Orinoco/ Ilustrado, y De-
fendido,/ Historia Natural,/ Civil, y Geographica/
de este Gran Rio,/ y de sus Caudalosas Vertien-

tes ;/ Govierno, Usos, y Costumbres de los Indios/
fus habitadores, con nuevas, y utiles noticias de
Animales, Arboles,/ Frutos, Aceytes, Refinas, Yer-
vas, y Raices medicinales ; y fobre/ todo, fe halla-
ràn converfiones muy fingulares à N. Santa Fé,/ y
cafos de mucha edificacion./ Escrita/ por el Padre
Joseph Gumilla, de la Compañia de Jesus ;/ Mif-
sionero, y Superior de las Mifsiones del Orinoco,
Meta, y Cafanare, Calificador, y/ Confultor del
Santo Tribunal de la Inquificion de Cartagena de
Indias, y Examinador/ Synodal del mifmo Obifpado, Provincial que fuè de fu Provincia del Nuevo
Reyno/ de Granada, y actual Procurador à entram-
bas Curias por fus dichas/ Mifsiones, y Provincia./
Segunda Impression, Revista, y Aumentada/ por
fu mifmo Autor, y dividida en dos Partes./ Tomo
Primero/ [y Segundo] En *Madrid:* Por Manuel
Fernandez, Impreffor de el Supremo/ Confejo de
la Inquificion, y de la Reverenda Camara Apoftolica,/ en la Caba Baxa. Año M.DCC.XLV. *Two Vo-*
lumes. Vol. I. 24 *prel. leaves and* 403 *pp.* ' Indice,'
4 *pp. Map at p.* 1. *and plate at p.* 209. *Vol. II.* 4
prel. leaves and 412 *pp.* '*Indice,*' 16 *pp. Plate at p.*
112. *Vellum.* 4*to.* (1*l.* 11*s.* 6*d.* 1302)

GUMILLA (JOSEPH). Histoire Naturelle, Civile
et Geographique de l'Orenoque ; Et des principales
Riviéres qui s'y jettent. Dans laquelle on traite
du Gouvernement, des Ufages & des Coûtumes
des Indiens qui l'habitent, des Animaux, des Arbres, des Fruits, des Réfines, des Herbes & des Ra-
cines Medicinales qui naiffent dans le Païs. Par
le P. Joseph Gumilla, de la Compagnie de Jefus,
Supérieur des Miffions de l'Orenoque. Traduite de
l'Efpagnol fur la feconde Edition, par M. Eidous,
ci devant Ingenieur des Armées de S. M. C. A
Avignon, Desaint & Saillant, M.DCC.LVIII. *Three*
Volumes. Tome I. *xviii pp. Advertissement* 7 &
Text 388 *pp. Table* 4 *pp. Copperplate map at p.* 1.
and plate at p. 303. Tome II. *Title and* 334 *pp.*
Table 4 *pp. plate at p.* 304. Tome III. *Title and* 332
pp. Table 4 *pp. Calf.* 12*mo.* (10*s.* 6*d.* 1303)

ACKE (William). A/ Collection/ of/ Original Voyages :/ Containing/ I. Capt. Cowley's Voyage round the Globe./ II. Captain Sharp's Journey over the Isthmus of/ Darien, and the Expedition into the South Seas,/ Written by himself./ III. Capt. Wood's Voyage thro' the Streights of/ Magellan./ IV. Mr. Roberts' Adventures among the Cor-/ fairs of the Levant ; his Account of their/ Way of Living ; Description of the Archi-/pelago Iflands, Taking of Scio, &c./ Illuftrated with feveral Maps and Draughts./ Publifhed by Capt. William Hacke. *London*, Printed for James Knapton, at the/ Crown in St. Paul's Church-Yard. 1699./ 8 *prel. leaves ; viz. Title, Dedication, Preface, and Index.* 'A New Map of the World.' 'Cowley's Voyage,' 45 *pp. Plate at pp.* 8, 9. 'Sharp's and Wood's Voyages.' 100 *pp. Plate at p.* 1. 'Roberts' Voyage' 53 *p. Map at pp.* 1. *Plate at p.* 18. *Calf. 8vo.* (8s. 6d. 1304)

HAERLEMS/ Schuyt-praetjen,/ O P't/ Redres/ Vande/ Weft-Indifche Compagnie./ Gedruct op't Jaer 1649./ 12 *leaves. Calf bound by Hayday.* 4*to.* (15s. 1305)

HAÏTI. The Rural Code of Haïti ; in French and English. With a Prefatory Letter to the Right Hon. The Earl Bathurst, K.G. &c. &c. &c. *London :* James Ridgway, 1827. *Half-title, title iii to xviii and 100 pp. 8vo.* (3s. 6d. 1306)

HAKLUYT (Richard). The Principall/ Navigations, Voia-/ges and Discoveries of the/ Englifh nation, made by Sea or ouer Land,/ to the most remote and fartheft distant Quarters of/ the earth at any time within the compaffe/ of thefe 1500 yeeres : Deuided into three/ feuerall parts, according to

the po-/fitions of the Regions wherun-/to they
were directed./   ***/ The firft, conteining the
perfonall trauels of the Englifh vnto Iudæa, Syria,
A-/rabia, the riuer Euphrates, Babylon, Balfara,
the Perfian Gulfe, Ormuz, Chaul,/ Goa, India,
and many Iflands adioyning to the South parts of
Afia : toge-/ther with the like vnto Egypt, the
chiefeft ports and places of Africa with-/in and
without the Streight of Gibralter, and about the
famous Promon-/torie of Buona Efperanza./   The
fecond, comprehending the worthy difcoueries of
the Englifh towards/ the North, and Northeaft by
Sea, as of Lapland, Scrikfinia, Corelia, the Baie/
of S. Nicholas, the Ifles of Colgoieue, Vaigats, and
Noua Zembla toward the/ great riuer Ob, with the
mightie Empire of Ruffia, the Cafpian Sea, Georgia,/ Armenia, Media, Perfia, Boghar in Bactria,
& diuers Kingdoms of Tartaria./   The third and
laft, including the Englifh valiant attempts in
fearching al-/moft all the corners of the vafte and
new world of America, from 73. de-/grees of
Northerly latitude Southward, to Meta Incognita,
Newfoundland,/ the maine of Virginia, the point
of Florida, the Baie of Mexico, all the In-/land of
Noua Hifpania, the coaft of Terrafirma, Brafill,
the riuer of Plate, to/ the Streight of Magellan :
and through it, and from it in the South Sea to/
Chili, Peru, Xalifco, the Gulfe of California, Noua
Albion vpon the backfide/ of Canada, further then
euer any Chriftian hitherto hath pierced./   Whereunto is added the last most renowmed Englifh Nauigation,/ round about the whole Globe of the Earth./
By Richard Hakluyt Mafter of Artes, and Student
fometime/ of Chrift-church in Oxford./   Imprinted
at *London* by George Bishop/ and Ralph Newberie,
Deputies to/ Christopher Barker, Printer to the/
Queenes moft excellent Maieftie./   1589./   8 *prel.
leaves; viz. Title reverse blank.*   'To the Right
Hono-/rable Sir Francis Walsingham/' *etc.*   3 *pp.*
' Richard Hakluyt to the fauourable Reader.' 3 *pp.*
1 *page of Epigrams.*   'The order of all the voyages
comprifed in this whole worke in/ generall,' *etc.* 7
pp. Text 825 *pp.*   ' A Table Alphabeticall,' *etc.* 9
pp.   [*Colophon*] Imprinted at London by the/ Deputies of Chriftopher Barker, Printer to/ the
Queenes moft excellent Maieftie./   Anno Dom.

1589./ 1 *page. Calf extra by Heyday. Fine tall
copy. Folio.* (10*l.* 10*s.* 1307)

This copy contains, between pages 490 and 506, the Voyage of Sir
Jerome Bowes, " printed this second time, according to the true
copie I received of a gentleman that went in the same voyage,
for the correction of the errours in the former impreffion," together with the eight original cancelled leaves. It also contains,
between pages 643 and 644, the six suppreffed leaves of Sir
Francis Drake's Voyage " about the whole Globe."

HAKLUYT (RICHARD). Virginia/ richly valued,/
By the defcription of the maine land of/ Florida,
her next neighbour :/ Out of the foure yeeres continuall trauell and difcouerie,/ for above one thoufand miles Eaft and Weft, of/ Don Ferdinando de
Soto, and fixe hundred/ able men in his companie./
Wherein are truly obferued the riches and fertilitie
of thofe parts,/ abounding with things neceffarie,
pleafant, and profitable/ for the life of man : with the
natures and difpo-/fitions of the Inhabitants./ Written by a Portugall gentleman of Eluas, emploied in/
all the action, and tranflated out of Portugefe/ by
Richard Haklvyt./ At *London*/ Printed by Felix
Kyngston for Matthew Lownes,/ and are to be
fold at the figne of the Bifhops/ head in Pauls
Churchyard./ 1609./ 4 *prel. leaves ; viz. Title,
reverse blank.* 'To the Right/ Honovrable, the/
Right Worfhipfull Counfellors, and/ others the
cheerefull aduenturors for/ the aduancement of
that Chriftian/ and noble plantation in/ Virginia.'/
6 *pp ; Text* 180 *pp. Fine clean copy in brown Calf.
4to.* (5*l.* 5*s.* 1308)

HALIBURTON (THOMAS C). An Historical and
Statistical Account of Nova-Scotia, in Two Volumes. Illustrated by a Map of the Province, and
several Engravings. By Thomas C. Haliburton,
Esq. Barrister at Law, and Member of the House
of Assembly of Nova-Scotia. *Halifax.* Joseph
Howe. 1829. *Two Volumes.* Vol. I. *viii and* 340
pp. Index viii pp. With Map and 2 *Plans at pp.*
100, 207. Vol. II. *Title and* 453 *pp. Index* 3 *pp.
Engravings and Plans at pp.* 1, 17, 29, 73, 103, 153,
239. *The Publisher's apology for the view of Halifax, on a small slip.* 3 *folded sheets, viz. Statement ;
Comparative State, etc. and Account, at page* 388.
Uncut. 8*vo.* (18*s.* 1309)

HALKETT (JOHN). Historical Notes respecting
the Indians of North America : With remarks on

the Attempts made to convert and civilize them.
By John Halkett, Esq. *London:* Archibald Constable and Co. 1825. *viii and* 408 *pp. Uncut.*
8*vo.* (6*s.* 6*d.* 1310)

HALL (JOSEPH). A/ Common/ Apologie of/ the
Chvrch of/ England:/ Againſt the vniuſt Chal-/
lenges of the ouer-iuſt Seɛt,/ commonly called/
Brownists./ Wherein the grounds and De-/fences,
of the Separation are/ largely diſcuſſed:/ Occasioned, by a/ Late Pamphlet publiſhed vnder the/
name, Of an Anſwer to a Cenſorious Epiſtle,/
Which the Reader ſhall finde/ in the Margent./
By J. H./ *London.*/ Printed for Samuel Mac-
ham, and/ are to be ſold at his Shop in Pauls/
Church-yard, at the Signe of/ the Bull-head./
1610./ *Title reverse blank, Dedication* 3 *pp;* Te t
145 *pp; A Table* 3 *pp; Errata* 1 *page. Half calf.*
4*to.* (1*l.* 1*s.* 1311)

The name of John Robinson, the Paſtor of the Church of the Pil-
grims, is ſigned at the bottom of page 145.

HALLIFAX (DUKE, *and others*). Letter of the Lords
of Trade to James Delancey Esq. Lt. Governor of
New York dated at Whitehall Dec 9, 1757, respecting Lord Loudon's affairs, and the Line of Partition between the Provinces of New York and the
Massachusett's-Bay. *Signed* by Duke Hallifax,
Soame Jenyns, Wm. Sloper, and W. G. Hamilton.
3 *pages. Manuscript. Folio.* (10*s.* 6*d.* 1312)

HAMILTON (ALEXANDER). Report of the Secretary of the Treasury of the United States, on the
subject of Manufactures. Presented to the House
of Representatives December 5, 1791. *London:*
J. Debrett. 1793. 2 *prel. leaves, and* 129 *pp. half
mor.* 8*vo.* (3*s.* 6*d.* 1313)

HAMILTON (ALEXANDER). Autograph Letter,
marked '*Private,*' to ' The Honble. Mr. Gilman,
dated at New York, Sept. 10, 1790,' desiring him
at the request of Gen. Washington, to name certain
persons to cruise in a revenue boat on the Eastern
Coast. "Prudence, activity, vigilance and strict integrity are the *desiderata.*" 1 *page.* 4*to.* (15*s.* 1314)

HAMILTON (ARCHIBALD, *Lord*). Articles Exhibited againſt Lord Archibald Hamilton, Late Governour of Jamaica. With Sundry Depositions

and Proofs relating to the fame. *London,* Printed
in the Year M.DCC.XVII. *Half-title, title, pp. v to
viii and 32 pp. 8vo.* (5s. 1315)

HAMILTON (ARCHIBALD, *Lord*). An Answer to
an Anonymous Libel, entitled, Articles exhibited
againſt Lord Archibald Hamilton, late Governour
of Jamaica; with ſundry Depoſitions and Proofs
relating to the fame. By Lord Archibald Hamilton. *London :* Printed in the Year MDCCXVIII. 92
pp. half mor. 8vo. (7s. 6d. 1316)

HAMMOND (JOHN). Leah and Rachel,/ Or,/ the
Two Fruitfull Siſters/ Virginia,/ and Mary-Land :/
Their Preſent Condition, Im-/partially ſtated and
related./ VVith/ A Removall of ſuch Imputations
as are ſcandalouſly/ caſt on thoſe Countries, whereby
many deceived/ Souls, choſe rather to Beg, Steal,
rot in Priſon,/ and come to ſhamefull deaths, then
to better their being/ by going thither, wherein is
plenty of all things/ neceſſary for Humane ſubſiſt-
ance./ By John Hammond./ *London,*/ Printed
by T. Mabb, and are/ to be ſold by Nich. Bourn,
neer the Royall/ Exchange, 1656./ *3 prel. leaves;
viz. Title the reverse blank;* ' To/ His Honoured and
Worthy Friends/ the Worſhipfull William Stone
Eſquire, Governour;/ and Leivt. General of the
Province of Mary-land./ And/ Mr. James William-
ſon of Rapahanock in/ Virginia Gentleman.'/ *2 pp.*
' To/ thoſe two worthy Commanders/ and Mariners,
Capt. Iohn Whittie, Commander/ of the good Ship,
the Freeman, now bound for Virginia ; And Capt.
Sam Tilghman, Commander/ of the Golden Fortune, now bound for the Province of Mary-Land./
2 pp; Text 28 pp. ' Poſt-ſcript' *in a large type pp.*
*29-32. Fine large copy with rough leaves, morocco by
Bedford. 4to.* (21l. 1317)

HAMOR (RAPHE). A Trve/ diſcovrse of the/ present estate of Vir-/ginia, and the ſucceſſe of the af-
faires/ there till the 18 of Iune. 1614. Together./
With a Relation of the/ ſeuerall Engliſh townes
and forts, the aſſu-/red hopes of that countrie and
the peace/ concluded with the Indians./ The Chriſ-
tening of Powhatans daughter/ and her mariage
with an Engliſh-man./ Written by Raphe Hamor
the yon-/ger, late Secretarie in that Colony./

Printed at *London* by Iohn Beale for Wil-/liam
Welby dwelling at the figne of the/ Swaune in
Pauls Church-Yard. 1615./ 4 *prel. leaves ; viz.
Title reverse blank* ' The Epiftle Dedicatory' 3 *pp.*
' To the Reader' 3 *pp. Text* 69 *pp.* ' Errata' 1 *page.
Fine large copy in blue morocco by Francis Bedford.*
4to.   (12l. 12s. 1318)

HAMOR (Raphe).   *Another Copy, the last two
leaves in facsimile.   Calf extra by Francis Bedford.*
4to.   (5l. 15s. 6d. 1319)

HANCOCK (John). Letter signed in the autograph
of Governor Hancock to His Excellency Samuel
Huntington Esq. Governor of Connecticut, dated
at Boston April 3, 1788, giving notice of the repeal
of the resolution offering a reward for apprehend-
ing Daniel Shays, Luke Day, Adam Wheeler, and
Eli Parsons, the principal abettors in the late Rebellion, and requesting Gov. Huntington to recall
his proclamation, etc.   1 *page, a good specimen.*
Folio.   (10s. 6d. 1320)

HANCOCK (John).   Observations on the Climate,
Soil, and Productions of British Guiana, and on the
Advantages of Emigration to, and Colonizing the
Interior of, that Country: Together with Inciden-
tal Remarks on the Diseases, their Treatment and
Prevention: Founded on a long experience within
the Tropics. By John Hancock, M.D. Second
Edition. *London:* Published for the Author. 1840.
2 *prel. leaves and* 92 *pp.* 8vo.   (2s. 6d. 1321)

HANSEN (Leonard).   [*Engraved title*] Rosa Per-
vana/ Vita Mirabilis et Mors/ Pretiosa/ Ven[lis].
Sororis Rosæ de S. Maria/ Limensis ex tertio Ordine S. P. Dominici/ Ad S[m]. D. N. Alex-
andrum VII./ Pont Max./ 1664/ [*Printed title*]
Vita mirabilis/ et Mors pretiosa/ venerabilis
Sororis/ Rosæ de S. Maria/ Limensis,/ Ex Tertio
Ordine S. P. Dominici,/ ad Sanctissimvm D. N./
Alexandrvm VII./ Pontificem Max. Excerpta &
collecta/ Per P. M. F. Leonardvm Hansen/ Pro-
uincialem Angliæ, & Socium/ Reueren-/diffimi P.
Magift. Generalis Ord. Præd./ *Romae,* Typis Nicolai Angeli Tinaffij m. dc. lxiv./ Superiorum permiffu./ 5 *prelim. leaves: Text breaks off abruptly
with the* 356*th page ; Index, Sphalmata & Protestatio,*
2 *leaves. Calf.* 4to.   (15s. 1322)

HANSEN (LEONARD). [*Engraved title*] Vita/ Bea-
tæ/ Rosæ/ Lovanij,/ Typis H. Nempei A : 1668./
[*Printed title*] Vita/ Mirabilis/ et/ mors pretiosa/
B. Rosæ/ de S. Maria/ Limensis,/ Ex Tertio Ordine S. P. Dominici,/ Excerpta & collecta,/ Per
Eximium/ P. F. Leonardum Hansen/ S. Th. Magift. Provincialem Angliæ, & So-/cium Reverend-
iffimi P. Magift./ Gener. Ord. Præd./ Poft Ro-
manam fecundam editio tertia./ *Lovanii,*/ Typis
H. Nempæi. 1668./ Superiorum permiffu./ 12
prel. leaves, and 549 *pp: Index, 3 pp. Old calf.*
12*mo.* (15*s.* 1323)

HANSON (ELIZABETH). An Account of the Captivity of Elizabeth Hanson, Late of Kachecky in
New-England : Who, with Four of her Children,
and Servant-Maid, was taken Captive by the Indians and carried into Canada. Setting forth The
various remarkable Occurrences, fore Trials, and
wonderful Deliverances which befel them after
their Departure, to the Time of their Redemption.
A New Edition. Taken in Subftance from her own
Mouth, by Samuel Bownas. *London* : James Phillips, 1782. 26 *pp.* ' Books,' 2 *pp. half mor. Uncut,
small* 8*vo.* (7*s.* 6*d.* 1324)

HANWAY (JONAS). An Account of the Society
For the Encouragement of the British Troops, In
Germany and North America. With the Motives
to the making a prefent to thofe troops, also to the
widows and orphans of fuch of them as have died
in defence of their country, particularly at the
battles of Thonhausen, Quebec &c. With an Alphabetical Lift of the Subfcribers to this benevolent
Defign ; and a State of the Receipts and Difburfe-
ments of the Society. *London.* M.DCC.LX. *viii*, 91,
and 55 *pp. Calf.* 8*vo.* (5*s.* 6*d.* 1325)

HARCOURT (ROBERT). A/ Relation/ of a Voyage/
to Gviana./ Describing the Climat,/ Scituation,
fertilitie, prouifions and commodities/ of that Country, containing feuen Prouinces, and/ other Signi-
ories within that Territory : Together,/ with the
manners, cuftomes, behauiors, and/ difpofitions of
the people./ Performed by Robert Harcovrt, of/
Stanton Harcourt Efquire./ The Pattent for the
Plantation of which Country,/ His Maieftie hath

granted to the faid Robert/ Harcovrt vnder the
Great Seale./ At *London*/ Printed by Iohn Beale,
for W. Welby, and/ are to be fold at his fhop in
Pauls Churchyard at the/ figne of the Swan. 1613./
8 *prel. leaves;* viz. *Title reverse blank,* ' ➋ To the
high and/ Mighty Prince, Charles, Prince/ of Great
Britaine.'/ 3 *pp. next page blank.* ' ➋ To the Readers,/ Adventvrers, Favorers,/ and wel-willers of
the Plantation/ in Gviana./ 10 *pp.* Text 71 *pp.*
Half-russia. 4to. (3*l.* 3*s.* 1326)

HARCOURT (Robert). The/ Relation/ of a Voy-
age/ To Gviana./ Defcribing the Climate, Situation,/ Fertilitie, & Commodities of that/ Country:
Together with the/ Manner, and Cuftomes of/ the
People./ Performed by Robert Harcovrt,/ of
Stanton Harcourt Efquier./ 1619./ Now newly reviewed, & enlarged, by addition/ of fome neceffary
Notes, for the more ample explai-/ning of fome
things mentioned in the faid Relation: Together,
with a larger declaration of the famous/ Riuer of
the Amazones and the Coun-/try thereabout./ Gathered from the moderne experience of/ our owne
Country-men./ The Patent for the Plantation of
which Country,/ His Maieftie hath lately Granted/
to a Corporation./ *London,*/ Printed by Edw:
Allde, dwelling neere Chrift-/Church. 1626./ 8
prel. leaves; viz. Title reverse blank, ' ¶ To the moft
high/ and mightie Monarch, Charles,'/ *etc.* 4 *pp.*
' To the High/ & Mighty Prince, Charles,/ Prince
of Great/ Britaine.'/ 2 *pp.* ' ➋ To the Readers,/
Adventvrers, Favorers,'/ *etc.* 8 *pp.* Text 84 *pp.*
Russia. 4to. (3*l.* 3*s.* 1327)

HARDIE (James). An Account of the Malignant
Fever, lately prevalent in the City of New-York.
Containing I. A Narrative of its Rise, Progress and
Decline, with the Opinions of fome Medical Gentlemen, with refpect to its Origin, &c. II. The
Manner in which the Poor were relieved during
this awful Calamity. III. A List of the Donations, which have been prefented to the Committee
for the Relief of the Sick and Indigent. IV. A
List of the Names of the Dead, arranged in alphabetical Order, with their Profeffions or Occupations, and as far as practicable to obtain Information, the Names of the Countries of which they

were Natives. V. A Comparative View of the Fever
of the Year 1798, with that of the Year 1795. By
James Hardie, A.M. Copy-Right secured according to Act of Congress. *New-York :* Printed by
Hurtin and M'Farlane, 1799. 148 *pp. Uncut.*
8vo. (10s. 6d. 1328)

HARDY (JOHN). A/ Description/ of the/ Laft Voy-
age/ to/ Bermudas,/ In the Ship/ Marygold,/ S. P.
Commander ;/ By J. H. φιλοχειρηρνεια./ Begun
November the twelfth, 1670. And ending/ May the
third, 1671./ With Allowance./ *London,* printed
for Rowland Reynald at the Sun and Bible/ in the
Poultrey 1671./ 4 *prel. leaves and Text pp.* 1 to 24
*in Verse. Wanting all after page 24. Calf by Bed-
ford.* 4to. (1l. 5s. 1329)

HARDY (R. W. H). Travels in the Interior of
Mexico, in 1825, 1826, 1827, & 1828. By Lieut.
R. W. H. Hardy, R.N. *London :* Henry Colburn
and Richard Bentley, 1829. *xiv and* 540 *pp. With
8 Illustrations. Cloth.* 8vo. (6s. 6d. 1330)

HARPER (ROBERT GOODLOE). Observations on the
Dispute between the United States and France, addressed By Robert Goodloe Harper, Esq. One of
the Representatives in Congress for the State of
South Carolina, to his Constituents, in May 1797.
Fifth Edition. Philadelphia Printed. *London* Reprinted John Stockdale, 1798./ *Title and Text pp.*
5-109. 8vo. (4s. 6d. 1331)

HARPER (ROBERT GOODLOE). Observations on the
Dispute between the United States and France, ad-
dressed By Robert Goodloe Harper, Esq. One of the
Representatives in Congress for the State of South
Carolina, to his Constituents, in May, 1797. The
Profits of this Pamphlet are devoted to the Benefit
of the Philanthropic Society, by the Editor. Fifth
Edition. Philadelphia printed. *London :* Reprint-
ed, 1798. 4 *prel. leaves, and Text pp.* 7 *to* 86 ; *half
morocco.* 12mo. (4s. 6d. 1332)

HARPER (ROBERT GOODLOE). Observations on the
Dispute between the United States and France, ad-
dressed By Robert Goodloe Harper, Esq. One of the
Representatives in Congress for the State of South
Carolina, to his Constituents, in May, 1797. The

Profits of this Pamphlet are devoted to the Benefit of the Philanthropic Society, by the Editor. Sixth Edition. Philadelphia Printed. *London :* Reprinted, 1798. *viii pp. and Text pp.* 5-110. *half morocco.* 8vo. (4s. 6d. 1333)

HARPER (ROBERT GOODLOE). Observations on the Dispute between the United States and France addressed By Robert Goodloe Harper, Esq. One of the Representatives in Congress for the State of South Carolina, to his Constituents, in May, 1797. Tenth Edition. Philadelphia printed. *Edinburgh* reprinted. Arch. Constable, Cross. 1798. 89 *pp.* 12mo. (4s. 6d. 1334)

HART (LEVI). The Christian Minister, or faithful Preacher of the Gospel described. A Sermon Delivered at the Ordination of the Reverend Mr. Joel Benedict, At Newent, in Norwich, On the 21ft of February, 1771. By Levi Hart, A.M. Pastor of the second Church in Preston. Also the Charge Given by the Rev. Mr. Rosseter, of Preston; And the Right-Hand of Fellowship Given by the Rev. Mr. Burroughs, of Killingly. Published at the general Defire of the People. *New-London :* Printed by Timothy Green, 1771. *Title and* 31 *pp. Uncut.* 8vo. (4s. 6d. 1335)

HART (LEVI). The Important Objects of the Evangelical Ministry considered; and Brief Hints suggested for the Improvement of the Christian Preacher, That his Labour may not be in Vain. In a Discourse at the Ordination of the Rev. Mr. Amos Chase, To the gospel Ministry, and paftoral Office, over the second Church in Litchfield, June 27th, 1787. By Levi Hart, A.M. Pastor of a Church in Preston. *Litchfield :* Printed by Thomas Collier, M.DCC.LXXXVIII. 26 *pp.* 8vo. (4s. 6d. 1336)

HART (LEVI). Autograph Letter ' For the Rev. Mr. James Cogswell, Canterbury. dated at Preston, 17th of Dec. 1767. 1 *page.* 4to. (7s. 6d. 1337)

HART (WILLIAM). Brief Remarks on a number of False Propositions, and Dangerous Errors, Which are spreading in the Country; Collected out of fundry Difcourfes publifh'd, wrote by Dr. Whitaker and Mr. Hopkins. Written by Way of Dialogue,

By William Hart, A.M. Paſtor of the Firſt Church
in Say-Brook. *New-London:* Printed and Sold by
Timothy Green. 1769. 72 *pp.* 8*vo.* (5*s.* 6*d.* 1338)

HARTGERTS (Joost). [*Engraved Title*] Ooſt en
Weſt-indiſche/ Voyagien :/ Met de/ Beſchrijvingen
van/ Indien./ Eerſte Deel./ t'Amsterdam, bij Iooſt
Hartgers. Inde Gasthuys=ſteech bij't Stad-huys.
1648./ [*Printed Title.*] Ooſt-Indiſche Voyagien/
Door dien/ Begin en Voortgangh, van de Vereen-
nighde/ Nederlandtſche Geoctroyeerde/ Ooſt-In-
diſche/ Compagnie./ Vervatende de voornaemſte
Reyſen, by de Inwoonderen der/ ſelver Provintien
derwaerts ghedaem./ Nevens de beſchrijvinghen
der Rijcken, Eylanden, Havenen, Revieren, Stroo=/
men, Rheeden, Winden, Diepten en Ondiepten;
Midtſgaders Religien, Manie=/ren Aerdt, Politie
ende Regeeringe der Volckeren; oock meede haer-
der Spe=/ceryen, Droogen, Gelt ende andere Koop-
manſchappen, met vele Diſcourſen/ over de gelegentheyt van Indien, nevens eenige kopere Platen
verciert./ Seer nut ende dienſtigh alle Curieuſe,
ende andere Zee-varende Lief hebbers./ Erſte Deel.
Daer in begrepen zijn 16 Voyagien./ t'*Amstelredam,*/ Voor Jooſt Hartgerts, Boeck-verkooper in de
Gaſthuys-Streegh, bezijden/ het Stadt-huys, in de
Boeck-winckel, Anno, 1648./ *12 prelim. leaves, including the engraved and printed titles, Inleydinge and
Register. Volume I.* 16 *Parts.* 4*to.* (10*l.* 10*s.* 1339)

The sixteen parts have the following titles and collations:—

PART I.

VERHAEL van de eerſte | Schip-vaert | der | Hollandiſche ende
Zeeuſche Schepen, | Door't | Way-Gat, | By Noorden Noorwegen,
Moſcovien ende Tar- | tarien om, na de Coninckrijcken Cathay
ende China. Met drie | Schepen, uyt Texel gezeylt inden Iare
1594. | Hier achter is by-ghevoeght de beſchrijvinghe van de
Landen | Siberia, Samoyeda, ende Tingœſa. Seer vreemt en
vermaac- | kelijck om leſen. T' *Amsterdam,* | Voor Ioost Hart-
gers, Boeck-verkooper in de Gaſthuys-ſteegh, in de | Boeck-
winckel, bezijden het Stadthuys. 1648. | *Title and* 57 *pp. with*
1 *copper-plate in* 6 *compartments at p.* 1.

PART II.

EERSTE | SCHIP-VAERT | Der Hollanders naer | Oost-Indien, |
Met vier Schepen onder 't beleydt van Corrnelis Houtman uyt |
Texel t'zeyl ghegaen, Anno 1595. | Waer in verhaelt werdt, al
wat haer ſonderlinghs onder wegen | bejegent is, als oock de
Conditien, Religien, Zeden en Huys-houdin- | gen der Volc-
keren, met den Aerdt, Vruchtbaerheyt, Gewaſ- | ſen Dieren en
andere eygenſchappen der Lan- | den, die ſy beſeylt hebben. |
Seer vermaeckelijck om leſen. T' *Amsterdam.* Voor Jooſt
Hartgers, Boeck-verkooper in de Gaſthuys-ſteegh, in de |
Boeck-winckel, bezijden het Stadt-huys, Anno 1648. | *Title
and* 102 *pp. with* 1 *copper-plate at page* 1 *in* 6 *compartments.*

PART III.

WAERACHTIGH VERHAEL | Van de Schip-vaert op | Oost-Indien, | Ghedaen | By de acht Schepen, onder den Heer Admi- | rael Jacob van Neck, en de Vice-Admirael Wybrand van | Warwijck, van Amfterdam gezeylt in den jare, 1598. | Hier achter is aen-ghevoeght | De Voyagie van Sebald de Weert, naer de Strate | Magalanes. | t' *Amstelredam*, | Voor looft Hartgerts, Boeck-verkooper in de Gaft-huys-fteegh, | in de Boeck-winckel, bezij-den 't Stadt-huys, Anno 1648. | *Title and pp.* 3 *to* 92, *with* 2 *copper-plates at p.* 1 *each in* 6 *compartments.*

PART IV.

WONDERLIJCKE VOAYGIE, | By de Hollanders gedaen, | Door de Strate | Magalanes, | Ende voorts den gantfchen kloot des Aert- | bodems om, met Schepen : onder den Admirael | Olivier van Noort, uytghevaren, Anno 1598. | Hier achter is byger-veght | De tweede Voyagie van Iacob van Neck, naer | Oost-Indien. | t' *Amstelredam*, | Voor looft Hartgerts, Boeck-ver-kooper in de Gaft-huys-fteegh, | in de Boeck-winckel, bezijden 'tStadt-huys, Anno 1648. | *Title and pp.* 3 *to* 88.

PART V.

HISTORIS JOURNAEL | Van de | Voyage | Gadaen met 3 Schepen uyt Zeelant naer d'Ooft-In- | dien onder het belevt van den Conmandeur Jores van Spil- | bergen, fyn eerfte Reyfe. Inden jare, 1601. 1602. 1603. 1604. | Als meede | Befchryvinge vande Tweede Voyage ghedaen | met 12 Schepen na d'Ooft-Indien onder den Admirael | Steven vander Hagen. t' *Amstelredam*, | Voor Jooft Hartgers Boeck-verkooper inde Gaft-huys-fteegh | bezijden het Stadt-huys, 1648. | *Title and pp.* 3 *to* 96, *with* 1 *copper-plate in* 6 *compartments.*

PART VI.

JOURNAEL, Ende Hiftorifche Verhael, van de | treffelijcke Reyfe, gedaen naer Ooft-Indien, ende | China, met elf Schepen. | Door den Manhaften Admirael | Cornelis Matelief | de Jonge. | Uyt-ghevaren in den Jare, 1605. En wat haer in de volghende Ja- | ren, 1606. 1607. ende 1608. weder varen is. | Een feer Vreemde en Wonderlijcke Reyfe. | t' *Amstelredam*. | Voor Jooft Hartgers, Boeck-verkooper in de Gafthuys-Steegh, | bezijden het Stadt-huys, in de Boeck-winckel, 1648. *Title and* 142 *pp. with* 1 *copper-plate in* 6 *compartments at p.* 1.

PART VII.

WONDERLIJCKE Hiftorifche | Ende | Journaelsche | aentey-ckeningh, | Van 't ghene | Pieter van den Broecke, op | fijne Reyfen, foo van Cabo Verde, Angola, Gunea, | Ooft-Indien : Waer in hem, foo in Schip-breuck, als m 't door-rey- | fen van't Landt, feer veel vreemde dingen ontmoet zijn, foovan | Religie, Manieren, Zeeden, en Huyf-houdingen der volc- | keren : En andere eygheufchappen der Landen | en kuften die fy bezeylt hebben. t' *Amstelredam*. | Voor Jooft Hartgerts, Boeck-ver-kooper in de Gafthuys-Steegh, | bezijden het Stadt-huys, in de Boeck-winckel, 1648. | *Title and pp.* 3 *to* 112, *with* 1 *copper-plate in* 6 *compartments.*

PART VIII. (1.)

OOST-EN WEST-INDISCHE Voyagie, | Door de | Strate Magal-lanes | Naer de Moluques, | Met fes Schepen onder den Com-mandeur Ioris Spilbergen. | Als mede | De wonderlijcke Reyfe ghedaen door Willem Cor- | nelifz Schouten van Hoorn, en Iacob le Maire, in den Jaere | 1615. 1616. 1617. | Hoe fy bezuy-den de Straet van Magallanes een Nieuwe paffagie | tot in de groote Zuydt-Zee ontdeckt, voort den gheheelen Aerd-kloot om-ghezeylt hebben. | Midtfgraders | Wat Eylanden, vreemde Volckeren, en wonderlijcke Avon- | tueren hun ontmoet zijn. | t' *Amstelredam*, | Voor Jooft Hartgerts, Boeck-verkooper in de Gafthuys-Steegh, | bezijdenhet Stadt-huys, in de Boeck-winckel. 1648. | 2 *prelim. leaves, and pp.* 5 *to* 66, *with* 1 *copper-plate in* 6 *compartments.*

PART VIII. (2.)

JOURNAEL, ofte | Befchrijvinge van de wonder- | lijcke Reyfe,

ghedaen door | Willem Cornelisz | Schouten van Hoorn. | In
de Iaren 1615. 1616. 1617. Hoe hy bezuyden de Straet Magel-
lanes eenen nieuwen door- | ganck gevonden heeft, ftreckende
tot in de Zuyd-Zee, met de | verklaringe van de vreemde Natien,
Volcken, Landen en Avonturen, | die fy gefien, ende haer weder-
varen zijn. | Hier is noch achter by-gevoeght eenighe Zee-
Vragen ende Antwoorden, | zijnde feer neet ende geheel dien-
ftigh alle Schippers, Stiermans ende Zeevarende maets. |
t'*Amstelredam*, | Voor Jooft Hartgers, Boeck-verkooper, in de
Gafthuys-Steegh, | bezijden het Stadt-huys, in de Boeck-winckel.
1648. | *Title-page and pp.* 68 *to* 120.

PART IX.

JOURNAEL | van de | Naffaufche Vloot, | ofte | Befchrijvingh van de
Voyagie om den gant chen Aert- | Kloot, Gedaen met elf Sche-
pen : | Onder 'tbeleydt van den Admirael | Iaques l' Heremite,
ende Vice-Admirael Gheen Huy- | gen Schapenham, inde Iaren
1623. 1624. 1625. en 1626. | Noch is hier by gevoegt een Bef-
chrijvinge vande Kegeeringe van Peru, door | Pedro de Madriga,
geboren tot Lima. Als mede een verhael van Pedro | Fernandez
de Quir, aengaende de ontdeckinge van 't on- | bekent Auftrialia,
fyn grooten Rijckdom ende | vruchtbaerheyt. | Oock mede
eenige Difcourfen de Ooft | Indifche Vaert en de Coopmanfchap
betreffende | t'*Amstelredam*, | Voor Jooft Hartgerifz. Boeck-
verkooper, woonende nide Gaft-huys- | fteegh naeft het Stadt-
huys, inde Boeck-winckel. Anno 1648- | *Title and* 76 *pp. with*
1 *copper-plate in* 6 *compartments at p.* 1.

PART X. (1.)

JOURNAEL | ofte | Gedenckwaerdige befchrijvin- | ge van de
Ooft-Indifche Reyfe van | Willem Ysbrantsz | Bontekoe van
Hoorn. | Begrijpende veel wonderlijcke en ghevaerlijcke faec- |
ken hun daer in weder varen. | Begonnen den 18. December
1618. en vol-eynd den 16. November 1625. | Waer by gevoeght
is het Journael van Dirck Albertfz Raven, als | oock verfcheyden
gedenckwaerdige gefchiedeniffen, op veel plaetfen | verbetert
en een groot deel vermeerdert. | t'*Amstelredam*, | Voor Jooft
Hartgers, Boeck-verkooper in de Gafthuys-Steegh, bezij- | den
het Stadt-huys, in de Boeck-winckel. 1648. 2 *prelim. leaves,*
and 58 *pp. with* 1 *copper-plate in* 6 *compartments.*

PART X. (2.)

JOURNAEL | ofte | Befchrijvinghe van de reyfe | ghedaen by den
Commandeur Dirck Albertfz. Ra- | ven, na Spitsberghen, in den
Jare 1639, ten dienfte vande | E. Heeren Bewind-thebbers van
de Groen- | landtfche Compagnie tot Hoorn. | Waer in ver-
haelt wort fijn droevige Schip-breuc- | ke; sijnellende op't
wrack, enfijnblijde verloffinghe. | Met noch eenige gedenck-
weerdige Gefchiedenifen. | Alles waerdigh om te lefen. t'*Am-
stelredam*, | Voor Jooft Hartgers, Boeck-verkooper in de
Gafthuys-Steegh, bezij- | den het Stadt-huys, in de Boeck-
winckel. 1648. | *Title-page and pp.* 60 *to* 76.

PART XI.

ONGELUCKIGE Voyagie, | Van't | Schip Batavia, | Nae | Ooft-In-
dien. | Uytgevaren onder de E. Françoys Pelfaert. | Ghebleven
op de Alrolhos van Frederick Houtman, op de hooch- | te van
28½ graden, by Zuyden de Sinie Æquinoctiael. | Vervattende 't
verongelucken des Schips, en de grouwelijcke. | Moorderyen
onder t' Scheepsvolck, op't Eylandt Bataviaes Kerck-hoff; |
nevens de ftraffe der handtdadighers in de Jaren | 1628 en 1629. |
Hier achter is by-gevoeght eenige difcourfen der Ooft-Indif-che
Zee-vaert, als mede de gantfche gelegentheydt der Koop- |
manfchappen diemen in Indien doet. t'*Amsterdam*, | Voor
Jooft Hartge:s, Boeck-verkooper in de Gafthuys-steegh, bezij-
den het | Stadt-huys, in de Boeck-winckel. Anno 1648. | *Title*
and 46 *pp. with* 1 *copper-plate in* 6 *compartments, followed by*
' *Diverfche Difcourfen, de Poft Indische Vaert betreffende.'*
8 *leaves not paged* (*signature* dd.)

PART XII.

GENERALE Befchrijvinge | Van | Indien. | Ende in 't befonder |
Kort verhael van de Regering, Ceremonien, Handel, Vruch-

ten en Geleghentheydt van't Koninckrijck van Gufuratten, |
ftaende onder de beheerfchinghe van den Groot-Machtighen
Koninck | Cajahan: anders genaemt den grooten | Mogor. |
Vyt Verfcheyden Autheuren ende eyghen onder-vindinge ver-
gadert | ende by een gheftell: | D*o*or | Johan van Twist, Gew-
efen Overhooft van de Nederlantfche Comtoo- | ren, Amadabat,
Cambaya, Brodera, ende Brotchia. | Hier achter is by-gevoeght
de aenwijfinge van meeft alle Kuften, Drooghten ende Reeden,
om | door gantfch Indien te zeplen. *t'Amstelredam,* | Voor
Jooft Hartgerts, Boeck-verkooper in de Gafthuys-Steegh,
bezij- | den het Stadt-huys, in de Boeck-winckel. 1648. | *Title
and* 94 *pp.*

PART XIII.

BESCHRIJVINGHE | Van het Machtigh Coninckrijcke | Japan, |
Vervattende | Den aert en eygenfchappen van't Landt, | man-
ieren der Volckeren, als mede hare grouwelijcke | wreedtheydt
teghen de Roomfche | Chriftenen, gefteldt | Door Françoys
Caron. | *t'Amstelredam,* Voor Joost Hartgers, Boeck-verkoo-
per in de Gafthuys-fteegh, in de | Boeck-winckel, bezijden
het Stadt-huys. 1648. | *Title and* 78 *pp.*

HARTLEY (DAVID). An Address to the Commit-
tee of Association of the County of York, on the
State of Public Affairs. [Chiefly the war with the
American Colonies.] By David Hartley, Efq. Ja-
nuary 3, 1781. The Second Edition. *York:* A.
Ward, 1781. 46 *pp. Half mor.* 8*vo.* (4*s.* 6*d.* 1340)

HARTLEY (DAVID). An Address to the Committee of the County of York, on the State of Public
Affairs. *London:* J. Stockdale, MDCCLXXXI. 63 *pp.*
half mor. 8*vo.* (4*s.* 6*d.* 1341)

This is a reprint of the preceding, with the addition, at the end, of
"The Address of the Committee of Association for the County
of York," pp. 53 to 63.

HARTLIB (SAMUEL). The Reformed/ Virginian/
Silk-Worm,/ Or, a Rare and New/ Discovery/ of/
A fpeedy way, and eafie means, found out/ by a
young Lady in England fhe having made/ full proof
thereof in May,/ Anno 1652./ For the feeding of
Silk-worms in the Woods, on the/ Mulberry-Tree-
leaves in Virginia: Who after fourty dayes/ time,
prefent their moft rich golden-coloured filken/
Fleece, to the inftant wonderful enriching of/ all
the Planters there, requiring from/ them neither
coft, labour, or hindrance/ in any of their other
employ-/ments whatfoever./ And alfo to the good
hopes, that the Indians, fee-/ing and finding that
there is neither Art, Skill, or Pains/ in the thing:
they will readily fet upon it, being/ by the benefit
thereof inabled to buy of the/ Englifh (in way of
Truck for their/ Silk-bottoms) all thofe things/ that
they moft defire./ *London,*/ Printed by John Strea-
ter, for Giles Calvert at the/ Black-Spread-Eagle

at the Weſt end/ of Pauls, 1655./ *2 prel. leaves; viz. Title in a narrow type metal border, reverse blank, ' To the Reader.' 2 pp. Text 40 pp. 4to.* (2l. 2s. 1342)

HARTWELL (HENRY). The Preſent State of Virginia, and the College: By Meſſieurs Hartwell, Blair, and Chilton. To which is added, The Charter for Erecting the ſaid College, granted by their late Majeſties King William and Queen Mary of Ever Glorious and Pious Memory. *London:* John Wyat, M.DCC.XXVII. *2 prel. leaves and 95 pp. half mor. 8vo.* (7s. 6d. 1343)

HATTERSLEY (JOHN). The Conquest of America, and Minor Poems, by John Hattersley. *London:* Baldwin and Cradock, MDCCCXXXI. *viii and 207 pp. Calf extra gilt by Hayday. 16mo.* (7s. 6d. 1344)

HAVEN (JASON). A Sermon Preached before his Excellency Sir Francis Bernard, Baronet, Governor: His honor Thomas Hutchinson, Esq; Lieutenant-Governor, The Honorable His Majesty's Council, And the Honorable House of Representatives, of the Province of the Maſſachuſetts-Bay in New-England, May 31ſt, 1769. Being the Anniverſary of the Election of His Majesty's Council for ſaid Province. By Jason Haven, A.M. Paſtor of the Firſt Church in Dedham. *Boston:* New-England: Printed by Richard Draper, Printer to His Excellency the Governor, and the Honorable His Majesty's Council. MDCCLXIX. *55 pp. half mor. small 8vo.* (5s. 6d. 1345)

HAWKESWORTH (JOHN). An Account of the Voyages undertaken by the order of his present Majesty, for making Diſcoveries in the Southern Hemiſphere, and successively performed by Commodore Byron, Captain Wallis, Captain Carteret, And Captain Cook, In the Dolphin, the Swallow, and the Endeavour: Drawn up from the Journals which were kept by the ſeveral Commanders, and from the Papers of Joseph Banks, Eſq; By John Hawkesworth, LL.D. To which is added a Voyage to the North Pole, By Commodore Phipps. In Two Volumes. Illuſtrated with Charts and elegant Copper-plates. *Dublin:* James Williams, M DCC LXXV. *2 Volumes. Vol. I. 6 prel. leaves; xxviii and pp. 3-489. Chart, and 5 Copperplates at*

pp. 76, 100, 197, 211, 263. Vol. II. 5 *prel. leaves;*
and 539 *pp.* ' A Voyage towards the North Pole :'
etc. 49 *pp. Chart and* 1 *copperplate, at page* 13.
Calf. 8vo. (12s. 6d. 1346)

HAWKESWORTH (John). An Account of the
Voyages undertaken by the order of his present
Majesty, for making Difcoveries in the Southern
Hemifphere, and successively performed by Commodore Byron, Captain Wallis, Captain Carteret,
And Captain Cook, In the Dolphin, the Swallow, and
the Endeavour : Drawn up from the Journals which
were kept by the feveral Commanders, and from
the Papers of Joseph Banks, Esq; By John Hawkesworth, LL.D. In Two Volumes. Illuftrated with
elegant Copper-Plates. *Dublin :* James Potts,
MDCCLXXV. *Two Volumes.* Vol. I. 6 *prel. leaves ;*
xxxviii pp ; and Text pp. 3-489. *With Chart of part*
of the South Sea. 3 *Copperplates at pp.* 23, 124, 196.
Vol. II. 5 *prel. leaves ; and* 539 *pp.* 4 *Copperplates*
at pp. 38, 101, 164, 289. *Calf.*
8vo. (10s. 6d. 1347)

HAWKINS (Sir Richard). The/ Observations/
of/ S^ir Richard Havv/kins Knight, in his/ Vojage
jnto the/ South Sea./ Anno Domini 1593./ *London/*
Printed by I. D. for Iohn Iaggard, and are to be/
fold at his fhop at the Hand and Starre in Fleete-
ftreete,/ neere the Temple Gate. 1622./ 3 *prel.*
leaves ; viz. Title reverse blank, ' To the/ Most Illvs-
triovs/ and Most Excellent/ Prince Charles,' *etc./*
1 *page.* ' ☟ To the Reader.' 1 *page. Text* 169 *pp.*
Errata 1 *page.* ' The Table,' *etc.* 5 *pp. Old Calf.*
Folio. (2l. 2s. 1348)

HAWLEY (Zerah). A Journal of a Tour through
Connecticut, Massachusetts, New York, the North
Part of Pennsylvania and Ohio, including a Year's
residence in that part of the State of Ohio, Styled
New Connecticut, or Western Reserve. In which
is given, a description of the Country, Climate,
Soil, Productions, Animals, Buildings, Manners of
the People, State of Society, Population, &c. From
actual and careful Observation. By Zerah Hawley,
A.M. *New-Haven :* Printed by S. Converse. 1822.
158 *pp. 12mo.* (4s. 6d. 1349)

HAYNE (Samuel). An/ Abstract/ of all the/ Sta-

tutes/ Made Concerning/ Aliens Trading/ in/ Eng-
land/ From the firſt year of K. Henry the VII./
Also,/ Of all the Laws made for Securing/ our
Plantation Trade to our Selves./ With Obſervations thereon, proving that the/ Jews (in their
practical way of Trade at this time)/ Break them
all, to the great Damage of the King in/ His Cuſtoms, the Merchants in their Trade, the/ whole
Kingdom, and His Majesties Plantations in/ America in their Staple./ Together with the Hardſhips
and Difficulties the Au-/thor hath already met with,
in his Endeavouring to find out/ and Detect the
Ways and method they take to Effect it./ By Samuel Hayne, ſometime Ryding-Surveyor for His
Majeſties/ Cuſtoms and Surveyor for the Act of
Navigation in the Coun-/ties of Devon and Corn-
wal./ [*London*] Printed by N. T. for the Author,
and are to be Sold by Walter/ Davis in Amen-
Corner, 1685. *3 prel. leaves; viz. Title and Dedication ; Text 38 pp. half mor. 4to.* (15s. 1350)

HAZARD (JOSEPH). The Conquest of Quebec. A
Poem. By Joseph Hazard, Of Lincoln College,
Oxford. *Oxford :* James Fletcher, 1769. *20 pp.
With Plan of Quebec. 4to.* (7s. 6d. 1351)

HECKEWELDER (JOHN). A Narrative of the
Mission of the United Brethren among the Delaware and Mohegan Indians, from its commencement, in the Year 1740, to the close of the Year
1808. Comprising all the remarkable incidents
which took place at their Missionary Stations during that period. Interspersed with Anecdotes, Historical Facts, Speeches of Indians, and other Interesting Matter. By John Heckewelder, Who was
many years in the service of that Mission. *Philadelphia,* M'Carty and Davis. 1820. *Portrait of
Zeisberger. xii pp. Text pp. 17 to 429. Errata 1
page. Calf. 8vo.* (10s. 6d. 1352)

HEIDELBERGH CATECHISM/ (THE)/ or/ Method of Inſtruction,/ in the/ Christian Religion,/
as/ The ſame is taught in the Reformed Churches/
and Schools of Holland./ Tranſlated for the Uſe of
the Reformed Proteſtant/ Dutch Church, of the City
of New-York./ *New-York :/* Printed and Sold by
John Holt, at the/ Exchange./ MDCCLXIV./ *46 pp.
half mor. 8vo.* (7s. 6d. 1353)

HELLENBROECK (A.) Specimen of Divine Truths, Fitted for the Ufe of thofe, of various Capacities, who defire to prepare themfelves for a due Confeffion of their Faith. By the Rev. Mr. A. Hellenbroeck, Late Minifter of the Gofpel at Rotterdam. Tranflated from the Dutch, for the Ufe of the Reformed Proteftant Dutch Church, of the City of New-York. *New-York:* Printed by John Holt, oppofite the Exchange. MDCCLXV. *95 pp. Half-calf. 8vo.* (7s. 6d. 1354)

HELLIER (THOMAS). The/ Vain Prodigal Life,/ and/ Tragical Penitent Death/ of/ Thomas Hellier/ Born at Whitchurch near Lyme/ in Dorset-shire :/ Who for Murdering his Master,/ Mistress, and a Maid, was Executed accor-/ding to Law at Weft-over in Charles City, in/ the Country of Virginia, neer the Plantation/ called Hard Labour, where he perpetrated/ the faid Murders./ He Suffer'd on Munday the 5th of Auguft, 1678./ And was after Hanged up in Chains at Windmill=/Point on James River./ *London :/* Printed for Sam. Crouch at the Princes Arms, a corner-fhop of/ Popes-head-alley in Cornhil. 1680./ *2 prel. leaves and 40 pp. Half calf. 4to.* (1l. 1s. 1355)

HENDERSON (GEORGE). An Account of the Britifh Settlement of Honduras ; being a brief view of its Commercial and Agricultural resources, Soil, Climate, Natural History, &c. To which are added, Sketches of the Manners and Customs of the Mosquito Indians, preceded by the Journal of a Voyage to the Mosquito shore, Illustrated by a Map. By Capt. Henderson, of his Majesty's 5th West India Regiment. *London:* C. and R. Baldwin, 1809. *xi, and 203 pp. Map. Uncut, in boards. 8vo.* (7s. 6d. 1356)

HENNEPIN (LOUIS). A/ New Difcovery/ of a/ Vaft Country in America,/ Extending above Four Thoufand Miles,/ between/ New France and New Mexico ;/ with a/ Defcription of the Great Lakes, Cata-/racts, Rivers, Plants, and Animals./ Alfo the Manners, Cuftoms, and Languages of the fe-/veral Native Indians ; and the Advantage of Com-/merce with thofe different Nations./ With a/ Continuation,/ giving an Account of the/ Attempts of the Sieur De la Salle upon the/ Mines of St. Barbe, &c. The taking of/ Quebec by the English; With the Advantages/ of a Shorter Cut to China and Japan./ Both Parts Illuftrated with Maps, and Figures,/ and Dedicated to His Majefty K. William./ By L. Hennepin, now Refident in Holland./ To which are added, Several New Difcoveries in North-America, not publifh'd in the French Edition./ *London*, Printed for M. Bentley, J. Tonson,/ H. Bonwick, T. Goodwin, and S. Manfhip. 1698./ *2 Parts in 1 Vol. Part I.* 12 *prelim. leaves and 243 pp. with map at p. 1 and 2 plates at pp. 24 and 90. Part II.* 16 *prelim. leaves and 228 pp. with map at p.* 1 *and 4 plates at pp.* 9, 33, 98, *and* 161. 8vo. (18s. 1357)

HENNEPIN (Louis). Voyage ou Nouvelle Decouverte d'un Tres-Grand Pays, dans L'Amerique, entre le Nouveau Mexique et la Mer Glaciale, Par le R. P. Louis Hennepin, Avec toutes les particularitez de ce Païs, & de celui connu fous le nom de La Louisiane; les avantages qu'on en peut tirer par l'etabliffement des Colonies enrichie de Cartes Geographiques. Augmenté de quelques figures en taille douce. Avec un Voyage Qui contient une Relation exacte de l'Origine, Mœurs, Coutûmes, Religion, Guerres & Voyages des Caraibes, Sauvages des Ifles Antilles de L'Amerique, Faite par la Sieur De la Borde, Tirée du Cabinet de Monfr. Blondel. *A Amsterdam*, Adriaan Braakman. MDCCIV. 18 *prelim. leaves including the engraved frontispiece. Text,* 604 *pp; Table,* 14 *leaves. 2 Maps at pp. 1 and 2; and copperplates at pp.* 44, 100, 187, 261, 352 *and* 449. *Old calf. Fine copy.* 12mo. (18s. 1358)

HENNEPIN (Louis). [*Engraved title*] Reyse/ door/ Nieuwe Ondekte/ Landen [*Printed title*] Aenmerckelycke/ Historische/ Reys - Beschryvinge/ Door verfcheyde Landen veel grooter als die van geheel/ Europa/ onlanghs ontdeckt./ Behelfende een nauwkeurige Befchrijvinge van gelegentheyd, natuur, en/ vrughtbaerheyd, van 't Zuyder, en Noorder gedeelte van America; mitsgaders/ de gedaente, aerd, manieren, kledingen, en 't geloove der talrijke Wilde Natien/ aldaer woonende. Het beleg en veroveringe van Quebek, de Hooft-ftad van Cana-/ da, door de Engelfchen. De gewigtige aenmer-

kingen op de onderneminge van de/ Heer de la
Salle, op de Goud-Mijnen van St. Barbara, met
veel meer andere/ waeragtige en feldfame gefchiedeniffen. En in't befonder de aenwijfingen om/ door
een korten wegh fonder de Linie Equinoctiael te
paffeeren, na China en/ Japan te komen; en de
groote voordeelen die men hier door, als mede door
de/ nieuwe Volckplantingen in defe vrughtbaare
Landen fou konnen trecken. Alles/ met een nette
Kaert tot defe/ aenwijfinge nodig, en kopere Platen
verciert./ Met Approbatie van/ Wilhelmus den
III./ Koningh/ van/ Groot-Britanie./ En aan de-
felve fijne Majefteyt opgedragen/ door/ Lodewyck
Hennepin,/ Miffionaris Recollect, en Notaris Apo-
ftolick./ Tot *Utrecht,*/ By Anthony Schouten. 1698./
16 *prel. leaves, and* 242 *pp.* (*for* 142), *Register* 18 *pp.*
Copperplate Map and 4 *Plates at pp.* 1, 8, 27, 74,
125. 4*to.* (1*l.* 11*s.* 6*d.* 1359)

HENRY (John Joseph). An Accurate and Interesting Account of the Hardships and Sufferings
of that Band of Heroes, who traversed the Wilder-
ness in the Campaign Against Quebec, In 1775.
By John Joseph Henry, Esq. Late President of the
Second Judicial District of Pennsylvania. *Lancaster :* Printed by William Greer. 1812. 225 *pp.*
Calf. 12*mo.* (8*s.* 6*d.* 1360)

HERMITE (Jaquis Le). A True Relation/ of the
Fleete which went vnder the/ Admirall Jaquis Le
Hermite through/ the Straights of Magellane towards the/ Coafts of Peru, and the Towne of/ Lima
in the Weft-Indies./ With a Letter, Containing the
prefent State/ of Caftile in Peru./ Herevnto is annexed an excellent Difcourfe/ which fheweth by
cleare and ftrong Arguments/ how that it was both
neceffary and profitable for/ the Vnited Provinces
to erect a Weft-India/ Company, and euery true
fubiect of/ the fame ought to aduance it accor-/ding
to his power./ Written by a Well-willer of the/
Common-wealth./ *London,*/ Printed for Mercu-
rius/ Britannicus. 1625./ *Title reverse blank ; Text*
33 *pp.* 4*to.* (5*l.* 5*s.* 1361)

HERRERA (Antonio de). Historia Gene/ral de
los hechos/ de los Castellanos/ en las Islas i tierra
fi=/rme del Mar oceano esc/rita por Antonio de/
Herrera coronista/ mayor de sv M^d. dlas/ Indias y

svrcoronis=/tade Castilia./ En quatro Decadas desde
el Ano de/1492. hasta el de 1531./ De Cada primera/
Al Rey Nu^{ro}. Señor./ En Ma^d. en la/ Emplentarea/
1061./ *Eight Decadas bound in 4 volumes. Dec.* i.
4 prel. leaves 371 *pp. and* 10 *leaves of table. Dec.* ii.
2 leaves, 368 *pp. and 8 leaves. Dec.* iii. *2 leaves,* 378
pp. and 8 leaves. Dec. iv. *2 leaves,* 293 *pp. and 7
leaves. Dec.* v. *4 leaves* 317 *pp. and* 10 *leaves. Dec.*
vi. *2 leaves* 302 *pp. and 9 leaves. Dec.* vii. *4 leaves*
316 *pp. and* 10 *leaves. Dec.* viii. *4 leaves* 342 *pp. and
8 leaves. 4 vols.* 1601-1615. *Folio.* (5*l.* 5*s.* 1362)
The first four Decadas were published in 1601, and the last four in
1615. There is an engraved title to each Decade.

HERRERA (Antonio de). Descripcion de/ las
Indias Occide=/ntales de Antonio de Herrera coro=/
nista Mayor de sv Mag^d. de las In=/dias y sv coro-
nista/ de Castilla./ Al Rey Nrō Señor./ En Mad:
enla emplen^{ta} Real 1601./ [*Colophon*] *En Madrid,/
Por Iuan Flamenco./ Año* m.dci./ *2 prelim. leaves
and* 96 *pp. The title is engraved on copper and there
are* 14 *copperplate maps. Folio.* (1363)
This work should go with the General History, and is usually
bound at the end of the second volume after the fourth Decade.
The price of this is included in the preceding.

HERRERA (Antonio de). Historia Gene/ral de
los hechos/ de los Castellanos/ en las Islas i Tierra
fi/rmed el Mar. Oceano. Es/crita por Antonio de/
Herrera Coronista/ Mayor de sv M^d. de las/ Indias
y sv Coronis=/ta de Castilla/ En quatro Decadas
des de el Año de/ 1492 hasta el de (1)531./ Decada
primera/ Al Rey Nu^{ro}. Señor./ *En Madrid/* en la
Imprenta/ Real/ de Nicolas Rodriguez/ franco/
Año de 1730./ *Eight Decades, bound in 4 Volumes.
Decade* i. *3 leaves and* 292 *pp ; Dec.* ii. 1726,*3 leaves
and* 288 *pp ; Dec.* iii. 1726, *2 leaves and* 296 *pp ;
Dec.* iv. 1730, *3 leaves and* 232 *pp ; Dec.* v. 1728, *4
leaves and* 252 *pp ; Dec.* vi. 1730, *3 leaves and* 236
pp ; Dec. vii. 1730, *3 leaves and* 245 *pp ; Dec.* viii.
1730, *3 leaves and* 251 *pp ;* ' Tabla General' *etc.* 226
leaves, ending with the Colophon. En Madrid : En
la Imprenta de Franci∫co/ Martinez Abad. Año de
m.dcc.xxviii. *Good copy in Spanish calf.*
Folio. (4*l.* 14*s.* 6*d.* 1364)

HERRERA (Antonio de). Descripcione de/ las
Indias Occide/ntales de Antonio/ de Herrera coro-
nista Mayor/ de sv Mag^d. de las/ Indias, ysu coro-
nista/ de Castilla. Al Rey Nrŏ. Señor./ En *Madrid*

en la Oficina Real/ de Nicolas Rodriguez Franco,
Año de 1730./ *20 prel. leaves; Text 70 pp;* ' Los
Presidentes' *etc. pp.* 71 *to* 78. *With copperplate
Maps numbered* 1 *to* 14. *Folio.* (1365)
This reprint of the first Edition usually accompanies the General
History, and forms part of that work.

HERRERA (ANTONIO DE). Histoire/ Generale/ des
Voyages et Conqvestes/ des Castillans dans les Isles
& Terre-ferme/ des Indes Occidentales./ Traduite
de l'Espagnol d'Antoine d'Herrera,/ Historiographe
de sa Majesté Catholique, tant/ des Indes, que des
Royaumes de Castille./ Par N. de la Coste./ Où
l'on voit la prise de la grande ville de Mexique, &
autres/ Provinces par Fernand Cortés; Sa fonda-
tion ; Le Rois qui/ la gouvernerent ; Le commencement & fin de cet Empire ;/ Leurs coûtumes & ceremonies ; Les grandes revoltes qui y/ sont arrivez;
Les contestations qu'eurent les Castillans &/ les
Portugais, sur l'affiette de la ligne de partarge de
leurs/ conquestes; La découverte des Isles Philippines par/ Hernando de Magellan; Sa mort & autres choses remar-/quables./ Dediée à Monseigneur
le premier President./ *A Paris,* [Chez La Veuve
Nicolas de la Coste, a l'Ecu/ de Bretagne./ François
Clovzier l'aisné, à l'Image nostre Dame/ et/ Pierre
Avboüin, à la Fleur de Lys./] demeurant tous/
proche l'Hostel/ de Monseigneur/ le premier Pre-/
sident./ M. DC. LXXI/ Avec Privilege dv Roy./ 9
prel. leaves, and 790 *pp. Table* 12 *pp. Calf.*
4to.   (15s.   1366)

This volume is a translation into French of Herrera's *Third Decade,* 1521 to 1526.

HERRERA (ANTONIO DE). Novvs Orbis,/ Sive
Descriptio/ Indiæ Occi-/dentalis,/Auctore/ Antonio
de Herrera,/ Supremo Castellæ & Indiarum autho-
ritate Philippi III./ Hispaniarum Regis Historio-
grapho./ Metaphraste C. Barlæo./ Accesserunt &
aliorum Indiæ Occidentalis Descriptiones, &/ Navi-
gationis nuperæ Australis Jacobi le Maire Histo-/
ria, uti & navigationum omnium per Fretum/
Magellanicum succincta narratio./ *Amstelodami,/*
Apud Michaelem Colinvm Bibliopolam, ad/ insigne
Libri Domestici. Anno M. D. C. XXII. Cum Privilegio./ 4 *prel. leaves including the engraved and
printed titles ; Text* 44 *folioed leaves ; followed by a
half-title* ' Ephemerides/ sive/ Descriptio Naviga-/

tionis Avstralis/ institutæ Anno M.D.C.XV./ Ductu
& moderamine fortifsimi Viri/ Iacobi Le Maire,'/
3 *leaves and text folioed 46 to* 83. *Then comes another
half-title* 'Descriptio/ Indiæ Occidentalis,'/ *etc.*
Avthore Petro Ordonnez de Cevallos,' 9 *leaves,
succeeded by a half-title* 'Brevis/ ac Succincta/ Americæ,'/ *etc.* 11 *leaves. Folio.* (*2l. 2s.* 1367)

The first part has the 14 maps copied from Herrera's, and Le Maire
is illustrated with the 3 maps taken from De Bry, together with
4 plates inserted in the text on fols. 60, 61, 65, 67. In the Preface to Barcia's reprint of Herrera's works at Madrid, 1726-30,
the editor repudiates this edition, as being full of typographical
errors, and saddled with matters not pertaining to Herrera.

HERRERA (ANTONIO DE). The General History
of the vast Continent and Islands of America, Commonly call'd, The West-Indies, from The First
Discovery thereof: With the Beſt Accounts the
People could give of their Antiquities. Collected
from the Original Relations ſent to the Kings of
Spain. By Antonio de Herrera, Historiographer
to His Catholick Majesty. Tranſlated into Engliſh
by Capt. John Stevens. Illuſtrated with Cutts and
Maps. *London:* Jer. Batley M.DCC.XXV. *Six
Volumes.* Vol. I. 4 *prel. leaves ; viz. Title and Preface; Text* 379 *pp. With 2 Maps, copperplate.
Portrait of Columbus and 2 copperplates at pp.* 63.
218. Vol. II. *Title and* 436 *pp.* 4 *copperplates at
pp.* 135, 372, 378, 380. Vol. III. M.DCC.XXVI.
Title and 418 *pp.* 3 *copperplates at pp.* 191, 194, 227.
Vol. IV. M.DCC.XXVI. *Title and* 422 *pp. copperplate Portrait of Cortes and* 2 *copperplates at pp.*
290, 357. Vol. V. M.DCC.XXVI. *Title and* 430 *pp.*
2 *copperplates at pp.* 1, 375. Vol. VI. M.DCC.XXVI.
Title and 408 *pp. Index* 30 *pp. copperplate at p.* 1.
Calf. 8vo. (*2l. 10s.* 1368)

HERRERA (ANTONIO DE). The General History
of the vast Continent and Islands of America,
Commonly call'd The West-Indies, from The First
Discovery thereof: With the beſt Accounts the
People could give of their Antiquities. Collected
from the Original Relations ſent to the Kings of
Spain. By Antonio de Herrera Hiſtoriographer to
His Catholick Majesty. Tranſlated into Engliſh
by Capt. John Stevens. Illuſtrated with Cuts and
Maps. The Second Edition. *London,* Wood and
Woodward MDCCXL. *Six Volumes.* Vol. I. 4 *prel.
leaves; viz. Title and Preface; Text* 379 *pp. With*

*Map; copperplate Portrait of Columbus and 2
copperplates at pp.* 63, 218. Vol. II. *Title and* 436
pp. Map and 4 copperplates at pp. 1, 135, 372, 378,
380. Vol. III. *Title and 418 pp. 3 copperplates at
pp.* 191, 194, 227. Vol. IV. *Title and 422 pp.
copperplate Portrait of Cortes and 2 copperplates at
pp.* 290, 357. Vol. V. *Title and 430 pp. 2 copper-
plates at pp.* 1, 375. Vol. VI. *Title and 408 pp.
Index. 30 pp. copperplate at p.* 1. *Calf extra by
Bedford. Fine copy. 8vo.* (3l. 3s. 1369)

This second Edition is the same as the preceding, with new title-
pages.

HEY (RICHARD). Observations On the Nature of
Civil Liberty, And the Principles of Government.
By Richard Hey, M. A. Fellow of Sidney Suffex
College, Cambridge; and Barrifter at Law of the
Middle Temple. *London*; T. Cadell, MDCCLXXVI.
*2 prel. leaves and text in 70 pp. Half. mor.
8vo.* (4s. 6d. 1370)

HICKERINGILL (EDMOND). Jamaica/ Viewed :/
With/ All the Ports, Harbours,/ and their feveral
Soundings,/ Towns, and Settlements/ thereunto
belonging/ Together,/ With the nature of it's Climate,/ fruitfulneffe of the Soile,/ and it's fuitable-
neffe to/ Englifh Complexions./ With feveral
other collateral/ Obfervations and Reflexions/ upon
the Island./ The fecond Edition./ By E. H./
London,/ Printed for Iohn Williams, at the Crown
in/ St. Paul's Church-yard, 1661./ *Eight prel.
leaves and 87 pp. with map of Jamaica on copper.
Calf. 16mo.* (1l. 1s. 1371)

HICKERINGILL (EDMOND). Jamaica/ Viewed :/
With/ All the Ports, Harbours, and their/ feveral
Soundings, Towns, and/ Settlements thereunto belonging./ Together,/ With the nature of its Climate, fruitfulnefs/ of the Soil, and its fuitablenefs
to Englifh/ Complexions./ With feveral other
collateral Obfervations/ and Reflections upon the
Island./ The Third Edition./ By Captain Hickeringill./ *London:/* Printed: and Sold by B. Bragg,
at the Blew Ball in/ Ave-Mary-Lane. MDCCV./
*4 prel. leaves, and 44 pp. With map of Jamaica.
Half mor. 4to.* (1l. 1s. 1372)

HIGGINS (BRYAN). Observations and Advices for

the Improvement of the Manufacture of Muscovado Sugar and Rum. Second Part. By Bryan Higgins, M. D. *St. Jago de la Vega*: Printed by Alexander Aikman, Printer to the Honourable the Assembly. M. DCCC. *2 prelim. leaves and 132 pp. with 9 copperplates. Half mor. 8vo.* (7s. 6d. 1373)

HIGGINSON (FRANCIS). New-Englands/ Plantation./ Or,/ a Short and Trve/ Description of the/ Commodities and/ Discommodities/ of that Covntrey./ Written by Mr. Higgeſon, a reuerend Diuine/ now there reſident./ Wherevnto is added a Letter, ſent by Mr. Graues/ an Enginere, out of New-England,/ The third Edition, enlarged./ London,/ Printed by T. and R. Cotes. for Michæl Sparke, dwelling/ at the Signe of the Blue Bible in Greene-/Arbor. 1630./ *On the reverse of the title* 'To the Reader' *18 lines in Italics signed,* M. S.; *Text* 12 *leaves, without pagination, with signatures* B C D *in fours.* 'Fine' *on the recto of the* 12*th leaf. Morocco by Bedford. 4to.* (7l. 7s. 1374)

HILL (ANTHONY). Afer Baptizatus: Or, the Negro turn'd Christian. Being a Short and Plain Discourse, shewing I. The Neceſſity of Inſtructing and Baptizing Slaves in English Plantations. II. The Folly of that Vulgar Opinion, That Slaves do ceaſe to be Slaves when once Baptized. Delivered (moſt of it) in a Sermon Preach'd at Stratford-le-Bow in Middleſex, March 15th. 170½. By Anthony Hill, Lecturer there, and Chaplain to His Grace the Duke of Richmond. *London*, Charles Broome, MDCCII. *3 prelim. leaves and 55 pp. Half mor. 8vo.* (10s. 6d. 1375)
With the autograph of White Kennett on the title-page.

HIPPISLEY (G). A Narrative of the Expedition to the Rivers Orinoco and Apuré, in South America; which sailed from England in November 1817, and joined the Patriotic forces in Venezuela and Caraccas. By G. Hippisley, Esq. Late Colonel of the first Venezuelian Hussars, in the service of the Republic, and Colonel-Commandant of the British Brigade in South America. *London*: John Murray, 1819. *xx and text in* 653 *pp* : *half calf. 8vo.* (5s. 6d. 1376)

HIRELING. Artifice Detected: Or, the Profit and

Loss of Great-Britain, in the Present War with
Spain, Set in its True Light; By laying before the
Publick, as Full, Compleat, and Regular a List as
can be had, of the Britiſh Ships taken ſince the
Beginning of the War; with proper Remarks upon
the List, and upon our Conduct both at Home and
Abroad. With An Appendix, containing a List
of the Ships taken ſince November 16. 1741. *London:* T. Cooper, 1742. *Title and 76 pp. half mor.*
8vo. (4s. 6d. 1377)

HISTOIRE des Tremblemens de Terre Arrive's a
Lima, Capitale du Perou, et Autres Lieux; Avec
la Description du Perou, Et des recherches ſur les
Cauſes Phiſiques des Tremblemens de Terre, par
M. Hales de la Société Royale de Londres, & autres Phiſiciens. Avec Cartes & Figures. Traduite
de L'Anglois, Premiere Partie. *A La Haye.*
M. DCC. LII. *xvi and 445 pp. With 7 Plates. Old
calf.* 12mo. (7s. 6d. 1378)

HISTOIRE de Kamschatka, des Isles Kurilski, et
des contrées voisines Publiée a Petersbourg, en
Langue Ruſſienne, par ordre de Sa Majeſté Impé-
riale. On y a joint deux Cartes, l'une de Kamschatka, & l'autre des Isles Kurilski. Traduite par
M. E * * *. *A Lyon,* Benoit Duplain, M.DCC.LXVII.
Two Volumes. Tome Premier. *4 prel. leaves; xv
and 327 pp. With* 'Carte de Kamtschatka.' Tome
Second. *4 prel. leaves, and 359 pp. With* 'Carte
des Isles Kurilski.' *Calf.* 12mo. (8s. 6d. 1379)

HISTOIRE des Navigations aux Terres Australes,
Contenant ce que l'on ſçait des mœurs & des productions des Contrées découvertes juſqu'à ce jour;
& où il eſt traité de l'utilité d'y faire de plus am-
ples découvertes, & des moyens d'y former un
etabliſſement. *A Paris,* Durand, M.DCC.LVI. *Two
Volumes.* Tome Premier. *Title, xiv and 463 pp.
Errata 4 pp.* Tome Second. *Title and 514 pp.
Errata 2 pp. With Charts, No.* I *to* VII. *Old calf.*
4to. (15s. 1380)

HISTORIA de America. Noticia de un Manuscrito
muy interesante. [*Habona* 1820?] *9 pp. Half mor.*
8vo. (4s. 6d. 1381)

HISTORICAL (AN) Account of the Discovery of

the Island of Madeira, Abridged from the Portugueze Original. To which is added An Account
of the prefent State of the Island in a Letter to a
Friend. *London :* J. Payne, and J. Boquet,
M,DCC,L. *Title, x and* 88 *pp.* 8vo. (4s. 6d. 1382)

HISTORICAL and Political Reflections on the Rise
and Progress of the American Rebellion. In which
The Caufes of that Rebellion are pointed out, and
the Policy and Neceffity of offering to the Americans a Syftem of Government founded in the Principles of the Britifh Conftitution, are clearly demonftrated. By the Author of Letters to a Nobleman on the Conduct of the American War.
London : G. Wilkie, MDCCLXXX. 4 *prel. leaves and*
135 *pp.* Half mor. 8vo. (6s. 6d. 1383)

HISTORICAL Anecdotes, Civil and Military : in a
Series of Letters, written From America, in the
years 1777 and 1778, to different Perfons in England; containing Obfervations on the General
Management of the War, and on the Conduct of
our Principal Commanders in the Revolted Colonies, During that Period. *London :* J. Bew,
M. DCC. LXXIX. 2 *prel. leaves and* 85 *pp.* Half mor.
8vo. (8s. 6d. 1384)

HISTORICAL (AN) Essay on the English Consti-
tution : Or, An impartial Inquiry into the Elective
Power of the People, from the firft Eftablifhment
of the Saxons in this Kingdom. Wherein The
Right of Parliament, to Tax our diftant Provinces,
is explained, and juftified, upon fuch conftitutional
Principles as will afford an equal Security to the
Colonifts, as to their Brethren at Home. *London :*
Edward and Charles Dilly. M. DCC. LXXI. *viii &*
210 *pp.* Half mor. 8vo. (6s. 6d. 1385)

HISTORICAL (AN) Memorial of the Negotiation
of France and England, From the 26th of March,
1761, to the 20th of September of the fame Year,
With the Vouchers. Tranflated from the French
Original, publifhed at Paris by Authority. *London :*
D. Wilson, MDCCLXI. 64 *pp.* 4to. (6s. 6d. 1386)

HISTORICAL REVIEW (AN) of the Constitution
and Government of Pennsylvania, From its Origin;
So far as regards the feveral Points of Controverfy,
which have, from Time to Time, arifen between

The feveral Governors of that Province, and Their
feveral Assemblies. Founded on authentic Documents. *London:* R. Griffiths, MDCCLIX. *viii,* 18,
and 444 *pp. Calf. 8vo.* (7s. 6d. 1387)

HISTORISCH=GEOGRAPHISCHE   Befchrei-
bung der in diefem Krieg von den Engländern
eroberten französischen Antillischen Infeln, befon-
ders von Guadaloupe und Martinique &c. Zur
Erläuterung der gegenwärtigen Kriegs=Staatsund
Handlungs=Geschichte. *Stutgart* bey Johann
Benedict Mezler, 1762. 4 *prel. leaves, and* 264 *pp.
Uncut. half mor. 8vo.* (7s. 6d. 1388)

HISTORY of North America; comprising, A Geographical and Statistical View of the United States,
and of the British Canadian Possessions ; including
a great variety of important information on the
subject of Emigration to that Country. In Two
Volumes. *Leeds:* Davies & Co. 1820. 2 *Volumes.*
Vol. I. *iv and* 498 *pp.* Vol. II. *Title and* 458 *pp.
Portrait of Thomas Jefferson, and* 2 *Plates of American Coins. 8vo.* (6s. 6d. 1389)

HISTORY (THE) of North and South America,
containing, An Account of the firft Difcoveries of
the New World, the Customs, Genius, and Persons
of the original Inhabitants, and a particular Defcription of the Air, Soil, natural Productions,
Manufactures and Commerce of each Settlement.
Including a Geographical, Commercial, and Historical Survey of the British Settlements, From the
earlieft Times to the prefent Period. With an
Account of the West Indies and the American
Iflands. To which is added, An impartial Enquiry
into the present American Disputes. *London :* J.
Whitaker, 1776. *Two Volumes.* Vol. I. 9 *prel.
leaves, including Frontispiece ; and pp.* 7-276. Vol.
II. 7 *prel. leaves, including Frontispiece ; and pp.*
5-280. *Calf. 12mo.* (7s. 6d. 1390)

HISTORY (THE) of North America. Containing An exact Account of their first Settlements;
Their Situation, Climate, Soil, Produce, Beasts,
Birds, Fishes, Commodities, Manufactures, Commerce, Religion, Charters, Laws, Governments,
Cities, Towns, Ports, Rivers, Lakes, Mountains,
and Fortifications. With The present State of the

different Colonies; and A large Introduction. Illuftrated with a Map of North America. *London*: Millar, *etc.* MDCCLXXVI. *2 prel. leaves, and* 284 *pp. With the Map.* 12*mo* (6s. 6d. 1391)

HISTORY of the Discovery of America, of the Landing of our Forefathers, at Plymouth, and of their most remarkable Engagements with the Indians, In New-England, From their first landing in 1620, until the final subjugation of the Natives in 1669. To which is annexed, the Defeat of Generals Braddock, Harmer & St. Clair, By the Indians at the Westward, &c. By a Citizen of Connecticut. *Norwich*: Published for the Author, (With Priviledge of Copy-Right.) 1810. *Title and pp.* 7-176. *Calf.* 8*vo.* (5s. 1392)

HISTORY of the United States, from their First Settlement as Colonies, to the Close of the War with Great Britain, in 1815. *London*: John Miller, 1826. *2 prel. leaves, and* 467 *pp. Uncut. Cloth.* 8*vo.* (5s. 6d. 1393)

HODGKINSON (JOHN). A Narrative of his Connection with the Old American Company, from the Fifth September, 1792, to the Thirty-First of March, 1797, By John Hodgkinson. *New-York*: Printed by J. Oram, No. 33, Liberty-Street, 1797. 28 *pp.* 'United States of America' 1 *page. half mor.* 8*vo.* (4s. 6d. 1394)

HODGSON (ADAM). Letters from North America, written During a Tour in the United States and Canada. By Adam Hodgson. In Two Volumes. *London*: Hurst, Robinson, & Co. 1824. *2 Volumes.* Vol. I. *xv and* 405 *pp. Errata on slip, and* 1 *Plate.* Vol. II. *Title, iv and* 473 *pp. Errata on slip, and* 1 *Plate. Half calf.* 8*vo.* (10s. 6d. 1395)

HOLM (THOMAS CAMPANIUS). [*Engraved Title*] Novæ Sveciæ/ feu/ Pensylvaniæ/ in America/ Descriptio./ [*Printed Title*] Kort Befkrifning/ Om/ Provincien/ Nya Swerige/ uti/ America,/ Som nu förtjden af the Engelfke kallas/ Pensylvania./ Af lärde och trowärdige Mäns fkrifter och berättelfer ihopale=/tad och fammanftrefwen, famt med äthfkillige Figurer/ utzirad af/ Thomas Campanius Holm./ Stockholm, Tryckt uti Kongl. Boktr. hos Sal. Wankijfs/ Ankia med egen bekoftnad,

af J. H. Werner. Ahr MDCCII./ 9 *prel. leaves, and*
text in 191 *pp. With copperplate maps and plates at*
pp. 1, 4, 27, 37, 52, 110. *Half calf.*
4to.   (3l. 3s.   1396)

HOLME (BENJAMIN). A Collection of the Epistles
and Works of Benjamin Holme.   To which is
prefix'd, An Account of his Life and Travels in the
Work of the Miniftry, through feveral Parts of
Europe and America : Written by Himself. *Lon-*
don: Luke Hinde, 1754. *vii and* 194 *pp. Old calf.*
8vo.   (4s. 6d.   1397)

HOLMES (ABIEL). The Life of Ezra Stiles, D.D.
LL.D.   A Fellow of the American Philosophical
Society ; of the American Academy of Arts and
Sciences; of the Connecticut Society of Arts and
Sciences ; a Corresponding Member of the Massa-
chusetts Historical Society ; Professor of Ecclesias-
tical History ; and President of Yale College. By
Abiel Holmes, A.M. Pastor of the First Church in
Cambridge.   Publifhed according to Act of Con-
grefs.   *Boston:* Printed by Thomas & Andrews,
Faust's Statue, No. 45 Newbury Street. May,
1798. 403 *pp. Calf.* 8vo.   (6s. 6d.   1398)

HOLMES (ABIEL). Autograph Letter to Dr.
Mason Folet Cogswell of Hartford, dated at Cambridge, Aug. 24, 1793.   3 *pages, a good specimen.*
4to.   (5s.   1399)

HOLYOKE (EDWARD). The Doctrine of Life,/ or
of Mans/ Redemtion,/ by The Seed of Eve, the
Seed of Abraham, the/ Seed of David, &c. as it
was taught in feverall/ Periods of Time, from Gen.
3. 15. till Chrift came in the Flefh,/ to fulfill all
Typicall Prefigurations of him by his Death./
Wherein also/ Sundry other Fundamentall Points
are difcuffed and cleared/ from fome common miftakes. As Daniels Chronologie of Se-/venty Sevens,
which is cleared from the uncertainty/ which too
many Expofitors have unadvifedly caft upon it./
And about the Jewes calling ; that it muft not be
underftood/ of any return to Canaan, or of their
Reftauration to a perfpicuous/ Common wealth any
more, but of he calling of a Remnant of them/ to
the Faith, in the Countries where they live dif-
perfed./   And with the true nature of our Lords
Sufferings : with/ fundry other fuch like Points, as

may be seen in the Table./ Propounded by way of Queftion and Anfwer, with Annota-/tions thereunto annexed; Divided into three Parts./ By Edward Holyoke of New-England./ *London*, Printed by T. R. for Nath. Ekins, and are to be/ fold at his Shop at the Gun in St. Pauls Church-yard, 1658./ 9 *prel. leaves; and* 426 *pp. Table* 17 *pp; Errata* 1 *page. Calf.* 4*to.* (15*s.* 1400)

HOLYOKE (EDWARD). Autograph Letter of Thanks dated Jan. 1, 1763 to Mr. T. Hollis, for his Present of Perry's Series of English Medalls, and two sets of Prints, one for the College, and one for himself. 1 *page.* 4*to.* (7*s.* 6*d.* 1401)
    The writer was President of Harvard College.

HOOKE (WILLIAM). New/ Englands/ Teares,/ for Old/ Englands/ Feares./ Preached in a Sermon on July 23./ 1640 being a day of Publike Humiliation,/ appointed by the Churches in behalfe of our/ native Countrey in time of/ feared dangers./ By William Hooke, Minifter of Gods/ Word; fometimes of Axmouth in Devonfhire,/ now of Taunton in New England./ Sent over to a worthy Member of the honourable/ Houfe of Commons, who defires it may be for/ publick good./ *London*,/ Printed by E. G. for Iohn Rothwell and Henry Overton, and/ are to be fould at the Sunne in Pauls Church-/ yard, and in Popes-head Alley. 1641./ 2 *prel. leaves and* 23 *pp. Fine copy in calf by Bedford.* 4*to.* (1*l.* 11*s.* 6*d.* 1402)
    There appear to have been two editions the same year.

HOOKER (NATHANAEL). Six Discourses, on different subjects; preached by The Rev. Nathanael Hooker, A.M. And late Paftor of the fourth Church of Chrift in Hartford. Being, a A Pofthumous Publication, from the Author's Original Manufcripts, At the Defire, and with the Advice of many judicious Perfons, both of the Clergy and Laity. *Hartford :* Printed and Sold by Ebenezer Watson, near the Great Bridge. 1771. 3 *prel. leaves and pp.* 7-99. 8*vo.* (7*s.* 6*d.* 1403)

HOOKER (THOMAS). The/ Eqvall/ Wayes of God :/ Tending to/ the Rectifying/ of the Crooked/ Wayes of Man./ The Paffages whereof are briefly/ and clearly drawne from the facred/ Scriptvres./ By T. H./ *London*,/ Printed for Iohn Clarke, and are

to be fold at his/ fhop under S[t] Peters Church in
Cornehill./　1632./　4 *prel. leaves and* 40 *pp.*
4*to.*　　　　　　　　　　　　　　(15*s.*　1404)

HOOKER (THOMAS). The/ Sovles/ Ingrafting/ into
Christ./　By T. H./　*London,*/ Printed by J. H.
for Andrew Crooke, at the/ figne of the Beare in
Pauls Church-yard./　1637./　*Title and* 30 *pp.*
4*to.*　　　　　　　　　　　　　　(10*s.* 6*d.*　1405)

HOOKER (THOMAS). The/ Sovles/ Vocation/ or/
Effectval/ Calling to Christ./　By T. H./ *London,*/
Printed by Iohn Haviland, for Andrew Crooke,/
and are to be fold at the Black Beare in S. Pauls/
Church-yard. 1638./ 12 *prel. leaves ; viz. Title, and
Table of Contents.* 2nd *Title* ' The/ Sovles/ Effec-
tvall/ Calling to Christ./　By T. H./　*London,*/
Printed by J. H. for Andrew Crooke, at the/ figne
of the Beare in Pauls Church-yard./　1637./　*Text
pp.* 33-668.　4*to.*　　　　　　　　　(15*s.*　1406)

HOOKER (THOMAS). The/ Sovles/ Exaltation./ A/
Treatife/ containing/ The Soules Vnion with
Christ, on 1 Cor. 6. 17./　The Soules Benefit from
Vnion/ with Christ, on 1 Cor. 1. 30./　The Soules
Justification, on/ 2 Cor. 5. 21./ By T. H./ *London,*/
Printed by Iohn Haviland, for Andrew Crooke,
and/ are to bee fold at the black Beare in S. Pauls/
Church-yard, 1638./ 8 *prel. leaves ; viz. Title, Table,
and Severall Treatises, etc.　Text* 311 *pp.　Old calf.*
4*to.*　　　　　　　　　　　　　　(15*s.*　1407)

HOOKER (THOMAS). The/ Sovles/ Preparation/
for Christ./ Or,/ A Treatise/ of Contrition./ Wherein is difcovered/ Hovv God breakes the heart,/ and
wounds the Soule, in the con-/verfion of a Sinner
to Himfelfe./ The fourth Edition/ *London,*/ Printed
by the Affignes of T. P. for T. Nickoles, and/ are
to bee fold at the figne of the Bible, in/ Popes-head
Ally, 1638./ 3 *prel. leaves ; viz. Title, and Table of
Contents ; Text* 242 *pp.*　4*to.*　　　(15*s.*　1408)

HOOKER (THOMAS). The/ Sovles/ Hvmiliation./
The fecond Edition./　*London,*/ Printed by I. L.
for Andrew Crooke, at the/ figne of the Beare in
Pauls Church-yard./　1638./ 223 *pp.　The Table* 4
pp.　The Scriptures, and Severall Treatises, etc. 4 *pp.
Old calf.* 4*to.*　　　　　　　　　　(15*s.*　1409)

HOOKER (Thomas). The/ Sovles/ Hvmiliation./ The third Edition. *London,*/ Printed by T. Cotes for Andrew Crooke, and/ Philip Nevill. 1640./ *223 pp.* The Table 4 pp. The Scriptures, & Severall Treatises, etc. 4 pp. a close reprint of the 2nd edition. Calf. 4to. (15s. 1410)

HOOKER (Thomas). The/ Sovles/ Hvmiliation./ *Amsterdam.*/ Printed for T. L. and are to be fould at his/ Chamber in Flowingburrow, neare/ unto the Englifh Church,/ Anno 1638./ *302 pp.* Old calf. 16mo. (15s. 1411)

HOOKER (Thomas). The/ Vnbeleevers/ Preparing for/ Chrift./ By T. H. *London,*/ Printed by Tho Cotes for Andrew Crooke and are to be/ fold at the Blacke Beare in Saint Pauls Church-/yard. 1638./ 2 prel. leaves; viz. Title, and Severall Treatises, etc. Text 204 pp. The First Table 4 pp. Second Part beginning on signature Aaa, 119 pp. The Table 4 pp. Old calf. 4to. (15s. 1412)

HOOKER (Thomas). The/ Christians/ Tvvo Chiefe/ Lessons,/ viz. [Selfe Deniall,/ and/ Selfe Tryall./ As Also/ the Priviledge of Adoption/ And Triall thereof./ In three Treatises on the Texts follow-ing :/ Viz.] Matt. 16. 24./ 2 Cor. 13. 5./ Iohn I. 12, 13./ By T. H./ *London,*/ Printed by T. B. for P. Stephens and C. Meredith, at the/ Golden Lion in S. Pauls Churchyard./ 1640./ 11 prel. leaves; viz. Title, Dedication, signed ' Z. S.' and Table of the Contents; Text 303 pp. Calf. 4to. (12s. 6d. 1413)

HOOKER (Thomas). The Soules/ Implantation/ into/ the Naturall Olive./ By T. H./ Carefully correćted, and much enlarged, with/ a Table of the Contents prefixed./ *London,*/ Printed by R. Young, and are to be fold by Fulke/ Clifton on New-Fifh-ftreet-hill. 1640./ 3 prel. leaves; viz. Title and The Contents; Text 320 pp. Calf. 4to. (15s. 1414)

HOOKER (Thomas). The/ Poore/ Doubting/ Chris-tian/ Drawn to/ Christ./ Wherein the main Lets and/ Hinderances which keep men/ from coming to Christ/ are difcovered./ With fpeciall Helps to re-/ cover Gods favor./ The fixth edition./ *London,*/ Printed by I. Raworth, for Luke Fawne,/ and are to be fold at his fhop, at the/ figne of the Parrot in

Pauls/ Church-yard. 1641./ *Title and* 163 *pp.*
12*mo.* (12*s.* 6*d.* 1415)

HOOKER (Thomas). The/ Sovles/ Preparation/ for
Christ./ Or,/ A Treatise of Contrition./ Wherein
is difcovered/ How God breakes the heart, and/
wounds the Soul, in the converfion/ of a Sinner to
Himfelfe./ The fixt Edition./ *London,/* Printed
by M. F. for R. Dawlman. 1643./ 4 *prel. leaves;
viz. Title,* ' *A Table of Contents,*' *and* ' *Sevcrall Treatises;*' *Text* 386 *pp.* 12*mo.* (10*s.* 6*d.* 1416)

HOOKER (Thomas). The/ Immortality/ of the/
Soule :/ The Excellencie of Christ/ Jesvs, treated
on./ Wherein the faithfull people of/ God may
finde comfort/ for their Souls./ By T. H./ Publifhed according to Order./ *London,/* Printed in the
yeer 1646./ *Title and* 21 *pp.* 4*to.* (10*s.* 6*d.* 1417)

HOOKER (Thomas). A/ Survey/ of the Summe of/
Church-Difcipline./ Wherein,/ The Way of the
Churches of/ New=England/ is warranted out of
the Word,/ and all Exceptions of weight, which/
are made againft it, anfwered: Whereby/ alfo it
will appear to the Judicious Reader,/ that fomething more muft be faid, then/ yet hath been, before their Prin-/ciples can be fhaken, or they/
fhould be unfetled in/ their practice./ By Tho.
Hooker, late Paftor of the Church at/ Hartford
upon Connecticott in N.E./ *London,/* Printed by
A. M. for John Bellamy at the three Golden Lions/
in Cornhill, near the Royall Exchange. M.DC.
XLVIII./ 18 *prelim. leaves. Text, Part I.* 139 *and* 185-
296 *pp. Part II.* 90 *pp. The third Part* 46 *pp.
Part IV.* 59 *pp.* 4*to.* (1*l.* 15*s.* 1418)

HOOKER (Thomas). The/ Saints/ Dignitie,/ and/
Dutie./ Together with/ The Danger of Ignorance/
and Hardnesse./ Delivered in Severall Sermons :/
By that Reverend Divine,/ Thomas Hooker,/ Late
Preacher in New-England./ *London,/* Printed by
G. D. for Francis Eglesfield, and are/ to be fold at
the Sign of the Marigold in Pauls/ Church-yard,
1651./ 3 *prel. leaves; viz. Title, and To the Reader.
Signed* ' T. S. [2*nd Title*] The Gift/ of /Gifts :/ Or,/
The End why/ Christ/ Gave Himself./ By that Re-
verend Divine,/ Thomas Hooker,/ Late Preacher in
New England./ *London,/* Printed by G. D. for

Francis Eglesfield, and are/ to be fold at the Sign
of the Marigold in Pauls/ Church-yard, 1651./
4 *prel. leaves, and Text* 248 *pp. The Contents* 4 *pp.
Calf.* 4*to.*   (15*s.* 1419)

HOOKER (THOMAS). The Souls/ Preparation/ for/
Christ./ Or,/ A Treatise/ of/ Contrition./ Wherein is difcovered/ How God breaks the Heart, and/
wounds the Soul in the converfion/ of a Sinner to
himfelf./ The feventh Edition./ *London,/* Printed
by J. G. for R. Dawlman, and are to be fold/ by
Hen. Cripps, at the entrance into Popes-head/
Alley, out of Lumbard-ftreet./ 1658./ 4 *prel. leaves;
viz. Title, A Table of the Contents, and Severall Treatises, Text* 386 *pp.* 12*mo.*   (10*s.* 6*d.* 1420)

HOOKER (THOMAS). The/ Poor Doubting/ Chris-
tian/ Drawn to/ Christ./ Wherein the main Lets/
and Hinderances, which keepe men/ from coming
to Chrift,/ are difcovered./ With fpeciall Helps
to recover/ Gods favour./ By Tho. Hooker./
London:/ Printed by John Macock, for Luke
Fawne,/ at the figne of the Parrot in Pauls/
Church-yard, 1659./ *Title and* 158 *for* 185 *pp.*
12*mo.*   (15*s.* 1421)

HOOKER (THOMAS). A Manuscript fragment in
the Autograph of this celebrated New-England
Father, containing 16 or 17 lines, apparently cut
from one of his religious treatises. The authenticity is vouched for in a letter attached, from Dr.
Sprague of Albany, than whom there is no better
authority.   (2*l.* 2*s.* 1422)

HOOPER (WILLIAM). The Apostles Neither Im-
postors nor Enthusiasts. A Sermon On Acts xxvi.
25. Preached at the Weft Church in Bofton,
September 1742. By William Hooper, A.M.
Paftor of the faid Church. *Boston,* Printed and
Sold by Rogers and Fowle below the Prifon in
Queen-ftreet near the Town-Houfe. 1742. *Title
and pp.* 5-48. 8*vo.*   (4*s.* 6*d.* 1423)

HOORNBEEK (JOHN). Johannis Hornbeek,/ S.
Literarum in Ecclefia & Academia, primum Tra-
jectina,/ deinde Lugduno-Batava, Doctoris &
Profefloris./ De/ Conversione/ Indorum & Gentil-
ium./ Libri Duo./ Accessit/ Ejufdem Vita ab

Amico edita./ *Amstelodami,/* Apud Johanném
Janssonium à Waesberge,/ & Viduam Elizæi Wey-
erstraet, Anno MDCLXIX./ 28 *prel. leaves, the last
blank; and* 259 *pp. Index,* 13 *pp;* ' Auctor Lectoris' 2 *pp;* ' Liber Secundus Caput XV. &
Ultimum' *pp.* 260 *to* 265. *With large folding copperplate portrait of Hoornbeek.* 4*to.*   (1*l.* 1*s.* 1424)

HOPKINS (SAMUEL). The Life and Character of
Miss Susanna Anthony, who died, in Newport,
(R.I.) June 23, MDCCXCI. in the Sixty-Fifth Year
of her Age. Consisting chiefly in Extracts from
her Writings, with some brief Observations on
them. Compiled By Samuel Hopkins, D.D. Pastor
of the First Congregational Church in Newport.
Printed at Worcester, Massachusetts. *Hartford :*
Re-printed by Hudson and Goodwin. 1799. 168
pp. Calf. 8*vo.*   (4*s.* 6*d.* 1425)

HOPKINS (SAMUEL). Memoirs of Miss Sufanna
Anthony, who died at Newport, Rhode-Island,
June 23, 1791, in the Sixty-fifth year of her age.
Consisting chiefly of Extracts from her Writings,
With some brief observations on them. Compiled
by Samuel Hopkins, D.D. Pastor of the first Con-
gregational Church in Newport. A New Edition,
with a recommendatory preface, By Dr. Ryland,
Mr. Fuller, and Mr. Sutcliff. *Clipstone :* J. W.
Morris. 1803. 2 *prel. leaves and* 241 *pp. unbound.*
8*vo.*   (4*s.* 6*d.* 1426)

HOPKINS (SAMUEL). Autograph Minutes of a
Sermon preached Friday Augt. 24, 1744. 4 *pp.
very closely written.* 16*mo.*   (7*s.* 6*d.* 1427)
Dr. Hopkins was a distinguished preacher at Newport, Rhode
Island, and was the father of Hopkinsonianism.

HOPKINS (SAMUEL). Autograph Letter to Rev.
Levi Hart, dated at Newport, Nov. 18, 1793.
1 *page, a fine specimen.* 4*to.*   (10*s.* 6*d.* 1428)

HOPKINS (SAMUEL). Autograph Letter ' To the
Rev^d Mr. Stephen Williams at Long Meadow,
dated at Springfield, June 11, 1741. 1 *page.*
4to.   (5*s.* 1429)
This Rev. S. Hopkins, of West Springfield, was uncle of the celebrated Dr. Samuel Hopkins of Newport.

HOPKIRK (J. G.) Second Edition. An Account
of the Insurrection in St Domingo, begun in Au-

gust 1791, taken from authentic sources, by J. G.
Hopkirk, LL.B. William Blackwood, *Edinburgh*;
MDCCCXXXIII. 59 *pp.* 8*vo.*   (2*s.* 6*d.* 1430)

HORNIUS (GEORGIUS.) GeorgI HornI/ De/
Originibvs/ Americanis/ Libri Qvatvor./ Hagæ
Comitis,/ Sumptibus Adriani Vlacq/ cIɔ Iɔ cLII./
[*Colophon*] Lvgdvni Batavorvm,/ Typis Philippi
de Cro-y,/ Arnhemo-Geldri, 1652./ 10 *prel. leaves,*
and 282 *pp. Calf.* 8*vo.*   (10*s.* 6*d.* 1431)

HORNIUS (GEORGIUS). [*Engraved Title*] Georgii
Hornii/ de Originibus Americanis/ Libri Quatuor./
Hemipoli./ Sumptibus Ioannis Mülleri. 1669./
[*Printed Title*] GeorgI HornI/ De/ Originibvs/
Americanis./ Libri Qvatvor./ Hemipoli./ Sump-
tibus Joannis Mülleri Bibl./ Anno 1669./ 12 *prel.*
leaves, and 503 *pp. Small* 12*mo.*   (15*s.* 1432)

HOUGHTON (THOMAS). The/ Alteration/ of the/
Coyn,/ with a/ Feaſible Method/ to do it,/ Moſt
Humbly Proposed to Both/ Houses of Parliament./
To which is Annexed,/ A Projection or Scheem/
of Reaſonable Terms, for Eſta-/bliſhing a Firm and
General/ Peace in Europe./ By Thomas Houghton,
of Lyme-ſtreet, Gent./ *London :* Printed for the
Author, 1695./ 50 *pp.* ' Europe's Glory :/ Or,/
Peace & Plenty/ to the/ People thereof./ Being a
Projection : Or, a Scheam of/ Reaſonable Terms,'
etc. 31 *pp. calf.* 4*to.*   (10*s.* 6*d.* 1433)

HOWE (ROBERT, *Lord*). A Candid and Impartial
Narrative of the Transactions of the Fleet, under
the Command of Lord Howe, from the arrival of
the Toulon Squadron, on the Coast of America, to
the time of his Lordship's Departure for England.
With Observations. By an Officer then serving in
the Fleet. The Second Edition, revised and corrected, with a plan of the Situation of the Fleet
within Sandy-Hook. *London :* J. Almon, [1779].
58 *pp. Plan. Half mor.* 8*vo.*   (7*s.* 6*d.* 1434)

HOWE (ROBERT, *Lord*). A Letter to the Right
Honourable Lord Viscount H—e, on his Naval
Conduct in the American War. The Second Edi-
tion, corrected. *London :* G. Wilkie, MDCCLXXXI.
Half-title, title, and text 50 *pp. half mor. Uncut.*
8*vo.*   (5*s.* 6*d.* 1435)

HOWE (ROBERT, *Lord*). A Letter from Cicero to The Right Hon. Lord Vifcount H—e: occasioned by His late Speech in the H—e of C—ns. *London* J. Bew, MDCCLXXXI. *Half-title, Title, and 43 pp. half mor. 8vo.* (5s. 6d. 1436)

HOWE (ROBERT, *Lord*). Three Letters to Lord Viscount Howe. With Remarks on the Attack at Bunker's Hill. The Second Edition. To which is added, A Comparative View of the Conduct of Lord Cornwallis and General Howe. *London:* G. Wilkie, MDCCLXXXI. *Title and 48 pp. half mor. 8vo.* (6s. 6d. 1437)

HOWE (F BERT, *Lord*). Autograph note to Col. Shrieve, dated Ringwood, 25 Jany 1781, wishing to see the Colonel :—" You will form some pretext to come up to me without letting it appear that this is your errand," *etc.* 1 *page. 8vo.* (15s. 1438)

HOWE (*Sir* WILLIAM). Remarks upon Gen. Howe's Account of his Proceedings on Long-Island, in the Extraordinary Gazette of October 10, 1776. The Second Edition. *London:* Fielding and Walker, 1778. *Half-title, title, and 54 pp. half mor. 8vo.* (5s. 6d. 1439)

HOWE (*Sir* WILLIAM). A View of the Evidence relative to the Conduct of the American War under Sir William Howe, Lord Viscount Howe, and General Burgoyne; As given before a Committee of the House of Commons Laft Session of Parliament. To which is added a Collection of the celebrated Fugitive Pieces That are faid to have given rife to that Important Enquiry. *London:* Richardson and Urquhart [1779] 3 *prel. leaves, and Text pp. 9-154. half mor. 8vo.* (15s. 1440)

HOWE (*Sir* WILLIAM). The Narrative of Lieut. Gen. Sir William Howe, in a Committee of the House of Commons, on the 29th of April, 1779, relative to his Conduct, during his late Command of the King's Troops in North America: To which are added, some observations upon a Pamphlet, entitled Letters to a Nobleman. The Second Edition. *London:* H. Baldwin, MDCCLXXX. *Half-title, Title, and Text in 110 pp. half morocco. 4to.* (7s. 6d. 1441)

HOWE (*Sir* WILLIAM). A Reply to the Observations of Lieut. Gen. Sir William Howe, on a pamphlet, entitled Letters to a Nobleman: in which His Misrepresentations are detected, and thofe Letters are fupported, by a Variety of New Matter and Argument. To which is added an Appendix, containing, I. A Letter to Sir William Howe upon his Strictures on Mr. Galloway's private Character. II. A Letter from Mr. Kirk to Sir William Howe, and his Anfwer. III. A Letter from a Committee to the Prefident, of the Congrefs, on the State of the Rebel Army at Valley Forge, found among the Papers of Henry Laurens, Esq. By the Author of Letters to a Nobleman. The Second Edition, with Additions. *London:* G. Wilkie, MDCCLXXXI. *Half-title, Title and* 157 *pp. half mor.* 8*vo.* (7*s.* 6*d.* 1442)

HOWGILL (FRANCIS). The Popifh/ Inquisition./ Newly Erected in/ New-England,/ whereby/ Their Church is manifefted to be a/ Daughter of Myfterie Babylon, which did drink the/ blood of the Saints, who bears the exprefs Image,/ of her Mother, demonftrated by her fruits./ Also,/ Their Rulers to be in the Beafts power/ upon whom the Whore rideth, manifeft by their/ wicked compulfary Laws againft the Lamb and his/ Followers, and their cruel and bloody practi-/fes againft the dear Servants of the Lord,/ who have deeply fuffered by this hy-/pocritical generation./ Some of their miferable fufferings for the Teftimony of/ Jefus, declared as follows, and fome of their unjuft/ and vvicked Lavvs fet dovvn by vvhich they have made the un-/godly to reioyce, and the righteous to lament, that all who/ fear the Lord, may come out of their foot-fteps./ Publifhed by a Lover of Mercy and Truth, and an Enemy to Envy/ and Cruelty. Francis Howgill./ *London,* Printed for Thomas Simmons, at the Bull and Mouth/ near Alderfgate, 1659./ *Title,* ' To the Reader,' 2 *pp. Text* 72 *pp.* (2*l.* 12*s.* 6*d.* 1443)

HOWGILL (FRANCIS). The/ Deceiver/ of the/ Nations/ Discovered:/ And his/ Cruelty/ Made Manifeft./ And/ How he hath deceived the Nations, and wrought his/ Works of Darknefs, more hiddenly under the Mask of Higher/ Power, and

Holy Church; and fo perfecutes the Righteous/
Seed, and makes them fuffer under the Name of
evil Doers,/ in thefe latter daies./ More efpecially
his cruel works of Darknefs laid open and re-/
proved in Maryland in Virginia, And the fad Sufferings of/ the Servants of the Lord there, by his
cruel Inftruments./ Sent back unto them again,
that they may view their Work a-/gain, and repent
and be afhamed; left the Wrath of God/ fink them
into the Pit, as it hath done many before them,/
who have oppofed the Lord./ By a Lover of Mercy
and Truth,/ Fra. Howgill./ *London:* Printed for
Thomas Simmons, at the fign of the Bull and/
Mouth, neer Alderfgate. 1660./ 27 *pp. half mor.*
4*to.*   (1*l.* 11*s.* 6*d.* 1444.)

HOWSE (Joseph). A Grammar of the Cree Language; with which is combined an Analysis of
the Chippeway Dialect. By Joseph Howse, Esq.
F.R.G.S. And Resident Twenty Years in Prince
Rupert's Land, in the Service of the Hon. Hudson's Bay Company. *London:* J. G. F. & J. Rivington, 1844. *xx and* 324 *pp. Cloth. Uncut.*
8*vo.*   (7*s.* 6*d.* 1445)

HOYO (Joseph del). Relacion Com-/pleta, y ex-
acta del Av-/to Publico de Fe, qve se Ce-/lebro en
esta Civdad de Lima/ A 20. de Diziembre de 1694.
Ad-/jvnto otro precedente del/ Ano de 1693./ Con
el Prelvdio Panegirico de/ Catholicos Progressos,
qve resve-/nan en los Numeros, y Clavsvlas de vn/
Historico compendio encomiastico./ Dedicala./ Al
Supremo/ Consejo de la Santa/ Inquisicion./ Y a
las Sagradasaras del Exc^mo. S^or./ Don Diego Sarmiento de/ Ualladres, Obispo de Plasencia,/ Inqvi-
sidor General de Espana. &c./ El Doct. D. Ioseph del Hoyo, Contador,/ Abogado de los Presos,
Secretario del Secreto,/ y qve de Presente Sirve,
Como en otras/ ocasionis de Promotor Fiscal. Del
S. Oficio/ Con Licencia; en *Lima* en la Imprenta
Real/ Por Joseph de Contreras, y Alvarado, Im-
pressor del/ Santo Officio. Año de 1695./ 44 *prel.
leaves; Text* 58 *folioed leaves;* ' Svmario de Al-/
gvnas Indvlgencias,' *etc.* 8 *pp.* 4*to.* (2*l.* 2*s.* 1446)

HUBBARD (William). A/ Narrative/ of the
Troubles with the/ Indians/ In New-England,

from the firſt planting thereof in the/ year 1607, to
this preſent year 1677. But chiefly of the late/
Troubles in the two laſt years, 1675 and 1676./ To
which is added a Diſcourſe about the Warre with
the/ Pequods/ In the year 1637./ By W. Hubbard, Miniſter of Ipſwich./ Publiſhed by Authority./ *Boston ;/* Printed by John Foſter, in the
year 1677./ 7 *prel. leaves ; viz. Licence Signed* ' Simeon Bradſtreet' *etc. Title, the reverse blank, Dedication* ' To the Honourable John Leveret, Josiah
VVinslow, William Leet,' 4 *pp. Signed* ' William
Hubbard.' ' An Advertiſement to the Reader,' 2
pp. ' To the Reverend Mr. William Hubbard on
his moſt exact Hiſtory of New-Englands Troubles.'
1 *p. Signed* ' J. S.' 'Upon The elaborate Survey of
New-Englands Paſſions from the Natives By the
impartial Pen of that worthy Divine Mr. William
Hubbard.' 2 *pp. Signed* ' B. T.' ' The Printer to
the Reader,' 1 *p.* ' A Map of New-England, Being
the firſt that ever was here cut,' *etc. inches by* .
' A Narrative,' *etc.* 132 *pp.* ' A Table ſhewing the
Towns and places which are inhabited by the Engliſh in New-England : *etc.* 7 *pp.* ' A Poſtſcript.' 1
p. & *pp* [7—12]. ' A Narrative of the Troubles
With the Indians in New-England, From Paſca-
taqua to Pemmaquid.' 88 *pp.* ' The Happineſs of
a People/ In the Wiſdome of their Rulers/ Direct-
ing/ And in the Obedience of their Brethren/ At-
tending/ Unto what Iſrael ougho to do :/ Recommended in a/ Sermon/ Before the Honourable Governour and Council, and/ the Reſpected Deputies
of the Mattachuſets Colony/ in New-England./
Preached at Boſton, May. 3d. 1676. being the day
of/ Election there./ By William Hvbbard Miniſter
of Ipſwich./ *Boston,* Printed by John Foſter.
1676./ *Title, reverse blank ; Dedication* ' To the
Honourable John Leveret Eſq :' *etc.* 5 *pp. Signed*
' W. H.' ' Some Faults,' *etc.* 1 *p. Text* 63 *pp.
Bound Together in Blue Morocco extra by Bedford.
Fine Copy.* 4*to.*   (5*l.* 15*s.* 6*d* 1447)

HUBBARD (WILLIAM). The Happineſs of a Peo-
ple/ in the Wiſdome of their Rulers/ Directing/ and
in the Obedience of their Brethren/ Attending/
unto what Iſrael ougho to do :/ Recommended in
a/ Sermon/ Before the Honourable Governour and
Council, and/ the Reſpected Deputies of the Mat-

tachufets Colony/ in New-England./   Preached at
Bolton, May. 3d. 1676. being the day of/ Election
there / By William Hvbbard Minifter of Ipfwich./
Boston, Printed by John Fofter. 1676./   *Title, re-
verse blank, Dedication* 'To the Honourable John
Leveret Efq :' *etc.* 5 *pp. Signed* 'W. H.' 'Some
Faults,' *etc* 1 *p. Text* 63 *pp ; Fine large copy with
rough leaves, half mor.* 4to.   (2*l.* 2*s.*   1448)
    This tract was the next year issued as a part of Hubbard's Narra-
    tive of the Troubles with the Indians in New England. *See* No.
    1447.

HUBBARD (William). The/ Prefent State/ of/
New-England./   Being a/ Narrative/ Of the
Troubles with the Indians/ in/ New-England, from
the firft planting/ thereof in the year 1607, to this
prefent year 1677 :/ But chiefly of the late Troubles
in the two laft/ years 1675, and 1676./ To which
is added a Difcourfe about the War/ with the
Peqvods in the year 1637./ By W. Hubbard
Minifter of Ipfwich /   *London :/* Printed for Tho.
Parkhurft at the Bible and Three Crowns in Cheap-
fide,/ near Mercers-Chappel, and at the Bible on
London-Bridg.   1677./ 7 *prelim. leaves; viz. Licence, Title, reverse blank, Dedication* 4 *pp. Signed*
'William Hubbard.' *An Advertisement to the Reader,*
2 *pp. To the Reverend* Mr. *William Hubbard* 2 *pp.
Signed* 'J. S.' *Vpon the elaborate Survey of New-
Englands Passions, etc.* 2 *pp. Signed* 'B. T.' 'A
Map of New-England, Being the firft that ever
was here cut,' *etc   inches by   Text* 131 *pp.* 'A
Table' *etc.* 7 *pp.* 'A Poftfcript.' 6 *pp.* 'A Narra-
tive,' *etc.* 88 *pp.   Blue Morocco extra by Bedford.*
4*to.*   (5*l.* 15*s.* 6*d.*   1449)

HUBBARD (William). A Narrative of the Indian
Wars in New England, From the firft Planting
thereof in the Year 1607, to the Year 1677, Containing A Relation of the Occasion Rise and Progress of the War with the Indians, in the Southern,
Weftern, Eaftern, and Northern Parts of the faid
Country. By William Hubbard, A. M. Minifter
of Ipfwich, Printed at *Worcester*, (Maffachufetts)
by Daniel Greenleaf, For Joseph Wilder. 1801.
410 *pp.* 12*mo.*   (15*s.*   1450)

HUBBARD (William). Autograph letter, of 12
lines, closely written, dated Feb. 27, 1670, ad-

dressed to Rev. Samuel Phillips of Rowley, giving
his opinion respecting certain church affairs, and
signed 'Your loving friend, W. H.' *A small 4to
sheet.*   (*5l. 5s.*   1451)

Beneath this letter there is in the autograph of Mr. Cobbet, of
Lynn, the following: " I fully Agree to what Brother Hubbard
here expresseth, *etc.* Thos. Cobbet." Mr. Cobbet then goes on
in a postscript and covers the whole page and margins. The
sheet was afterwards folded into an octavo shape, and Mr. Paper-
Saving Phillips has covered the other side very closely with a
sermon on Eccl. ix. 10, preached Feb. 19, 1670.

HUDSON (SAMUEL). The/ Essence/ and/ Unitie/
of the/ Church Catholike/ Visible,/ And the
Prioritie thereof in regard/ of Particular Churches/
Discussed./ By Samuel Hudson Minister of the
Gospell./ *London,/* Printed by George Miller
for Christopher Meredith at the/ Signe of the Crane
in Pauls Church-/yard. 1645./ *Title, and* 'To the
Reader,' *2 leaves; Text 52 pp. 4to.* (*7s. 6d.*   1452)

HUDSON (SAMUEL). A/ Vindication/ of the/ Essence and Unity/ of the/ Chvrch Catholike Visible./ And/ The Priority thereof in regard of/
Particular Churches./ In answer to the Objections
made against it, both/ by Mr John Ellis junior,
and by that Reverend and/ worthy Divine Mr
Hooker, in his Survey/ of Church Discipline./ By
Samuel Hudson Minister of the Gospel/ at Capell
in Suff./ *London,/* Printed by A. M. for Christopher Meredith at the Signe of the/ Crane in Pauls
Church-yard. 1650./ *15 prel. leaves; viz. Title,
Dedication, Epistle to the Reader, Errata, Table, and
This Leaf, etc. Text 265 pp. 4to.* (*15s.*   1453)

HUDSON (SAMUEL). An/ Addition or Postscript/
to the/ Vindication/ of the/ Essence and Unity/ or
the/ Church-Catholick visible,/ And the Priority
thereof in regard of/ Particular Churches./ In
answer to the Objections made against it,/ both by
Mr Stone, and some others./ By Samuel Hudson,
Minister of the Gospel/ at Capell in Suff./ *London,/*
Printed by J. B. for Andrew Kembe, and are to be
sold/ at his shop neer S. Margarets hill in Southwark and by Ed-/ward Brewster at the Crane in
Paul's Church-yard,/ and Thomas Basset under
Dunstanes Church/ Fleet-street, 1658./ *2 prel.
leaves; viz. Title and To the Christian Reader. Text
52 pp. 4to.*   (*8s. 6d.*   1454)

HUIT (Ephraim). The whole/ Prophecie/ of/ Daniel/ explained,/ By a Paraphrase, Analysis/ and briefe Comment:/ Wherein the feverall Vifions fhewed to the Prophet, are/ clearely Interpreted, and the Application thereof vindi-/cated againft diffenting Opinions./ By Ephraim Huit somtime Preacher at Roxall in Warwickfhire,/ now Paftor to the Church at Windfor in New-England./ Imprimatur, Jam : Cranford./ [*London*]/ Printed for Henry Overton, and are to be fold at his Shop,/ entering into Popes-head Alley out of Lumbard/ Street. MDCXLIV./ *2 prel. leaves, and 358 pp. With* 'Analifis' *at page* 4; *and 10 folio folded sheets of Analyses at pp.* 20, 70, 95, 131, 151, 171, 217, 241, 269 *and* 283. *Old calf. 4to.* (15s. 1455)

HUMBLE (An) Apology for the Quakers, Addreffed to Great and Small. Occasiond By certain grofs Abuses and Imperfect Vindications Of that People, relative to the late Public Fast. To which are added Obfervations on a New Pamphlet, intituled A Brief View of the Conduct of Pennsylvania For the Year 1755. So far as to fhew the real Spirit and Defign, of that Angry Writer. And also A much Fairer Method pointed out, Than That contained in the Brief State of Penfylvania, to prevent the Incroachments of the French, and reftore Quiet to the Province. Stanley Crowder, and Henry Woodgate, *London*. MDCCLVI. *38 pp. Advertisement* 1 *page. 12mo.* (7s. 6d. 1456)

HUMBOLDT (Alexandre de). Essai Politique sur le Royaume de la Nouvelle-Espagne. Par Al. de Humboldt. A *Paris*, F. Schoell, 1811. *Five Volumes.* Tome Premier. *Half-title, Title, iii and* 456 *pp. With Map.* Tome Deuxième. *Half-title, Title, and* 522 *pp. With Tableau.* Tome Troisième. *Half-title, Title, and* 420 *pp.* Tome Quatrième. *Half-title, Title, and* 365 *pp.* Tome Cinquième. *Half-title, Title, and* 352 *pp. Half-calf, gilt backs.* 8vo. (1l. 5s. 1457)

HUME (Sophia). An Exhortation to the Inhabitants Of the Province of South-Carolina, To bring their Deeds to the Light of Christ, in their own Confciences. By S. H. In which is inferted, Some Account of the Author's Experience in the Important Business of Religion. *Philadelphia:* Printed by William Bradford. [1747] 158 *pp.*

(10*s.* 6*d.* 1458)

HUME (SOPHIA). An Exhortation to the Inhabitants Of the Province of South-Carolina, To bring their Deeds to the Light of Christ, in their own Confciences. By S. H. In which is inferted, Some Account of the Author's Experience in the Important Business of Religion. *Briftol:* Samuel Farley, M.DCC.L. 80 *pp. calf.* 8*vo.* (6*s.* 1459)

HUME (SOPHIA). An Exhortation to the Inhabitants Of the Province of South-Carolina, To bring their Deeds to the Light of Christ, in their own Confciences. By Sophia Hume. In which is inferted, Some Account of the Author's Experience in the Important Business of Religion. *London:* Luke Hinde, 1752. 152 *pp.* 8*vo.* (5*s.* 1460)

HUME (SOPHIA). An Epistle to the Inhabitants of South=Carolina; Containing Sundry Obfervations proper to be confider'd by every Profeffor of Chriftianity in general. By Sophia Hume. *London:* Luke Hinde, 1754. 114 *pp.* 8*vo.* (5*s.* 1461)

HUMPHREYS (DAVID). An Historical Account of the Incorporated Society for the Propagation of the Gofpel in Foreign Parts. Containing their Foundation, Proceedings, and the Succefs of their Miffionaries in the Britifh Colonies, to the Year 1728. By David Humphreys, D.D. Secretary to the Honorable Society. *London:* Joseph Downing, M.DCC.XXX. *xxxi and* 356 *pp.* 2 *Copperplate Maps. Calf.* 8*vo.* (15*s.* 1462)

HUMPHREYS (DAVID). An Account of the Endeavours Used by the Society for the Propagation of the Gospel in Foreign Parts, To inftruct the Negroe Slaves in New York. Together with Two of Bp. Gibson's Letters on that subject. Being an Extract from Dr. Humphreys's Hiftorical Account of the Incorporated Society fro the Propagation of the Gofpel in Foreign Parts, from its Foundation to the Year 1728. Printed at *London* in 1730. 45 *pp.* 8*vo.* (4*s.* 6*d.* 1463)

HUMPHRIES (DAVID). A Poem addressed to the Armies of the United States of America. By

David Humphries, Esq; Colonel in the Service of
the United States, and Aid-de-Camp to His Excellency the Commander in Chief.   New-Haven:
Printed by T. and S. Green, 1784. Paris, reprinted
1785: And, at *London*, in the same Year, for G.
Kearsley, at No. 46 Fleet Street. 28 *pp. half mor.*
4*to.*   (5*s.* 6*d.*   1464)

HUMPHREYS (David).   The Miscellaneous
Works of Colonel Humphreys. *New-York:* Printed
by Hodge, Allen, and Campbell; and Sold at their
respective Book-Stores. M.DCC.XC. 348 *pp. half
calf.* 8*vo.*   (7*s.* 6*d.*   1465)

HUNTER (John).   Memoirs of a Captivity among
the Indians of North America, from Childhood to
the age of Nineteen: With Anecdotes descriptive
of their Manners and Customs. To which is added,
some account of the Soil, Climate, and Vegetable
productions of the Territory Westward of the
Mississippi. By John D. Hunter. A New Edition,
with Portrait. *London:* Longman, 1823. 8 *prel.
leaves including Portrait and pp.* 3-447 : *half calf.*
8*vo.*   (5*s.* 6*d.*   1466)

HUNTINGTON (Joseph).   Autograph Letter to
Rev. Levi Hart, V.D.M. Preston, dated at Coventry, 18 Jan. 1783. 3 *pp.* 4*to.* (5*s.* 6*d.* 1467)
    Dr. Huntington was a popular preacher at Coventry, Connecticut,
    and is distinguished for having written towards the close of his
    life a work in defence of Universalism, which was published
    after his death.

HUNTINGTON (Samuel).   Letter signed in the
Autograph of Gov. Huntington to the Governor of
New-York, dated Norwich, Nov. 11, 1791, respecting the apprehension of certain Criminals.
1 *page. Folio.*   (10*s.* 6*d.*   1468)
    Samuel Huntington was President of Congress. Signer of the De-
    claration of Independence, and Governor of Connecticut.

HUTCHINS (Thomas).   A Topographical Description of Virginia, Pennsylvania, Maryland,
and North Carolina, comprehending the Rivers
Ohio, Kenhawa, Sioto, Cherokee, Wabash, Illinois,
Mississippi, &c. The Climate, Soil and Produce,
whether Animal, Vegetable, or Mineral ; the
Mountains, Creeks, Roads, Distances, Latitudes,
&c. and of every Part, laid down in the annexed
Map. Published by Thomas Hutchins, Captain in
the 60th Regiment of Foot. With a Plan of the

Rapids of the Ohio, a Plan of the feveral Villages
in the Illinois Country, a Table of the Distances
between Fort Pitt and the Mouth of the Ohio, all
Engraved upon Copper. And An Appendix, containing Mr. Patrick Kennedy's Journal up the
Illinois River, and a correct Lift of the different
Nations and Tribes of Indians, with the Number
of Fighting Men, &c. *London:* J. Almon,
MDCCLXXVIII. *2 prel. leaves, and 67 pp. With 2
plans and a Table of Distances. 8vo.* (10s. 6d. 1469)

HUTCHINSON (SAMUEL). A Declaration of a
Future Glori-/ous Eftate of a Church to be here/
upon Earth, at Chrifts Perso-/nal Appearance for
the Reftitu-/tion of all things, a Thousand/ Years
before the Ultimate Day/ of the General Judgement./ Set forth by a Letter to a Friend./ As
alfo further proved by divers Scriptures, together
with/ the Teftimony of many Godly Divines, both/
Ancient and Modern./ By S. H. of Bofton in
New-England./ *London:* Printed in the year
1667./ *36 pp. Half mor. 4to.* (1l. 1s. 1470)

HUTCHINSON (THOMAS). Copy of Letters Sent
to Great Britain, by his Excellency Thomas Hut-
chinfon, the Hon. Andrew Oliver, and feveral other
Perfons, born and educated among us. Which
original Letters have been returned to America,
and laid before the honorable Houfe of Reprefentatives of this Province. In which (notwithftanding his Excellency's Declaration to the Houfe, that
the Tendency and Defign of them was not to fub-
vert the Conftitution, but rather to preferve it
entire) the judicious Reader will difcover the fatal
Source of the Confufion and Bloodfhed in which
this Province efpecially has been involved, and
which threatned total Deftruction to the Liberties
of all America. *Boston:* Printed by Edes and
Gill, in Queen-Street: 1773. *40 pp. Half mor.
8vo.* (10s. 6d. 1471)

HUTCHINSON (THOMAS). The Representations
of Governor Hutchinson and others, contained in
certain Letters Tranfmitted to England, And afterwards returned from thence, And laid before the
General-Affembly of the Maffachusetts-Bay. Together with the Resolves Of the two Houfes thereon.

Boston: N. E. Printed and Sold by Edes and Gill, in Queen-Street, 1773. *Title and 94 pp. Half mor. 8vo.* (10s. 6d. 1472)

HUTCHINSON (Thomas). The Speeches of His Excellency Governor Hutchinson, to the General Assembly Of the Massachusetts-Bay. At a Seffion begun and held on the Sixth of January, 1773. With the Answers of His Majesty's Council and the House of Representatives respectively. [Publifh'd by Order of the Houfe.] *Boston;* New-England: Printed by Edes and Gill, Printers to the Honourable House of Representatives. M,DCC,LXXIII. *Title and pp. 3-126. Half mor. 8vo.* (10s. 6d. 1473)

HUTCHINSON (Thomas). The Letters of Governor Hutchinson, and Lieut. Governor Oliver, &c. Printed at Boston. And Remarks thereon. With the Assembly's Address, and the Proceedings of the Lords Committee of Council. Together with the Substance of Mr. Wedderburn's Speech relating to those Letters. *London:* J. Wilkie, MDCCLXXIV. *Title and 134 pp. Half morocco. 8vo.* (5s. 6d. 1474)

HUTCHINSON (Thomas). The Letters of Governor Hutchinson, and Lieut. Governor Oliver, &c. Printed at Boston. And Remarks thereon. With the Afsembly's Address And the proceedings Of the Lords Committee of Council. Together with The Substance of Mr. Wedderburn's Speech relating to thofe Letters. And the Report of the Lords Committee to his Majesty in Council. The Second Edition. *London:* J. Wilkie, MDCCLXXIV. *Half title, title and 142 pp. Half mor. 8vo.* (5s. 6d. 1475)

HUTCHINSON (Thomas). The History of the Colony of Massachusets-Bay, from the first Settlement thereof in 1628, until its Incorporation with the Colony of Plimouth, Province of Main, &c. by the Charter of King William and Queen Mary, in 1691. By Mr. Hutchinson, Lieutenant-Governor of the Massachusets Province. *Boston,* New-England: Printed by Thomas and John Fleet, at the Heart and Crown in Cornhill. MDCCLXIV. *Two Volumes. Vol. I. Title; Contents 2 pp; The Preface iv pp; Text 566 pp; Volume II. The History* of the Province of Massachusets-Bay, from the Charter of King William and Queen Mary, in 1691, Until the Year 1750. By Mr. Hutchinson, Lieutenant-Governor of the Province. *Boston,* New-England: Printed by Thomas & John Fleet, in Cornhill, and sold in Union-Street, opposite to the Cornfield. MDCCLXVII. *Title, Contents and Preface,* 4 *leaves; Text* 520 *pp. Index pp.* 521 *to* 539. *First Edition.* 8*vo.*   (1*l.* 11*s.* 6*d.*   1476)

HUTCHINSON (Thomas). The History of the Colony of Massachusett's Bay, from the First Settlement thereof in 1628, until its Incorporation with the Colony of Plimouth, Province of Main, &c. By the Charter of King William and Queen Mary, in 1691. By Mr. Hutchinson, Lieutenant-Governor of the Massachuset's Province. The Second Edition. *London :* M. Richardson, MDCCLXV. *Two Volumes.* Vol. I. 3 *prel. leaves; iv and* 566 *pp.* Vol. II. The History of the Province of Massachusetts-Bay, from the Charter of King William and Queen Mary, in 1691, Until the Year 1750. By Mr. Hutchinson, Lieutenant Governor of the Province. Vol. II. The Second Edition. *London:* J. Smith, MDCCLXVIII. 2 *prel. leaves; iv, and* 539 *pp.* 8*vo.*   (1*l.* 11*s.* 6*d.*   1477)
This second edition was issued in London at first with the date MDCCLX. in error for 1765, but the title was cancelled, and the date corrected. I have copies with both titles.

HUTCHINSON (Thomas). A Collection of Original Papers Relative to the History of the Colony of Maffachusets-Bay. *Boston,* New-England: Printed by Thomas and John Fleet, 1769. *Title and* 576 *pp. Calf.* 8*vo.*   (2*l.* 2*s.*   1478)

HUTCHINSON (Thomas). The History of the Province of Massachusetts Bay, from 1749 to 1774, comprising a detailed Narrative of the origin and early stages of the American Revolution. By Thomas Hutchinson, Esq., L.L.D. formerly Governor of the Province. Edited from the Author's MS., by his Grandson, The Rev. John Hutchinson, M.A. *London:* John Murray, MDCCCXXVIII. *xx and* 551 *pp; Boards.* 8*vo.*   (7*s.* 6*d.*   1479)

HUTCHINSON (Thomas). Autograph Letter to Sir William Johnson Bart. dated at Boston, 8

October 1771. 1 *page.* *A fine specimen.*
4*to.* (1*l.* 1*s.* 1480)

HUTTEN (ULRICH). Of the VVood/ called Gvaia-
cvm,/ that healeth/ the Frenche/ Pockes,/ and alſo
helpeth the goute in the/ feete, the ſtoone, the/
palſey, lepree,/ dropſy,/ fallynge euyll, and o=/ther
dyſeaſes./ ⅋/ *Londini* in Aedibvs/ Tho. Berthe-
leti/ M.D.XXXVI. Cvm Privilegio./ *Title, reverse
blank;* 'The preface./ ❧ The preface of Thomas
Paynal cha-/non of Marten abbey, tranſla-/tour of
this boke.'/ *and* '❧ The table of this boke.'/ *together 5 pp. Text 82 folived leaves for* 79. *Wanting
the* 24*th leaf.* 16*mo.* (1*l.* 11*s.* 6*d.* 1481)

HUTTEN (ULRICH). ⅋ Of the/ VVood cal=/led
Gvaia/-cvm,/that healeth the frenche pockes, and
alſo/ helpeth the goute in the feete,/ the ſtone,
palſey, lepre,/ dropſy, fallynge/ euyll, and o=/ther
diſ-/eſes. Made in latyn by Ulrich Hutten/ knyght,
and tranſlated in/to englyſh by Tho=/mas Paynel./
⅋/ *Londini./* Ex Officina Thomæ Bertheleti
regii/ impreſſoris. Cum priuilegio/ ad imprimen-
dum ſolum./ Anno. M.D.XL./ *Title, reverse blank;*
'The Preface./ ❧ The preface of Thomas Pay-
nell,/ tranſlatour of this boke.'/ 2 *pp.* 'The Table.'
2 *pp. Text* 58 *folived leaves. Black Letter. Boards.*
4*to.* (2*l.* 2*s.* 1482)

HYPOCRISY Unmaſked; or a Short Inquiry into
the Religious Complaints of our American Colonies. To which is added, a Word on the Laws
against Popery in Great Britain and Ireland. The
Third Edition. *London:* W. Nicoll, MDCCLXXVI.
24 *pp. Half mor.* 12*mo.* (4*s.* 6*d.* 1483)

MLAY (GEORGE). A Topographical Description of the Western Territory of North America: Containing A Succinct Account of its Soil, Climate, Natural Hiſtory, Population, Agriculture, Manners, and Cuſtoms. With an ample Deſcription of the ſeveral Diviſions into which that Country is partitioned; to which are added, the Discovery, Settlement, and Present State of Kentucky. And An Essay towards the Topography, and Natural History of that important Country. By John Filson. To which is added I. The Adventures of Col. Daniel Boon, one of the Firſt Settlers, comprehending every important Occurence in the Political Hiſtory of that Province. II. The Minutes of the Piankashaw Council, held at Post St. Vincent's, April 15, 1784. III. An Account of the Indian Nations inhabiting within the Limits of the Thirteen United States; their Manners and Cuſtoms; and Reflections on their Origin. By George Imlay, A Captain in the American Army during the War, and Commiſſioner for laying out Lands in the Back Settlements. Illuſtrated with correct Maps of the Weſtern Territory of North America; of the State of Kentucky, as divided into Counties, from the latent Surveys; and a plan of the Rapids of the Ohio. The Second Edition, with considerable Additions. *London:* J. Debrett, MDCCXCIII. *Title, xvi and* 433 *pp. Index* 19 *pp; Errata* 1 *page.* 2 *Maps, Plan, and Table.* 8*vo.* (7s. 6d. 1484)

IMPARTIAL (AN) and correct History of the War between the United States of America, and Great Britain; Declared by a Law of Congress, June 18, 1812, and concluded by a ratification and exchange

D D

of a Treaty of Peace, at the City of Washington, Feb. 17, 1815. Comprising a particular detail of the Naval and Military Operations, and a faithful record of the Events produced during the Contest. And including the following important Documents: 1. The President's Message to Congress of 1st June, 1812. 2. The Report of the Committee of Foreign Relations of 3d June, 1812. 3. The Act declaring War between the United States and Great Britain. 4. The Treaty of Peace. 5. Niles's List of Prizes, captured during the War. 6. The Treaty of Peace of 1783. Carefully compiled from Official Documents. *New-York:* John Low, 1815. 304 *pp. Frontispiece.* 12*mo.* (5*s.* 6*d.* 1485)

IMPARTIAL (An) History of the War in America, between Great Britain and Her Colonies, from Its Commencement to the end of the Year 1779. Exhibiting a circumſtantial, connected and complete Account of the real Causes, Rise, and Progress of the War, interſperſed with Anecdotes and Characters of the different Commanders, and Accounts of ſuch Perſonages in Congreſs as have diſtinguiſhed themſelves during the Conteſt. With an Appendix, containing A Collection of Intereſting and Authentic Papers tending to elucidate the Hiſtory. *London:* R. Faulder, and J. Milliken, M,DCC, LXXX. *xi and* 608 *pp. Appendix* 44 *pp. Map of North America and* 13 *copperplate portraits at pp.* 205, 207, 208, 212, 221, 241, 310, 319, 327, 336, 345, 400, 494. *Half calf.* 8*vo.* (1*l.* 1*s.* 1486)

IMPARTIAL (An) History of the War, *etc. Another copy wanting the Map and Portraits. Calf.* 8*vo.* (7*s.* 6*d.* 1487)

IMPARTIAL (An) Sketch of the Various Indulgences granted by Great-Britain to her Colonies, upon which They have founded their Presumption of ſoaring towards Independence. By an Officer. *London:* W. Davenhill, M.DCC.LXXXVIII. 2 *prel. leaves, and* 43 *pp.* 8*vo.* (4*s.* 6*d.* 1488)

IMPORTANCE (The) and advantage of Cape Breton, Truly Stated, and Impartially Conſidered. With Proper Maps. *London:* John and Paul Knapton, MDCCXLVI. 4 *prel. leaves and* 156 *pp.* 2 *copperplate maps. Half mor.* (10*s.* 6*d.* 1489)

IMPORTANCE (THE) of Effectually Supporting the Royal African Company of England Impartially confidered; shewing That a Free and Open Trade to Africa, and the Support and Preservation of the Britifh Colonies and Plantations in America, depend upon Maintaining the Forts and Settlements, Rights and Privileges belonging to that Corporation, againft the Encroachments of the French and all other Foreign Rivals in that Trade. The Second Edition. With a New and more Correct Map than any hitherto publifhed fhewing the Situation of the feveral European Forts and Settlements in that Country. In a Letter to a Member of the House of Commons. *London:* E. Say, 1745. *Half-title, Title, and* 47 *pp. Map of the Gold Coast of Africa* 1744. 4to.   (7s. 6d. 1490)

IMPORTANCE (THE) of Gaining and Preserving the Friendship of the Indians to the British Interest considered. *London:* E. Cave, M.DCC.LII. *Title and* 46 *pp.* 8vo.   (10s. 6d. 1491)
By Archibald Kennedy.

IMPORTANCE (THE) of the British Dominion in India, compared with that in America. *London:* J. Almon, MDCCLXX. *Title, and Text pp.* 5-60. 16mo.   (4s. 6d. 1492)

IMPORTANCE (THE) of the British Plantations in America to this Kingdom; with The State of their Trade, and Methods for Improving it; as also A Defcription of the feveral Colonies there. *London:* J. Peele. MDCCXXXI. *3 prel. leaves, and* 114 *pp. Uncut, half mor.* 8vo.   (7s. 6d. 1493)

IMPORTANCE (THE) of the Sugar Colonies to Great-Britain Stated, and Some Objections against the Sugar Colony Bill anfwer'd. In a Letter to a Member of the Houfe of Commons. *London:* Printed for J. Roberts, 1731. 40 *pp. Half mor.* 8vo.   (4s. 6d. 1494)

INC'WADI/ Yokuqala Ka-Yowannes/ Intloko Yokuqala/ [*Colophon*] Ibishicilelwe/ E -Chumie/ *Emaxoseni,*/ 1832./ 16 *pp. Uncut. Half mor. Small* 8vo.   (15s. 1495)

INDARTE (JOSE RIVERA). Efemerides de los Deguellos. Asesinatos y Matanzas del Degollador Juan Manuel Rosas. Por Jose Rivera Indarte.

Montevideo, Imprenta del Nacional. [1829] *32 pp.*
8*vo.* (*2s. 6d.* 1496)

INDEPENDENT WHIG (The) [*Colophon*] Printed and sold by Samuel Keimer, in *Philadelphia.*
[1720]. 8 *prel. leaves; and Text* 227 *pages. Old
Calf.* 4*to.* (*2l. 2s.* 1497)

This *Independent Whig* consists of an Introduction of 16 pages,
and 53 numbers, generally of four pages each, reprinted from
the London edition.

INFORMATIONS concerning the Province of
North Carolina addressed to Emigrants from the
Highlands and Western Isles of Scotland. By an Impartial hand. *Glasgow :* James Knox, MDCCLXXIII.
32 *pp. Signed,* 'Scotus Americanus.' *Uncut.*
8*vo.* (*7s. 6d.* 1498)

INGLIS (Charles). Long and interesting autograph Letter of Rev. Charles Inglis to Sir William
Johnson, dated at New York June 21, 1770, concerning a plan for extending Christianity among
the Indians. *6 pages closely written.*
4*to.* (*1l. 1s.* 1499)

INQUIRY (An) into the Causes of the Insurrection
of the Negroes in the Island of St. Domingo. To
which are added Observations of M. Garran-Cou-
lon on the same subject, Read in his Abſence by
M. Guadet, before the National Aſſembly 29th
Feb. 1792. *London :* J. Johnson, MDCCXCII. 32
pp. half mor. 8*vo.* (*4s. 6d.* 1500)

INQUIRY (An) into the Nature and Causes of the
Present Disputes between the British Colonies in
America and their Mother-Country ; And their reciprocal Claims and juſt Rights impartially examined, and fairly ſtated. *London :* J. Wilkie,
MDCCLXIX. *Half-title, title, & 76 pp. half mor.*
8*vo.* (*5s. 6d.* 1501)

INSIGNE victoria que el Señor Marquez de Guadalcazar, Vir-/rey en el Reyno del Pirû, ha alcançado en los puertos de Lima,/ y Callao, contra vna
armada poderoſa de Olanda, deſpachada/ por orden
del Conde Mauricio. Daſe cuenta de como el ene-/
migo lleuaua intento de coger la plata de ſu Magestad : y el de=/ſastrado fin que tuuo por mano de
los Eſpañoles. Auiſaſe tam=/bien de vna declaracion que hizo vn ſoldado del enemigo,/ Frances de
nacion, y en ſu profeſsion Catolico, llama-/do Iuan

de Bulas, que huyò de fu exer-/cito, ante el feñor
Virrey, a ocho/de Enéro defte año/ de 1625. [*Colophon*] Em *Lisboa.* Por Geraldo da Vinha./ [1625].
4 unnumbered pages. Folio. (1*l.* 11*s.* 6*d.* 1502)

INSTRUCTIONS/ By the Commiffioners of his Majefty's/ Cuftoms in America, to/   / who is ap-
pointed/   / of the Cuftoms at the Port of/
        / in America./ [*Boston?* 1770?] 40 *pp.*
Half mor. 8vo.   (10*s.* 6*d.* 1503)

INTEREST (THE) of the Merchants and Manufacturers of Great Britain, in the present contest with
the Colonies, Stated and Considered. *London*:
T. Cadell. M,DCC,LXXIV. *Title and* 50 *pp. Half
mor. 8vo.*   (5*s.* 6*d.* 1504)

INTEREST (THE) of Great Britain Considered,
With Regard to her Colonies, And the Acquisitions
of Canada and Guadaloupe. To which are added,
Observations concerning the Increafe of Mankind,
Peopling of Countries, &c. The Second Edition.
London: T. Becket, MDCCLXI. *Title, and* 58 *pp.*
8vo.   (5*s.* 6*d.* 1505)

INTRODUCTION to the Observations made by the
Judges of the Court of Common Pleas for the District of Quebec, upon the Oral and Written Testimony adduced upon the Investigation into the Past
Administration of Justice. Ordered in consequence
of an Address of the Legislative Council. *London*:
J. Stockdale, MDCCXC. *iv. and* 50 *pp. half mor.*
8vo.   (4*s.* 6*d.* 1506)

IRENICVM ;/ or, an/ Essay/ Towards a Brotherly/
Peace & Vnion,/

Between thofe of the $\left\{ \begin{array}{c} \text{Congregational} \\ \text{and} \\ \text{Presbyterian} \end{array} \right\}$ Way ;/

Shewing out of the moft Learned and Renowned
Di-/vines of the Congregational Way, that their
Pofitions/

Concerning $\left\{ \begin{array}{l} \text{1. Church Matters and Members.} \\ \text{2. Church Conftitution and Form.} \\ \text{3. Church State.} \\ \text{4. Church Officers and Ordination.} \\ \text{5. Church Government and Cenfures.} \\ \text{6. Church Combinations and Synods.} \\ \text{7. Communion with} \\ \text{\quad and Separation from} \end{array} \right.$ $\left. \begin{array}{l} \\ \\ \\ \\ \\ \\ \text{Churches.} \end{array} \right\}$

Are fufficient for the eftablifhing a firme and laft-
ing/ Peace between them and the Presbyterians./
Drawn up and publifhed by/ Difcipulus De Tempore Junior./ In purfuance of the good defign begun at the Savoy, where it was agreed, and declared, That fuch Reforming Churches as/confift of
Perfons found in the Faith, and of converfation be-/
coming the Gofpel, ought not to refufe the communion of each o-/ther, fo far as may confift, With
their own principles refpe-/ctively, though they
walk not in all things according to the fame/ Rules
of Church Order, Canon 29./ *London,* Printed for
Nathanael Webb and William Grantham,/ at the
black Bear in Pauls Church-yard, near the little
North-door. 1659./ *7 prel. leaves ; viz. Title, reverse blank ; The Preface ; The Attestation ; To the
Judicious Reader ; and An Advertisement to the
Reader. Text 75 pp. 4to.* (15s. 1507)

A great part of this book pertains to the Church affairs of New
England. Mr. Cotton's, Mr. Hook's, and Mr. Shepard's books
are frequently quoted.

ISRAEL (Menasseh Ben). **מקוה ישראל**/
Hoc eft,/ Spes Israelis./ Authore/ Menasseh Ben
Israel./ Theologo & Philofopho Hebræo./ *Am-
stelodami./ Anno 1650./ 6 prel. leaves and 111 pp.
Calf by Bedford. 12mo.* (1l. 1s. 1508)

IZQUIERDO (Sebastian)./✥/ El Padre Sebastian
Izquierdo,/ Afsiftente en Roma por las Provincias
de Efpaña,/ mandò al Procurado General de Indias
en efta Corte,/ el año de 1673. dar à la eftampa,
efte Papel./ [*Lima* 1673 ?] *8 folioed leaves. Unbound. Folio.* (1l. 11s. 6d. 1509)

ACQUIN (Nic. Joseph). Selectarum Stirpium Americanarum Historia in qua ad Linnaeanum Systema Determinatae Descriptaeque sistunter Plantae illae, quas in Insulus Martinica, Jamaica, Domingo, Aliisque, et in Vicina Continentis Parte Observavit Rariores. Cum Approbatione Auctoris ad exemplar Majoris Operis Vindobonae Editi Recusum. *Manhemii* In Bibliopolio Novo Aul. & Acad. MDCCLXXXVIII. *xv and 363 pp. Uncut.* 8*vo.* (*7s. 6d.* 1510)

JAMAICA. The/ Present State/ of/ Jamaica./ With the/ Life/ Of the Great Columbus/ The firſt Discoverer :/ To which is Added/ An ExaČt Account of Sir Hen. Morgan's/ Voyage to, and famous Siege and ta-/king of Panama from the Spaniards./ *London,/* Printed by Fr. Clark for Tho. Malthus/ at the Sun in the Poultry, 1683./ 5 *prel. leaves*; *viz. Title, reverse blank,* 'To the Reader.' 4 *pp. Books sold by Tho. Malthus* 4 *pp. Text* 54 *pp. Title.* 'Sir Henry Morgan's/ Voyage/ to/ Panama,/ 1670./ *London,* Printed for Thomas Malthus at the/ Sun in the Poultry, 1683./ *Text pp.* 57 *to* 117. 12*mo.* (*1l. 11s. 6d.* 1511)
See the note under Nº. 1002.

JAMAICA. A/ Narrative/ of/ Affairs/ Lately received from his Majesties/ Iſland of Jamaica :/ viz./ I. His Excellency the Governour Sir Thomas Linch's/ Speech to the Aſſembly met Sept. 21. 1682./ II. Samuel Bernard Eſq ; Speaker of the ſaid Aſſembly, his/ Speech to the Governour./ III. An humble Addreſs from his Majeſties Council, and/ the Gentlemen of the Aſſembly, to his moſt Sacred Majeſty./ IV. The Governour's

Speech at the Prorouging the Af-/fembly./ *London:/* Printed for Randal Taylor, near Stationers Hall. 1683./ *Title and 6 pp. Folio.* (1*l.* 1*s.* 1512)

JAMAICA. Account/ of the/ Late Earthquake/ in/ Jamaica./ June the 7th. 1692./ Written by a Reverend Divine there to his/ Friend in London./ With fome Improvement thereof by another Hand./ *London,/* Printed for Tho. Parkhurft, at the Bible and three Crowns/ at the lower End of Cheapfide, near Mercers-Chappel. 1693./ *4 prel. leaves; viz. Title, and Preface; Signed* 'H. L.' *Text 26 pp. Calf extra by* Bedford. *4to.* (1*l.* 11*s.* 6*d.* 1513)
With the Autograph of White Kennett on the Title.

JAMAICA. The Trueft and Largeft/ Account/ of the/ Late Earthquake/ in/ Jamaica,/ June the 7th, 1692./ Written by a Reverend Divine there to his/ Friend in London./ With fome Improvement thereof by another Hand./ *London,* Printed, and are to be Sold by *J. Buttler* Bookfeller at/ Worcefter, 1693./ *4 prel. leaves; viz. Title, and Preface; Signed* 'H. L.' *Text 26 pp. Half morocco.* *4to.* (1*l.* 1*s.* 1514)

JAMAICA. The following Addrefs, and particular Inftances as to the Duties demanded on Prize Goods brought into Jamaica, were fent from that Ifland by the Governor, Council and Affembly, in March 17$\frac{9}{10}$: Whereupon an Act pafs'd in the Ninth Year of Her Majefty's Reign, That Prize Goods fhould not be liable to the Demand of Duties by Vertue of an Act, Entituled, An Act to Encourage to Trade to America for the future: And all Proceedings upon the Bonds enter'd into were ordered to be ftaid until a clear State of thofe Bonds could be had from Jamaica, and laid before this prefent Parliament. Since then an Account of the faid Bonds has been tranfmitted by the Governor, Council and Affembly of Jamaica to the Lords Commiffioners of Trade and Plantations, as well as by the Collector of Her Majefty's Duties in the faid Ifland to the Commiffioners of Her Majefty's Cuftoms in Great Britain; which Account is hereunto annexed. *4 pp. With the Account, a folded Sheet.* 'An Answer to fome Falfe and Malicious Objections given out, to prevent the Duties on Prize Goods being remitted, with fome Obferva-

tions.' *2 pp. Bound together. Half morocco.*
Folio. (*7s. 6d.* 1515)

JAMAICA. The Trade Granted to the South-Sea-
Company : Confidered with Relation to Jamaica.
In a Letter to one of the Directors of the South-
Sea-Company; By a Gentleman who has refided
feveral Years in Jamaica. *London:* Samuel Crouch,
1714. *30 pp. half mor. 8vo.* (*5s. 6d.* 1516)

JAMAICA. A View of the Proceedings of the
Affemblies of Jamaica, For fome Years paft. With
fome Confiderations on the Prefent State of that
Island ; In Several Occafional Papers. Earneftly
Recommended to the Planters, Traders, and Free-
holders of Jamaica. *London:* Printed in the Year
M.DCC.XVI. *vi and 42 pp. 8vo.* (*7s. 6d.* 1517)

JAMAICA. A Vindication Of the Late Governor
and Council of Jamaica. Occafion'd by A Letter
in the St. James's Poft of the 23d of July laft, as
from Bath. In a Letter to —— *London:* W. Wilkins, 1716. *32 pp. 8vo.* (*7s. 6d.* 1518)

JAMAICA. A True Account Of the Late Pyracies
of Jamaica; the Authors, Abettors, and Encou-
ragers thereof. With other Transactions relating
thereto. By One juft arrived from that Island.
To which is added, A Genuine Letter to a very
Eminent Perfonage concern'd. *London :* J. Moore,
1716. *36 pp. signed* ' A. Wagftaffe.' *half morocco.*
8vo. (*7s. 6d.* 1519)

JAMAICA. The Politicks and Patriots of Jamaica.
A Poem. *London:* T. Warner, 1718. *20 pp. half*
mor. 8vo. (*7s. 6d.* 1520)

JAMAICA. The State of The Island of Jamaica.
Chiefly in Relation to its Commerce, and the Conduct of the Spaniards in the West-Indies. Addrefs'd to a Member of Parliament. By a Perfon
who refided feveral Years at Jamaica. *London :*
H. Whitridge, 1726. *Title & pp.* 3-79. *half mor.*
8vo. (*7s. 6d.* 1521)

JAMAICA. A New Hiftory of Jamaica, from the
Earliest Accounts, to the Taking of Porto Bello by
Vice Admiral Vernon. In Thirteen Letters from
a Gentleman to his Friend. Containing, I. The
Author's Voyage to that Ifland ; with an Account

of feveral Curious Particulars which he met with
in his Paffage. II. A Defcription of Jamaica; its
Natural Advantages, Manners of the People, &c.
III. Spanifh Cruelty on firft Settling there, Expedition of Sir Anthony Shirley and Col. Jackfon
againft them. Its Conqueft by the Englifh. IV.
The Enterprizes of the famous Buccaneers Bartholomew, Brafiliano, Lewis Scot, and John Davis,
who took St. Auguftine. V. The Life and gallant
Actions of the ever memorable Sir Henry Morgan,
and his almoft incredible Enterprizes and Succeffes
againft the Spaniards. VI. Inftitution of the General Affembly, and other Curious Particulars.
VII. Abftract of all the Laws and Statutes in force
in Jamaica. VIII. The firft Affiento Contract.
Enterprizes of the Rebel Negroes. Dreadful
Earthquake. French Invafions. Col. Lillingftone's
Expedition againft Hifpaniola. The Scots Settlement at Darien. Gallant Actions and Death of
Admiral Bembow, &c. IX. Port-Royal burnt to
the Ground. A dreadful Hurricane. Of Black-
beard, a famous Pyrate. Character and Importance
of the Mofqueto Indians. Formidable Power of
the Rebel Negroes. X. The Rebels fubmit to
Terms. Admiral Vernon's Succefs againft Porto-
Bello. XI. Of the Government, Ecclefiaftical,
Civil and Military, of Jamaica. Cuftoms of the
Inhabitants. The Sacrifices, Libations, Exercifes,
and Diverfions of the Negroes, &c. XII. Of the
Products of Jamaica; of its Trees, Plants, Birds,
Beafts, Fifh, Infects, &c. XIII. Its Trade and
Commerce. Its Importance to Great Britain.
Number of its People. Money it returns to Great
Britain. Directions to new Settlers, in relation to
their Healths, &c. In which are briefly inter-
fperfed, The Characters of its Governors and Lieu-
tenant-Governors; viz. Colonel D'Oyley. Major
Sedgewick. Colonel Brayne. Lord Windfor. Sir
Tho. Moddiford. Sir Tho. Lynch. Lord Vaughan.
Earl of Carlifle. Sir Henry Morgan. Colonel
Molefworth. Duke of Albemarle. Earl of Inchi-
quin. Sir William Beefton. General Selwyn.
Peter Beckford, Efq; Earl of Peterborough.
Colonel Handafyde. Ld. Arch. Hamilton. Sir
Nicolas Lawes. Duke of Portland. Major Gen.
Hunter. John Ayfcough, Efq; John Gregory, Efq;

H. Cunningham, Efq; And the prefent Governor, Edward Trelawney, Efq; With Two Maps, one of the Ifland, and the other of the circumjacent Iflands and Territories belonging to France, Spain, &c. The Second Edition. *London*: J. Hodges, 1740. *iv and* 340 *pp. With the two Maps. Calf.* 8*vo.* (7*s.* 6*d.* 1522)

JAMAICA. The Importance of Jamaica to Great Britain, confider'd With fome Account of that Ifland, from its Difcovery in 1492 to this Time: and a Lift of the Governors and Prefidents, with an Account of their Towns, Harbours, Bays, Buildings, Inhabitants, Whites and Negroes, &c. The Country and People cleared from Mifreprefentations; the Mifbehaviour of Spanifh Governors by entertaining Pirates, and plundering the Inhabitants and Merchants of Jamaica, and the Rife of the Pirates among them. An Account of their Fruits, Drugs, Timber and Dying-Woods, and of the Ufes they are apply'd to there: With a Defcription of Exotick Plants, preferved in the Gardens of the Curious in England; and of the Kitchen and Flower-Gardens in the Weft-Indies. Alfo of their Beafts, Birds, Fifhes, and Infects; with their Eatables and Potables, Diftempers and Remedies. With an Account of their Trade and Produce; with the Advantages they are of to Great-Britain, Ireland, and the Colonies in North-America, and the Commodities they take in Return from them, with the Danger they are in from the French at Hifpaniola, and their other Iflands and Settlements on the Continent, by the Encouragements they have over the Britifh Planters. With Inftances of Infults they have given his Majefty's Subjects in the Weft-Indies and on the Main. With the Reprefentations of his late Majefty when Elector of Hanover, and of the Houfe of Lords, againft a Peace, which could not be fafe or honourable if Spain or the Weft-Indies were allotted to any branch of the Houfe of Bourbon. In a Letter to a Gentleman. In which is Added, A Poftfcript, of the Benefits which may arife by keeping of Carthagena, to Great-Britain and our American Colonies; with an Account of what Goods are ufed in the Spanifh Trade, and Hints of fettling it after the French Method (by fending of Women there) and of the Trade and Method of living of the Spaniards and the Englifh South-Sea Company's Factors there. *London:* A. Dodd, [1744]. *Title and 81 pp. half mor. 8vo.* (7s. 6d. 1523)

JAMAICA. Acts of Assembly, passed in the Island of Jamaica; From 1681, to 1754, inclufive. *London:* Curtis Brett and Comp^y. MDCCLVI. *2 prel. leaves; 27 and 358 pp; followed by one leaf of Forms.* 'An Abridgment of the Laws of Jamaica,' *etc. 2 prelim. leaves and 43 pp. Old calf. Fine copy. Folio.* (14s. 6d. 1524)

JAMAICA. An Hiftorical Account of the Seffions of Assembly, for the Island of Jamaica: Which began on Tuefday the 23d of Sept. 1755, Being the Second Seffions of that Affembly. Containing a Vindication of his Excellency Charles Knowles, Efq; Then Governor of that Island; Against feveral groundlefs Accusations that have been brought againft him, particularly from thofe contain'd in a Petition, which has been prefented to his Majesty, by feveral Perfons who called themfelves Members of that Assembly, the Matter of which Petition is now depending. *London:* Printed in the Year MDCCLVII. *76 pp. half mor. 8vo.* (7s. 6d. 1525)

JAMAICA. The Jamaica Association Develop'd. Jamaica: Printed in the Year 1755. *London:* Reprinted 1757. *26 pp. Signed* 'Jamaicanus.' *Half mor. 8vo.* (7s. 6d. 1526)

JAMAICA. The History of Jamaica or General Survey of the Antient and Modern State of that Island: With Reflections on its Situation, Settlements, Inhabitants, Climate, Products, Commerce, Laws, and Government. In Three Volumes. Illustrated with Copper Plates. *London:* T. Lowndes, MDCCLXXIV. *3 Volumes. Vol. I. Title, and 628 pp. Copperplates numbered 1 to 4. Vol. II. Title, and 601 pp. plates numbered 5 to 15. Vol. III. Title viii and pp. 595-976. plate numbered 16. Fine copy. Calf. 4to.* (2l. 12s. 6d. 1527)

JAMAICA. Acts of Assembly Passed in the Island of Jamaica, From 1770, to 1783, inclufive. *Kingston, - - - Jamaica:* Printed for James Jones, Efq: by Lewis and Eberall. M,DCC,LXXXVI. *3 prel. leaves; 31 pp. and pp. 3-424.* ' An Abridgment of the Laws of Jamaica: *etc.* by way of Index,' *etc.* 40 *pp. half calf.* 4*to.* (15*s.* 1528)

JAMAICA. The New Jamaica Almanack, and Register, Calculated to the Meridian of the Island for the Year of our Lord 1798. Being the Second after Bissextile or Leap Year. [Second Edition—Carefully Corrected.] *Kingston:* Printed by Stevenson and Aikman. [1798]. 157 *pp. Index etc.* 15 *pp. Map of Martinico. Morocco.* 12*mo.* (7*s.* 6*d.* 1529)

JAMAICA. The Revised Statutes of Jamaica, as to Crimes and Misdemeanors: Analytically and Alphabetically arranged, down to the Session 6th of Victoria, Anno 1842-3, inclusive. *London:* J. Haddon, 1844. *viii and* 376 *pp.* 8*vo.* (10*s.* 6*d.* 1530)

JAMAICA. Appendix to the Report of the Central Board of Health of Jamaica. Presented to the Legislature under the provisions of the 14th Vic. chap. 60, and printed by order of the Assembly. *Spanish-Town:* F. M. Wilson. 1852. 3 *prel. leaves, and* 282 *pp. Uncut.* 8*vo.* (3*s.* 6*d.* 1531)

JAMES (THOMAS). The/ Strange/ and Dange-/rous Voyage of/ Captaine Thomas Iames, in/ his intended Difcouery of the Northweft/ Paffage into the South Sea./ Wherein The Miseries indvred both/ Going, Wintering, Returning; and the Rarities/ obferued, both Philofophicall and Mathematical,/ are related in this Iournall of it./ Publifhed by His Maiesties/ command./ To which are added, A Plat or Card for the/ Sayling in thofe Seas./ Diuers little Tables of the Author's, of the Va-/riation of the Compaffe, &c./ With/ An Appendix concerning Longitude, by Mafter/ Henry Gellibrand Aftronomy Reader/ of Grefham Colledge in London./ And/ An Aduife concerning the Philofophy of thefe late/ Difco-ueryes, By W. W./ *London,*/ Printed by Iohn Legatt, for Iohn Partridge./ 1633./ 3 *prel. leaves; viz. Title. reverse blank*, ' To the Kings Most/ excellent and Sacred/ Maiestie.'/ 2 *pp.* ' To my worthy friend and fellow-/Templar Captaine Iames.'/ *Signed* 'Thomas Nash.' 1 *page;* ' The Printer de-fires' *etc.* 1 *page; Text* 120 *pp.* ' The Names of the/ feuerall Inftruments, I prouided/ and bought for this Voyage.'/ 2 *pp;* ' This was the manner that we tooke the variation of/ the Compaffe,' *etc.* 4 *pp;*

& blank leaf; 'An Appendix touching/ Longitude./
6 *pp. Signed* ' H. Gellibrand.' 'To the venerable
Artifts and youn-/ger Students in Divinity, in the
famous Vni-/uerfity of Cambridge.'/ 10 *pp. Signed*
' X. Z.' *Green morocco extra by Heyday. The Map
wanting.* 4*to.*   (3*l.* 3*s.* 1532)

JAMES (Thomas). The Dangerous Voyage of
Capt. Thomas James, In his intended Difcovery
of a North West Passage into the South Sea:
Wherein The Miferies indured, both Going, Wintering and Returning, and the Rarities obferv'd
Philofophical, Mathematical and Natural are related in this Journal of it, publifh'd by the Special
Command of King Charles I. To which is added, A
Map for Sailing in thofe Seas: Alfo divers Tables
of the Author's of the Variation of the Compafs,
&c. With an Appendix concerning the Longitude, by Mafter Gellibrand, Aftronomy Reader at
Gresham College. The Second Edition, Revifed
and Corrected. *London:* Printed in 1633, and now
Reprinted for O. Payne, MDCCXL. 5 *prel. leaves,
and* 142 *pp. Map.* 8*vo.*   (16*s.* 1533)

JANEWAY (James.) Mr. James Janeway's/ Le-
gacy/ to his/ Friends,/ Containing Twenty Seven
Fa-/mous Inftances of God's Providen-/ces in and
about Sea Dangers and/ Deliverances, with the
Names of Se-/veral that were Eye-witneffes to
many/ of them./ Whereunto is Added a Sermon
on the/ fame Subject./ *London,* Printed for Dorman Newman, at/ the Kings Armes in the Poultry,
1674./ 4 *prel. leaves; viz. Title and* ' The Epistle
to the Reader,' *Signed* ' John Ryther.' *Text* 134 *pp.
Old calf.* 16*mo.*   (10*s.* 6*d.* 1534)

A great part of this book relates to New England, and other parts
of America.

JANNEY (Thomas.) An/ Epistle/ from Thomas
Janney,/ to/ Friends of Cheshire,/ And by them
defired to be made Publick./ [*Signed*] Thomas
Janney./ From my Houfe near the/ Falls of
Delaware in/ the County of Bucks in/ Penfylvania,
the 16th/ day of the 10th./ Month, 1693./ [*Colophon*] *London,*/ Printed and Sold by T. Sowle,
near the Meeting-Houfe in/ White-hart-court in
Gracious-ftreet, 1694./ 8 *pp. Front margin mutilated.* 4*to.*   (7*s.* 6*d.* 1535)

JAPAN. A Briefe/ Relation/ of the Persecvtion lately made/ Againſt the Catholike Chriſtians in the/ Kingdome of Iaponia,/ Deuided into two Bookes./ Taken out of the Annuall Letters of the Fathers of/ the Society of Iesvs, and other Authenticall/ Informations. Written in Spaniſh, and prin-/ ted firſt at Mexico in the Weſt Indies, the/ yeare of Chriſt M.DC.XVI./ And/ Newly tranſlated into English by W. W. Gent./ The Firſt Part./ Permiſſu Superiorum, M.DC.XIX./ 350 *pp.* 'The Table.' 2 *pp. Old calf. 16mo.* (1*l.* 11*s.* 6*d.* 1536)

JARDINE (L. J.) A Letter from Pennsylvania to a Friend in England : containing Valuable Information with respect to America. By L. J. Jardine, M.D. *Bath*, R. Cruttwell; MDCCXCV. 2 *prel. leaves, and* 31 *pp. 8vo.* (3*s.* 6*d.* 1537)

JAY (JAMES). Dissertatio Medica Inauguralis, de Fluore Albo : Quam annuente summo numine, Ex auctoritate Amplissimi Senatus Academici Edinburgeni, et nobiliſſimæ Facultatis Medicæ decreto; pro gradu Doctoratus, Summisque in Medicina Honoribus et Privilegiis rite et legitime Consequendis, eruditorum examini subjicit Jacobus Jay, Novi Eboracensis. *Edinburgi :* Hamilton, Balfour, et Neill. M,DCC,LIII. 2 *prel. leaves, and* 28 *pp. Half mor. 4to.* (4*s.* 6*d.* 1538)

JAY (*Sir* JAMES.) A Letter to the Universities of Oxford and Cambridge, &c. In reſpect to the Collection that was made for the Colleges of New York and Philadelphia. By Sir James Jay, Knt. M.D. Being A Vindication of the Author, occaſioned by the groundleſs Inſinuations, and very illiberal Behaviour of Mr. Alderman Trecothick, with authentic Evidence. *London:* G. Kearsly, M,DCC,LXXIV. *Title, and* 20 *pp. Half morocco. 8vo.* (4*s.* 6*d.* 1539)

JAY (JOHN). Autograph Address to the Legislature of New York, dated, Albany, 8 Jan. 1798. 1 *page, a fine specimen. 4to.* (10*s.* 6*d.* 1540)

JAY (WILLIAM). A Review of The Causes and Consequences of The Mexican War. By William Jay. *Boston:* Benjamin B. Mussey & Co.; 1849. 333 *pp. Calf. 12mo.* (7*s.* 6*d.* 1541)

JEFFERSON (Thomas). Authentic Copies of the
Correspondence of Thomas Jefferson, Esq. Secretary of State to the United States of America, and
George Hammond, Esq. Minister Plenipotentiary
of Great-Britain, on the Non-Execution of Existing Treaties, the delivering the Frontier Posts,
and on the Propriety of a Commercial Intercourse
between Great-Britain and the United States.
Philadelphia, Printed: *London:* Reprinted J.
Debrett, 1794. *2 Parts.* Part I. *Title and 89 pp.*
Part. II. *Title and* 11 *pp.* 'Papers relative to
Great Britain.' 59 *pp. Half morocco.*
8vo.   (*4s. 6d.* 1542)

JEFFERSON (Thomas). Autograph Letter to
Paul Jones, dated [at Paris] June 24, 1785, respecting an interview with the Count de Vergennes.
page, a fine specimen, with Portrait attached, en-
graved by W. Hall. 4to.   (*1l. 1s.* 1543)

JEFFERYS (Thomas). The Natural and Civil
History of the French Dominions in North and
South America. Giving a particular Account of
the Climate, Soil, Minerals, Animals, Vegetables,
Manufactures, Trade, Commerce and Languages,
together with The Religion, Government, Genius,
Character, Manners and Customs of the Indians
and other Inhabitants. Illustrated by Maps and
Plans of the principal Places, Collected from the
best Authorities, and engraved by T. Jefferys,
Geographer to his Royal Highness the Prince of
Wales. Part I. Containing A Description of
Canada and Louisiana. *London,* Thomas Jefferys,
MDCCLX. Part I. 4 *prel. leaves, and* 168 *pp.* 8 *Maps.*
Part II. 2 *prel. leaves, and* 246 *pp. With* 10 *Maps.*
Folio.   (*1l. 1s.* 1544)

JEFFERYS (Thomas). A Description of the Spa-
nish Islands and Settlements On the Coast of the
West Indies, Compiled from authentic Memoirs,
Revised by Gentlemen who have resided many
Years in the Spanish Settlements; and Illustrated
With Thirty-two Maps and Plans, Chiefly from
original Drawings taken from the Spaniards in
the last War, And Engraved by Thomas Jefferys,
Geographer to His Majesty. *London:* T. Jefferys,
1762. 3 *prel. leaves. xxiv and* 106 *pp. Index 2 pp.*

With the 32 Maps and Plans. Old Calf.
4to. (12s. 6d. 1545)

JEFFERYS (Thomas). Voyages from Asia to
America, For Completing the Discoveries of the
North Weſt Coaſt of America. To which is pre-
fixed, a Summary of the Voyages Made by the
Russians on the Frozen Sea, In Search of a North
East Paſſage. Serving as an Explanation of a Map
of the Ruſſian Diſcoveries, publiſhed by the Acade-
my of Sciences at Peterſburgh. Translated from
the High Dutch of S. Muller, of the Royal
Academy of Peterſburgh. With the Addition of
Three New Maps ; 1. A Copy of Part of the
Japaneſe Map of the World. 2. A Copy of De
Liſle's and Buache's fictitious Map. And 3. A
Large Map of Canada, extending to the Pacific
Ocean, containing the New Diſcoveries made by
the Russians and French. By Thomas Jefferys,
Geographer to his Majeſty. The Second Edition.
London: T. Jefferys, M.DCC.LXIV. *viii and* 120 *pp.*
2 *Maps.* 4to. (8s. 6d. 1546)

JEFFERYS (Thomas). The Great Probability of
a North West Passage: deducted from Observations on the Letter of Admiral De Fonte, Who
ſailed from the Callao of Lima on the Diſcovery of
a Communication between the South Sea and the
Atlantic Ocean ; And to intercept ſome Navigators
from Boſton in New England, whom he met with,
Then in Search of a North West Passage. Proving the Authenticity of the Admiral's Letter.
With Three Explanatory Maps. 1ſt. A Copy of
an authentic Spaniſh Map of America, publiſhed
in 1608. 2d. The Diſcoveries made in Hudſon's
Bay, by Capt. Smith, in 1746 and 1747. 3d. A
General Map of the Diſcoveries of Admiral de
Fonte. By Thomas Jefferys, Geographer to the
King. With an Appendix. Containing the Account of a Discovery of Part of the Coaſt and In-
land Country of Labrador, made in 1753. The
Whole intended for The Advancement of Trade
and Commerce. *London*: Thomas Jefferys, MDCC
LXVIII. *xxiv and text in* 154 *pp. With 3 Maps.*
4to. (10s. 6d. 1547)

JEFFERYS (Thomas). A Description of the Spanish Islands and Settlements On the Coaſt of the

West Indies, Compiled from authentic Memoirs,
Revifed by Gentlemen who have refided many
Years in the Spanish Settlements; and Illustrated
With Thirty-two Maps and Plans, Chiefly from
original Drawings taken from the Spaniards in the
laft War, and Engraved by the late Thomas Jefferys. The Second Edition. *London,* Faden and
Jefferys, 1774. 3 *prel. leaves, xxiv and* 106 *pp. Index*
2 *pp. With the* 32 *maps and plans. Half calf.*
4*to.* (10s. 6d. 1548)

JEVERUM (Jo.) Verzeichnifs Allerhand Pietif-
tifcher Intriguen und Unordnungen, in Litthauen,
vielen Städten Teutfchlandes, Hungarn, und America: Durch Jo. Jeverum, Wiburgenfem. A. C.
MDCCXXIX. *Title and* 173 *pp.* 8*vo.* (10s. 6d. 1549)

JOHN *the Painter.* A Short Account of the Motives
which determined the Man, called John the Painter;
and a justification of his conduct; written by himself, And fent to his Friend, Mr. A. Tomkins, with
a request to publish it after his Execution. *London,*
John Williams M,DCC,LXXVII. *Half-title, title, and*
15 *pp.* 4*to.* (7s. 6d. 1550)

JOHNSON (CHARLES). A General History of the
Robberies and Murders Of the moft notorious Pyrates, and also Their Policies, Difcipline, and Government, From their firft Rise and Settlement in
the Ifland of Providence, in 1717, to the prefent
Year 1724. With The remarkable Actions and Adventures of the two Female Pyrates, Mary Read
and Anne Bonny. To which is prefix'd An Account of the famous Captain Avery and his Companions; with the Manner of his Death in England. The Whole digefted into the following Chapters; Chap. I. Of Captain Avery. II. The Rise of
Pyrates. III. Of Captain Martel. IV. Of Captain Bonnet. V. Of Captain Thatch. VI. Of Captain Vane. VII. Of Captain Rackam. VIII. Of
Captain England. IX. Of Captain Davis. X. Of
Captain Roberts. XI. Of Captain Worley. XII.
Of Captain Lowther. XIII. Of Captain Low.
XIV. Of Captain Evans. And their feveral Crews.
To which is added, A fhort Abstract of the Statute
and Civil Law, in Relation to Pyracy. By Cap-
tain Charles Johnson. *London,* Ch. Rivington

1724. 11 *prel. leaves; and pp.* 17-320. 3 *Copper-*
plates at pp. 86, 117, 202. *Calf. 8vo.* (10s. 6d. 1551)

JOHNSON (Mʳˢ. Jᴀᴍᴇꜱ). The Captive American;
containing an Account of the Sufferings of Mʳˢ.
Johnson, during four years with the Indians and
French. The author, Mrs. Johnson, now Mrs. Haf-
tings, is ftill living in Charleftown, Newhampshire,
and first publifhed her Narrative at Walpole in
Newhampfhire, in the year 1796.—The fufferings
fhe met with during her captivity, fhe bore with a
degree of magnanimity that will aftonifh the reader
while he perufes the following pages. *Air*, Printed
by *J. and P. Wilson*, 1802. 24 *pp. Half mor.*
12*mo.* (4s. 6d. 1552)

JOHNSON (Sᴀᴍᴜᴇʟ). A Letter to Mr. Jonathan
Dickinson, In defence of Ariftocles to Authades,
Concerning the Sovereignty & Promifes Of God.
From Samuel Johnson, D.D. *Boston:* N. E.
Printed and Sold by Rogers and Fowle in Queen-
Street. ᴍᴅᴄᴄxʟᴠɪɪ. 28 *pp. Half morocco.*
8*vo.* (7s. 6d. 1553)

JOHNSON (Sᴀᴍᴜᴇʟ). The Christian indeed; Ex-
plained, in Two Sermons, of Humility and Charity.
Preached at New-Haven, June 28, 1767. And
publifhed at the Defire of Some that heard them.
By Samuel Johnson, D.D. Late Prefident of King's-
College at New-York now Miffionary from the
Society for propagating the Gofpel, and Rector of
Christ's-Church, at Stratford. *New Haven;* Printed
by Thomas and Samuel Green. ᴍ,ᴅᴄᴄ,ʟxᴠɪɪɪ. 24
pp. half mor. 8*vo.* (6s. 6d. 1554)

JOHNSON (Sᴀᴍᴜᴇʟ). A Demonstration of the
Reafonablenefs, Ufefulnefs, and Great Duty of
Prayer. By Samuel Johnfon, D.D. Prefident of
King's College, and Lecturer of Trinity Church,
in New-York. *New-York:* Printed by W. Weyman, in Broad-ftreet, not far from the Exchange,
1760. 28 *pp.* ' A Letter to a Friend, relating to
the fame Subject.' 6 *pp.* ' Advertisement,' *and* ' A
fhort Tract on Mysteries.' 4 *pp. Half morocco.*
8*vo.* (7s. 6d. 1555)

JOHNSON (*Sir* Wɪʟʟɪᴀᴍ). Autograph Letter to
Governor Shirley, May 4th, 1755, respecting the

imployment of the Indians in military services and
money affairs. *2 pages. An important Letter.*
Folio. (15s. 1556)

JOHNSON (*Sir* WILLIAM). Autograph draft of a
Letter to General Gage, dated at Johnson's hall,
Nov. 23, 1769, on public and Indian Affairs. *2
large pages, not signed. Folio.* (7s. 6d. 1557)

JOHNSTON (THOMAS). Travels through Lower
Canada, interspersed with Canadian Tales & Anec-
dotes, and Interesting Information to intending
Emigrants. By Thomas Johnston. *Edinburgh:*
J. Glass, 1827. *Frontispiece and 96 pp. Unbound.*
12mo. (3s. 6d. 1558)

JOHNSTONE (WALTER). A Series of Letters descriptive of Prince Edward Island, in the Gulph
of St. Laurence, addressed to the Rev. John
Wightman, Minister of Kirkmahoe, Dumfries-
Shire. By Walter Johnstone, a Native of the
same Country. The Author of these Letters went
out for the express purpose of surveying Prince
Edward Island, and collecting information on the
subject of Emigration. During two Summers, and
one Winter, he was assiduously engaged in the
prosecution of this object; and the small Volume
now presented to the Public, will be found to contain a full and particular Account of the Climate,
Soil, Natural Productions, and Mode of Husbandry adopted in the Island; together with
Sketches of Scenery, Manners of the Inhabitants,
&c. &c.; the whole being intended for the guid-
ance of future Emigrants, particularly as to what
Implements and Necessaries it may be proper to
provide themselves with before crossing the Atlantic. *Dumfries:* J. Swan. 1822. *72 pp. Uncut.*
12mo. (4s. 6d. 1559)

JOHNSTONE (WALTER). Travels in Prince Edward Island, Gulf of St. Lawrence, North-America, In the Years 1820-21. Undertaken with a
Design to Establish Sabbath Schools, And Inves-
tigate the Religious State of the Country: Wherein
is given a Short Account of the Different Denominations of Christians, their Former History and
Present Condition, interspersed with Notes relative to the various Clergymen that have officiated

on the Island. By Walter Johnstone, Author of
" A Series of Letters " descriptive of that Island.
Edinburgh: David Brown, 1823. 132 *pp. With
map.* 12*mo.* (4*s.* 6*d.* 1560)

JONES (JAMES ATHEARN). Traditions of the North
American Indians : Being a second and revised
Edition of " Tales of an Indian Camp." By John
Athearn Jones. In Three Volumes. *London:*
Henry Colburn and Richard Bentley, 1830. 3
Volumes. Vol. I. 30 *prel. leaves, and* 312 *pp.
Frontispiece, and Plate at page* 158. Vol. II. 3
prel. leaves, and 336 *pp. Frontispiece, and Plate at*
page 204. Vol. III. 3 *prel. leaves, and* 341 *pp.
Frontispiece and Plate at page* 204. *Uncut, in boards.*
8*vo.* (7*s.* 6*d.* 1561)

JONES (PAUL). Paul-Jones ou Prophéties sur
L'Amérique, L'Angleterre, La France, L'Espagne,
La Hollande, &c. Par Paul-Jones Corsaire, Pro-
phéte & Sorcier comme il n'en fût jamais. Y Joint
Le Rêve d'un Suisse sur La Révolution de
L'Amérique, Dédié à Son Excellence Mgneur
l'Ambaffadeur Franklin, & à leurs Nobles &
Hautes Puissances Messeigneurs du Congrès. De
L'Ere de L'Independance de L'Amerique L'An
V. [1797] 120 *pp. Half morocco. Uncut.*
8*vo.* (5*s.* 6*d.* 1562)

JONES (PAUL). Retained copies of two autograph
Letters addressed to the Baron Vander Capellan
&c. at Amsterdam, dated on board the Serapis at
the Texel, Oct. 19, 1779, and on board the Alliance,
Nov. 29, 1779. 3 *pages, in the autograph of Paul
Jones, but not signed.* 4*to.* (15*s.* 1563)

JORGENSEN (JORGEN). State of Christianity in
the Island of Otaheite, and a defence of the pure
precepts of the Gospel, against Modern Anti-
christs, with reasons for the ill success which
attends Christian Missionaries in their attempts to
convert the Heathens. By a Foreign Traveller.
London, J. Richardson, 1811. *Title and* 175 *pp.*
8*vo.* (3*s.* 6*d.* 1564)

JOSEPH (E. L.) History of Trinidad, by E. L.
Joseph. *Trinidad.* Henry James Mills. [1838]
ix and 272 *pp.* 12*mo.* (4*s.* 6*d.* 1565)

JOSEPH and BENJAMIN, a Conversation. Translated from a French Manuscript. *London :* Printed
at the Logographic Press for J. Murray,
MDCCLXXXVII. *2 prel. leaves; xv and 238 pp. Uncut.*
12mo. (10s. 6d. 1566)

JOSSELYN (JOHN). An/ Account/ of two/ Voy-
ages/ to/ New-England./ Wherein you have the
fetting out of a Ship,/ with the charges ;/ The prices
of all neceffaries for/ furnifhing a Planter and his
Family at his firft com-/ing; A Defcription of the
Countrey, Natives and/ Creatures, with their Mer-
chantil and Phyfical ufe; The Government of the
Countrey as it is now pof-/feffed by the Englifh,
&c. A large Chronological Ta-/ble of the moft
remarkable paffages, from the firft dif-/covering of
the Continent of America, to the year/ 1673. By
John Joffelyn Gent./ *London,* Printed for Giles
Widdows, at the Green-Dragon/ in St. Paul's-
Church-yard, 1674./ *4 prel. leaves; viz. License,
Title, Dedication, To the Reader, and Errata; Text
279 pp. Books, etc. 3 pp. 16mo.* (2l. 2s. 1567)

JOURDAN. A Plaine/ Description/ of the Bar-
mvdas,/ now called Sommer/ Ilands./ With the
manner of their difcouerie/ Anno 1609. by the fhip-
wrack and admirable deliuerance/ of Sir Thomas
Gates, and Sir George Sommers, wherein/ are
truly fet forth the commodities and profits of/ that
Rich, Pleafant, and Healthfull/ Covntrie./ With/
An Addition, or more ample relation of diuers other
remarkable matters concerning thofe/ Iflands fince
then experienced, lately fent/ from thence by one
of the Colonie now/ there refident./ *London,/*
Printed by W. Stansby, for W. Welby./ 1613./
4 prel. leaves ; viz. Title, the reverse blank, ' To the
trvly Honorable and Right Worthy Knight Sir
Thomas Smith,' *etc. 6 pp. in roman letter, signed
'W. C.' Text in large Black Letter in 20 unnumbered leaves,* ' A Copie of the Articles which Mafter
R. More, Gouernour Deputie of the Sommer Ilands,
propounded to the Companie *etc.* Anno 1612.' *3 pp.
in roman type. Olive morocco extra gilt by Bedford.*
4to. (8l. 8s. 1568)

JOURNAL of the Expedition to La Guira and Porto
Cavallos in the West-Indies, Under the Command

of Commodore Knowles. In a Letter from an Officer on board the Burford to his Friend at London. *London:* J. Robinson, 1744. *63 pp. half mor.* *8vo.* (7s. 6d. 1569)

JOURNAL of the Proceedings of the Congress, Held at Philadelphia, September 5th, 1774. Containing, The Bill of Rights; A Lift of Grievances; Occafional Refolves; The Affociation; An Addrefs to the People of Great Britain; A Memorial to the Inhabitants of the Britifh American Colonies; and, An Addrefs to the Inhabitants of the Province of Quebec. Publifhed by Order of the Congress. To which is added, (Being now first printed by Authority) an Authentic Copy of the Petition to the King. *London:* E. and C. Dilly. M.DCC.LXXV. *Half-title and 66 pp. Half mor. 8vo.* (4s. 6d. 1570)

This Pamphlet contains only that part of the Journal of the proceedings of the Congress that was omitted in the Pamphlet entitled, " Extracts from the Votes and Proceedings of the Congress."

JOUTEL. A Journal Of the Last Voyage Perform'd by Monfr. de la Sale, to the Gulph of Mexico, To find out the Mouth of the Miffifipi River; Containing An Account of the Settlements he endeavour'd to make on the Coaft of the aforefaid Bay, his unfortunate Death, and the Travels of his Companions for the Space of Eight Hundred Leagues acrofs that Inland Country of America, now call'd Louifiana, (and given by the King of France to M. Crozat,) till they came into Canada. Written in French by Monfieur Joutel, A Commander in that Expedition; And Translated from the Edition just publifh'd at Paris. With an exact Map of that vaft Country, and a Copy of the Letters Patents granted by the K. of France to M. Crozat. *London,* A. Bell, 1714. *16 prel. leaves, 205 pp. and 5 pp. of Index. Calf. 8vo.* (15s. 1571)

JUSTICE (THE) and Necessity of Taxing the American Colonies, Demonftrated. Together with a Vindication of the Authority of Parliament. *London:* J. Almon, 1766. *36 pp. Half morocco.* *8vo.* (4s. 6d. 1572)

JUSTICE (THE) and Policy of the late Act of Parliament for Making more effectual Provision for the Government of the Province of Quebec, As-

serted and Proved: And the Conduct of Administration respecting that Province Stated and Vindicated. *London:* Printed in the Year 1774. *32 pp.
Half mor. 8vo.* (5s. 6d. 1573)

JUSTICE (The) and Policy of the late Act of Parliament, for Making more Effectual Provifion for
the Government of the Province of Quebec, Asserted and Proved; and the Conduct of Administration respecting that Province, stated and Vindicated. *London:* J. Wilkie, MDCCLXXIV. *90 pp.
Half mor. 8vo.* (5s. 6d. 1574)

JUAN (George). A Voyage to South America:
Describing at large The Spanish Cities, Towns,
Provinces, &c. on that extenfive Continent. In-
terspersed throughout With Reflections on the
Genius, Customs, Manners, and Trade of the In-
habitants; together with The Natural History of
the Country. And An Account of their Gold and
Silver Mines. Undertaken by Command of his
Majefty the King of Spain, By Don George Juan,
and Don Antonio de Ulloa, Both Captains of the
Spanish Navy, Members of the Royal Societies of
London and Berlin, And correfponding Members
of the Royal Academy at Paris. Tranflated from
the Original Spanish. Illuftrated with Copper
Plates. In Two Volumes. *London:* L. Davis and
C. Reymers, MDCCLVIII. *Two Volumes.* Vol. I.
xxiv and 509 pp. Vol. II. *3 prel. leaves; and 420
pp. Index 18 pp. Copperplates in the two volumes
numbered I to VII. Calf. 8vo.* (8s. 6d. 1575)

JUAN (George). A Voyage to South-America:
Defcribing at Large The Spanish Cities, Towns,
Provinces, &c. on that extenfive Continent. In-
terfperfed throughout with Reflections on the
Genius, Cuftoms, Manners, and Trade of the In-
habitants; Together with the Natural History of
the Country. And an Account of Their Gold and
Silver Mines. Undertaken by Command of His
Majefty tLe King of Spain, by Don George Juan,
and Don Antonio de Ulloa, Both Captains of the
Spanish Navy, Members of the Royal Societies of
London and Berlin, And Correfponding Members
of the Royal Academy at Paris. Tranflated from
the Original Spanish. Illuftrated with Copper-
Plates. In Two Volumes. *Dublin:* William

Williamson, MDCCLVIII. *Two Volumes.* Vol. I.
378 pp. Plates at pp. 127, 159, 341. *Vol. II.* 2 *prel.
leaves, and Text pp.* 9-356. *Plates at pp.* 15, 192.
Calf. 8vo. (8s. 6d. 1576)

JUAN (GEORGE). A Voyage to South America.
Describing at large, The Spanish Cities, Towns,
Provinces, &c. on that extenfive Continent. Interspersed throughout With Reflections on whatever is peculiar in the Religion and Civil Policy;
in the Genius, Customs, Manners, Dress, &c. &c.
of the feveral Inhabitants; whether Natives,
Spaniards, Creoles, Indians, Mulattoes, or Negroes.
Together with The Natural as well as the Com-
mercial History of the Country. And an Account
of their Gold and Silver Mines. Undertaken by
Command of the King of Spain, By Don George
Juan, and Don Antonio de Ulloa, Both Captains
of the Spanish Navy; and Members of the Royal
Societies of London and Berlin; and of the Royal
Academy at Paris. Tranflated from the Original
Spanifh. Illuftrated with Copper Plates In Two
Volumes. The Second Edition, revifed and cor-
rected. *London:* L. Davis and C. Reymers, MDCC
LX. *Two Volumes.* Vol. I. xxiv *and* 498. *Plates
numbered* I *to* v. Vol. II. 2 *prel. leaves; and* 410 *pp.
Index* 18 *pp. Plates numbered* VI *and* VII. *Calf.*
8vo. (7s. 6d. 1577)

JUAN (GEORGE). A Voyage to South America.
Described at large, The Spanish Cities, Towns,
Provinces, &c. on that extenfive Continent. Un-
dertaken by Command of the King of Spain, By
Don George Juan, and Don Antonio de Ulloa,
Both Captains of the Spanish Navy; Fellows of
the Royal Society of London; Members of the
Royal Academy at Paris, &c. &c. Tranflated from
the Original Spanish. The Third Edition: To
which are added, By Mr. John Adams, of Wal-
tham-Abbey, who refided feveral Years in thofe
Parts, Occasional Notes and Observations; an
Account of fome Parts of the Brazils, hitherto un-
known to the English Nation; and a Map of South
America corrected. *London:* Lockyer Davis,
MDCCLXXII. *Two Volumes.* Vol. I. xxiv *and* 479 *pp.
Plates numbered* I *to* v. Vol. II. 2 *prel. leaves, and*
419 *pp. Index* 14 *pp. Plates numbered* VI *and* VII.
Calf. 8vo. (8s. 6d. 1578)

JUAN (GEORGE). A Voyage to South America:
describing at large the Spanish Cities, Towns,
Provinces, &c. on that Extensive Continent; un-
dertaken, by command of the King of Spain, by
Don George Juan, and Don Antonio de Ulloa,
Captains of the Spanish Navy, Fellows of the
Royal Society of London, Members of the Royal
Academy at Paris, &c. &c. Translated from the
Original Spanish with Notes and Observations: and
An Account of the Brazils. By John Adams, Esq.
of Waltham Abbey; Who resided several Years
in those Parts. The Fifth Edition. Illustrated
with Plates. *London :* John Stockdale, 1807. *Two
Volumes.* Vol. I. *xxvii and* 479 *pp. Plates numbered*
I *to* v. Vol. II. *iv and* 419 *pp. Index* 14 *pp. Plates
numbered* vi *and* vii. 8vo.　　　(7s. 6d. 1579)

JUAN (GEORGE). Historiche Reisbeschryving van
geheel Zuid-America; gedaan op bevel des Kon-
ings van Spanje, door Don George Juan, Comman-
deur van Aliaga, Ridder van Maltha, en Bevel-
hebber van de Compagnie der Edele Opzieneren
over de Scheepsvaart; en door Don Antonio de
Ulloa, Luitenant van dezelfde Compagnie; Beiden,
Opperbevelhebberen der Spaanfche Zeemagt; Le-
den van de Koninglyke Genootfchappen van Lon-
den en Berlin; en, Correspondenten van der Koninglyke Maatfchappye der Wetenfchappen te
Parys. Verfierd met zeer fraaije Afbeeldingen,
Platte Gronden en Kaarten, door voorname
Meefters gegraveerd, en voorzien van de vere-
ifchte Bladwyzers. Te Goes, By Jacobus Huys-
man, M.DCC.LXXI. [*Colophon*] *In's Gravenhage,*
Jacobus van Karnebeek, 1771. *Two Volumes.*
Eerste Deel. 4 *prel. leaves; xxiv and* 428 *pp. Frontispiece, and Plates numbered* I *to* xii. Tweede Deel.
M.DCC.LXXII. [*Colophon*] 1773. *viii, iv, and* 407
pp. Plates numbered xiii *to* xxv. *Uncut & unbound.*
4to.　　　　　　　　　(12s. 6d. 1580)

JULIUS (N. H.) Nordamerikas fittliche Zuftände.
Nach eigenen Anfchauungen in den Jahren 1834,
1835, und 1836, von Dr. N. H. Julius. Boden
und Gefchichte Religiöfes Erziehung und Un-
terricht. Armuth und Mildthätigkeit. Volk und
Gefellfchaft. Mit einer von Nordamerika und zwei
Mufikbeilagen. *Leipzig:* F. A. Brockhaus. 1839.

2 *Volumes.* Erster Band. *xxviii and* 514 *pp. Map.*
Zweiter Band. *xii and* 504 *pp.* 67 'Tafel' *and*
13 *Plates. Uncut. 8vo.* (7s. 6d. 1581)

JULIAN (Antonio). La Perla de la America,
Provincia de Santa Marta, reconocida, obser-
vada, y expuefta en discursos historicos por el
Sacerdote Don Antonio Julian, á mayor bien de
la Católica Monarquia, fomento del comercio de
España, y de todo el Nuevo Reyno de Granada, é
incremento .de la Christiana Religion entre las
naciones barbaras, que subsisten todavia rebeldes
en la Provincia. *Madrid*, MDCCLXXXVII. Don
Antonio de Sancha. *Title, xxx and* 280 *pp. Half
calf. 4to.* (10s. 6d. 1582)

JULIAN (Antonio). Trasformazione dell' Ame-
rica o sia Trionfo della S. Chiesa Su la Rovina
della Monarchìa del Demonio in America dopo la
Conquista fattane da' Monarchi delle Spagne : Con
Riflessioni Apologetiche, E coll' aggiunta di una
Dissertazione Critico-Espositiva, nella quale spieg-
andosi le parole di S. Pietro Epi. I. c. 3. Qui in-
creduli fuerant in diebus Noe, cum fabricaretur
Arca. vv. 18. 19. 20. Dimostrasi con valide ragioni,
essere tutto ciò accaduto nell' America. Opera del
Sacerdote Antonio Juliàn Stato per molti anni
Missionario in quelle parti. In *Roma* MDCCXC.
xii and 286 *pp. With copperplate Frontispiece. Calf.
8vo.* (10s. 6d. 1583)

JUDSON (L. Carroll). A Biography of the Sign-
ers of the Declaration of Independance, and of
Washington and Patrick Henry. With an Appendix, containing the Constitution of the United
States and other Documents. By L. Carroll Judson, a Member of the Philadelphia Bar. *Philadelphia*: J. Dobson, and Thomas Cowperthwait &
Co. 1839. *ix and pp.* 9-354. *8vo.* (6s. 1584)

KALM (Peter). Travels into North
America; containing Its Natural
History, and A circumſtantial Account of its Plantations and Agri-
culture in general, with the Civil,
Ecclesiastical and Commercial State
of the Country, The Manners of
the Inhabitants, and ſeveral curious and Important
Remarks on various Subjeċts. By Peter Kalm,
Profeſſor of Oeconomy in the Univerſity of Aobo
in Swediſh Findland, and Member of the Swediſh
Royal Academy of Sciences. Translated into
Engliſh By John Reinhold Forster, F.A.S. En-
riched with a Map, ſeveral Cuts for the Illuſtration
of Natural Hiſtory, and ſome additional Notes.
Warrington: William Eyres. MDCCLXX. *3 Volumes.*
Vol. I. *xvi and* 400 *pp.* 'Advertisement.' 1 *page.*
Copperplates at pp. 273, & 322. Vol. II. *London:*
T. Lowndes, MDCCLXXI. 352 *pp. Copperplates at pp.*
79, 82, 90, 274. Vol. III. *London:* T. Lowndes,
MDCCLXXI. *viii and* 310 *pp. Index* 14 *pp. List of
Subscribers,* 8 *pp. Map of North America.*
8*vo.*   (15s. 1585)

KEATH (*Sir* William). A Collection of Papers
and other Tracts, Written occaſionally; containing,
I. An Essay on the Nature of a Public Spirit.
II. The Citizen. Containing Twenty-five Diſcourſes on Trade, with other Praċtical and Moral
Subjeċts, tending to encourage and promote both
publick and private Virtue. III. A Dissertation
on the Liberty of the Subject in Great-Britain.
IV. An Essay on the Education of a Young
Britiſh Nobleman. V. Observations on the Office
of an Ambassador. VI. A Discourse on the preſent State of the Britiſh Plantations in America,
with Reſpeċt to the Intereſt of Great-Britain.
VII. A Report to the Right Hon. the Lords Com-

miffioners of Trade and Plantations in the Year 1718. VIII. A Discourse on the Medium of Commerce. IX. Some ufeful Obfervations on the Confequences of the War with Spain, 1740. By Sir William Keath, Bart. The Second Edition. *London* : Jacob Loyseau, MDCCXLIX. *xxiv and 228 pp.* 12*mo.* (7*s.* 6*d.* 1586)

KEATING (MAURICE). The Genuine Narrative Of the Life and Tranfactions of Major Maurice Keating, The noted Pirate and Murderer, Who was executed on Monday the 27th of December, 1784, at Cuckold's Point, near Port-Royal, in the Ifland of Jamaica. Which contains a particular account of his being fhipwrecked and reduced to the greateft neceffities, and afterwards being concerned with three others in feizing the fchooner Friendfhip, Captain William Lewis, bound from Virginia to St. Thomas's, in which they had agreed to take their paffage, with the fixt refolution to feize the veffel the firft opportunity, and to murder all the perfons belonging to her, without diftinction ; in which diabolical fcheme they too well succeeded.—On the Captain, Mate, and particularly on a Mr. Wilkinfon, who was alfo a paffenger, they exercifed the moft unheard of cruelty, although the unhappy gentleman begged earneftly for his life in the moft pathetic manner.—The particulars of the extraordinary manner of his being difcovered, and his confeffion of the whole tranfaction before the magiftrates at Kingfton.—Likewife an account of his behaviour at the place of execution, and a particular narration of his life, which he delivered to a gentleman the night before he fuffered. N.B. This Narrative is publifhed as a caution to captains of fhips to be particularly careful what paffengers they take on board ; and is one of the moft bloody fcenes of villainy ever heard of fince the time of the noted pirate Blackbeard. To which is added, A True and Faithful Account of the Loss of the Brigantine Tyrrell, And the uncommon Hardfhips fuffered by the Crew. *London* : Printed by J. Miller, No. 74, Rofemary-lane. [1784] 16 *pp. half mor.* 8*vo.* (10*s.* 6*d.* 1587)

KEATING (WILLIAM H.) Narrative of an Expedition to the Source of St. Peter's River, Lake

Winnepeek, Lake of the Woods, &c. &c. Performed in the year 1823, by order of the Hon. J. C. Calhoun, Secretary of War, under the Command of Stephen H. Long, Major U. S. T. E. Compiled from the Notes of Major Long, Messrs. Say, Keating, and Colhoun, by William H. Keating, A.M. &c. Professor of Mineralogy and Chemistry as applied to the Arts, in the University of Pennsylvania; Geologist and Historigrapher to the Expedition. In Two Volumes. *Philadelphia :* H. C. Carey & J. Lea. 1824. 2 *Volumes.* Vol. I. 7 *prel. leaves, and pp.* 9-439. *With 5 plates.* Vol. II. 3 *prel. leaves, and pp.* 5-459. *With* 10 *plates. Uncut.* 8*vo.* (12*s.* 6*d.* 1588)

KEATING (William H.) Narrative of an Expedition to the Source of St. Peter's River, Lake Winnepeek, Lake of the Woods, &c. Performed in the year 1823, by order of the Hon. J. C. Calhoun, Secretary of War, under the Command of Stephen H. Long, U. S. T. E. Compiled from the Notes of Major Long, Messrs. Say, Keating, & Colhoun, By William H. Keating, A.M. &c. Professor of Mineralogy and Chemistry, as applied to the Arts, in the University of Pennsylvania; Geologist and Historiographer to the Expedition. In Two Volumes. *London :* Geo. B. Whittaker, 1825. 2 *Volumes.* Vol. I. *xvi and* 458 *pp. With* 5 *plates.* Vol. II. *vi and* 248 *pp.* 'Appendix.' 156 *pp.* 3 *folded Sheets and* 10 *plates. Uncut.* 8*vo.* (10*s.* 6*d.* 1589)

KEENE (Richard Raynal). A Letter of Vindication to Colonel Munroe, President of the United States: By Richard Raynal Keene, Colonel in the late Constitutional Service of Spain. *London :* Printed by Ambrose Cuddon, 1824. 86 *pp. Uncut.* 8*vo.* (2*s.* 6*d.* 1590)

KEITH (George). The/ Presbyterian and Independent/ Vifible Churches/ in/ New-England/ And elfe-where,/ Brought to the Teft, and examined accor-/ding to the Doctrine of the holy Scriptures,/ in their Doctrine, Miniftry, Worfhip, Confti-/tution, Government, Sacraments and Sabbath/ Day, and found to be No True Church of/ Chrift./ More particularly directed to thefe in

New-Eng-/land, and more generally to thofe in Old-/England, Scotland, Ireland, &c./ With/ A Call and Warning from the Lord to the People/ of Bofton and New-England, to Repent, &c. And two/ Letters to the Preachers in Bofton; and an Anfwer to the/ grofs Abufes, Lyes and Slanders of Increase Mather and Samuel Norton, &c./ By George Keith./ *Philadelphia*, Printed and Sold by Will. Bradford,/ Anno 1689./ *6 prel. leaves; viz. Texts* 1 *page. Title, reverse blank.* 'A Friendly Epistle.' *etc.* 7 *pp.* 'Errata.' 1 *page. Text* 232 *pp. Small 8vo.* (5*l.* 5*s.* 1591)

KEITH (George). The/ Presbyterian and Inde-pendent/ visible/ Churches/ in/ New=England/ And elfe-where,/ Brought to the Teft, and ex-amined according to the/ Doctrin of the holy Scriptures, in their Doctrin,/ Miniftry, Worfhip, Conftitution, Government, Sacraments,/ and Sab-bath Day./ More particularly directed to thofe in New-England, and/ more generally to thofe in Old-England, Scotland,/ Ireland, &c./ With/ A Call and Warning from the Lord to the People of/ Bofton and New-England, to Repent, &c. And two/ Letters to the Preachers in Bofton; and an Anfwer to/ the grofs Abufes, Lies and Slanders, of Increase Mather/ and Nath. Morton, &c,/ By George Keith./ *London:*/ Printed for Thomas Northcott, in George-Yard/ in Lombard-ftreet, 1691./ *5 prel. leaves, and* 230 *pp. Calf. Small 8vo.* (2*l.* 2*s.* 1592)

KEITH (George). A/ Serious Appeal/ To all the more Sober, Impartial & Judicious People/ in/ Nevv-England/ To whofe Hands this may come,/ Whether Cotton Mather in his late Addrefs, &c. hath not/ extreamly failed in proving the People call'd Quakers guilty/ of manifold Herefies, Blaf-phemies and ftrong Delufions,/ and whether he hath not much rather proved himfelf ex-/treamly Ignorant and greatly poffeffed with a Spirit of/ Perverfion, Error, Prejudice and envious Zeal againft them/ in general, and G. K. in particular, in his moft uncharit-/able and rafh Judgment againft him./ Together with a Vindication of our/ Christian Faith/ In thofe Things Sincerely Be-lieved by us, efpecially refpect-/ing the Funda-

mental Doctrines and Principles of/ Christian
Religion./ By George Keith./ Printed and Sold
by William Bradford at *Philadelphia* in Pennfyl-/
vania, in the Year 1692./ *Title reverse blank,* 'A
few Words of Preface.' 2 *pp.* *Text* 67 *pp.* *half
calf.* 4*to.* (3*l.* 3*s.* 1593)

KEITH (GEORGE). The/ Doctrine/ of the Holy/
Apoftles and Prophets the Foundation/ of the
Church of Chrift,/ As it was Delivered in a/ Ser-
mon/ At Her Majefties Chappel, at/ Boston in
New-England, the/ 14th. of June 1702./ By George
Keith, M.A./ *Boston:/* Printed for Samuel Phil-
lips at the Brick Shop. 1702./ *Title, and* 17 *pp.*
half mor. 4*to.* (1*l.* 1*s.* 1594)

KEITH (GEORGE). The Notes of the/ True Church/
With the Application of them to the/ Church of
England,/ And the great Sin of Seperation from
Her./ Delivered in A/ Sermon Preached at/
Trinity Church in New-York,/ Before the Ad-
miniftration of the holy Sacrament/ of the Lords
Supper./ The 7th of November, 1703./ By George
Keith, M.A./ Printed and Sold by William Brad-
ford at the Sign of the Bible/ in *New-York,* 1704./
4 *prel. leaves; viz. Title and Epistle, and* 20 *pp. half
morocco.* 4*to.* (1*l.* 1*s.* 1595)

KEITH (GEORGE). The/ Power/ of the/ Gospel,/
in the/ Conversion of Sinners/ in a/ Sermon/
Preach'd at/ Annapolis In Maryland,/ By George
Keith, M.A./ July the 4th/ [*Annapolis?*] Printed
and are to be Sold by Thomas Reading,/ at the
Sign of the George, Anno Domini MDCCIII./ *Title
and* 19 *pp. half mor.* 4*to.* (1*l.* 11*s.* 6*d.* 1596)

KEITH (GEORGE). The great Neceffity & Ufe/ of
the/ Holy Sacraments/ of/ Baptifm & the Lords
Supper,/ Delivered In A/ Sermon/ Preached at/
Trinity-Church in New-York,/ The 28th of November, 1703./ By George Keith, M.A./ Printed
and Sold by William Bradford at the Sign of the
Bible in/ *New-York,* 1704./ 24 *pp. half morocco.*
4*to.* (1*l.* 11*s.* 6*d.* 1597)

KEITH (GEORGE). Some brief Remarks upon a
late Book, en-/tituled, George Keith once more
brought to/ the Teft, &c. having the Name of

F F

Caleb/ Pufey at the end of the Preface, and C. P./ at the end of the Book./ [*New-York*, 1704]. 20 *pp. half mor.* 4to. (1*l.* 11*s.* 6*d.* 1598)

KENNEDY (Archibald). Serious Considerations on the Prefent State of the Affairs of the Northern Colonies. By Archibald Kennedy, Efq; Author of *The Importance of Gaining and Preserving the Friendſhip of the Indians of the Six Nations, to the British Interest, considered.* New York, Printed: *London,* Reprinted for R. Griffiths, [1754.] 24 *pp. half mor.* 8*vo.* (7*s.* 6*d.* 1599)

KENTUCKY. A Description of Kentucky, in North America: To which are prefixed Miscellaneous Observations respecting the United States. [*London*], Printed in November, 1792. 124 *pp.* 8*vo.* (6*s.* 6*d.* 1600)

KER, of KERSLAND (John). The Memoirs of John Ker, of Kerfland, in North Britain, Efq; Relating to Politicks, Trade, and History. In Three Parts. Containing his Secret Tranſactions and Negotiations in Scotland, England, the Courts of Vienna, Hanover and other Foreign Parts. With An Account of the Rife and Progreſs of the Oſtend Company in the Auſtrian Netherlands. Publiſhed by Himſelf. The Third Edition. *London:* Printed in the year M.DCC.XXVII. *Three Parts in Two Volumes.* Part I. 8 *prel. leaves,* 180 *pp. Index* 4 *pp.* Part II. M.DCC.XXVI. *Title, viii* and 184 *pp. Index* 6 *pp.* Part III and Last. 2 *prel. leaves, vi and* 221 *pp.* 'Remarks,' *etc.* 1727. 160 *pp.* 'Appendix.' 16 *pp. Fine copy in old calf gilt.* 8*vo.* (10*s.* 6*d.* 1601)

KIDD (*Captain* William). A full/ Account/ of the/ Proceedings/ In Relation to/ Capt. Kidd./ In two Letters./ Written by a Perſon of Quality to a/ Kinſman of the Earl of Bellomont/ in Ireland./ *London,*/ Printed and Sold by the Bookſellers of London and/ Weſtminſter. MDCCI./ 4 *prel. leaves,* and 51 *pp.* 4to. (12*s.* 6*d.* 1602)

KIDD (*Captain* William). A full/ Account/ of the/ Proceedings/ In Relation to/ Capt. Kidd./ In Two Letters./ Written by a Perſon of Quality to a/ Kinſman of the Earl of Bellomont in Ireland./ The Second Edition./ *London,*/ Printed and Sold

by the Bookfellers of London/ and Weftminfter.
1701./ 41 *pp. Half mor. 8vo.* (12s. 6d. 1603)

KINGSLEY (JAMES LUCE). A Historical Dis-
course, delivered by request before the Citizens of
New Haven, April 25, 1838, the Two Hundredth
Anniversary of the First Settlement of the Town
and Colony. By James L. Kingsley. *New Haven:*
B. & W. Noyes. 1838. 115 *pp. 8vo.* (3s. 6d. 1604)

KIRKLAND (SAMUEL). Autograph Letter to Sir
William Johnson, dated at Kannandausaga, Feb.
21, 1766. 1 *page, large Folio.* (10s. 6d. 1605)

Mr. Kirkland was one of the earliest American Missionaries among
the Indians.

KIRKLAND (SAMUEL). Autograph Letter 'For
Mr. David McCluer, Student at Rev. Mr. Whee-
locks School in New England' dated at Kannandausaga, 11 March 1766. 2 *pp. 4to.* (7s. 6d. 1606)

KIRKBY (RICHARD). An Account of the Arraign-
ments and Tryals of Col. Richard Kirkby, Capt.
John Conftable, Capt. Cooper Wadé, Capt. Sa-
muel Vincent, and Capt. Chriftopher Fogg, on A
Complaint exhibited by the Judge-Advocate on be-
half of Her Majesty, at a Court-Martial held on
Board the Ship Breda in Port-Royal Harbour in
Jamaica in America, the 8th, 9th, 10th, and 12th
Days of October, 1702. For Cowardice, Neglect of
Duty, Breach of Orders, and Other Crimes, Com-
mitted by them in a Fight at Sea, commenced the
19th of Auguft 1702, off of St. Martha, in the
Latitude of Ten Degrees North ,near the Main-
Land of America, Between the Honourable John
Benbow Efq; and Admiral Du Caffe with Four
French Ships of War. For which Col. Kirkby and
Capt. Wade were Sentenc'd to be Shot to Death.
Transmitted from Two Eminent Merchants at Port-
Royal in Jamaica, to a Perfon of Quality in the
City of London. *London:* John Gellibrand. *Title*
& 10 *pp. half mor. Folio.* (10s. 6d. 1607)

KNOWLES (*Sir* CHARLES). Autograph Letter dated
at Jamaica Nov. 24, 1752. 2 *pages.*
4to. (7s. 6d. 1608)

KNOX (JOHN). An Historical Journal of the Campaigns in North-America, for The Years 1757, 1758,
1759, and 1760: Containing The Moft Remarkable

Occurrences of that Period ; Particularly The Two
Sieges of Quebec, &c. &c. The Orders of the Ad-
mirals and General Officers; Defcriptions of the
Countries where the Author has ferved, with their
Forts and Garrifons; their Climates, Soil, Produce ; and A Regular Diary of the Weather. As
also Several Manifesto's, a Mandate of the late
Bishop of Canada ; The French Orders and Disposition for the Defence of the Colony, &c. &c. &c.
By Captain John Knox. Dedicated by Permission
To Lieutenant-General Sir Jeffery Amherst. *London :* Printed for the Author ; And Sold by W.
Johnston, MDCCLXIX. *Two Volumes. Vol. I. 8 prelim. leaves 405 pp. and 1 leaf of errata. Large Map
and Portrait of Gen. Amherst. Vol. II. Title and
465 pp. with 1 leaf of Errata. Portrait of Wolfe.
Half calf. 4to.* (1*l.* 11*s.* 6*d.* 1609)

KOSCIUSZKO (THADDEUS). Autograph Letter ad-
dressed to ' The Honourable Vice Admiral Paul
Jones, Amsterdam ' dated at Warsaw 15 Feb. 1790.
Written in English. 1 page. 4to. (2*l.* 2*s.* 1610)

KOSTER (HENRY). Travels in Brazil. By Henry
Koster. *London :* Longman, 1816. *xi and 502 pp.
With 10 plates. Calf. 4to.* (10*s.* 6*d.* 1611)

KOSTER (HENRY). Travels in Brazil. By Henry
Koster. Second Edition. In Two Volumes. *London :* Longman, 1817. *2 Volumes. Vol. I. xii and
406 pp. 8 plates. Vol. II. iv and 380 pp. 2 plates.
Uncut.* (7*s.* 6*d.* 1612)

END OF VOL I.

BIBLIOTHECA AMERICANA

VOLUME II

BIBLIOTHECA AMERICANA.

ABAT (JEAN BAPTISTE). Nouveau Voyage aux Isles de l'Amerique. Contenant l'Histoire Naturelle de ces Pays, l'Origine, les Mœurs, la Religion & le Gouvernement des Habitans anciens & modernes : Les Guerres & les Evenemens singuliers qui y sont arrivez pendant le long séjour que l'Auteur y a fait. Le Commerce et les Manufactures qui sont établies, & les moyens de les augmenter. Avec une Description exacte & curieuse de toutes ces Isles. Ouvrage enrichi d'un grand nombre de Cartes, Plans, & Figures en Taille-douce. *A La Haye*, P. Husson, *etc.* M.DCC.XXIV. *Six Volumes.* Tome Premier. 15 *prel. leaves ; viz. Collective title, Title, Table des Chapitres, and Preface. Text* 504 *pp. Map at p.* 1 *and plates at pp.* 45, 75, 200, 269, 297, 312, 315, 343, 376, 379, 380, 402, 432, 475. Tome Second. 4 *prel. leaves, and* 576 *pp. Plates at pp.* 9, 12, 15, 29, 39, 46, 48, 54, 200, 212, 251, 257, 326, 349, 379, 380, 387, 398, 414, 463, 553. Tome Troisième. 3 *prel. leaves, and* 528 *pp. Plates at pp.* 21, 32, 57, 63, 65 (2), 68 (2), 69, 74, 79, 86, 93, 98, 104, 109, 114, 116, 132, 178, 181, 222, 223, 234, 246, 255, 275, 278, 333. Tome Quatrième. 4 *prel. leaves, and* 539 *pp. Plates at pp.* 36, 37, 54, 59, 202, 203, 207, 346, 356, 387, 420, 504, 510. Tome Cinquième. 4 *prel. leaves, and* 504 *pp. Plates at pp.* 1, 35, 55, 262, 380. Tome Sixième. 3 *prel. leaves, and* 514 *pp. Table des Matieres,* 58 *pp. Plates at pp.* 1, (3), 110, 143, 312, 382, 404, 406. *Old calf.* 12mo.   (1*l.* 11*s.* 6*d.*   1613)

LABAT (JEAN BAPTISTE). Nouveau Voyage aux
Isles de l'Amerique. Contenant l'Histoire Naturelle de ces Pays, l'Origine, les Mœurs, la Re-
ligion & le Gouvernement des Habitans anciens &
modernes : Les Guerres & les Evenemens singuliers
qui y font arrivez pendant le long féjour que
l'Auteur y a fait : Le Commerce et les Manufactures
qui y font établies, & les moyens de les augmenter.
Ouvrage enrichi d'un grand nombre de Cartes,
Plans, & Figures en Taille-douce. A *La Haye*,
P. Husson, *etc.* M.DCC.XXIV. *Two Volumes.* Tome
Premier. 11 *prel. leaves; viz. Collective Title,*
'Voyage du Pere Labat, aux Isles de l'Amerique.
Contenant Une exacte Defcription de toutes ces
Ifles ; *etc.* En II. Volumes.' *Title;* 'Epitre,' 3 *pp.*
'Preface,' *viii. pp.* 'Avis au Relieur,' 2 *pp. con-
taining a list of the maps and plates in the 2 volumes;
viz.* 'Tome I. Premiere Partie, 11 *maps and plates.*
Seconde Partie, 13 *plates.* Troisieme Partie, 23
plates. Tom. II. Quatrieme Partie, 9 *plates.* Cin-
quieme Partie, 6 *plates.* Sixieme Partie, 4 *plates.*
'Table,' 3 *pp. Text Premiere Partie,* 175 *pp. Sec-
conde Partie,* 360 *pp.* Tome Second, 4 *prel. leaves;
viz. Collective title, Title,* 'Table,' 3 *pp. Text* 520
pp. 'Table des Matieres,' 20 *pp. With the maps
and plates. Old calf.* 4to. (1*l.* 4*s.* 1614)

LABAT (JEAN BAPTISTE). Nouveau Voyage aux
Isles de l'Amerique, Contenant l'Histoire Naturelle de ces Pays, l'Origine, les Mœurs, la Religion & le Gouvernement des Habitans anciens &
modernes. Les Guerres & les Evenemens singuliers
qui y font arrivez pendant le féjour que l'Auteur y
a fait. Par le R. P. Labat, de l'Ordre des Freres
Prêcheurs. Nouvelle Edition augmentée con-
fidérablement, & enrichie de Figures en Tailles-
douces. A *Paris*, Ch. J. B. Delespine, M.DCC.XLII.
Eight Volumes. Tome Premier, *xxxvi pp. and* 7
prel. leaves, Text 472 *pp. Portrait,* 20 *maps and
plates.* Tome Second, 3 *prel. leaves, and* 444 *pp.*
17 *maps and plates.* Tome Troisième, 3 *prel. leaves,
and* 475 *pp.* 31 *plates.* Tome Quatrième, 2 *prel.
leaves, and* 533 *pp.* 12 *plates.* Tome Cinquième, 3
prel. leaves, and 418 *pp.* Tome Sixième, 2 *prel.
leaves, and* 502 *pp.* 14 *plates.* Tome Septième, *vi
and* 516 *pp.* 5 *plates.* Tome Huitième, 3 *prel. leaves,*

and 437 *pp. Privilege du Roi.* 7 *pp.* 4 *plates. Old
calf.* 12*mo.* (1*l.* 11*s.* 6*d.* 1615)

LAET (Jean de). Befchrijvinghe/ van/ West-
Indien/ door/ Ioannes de Laet/ Tweede druck:/ In
ontallijcke plaetfen ver=/betert, vermeerdert, met
eenige/ nieuwe Caerten, beelden van/ verfchyden
dieren ende/ planten verciert./ Tot *Leyden*, bij de
Elzeviers. A°.1630./ 14 *prel. leaves, including half-
title, Engraved title, and Register of Maps (of which
there are* 14), *on the reverse Errata; Text* 622 *pp.*
' Register.' 17 *pp. Fine copy. Half calf.
Folio.* (2*l.* 2*s.* 1616)

LAET (Jean de). Novvs Orbis/ feu/ Descriptionis/
Indiæ Occidentalis/ Libri XVIII./ Authore/
Ioanne de Laet Antverp./ Novis Tabulis Geo-
graphicis et variis/ Animantium, Plantarum,
Fructumque/ Iconibus illuftrati./ Cvm Privilegio./
Lvgd. Batav. apud Elzevirius. A°. 1633./ 16 *prel.
leaves, including the Half-title, Engraved title, and
list of Maps (of which there are* 14). *Text* 690 *pp.
Index,* 17 *pp. Folio.* (1*l.* 11*s.* 6*d.* 1618)

LAET (Jean de). L'histoire/ dv/ Nouvean Monde/
ou/ description/ des Indes/ Occidentales,/ Contenant dix-huict Liures,/ Par le Sieur Iean de
Laet, d'Anuers;/ Enrichi de nouuelles Tables
Geographiques, & Figures des/ Animaux,
Plantes, & Fruicts./ A *Leyde*,/ Chez Bona-
uenture & Abraham Elfeuiers, Imprimeurs/ ordi-
naires de l'Vniuerfité./ cIↃ IↃcxl./ 14 *prel.
leaves, including Title, list of Maps, (of which there
are* 14), *Preface, Table of Chapters and List of
illustrations; Text* 632 *pp. and Index* 6 *leaves. Old
calf. Folio.* (1*l.* 10*s.* 1619)

LAFITAU (Joseph François). Histoire des De-
couvertes et Conquestes des Portugais dans le
Nouveau Monde, Avec des Figures en taille-douce.
Par le R. P. Joseph-François Lafitau de la Com-
pagnie de Jesus. A *Paris*, Saugrain, & Jean-Bap-
tiste Coignard. mdccxxxiv. *Four Volumes.* Tome
Premier. *Frontispiece,* 3 *prel. leaves, xl and* 432 *pp.
Copperplate map and plates, at pp.* 1, 38, 74, 302,
320. Tome Second. *Title and* 381 *pp.* 'Table,
I & II Tomes.' 79 *pp. Plates at pp.* 52, 206, 254.

Tome Troisième. *Title and* 512 *pp. Plates at pp.*
66, 334. Tome Quatrième. *Title and* 388 *pp.*
'Table,' III & IV Tomes, *Approbation, Privilege,
and Errata,* 149 *pp. Plates at pp.* 16, 32, 190, 200,
379. *Uncut. Small 8vo.* (1*l.* 5*s.* 1620)

[LAFITAU (Joseph François)]. Algemeine Gefchichte der Länder und Völker von America.
Nebft einer Vorrede Siegmund Jacob Baumgartens
der h. Schrift Doctors und öffentl. Lehrers, auch
des theologifchen Seminarii Directors auf der
königl. preufzl. Friedrichs univerfität in Halle.
Mit vielen Kupfern. *Halle,* bey Johann Juftinus
Gebauer. 1752. *Two Volumes.* Erfter Theil.
Frontispiece and 23 *prel. leaves; Text* 688 *pp. Copperplate Map at p.* 13, *and plates numbered* I *to* XLI.
Zweiter Theil. 11 *prel. leaves, and* 905 *pp. Register*
63 *pp.* 25 *Copperplate maps and plates. Vellum.*
4*to.* (15*s.* 1621)

LA HONTAN (Baron de). New Voyages to North-
America. Containing An Account of the feveral
Nations of that vaft Continent; their Cuftoms, Commerce, and Way of Navigation upon the Lakes
and Rivers; the feveral Attempts of the Englifh
and French to difpoffefs one another; with the
Reafons of the Mifcarriage of the former; and the
various Adventures between the French, and the
Iroquefe Confederates of England, from 1683 to
1694. A Geographical Defcription of Canada, and
a Natural Hiftory of the Country, with Remarks
upon their Government, and the Intereft of the
Englifh and French in their Commerce. Also a
Dialogue between the Author and a General of the
Savages, giving a full View of the Religion and
ftrange Opinions of thofe People : With an Account of the Authors Retreat to Portugal and
Denmark and his Remarks on thofe Courts. To
which is added, A Dictionary of the Algonkine
Language, which is generally fpoke in North-
America. Illuftrated with Twenty Three Mapps
and Cuts. Written in French By the Baron La-
hontan, Lord Lievtenant of the French Colony at
Placentia in New-foundland, now in England.
Done into Englifh. In Two Volumes. A great
part of which never Printed in the Original. *London :* H. Bonwicke, 1703. Vol. I. 12 *prel. leaves*

and 280 pp. 13 copperplate maps and plates. Vol.
II. *wanting. Old calf. 8vo.* (7s. 6d. 1622)

LA HONTAN (Baron de). Nouveaux Voyages de
Mr. Le Baron de Lahontan, dans l'Amerique
Septentrionale, Qui contiennent une Relation des
differens Peuples qui y habitent; la nature de leur
Gouvernement; leur Commerce, leurs Coûtumes,
leur Religion, & leur maniére de faire la Guerre.
L'intérêt des François & des Anglois dans le Commerce qu'ils font avec ces Nations; l'avantage que
l'Angleterre peut retirer dans ce Pais, étant en
Guerre avec la France. Le tout enrichi de Cartes
& de Figures. Tome Premier. *A la Haye,* Chez les
Fréres l'Honoré, Marchands Libraires. m.dcc.iii.
Two Volumes. Tom. I. *12 prel. leaves, and 279 pp.*
15 copperplate maps and plates. Tom. II. 'Memoires de l'Amerique Septentrionale, ou la suite
des Voyages de Mr. Le Baron de Lahontan. Qui
contiennent la Defcription d'une grande étenduë
de Païs de ce Continent, l'intérêt des François &
des Anglois, leurs Commerces, leurs Navigations,
les Mœurs & les Coutumes des Sauvages, &c.
Avec un petit Dictionaire de la Langue du Pais.
Le tout enrichi de Cartes & de Figures. Tome
Second. *A La Haye,* Chez les Fréres l'Honoré,
Marchands Libraires. mdcciii. *220 pp. Table 16*
pp. Copperplate map and 13 plates. Old Calf.
12mo. (18s. 1623)

LA HONTAN (Baron de). Dialogues De Monfieur le Baron de La Hontan Et d'un Sauvage,
Dans l'Amerique. Contenant une defcription
exacte des mœurs & des coutumes de ces Peuples
Sauvages. *A Amsterdam,* Boeteman, m.dcciv.
8 prel. leaves, and 103 pp. Copperplate at page 1.
12mo. (1l. 1s. 1624)

LA HONTAN (Baron de). Voyages du Baron de
La Hontan dans l'Amerique Septentrionale, Qui
contiennent une Rélation des différens Peuples qui
y habitent; la nature de leur Gouvernment; leur
Commerce, leurs Coûtumes, leur Religion, & leur
maniére de faire la Guerre: L'Intérêt des François
& des Anglois dans le Commerce qu'ils font avec
ces Nations; l'avantage que l'Angleterre peut
reteirer de ce Païs, étant en Guerre avec la France.

Le tout enrichi de Cartes & de Figures. Tome
Premier, Seconde Edition, revuë, corrigée & augmentée. A *Amsterdam*, Chez François l' Honoré,
vis-à-vis de la Bourſe. MDCCV. *Two Volumes.*
Tom. I. 10 *prel. leaves including Frontispiece, and
376 pp. 2 copperplate maps and 11 plates.* Tom.
II. 'Memoires de l'Amerique Septentrionale, ou
la suite des Voyages de Mr. Le Baron de La Hontan: Qui contiennant la Deſcription d'une grande
étenduë de Païs de ce Continent, l'intérêt des
François & des Anglois, leurs Commerces, leurs
Navigations, les Mœurs & les Coutumes des Sauvages, &c. Avec un petit Dictionaire de la Langue
du Païs. Le tout enrichi de Cartes & de Figures.
Tome Second. Second Edition, augmentée des
Conversations de l'Auteur avec un Sauvage diſ-
tingué. A *Amsterdam*, Chez Francois l'Honoré &
Compagnie. MDCCV. *Title, and pp. 5-336. Table
2 pp. Small copperplate map and 9 plates. Old calf.
12mo.* (18s. 1625)

LA HONTAN (BARON DE). New Voyages to North-
America. Containing An Account of the ſeveral
Nations of that vaſt Continent; their Cuſtoms,
Commerce, and Way of Navigation upon the
Lakes and Rivers; the ſeveral Attempts of the
Engliſh and French to diſpoſſeſs one another; with
the Reaſons of the Miſcarriage of the former; and
the various Adventures between the French, and
the Iroqueſe Confederates of England, from 1683
to 1694. A Geographical Deſcription of Canada,
and a Natural Hiſtory of the Country, with Remarks upon their Government, and the Intereſt of
the Engliſh and French in their Commerce. Alſo
a Dialogue between the Author and a General of
the Savages, giving a full View of the Religion
and ſtrange Opinions of thoſe People: With an
Account of the Author's Retreat to Portugal and
Denmark, and his Remarks on thoſe Courts. To
which is added, A Dictionary of the Algonkine
Language, which is generally ſpoke in North-
America. Illuſtrated with Twenty-Three Maps
and Cuts. Written in French By the Baron Lahontan, Lord Lieutenant of the French Colony at
Placentia in Newfoundland, at that Time in England. Done into Engliſh. The Second Edition.
In Two Volumes. A great Part of which never

Printed in the Original. *London:* J. and J. Bonwicke, M,DCC,XXXV. *Two Volumes.* Vol. I. 12 *prel.
leaves, and* 280 *pp.* 10 *copperplate maps and plates.*
Vol. II. ' New Voyages to North-America. Giving
a full Account of the Cuftoms, Commerce, Religion, and ftrange Opinions of the Savages of that
Country. With Political Remarks upon the Courts
of Portugal and Denmark, and the Prefent State
of the Commerce of thofe Countries. The Second
Edition. Written By the Baron Lahontan, Lord-
Lieutenant of the French Colony at Placentia in
Newfoundland: Now in England. *London:* J.
Walthoe, 1735.' 304 *pp.* 10 *Copperplates. Old
calf.* 8vo. (18s. 1626)

LAMB (R.) An Original and Authentic Journal
of Occurrences during the late American War, from
its commencement to the year 1783. By R. Lamb,
late Serjeant in the Royal Welch Fuzileers.
Dublin: Wilkinson & Courtney, 1809. 6 *prel.
leaves, and pp.* 5-438. ' Order,' 1 *page, at page* 158.
Calf. 8vo. (10s. 6d. 1627)

LAMBRECHTSEN (N. C.) Korte Beschrijving
van de ontdekking en der verdere lotgevallen van
Nieuw-Nederland, weleer eene volkplanting van
het gemeenebest der vereenigde Nederlanden in
America, door Mr. N. C. Lambrechtsen van Ritt-
hem, ridder der orde van den Nederlandschen
leeuw, President van het Zeeuwsch Genootschap
der Wetenschappen. Te *Middelburg,* bij S. Van
Benthem, MDCCCXVIII. 2 *prel. leaves, and* 102 *pp.
With Map. Uncut.* 8vo. (10s. 6d. 1628)

LARRANAGA (BRUNO FRANCISCO). Prospecto
de una Eneida Apostólica, ô Epopeya, que celebra
la predicacion del V. Apóstol del Occidente P. Fr.
Antonio Margil de Jesus: Intitulada Margileida.
Escrita con puros versos de P. Virgilio Maron, y
traducida a verso Castellano: La que se propone al
público de esta America septentrional por Sub-
scripcion: Para que colectados anticipadamente
los gastos necesarios, se proceda inmediatamente
â su impresion. Su Autor Don Bruno Francisco
Larrañaga. Impresa en *México* en la Imprenta
nueva Madrileña de los Herederos del Lic. D.
Joseph de Jauregui. Calle de S. Bernardo. Año

de 1788. *2 prel. leaves and* 28 *pp. Half morocco.*
4*to.*   (1*l.* 1*s.* 1629)

LAS CASAS (Bartholome de). ℈Aqui ſe con-
tiene/ vna diſputa, o controuerſia : entre el/ Obiſpo
dõ fray Bartholome de las/ Caſas, o Caſaus, obiſpo
q fue de la/ ciudad Real de Chiapa, que es en=/
las Indias, parte de la nueua Eſpa=/ña : y el doctor Gines de Sepulueda/ Coroniſta del Emperador
nueſtro ſe/ñor : ſobre q el doctor contendia : q las/
conquiſtas de las Indias contra los/ Indios eran li-
citas : y el obiſpo por/ el cõtrario d'fendio y affirmo
auer ſi/ do y ſer ĩpoſſible no ſerlo : tiranicas,/ in-
juſtas ⟨ iniquas. La qual queſtiõ/ ſe vẽtilo ⟨ diſ-
puto en preſ-ncia d'mu/ chos letrados theologos ⟨
juriſtas/ en vna cõgregacion q mando ſu ma=/geſtad
juntar el año de mil ⟨ qniẽtos/ y cincuẽta en la
villa de Valladolid./ Año. 1552./ [*Colophon*]
℘Aloor y gloria de nueſtro ſe/ñor Jeſu Chriſto y
dela ſacratiſſima virgen ſancta/ Maria ſu madre.
Fue impreſſa la preſente obra/ enla muy noble ⟨
muy leal ciudad de *Seuilla* :/ en caſa de Sebaſtian
Trugillo impreſſor de/ libros. Frõtero de nueſtra
ſeñora de Gra/cia. Acaboſſe a. x. dias del mes de
Se=/tiembre. Año de mil ⟨ quinien/tos ⟨ cin-
cuenta y dos./ ✤/ (Here is contained a dispute or
controversy between the Bishop Friar Bartholomew
de Las Casas, or Casaus, formerly Bishop of the
royal City of Chiapa which is in the Indies a part
of New Spain, and the Doctor Gines de Sepulveda
Chronicler to the Emperor our Lord, in which the
Doctor contended that the conquests of the Indies
against the Indians were lawful, and the bishop
on the contrary defended and affirmed them to
have been and to be impossible to be so, but
tyrannical, unjust and iniquitous. Which question
was examined and disputed in the presence of
many learned theologians and jurists in a meeting
which his Majesty ordered to be held in the year
one thousand five hundred and fifty in the City of
Valladolid. In the year 1552. [*Colophon*] To the
honor and glory of our Lord Jesus Christ and of
the most holy Virgin Saint Mary his Mother.
The present work was printed in the very noble
and very loyal City of Seville ; at Sebastian Trugillo's, printer of books, and Opposite Lady of
Grace. Finished the 10th day of the month of

September. In the 1552. *62 leaves, signatures* a
to g *in eights and* h *in* 6 *leaves, the last being blank.*
4*to.*   (*2l. 2s.* 1629*)

LAS CASAS (BARTHOLOME DE). ❡ Aqui ſe cõtienē
tre/ynta propoſiciones muy juridicas: en/ las quales
ſumaria y ſuccintamente ſe/tocã muchas cosas per-
teneciētes al de/recho q la ygleſia y los principes
chri=/ſtianos tienen, o puedē tener ſobre los/ infieles
de qual quier eſpecie que ſean./ Mayormente ſe
aſſigna el verdadero/ y fortiſſimo fundamento en
que ſe aſſi/ęnta y eſtriba: el titulo y ſeñorio ſupre=/
mo y vniuerſal que los Reyes d'Caſti/lla y Leon
tienen al orbe de las que lla/mamos occidētales
Indias. Por el ql/ſon conſtituydos vniuerſales
ſeñores y/Emperadores enellas ſobre muchos re-/
yes. Apuntã ſe tambien otras coſas cõ/cernientes
al hecho acaecido en aql or/be notabiliſſimas : y
dignas d'ſer viſtas/ y ſabidas. Colijo las dichas
treynta p/ poſiciones El obiſpo dõ Fray Bartho-/
lome de las Caſas, o Caſaus : Obiſpo/ q fue d'la
ciudad Real de Chiapa : cier/to Reyno de los de la
nueua Eſpaña./ Ano. 1552./ [*Colophon*] ❡ Impreſſo en *ſeuilla* en caſa de ſebaſtiã trugillo./ (Here
are contained thirty most lawful propositions, in
which are summarily and succinctly treated of,
many things appertaining to the right which the
church and the christian princes have, or may have
over the infidels of whatever kind they may be.
Chiefly the true and strongest foundation is assigned
on which is based and supported the title and
supreme and universal lordship which the kings of
Castile and Leon hold over the world of what we
call the West Indies. By the which they are con-
stituted universal lords and emperors in them,
over many kings. Other most remarkable things
are also pointed out relative to the transaction
which has taken place in that world, and worthy
to be seen and known. The Bishop Don Friar
Bartholomew de Las Casas or Casaus, formerly
Bishop of the royal City of Chiapa a certain kingdom of the new Spain, collected the said thirty
propositions.—In the year 1552.) 10 *leaves, signature* a. 4*to.*   (*2l. 2s.* 1630)

LAS CASAS (BARTHOLOME DE). ❡ Aqui ſe cõtienē
vnos/ auiſos y reglas para los confeſſores q/ oyeren

confeſſiones de los Eſpaño/ les que ſon, o han ſido
en cargo a/ los Indios de las Indias del/ mar
Oceano: colegidas por/ el obiſpo de Chiapa don/
fray Bartholome d'las/ caſas, o caſaus dela/ orden
de Sancto/ Domingo./ [*Colophon.*] ⸿ Aloor y
gloria de nueſtro ſe/ñor Jeſu Chriſto y dela ſacratiſſima virgen ſancta/ Maria. Fue impreſſa la preſente obra en la muy/ noble ⸿ muy leal ciudad de
Seuilla, en caſa/ de Sebaſtian Trugillo impreſſor de
li/bros. Frōtero de nueſtra ſeñora de/ Gracia.
Acaboſſe a. xx. dias del/ mes de Setiembre. Año
de/ mil ⸿ quinientos ⸿ cin/cuenta y dos./ ✤ /
(Here are contained some devices and rules for the
confessors who have heard the confessions of the
Spaniards who have or have had the charge of the
Indians of the Indies of the Ocean Sea; collected
by the Bishop of Chiapa Don Bartholomew de
Las Casas, or Casaus, Friar of the Order of Saint
Dominick. [*Colophon*] To the honor and glory of
Our Lord Jesus Christ and of the most Holy
Virgin Saint Mary. The present work was
printed in the very noble and very loyal City of
Seville, at Sebastian Trugillo's, printer of books.
Opposite Our Lady of Grace: finished the 20th
day of the month of September. In the year one
thousand five hundred and fifty-two.) 16 *leaves,
signature* a, *the reverse of the last leaf blank.*
4*to.* (2*l.* 2*s.* 1631)

LAS CASAS (BARTHOLOME DE). ⸿ Breuiſſima
rela/cion de la deſtruycion de las In=/dias: colegida
por el Obiſpo dō/ fray Bartolome de las Caſas, o/
Caſaus de la orden de Sācto Do/mingo./ Año.
1552./ [*Colophon*] ⸿ Fue impreſſa la preſente o=/
bra enla muy noble ⸿ muy leal ciudad de *Seuilla*/
en caſa de Sebaſtian Trugillo impreſſor de/ libros.
A nueſtra ſeñora de Gracia./ Año de M. D. L ij./
(A very brief account of the Destruction of the Indies; collected by the Bishop Don Bartholomew
de Las Casas, or Casaus, Friar of the Order of Saint
Dominick. In the year 1552. [*Colophon*] The
present work was printed in the most noble and
loyal city of Seville at Sebastian Trugillo's, printer
of books. At our Lady of Grace's. In the year
1552.) 54 *leaves, signatures* a *to* e *in eights,* f *ten,
and* g *in four leaves being a separate tract commenc-*

ing ❡ Lo que fe figue es vn pedaço de vna carta, *etc.* 4*to.* (*2l. 2s.* 1632)

LAS CASAS (Bartholome de). ✤ Entre los re=/ medios q dõ fray Bartolome de las caſas :/ obiſpo d'la ciudad real de Chiapa : refirio/ por mandado del Emperador rey nro ſe=/nor: en los ayuntamiẽtos q mãdo hazer ſu/ mageſtad de perlados y letrados y perſo/nas grãdes en Valladolid el año de mill 𝑟/ quiniẽtos y quarẽta y dos: para reforma=/ciõ de las Indias. El octauo en ordẽ es el/ ſiguiẽte. Dõde fe afignã veynte razones :/ por las qles prueua no deuerſe dar los in=/dios a los Eſpañales en encomiẽda: ni en/ feudo : ni en vaſſallaje : ni d'otra manera al/gũa. Si ſu majeſtad como deſſea quiere li/brarlos de la tyrania y perdicio q padecẽ/ como de la boca de los dragones : y q total=/mẽte no los cõſumã y matẽ y q de vazio to=/do aql orbe d'ſus tã infinitos naturales ha/bitadores como eſtaua y lo vimos poblado/ [*Colophon.*] ❡Fue impreſſa la preſente obra en/ la muy noble y opulentiſſima y muy leal ciudad/ de *Seuilla*, en las caſas de Jacome Crõ/berger. Acaboſe a diez 𝑟 ſiete dias/ del mes de Agoſto, año de mill/ 𝑟 quinientos 𝑟 cinquen=/ta y dos años./ (Among the remedies which Brother Don Bartholomew de Las Casas Bishop of the Royal City of Chiapa reported by order of the Emperor, the King, our Lord, in the meetings which his Majesty ordered to be held by the prelates and learned men and grandees of Valladolid, in the year one thousand five hundred and forty two, for the reformation of the Indies ; the eighth in order is the following, wherein twenty reasons are assigned, by which it is proved that the Indians should not be given to the Spaniards, neither in commission, nor in fief, nor in vassalage, nor in any other way whatsoever, if His Majesty according to his desire would free them from the tyranny and perdition which they suffer, as from the mouth of the dragons, and that they may not 'otally consume and kill them, and devastate that world of its so infinite natural inhabitants, with whom it was, and we saw it, peopled. [*Colophon.*] The present work was printed in the very noble and most opulent and very loyal city of Seville at Jacob Cromberger's ; finished on the seventeenth day of

the month of August in the year 1552.) 54 *leaves,*
signatures a *to* f *in eights, and* g *in six leaves, the last*
being blank. 4*to.*   (2*l.* 2*s.*   1633)

LAS CASAS (Bartholome de). ℭ Efte es vn tratado q/ el obifpo de la cuidad Real de Chiapa dõ/
fray Bartholome de las Cafas, o Cafaus/ compufo,
por comiffion del Confejo Real/ de las Indias : fobre
la materia de los yn=/dios que fe han hecho en ellas
efclauos.   El/ qual contiene muchas razones y
aucto=/ridades juridicas : que pueden apro/uechar
a los lectores para deter=/minar muchas y diuerfas/
queftiones dudofas/ en materia de re=/ftitucion : y
de/ otras que al/ qfente los/ hõbres/ el tiẽpo de
agora tratan./   Año 1552./   [*Colophon*] ℭ Aloor
y gloria de nueftro fe/ñor Jefu Chrifto y dela fac-
ratiffima virgen fancta/ Maria.   Fue impreffa la
prefente obra en la muy/ noble ꝝ muy leal ciudad
de *Seuilla,* en cafa/ de Sebaftian Trugillo impreffor
de li/bros.   Frontero de nueftra feñora/ de Gracia.
Acaboffe a doze/ dias del mes de Setiem/bre.   Año
de mil ꝝ qui/nientos y cincuẽ/ta y dos./   (This is
a treatise which the Bishop of the Royal City of
Chiapa, Friar Don Bartholomew de Las Casas or
Casaus composed by commission of the Royal
Council of the Indies : upon the subject of the Indians who have been made slaves there ; which contains many reasons and lawful authorities, which
may profit the readers for the determination of many
and different doubtful questions in the matter of
restitution, and of others which now the men of
the present day treat of.   In the year 1552.
[*Colophon*] To the honor and glory of Our Lord
Jesus Christ and of the most Holy Virgin Saint
Mary.   The present work was printed in the most
noble and most loyal City of Seville, at Sebastian
Trugillo's, printer of books.   Opposite Our Lady
of Grace.   Finished the twelfth day of the month
of September.   In the year one thousand five
hundred and fifty-two.) 36 *leaves, signatures* a *to* c
in eights, d *in* 12 *leaves, the reverse of the last leaf*
blank. 4*to.*   (2*l.* 2*s.*   1634)

LAS CASAS (Bartholome de). ℭ Principia
quedã ex quibus/ procedendum eft in difputatione
ad manifeftan/dam et defendendam iufticiam Yn-
dorum :/ Per Epifcopũ. F. Bartholomeũ a Ca/faus

ordinis predicatorū, collecta./ [*Colophon*] ℂ Impreſſum Hiſpali in edibus Sebaſtiani Trugilli./
(Certain principles from which we are to proceed
in disputation to the manifeſtation and defence of
the juriſdiction of the Indians. Collected by bishop
Bartholomew de Las Casas, Friar of the Order
of Preachers. [*Colophon*] Printed at Seville, at
Sebaſtian Trugillo's, [1552].) 10 *leaves, signature*
A. 4*to.* (3*l.* 3*s.* 1635)

LAS CASAS (BARTHOLOME DE). ℂ Tratado cōpro/
batorio del Imperio ſoberano y/ principado vniuerſal
que los Re/yes de Caſtilla y Leon tienen ſo=/bre
las indias : compueſto por el/ Obiſpo don fray
Bartholome d'/ las Caſas, o Caſaus de la orden d'/
Sancto Domingo. Año. 1552./ [*Colophon*] ℂ A loor
y gloria de nueſtro ſe/ñor Jeſu Chriſto y de la
ſacratiſſima virgen ſancta/ Maria ſu madre. Fue
impreſſa la preſente o=/bra en la muy noble ϒ muy
leal cuidad/ d' *Seuilla* en caſa d Sebaſtiā Tru/ gillo
impreſſor de libros. Aca/ boſſe a ocho dias d'l mes/
de Enero. Año./ 1553./ 84 *leaves, signatures* a *to*
k, *in eights.* 4*to.* (3*l.* 3*s.* 1636)

LAS CASAS (BARTHOLOME DE). Tyrannies/ et
Crvavtez/ des/ Espagnols,/ perpetrees/ és/ Indes
Occidentales,/ qu'on dit Le Nouueau monde ;/
Brieuement deſcrites en langue Castillane par
l'Eueſque/ Don Frere Bartelemy de Las Casas ou/
Casavs, Espagnol, de l'ordre de S. Dominique ;
fide-/lement traduictes par Iaqves de Miggrode :/
Pour seruir d'exemple & aduertiſſement/ aux xvII
Prouinces du pais bas./ Heureux celuy qui deui-
ent ſage/ En voyant d'autruy le dommage./ A
Anvers,/ Chez François de Ravelenghien ioignant
le por-/tail Septentrional de l'Egliſe noſtre Dame./
M.D.LXXIX./ (Tyrannies and cruelties of the Spa-
nish, perpetrated in the West Indies which are
called the New World; briefly described in the
Castilian tongue, by the Bishop Don Bartholomew
de Las Casas or Casaus, Spaniard, Friar of the
Order of St. Dominick; faithfully translated by
James de Miggrode; to serve as an example and
warning to the seventeen provinces of the Low
Countries. Happy is he who becomes wise in wit-
nessing another's disadvantage. Antwerp, at
Francis de Ravelingen's, adjoining the northern

entrance of the Church of our Lady. 1579.) 8 *prel.*
leaves, and 184 *pp.* 8*vo.* (2*l.* 2*s.* 1637)

LAS CASAS (Bartholome de). The/ Spanifh
Colonie,/ or/ Briefe Chronicle of the Acts and/
geftes of the Spaniardes in the Weft In-/dies, called
the newe World, for the/ fpace of xl. yeeres:
written in the Ca-/ftilian tongue by the reuerend
Bi=/fhop Bartholomew de las Cafas or Cafaus, a
Friar of the or-/der of St. Dominicke./ And nowe
firft tranflated into/ Englifh, by M. M. S./ ❡ Im-
printed at *London* for/ William Brome./ 1583./
[*Colophon*] Imprinted at London at the three/
Cranes in the Vintree by Thomas/ Dawfon, for
William Broome./ 1583./ 8 *prel. leaves; viz. Title*
in a broad type metal border, the reverse blank; ' To
the Reader.' 7 *pp.* 'The Argument of this prefent/
Summarie.'/ 2 *pp.* 'The Prologue of the Bifhop
Frier/ Bartholomewe de las Cafas or Cafaus,/ to
the moft high and mightie prince,/ Our Lord Don
Philip Prince/ of Spaine.'/ 4 *pp. in roman type.*
Text 52 *leaves in Black letter; Signatures* A. *to* N.
in fours. ' To the Reader.' 14 *leaves in roman type;*
signatures O. *to* Q. *in fours,* R. *in two.* [*Colophon*]
Imprinted at London at the three/ Cranes in the
Vintree by Thomas/ Dawfon, for William Broome./
1583./ *Russia extra.* 4*to.* (10*l.* 10*s.* 1638)

LAS CASAS (Bartholome de). Newe Welt./
Warhafftige Anzeigung/ Der Hifpanier grewli=/
chen, abfchewlichen vnd vnmenfchlichen Ty=/
ranney, von ihnen inn den Indianifchen Ländern,/
fo gegen Nidergang der Sonnen gelegen, vnd die/
Newe Welt gennet wird, begangen./ Erftlich/
Caftilianifch, durch Bifchoff Bartholomeum de las
Cafas oder/ Cafaus, gebornen Hifpaniern, Prediger
Ordens, befchrieben : Vnd/ im Jahr 1552 in der
Königlichen Staat Hifpalis oder/ Sevilia in Spanien
gedruckt :/ Hernacher in die/ Frantzöfifche Sprach,
durch Jacoben von Miggrode, den 17/ Provincien
defz Niderlands, zur Warnung/ und Beyfpiel,
gebracht :/ Jetzt aber erft ins/ Hochteutfch, durch
einen Liebhaber defz Vatterlands, vmb ebenmäffiger/
vrfachen wiffen, vbergefetzt./ Jm Jhar/ 1597./ 8
prel. leaves and 158 *pp. Register* 12 *pp. unbound.*
4*to.* (3*l.* 3*s.* 1639)

LAS CASAS (Bartholome de). Spieghel der
Spaenſcher ty=/rannye, in Weſt-Indien. Waer inne
verhaelt wordt de moorda=/dighe, ſchandelijcke,
lende grouweijcke feyten, die deſelve Spaen-/
jaerden ghebruyckt hebben inde ſelve Landen./
Mitſgaders de beſchryvinghe vander ghelegentheyt,
zeden/ ende aert van de ſelfde Landen ende Volcken./ In Spaenſcher Talen beſchreven, door den
E. Biſſchop Don Fray Bartholome de las Caſas, van
S. Dominicus Oorden./ t'*Amstelredam*,/ By Cornelis Claeſz. Boeckvercooper woonende opt Water,/
int Schrijfboeck. Anno 1607./ 44 *leaves including
title, with map of America engraved on the title, the
reverse blank. Black letter. Signatures* A. *to* L. *in
fours, the last blank.* 4*to.* (1*l.* 10*s.* 1640)

LAS CASAS (Bartholome de). Den/ Spieghel/
Vande Spaenſche Tyrannie beeldelijcken af=/ge-
maelt, leeſt breederen in-hout door het schrijven
van den E. Biſſchop/ van Chiapa in nieu Spaengien,
ghenaemt Don Fray Bartholome de/ las Caſas,
van S. Dominicus Oorden, aen den grootmach-/
tigen Coninck van Spaengien Philips de tweede./
Ghedruckt tot *Amstelredam* by Cornelis Claeſz.
1609./ *Title with copperplate engraving the reverse
blank, and copperplates numbered* 1 *to* xvii, *with
letter-press description at foot of each. Black letter.*
4*to.* (1*l.* 10*s.* 1641)

LAS CASAS (Bartholome de). Le Miroir/ De
la/ Tyrannie Eſpagnole/ Perpetree aux Indes/
Occidentales./ On verra icy la cruaute plus/ que
inhumaine, commiſe par les/ Eſpagnols, auſsi la
deſcription de/ ces terres, peuples, et leur nature./
Miſe en lumiere par un/ Eveſque Bartholome de las
Caſas,/ de l'Ordre de S. Dominic./ Nouvellement
refaicte, avec les/ Figurs en cuyvre./ tot/ *Amsterdam*/ Ghedruckt by Ian Evertſs,/ Cloppenburg,
op't Water,/tegen over de Koor-Beur/ in vergulden
Bijbel./ 1620./ 68 *folioed leaves including title
within an engraved border of Figures, and copperplates
with the text on folios* 5, 6, 8, 11, 14, 18, 20, 21, 24,
27, 29, 30, 33, 49, 53, 55, 65. *Old calf.*
4*to.* (1*l.* 11*s.* 6*d.* 1642)

LAS CASAS (Bartholome de). Istoria/ ò breuiſ-
sima relatione/ Della Distrvttione/ dell' Indie Oc-

cidentali/ di Monsig. Reverendiss./ Don Bartolomeo dalle Cafe, ò Cafaus, Siuigliano/ Vefcouo
di Chiapa Città Regale nell' Indie./ Conforme al
svo vero originale/ Spagnuolo, già ftampato in
Siuiglia./ Con la traduttione in Italiano de Francefco Berfabita./ Dedicata all' Amicitia./ In
Venetia Preffo Marco Ginammi. M.DC.XXVI./ Con
licenza de' Superjori, & Priuilegio./ (History or
very short account of the destruction of the West
Indies; by My Lord the most reverend Don Bartholomew de Las Casas, or Casaus, of Seville,
Bishop of Chiapa, a royal City in the Indies. According to his true original Spanish, formerly
printed in Seville, with the translation in Italian
of Francis Bersabita. Dedicated to Friendship.
Venice, at Mark Ginammi's, 1626. With license
of the Superiors and privilege.) 8 *prel. leaves and*
154 *pp. Libri Stampati & Errori* 2 *pp. Vellum.*
4*to.*   (1*l.* 1*s.*   1643)

LAS CASAS (BARTHOLOME DE).   Tyrannies/ et/
Crvavtez/ des/ Espagnols,/ Commises es Indes/
Occidentales, qu'on/ dit le Nouueau Monde./
Briefvement descrite en/ Espagnol, par Dom Frere
Barthelemy de/ las Casas de l'Ordre de S. Do-
minique, &/ Euefque de la ville Royalle de
Chiappa./ Traduitte fidellement en François par
Iacques de Miggrode/ sur la Coppie Espagnolle :
Imprimée à la ville de Seuille./ A *Rouen,*/ Chez
Iacques Cailloüé à la Court du Palais:/
M.DC.XXX./ Iouxte la Coppie Imprimée à
Paris, par Guillaume Iulien./ Avec Privilege dv
Roy./ (Tyranny and Cruelties of the Spaniards,
committed in the West Indies, called the New
World. Briefly described in Spanish by Don Fr.
Bartholomew de Las Casas of the Order of St.
Dominic and Bishop of the Royal City of Chiapa.
Faithfully translated into French by James de
Miggrode from the Spanish original, printed in the
city of Seville. At Rouen, at James Cailloüé's,
in the Palace Court. 1630.) 11 *prel. leaves; viz.*
Title, the reverse blank, 'Advertissement av Lec-
tevr tovchant le present Livre.' 12 *pp.* 'Sonnet.' 1
page. 'Argvment dv prefent Liure.' 2 *pp.* 'Pro-
logve de L'evesqve dom Frere Barthelemy de las
Casas,' *etc.* 5 *pp : Text* 214 *pp. Old calf extra.*
4*to.*   (1*l.* 11*s.* 6*d.*   1644)

LAS CASAS (Bartholomeo de). La Libertà/ Pre-
tesa/ Dal fupplice Schiauo Indiano/ di Monsignor
Reverendiss./ D. Bartolomeo dalle Cafe,/ ò
Cafaus, Siuigliano, dell' Ordine de' Predicatori, &
Vefcouo/ di Chiapa, Città Regale dell' Indie./
Conforme al fuo vero Originale Spagnuolo già
ftampato in Siuiglia./ Tradotto in Italiano per
opera di Marco Ginammi./ All' Altezza Serenif-
sima di/ Odoardo Farnese/ Dvca di Parma, et
Piacenza, &c./ In *Venetia*, Preffo Marco Gin-
ammi. m dc xxxx./ Con Licenza de' Superiori, &
Priuilegio./ (The pretended liberty of the sup-
pliant Indian slave, by My Lord the most reverend
D. Bartholomew de Las Casas, or Casaus, of Se-
ville, of the order of Preachers and Bishop of
Chiapa, a royal city of India. According to the
true Spanish original, formerly printed at Seville.
Translated into Italian by the industry of Mark
Ginammi. To His Most Serene Highness Edward
Farnese, Duke of Parma and Piacenza, etc.
Venice. At Mark Ginammi's, 1640. With license
of the Superiors, and privilege.) 158 *pp. Vellum.*
4*to.*   (1*l.* 1*s.* 1645)

LAS CASAS (Bartholome de). Histoire/ des In-
des/ Occidentales./ Ov l'on reconnoit/ la bonté
de ces pais, & de leurs/ peuples ; & les cruautez
Tyran/niques des Espagnols./ Décrite premierement en langue Caftillane par/ Dom Barthelemy
de las Casas,/ de l'Ordre de S. Dominique, &
Euefque/ de Chappa ; & depuis fidellement/ traduite en François./ A *Lyon*,/ Chez Iean Caffin,
& F. Plaignard,/ en ruë Merciere, au Nom de
Iesvs./ m.dc.xlii./ Auec Approbation, & Permiffion./ (History of the West Indies. Where
are recognised the excellence of those countries
and of their people, and the tyrannical cruelties of
the Spaniards. First described in the Castilian
tongue by Don Bartholomew de Las Casas, of the
Order of Saint Dominic, and Bishop of Chiapa,
and since faithfully translated into French. Lyons.
At John Caffin and F. Plaignard's, in Mercer
Street, at the name of Jesus. 1642. With approbation and permission.) 4 *prel. leaves ; viz. Title on
the reverse, Approbation, and Permission.* ' Preface
av Lectevr.' 6 *pp. Text* 299 *pp. Vellum. Small*
8*vo.*   (1*l.* 1*s.* 1646)

LAS CASAS (Bartholome de). Istoria,/ ò
Breuifsima Relatione/ della Distrvttione/ dell' In-
die Occidentali/ di Monsig. Reverendiss./ Don
Bartolomeo dalle Cafe, ò Cafaus, Siuigliano dell'
Ordine/ de' Predicatori; & Vefcouo di Chiapa./
Conforme al fuo vero Originale Spagnuolo già
ftampato in Siuiglia./ Tradotta in Italiano dall
Eccell. Sig. Giacomo Castellani,/ già fotto nome
di Francesco Berfabita. Al Molt' Ill.re, & Ecc.mo.
Sig.re Sig.r mio Col.mo Il Sig./ Nicolo' Persico./
In *Venetia* Preffo Marco Ginammi. m.dc.xliii./
Con Licenza de' Superiori, & Priuilegio./ (His-
tory or very short account of the destruction of
the West Indies. By My Lord the most reverend
Don Bartholomew de Las Casas, or Casaus, of
Seville, of the order of Preachers, and bishop of
Chiapa. According to the true Spanish original
formerly printed in Seville. Translated into Italian by His Excellency Signor James Castellani,
formerly under the name of Francis Bers-abita.
To the most Illustrious and most excellent Signor,
my most Honored Lord, Signor Nicholas Persico.
Venice, At Mark Ginammi's. 1643. With license
of the Superiors, and privilege.) 3 *prel. leaves and*
150 *pp.* 4*to.* (1*l.* 1*s.* 1647)

LAS CASAS (Bartholomeo de). Conqvista/ dell'
Indie/ Occidentali/ di Monsignor/ Fra Bartolomeo
dalle Case,/ ò Cafaus, Siuigliano, Vofcouo di
Chiapa./ Tradotta in Italiano per opera di Marco
Ginammi./ All' Ill.mo & Ecc.mo Sig.re Sig.or/ &
mio Padron Col.mo/ Il Sig.or Pietro Sagredo/ Pro-
cvratore di S. Marco./ In *Venetia*, m dc xxxxv./
Preffo Marco Ginammi./ Con Licenza de' Su-
periori, & Privilegio./ (Conquest of the West
Indies by My Lord, Brother Bartholomew de Las
Casas or Casaus, of Seville, Bishop of Chiapa.
Translated into Italian by the labours of Mark
Ginammi. To the most Illustrious and excellent
Lord, My Lord and most honoured patron the Lord
Peter Sagredo, Procurator of Saint Mark. Venice,
1645. At Mark Ginammi's. With the license of
the Superiors and privilege.) 184 *pp. Vellum.*
4*to.* (1*l.* 1*s.* 1647*)

LAS CASAS (Bartholome de). The Tears of the
Indians :/ Being/ An Hiftorical and true Account/

Of the Cruel/ Maſſacres and Slaughters/ of above
Twenty Millions/ of innocent People ;/ Committed
by the Spaniards/ In the Iſlands of/ Hiſpaniola,
Cuba, Jamaica, &c./ As alſo, in the Continent
of/ Mexico, Peru, and other Places of the/ Weſt-
Indies,/ To the total deſtruction of thoſe Countries./
Written in Spaniſh by Caſaus,/ an Eye-witneſs of
thoſe things ;/ And made Engliſh by J. P./ *London*,/ Printed by J. C. for Nath. Brook, at the An-
gel/ in Cornhil. 1656./ 15 *prel. leaves; viz.* 1*st
blank, Title the reverse blank*, 'To His Highneſs,
Oliver Lord Protector of the Commonwealth of
England, Scotland and Ireland, With the Dominions thereto belonging.' 7 *pp. Signed* 'J.
Phillips.' 'To all true Engliſh-men.' 18 *pp. Text*
134 *pp. Copper plate by* 'R. Gaywood.' *Old calf.
Small* 8*vo.* (1*l.* 1*s.* 1648)

LAS CASAS (Bartholome de). Popery/ Truly
Diſplay'd in its/ Bloody Colours :/ Or, a Faithful/
Narrative/ of the/ Horrid and Unexampled Maſſacres, But-/cheries, and all manner of Cruelties,
that Hell and/ Malice could invent, committed by
the Popiſh Spaniſh/ Party on the Inhabitants of
West-India :/ Together/ With the Devaſtations of
ſeveral Kingdoms in America/ by Fire and Sword,
for the ſpace of Forty and Two/ Years, from the
time of its firſt Diſcovery by them./ Compoſed
firſt in Spaniſh by Bartholomew de las Caſas, a
Biſhop/ there, and an Eye-Witneſs of moſt of theſe
Barbarous Cruelties ;/ afterward Tranſlated by him
into Latin, then by other hands, into/ High-Dutch,
Low-Dutch, French, and now Taught to ſpeak/
Modern Engliſh./ *London*, Printed for R. Hewſon
at the Crown in Cornhil,/ near the Stocks-Market.
1689./ 4 *prel. leaves and* 80 *pp.* 4*to.* (2*l.* 2*s.* 1649)

LAS CASAS (Bartholome de). La Decouverte/
des/ Indes Occidentales,/ par/ les Espagnols./
Ecrite par Dom Balthazar de Las-/Casas, Evêque
de Chiapa./ Dedié à Monſeigneur le Comte/ de
Toulouse./ A *Paris*,/ Chez Andrè Prelard, ruë
Saint Jacques, à l'Occaſion/ m.dc.xcvii./ Avec
Privilege du Roi./ (The Discovery of the East
Indies by the Spaniards. Written by Don Bal-
thasar de Las Casas, Bishop of Chiapa. Dedicated
to my Lord, the Count of Toulouse. Paris, At

Andrew Prelard's, St. James Street, at the Opportunity, 1697. With the King's privilege). 6 *prel.
leaves including engraved title; Text* 382 *pp ; Table*
2 *pp. Old calf.* 12*mo.*   (12*s.* 6*d.* 1650)

LAS CASAS (BARTHOLOME DE). Relation/ des/
Voyages/ et des/ découvertes/ Que les Espagnols
ont fait dans les/ Indes Occidentales ;/ Ecrite par
Dom B. de Las-Casas, Evê-/que de Chiapa./ Avec
la Relation curieuse des Voyages du/ Sieur de
Montauban, Capitaine des/ Filbustiers, en Guinée
l'an 1695./ A *Amsterdam*,/ Chez J. Louis de Lorme
Libraire sur le/ Rockin, à l'enseigne de la Liberte.'/
M.DCXCVIII./ 6 *prel. leaves, including Frontispiece ;
Text* 402 *pp. Catalogue,* 2 *pp. blank leaf ; Followed
by* L'Art/ de/ Voyager/ Utilement./ Suivant la
Copie de Paris./ A *Amsterdam*,/ Chez J. Louis de
Lorme Libraire sur le/ Rockin, à l'enseigne de la
Liberte.'/ M.DC.XCVIII./ 2 *prel. leaves and* 52 *pp.
Old calf.* 12*mo.*   (10*s.* 6*d.* 1651)

LAS CASAS (BARTHOLOME DE). An/ Account/ Of
the First/ Voyages and Discoveries/ Made by the
Spaniards in America./ Containing/ The most
Exact Relation hitherto pub/lish'd, of their unparallel'd Cruelties/ on the Indians, in the destruction of a-/bove Forty Millions of People./ With
the Propositions offer'd to the King of Spain,/ to
prevent the further Ruin of the West-Indies./ By
Don Bartholomew de las Casas, Bishop of Chiapa,/
who was an Eye-witness of their Cruelties./ Illustrated with Cuts./ To which is added,/ The Art
of Travelling, shewing how a Man may/ dispose his
Travels to the best advantage./ *London*,/ Printed
by J. Darby for D. Brown at the Black Swan/ and
Bible without Temple-Bar, J. Harris at the/ Har-
row in Little Britain, and Andr. Bell at the/
Cross-keys and Bible in Cornhil. M.DC.XC.IX./ 4
prel. leaves ; viz. Title, Preface, and Contents : Text
248 *pp.* 'The Art of Travelling to Advantage.' 40
pp. 2 *copperplates, each in two leaves at page* 1. *Old
calf.* 8*vo.*   (12*s.* 6*d.* 1652)

LAS CASAS (BARTHOLOME DE). Breve Relacion
de la Destruccion de las Indias Occidentales, Pre-
sentada a Felipe II siendo Principe de Asturias
por D. Fr. Bartolomé de las Casas, Del Orden de

Predicadores, Obispo de Chiapa. Impresa en
Sevilla en 1552. Reimpresa en *Londres* Por Schulze
y Dean, 13, Poland Street. 1812. *Half-title, title,
and* 140 *pp. Uncut.* 12*mo.*   (10*s.* 6*d.*   1653)

LASO DE LA VEGA (Antonio de Cordova).
✢ / Por/ D. Antonio de Cordova/ Laſo de la Vega,
Capitan de las Guardas/ de el Governador, y
Teniente Gene-/ral de la Cavalleria del Reyno/ de
Chile./ Con/ El Señor Fiscal del/ Conſejo de
Indias, y el Promotor Fiſcal/ de Cobranças de él./
[*Lima* 1620?]   4 *unnumbered leaves, unbound.*
Folio.   (1*l.* 1*s.*   1654)

LASSO DE LA VEGA (Gabriel). Elogios/ en
loor de/ los Tres Famosos Varo-/nes Don Iayme Rey
de Aragon, Don Fernan-/do Cortes Marques del
Valle, y Don/ Aluaro de Baçan Marques de/ Santa-
cruz./ Cõpueſtos por Gabriel Laſſo dela Vega
Cõtino del R. N. S./ Dirigidos a Don Gaſpar Gal-
çaran de Caſtro y Pi-/nos, Cõde de Guimaran,
Vizcõde de Ebol, &c./ Año 1601/. Con priuilegio, En *Caragoça* por Alonſo Rodriguez./ 8 *prel.
leaves and* 144 *folioed leaves. Fine copy. Old calf.*
16*mo.*   (3*l.* 13*s.* 6*d.*   1655)

LAST (The)/ Eaſt-Indian/ Voyage./ Containing
Mvch/ varietie of the State of the ſeuerall/ king-
domes where they haue traded :/ with the Letters of
three ſeuerall Kings/ to the Kings Maieſtie of
England,/ begun by one of the Voyage : ſince con-
tinued/ out of the faithfull obſeruations of/ them
that are come home./ At *London,*/ Printed by T.
P. for Walter Burre./ 1606./ *Title, reverse blank ;*
'To the Reader.' 1 *page, Signed* 'W. B.' *Text, sig.*
B *to* K *in fours. Half mor.* 4*to.*   (3*l.* 3*s.*   1656)

LATHROP (John). A Discourse Preached, December 15th 1774. Being the day recommended
By the Provincial Congreſs, To be Observed In
thankſgiving to God for the Bleſſings enjoyed ; and
humiliation on account of public Calamities. By
John Lathrop, A.M. Pastor of the Second Church
in Boston. *Boston :* Printed by D. Kneeland ;
and Sold by Samuel Webb, in Queen-Street. 1774.
39 *pp. Uncut.* 8*vo.*   (4*s.* 6*d.*   1657)

LATHROP (Joseph). Two Sermons, on the
Chriſtian Sabbath, for Distribution in the New

Settlements of the United States. By Joseph La-throp, D.D. Paſtor of the firſt Church in Weſt-Springfield. *Northampton,* (Maſſachuſetts.) Printed By William Butler, (For the Hampſhire Miſſionary Society.) 1803. *28 pp. Uncut.*
8vo. (2s. 6d. 1658)

LATOUR (A. LACARRIERE). Historical Memoir of the War in West Florida and Louisiana in 1814-15. With an Atlas. By Major A. Lacarriere Latour, Principal Engineer in the Seventh Mili-tary District United States' Army. Written Originally in French, and translated for the Au-thor, by H. P. Nugent, Esq. *Philadelphia:* Pub-lished by John Conrad and Co. J. Maxwell, printer 1816. *xx and 264 pp.* 'Appendix,' *cxc pp. With 7 colored maps and plans. Boards, uncut.*
8vo. (15s. 1659)

LAW (WILLIAM). An Extract from a Treatise By William Law, M.A. Called, The Spirit of Prayer; or, The Soul riſing out of the Vanity of Time, into the Riches of Eternity. Diſcovering the true Way of turning to God, and of finding the King-dom of Heaven the Riches of Eternity in our Souls. *Philadelphia:* Printed by B. Franklin, and D. Hall. 1760. *47 pp. 8vo.* (10s. 6d. 1660)

LAWSON (DEODAT). Christ's Fidelity/ the only/ Shield/ against/ Satan's Malignity./ Asserted in a/ Sermon/ Deliver'd at Salem-Village the/ 24th of March, 1692. Being Lecture-/day there, and a time of Publick Examination, of ſome Suſpected/ for Witchcraft./ By Deodat Lawson, Miniſter/ of the Goſpel./ The Second Edition./ Printed at Boſton in New-England, and Reprinted/ in *Lon-don* by R. Tokey for the Author; *etc.* 1704./ *6 prel. leaves, and 120 pp. Fine copy, half calf.*
12mo. (2l. 2s. 1661)

LAWSON (JOHN). A New Voyage to Carolina; Containing the Exact Deſcription and Natural Hiſtory of that Country: Together with the Pre-ſent State thereof. And A Journal Of a Thousand Miles, Travel'd thro' ſeveral Nations of Indians. Giving a particular Account of their Cuſtoms, Manners, &c. By John Lawson, Gent. Surveyor-General of North-Carolina. *London:* Printed in the Year 1709. *Title, reverse blank; Dedication to Lord Craven* 2 *pp; Preface* 2 *pp; Introduction & Journal,* 60 *pp; Description of North Carolina, pp.* 61 *to* 258 ; *Lately published etc.* 1 *page. Map at p.* 61. & *plate of animals at p.* 125. *Fine copy. Calf.* 4*to.* (2*l.* 12*s.* 6*d.* 1662)

This copy is as it was originally published in numbers, having the several titles to the April, May, June, and July numbers, 1709.

LECHFORD (Thomas). Plain Dealing:/ Or,/ Nevves/ from/ New-England./ A fhort view of New-Englands/ prefent Government, both Ecclefiafticall and Civil,/ compared with the anciently-received and efta-/blifhed Government of England, in/ fome materiall points ; fit for the gravest/ confideration in thefe times./ By Thomas Lechford of Clements Inne,/ in the County of Middlefex, Gent./ *London,*/ Printed by W. E. and I. G. for Nath: Butter, at the figne/ of the pyde Bull neere S. Auftins gate. 1642./ 4 *prel. leaves ; viz. Title, on the reverse Royal Arms;* 'To the Reader.' 5 *pp.* 'A Table' *etc.* 1 *page ; Text* 80 *pp. Fine copy, calf extra by Bedford.* 4*to.* (5*l.* 5*s.* 1663)

LEDERER (John). The/ Discoveries/ of/ John Lederer,/ In three feveral Marches from/ Virginia,/ To the Weft of/ Carolina,/ And other parts of the Continent:/ Begun in March 1669, and ended in September 1670./ Together with/ A General Map of the whole Territory/ which he traverfd./ Collected and Tranflated out of Latine from his Difcourfe/ and Writings,/ By Sir William Talbot Baronet./ *London,* Printed by J. C. for Samuel Heyrick, at Grays-/Inne-gate in Holborn. 1672./ 3 *prel. leaves ; viz. Title reverse blank,* 'To the Right Honourable Anthony Lord Ashley,' *etc.* 2 *pp, signed* 'William Talbot.' 'To the Reader.' 2 *pp, signed* 'William Talbot.' 'A Map of the whole Territory Traversed by Iohn Lederer in his three Marches.' *Text* 27 *pp. Fine copy. Green morocco extra.* 4*to.* (3*l.* 3*s.* 1664)

LEE (Charles). Memoirs of the life of the late Charles Lee, Esq. Lieutenant Colonel of the Forty Fourth Regiment, Colonel in the Portuguese service, Major General, and Aid du Camp to the King of Poland, and Second in Command in the Service of the United States of America during the Revolution : To which are added his Political and Military Essays ; also, Letters to, and from many distinguished Characters, both in Europe and America. *Dublin:* P. Byrne, *etc.* 1792. *xii and* 439 *pp. Old calf. 8vo.* (10s. 6d. 1665)

LEE (CHARLES). The Life and Memoirs of the late Major General Lee, Second in Command to General Washington, during the American Revolution, to which are added, his Political and Military Essays. Also, Letters to and from many distinguished Characters both in Europe and America. *New-York;* Richard Scott, 1813. 4 *prel. leaves and pp.* 13-352. *Calf. 12mo.* (7s. 6d. 1666)

LEEDS (DANIEL). An Almanack For the Year of Christian Account 1687. Particularly respecting the Meridian and Latitude of Burlington, but may indifferently serve all places adjacent By Daniel Leeds, Student in Agriculture. Printed and Sold by William Bradford, near *Philadelphia* in Pennsylvania, pro Anno 1687. *A broadside.* *Folio.* (2l. 2s. 1667)

This sheet Almanac is said to have been the first piece printed at Philadelphia. The present copy is only a fragment of about three-eighths of the whole, but it has the lower right-hand corner, with the date 1687.

LEEDS (DANIEL). *The same, a reprint. A broadside.* *Folio.* (2s. 6d. 1668)

LEEVEN EN DADEN/ der Doorluchtighfte/ Zee-Helden/ en/ Ontdeckers van Landen,/ deser eeuwen./ Beginnende met/ Christoffel Colombus,/ Vinder van de Nieuwe Wereldt./ En eyndigende met den Roemruchtigen Admirael/ M. A. de Ruyter, Ridd, &c./ Vertoonende veel vreemde Voorvallen, dappere Verrichtingen,/ ftoutmoedige Beftieringen, en fwaere Zee-flagen, &c./ Naeukeurigh, uyt veele geloofwaerdige Schriften, en Authentijcke/ Stucken, by een gebracht, en befchreven,/ Door V. D. B./ t'*Amsterdam,*/ By Jan Claesz. ten Hoorn, en Jan Bouman,/ Boeckverkoopers. Anno 1676./ Met Privilegie voor 15. Jaren./ 5 *prel. leaves; viz. Engraved title* ' Leeven. en Daden./ der Doorlughtige/ Zee-Helden./' *title on the reverse* ' Privilegie.' *Portrait of De Ruyter.* ' Op-dracht' 2 *pp.* ' Aen den Lezer.' *and* ' Register.' 2 *pp. Text* 350 *pp. Copperplates at pp.* 1, 20, 45, 79, 89, 108,

128, 153, 183, 210, 235, 258, 280. Tweede Deel. 2 *and* 303 *pp.* 'Register.' 7 *pp. Copperplates at pp.* 1, 7, 43, 50, 71, 85, 92, 121, 166, 173, 179, 185, 251, 271, 281, 295, 299. *Calf extra by Clarke and Bedford.* 4*to.* (1*l.* 11*s.* 6*d.* 1669)

LEEVEN EN DAADEN/ der Doorluchtigſte/ Zee-Helden,/ Beginnende met de Tocht na/ Damiaten,/ Voorgevallen in den Jare 1217./ En eindigende met den beroemden Admirael/ M. A. de Ruyter, Hartog, Ridd, &c./ Vertoonende alle de voorna-emſte Zeedaden die de Hollanders en Zee-/landers &c. van haer begin aen, loffelijck tegens hun vy-anden ver-/richt hebben ; nevens veel vreemde Voorvallen, dappere Helde-/daden, ſtoutmoedige Beſtieringen, en ſwaere Zee-ſlagen, &c./ Naeukeu-righ, uyt veele geloofwaerdige Schriften, en Au-thentijcke/ Stucken, by een gebracht, en beſchre-ven,/ Door V. D. B./ Met veele curieuſe koopere Plaeten verciert./ t'*Amsteldam*,/ By Jan ten Hoorn, en Jan Bouman,/ Boekverkoopers, in Compagnie. Anno 1683./ 8 *prel. leaves; viz. Engraved title,* 'Leeven. en Daden./ der Doorlughtige/ Zee-Hel-den./ T'*Amsterdam*/ By Jan ten Hoorn, en Jan Bouman,/ Boekverkópers in Compani 1683./ *Title, on the reverse* ' Privilegie.' ' Opdracht ' 2 *pp.* ' Aan den Leezer.' 2 *pp.* ' Register Der Hooft-Deelen ' 8 *pp. Text* 784 *pp.* 'Register.' 7 *pp. Copperplates at pp.* 3, 39, 93, 123, 127, 150, 193, 203, 224, 282, 293, 326, 412, 482, 489, 512, 519, 548, 558, 587, 593, 601, 633, 721, 749, 773, 778, 781. *Vellum.* 4*to.* (1*l.* 11*s.* 6*d.* 1670)

LEIGH (EGERTON). Extracts from the Proceedings of the High Court of Vice-Admiralty, in Charles-town, South Carolina, upon Six several Informa-tions, adjudged by The Honourable Egerton Leigh, Esq ; Sole Judge of that Court, and His Majesty's Attorney-General in the ſaid Province, In the Years 1767 and 1768. With explanatory Remarks, &c. And copies of two extraordinary Oaths. To which are subjoined, Recapitulation, reflections arising from a retrospect of a late Case, and some General Observations on American Custom-House Officers, And Courts of Vice-Admiralty. The Se-cond Edition, with an Appendix. *Charlestown:* Printed by David Bruce. MDCCLXIX. *iv and* 64 *pp. Folio.* (2*l.* 12*s.* 6*d.* 1671)

LEJARZA (Juan Jose Martinez de). Análsis Estadístico. De la Provincia de Michuacan, en 1822. Por J. J. L. *Mexico*: 1824. *2 prel. leaves, ix and* 281 *pp. Tabla Num.* 1-7. *4to.* (15s. 1672)

LEO AFRICANUS (Jean). Historiale/ Description/ de l'Afriqve, Tier=/ce partie dv/ Monde,/ Contenant fes Royaumes, Regions, Viles, Citez,/ Chateaus & forterefles: Iles, Fleuues, Ani-/maus, tant aquatiques, que terreftres: coutu-/mes, loix, religion & façon de faire des habitãs,/ auec pourtraits de leurs habis: enfemble autres/ chofes memorables, & fingulieres nouueautez :/ Efcrite de nôtre temps par Iean Leon, African,/ premierement en langue Arabefque, puis en Tof-/cane, & à present mife en François./ *En Anvers./* Ches Iean Bellere./ 1556./ 16 *prel. leaves: Text* 412 *folioed leaves.* 'Indice des principales matieres' *etc.* 48 *pp. Calf extra.* 8vo. (1l. 1s. 1673)

LEON (Antonio de). Epitome/ de la/ Biblioteca/ Oriental i Occidental, Nautica/ i Geografica./ Al Excelentiff. Señor D. Ramiro Nuñez/ Perez Felipe de Guzman, Señor de la Cafa/ de Guzman, Duque de Medina de las Tor=/res Marques de Toral i Monafterio, Conde/ de Parmaccello i Valdorce, Comendador/ de Valdepeñas, Gran Canciller de las In=/ dias, Teforero General de la Corona de Ara,/=gon i Confejo de Italia, Capitan de los cien/ Hijosdalgo de la guarda de la Real per=/fona i Sumiller de Corps./ Por el Licenciado Antonio de Leon/ Relator del Supremo i Real/ Consejo de las Indias./ Con Priuilegio./ *En Madrid,* Por Iuan Gonzalez./ Año de M.DCXXIX. *Engraved title and* 43 *prel. leaves; Text* 186 *pp.* 'Appendice.' *xii pp, and Colophon leaf. Half calf.* 4to. (2l. 2s. 1674)

LEON (Antonio de). Politica/ de las Grandezas/ y Govierno del Svpremo/ y Real Consejo de/ las Indias./ Dirigida/ Al Rey Nvestro Señor en el/ mifmo Real Confejo, Prefidente el Licenciado D. Iuan de Vi-/lela del Ábito de Santiago; Gran Can ciller el Côde Duque dõ/ Gafpar de Guzman, Comendador mayor de Alcantara; Confe-/jeros, el Lic. don Francifco Arias Maldonado, Maeftre-efcuela/ de Salamanca, Lic. Iuan Gonçalez de Solorçano, Lic. don Ro-/drigo de Aguiar y Acuña, Lic.

Alonſo Maldonado de Torres,/ Lic. Fernando de Villa ſeñor, Preſidente de la Contratacion,/ Lic. Sancho Florez del Conſejo de Cruzada, Lic. don Diego de/ Cardenas, Lic. don Franciſco Manſo y Zuñiga, Lic. don Pedro/ de Bibanco, del Abito de Santiago, Lic. don Diego Gonçalez/ de Cuenca y Contreras, Lic. don Franciſco Antonio de Alarcō/ del Abito de Santiago ; Fiſcal el Lic. don Antonio de la/ Cueva y Silva, Secretarios, Pedro de Ledeſ-ma, y/ don Ferdinando de Contreras ; Teniente de/ Gran Canciller D. Antonio de/ Aguiar y Acuña, del Abito/ de Santiago./ Por el Licenciado Antonio de Leon./ [*Lima*, 1658 ?] *Title and* 20 *folioed leaves. Vellum.* 4*to.*   (1*l.* 1*s.* 1675)

LEON PINELO (Antonio de). [*Printed Title*] Vida/ del Ilvstr. i Reverend./ Don Toribio/ Alfonso Mogrovejo/ Arzobispo de Lima./ [*Engraved Title*] Vida/ del Ilvstrissimo/ i Reverendiſſimo D. Toribio/ Alfonso Mogrovejo./ Arcobispo de la Civdad/ de los Reyes Lima/ Cabeza de las Provincias del Piru./ Dedicase./ Al Eminentissimo S.ʳ/ Don Baltasar de Moscoso/ y Sandoval, Presbitero Cardenal de la/ S.ª Igleſia de Roma del Titulo de S.ª Cruz/ en Gerusalen Arcobiſpo de Toledo Pri/-mado de las Eſpañas Chanciller/ mayor de Caſtilla del Con-/ſejo de Eſtado. &/ Por el Licenciado Antonio/ de Leon Pinelo, Relator del Conſejo Supre-/mo de las Indias, y del de la/ Camara dellas./ [*Lima*] 1653. 24 *prel. leaves and* 421 *pp. With Portrait of Toribius Alfonsus Mogrovejo. Calf.* 4*to.*   (2*l.* 2*s.* 1676)

LEON Y GAMA (Antonio de). Disertacion Fisica sobre la Materia y Formacion de las Auroras Boreales, que con ocasion de la que aparecio en Mexico y otros Sugares de la Nueva España el dia 14 de Noviembre de 1789. Escribió D. Antonio de Leon y Gama. Con las Licencias Necesarias. *Mexico:* Por D. Felipe de Zuñiga y Ontiveros, calle del Espíritu Santo, año de 1790. *Title and* 37 *pp. Half mor.* 4*to.*   (10*s.* 6*d.* 1677)

LEON Y GAMA (Antonio de). Descripcion Histórica y Cronológica de las dos Piedras que con ocasion del nuevo Empedrado que se está form-ando en la Plaza Principal de México, se hallaron

en ella el Año de 1790. Explícase el sistema de
los Calendarios de los Indios, el método que tenian
de dividir el tiempo, y la correccion que hacian de él
para igualar el año civil, de que usaban, con el
año solar trópico. Noticia muy necesaria para la
perfecta inteligencia de la segunda piedra: á que
se añaden otras curiosas é instructivas sobre la
Mitología de los Mexicanos, sobre su Astronomía,
y sobre los ritos y ceremonias que acostumbraban
en tiempo de su Gentilidad. Por Don Antonio de
Leon y Gama. *México.* En la Imprenta de Don
Felipe de Zúñiga y Ontiveros Año de M.DCC.XCII.
3 *prel. leaves and* 116 *pp. Lista, etc.* 2 *pp. and* 3
plates. Calf. 4*to.*   (15*s.* 1678)

LE PAGE DU PRATZ (M.)   Histoire de la
Louisiane, Contenant la Découverte de ce vaste
Pays; sa Description géographique; un Voyage
dans les Terres; l'Histoire Naturelle; les Mœurs,
Coûtumes & Religion des Naturels, avec leurs
Origines; deux Voyages dans le Nord du nouveau
Mexique, dont un jusqu'à la Mer du Sud; ornée
de deux Cartes & de 40 Planches en Taille douce.
Par M. Le Page du Pratz. A *Paris,* M.DCC.LVIII.
Three Volumes. Tome Premier, *xvj and* 358 *pp.*
2 *copperplate maps at pp.* 138, 139. Tome Second,
Half-title, title, and 441 *pp.* 34 *copperplates.* Tome
Troisieme, *Half-title, title, and* 451 *pp. Approba-
tion and Privilege* 3 *pp. Errata* 1 *page.* 4 *copper-
plates. Old calf.* 12*mo.*   (15*s.* 1679)

LE PAGE DU PRATZ (M.)   The History of
Louisiana, or of The Western Parts of Virginia
and Carolina: Containing A Description of the
Countries that lye on both Sides of the River
Missisipi: With An Account of the Settlements,
Inhabitants, Soil, Climate, and Products. Trans-
lated from the French, (lately published,) By M.
Le Page Du Pratz; with Some Notes and Obser-
vations relating to our Colonies. In Two Volumes.
London, T. Becket and P. A. De Hondt. MDCC
LXIII. *Two Volumes.* Vol. I. *Half-title, title, l pp.
vii and* 368 *pp.* 2 *maps.* Vol. II. 4 *prel. leaves,
and* 272 *pp. Old calf.* 12*mo.*   (15*s.* 1680)

LE ROY (P. L.)   A Narrative of the singular
Adventures of Four Russian Sailors, Who were

caſt away on the deſert Iſland of East-Spitzbergen.
Together with some Observations on the Productions of that Iſland, &c. By Mr. P. L. Le Roy,
Profeſſor of Hiſtory, and Member of the Imperial
Academy of Sciences at St. Peterſburg. Tranſlated from the German Original, at the deſire of
ſeveral Members of the Royal Society. [*London,*
1774?] *Title and pp.* 43-118. *Half morocco.*
8*vo.* (4*s.* 6*d.* 1681)

LERY (JEAN DE). Histoire/ d'vn Voyage/ fait en
la terre/ dv Bresil, avtre-/ment dite Ame-/rique./
Contenant la nauigation, & choſes remar-/quables,
veuës ſur mer par l'auĉteur : Le compor/ tement
de Villegagnon, en ce païs là. Les meurs/ & façons
de viure eſtranges des Sauuages A-/meriquains :
auec vn colloque de leur langage./ Enſemble la
deſcription de pluſieurs Animaux,/ Arbres, Herbes,
& autres choſes ſingulieres,/ & du tout inconues par
deçà, dont on verra les/ ſommaires des chapitres
au commencement du/ liure./ Non encores mis en
lumiere, pour les cauſes/ contenues en la preface./
Le tout recueilli ſur les lieux par Iean de/ Lery
natif de la Margelle, terre/ de ſainĉt Sene au Duché
de/ Bourgongne./ Seigneur, ie te celebreray entre
les peu-/ples & te diray Pſeaumes entre les na-/
tions. Pseav. cviii. [*A la Rochelle.*] Pour Antoine Chuppin. M.D.LXXVIII./ *First Edition.* 24
prel. leaves, and 424 *pp. Table* 12 *pp. Errata* 1 *page.*
Vellum. 8*vo.* (2*l.* 2*s.* 1682)

LERY (JEAN DE). Histoire/ d'vn Voyage/ faict en
la terre dv/ Bresil, avtrement/ dite Amerique./
Contenant la navigation,/ & choſes remarquables,
veuës ſur mer par l'auĉteur : Le com-/portement de
Villegagnon en ce pays-/la. Les mœurs & façons/
de viure eſtranges des Sauuages Ameriquains :
auec vn collo/-que de leur langage. Enſemble
la deſcription de pluſieurs A-/nimaux, Arbres,
Herbes, & autres choſes ſingulieres, & du/ tout incõ-
nues par deçà : dont on verra les ſommaires des
cha-/pitres au commencement du liure./ Reveve
corrigee, et bien/ augmentee en ceſte ſeconde
Edition, tant de fi-/gures, qu'autres chſoes notables
ſur le/ ſuiet de l'auteur. Le tout recueilli ſur les
lieux par Iean de/ Lery, natif de la Margelle,
terre/ de ſainĉt Sene, au Duché de/ Bourgongne./

[*A la Rochelle*] Pour Antoine Chuppin./ M.D.LXXX./ 22 *prel. leaves, and* 382 *pp.* *Table* 10 *pp.* *Errata* 1 *page.* *Vellum.* 8*vo.*   (1*l.* 5*s.* 1683)

LERY (JEAN DE). Historia/ Navigationis/ in Bra-siliam,/ quæ et America/ dicitvr./ Qva describitvr avtoris/ nauigatio, quæque in mari vidit memoriæ pro-/denda: Villagagnonis in America gesta: Brasi-/liensium victus & mores, à nostris admodum a-/lieni, cum eorum linguæ dialogo: animalia etiam,/ arbores, atque herbæ, reliquáque singularia & no-/bis penitùs incognita./ A Ioanne Lerio Bvrgvndo/ Gallicè scripta. Nunc verò primum Latinitate/ donata, & variis figuris illustrata./ Excvdebat/ Evstathivs Vignon./ Anno cɪɔ ɪɔ LXXXVI./ [*Genevæ*] 32 *prel. leaves, the last blank; Text* 342 *pp. Index* 16 *pp. At page* 178 *is a wood-cut* 6¼ *by* 9 *inches. Vellum.* 8*vo.*   (1*l.* 10*s.* 1684)

LERY (JEAN DE). Historia/ Navigationis/ in Bra-siliam/ quæ et America/ dicitur./ Qva describitvr avthoris/ nauigatio, quæque in mari vidit me-moriæ prodenda: Villa-/gagnonis in America gesta: Brasiliensium victus & mores, à/ nostris ad-modum alieni, cum eorum linguæ dialogo: ani-/malia etiam, arbores, atque herbæ, reliquáque singularia &/ nobis penitus incognita./ A Joanne Lerio Bvrgundo/ Gallicè scripta. Nunc verò pri-mùm Latinitate/ donata, & varijs figuris illustrata./ Secvnda Editio./ *Genevæ.*/ Apud hæredes Eusta-thij Vignon./ cɪɔ ɪɔ xcIIII. *Title, reverse blank;* 'Epistola,' 3 *leaves;* *Epigrams* 2 *leaves;* 'Totivs Historiæ Svmma Capita,' 2 *leaves;* 'Praefatio,' 21 *leaves; text* 340 *pp.* 'Index,' 8 *leaves; with folding woodcut to face p.* 178. *Fine copy. Old calf.* 8*vo.*   (1*l.* 10*s.* 1685)

LE SAGE (M.) The Adventures of Robert Che-valier, call'd De Beauchene, Captain of a Priva-teer in New-France. By Monsieur Le Sage, Author of Gil-Blas. In Two Volumes. *London :* T. Gardner, M,DCC,XLV. *Two Volumes.* Vol I. 4 *prel. leaves, and* 307 *pp.* Vol. II. 4 *prel. leaves, and* 287 *pp.* 12*mo.*   (10*s.* 6*d.* 1686)

LESLIE (CHARLES). A New and Exact Account of Jamaica, wherein The Antient and Present State of that Colony, its Importance to Great Britain,

Laws, Trade, Manners and Religion, together with the moſt remarkable and curious Animals, Plants, Trees, &c. are deſcribed : With a particular Account of the Sacrifices, Libations, &c. at this Day in Uſe among the Negroes. The Third Edition. To which is added, An Appendix, containing an Account of Admiral Vernon's Success at Porto Bello and Chagre. *Edinburgh :* R. Fleming, Mdccxl. 4 *prel. leaves, and* 376 *pp. Calf.* 8vo. (10s. 6d. 1687)

LESSEPS (M. de). Travels in Kamtschatka, during the years 1787 and 1788. Translated from the French of M. De Lesseps, Consul of France, and Interpreter to the Count de la Perouse, now engaged in a Voyage round the World, by Command of his most Christian Majesty. In Two Volumes. *London:* J. Johnson, 1790. *Two Volumes.* Vol. I. *xvi and* 283 *pp. Map.* Vol. II. *viii and* 408 *pp. Calf.* 8vo. (10s. 6d. 1688)

LETERA de la nobil cipta: nouamente ritrouata alle Indie con li coſtumi & modi del ſuo Re & ſoi populi : Li modi del ſuo adorate con la bella vſanza de le donne loro : & de le dua perſone ermafrodite donate da quel Re al Capitano de larmata. [*at the end*] Data in Peru adi. xxv. de Nouembre. Del mdxxxiiii. [*Reprint, Milan,* 1830 ?] 8 *pp. boards.* 4to. (1l. 1s. 1689)

LETRAS Anvas/ de la Compania/ de Iesvs/ de la Provincia/ del Nvevo Reyno/ de Granada./ Desde el Ano de Mil y Seys cientos/ y treinta y ocho,/ hasta el Ano de Mil y Seys cientos/ y quaranta y tres./ En *Zaragoza* Año de 1645./ Impreſas con licencia delos Superiores./ 239 *pp. Old calf.* 4to. (1l. 11s. 6d. 1690)

LETTER (A) from a Merchant at Jamaica to a Member of Parliament in London, Touching the African Trade. To which is added, A Speech made by a Black of Gardaloupe, at the Funeral of a Fellow-Negro, *London*, A. Baldwin. mdccix. 31 *pp. Uncut. Half mor. Small* 8vo. (4s. 6d. 1691)

LETTER (A) from South Carolina; giving an Account of the Soil, Air, Product, Trade, Government, Laws, Religion, People, Military Strength, &c., of that Province; Together with the manner

and neceſſary Charges of Settling a Plantation there, and the Annual Profit it will produce. Written by a Swiſs Gentleman, to his friend at Bern. *London*, A. Baldwin, 1710. *63 pp. Half morocco.*
8vo.   (10s. 6d.   1692)

LETTER (A) To the Right Honourable The Lords Commiſſioners of Trade & Plantations: Or, A ſhort Essay on the Principal Branches of the Trade of New-England, with the Difficulties they labour under; and Some Methods of Improvement. *London:* 1715. *2 prel. leaves; viz. Title and Dedication, Signed* 'T. B.' *Text 19 pp. Half morocco.*
8vo.   (12s. 6d.   1693)

LETTER (A) To the Right Reverend the Lord Biſhop of London, from An Inhabitant of his Majesty's Leeward-Caribbee-Iſlands. Containing ſome Considerations on His Lordſhip's Two Letters of May 19, 1727. The first To the Masters and Mistresses of Families in the Engliſh Plantations abroad; The second To the Missionaries there. In which is Inſerted, A Short Essay concerning the Conversion of the Negro-Slaves in our Sugar-Colonies; Written in the Month of June, 1727, by the ſame Inhabitant. *London:* J. Wilford, 1730. *Half-title, title, and text 103 pp. Half morocco.*
8vo.   (7s. 6d.   1694)

LETTER (A Second) From a Miniſter of the Church of England To his Diſſenting Pariſhioners, In Anſwer to Some Remarks made on the former, by one J. G. *Boston:* Printed in the Year 1734. *Half-title, title and 113 pp. Errata 1 page, half mor.*
8vo.   (7s. 6d.   1695)

LETTER (A) To a certain Eminent British Sailor. Occaſion'd by his Specimen of Naked Truth. From a zealous Aſſertor of his Merit, and ſincere Well-wiſher to his Person. *London:* M. Moore, M.DCCXLVI. *32 pp. half mor. 8vo.*   (6s.   1696)

LETTER (A) to Mrs. P------- S. In which ſome Facts in her laſt Number are reſcued from the falſe Light ſhe has put them in, and ſome others which ſhe has omitted, are ſupply'd. *London:* H. Carpenter, M.DCC.XLIX. *Title and 21 pp. half mor.*
8vo.   (7s. 6d.   1697)

LETTER (A) to the People of England, on the Prefent Situation and Conduct of National Affairs. Letter I. The Third Edition. *London:* Printed in the Year, 1756. *56 pages. Half morocco.* 8vo. (4s. 6d. 1698)

LETTER (A Second) to the People of England on Foreign Subsidies, Subsidiary Armies, and Their Confequences to this Nation. The Third Edition. *London:* J. Scott, MDCCLVI. *56 pp. Half morocco.* 8vo. (4s. 6d. 1699)

LETTER (A Third) to the People of England, on Liberty, Taxes, And the Application of Publick Money. The Third Edition. *London:* Printed in the Year, 1756. *Title and pp. 5-54. half morocco.* 8vo. (4s. 6d. 1700)

LETTER (A Fourth) to the People of England. On the conduct of the M——rs in Alliances, Fleets, and Armies, fince the firft Differences on the Ohio, to the taking of Minorca by the French. *London:* M. Collier, 1756. *Half-title, title, and* 111 *pp. half mor.* 8vo. (4s. 6d. 1701)

LETTER (A) to a Clergyman, in the Colony of Connecticut, from his Friend. In which, the true Notion of Orthodoxy is enquired into; and fome Thoughts are fuggefted concerning publick Tefts of Orthodoxy, and the mifchievous Effects of fetting up falfe Tefts thereof. *New-Haven:* Printed by James Parker, and Company. MDCCLVII. *24 pp. signed* 'Catholicus.' 8vo. (4s. 6d. 1702)

LETTER (A) to the Right Honourable William Pitt, Esq; from an Officer at Fort Frontenac. *London:* J. Fleming, MDCCLIX. *Half-title, title, and* 38 *pp.* 8vo. (7s. 6d. 1703)

LETTER (A) to the Clergy of the Colony of Connecticut, from an Aged Layman of faid Colony. [*New-Haven?*] Printed in the Year 1760. *22 pp.* 8vo. (4s. 6d. 1704)

LETTER (A) Addressed to Two Great Men, on the Prospect of Peace; And on the Terms neceffary to be infifted upon in the Negociation. *London:* A. Millar, MDCCLX. *Title and 56 pp. Half morocco.* 8vo. (5s. 6d. 1705)

LETTER (A) Addressed to Two Great Men, on the
Prospect of Peace ; And on the Terms neceſſary to
be inſiſted upon in the Negociation. The Second
Edition, corrected. *London :* A Millar, MDCCLX.
Half-title, title, and text 56 pp. Half morocco.
8vo. (5s. 6d. 1706)

LETTER (A) To an Honourable Brigadier General,
Commander in Chief of his Majeſty's Forces in
Canada. *London,* J. Burd, 1760. *Title and 32 pp.*
half mor. 8vo. (5s. 6d. 1707)
<small>Now generally acknowledged to be by Junius. It has been re-
printed by Mr. Simons of the British Museum.</small>

LETTER (A) to the People of England, on the Necessity of putting an Immediate End to the War ;
and The Means of obtaining an Advantageous
Peace. *London :* R. Griffiths, MDCCLX. *Title and*
52 pp. half mor. 8vo. (4s. 6d. 1708)

LETTER (A) to a Great M --------- R, on the
Proſpect of a Peace ; Wherein the Demolition of
the Fortifications of Louisbourg Is ſhewn to be
abſurd ; The Importance of Canada fully refuted ;
The proper Barrier pointed out in North America ;
and the Reaſonableneſs and Neceſſity of retaining
the French Sugar Islands. Containing Remarks
on ſome preceding Pamphlets that have treated of
the Subject, and a ſuccinct View of the whole
Terms that ought to be inſiſted on from France at
a future Negociation. By an unprejudiced Observer. *London :* G. Kearsly, MDCCLXI. *Title and*
148 pp. half mor. (7s. 6d. 1709)

LETTER (A) to G. G. *Stiff in Opinions, always in*
the wrong. London : J. Williams, MDCCLXVII.
Half-title, title, and text 96 pp. Half morocco.
8vo. (7s. 6d. 1710)
<small>This letter is signed *L*, at the end, and is dated " Richmond, Jan.
18, 1767." It was addressed to George Grenville, the Minister,
and relates entirely to American Affairs.</small>

LETTER, (A) concerning an American Bishop,
&c. To Dr. Bradbury Chandler, Ruler of St.
John's Church, in Elizabeth-Town. In Anſwer to
the Appendix Of His 'Appeal to the Public, &c.
Printed, A.D. 1768. *19 pp. Half morocco.*
8vo. (7s. 6d. 1711)

LETTER (A) To the Right Honourable The Earl
of H ---- B ----- H, His M——y's S——y of

S—te for the C—l——s, on the Present Situation
of Affairs in the Island of Gr—n—da. *London:*
J. Wilkie, M.DCC.LXIX. *54 pp. Half morocco.*
8vo. (4s. 6d. 1712)

LETTER (A) to Samuel Johnson, L.L.D. [in answer to the False Alarm,] J. Almon, 1770. *Title,
and pp. 5-54. half mor. 8vo.* (3s. 6d. 1713)

LETTER (A) from a Virginian to the Members of
the Congrefs to be held at Philadelphia, on The Firſt
of September, 1774. Boston, printed: *London,* reprinted ; J. Wilkie 1774. *Title, 4 and 60 pp. half
mor. 8vo.* (5s. 6d. 1713*)

LETTER (A) to Doctor Tucker on his proposal of
a Separation between Great Britain and her American Colonies. *London.* J. Becket, MDCCLXXIV.
Title and 36 pp. half mor. 8vo. (5s. 6d. 1714)

LETTER (A) to a Member of Parliament on the
Present Unhappy Dispute between Great-Britain
and her Colonies. Wherein the Supremacy of the
Former is Aſſerted and Proved; and the Necessity of Compelling the Latter to pay due Obedience
to the Sovereign State, is Enforced, upon Principles
of Sound Policy, Reason, and Justice. *London:*
J. Walter, MDCCLXXIV. *Title and 47 pp. half mor.
8vo.* (5s. 6d. 1715)

LETTER (A) to [William Pitt] the Earl of Chat
ham, on the Quebec Bill. *London:* T. Cadell,
MDCCLXXIV. *Title and 36 pp. Half morocco.*
8vo. (4s. 6d. 1716)

LETTER (A) to the People of Great-Britain, in
Answer to that published by the American Congress. *London:* F. Newbery, MDCCLXXV. *59 pp.
half mor. 8vo.* (5s. 6d. 1717)

LETTER (A) to the Right Honourable Lord Cam-
den, on the Bill for restraining the Trade and
Fishery of the Four Provinces of New England.
London: T. Cadell, MDCCLXXV. *Title and 44 pp.
half mor. 8vo.* (7s. 6d. 1718)

LETTER (A) to Doctor Mather. Occaſioned by
his diſingenuous Reflexions upon a certain Pamphlet, entitled, Salvation for all Men. By One
who wiſhes well to Him in common with Mankind.

[*Rev. John Clark, of Boston.*] *Boston:* Printed and fold by T. and J. Fleet at the Bible and Heart in Cornhill, 1782. *Title, and text* 9 *pp. Unbound.* 8*vo.* (2*s.* 6*d.* 1719)

LETTERS (Two) of the Lord Bifhop of London: The First, To the Mafters and Miftreffes of Families in the Englifh Plantations abroad; Exhorting them to Encourage and Promote the Inftruction of their Negroes in the Chriftian Faith. The Second, To the Missionaries there; Directing them to diftribute the faid Letter, and Exhorting them to give their Affiftance towards the Inftruction of the Negroes within their feveral Parifhes. *London:* Joseph Downing, M.DCC.XXVII. 20 *pp. Half mor.* 4*to.* (7*s.* 6*d.* 1720)

LETTERS from a Farmer in Pennfylvania, To the Inhabitants of the British Colonies. *Boston:* Printed by Mein and Fleeming, and to be sold by John Mein, at the London Book-Store, North-Side of King-Street. MDCCLXVIII. *Title and pp.* 5-146. 'To the ingenious Author,' *etc.* 2 *pp. Half morocco.* 8*vo.* (5*s.* 6*d.* 1721)

LETTERS and other Papers relating to the Proceedings of his Majefty's Commiffioners. By the Earl of Carlisle, Sir Henry Clinton, William Eden, Esquire, and George Johnstone, Esquire, Commiffioners appointed by his Majefty in Purfuance of an Act of Parliament, to treat, confult, and agree upon the Means of quieting the Diforders now subfifting in certain of the Colonies, Plantations, and Provinces of North-America. 55 *pp.* Propofed Appendix to the feveral Publications relating to the Proceedings of His Majesty's Commissioners. By a Well Wifher to the Profperity both of Great-Britain and North-America. [Rivington, *New-York,* 1778] 10 *leaves. Privately printed. Half mor.* 8*vo.* (10*s.* 6*d.* 1722)

LETTERS of Papinian: In which The Conduct, prefent State, and Profpects of the American Congress are Examined. New-York, Printed: *London:* Reprinted for J. Wilkie, MDCCLXXIX. 3 *prel. leaves, and text* 86 *pp. uncut. Half morocco.* 8*vo.* (5*s.* 6*d.* 1723)

LETTERS to a Nobleman, on the Conduct of the War in the Middle Colonies. *London:* J. Wilkie, MDCCLXXIX. *3 prel. leaves, and* 101 *pp. With a Plan. 8vo.* (5s. 6d. 1724)

LETTERS to a Nobleman, on the Conduct of the War in the Middle Colonies. The Fourth Edition. *London:* G. Wilkie, MDCCLXXX. *3 prel. leaves, and* 101 *pp. With the Plan. 8vo.* (5s. 6d. 1725)

LETTERS and Dissertations, by the Author of the Letter Analysis A. P. On the Disputes between Great Britain and America. *London:* Printed for the Author. M.DCC.LXXXII. 130 *pp. half mor.* 12*mo.* (7s. 6d. 1726)

LETTERS and Papers on Agriculture: Extracted from the Correspondence of a Society instituted at Halifax, for Promoting Agriculture in the Province of Nova-Scotia. To which is added a selection of Papers on various branches of Husbandry, from some of the best publications on the subject in Europe and America. Vol. I. [*all published?*] *Halifax:* Printed by John Howe, in Barrington-Street. M.DCC.XCI. 139 *pp. Contents 2 pp. Old green morocco extra. 8vo.* (7s. 6d. 1727)
With the Autograph of John Inglis, Bishop of Nova Scotia, on the title-page.

LETTRES/ à un Amériquain/ sur l'histoire naturelle, générale et par-/ticuliere de monsieur de Buffon./ troisiéme partie./ à *Hamburg*/ 1. 7. 5. 1./ *Title,* 31, 96, *and* 69 *pp. Small 8vo.* (10s. 6d. 1728)

LEWIS (MERRIWETHER.) The Travels of Capts. Lewis & Clarke, from St. Louis, by way of the Missouri and Columbia Rivers, to the Pacific Ocean; performed in the years 1804, 1805, & 1806, by Order of the Government of the United States. Containing delineations of the Manners, Customs, Religion, &c. Of the Indians, compiled from Various Authentic Sources, and Original Documents, and a Summary of the Statistical View of the Indian Nations, from the Official communications of Merriwether Lewis. Illustrated with a Map of the Country, inhabited by the Western Tribes of Indians. *London:* Longman, 1809. *ix and* 309 *pp. Map. 8vo.* (7s. 6d. 1729)

LEWIS (Merriweather.) Travels to the Source
of the Missouri River and across the American
Continent to the Pacific Ocean. Performed by
Order of the Government of the United States, in
the Years 1804, 1805, and 1806. By Captains
Lewis and Clarke. Published from the Official
Report and Illustrated by a Map of the Route, and
other Maps. *London:* Longman, 1814. *xxiv and
663 pp. Large map and 2 small maps at page 379.
Calf. 4to.* (15s. 1730)

LEYES y ordenanzas nuevamente hechas/ por su
Magestad, para la gobernacion de las/ Indias y
buen tratamiento y conservacion de los/ Indios;
que se han da guardar en el consejo y au-/diencias
reales que en ellas residen: y por todos/ los otros
gobernadores, juezes y personas particu-/lares de
ellas./ Con privilegio imperial./ [*Colophon*] Las
presentes leyes, y nuevas/ ordenanzas y declaracion
dellas/ para la governacion de las In-/dias, y buen
tratamiento de los/ naturales dellas. Fueron im-/
presas por mandado de/ los señores: presidente,
y/ del consejo de las In-/dias: en la villa/ de
Alcala/ de/ Henares: en casa de Joan/ de Brocar
á ocho dias del/ mes de Julio del año/ de nro sal-
vador/ Jesu cris-/to./ M.D.XLIII./ *Black letter.
Folio.* (7l. 7s. 1731)

This copy is MS. except folios 2 to 9, which are original.

LIBERTY (The) and Property of British Subjects
Asserted: In a Letter from An Assembly-Man in
Carolina, To his Friend in London. *London:*
Printed for J. Roberts in Warwick-lane, M.DCC.
XXVI. *39 pp. Signed '* J---- N----.' *unbound.
8vo.* (4s. 6d. 1732)

LIGON (Richard). A True & Exact/ History/
Of the Island of/ Barbadoes./ Illustrated with a
Map of the Island, as also the/ Principal Trees and
Plants there, set forth in/ their due Proportions
and Shapes, drawn out by their several and respective Scales./ Together with the Ingenio that
makes the Sugar, with/ the Plots of the several
Houses, Rooms, and other places, that/ are used
in the whole process of Sugar-making; viz. the
Grinding-/room, the Boyling-room, the Filling-
room, the Curing-/house, Still-house, and Fur-
naces;/ All cut in Copper./ By Richard Ligon,

Gent./ *London,*/ Printed and are to be fold by
Peter Parker, at his Shop at the Leg and Star/
over againſt the Royal Exchange, and Thomas
Guy at the corner/ Shop of Little Lumbard-ſtreet
and Cornhill, 1673./ *Title reverse blank, and* 122 *pp.*
Contents 2 *pp. An Index, etc. after folio* 84, 1 *page.*
With 'A topographicall Description and/ Admea-
surement of the Yland of/ Barbados in the Weſt
Indyaes/ With the M^{rs}. Names of the Severall
plantacons/' 6 *copperplates at pp.* 70, 76, 78, 80,
82, 84, *and* 3 *Engraved Plans. Half russia.*
Folio. (1*l.* 10*s.* 1733)

LIMA. A True and Particular Relation Of the
Dreadful Earthquake Which happen'd At Lima,
the Capital of Peru, and the neighbouring Port of
Callao, On the 28th of October, 1746. With an
Account likewiſe of every Thing material that
paſſed there afterwards to the End of November
following. Publiſhed at Lima by Command of the
Viceroy, And tranſlated from the Original Spaniſh,
By a Gentleman who reſided many Years in thoſe
Countries. To which is added, A Deſcription of
Callao and Lima before their Deſtruction; and of
the Kingdom of Peru in General, with its Inhabi-
tants; ſetting forth their Manners, Cuſtoms, Re-
ligion, Government, Commerce, &c. Interſperſed
with Paſſages of Natural Hiſtory and phyſiological
Diſquiſitions; particularly an Enquiry into the
Cause of Earth-quakes. The whole illuſtrated with
A Map of the Country about Lima; Plans of the
Road and Town of Callao, another of Lima; and
ſeveral Cuts of the Natives drawn on the Spot by
the Tranſlator. The Second Edition. *London:* T.
Osborne, MDCCXLVIII. *xxiii and* 341 *pp.* •*Copper-*
plates numbered I-IX. *Calf.* 8*vo.* (8*s.* 6*d.* 1734)

LINSCHOTEN (JAN HUYGEN VAN). Semper
Eadem/ Iohn/ Hvighen Van/ Linschoten./ his
Diſcours of Voyages/ into ye East & West/ Indies/
Diuided into foure Bookes/ Printed at *London* by/
Iohn Wolfe/ Printer to y^c Honorable Cittie of/
London/ [1598] Willms Rogers/ ciuis Londi-/
nenſis Inuentor/ et ſculptor./ 1 W/ 5 *prel. leaves;*
viz. Engraved title, the reverse blank. 'To the Right
VVorſhipfull/ Ivlivs Caesar Doctor of the Lawes,/
Iudge of the High Court of Admiralty,/ Maſter

of Requefts to the Queenes/ Maiefty, and Mafter of
Saint Katherines./ 3 *pp. signed* 'Iohn VVolfe.'
'To the Reader.' 4 *pp. Text* 197 *pp.* 'The Second
Booke, *etc.* 1598.' *Title, reverse blank, and Text*
pp. 197-259. 'The Thirde Booke, *etc.* 1598.' *Title,*
reverse blank, and Text pp. 307-447. 'The Fovrth
Booke, *etc,* 1598.' *Title, reverse blank, and Text*
pp. 451-462. *Fine copy. Folio.* (7*l.* 7*s.* 1735)
With Twelve Copperplate Maps. viz.—

   I. Τγρνς Orbis Terrarvm. *at p.* 1.
   II. The description of the Islandes and Caftle of Mozambique,
     etc. Grauen by William Rogers. *at p.* 8.
   III. The defcription or Caerd of the Coaftes, *etc.* called Terrado
     Natal, *etc.* Robertus Beckit. *at p.* 12.
   IV. The defcription of the Coaft of Abex, The Streaights of
     Meca, *etc.* Grauen by Robert Beckit. *at p.* 12.
   V. The trew defcription of all the Coafts of China, *etc.* Grauen
     by Robert Beckit. *at p.* 32.
   VI. The Ifland of Sct Helena, *etc.* Grauen by Raygnald Elft-
     rake. *at p.* 172,
   VII. The true defcription and fcituation of the Ifland St Helena
     on the Eaft, North, and Weft fydes, *etc.* Grauen by Ray-
     gnald Elftrak. *at p.* 172.
   VIII. The Trve Defcription of the Island of Ascention, *etc.* Grauen
     by William Rogers. *at p.* 174.
   IX. A difcription of Ægipt from Cair downeward, *etc.* Grauen
     by William Rogers. *at p.* 197.
   X. The defcription of the Coaft of Guinea, Manicongo, and An-
     gola, *etc.* R. E. fculpfit. *at p.* 197.
   XI. The defcription of the whole coaft lying in the South feas of
     America called Peru, *etc.* Grauen by Robert Becket. *at*
     p. 216.
   XII. Insvlae Molvccae, *etc.* Grauen by Robert Beckit. *at p.* 328.

LINSCHOTEN (Jan Huygen van). Navigatio/
ac Itinerarivm/ Iohannis Hvgonis Lin-/scotani in
Orientalem sive Lvsitano-/rvm Indiam. Descriptiones eivsdem Terræ ac Tractvm/ Littoralium.
Præcipuorum Portuum, Fluminum, Capitum, Lo-
corumque, Lufita-/norum hactenus navigationibus
detectorum, figna & notæ. Imagines habi-/tus
geftufque Indorum ac Lufitanorum per Indiam
viventium, Tem-/plorum, Idolorum, Ædium, Ar-
borum, Fructuum, Herbarum,/ Aromatum, &c.
Mores genitum circa facrificia, Poli-/tiam ac rem
familiarē. Enarratio Mercature, quo-/modo &
vbi ea exerccatur. Memorabilia/ gefta fuo tempore
iis in partibus./ Collecta omnia ac defcripta per
eundem Belgicè; Nunc vero Latinè reddita, in
vfum/ commodum ac voluptatem ftudiofi Lectoris
novarum memoriáque/ dignarum rerum, diligenti
studio ac operâ./ *Hagæ-Comitis*/ Ex officinâ Alberti
Henrici. Impenfis Authoris & Cornelii Nicolai,/
proftantque apud Ægidium Elfevirum. Anno1599./
4 *prel. leaves; viz. Title, on the reverse* 'Ad Illvs-

trissimvm' *etc. Engraved Coat of Arms* 1 *leaf.*
' Illvstrissimo atqve Serenissimo Principi ac Domino
D. Mavritio Lantgravio Hessiæ, Comiti in Cat-
zenelnbogen, Dietz, Zigenhain, Nidda, &c.' 2 *pp.*
' Praefatio ad Lectorem.' 1 *page, on the reverse Por-
trait of Linschoten. Text* 124 *pp.* ' Descriptio Totivs
Gvineae Trac-/tvs, Congi, Angolae,' *etc.* 45 *pp.*
' Index ' 3 *pp. With* 37 *Maps and Plates. Unbound.
Folio.* (2*l.* 2*s.* 1736)

LINSCHOTEN (JAN HUYGEN VAN). Histoire/ de
la Navi-/gation de Iean Hv-/gves de Linscot Hollandois et de/ son voyagees Indes Orientales ; con-
tenante diuerses descriptions des/ Pays, Costes,
Haures, Riuieres, Caps, & autres lieux iusques à
present/ descouuerts par les Portugais : Obserua-
tions des coustumes des na-/tions de delà quant à
la Religion, Estat Politic & Domestic, de leurs/
Commerces, des Arbes, Fruicts, Herbes, Espiceries,
& autres/ singularitez qui s'y trouuent : Et narra-
tions des choses/ memorables qui y sont aduenues
de/ son temps./ Avec Annotations de Bernard
Palv-/danus Docteur en Medecine, specialement
sur la matiere des plantes &/ espiceries : & diuerses
figures en taille douce, pour illu-/stration de
l'œuure./ A Qvoy sont adiovstees qvel qves av-/
tres description tant du pays de Guinee, & autres
costes d'Ethiopie,/ que des nauigations des Hollandois vers le Nord au Vay-/gat & en la nouuelle
Zembla./ Le Tovt recveilli et descript par le
mesme/ de Linscot en bas Alleman, & nouuellement traduict/ en François./ A *Amstelredam,*/ De
l'Imprimerie de Theodore Pierre./ M DC. X./ 2
prel. leaves ; viz. Title, reverse blank, ' Preface av
Lectevr.' 1 *page ; Text* 275 *pp. With* 8 *copperplate
Maps and numerous Engravings with the text.
Folio.* (2*l.* 12*s.* 6*d.* 1737)

LINSCHOTEN (JAN HUYGEN VAN). Itinerario./
Voyage ofte Schipvaert, van Jan/ Huygen van
Linschoten naer Oost ofte Portugaels Jn=/dien, in-
houdende een corte beschryvinghe der selver Landen ende Zee-custen, met aen=/wysinge van alle de
voornaemde principale Havens, Revieren, hoecken
ende plaetsen, tot noch/ toe vande Portugesen
ontdeckt ende bekent : Waer by ghevoecht zijn,
met alleen die Conter=/seytsels vande habyten,

drachten ende wefen, fo vande Portugefen aldaer, refiderende, als van=/de ingeboornen Indianen, ende huere Tempels, Afgoden, Huyfinge, met die voornaemfte/ Boomen, Vruchten, Kruyden, Speceryen, ende diergelijcke materialen, als oot die/ manieren des felkden Volckes, fo in hunnen Godtsdienften, als in Politie/ eñ Huijf-hondinghe : maer ooc een corte verhalinge van de Coophan=/ delingen, hoe eñ waer die ghedreven eñ ghevonden worden,/ met die ghedenck weerdichfte gefchiedeniffen,/ voorghevallen den tijt zijnder/ refidentie aldaer./ Alles befchreven ende by een vergadert, door den felfden, feer nut, oorbaer,/ ende oock vermakelijcken voor alle curieute ende Lief-/hebbers van vreemdigheden./ t'*Amstelredam.*/ By Cornelis Claefz. op't VVater, in't Schrijf-boeck, by de oude Brugghe./ Anno cɪɔ. ɪɔ. xcvɪ./ *First Edition. Three Parts.* Part I. 4 *prel. leaves; viz. Title, on the reverse* ' Extract uyt't Regifter ' *etc.* ' Aende Hooghende VVelghe borene,' *etc.* 2 *pp.* ' Prohemio ofte voorreden totten leser.' 1 *page.* ' Sonnet.' 1 *page.* ' Ode.' 1 *page, on the reverse Portrait of Linschoten. Text* 160 *pp.* Part II. Reysgheschrift *etc.* M. D. xcv. 134 *pp.* ' Een feker Extract ende etc.* cɪɔ. ɪɔ. xcvɪ.' *Title reverse blank,* ' Aende VVelgheborene,' *etc.* 1 *page on the reverse* ' Ad Io. Hvg. Linscotvm ' *etc. Text pp.* 135-147. Part III. ' Befchryvinghe *etc.* M.D.xcvɪ.' 82 *pp. followed by 5 leaves containing lists of Plates and Maps, Register etc.* 42 *maps and plates. Fine copy. Folio.*   (3*l.* 3*s.* 1738)

LIST (A) of Copies of Charters, from the Commiffioners for Trade and Plantations, Prefented to the Honourable the Houfe of Commons, in Purfuance of their Address to His Majesty, of the 25th of April 1740. viz. Maryland Charter, granted by King Charles I. in the 8th Year of His Reign. Connecticut Charter granted by King Charles II. in the 14th Year of His Reign. Rhode-Island Charter, granted by King Charles II. in the 15th Year of His Reign. Penfylvania Charter, granted by King Charles II. in the 33d Year of His Reign. Massachusets Bay Charter, granted by King William and Queen Mary, in the 3d Year of Their Reign. Georgia Charter, granted by His Majesty, in the 5th Year of His Reign. *London :*

Printed in the Year M.DCC.XLI. *Title :* 12, 10, 14, 12, 21, *and* 18 *pp. half mor.* 4to. (7s. 6d. 1739)

LITERARY AND HISTORICAL SOCIETY. Transactions of the Literary and Historical Society of Quebec : founded, January 6, 1824. Volume I. *Quebec :* Printed for the Literary and Historical Society ; by François Le Maitre, Star office. 1829. 3 *prel. leaves, xxxvi and* 261 *pp ; Errata* 1 *page.* 'Catalogue of the Mineralogical Collection belonging to the Literary and Historical Society of Quebec.' 72 *pp.* 'Solar Spots.' 1 *page. With* 12 *plates.* 8*vo.* (10s. 6d. 1740)

LITTLE (OTIS). State of Trade in the Northern Colonies considered ; with An Account of their Produce, And a Particular Description of Nova Scotia. *London :* G. Woodfall M.DCC.XLVIII. *viii and* 84 *pp. half mor.* 8*vo.* (7s. 6d. 1741)

LITTLE (OTIS). The State of Trade in the Northern Colonies considered ; with An Account of their Produce, And a particular Description of Nova Scotia. London Printed, 1748. *Boston* Re-printed and fold by Thomas Fleet, at the Heart and Crown in Cornhill. 1749. 43 *pp.* 8*vo.* (7s. 6d. 1742)

LITURGY. A/ Liturgy,/ collected principally from the/ Book of Common Prayer,/ for the use of the/ First Episcopal Church/ in/ Boston ;/ together with the/ Psalter, or Psalms/ of/ David./ *Boston,*/ Printed by Peter Edes, in State-Street./ MDCC LXXXV. 4 *prel. leaves and signatures,* A *to* B bb *in fours. Fine clean copy uncut.* 8*vo.* (12s. 6d. 1743)

LITURGY. The Book of Common Prayer, And Administration of the Sacraments, and other Rites and Ceremonies of the Church, according to the use of the Church of England : Together with a Collection of Occasional Prayers, and divers Sentences of Holy Scripture, Neceffary for Knowledge and Practice. Formerly collected, and tranflated into the Mohawk Language under the direction of the Miffionaries of the Society for the Propagation of the Gofpel in Foreign Parts, to the Mohawk Indians. A New Edition : To which is added The Gofpel according to St. Mark, Tranflated into the Mohawk Language, By Captn. Joseph Brant, An

Indian of the Mohawk Nation. *London* : C. Buckton 1787. Ne Yakawea Yondereanayendaghkwa Oghseragwegouh, neoni yakawea ne orighwa dogeaghty Yondatnekosseraghs neoni Tekarighwagehhadont, oya oni Adereanayent, ne teas nikariwake Raditsihuhstatsygowa Ronaderighwissoh Goraghgowa a-onea Rodanhaouh. Oni, watkanissaaghtoh Oddyake Adereanayent, neoni tsiniyoghthare ne Kaghyadoghseradogeaghty, Newahòeny Akoyendarake neoni Ahhondatterihhonny. A-onea wadiròroghkwe, neoni Tekaweanadènnyoh Kanyenkehàga Tfikaweanondaghko, ne neane Raditfihuhftatfy ne Radirighwawakoughkgòwa ronadanhà-outh, Kanyenkewaondye tfi-radinakeronnyo Ongwe-oewe. Keagaye ase yondereanayendaghkwa. Oni tahoghsonderoh St. Mark Raorighwadogeaghty, Tekaweanadennyoh Kanyenkehàga Rakowànea T'Hayen danegea, Roewayats. *London :* C. Buckton, 1787. *Two Titles, iii and 506 pp ; 18 copperplates, old calf. 8vo.* (15s. 1744)

LOCKE (JOHN). A Collection of several Pieces of Mr. John Locke, Never before printed, or not extant in his Works. Publifh'd by the Author of the Life of the ever-memorable Mr. John Hales, &c. *London :* J. Bettenham for R. Francklin, M.DCC.XX. *31 prel. leaves and 362 pp. Index and Errata 19 pp. Calf. 8vo.* (5s. 6d. 1745)
The Fundamental Constitution of Carolina, drawn up by Locke, fills pages 1 to 53 of this volume.

LOCKMAN (JOHN). Travels of the Jesuits, into Various Parts of the World: Particularly China and the East-Indies. Intermix'd with an Account of the Manners, Government, Civil and Religious Ceremonies, Natural History, and Curiosities, of the feveral Nations vifited by thofe Fathers. Translated from the celebrated *Lettres edifiantes & curieuses, ecrites des Missions etrangeres, par les Missionaires de la Compagnie de Jesus.* A Work fo entertaining and curious, that it has already been tranflated into moft of the European Languages. This Work is illuftrated with Maps and Sculptures, engraved by the beft Mafters. To which is now prefixed, An Account of the Spanish Settlements in America, with a general Index to the whole Work. By Mr. Lockman. Second Edition, cor-

rected. T. Piety, [*London*] 1762. *Two Volumes.*
Vol. I. 16 *prel. leaves, and* 488 *pp.* Vol. II. 5 *prel.
leaves, and* 508 *pp. General Index* 19 *pp.* ' A Concise
Account of the Spanish Dominions in America.'
24 *pp.* 8*vo.* (18*s.* 1746)

LONG (J.) Voyages and Travels of an Indian In-
terpreter and Trader, describing The Manners and
Customs of the North American Indians ; with an
Account of the Posts situated on the River Saint
Laurence, Lake Ontario, &c. To which is added
a Vocabulary of The Chippeway Language. Names
of Furs and Skins, in English and French. A List
of Words in the Iroquis, Mohegan, Shawanee, and
Esquimeaux Tongues, and a Table, shewing The
Analogy between the Algonkin and Chippeway
Languages. By J. Long. *London :* Printed for
the Author ; M,DCC,XCI. 7 *prel leaves, and* 295 *pp.
With Sketch of the Western Countries of Canada.*
4*to.* (15*s.* 1747)

LONGACRE (JAMES B.) The National Portrait
Gallery of Distinguished Americans. Conducted
by James B. Longacre, Philadelphia ; and James
Herring, New York : Under the Superintendence
of the American Academy of the Fine Arts. *Philadelphia,* Henry Perkins, 1834. *Four Volumes.*
Vol. I. 5 *prel. leaves, the contents stating the number
of pages to each Portrait. 36 Portraits.* Vol. II.
1835. 5 *prel. leaves, the contents stating the number
of pages to each Portrait. 36 Portraits.* Vol. III.
1836. 5 *prel. leaves, the contents stating the number of
pages to each Portrait. 36 Portraits.* Vol. IV.
James B. Longacre, 1839. 5 *prel. leaves, the contents stating the number of pages to each Portrait. 39
Portraits. Large paper copy. Half morocco extra.*
4*to.* (6*l.* 6*s.* 1748)

LOOKING-GLASS (A) for Presbyterians. Or,
A brief Examination of their Loyalty, Merit, and
other Qualifications for Government. With some
Animadversions on the Quaker unmask'd. Humbly
Addrefs'd to the Confideration of the Royal Freemen of Pennsylvania. *Philadelphia.* Printed in
the Year M,DCC,LXIV. 18 *pp. Signed* ' Philo-Liber-
tatis.' *Uncut.* 8*vo.* (7*s.* 6*d.* 1749)
This piece is marked " Numb. 1" at the top of the title.

LOPEZ DE ESCOBAR (Diego). Relacion/ de los
Particvlares/ feruicios que ha hecho a V. Mageſtad
Don/ Diego Lopez de Eſcobar Gouernador y Ca-/
pitan general de la Isla de la Trinidad, y de las/
Prouincias del Dorado, hijo del Capitan/ Diego
Lopez de la Fuente, en/ el año de 1636./ Con Li-
cencia/ En *Madrid.* Por la vuida de Iuan Gonçalez./ Año M.DC.XXXVII./ *Title reverse blank,
and 8 pp. half morocco. Folio.*   (18s. 1750)

LORD (Joseph). Reaſon Why, not Anabaptiſt
Plunging but Infants-Believer's Baptism Ought
to be approved, Is becauſe the Lord Jesus Christ,
and His Apoſtles, Preached it and Practiced it. In
Anſwer to the Anabaptiſt Reaſon Why. With Remarks pointing at the Notable Fallacies that are
every where to be found, in the Notes on the Forty
one Texts of Scripture ; The Arguments and Anſwers to Objections, and other things contained in
that Book, Together with ſundry Evidences of the
Churchmemberſhip of Infants of Believers, and
regularity of Sprinking, In Old Testament Scriptures atteſted to in the New-Teſtament. Old-
Testament Prophecies relating to New-Teſtament
Times, and New-Testament Testimonies. By
Joseph Lord. *Boston :* Printed by S. Kneeland,
for Samuel Gerriſh, at his Shop in Cornhill, 1719.
Title, viii and 170 *pp. Old calf.* 12mo. (16s. 1751)

LORENZANA (Francisco Antonio). Concilios
Provinciales Primero, y Segundo, celebrados en
la muy Noble, y muy leal Ciudad de México,
Presidiendo en Illmo. y Rmo. Señor D. Fa.
Alonso de Montufar, En los años de 1555, y
1565. Dalos a luz El Ill.ᵐᵒ S.ʳ D. Francisco Antonio Lorenzana, Arzobiſpo de eſta Santa Metropo-
litana Igleſia. Con las Licencias Necesarias En
México, en la Imprenta de el Superior Gobierno,
de el Br. D. Joſeph Antonio de Hogal, en la Calle
de Tiburcio, Año de 1769, 5 *prel. leaves,* 184 *pp.*
' CIƆIƆLXV. Años. Concilio Provincial,' *etc.* 1 *page ;*
pp. 185-396. ' Indice de los Capitulos.' 12 *pp.* ' Con-
cilium Mexicanum Provinciale III. Celebratum
Mexici anno MDLXXXV. Præside D. D. Petro
Moya, et Contreras Archiepiscopo ejusdem urbis.
Confirmatum Romæ die XXVII. Octobris Anno
MDLXXXIX. Poſtea Juſſu Regio editum Mexici

Anno MDCXXII. fumptibus D. D. Joannis Perez de
la Serna Archiepiscopi. Demum typis mandatum
cura, & expenfis D. D. Francisci Antonij A Lorenzana Archipræsulis. Mexici Anno MDCCLXX. Superiorum Permissu. Ex Typographia Bac. Jofephi
Antonij de Hogal. 6 *prel. leaves and* 328 *pp.* ' Index ' 4 *pp.* ' Statuta Ordinata a Sancto Concilio
Provinciali Mexicano III. Anno Domini MDLXXXV.
Ex Præscripto Sacrosancti Concilij Tridentini
Decreto Seff. 24. Cap. 12. de Reform. verbo
Cetera. Revisa a Catholica Majestate, et a Sacro-
sancta sede Apostolica Confirmata Anno Domini
milleffimo quingentiffimo octuageffimo nono. *Title
and* 141 *pp. Index* 3 *pp. Two Volumes. Vellum.*
Folio.   (*2l. 12s. 6d.* 1752)

LORENZO DE SAN MILIAN (FRANCISCO). Por/
D. Francisco Lorenzo/ de San Milian,/ Iuez oficial
de la Cafa de/ la Contratacion de la Ciudad de
Seuilla,/ y Contador de la Vifita del Tribunal de/
Quentas de la Ciudad de Mexico, y/ de las caxas
Reales della, y de las de-/mas del Reyno de
Nueua/ Efpaña./ En la Cavsa/ qve en virtvd de
cedvla de sv/ Mageftad fe ha actuado, contra el
dicho Don Fran-/cifco, fobre fus procedimientos
en el juizio de vi-/fita de las caxas, y Minas de la
Ciudad/ da Zacatecas./ [1672?] 19 *folioed leaves.*
half mor. Folio.   (*1l. 1s.* 1753)

LORING (ISRAEL). Juftification not by Works,
but by Faith in Jesus Christ. A Practical Difcourfe Exhibited on Gal. II. 16. By Ifrael Loring,
M.A. And Paftor of the Weft Church in Sudbury.
Boston : Printed & Sold by Kneeland and Green,
in Queen-Street, 1749. *Title and* 93 *pp. Uncut.*
12mo.   (*10s. 6d.* 1754)

LORT (MICHAEL). Account of an antient Infcrip-
tion in North America. By the Rev. Michael
Lort, D.D. V.P.A.S. [With Col. Vallancey's Ob-
servations] 17 *pp; and* 2 *plates. Half morocco.*
4to.   (*4s. 6d.* 1755)

LOSA (FRANCISCO). La Vie/ de/ Gregoire/ Lopez/
dans la Novvelle/ Espagne,/ composee en Espag-
nol/ par François Losa Preftre,/ Licentié, & iadis
Curé de l'Eglife/ Cathedrale de Mexico./ Et

traduite nouuellement en François, par vn Pere de
la Compagnie de/ Iesvs./   Seconde Edition./   A
Paris,/ Chez Iean Henavlt, Libraire Iuré,/ ruë S.
Iacques, à l'Ange Gardien/ & fainƈt Raphaël./
M.DC.LVI./ Auec Priuilege dv Roy./ *12 prel. leaves
and text 260 pp.   Table des Chapitres 3 pp.   Old calf.*
12mo.   (10s. 6d.   1756)

LOSKIEL (George Henry).   History of the Mif-
sion of the United Brethren among the Indians in
North America. In Three Parts. By George
Henry Loskiel. Translated from the German. By
Christian Ignatius La Trobe. *London*: Printed
for the Brethren's Society for the furtherance of
the Gospel: 1794. *xii pp. Map. Part I. 159 pp.
Part II. 234 pp. Part III. 233 pp. Index 21 pp.
Uncut. 8vo.*   (12s. 6d.   1757)

LOTTERY MAGAZINE (The); Or, Compleat
Fund of Literary, Political and Commercial Know-
ledge. For August and September, 1776. *London :*
Johnson and Co. [1776] *8vo.*   (2s. 6d.   1758)
The Number for August contains the Declaration of Independence,
    probably the earliest publication of it in England. The Septem-
    ber Number has a description of the City of New York, with a
    plan.

LOUISBOURG.   An Authentic Account of the
Reduction of Louisbourg, In June and July 1758.
By a Spectator. *London*: W. Owen, 1758. *60 pp.
half mor. 8vo.*   (10s. 6d.   1759)

LOUISIANA.   Voyage a la Louisiane, et sur le
Continent de L'Amérique Septentrionale, fait dans
les années 1794 à 1798 ; Contenant un Tableau
historique de la Louisiane, des observations sur son
climat, ses riches productions, le caractère et le
nom des Sauvages ; des remarques importantes sur
la navigation ; des principes d'administration, de
législation et de gouvernement propres à cette
Colonie, etc. etc. Par B*** D***. [Baudry les
Lozieres] Orné d'une belle carte. *Paris*, Dentu,
An XI-1802. *3 prel. leaves, and 382 pp. Map. mor.
8vo.*   (10s. 6d.   1760)

LÖW (Conrad).   Meer oder Seehanen Buch,/
Darinn/ Verzeichnet feind, die Wun=/derbare, Gedenckwürdige Reife vnd Schiffarhten, fo/ recht vnd
billich geheiffen Meer vnd Seehanen, der Königen
von Hi=/fpania, Portugal, Engellandt vnd Franck-
reich, inwendig den letſt vergangnen hun=/dert

Jahren, gethan. Auff vnd durch welche Schiffarten, ein Newe Welt gegen/ Nidergang, vnd grosse
Königreichen, Landtschafften vnd Insulen,/ gegen
Auffgang gelegen, erfunden vnd/ entdeckt seind./
Hierzu seind noch gesetzt zwey seltzame vnd
gedenckwürdige Stück./ Das eine ist,/ Die Erzehlung der Schiffart, so im Jahr 1594. gethan siben
Schiff,/ welche die Vnierte Niderländische Ständ
geschickt gegen Mitternacht, vmb von/ dannen
jren lauff nach China zu nemen. Dieselbige Schiff
seind gefahren, durch die Enge oder/ Strasz zwischen
den Landtschafften des Grofzfürsten von der Moscow, vnd der Insel Waigatz,/ bey Noua Zembla
gelegen, bisz ins grosse Tartarische Meer, Welches
auff Latein Oceanus/ Scythicus oder Mare Tabin
genennet wirt, vnd haben entdeckt den Flusz/
Gilissy nur 13. Meil vom grossen Flusz/ Obij gelegen./ Das ander stück ist./ Ein Warhaffter,
klarer, eigentlicher Bericht, von der weiten vn
wun=/derbaren Reise oder Schiff fahrt, so drey Schiff
vnd ein Pinasz, aufz Holland, bisz in/ Indien gegen
Auffgang gethan. Dieselbe Schiff seind von
Texel in Hollandt abgefaoren am an-/dern tag
Aprilis, im Jar 1595. Haben vmbgesägelt das
Vorhaupt Bonæ Spei, vnd seind ahn der/ grossen
Insel Madagascar jetzt S. Laurentz Insel geheissen,
angefahren. Von dannen seind sie/ gesagelt gen
Samatra, vorzeïten Taprobana, vnd fehrner gen
Bantam, ein grosse Gewerbstatt/ in der Insel Iaua
Maior, weiter gen Sidaya, vnd der Insel Bally.
Von dannen seind sie am 26./ Februarij 1597. wider
nach Hollandt gefahren, vnd ohn jrgendts ahnzu-
länden, am 10. tag/ Augstmonats desselben Jars mit
freuden zu Hausz amkomen. Haben mitbracht/
Pfeffer, Nägelein, Muscat Nüsz vnd Blumen.
Neben dem einen/ wunderbarlichen Vogel, der
Fewrkolen verschlucket./ Gantz lustig zulesen./
Dise Reisen vnd Schiffahrten seind zusamen, aufz
an=/dern Spraachen ins Teutsch gebracht,/ Durch/
Conrad Löw der Historien Liebhaber./ Getruckt
zu Cölln, auff der Burgmauren. Bey/ Bertram
Buchholtz, Im Jahr/ 1598. *Title reverse blank,
and text* 110 *pp. With Map. Vellum.* (Book
of the Ocean or sea-cocks In which are related the
wonderful memorable travels and voyages which
the rightly and justly called Ocean or Sea-cocks of

the Kings of Spain, Portugal, England, and France
have made within the last past hundred years. In
and by means of which voyages a New World
situated towards the West and great Kingdoms,
countries, and islands towards the east have been
found and discovered. Hereto are yet added two
curious & remarkable pieces. One is the relation
of the voyage which seven ships, which the United
States of the Netherlands sent to the North in order
to take thence their course to China, performed in
the year 1594. The said ships proceeded through
the pass or straits between the territories of the
Great Prince of Moscow and the Island Waigatz
situated near Nova Zembla, into the great Tartaric
Sea, which is called in Latin Oceanus Scythicus or
Mare Tabin ; and have discovered the River Gilissy
situated only 13 miles from the great River Obij.
The other piece is a true, clear, and accurate account of the distant and wonderful voyage which
three ships and a pinnace made from Holland to
India towards the East. These ships proceeded
from Texel in Holland on the second day of April
in the year 1595. They sailed round the Cape of Good
Hope and proceeded to the great Island Madagas
car, now called St. Lawrence Island. Hence they
sailed to Sumatra, formerly Taprobana and further
to Bantam a great trading city in the Island of
Java Major, further to Sidaya and the island Bally.
Thence they proceeded on the 26th of February
1597 again towards Holland, and arrived at home
with joy on the 10th day of August in the same
year without landing any where. They have
brought with them pepper, cloves, nutmeg, nuts,
and flowers, together with a wonderful bird which
swallows red-hot Coals. Very pleasant to read.
These travels and voyages have been collected in
German, out of other languages, by Conrad Low,
a lover of histories. Printed at Cologne on the
Castle-walls by Bertram Buchholz. In the year
1598.) *Folio.* (*5l. 15s. 6d.* 1761)

LUSSAN (Raveneau de). Journal/ du Voyage/
fait a la mer de Sud,/ avec les Flibustiers/ De
L'Amerique en 1684./ & années fuivantes./ Seconde Edition./ Par le Sieur Raveneau De Lussan./ A *Paris,*/ Jean Bapt. Coignard,/ et/ Jean
Baptiste Coignard, Fils,/ MDCLXXXXIII. Avec pri-

vilege de sa Majeste./ *8 prel. leaves, and* 448 *pp. Privilege and Colophon* 2 *leaves. Old calf.* 12*mo.*   (10*s.* 6*d.* 1762)

LYNE (CHARLES). A Letter to the Right Honourable Lord Castlereagh, &c. &c. &c. on the North American Export Trade During the War, and during any time the Import and use of our Manufactures are interdicted in the United States. To which is added, the resolutions of the Manufacturers, Exporters of Goods, and Merchants, of the City of Glasgow. By Charles Lyne. *London :* J. M. Richardson, 1813. *Title and* 46 *pp. unbound.* 8*vo.*   (3*s.* 6*d.* 1763)

LYTTELTON (THOMAS, *Lord*). A Letter from Thomas Lord Lyttelton to William Pitt, Earl of Chatham, on the Quebec Bill. *Boston :* Printed by Mills and Hicks, for Cox and Berry, in King-Street. M,DCC,LXXIV. 17 *pp. Half morocco.* 8*vo.*   (5*s.* 6*d.* 1764)

LYTTELTON (THOMAS, *Lord*). A Letter from Thomas Lord Lyttelton, to William Pitt, Earl of Chatham, on the Quebec Bill. *New-York :* Reprinted by James Rivington. M,DCC,LXXIV. 20 *pp. half mor.* 8*vo.*   (4*s.* 6*d.* 1765)

ABLY (ABBE DE). Remarks concerning the Government and the Laws of the United States of America: In Four Letters, addressed to Mr. Adams; Minister Plenipotentiary from the United States of America to those of Holland; and one of the Negociators for the purpose of concluding a general Peace, from the French of the Abbé de Mably: With Notes, by the Translator. *London:* J. Debrett, M,DCC,LXXXIV. *Half-title, title, and* 280 *pp.* 8vo. (4s. 6d. 1766)

MABLY (ABBE DE). Remarks concerning the Government and the Laws of the United States of America: In four Letters, addressed to Mr. Adams, Minister Plenipotentiary from the United States of America to those of Holland; and one of the Negociators for the purpose of concluding a general peace, from the French of the Abbé de Mably: With Notes, by the Translator. *Dublin:* Moncrieffe, *etc.* MDCCLXXXV. *Half-title, title, and* 280 *pp. Old calf.* 8vo. (4s. 6d. 1767)

MACAULAY (CATHARINE). Observations on a Pamphlet, entitled, Thoughts on the Cause of the Present Discontents. By Catharine Macaulay. The Third Edition, Corrected. *London:* Edward and Charles Dilly. MDCCLXX. 31 *pp. Half mor.* 8vo. (4s. 6d. 1768)

MACAULAY (CATHARINE). An Address to the People of England, Scotland, and Ireland, on the present Important Crifis of Affairs. By Catharine Macaulay. R. Cruttwel, *Bath,* MDCCLXXV. 29 *pp. Half mor.* 8vo. (4s. 6d. 1769)

MAC CLURE (DAVID). Memoirs of the Rev.

Eleazar Wheelock, D.D. Founder and President of Dartmouth College and Moor's Charity School; with a summary history of the College and School. To which are added, copious Extracts from Dr. Wheelock's Correspondence. By david M'Clure, D.D., S.H.S. Pastor of a Church in East Windsor, Con. and Elijah Parish, D.D. Pastor of the Church in Byfield, Mass. *Newburyport:* Edward Little & Co. 1811. *336 pp. Portrait of Eleazar Wheelock. Calf. 8vo.* (7s. 6d. 1770)

MAC DONALD (John). Emigration to Canada. Narrative of a Voyage to Quebec, and Journey from thence to New Lanark, in Upper Canada. Detailing the hardships and difficulties which an Emigrant has to encounter, before and after his settlement; With an Account of the Country, as it regards its climate, soil, and the actual condition of its inhabitants. By John M'Donald. Eighth Edition. *London:* H. Arliss. 1826. *36 pp. half mor. 8vo.* (3s. 6d. 1771)

MACER (John). Les trois liures de/ l'Histoire des/ Indes, acomplie/ de plufieurs chofes memorables, autant fidelement que fommaire-/ment compofez en Latin, & depuis/ nagueres faictz en Françoys./ Par Maiftre Iehan Macer,/ licencié en droict./ Avec Privilege./ A *Paris./* Chez Guillaume Guillard en la rue/ Sainct Iacques à l'enfeigne/ Saincte Barbe./ 1555./ *96 folioed leaves. Vellum. 16mo.* (1l. 10s. 1772)

MAC GREGOR (James). Letter from the Reverend Mr. James M'Gregor, Minister, at Pictou, Nova, Scotia, to the General Associate Synod, April 30th, 1793. Published by order of Synod. *Paisley:* Printed by John Neilson. m.dcc.xciii. *16 pp. 8vo.* (4s. 6d. 1773)

MAC KENNEY (Thomas L.) Sketches of a Tour to the Lakes, of the character and customs of the Chippeway Indians, and of incidents connected with the Treaty of Fond du Lac. By Thomas L. Mc Kenney, of the Indian Department, And joint Commissioner with his Excellency Gov. Cass, in negotiating the Treaty. Also, a Vocabulary of the Algic, or Chippeway Language, formed in part, and as far as it goes, upon the basis of one furnished by the Hon. Albert Gallatin. Ornamented with twenty-nine Engravings, of Lake Superior, and other Scenery, Indian Likenesses, Costumes, &c. *Baltimore:* Fielding Lucas, Jun'r. 1827. *294 pp. 29 plates. 8vo.* (7s. 6d. 1774)

MACKENZIE (ALEXANDER). Voyages from Montreal, on the River St. Lawrence, through the Continent of North America, to the Frozen and Pacific Oceans; In the Years 1789 and 1793. With a preliminary account of the Rise, Progress, and Present State of the Fur Trade of that Country. Illustrated with Maps. By Alexander Mackenzie, Esq. *London:* T. Cadell, Jun. M.DCCC.I. *Half-title, title, viii and cxxxii pp: Text 412 pp. Errata 2 pp. With Portrait of the Author, and 3 Copperplate Maps. 4to.* (10s. 6d. 1775)

MAC KINNEN (DANIEL). A Tour through the British West Indies, in the Years 1802 and 1803, giving a particular Account of the Bahama Islands. By Daniel McKinnen, Esq. *London:* J. White. 1804. *Half-title, title, viii and 272 pp. With Map. 8vo.* (5s. 6d. 1776)

MAC LANE (DAVID). The Trial of David M'Lane for High Treason, before a Special Court of Oyer and Terminer at Quebec, on the 7th July 1797. *Quebec:* Printed and Sold by J. Neilson, 1797. *21 pp. half mor. 8vo.* (5s. 6d. 1777)

MAC MAHON (JOHN V. L.) An Historical View of the Government of Maryland, from its Colonization to the present day. By John V. L. McMahon. *Baltimore:* F. Lucas, Jr. 1831. Vol. I. *xvi and 539 pp.* (12s. 6d. 1778)

MAC NEILL (HECTOR). Observations on the Treatment of the Negroes, in the Island of Jamaica, including some Account of their Temper and Character, with Remarks on the Importation of Slaves from the Coast of Africa. In a Letter to a Physician in England, from Hector M'Neill. *London:* G. G. and J. Robinson, *vi and 46 pp. half morocco. 8vo.* (3s. 6d. 1779)

MACQUEEN (JAMES). The Colonial Controversy containing a Refutation of the Calumnies of the Anticolonists: the State of Hayti, Sierra Leone,

India, China, Cochin China, Java, &c. &c.; the
Production of Sugar, &c. and the state of the Free
and Slave Labourers in those Countries; fully considered in a Series of Letters, addressed to The Earl
of Liverpool; with a supplementary Letter to Mr.
Macaulay. By James Macqueen. *Glasgow:*
Khull, Blackie, & Co. 1825. *223 pp. half mor.*
8vo. (4s. 6d. 1780)

MADRE DE DEOS (Gaspar da). Memorias para
a Historia da Capitania de S. Vicente, hoje chamada
de S. Paulo, do estado do Brazil publicadas de
Ordem da Academia R. das Sciencias por Fr.
Gaspar da Madre de Deos, Monge Benedictino, e
correspondente da mesma Academia. *Lisboa:* Na
Typografia da Academia. 1797. *4 prel. leaves, and
text 242 pp.* ' Catalogo' *etc. 2 pp. Half calf.*
4to. (7s. 6d. 1781)

MAFFEIUS (Joannes Petrus). Ioan. Petri/
Maffeii,/ Bergomatis,/ e Societate Iesv,/ Histori-
arvm/ Indicarvm/ Libri XVI./ Selectarvm, item,
ex India/ Epistolarum, eodem interprete, Libri
IV./ Accessit Ignatii Loiolæ vita./ Omnia ab
Auctore recognita, & nunc primùm in Germania
excufa./ Item, in fingula opera copiofus Index./
His nunc recèns adiecta est charta geographica,
x renitidiffimè expreffa, qua Lectori vtriufq;/ Indiæ fitus, & longinqua ad eas nauigatio, accuratè
ob oculos fpectanda pro-/ponitur, non minus ad-
fpectu, quàm historia ipfa lectu iucunda./ *Coloniæ
Agrippinæ,/* In Officina Birckmannica, fumptibus/
Arnoldi Mylij./ Anno m. d.xciii./ Cum Gratia &
Priuilegio S. Cæfarea Maiestatis./ *2 prel. leaves;
viz. Title, reverse blank,* 'Philippo Re=/gi Catho=/
lico.' *2 pp; Text 541 pp.* ' Compendiosvs Index,'
etc. 35 pp. Pigskin. Folio. (15s. 1782)

MAFFEIUS (Joannes Petrus). Ioan. Petri/
Maffeii,/ Bergomatis,/ e Societate/ Iesv,/ Histori-
arvm/ Indicarvm/ Libri XVI./ Selectarvm, Item,
ex In-/dia Epistolarvm Libri IV./ Acceffit liber
recentiorum Epistolarvm, a Ioanne Hayo Dalgat-
tienfi/ Scoto ex eadem Societate nunc primùm excufus, cum/ Indice accurato./ Dvobvs Tomis Dis-
tribvti./ Omnia ab Auctore recognita & emendata./
In fingula copiofus Index./ *Antverpiæ,* Ex Officina

Martini Nutij, ad infigne dua-/rum Ciconiarum, Anno M. DC. V./ 36 *prel. leaves;* Text ' Liber Primvs' 478 *pp;* 1 *blank leaf.* ' Selectarvm Epistolarvm ex India Libri Qvatvor,' *etc.* 402 *pp. Index* 6 *pp. Pigskin. 8vo.* (15s. 1783)

MAGELLANS. Appendice a la Relacion del Viage al Magallanes de la Fragata de Guerra Santa María de la Cabeza, que contiene el de los Paquebotes Santa Casilda y Santa Eulalia para completar el Reconocimiento del estrecho en los Años de 1788 y 1789. Trabajado de Orden Superior. *Madrid* MDCCLXXXXIII. En la Imprenta de la Viuda de D. Joaquin Ibarra. 2 *prel. leaves and* 128 *pp. Carta Estrecho de Magallanes,* 1786, *y* 1789.* 4*to.* (10s. 6d. 1783*)

MALOUET (V. P.) Examen de cette question : Quel sera pour les Colonies de l'Amérique le Résultat de la Révolution Françoise, de la Guerre qui en est la Suite, & de la Paix qui doit la terminer ? Par M. Malouet, Député de la Colonie de St. Domingue. *A Londres:* Baylis, 1797. 29 *pp. half mor. 8vo.* (3s. 6d. 1784)

MALOUET (V. P.) Lettre à M.S.D., Membre du Parlement, sur l'Intérêt de l'Europe, au Salut des Colonies de l'Amérique. Par M. Malouet, Député de la Colonie de St. Domingue. *Londres:* Baylis, 1797. *Half-title, title, and* 36 *pp. Uncut.* 8*vo.* (3s. 6d. 1785)

MALOUET (V. P.) Collection de Mémoires et Correspondances Officielles sur l'Administration des Colonies, Et notamment sur la Guiane française et hollandaise, par V. P. Malouet, ancien administrateur des Colonies et de la Marine. *Paris,* Baudouin, An X. [1802] *Four Volumes.* Tome Premier. *Half-title, title, and* 484 *pp.* Tome II. *Half-title, title, and* 379 *pp.* Tome III. *Half-title, title, and* 388 *pp.* Tome IV. *Half-title, title, and* 378 *pp. half calf. 8vo.* (10s. 6d. 1786)

MANSIE (ALEXANDER). Dedicated by permission to his Excellency the Governor. The Apprenticed Labourer's Manual : Or An Essay on the Apprenticeship System, and the Duties of the Apprenticed Labourers, Including several of the Personal and Relative Duties binding on Mankind in general.

By Alexander Mansie, Wesleyan Minister. *British Guiana :* Published by the Society for the Instruction of the Labouring Classes. 1837. *xiv and* 217 *pp.* ' A Catechism of certain Moral, Social, and Civil Duties ; adapted to existing circumstances. By the Wesleyan Missionaries of Antigua. Originally printed by Order of the Legislature of that Colony.' 13 *pp.*   *8vo.*   (5*s.* 1787)

MASON (J. M.) An Oration commemorative of the late Major-General Alex[r]. Hamilton ; pronounced before the New-York State Society of the Cincinnati, on Tuesday, July 31, 1804. By J. M. Mason, D.D. Pastor of the first Associate Reformed Church in the City of New York. With an Appendix, containing the Particulars of the Duel between General Hamilton and Colonel Burr, a Copy of the Paper left by the General, and The Rev. Dr. Mason's Letter to the Editor of the Commercial Advertiser, Giving an Account of the General's last Moments. *London :* R. Edwards, 1804. 38 *pp. Uncut.* *8vo.*   (2*s.* 6*d.* 1788)

MARBAN (Pedro). Arte/ de la Lengva/ Moxa,/ consu Vocabulario, y Cathecismo./ Compuesto/ por el M. R. P. Pedro Marban/ de la Compañia de Jesvs, Superior, que fue,/ de las Mifsiones de Infieles, que tiene la Com=/pañia de efta Provincia de el Perù en las/ dilatadas Regiones de los Indios/ Moxos, y Chiquitos./ Dirigido./ Al Exc.[mo] Sor D. Melchor/ Portocarrero Laffo, de la Vega. Conde/ de la Monclova, Comendador de la/ Zarza, del Ordẽ de Alcantara, del Con-/fejo de Guerra, y Junta de Guerra de Indias, Virrey, Governando, y Capitan/ General, que fue del Reyno de la Nueva/ Efpaña, y actual, q es de eftos Rey=/nos, y Provincias del Peru./ [*Lima* 1701] Con Licencia de los Svperiores. En la Imprenta Real de Jofeph de Contreras. 8 *prel. leaves, and* 664 *pp;* ' Cathecismo Meno' *etc.* 202 *pp;* ' Indice' 1 *page. Vellum. Small 8vo.*   (3*l.* 13*s.* 6*d.* 1789)

MARKHAM (William). A Sermon Preached before the Incorporated Society for the Propagation of the Gofpel in Foreign Parts ; at their Anniversary Meeting in the Parifh Church of St. Mary-le-Bow, On Friday February 21. 1777. By the Moft

Reverend Father in God, William Lord Archbifhop
of York. *London:* T. Harrison and S. Brooke,
MDCCLXXVII. 104 *pp.* 'The Form of a Legacy to
this Society.' 1 *page. half mor.* 8vo. (3s. 6d. 1790)

MARQUETTE (Le P.) Voyage et découverte de
quelques Pays et Nations de l'Amérique Septen-
trionale par Le P. Marquette et Sr. Joliet. À Paris,
Chez Estienne Michallet ruë S. Jaques à l'Image
S. Paul. M.DC.LXXXI. Avec privilege du Roy.
Paris. Maulde et Renou, 1845. *Half-title, title;
and* 43 *pp. Map. Morocco extra. A reprint for Mr.
O. Rich. Small 8vo.* (12s. 6d. 1791)

MARRANT (John). A Narrative of the Lord's
wonderful Dealings with John Marrant, a Black,
(Now going to Preach the Gospel in Nova-Scotia)
Born in New-York, in North-America. Taken
down from his own Relation, Arranged, Corrected,
and Published By the Rev. Mr. Aldridge. The
Second Edition. *London:* Gilbert and Plummer.
1785; 38 *pp.* 8vo. (4s. 6d. 1792)

MARSHALL (Humphry). Arbustrum Americanum: The American Grove, or, an Alphabetical
Catalogue of Forest Trees and Shrubs, natives of
the American United States, arranged according to
the Linnæan System. Containing, The particular
diftinguifhing Charaĉters of each Genus, with plain,
fimple and familiar Defcriptions of the Manner of
Growth, Appearance, &c. of their feveral Species
and Varieties. Also some hints of their uses in
Medicine, Dyes, and Domestic Oeconomy. Compiled from actual knowledge and observation, and
the assistance of Botanical Authors, By Humphry
Marshall. *Philadelphia:* Printed by Joseph Crukshank, in Market-Street, between Second and Third-
Streets. MDCCLXXXV. *xx and* 174 *pp. unbound.*
8vo. (7s. 6d. 1793)

MARSTON (Edward). To The Moft Noble Prince
Henry Duke of Beaufort, Marquifs and Earl of
Worcefter, Baron Herbert, Lord of Ragland, Chep-
ftow and Gower. Palatine of the Province of South
Carolina in America. [*London,* 1712.] 12 *pp. half
mor.* 4to. (18s. 1794)

MARTENS (Friderich). Friderich Martens/ von
Hamburg/ Spitzbergifche oder Groenlandifche/

Reife Befchreibung/ gethan im Jahr 1671./ Aus/
eigner Erfahrunge befchrieben, die dazu erforderte/
Figuren nach dem Leben felbft abgeriffen, (fo hier-
bey in/ Kupfferzufehen) und jetzo durch den/ Druck
mitgetheilet./ Hamburg,/ Auff Gottfried, Schult-
zens Koften, gedruckt, Im Jahr 1675./ 4 *prel.*
leaves and 132 *pp.* 'Regifter' 2 *pp.* 'Errata.' 1
page. 15 *Copperplates.* 4*to.*　　　(1*l.* 5*s.* 1795)

MARTENS (FREDERICH). [*Engraved title*] Vojagie
naar/ Groenland of Spitsbergen/ mits gaders een
net verhaal der/ Walvis vanghst/ en der zelve be-
handeling./ Met veel Avontuurlyke voorvallen
door F. Martens./ Te Dordrecht,/ Gedrukt by
Hendrik Walpot, boekverkooper overt Stadhuys./
[*Printed title*] Fredrik Martens/ Naukeurige Besch-
ryvinge/ van/ Groenland/ of/ Spitsbergen,/ Waer
in de Walvifch-Vangft, gelogentheyd van/ 't Ys,
en haer wonderlyke kragt en Figuren duydelyk
worden/ aengewefen:/ Nevens/ Den Aard van't
Land, Gewaffen, Ys-Bergen, Gevogelte,/ Viervoe-
tige Dieren, en Viffchen defer Contryen./ Ook hoe
de Walviffchen gevangen, gekapt en gefneden worden :/ Benevens verfcheyde Avontuurlyke voorvallen in Groenland./ Met een Verhael van de ge-
vange Walvifch by St. Anne-Land./ Als mede een
Gevegt en fpringen van twee Schepen, een Frans
en een En-/gels: Nevens alle de Gevaaren haar
overgekomen./ Met Kopere Platen Verçiert./ Te
Dordrecht,/ Gedrukt by Hendrik Walpot, Boek-
drukker en Boekverkooper/ over 't Stadthuys./
[1710 ?] 5 *prel. leaves, and* 88 *pp.* *Copperplates at*
pp. 46, 58, 68. 4*to.*　　　(1*l.* 11*s.* 6*d.* 1796)

MARTINI (FRANCIS). Argo-Navta/ Batavvs,/ Sive
expeditionis Navalis, quam alter nofter/ Jason, &
Heros fortiffimus, Petrvs/ Heinivs, fub aufpicijs
Illuftriffimorum &/ potentiffimorum DD. Ordd: &/
Illuftriffimi Principis Auraici, In-/clytæq; Socie-
tatis Indiæ Occi-/dentalis duĉtu nuper/ fufcepit :/
Et Viĉtoriæ in finu Matanzæ divinitus/ reportatæ/
Historia/ Carmine heroico defcripta, & publicé re-
citata,/ à/ Francisco Martini/ Scholæ Campenfis
Difcipulo./ *Campis./* Ex officina Petri Henrici
Wyringani,/ fub figno Typographiæ./ CIƆIƆ CXXIX/
Title and 28 *pp.* 4*to.*　　　(2*l.* 2*s.* 1797)

MARTINIERE (Sieur de la). A New/ Voyage/ into the/ Northern Countries/ Being a Difcription of the Manners,/ Cuftoms, Superftition, Buildings,/ and Habits of the Norwegians, La-/ponians, Kilops, Borandians, Sib-/erians, Samojedes, Zemblans and Iflanders./ With Reflexions upon an Error in/ our Geographers about the fcitua-/tion and Extent of Greenland and/ Nova Zembla./ *London*/ Printed for John Starkey, at the Miter/ in Fleetftreet near Temple-/Bar. 1674./ *5 prel. leaves and 153 pp. Old calf. 12mo.* (1*l.* 1*s.* 1798)

MARTINIERE (Sieur de la). [*Engraved title*] Voyage/ Des Pais/ Septentrionavx/ Par le Sʳ. D. L M./ A Paris/ Chez Louis Vandosme proche/ Monfeigʳ. le Premier Prefident./ G. Ladame [*Printed title*] Voyage/ des Pays/ Septentrionavx./ Dans lequel fe void les mœurs, maniere de vivre, & fuperfti-/tions des Norweguiens, Lap-/pons, Kiloppes, Borandiens,/ Syberiens, Samojedes, Zem-/bliens, Iflandois./ Par le fieur de la Martiniere,/ Seconde Edition, reveuë & augmentée/ de nouveau./ A *Paris*,/ Chez Louis Vendosme, Libraire/ au Palais dans la Salle Royalle,/ au Sacrifice d'Abraham 1676./ Avec Privilege dv Roy./ *6 prel. leaves, and 322 pp.* ' Extraict du Privilege du Roy.' *2 pp. Old calf. 12mo.* (15*s.* 1799)

MARTYN (Benjamin). Reasons For Establishing the Colony of Georgia, With Regard to the Trade of Great Britain, the Increafe of our People, and the Employment and Support it will afford to great Numbers of our own Poor, as well as foreign perfecuted Protestants. With fome Account of the Country and the Defign of the Trustees. By Benjamin Martyn Efq. The Second Edition. *London* : W. Meadows, MDCCXXXIII. *48 pp. Frontispiece & Map, both engraved on copper. Half morocco. 4to.* (15*s.* 1800)

MARTYR (Peter). De orbe nouo Decades. [*tres. Colophon*] Cura & diligentia uiri celebris Magiftri Antonii Ne=/briffenfis historici regii fuerunt hæ tres protono/tarii Petri martyris decades Impreffæ in/ contubernio Arnaldi Guillelmi in/ Illustri oppido carpetanæ puī-/ciæ cōpluto quod uulgari/ter diciter *Alcala* pfe/ctū eft nonis No/uébris An./ 1516./ *Without pagination or catchwords. On the*

2   L L

reverse of the Title "Clarissimo Principi Carolo Regi Catholico:" *The Preface occupies the next page* a ii, *on the reverse of which begins the text which ends on the reverse of* i. iii; 'Ad Lectorem de qvibusdam locis leviter depravatis" *2 pages followed by one blank leaf:* "Vocabula Barbara," *5 pages ending with the Colophon, reverse blank; Signatures* a to i *in eights, except* a *and* h, *which have only six leaves each.* "Incipitur Legatio Babylonica " 16 *leaves, signatures* A *and* B. *Splendid copy with rough leaves in red morocco extra by Bedford. Folio.* (10l. 10s. 1801)

MARTYR (Peter). De Nvper/ svb D. Carolo Reper-/tis Inſulis, ſimulque incolarum/ moribus, R. Petri Marty-/ris, Enchiridion, Domi-/næ Margaritæ, Diui/ Max. Cæf. filiæ/ dicatum./ *Basileæ,* Anno/ M.D.XXI. 43 *pp.* 4*to.* (2l. 2s. 1802)

MARTYR (Peter). Petri Martyris/ ab Angleria Mediolanen. Oratoris/ clariſſimi, Fernandi & Heliſabeth Hiſpaniarum quondam regum/ à conſilijs, de rebus Oceanicis & Orbe nouo decades tres : quibus/ quicquid de inuentis nuper terris traditum, nouarum rerum cupi=/dum leċtorem retinere poſſit, copioſe, fideliter, eruditeque docetur./ Eivsdem praeterea/ Legationis Babylonicae li/bri tres : vbi praeter oratorii mvneris pulcherrimum exemplum, etiam quicquid in uariarum gentium mori=/bus & inſtitutis inſigniter præclarum uidit, quæque terra marique acciderunt,/ omnia lectu mirè iucunda, genere dicendi politiſſimo traduntur. *Basileae,/* apud Ioannem Bebelium./ M.D.XXXIII. 12 *prel. leaves and* 92 *folioed leaves. Fine copy in Spanish morocco by Leighton. Folio.* (1l. 11s. 6d. 1803)

MARTYR (Peter). Relationi/ del S. Pietro Martire/ Milanese./ Dell coſe notabili della prouincia dell' E-/gitto ſcritte in lingua Latina alli Sereniſs,/ di felice memoria Re Catolici D. Fernando,/ e D. Iſabella, & hora recate nella Italiana./ Da Carlo Paſsi./ Con Privilegio./ In *Venetia* appreſſo Giorgio de' Caualli 1564. 7 *prel. leaves ; viz. Title reverse blank,* 'All' Illustriss. et Eccellentiss. Signora Givlia Sforza Pallavicina,' *etc.* 5 *pp* ; 'Discorso di Carlo Paſsi,' *etc.* 6 *pp. Text* 71 *folioed leaves,* 'Tavola,' *etc.* 12 *pp* ; 'Errori fatti nello ſtamparſi,' *etc.* 3 *pp. calf. Small* 8*vo.* (1l. 1s. 1804)

MARTYR (PETER). De Rebus/ Oceanicis/ et Novo
Orbe, de-/cades tres, Petri Mar-/tyris ab Angleria/
Mediolanensis./ Item eivsdem,/ de Babylonica/
Legatione, Libri III./ et item/ de Rebvs Aethiopi-
cis,/ Indicîs Lufitanicis & Hifpanicis, opufcula quæ-
dã/ Hiftorica doctiffima, quæ hodiè non facilè/ alibì
reperiuntur, Damiani/ A Goes Equitis/ Lufitani./
Quæ omnia fequens pagina lattùs demonftrat./
Cum duplici locupletiffimo Indice./ *Coloniæ,* Apud
Geruinum Calenium & hæredes/ Quentelios. M.D.
LXXIIII./ Cum gratia & Privilegio Cæsareo./ 24
prel. leaves and 655 *pp.* 'Index,' 28 *pp. Fine copy,*
Vellum. Small 8*vo.*   (1*l.* 10*s.* 6*d.* 1805)

MARTYR (PETER). De Novo Orbe,/ or/ the Historie of/ the weft Indies, Contaying the actes/ and aduentures of the Spanyardes, which haue/ conquered
and peopled thofe Countries,/ inriched with varietie
of pleafant re-/lation of the Manners, Ceremonies,/
Lawes, Gouernments, and/ Warres of the Indians./
Comprifed in eight Decades./ Written by Peter
Martyr a Millanoife of Algeria, Cheife/ Secretary
to the Emperour Charles the fift,/ and of his Priuie Councell./ Whereof three, haue beene formerly
tranflated in-/to Englifh, by R. Eden, whereunto
the other/ fiue, are newly added by the Induftrie,
and/ painefull Trauaile of M. Lok Gent./ *London*/
Printed for Thomas Adams./ 1612./ 5 *prel. leaves ;*
viz. Title, reverse blank ' Epistola Dedicatoria' 4 *pp.*
Signed ' Michael Lok.' To the Reader' 4 *pp. Signed*
' M. Lok.' *Text* 318 *folioed leaves. Wanting leaf*
folioed 158. 4*to.*   (2*l.* 12*s.* 6*d.* 1806)

MARTYR (PETER). The/ famovs/ Historie of/ the
Indies :/ Declaring the aduentures of/ the Spa-
niards, which haue conque-/red thefe Countries,
with varietie of Relations/ of the Religions, Lawes,
Gouernments, Manners,/ Ceremonies, Cuftomes,
Rites, Warres,/ and Funerals of the People./ Com-
prifed into fundry Decads./ Set forth firft by M[r]
Hackluyt, and now pub-/lifhed by *L. M.* Gent./
The fecond Edition./ *London :* Printed for Michael
Sparke dwelling at the figne/ of the blue Bible in
Green-Arbor. 1628./ *3 prel. leaves ; viz. Title the*
reverse blank ; 'To the Reader' *Signed* ' M. Lok.' 4
pp. Text 318 *folioed leaves. Calf extra by Bedford.*
4*to.*   (4*l.* 14*s.* 6*d.* 1807)

MARTYR; OVIEDO & XERES. Libro Primo/
della Histo/ria de l'In/die Oc/ciden/tali ♊/ [*verso*]
Svmmario de la Generale/ Historia de l'Indie Oc=
ci=/dentali cavato da li=/bri scritti dal si=/gnor don
Pietro/ Martyre del consi/glio delle Indie/ della
Maesta/ de l'Imperadore,/ et da molte/ altre par=/
ticvla=/ri rela=/tioni./ 79 *folioed leaves, the 80th
blank.* Libro Secon/do delle In/die Oc/ciden/tali/
✠ MDXXXIIII./ Con gratia & priuilegio./ [*verso*]
Svmmario de la/ Naturale et General Histo/ria de
l'Indie occidentali, compofta da Gonzalo ferdi=/
nando del Ouiedo altrimenti di valde, natio de/ la
terra di Madril : habitatore & rettore de/ la citta
di fanta Maria antica del Darien,/ in terra ferma del'
indie : ilqual fu riue/duto & corretto per ordine
de la/ Maefta del Imperadore, pel fuo/ real config-
lio, de la dette In/die. & tradotto di lingua/ caftig-
liana in Italia=/na. Cõ priuilegio/ de la Illuftriff./
Signoria di/ Vinegia,/ per ãni xx. 64 *folioed leaves,
the 65th containing the Table and the 66th the explanation of the maps.* Libro vltimo del svmma/rio
delle/ Indie Oc/ciden/tali/ MDXXXIIII. [*Colophon*]
❡ In *Venegia*, Del mefe d'Ottobre./ MDXXXIIII./
16 *leaves, the 16th being blank. The three Parts
complete, a very large copy, with the Map of* 'Isola
Spagnvola' *and* 'La carta uniuersale della terra
firme,' *both of which are here inserted in facsimile.*
4to.   (2*l.* 12*s.* 6*d.*   1808)

MARYLAND. A/ Relation/ of/ Maryland ;/ Together,/ With [A Map of the Countrey,/ The Conditions of Plantation,/ His Majefties Charter to the/
Lord Baltemore, tranflated/ into Englifh./ Thefe
Bookes are to bee had, at Mafter William/ Peafley
Efq ; his houfe ; on the back-fide of Dru-/ry-Lane,
neere the Cock-pit Playhoufe ; or in/ his abfence ;
at Mafter Iohn Morgans houfe in/ high Holbourn,
over againft the Dolphin, *London.*/ September the
8. Anno Dom. 1635./ *Title reverse blank, and 56 pp.*
'The Charter of Maryland.' 25 *pp.*` *Blue morocco
extra by Hayday. Map* 15¾ *by* 11¾ *inch. wanting.*
4to.   (3*l.* 3*s.*   1809)

MARYLAND. The/ Declaration/ of the/ Reasons
and Motives/ For the Present/ Appearing in Arms/
of/ Their Majesties/ Protestant Subjects/ In the
Province of/ Maryland./ Licens'd, November

28th 1689. J. F./ [*Colophon*] Maryland, Printed by William Nuthead at the City of St./ Maries./ Reprinted in London, and Sold by Randal Tay-/lor near Stationers Hall, 1689./ 8 *pp. unbound.*
Folio. (1*l.* 11*s.* 6*d.* 1810)

MARYLAND. The Charter/ of/ Maryland./ [*London*] 23 *pp.* 8*vo.* (10*s.* 6*d.* 1811)

MASSACHUSETTENSIS. *Letters numbered* I *to* XVII. [*Boston*, 1775.] 118 *pp. First Edition. half mor.* 8*vo.* (10*s.* 6*d.* 1812)

MASSACHUSETTENSIS: Or a Series of Letters, containing a faithful state of many important and striking facts, which laid the foundation of the present Troubles in the Province of the Maſſachuſetts-Bay; interspersed with Animadversions and Reflections, originally Addreſſed to the People of that Province, and worthy the conſideration of the True Patriots of this Country. By a Person of Honor upon the Spot. The Third Edition. Boston printed. *London* reprinted for J. Mathews, MDCCLXXVI. *viii and* 118 *pp. half mor.* 8*vo.* (7*s.* 6*d.* 1812*)

MASSACHUSETTENSIS: Or a Series of Letters, containing a faithful state of many important and striking facts, which laid the foundation of the present Troubles in the Province of the Maſſachuſetts-Bay; interspersed with Animadversions and Reflections, originally Addreſſed to the People of that Province, and worthy the Conſideration of the True Patriots of this Country. By a Person of Honor upon the Spot. The Fourth Edition. Boston printed: *London* reprinted for J. Mathews, MDCCLXXVI. *viii and* 118 *pp. Half morocco.*
8*vo.* (7*s.* 6*d.* 1813)

MASSACHUSETTS. An Account of the Massachusetts State Prison. Containing a description and Plan of the Edifice; the Law, Regulations, Rules and Orders: With a view of the present State of the Institution. By the Board of Visitors. *Charlestown:* Printed by Samuel Etheridge. 1806. 48 *pp. With 2 folded plates.* 8*vo.* (2*s.* 6*d.* 1814)

MASSACHUSETTS-BAY. A/ Collection/ Of the Proceedings of the/ Great and General Court or Aſſembly/ Of His Majesty's Province of the/ Maſſachuſetts-Bay,/ in/ New-England ;/ Containing feveral Inftructions from the Crown, to the/ Council and Affembly of that Province, for fixing a/ Salary on the Governour, and their Determinations/ thereon./ As also,/ The Methods taken by the Court for Supporting the feveral/ Governours, fince the Arrival of the prefent Charter./ Printed by Order of the Houfe of Reprefentatives./ *Boston:* Printed by T. Fleet, in Pudding-Lane./ 1729./ 112 *pp. half calf. 4to.*　　　　　(1*l.* 1*s.*　1815)

MASSACHUSETTS BAY. A Brief State of the Services and Expences of the Province of the Maffachusett's Bay, In the Common Cause. *London:* J. Wilkie, MDCCLXV. 24 *pp. Half morocco. 8vo.*　　　　　(7*s.* 6*d.*　1816)

MASSACHUSETTS BAY. The Proceedings of the Council, and the House of Representatives Of the Province of the Mafsachusetts-Bay, relative to the Convening, holding and keeping The General Affembly At Harvard-College in Cambridge: And The feveral Meffages which pafsed between His Honor the Lieutenant Governor and The Two Houfes, Upon the Subject. Publifhed by Order of the Houfe of Representatives. *Boston:* Printed by Edes and Gill, Printers to the Honorable Houfe of Representatives, 1770. *Title, and pp.* 5-83. *half mor. 8vo.*　　　　　(7*s.* 6*d.*　1817)

MASSIE (J.) Calculations and Observations relating to an Additional Duty upon Sugar. *Dated Westminster,* 20th January 1759. 2 *pp. single sheet. Folio.*　　　　　(4*s.* 6*d.*　1818)

MASSIE (J.) A State of the British Sugar-Colony Trade; shewing, That an Additional Duty of Twelve Shillings per 112 Pounds Weight may be laid upon Brown or Muscovado Sugar (and proportionably higher Duties upon Sugar refined before imported) without making Sugar dearer in this Kingdom than it hath been of late Years, and without Diftreffing the Britifh Sugar-Planters; for their Profits will then be Twice as much Money per acre of Land, as the Landholders of England receive for their Eftates. All which Matters are plainly made appear, and the vaft loffes which this Kingdom hath fuffered by the Sugar-Colony Trade, written Thirty Years laft paft, are particularly

pointed out. Moſt humbly ſubmitted to the conſideration of the Honourable House of Commons.
By J. Maſſie. *London*, T. Payne, MDCCLIX. *Title
and* 40 *pp. half calf.* 4*to.* (5*s.* 6*d.* 1818*)

MATHER (COTTON). Late/ Memorable Provi-
dences/ Relating to/ Witchcrafts and Poſſeſſions,/
Clearly Manifeſting,/ Not only that there are
Witches, but that Good Men (as well as others)
may poſſibly have their Lives ſhortned/ by ſuch
evil Inſtruments of Satan./ Written by Cotton
Mather Miniſter of the/ Goſpel at Boſton in New-
England./ The Second· Impreſſion./ Recommended by the Reverend Mr. Richard/ Baxter in
London, and by the Miniſters of/ Boſton and
Charleſtown in New-England./ *London*, Printed
for Tho. Parkhurſt at the Bible and/ Three Crowns
in Cheapſide near Mercers-/Chapel. 1691./ 11 *prel.
leaves, viz. Title reverse blank*, 'To the Honourable
Wait Winthrop Eſq;' 2 *pp.* 'To the Reader.' 4
pp. 'The Preface.' 9 *pp.* 'A Catalogue of Books'
etc. 3 *pp.* 'The Introduction.' 2 *pp. Text* 144 *pp.
Small* 8*vo.* (2*l.* 2*s.* 1819)

MATHER (COTTON). The/ Life and Death/ Of
The Renown'd/ Mr. John Eliot,/ Who was the/
Firſt Preacher/ of the/ Gospel/ to the/ Indians in
America./ With an Account of the Wonderful
Suc-/ceſs which the Goſpel has had amongſt the
Hea-/then in that part of the World : And of the/
many ſtrange Cuſtomes of the Pagan Indians,/ In
New-England./ Written by Cotton Mather./
The Second Edition carefully correċted./ *London* :/
Printed for John Dunton, at the Raven/ in the
Poultrey. MDCXCÍ./ 3 *prel. leaves, and* 138 *pp. calf.
Small* 8*vo.* (1*l.* 5*s.* 1820)

MATHER (COTTON). A/ True Account/ of the
Tryals, Examinations,/ Confeſſions, Condemna-
tions,/ and Executions of divers/ Witches,/ At
Salem, in New-England,/ for/ Their Bewitching
of ſundry People and Cattel/ to Death, and doing
other great Miſchiefs,/ to the Ruine of many People about them./ With/ The Strange Circumſtances that attended/ their Enchantments :/ And/
Their Converſation with Devils, and other/ Infer-
nal Spirits./ In a Letter to a Friend in London./

Licenfed according to Order./ *London*, Printed for
J. Conyers, in Holbourn./ 8 *pp.* 'Salem, 8th.
Month, 1692. Signed C. M.' *4to.* (*2l. 2s.* 1821)

MATHER (Cotton). The Wonders of the Invifible World :/ Being an Account of the/ Tryals/
of Several Witches,/ Lately Executed in/ New-
England :/ And of several remarkable Curiofities
therein Occurring./ Together with,/ I. Obfervations upon the Nature, the Number, and the Operations of the Devils./ II. A fhort Narrative of a
late outrage committed by a knot of Witches in/
Swede-Land, very much refembling, and fo far explaining, that under which/ New-England has
laboured./ III. Some Councels directing a due
Improvement of the Terrible things lately/ done
by the unufual and amazing Range of Evil-Spirits
in New-England./ IV. A brief Difcourfe upon
thofe Temptations which are the more ordinary
Devi-/ces of Satan./ By Cotton Mather./ Publifhed by the Special command of his Excellency
the Governour of/ the Province of the Maffachufetts-Bay in New-England./ Printed firft, at Bofton in New-England ; and Reprinted at *Lon-/don*,
for John Dunton, at the Raven in the Poultry.
1693./ *First Edition. Title, and* 98 *pp. unbound.*
4to. (*2l. 2s.* 1822)

MATHER (Cotton). The Wonders of the Invifible World :/ Being an Account of the/ Tryals/
of/ Several Witches/ Lately Executed in/ New-
England :/ And of feveral Remarkable Curiofities
therein Occurring./ By Cotton Mather./ Publifhed by the Special Command of his Excellency
the/ Governour of the Province of the Maffachufetts-Bay in New-/England./ The Second Edition./
Printed firft, at Bofton in New-England, and reprinted at *London*, for/ John Dunton, at the Raven
in the Poultrey. 1693./ *3 prel. leaves, and pp.* 9-62.
half mor. 4to. (*2l. 2s.* 1823)

MATHER (Cotton). The Wonders of the Invifible World :/ Being an Account of the/ Tryals/ of/
Several Witches/ Lately Executed in/ New-England :/ And of feveral Remarkable Curiofities/
therein Occurring./ By Cotton Mather./ Publifhed by the Special Command of his Excellency/

the Governour of the Province of the Maſſachuſetts-Bay in/ New-England./ The Third Edition./
Printed firſt at Boſton in New-England, and reprinted at *London,*/ for John Duneon, at the Raven
in the Poultrey. 1693./ 4 *prel. leaves, and pp.* 9-64.
half mor. 4*to.* (2*l.* 2*s.* 1824)

MATHER (Cotton). The Order of the Churches
in New-England. Vindicated. [*Boston* 1700 ?]
pp. 13-144. *Wanting the title and prel. leaves.*
12*mo.* (7*s.* 6*d.* 1825)

MATHER (Cotton). Magnalia Chriſti Americana :
Or, the Eccleſiaſtical Hiſtory of New-England,
from Its Firſt Planting in the Year 1620. unto the
Year of our Lord, 1698. In Seven Books. I. An-
tiquities : In Seven Chapters. With an Appendix.
II. Containing the Lives of the Governours, and
Names of the Magiſtrates of New-England : In
Thirteen Chapters. With an Appendix. III. The
Lives of Sixty Famous Divines, by whoſe Miniſtry
the Churches of New-England have been Planted
and Continued. IV. An Account of the Univer-
ſity of Cambridge in New-England ; in Two Parts.
The Firſt contains the Laws, the Benefaċtors, and
Viciſſitudes of Harvard College ; with Remarks
upon it. The Second Part contains the Lives of
ſome Eminent Perſons Educated in it. V. Aċts
and Monuments of the Faith and Order in the
Churches of New-England, paſſed in their Synods ;
with Hiſtorical Remarks upon thoſe Venerable
Aſſemblies ; and a great Variety of Church-Caſes
occurring, and reſolved by the Synods of thoſe
Churches : In Four Parts. VI. A Faithful Record of many Illuſtrious, Wonderful Providences,
both of Mercies and Judgments, on divers Perſons
in New-England : In Eight Chapters. VII. The
Wars of the Lord. Being an Hiſtory of the Manifold Afflictions and Diſturbances of the Churches
in New-England, from their Various Adverſaries,
and the Wonderful Methods and Mercies of God
in their Deliverance : In Six Chapters : To which
is ſubjoined, An Appendix of Remarkable Occurrences which New-England had in the Wars with
the Indian Salvages, from the Year 1688, to the
Year 1698. By the Reverend and Learned Cotton
Mather, M.A. And Paſtor of the North Church in

Bofton, New-England. *London :* Printed for Thomas Parkhurft, at the Bible and Three Crowns in
Cheapfide. MDCCII. 14 *prel. leaves ; viz. Title, Attestation, Poems, General Introduction, and Contents.*
' Antiquities. The First Book.' *Title and* 38 *pp.*
' Ecclefiarum Clypei. The Second Book.' *Title
and* 75 *pp.* ' Polybius. The Third Book.' *Title and*
238 *pp.* 'Sal Gentium. The Fourth Book.' *Title
and pp.* 125-222. ' Acts and Monuments. The Fifth
Book.' *Title and pp.* 3-100. ' Thaumaturgus. The
Sixth Book.' *Title and* 88 *pp. blank leaf.* ' Eccle-
siarum Prœlia : The Seventh Book.' *Title and pp.*
3-118. ' Books,' *etc.* 2 *pp. With map. Old calf.
Folio.*   (*3l. 3s.* 1826)

MATHER (COTTON). The Curbed Sinner. A Dis-
course Upon the Gracious and Wondrous Reftraints
Laid by the Providence Of the Glorious God, On
the Sinful Children of Men, to Withold them from
Sinning againft Him. Occafioned by a Sentence
of Death, paffed on a poor Young Man, for the
Murder of his Companion. With fome Hiftorical
Paffages referring to that Unhappy Spectacle. By
Cotton Mather, D.D. *Boston, N.E.* Printed by
John Allen, for Nicholas Boone, at the Sign of the
Bible in Cornhil. 1713. *Title, xiv and* 64 *pp.
Vellum.* 12*mo.*   (10*s.* 6*d.* 1827)

MATHER (COTTON). A Prefent of Summer Fruit.
A very brief Essay To Offer Some Instructions of
Piety, Which the Summer-Season more Particularly and Emphatically Leads us to ; But fuch alfo
as are never out of Seafon. Being The fhort Entertainment of an Auditory in Bofton, on a Day
diftinguifhed with the Heat of the Summer ; 5d.
5m. 1713. By Cotton Mather, D.D. *Boston :*
Printed and Sold by B. Green, in Newbury Street.
1713. *Title, and text* 29 *pp. Vellum.*
12*mo.*   (10*s.* 6*d.* 1828)

MATHER (COTTON). The Grand Point of Solici-
tude. A very brief Essay upon Divine Defertions ;
the Symptoms of them, and The Methods of Preventing them. A Sermon Publifhed for the Service
of Others, by One of the Hearers, more particularly
affected in the Hearing of it. *Boston :* Printed by
B. Green. 1715. *Blank leaf, Title, and* 31 *pp.*
12*mo.*   (7*s.* 6*d.* 1829)

MATHER (Cotton). Fair Dealing between Debtor and Creditor. A very brief Essay upon The Caution to be uſed, about coming in to Debt, And getting out of it. Offered at Boston-Lecture; 5. d. xi. m. 17$\frac{15}{16}$. By Cotton Mather, D.D. & F.R.S. *Boston:* Printed by B. Green, for Samuel Gerriſh, at his Shop over againſt the North ſide of the Town-Houſe. 1716. *Title and 30 pp. unbound.* 16mo. (15s. 1830)

MATHER (Cotton). Desiderius. Or, A Deſireable Man Deſcrib'd; In the Characters of One Worthy to be, a Man Greatly Beloved. And An Example ˙of One, who Lived very much Deſired, and has Dyed as much Lamented; Given in ſome Commemoration of the very Valuable and Memorable Mr. James Keith, Late Miniſter of the Gospel in Bridgwater; Who Expired, on 23. d. V. m. 1719. In the Seventy Sixth Year of his Age. By Cotton Mather, D.D. & F.R.S. *Boston:* Printed by S. Kneeland, 1719. *Title, and text 34 pp. Vellum.* 12mo. (10s. 6d. 1831)

MATHER (Cotton). A Year and a Life Well Concluded. A brief Essay, On the Good Things Wherein The Last Works Of a Christian, may be, and ſhould be, His Best Works. A Sermon Preached on the Last Day of the Year, 1719. *Boston:* Printed by S. Kneeland, for B. Gray, at the Corner Shop on the North ſide of the Town-Houſe, 1719-20. 24 pp. 12mo. (10s. 6d. 1832)

MATHER (Cotton). Coheleth. A Soul ˙ ꝑon Recollection; Coming into Inconteſtible Sentiments of Religion; Such as all the Sons of Wisdom, will and muſt forever Justify. Written by a Fellow of the Royal Society. Offering the Advice of a Father going out of the World, unto a Son coming into it. *Boston:* Printed by S. Kneeland, for S. Gerrish, and Sold at his Shop. 1720. *Title and 46 pp.* 12mo. (10s. 6d. 1833)

MATHER (Cotton). India Chriſtiana. A diſcourſe, Delivered unto the Commiſſioners, for the Propagation of the Gospel among the American Indians which is Accompanied with ſeveral Instruments relating to the Glorious Design of Propagating our Holy Religion, in the Eastern as well as the West-

ern, Indies. An Entertainment which they that
are Waiting for the Kingdom of God will receive
as Good News from a far Country. By Cotton
Mather, D.D. and F.R.S. *Boston* in New-England:
Printed by B. Green. 1721. *Title, Dedication ii
pp. Text 94 pp.* 'Corrigenda,' 1 *page.* *Old calf.
Small 8vo.*   (1*l.* 1*s.*   1834)

MATHER (Cotton). A Paſtoral Letter, to Families Viſited with Sickneſs. From ſeveral Ministers
of Boston, At a time of Epidemical Sickneſs Dif-
treſſing of the Town. The Third Impreſſion. [*Colophon*] *Boston:* Printed by R. Green, for S. Gerriſh, at his Shop near the Brick Meeting-Houſe in
Cornhill. 1721. *Half-title, and 24 pp. half morocco.*
12*mo.*   (7*s.* 6*d.*   1835)

MATHER (Cotton). Silentiarius. A brief Essay on
the Holy Silence and Godly Patience, that Sad
Things are to be Entertained withal. A Sermon at
Boſton-Lecture, On the Death of Mrs. Abigail Willard, And the Day before her Interment; who Expired Septemb. 26.1721. By her Father. Whereto
there is added, A Sermon on, The Refuge of the
Diſtreſſed, which was Preached on the Lord's-Day
preceeding. *Boston:* Printed by S. Kneeland,
1721. *On the reverse of the Title,* Introduction.'
signed 'Cotton Mather.' 'The Silent Sufferer,' 34
pp. ' The Refuge of the Diſtreſſed.' 28 *pp. unbound.*
12*mo.*   (15*s.*   1836)

MATHER (Cotton). Bethiah. The Glory Which
Adorns the Daughters of God. And the Piety,
Wherewith Zion wiſhes to ſee her Daughters Glo-
rious. *Boston:* Printed by J. Franklin, for S.
Gerriſh, at his Shop in Cornhill. 1722. 60 *pp.*
12*mo.*   (10*s.* 6*d.*   1837)

MATHER (Cotton). Columbanus. Or, The Doves
Flying to the Windows of their Saviour. A Sermon to a Religious Society of Young People. June
4th. 1722. *Boston:* Printed by S. Kneeland, for J.
Edwards, Sold at his Shop. 1722. *Title and 22 pp.*
12*mo.*   (10*s.* 6*d.*   1838)

MATHER (Cotton). Honeſta Parſimonia: Or,
Time Spent as it ſhould be. Proposals, To prevent
that Great Folly and Mischief, The Loſs of Time ;

And Employ the Talent of Time So Watchfully and Fruitfully that a Good Account may at Laſt be given of it. *Boston:* Printed by S. Kneeland, for J. Edwards, and Sold at his Shop. 172[2?] *Half-title, Title, and* 23 *pp.* 12*mo.* (10*s.* 6*d.* 1839)

MATHER (COTTON). The Minister. A Sermon, Offer'd unto the Anniverſary Convention of Min-isters, From ſeveral Parts of New-England, Met at Boston, 31 d. III m. 1722. By One of their Number. And publiſhed at the Requeſt of them that heard it. *Boston:* Printed in the Year 1722. *Half-title* ' Dr. Cotton Mather's Sermon, at the Anniversary Convention of Ministers, May 31ſt. 1722.' *and* 45 *pp.* 8*vo.* (10*s.* 6*d.* 1840)

MATHER (COTTON). Pia Diſideria. Or, The Smoaking Flax, raiſed into a Sacred Flame; In a Short and Plain Essay upon thoſe Pious Deſires, Which are the Introduction and Inchoation of all Vital Piety, Delivered unto a Religious Society of Young People; On the Lord's-Day-Evening, Aug. 5. 1722. *Boston:* Printed by S. Kneeland for S. Gerriſh, at his Shop in Cornhill. 1722. *Title and* 22 *pp.* 12*mo.* (10*s.* 6*d.* 1841)

MATHER (INCREASE). The/ Mystery/ of/ Iſrael's Salvation,/ Explained and Applyed :/ Or,/ A Dis-course/ Concerning the General Converſion of the/ Israelitish Nation./ Wherein is Shewed,/ 1. That the twelve Tribes ſhall be ſaved./ 2. When this is to be expected./ 3. Why this muſt be./ 4. What kind of Salvation the Tribes of Israel/ ſhall partake of. (viz.) A Glorious, Wonder-/ful, Spi-ritual, Temporal Salvation./ Being the Subſtance of ſeveral Ser-/mons Preached./ By Increase Ma-ther, M.A./ Teacher of a Church in Boſton in New-England./ *London,* Printed for John Allen in Wentworth-ſtreet, near/ Bell-Lane, 1669. 23 *prel. leaves; viz. Title reverse blank,* ' An Epistle to the Reader.' *signed* ' John Davenporte.' 11 *pp.* ' To the Reader.' *signed* ' W. G.' 4 *pp.* ' To the Reader.' *signed* ' W. H.' 14 *pp.* ' The Authors Preface To The Reader.' *signed* ' J. M.' 14 *pp: Text* 181 *pp.* ' The Names of Writers,' *etc. being* ' The Table.' 5 *pp.* ' Places of Scripture opened,' *etc.* 4 *pp. Calf extra by Bedford. Small* 8*vo.* (1*l.* 16*s.* 6*d.* 1842)

MATHER (Increase). The/ First Principles/ of/
New-England,/ Concerning/ The Subject of Bap-
tifme/ &/ Communion of Churches./ Collected
partly out of the Printed Books, but chiefly/ out
of the Original Manufcripts of the Firft and chiefe/
Fathers in the New-Englifh Churches; With the
Judg-/ment of Sundry Learned Divines of the
Congregational/ Way in England, Concerning the
faid Queftions./ Publifhed for the Benefit of thofe
who are of the Rifing Gene-/ration in New-England./ By Increase Mather, Teacher of a Church/
in Bofton in New-England/ *Cambridge/* Printed
by Samuel Green, 1675./ *4 prel. leaves; viz. Title
in a narrow metal type border, the reverse blank,* 'To
the Reader.' *signed* 'Increase Mather.' *6 pp; Text*
40 *pp.* 'Postscript' *signed* 'Iohn Allin.' *1 page.*
'A Letter concerning the Subject of Baptifme,' *etc.
signed* 'Jonathan Mitchel.' *pp.* 2-7. *Calf extra by
Bedford.* 4to. (4*l.* 4*s.* 1843)
With the Autograph of White Kennett on the Title.

MATHER (Increase). The/ Divine Right/ of/
Infant-Baptifme/ Afferted and Proved from/ Scrip-
ture/ And/ Antiquity. By Increase Mather,/
Teacher of a Church of Chrift in Bofton in New-
England./ *Boston,/* Printed by John Fofter, in the
Year 1680./ *4 prel. leaves; viz. Title the reverse
blank;* 'Christian Reader.' *5 pp. Signed* 'Urian
Oakes.' *Text* 27 *pp. Calf extra, gilt by Bedford.*
4to. (4*l.* 4*s.* 1844)

MATHER (Increase). Returning unto God the
great concernment/ of a Covenant People./ Or/
A Sermon/ Preached to the fecond Church in
Boston in/ New-England, March 17. 16$\frac{79}{80}$. when/
that Church did folemnly and explicitly/ Renew
their Covenant with/ God, and one with another./
By Increase Mather Teacher of that Church./
Boston, Printed by John Fofter. 1680./ *3 prel.
leaves; viz. Title, reverse blank;* 'To the fecond
Church of Chrift in Boston in New-England.' 4
pp. Text 21 *pp. Fine copy in morocco by Bedford.*
4to. (3*l.* 3*s.* 1845)

MATHER (Increase). Diatriba/ de signo/ Filii
Hominis/ et de/ Secundo Messiæ Adventu;/ Ubi
de modo futuræ Judæorum Converfionis:/ Nec non
de fignis Novifsimi diei, differitur./ Authore/ Cres-

centio Mathero/ V.D.M. apud Boftonienfis in Novâ
Angliâ. *Amstelodami*,/ Apud Mercy Browning
Juxta Burfam. 1682./ *4 prel. leaves and 98 pp.
Index 5 pp. Corrigenda*, 1 *page. Calf extra by Bed-
ford. 8vo.* (1*l.* 11*s.* 6*d.* 1846)

MATHER (INCREASE). KOMHTOΓPAΦIA./ Or
a/ Difcourfe Concerning/ Comets ;/ Wherein the
Nature of Blazing Stars/ is Enquired into :/ With
an Hiftorical Account of all the Comets/ which
have appeared from the Beginning of the/ World
unto this prefent Year, M.DC.LXXXIII./ Expreffing/
The Place in the Heavens, where they were seen,/
Their Motion, Forms, Duration ; and the Re-/
markable Events which have followed/ in the
World, fo far as they have been/ by Learned Men
Obferved./ As alfo two Sermons,/ Occafioned by
the late Blazing Stars./ By Increase Mather,
Teacher of a Church/ at Bofton in New-England./
Boston In New-England./ Printed by S. G. for
S. S. And fold by J. Browning/ At the corner of
the Prifon Lane next the Town-/Houfe. 1683./ *6
prel. leaves* ; *viz. Title.* ' To the Reader ' 4 *pp. signed*
' John Sherman.' ' To the Reader,' 3 *pp.* ' The
Contents' 2 *pp. Text* 143 *pp. Errata* 1 *page.* Hea-
ven's/ Alarm/ to the/ World./ Or/ A Sermon,
wherein is shewed,/ That Fearful/ Sights/ And
Signs in Heaven, are the Presa-/ges of great Calamities at hand./ Preached at the Lecture of Bofton
in New-England ;/ January, 20. 1680./ By Mr.
Increase Mather./ The Second Impression./ *Boston*
in New-England,/ Printed for Samuel Sewall.
And are to be fold by/ Jofeph Browning at the
Corner of the Prifon-Lane/, Next the Town-Houfe.
1682./ *4 prel. leaves* ; *viz. Title*, ' To the Reader.'
6 *pp* ; *Text* 38 *pp.* ' The Latter/ Sign/ Difcourfed
of,/ in a Sermon/ Preached at the Lecture of Bofton in/ New-England ;/ August, 31. 1682./ Wherein is fhewed, that the Voice of/ God in Signal Providences, efpecially/ when repeated and Iterated,
ought to be/ Hearkned unto/ By Increase Mather./
Title and 32 *pp. small 8vo.* (2*l.* 2*s.* 1847)

MATHER (INCREASE). The/ Mystery/ of/ Christ/
opened and applyed./ In several Sermons, Concerning the/ Perfon, Office, and Glory of Jefus
Chrift./ By Increase Mather,/ Teacher of a Church

at Bofton in N. England./ [*Boston*] Printed in
the year MDCLXXXVI. *Title 6 and* 212 *pp. The
Contents* 1 *page. Books printed, etc. Calf extra by
Bedford.* 12*mo.*   (1*l.* 11*s.* 6*d.*   1848)

MATHER (INCREASE). De/ Succeffu Evangelij/
Apud Indos/ in/ Novâ-Angliâ/ Epistola./ Ad Cl.
Virum/ D. Johannem Leufdenum,/ Linguæ Sanctæ
in Ultra-/jectinâ Academiâ Pro-/fefforem, Scripta./
A Crefcentio Mathero/ Apud Boftonienfes V.D.M.
nec non/ Collegij Harvardini quod eft Canta-/
brigiæ Nov-Anglorum, Rectore./ *Londini*, Typis
J. G. 1688./ *Title and* 13 *pp. Green morocco.*
12*mo.*   (1*l.* 1*s.*   1849)

MATHER (INCREASE). De/ Succeffu Evangelii/
Apud/ Indos/ occidentales,/ In Novâ-Angliâ ;/
Epistola./ Ad Cl. Virum/ D. Johannem Leus-
denum/ Linguæ Sanctæ in Ultrajectinâ Acade-/
miâ Profefforem, Scripta,/ A Crefcentio Mathero./
Apud Boftonienfes V. D. M. nec non Collegii/
Harvardini quod eft Cantabrigia Nov-An-/glorum,
Rectore./ Londini, Typis J. G. 1688,/ Jam recu-
fua, & fuccefsu Evangelii apud In-/dos Orientales
aucta./ *Ultrajecti*, /Apud Wilhelmum Broedeleth,/
Anno 1699./ 16 *pp.* 8*vo.*   (12*s.* 6*d.*   1850.)

MATHER (INCREASE). A Further/ Account/ of
the/ Tryals/ of the/ New-England Witches./ With
the Obfervations/ Of a Perfon who was upon the
Place feveral/ Days when the fufpected Witches
were/ firft taken into Examination./ To which is
added,/ Cafes of Confcience/ Concerning Witchcrafts and Evil Spirits Per-/fonating men./ Written
at the Requeft of the Minifters of New-England./
By Increafe Mather, Prefident of Harvard Colledge./ Licenfed and Entred according to Order./
London: Printed for **J.** Dunton, at the Raven in
the Poultrey/ 1693. Of whom may be had the
Third Edition of Mr. Cotton/ Mather's Firft Account of the Tryals of the New-England/ Witches,
Printed on the fame fize with this Laft Account,/
that they may bind up together./ *Title and* 10 *pp :*
" Cases of Conscience " *etc. Title ; and* ' Chriftian
Reader' 2 *pp : Text* 40 *pp.* ' Postscript' 4 *pp. half
mor.* 4*to.*   (2*l.* 2*s.*   1851)

MATHER (INCREASE). Angelographia,/ or/ A Difcourfe/ Concerning the Nature and Power of the/ Holy Angels, and the Great Benefit/ which the True Fearers of God Receive/ by their Miniftry :/ Delivered in feveral/ Sermons :/ To which is added, A Sermon concerning the Sin and/ Mifery of the Fallen Angels :/ Alfo a Difquifition concerning/ Angelical Apparitions./ By Increase Mather, Pre-fident of Harvard/ Colledge, in Cambridge, and Preacher of the/ Gofpel at Bofton in New-England./ *Boston* in N. E. Printed by B. Green & J. Allen,/ for Samuel Phillips at the Brick Shop. 1696./ 8 *prel. leaves; viz. Title,* ' The Epiftle Dedicatory,' 2 *pp.* ' To the Reader,' 12 *pp : Text* 132 *pp.* ' A Difquifition' *etc.* 44 *pp. Portrait of Increase Mather. Calf extra by Bedford. Small 8vo.* (2*l.* 2*s.* 1852)

MATHER (INCREASE). Two Plain and Practical/ Difcourfes/ Concerning/ I. Hardnefs of Heart./ Shewing,/ That fome, who live under the Gofpel,/ are by a Judicial Difpenfation, given/ up to that Judgment; and the Signs/ thereof./ II./ The Sin and Danger/ of/ Difobedience to the Gofpel./ By Increafe Mather, Prefident of Harvard-/College in Cambridge, and Preacher of/ the Gofpel at Bofton in New-England./ *London.* Printed for J. Ro-binfon, and are to/ be Sold by Samuel Phillips, Bookfeller in Bofton,/ in New-England. 1699./ 187 *pp. Books lately Printed, etc.* 5 *pp. Calf extra by Bedford.* 12*mo.* (18*s.* 1853)

MATHER (INCREASE). Meditations on the Glory of the Lord Jefus Chrift : Delivered in feveral Ser-mons. By Increafe Mather. Boston in New-England. Printed by Bartholomew Green, for Benj. Eliot, at his Shop under the Weft-End of the Town-houfe, 1705. *viii. and* 162 *pp. (wanting all after page* 162). 16*mo.* (7*s.* 6*d.* 1854)

MATHER (INCREASE). The Doctrine of Singular Obedience, As the Duty and Property of the True Chriftian : Opened & Applied. In a Sermon, Preached by I. Mather, D.D. *Boston* in New-England, Printed & Sold by Timothy Green, at the North End of the Town, 1707. 29 *pp ; Adver-tisement,* 1 *page. Vellum.* 12*mo.* (1*l.* 1*s.* 1855)
A presentation copy " To Mr. Samuel Mather."

MATHER (INCREASE). A Discourse Concerning

2　　　　　　　　M M

the Maintenance, Due to thofe that Preach the
Gofpel: In which The Question, Whether Tithes
Are by the Divine Law, the Minifters Due? is
considered: and the Negative Prov'd. By J.
Mather, D.D. Bofton, N. E. Printed 1706, and
Reprinted at *London*, 1709. *2 prel. leaves; and 32
pp. Small 8vo.* (12s. 6d. 1856)

MATHER (Increase). Practical Truths, Plainly
Delivered. Wherein is Shewed, I. That true Believers on Jefus Chrift, fhall as certainly enjoy
Everlasting Life in Heaven, as if they were there
already. II. That there is a bleffed Marriage between Jefus Chrift the Son of God, and the true
Believer. III. That Men are Infinitely concerned,
not only to hear the Voice of Chrift, but that they
do it, To Day. IV. The Work of the Miniftry,
defcribed, in an Ordination Sermon. By Increafe
Mather, D.D. *Boston*, N. E. Printed by B. Green,
for Daniel Henchman, and Sold at his Shop, 1718.
*2 prel. leaves, and 134 pp. (Wanting all after page
134.) 16mo.* (16s. 1857)

MATHER (Increase). Memoirs of the Life Of
the late Reverend Increafe Mather, D.D. Who
died Auguft 23, 1723. With a Preface by the
Reverend Edmund Calamy, D.D. *London:* John
Clark and Richard Hett, MDCCXXV. *4 prel. leaves,
and 88 pp. 8vo.* (16s. 1858)

MATHER (Nathanael). Twenty-Three Select
Sermons Preached at the Merchants-Lecture, at
Pinners-Hall, and in Lime-ftreet. Wherein several
Cafes of Confcience, and Other Weighty Matters,
are propounded, and handled. By the Judicious
and Learned Mr. Nathanael Mather. *London:*
N. Hiller, 1701. *4 prel. leaves, and 480 pp. calf.
8vo.* (10s. 6d. 1859)

MATHER (Richard). A/ Modeft & Brotherly/
Answer/ To Mr. Charles Herle his Book,/ againft
the Independency of Churches./ Wherein his foure
Arguments for the Govern-/ment of Synods over
particular Congregati-/ons, are friendly Examined,
and/ clearly Anfwered./ Together, with Chriftian
and Loving Ani-/madverfions upon fundry other
obfervable paffa-/ges in the faid Booke./ All tending to declare the true ufe of Synods, and the/

power of Congregationall Churches in the points
of/ electing and ordaining their owne Officers,/
and cenfuring their Offendors./ By Richard Mather Teacher of the Church at Dorchefter; And
William Tompson Paftor of the Church at/ Brain-
tree in New-England./ Sent from thence after
the Affembly of Elders were diffolved that/ laft met
at Cambridg to debate matters about Church-government./ *London*, Printed for Henry Overton
in Popes-head alley, 1644./ *2 prel. leaves, and 58
pp. 4to.* (15s. 1860)

MATHER (Richard). A/ Reply/ to/ Mr. Rutherfurd,/ or,/ A defence of the Anfwer to Re-/verend
Mr. Herlès Booke againft the/ Independency of
Churches./ Wherein fuch Objections and/ Anfwers, as are returned to fundry paffages/ in the
faid Anfwer by Mr. Samuel Rutherfurd,/ a godly
and learned Brother of the Church of Scotland, in
his Booke Entituled The Due/ Right of Presbyters,
are examined and removed, and the Anfwer jufti-
fied/ and cleared./ By Richard Macher Teacher
to/ the Church at Dorchefter in New/ England.
1646./ *London*,/ Printed for J. Rothwell, and H.
Allen at the Sun/ and Fountaine in Pauls Church-
yard, and/ the Crown in Popes-head Alley, 1647,/
4 prel. leaves, and 109 *pp. 4to.* (15s. 1861)

MATHER (Samuel). Early Piety,/ exemplified/
in the/ Life and Death/ of Mr. Nathanael Mather,/
who/ Having become at the Age of/ Nineteen, an
Inftance of more/ than common/ Learning and
Virtue,/ Changed Earth for Heaven, Oct. 17. 1688./
Whereto are added/ Some Difcourfes on the true
Nat   /the great Reward, and the   /Seafon of fuch/
A Walk With Go   /as he left a Pattern of./ *Lon-
don*,/ Printed by J. Aftwood for J. Dun [*date cut
off*]/ *5 prel. leaves, and* 60 *pp.* 'Several Sermons/
Concerning,/ Walking/ with/ God,/ and that/ In
the Dayes of Youth :/ Preached/ At Bofton in
New-England./ By Cotton Mather, Paftor of a
Church there./ *London*, Printed by J. Aftwood
for J. Dunton, at the Black/ Raven in the Poultrey,
over againft the Compter. 1689.'/ *Title and 86 pp.
Old calf. Small 8vo.* (15s. 1861*)

MATHER (Samuel). The/ Figures/ or/ Types/

of the/ Old Teſtament,/ by which/ Christ and the
Heavenly Things of the/ Goſpel were Preached
and Shadowed to the/ People of God of Old./ Ex-
plain'd and Improv'd in ſundry/ Sermons./ By
Samuel Mather, ſometime Paſtor/ of a Church in
Dublin./ The Second Edition, To which is annex'd,
(more than/ was in the former Edition) a Scheme
and Table of the whole,/ whereby the Reader may
readily turn to any Subjeƈt treated/ of in this Book./
London,/ Printed for Nath. Hillier, at the Prince's
Arms in Leaden-/hall-ſtreet, over againſt St. Mary
Axe, 1705./ *6 prel. leaves ; viz. Title, and To the
Reader, vii pp. Signed* ʻNathanael Mather.' *Books
&c.* 1 *page, Scheme* 4 *pp. Text* 540 *pp. Table* 11 *pp.
Errata* 1 *page. Old calf.* 4*to.*   (1*l.* 5*s.*   1862)

MATHER (Samuel).   An Apology For the Liberties of the Churches in New England : To which
is prefix'd, A Diſcourſe concerning Congregational
Churches.   By Samuel Mather, M.A. Paſtor of a
Church in Boſton, New England. *Boston :* Printed
by T. Fleet, for Daniel Henchman, over againſt the
Brick Meeting Houſe in Cornhill. 1738. *4 prel.
leaves, ix pp. Errata* 1 *page, and text* 116 *pp. Old
calf.* 8*vo.*   (12*s.* 6*d.*   1863)

MAUDUIT (Israel).   A Short View of the History
of the Colony of Massachusett's Bay, With Reſpeƈt
to their Original Charter and Constitution. *London :*
J. Wilkie, 1769. *Title and* 71 *pp. half morocco.*
8*vo.*   (7*s.* 6*d.*   1864)

MAUDUIT (Israel).   A Short View of the History
of the Colony of Maſſachuſetts Bay, With Reſpeƈt
to their Charters and Constitution. By Israel Mauduit.   The Third Edition, To which is now added
the Original Charter granted to that Province in
the 4th of Charles I. and neyer before printed in
England. *London :* J. Wilkie, mdcclxxiv. *Title,
and pp.* 5-93. *half mor.* 8*vo.*   (7*s.* 6*d.*   1865)

MAUDUIT (Israel).   A Short View of the History
of the New England Colonies, With Reſpeƈt to
their Charters and Constitution. By Israel Mauduit.   The Fourth Edition, To which is now added,
An Account of a Conference between the late Mr.
Grenville and the ſeveral Colony Agents, in the
Year 1764, previous to the paſſing the Stamp Aƈt.

Alfo the Original Charter granted in the 4th of Charles I. and never before printed in England. *London:* J. Wilkie, MDCCLXXVI. *Title, and pp.* 5-100. *half mor.* *8vo.* (*7s. 6d.* 1866)

MAW (HENRY LISTER). Journal of a Passage from the Pacific to the Atlantic, crossing the Andes in the Northern Provinces of Peru, and descending the River Marañon, or Amazon. By Henry Lister Maw, Lieut. R. N. *London:* John Murray, MDCCCXXIX. *xv and* 486 *pp. With Map. Unbound.* *8vo.* (*5s. 6d.* 1867)

MAXIMILIANUS (TRANSYLVANUS). De Molvccis in/ fulis, itemq; alijs pluribus mirādis, quæ/ nouif-fima Caftellanorum nauigatio Se-/renifs. Impera-toris Caroli. V. aufpicio/ fufcepta, nuper inuenit: Maximiliani/ Tranfyluani ad Reuerendifs. Car-dina-/lem Saltzburgenfem epiftola lectu per-/quam iucunda./ [*Colophon*] *Coloniæ* in ædibus Eucharij Ceruicorni. Anno uir-/ginei partus. M. D. XXIII. menfe/ Ianuario.·./ 15 *unfolioed leaves; Signature* A. *in eight,* B. *in seven leaves. Red morocco extra by Bedford. Small 8vo.* (*4l. 14s. 6d.* 1868)

MAYHEW (EXPERIENCE). Grace Defended, in a Modeft Plea for an Important Truth; Namely, That the Offer of Salvation made to Sinners in the Gofpel, comprifes in it an Offer of the Grace given in Regeneration. And Shewing the Confiftency of this Truth with the Free and Sovereign Grace of God, in the whole Work of Man's Salvation. In Which The Doctrine of Original Sin and Hu-mane Impotence, the Object and Extent of Re-demption, the Nature of Regeneration, the Differ-ence between Common and Special Grace, the Nature of juftifying Faith, and other Important Points, are confidered and cleared. By Experience Mayhew. *Boston:* Printed by B. Green, and Com-pany, for D. Henchman, in Cornhil. 1744. *Title, vi and* 208 *pp.* *8vo.* (*10s. 6d.* 1869)

MAYHEW (JONATHAN). Seven Sermons Upon the following Subjects; viz. I. The Difference betwixt Truth and Falfhood, Right and Wrong. II. The natural Abilities of Men for discerning thefe Differences. III. The Right and Duty of private Judgment. IV. Objections confidered.

V. The Love of God. VI. The Love of our Neigh-
bour. VII. The firſt and great Commandment,
&c. Preached at a Lecture in the Weſt Meeting-
Houſe in Boston, Begun the firſt Thurſday in June,
and ended the laſt Thurſday in Auguſt, 1748. By
Jonathan Mayhew, D.D. Paſtor of the Weſt
Church in Boſton. Firſt Printed at Boston in
New-England. *London* Reprinted, John Noon,
Mdccl. 3 *prel. leaves and* text 132 *pp. Unbound.*
8*vo.*   (4*s.* 6*d.*   1870)

MAYHEW (Jonathan). A Discourse Occaſioned
by the Death of The Honourable Stephen Sewall,
Eſq; Chief-Juſtice of the Superiour Court of Ju-
dicatnre, Court of Aſſize, and General-Goal-De-
livery; as alſo A Member of His Majesty's Council
for the Province of the Massachusetts-Bay in New-
England : Who departed this Life On Wedneſday-
Night, September 10. 1760. Ætatis 58. Delivered
the Lord's-Day after his Deceaſe. By Jonathan
Mayhew, D.D. Paſtor of the Weſt-Church in Bos-
ton. *Boston*: Printed by Richard Draper, in
Newbury-Street: Edes and Gill, in Queen-Street:
And Thomas and John Fleet, in Cornhill. mdcclx.
Title, and pp. 5-66. *half mor.* 8*vo.* (5*s.* 6*d.*   1871)

MAYHEW (Jonathan). Observations on the
Charter and Conduct of the Society for the Propa-
gation of the Gospel in Foreign Parts ; designed
to shew Their Non-conformity to each other. With
Remarks on the Mistakes of East Apthorp, M.A.
Miſſionary at Cambridge, in Quoting and Repre-
ſenting the Senſe of ſaid Charter, &c. As also
Various incidental Reflections relative to the
Church of England, and the State of Religion in
North-America, particularly in New-England. By
Jonathan Mayhew, D.D. Paſtor of the Weſt-
Church in Boston, To which is subjoined Apthorp's
Considerations. Boston, in New-England, printed :
London, reprinted for W. Nicoll, mdcclxiii. 164
pp. half mor. 8*vo.*   (5*s.* 6*d.*   1872)

MAYHEW (Jonathan). An Answer to Dr. Mayhew's Obſervations on the Charter and Conduct of
the Society for the Propagation of the Gospel in
Foreign Parts. *London*, John Rivington, m.dcc.
lxiv. 68 *pp. half mor.* 8*vo.*   (4*s.* 6*d.*   1873)

MAYHEW (JONATHAN). The Claims of the Church
of England feriously examined : In a letter to the
Author of an Answer to Dr. Mayhew's observations on the Charter and Conduct of the Society
for Propagating the Gofpel in Foreign Parts. By
a Protestant Dissenter of Old England. *London :*
W. Nicholl, 1764. *28 pages. Half morocco.*
8vo. (4s. 6d. 1874)

MAYHEW (JONATHAN). A Defence Of the Observations on the Charter and Conduct of the Society
for the Propagation of the Gofpel in Foreign
Parts, against An anonymous Pamphlet falfly intitled, a Candid Examination Of Dr. Mayhew's
Obfervations, &c. And also against The Letter to
a Friend annexed thereto, faid to contain a short
Vindication of faid Society. By one of its Members.
By Jonathan Mayhew, D.D. Paftor of the West
Church in Bofton. Boston printed : *London :* reprinted for W. Nicoll, M.DCC.LXIV. 120 *pp. half*
mor. 8vo. (5s. 6d. 1875)

MAYHEW (JONATHAN). Remarks on an Anony-
mous Tract, entitled An Answer to Dr. Mayhew's
Observations On the Charter and Conduct of the
Society for the Propagation of the Gofpel in Foreign
Parts. Being a Second Defence of the faid Obser-
vations. By Jonathan Mayhew, D.D. Paftor of
the West Church in Bofton. *Boston :* Printed and
Sold by R. and S. Draper, in Newbury Street ;
Edes and Gill, in Queen-Street ; and T. & J. Fleet,
in Cornhill. 1764. 86 *pp.* ' Advertifement.' 1 *page*
Signed ' J. Mayhew.' *Soliciting contributions in Eu-*
rope, for the loss of the Library of Harvard College by
Fire. Half mor. 8vo. (5s. 6d. 1876)

MAYHEW (JONATHAN). Sermons to Young Men.
In Two Volumes. By Jonathan Mayhew, D.D.
London, T. Becket MDCCLXVII. *Two Volumes.*
Volume the First. *xx and* 275 *pp.* Volume the
Second. *Title, iv and text* 304 *pp. Old calf.*
12mo. (8s. 6d. 1877)

MAYNAS. Copia de dos Cartas Escritas de vn/
Mifsionero, y del Superior de las Mifsiones de los
Maynas,/ en el Rio Marañon, jurifdiccion de la
Real Audiencia de Qui-/to, avifando al Padre Vice-
Provincial de la Compañia de/ Iesvs, del Nuevo

Reyno de Granada; el vno, el eftado del/ Pueblo
en que afsifte; y el otro, el que tiene parte de
aquella/ gloriofa Mifsion, que avia vifitado el año
paffado de 1681./ Primera Carta./ 4 *unfolioed pp.*
Folio. (1*l.* 11*s.* 6*d.* 1878)

MEAD (Joseph). An Essay on Currents at Sea;
By which it appears, There is Reafon to apprehend, that the Sea is not a Fluid in a State of Reft,
except thofe Motions which are caufed by the Impulse of Winds, and that known by the Name of
Tides: And consequently, That this Earth is not
of a uniform Denfity, according to the Suppofition
of Sir Isaac Newton; but that the Currents of the
Gulph of Florida, alfo on the Coaft of Brasil, and
the Northern In-draught on this Weftern Coaft,
are Currents of Circulation, kept up by different
Denfities in this Earth, and its Motion round its
Axis. By Joseph Mead. *London:* J. Marshall,
m,dcc,lvii. *Title having on the reverse* 'Errata.' 5
lines, Text 48 *pp. half mor.* 8*vo.* (7*s.* 6*d.* 1879)

MEAD (Matthew). The Almoft Chriftian Dis-
covered or, the Falfe Profeffor Tryed and Cast.
Being the Subftance of Seven Sermons, Firft
Preached at Sepulchers, London, 1661 And now
at the Importunity of Friends made Publick. The
Fourteenth Edition. By Matthew Mead. *Boston:*
Printed for Jofeph Edwards at the corner Shop on
the North fide of the Town-Houfe, & Hopeftill
Fofter in Cornhill. 1730. 4 *prel. leaves and* 194 *pp.*
12*mo.* (10*s.* 6*d.* 1880)

MEDINA (Antonio de). Sermon/ predicado en/
el Castillo de San Felipe/ del Puerto del Callao, a
fu Dedicacion y benedi-/cion; eftando defcubierto
el Santifsimo Sacra-/mento, y en prefencia de todo
el/ Prefidio./ Por el P. F. Antonio de Medina del
Orden/ de Predicadores, Letor de Teologia del
Conuento del Cuzco, à onze/ de Mayo de 1625.
años./ ¶ A Don Fernando de Castro Cavallero/ del
Abito de Santiago, y Teniente de Capitan General,
por el/ Excellentifsimo Señor Marques de Guadal-
caçar./ Virrey deftos Reynos del Pirù./ Con licencia./ Impreffo en *Lima;* por Geronymo de
Contreras./ Año de 1625./ 18 *folioed leaves, half*
mor. 4*to.* (10*s.* 6*d.* 1881)

MEDRANO (SEBASTIAN FERNANDEZ DE). Breve/ descripcion del/ Mundo/ o Guia Geographica/ de Medrano./ Lo mas principal de ella en Verſo., Dirigida/ A la Catholica Mageſtad del Rey Nu-eſtro Señor/ Don Carlos Segundo,/ Monarcha de las Eſpañas./ Debajo/ De la protecion del Excel-entiſſimo Señor/ Marques de Jodar./ En *Brusselas*,/ En caſa de Lamberto Marchant,/ Mercader de Li-bros/ M.DC.LXXXVIII./ 108 *pp. Old calf.* 12mo. (10s. 6d. 1882)

MEMOIRES/ tovchant/ l'Etablissement/ d'vne/ Mission Chrestienne/ dans/ le Troisieme Monde,/ Autrement appellé,/ La Terre Auſtrale, Meridio-nale,/ Antartique, & Inconnuë./ Dediez à Noſtre S. Pere le Pape/ Alexandre VII./ Par vn Ecclefi-aſtique Originaire de cette/ meſme Terre. [Juan Paulymer]/ A *Paris*,/ Chez Clavde Cramoisy, ruë Saint/ Victor, proche la place Maubert,/ au Sacri-fice d'Abel./ M.DC.LXIII./ Avec privilege dv Roy./ 18 *prel. leaves and* 216 *pp. With copperplate map of the World. Old calf.* 8vo. (1l. 11s. 6d. 1883)

MEMOIRES des Commissaires du Roi et de ceux de sa Majesté Britannique, Sur les poſſeſſions & les droits reſpectifs des deux Couronnes en Amé-rique; Avec les Actes publics & Piéces juſtifica-tives. Contenant les Mémoires ſur l'Acadie & ſur l'iſle de Sainte-Lucie. A *Paris*, de l'Imprimerie Royale. M.DCCLV. *Four Volumes.* Tome Premier. *viii; lxxv; and* 181 *pp.* ' Premier Memoire' *etc.* 61 *pp.* ' Memoire de Messieurs les Commissaires Anglois,' *etc. cvii pp.* 'Second Memoire,' *etc.* 120 *pp. Map.* Tome Second. *xiii and* 646 *pp.* Tome Troisième. *xvi and* 319 *pp.* Tome Quatrième, M.DCCLVII. 3 *prel. leaves; xxv and* 654 *pp. Map. Fine copy. Calf extra.* 4to. (3l. 13s. 6d. 1884)

MEMOIRS of an Unfortunate Young Nobleman, Return'd from a Thirteen Years Slavery in Ame-rica, Where he had been ſent by the Wicked Con-trivances of his Cruel Uncle. A Story founded on Truth, and addreſs'd equally to the Head and Heart. *London:* J. Freeman, MDCCXLIII. *Half-title, title, and* 277 *pp. Old calf.* 12mo. (8s. 6d. 1885)

MEMOIRS of the Principal Tranſactions of the Last War between the English and French in North

America. From the Commencement of it in 1744, to the Conclufion of the Treaty at Aix la Chapelle. Containing in Particular An Account of the Importance of Nova Scotia or Acadie and Ifland of Cape Breton to both Nations. [By William Shirley.] *London:* R. and J. Dodsley, M.DCC.LVII. *viii and* 102 *pp. half mor.* 8*vo.* (7*s.* 6*d.* 1886)

MEMOIRS of the Principal Tranfactions of the Last War between the Englifh and French in North-America. From the Commencement of it in 1744, to the Conclufion of the Treaty at Aix la Chapelle. Containing in Particular An Account of the Importance of Nova Scotia or Acadie, and the Ifland of Cape Breton to both Nations. The Third Edition. London, Printed. *Boston,* New-England; Re-printed and Sold by Green and Russell, at their Printing-Office in Queen-ftreet. MDCCLVIII. *iv and pp.* 9-80. 8*vo.* (7*s.* 6*d.* 1888)

MEMORIAL/ (✣)/ de lo Svcedido en/ la ciudad de Mexico, defde el dia pri/mero de Nouiembre, de 1623. haf/ta quienze de Enero de/ 1624./ 28 *folioed leaves. Folio.* (1*l.* 1*s.* 1889)

MEMORIAL (A) Relating to the Tobacco-Trade. Offer'd to The Confideration of the Planters of Virginia and Maryland. *Williamsburgh:* Printed by William Parks, M,DCC,XXXVII. 25 *pp. Signed* 'Daniel Mac Kercher.' *half mor.* 8*vo.* (10*s.* 6*d.* 1890)

MEMORIALS (THE) of the Englifh and French Commissaries concerning St. Lucia. *London;* Printed in the Year MDCCLV. *Title and* 550 *pp. Fine copy. Old calf.* 4*to.* (1*l.* 1*s.* 1891)

MEMORIALS (THE) of the Englifh and French Commissaries Concerning the Limits of Nova Scotia or Acadia. *London:* Printed in the Year MDCCLV. 2 *prel. leaves, and* 771 *pp. Map. Fine copy. Old calf.* 4*to.* (1*l.* 10*s.* 1892)

MENDOCA (JUAN GONÇALES DE). Historia/ de las Cosas/ mas Notables,/ Ritos y Costvmbres,/ Del gran Reyno dela China, fabidas affi por los libros/ delos mefmos Chinas, como por relacion de Religio-/fos y otras perfonas que an eftado en el dicho Reyno./ Hecha y ordenada por el mvy R. P. Maestro Fr. Ioan Gonçalez de Mendoça dela Orden

de S. Auguſtin, y peniten-/ciatio Appoſtolico a quien
la Mageſtad Catholica embio con ſu real/ carta y
otras coſas para el Rey de aquel Reyno el año.
1580./ Al Illvstrissimo S. Fernando/ de Vega y
Fonſeca del conſejo de ſu Mageſtad y ſu/ preſidente
en el Real delas Indias./ Con vn Itinerario del
nueuo Mundo./ Con Priuilegio y Licencia de ſu
Sanctidad./ En *Roma*, a coſta de Bartholome
Graffi. 1585/ en la Stampa de Vincentio Accolti./
*16 prel. leaves, the 16th blank; and 440 pp. Vellum.
8vo.* (15s. 1893)

MENDOCA (Juan Gonçales de). Dell' Historia/
della China,/ Deſcritta nella lingua Spagnuola, dal
P. Maeſtro/ Giouanni Gonzalez di Mendozza,/
dell' Ord. di S. Agoſtino./ Et tradotta nell' Italiana,
dal Magn. M. Franceſco/ Auanzo, cittadino ori-
ginario di Venetia./ Parti dve,/ Diuiſe in tre libri,
& in tre viaggi, fatti in quei paeſi,/ da i Padri Ago-
ſtiniani & Franciſcani./ Doue ſi deſcriue il ſito, &
lo ſtato di quel gran Regno,/ & ſi tratta della reli-
gione, de i coſtumi, & della/ diſpoſition de ſuoi po-
poli, & d'altri luochi/ più conoſciuti del mondo
nuouo./ Con due Tauole, l'vna de' Capitoli, & l'altra delle coſe notabili./ In *Venetia,* MDLXXXVI./
Appreſſo Andrea Muſchio./ *16 prel. leaves, the
16th blank, and 462 pp; 1 blank leaf, and* 'Tavola,'
etc. 40 *pp. Vellum. 8vo.* (15s. 1894)

MENDOCA (Juan Gonçales de). L'Historia/ del
gran Regno/ della China,/ Compoſta primier
amente in iſpagnuolo da/ maeſtro Giouanni Gonzalez di Men-/dozza, monaco dell' ordine di/ S.
Agoſtino :/ Et poi fatta vulgare da Franceſco Au-
anzi/ cittadino Vinetiano./ Stampata la terza volta,
& molto più dell' al-/tre emendata./ Con due
tauole l'una dé Capitoli, & l'altra delle/ coſe più
notabili./ In *Vinegia.* 1587./ Per Andrea Muſchio./ 508 *pp.* 'Lo ſtampatore,' *etc.* 1 *page* ; 'Tavola,' *etc.* 77 *pp.* 'Errori' *etc.* 1 *page. Old calf.*
12mo. (15s. 1895)

MENDOCA (Juan Gonçales de). Histoire/ dv
Grand/ Royavme de la/Chine, sitvé avx/ Indes
orientales, diuiſée/ en deux parties./ Contenant en
la Premiere, la ſituation, antiquité, fertilité,/ religion, ceremonies, ſacrifices, rois magiſtrats, mœurs,/

vs, loix, & autres chofes memorables dudit royaume./ Et en la Seconde, trois voyages faits vers
iceluy en l'an/ 1577, 1579 & 1581. auec les fin-
gularitez plus remarqua-/bles y veües & entendües :
enfemble vn Itinerarie/ du nouueau monde, & le
defcouurement du/ nouueau Mexique en l'an 1583./
Faite en efpagnol par R. P. Ivan Gonçales de
Men-/doce, de l'ordre de S. Auguftin : & mife en
François auec/ des additions en marge, & deux Indices./ Par Lvc de la Porte, Parifien,/ docteur és
droits./ A/ Monseignevr le Chancelier./ A *Paris,*
Chez Ieremie Perier, ruë S. Iean de/ Beuuais, au
franc Meurier./ 1589./ Avec privilege dv Roy./
12 *prel. leaves, and* 323 *folioed leaves;* ' Indice des
choses Notables,' *etc.* 48 *pp.* ' Tautes,' *etc.* 1 *page.*
Old calf. 8*vo.*   (1*l.* 1*s.* 1896)

MENDOZA (Diego de).   Chronica/ de la Provincia de S. Antonio/ de los Charcas/ del orden de Nrõ.
Seraphico P./ S. Francisco/ En la Indias Occidentales Reyno del Peru/ Escrita/ por el R. P. Predicador F. Diego de Mendoza/ Chronifta y Padre
de la mesma Prouincia./ Dedicala/ Al Illᵐᵒ. Yrᵐᵒ.
S. D. F. Gabriel/ de Guillestegui del Confejo de
fu Magᵈ./ y Obifpo del Paraguay./ P'a Villafranca
fculptor Regius, fculpfit *Matriti,* 1664./ *Engraved
title,* 14 *prel. leaves, and* 601 *pp.* ' Protesta de el
Autor.' 1 *page;* ' Indice de los Capitvlos,' *etc.* 6 *pp.*
Vellum. Folio.   (2*l.* 2*s.* 1897)

MERCATOR (Gerardus).   Gerardi Mercatoris/
Atlas/ sive/ Cosmographicæ/ Meditationes/ de/ fa-
brici Mundi et/ fabricati Figvra./ Iam tandem ad
finem perductus, quamplurimus æneis ta=/bulis His-
paniæ, Africæ, Afiæ & Americæ auctus ac/ illuftratus à Iudoco Hondio. Quibus etiam additæ (præter
Mercatoris) dilucidæ & accuratæ omnium tabu=/
larum defcriptiones novæ, ftudio et opera Pet. Mon-
tani./ Excufum in ædibus Iudoci Hondij *Amsterodami.* 1606. 10 *prel. leaves, and* 354 *pp. Index
etc.* 18 *leaves. Maps with the text. Fine copy. Old
culf. Large Folio.*   (1*l.* 11*s.* 6*d.* 1898)

MERCATOR (Gerardus).   Atlas/ Minor/ Gerardi
Mercatoris/ à I. Hondio plurimis æneis tabulis/
auctus atque illuftratus./ *Amsterodami*/ Excusum
in ædibus Iudoci Hondij./ veneunt etiam apud

Corneliũ Nicolai./ item apud Ioannem Ianſoniũ
Arnhemi./ [*Colophon*] *Dordrechti*/ Excudebat Adri-
anus Bottius/ Anno CIƆ IƆ CX./ 4 *prel. leaves, and*
684 *pp.* *Vellum.* *Oblong 4to.* (15s. 1899)

MERCATOR (GERARDUS). [*Engraved title*] Historia lvx ævi/ Geographia Mvndi./ Historia Mvndi/
or Mercators Atlas. Containing his Cosmographi-
call Descriptions/ of the Fabricke and Figure of the
world./ Latelij rectified in diuers places, as alſo
beutiñed/ and enlarged with new Mapps and
Tables/ by the Studious industrie of Iodocvs Hon-
dy/ Englished by W. S. Generosus & Regin: Oxoniæ./ London/ Printed for/ Michaell/ Sparke, and
are to be ſowld in/ greene Arbowre/ 1637/ Second
Edytion/ [*Printed title*] Historia Mvndi´:/ Or/ Mercator's/ Atlas./ Containing his Cosmographicall/
Deſcription of the Fabricke and/ Figure of the
World./ Lately reĉtified in divers places, as alſo
beautified/ and enlarged with new Mappes and
Tables;/ By the Studious induſtry,/ Of/ Ivdocvs
Hondy./ Englished/ By/ W. S./ Generoſus, &
Coll. Regin. Oxoniæ./ *London*/ Printed by T.
Cotes, for Michael Sparke and/ Samuel Cartwright.
1635./ 12 *prel. leaves;* 56 *pp;* *The Preface upon*
Atlas 2 *pp. and* 930 *pp.* *Tables etc.* 32 *pp.* *Old calf.*
Folio. (1l. 1s. 1900)

MESSAGES (THREE) from the President of the
United States, to the Congress, in November 1811,
Together with Documents accompanying the same.
Washington; Printed 1811: *London:* Reprinted
for J. Hatchard, 1812. 260 *pp.* *8vo.* (4s. 6d. 1901)

MEXICO. Album Méjicano Tributo de gratitud al
Civismo nacional Retratos de los Personages ilus
tres de la primera y segunda época de la Independencia Mejicana y notabilidades de la présente.
Méjico C. L. Prudhomme Editor 2ª Calle de los
Plateros Nº. 12. 1843. *Title, Advertencia, and* 21
plates, each with 4 *portraits.* 4to. (10s. 6d. 1902)

M'FINGAL: A Modern Epic Poem, in Four Cantos.
By John Trumbull. The Fifth Edition, With Explanatory Notes. *London:* J. S. Jordan, M,DCCXCII.
xv and 142 *pp.* *8vo.* (7s. 6d. 1903)

MICHAUX (F. A.). Travels to the Westward of

the Allegany Mountains, in the States of the Ohio, Kentucky, and Tennessee, and return to Charlestown, through the Upper Carolinas; containing details on the present State of Agriculture and the Natural Productions of these Countries; as well as information relative to the commercial connections of these States with those situated to the Eastward of the Mountains and with Lower Louisiana. Undertaken in the year X, 1832, under the auspices of His Excellency M. Chaptal, Minister of the Interior. With a very correct Map of the States in the Centre, West and South of the United States. By F. A. Michaux, M.D. Member of the Society of Natural History of Paris, and Correspondent of the Society of Agriculture of the Department of the Seine and Oise. Faithfully Translated from the Original French, by B. Lambert. *London:* J. Mawman, 1805. *xvi and* 350 *pp. Map, boards.* 8vo.   (7s. 6d.   1904)

MICHAUX (F. A.). Travels to the West of the Alleghany Mountains, in the States of Ohio, Kentucky, and Tennessea, and back to Charleston, by the Upper Carolines; comprising The most interesting Details on the present State of Agriculture, and the Natural produce of those Countries: Together with Particulars relative to the Commerce that exists between the above-mentioned States, and those situated East of the Mountains and Low Louisiana, Undertaken, in the Year 1802, under the auspices of His Excellancy M. Chaptal, Minister of the Interior, By F. A. Michaux, Member of the Society of Natural History at Paris; Correspondent of the Agricultural Society in the Department of the Seine and Oise. Second Edition. *London:* B. Crosby & Co. 1805. *xii and* 294 *pp. Calf.* 8vo.   (7s. 6d.   1905)

MIDDLETON (Christopher). A Vindication of the Conduct of Captain Chriſtopher Middleton, in a Late Voyage on Board His Majeſty's Ship the Furnace, for Diſcovering a North-weſt Paſſage to the Weſtern American Ocean. In Answer To certain Objeƈtions and Aſperſions of Arthur Dobbs, Eſq; with an Appendix: Containing The Captain's Inſtruƈtions; Councils held; Reports of the Inferior Officers; Letters between Mr. Dobbs, Capt.

Middleton, &c. Affidavits and other Vouchers re-
fer'd to in the Captain's Anfwers, &c. With as
much of the Log-Journal as relates to the Discovery. The Whole as lately deliver'd to the Lords
Commiffioners of the Admiralty. To which is annex'd, An Account of the Extraordinary Degrees
and Surprizing Effects of Cold in Hudfon's-Bay,
North America, read before the Royal Society. By
Christopher Middleton, Late Commander of the
Furnace, and F.R.S. *London:* Jacob Robinfon,
1743. *2 prel. leaves, and* 206 *pp.* 'Several Abbre-
viations,' *etc.* 1 *page. Log-Journal* 48 *pp. Old calf.*
8*vo.*   (7*s.* 6*d.* 1906)

MIDDLETON (CHRISTOPHER). A Vindication of
the Conduct of Captain Chriftopher Middleton, in
a Late Voyage on Board His Majesty's Ship the
Furnace. For Difcovering a North-Weft Paffage to
the Weftern American Ocean. In Answer To certain Objections and Afperfions of Arthur Dobbs,
Efq; with an Appendix: Containing The Captain's
Inftructions; Councils held; Reports of the Inferior Officers, Letters between Mr. Dobbs, Capt.
Middleton, &c. Affidavits and other Vouchers re-
fer'd to in the Captain's Anfwers, &c. With as
much of the Log-Journal as relates to the Discovery. The Whole as lately deliver'd to the Lords
Commiffioners of the Admiralty. To which is Annex'd, An Account of the Extraordinary Degrees
and Surprizing Effects of Cold in Hudfon's-Bay,
North-America, read before the Royal Society. By
Christopher Middleton, Late Commander of the
Furnace, and F.R.S. *Dublin:* J. Jackson, M,DCC,
XLIV. 168 *and* 48 *pp. half mor.* 8*vo.* (7*s.* 6*d.* 1907)

MIDDLETON (CHRISTOPHER). A Reply to the Remarks of Arthur Dobbs, Efq; on Capt. Middleton's Vindication of his Conduct on board his Majesty's Ship the Furnace, when Sent in Search of
a North-weft Passage, by Hudson's-Bay, to the
Weftern American Ocean. Humbly Infcribed to
the Right Honorable the Lords Commissioners for
executing the Office of Lord High Admiral of
Great-Britain and Ireland, &c. By Christopher
Middleton, Efq; *London:* George Brett, MDCCXLIV.
x and 192 *pp.* 'Appendix' 94 *pp. Errata and Index,* 8 *pp.* 8*vo.*   (7*s.* 6*d.* 1908)

MIDDLETON (Christopher). Forgery Detected.
By which is evinced how groundless are All the Ca-
lumnies caft upon the Editor, in a Pamphlet pub-
lifhed under the Name of Arthur Dobbs, Esq; By
Capt. Christopher Middleton, late Commander of
his Majefty's Ship, Furnace, when fent upon the
Search of a North-Weft Paffage to the Weftern
American Ocean. *London:* M.Cooper, M.DCC.XLV.
Title, v and 35 pp. half mor. 8vo. (10s. 6d.   1909)

MILIUS (Abraham). De Origine/ Animalium,/ et
Migratione/ Populorum,/ Scriptum Abrahami Mi-
lii./ Ubi inquiritur, quomodo quaque via Homines
cætera-/que Animalia Terreftria provenerint; &
poft De-/luvium in omnes Orbis terrarum partes &
regiones:/ Afiam, Europam, Africam, utramque
Americam,/ & Terram Auftralem, five Magellani-
cam pervene-/rint./ *Genevæ:/* Apud Petrum Colu-
mesium. M.DC.LXVII./ *68 pp.   Calf extra by Bedford.   12mo.* (15s.   1910)

MILLS (Henry James). Mills's Trinidad Almanac
and Pocket Register for the Year of our Lord 1840,
Being Bissextile or Leap Year. Calculated to the
Meridian of Port of Spain. Port of Spain is situated in Latitude 10 deg. 39 m. N. Longitude 61
deg, 34 m. W. *Port of Spain.* Henry James Mills,
[1840] *62 pp.   With Plan.* 'Trinidad imports *etc.*
1839.' *folded sheet at page* 60. *12mo.* (2s. 6d.   1911)

MILLS (Samuel J.) Report of a Missionary Tour
through that part of the United States which lies
West of the Allegany Mountains; performed under
the direction of the Massachusetts Missionary Society. By Samuel J. Mills and Daniel Smith.
Andover: Flagg and Gould. 1815. *64 pp.   Uncut.
8vo.* (2s. 6d.   1912)

MILTON (Charles William). Narrative of the
Gracious dealings of God in the Conversion of W.
Mooney Fitzgerald and John Clark, two malefac-
tors, Who were Executed on Friday, Dec. 18,1789,
At St. John's New Brunfwick, Nova Scotia, for
Burglary; in a Letter from The Reverend Mr. Milton to the Right Honourable the Countess Dowager
of Huntingdon. *London:* Printed in the year 1790.
22 pp.   12mo. (4s. 6d.   1913)

MINISTERIAL (A) Catechise, Suitable to be Learned by all Modern Provincial Governors, Penfioners, Placemen, &c. Dedicated to T ------ H --------, Efq. *Boston :* Printed and Sold by Isaiah Thomas, near the Mill-Bridge. MDCCLXXI. 8 *pp. half mor. 8vo.*   (10s. 6d. 1914)

MINOT (George Richards). The History of the Insurrections, in Massachusetts, in the Year MDCCLXXXVI, and the Rebellion consequent thereon. By George Richards Minot, A.M. Printed at Worcester, Massachusetts, by Isaiah Thomas. MDCCLXXXVIII. 192 *pp. 8vo.*   (7s. 6d. 1915)

MISSA Gothica seù Mozarabica, et Officium itidèm Gothicum diligentèr ac dilucidè explanata ad Usum Percelebris Mozárabum Sacelli Toleti á Munificentissimo Cardinali Ximenio erecti ; et in Obsequium Ill^{mi}. Perindè ac Venerab. D. Decani et Capituli Sanctae Ecclesiae Toletanae, Hispaniarum et Indiarum Primátis. *Angelopoli :* Typis Seminarii Palafoxiani Anno Domini M.DCC.LXX. 4 *prel. leaves;* 137 *and* 198 *pp.* 2 *Copperplates. Old red morocco. Folio.*   (3l. 13s. 6d. 1916)

MITCHIL (Jonathan). A/ Discourse/ of the/ Glory/ To which God hath called/ Believers/ By Jesus Christ./ Delivered in fome Sermons out/ of the 1 Pet. 5 Chap. 10 Ver./ Together with an annexed Letter./ Both, by that Eminent and Worthy Mi/nifter of the Gofpel, Mr. Jonathan/ Mitchil, late Paftor to the Church/ at Cambridge in New-England. *London :* Printed for Nathaniel Ponder at the/ Peacock in the Poultry, Anno Dom. 1677./ 8 *prel. leaves; viz. Title,* 'To the Reader.' 11 *pp. signed* 'John Collins.' *Text* 263 *pp.* 'A Letter,' *etc.* 20 *pp. Small 8vo.*   (15s. 1917)

MOCQUET (Jan). Wunderbare/ Jedoch/ Gründlich=und warhaffte Gefchichte/ und/ Reife Begebniffe/ In Africa, Afia, Oft=und/ West=Indien/ von/ Jan Mocquet aus Frankreich,/ Ihrer Königlichen Majeftät Heinrichs des Groffen oder IV./ und Ludwigs des XIII. dafelbft gewefnen geheimen Hof= und Cammer=/Apotheckers, wie auch wolbeftellten Verwefers, derer dafelbft befindlichen frem=den,/ ausländifchen, und in unfern Landen unbekannten Früchten, Gewächfen, Kräutern/ und Blumen, in

2   N N

dero Königlichen Refidenz=Stadt zu Paris,/ in der
Tuillerie./ Nebft eigent=licher Befchreibung derer
Städte, Königreiche, Infeln und/ Provinzen, wie
felbige itziger Zeit annoch zu befinden, und Er zu
verfchiednen/ malen mit langwirigen Sorgen, Mühe
und Befchwerniffen zu Waffer und Lande, in Hitz
und/ Froft, Hunger und Durft, Armuth und Man=
gel, nach unzehlich erdultetem Elend und/ Unge-
mach, in höchfter Lebens=Gefahr, Krankheit und
Gefängniffen, auch endlich erlittnen/ Schiffbruch,
ganzer zwanzig Jahr, durch Gottes Gnade, durch-
zureifen/ über fich genommen, ausgeftanden und
geendiget./ Allen Liebhabern verwun=derfamer
Begebniffen und Reife=Gefchichten/ zu angeneh-
mer Ergötzlichkeit in unterfchiednen Büchern aus
dem Französichen/ in Hochteutfche Sprache überfetzet und entdecket/ durch/ Johann Georg Schoe-
hen. *Lüneburg,/* [1688.] In Verlegung Johann
Georg Lippers./ *30 prel. leaves ; Engraved Frontispiece ; and Text 632 pp. Copperplates numbered I to
X, and plan of* ' Ierusalem.' *4to.* (1*l.* 1*s.* 1918)

MODEST (A) Proof of the Order and Government
Settled by Chrift and his Apoftles in the Church.
By Shewing I. What Sacred Offices were inftituted
by them. II. How thofe Offices were Diftinguifhed.
III. That they were to be Perpetual Standing in
the Church. And, IV. Who Succeed in them, and
rightly Execute them to this Day. *Boston :* Reprinted by Tho. Fleet, and are to be Sold by Benjamin Eliot in Bofton, Daniel Aurault in Newport,
Gabriel Bernon in Providence, Mr. Gallop in Briftol, Mr. Jean in Stratford, and in moft other Towns
within the Colonies of Connecticut and Rhode-
Ifland. 1723. *Title, v pp. and text 63 pp. Unbound.*
16*mo.* (1*l.* 1*s.* 1919)

MOLINA (ALONSO DE). Vocabvlario/ en lengva
Castellana y Mexicana, [y Mexicana y Castellana]
com=/puefto por el muy Reuerendo Padre Fray
Alonfo de Molina, dela/ Orden del bienauenturado
nueftro Padre fant Francifco./ Dirigido al mvy
Excelente Senor/ Don Martin Enriquez, Viforrey
deftanueua Efpaña./ En *Mexico,/* En Cafa de Antonio de Spinofa./ 1571./ [*Colophon*]. ¶ Soli Deo
honor et Gloria./ ¶ Aqvi hazen fin los dos voca-
bvlarios, en lengva Caste/ llana y nahual o Mexi-

cana que hizo y recopilo el muy Reuerendo padre,
fray Alonſo de Mo-/lina : de la orden de ſeñor ſan
Franciſco. Imprimieronſe enla muy inſigne y gran
ciudad/ de Mexico : en caſa de Antonio de Spinoſa.
enel Año de nueſtra redẽpcion. de. 1571./ ¶ Ni-
cantzon qvi ça yn ontetl vocabvlario Sy-/pan Caſ-
tillan tlatolli yuan nauatlatolli, y oquimotlalili cen-
ca mauiztililoni, to/ tatzin fray Alonſo de Molina,
teupixqui Sant Franciſco. Omicuilo/ nican ypan
vey altepetl ciudad Mexico : ychã/ Antonio de Spi-
noſo. Ypan xiuitl./ 1571. Años./ *Two Parts. Part*
I. 4 *prel. leaves; viz. Title, on the reverse, '* Licencias.' ' *Epistola* Nvncvpatoria.' 2 *pp ;* '¶ *Prologo*
al *Lector.'* 2 *pp ;* ' *Avisos.'* 2 *pp ; Text* 121 *folioed
leaves,* 'DirigatvrOratiomea,' *etc. with woodcut figure*
1 *page, on the reverse woodcut device. Part* II. *Title,
with woodcut of Saint Francis; on the reverse,* '¶ *Prologo ul Lector,' and '* Avisos.' 2 *pp ; Text* 162 *folioed
leaves ; the last leaf containing the colophon as above,
and on the reverse a large woodcut device. Old calf.
Folio.* (21*l.* 1920)

MOLINA (JUAN IGNATIUS). Essai sur l'Histoire
Naturelle du Chili, Par M. l'Abbé Molina; Traduit de l'Italien, & enrichi de notes, Par M. Gru-
vel, D. M. A *Paris,* Née de la Rochelle, M.DCC.
LXXXIX. *xvi pp. and text* 352 *pp. Old calf, gilt back.*
8*vo.* (7*s.* 6*d.* 1921)

MOLINA (JUAN IGNATIUS). The Geographical Natural, and Civil History of Chili. Translated from
the original Italian of the Abbe Don J. Ignatius
Molina. To which are added, Notes from the
Spanish and French Versions, and two Appendixes,
by the English Editor ; the first, an Account of the
Archipelago of Chiloe, from the Descripcion His-
torial of P. F. Pedro Gonzalez de Agueros ; the
second, an Account of the Native Tribes who inhabit the Southern extremity of South America,
extracted chiefly from Falkner's description of Patagonia. In Two Volumes. Longman, 1809. *Two
Volumes.* Vol. I. *xx and* 321 *pp. Map.* Vol. II.
xii and 385 *pp.* 8*vo.* (8*s.* 6*d.* 1922)

MONARDES (NICOLO). Primera y/ Segvnda y
Tercera/ Partes de la Historia/ Medicinal de las
cosas/ que ſe traen de nueſtras Indias Occi-/dentales

que firuen en/ Medicina./ Tratado de la Piedra/
Bezaar, y dela yerua Efcuerconera./ Dialogo de
las Gran-/dezas del Hierro, y de fus virtudes/ Me-
dicinales/ Tratado de la Nieve y del beuer frio./
Hechos por el Do-/ĉtor Monardes Medico/ de Seuilla./ Van en esta impression/ la Tercera parte
y el Dialogo del Hierro nueua-/mente hechos, que
no han fido impreffos/ hafta agora. Do ay cofas
grandes/ y dignas de faber./ ¶ Con licencia y Preuilegio de fu Mageftad./ En *Sevilla*/ En cafa de
Alonfo Efcriuano./ 1574./ 6 *prel. leaves; viz. Title
reverse blank;* ' Licencia y Previlegio.' 2 *pp ;* ' Elo-
gio hecho,' *etc.* 4 *pp.* 'Sanctis D. N. Gregorio
XIII. Pont. Opt. Max. Doct. Nicolaus Monardus
Medicus Hifpalenfis. S.P.D.' 3 *pp ; Text 206 folioed leaves; Woodcut and Colophon on the reverse of
folio 206,* ' In Lavdem Dotiffimi Nicolai Monardis
Medici Hifpalensis.' 1 *page.* ' Erratas.' 1 *page.
Vellum. 4to.*   (2*l.* 2*s.* 1923)

MONARDES (NICOLO). ¶ Ioyfvll/ Nevves ovt of/
the newe founde worlde, wherein is/ declared the
rare and fingular vertues of diuerfe/ and fundrie
Hearbes, Trees, Oyles, Plantes, and Stones, with
their aplications, af well for Phificke as Chirurge-
rie, the faied be/yng well applied bryngeth fuche
prefent remedie for/ all defeafes, as maie feme altogether incredible:/ notwithftandyny by practize
founde out,/ to bee true : Alfo the portrature of the
faied Hearbes, very apt=/ly difcribed : Engli=/fhed
by Jhon/ Framp=/ton/ Marchaunt./ ¶ Imprinted
at *London* in/ Poules Churche-yarde, by/ Willyam
Norton./ Anno Domini./ 1577./ 3 *prel. leaves;
viz. Title, reverse blank,* ' ¶ To the right worfhipfull
Maifter/ Edvvarde Dier Efquire, Jhon Framp-/ton
wifheth muche healthe, with profpe-/rous and per-
fite felicitie./ 3 *pp. in Italics. Text in 109 folioed
leaves ;* ' The Table of the/ thinges that thefe three
Bookes/ doe containe./` 2 *pp. Black Letter. First
Edition. 4to.*   (3*l.* 13*s.* 6*d.* 1924)

MONARDES (NICOLO). Delle cose,/ che vengono/
portate dall' Indie/ Occidentali pertinenti all' vfo/
della Medicina./ Raccolte, & trattate dal Dottor
Nicolò/ Monardes, Medico in Siuiglia,/ Parte Prima./ Nouamente recata dalla Spagnola nella nos-
tra/ lingua Italiana./ Doue ancho tratta de Veneni,

& della lor cura./ Aggiuntiui doi Indici; vno de'
Capi principali; l'altro delle cofe piu ri-/leuanti,
che fi ritrouano in tutta l'opera./ Con privilegio./
In Venetia, Appreffo Giordan Ziletti. 1582./ 8
prel. leaves; viz. Title the reverse blank, 'Al Clarissimo mio Sig. osservand. Il Sig. Andrea Conta-
rini, fu del Clarifs. M. Dionigi.' 6 *pp.* 'Giordan
Ziletti a' Lettori.' 3 *pp. the reverse blank;* 'Capi
del primo libro.' 1 *page; and one blank leaf. Text*
249 *pp.* 'Tavola.' 13 *pp.* 'Dve Libri/ dell' His-
toria/ de i Semplici, Aromati,/ et altre cose; che
venegono/ portate dall' Indie Orientali pertinenti/
all' vfo dell Medicina./ Di. Don Garzia dall' Hor-
to,/ Medico Portughefe; con alcune breui Anno-
tationi/ di Carlo Clvsio./ Et dve Altri Libri/ Pari-
mente di quelle che fi portano dall' Indie Occidentali,/ Di Nicolò Monardes, Medico di Siuiglia./
Hora tutti tradotti dalle loro lingue nella noftra Italiana da M./ Annibale Briganti, Marrucino da Ciu-
ità di Chieti, Dottore & Medico excellentiffimo./
Con Privilegio./ In *Venetia,* Appreffo Francefco
Ziletti. 1582./ 12 *prel. leaves; viz. Title the reverse
blank,* 'All' Illvstriss. Signore il Signor Don Fer-
rante de Alarcon, e di Mendoza, Marchefe della
Valle.' 9 *pp. the reverse blank;* 'Tavola' 12 *pp;
Text* 347 *pp. Vellum. 8vo.* (1*l.* 11*s.* 6*d.* 1925)

MONARDES (NICOLO). Ioyfvll Newes/ Out of
the New-found/ VVorlde./ Wherein are declared,
the rare and/ finguler vertues of diuers Herbs,
Trees,/ Plantes, Oyles & Stones, with their ap-/
plications, af well to the vfe of Phificke, as of/
Chirurgery: which being well applyed, bring/
fuch prefent remedie for all difeafes, as may/ feeme
altogether incredible: notwith-/ftanding by practice found out/ to be true./ Alfo the portrature of
the faid Hearbs,/ verie aptly defcribed:/ Englifhed
by John Frampton Marchant./ Newly corrected
as by conference with/ the olde copies may appeare.
Wher=/vnto are added three other bookes/ treating
of the Bezaar ftone, the herb/ Efcuerconera, the
properties of Iron/ and Steele in Medicine, and the
be=/nefit of Snow./ *London,/* Printed by E. Allde.
by the afsigne of/ Bonham Norton./ 1596./ 3 *prel.
leaves; viz. Title in a broad type metal border, the reverse blank,* '¶ To the right worfhipful Mayfter/
Edwarde Dier Efquier, Iohn Frampton wi-/fheth

much health, with profperous and/ perfect felicitie./
Signed ' John Frampton.' *3 pp. in roman type ;
Text in 187 folioed leaves. Black Letter. Green
Morocco extra. Fine copy. 4to.* (*2l. 12s. 6d.* 1926)

MONARDES (Nicolo). Histoire des/ Simples
Medica-/mens Apportés de l'A-meriqve, defqvels/
on fe fert en la Medicine./ Efcrite premierement en
Efpangnol, par M. Nicolas/ Monard, Medecin de
Siuille./ Du defpuis mife en Latin, & illuftrée de
plufieurs Annota-/tions, par Charles l'Eclufe d'
Arras./ Et nouuellement traduicte en François
par Anthoine Colin/ Maiftre Apoticaire Iuré de la
ville de Lyon./ Edition feconde augmentée de
plufieurs fi-/gures & Annotations./ *A Lyon,*/ Aux
defpens de Iean Pillehotte,/ à l'enfeigne du nom
de Iesvs./ M.DC.XIX./ Auec Priuilege du Roy./
262 pp. Table, etc. 6 pp. 8vo. (*10s. 6d.* 1927)

MONROE (James). A View of the Conduct of the
Executive in the Foreign Affairs of the United
States, as connected with the Mission to the French
Republic, during the years 1794, 5, and 6. By
James Monroe, late Minister Plenipotentiary to
the said Republic. Illustrated by his Instructions
and Correspondence, and other Authentic Docu-
ments. The Second Edition. Philadelphia, Printed.
London: Reprinted for James Ridgway, 1798.
viii and 117 pp. 8vo. (*2s. 6d.* 1928)

MONTANO (Benito Arias). Relacion Cierta y
Verdadera,/ del famofo fuceffo y vitoria que tuvo
el Capitan/ Benito Arias Montano, fobrino del
doctifsimo Arias Montano, natural de Eftremadura,
Gover-/nador y Capitan general de la Provincia de
la nue/va Andaluzia, y ciudad de Cumana, y Alcayde de/ la fuerea de Araya, por el Rey nueftro
feñor, con/tra los enemigos Oládefes, q eftavan forti-
ficados/ en una falina que eftá riberas del rio Vnare,
que es/ en efta governacion, veynte y quatro leguas
de la/ ciudad de Cumana, efte año de 1633./ [*Colophon*] Con licencia, impreffo en Sevilla por Francifco de Lyra,/ Año de 1634./ *4 pp. half morocco.
Folio.* (*1l. 11s. 6d.* 1929)

MONTANUS (Arnold). [*Engraved title*] America/
T'Amsterdam/ By Jacob van Meurs, Plaetfnyder

en Boeckverkooper op de Keyſers graft in de Stadt
Meurs. 1671./ [*Printed title*] De Nieuwe en On-
bekende/ Weereld :/ Of/ Beſchryving/ van/ Ame-
rica/ in 't Zuid-Land,/ Vervaetende/ d'Oorſprong
der Americaenen en Zuid-/landers, gedenkwaerdige
tegten derwaerds,/ Gelegendheid/ Der vaſte Kuſten,
Eilanden, Steden, Sterkten, Dorpen, Tempels,/
Bergen, Fonteinen, Stroomen, Huiſen, de natuur
van Beeſten, Boomen, Planten en vreemde Ge-
waſſchen, Gods-dienſt en Zeden, Wonderlijke/
Voorvallen, Vereeuwde en Nieuwe Oorloogen :/
Verciert met Af-beeldſels na 't leven in America
gemaekt, en beſchreeven/ Door/ Arnoldus Montanus./ t'*Amsterdam*,/ By Jacob Meurs Boek-ver-
kooper en Plaet-ſnyder, op de Kaiſars-graft,/ ſchuin
over der Weſter-markt, in de ſtad Meurs. Anno
1671. Met Privilegie./ *4 prel. leaves and 585 pp :*
' Blad-Wyzer,' *etc.* 25 *pp* ; ' Naemen der Schry-
vers,' *etc.* 1 *page* ; ' Aenwyzing Voor der Boek-
binders' *etc.* 1 *page.* Portrait of ' Ioan Maurits,
Prius van Nassouw.' *and* 54 *Maps and Plates.*
Folio. (1*l.* 1*s.* 1930)

MONTCALM (MARQUIS DE). Lettres de Monsieur
Le Marquis de Montcalm, Gouverneur-General en
Canada; a Messieurs de Berryer & de la Molé,
Ecrites dans les Années 1757, 1758, & 1759. Avec
une Verſion Angloiſe. A *Londres :* J. Almon,
M.DCC.LXXVII. Letters from the Marquis de Mont-
calm, Governor-General of Canada; to Meſſrs. De
Berryer & de la Molé, In the Years 1757, 1758,
and 1759. With an Engliſh Tranſlation. *London :*
J. Almon, M.DCC.LXXVII. *Title, and 28 pp. doubly
numerated. French and English. Half morocco.*
8*vo.* (7*s.* 6*d.* 1931)

MONTESINOS (FERNANDO DE). Avto/ de la Fe/
celebrado en/ Lima a 23. de Enero/ de 1639./ Al
Tribvnal del Santo Ofi-/cio de la Inquiſicion, de los
Reynos del Perù,/ Chili, Paraguay, y Tucuman./
Por el licenciado D. Fer-/nando de Monteſinos
Presbitero, natural de Oſſuna./ Con Licencia/ de
sv Excelencia, del Ordi-/nario, y del ſanto Oficio.
Impreſſo en *Lima*,/ por Pedro de Cabrera; Año de
1639./ Vendenſe en la tienda de Simon Chirinos,
Mercader de Libros./ *4 prel. leaves, and Text, sig-
natures A to G in fours.* 4*to.* (1*l.* 1*s.* 1932)

MOODY (James). Lieut. James Moody's Narrative of his Exertions and Sufferings in the Cause of Government, Since the Year 1776; Authenticated by proper Certificates. The Second Edition. *London:* Richardson and Urquhart, MDCCLXXXIII. *Title and* 57 *pp.* 'Appendix' 7 *pp. half morocco.* 8vo.   (7s. 6d. 1933)

MOORE (Daniel). A Representation of Facts, Relative to the Conduct of Daniel Moore Eſquire, Collector of His Majeſtys Cuſtoms at Charles-Town, In South Carolina. From the Time of his Arrival in March, 1767, to the Time of his Departure in September following. Transmitted By the Merchants of Charles-Town, to Charles Garth, Eſquire, in London, Agent for the Province of South-Carolina: and, Recommended in a Letter from the Honourable The Committee of Correſpondence. *Charlestown, South Carolina:* Printed by Charles Crouch, at his Printing-Office in Elliott-ſtreet. 1767. *viii and pp.* 3-43. *Folio.* (2l. 2s. 1934)

MOORE (Francis). A Voyage to Georgia. Begun in the Year 1735. Containing An Account of the Settling the Town of Frederica, in the Southern Part of the Province; and a Deſcription of the Soil, Air, Birds, Beasts, Trees, Rivers, Islands, &c. With The Rules and Orders made by the Honourable the Trustees for that Settlement; including the Allowances of Proviſions, Cloathing, and other Neceſſaries to the Families and Servants which went thither. Also a Deſcription of the Town and County of Savannah, in the Northern Part of the Province; the manner of dividing and granting the Lands, and the Improvements there: With an Account of the Air, Soil, Rivers, and Islands in that Part. By Francis Moore, Author of Travels into the Inland Parts of Africa. *London:* Jacob Robinson, 1744. 108 *pp. & 1 leaf at end with Author's advertisement of voyage to Georgia in 1738, etc. half mor.* 8vo.   (7s. 6d. 1935)

MOORE (JAMES L.) The Columbiad: An Epic Poem on the Discovery of America and the West Indies by Columbus. In Twelve Books. By the Rev. James L. Moore, Master of the Free Grammar School, in Hertford, Herts. *London:* F. and

C. Rivington, 1798. *Title and* 455 *pp. Russia extra.*
8*vo.* (10*s.* 6*d.* 1936)

MOORE (*Sir* THOMAS). Mangora, King of the
Timbusians. Or the Faithful Couple. A Tragedy.
By Sir Thomas Moore. *London:* W. Harvey, 1718.
4 *prel. leaves and text* 54 *pp. Half morocco.*
4*to.* (10*s.* 6*d.* 1937)

MORETON (J. B.) West India Customs and Manners, containing strictures on the soil, cultivation,
produce, trade, officers, and inhabitants; with the
method of establishing and conducting a Sugar
Plantation. To which is added, the Practice of
training new Slaves. By J. B. Moreton, Esq. A
new edition. *London:* J. Parsons, 1793. 192 *pp.*
half mor. 8*vo.* (4*s.* 6*d.* 1938)

MORGAN (JOHN). A Discourse Upon the Institu-
tion of Medical Schools In America; Delivered at
a Public Anniversary Commencement, held in the
College of Philadelphia May 30 and 31, 1765.
With a Preface Containing, amongſt other things,
The Author's Apology For attempting to introduce
the regular mode of praſtiſing Physic in Philadelphia: By John Morgan, M.D. Fellow of the Royal
Society at London; Correſpondent of the Royal
Academy of Surgery at Paris; Member of the
Arcadian Belles Lettres Society at Rome; Licen-
tiate of the Royal Colleges of Phyſicians in London
and in Edinburgh; and Profeſſor of the Theory
and Praſtice of Medicine in the College of Philadelphia. *Philadelphia:* Printed and ſold by William Bradford, at the Corner of Market and Front-
Streets, MDCC,LXV. 18 *prel. leaves and* 63 *pp. calf.*
8*vo.* (1*l.* 1*s.* 1939)

MORNING (THE) and Evening Prayer. The Li-
tany, and Church Catechiſm. Ne Orhoengene
neoni Yogaraskhagh Yondereanayendaghkwa, Ne
Ene Niyoh Raodeweyena, neoni Onoghſadogeagh-
tige Yondadderighwanondoenthia. *Boston,* New-
England: Printed by Richard and Samuel Draper.
1763. *Title and* 24 *pp.* 'The Church Catechiſm.'
18 *pp. half mor.* 4*to.* (3*l.* 3*s.* 1940)

MORRIS (VALENTINE). A Narrative Of the Official Conduct of Valentine Morris, Eſq. late Cap-

tain General, Governor in Chief, &c. &c. of the
Island of St. Vincent and its Dependencies. Written by himself. Supported by his Official Corre-
fpondence with the Secretary of State, Lords of the
Treafury, and other of his Majefty's Servants, Admirals, Governors, &c. The Originals to be found
in the refpective Offices, and the Duplicates now
in his Poffeffion. Alfo by other Documents equally
Authentic. *London*: Printed at the Logographic
Prefs, by J. Walter, Printing-House-Square, Black-
Friars, MDCCLXXXVII. *Half-title, title, xvii, 3, and*
467 pp. (6s. 6d. 1941)

MORSE (JEDIDIAH). The American Geography;
or, A View of the Present Situation of the United
States of America. Containing Aftronomical Geography. Geographical Definitions. Difcovery,
and General Defcription of America. Summary
account of the Difcoveries and Settlements of North
America; General View of the United States; Of
their Boundaries; Lakes; Bays and Rivers; Mountains; Productions; Population; Government;
Agriculture; Commerce; Manufactures; Hiftory;
Concife Account of the War, and of the important
Events which have fucceeded. Biographical Sketches of feveral illuftrious Heroes. General account
of New England; Of its Boundaries; Extent;
Divifions; Mountains; Rivers; Natural History;
Productions; Population; Character; Trade;
Hiftory. Particular Defcriptions of the Thirteen
United States, and of Kentucky, The Weftern Ter-
ritory and Vermont.—Of their Extent; Civil Di-
vifions; Chief Towns; Climates: Rivers; Moun-
tains; Soils; Productions; Trade; Manufactures;
Agriculture; Population; Character; Conftitu-
tions; Courts of Juftice; Colleges; Academies and
Schools; Religion; Iflands; Indians; Literary
and Humane Societies; Societies; Springs; Curi-
ofities; Hiftories. Illuftrated with two Sheet Maps
—One of the Southern, the other of the Northern
States, neatly and elegantly engraved, and more
correct than any that have hitherto been publifhed.
To which is added, a concife Abridgment of the
Geography of the Britifh, Spanifh, French and
Dutch Dominions in America, and the Weft-Indies
—Of Europe, Afia, and Africa. By Jedidiah

Morse. *Elizabeth Town :* Printed by Shepard Kollock, for the Author. M,DCC,LXXXIX. *xii and* 534
pp. 'The Reader' *etc.* 1 *page. Without the maps.*
Calf. 8vo. (12*s.* 6*d.* 1942)

MORSE (JEDIDIAH). A Sermon, exhibiting the
present dangers, and consequent duties of the Citizens of the United States of America. Delivered
at Charlestown, April 25, 1799. The day of the
National Fast, By Jedidiah Morse, D.D. Paſtor of
the Church in Charleſtown. Published at the request of the hearers. *Charlestown :* Printed and
sold by Samuel Etheridge, next door to Warren-
Tavern./ 1799. 50 *pp.* 8*vo.* (2*s.* 6*d.* 1943)

MORSE (JEDIDIAH). A Sermon, delivered before
the Ancient & Honourable Artillery Company, In
Boston, June 6, 1803, being the Anniversary of
their Election of Officers. By Jedidiah Morse,
D.D. Minister of the Congregational Church in
Charlestown. *Charlestown :* Samuel Etheridge,
1803. 32 *pp.* 8*vo.* (2*s.* 6*d.* 1944)

MORSE (JEDIDIAH). A Compendious History of
New England, exhibiting an interesting view of
the first settlers of that Country, their Character,
their Sufferings, and their Ultimate Prosperity.
Collected and arranged, from authentic sources of
information, By Jedidiah Morse, D.D. and Rev.
Elijah Parish, A. M. of Boston, New England.
London : William Burton, 1808. 6 *prel. leaves, and*
207 *pp. Calf.* 8*vo.* (5*s.* 1945)

MORSE (JEDIDIAH). A Report to the Secretary of
War of the United States, on Indian Affairs, comprising a Narrative of a Tour performed in the
Summer of 1820, under a Commission from the
President of the United States, for the purpose of
ascertaining for the use of the Government, the
actual state of the Indian Tribes in our Country :
Illustrated by a Map of the United States ; ornamented by a correct Portrait of a Pawnee Indian.
By the Rev. Jedidiah Morse, D.D. Late Minister
of the First Congregational Church in Charlestown,
near Boston, now resident in New Haven. *New-*
Haven : 1822. 400 *pp. Errata* 1 *page. Colored Map ;*
and Portrait. Uncut. 8*vo.* (6*s.* 6*d.* 1946)

MORTON (THOMAS). New English Canaan/ or/ New Canaan./ Containing an Abftract of New England,/ Compofed in three Bookes./ The firft Booke fetting forth the originall of the Natives, their/ Manners and Cuftomes, together with their tractable Nature and/ Love towards the Englifh./ The fecond Booke fetting forth the naturall Indowments of the/ Country, and what ftaple Commodities it/ yealdeth./ The third Booke fetting forth, what people are planted there,/ their profperity, what remarkable accidents have happened fince the firft/ planting of it, together with their Tenents and practife/ of their Church./ Written by Thomas Morton, of Cliffords Inne gent, upon tenne/ yeares knowledge and experiment of the/ Country./ Printed at *Amsterdam,*/ By Jacob Frederick Stam./ In the yeare 1637./ 188 *pp.* 'A Table' *etc. 3 pp.* 4*to.*   (4*l.* 4*s.* 1947)

MOST (A/) Exact and Accurate/ Map/ of the/ Whole World:/ Or the/ Orb Terreftrial defcribed in Four plain Maps,/ (viz.)/ Asia, Evrope, Africa, America./ Containing all the known and moft Remarkable/ Capes, Ports, Bayes and Ifles, Rocks, Rivers, Towns,/ and Cities; together with their Scituation, Commodities,/ Hiftory, Cuftomes, Government; and a new and exact Geography,/ efpecially their Longitudes and Latitudes, in Alphabetical Order, and fitted/ to all Capacities./ A Work, as well ufeful as delightful, for all Schollars,/ Merchants, Mariners, and all fuch as defire to know Forreign/ parts, and is very helpful for the ready finding out any place mentioned in/ large Maps./ D. L. M.A./ *London,* Printed for John Garrett, at his Shop as you go/ up the Stairs of the Royal Exchange in Cornhil: where is Printed,/ Coloured and Sold, a Map of the World in four Sheets with Englifh de-/fcriptions: And where you may have alfo choice of all forts of Maps,/ and Pictures for Houfes, Studies, or Clofets. 4 *prel. leaves, and* 192 *pp. Poor copy, wanting several leaves.* 4*to.*   (5*s.* 1948)

MOULTRIE (JOHN). Dissertatio Medica Inauguralis, de Febre maligna biliofa Americæ; quam. Annuente deo ter opt. max. Ex auctoritate reverendi admodum Viri. D. Gulielmi Wishart

S. T. D. Academiae Edinburgenæ præfecti, nec
non Amplissimi Senatus Academici consensu, et
nobilissimae Facultatis Medicinae decreto; pro
gradu doctoratus, summisque in Medicina honoribus ac priviligüs rite et legitime consequendis,
Eruditorum Examini Subjicit Joannes Moultrie
ex Meridionali Carolinæ provincia, A et R. Ex
officina Roberti Flaminii. M.DCCXLIX. *2 prel. leaves,
and 24 pp;* 'Ephemerides Meteorologicae,' *etc.* 8 *pp.*
4*to.* (4*s.* 6*d.* 1949)

MOUNTGOMERY (*Sir* ROBERT). A Discourse
Concerning the defign'd Establishment of a New
Colony to the South of Carolina, in the Moft de-
lightful Country of the Univerfe. By Sir Robert
Mountgomery Baronet. *London :* Printed in the
Year. 1717. *Title and* 30 *pp. Large Copperplate
Plan at page* 11. *half mor.* 8*vo.* (10*s.* 6*d.* 1950)

MUHLENBERG (HENRY). Descriptio Uberior
Graminum et Plantarum Calamariarum Americæ
Septentrionalis indigenarum et cicurum. Auctore
D. Henrico Muhlenberg, Societ. Physic. Gotting.
—Berolini Imperalis Naturæ Curiosorum-Phytogr.
Gotting.—Physiogr. Lund.—Americ. Philosoph.
etc. Membro. *Philadelphiæ :* Solomon W. Conrad,
1817. *Title, ii and* 295 *pp.* 8*vo.* (7*s.* 6*d.* 1951)

MUNOZ (JUAN BAUTISTA). Historia del Nuevo-
Mundo escribíala D. Juan Baut. Muñoz. Tomo I.
en *Madrid* por la Viuda de Ibarra MDCCXCIII. 3
prel. leaves, xxx and 364 *pp. Portrait and Map.
Large Paper. half calf.* 8*vo.* (15*s.* 1952)
No second Volume was ever published.

MUNOZ (JUAN BAPTISTA). The History of the
New World, by Don Juan Baptista Munoz. Translated from the Spanish, with Notes by the Translator, an Engraved Portrait of Columbus, and a
Map of Espanola. *London :* G. G. and J. Robinson, 1797. Vol. I. *xv and* 552 *pp. Map & Portrait.*
8*vo.* (8*s.* 6*d.* 1953)

MUNSTER (SEBASTIAN). Cosmographia./ Bfch-
reibüg/ aller Lender Dürch/ Sebaftianum Munf-
terum/ in welcher begriffen,/ Aller völcker, Herr-
fchafften,/ Stetten, vnd namhafftiger flecken her-
komen :/ Sitten gebreüch, ordnung, glauben,
fecten, vnd hautie-/rung, durch die gantze welt,

vnd fürnem=/lich Teütfcher nation./ Was auch
befunders in iedem landt gefunden,/ vnnd darin
befchenfey./ Alles mit figuren vnd fchönen landt
taflen erklert,/ vnd für augen geftelt./ Getruckt
zü *Basel* durch Henrichum/ Petri. Anno M. D.
xliiij./ *6 prel. leaves; 24 woodcut Maps of 2 leaves
each, and Text* dclix *pp. Woodcut maps at pp. 546,
554. and 2 plates at pp. 630, & 631. Pigskin.
Folio.*   (*2l. 12s. 6d.*   1954)

MURRAY (James). An Impartial History of the
present War in America; Containing An Account
of its Rise and Progress, The Political Springs
thereof, with its various Successes and Disapoint-
ments on both sides. By the Rev. James Murray,
of Newcastle. *London:* R. Baldwin, [1778.]
Two Volumes. Vol. I. 373 *pp.* Vol. II. 376 *pp. 22
Copperplate Portraits, and Plan of the Town of Boston. Calf. 8vo.*   (*1l. 10s.*   1955)

MURRAY (William, *Earl of Mansfield*). Lord
Mansfield's Speech In giving the Judgment of the
Court of King's-Bench, On Monday, November
28, 1774, In the Cause of Campbell againft Hall,
respecting the King's Letters Patent, of the 20th
of July, 1764; for raising a Duty of Four and an
Half per Cent. On all the Exports from the Island
of Granada. Accurately taken by a Barrister. A
New Edition Corrected. *London:* G. Kearsly.
m.dcc.lxxv. *Title, and text 23 pp. Half morocco.
8vo.*   (*3s. 6d.*   1956)

MYSTERY (The) Reveal'd; or, Truth brought to
Light. Being a Difcovery of fome Facts, in Relation to the Conduct of the late M——y, which however extraordinary they may appear, are yet fupported by fuch Teftimonies of authentick Papers
and Memoirs as neither Confidence, can, out-brave;
nor Cunning invalidate. By a Patriot. *London:*
W. Cater, 1759. *Title and 319 pp. Half morocco.
8vo.*   (*4s. 6d.*   1957)

ARBOROUGH (*Sir* John *and Others*). An/ Account/ Of Several Late/ Voyages & Diſcoveries/ To the Sovth and North./ Towards The Streights of Magellan, the South Seas, the vaſt/ Tracts of Land beyond Hollandia Nova &c./ Also/ Towards Nova Zembla, Greenland or Spitsberg,/ Groynland or Engrondland, &c./ By Sir John Narborough, Captain Jasmen/ Tasman, Captain John Wood, and/ Frederick Marten of Hamburgh./ To which are Annexed a Large/ Introduction and Supplement,/ giving/ An Account of other Navigations/ to thoſe Regions of the Globe./ The Whole Illuſtrated with/ Charts and Figures./ *London:* Printed for Sam Smith and Benj. Walford, Printers to the/ Royal Society, at the Prince's Arms in S. Paul's Churchyards, 1694./ 18 *prel. leaves, Map of the Streights of Magellan, and* 196 *pp. Map of the North East, etc. at page* 143. 'The First Part of the Voyage into Spitzbergen,' *etc.* 207 *pp. Table at page* 1; *and Plates lettered A to S,* 2 *of the letter P. Fine copy. Old calf.* 8vo. (12s. 6d. 1958)

NARRATIVE (A) of Occurrences in the Indian Countries of North America, since the Connexion of the Right Hon. The Earl of Selkirk with the Hudson's Bay Company, and his attempt to Establish a Colony on the Red River; with a detailed account of his Lordſhip's Military Expedition to, and subsequent proceedings at Fort William, in Upper Canada. *London:* B. McMillan, 1817. xiv *and* 152 *pp.* 'Appendix.' 2 *prel. leaves and* 87 *pp.* 8vo. (6s. 6d. 1959)

NEAL (Daniel). The History of New-England, Containing an Impartial Account of the Civil and

Ecclefiaftical Affairs Of the Country, To the Year
of our Lord, 1700. To which is added, The Pre-
sent State of New-England. With a New and
Accurate Map of the Country. And an Appendix
Containing their Prefent Charter, their Ecclefiaf-
tical Difcipline, and their Municipal-Laws. In
Two Volumes. The Second Edition. With many
Additions by the Author. By Daniel Neal, A.M.
London: A. Ward, MDCCXLVII. *Two Volumes.* Vol.
I. 8 *prel. leaves and* 392 *pp. Map.* Vol. II. 2 *prel.
leaves and text* 380 *pp. Index.* 15 *pp. Old calf.*
8*vo.* (18*s.* 1960)

NECK (JACOB CORNELIUS). The/ Iovrnall, or Day-/
ly Regifter,/ Contayning a Trve/ manifeftation, and
Hiftoricall declaration of the/ voyage, accomplifhed
by eight fhippes of Amfterdam, vnder/ the conduct
of Iacob Cornelifzen Neck Admirall, & Wybrandt/
van Warwick Vice-Admirall, which fayled from
Amfter-/dam the firft day of March,/ 1598./ Shewing the covrse they/ kept, and what other notable
matters happened/ unto them in the fayd voyage./
Imprinted at *London* for Cuthbert Burby & Iohn
Flafket:/ And are to be fold at the Royall Exchange, & at the figne/ of the blacke beare in
Paules Church-yard./ 1601./ *Title, with Woodcut
of Ship in full sail, the reverse blank.* 'To the Right
Worship-/fvll, Master Thomas Smith,/ Sheriffe of
the honorable Citie of London, and/ Gouernor of
the famous companie of the Englifh Marchants/
trading to the Eaft Jndies, Sumatra, Iava, the Ifles
of the Malucos,/ Banda, and the Rich and Mightie
Kingdome of Chyna : and to the/ right VVorfhip-
full the Aldermen, and the reft of the Commit-/ties
and focietie of the faid corporation. William/
Walker vvifheth all profperitie and/ happie fucceffe./ 2 *pp. signed* 'William Walker.' *Text in* 58
folioed leaves. 'Some words of the Malifh fpeech,
which/ language is vfed throughout the Eaft Indies, as/ French is in our Countrie, wherewith a
man may trauell/ ouer all the Land. The Portugals fpeech is apt and pro-/fitable in thefe Iflands,
for there are many Inter-/preters which fpeake
Portugall./ 9 *pp.* 4*to.* (2*l.* 2*s.* 1961)
This copy is imperfect, wanting several leaves.

NECESSITY (THE) of Repealing the American

Stamp-Act demonstrated: Or, a Proof that Great-Britain muſt be injured by that Act. In a Letter to a Member of the British House of Commons. *London* : J. Almon, MDCCLXVI. 46 *pp. half mor.* 8vo. (4s. 6d. 1962)

NEILSON (John). Second Series of The Present and Future Prospects of Jamaica considered, Pointing out the Advantages which may be derived from the Extinction of Slavery, and Shewing the causes which oppose themselves to the successful Working of the Apprenticeship system, in accelerating that object, and proposing a remedy, Suggesting the means for establishing a Bank, on a solid basis, by John Neilson. *Kingston-Jamaica:* Printed at the office of the Commercial Advertiser. 1834. 20 *pp.* 8vo. (2s. 6d. 1963)

NEUE NACHRICHTEN von denen neuentdekten Inſuln in der See zwiſchen Aſien und Amerika; aus mitgetheilten Urkunden und Auszügen verfaſſet von J. L. S. * * *Hamburg* und *Leipzig*, bey Friedrich Lugo Ludwig Gleditſch. 1776. *Title and* 173 *pp.* 8vo. (4s. 6d. 1964)

NEU=EROFFNETES Amphitheatrvm, Worinnen Nach dem uns bekanten gantzen Welt=Greiſz, Alle Nationen Nach ihrem Habit, inſaubern Figuren repräſentiret. Anbey Die Länder nach ihrer Situation, Climate, Fruchtbarkeit, Inclination und Beſchaffenheit der Einwohner, Religion, vornehmſten Städten, Ertz=Biſthümern, Univerſitäten, Häfen, Veſtungen, Commercien, Macht, Staats= Intereſſe, Regierungs=Form, Raritäten, Müntzen, Prætensionibus, vornehmſten Ritter=Orden und Mappen aufgeführet ſind, Und welches, mit Zuziehung der Land=Charten, zu vieler Beluſtigung, vornehmlich aber der ſtudierenden Jugend, als ein ſehr nützliches und anmuthiges Compendium Geographicum, Genealogicum, Heraldicum, Curioſum, Numiſmaticum, kangebrauchet werden. *Erffurth*, Gedruckt und verlegt von Johann Michael Funcken, 1723. *Five Parts. General Title, Vorrede,* 2 *pp.* 'I. Aus dem gantzen Europa, *etc.* 1722.' 66 *leaves.* 'II. Aus dem gantzen Africa, *etc.* 1723.' 2 *prel. leaves, and* 96 *pp.* 'III. Aus dem gantzen America, *etc.* 1723.' 2 *prel. leaves and* 124 *pp.* 'Aus dem Stüdlichen Asia, *etc.* 1728.' *Title and* 142 *pp.* 'Turcicum, *etc.* 1724.' 172 *pp. Register* 4 *pp. Woodcuts with the text. Folio.* (1*l.* 10*s.* 1965)

NEVE, Y MOLINA (Luis de). Reglas de Orthographia, Diccionario, y Arte del Idioma Othomi breve instruccion para los principiantes, qve dictó el L. D. Lvis de Neve, y Molina, Cathedratico Proprietario de dicho Idioma en el Real, y Pontificio Colegio Seminario, Examinador Synodal, è Interprete de el Tribunal de Fé en el Proviforato de Indios de efte Arzobifpado, y Capellan del Hofpital Real de efta Corte. Dedicalo al Gloriosissimo Señor San Joseph, Padre Putativo del Verbo Eterno, y bajo fu Proteccion lo faca a luz. Impreffas en *Mexico*, con las licencias neceffarias, en la Imprenta de la Bibliotheca Mexicana, en el Puente del Efpiritu Santo. Año de 1767. 12 *prel. leaves and* 160 *pp. at page* 12 *Engraved leaf* 'Antes de leer el Diccionario, &c,' *etc.* 1 *page. Old calf. Small 8vo.* (3*l.* 3*s.* 1966)

NEVIS and ST. CHRISTOPHERS. To the Honourable the Knights, Citizens, and Burgeffes in Parliament Affembled. The humble Petition of feveral Proprietors of Plantations in the Iflands of Nevis and St. Chriftophers in America, and Merchants Trading to the fame; on behalf of themfelves and other Inhabitants and Traders to the aforefaid Iflands. [*London*] *A single sheet. Folio.* (2*s.* 6*d.* 1967)

NEW (A) Essay [By the Pennfylvanian Farmer] on the Constitutional Power of Great-Britain over the Colonies in America; with the Resolves of the Committee for the Province of Pennsylvania, and their Instructions To their Representatives in Assembly. Philadelphia Printed, and *London* Reprinted for J. Almon, 1774. *viii and* 126 *pp. half mor. 8vo.* (5*s.* 6*d.* 1968)

NEW BRUNSWICK. Hand Book for Emigrants to the Province of New Brunswick, Containing the average price of Land, Provisions, Clothing, Farm Stock, Building and other Materials, &c., and the rate of Wages to Mechanics, Labourers, &c. With other necessary information for persons with Capital, as well as for Mechanics, Farm Servants, Labourers, &c. intending to settle in the Province. Compiled From Returns in the Office of the Provincial Secretary. *Fredericton:* John Simpson, Printer to the Queen's Most Excellent Majesty. 1841. 15 *pp.* 8*vo.* (*2s.* 6*d.* 1969)

NEWE/ vnbekanthe/ landte/ Und/ ein/ newe/ Weldte/ in/ kurtz/ verganger/ zeythe/ erfunden/ [*Colophon*] ¶ Alſo hat ein endte dieſes Büchlein, wel=/ches aufz welliſcher ſprach, in die dewtſchen/ gebrachte vnd gemachte iſt worden, durch/den wirdigē vnd hochgelarthen herrē Job-/ſten Ruchamer der freyen künſte, vnd artz-/enncien Doctorē rc. Vnd durch mich Geor=/gen Stüchſzen zu *Nüreinberghk,* Gedrückte/ vnd volendte nach Chriſti vnſers lieben her/ren geburdte. M.cccc.vɪɪɟ. Jare, am Mit-/ woch ſanctii Mathei, des heiligen apoſtols/ abenthe, der do was der zweigntzigiſte tage/ des Monadts Septembris./ 68 *leaves, in double columns without catchwords or pagination, but with signatures* a *to* k *in sixes, and* l *in four leaves, with* 4 *leaves of register. Vellum. Folio.* (5*l.* 5*s.* 1970)

NEW-ENGLAND. An/ Abstract/ of the/ Lawes/ of/ New England,/ As they are now eſtablished./ *London,/* Printed for F. Coules, and W. Ley at Paules Chain,/ 1641./ *Title reverse blank, and* 15 *pp.* 'The Table of the Chapters.' 2 *pp. Unbound.* 4*to.* (2*l.* 2*s.* 1971)

NEVV/ ENGLANDS/ First Fruits ;/ in reſpect,/ Firſt of the ⎰ Converſion of ſome, ⎱ of the Indians. ⎱ Conviĉton of divers, ⎰ ⎱ Preparation of ſundry ⎰

2. Of the progreſſe of Learning, in the Colledge at/ Cambridge in Maſſachuſetts Bay./ With/ Divers other ſpeciall Matters concerning that Countrey./ Publiſhed by the inſtant requeſt of ſundry Friends, who deſire/ to be ſatisfied in theſe points by many New-England Men/ who are here preſent, and were eye or eare-/witneſſes of the ſame./ *London,* Printed by R. O. and G. D. for Henry Overton, and are to be/ ſold at his Shop in Popes-head Alley. 1643./ *Title reverse blank, and* 26 *pp. Calf extra, by Bedford.* 4*to.* (2*l.* 2*s.* 1972)

NEW-ENGLAND. A Brief/ Narration/ of the/ Practices/ of the/ Churches in New-England./ Written in private to one that deſired/ information

therein ; by an Inhabitant there,/ a Friend to Truth
and Peace./ Publifhed according to Order./ *London*,/ Printed by Matth. Simmons for John Rothwell, and/ are to be fold at his Shop, at the figne
of the Sunne/ in Pauls Churchyard, 1645./ *Title
and* 18 *pp.* (1*l.* 11*s.* 6*d.* 1973)

NEW-ENGLAND. A Brief/ Narration/ of the/
Practices/ of the/ Churches in New-England, in/
their folemne Worfhip of God./ Written to one
that defired infor-/mation therein ; by an Inhabitant there ;/ a Friend to Truth and Peace./ Publifhed according to Order./ *London ;* Printed by
Matthew Simmons, and are to be fold by/ John
Pounfet at the lower end of Budge-Row/ neere
Canning-streete. 1647./ *Title and Text in* 18 *pp.*
4*to.* (1*l.* 11*s.* 6*d.* 1974)
This differs from the preceding only in the title.

NEW-ENGLAND. The/ Day-Breaking,/ if not/
The Sun-Rifing/ of the/ Gospell/ With the/ Indians
in New-England./ *London*,/ Printed by Rich.
Cotes, for Fulk Clifton, and are to bee/ fold at his
fhop under Saint Margarets Church on/ New-fifh-
ftreet Hill, 1647./ *Title in a narrow type metal
border, on the reverse* ' To the Reader. *signed* ' Nathan. Warde.' *Text* 25 *pp. Calf extra by Bedford.*
4*to.* (2*l.* 2*s.* 1795)

NEW-ENGLAND. An Act/ For the promoting
and propagating the/ Gospel/ of/ Jefus Chrift/ in/
New-England./ *London,* Printed for Edward Huf-
band, Printer to the Parliament of England, and
are to be fold at his Shop in Fleetftreet, at the Sign
of the Golden-/Dragon, near the Inner-Temple,
1649./ *Title and pp.* 407-412. *Black Letter, half
mor. Folio.* (15*s.* 1976)

NEW-ENGLAND. The Light appearing more
and more to-/wards the perfect Day./ Or,/ A farther Difcovery of the prefent ftate/ of the Indians/
in/ New-England,/ Concerning the Progreffe of
the Gofpel/ amongft them./ Manifefted by Letters
from fuch as preacht/ to them there./ Publifhed
by H. Whitfield, late Paftor to the Chuch/ of
Chrift at Gilford in New-England, who came/ late
thence./ *London,* Printed by T. R. & E. M. for
John Bartlet, and are to be/ fold at the Gilt Cup,

near St. Auftins gate in Pauls/ Church-yard. 1651./ 4 *prel. leaves;* viz. 'The Lord, who is wonderful in Councel,' *etc. signed* 'Jofeph Caryl.' *on the reverse of the first leaf; Title in a type metal border, the reverse blank.* 'To the Right Honorable the Parliament of England and the Councel of State.' *Signed* 'Henry Whitfeld.' 4 *pp: Text* 46 *pp. Calf extra by Bedford.* 4to. (2*l.* 2*s.* 1977)

NEW-ENGLAND. Strength/ ovt of/ Weakneffe; Or a Glorious/ Manifeftation/ Of the further Progreffe of/ the Gofpel among the Indians/ in Nevv-England./ Held forth in Sundry Letters/ from divers Minifters and others to the/ Corporation eftablifhed by Parliament for/ promoting the Gofpel among the Hea-/then in New-England; and to particular/ Members thereof fince the laft Trea-/tife to that effect, Published by/ Mr. Henry Whitfield late Paftor/ of Gilford in New-England./ *London ;/* Printed by M. Simmons for John Blague and/ Samuel Howes, and are to be fold at their/ fhop in Popes-Head-Alley. 1652./ 8 *prel. leaves; viz. Title in a type metal border, the reverse blank;* 'To the Supreame Authoritie of this Nation, The Parliament of the Common-Wealth of England.' *Signed by* 'John Owen' *and* 11 *others,* 4 *pp ;* 'To the Reader. *Signed* ' W. Gouge.' *and* 13 *others,* 5 *pp.* 'To the Chriftian Reader.' 3 *pp. Text* 40 *pp.* 4to. (1*l.* 11*s.* 6*d.* 1978)

NEW-ENGLAND. Strength out of Weaknefs./ Or a Glorious/ Manifeftation/ Of the further Progreffe of the/ Gospel/ amongft/ the Indians/ in/ New-England./ Held forth in fundry Letters/ from divers Minifters and others to the/ Corporation eftablifhed by Parliament for/ promoting the Gofpel among the Hea-/then in New-England; and to particular/ Members thereof fince the laft Trea-/tife to that effect, formerly fet/ forth by Mr Henry Whitfield/ late Paftor of Gilford in/ New-England./ Publifhed by the aforefaid Corporation./ *London,/* Printed by M. Simmons for John Blague/ and Samuel Howes, and are to be fold at their/ Shop in Popes Head Alley. 1652./ 8 *prel. leaves ; viz. Title in a type metal border, the reverse blank,* 'To the Supreame Authoritie of this Nation, The Parliament of the Common-Wealth of England.' *Signed*

' William Steele, Prefident.' *4 pp* ; ' To the Reader.'
signed ' William Gouge.' *and* 17 *others,* 5 *pp.* ' To
the Chriftian Reader.' 3 *pp* : *Text* 40 *pp. Calf extra
by Bedford.* 4*to.* (2*l.* 2*s.* 1979)

NEW-ENGLAND. Strength/ ovt of/ Weakneffe;/
Or a Glorious/ Manifeftation/ Of the further Progreffe of/ the Gofpel among the Indians/ in Nevv-
England./ Held forth in Sundry Letters/ from
divers Minifters and others to the/ Corporation
eftablifhed by Parliament for/ Promoting the Gofpel
among the Hea-/then in New-England ; and to
particular/ Members thereof fince the laft Trea-/
tife to that effect, formerly fet forth by M͏ʳ Henry
Whitfield/ late Paftor of Gilford in New-England./ Publifhed by the aforefaid Corporation./
London ; Printed by M. Simmons for John Blague
and/ Samuel Howes, and are to be fold at their/
Shop in Popes-Head-Alley. 1652./ 8 *prel. leaves ;
viz. Title in a metal type border, the reverse blank ;*
' To the fupreame Authoritie of this Nation, The
Parliament of the Common-Wealth of England.'
signed ' William Steele, Prefident.' 4 *pp* ; ' To the
Reader.' *signed* ' William Gouge ' *and* 13 *others,* 5
pp. Strength ovt of Weakneffe ; Or a Glorious
Manifeftation Of the further Progreffe of the Gofpel among the Indians in New-England.' 4 *pp* :
Text 40 *pp. Fine copy in calf extra by Bedford.*
4*to.* (2*l.* 2*s.* 1980)

NEW-ENGLAND. A/ History/ of/ New-England./ From the Englifh planting in the Yeere/
1628. untill the Yeere 1652./ Declaring the form
of their Government,/ Civill, Military, and Ecclefiaftique. Their Wars with/ the Indians, their
Troubles with the Gortonifts,/ and other Here-
tiques. Their manner of gathering/ of Churches,
the commodities of the Country,/ and defcription
of the principall Towns/ and Havens, with the
great encou-/ragements to increafe Trade/ betwixt
them and Old/ England. With the names of all
their Governours, Magiftrates,/ and eminent
Minifters./ *London,/* Printed for Nath: Brooke
at the Angel/ in Corn-hill. 1654./ 2 *prel. leaves ;
viz. Title, and* ' To the Reader.' *signed* ' T. H.' 2
pp : *Text* 236 *pp.* ' Brooke's Catalogue ' 4 *pp.*
4*to.* (4*l.* 14*s.* 6*d.* 1981)

NEW-ENGLAND. The/ Secret Workes/ Of a Cruel/ People/ Made manifest;/ Whofe little finger is become he-/vier then their persecutors the bishops Loyns, who have/ fet up an Image amongst them in New-England, which/ all that will not bow down unto, and worship, must un-/dergo all fuch Sufferings as can be invented and/ inflicted by the hearts and hands of such/ men whofe tender mercies are cruel./ Which may be feen in this fhort relation of their cruelty,/ which was pre-sented to Parliament, and now recom-/mended to the consideration of all fober people, that/ they may fee how these profeffors of New-England have/ loft their former tendernefs, who fled from perfe-cution,/ and now are become the chiefeft of Perfe-cutors./ Whereunto is annexed a Copy of a Letter which came/ from one who had been a Magiftrate among them,/ to a friend of his in London, wherein he gives an/ account of the cruel fufferings of the/ people of God in those parts under the/ Rulers of New-England and their un-/righteous Laws./ *London,* Printed in the Year 1659./ *Title, reverse blank, and 26 pp : at page 18 signed '* John Rous.*'* 4*to.* (2*l.* 2*s.* 1982)

The title is in manuscript.

NEW-ENGLAND. The Humble/ Petition/ and/ Address/ Of the General Court fitting at/ Bofton in New-England,/ unto/ The High and Mighty/ Prince/ Charles/ the Second./ And prefented unto His Moft-Gracious/ Majefty Feb. 11. 1660./ [*London*] Printed in the Year 1660./ *8 pp. signed '* John Endecot Gov[r]./ In the Name, and with the con-/fent of the General Court.*' Calf extra by Bedford.* 4*to.* (2*l.* 2*s.* 1983)

NEW ENGLAND. The Necessity/ of/ Reforma-tion/ With the Expedients fubfervient/ thereunto, afferted ;/ in Anfwer to two/ Qveftions/ I. What are the Evils that have provoked the Lord to bring his Judg-/ments on New-England ?/ II. What is to be done that fo thofe Evils may be Reformed ?/ Agreed upon by the/ Elders and Messengers/ Of the Churches affembled in the/ Synod/ At Bofton in New-England,/ Sept. 10. 1679./ *Boston ;/* Printed by John Fofter. In the Year 1679./ *4 prel. leaves ; viz.* 1*st,* ' At a General Court held at Bofton

in New-England, 15th. of October 1679.' *signed*
'By the Court Edward Rawſon Secr.' *2nd, Title
the reverse blank. 3rd, and 4th,* ' The Epiſtle Dedicatory.' *Text* 15 *pp. Fine copy in morocco by Bedford.* 4*to.* (4*l.* 4*s.* 1984)

NEW-ENGLAND'S Faction Discovered;/ Or,/ A
Brief and True Account of their Perſecution of the
Church/ of England; the Beginning and Progreſs
of the War/ with the Indians; and other Late Proceedings there, in/ a Letter from a Gentleman of
that Country, to a Perſon/ of Quality./ Being, an
Anſwer to a moſt falſe and ſcandalous Pamphlet
late-/ly Publiſhed; Intituled, News from New-
England, &c./ [*Colophon*] *London,*/ Printed for J.
Hindmarſh, at the Sign of the Golden Ball, over
againſt/ the Royal Exchange in Cornhill. 1690./
8 *pp. signed* ' C. D.' *Poor copy closely cut. Unbound.*
4*to.* (1*l.* 1*s.* 1985)

NEW-ENGLAND. The/ Humble Addreſs/ of the/
Publicans/ of/ New-England,/ To which King you
pleaſe./ With some Remarks/ Upon it./ *London:*
Printed in the Year, 1691./ 35 *pp. Fine copy. calf
extra by Bedford.* 4*to.* (2*l.* 2*s.* 1986)

NEW-ENGLAND. A brief Review of the Rise
and Progress, Services and Sufferings, of New
England, especially the Province of Massachuset's-
Bay. Humbly ſubmitted to the Conſideration of
both Houſes of Parliament. *London:* J. Buckland,
MDCCLXXIV. 32 *pp. half mor.* 8*vo.* (7*s.* 6*d.* 1987)

NEW-ENGLAND, and her Institutions: By One
of her Sons. [Jacob Abbot.] R. B. Seeley and W.
Burnside: *London.* MDCCCXXXV. 4 *prel. leaves and*
393 *pp.* 8*vo.* (4*s.* 6*d.* 1988)

NEW-JERSEY An/ Abstract,/ or/ Abbreviation/
Of ſome Few of the/ Many (Later and Former)
Testimonys/ from the/ Inhabitants of/ New-Jersey,/
And Other/ Eminent Perſons,/ Who have Wrote
particularly concerning/ That Place./ *London,*
Printed by Thomas Milbourn, in the Year, 1681./
32 *pp.* 4*to.* (3*l.* 13*s.* 6*d.* 1989)

NEW-JERSEY. The Acts Of the General Assembly Of the Province of New-Jersey, From the
Time of the Surrender of the Government of the

faid Province, to the Fourth Year of the Reign of King George the Second. Collected and Published by Order of the faid Assembly. With a Table of the Principal Matters therein contained. *Philadelphia:* Printed and Sold by William and Andrew Bradford, Printers to the King's Moft Excellent Majefty, for the Province of New-Jerfey, MDCC XXXII. *7 prel leaves and wanting all after p. 332. Old calf. Folio.* (15s. 1990)

NEW-JERSEY. The Acts of the General Assembly of the Province of New-Jersey, From the Year 1753, being the Twenty-fixth of the Reign of King George the Second, where the Firft Volume ends, to the Year 1761, being the Firft of King George the Third. With proper Tables; and an alphabetical Index; containing all the principal Matters in the Body of the Book: Together with an Appendix; containing the feveral Acts of Parliament now in Force in America, relating to his Majefty's Forces, and the Articles of War. Collected and publifhed by Order of the General Assembly of the faid Province. By Samuel Nevill, Efq; Second Juftice of the Supreme Court of Judicature of the faid Province. Volume the Second. *Woodbridge,* in New-Jersey: Printed by James Parker, Printer to the King's Moft Excellent Majefty, for the Province. M.DCC.LXI. *xvi and 401 pp. Index 56 pp; Appendix 59 pp; Index to the Appendix pp. 61-64. Old calf. Folio.* (1l. 10s. 1991)

NEW-YORK. Laws, Statutes, Ordinances and Constitutions, Ordained, made and Established, by the Mayor, Alderman, and Commonalty, of the City of New-York, Convened in Common-Council, for The good Rule and Government of the Inhabitants and Refidents of the faid City. Published the Ninth Day of November, in the third Year of the Reign of our Sovereign Lord, George the Third, by the Grace of God, of Great Britain, France and Ireland, King, Defender of the Faith, &c. Annoque Domini 1762. And in the Mayoralty of John Cruger, Efq; To which is added, An Appendix, containing Extracts of fundry Acts of the General Affembly, of the Colony of New-York, immediately relating to the good government of the faid City and Corporation. [*New-York*] Printed and Sold, by John Holt, at the Printing Office, at the lower End of Broad Street, oppofite the Exchange, 1763. *2 prel. leaves and pp.* 3-108. *Table* *2 pp. Folio.* (1*l.* 11*s.* 6*d.* 1992)

NEW-YORK. The Charter of the City of New-York; Printed by Order of the Mayor, Recorder, Aldermen and Commonalty of the City aforefaid. To which is annexed, The Act of the General Affembly confirming the fame. *New York,* Printed by W. Weyman, in Broad-Street, 1765. *50 pp.* *Folio.* (1*l.* 11*s.* 6*d.* 1993)

NEW-YORK. Authentic Account of the Proceedings of the Congress held at New-York, In MDCCLXV, On the Subject of the American Stamp Act. MDCCLXVII. *Title and 37 pp. Half morocco.* *8vo.* (7*s.* 6*d.* 1993*)

NEW-YORK. The Constitution of the State of New-York. *Philadelphia:* Printed and Sold by Styner and Cist, in Second-ftreet, fix Doors above Arch-ftreet. MDCCLXXVII. *32 pp. Half calf.* *8vo.* (7*s.* 6*d.* 1994)

NEW-YORK. The Charter of the City of New-York. Printed by Order of the Mayor, Recorder, Aldermen and Commonalty Of the City aforefaid. To which is annexed, The Act of the General Affembly confirming the fame. *New-York:* Printed by Samuel and John Loudon, Printers to the State. M,DCC,LXXXVI. *Title and pp.* 3-44. *Folio.* (1*l.* 10*s.* 1995)

NEW-YORK. Laws and Ordinances, Ordained and Established by the Mayor, Aldermen and Commonalty of the City of New-York, In Common Council convened; For the good Rule and Government of the Inhabitants and Residents of the faid City. Published the Twenty-Ninth Day of March, 1786, in the Tenth Year of our Independence, And in the Mayoralty of James Duane, Efq. *New-York:* Printed by Samuel and John Loudon, Printers to the State. M,DCC, LXXXVI. *29 pp. Folio.* (1*l.* 10*s.* 1996)

NICHOLSON (FRANCIS). A Modeft Answer To a Malicious Libel Againft his Excellency Francis Nicholfon, Efq; &c. Or An Examination of that Part of Mr. Blair's Affidavit, relating to the

School-Boys of the Grammar-School, in her Majefty's Royal College of William and Mary in Virginia. Written in Virginia, in the Year 1704.
[*London.* 1706.] *Privately printed, beginning with
page* 1, *without separate title.* 55 *pp. Calf extra by
Bedford. 8vo.* (1*l.* 1*s.* 1997)

NICHOLSON (FRANCIS). An Apology or Vindication of Francis Nicholfon, Efq ; His Majesty's
Governor of South-Carolina, From the Unjuft Afperfions caft on Him by fome of the Members of
the Bahama-Company. *London,* Printed in the
Year 1724. 62 *pp. Calf extra by Francis Bedford.*
8*vo.* (1*l.* 1*s.* 1998)

NICHOLSON (FRANCIS). Papers Relating to An
Affidavit Made by His Reverence James Blair,
Clerk, pretended Prefident of William and Mary
College, and fuppofed Commiffary to the Bifhop of
London in Virginia, against Francis Nicholfon,
Efq ; Governour of the faid Province. Wherein
His Reverence's great Refpect to Government, and
obedience to the Ninth Commandment, *Thou shalt
not bear false Witness,* &c. will plainly appear ; as
will alfo his Gratitude to the faid Governour, from
whom he had received fo many Favours, and to
whom he was himfelf fo highly obliged, in feveral
original Letters under his own Hand, fome whereof
are here publifhed, and more (God willing) fhall
hereafter. [*London.*] Printed in the Year 1727. 2
prel. leaves and 104 *pp. Calf extra by Bedford.*
8*vo.* (1*l.* 1*s.* 1999)

NISBET (CHARLES). Monody to the Memory of
the Rev. Dr. Charles Nisbet, many years first
Minister of Montrose, and late President of the
College of Carlisle in Pennsylvania. *Edinburgh:*
James Ballantyne, 1805. 23 *pp. Half morocco.*
8*vo.* (3*s.* 6*d.* 2000)

NODAL (BARTOLOME GARCIA DE, *and* GONÇALO DE).
Relacion/ del Viaje qve por/ orden de sv Mag.[d]/
y acverdo del Real Consejo/ de Indias Hezieron los
Capitanes/ Bartolome Garcia de Nodal, y Gon-
çalo/ de Nodal hermanos, naturales de Ponte/
Vedra, al defcubrimiento del Estrecho/ nuebo de
S. Vicente y reconofinj°:/ del de Magallanes./ A
Don Fernando Carrillo/ Cauallero del abito de

Santiago Prefidente/ en el mifmo Confejo./ Con
Privilegio/ En *Madrid*. Por Fernando Correa-/ de
Montenegro. Año. 1621./ N. S. de Atocha N. S.
del becen Suceffo./ I de Courbes Sculpfit./ 12 *prel.
leaves; viz. Engraved title with Portraits of the two
brothers Nodal, the reverse blank* ; ' Fee de aproua-
cion.' 3 *pp* ; ' Suma del priuilegio.' 1 *page* ; ' Tassa.'
1 *page* ; ' Erratas.' 1 *page* ; ' A Don Fernando
Carrillo, Cauallero del Abito de Sãtiago, Prefidente
del Real Confejo de Indias.' 3 *pp* ; ' Al Lector.'
5 *pp* ; ' Advertencias.' 3 *pp* ; ' Variacion de la
aguja' 3 *pp* ; Reglas para faber la variacion de la
aguja al nacer y pouer del Sol.' 2 *pp* ; *Text* 65
folioed leaves : ' Tabla Para Saler Las horas ' *etc.* 1
leaf : ' Relacion svmaria de los Servicios de los
Capitanes Bartolome Garcia de Nodal, y Gonçalo
de Nodal hermanos.' *folioed leaves* 2-15. *At fol.
35 is a copperplate Map entitled* ' Reconocimiento de
los Estrechos de Magallanes ' *etc.* ' I de Courbes
fculpfit.' 13½ *by* 15½ *inches. Fine copy in morocco by
Bedford. 4to.* (10*l.* 10*s.* 2001)

NOMENCLATURA Brevis Anglo=Latino in usum
Scholarum. Together with Examples of the Five
Declenfions of Nouns: With the Words in Pro-
pria quæ Maribus and Quæ Genus reduced to each
Declenfion. Per F. G. *Boston*, in New-England:
Printed by J. Draper, for J. Edwards and H.
Fofter in Cornhil. 1735. *2 prel. leaves and* 88 *pp.
Calf.* 12*mo.* (10*s.* 6*d.* 2002)

NOOTKA SOUND. An Authentic Statement of
all the Facts relative to Nootka Sound; its discovery, history, settlement, trade, and the probable
advantages to be derived from it ; in an Address to
the King. *London :* J. Debrett, MDCCXC. *Title and*
26 *pp : signed* ' Argonaut.' 8*vo.* (4*s.* 6*d.* 2003)

NORGATE (E.) Mr. John Dunn Hunter defended:
Or, some Remarks on an Article in the North
American Review, in which that Gentleman is
branded as an impostor. By E. Norgate. *London:*
John Miller, 1826. 38 *pp.* 8*vo.* (2*s.* 6*d.* 2004)

NORTH-AMERICAN (THE) and the West-Indian
Gazetteer. Containing An Authentic Defcription
of the Colonies and Islands in that part of the
Globe, Shewing their Situation, Climate, Soil, Pro-

duce, and Trade: With their Former and Prefent
Condition. Also an exact Account of the Cities,
Towns, Harbours, Ports, Bays, Rivers, Lakes,
Mountains, Number of Inhabitants, &c. Illustrated with maps. *London*,G.Robinson,MDCCLXXVI.
3 *prel. leaves; Introduction xxiv pp ; Text, signatures B. to T, in sixes & U.* 1. *Addenda* 2 *pp.* 2
maps. Old calf. 12*mo.* (4s. 6d. 2005)

NORTH-AMERICAN (THE) and the West-Indian
Gazetteer. Containing An Authentic Defcription
of the Colonies and Islands in that part of the
Globe, shewing their Situation, Climate, Soil, Pro-
duce, and Trade; With their Former and Prefent
Condition. Also An exact Account of the Cities,
Towns, Harbours, Ports, Bays, Rivers, Lakes,
Mountains, Number of Inhabitants, &c. Illus-
trated with Maps. The Second Edition. *London :*
G. Robinson, MDCCLXXVIII. 3 *prel. leaves. Intro-
duction xxiv pp. Text, signatures B. to T. in sixes &
U.* 1. 2 *Maps.* 12*mo.* (4s. 6d. 2006)

NORTHERN TOUR (A): Being A Guide to Sa-
ratoga, Lake George, Niagara, Canada, Boston,
&c.&c. Through the States of Pennsylvania, New
Jersey, New York, Vermont, New Hampshire,
Massachusetts, Rhode Island, and Connecticut;
embracing an account of the Canals, Colleges,
Public Institutions, Natural Curiosities, and interesting objects therein. *Philadelphia :* H. C. Carey
& I. Lea. 1825. 4 *prel. leaves and* 279 *pp. Half
calf.* 12*mo.* (5s. 2007)

NORTON (JOHN). A/ Discussion/ of that Great
Point in/ Divinity,/ the/ Sufferings of Christ;/
And the Questions about his/ Righteoufneffe Active,
Paffive :/ and the Imputation thereof./ Being an
Answer to a Dialogue/ Intituled/ The Meritorious
Price of our Redemption,/ Juftification, &c./ By
John Norton Teacher of the Church/ at Ipfwich
in New-England./ Who was appointed to draw
up this Anfwer by the Generall Court./ *London,*
Printed by A. M. for Geo. Calvert at the Sign of
the half/ Moon, and Jofeph Nevill at the Sign of
the Plough in the/ new Buildings in Pauls Church-
yard. 1653./ 8 *prel. leaves and* 270 *pp. Mottoes* 1
page. 'The Copy of a Letter,' *etc.* 3 *pp. Unbound.*
8*vo.* (10s. 6d. 2008)

NORTON (John). The/ Orthodox Evangelift./ Or a/ Treatise/ Wherein many Great/ Evangelical Truths/ (Not a few whereof are much oppofed and Eclipfed/ in this perillous hour of the Paffion of the Gofpel)/ Are briefly Difcuffed, cleared, and con-/firmed : As a further help, for the Begeting, and Eftablifhing of the Faith which is in Jefus./ As also the State of the Bleffed, Where;/ Of the condition of their Souls from the/ inftant of their Diffolution : and of their/ Perfons after their Re-furrection./ By John Norton, Teacher of the Church/ at Ipfwich in New England./ *London,/* Printed by John Macock, for Henry Cripps, and Lodowick Lloyd,/ and are to be fold at their fhop in Popes head Alley,/ neer Lombard ftreet. 1654./ 8 *prel. leaves and* 356 *pp.* 'An Alphabetical Table,' etc. 14 *pp.* 4*to.* (18*s.* 2009)

NORTON (John). Abel being Dead yet fpeaketh;/ or, the/ Life & Death/ Of that defervedly Famous Man of God,/ Mʳ John Cotton,/ Late Teacher of the Church of/ Christ, at Boston in/ New-Eng-land./ By John Norton, Teacher/ of the fame Church./ *London,/* Printed by Tho. Newcomb for Lodowick Lloyd, and/ are to be fold at his Shop next the Caftle-/Tavern in Cornhill. 1658./ 51 *pp.* 'A Catalogue of fome Books *etc.*' 5 *pp. Calf extra, by Bedford.* 4*to.* (2*l.* 2*s.* 2010)

NORTON (John). The/ Heart of New England/ Rent at the/ Blasphemies/ of the prefent Genera-tion./ Or a brief/ Tractate,/ Concerning the/ Doc-trine of the Quakers,/ Demonftrating the deftruc-tive nature/ thereof, to Religion, the Churches, and/ the State; with confideration of the Re-/medy againft it./ Occafional Satisfaction to Objections, and Confirmation of the contrary Truth./ By John Norton, Teacher of the Church of/ Chrift at Bof-ton./ Who was appointed thereunto by the Order of the/ General Court./ *London,* Printed by J. H. for John Allen at the Rifing-/Sunne in St. Pauls Church-yard. 1660./ *Title and* 83 *pp. Unbound.* 16*mo.* (3*l.* 3*s.* 2011)

NOVA SCOTIA. A Genuine Account of Nova Scotia : Containing a Defcription of its Situation, Air, Climate, Soil and its Produce ; alfo Rivers,

Bays, Harbours, and Fiſh, with which they abound
in very great Plenty. To which is Added His Majeſty's Proposals, as an Encouragement to thoſe
who are willing to ſettle there. London Printed:
And *Dublin*, Re-printed for Philip Bowes, Mᴅᴄᴄʟ.
16 *pp. half mor. 8vo.*   (5*s.* 6*d.* 2012)

NOVA SCOTIA. The Conduct of the French, With
Regard to Nova Scotia, From its firſt Settlement to
the preſent Time. In which are expoſed the Falſe-
hood and Abſurdity of their Arguments made uſe
of to elude the Force of the Treaty of Utrecht, and
ſupport their unjuſt Proceedings. In a Letter to
a Member of Parliament. *London:* T. Jefferys.
ᴍᴅᴄᴄʟɪᴠ. *Title, and text* 77 *pp. Half morocco.*
8vo.   (7*s.* 6*d.* 2013)

NOVA SCOTIA. A fair Representation of His Majeſty's Right to Nova Scotia or Acadie. Briefly
ſtated from the Memorials of the English Commiſ-
ſaries; with an Answer to the Objections Contained
In the French Memorials, and In a Treatise, Entitled, Diſcuſſion Sommaire ſur les anciennes Limites de l'Acadie. *London:* Edward Owen,
ᴍᴅᴄᴄʟᴠɪ. 64 *pp. half mor.* 8*vo.* (7*s.* 6*d.* 2014)

NOVA SCOTIA. An Account of the Present State
of Nova Scotia. *Edinburgh:* William Creech;
ᴍ,ᴅᴄᴄ,ʟxxxᴠɪ. *viii and text* 157 *pp. Uncut.*
8vo.   (7*s.* 6*d.* 2015)

NOVVS ORBIS Regio-/nvm ac Insvlarvm veteribvs
incognitarvm,/ unà cum tabula coſmographica, &
aliquot alijs confimilis/ argumenti libellis, quorum
omnium catalogus/ ſequenti patebit pagina./ His
acceſſit copioſus rerum memorabilium index./ *Basileae* apvd Io. Hervagivm, mense Martio, Anno
ᴍ.ᴅ.xxxɪɪ./ 24 *prel. leaves; viz. Title, on the reverse,*
' Catalogvs eorvm qvae hoc' *etc.* ' Excellenti viro
Georgio Collimitio Danstettero Artis Medicae et
disciplinarū Mathematicarū omnium facile principi,
Simon Grynaevs S.' 3 *pp.* ' Index rervm' *etc.* 18
pp. 'Index e Brocardo,' *etc.* 13 *pp.* 'Typi Cosmographici et declaratio et uſus Sebaſtianum Mun-
ſterum.' 12 *pp. Text* 584 *pp. and Colophon leaf.
Fine copy. Old stamped calf. Folio.* (1*l.* 10*s.* 2016)

NOVVS ORBIS Re-/gionvm ac Insvlarvm ve-/teri-
bus incognitarum, unà cum tabula coſmographica,

&/ aliquot aliis confimilis argumenti libellis, quo-
rum/ omnium catalogus fequenti patebit pagina./
His acceffit copiofus rerum memorabilium index./
Parisiis apvd Galeotvm à/ Prato, in aula maiore regii Palatii ad primam columnam/ [*Colophon*] Im-
preffum Parifiis apud Antonium Augerellum, impenfis Ioannis/ Parui & Galeoti à Prato. Anno
M. D. XXXII. VII./ Calen. Nouembris./ 26 *prel.*
leaves; viz. Title, on the reverse, 'Catalogvs' *etc.*
'Excellenti viro Georgio' *etc.* 3*pp.* 'Index rervm'
etc. 37 *pp.* 'Typi Cosmographici et Declaratio,'
etc. 10 *pp.* Text 507 *pp.* [*for* 514] *colophon leaf as*
above. Vellum. Folio.   (1*l.* 10*s.* 2017)

NOVVS ORBIS. Die New/Welt, der landfchaf=/
ten vnnd Infulen, fo/bis hie her allen Altweltbe-
fchrybern vnbekant,/ Jungft aber von den Portu-
galefern vnnd Hifpaniern jm/ Nider=/genglichen
Meer herfunden. Sambt den fitten vnnd gebreuchen
der Inwonenden/ völcker. Auch was Gütter oder
Waren man bey jnen funden, vnd jnn/ vnfere
Landtbrachthab. Do bey findt man auch hie den
vrfprung vnd/ altherkummen Fürnembften Gwal-
tigften Völcker der Alt=/bekanten Welt, als do
feind die Tartern, Mofcouiten,/ Reuffen, Preuffen,
Hungern, Sfchlafen. etc./ nach anzeygung vnd jnn-
halt difs vmb=/gewenten blats./ Gedruckt zü
Straszburg durch Georgen Vlricher,/ von Andla, am
viertzehenden tag des Mertzens./ An. M.D.XXXIIII.
6 *prel. leaves; viz. Title, on the reverse,* ' Anzeygung
vnd Iñhalt diffes Büchs der Newen Welt.' ' Dem
Wolgebornen Herrn Herrn Reynharten Graffen zü
Hanaw, Herrn zü Lichtenberg, des Hohen Stiffts zü
Strafzburg Thümcufter feinem Gnedigen Herrn.
etc." 10 *pp.*   Text 242 [*for* 252] *folioed leaves.*
Folio.   (1*l.* 10*s.* 2018)

NOVVS ORBIS Regio-/nvm ac Insvlarvm veteribvs
incognitarvm/ unà cum tabula cofmographica, &
aliquot alijs confimilis/ argumenti libellis, quorum
omnium catalogus/ fequenti patebit pagina./ His
acceffit copiofus rerum memorabilium index./ Adiecta est hvic postremae Editioni/ Nauigatio Caroli
Cæfaris aufpicio in comi-/tijs Auguftanis inftituta./
Basileae apvd Io. Hervagivm mense/ Martio Anno
M.D.XXXVII. 24 *prel. leaves; viz. Title, on the re-*
verse, 'Catalogus' *etc.* ' Excellenti viro Georgio,'

etc. 3 *pp.* 'Index rervm' *etc.* 18 *pp.* 'Index e Brocardo,' *etc.* 13 *pp.* 'Typi Cosmographici' *etc.* 12
pp. *Text* 600 *pp ; and blank leaf with woodcut on
verso. Old stamped calf. Folio.* (1*l.* 10*s.* 2019)

NOVVS ORBIS Re-/gionvm ac Insvlarvm vete=/ri-
bvs incognitarvm vna cvm Tabvla Cos-/mographi-
ca, & aliquot alijs confimilis argumenti libellis,
nunc no-/nis navigationibvs auctus, quorum omnium catalogus/ fequenti patebit pagina./ His ac-
cefsit copiofus rerum memorabilium index./ Adiecta est hvic postremae Editioni/ Nauigatio Caroli
Cæsaris aufpicio in comi-/tijs Auguftanis inftituta./
Basileæ apvd Io. Hervagivm, Anno M.D.LV./ 26
prel. leaves ; viz. Title, on the reverse, 'Catalogvs'
etc. 'Excellenti viro Georgio,' *etc.* 3 *pp.* 'Index
rerum' *etc.* 33 *pp. Errata on the last page ; blank
leaf ;* 'Typi cosmographici' *etc.* 12 *pp. Text* 677 *pp ;
blank leaf with woodcut on the reverse. With Map.
Fine copy. Best Edition. Folio.* (1*l.* 10*s.* 2020)

NOVUS ORBIS./ id eft,/ Navigationes/ Primæ in
Americam :/ quibus adjunximus/ Casparis Varrerii
discvrsvm/ fuper Ophyra Regione./ Elenchum
Autorem verfa pagina/ Lector inveniet./ *Rotero-
dami,*/ Apud Iohannem Leonardi Berewout/ Anno
cIↄ. Iↄ. cxvi./ 8 *prel. leaves ; viz. Title, on the reverse* 'Elenchvs Avtorvm.' 'Ornatifsimis, Pruden-
tifsimisque viris in Collegio Thalassiarchico vrbis
Roterod. Dominis fuis.' 13 *pp : Text* 570 *pp ; and*
1 *blank leaf./* 'Casparis/ Varrerii Lvsitani/ Com-
mentarius/ de Ophyra/ Regione,/ In facris litteris
Lib. III. Regum/ & II. Paralipomenon./ Rotero-
dami,/ Apud Ioannem Leonardi Berevvout,/ Anno
1616./ *Title. and* 82 *unnumbered pages. Fine copy.
Small* 8*vo.* (2*l.* 12*s.* 6*d.* 2021)

NUEVA ESPANA. Continente/ Americano,/ Ar-
gonauta/ de las Costas/ de/ Nueva-España,/ y/
Tierra-Firme,/ Islas, y Baxos/ de esta Navegacion,/ Longitud,/ y Altura de Polo,/ de sus Puertos,/ y Noticias de estas Habitaciones. [*Cadiz
1728 ?*] 3 *prel. leaves and* 161 *pp. Old red morocco.*
8*vo.* (12*s.* 6*d.* 2022)

NUNEZ CABECA DE VACA (ALVAR). ⁊ La
relacion y comentarios del gouerna/ dor Aluar nuñez cabeça de vaça, de lo acaefcido en las/ dos jor-

nadas quebizo a las Indias./ Con priuilegio./
¶ Esta tassada por los señores del consejo en Ocheta
y cinco mr̃s./ [*Colophon*] ꝛ Impresso en *Valladolid*, por Francisco fer-ꝛ/nandez de Cordoua. Año
de mil y quinien-/nientos y cinquenta y cinco años./
146 *leaves; viz. Title with engraved coat of Arms;
on the reverse* ' El Rey.' *signed* ' Francisco de Le-
desma.' *and* fol. ij. *to* fol. lvj. *the reverse blank.*ꝛ
Commentaꝛ/rios de Alvar Nvnez Cabe/ça de
vaca, adelantado y gouernador dela pro/uinca del
Rio de la Plata./ Scriptos por Pero hernandez
scriuano y secre-/tario de la prouincia. Y dirigidos
al sereniss./ muy alto y muy poderoso señor/ el In-
fante don Carlos. N. S./ 1 *page.* 'Prohemio.' 5 *pp;
the 4th page of the Prohemis is* ' Fol. lvij.' *and* fol.
lviij. *to* fol. clxiiii. [*for* cxliiii.] fol. xxv. [*for* xv.]
fol. lxi. [*for* lxii.] fol. lxxxiii. [*for* lxxxv.] *Black
letter. Fine large copy in blue mor. by Bedford.*
4to.   (10*l.* 10*s.* 2023)

NUNEZ CASTANO (Diego). Breve compendivm/
Hostivm Haere-/ticorvm Olandensivm/ aduentum
in Valdiuian, explorato/rem missum, & narrationem
eius,/ fugam illorum cum pacto redeun-/di : proui-
das dispositiones Prorregis :/ Classim expeditam ad
conditum e-/ius cum rebus necessarijs,/ & alia continens./ Gvbernante Exc. D.D./ Petro à Toleto &
Ley va Prorrege./ Regnante Philippo IIII./ Hispaniarum Rege./ Stvdio, et Labore/ Didaci Nuñes
Castaño Presbyteri./ *Limæ*, Anno 1645./ *Title, on
the reverse* ' Ad Oblationem Libri.' *and folioed leaves*
2-36. 16*mo.*   (2*l.* 12*s.* 6*d.* 2024)

NUNEZ DE HARO (Alonso). Nos el Dᴿ. D. Alonso Nuñez de Haro, y Peralta, por la Gracia de Dios,
y de la Santa Sede Apóstolica, Arzobispo de Mé-
gico, del Consejo de su Magestad, &ᴄ. [*Mexico*]. *a
Broadside in 2 Sheets. Folio.* (7*s.* 6*d.* 2025)

BJECTIONS (The) to the Taxation of our American Colonies, by the Legislature of Great Britain, Briefly Confider'd. *London*: J. Wilkie, 1765. *Title, and pp. 3-20.* 4to. (7s. 6d. 2026)

OBSERVATIONS on American Independency. *24 pp. signed* 'T. T. B.' 8vo. (4s. 6d. 2027)

OBSERVATIONS on the Conduct of Great Britain, with Regard to the Negociations and other Transactions Abroad. *London*, J. Roberts. 1729. *61 pp.* 8vo. (5s. 6d. 2028)

OBSERVATIONS on the Case of the Northern Colonies. *London*: J. Roberts, 1731. *31 pp. half mor.* 8vo. (7s. 6d. 2029)

OBSERVATIONS Occafion'd by reading a Pamphlet, intitled a Discourse concerning The Currencies of the Britifh Plantations in America. In a Letter to * * * * *. *London*: T. Cooper, 1741. *23 pp. half mor.* 8vo. (4s. 6d. 2030)

OBSERVATIONS On the Inflaving, importing and purchafing of Negroes; With fome Advice thereon, extracted from the Epiftle of the Yearly-Meeting of the People called Quakers held at London in the Year 1748. Second Edition. *Germantown* Printed by Christopher Sower. 1760. *16 pp.* 8vo. (7s. 6d. 2031)

OBSERVATIONS on a late State of the Nation. *London*: J. Dodsley, MDCCLXIX. *Title and 97 pp.* 4to. (4s. 6d. 2032)

OBSERVATIONS on a Late State of the Nation. The Fourth Edition. *London*, J. Dodsley, MDCC

LXIX. *Half-title, title, & 155 pp. Half morocco.*
8*vo.*   (4*s.* 6*d.* 2033)

OBSERVATIONS on Several Acts of Parliament,
passed In the Fourth, Sixth and Seventh Years of
His Present Majesty's Reign. Publifhed by the
Merchants of Boston: Boston: Printed by Edes
and Gill. *London:* Reprinted for G. Kearsly,
M.DCC.LXX. *Title and text 37 pp. half morocco.*
8*vo.*   (5*s.* 6*d.* 2034)

OBSERVATIONS: On the Reconciliation of Great-
Btitain, and the Colonies; In which are exhibited
Arguments for, and againft, that Measure. By a
Friend of American Liberty. *Philadelphia;* Print-
ed, by Robert Bell, in Third-Street. MDCCLXXVI.
32 pp. ' The Plan of an American Compact, with
Great-Britain. Firft Publifhed at New-York.' *pp*
33-40. *half mor.* 8*vo.*   (5*s.* 6*d.* 2035)

OBSERVATIONS on the Dutch Manifesto, addressed to the Earl of Shelburn. *London:* G.
Kearsly, [1781]. *iv and 27 pp.* 8*vo.* (4*s.* 6*d.* 2036)

OBSERVATIONS on the Commerce of the American States. With an Appendix; containing An
Account of all Rice, Indigo, Cochineal, Tobacco,
Sugar, Molaffes, and Rum imported into and exported from Great Britain the laft ten Years. Of
the Value of all Merchandize imported into and
exported from England. Of the Imports and Exports of Philadelphia, New-York, &c. Alfo an
Account of the Shipping employed in America
previous to the War. The Second Edition. *London:* J. Debrett, MDCCLXXXIII. *2 prel. leaves and
122 pp.* ' The Tables ' *etc.* 1 *page,* ' Contents of the
Appendix ' *iv pp.* ' Appendix.' No. I to XVIII.
Tables. Half mor. 8*vo.*   (5*s.* 6*d.* 2037)

OBSERVATIONS on the Fift Article of the Treaty
with America: And on The Neceffity of appointing a Judicial Enquiry into the Merits and Losses
of the American Loyalists. Printed by Order of
their Agents. *London:* G. Wilkie, MDCCLXXXIII.
19 pp. half mor. 8*vo.*   (4*s.* 6*d.* 2038)

OBSERVATIONS on a Pamphlet, entitled A State
of the Present Form of Government of the Province of Quebec; circulated in London, during the

last summer. With an Appendix, containing information on the subject. By a Citizen of Quebec. *London:* J. Stockdale, MDCCXC. *Title & 78 pp. Half mor.* 8vo.   (4s. 6d. 2039)

OBSERVATIONS on the Present War, the Projected Invasion, and a Decree of the National Convention, for the Emancipation of the Slaves in the French Colonies. [By the Rev. John Hampson]. *Sunderland:* [1793]. *Half-title, title, and pp. 3-61. half mor.* 8vo.   (3s. 6d. 2040)

OBSERVATIONS on the System by which Estates have been and are still Managed in Jamaica; and on the Apprenticeship introduced by the recent Abolition Act. By a Proprietor. *Edinburgh:* Maclachlan and Stewart. MDCCCXXXVI. *27 pp.* 8vo.   (2s. 6d. 2041)

O'CALLAGHAN (E. B.) Jesuit Relations of discoveries and other occurrences in Canada and the Northern and Western States of the Union. 1632-1672. By E. B. O'Callaghan, M.D. Corresponding Member of the New York Historical Society, and Honorary Member of the Historical Society of Connecticut. From the Proceedings of the New York Historical Society, Nov. 1847. *New York:* Press of the Historical Society. MDCCXLVII. *22 pp. calf.* 8vo.   (7s. 6d. 2042)

OCCASIONAL Reflections on the Importance of the War in America, And the Reasonableness and Justice of Supporting the King of Prussia, &c. In Defence of the Common Cause. Founded on a general View of the State and Connections of this Country; the General Syſtem of Europe; and the ambitious Deſigns of French Policy for overturning the Ballance of Power and Liberties of Europe. In a Letter to a Member of Parliament. *London:* J. Whiston and B. White. M.DCC.LVIII. *Half-title, title, and 139 pp. half mor.* 8vo.   (7s. 6d. 2043)

OCCOM (SAMPSON). A Sermon at the Execution of Moses Paul, an Indian; Who had been guilty of Murder, Preached at New Haven in America. By Samson Occom, A native Indian, and Miſſionary to the Indians, who was in England in 1776 [1766] and 1777, [1767] collecting for the

Indian Charity Schools. To which is added a
short Account of the Late Spread of the Gospel,
among the Indians. Also Observations on the
Language of the Muhhekaneew Indians; communicated to the Connecticut Society of Arts and
Sciences, by Jonathan Edwards, D.D. New
Haven, Connecticut: Printed 1788. *London:* Reprinted, 1788, *24 pp.* 'Observations,' *etc.* 16 *pp.*
8vo.   (5s. 6d.   2044)

OCKANICKON. A True/ Account/ of the/ Dying
Words/ of/ Ockanickon,/ an Indian/King./ Spoken
to/ Jahkursoe,/ His Brother's Son, whom he ap-
pointed/ King/ after him./ [*London*] Printed in
the Year 1683. 6 *pp. On the reverse of the title,*
'A Letter' *etc. dated* 'Burlington the 12th, of the
5th. Month, 1682.' *signed* 'John Cripps.'
4to.   (1l. 11s. 6d.   2045)

O'DONOJU (JUAN). Correspondencia entre el
General D. Juan O-Donoju, y el Brigadier D.
Francisco Lemaur, Y las últimas cartas de aquel al
general Dávila, con las respuestas de éste. [*Colophon*] *Habana.* 1821. Diaz de Castro. 25 *pp. half
mor.* 8vo.   (3s. 6d.   2046)

O'DONOJU (JUAN). Refutacion, con notas interes-
tantes, al parte que dirigio a Superior Gobierno el
Teniente General Don Juan O-Donoju sobre el
Tratado que Firmó en Córdoba. *Habana.*—1822.
Pedro Nolásce Boloña, *Title and* 15 *pp. half mor.*
8vo.   (3s. 6d.   2047)

OEXMELIN (ALEXANDRE OLIVIER). Histoire/ des/
Avanturiers/ qui se sont signalez dans les Indes,/
contenant/ ce qu'ils ont fait de plus remarquable/ de
puis vingt Anne'es./ Avec/ La Vie, les Mœurs, les
Coûtumes des Habitans de Saint Do-/mingue & de
la Tortuë, & une defcription exaɛte de ces/ lieux ;/
Où l'on voit/ L'etabliffement d'une Chambre des
Comptes dans les Indes,/ & un Etat, tiré de cette
Chambre, des Offices tant Eccle-/fiaftiques que Se-
culiers, où le Roy d'Efpagne pourvoit, les/ Re-
venus qu'il tire de l'Amerique, & ce que les plus
grands/ Princes de l'Europe y poffedent./ Le tout
enrichi de Cartes Geographiques & de Figures/ en
Taille-douce./ Par Alexandre Olivier Oexmelin./
A Paris,/ Jacques le Febure,/ M.DC.LXXXVIII./ Avec

Privilege du Roy./ *Two Volumes.* Tome Prémier.
12 prel. leaves including Engraved title, and 448 pp.
[*for* 248] *Table* 16 *pp. Maps at pp.* 1, 179. Tome
Second. 3 *prel. leaves and* 285 *pp. Table* 16 *pp.* 'Extrait du Privilege.' 1 *page. Map at page* 133. *Old
calf.* 12*mo.* (8*s.* 6*d* 2048)

OGDEN (UZAL). The Theological Preceptor; or
Youth's Religious Instructor. Containing a Summary of the Principles, Rise, and Progrefs of Religion, from the Creation of the World, to the Con-
fumation thereof;—together with moral Reflections,&c. and a Sketch of the Arguments in Favour
of Chriftianity. In a Series of Dialogues. By
Uzal Ogden Jun. a Candidate for Holy Orders.
New York: Printed by John Holt, M,DCC,LXXII.
xii and 259 *pp.* 12*mo.* (10*s.* 6*d.* 2049)

OGLE (*Sir* CHALONER). The Tryal of Sir Chaloner
Ogle, Kt. Rear-Admiral of the Blue, before the
Chief Juftice of Jamaica, For an Affault on the
Perfon of his Excellency Mr. Trelawney the Go-
vernor, committed in his own Houfe in Spanifh
Town on the 22d Day of July laft. With Authentic
Copies of the feveral Letters that paffed on that
Occafion, between Mr. Concanen, now Attorney-
General of the Ifland, Sir Chaloner Ogle, the Go-
vernor, and A—l V—. [Admiral Vernon.] Lon-
don Printed: *Dublin* Reprinted MDCCXLII. 16 *pp.
Half morocco.* 8*vo.* (7*s.* 6*d.* 2050)

OGLE (*Sir* CHALONER). The Tryal of Sir Chaloner
Ogle, Kt. Rear Admiral of the Blue. Before the
Chief Justice of Jamaica, For an Affault on the
Perfon of his Excellency Mr. Trelawney the Go-
vernor, committed in his own Houfe in Spanifh
Town, on the 22d Day of July laft. With Authen-
tic Copies of the feveral Letters that paffed on that
Occafion, between Mr. Concanen, now Attorney
General of the Ifland, Sir Chaloner Ogle, the Go-
vernor, and A—l V—. *London:* W. Webb,
M,DCCXLIII. 32 *pp. half mor.* 8*vo.* (7*s.* 6*d.* 2051)

OGLETHORPE (GENERAL). An Impartial Account Of the late Expedition Againft St. Augustine
Under General Oglethorpe. Occafioned by The
Suppreffion of the Report, made by a Committee
of the General Affembly in South-Carolina, tranf-

mitted, under the Great Seal of that Province, to
their Agent in England, in order to be printed.
With an Exact Plan of the Town, Caftle and Harbour of St. Auguftine, and the adjacent Coaft of
Florida; fhewing the Difpofition of our Forces on
that Enterprize. *London:* J. Huggonson, 1742.
68 pp. With Plan of St. Augustine. Half mor.
8vo. (10s. 6d. 2052)

OLD ENGLAND for Ever, or, Spanifh Cruelty
difplay'd. [*London*, 1741?] *pp.* 7-320. *Title and
prel. leaves wanting. Old calf.* 8vo. (7s. 6d. 2053)

ONA (PEDRO DE). Aravco/ donado./ Compvesto
por el/ Licenciado Pedro de Oña, natural de los/
Infantes de Engol en Chile, Colegial del/ Real
Colegio Mayor de San Felipe, y/ San Marcos
fundado en la Ciu-/dad de Lima./ Dirigido a Don
Hvrtado/ de Mendoça, Primogenito de don Garcia
Hur-/tado de Mendoça, Marques de/ Cañete, &c./
Año, 1605./ Con privilegio ;/ En *Madrid*, por Ivan
de la Cuefta./ Vendefe en cafa de Francifco Lopez./
16 prel. leaves; Text 342 folioed leaves. 'Tabla' 3
pp. Old calf. 8vo. (3l. 13s. 6d. 2054)

OPPORTUNITY (THE), or Reasons for an Immediate Alliance with St. Domingo. By the Author
of " The Crisis of the Sugar Colonies." *London:*
J. Hatchard, 1804. *viii and text* 156 *pp. Unbound.*
8vo. (3s. 6d. 2055)

ORDERS in Council; or, an Examination of the
Justice, Legality, and Policy of the New System
of Commercial Regulations. With an Appendix
of State Papers, Statutes, and Authorities. The
Second Edition. *London:* Longman, 1808. *Half-
title, title, and* 120 *pp.* 8vo. (3s. 6d. 2056)

ORFORD (ROBERT, *Earl of*). A Further Report
from the Committee of Secrecy, Appointed to Enquire into the Conduct of Robert, Earl of Orford;
During the laft Ten Years of his being Firft Commissioner of the Treasury, and Chancellor and
Under-Treafurer of his Majesty's Exchequer. Delivered the 30th of June 1742. *London:* T. Leech,
1742. *132 pp.* ' No. 13' *a folded sheet between pp.*
128 & 129. half mor. 8vo. (4s. 6d. 2057)

ORIGIN (THE) of the Whale bone-petticoat. A

Satyr. *Boston*, Auguſt 2d. 1714. 8 *pp. in Verse.*
8*vo.* (10*s.* 6*d.* 2058)

OSORIO (Hieronymo). De Rebvs,/ Emmanvelis
Regis Lv-/sitaniæ Invictissimi Virtvte/ et Avspicio
gestis libri/ dvodecim./ Auctore Hieronymo Oſorio/
Episcopo Sylvensi./ *Olysippone.*/ Apud Antonium
Gondiſaluũ Typographum./ Anno Domini m.d.
lxxj./ Cvm Privilegio Regio./ 480 *pp. including
the title. Privilege and Errata* 2 *pp. Fine copy, Old
calf. Folio.* (1*l.* 1*s.* 2059)

OTHER (The) Side of the Queſtion: Or a Defence
of the Liberties of North-America. In Answer to
a late Friendly Address to All Reaſonable Americans, on The Subject of Our Political Confusions.
By a Citizen. *New York:* Printed by James Rivington, fronting Hanover-Square. m,dcc,lxxiv.
30 *pp. half mor.* 8*vo.* (7*s.* 6*d.* 2060)

OTIS (James). The Rights of the Britiſh Colonies
Aſſerted and proved. By James Otis Eſq, *Boston:*
Printed and Sold by Edes and Gill, in Queen-
Street. M,dcc,lxiv. 80 *pp. Half morocco.*
8*vo.* (5*s.* 6*d.* 2061)

OTIS (James). The Rights of the Britiſh Colonies
Aſſerted and proved. By James Otis, Eſq; The
Second Edition. Boston, New England, Printed;
London Reprinted for J. Almon, [1765?] 120 *pp.
half mor.* 8*vo.* (5*s.* 6*d.* 2062)

OTIS (James). The Rights of the Britiſh Colonies
Aſſerted and proved. By James Otis, Eſq; The
Third Edition, corrected. Boston, New-England,
Printed: *London* Reprinted, for J. Williams, 1766.
120 *pp. half mor.* 8*vo.* (5*s.* 6*d.* 2063)

OTIS (James). A Vindication of the Britiſh Colonies. By James Otis, Eſq; Of Boston. Boston,
printed: *London*, reprinted for J. Almon, 1769. 2
prel. leaves and text 48 *pp. Half morocco.*
8*vo.* (6*s.* 6*d.* 2064)

OUSELEY (William Gore). Remarks on the Sta-
tistics and Political Institutions of the United
States, with some Observations on the Ecclesiastical System of America, her Sources of Revenue,
&c. To which are added Statistical Tables, &c.
By William Gore Ouseley, Esq. Attaché to his Ma-

jesty's Legation at Washington. *London :* J. Rodwell, 1832. *xv and* 208 *pp.* 8*vo.* (3*s.* 6*d.* 2065)

OVALLE (ALONSO DE). Historica/ Relacion/ Del Reyno de Chile,/ Y delas miſſiones, y miniſterios que exercita en el/ la Compañia de Ieſvs./ A Nvestro Senor/ Ieſv Christo/ Dios Hombre,/ Y ala Santiſsima Virgen, y Madre/ Maria/ Señora del Cielo, y dela Tierra,/ y alos Santos/ Ioseph, Ioachin, Ana/ ſus Padres, y Aguelos./ Alonso de Ovalle/ Dela Compañia de Ieſvs Natural de Santia-/go de Chile, y ſu Procurador à Roma. En *Roma,* por Franciſco Cauallo. M.DC.XLVI./ Con licencia delos Superiores./ 5 *prel. leaves ; viz.* [*Advertisement*] Varias, y Cvriosas Noticias del Reino de Chile,' *etc,* 1 *page the reverse blank ; Title on the reverse* 'Qveſta Relatione del Chile,' *etc.* ' Prologo al letor.' 3 *pp.* ' Aduertencia para no errar en poner las Imagenes,' *etc.* 2 *pp :* ' Protesta del Avtor.' 1 *page. Text* 456 *pp. With Map of Chile, and* 37 *Copperplates at pp.* 51, 58, 88, 90, 91, 92, 104, 107, 186 (3), 288, 302, 322 (23), 393. *With* 18 *woodcuts at the end. Vellum. Folio.* (3*l.* 3*s.* 2066)

OVIEDO (HERNANDEZ DE). La hiſtoria general/ delas Indias./ ৯৶ Con priuilegio imperial ৯৶/ [*Colophon*] De *Seuilla* a treynta/ dias del mes de Setiembre: de M. d. ɼ treynta ɼ cinco años [1535]. *Title in black and red, having on the reverse* 11 *lines giving a fuller description of the book ; Preface* ' Libro primero' 6 *pp ; Text in* cxciij *folioed leaves. Very fine copy in Black Letter. Folio.* (10*l.* 10*s.* 2067)
At the end of the book is the autograph of the author.

OVIEDO Y VALDES (GONÇALO FERNANDEZ DE). ⁋ Libro. XX. De la ſegunda parte de la general/ hiſtoría de las Indías. Eſcrípta por el Capítan/ Gonçalo Fernandez de Ouíedo, y Valdes. Al=/cayde de la fortaleza y puerto de Sācto Domín/go, d'la iſla Eſpañola. Croniſta d' ſu Mageſtad./ Que trata del eſtrecho de Magallans./ ⁋ En *Valladolid.* Por Franciſco Fernandez de Cordoua,/ Impreſſor de su Mageſtad. Año de M.D.LVII./ [*Colophon*] ⁋ Impreſſo en Valladolid, por frā=/cisco fernandez de Cordoua./ En eſte año de M.D.LVII./ 64 *folioed leaves including title. Black letter. Fine copy. Folio.* (4*l.* 14*s.* 6*d.* 2068)

AINE (Robert Treat). The Works,
in Verse and Prose, of the late
Robert Treat Paine, Jun. Esq.
With Notes. To which are prefixed, Sketches of his Life, Character, and Writings. *Boston:* J.
Belcher. 1812. *xc and 464 pp. Er-*
rata 1 *page. With Portrait of Paine. Green mo-*
rocco extra gilt. 8vo.   (10s. 6d.   2069)

PAINE (Thomas). The American Crisis, and a
Letter to Sir Guy Carleton, on the murder of Captain Huddy, and the intended retaliation on Captain Asgill, of the Guards. By Thomas Paine,
Author of Common Sense—Rights of Man—Age
of Reason—and the Decline and Fall of the English System of Finance. *London:* Daniel Isaac
Eaton, *Title and* 293 *pp.* 8vo.   (7s. 6d.   2070)

PAINE (Thomas). Observations on Paine's Rights
of Man, in a Series of Letters, By Publicola,
[John Adams]. *Newcastle:* Hall and Elliot. 36
pp. 12mo.   (3s. 6d.   2071)

PAINE (Thomas). A Letter addressed to the Abbe
Raynal of the Affairs of North-America. In which
The Miſtakes in the Abbe's Account of the Revo-
lution of America are corrected and cleared up.
By Thomas Paine, M.A. Of the University of
Pennsylvania, and Author of a Tract, entitled
" Common Sense." Philadelphia, printed: *Lon-*
don, reprinted, C. Dilly, M.DCC.LXXXII. *viii and* 76
pp. half mor. 8vo.   (3s. 6d.   2072)

PAINE (Thomas). Common Sense: Addreſſed to
the Inhabitants of America, On the following Interesting Subjects. I. Of the Origin and Deſign of
Government in general, with conciſe Remarks on

the Englifh Conftitution. II. Of Monarchy and
Hereditary Succession. III. Thoughts on the
prefent State of American Affairs. IV. Of the
prefent State of America, with fome Mifcellaneous
Reflections. A New Edition. With feveral Additions in the Body of the Work. To which is
added, an Appendix; together with an Addrefs to
the People called Quakers. The New Edition
here given increafes the Work upwards of One
Third. By Thomas Paine. Secretary to the Committee for Foreign Affairs to Congrefs during the
American War, and Author of the Rights of Man,
and a Letter to the Abbé Raynal. *London:* Printed
and sold by all the Booksellers. M.DCC.XCII. 58 *pp.*
12*mo.*   (3*s.* 6*d.* 2073)

PAINE (THOMAS). Common Sense; addressed to
the Inhabitants of America, On the following interefting Subjects: I. Of the Origin and Defign of
Government in general, with concife Remarks on
the Englifh Conftitution. II. Of Monarchy and
Hereditary Succeffion. III. Thoughts on the
Prefent State of American Affairs. IV. Of the
prefent Ability of America, with fome mifcellaneous Reflections. A New Edition with feveral Additions in the Body of the Work. To which is
added, an Appendix; together with an Addrefs
to the People called Quakers. N. B. The New
Edition here given increafes the Work upwards of
One-Third. By Thomas Paine, Secretary to the
Committee for Foreign Affairs to Congrefs, during
the American War, and Author of the Rights of
Man, and a Letter to the Abbe Raynal. *London:*
H. D. Symonds, 1792. 36 *pp. With Portrait of
Thomas Paine.* 12*mo.*   (4*s.* 6*d.* 2074)

PAINE (THOMAS). A Letter addressed to the Abbe
Raynal, on the affairs of North-America. In which
the mistakes in the Abbe's Account of the Revolution of America are corrected and cleared up. By
Thomas Paine, Secretary for Foreign Affairs to
Congress during the American War, and Author
of Common Sense, and the Rights of Man. *London:* J. Ridgway, M,DCC,XCII. 46 *pp. Unbound.*
12*mo.*   (4*s.* 6*d.* 2075)

PAINE (THOMAS). Letter addressed to the Addressers, of the late Proclamation. By Thomas Paine, Secretary for Foreign Affairs to Congress in the American War, and Author of the Works intitled " Common Sense," " Rights of Man, Two Parts," &c. *London:* H. D. Symonds, 1792. 40 *pp.* 12*mo.* (3*s.* 6*d.* 2076)

PAINE (Thomas). Miscellaneous Articles, by Thomas Paine. Consisting of A Letter to the Marquis of Lansdowne. A Letter to the Authors of the Republican. A Letter to the Abbe Syeyes. Thoughts on the Peace, and the Probable Advantages thereof. First Letter to Mr. Secretary Dundas. Letter to Lord Onslow. Second Letter to Mr. Dundas. And A Letter to the People of France. *London:* J. Ridgway, M.DCCXCII. 36 *pp.* 12*mo.* (3*s.* 6*d.* 2077)

PAINE (Thomas). Rights of Man: Being an Answer to Mr. Burke's Attack on the French Revolution. By Thomas Paine, Secretary for Foreign Affairs to Congress in the American War, and Author of the Works intitled " Common Sense," and " A Letter to the Abbe Raynal." Part I. *London:* H. D. Symonds, M,DCC,XCII. *iv and* 78 *pp. and* 1 *p.* 12*mo.* (4*s.* 6*d.* 2078)

PAINE (Thomas). Rights of Man; part the Second. Combining Principle and Practice. By Thomas Paine, Secretary for Foreign Affairs to Congress in the American War, and Author of the Works entitled " Common Sense," and the " First Part of the Rights of Man." *London:* H. D. Symonds, 1792. 94 *pp. and* 1 *p.* 12*mo.* (4*s.* 6*d.* 2079)

PAINE (Thomas). Rights of Man : Part the Second combining Principle and Practice. By Thomas Paine, Secretary for Foreign Affairs to Congress in the American War, and Author of the Works intitled " Common Sense," And the " First Part of the Rights of Man." *London:* Printed for the Booksellers. M,DCC,XCII. 82 *pp. Unbound.* 12*mo.* (3*s.* 6*d.* 2080)

PAINE (Thomas). Mr. Paine's Principles and Schemes of Government examined, and his errors detected. *Edinburgh:* J. & J. Fairbairn, 1792. 2 *prel. leaves and* 60 *pp.* 8*vo.* (3*s.* 6*d.* 2081)

PAINE (Thomas). Paine's Political and Moral
Maxims; selected from the Fifth Edition of Rights
of Man, Part I. and II. With Explanatory Notes
and Elucidations; additional interefting Óbferva-
tions on the prefent State of Public Affairs; and
important information for the benefit, not of the
Houfe of Commons at Weftminfter but of the whole
Commons of Great Britain and Ireland. And an
Intro-duétory Letter to Mr. Paine. By a Free-
Born Englishman. *London:* Printed for the Booksellers. 1792. 47 *pp.* 8*vo.*   (3*s.* 6*d.*   2082)

PALAFOX (Juan de, *El Obispo de la Puebla de los
Angeles*). Al/ Rey Nvestro Señor./ Satisfacion/
al Memorial de los/ Religiosos de la Compañia/
del nombre de Iesvs de la/ Nveva-España./ Por/
La Dignidad Epifcopal de la Puebla de los Angeles./ Sobre la Execvcion, y Obediencia/ del
Breue Apoftolico de N. Santifsimo Padre/ Inno-
cencio X./ Expedido en sv favor a XIIII./ de
Mayo de m.dc.xlviii./ Y/ Paffado repetidamente,
y mandado executar por el/ Supremo Confejo de
las Indias./ En el qual determinò fu Santidad
veinte y feis Decretos/ Sacramentales, y Iurifdic-
cionales, importantes/ al bien de las almas./ Año
de m.dc.lii./ *Title, reverse blank; 3 leaves and
folioed leaves* 4 *to* 157. *Fine copy. Vellum.*
Folio.   (1*l.* 1*s.*   2083)

PALAFOX (Juan de, *El Obispo de la Puebla de los
Angeles*). [Memorial del Dr. Palafox al Rey Sobre
el Tratamiento de los Indios] *Running title*, Vir-
tudes/ del Indio./ [*Puebla*, 1634?] *Vellum.*
4*to.*   (10*l.* 10*s.*   2084)

This Memorial, respecting the Virtues of the Indians, was probably privately printed for the use of the King and the Council
  of the Indies, as it is without date, place of printing, name of
  Printer, title or any of the usual ' *Privileges.*' It fills 93 pages,
  and is divided into 21 Chapters preceded by an Introductory Address to the King. The work is a panegyric of the Indians, as
  will appear by the heading of the Chapters; viz.
    Cap. I. Quam dignos fon los Indios del amparo Real | de
      V. Mageftad, por la fu auidad con que re- | cibieron la Ley
      de Chrifto Señor Nueftro | con el caler de fus Catolicas |
      vanderas. |
    Cap. II. De lo que merecen los Indios el amparo Real | de
      V. Mageftad, por el fauor grande con que | fe exercitan en
      la Religion Chrif- | tiana. |
    Cap. III. De lo que merecen el amparo Real de V. M. | los
      Indios, por la fu auidad con que han en- | trado en fu Real
      Corona, y fu fide- | lidad conftantif- | fima. |
    Cap. IV. Del valor, y esfuerço de los Indios, y que fu |
      lealtad, y rendimiento a la Corona de V. | Mageftad, no
      procedo de bajez a de | animo, fino de vir- | tud. |

Cap. V. Quandignos fon los Indios de la proteccion ¦ Real, por las vtilidades que han caufædo | a la Corona de Ef- | paña. |

Cap. VI. De la innocencia de los Indios, y que fe hallan | comumente eſſentos de los vicios de foberuia, | ambicion, codicia, auaricia, ira è embidia, | juegos, blasfemias, jur amentos, y mur- | muraciones. |

Cap. VII. De otros tres vicios de Senfualidad, Gule, | y Perez a, en que fuelen incurrir los | Indios. |

Cap. VIII. De la pobreza del Indio. |

Cap. IX. De la paciencia del Indio. |

Cap. X. De la Liberalidad del Indio. |

Cap. XI. De la honeſtidad del Indio. |

Cap. XII. De la parfimonia del Indio en fu comida. |

Cap. XIII. De la obediencia del Indio. |

Cap. XIIII. De la difcrecion, y elegancia del Indio. |

Cap. XV. De la agudez, y promptitud del Indio. |

Cap. XVI. De la induſtria del Indio, feñaladamente en | las Artes mecanicas. |

Cap. XVII. De la juſticia del Indio. |

Cap. XVIII. De la valentia del Indio. |

Cap. XIX. De la Humildad, Cortefia Silencio, y Maña | del Indio. |

Cap. XX. De la Limpieça del Indio, y de fu Paz. |

Cap. XXI. Refpondefe à algunas objeciones que fe pueden | oponer. |

PALAFOX (JUAN DE, *El Obispo de la Puebla de los Angeles*). Carta Pastoral/ del Illvst.mo y R.mo Señor Obispo/ de la Pvebla de los Angeles,/ que oy es de osma./ A las Religiosas/ de aqvel Obis-pado,/ sir viendo aqvella Santa Iglesia/ Año de 1641./ Es muy vtil para el conocimiento de las obligacio-/nes de las Efpofas de Jefu Chrifto bien nueſtro,/ alteza de fu Dignidad, y atencion que/ deuen tener a fer-/uirle./ Imprimefe por orden de fu Eminencia, y concede cien/ dias de Indulgencia à quien leyere, ò oyere esta/ Carta Pastoral, tan docta, y efpiritual, En To-/*ledo* à 25. de Março de 1659. años./ *Title reverse blank, and folioed leaves* 2-10. *4to.* (1*l.* 1*s.* 2085)

PALOU (FRANCISCO). Relacion Historica de la vida y Apostolicas Tareas del venerable Padre Fray Junipero Serra, Y de las Misiones que fundó en la California Septentrional, y nuevos estable-cimientos de Monterey. Escrita Por el R. P. L. Fr. Francisco Palou, Guardian actual del Colegio Apostólico de S. Fernando de México, y Discipulo del Venerable Fundador: Dirigida a su Santa Pro-vincia de la Regular observancia de Nrô. S. P. S. Francisco de la Isla de Mallorca. A Expensas de Don Miguel Gonzalez Calderon Sindico de dicho Apostolico Colegio. Impresa en *Mexico*, en la Im-prenta de Don Felipe de Zúñiga y Ontiveros, calle del Espiritu Santo, año de 1787. 14 *prel. leaves,*

and 344 pp. plate at p. 1 & Map of California en-
graved on Copper by Diego Froncoso in Mexico 1787.
Fine copy. Vellum. 4to.   (*2l. 2s.* 2086)

PANAMA. Original Papers Relating to the Expedition to Panama. *London:* M. Cooper, M.DCC.
XLIV. *Title and* 224 *pp. Wanting pp.* 207-8. *half*
mor. 8vo.   (*7s. 6d.* 2087)

PAPERS and Letters on Agriculture, Recommended
to the Attention of the Canadian Farmers, By the
Agricultural Society in Canada. *Quebec:* Printed
by Samuel Neilson, Nº. 3 Mountain-street.
M.DCC.XC. *In English and French on opposite pages*
5 *prel. leaves and* 34 *doubly numbered pp. Thick*
paper: old green morocco extra, tooled sides. With
the Autograph of Bishop Inglis of Nova Scotia on the
title page. 8vo.   (*7s. 6d.* 2088)

PARISH (ELIJAH). A Sermon preached at Boston,
November 3, 1814, before the Society for Propa-
gating the Gospel among the Indians and others in
North-America. By Elijah Parish, D.D. S.A.S.
Boston: Nathaniel Willis, 1814. 44 *pp. Unbound.*
8vo.   (*2s. 6d.* 2089)

PARKER (THOMAS). The/ Visions and Prophecies/
of/ Daniel expounded :/ Wherein the Miſtakes of
former/ Interpreters are modeſtly diſcovered, and
the true/ meaning of the Text made plain by/ the
Words and Circumſtances of it./ The ſame alſo illuſtrated by clear inſtances taken/ out of Histories,
which relate the Events/ of time, myſtically fore-
told by the Holy Prophet./ Amongſt other things
of Note, touching/ The Two Witneſſes, the New
Jeruſalem, the Thouſand/ yeers, etc. Here is propounded a new Way for the finding out of the/ de-
terminate time ſignified by Daniel in his Seventy
Weeks :/ When it did begin, and when we are to
expeᴄt the end thereof,/ Very confiderable, in re-
ſpeᴄt of the great ſtirs and tumults/ of this preſent
Age wherein we live./ By Thomas Parker of Newbery in Berkſhire, and now Paſtor to the/ Church
at Newbery in New-England./ *London,* Printed
by Ruth Raworth and John Field, for Edmund
Paxton, dwelling/ at Pauls chain neer Doᴄtors
Commons. 1646./ 2 *prel. leaves and* 156 *pp. Old*
calf. 4to.   (*2l. 2s.* 2090)

PARKINSON (SYDNEY). A Journal of a Voyage to the South Seas, in his Majefty's Ship, The Endeavour. Faithfully tranfcribed from the Papers of the late Sydney Parkinson, Draughtfman to Joseph Banks, Efq. on his late Expedition, with Dr. Solander, round the World. Embellished with Views and Defigns, delineated by the Author, and engraved by capital Artifts. *London:* Stanfield Parkinson, M.DCC.LXXIII. *xxiii and 212 pp. Errata 2 pp. Portrait and 27 Plates. Large Paper. Calf. 4to.* (10s. 6d. 2091)

PARSONS (JONATHAN). Good News From a Far Country. In Seven Discourses From 1 Tim I. 15. Deliveredat the Presbyterian Church in Newbury: And now publifhed at the Defire of many of the Hearers and Others. By Jonathan Parsons, A.M. And Minifter of the Gofpel there. *Portsmouth,* in New-Hampshire: Printed and Sold by Daniel Fowle. 1756. *viii and 168 pp. 8vo.* (7s. 6d. 2092)

PARSONS (JONATHAN). To live is Christ, to die is Gain. A Funeral Sermon On the Death of the Rev. Mr. George Whitefield, Chaplain to the Countefs of Huntington, Who died fuddenly of a fit of the Afthma, at New-bury Port, at Six of the Clock Lord's Day Morning, Sept. 30th, 1770. The Sermon preached the fame Day, Afternoon. By Jonathan Parsons, A.M. And Minifter of the Prefbyterian Church there. To which are added, An Account of his Interment; The Speech over his Grave, By the Rev. Mr. Jewet; And fome Verses to his Memory, By the Rev. Tho. Gibbons, D.D. Poitsmouth, New-Hampshire, Printed, *London* Reprinted, For James Buckland, 1771. *2 prel. leaves and 36 pp. 8vo.* (4s. 6d. 2093)

PARSONS (MOSES). A Sermon preached at Cambridge, Before his Excellency Thomas Hutchinson, Esq; Governor: His Honor Andrew Oliver, Esq; Lieutenant-Governor, The Honorable his Majesty's Council, and the honorable House of Representatives, Of the Province of the Massachusetts-Bay in New-England, May 27th 1772. Being the Anniverfary for the Election of His Majesty's Council for faid Province. By Moses Parsons, A.M. Paftor of the Church at Newbury Falls,

Boston: Printed by Edes and Gill, Printers to the Honorable House of Representatives. M,DCC,LXXII. 43 pp. half mor. 8vo. (3s. 6d. 2094)

PARTICULAR (A) Account of the Commencement and Progress of the Insurrection of the Negroes in St. Domingo, which began in August, 1791: Being a Translation of the Speech made to the National Assembly, The 3d of November, 1791, by the Deputies from the General Assembly of the French Part of St. Domingo. The Second Edition, With Notes and an Appendix, containing Extracts from authentic Papers. *London:* J. Sewell, M.DCC. XCII. *iv and* 47 pp. 8vo. (4s. 6d. 2095)

PASCHOUD (MR.) Historico-Political Geography: Or, A Particular Description Of the Several Countries in the World; in their Situation, Extent, Air, Soil, Divisions, Provinces, Rivers, Commodities, Rarities, Capital Cities, Chief Towns, Inhabitants, Manners, Languages, Populousness, &c. The Genealogy, Pretensions, Government, Titles, Revenues, Residence, &c. of their Kings and Princes. Their respective States, Courts of Justice, Laws, Nobility, Orders of Knighthood, Clergy, Archbishopricks, Bishopricks, Universities, and Religion. The Second Edition, with Additions. *London:* William France, 1729. *Title xiv and* 395 *pp; Index* 5 *pp. Old calf.* 8vo. (7s. 6d. 2096)

PATRIOT (THE). Addressed to the Electors of Great Britain. *London:* MDCCLXXIV. *Title and* 33 pp. half mor. 8vo. (4s. 6d. 2097)

PATRIOTS (THE) of North-America: A Sketch [*in verse*]. With Explanatory Notes. *New-York:* Printed in the Year M,DCC,LXXV. *iv and* 48 pp. half mor. 8vo. (10s. 6d. 2098)

PATTERSON (WALTER). Some Facts stated, relative to the conduct of Walter Patterson, Esq; Late Governor and Lieutenant-Governor of the Island St. John. Of Edmund Fanning, Esq; The present Lieutenant-Governor; and of Peter Stewart, Esq; Chief Justice of the said Island; Occasioned by some Notes, contained in a Pamphlet, entitled The Criminating Complaint, &c. &c. *Title and* 40 *pp. half mor.* 8vo. (4s. 6d. 2099)

PAULLI (SIMON). Simonis Paulli, D./ Medici Re-

gii, ac Prælati Aarhufienfis/ Commentarius/ De/
Abusu Tabaci/ Americanorum Veteri,/ et/ Herbæ
Thee/ Asiasticorum in Europa Novo,/ Quæ ipfiffi-
ma eft Chamæleagnos Dodonæi,/ Editio Secunda
priori auctior & correctior./ *Argentorati/* Sumptibus B. Authoris Filii Simonis Paulli Bibliop./
Anno Salutis M.DC.LXXXI./ *30 prel. leaves including Portrait & Arms, &c. of Author, and* 88 *pp.* 'Syl-
labus Auctorum.' 4 *pp.* ' Index Rerum.' 7 *pp.* 2
foiding plates at pp. 76 & 77. *4to.* (10s. 6d. 2100)

PAUW (*Mr.* DE). Recherches Philosophiques sur
les Americains, ou Mémoires intéreffants pour servir à l'Hiftoire de l'Efpece Humaine. Par Mr. de
P***. Avec une Differtation fur l'Amérique &
les Américains, par Don Pernety. Et la Défenfe
de l'Auteur des Recherches contre cette Differtation. A *Berlin,* M.DCC.LXX. *Three Volumes.* Tome
I. *xxiv and* 326 *pp. Table* 25 *pp.* Tome II. *Title and*
366 *pp. Table* 31 *pp.* Tome III. 136 *pp.* '*Defense,*'
etc. 256 *pp. Old calf. Small* 8*vo.* (10s. 6d. 2101)

PAUW (*Mr.* DE). Recherches Philosophiques sur
les Americains, ou Mémoires intéreffants pour
fervir à l'Hiftoire de l'Efpece Humaine. Par M.
de P***. Avec une Differtation fur l'Amérique
& les Américains, par Dom Pernety. A *Londres.*
M.D.CC.LXXI. *Three Volumes.* Tome Premier. *xx
and* 276 *pp. Table* 26 *pp. The 2nd and 3rd are of the
edition above.* 12*mo.* (10s. 6d. 2102)

PAUW (*Mr.* DE). Selections from les Recherches
Philosophiques sur les Americains of M. Pauw.
By Mr. W***. [Webb.] *Bath,* Printed by R.
Cruttwell. MDCCLXXXIX. *2 prel. leaves and* 211 *pp.*
8*vo.* (15s. 2103)

Fifty copies only of this work were printed, and given to the Author's friends.

PAYNE (JOHN HOWARD). Memoirs of John Howard Payne, the American Roscius: With Criti-
cisms on his Acting, in the various Theatres of
America, England and Ireland. Compiled from
Authentic Documents. *London:* John Miller,
1815. *2 prel. leaves and* 131 *pp. With Portrait of
Payne.* 8*vo.* (4s. 6d. 2104)

PEALE (REMBRANDT). Account of the Skeleton
of The Mammoth, a non-descript Carnivorous

Animal of Immense Size, Found in America. By Rembrandt Peale, the Proprietor. *London:* E. Lawrence, 1802. *46 pp. 8vo.*   (*4s. 6d.* 2105)

PECKARD (P.) Memoirs of the Life of Mr. Nicholas Ferrar. By P. Peckard, D.D. Master of Magdalen College, Cambridge. *Cambridge,* J. Archdeacon, MDCCXC. *xvi and* 316 *pp. With Portrait and Pedigree of Nicholas Ferrar.* 8vo.   (*12s. 6d.* 2106)

PEMBERTON (EBENEZER). Sermons and Discourses on Several Occasions. By the late Reverend and Learned Ebenezer Pemberton, A. M. Pastor of the South Church in Bofton, and Fellow of Harvard College in Cambridge, New-England. To which is added, A Sermon after his Funeral preached by the Reverend Mr. Colman, Pastor of a Church in Bofton: Containing fome Account of Mr. Pemberton's Life and Character. Now first Collected into One Volume. *London:* J. Batley, MDCCXXVII. *4 prel. leaves and* 310 *pp. Old calf.* 8vo.   (*7s. 6d.* 2107)

PEMBERTON (EBENEZER). Heaven the Refidence of the Saints. A Sermon Occafioned by the fudden and much lamented Death of the Rev. George Whitefield, A.M. Chaplain to the Right Honourable the Countefs of Huntington. Delivered at the Thurfday Lecture at Boston, in America, October 11, 1770. By Ebenezer Pemberton, D.D. Pastor of a Church in Bofton. To which is added, An Elegiac Poem on his Death, By Phillis, a Negro Girl, of Seventeen Years of Age, Belonging to Mr. J. Wheatley of Bofton. Bofton, Printed: *London,* Reprinted, For E. and C. Dilly. M.DCC. LXXI. *31 pp. half mor. 8vo.*   (*4s. 6d.* 2108)

PEMBERTON (JOHN). A Testimony of the Monthly Meeting of Friends, at Pyrmont in Westphalia, Germany, concerning John Pemberton, of Philadelphia in North America: With his Epistle to the Inhabitants of Amsterdam. Philadelphia printed: *London* reprinted James Phillips & Son, 1798. *36 pp. 12mo.*   (*1s. 6d.* 2109)

PEMBERTON (JOHN). A Testimony of the Monthly Meeting of Friends, at Pyrmont in Westphalia, Germany, concerning John Pemberton, of Phila-

delphia in North America : With his Epistle to the
Inhabitants of Amsterdam. *Philadelphia :* Printed
by Henry Tuckniss. 1798. *v and pp.* 7-36.
12*mo.* (4*s.* 6*d.* 2110)

PENA MONTENEGRO (Alonso de la). Itine-
rario/ para/ Parochos/ de Indios,/ en que se tratan
las materias/ mas particulares, tocantes à ellos,
para fu/ buena Adminiftracion :/ Compuefto/ por
El llustrissimo, y Reverendissimo/ Señor Doctor
Don Alonso/ de la Peña Montenegro,/ Obispo del
Obispado de San Francisco del Quito,/ del confejo
de fu Mageftad, Colegial que fue del Colegio mayor/
de la Univerfidad de Santiago, &c./ Nueva Edicion Purgada de muchos Yerros./ En *Amberes.*/
Por Henrico y Cornelio Verdussen./ Año m.dc.
xcviii./ Con Licencia./ *28 prel. leaves: Text 697
pp. double columns, followed by Indice 43 leaves & 1
page. Old calf. 4to.* (1*l.* 1*s.* 2111)

PENHALLOW (Samuel). The History of the
Wars of New-England, With the Eaftern Indians.
Or, a Narrative Of their continued Perfidy and
Cruelty, from the 10th of Auguft, 1703. To the
Peace renewed 13th of July, 1713. And from the
25th of July, 1722. To their Submiffion 15th December, 1725. Which was Ratified Auguft 5th,
1726. By Samuel Penhallow, Esq. *Boston :*
Printed by T. Fleet, for S. Gerrifh at the lower
end of Cornhill, and D. Henchman over-againft
the Brick Meeting-Houfe in Cornhill, 1726. 4
prel. leaves and 134 *pp.* ' Advertifement.' 1 *page.
Red mor. by Bedford. Small* 8*vo.* (10*l.* 10*s.* 2112)

PENINGTON (Isaac). An/ Examination/ of
the/ Grounds or Caufes,/ Which are faid to induce
the Court of/ Bofton in New=England to make
that Order or Law/ of Banifhment upon pain of
Death againft the Quakers ;/ As alfo of the Grounds
and Confiderations by them pro-/duced to manifeft
the warrantablenefs and juftnefs both of/ their
making and executing the fame, which they now
ftand/ deeply engaged to defend, having already
thereupon put/ two of them to death./ As alfo of
fome further Grounds for juftifying of/ the fame,
in an Appendix to John Norton's Book (which/
was Printed after the Book it felf, yet as part
thereof) whereto/ he is faid to be appointed by the

General Court./ And likewiſe of the Arguments
briefly hinted in that which/ is called, A true Relation of the Proceedings againſt the Quakers, &c./
Whereunto ſomewhat is added about the Authority
and Go-/vernment which Chriſt excluded out of
his Church, which occaſi-/oneth ſomewhat concerning the true Church-Government./ By Iſaac Penington, the Younger./ *London*, Printed for L.
Lloyd, next to the Sign of/ the Caſtle in Cornhill,
1660./ *2 prel. leaves and 99 pp.* 4*to.* (3*l.* 3*s.* 2113)

PENINGTON (JOHN). An/ Apoſtate/ Expoſed :/
Or,/ George Keith/ Contradicting himſelf and his
Brother Bradford. Wherein Their Teſtimony to
the Chriſtian Faith of the People called Qua-/kers,
is oppoſed to G. K's late/ Pamphlet, Stiled, Groſs
Error/ and Hypocriſe detected./ By John Penington./ *London*, Printed and Sold by T. Sowle,
near the Meeting-/Houſe in White-Hart-Court in
Grace-Church-ſtreet, 1695./ *Title and pp.* 3-29.
12*mo.* (2*l.* 2*s.* 2114)

PENN (WILLIAM). A/ Letter/ from/ William
Penn/ Proprietary and Governour of/· Pennſyl-
vania/ In America, to the Committee/ of the/ Free
Society of Traders/ of that Province, reſiding in
London./ Containing/ A General Deſcription of
the ſaid Province, its Soil, Air, Water, Seaſons
and Produce,/ both Natural and Artificial, and the
good Encreaſe thereof./ Of the Natives or Abori-
gines, their Language, Cuſtoms and Manners, Diet,
Houſes or Wig-/wams, Liberality, eaſie way of
Living, Phyſick, Burial, Religion, Sacrifices and
Cantico,/ Feſtivals, Government, and their order
in Council upon Treaties for/ Land, &c. their
Juſtice upon Evil Doers./ Of the firſt Planters,
the Dutch, &c. and the preſent Condition and
Settlement of the ſaid Province,/ and Courts of
Juſtices, &c./ To which is added, An Account of
the City of/ Philadelphia/ Newly laid out. Its
Scituation between two Navigable Rivers, Dela-
ware and Skulkill,/ with a/ Portraiture or Plat-
form thereof,/ Wherein the Purchaſers Lots are
Diſtinguiſhed by certain Numbers inſerted./ And
the Proſperous and Advantagious Settlements of
the Society aforeſaid, within/ the ſaid City and
Country, &c./ Printed and Sold by Andrew

Sowle, at the Crooked-Billet in Holloway-Lane in/ Shoreditch, and at feveral Stationers in *London,* 1683./ 10 *pp. With the Portraiture of the City of Philadelphia. Folio.*   (2*l.* 12*s.* 6*d.* 2115)

PENNSYLVANIA. A/ Further Account/ Of the Province of/ Pennsylvania/ and its/ Improvements./   For the Satisfaction of thofe that are Adventurers, and/ enclined to be so. [*London* 1685.] *At the end Dated* 'Worminghurft-Place, 12fth of the 10th Month 85.' *Signed* 'William Penn.' 20 *pp. Half mor.* 4*to.*   (1*l.* 11*s.* 6*d.* 2116)

PENNSYLVANIA. Some/ Letters/ and an/ Abftract of Letters/ from Pennsylvania,/ Containing/ The State and Improvement of that/ Province./ Publifhed to prevent Mif-Reports./   [*London*] Printed and Sold by Andrew Sowe, at the Crooked-Billet in Hollo-/way-Lane, in Shoreditch, 1691./ 12 *pp. Uncut.* 4*to.*   (2*l.* 2*s.* 2117)

PENNSYLVANIA. The Charters of the Province of Pennsylvania and City of Philadelphia. *Philadelphia :* Printed and Sold by B. Franklin. MDCC XLII. 30 *pp. Folio.*   (1*s.* 11*s.* 6*d.* 2118)

PENNSYLVANIA. A Collection of all the Laws Of the Province of Pennsylvania : Now in Force. Publifhed by Order of Assembly. *Philadelphia :* Printed and Sold by B. Franklin. M,DCC,XLII. 562 *pp.* 'An Appendix ; containing a Summary of such Acts of Assembly As have been formerly in Force within this Province, For Regulating of Defcents, And Transfering the Property of Lands, &c. But fince expired, altered or repealed. *Philadelphia :* Printed by B. Franklin. M,DCC,XLII. *iv pp. and wanting all after p.* 16. *Folio.*   (18*s.* 2119)

PENNSYLVANIA. A Brief State of the Province of Pennsylvania, in which The Conduct of their Assemblies for feveral Years paft is impartially examined, and the true Caufe of the continual Encroachments of the French difplayed, more efpecially the fecret Defign of their late unwarrantable Invafion and Settlement upon the River Ohio. To which is annexed, An eafy Plan for Reftoring Quiet in the Public Meafures of that Province, and defeating the ambitious Views of the French in time to come. In a Letter from a

Gentleman who has refided many Years in Pennfylvania to his Friend in London [Benjamin
Franklin]. *London*: R. Griffiths. 1755. *Half-
title, title, and text pp.* 3-45. *Half morocco.*
8vo.   (10s. 6d.   2120)

PENNSYLVANIA. A brief State of the Province
of Pennsylvania, in which The Conduct of their
Assemblies for feveral Years paft is impartially
examined, and the true Caufe of the continual
Encroachments of The French difplayed, more
efpecially the fecret Defign of their late unwarrantable Invafion and Settlement upon the River Ohio.
To which is annexed, An eafy Plan for reftoring
Quiet in the public Meafures of that Province, and
defeating the ambitious Views of the French in
time to come. In a Letter from a Gentleman who
has refided many Years in Pennfylvania to his
Friend in London. The Second Edition. *London*:
R. Griffiths, 1755. *Half-title, title, and text pp.*
3-45. *Half mor.* 8vo.   (10s. 6d.   2121)

PENNSYLVANIA. An Answer To an invidious
Pamphlet, intituled, *A Brief State of the Province of
Pensylvania.* Wherein are expofed The many
falfe Affertions of the Author or Authors, of the
faid Pamphlet, with a View to render the Quakers
of Penfylvania and their Government obnoxious
to the Britifh Parliament and Miniftry; and the
Several Tranfactions, moft grofly mifreprefented
therein, fet in their true light. *London*; S. Blan-
don, MDCCLV. *Title and 80 pp. Half morocco.*
8vo.   (10s. 6d.   2122)

PENNSYLVANIA. A Brief View Of the Conduct
of Pennsylvania, For the Year 1755; So far as it
affected the General Service of the British Colonies,
particularly the expedition under the late General
Braddock. With an Account of the fhocking In-
humanities, committed by the Incurfions of the
Indians upon the Province in October and November; which occafioned a Body of the Inhabitants
to come down, while the Affembly were fitting,
and to infift upon an immediate Sufpenfion of all
Difputes, and the Paffing of a Law for the Defence
of the Country. Interfpers'd with feveral interefting Anecdotes and original Papers, relating to

the Politics and Principles of the People called
Quakers: Being a Sequel to a late well known
Pamphlet, Intitled, A Brief State of Pennsylvania.
In a Second Letter to a Friend in London. *Lon-
don*: R. Griffiths. 1756. *88 pp. Half morocco.*
8vo. (10s. 6d. 2123)

PENNSYLVANIA. An Historical Review of the
Constitution and Government of Pennsylvania
From its Origin; So far as regards the feveral
Points of Controverfy, which have, from Time to
Time, arifen between The feveral Governors of
that Province, and Their feveral Assemblies.
Founded on authentic Documents. [By Dr.
Franklin] *London*: R. Griffiths, MDCCLIX. *viii*
pp. Contents 18 pp; and Text 444 pp. Old calf.
8vo. (7s. 6d. 2124)

PENNSYLVANIA. A New Essay [By the Pennfylvanian Farmer] On the Constitutional Power
of Great-Britain over the Colonies in America;
with the Resolves of the Committee for the Province of Pennsylvania, and their Instructions To
their Representatives in Assembly. Philadelphia
Printed; and *London* Re-printed for J. Almon, 1774.
viii and 126 pp. Half mor. 8vo. (5s. 6d. 2125)

PENNSYLVANIA. The Acts of the General Affembly of the Commonwealth of Pensylvania,
Carefully compared with the Originals. And an
Appendix, Containing the Laws now in Force,
paffed between the 30th Day of September, 1775,
and the Revolution. Together with The Declaration of Independence; the Conftitution of the State
of Pennsylvania; and the Articles of Confederation
of the United States of America. Publifhed by
order of the General Affembly. *Philadelphia*:
Printed and Sold by Francis Bailey, in Market-
Street, M,DCC,LXXXII. *Two Volumes.* Vol. I. *2*
prel. leaves, xxxii and 527 pp. Index or Table viii pp.
Vol. II. Hall and Sellers, *Title and pp. 3-704.*
Tables at pp. 82-3, 110, 254, 270, 369, 400, 588, 704.
Volumes IV. V. *and* VI. *400 pp. Tables at pp. 8, 88,*
180, 194, 314, 400. Fine copy in Old calf.
Folio (1l. 11s. 6d. 2126)

PENNSYLVANIA. Proceedings and Debates of
the General Assembly of Pennsylvania, As taken

in short-hand by Thomas Lloyd. *Philadelphia:* Printed by Joseph James, in Chesnut-Street. M,DCC,LXXXVII. Volume the Second. *Title and* 189 *pp. Errata* 1 *page.* 8*vo.* (3*s.* 6*d.* 2127)

PENNSYLVANIA. Observations upon the present Government of Pennsylvania. In four letters to the People of Pennsylvania. *Philadelphia:* Printed and Sold by Styner and Cist, in Second-ſtreet, five doors above Arch-ſtreet. MDCCLXXVII. 24 *pp. Half mor.* 8*vo.* (5*s.* 2128)

PENNSYLVANIA. An Historical Review of the Constitution and Government of Pennsylvania, from its origin; so far as regards the several points of controversy which have from time to time arisen between the several Governors of Pennsylvania and their several Assemblies. Founded on Authentic Documents. [By Dr. Franklin] 1808, Reprinted at Philadelphia by Wm. Duane, from the London Edition of 1759. *Title and pp. xv-xxxvi. Text* 431 *pp.* 8*vo.* (7*s.* 6*d.* 2129)

PENNSYLVANIA HOSPITAL. Continuation of the Account of the Pennſylvania Hoſpital; From the Firſt of May 1754, to the Fifth of May 1761. With an alphabetical List of the Contributors, and of the Legacies which have been bequeathed, for Promotion and Support thereof, from its firſt Rise to that Time. *Philadelphia:* Printed by B. Franklin, and D. Hall. MDCCLXI. *Title and pp.* 41-77. 4*to.* (1*l.* 10*s.* 2130)

PENNSYLVANIA MAGAZINE (THE): Or, American Monthly Museum. MDCCLXXV. Volume I. *Philadelphia:* Printed and sold by R. Aitken, Printer and Bookseller, opposite the London Coffee-House, Front-Street. 4 *prel. leaves and text pp.* 9-625. *Index* 5 *pp. With several copperplates. Old calf.* 8*vo.* (15*s.* 2131)

PEREZ (FRANCISCO). Catecismo de la Doctrina Cristiana en lengua Otomi, traducida literalmente al Castellano por el Presbitero D. Francisco Perez, catedratico propietario de dicho idioma en la nacional y pontificia universidad de la Ciudad federal de los estados Mexicanos, examinador ſinodal de dicho Idioma de este arzobispado.

Mexico: Imprenta de la Testamentaria de Valdés, a cargo de José Maria Gallegos 1834. 5 *prel. leaves and* 17 *pp.* 'Manualito' *etc.* 46 *pp. Half mor.* 8*vo.* (1*l.* 1*s.* 2132)

PEREZ (Manuel). Arte de el Idioma Mexicano. Por el P. Fr. Manuel Perez, del Orden de N. P. San Auguſtin, hijo de la Santa Provincia del Santiſſimo Nombre de Jesvs, actual Viſitador en ella. Cura Miniſtro, por ſu Mageſtad, de la Parroquia de los Naturales del Real Collegio de San Pablo, y Cathedratico de dicho Idioma en la Real Vniverſidad de Mexico. Dedicalo a la dicha Santiſſima Provincia. Con Licencia. En *Mexico,* por Francisco de Ribera Calderon, en la calle de San Auguſtin. Año de 1713. 8 *prel. leaves and* 80 *pp.* 'Indice,' 3 *pp.* 4*to.* (4*l.* 14*s.* 6*d.* 2133)

PEREZ (Manuel). Farol Indiano, y Gvia de Curas de Indios. Summa de los Cinco Sacramentos que adminiſtran los Miniſtros Evangelicos en eſta America. Con todos los caſos morales que ſuceden entre Indios. Deducidos de los mas claſicos Authores, y amoldados à las coſtumbres, y privilegios de los Naturales. Por el P. Fr. Manuel Perez, del Orden de N. P. S. Auguſtin, hijo de eſta Provincia del Santiſſimo Nombre de Jesus. Viſitador actual de ella, Cura-Miniſtro, por ſu Mageſtad, de la Parroquia de Naturales de S Pablo de Mexico, y Cathedratico de Lengua Mexicana en la Vniverſidad. Dedicala Al Santiſſimo Eſpoſo de la Eſpoſa, y Madre de Dios, y Patron de Eſta Nueva-Eſpaña, Señor SanJoseph. Con Licencia de los Svperiores. En *Mexico,* por Franciſco de Rivera Calderon, en la calle de San Auguſtin. Año de 1713. 24 *prel. leaves and* 192 *pp.* 'Indice de los Capitulos,' 3 *pp.* 4*to.* (2*l.* 2*s.* 2134)

PERNETTY (Dom). Histoire d'un Voyage aux Isles Malouines, Fait en 1763 & 1764; avec des Observations sur le Detroit de Magellan, et sur les Patagons, Par Dom Pernetty, Abbé de l'Abbaye de Burgel, Membre de l'Académie Royale des Sciences & Belles-Lettres de Pruſſe ; Aſſocié Correſpondant de calle de Florence, & Bibliothécaire de Sa Majeſté le Roi de Pruſſe. Nouvelle Edition. Refondue & augmentée d'un Diſcours Préliminaire, de Remarques ſur l'Histoire Natu-

relle, &c. A *Paris*, Saillant & Nyon, M.DCC.LXX.
Two Volumes. Tome Premier. *iv and* 385 *pp.*
Tome Second. *Title and* 334 *pp. Approbation and
Privilege* 2 *pp. With* 18 *folded plates at end. Old
calf.* 8*vo.*   (8*s.* 6*d.*   2135)

PERU. Conquefte van Indien./ De wonderlijcke
ende warach=/tighe Hiftorie vant Coninckrijck van
Peru,/ ghelegen in Indien, inde welcke verhaelt
wordt de gheleghenthept,/ coftuymen, manieren
van leven, overuloedicheyt des Goudts ende
Silvers,/ ende voorts alle de fonderlingfte dinghen
van den felven lande./ Infghelijcks van den/
fteden, plaetfen ende inwoonders deffelfs Con-
inckrijcx, daer beneven, hoet ghevonden/ ende
eerft by de Keyferlijcke Mayefteyt hochloflijcker
memorien gheconque=/fteert ende vercreghen is,
met alle de Oorloghen, ende ftrijden, die ghe=/
buert zijn, foo teghens d' Indianen, als oock om
tgoe=/vernement d'een teghens den anderen./ De
Caerte van America./ [*Engraved on Copper on the
title.*] *t' Amstelredam.*/ By Cornelis Claefz, woonende opt Water, by de Oude Brugghe,/ Int
Schrijf Boeck. Anno. 1598./ *Title, on the reverse,*
'Tot den Lefer.' *Text in* 148 *leaves very irregu-
larly folioed ; copperplate engraving of* 'Cerro de
Potosi' *on the reverse of sig.* E e ij. 'Tafel oft Regifter des boeckx' 20 *pp. Fine copy. Old calf.*
4*to.*   (2*l.* 2*s.*   2136)

PERU. Constitucion. Politica de la Republica
Peruana Jurada en Lima el 20 de Noviembre de
1823. *Lima :* 1825. Imprenta del estado por J.
Gonzalez. *cxii and* 52 *pp. Indice* 2 *pp. Unbound.*
16*mo.*   (5*s.*   2137)

PETERS (BERNHARD MICHAEL). Eine befonders
merkwürdige Reife von Amfterdam nach Surinam,
und von da zurück nach Bremen, in den Jahren
1783 und 1784. von Bernhard Michael Peters,
einem Jeverländer. Wobei die Reifen und Le-
bensgefchichte John Thomfons eines Engländers,
feines vertrauten Freundes und Reifegefährten auf
der See. *Bremen*, 1788. *Two Volumes.* Erfter
Theil. 4 *prel. leaves and* 214 *pp.* Zweyte und letzte
Theil. 1790. 6 *prel. leaves and* 188 *pp. boards.*
8*vo.*   (7*s.* 6*d.*   2138)

PETERS (Hugh). An Historical and Critical
Account of Hugh Peters. After the Manner of
Mr. Bayle. *London:* J. Noon. MDCCLI. 72 *pp.*
Half mor. 8*vo.* (4*s.* 6*d.* 2139)

PETITIONS from the Old and New Subjects, Inhabitants of the Province of Quebec, to the Right
Honourable the Lords Spiritual and Temporal.
London: Printed in the Year 1791. 2 *prel. leaves
and 55 pp. Half mor.* 8*vo.* (4*s.* 6*d.* 2140)

PHILIPOT (Thomas). The Original and Growth/
of/ The Spanifh/ Monarchy/ United with the
House of/ Austria./ Extracted from thofe Chro-
nicles,/ Annals, Regifters and Genealogies,/ that
yeild any faithful Reprefentation/ how the Houfes
of Caftile, Aragon and/ Burgundy became knit and
combin'd/ into one Body./ To which are added
feveral Difcourfes of thofe/ Acceffions and Improvements in Italy,/ Africk, with the Eaft and
Weft-Indies,/ that are now annexed by Alliance
or Con-/queft to the Diadem of Spain./ By
Thomas Philipot, M.A./ Formerly of Clare-Hall in
Cambridge./ *London,* Printed by W. G. for R.
Taylor, in St. Martins le/ Grand neer St. Leonards
Church yard. 1664./ 4 *prel. leaves and text* 264
pp. With portrait of Phillip the IV. of Spain.
Small 8*vo.* (18*s.* 2141)

PHILIPS (Miles). The Voyages and Adventures
of Miles Philips, A Weft-Country Sailor. Containing A Relation of his various Fortune both by
Sea and Land; the inhuman Ufage he met with
from the Spaniards at Mexico, and the Salvage
Indians of Canada and other barbarous Nations;
and the Sufferings he and his Companions underwent by their Confinement and Sentence in the
Spanifh Inquifition. Together with A Natural
Defcription of the Countries he vifited, and particular Obfervations on the Religion, Cuftoms and
Manners of their refpective Inhabitants. Written
by Himself in the plain Stile of an Englifh Sailor.
London: T. Payne, 1724. 6 *prel. leaves and* 216 *pp.*
Wanting pages 17, 18, 101, *to* 116, 203, *to* 206,
inclusive. Old calf. 12*mo.* (14*s.* 6*d.* 2142)

PHILLIP (William). The/ True and perfect De-/
fcription of three Voy-/ages fo ftrange and woon-

590 Bibliotheca Americana.

derfull,/ that the like hath neuer been/ heard of
before:/ Done and performed three yeares, one after
the other by the Ships of/ Holland and Zeland, on
the North fides of Norway, Mufcouia and/ Tartaria,
towards the Kingdomes of Cathaia and China;
fhewing/ the difcouerie of the Straights of Weigates
Noua Zembla,/ and the Countrie lying vnder 80
degrees; which is/ thought to be Greenland;
where neuer any man had/ bin before; with the
cruell Beares, and other/ Monfters of the Sea, and
the vnfup-/portable and extreame cold/ that is
found to be in/ thofe places./ And how that in
the laft Voyage, the Shippe was fo inclofed by the/
Ice, that it was left there, whereby the men were
forced to build a/ houfe in the cold and defart
Countrie of Noua Zembla wherin/ they continued
10 monthes togeather, and neuer faw nor/ heard of
any man, in moft great cold and extreame/ miferie;
and how after that, to faue their liues, they/ were
conftrained to sayle aboue 350 Duch-/miles, which
is above 1000 miles Englifh,/ in little open boates,
along and ouer the/ maine Seas, in moft great
dannger,/ and with extreame labour, vn-/fpeakable
troubles, and/ great hunger./ Imprinted at *London*, for T. Pauier./ 1609./ *2 prel. leaves; viz.
Title the reverse blank,* ' To the Right Wor-/fhip-
full, Sir Thomas Smith Knight, Gouer-/nour of
the Mufcouy Company, &c.' *Signed* 'William
Phillip.' *2 pp. Text in 97 unfolioed leaves. Signatures* B. *to* V. *in fours, and* X. *in* 3 *leaves. Morocco
extra, by Riviere.* 4*to.*   (4*l.* 4*s.* 2143)

PHILOPONUS (HONORIUS). Nova Typis/ Trans-
acta Na-/vigatio./ Novi Orbis Indiæ Occi-/den-
talis/ Admodvm Re-/verendissimorvm P.P./ ac
F.F. Reverendffimi ac Illustriffimi Domini,/ Dn.
Bvellii Cataloni Abbatis montis/ Serrati, & in vni-
verfam Americam, five Novum,/ Orbem Sacræ
Sedis Apoftolicæ Romanæ à Latere/ Legati, Vicarij,
ac Patriarchæ Sociorumq; Mo-/nachorum ex Ordine
S. P. N. Benedicti ad fuprà/ dicti Novi Mundi
barbaras gentes Chrifti S. Evan-/gelium prædicandi
gratia delegatorum Sacerdo-/tum.   Dimiffi per
S. D. D. Papam Alexandrum/ VI. Anno Chrifti,
1492./ Nvnc Primvm/ E varijs Scriptoribus in
vnum colle-/cta, & figuris ornata./ Avthore/
Venerando Fr. Don Honorio Philopono/ Ordinis

S. Benedicti Monacho. 1621./ *3 prel. leaves in-
cluding the engraved title, and* 101 *pp. with 3 seq. pp.
There are 18 copperplate engravings. Vellum.
Folio.*   (*2l. 12s. 6d.* 2144)

PHILOSOPHIC SOLITUDE: Or, the choice of
a rural life: A Poem. By a Gentleman educated
at Yale College. The Third Edition. *New-York:*
Printed by John Holt at the Exchange. [1769?]
40 *pp. Half mor. 8vo.*   (10*s. 6d.* 2145)

PHILOTHEUS. A True and Particular History of
Earthquakes. Containing A Relation of that
dreadful Earthquake which happen'd at Lima and
Callaó, in Peru, October 28, 1746; publifh'd at
Lima by Command of the Vice-Roy, and now
tranflated from the Original Spanifh; alfo of that
which happen'd in Jamaica in 1692, and of others
in different Parts of the World. Accurately
defcribing The dreadful Devaftations that have
been made by thofe horrible Convulfions of the
Earth; whereby Mountains have been thrown
down, or remov'd to great Diftances; Cities, with
all their Inhabitants, fwallow'd up in a Moment;
whole Flocks and Herds, with their Keepers, in-
gulph'd in the termendous Chafms and Openings
of Valleys; large Forefts funk, and for ever buried
in an Inftant. Extracted from Authors of the
moft unexceptionable Credit and Reputation. By
Philotheus. *London:* for the Author, 1748. *xvi
and* 176 *pp. Old calf. 8vo.*   (7*s. 6d.* 2146)

PIECES Justificatives des Mémoires concernant les
Limites de L'Acadie. A *Paris,* de L'Imprimerie
Royale. M.DCCLIV. *Title and* 646 *pp. Old calf.
4to.*   (1*l. 5s.* 2147)

PIGGOTT (S.) An Authentic Narrative of four
years residence at Tongataboo, One of the Friendly
Islands, by Geo. V—— Who together with 28
other Missionaries was sent thither by the London
Society in the Ship Duff, under Captain Wilson
in 1796, and survived them all; and lived as one
of the Natives for two Years. With an Appendix
by an Eminent Writer, By the Rev. S. Piggott,
A.M. Domestic Chaplain to the Right Hon. Viscount
Lord Galway, and perpetual Curate of St. James'
Church, Latchford, Warrington. *London:* Long•

man & Co. 1815. *xv and* 234 *pp.   Errata* 1 *page.
With plate and chart.* 8*vo.*   (5*s.* 6*d.* 2148)

PIKE (Zebulon Montgomery).   Exploratory
Travels through the Western Territories of North
America: Comprising a Voyage from St. Louis,
on the Mississipi, to the Source of that River, and
a Journey through the Interior of Louisiana, and
the North-Eastern Provinces of New Spain. Performed in the years 1805, 1806, 1807, by Order of
the Government of the United States. By Zebulon
Montgomery Pike, Major 6th Regt. United
States Infantry. *London:* Longman, 1811. *xx pp.
and text* 436 *pp.   With* 2 *Maps.   Half calf.*
4*to.*   (10*s.* 6*d.* 2149)

PIMIENTA (Francisco Diaz).   Relacion del
Svcesso Qve/ Tvvo Francisco Diaz Pimienta,
General de la Real/ Armada de las Indias, en la
Isla de santa Catalina. Dase cuenta como la/ tomò
a los enemigos que la posseìan, echandolos della, y
de la/ estimacion de los despojos, y numero de los/
prisioneros./ [*Colophon*] Con licencia. En Madrid, Por Iuan Sanchez. Año 1642./ 6 *unnumbered pages.   Half mor.   Folio.* (1*l.* 11*s.* 6*d.* 2150)

PIMIENTA (Francisco Diaz).   Relacion del
svcesso qve tvvo Francisco/ Diaz Pimienta,
General de la Real Armada de las Indias, en la
Is-/la de S. Catalina. Dase cuenta de como la
tomò a los enemigos que/ la posseian, èchandolos
della, y la estimacion de los despojos, y nu-/mero
de prisioneros./ [*Colophon*] Con licència del señor
don Miguel de Luna y Arellano, Cavallero del
Abito de San-/tiago, del Consejo de su Magestad, y
su Oydor en la Real Audiencia de Sevi-/lla lo im-
primio Francisco de Lyra, Año 1642./ 12 *unnumbered pages.   Half mor.* 4*to.* (1*l.* 11*s.* 6*d.* 2151)

PINES. The Isle of/ Pines,/ or,/ A late Discovery
of a fourth Island in/ Terra Austral, Incognita./
Being/ A True Relation of certain Englifh perfons,/ Who in the dayes of Queen Elizabeth,
making a/ Voyage to the East India, were cast
away, and wrack-/ed upon the Island near to the
Coast of Terra Austra-/lis Incognita, and all
drowned, except one Man and/ four Women,

whereof one was a Negro. And now/ lately Anno
Dom. 1667. a Dutch ship driven by foul/ weather
there by chance have found their Posterity/ (speak-
ing good English) to amount to ten or twelve/ thousand persons, as they suppose. The whole Rela-/
tion follows, written, and left by the Man himself a/
little before his death, and declared to the Dutch
by/ his Grandchild./ Licensed June 27. 1668./
London,/ Printed by S. G. for Allen Banks and
Charles Harper/ at the Flower-Deluice near Cripplegate Church,/ 1668./ *Title and 9 pp. half mor.*
4to.   (1*l*. 1*s*. 2152)

PINTO (FERDINAND MENDEZ). Wunderliche und
Merckwürdige/ Reisen/ Ferdinandi/ Mendez Pinto,/ Welche er inerhalb ein und zwantzig Jah=/ren,
durch Europa, Asia, und Africa, und deren König-
reiche/ und Länder; als Abyssina, China, Japon,
Tartarey, Siam, Calamin-/ham, Pegu, Martabane,
Bengale, Brama, Ormus, Batas, Queda,/ Aru, Pan,
Ainan, Calempluy, Cauchenchina,/ und andere
Oerter verrichtet. Darinnen er beschreibet/ Die
ihme zu Wasser und Land zugestossene grosse/
Noht und Gefahr; wie er nemlich sey dreyzehn-
mal gefangen genom=/men und siebenzehnmal ver-
aufft worden; auch vielfältigen/ Schiffbruch er-
litten habe:/ Dabey zugleich befindlich eine gar
genaue Entwerffung der/ Wunder und Raritäten
erwehnter Länder; der Gesetze, Sitten, und Ge-
won=/heiten derselben Völcker; und der grosse
Macht und Heeres=Krafft/ der Einwohner./ Nun
erst ins Hochteutsche übersetzet, und mit unter=/
schiedlichen Kupferstükken gezieret./ *Amsterdam,*/
Bey Henrich und Dietrich Boom, Buchhändlern,/
Im Jahr Christi 1671./ *4 prel. leaves including*
Frontispiece title; and 393 pp. Maps & Plates at pp.
1, 13, 30, 98, 159, 217, 256, 267. Pagination very
irregular, 4to.   (10*s*. 6*d*. 2153)

PINTO (J. DE). Reponse de M^r. J. de Pinto, aux
observations d'un homme impartial, Sur sa Lettre
à Mr. S. B., Docteur en Médecine à Kingston dans
la Jamaïque, au sujet des Troubles qui agitent ac-
tuellement toute l'Amérique Septentrionale. A
La Haye, Pierre-Frederic Gosse, MDCCLXXVI. 60
pp. half mor. 8vo.   (4*s*. 6*d*. 2154)

PIRATAS/ de la/ America./ Y Luz à la defensa de

las Coftas/ de Indias Occidentales/ Dedicado/ Al
muy Noble Señor Don/ Francisco Lopez Suazo./
Traducido/ De la lengua Flamenca en Efpañola,
por/ el D^or. de Buena-Maifon Medico/ Practico en
la opulentifsima/ Ciudad de Amfterdam./ Segunda
Impression./ En *Colonia Agrippina,*/ En cafa de
Lorenço Struik-/Man Año de 1682./ *24 prel. leaves
and* 490 *pp.* 'Tabla De los Capitulos' 8 *pp. Vellum.* 12*mo.*   (1*l*. 1*s*. 2155)

PIRATAS (✠) de la/ America./ Y Luz à la defenfa de las Coftas/ de Indias Occidentales/ Dedi-
cado/ Al muy Noble Señor Don/ Ricardo de
Whyte,/ Cavellero del Orden Militar/ de Calatrava
&c^a./ Traducido/ De la lengua Flamenca en Efpañola,/ por el D^or. de Bonne-Maifon./ Impression
Segunda./ En *Colonia Agrippina,*/ En cafa de Lorenço Struik-/Man, Año de 1682./ *28 prel. leaves
and* 490 *pp.* 'Tabla De los Capitulos' 8 *pp. Vellum.* 12*mo.*   (1*l*. 1*s*. 2156)

PISO (Gulielmus). Gulielmi Pisonis/ Medici Am-
ftelædamensis/ de/ Indiæ Utriusque/ re Naturali
et Medica/ Libri Qvatvordecim/ Quorum contenta
pagina fequens/ exhibet./ [Gvlielmi Pisonis,/ Medici Amftelædamenfis,/ I. De Aëribus, Aquis, &
Locis./ II. De Natura & cura Morborum, Occidentali Indiæ, imprimis/ Brafiliæ, familiarium./
III. De Animalibus, aquatilibus, volatilibus, &
terreftibus, edulibus./ IV. De Arboribus, fructi-
bus, & herbis medicis, atque alimentariis,/ nafcen-
tibus in Brafilia & regionibus vicinis./ V. De
Noxiis & venenatis, eorumque Antidotis. Quibus
infertæ funt/ Animalium quorundam vivæ fectiones;
Tum & aliquot Me-/tamorphofes Infectorim./ VI.
Mantiffa aromatica &c. Pofita poft Bontii tracta-
tus./ Georgii Margravii De Liepftadt/ I. Tracta-
tus Topographicus & Meteorologicus Brafiliæ, cum
Ob-/fervatione Eclipfis Solaris./ II. Commentarius
de Brafilienfium & Chilenfium indole ac lingua
&c./ Iacobi Bontii, Bataviæ in majore Java novæ
Medici ordinarii,/ I. De Confervanda valetudine./
II. Methodus medendi./ III. Obfervationes in
cadaveribus./ IV. Notæ in Garciam ab Orta. V.
Hiftoria Animalium. VI. Hiftoria Plantarum.]
Quibus fparfim inferuit G. Piso Annotatio-/nes &
Additiones quà icones atque res ne-/ceffarias./]

Amstelædami,/ Apud Ludovicum et Danielem/ El-
zevirios./ A°. cIↃ Iↄ cLVIII./ 13 *prel. leaves ; viz.
Engraved title,* 'Avtores et Titvli,' 1 *page ;* 'Dedi-
catoria,' 4 *pp ;* 'Præfatio,' 4 *pp ; Verses, etc.* 12 *pp.
Half-title ; Text pp.* 3-327. 'Index' 5 *pp.* 'Georgii
Marcgravii' *etc.* 39 *pp.* 'Jacobi Bontii,' *etc.* 326
pp. 'Index rervm' 2 *pp. Fine copy. Vellum.
Folio.* (18*s.* 2157)

PITMAN (HENRY). A/ Relation/ of the/ Great
Sufferings/ and/ Strange Adventures/ Of Henry
Pitman,/ Chyrurgion to the late Duke of Mon-
mouth, contain-/ing an Account;/ 1. Of the occafion of his being engaged in the Duke's Service.
2. Of/ his Tryal, Condemnation, and Tranfportation
to Barbadoes, with/ the moft fevere and Unchrif-
tian Acts made againft him and his Fellow-fuf-
ferers, by the/ Governour and General Affembly
of that Ifland. 3. How he made his efcape in a
fmall/ open Boat with fome of his fellow Captives,
namely, Jo. Whicker, Peter Begwell, William/
Woodcock, Jo. Cooke, Jeremiah Atkins, &c. And
how miraculoufly they were preferved/ on the Sea.
4. How they went afhore on a uninhabitable Ifland,
where they met/ with fome Privateers that burnt
their Boat, and left them on that defolate place to
fhift/ for themfelves. 5. After what manner they
lived there for about three Months until/ the faid
Henry Pitman was taken aboard a Privateer, and
at length arrived fafe in En-/gland. 6. How his
Companions were received aboard another Priva-
teer that was after-/wards taken by the Spaniards,
and they all made Slaves; And how aftar fix
Moneths/ Captivity they were delivered, and returned to England alfo./ Licenfed, June 13th,
1689. *London,* Printed by Andrew Sowle: And
are to be Sold by John Taylor, at the Sign/ of the
Ship in Paul's Church-Yard, 1689./ *Title and pp.*
3-38. *Advertisements* 1 *page. Calf extra by Bedford.*
4*to.* (1*l.* 11*s.* 6*d.* 2158)

PITMAN (ROBERT BIRKS). A Succinct View and
Analysis of Authentic Information extant in Ori-
ginal Works, on the practicability of joining the
Atlantic and Pacific Oceans, by a Ship Canal acrofs
the Isthmus of America. By Robert Birks Pitman.
London: J. M. Richardson, 1825. *viii and* 229 *pp.*

Errata 1 *page. Map of the Isthmus of America facing Title.* 8vo. (7s. 6d. 2159)

PLAIN TRUTH: Addressed to the Inhabitants of America. Containing Remarks on a late Pamphlet, intitled Common Sense: Wherein are ſhewn, that the Scheme of Independence is ruinous, deluſive, and impracticable; that were the Author's Aſſeverations, reſpecting the Power of America, as real as nugatory, Reconciliation on liberal Principles with Great Britain would be exalted Policy; and that, circumſtanced as we are, permanent Liberty and true Happineſs can only be obtained by Reconciliation with that Kingdom. Written by Candidus. Philadelphia, Printed. *London,* Reprinted for J. Almon, M.DCC.LXXVI. *2 prel. leaves and* 47 *pp. half mor.* 8vo. (4s. 6d. 2160)

PLAIN TRUTH: Or, a Letter to the Author of Dispassionate Thoughts on the American War. In which The Principles and Arguments of that Author are refuted, and the Neceſſity of carrying on that War clearly demonſtrated. By the Author of Letters to a Nobleman on the Conduct of the American War; and of Cool Thoughts on the Consequences of American Independence. *London:* G. Wilkie, MDCCLXXX. *vii and* 76 *pp. half morocco.* 8vo. (4s. 6d. 2161)

PLAIN TRUTH, in a Series of Numbers from the New-York Daily Advertiser. *New-York.* Daniel Fanshaw, 1821. 56 *pp.* 12*mo.* (2s. 6d. 2162)

PLAN (A) of a Proposed Union between Great-Britain and The Colonies of New-Hampſhire, Maſſachuſetts-Bay, Rhode-Iſland, New-York, New-Jerſey, Pennſylvania, Maryland, Delaware Counties, Virginia, North Carolina, South Carolina, and Georgia. Which was produced by one of the Delegates from Pennſylvania, in Congreſs, as mentioned in the preceeding Work. 4 *pp. half mor.* 8vo. (2s. 6d. 2163)

PLAN (A) to reconcile Great Britain & her Colonies, and preserve the Dependency of America. *London:* J. Almon, MDCCLXXIV. [1774]. *xvi prel. pp. Signed* 'Cosmopolite.' *Text* 40 *pp. half mor.* 8vo. (5s. 6d. 2164)

PLAN (A) for conciliating the Jarring Political In-
terests of Great Britain and her North American
Colonies, and For promoting a general Re-union
throughout the Whole of the British Empire.
London: J. Ridley, 1775. *xviii pp. Uncut and
Unbound.* 8*vo.* (4*s.* 6*d.* 2165)

PLAN (A) for conciliating the Jarring Interests of
Great Britain and her North American Colonies,
and For promoting a general Re-union throughout
the Whole of the British Empire. *London:* J.
Ridley, 1775. *xviii pp.* 'Letters, &c.' [*Boston*,
1775.] 127 *pp. half mor.* 8*vo.* (10*s.* 6*d.* 2166)

PLANTAGANET (BEAUCHAMP). A/ Description/
of the/ Province/ of/ New Albion./ And a Direction for Adventurers/ with fmall ftock to get two
for one, and good land freely./ And for Gentlemen, and all Servants, Labourers,/ and Artificers,
to live Plentifully./ And a former Defcription Reprinted of the healthieft, plea-/fanteft, and richeft
Plantation of Nevv Albion in/ North Virginia,
proved by thirteen Witneffes./ Together with/ A
Letter from Mafter Robert Evelin, that lived/ there
many yeers, fhewing the particularities, and ex-/
cellency thereof./ With a Brief of the Charge of
Victual, and Neceffaries, to tranf-/port and buy
ftock for each Planter, or Labourer, there to get/
his Mafter fifty pounds per Annum, or more, in
twelve Trades,/ and at ten pounds charges only a
man./ *London,/* Printed by James Moxon, in the
Yeer MDCL./ *4 prel. leaves; viz. Title having on the
reverse 3 woodcuts of the* ' Ploydens Armes. Albions
Armes. The Order, Medall and Riban of the Albion Knights,' *etc.* 'This Epiftle and Preface
fhews Cato's beft Rules for a Plantation.' *etc. at
the end dated* ' Middleboro this 5 of Decemb. 1641.'
Signed ' Beauchamp Plantagenet.' *6 pp: Text* 32
*pp. Fine large copy, with rough leaves; morocco by
Bedford.* 4*to.* (21*l.* 2167)

PLANTATION WCRK/ the/ Work/ of this/ Generation./ Written in True-Love/ To all fuch as are
weightily inclined to Transplant themfelves and
Fami-/lies to any of the Englifh Plantati-/ons in/
America./ The/ Moft material Doubts and Objections againft it/ being removed, they may more

cheerfully pro-/ceed to the Glory and Renown of
the God of/ the whole Earth, who in all Undertakings is to/ be looked unto, Praised and Feared
for Ever./ *London*, Printed for Benjamin Clark
in George-Yard in/ Lombard-ftreet, 1682./ *Title
and* 18 *pp.* 4*to.*   (1*l.* 11*s.* 6*d.*   2168)

PLANTERS/ PLEA/ (The)./ Or/ the Grovnds of
Plan-/tations Examined,/ And vfuall Objections
anfwered./ Together with a manifeftation of the
caufes mooving/ fuch as have lately vndertaken a
Plantation in/ Nevv-England :/ For the fatiffaction
of thofe that queftion/ the lawfulneffe of the Action./
London,/ Printed by William Iones./ 1630./ *Title,
reverse blank*; ' To the Reader.' 2 *pp.* Text 84 *pp.
Fine copy.* 4*to.*   (6*l.* 6*s.*   2169)

PLATFORM (A) of Church Discipline : Gathered
out of the Word of God and agreed upon by the
Elders and Messengers of the Churches Assembled
in the Synod at Cambridge, in New-England : To
be presented to the Churches and General Court,
for their consideration and acceptance in the Lord,
the eighth month, Anno 1648. *Boston* : Belcher and
Armstrong, 1808. 118 *pp.* ' Confession of Faith '
etc. 36 *pp. Calf.* 12*mo.*   (4*s.* 6*d.*   2170)

POINTIS (Louis de). Relation/ de ce qui s'est fait
a la prise/ de Cartagene,/ scitue'e aux/ Indes Espagnoles,/ par l'Escadre Commande'e/ par Mr. de
Pointis./ *A Bruxelles*,/ Chez Jean Fricx, Imp./ &
Marchand Libraire./ m.dc.xcviii./ *Title and* 141
pp. Old calf. 12*mo.*   (10*s.* 6*d.*   2171)

POINTIS (Louis de). Monfieur De Pointi's/ Expe-
dition/ to/ Cartagena :/ Being/ A particular Relation,/ I. Of the Taking and Plundering of that/ City,
by the French, in the/ Year 1697./ II. Of their
Meeting with Admiral Nevil,/ in their Return, and
the Courfe they/ fteer'd to get clear of him./ III.
Of their Paffing by Commadore Norris,/ at New-
found-Land./ IV. Of their Encounter with Capt.
Harlow,/ at their going into Brest./ Englifh'd from
the Original publifh'd at Paris/ by Monfieur De
Pointis himfelf. And/ Illuftrated with a large
Draught of the City/ of Cartagena, its Harbour
and Forts./ *London :*/ Sold by S. Crouch, at the

Corner of Pope's Head-Alley, in Cornhil ;/ Richard
Mount at the Poſtern, upon Tower-hill ;/ S. Buckley, againſt St. Dunſtan's Church, in Fleet-ſtreet ;
and/ A. Feltham, at the foot of the Parliament
Stairs, Weſtminster, 1699./ 4 *prel. leaves, including
title and text* 134 *pp. Plan wanting. Old calf.*
8vo. (1*l*. 1*s*. 2172)

POINTIS (Louis de). A Genuine and Particular
Account of the Taking of Carthagena by the French
and Buccaniers, In the Year 1697. Containing an
Exaĉt Relation of that Expedition, from their firſt
ſetting out, to their Return to Breſt ; wherein are
deſcrib'd their ſeveral Engagements with the Engliſh, in their Paſſage home. By the Sieur Pointis,
Commander in Chief. With a Preface, giving an
Account of the Original of Carthagena in 1532, to
the preſent time : Alſo an Account of the Climate
and Produĉt of that Place, and the Country adjacent. *London*, Olive Payne, 1740. *viii and* 86 *pp.*
half mor. 8vo. (10*s*. 6*d*. 2173)

POINTIS (Louis de). An Authentick and Particular Account Of the Taking of Carthagena by the
French In the Year 1697. Containing An exact
Relation of that Expedition, (in all its Circumſtances) from their firſt Setting out, to their Return
to Breſt ; wherein are deſcrib'd their ſeveral Engagements with the Engliſh Fleets, in their Paſſage home. By the Sieur Pointis, Commander
in Chief. With a Preface, giving an Account of
the Original of Carthagena in 1532, to the preſent
Time ; alſo an Account of the Climate and Product
of that Place, and the Country adjacent. The
Second Edition. *London:* Olive Payne, 1740.
viii and 86 *pp. With plan of Carthagena. Half*
morocco. 8vo. (10*s*. 6*d*. 2174)

POLITICAL (A) Analysis of the War : The Principles of the preſent political Parties examined ;
and A juſt, natural and perfeĉt Coalition propos'd
between Two Great Men, whoſe Conduĉt is particularly conſider'd. The Second Edition. With an
Appendix, Enforcing the Coalition propos'd ; and
proving, from our late Acquiſition of the Havanna,
that we are now in the moſt happy Situation for
continuing the War, or concluding a Peace. *Lon-*

don: Tho. Payne, 1762. *Title and 86 pp. half mor.*
8*vo.*   (7*s.* 6*d.*   2175)

POLITICAL DEBATES [on American Affairs]·
A *Paris,* J. W. MDCCLXVI. *Title and* 13 *pp.   half
mor.* 8*vo.*   (4*s.* 6*d.*   2176)

POLITICAL (THE) Detection; or the Treachery
and Tyranny of Administration, both at Home and
Abroad; displayed in a Series of Letters, signed
Junius Americanus. *London:* J. and W. Oliver,
MDCCLXX. *Title and text* 151 *pp. half morocco.*
8*vo.*   (6*s.*   2177)

POLITICAL Electricity, or, An Historical & Prophetical Print in the Year 1770.   Bute & Wilkes
invent. Mercurius & Apelles fect. Publish'd according to Act of Parliament.   [*London,* 1770.]
Large sheet, Folio.   (4*s.* 6*d.*   2178)

POLITICAL Reflections on the late Colonial Go-
vernments : In which Their original Constitutional
Defects are pointed out, and fhown to have natu-
rally produced the Rebellion, which has unfortu-
nately terminated in the Difmemberment of the
British Empire. By An American. *London:* G.
Wilkie, MDCCLXXXIII. *3 prel. leaves and* 259 *pp.
Calf extra by Bedford.* 8*vo.*   (15*s.*   2179)

PONCE DE LEON (FRANCISCO). Descripcion/ del
Reynode Chile,/ de fus Puertos, Caletas, y fitio de
Val-/diuia, con algunos difcurfos para fu/ mayor
defenfa, Conquifta,/ y duracion./   Consagrale al
Rey Nvestro/ Señor, en fu Real Confejo de/ las Indias,/ El Maestro Fray Francisco/ Ponce de Leon,
del Orden de nueftra Señora de la Mer-/ced, Procurador General del Reyno de Chile, y del/ Real
Exercito que fu Mageftad tiene en el Conquif-/ta-
dor, y Defcubridor de las Prouincias del Rio Ma-
ra-/ñon, Fundador de la ciudad de fan Francifco de
Borja,/ Prouifor, Gouernado, Vicario General, y
Iuez Ecle-/fiaftico en los Obifpados, de Quito,
Truxillo, y Chile, Vi-/cario Prouincial de la Prouincia de Lima, y fu Vifita-dor : y Reformador General de las de Chile,/ y Tucuman : Prouincial de
la de Chile, Capellan/ Mayor de los Reynos del
Peru, y Chile, y/ Comiffario del fanto Oficio./

[*Madrid* 1644]. *Title and* 15 *folioed leaves. Unbound.* 4*to.* (3*l.* 3*s.* 2180)

POOR SOLDIER (The); an American Tale: Founded on a recent Fact. Inscribed to Mrs. Crespigny. The Second Edition. *London:* J. Walter, M.DCC.LXXXIX. 3 *prel. leaves and* 43 *pp. half morocco.* 4*to.* (4*s.* 6*d.* 2181)

PORCACCHI (Tomaso). L'Isole/ piv Famose/ del Mondo,/ descritto da/ Tomaso Porcacchi/ da Castiglione Arretino,/ et intagliate/ da Girolamo Porro/ Padovano./ Di nuovo corrette, & illuſtrate con l'aggiunta dell' Iſtria, &/ altre Iſole, Scogli, e nuove curioſità. Eſſendovi una/ diſtinta deſcrittione della Città di Conſtantino-/poli, e della Peniſola di Morea./ Conſecrate/ All' Illuſtriſſimo, & Eccelentiſſimo Sign. il Sign./ Pietro Gritti/ Q. Lvigi, Q. Raimondo,/ nobile Veneto./ In *Venetia,* M.DC. LXXXVI. Preſſo Pietr' Antonio Brigonci. Con Licenza de' Superiori, e Privilegio./ 2 *prel. leaves and* 200 *pp. Small copperplate Maps at pp.* 1, 93, 95, 102, 104, 107, 108, 111, 112, 114, 115, 117, 119, 127, 128, 130, 143, 156, 160, 166, 169, 171, 174, 176, 179. 4*to.* (10*s.* 6*d.* 2182)

PORCEL (Francisco Moreno). Retrato de Manuel de Faria y Sousa, Cavallero del Orden Militar de Chriſto, y de la Caſa Real. Contiene una Relacion de ſua Vida, un Catalogo de ſus Eſcritos, y un ſumario de ſus Elogios, recogidos de varios Autores, por D. Francisco Moreno Porcel; Aora nuevamenta acreſcentado con un Juiſio Hiſtorico, que compuzo el Excellentiſſimo Senhor Don Franciſco Xavier de Meneſes, Conde de la Erizeira. Ofrecido al Excellentissimo Senhor D. Luis de Meneses Quinto Conde de la Erizeira, del Concejo Su Mageſtad, Coronel, y Brigadero de Infanteria, Vi-Rey, y Capitan General que fue en los Eſtados de la India, &c. *Lisboa* Occidental, en la Officina Ferreiriana. M.DCC.XXXIII. Com todas las licencias neceſſarias. 8 *prel. leaves, and* 103 *pp. Unbound. Folio.* (2*l.* 2*s.* 2183)

PORCUPINE (Peter). Observations on the Debates of the American Congress, or the Addresses presented to General Washington, on his resignation: With remarks on the Timidity of the

Language held towards France; The Seizures
of American Veſſels by Great Britain and
France; and on the relative situations of those
countries with America. By Peter Porcupine,
Author of the Bone to gnaw for Democrats,—
Letter to Tom Paine, &c. &c. To which is prefixed, General Washington's Address to Congress;
and the answers of the Senate and House of
Representatives. Philadelphia printed: *London*
reprinted, David Ogilvy and Son, 1797. *Title
and* 38 *pp.* 8*vo.* (2s. 6d. 2184)

PORCUPINE'S WORKS; containing various
Writings and Selections, exhibiting a faithful
Picture of the United States of America; of their
Governments, Laws, Politics, and Rescources; of
the characters of their Presidents, Governors,
Legislators, Magistrates, and Military Men; and
of the Customs, Manners, Morals, Religion, Virtues and Vices of the People: Comprising also a
complete series of historical documents and remarks, from the end of the War, in 1783, to the
Election of the President, in March, 1801. By
William Cobbett. In Twelve Volumes. (*A Volume
to be added annually.*) *London:* Cobbett and
Morgan, May, 1801. *Twelve Volumes.* Vol. I.
400 *pp.* Vol. II. 2 *prel. leaves and* 472 *pp.* Vol.
III. 2 *prel. leaves and* 440 *pp.* Vol. IV. 2 *prel.
leaves and* 444 *pp.* Vol. V. 2 *prel. leaves and* 432
pp. Vol. VI. 2 *prel. leaves and* 432 *pp.* Vol. VII.
2 *prel. leaves and* 430 *pp.* Vol. VIII. 2 *prel. leaves
and* 480 *pp.* Vol. IX. 2 *prel. leaves and* 412 *pp.*
Vol. X. 2 *prel. leaves and* 449 *pp.* 'Postscript.—To
the Public.' 3 *pp.* Vol. XI. 2 *prel. leaves and* 434
pp. Vol. XII. 2 *prel. leaves and* 252 *pp.* 'Index'
81 *pp. Half calf.* 8*vo.* (2*l.* 2*s.* 2185)

PORTER (ELIPHALET). A Discourse before the
Society for Propagating the Gospel among the
Indians and others in North-America, delivered
November 5th, 1807. By Eliphalet Porter, D.D.
Pastor of the first Church in Roxbury. *Boston :*
Munroe, Francis, & Parker, 1808. 24 *pp.*
Uncut 8*vo.* (2s. 6d. 2186)

PORTEUS (BEILBY). A Letter to the Governors,
Legislatures, and Proprietors of Plantations, in the

British West-India Islands. By the Right Reverend Beilby Porteus, D.D. Bishop of London. *London:* T. Cadell and W. Davies, 1808. 48 *pp.* 8*vo.* (3*s.* 6*d.* 2187)

POTENT (The) Enemies of America laid open: Being Some account of the baneful effects attending the ufe of Distilled Spirituous Liquors, and the Slavery of the Negroes; To which is added, The happinefs attending life, when dedicated to the honour of God, and good of mankind, in the fentiments of fome perfons of eminence near the clofe of their lives, viz. the earl of Effex, count Oxciftern, H. Grotius, D. Brainard, John Lock, &c. *Philadelphia:* Printed by Joseph Crukshank in Market-Street, between Second and Third Streets. *A Collective title of the following:*—1*st.* 'The Mighty Destroyer displayed, In some Account of the Dreadful Havock made by the miftaken Use as well as Abuse of Distilled Spirituous Liquors. By a Lover of Mankind. *Philadelphia:* Printed by Joseph Crukshank, between Second and Third Streets, in Market-Street. M.DCC.LXXIV.' 48 *pp.* 2*nd.* 'Thoughts upon Slavery. By John Wesley, A. M. London Printed: Re-printed in *Philadelphia*, with notes and fold by Joseph Crukshank. MD,CC,LXXIV.' 83 *pp.* 3*rd.* 'To the foregoing teftimonies of the happinefs of a life fpent in the fervice of God, may be added that of a faithful fervant of Christ from amongft ourfelves, to wit, David Brainard,' *etc.* 16 *pp.* 4*th.* 'The Dreadful Visitation, in a short Account of the Progress and Effects of the Plague, The laft time it fpread in the city of London, in the year 1665, extracted from the memoirs of a perfon who refided there during the whole time of that infection. *Philadelphia:* Printed by Joseph Crukshank on the North fide of Market-Street, between Second and Third Streets. MDCC LXXIV.' 16 *pp. Small* 8*vo.* (15*s.* 2188)

POTHERIE (Bacqueville de la). Histoire de L'Amerique Septentrionale. Divifée en quatre Tomes. Tome Premier. Contenant le Voyage du Fort de Nelfon, dans la Baye d'Hudfon, a l'extrémité de l'Amerique. Le premier établiffement des François dans ce vafte païs, la prife

dudit Fort de Nelſon, la Deſcription du Fleuve de
faint Laurent, le gouvernement de Quebec, des
trois Rivieres & de Montreal, depuis 1534. juſqu'
à 1701. Par Mr. de Bacqueville de la Potherie,
né à la Guadaloupe, dans l'Amerique Meridionale,
Aide Major de la dite Iſle. Enrichie de Figures.
A Paris Jean-Luc Nion et Francois Didot, M.DCC.
XXII. Tome I. *7 prel. leaves including Engraved
title, and 370 pp. Table 4 pp. Copperplates at pp.*
16, 17, (2) 51, 56, 66, 67, 76, 80, 81, 100, 105,
132, 232, 311, 334, 351. *Vol. I. only. Old calf.*
12*mo.*   (4s. 6d.   2189)

POTTER (Lyman). A Sermon preached before
the General Aſſembly of the State of Vermont, On
the Day of their Anniversary Election, October 11,
1787, at Newbury. By Lyman Potter, A.M.
Pastor of the Church in Norwich. *Windsor [Ver-
mont]* Printed by Hough & Spooner. M.DCC.
LXXXVIII. *23 pp. 8vo.*   (4s. 6d.   2190)

POWNALL (Thomas). Principles of Polity, being
the Grounds and Reasons of Civil Empire. In
Three Parts. By Thomas Pownall, Eſq ; *London :* Edward Owen, MDCCLII. *viii, and text 142
pp. With 1 leaf of errata. Half morocco.*
4*to.*   (10s. 6d.   2191)

POWNALL (Thomas). Speedily will be Publiſhed,
[Sold by J. Almon, opposite Burlington-House,
Piccadilly] A Map of the Middle Britiſh Colonies
in North-America. First published by Mr. Lewis
Evans, of Philadelphia, in 1755; and ſince cor-
rected and improved, as alſo extended, with the
Addition of New-England, &c. and bordering
Parts of Canada; from actual Surveys now lying
at the Board of Trade. By T. Pownall, M.P.
Late Governor, &c. &c. of his Majeſty's Provinces
of Massachusets-Bay and South-Carolina, and
Lieutenant-Governor of New-Jersey. *4 pp. followed by* ' Books printed for J. Almon in Piccadilly,' *pp. 4-8. Half mor. 8vo.*   (4s. 6d.   2192)

POWNALL (Thomas). The Administration of the
Colonies. By Thomas Pownall, Late Governor
and Commander in Chief of his Majeſty's Provinces, Maſſachuſets-Bay and South-Carolina, and

Lieutenant-Governor of New-Jersey. The Second
Edition, Revifed, Corrected, and Enlarged. *London :* J. Dodsley, MDCCLXV. 13 *prel. leaves and*
202 *pp.* 'Appendix. Section 1. *and* II.' 60 *pp.*
Half-mor. 8*vo.* (7*s.* 6*d.* 2192*)

POWNALL (THOMAS). The Administration of the
Colonies. By Thomas Pownall, Late Governor
and Commander in Chief of his Majefty's Provinces, Maffachufets-Bay, and South-Carolina, and
Lieutenant-Governor of New-Jerfey. The Third
Edition, Revifed, Corrected and Enlarged. To
which is added, An Appendix, N°. III, containing, Confiderations on the Points lately brought
into Queftion as to the Parliament's Right of taxing the Colonies, and of the Meafures neceffary
to be taken at this Crifis. *London :* J. Dodsley,
MDCCLXVI. 14 *prel. leaves and* 202 *pp.* 'Appendix.
Section I. *and* II.' 60 *pp.* 'Appendix. Section
III.' 52 *pp. Calf.* 8*vo.* (9*s.* 2193)

POWNALL (THOMAS). The Administration of
the Colonies. (The Fourth Edition.) Wherein
their Rights and Constitution Are difcuffed and
ftated, By Thomas Pownall, Late Governor and
Commander in Chief of his Majefty's Provinces,
Maffachufetts-Bay and South-Carolina, and Lieutenant-Governor of New-Jerfey. *London :* J.
Walter, MDCCLXVIII. *Title, v to* xxxi *and* 318 *pp.*
'Appendix' 73 *pp. Calf.* 8*vo.* (10*s.* 6*d.* 2194)

POWNALL (THOMAS). The Administration of the
British Colonies. The Fifth Edition. Wherein
their Rights and Constitution Are difcuffed and
ftated. By Thomas Pownall, Late Governor,
Captain General, Commander in Chief, and Vice
Admiral of His Majefty's Provinces, Maffachufetts-Bay, and South-Carolina ; and Lieutenant-
Governor of New-Jerfey. In Two Volumes.
London : J. Walter, M.DCC.LXXIV. *Two Volumes.*
Vol. I. xi, *and* xv *prel. pp. Text* 288 *pp.* Vol. II.
xi *and* 171 *pp. followed by Half-title, errata, title,*
and 308 *pp. Fine copy in Old calf. Best Edition.*
8*vo.* (15*s.* 2195)

POWNALL (THOMAS). A Topographical description of such Parts of North America as are con-

tained in the (annexed) Map of the Middle British
Colonies, &c. In North America. By T. Pownall,
M.P. Late Governor, &c. &c. of his Majesty's
Provinces of Massachusetts Bay and South Caro-
lina, and Lieutenant Governor of New Jersey.
London: J. Almon, MDCCLXXVI. *vi,* 46 *and
Appendix* 16 *pp. With Map. Folio.* (1*l.* 1*s.* 2196)

POYNTZ (JOHN). The/ Prefent Profpect/ of the/
Famous and Fertile Island/ of/ Tobago,/ To the
Southward of/ The Ifland of Barbadoes./ With/
A Defcription of the Scituation, Growth, Fertility/
and Manufacture of the faid Ifland : Setting forth/
how that 100*l.* Stock in feven Years may be im-
proved to 5000*l.* per Annum./ To which is added/
Proposals for an Encouragement of all thofe that/
are minded to fettle there./ By Captain John
Poyntz./ The Second Edition./ *London,*/ Printed
by John Attwood for the Author, and fold/ by
William Starefmore at the Half Moon and Seven
Stars in/ Cornhill, and at the Marine Coffee-houfe
in Birchin-lane, 1695./ 3 *prel. leaves; viz. Title
reverse blank.* ' To The Ever Honoured Sr Jofeph
Herne.' 2 *pp.* ' To the Reader.' 2 *pp. Text* 50 *pp.
Calf extra by Bedford.* 4*to.* (1*l.* 15*s.* 6*d.* 2197)
With the Autograph of White Kennett on the title.

PRADT (M. DE). Des Colonies, et de la Révolution Actuelle de l'Amerique ; par M. de Pradt, ancien Archevêque de Malines. *Paris,* F. Bechet, A.
Egron, M.DCCC.XVII. *Two Volumes.* Tome Premier.
Half-title, title xxxii and 403 *pp. Errata* 1 *page.*
Tome Second. *Half-title, title, and* 394 *pp. Errata*
2 *pp. Calf extra.* 8*vo.* (8*s.* 6*d.* 2198)

PRECIOUS MORSELS. I. Features of Sundry
great Personages ; viz. His Majesty, George the
Third ; the late Earl of Bute, and present Lord
Hawkesbury ; King Midas marched from home ;
the Bamboozled Mynheers ; his Serene Highness,
John Bull, Pay Master General, &c. &c. II. A
Tit-Bit for Billy Pitt, &c. &c. III. America fast
A-Sleep. IV. The Wonders of the hatred of Liberty ; a raree-show. [*London* 1794.] 4 *prel. leaves
and* 44 *pp. Signed* ' Wm. Belcher.' *Unbound.*
8*vo.* (2*s.* 6*d.* 2199)

PRESENT (THE) Crisis, with respect to America,

considered. *London:* 1775. *Title and 46 pp. half mor. 8vo.* (4s. 6d. 2200)

PRESENT STATE (The) of the Britiſh Sugar Colonies Conſider'd: In a Letter From a Gentleman of Barbadoes to his Friend in London. *London:* Printed in the Year M.DCC.XXXI. *28 pp. half mor. 4to.* (5s. 6d. 2201)

PRESENT STATE (The) of the Country and Inhabitants, Europeans and Indians, of Louisiana, On the North Continent of America. By an Officer at New Orleans to his Friend at Paris. Containing The Garriſons, Forts and Forces, Price of all Manner of Proviſions and Liquors, &c. alſo an Account of their drunken lewd Lives, which lead them to Exceſſes of Debauchery and Villany. To which are added, Letters from the Governor of that Province on the Trade of the French and Engliſh with the Natives. Alſo Propoſals to them to put an end to their Traffick with the Engliſh. Annual Preſents to the Savages; a Liſt of the Country goods, and thoſe proper to be ſent there, &c. Tranſlated from the French Originals, taken in the Golden Lyon Prize, Raſteaux, Maſter, by the Hon. Capt. Aylmer, Commander of his Majeſty's Ship the Portmahon, and by him sent to the Admiralty Office. *London:* J. Millan, 1744. *55 pp. half mor. 8vo.* (7s. 6d. 2202)

PRESENT STATE (The) of North América, &c. Part 1. The Second Edition, with Emendations. *London:* J. Dodsley. MDCCLV. *2 prel. leaves and 88 pp. Half mor.* (7s. 6d. 2203)

RESENT STATE (The) of Great Britain and North America, with regard to Agriculture, Population, Trade, and Manufactures, impartially conſidered. Containing a particular Account of The dearth and ſcarcity of the neceſſaries of life in England; the want of staple commodities in the Colonies; the decline of their trade; increase of people; and neceſſity of manufaĉtures, as well as of a trade in them hereafter. In which The cauſes and conſequences of theſe growing evils, and methods of preventing them, are ſuggeſted; The proper Regulations for the Colonies, and the taxes impoſed upon them, are conſidered, and compared

with their condition and circumstances. *London :*
T. Becket. MDCCLXVII. 12 *prel. leaves & 364 pages.*
Old calf. 8vo. (7s. 6d. 2204)

PRESENT STATE (THE) of the Nation: Particularly with respect to its Trade, Finances, &c. &c.
Addressed to The King and both Houses of Parliament. *London:* J. Almon, MDCCLXIX. *Title, iv
and pp.* 9-107. *half mor. 8vo.* (4s. 6d. 2205)

PRICE (RICHARD). Cursory Remarks on Dr. Price's
Observations on the Nature of Civil Liberty. In
a Letter to a Friend. By a Merchant. *London :*
W. Nicoll, M,DCC,LXX,VI. *3 prel. leaves and 23 pp.*
half mor. (3s. 6d. 2206)

PRICE (RICHARD). Observations on the Nature of
Civil Liberty, the Principles of Government, and
the Justice and Policy of the War with America,
etc. London, Printed: *New-York,* Re-printed by
S. Loudon, in Water-Street. 1776. 107 *pp. half
mor. 8vo.* (3s. 6d. 2207)

PRICE (RICHARD). Observations on the Nature of
Civil Liberty, the Principles of Government, and
the Justice and Policy of the War with America,
etc. By Richard Price, D. D. F. R. S. The Third
Edition. *London :* T. Cadell, M.DCC.LXXVI. 4 *prel.*
leaves & 128 pp. half mor. 8vo. (3s. 6d. 2208)

PRICE (RICHARD). Observations on the Nature of
Civil Liberty, the Principles of Government, and
the Justice and Policy of the War with America.
To which is added An Appendix, Containing a
State of the National Debt, an Estimate of the
Money drawn from the Public by the Taxes, and
an Account of the National Income and Expendi-
ture since the last War. By Richard Price, D.D.
F.R.S. The Fourth Edition. *London :* T. Cadell,
M.DCC.LXXVI. 4 *prel. leaves and* 128 *pp. Unbound.*
8vo. (4s. 6d. 2209)

PRICE (RICHARD). Observations on the Nature of
Civil Liberty, the Principles of Government, and
the Justice and Policy of the War in America. To
which are added an Appendix and Postscript, containing a State of the National Debt, an Estimate
of the Money drawn from the Public by the Taxes,
and an Account of the National Income and Ex-

penditure fince the laft War. By Richard Price,
D. D. F. R. S. The Sixth Edition. *London :* T.
Cadell, MDCC.LXXVI. *4 prel. leaves and* 132 *pp. half*
mor. 8*vo.* (4*s.* 6*d.* 2210)

PRICE (RICHARD). Observations on the Nature of
Civil Liberty, the Principles of Government, and
the Justice and Policy of the War with America,
etc. By Richard Price, D.D. F.R.S. The Seventh
Edition. With Corrections and Additions. *Lon-*
don : T. Cadell, M.DCC.LXXVI. *4 prel. leaves and*
134 *pp.* 8*vo.* (2*s.* 6*d.* 2211)

PRICE (RICHARD). Observations on the Nature of
Civil Liberty, the Principles of Government, and
the Justice and Policy of the War with America.
To which are added, An Appendix and Postscript,
Containing a State of the National Debt, an Efti-
mate of the Money drawn from the Public by the
Taxes, and an Account of the National Income and
Expenditure fince the laft War. By Richard Price,
D.D. F.R.S. The Eighth Edition, newly corrected
by the Author. *Edinburgh :* [By permiffion of the
Author.] J. Wood and J. Dickson. M,DCC,LXXVI.
4 prel. leaves and 94 *pp.* 12*mo.* (3*s.* 6*d.* 2212)

PRICE (RICHARD). Observations on the Nature of
Civil Liberty, the Principles of Government, and
the Justice and Policy of the War with America.
To which is added, An Appendix and Postscript,
containing A State of the National Debt, An Estimate of the Money drawn from the Public by the
Taxes, and An Account of the National Income
and Expenditure fince the laft War. By Richard
Price, D.D. F.R.S. The Ninth Edition. *London :*
Edward and Charles Dilly, M.DCC.LXXVI. 48 *pp.*
half. mor. 8*vo.* (3*s.* 6*d.* 2213)

PRICE (RICHARD). Observations on Dr. Price's
Theory and Principles of Civil Liberty and Government, Preceded by a Letter to a Friend, on
the Pretenfions of the American Colonies, In refpect of Right and Equity. *York :* A. Ward, 1776.
4 prel. leaves and 147 *pp.* 8*vo.* (3*s.* 6*d.* 2214)

PRICE (RICHARD). Remarks on a Pamphlet lately
published by Dr. Price, intitled, Observations on
the Nature of Civil Liberty, the Principles of Government, and the Justice and Policy of the War

with America, &c. In a Letter from a Gentleman
in the Country to a Member of Parliament. *London:* T. Cadell, MDCCLXXVI. *Title and 61 pp. half
mor. 8vo.*   (4s. 6d. 2215)

PRICE (RICHARD). Remarks on Dr. Price's Observations on the Nature of Civil Liberty, &c.
London: G. Kearsley, MDCCLXXVI. *2 prel. leaves and
76 pp. Half mor. 8vo.*   (4s. 6d. 2216)

PRICE (RICHARD). Three Letters to Dr. Price, containing Remarks on his Observations on the Nature of Civil Liberty, the Principles of Government,
and the Juſtice and Policy of the War with America. By a Member of Lincoln's Inn, F.R.S. F.S.A.
London, T. Payne, MDCCLXXVI. *Half-title, title, xxii
and 163 pp. Half mor. 8vo.*   (4s. 6d. 2217)

PRICE (RICHARD). Additional Observations On the
Nature and Value of Civil Liberty, and the War
with America: Also Observations on Schemes for
raiſing Money by Public Loans; An Hiſtorical Deduction and Analyſis of the National Debt; And
a brief Account of the Debts and Resources of
France. By Richard Price, D.D. F.R.S. *London:* T. Cadell, M.DCC.LXXVII. *xvi and 176 pp.
8vo.*   (2s. 6d. 2218)

PRICE (RICHARD). Additional Observations On the
Nature and Value of Civil Liberty, and the War
with America: Also Observations on Schemes for
raiſing Money by Public Loans; An Hiſtorical Deduction and Analyſis of the National Debt; And
a brief Account of the Debts and Resources of
France. By Richard Price, D.D. F.R.S. The Second Edition. *London:* T. Cadell, M.DCC.LXXVII.
xvi and 176 pp. half mor. 8vo.   (4s. 6d. 2219)

PRICE (RICHARD). Additional Observations On the
Nature and Value of Civil Liberty, and the War
with America: Also Observations on Schemes for
raiſing Money by Public Loans; An Hiſtorical Deduction and Analyſis of the National Debt; And
a brief Account of the Debts and Resources of
France. Ry Richard Price, D.D. F.R.S. The
Third Edition, with Additions. *London:* T. Cadell,
M.DCCLXXVIII. *xxii and 176 pp. 8vo.* (4s. 6d. 2220)

PRICE (RICHARD). The General Introduction and

Supplement to The Two Tracts on Civil Liberty,
the War with America, and the Finances of the
Kingdom. By Richard Price, D.D. F.R.S. *London:*
Printed for T. Cadell, in the Strand. MDCCLXXVIII.
Title, xxvi and pp. 181-216. ' A Summary View '
etc. a folded sheet. 8vo.   (4s. 6d.   2221)

PRICE (RICHARD). A Sermon delivered to a Congregation of Protestant Dissenters, at Hackney,
On the 10th of February laft, Being the Day appointed for a General Fast. By Richard Price,
D.D. F.R.S. The Third Edition. To which are
added, Remarks on a Passage in the Bishop of
London's Sermon on Ash-Wednesday, 1779. *London:* T. Cadell, M.DCC.LXXIX. *2 prel. leaves and* 45
pp. Half mor. 8vo.   (2s. 6d.   2222)

PRICE (RICHARD). Three Letters to the Rev. Dr.
Price: Containing Remarks upon his Fast-Sermon.
By a Cobler. *London:* S. Bladon, MDCCLXXIX.
Half-title, title, and 35 pp.   (3s. 6d.   2223)

PRICE (RICHARD). Observations on the Importance
of the American Revolution, and The Means of
making it a Benefit to the World. To which is
added, A Letter from M. Turgot, late Comptroller-
General of the Finances of France : With An Ap-
pendix, containing a Tranflation of the Will of M.
Fortune Ricard, lately publifhed in France. By
Richard Price, D.D. L.L.D. And Fellow of the
Royal Society of London, and of the Academy of
Arts and Sciences in New-England. *London* : T.
Cadell, M.DCC.LXXXV. *viii and* 156 *pp. Errata* 4
lines. half mor. 8vo.   (4s. 6d.   2224)

PRIEST (WILLIAM). Travels in the United States
of America; commencing in the year 1793, and
ending in 1797. With the Author's Journals of
his two Voyages across the Atlantic. By William
Priest, Musician, late of the Theatres Philadelphia,
Baltimore and Boston. *London* : J. Johnson, 1802.
x and 214 *pp. Frontispiece. 8vo.*   (5s.   2225)

PRIESTLEY (JOSEPH). Observations on the Emigration of Dr. Joseph Priestley, and on the several
addresses delivered to him on his arrival at New-
York. New Edition. Philadelphia, printed. *London:* Re-printed for John Stockdale, 1794.   63 *pp.*
8vo.   (2s. 6d.   2226)

PRIMER,/ (A)/ for the Use of the/ Mohawk Children,/ To acquire the Spelling and Reading of
their/ own, as well as to get acquainted with the/
English Tongue; which for that Purpose is put/
on the oppofite Page./ Waerighwaghsawe/ Iksa-
ongvenwa/Tfiwaondad-derighhonny Kaghyadogh=
fera; Nayon-/deweyeftaghk ayeweanaghnòdon ay-
eghyàdow Ka-/niyenkehàga Kaweanondaghkouh :
Dyorheaf-hàga/ oni tfinihadiweanotea./ *London,/*
Printed by C. Buckton, Great Pultney-Street/.
1786. *Frontispiece, and* 98 *pp. including Title. Old
tree calf./ 24mo.* (*3l.* 13*s.* 6*d.* 2227)

PRINCE (DEBORAH). Dying Exercises of Mrs.
Deborah Prince : And Devout Meditations of Mrs.
Sarah Gill, Daughters of the late Rev. Mr. Thomas
Prince, Minifter of the South Church, Boston.
Edinburgh : D. Paterson, MDCCLXXXV. 46 *pp.*
12*mo.* (7*s.* 6*d.* 2228)

PRINCE (THOMAS). A Sermon Delivered By Thomas Prince, M.A. On Wenfday Octoober 1. 1718.
At his Ordination to the Pastoral Charge Of the
South Church in Bofton, N. E. In Conjunction
with the Re-verend Mr. Joseph Sewall. Together
with The Charge, By the Reverend Increase Mather, D.D. And a Copy of what was faid at giving
the Right Hand of Fellowfhip : By the Reverend
Cotton Mather, D.D. To which is added, A Discourse Of the Validity of Ordination by the Hands
of Presbyters, Previous to Mr. Sewall's on September 16. 1713. By the Late Reverend and Learned
Mr. Ebenezer Pemberton, Paftor of the fame
Church. *Boston :* Printed by J. Franklin for S.
Gerrish, and Sold at his Shop, near the Old Meeting-Houfe. 1718. 4 *prel. leaves and* 76 *pp.* ' A
Discourse had By the late Reverend and Learned
Mr. Ebenezer Pemberton, Previous to the Ordination Of the Reverend Mr. Jofeph Sewall, At Boston, September 16. 1713. Affirming and proving
the Validity of Presbyterial Ordination. *Boston :*
Printed by J. Franklin, for S. Gerrish, and Sold at
his Shop near the Old Meeting Houfe. 1718.' 2
prel. leaves and 15 *pp. Small 8vo.* (1*l.* 11*s.* 6*d.* 2229)

PRINCE (THOMAS). The Departure of Elijah lamented A Sermon Occafioned By the Great & Pub-

lick Lofs In the Deceafe of the very Reverend &
Learned Cotton Mather, D.D. F.R.S. And Senior
Paftor of the North Church in Boston: Who left
this Life on Feb. 13th 1727, 8. The Morning after
He finifhed the LXV Year of his Age. By Thomas
Prince, M.A. And one of the Paftors of the South
Church. *Boston* in New-England: Printed for D.
Henchman, near the Brick Meeting Houfe in Corn-
hil. MDCCXXVIII. *Half-title, title, and 26 pp.*
8*vo.*   (7*s.* 6*d.* 2230)

PRINCE (THOMAS). A Chronological Hiftory of
New-England In the Form of Annals: Being A
fummary and exaɛt Account of the moft material
Tranfaɛtions and Occurrences relating to This
Country, in the Order of Time wherein they happened, from the Difcovery by Capt. Gosnold in
1602, to the Arrival of Governor Belcher, in 1730.
With an Introduction, Containing A brief Epitome
of the moft remarkable Tranfaɛtions and Events
Abroad, from the Creation: Including the con-
neɛted Line of Time, the Succeffion of Patriarchs
and Sovereigns of the moft famous Kingdoms and
Empires, the gradual Difcoveries of America, and
the Progress of the Reformation to the Difcovery
of New England. By Thomas Prince, M.A. *Boston,* N. E. Printed by Kneeland & Green for S.
Gerrish, MDCCXXXVI. Vol. I. *5 prel. leaves, xii, and*
20 *pp.* 'The Introduction' 104 *pp.* 'The New-
England Chronology' Part I. *and* Part II. 254 *pp.*
Old calf. Small 8*vo.*   (15*s.* 2231)

PRINCE (THOMAS). Extraordinary Events the Do-
ings of God, and marvellous in pious Eyes. Illuftrated In a Sermon At the South Church in Bofton,
N. E. On the General Thanksgiving, Thurfday,
July 18. 1745. Occafion'd By taking the City of
Louifbourg on the Ifle of Cape-Breton, by New-
England Soldiers, affifted by a Britifh Squadron.
By Thomas Prince, M.A. And one of the Paftors
of faid Church. *Boston:* Printed for D. Henchman in Cornhil. 1745. *2 prel. leaves and pp.* 7-35.
8*vo.*   (7*s.* 6*d.* 2232)

PRINCE (THOMAS). Extraordinary Events the Do-
ings of God, and marvellous in pious Eyes. Illustrated in a Sermon At the South Church in Bofton,

N. E. On the General Thanksgiving, Thursday,
July 18, 1745. Occafion'd By Taking the City of
Louifbourg on the Ifle of Cape-Breton, by New-
England Soldiers, affifted by a Britifh Squadron.
By Thomas Prince, M.A. And one of the Paftors
of the faid Church. The Third Edition. Boston,
Printed: *London,* Reprinted; J. Lewis, 1746. 32
pp. 8vo. (*7s. 6d.* 2233)

PRINCE (Thomas). Extraordinary Events the Do-
ings of God, and marvellous in pious Eyes. Illuftrated in a Sermon at the South Church in Bofton,
N. E. On the General Thanksgiving, Thursday,
July 18. 1745. Occafion'd By taking the City of
Louifbourg on the Ifle of Cape-Breton, by New-
England Soldiers, affifted by a Britifh Squadron.
By Thomas Prince, M.A. And one of the Paftors
of faid Church. *Edinburgh:* R. Fleming and Company. 1746. 3 *prel. leaves and pp.* 5-38. *Unbound.*
8vo. (*5s. 6d.* 2234)

PRINCE (Thomas). The Salvation of God in 1746.
In Part fet forth in a Sermon At the South Church
in Bofton, Nov. 27. 1746. Being the Day of the
Anniversary Thanksgiving In the Province of the
Maffachufetts Bay in N. E. Wherein The moft remarkable Salvations of the Year paft, both in Europe and North-America, as far as they are come
to our Knowledge, are briefly confidered. By Thomas Prince, M.A. And a Paftor of the faid Church.
Boston: Printed for D. Henchman in Cornhil.
1746. *Title and pp.* 5-35. *8vo.* (*7s. 6d.* 2235)

PRINCE (Thomas). A Sermon Delivered At the
South Church in Bofton, N. E. Auguft 14. 1746.
Being the Day of General Thanksgiving for The
great Deliverance of the Britifh Nations by The
glorious and happy Victory near Culloden. Ob-
tained by His Royal Highnefs Prince William
Duke of Cumberland April 16. laft. Wherein The
Greatnefs of the Publick Danger and Deliverance
is in Part fet forth, to excite their moft grateful
Praifes to the God of their Salvation. By Thomas
Prince, M.A. And a Paftor of the faid Church.
Boston: Printed for D. Henchman in Cornhil, and
S. Kneeland and T. Green in Queen-ftreet. 1746.
Title and pp. 5-39. *8vo.* (*7s. 6d.* 2236)

PRINCE (Thomas). A Sermon Deliver'd at the South Church in Boston, New-England, Auguft 14, 1746. Being the Day of General Thanksgiving for the Great Deliverance of the Britifh Nations, by the Glorious and Happy Victory near Culloden. Obtained by His Royal Highness Prince William Duke of Cumberland, April 16, in the fame Year. Wherein the Greatness of the Publick Danger and Deliverance is in Part fet forth, to excite their moft grateful Praifes to the God of their Salvation. By Thomas Prince, M.A. And a Paftor of the faid Church. Boston Printed: *London*, Re-printed, John Lewis, 1747. *39 pp. 8vo.* (*7s. 6d. 2237*)

PRINCE (Thomas). The natural and moral Government and Agency of God in caufing Droughts and Rains. A Sermon At the South Church in Boston, Thurfday, Aug. 24. 1749. Being the Day of the General Thanksgiving, In the Province of the Massachusetts, For the extraordinary reviving Rains, after the moft diftreffing Drought which have been known among us in the Memory of any Living. By Thomas Prince, A.M. And a Paftor of the faid Church. *Boston:* Printed and Sold at Kneeland and Green's, in Queen Street, 1749. *3 prel. leaves and 40 pp. 8vo.* (*4s. 6d. 2238*)

PRINCE (Thomas). Six Sermons by the late Thomas Prince, A.M. one of the Ministers of the South Church In Boston. Publifhed from his Manuscripts, By John Erskine, D.D. one of the Ministers of Edinburgh. *Edinburgh:* David Paterson, MDCCLXXXV. *xvi and text 156 pp. Half morocco. 12mo.* (*7s. 6d. 2239*)

The 16 preliminary pages are occupied with an interesting Memoir of Thomas Prince and the Prince family, By Dr. John Erskine.

PRINCE (Thomas). A Chronological History of New-England, in the form of Annals: Being A Summary and exact Account of the most material Transactions and Occurrences relating to this Country, in the order of Time wherein they happened, from the Discovery of Capt. Gosnold, in 1602, to the Arrival of Governor Belcher, in 1730. With an Introduction containing A brief Epitome of the most considerable Transactions and Events abroad, From the Creation. Including the con-

nected line of Time, the succession of Patriarchs
and Sovereigns of the most famous Kingdoms and
Empires; the gradual Discoveries of America, and
the Progress of the Reformation, to the Discovery
of New-England. By Thomas Prince, M.A. *Boston*, N. E. Printed by Kneeland & Green, for S.
Gerrish. MDCCXXXVI. A New Edition, published
by Cummings, Hilliard, and Company. 1826. 439
pp. 8vo.   (8s. 6d. 2240)

PRINCIPLES of Trade. Freedom and Protection
are its beſt Suport : Induſtry, the only Means to
render Manufactures cheap. Of Coins; Exchange;
and Bountys; particularly on Corn. By a Well-
Wiſher to his King and Country. With an Appendix. Containing Reflections on Gold, Silver,
and Paper paſſing as Mony. The Second Edition
corected and enlarg'd. *London*, Brotherton and
Sewell, MDCCLXXIV. *3 prel. leaves and* 48 *pp.* ' Appendix' 16 *pp. Old tree calf. 8vo.*   (15s. 2241)
This copy once belonged to William Vaughan, who has written on
its fly leaf " N.B. The Notes by Dr. Franklin."

PRINCIPLES of Law and Government with an inquiry into the Justice and Policy of the Present
War, [with America], and most effectual means of
obtaining an honourable, permanent, and advantageous Peace. *London* : J. Murray, MDCCLXXXI.
Two Parts. Part I. *3 prel. leaves and 202 pp.* Part
II. *Half-title and 127 pp. Errata* 1 *page. Old calf.
4to.*   (7s. 6d. 2242)

PROCLAMATION. By the Queen, a Proclamation, For Settling and Aſcertaining the Current
Rates of Foreign Coins in Her Majeſties Colonies
and Plantations in America : [*Colophon*]. *London*,
Printed by Charles Bill, and the Executrix of Thomas Newcomb, deceas'd ; Printers to the Queens
moſt Excellent Majeſty. 1704. *A Broadside. half
mor. Folio.*   (4s. 6d. 2243)

PROGRESS (THE) of the French In their Views of
Univerſal Monarchy. *London* : W. Owen, M.D.CC.
LVI. *vi and 58 pp. 8vo.*   (4s. 6d. 2244)

PROPOSAL (A) For putting a Speedy End to the
War, By Ruining the Commerce of the French and
Spaniards, And Securing our Own, Without any
additional Expence to the Nation. *London*, Daniel
Brown, MDCCIII, *viii and pp.* 5-18. *Half morocco.
4to.*   (7s. 6d. 2245)

PROPOSAL (A) For Humbling Spain. Written in 1711. By a Perſon of Diſtinction. And now firſt printed from the Manuscript. To which are added, Some Conſiderations on the Means of Indemnifying Great Britain from the Expences of the Preſent War. *London:* J. Roberts, [1739?] *viii and 72 pp. half mor. 8vo.* (*7s. 6d.* 2246)

PROPOSAL (A) For Humbling Spain. Written in 1711. By a Perſon of Diſtinction. And now firſt printed from the Manuscript. To which are added Some Conſiderations on the Means of Indemnifying Great Britain from the Expences of the Preſent War. The Second Edition. *London:* J. Roberts [1739?] *viii and 72 pp. half mor. 8vo.* (*7s. 6d.* 2247)

PROPOSALS Offered for the Sugar Planters Redress, And for Reviving the Britiſh Sugar Commerce. In a further Letter from a Gentleman of Barbadoes, To his Friend in London. *London,* J. Wilford, M.DCC.XXXIII. *35 pp. Half morocco. 4to.* (*4s. 6d.* 2248)

PROPOSALS For Uniting the English Colonies on the Continent of America So as to enable them to act with Force and Vigour againſt their Enemies. *London:* J. Wilkie, M.DCC.LVII. *Title, vi and 38 pp. half mor. 8vo.* (*7s. 6d.* 2249)

PROSPECT (A) of the Consequences of the Preſent Conduct of Great Britain towards America. *London:* J. Almon, 1776. *98 pp. Half morocco. 8vo.* (*5s. 6d.* 2250)

PROSPECTS on the Rubicon: Or, an Investigation into the Causes and Consequences of the Politics to be agitated at the Meeting of Parliament. *London:* MDCCLXXXVII. *iv and 68 pp. Half morocco. 8vo.* (*4s. 6d.* 2251)

PROTEST Against the Bill To repeal the American Stamp Act, of Last Session. A *Paris,* J. W. M.DCC. LXVI. *16 pp. 8vo.* (*4s. 6d.* 2252)

PROTEST (SECOND), with a List of the Voters against the Bill To Repeal the American Stamp Act, of Last Session. A *Paris,* J. W. 1766. *15 pp. With Errata to the 1st and 2nd Protest 14 lines. 8vo.* (*4s. 6d.* 2253)

PROTESTS. Correct Copies Of the Two Protests against the Bill To Repeal the American Stamp Act, of Last Session. With Lists of the Speakers and Voters. A *Paris*, J. W. M.DCC.LXVI. *22 pp.* ' A List' *etc.* 8 *pp. 8vo.*   (4s. 6d.   2254)

PROUD (Robert). The History of Pennsylvania, in North America, from the Original Institution and Settlement of that Province, under the first Proprietor and Governor William Penn, in 1681, till after the Year 1742 ; with an Introduction respecting The Life of W. Penn, prior to the grant of the Province, and the religious Society of the People called Quakers ;—with the first rise of the neighbouring Colonies, more particularly of West-New-Jersey, and the Settlement of the Dutch and Swedes on Delaware. To which is added, A brief Description of the said Province, and of the General State, in which it flourished, principally between the Years 1760 and 1770. The whole including a Variety of Things Useful and interesting to be known, respecting that Country in early Time, &c. With an Appendix. Written principally between the Years 1776 and 1780, By Robert Proud. *Philadelphia*, Printed and Sold by Zachariah Poulson, Junior, Number Eighty, Chesnut Street, 1797. *Two Volumes.* Volume I. 508 *pp. With Portrait of Penn, and Map of Pennsylvania.* Volume II. ' Printed *etc.* No. 106, Chesnut street, Nearly opposite to the Bank of North America. 1798.' *373 pp.* 'Appendix' *etc.* 146 *pp. 8vo.*   (1l. 1s.   2255)

PSALMS. The/ Psalms,/ Hymns,/ and/ Spiritual Songs/ of the/ Old and New Testament,/ Faithfully Translated into/ English Metre./ For the use, edification, and comfort of the/ Saints in publick and private, espe-/cially in New-England./ *Cambridge,*/ Printed for Hezekiah Usher, of Bostoo./ [1664]. 94 *pp. including the title. Imperfect, wanting all after page* 94. *Red morocco extra by Francis Bedford.* 12*mo.*   (10l. 10s.   2256)

PSALTERIUM AMERICANUM. The' Book of Psalms, In a Translation Exactly conformed unto the Original; but all in Blank Verse, Fitted unto the Tunes commonly used in our Churches. Which Pure Offering is accompanied with Illustrations, digging for Hidden Treasures in it; And Rules to

Employ it upon the Glorious and Various Inten-
tions of it. Whereto are added, Some other Por-
tions of the Sacred Scripture, to Enrich the Can-
tional. *Boston :* in N. E. Printed by S. Kneeland,
for B. Eliot, S. Gerrish, D. Henchman, and J. Edwards, and Sold at their Shop, 1718. *Title, xxxvi and
426 pp. Imperfect, wanting pages iii and iv. Bound.
Small 8vo.* (2*l.* 2*s.* 2257)

PTOLEMÆUS (Claudius). In hoc Opere/ hæc con-
ti/nentvr Geographiæ Cl. Ptolemæi a plurimis uiris
utriusſq3 linguæ doctiſſ./ emēdata : & cū archetypo
græco ab ipſis collata./ Schemata cū demonſtra-
tionibus ſuis correcta a Marco Beneuentano/ Monacho cœleſtino & Joanne Cotta Veronenſi uiris
Mathematicis/ conſultiſſimis./ Figura de proiectione
ſpheræ in plano quæ in libro octauo deſidera/ batur
ad ipſis nōdum inſtaurata ſed fere ad inuenta eius.
n. ueſtigia/ in nullo etiam græco codice extabant./
Maxima quantitas diert ciuitatū : & diſtantiæ locon
ab Alexâdria/ Aegypti cuiuſq3 ciuitatis : quæ malijs
codicibus nō erant./ Planiſphærium Cl. Ptolemei
nouiter recognitū & diligentiſſ. emen-/datum a
Marco Beneuentano Monacho celeſtino./ Noua
orbis deſcriptio ac noua Oceani nauigatio qua Liſ-
bona ad/ Indicū peruenitur pelagus Marco Beneuentano monacho cæle-/ſtino ædita./ Noua & uni-
uerſalior Orbis cogniti tabula Ioā. Ruyſch Germano/
elaborata./ Sex Tabulæ nouiter confectæ uidelicet
Liuoniæ : Hyſpaniæ Galliæ :/ Germaniæ : Italiæ :
& Iudeæ./ Cavtvm est edicto Ivlii. II. Pont. Max./
ne q vis Imprimere avt Imprimi/ facere avdeat hoc
ipsvm opvs/ pena excommvnicationis latæ Senten-
tiae/ his qvi contra Mandatvm Ivssvmqve/ conari
avdebvnt./ Anno Virginei Partvs/ MDVIII./
Rome. Signatures A. [D & E *in six*] *to* N. *in
eights, O. in seven, followed by 34 copperplate Maps.*
' Incipit Regiſtrum' *etc; signatures* Aa & Bb *in eights,*
Cc *in four.* ' Reuerendiſſimo in Chriſto' *etc. signatures* a *in six* b *in eight. Fine copy. Vellum.
Folio.* (3*l.* 3*s.* 2258)

PTOLEMÆUS (Claudius). Geo-/graphiæ/ vni-
versæ/ tvm veteris, tvm/ novæ absolvtissimum/
opus, duobus voluminibus distinctum,/ In quorum
priore habentur/ Cl. Ptolemæi Pelvsiensis/ Geo-
graphicæ enarrationis Libri octo :/ Quorum primus,
qui præcepta ipſius facultatis omnia complectitur,/

commentarijs vberrimis illuftratus est à/ Io. Antonio Magino Patavino./ In fecundo volumine in
funt/ Cl. Ptolemaei, antiquæ orbis tabulæ xxvii. ad
prifcas hi-/ftorias intelligendas fummè neceffariæ.
Et tabulæ xxxvii. recen-/tiores, quibus vniuerfi
orbis pictura, ac facies, fingularumqӡ/ eius partium,
regionum, ac prouinciarum ob ocu-/los patet noftro
sæculo congruens. Vnà cum ipfarum tabularum
copiofiffimis expofitionibus, quibus fingulæ/ orbis
partes, prouinciæ, regiones, imperia, regna, duca-
tus, &/ alia dominia, prout nostro tempore fe habent,/ exactè defcribuntur/ Auctore eodem Io. Ant.
Magino/ Patavino, Mathematicarum in/ Almo Bo-
nonienfi Gymnafio publico profeffore./ Anno 1597./
In celeberrima Agrippinensivm *Coloniæ* excvdebat/
Petrvs Keschedt./ *Two Parts.* [Part I.] 4 *prel.
leaves*, 47 *and* 184 *pp. Index* 38 *pp.* [Part II]. *Title
and folived leaves* 2-292. *Index* 56 *pp. Vellum.
4to.*   (12s. 6d. 2259)

PUGH (Ellis). A Salutation to the Britains, To
  Call them From the Many Things, to the One
  Thing needful, for the Saving of their Souls; Especially, To the poor unlearned Tradefmen, Plow-
  men and Shepherds, thofe that are of a low Degree
  like my felf, This, in Order to direct you to know
  God and Chrift, the only wife God, which is Life
  eternal, and to learn of him, that you may become
  wifer than your Teachers. By Ellis Pvgh. Tranflated from the Britifh Language by Rowland Ellis,
  Revis'd and Corrected by David Lloyd. *Philadelphia:* Printed by S. Keimer, for W. Davies,
  Bookbinder, in Chefnut-Street. 1727. *xv and* 222
  pp. Old calf. 16*mo.*   (1*l.* 1s. 2260)

PULLEIN (Samuel). The Culture of Silk: Or,
  an Essay on its rational Practice and Improvement. In Four Parts. I. On the raifing and planting of Mulberry Trees. II. On hatching and rear-
  ing the Silk-Worms. III. On obtaining their Silk
  and Breed. IV. On reeling their Silk-Pods. For
  the ufe of the American Colonies. By the Rev.
  Samuel Pullein. M.A. *London:* A. Millar, mdcc
  lviii. *xv and* 399 *pp. With two plates. Old calf.*
  8*vo.*   (7s. 6d. 2261)

PULTENEY (William). Thoughts on the present

State of Affairs with America, and the means of Conciliation. By William Pulteney, Esq : The Third Edition. *London :* J. Dodsley, MDCCLXXVIII. *Title and* 102 *pp. half mor.* 8*vo.* (4*s.* 6*d.* 2262)

PULTENEY (WILLIAM). Thoughts on the present state of affairs with America, and the means of conciliation. By William Pulteney, Esq. The fourth edition. *London:* J. Dodsley, MDCCLXXVIII. *Title and* 102 *pp. half mor.* 8*vo.* (4*s.* 6*d.* 2263)

PULTENEY (WILLIAM). Considerations on the Present State of Public Affairs, and the means of raising the necessary Supplies. By William Pulteney, Esq. The Second Edition. *London :* J. Dodsley, MDCCLXXIX. *Title and* 51 *pp. half mor.* 8*vo.* (4*s.* 6*d.* 2264)

PURCHAS (SAMUEL). Pvrchas his Pilgrimage./ Or/ Relations/ of the World/ and the Religions/ observed in all Ages/ And places difcouered, from the/ Creation vnto this/ present./ In foure Partes./ This first contai-/neth A Theological and/ Geographical Hiftorie of Afia, Africa,/ and America, with the Iflands/ Adiacent./ Declaring the Ancient Religions before the Flovd, the/ Heathnifh, Jewifh, and Saracenicall in all Ages fince, in thofe/ parts profeffed, with their feuerall Opinions, Idols, Oracles, Temples,/ Prieftes, Fafts, Feafts, Sacrifices, and Rites Religious : Their/ beginnings, Proceedings, Alterations, Se&ts,/ Orders and Succeffions./ With briefe Defcriptions of the Countries, Nations, States, Difcoueries,/ Priuate and Publike Cuftomes, and the moft Remarkable Rarities of/ Nature, or Humane Induftrie, in the fame./ By Samvel Pvrchas, Minifter at Eftwood in Effex./ *London,*/ Printed by William Stansby for Henrie Fetherftone, and are to be/ fold at his Shoppe in Pauls Church-yard at the/ Signe of the Rofe 1613./ 14 *prel. leaves ; viz. Title reverse blank ;* 'The Epistle Dedicatorie.' 4 *pp :* 'To the Reader.' 4 *pp. Epigrams* 2 *pp ;* 'The Contents' *etc.* 9 *pp ;* 'The Catalogue of the Authors.' 6 *pp ; Text* 752 *pp.* 'Table of the principall Matters' *etc.* 20 *pp. Fine copy. Old calf. Folio.* (18*s.* 2265)

PURCHAS (SAMUEL). Pvrchas his Pilgrim./ Mi-

crocosmvs,/ or/ the Historie/ Of Man./　Relating
the ⎰ Wonders of his Generation,/　⎱
⎱ Vanities in his Degeneration,/ ⎰
⎰ Neceffity of his Regeneration./ ⎱
Meditated on the words of David.　By Samuel
Pvrchas, Parfon of S. Martins/ neere Lvdgate, London./　*London,*/ Printed by W. S. for Henry Fetherftone./　1619./　14 *prel. leaves and* 818 *pp.　Old
calf.　Small 8vo.*　　　　　　　(15s.　2266)

PURNELL (THOMAS).　The following is a true and
faithful Account of the Loss of the Brigantine Tyrrell, Arthur Coghlan, Commander; with the Misfortunes attending the faid Veffel's Crew.　By Thomas Purnell, Chief Mate thereof.　[*London.*] *Dated*
' Hoxton Sept. 1766.'　*Signed* ' Thomas Purnell.'
8 *pp.　4to.*　　　　　　　　　(7s. 6d.　2267)

PURRY (JOHN PETER).　A Method For Determining the best Climate of the Earth, On a Principle
to which All Geographers and Historians have been
hitherto Strangers.　In a Memorial prefented to
the Governors of the East-India Company in Holland, for which The Author was obliged to leave
that Country, By John Peter Purry.　Translated
from the French.　*London*, M. Cooper, MDCCXLIV.
2 *prel. leaves and text* 60 *pp.　Half morocco.*
8vo.　　　　　　　　　　　(4s. 6d.　2268)

PYNCHON (WILLIAM).　I The Time when the/
First Sabbath/ was Ordained./　1 Negatively, Not
in the Time of Adams Innocency,/ as many fay it
was./　2 Affirmatively, It was Ordained after the
Time of/ Adams Fall and Re-creation./　II The
Manner how the Firft Sabbath was Ordained./　1
By bleffing the Seventh Day with many Spiritual
Or-/dinances, both for publick and private ufe./
2 By Sanctifying that Day for the Exercife of the
faid Or-/dinances./　3 By Sanctifying the outward
Reft of that Day, to be a Ty-/pical Sign both of
Gods Refting, and of mans Refting/ in the Seed of
the Woman, that was promifed to break/ the Devils
Head-plot, namely, by his Propitiatory Sacrifice./
And hence it follows,/ 1 That as the Sabbath was
Ordained to be a typical Sign,/ fo it muft be abo-
lifhed; as foon as Chrift had performed/ his faid
Propitiatory Sacrifice./　2 As it was Ordained to
be the Sanctified time, for the/ Exercife of the faid

bleſſed Ordinances; ſo the next day of/ the week,
into which it was changed, muſt continue with-/out
intermiſſion to the end of the world./ Part II.
III A Treatiſe of Holy Time, concerning the true
limits/ of the Lords Day, when it begins, and when
it ends, is/ hereunto annexed/ By William Pynchon Eſq./ Publiſhed by Authority./ *London,*
Printed by R. I. and are to be ſold by T. N. at the
three Lions/ in Cornhil, near the Royal Exchange
1654./ *Two Parts.* Part I. 8 *prel. leaves and* 143
pp: Part II. 8 *prel. leaves and* 120 *pp. Old calf.*
4to. (15*s.* 2269)

PYNCHON (William). The Meritorious Price/
of/ Mans Redemption,/ or/ Chriſts Satisfaction diſcuſſed and explained./ 1 By ſhewing how the Sufferings and the Sacrifice of Chriſt, did ſatisfie Gods/
Juſtice, pacifie his Wrath, and procure his Reconciliation for mans Redemp-/tion, from Satans Head-
plot./ 2 By vindicating the Sufferings and the Sacrifice of Chriſt, from that moſt dan-/gerous Scrip-
ture-leſs Tenent, that is held forth by Mr. Norton of
New-England/ in his Book of *Chriſts Sufferings,*
affirming that he ſuffered the Eſſential Tor-/ments
of Hell, and the ſecond death from Gods immediate
vindicative wrath. 3 By ſhewing that the Righteouſneſs and Obedience of Christ in relation to his/
Office of Madiatorſhip, is a diſtinct ſort of obedience,
from his moral obedience,/ in Chapter the third and
elſewhere./ 4 By ſhewing that the Righteouſneſs
of God (ſo called in Rom. 3. 21, 22, 26/ in Rom.
10. 3, in 2 Cor. 5. 21. and in Phil. 3. 9.) is to be
underſtood of God the/ Fathers performance of his
Covenant with Christ;/ namely, that upon Chriſts/
performance of his Covenant (by combating with
Satan, and at laſt by making/ his death a ſacrifice)
he would be reconciled to beleeving ſinners, and
not im-/pute their ſins to them. And therefore I.
This Righteouſneſs of God muſt/ needs be the formal cauſe of a ſinners juſtification. And 2. It muſt
needs be/ a diſtinct ſort of Righteouſneſs from the
Righteouſneſs of Christ contrary to/ Mr Nortons
Tenent. This is evidenced in Chap. 14. and elſewhere./ 5 By Explaining Gods Declaration of the
combate between the Devil and the ſeed/ of the woman in Gen. 3. 15. from whence (as from the foun-

dation-principle)/ this prefent Reply doth explain
all the after prophecies of Chrifts Sufferings./ 6 By
clearing feveral other Scriptures of the greateft
note in thefe Controverfies,/ from Mr. Nortons cor-
rupt Expofitions, and by expounding them in their
right/ fenfe; Both according to the Context, and
according to fundry eminent Or-/thodox Writers./
By William Pynchon Efq ; late of New England./
London, Printed by R. I. for Thom. Newberry, and
are to be fold at his Shop in/ Cornhil, over againft
the Conduit near the Royal Exchange, 1655./ 26
prelim. leaves and text 439 *pp. Errata* 1 *page. Old
calf.* 4*to.*   (3*l.* 3*s.*   2270)

UINTANA Y GUIDO (Antonio
de). Epitafios/ Originales con/qve
el Real Convento de Iesvs/ Maria, de
esta Noble Civdad de Mexico,/ facò
a luz parte del juſtiſſimo ſentimiento,
que ocultauan los generoſos/ pechos
de ſus Religioſas hijas; los quales, en
viſtoſas tarjas eſtauan repar-/tidos por los pedeſtales
de doze viſtoſas piramides, y ſeis eſpacioſas/ gradas
(que hazian exquiſita armonia) ſobre que eſtaua vna
bien diſ-/pueſta Pyra que ſubſtituya el depoſito del
Mageſtuoſo cuerpo, con ſu tum/ ba cubierta de vn
paño, y dos almoadas de rica tela, ornato (ſi de-
cen-/te) deuido a la Real Corona, de que le conſti-
tuyò, y compuſſo el/ ſumptuoſiſsimo Panteon, que
poblado de eſquadrones de/ brillantes luzes, erigiò
in honra de ſu Patrona la Se-/reniſſima D. Isabel de
Borbon,/ Reyna de Eſpaña, y Señora nueſtra, a/ los
26. y 27. de Iulio del Año/ de 1645./ Al Señor
Doctor Don Pedro de Barrientos/ Lomelin, del
Conſejo de ſu Mageſtad, &c./ Por el Bachiller
Antonio de Qvintana/ y Guido, Capellan del Choro
deſta Santa Igleſia Cathedral./ Con Licencia :/ En
Mexico, por la Viuda de Bernardo Calderon. Año
de 1645./ *Title on the reverse, Woodcut Arms.* ' Ap-
rvacion del Padre/ Iuan de S. Miguel, de la Com-
pañia/ de Iesvs./ 1 *puge, reverse blank.* ' Al Señor
Doctor D. Pedro/ de Barrientos Lomelin,' *etc.* 2
pp. Text commencing ' Titulo Dedicatorio que ocu-
paua la quarta' *etc. folioed leaves* 3-8, *the reverse
blank.* 4to. (1*l.* 11*s.* 6*d.* 2271)

QUIR (Peter Ferdinand de). Terra Auſtralis incognita,/ or/ A new Southerne/ Discoverie,/ con-
taining/ A fifth part of the World./ Lately found
out/ By Ferdinand De Qvir,/ a Spaniſh Captaine./

2   T T

Neuer before publifhed./ Tranflated by W. B./
London/ Printed for Iohn Hodgetts./ 1617. *Title,
reverse blank, and 27 pp.* 4*to.* (4*l.* 14*s.* 6*d.*   2272)

QUEBEC. State of the present form of Government
of the Province of Quebec. With a large Appendix; containing Extracts from the Minutes of an
investigation into the past administration of justice in that province, instituted by order of Lord
Dorchester in 1787, and from other original Papers.
London, J. Debrett, MDCCLXXXIX. *Title, Errata,
and 176 pp. Half morocco.* 8*vo.*   (5*s.* 6*d.*   2273)

QUINCY (JOSIAH, *Junior*). Observations on the
Act of Parliament, commonly called the Boston
Port-Bill; with Thoughts on Civil Society and
Standing Armies. By Josiah Quincy, Junior,
Counfellor at Law, in Boston. Boston, N. E.
Printed. *London:* Re-printed for Edward and
Charles Dilly, MDCCLXXIV. *3 prel. leaves and* 80
pp. Half morocco. 8*vo.*   (5*s.* 6*d.*   2274)

ALEIGH (*Sir* WALTER). The/ Disco-
verie/ of the Large,/ Rich and Bevv-
tifvl/ Empire of Gviana, with/ a re-
lation of the Great and Golden Citie/
of Manoa (which the ſpaniards call
El/ Dorado) And the provinces of
Emeria,/ Arromaia, Amapaia and
other Coun-/tries, with their riuers, ad-/ioyning/
Performed in the yeare 1595. by Sir/ W. Ralegh
Knight, Captaine of her/ Majeſties Guard, Lo.
Warden/ of the Stanneries, and her High-/neſſe
Lieutenant generall/ of the Countie of/ Cornewall./
Imprinted at *London* by Robert Robinſon/ 1596./
8 *prel. leaves ; viz. Title, reverse blank,* 'To the Right/
Honorable my/ ſingular good Lord and kinſman,/
Charles Howard, Knight of the Gar-/ter Barron,
and Counceller, and of the Ad-/miralls of England
the moſt renow-/med : And to the Right Honorable/
Sr Robert Cecyll Knight, Councel-/ler in her High-
nes priuie/ Councels.' 8 *pp :* 'To the Reader.' 6
pp : Text 112 *pp. Vellum.* 4to. (3*l.* 3*s.* 2275)

RALEIGH (*Sir* WALTER). A/ Declaration/ of the
Demea-/nor and Cariage of/ Sir Walter Raleigh,/
Knight, aſwell in his Voyage, as/ in, and ſithence
his Returne ;/ And of the true motiues and induce-/
ments which occaſioned His Maieſtie/ to Proceed in
doing Iuſtice upon him,/ as hath bene done./ *London*, Printed by Bonham Norton/ and Iohn Bill,
deputie Printers for/ the Kings moſt Excellent Maieſtie./ M.DC.XVIII. *Title, having on the reverse a
woodcut of the Royal Arms; Text* 68 *pp. Half calf.*
4*to.* (10*s.* 6*d.* 2276)

RALEIGH (*Sir* WALTER). Sir Walter/ Ravvleighs/
Ghost,/ or/ Englands Forewarner./ Diſcouering

a fecret Confultation, newly hol-/den in the Court of Spaine./ Together, with his tormenting of Count de/ Gondomar; and his ftrange affrightment, Con-/feffion/ and publique recantation: laying open many/ treacheries intended for the fubuer-/fion of England./ *Vtricht,*/ Printed by John Sehellem./ 1626./ *Title, reverse blank, and* 41 *pp. Wanting pages* 7 *to* 22, *inclusive.* 4*to.* (3*s.* 6*d.* 2277)

RALEIGH (*Sir* WALTER). The/ Prerogatiue/ of Par-laments/ in England :/ Proued in a Dialogue (pro &/ contra) betweene a Councellour/ of State and a Iuftice/ of Peace./ Written by the Worthy (much lacked/ and lamented) Sir W. R. Kᵗ. deceafed./ Dedicated to the Kings Maiefty, and to/ the Houfe of Parlament now affembled./ Preferued to be now happily/ (in thefe diftracted Times)/ Publifhed, and/ Printed at *Hamburgh./* 1628./ 4 *prel. leaves; viz. Title, reverse blank,* 'To the King.' 5 *pp. Text* 66 *pp. half mor.* 4*to.* (10*s.* 6*d.* 2278)

RALEIGH (*Sir* WALTER). The/ Prerogative/ of/ Parliaments/ in England :/ Proued in a Dialogue (pro &/ contra) betweene a Councellour/ of State and a Iuftice/ of Peace./ Written by the worthy (much lacked and/ lamented) Sir Walter Raleigh Knight,/ deceafed./ Dedicated to the King's Ma-ieftie, and to the/ Houfe of Parlament now affem-bled./ Preferued to be now happily/ (in thefe dif-tracted Times)/ Publifhed, and/ Printed at *Midel-burge./* 1628./ 4 *prel. leaves; viz. Title, reverse blank,* 'To the King.' 5*pp : Text* 66 *pp. half mor.* 4*to.* (7*s.* 6*d.* 2279)

RALEIGH (*Sir* WALTER). Tvbvs Historicvs :/ An Hiftoricall Perfpective ;/ Difcovering all the Em-pires and King-/domes of the World, as they/ flou-rifht refpectively under/ the foure Imperiall/ Mo-narchies./ Faithfully compofed out of the moft ap-/proved Authours, and exactly di-/gefted accord-ing to the fup-/putation of the beft/ Chronologers./ (With a Catalogue of the Kings and Emperours of/ the chiefe Nations of the World.)/ By the late famous and learned Knight/ Sir Walter Raleigh./ *London,*/ Printed by Thomas Harper, for Benjamin Fifher, 1636./ 13 *unnumbered leaves; viz. Title, re-verse blank,* 'To the most Illuftrious and hopefull

Prince Charles,' *etc.* 1 *page, the reverse blank ;* ' The Publisher's Advertisement to the Reader.' *3 pp. the reverse blank ;* ' Tubus Historicus.' *running title* ' Sir Walter Raleigh's/ Chronologicall Tables.' 9 *pp. the reverse blank ;* ' A Catalogue of the Kings and Em-/perours of the chiefe Nations/ of the World.' 7 *pp. the reverse blank.* 4*to.* (10*s.* 6*d.* 2280)

RALEIGH (*Sir* WALTER). The/ Prince,/ or/ Max-ims/ of/ State./ Written/ by Sir Walter Ravvley,/ and presented to Prince Henry./ *London,* Printed, MDCXLII. 3 *prel. leaves and* 46 *pp. Half morocco.* 4*to.* (7*s.* 6*d.* 2281)

RALEIGH (*Sir* WALTER). Judicious/ and/ Select Essayes/ and/ Observations,/ By that Renowned and/ Learned Knight./ Sir Walter Raleigh./ upon/ The first Invention of Shipping./ The Misery of Invasive Warre./ The Navy Royall and Sea-Service./ With his/ Apologie for his voyage to Guiana./ *London,*/ Printed by T. W. for Humphrey Moseley/ and are to be Sold at the Princes Armes in/ St. Pauls-Church-yard, 1650./ 5 *prel. leaves and* 42 *pp ; Title,* 4 *pp. and* 31 *unpaged leaves;* 1 *blank leaf ; Title and* 46 *pp ; Title and* 69 *pp. With Portrait. Calf extra by Riviere.* 12*mo.* (12*s.* 6*d.* 2282)

RALEIGH (*Sir* WALTER). The Cabinet-Council :/ Containing the Chief Arts/ of/ Empire,/ And Mys-teries of/ State ;/ discabineted/ In Political and Po-lemical Aphorisms,/ grounded on Authority, and Experience ;/ And illustrated with the choicest/ Examples and Historical/ Observations./ By the Ever-renowned Knight,/ Sir Walter Raleigh,/ Published By John Milton, Esq ;/ *London,* Printed by Tho. Newcomb for Tho. John-/son at the sign of the Key in St. Pauls Churchyard,/ near the West-end. 1658./ 4 *prel. leaves and* 199 *pp. Portrait of Raleigh. Old calf.* 16*mo.* (10*s.* 6*d.* 2283)

RALEIGH (*Sir* WALTER). The/ Life/ of the/ Valiant and Learned/ Sir Walter Raleigh, Knight./ With his/ Tryal/ at/ Winchester./ The Third Edition./ *London,*/ Printed for George Dawes, and Richard Tonson within Grays-Inn-/ Gate next Grays-Inn-Lane. MDCLXXXVII. *Title and* 41 *pp. half mor. Folio.* (10*s.* 6*d.* 2284)

RALEIGH (*Sir* WALTER). An Introduction to a/
Breviary of the/ History of England/ With the/
Reign/ of/ King William the I./Entitled the/ Con-
queror./ Written by Sr. Walter Raleigh, Kt. And/
Dedicated to the then Earl of Salisbury./ *London*,/
Printed for Sam. Keble at the Great-Turks-/Head
in Fleet-street. And Dan. Brown/ at the Black-
Swan and Bible without/ Temple-Bar. 1693./ 4
prel. leaves including the Portrait, and 77 *pp. Calf.*
Small 8vo. (6s. 6d. 2285)

RAMSAY (DAVID). The History of the Revolution
of South-Carolina, from a British Province to an
Independent State. By David Ramsay, M.D.
Member of the American Congress. In Two Volumes. *Trenton:* Printed by Isaac Collins. M.DCC.
LXXXV. *Two Volumes.* Vol. I. *xx and* 453 *pp. Map*
and Sketch at pp. 1, *and* 145. Vol. II. *xx and* 574
pp. Sketches and plan at pp. 52, 58, *and* 326.
8vo. (10s. 6d. 2286)

RAMSAY (DAVID). The History of the American
Revolution. By David Ramsay, M.D. of South-
Carolina. A New Edition. In Two Volumes.
London: John Stockdale, 1793. *Two Volumes.*
Volume I. 2 *prel. leaves and* 357 *pp.* Volume II.
xii and 360 *pp. 8vo.* (8s. 6d. 2287)

RANDALL (JOHN). A brief Account of the Rise,
Principles, and Discipline of the People call'd
Quakers, In America, and elsewhere. Extracted
from A System of Geography Lately Publish'd.
By John Randall. *Bristol:* Sam. Farley, 1747. 24
pp. 12mo. (4s. 6d. 2288)

RANGEL (JOSEPH FRANCISCO DIMAS). Discurso
fisico sobre la Formacion de las Auroras Boreales.
Por D. Joseph Francisco Dimas Rangel, Reloxero
en esta Corte. [*Colophon*] Con las Licencias Necesarias: Impreso en *México* en la Oficina de los
Herederos del Lic. D. Joseph de Jauregui, Calle de
San Bernardo. Año de 1789. '1. *to* VII.' *pp. Half*
mor. 4to. (10s. 6d. 2289)

RAYNAL (ABBE). A Philosophical and Political
History of the British Settlements and Trade in
North America. From the French of Abbé Raynal.
In Two Volumes. *Edinburgh:* C. Macfarquhar,

M.DCC.LXXVI. *Two Volumes.* Vol. I. 240 *pp. Map of North America.* Vol. II. 231 *pp.* 12*mo.* (7*s.* 6*d.* 2290)

RAYNAL (ABBE). Révolution de l'Amérique, par M. L'Abbé Raynal, Auteur de l'Hiftoire Philofophique & Politique des Etabliffemens, & du Commerce des Européens dans les deux Indes. A *Londres,* Lockier Davis, M.DCC.LXXXI. *xvi and* 183 *pp. With Portrait of Raynal. Half morocco.* 8*vo.* (4*s.* 6*d.* 2291)

RAYNAL (ABBE). The Revolution of America. By the Abbé Raynal, Author of the Philosophical and Political History of the Establishments and Commerce of the Europeans in both the Indies. *Dublin :* C. Talbot, M,DCC,LXXXI. *xx and* 244 *pp. Old calf.* 12*mo.* (5*s.* 2292)

RAYNAL (ABBE). The Revolution of America. By The Abbé Raynal, Author of the Philosophical and Political History of the Establishments and Commerce of the Europeans in both the Indies. *London :* Lockyer Davis, MDCCLXXXI. *xvi and* 181 *pp.* 8*vo.* (4*s.* 6*d.* 2293)

RAYNAL (ABBE). The Revolution of America. By The Abbé Raynal, Author of the Philosophical and Political History of the Establishments and Commerce of the Europeans in both the Indies. A New Translation. *London :* Lockyer Davis. M.DCC. LXXXI. *2 prel. leaves and* 199 *pp. Half morocco.* 12*mo.* (3*s.* 6*d.* 2294)

REAL Compañia de Comercio Para las Islas de Santo Domingo, Puerto-Rico, y la Margarita, que se ha dignado su Magestad conceder con diez Regiftros para Honduras, y Provincias de Guathemala, al Comercio de la Ciudad de Barcelona, y fu Eftablecimiento en la mifma, baxo el Patrocinio de Nueftra Señora de Monferrate, y de la Real Protecion de fu Mageftad. En *Madrid :* Joseph Rico, 1755. *2 prel. leaves and text 33 pp. Calf.* 16*mo.* (14*s.* 2295)

REALES Ordenanzas para la direccion, Régimen y Gobierno del Importante cuerpo de la Mineria de Nueva-España, y de su Real Tribunal General. De Orden de su Mageftad. *Madrid.* Año de 1783. *Frontispiece, Title, xlvi and* 214 *pp. In boards. Folio.* (12*s.* 6*d.* 2296)

REALES (Juras). Entretenimientos de un Prisio-
nero en las Provincias del Rio dé la Plata : Por el
Baron de Juras Reales, siendo Fiscal de S. M. en
el Reino de Chile. *Barcelona:* José Torner. 1828.
Two Volumes. Tomo Primero. *4 prel. leaves, viii
and 334 pp. Wanting pp. 295—302 inclusive.* Tomo
Segundo. *2 prel. leaves, and 391 pp.* ' Appendice.'
16 pp. 4to. (12s. 6d. 2297)

REASONS For Establishing the Colony of Georgia,
With Regard to the Trade of Great Britain, the
Increafe of our People, and the Employment and
Support it will afford to great Numbers of our own
Poor, as well as foreign perfecuted Protestants.
With fome Account of the Country, and the De-
fign of the Trustees. *London:* W. Meadows,
MDCCXXXIII. *39 pp. Plate and Map. Half morocco.
4to.* (10s. 6d. 2298)

REASONS grounded on facts. Shewing, I. That a
new Duty on Sugar muft fall on the Planter. II.
That the Liberty of a direct Exportation to Foreign
Markets will not help him in this Cafe. III. That a
new Duty will not certainly increafe the Revenue.
And, IV. That it will probably occafion the Defer-
tion of our Sugar Iflands. *London:* M. Cooper,
M,DCC,XLVIII. *Title and pp. 3—21. Half morocco.
8vo.* (4s. 6d. 2299)

RECENTES/ Novi Orbis/ Historiæ,/ Hoc eft,/ I.
Inquifitio nauigationis Septentrionalis, an & quomodo ea feliciter perfici poffit, eáque/ figuris æneis
demonftrata./ II. Relatio fuper detectione noui ad
Caurum tranfitus ad terras Americanas in Chinam
at-/que Iaponem ducturi./ III. Memorialis libellus
Sereniffimo Hifpa-/niarum Regi oblatus fuper Detectione quar-/tæ orbis terrarum partis cui nomen
Av-/stralis Incognita, eiúfque im-/menfis opibus
& fertilitate./ IIII. Rerum ab Hispanis in India
Occiden-/tali hactenus geftarum, libri tres./ *Coloniæ Allobrovm,/* Apud Petrvm de la Rouiere./
Anno M DCXII./ *Title reverse blank,* 51 *and Text*
480 *pp.* ' Elenchvs, sive Index,' 12 *pp. With 2
copperplate maps. Vellum. 8vo.* (3l. 3s. 2300)

RECIO DE LEON (Juan). *[Begins]* Ivan Recio
de Leon Maeffe de Campo, *etc.* [Account of the
discovery of a new route for the conveyance of

Silver from Potosi in Peru to Spain in lefs than
half the time and expense of the ordinary route].
[*Madrid*, 1626.] 10 *leaves. Half morocco. Folio.*
(1*l.* 11*s.* 6*d.* 2301)

RECUEIL des Plans de L'Amerique Septentrionale,
A Paris Chez Le S.ᵣ Le Rouge Ingenieur Geographe
du Roy, Et de S. A. S. M. le Comte de Clermont,
Ruë des Augustins. 1755. *Engraved Title and* 16
Plans. 4*to.* (12*s.* 6*d.* 2302)

REDMAN (JOHN). Dissertatio Medica Inauguralis
de Abortu. Qvam favente Deo ter Opt. Max. Ex
Auctoritate Magnifici Rectoris D. Joannis Alberti,
S. S. Theologiæ Doctoris, ejusdemque facultatis in
Academia Lugduno Batava Professoris Ordinarii.
Nec non Ampliffimi Senatus Academici Confenfu,
& Nobiliffimæ Facultatis Medicæ Decreto, pro
Grandu Doctoratus, Summifque in Medicina Honoribus, & Privilegiis rite, ac legitime confequendis,
Eruditorum Examini fubjicit Johannes Redman,
Penfylvanienfis. Ad diem 15 . Julii 1748 hora lo-
coque folitis. Nulla eft quæ pulchriora laborum
præmia cultoribus perfolvit, quam medica fapi-
entia. H. Boerhaav. De ufu ratiocin. Mechan.
in Medicina p. 54. Constantia Triumphans *Lugduni Batavorum* Apud Conradum Wishoff. 3 *prel.
leaves and* 31 *pp. half morocco.* 4*to.* (7*s.* 6*d.* 2304)

REED (JOHN). An Explanation of the Map of the
City and Liberties of Philadelphia. By John
Reed. *Philadelphia:* Printed for the Author, and
Sold by Mr. Nicholas Brooks, in Second-Street,
between Market and Chesnut Streets, M.DCC.LXXIV.
24 *pp:* ' An Alphabetical List of the First Pur-
chasers Names,' *etc.* 8 *and* 23 *pp:* 'The Date of
Surveys' *etc.* 9 *pp.* 4*to.* (18*s.* 2305)

REED (JOSEPH). Joseph Reed Defendant, Ad.
John Reed.} Argument for the Defendant in
Error. 28 *pp.* 4*to.* (7*s.* 6*d.* 2306)

REEVES (JOHN). History of the Government of
the Island of Newfoundland. With an Appendix ;
containing the Acts of Parliament made respecting
the Trade and Fishery. By John Reeves, Esq.,
Chief Justice of the Island. *London:* J. Sewell,
1793. 4 *prel. leaves and* 167 *pp.* 'Appendix.' 2
prel. leaves and cxvi *pp.* 8*vo.* (7*s.* 6*d.* 2307)

REFLECTIONS on the Importation of Bar-Iron,
From our own Colonies of North-America. In
Anſwer to a late Pamphlet on that Subjeƈt. Humbly Submitted to the Conſideration of the Honourable the House of Commons, March 14, 1757.   23
pp. Half morocco. 8vo.   (10s. 6d.   2308)

REFLECTIONS Moral and Political on Great
Britain and her Colonies. *London:* T. Becket.
M.DCC.LXX. *3 prel. leaves and 66 pp. Half morocco.
8vo.*   (4s. 6d.   2309)

REFLECTIONS on the Rise, Progress, and probable consequences, of the present contentions
with the Colonies. By a Freeholder. *Edinburgh:*
Printed in the Year MDCCLXXVI. *iv and 53 pp.
12mo.*   (4s. 6d.   2310)

REFUTATION (A) of the Letter to an Hon[ble]
Brigadier-General, Commander of His Majeſty's
Forces in Canada. By an Officer. The Second
Edition. *London:* R. Stevens, MDCCLX. [*See*
LETTER]. *Half-title, title, and 52 pp. Half morocco.
8vo.*   (4s. 6d.   2311)

REGIL (PEDRO MANUEL). Memoria Instructiva
sobre el comercio general de la Provincia de
Yucatan, y particular del puerto de Campeche,
formada por el Señor don Pedro Manuel Regil,
diputado electo para las Cortes Ordinarias por
dicha Provincia. La Publica don Angel Alonso y
Pantiga, diputado de las actuales Cortes, y cura
Territorial y Castrense de la Parroquia de Campeche. *Madrid:* Año MDCCCXIV. En la Imprenta
de Vega y Compañía. Calle de Capellanes. *Title;
and 56 pp. Folded sheets at pp. 42, and 45 (2).
Half calf. 8vo.*   (15s.   2312)

REGIMENTO, & Leys sobre as Missonens do
Eſtado do Maranhaõ, & Parà, & ſobre a liberdade
dos Indios. Impreſſo por ordem de El-Rey
noſſo Senhor. *Lisboa Occidental,* Antonio Manescal,
M.DCCXXIV. *2 prel. leaves and text 82 pp. Calf.
Folio.*   (1l. 11s. 6d.   2313)

REGISTER (A) for The State of Connecticut:
With an Almanack, For the Year of our Lord,
1785. Calculated for the Meridian of New-London, Lat. 41. 25. North, By Nathan Daboll,
Teacher of the Mathematics at the Academic

School in Plainfield. *New-London:* Printed and
Sold by T. Green, near the Court-House. [1785].
48 *pp.* [Almanac] 12 *pp.* 16*mo.*   (2*s.* 6*d.* 2314)

REGULATIONS (The) Lately Made concerning
the Colonies, and the Taxes Impoſed upon Them,
conſidered. [By George Grenville.] *London:* J.
Wilkie, 1765. *Half-title, title, and pp.* 3—114.
8*vo.*   (6*s.* 6*d.* 2315)

RELACAM/ Verdadeira,/ e breve datomada da/
Villa de Olinda, Elvgardo Recife na Costa/ do
Brazil pellos rebeldes de Olanda, tirada de huma
carta que eſcreueo/ hum Religioſo de muyta autho-
ridade, & que ſoy teſtemunha de viſta/ de quaſi todo
ſocedido : & aſſi o affirma, & jura ; & do mais/ que
depois diſſo ſocedeo tè os dezoito de Abril/ deſte
prezente, & fatal anno de 1630./ [*Colophon*] En
Lisboa. Com todas as licenças neceſſarias Por
Mathias/ Rodrigues Anno 1630./ Taixão eſta Re-
lação em reis./ *6 unnumbered pages. Half morocco.*
Folio.   (1*l.* 11*s.* 6*d.* 2316)

RELACAŌ Abbreviada Da Republica, que os Religioſos Jeſuitas das Provincias de Portugal, e
Heſpanha, eſtabelecerão nos Dominios Ultramarinos
das duas Monarchias, e da Guerra, que nelles tem
movido, e ſuſtentado contra os Exercitos Heſpan-
hoes, e Portuguezes : Formada pelos regiſtos das
Secretarias dos dous reſpectivos Principaes Com-
miſſarios, e Plenipotentiarios ; e por outros Documentos authenticos. Relation Abregée, Concernant
la République que les Religieux, nommés Jéſuites,
des Provinces de Portugal & d'Eſpagne, ont établie
dans les Pays & Domaines d'outre mer de ces deux
Monarchies, & de la Guerre qu'ils y ont excitée &
ſoutenue contre les Armées Eſpagnoles & Portu-
gaiſes : Dreſſée ſur les Regiſtres de Secrétariat des
deux Commiſſaires reſpectifs Principaux & Pléni-
potentiaires des deux Couronnes, & ſur d'autres
Pieces authentiques. [1758]. 68 *pp.* Memoire
Pour ſervir d'addition & d'éclairciſſement à la Relation abrégée, &c. qu'on vient de donner au Public,
ſur l'abominable conduite des Jéſuites, dans les
pays & domaines d'outre-mer dépendans des Royaumes d'Eſpagne & de Portugal.' 30 *pp. Old calf.*
12*mo.*   (8*s.* 6*d.* 2317)

RELACION de lo Svcedido/ en los Galeones y Flota
de Terrafirme. [1622] 5 *folioed leaves. Unbound.*
Folio. (1*l.* 11*s.* 6*d.* 2318)

RELACION de las Vito-/rias qve Don Diego de
Arroy o/ y Daça, Governador y Capitan general
de la prouinci/ de Cumana, tuuo en la gran Salina
de Arraya, a 30. de No-/uiembre, del año paſſado
de 622. y a treze de/ Enero deſte año, contra ciento
y/ quatro nauios de Olan-/deſes./ [*Colophon*] Con
Licencia/ En *Madrid*, Por la viuda de Alonſo
Martin./ [1623] 4 *unnumbered pages. Unbound.*
Folio. (1*l.* 1*s.* 2319)

RELACION/ de Como Martirizaron/ los Hereges
Olandeses, Gelandeses,/ y Pechilingues, en odio de
nueſtra ſanta Fè Catolica, al Religio-/ſo y ob-
ſeruante varon el Padre Preſentado fray Alonſo
Gomez/ de Enzinas, del Orden de nueſtra Señora
de·la Merced, Reden-/cion de Cautinos, y natural
de la villa de Cuellar, en la entrada/ que hizieron
eſte mes paſſado de Iunio de 1624. en la cuidad/ de
Guayaquil, en la Prouincia de Quito, que es en/
las Indias, y Reynos del Perù./ [*Colophon*] Con
Licencia, En *Madrid* por Iuan Delgado. Año
1625./ 4 *unnumbered pages. Folio.* (1*l.* 1*s.* 2320)

RELACION del Svcesso del Armada, y/ excercito
que fue al ſocorro del Brazil, deſde que entrò en la
Bahia de Todos-/ Santos, haſta que entrò en la
ciudad del Saluador, que poſſeian los Rebeldes de/
Olanda, ſacada de vna carta que el ſeñor don
Fadrique de Toledo eſcriuio a ſu/ Mageſtad./
[1625.] 4 *unnumbered pages. Folio.* (1*l.* 1*s.* 2321)

RELACION/ y Copia de vna Car/ ta, de las Com-
panias de/ Infanteria, y de Acauallo, que ſu Mageſtad tiene en/ el puerto de Callao, para defenſa
del dicho puerto, y/ de la Isla del Braſil. Iunta-
mente ſe haze rela-/cion de las nōbres de los Capitanes, y la gen/te que cada vno tiene, con las demas
pre/uenciones para el dicho efeto./ [*Colophon*]
Con Licencia./ Impreſſo en *Madrid*: en casa de
Ber-/nardino de Guzman. Año/ de 1625./ 4 *unnumbered pages. Folio.* (1*l.* 11*s.* 6*d.* 2322)

RELACION de la Iornada qve la/ Armada de ſu
Mageſtad à hecho al ſocorro del Brazil, y/ batalla
que entre ella, y la de los Eſtados de Olāda ſe

die/ron en doze de Septiembre defte año de 1631.
en diez y/ ocho grados de altura a la bāda del Sur
de la equinocial,/ y paraje de los Abrojos. [*Colophon*] Con licencia del feñor Alcalde don Alonfo
de Bolañoz, En *Sevilla* por Francifco de Lyra.
Año de 1631./ *4 unnumbered pages. Half morocco.
Folio.* (1*l.* 11*s.* 6*d.* 2323)

RELACION cierta y Verdadera,/ del famofo fuceffo
y vitoria que tuvo el Capitan/ Benito Arias Montano, fobrino del doctifsimo/ Arias Montano, natural
de Eftremadura, Gover-/nador y Capitan general
de la Provincia de la nue/va Andaluzia, y cuidad
de Cumana, y Alcayde de/ la fuerea de Araya, por
el Rey nueftro feñor, con/tra los enemigos Olādefes,
q eftavan fortificados/ en una falina que eftà riberas
del rio Vnare, que es/ en efta governacion, veynte
y quatro leguas de la/ ciudad de Cumana, efte año
de 1633./ [*Colophon*] Con licencia, impreffo en
Sevilla por Francifco de Lyra,/ Año de 1634./ 4
unnumbered pages. Folio. (1*l.* 1*s.* 2324)

RELACION de los/ muertos, y heridos que huuo en
la Real/ Armada de la guardia de las Indias, las/
dos vezes que peleò con el enemigo,/ fobre Pan de
Cauañas, año/ de 1638./ *4 unnumbered pages.
4to.* (1*l.* 1*s.* 2325)

RELACION de lo Svcedido a/ la Armada Real de
la guarda de la carrera de las In-/dias, defde el dia
que fe hizo a la vela en la Vaia de Ca-/diz, hafta el
en que dio fondo en el puerto de la Vera Cruz/ en
la Nueua Efpaña. Recopilada de cartas de algunas
per/fonas fidedignas y de auctoridad, que vinieron
a manos de/ vna perfona graue defta Ciudad. En
efte año de mil y feif-/cientos y treinta y ocho./
[*Mexico*, 1638.] *8 folioed leaves. 4to.* (1*l.* 1*s.* 2326)

RELACION. Mverte de Pie de Palo./ Segvnda/
Relacion, y mvy co-/ piofa de vna carta que embiò
el/feñor Duque de Medina/ a la contraftacion de/
Seuilla./ Dafe cuenta de la batalla que han tenido
los Galeones con/ 40 Nauios de Olandefes, fiendo
General de ellos Pie de/ Palo. Afsi mifmo fe da
cuenta de fu muerte, con/ perdida de fiete nauios,
en el cabo de S. Anton./ [*Colophon*] Con licencia,
en *Madrid*, por Antonio Duplaftre,/ Año 1638./
4 unnumbered pages. 4to. (1*l.* 1*s.* 2327)

RELACION/ Verdadera,/ de la Gran Vitoria qve han/ alcançado en el Brafil la gente de la Baia de/Todos Santos, contra los Olandefes. Dafe/ cuenta como les mataron dos mil hombres,/ y de la gran preffa que les tomaron, haziendo-/los embarcar, y dexar el puerto, quitando-/les todo el bagaje que/ Ileuauan./ [*Colophon*] Impreffa con licencia en *Seuilla*, por Nicolas Ro-/driguez, en calle de Genoua. Año de 1638./ 4 *unnumbered pages.* 4*to.*   (1*l.* 1*s.* 2328)

RELACION/ Verdadera de la/ Refriega qve Tvvieron/ nueftros Galeones de la Plata en el Ca-/bo de fan Anton, con catorze navios/ de Olãda, de que era general Pie de Pa-/lo, y da la vitoria que dellos alcançarõ,/ fucedido en el mes de Agofto paffado defte prefente año de mil y feif-/cientos y treinta y/ ocho./ [*Colophon*] Con Licencia./ Impreffo en *Sevilla*, por Francifco de Lyra, Año de 1638./ 4 *unnumbered pages.* 4*to.*   (1*l.* 1*s.* 2329)

RELACION Verda-/dera del viaje de los Galeones, y de las/ dos batallas que ruuieron fobre Pan de Cauañas, con los/ Olandefes, en efte año de 1638./ [*Colophon*] Con licencia, en *Seuilla* por Nicolas Rodriguez, en calle de Genoua, en efte año de 1638./ 4 *unnumbered pages.* 4*to.*   (1*l.* 1*s.* 2330)

RELACION/ de la Vitoria qve/ Alcanzaron las Armas/ Catolicas en la Baía de Todos Santos, con-/tra Olandefes, que fueron a fitiar aquella Pla-/ça, en 14. de Iunio de 1638. Siendo Go-/uernador del Eftado del Brafil/ Pedro de Silua./ [*Colophon*] En *Madrid*, Por Francifco Martinez, año 1638./ 6 *folioed leaves. Half morocco.*
Folio.   (1*l.* 11*s.* 6*d.* 2331)

RELACION Verdadera de las Pazes/ que Capitvlo con el Aravcano Rebelado, el/ Marques de Baides, Conde de Pedrofo, Gouernador, y Capitan Gene-/ral del Reyno de Chile, y Prefidente de la Real Audiencia. Sacada de/ fus informes, y cartas, y de los Padres de la Compañia de Iefus, que acõ-/pañaron el Real excerito en la jornada que hizo para efte efeto/ el Año paffado de 1641./ [*Colophon*] En *Madrid*, por Francifco Maroto, año de 1642./ 8 *unnumbered pages. Folio.*   (1*l.* 11*s.* 6*d.* 2332)

RELACION de Todo lo Sv-/cedido en estas Provincias de la Nveva/ Eſpaña, deſde la formacion de
la Armada Real de Barlovento, deſpacho/ de Flota,
y ſuceſſo della, haſta la ſalida deſte primer Aviſo
del año de/ 1642./ *4 unnumbered pages. Half
morocco. Folio.*   (1*l.* 11*s.* 6*d.*   2333)

RELACION de/ los Socorros,/ que ha/remitido à
Tierra-Firme el Excelentiſsi-/mo ſeñor Conde de
Lemos, Virrey, Go-/vernador, y Capitan General
de los Rey-/nos, y Provincias del Perù, para la
reſtau-/racion del Caſtillo de Chagre, y/ Ciudad de
Panamà, de que ſe/ apoderò el Enemigo/ Inglés./
[1671]. *4 unnumbered pages. Half morocco.*
Folio.   (1*l.* 11*s.* 6*d.*   2334)

RELACION de la/ Salvd Milagrosa, qve dio/ el
Bienaventurado Stanislao Koſt Ka, Novicio/ de la
Compañia de Ieſus, à otro Novicio de/ la miſma
Compañia, en la Caſa de Provacion/ de San Antonio
Abad de la Ciudad de/ Lima, el dia 13. de Noviembre de/ el año de 1673./   Y conſta de la Pro-
ceſſo,/ que ſe hizo por orden de el ſeñor Doctor
Don/ Ioſeph Davila Falcon. Proviſor, y Vicario/
General de el Arçobiſpado de Lima en Sede-/va-
cante, Canonigo Doctor al, y Catredatico/ de Prima
de Canones en la Real/ Vniverſidad./ Con licencia
en *Madrid* : Año de 1674./ *6 folioed leaves. Un-*
bound. 4to.   (1*l.* 1*s.*   2335)

RELACION/ del Exemplar Castigo qve/ embiò
Dios a la Ciudad de Lima Cabeza del Perù,/ y ſu
Coſta de Barlouento con los eſpantoſos/ Temblores
del dia 20. de Octubre/ del Año de 1687./ [*Colo-*
phon] Con Licencia En *Lima*,/ Por Ioſeph de
Contreras. Año de 1687./ *8 unnumbered pages.*
Folio.   (1*l.* 1*s.*   2336)

RELACION/ de lo Svcedido a la Armada de/ Barlovento à fines del año paſſado, y/ principios de eſte
de 1691./ Victoria, que contra los Franceſes, que
ocupan la Coſta/ del morte de la Iſla de Santo
Domingo tuvieron,/ con el ayuda de dicha Armada,
los Lauzeros, y/ milicia Eſpañola de aquella Iſla,
abraſando el/ Puerto de Guarico, y otras Pobla-
ciones./ Debido todo al influxo, y providentiſſimos/
ordenes del Excellentiſſimo Señor/ D. Gaspar de
Sandoval, Cer-/da, Silva, y Mendoza, Conde de/
Galve, &c. meritiſſimo Virrey, Governador, y/

Capitan General de efta Nueva-Efpaña./ Con
licencia de los Superiores en *Mexico* por los Here-
deros/ de la Viuda de Bernardo Calderon año de
1691./ 16 *unnumbered pages.* *Uncut and unbound.*
4*to.* (2*l.* 2*s.* 2337)

RELACION./ Del Espantoso Terre-/moto que
padecio efta Ciudad de los Reyes/ Lima, y fus con-
tornos el dia 14. de Iulio de/ efte prefente año de
1699. fus laftimofos/ efectos, de muertes, y ruynas./
7 *unnumbered pages.* 4*to.* (1*l.* 11*s.* 6*d.* 2338)

RELATIONS/ Veritables/ et Cvrievses/ de l'Isle/
de Madagascar,/ et dv Bresil./ Auec l'hiftoire de
la derniere Guerre faite au Brefil,/ entre les Portugais & les Hollandois./ Trois Relations d'Egypte,/
& vne du Royaume de Perfe./ *A Paris,*/ Chez
Avgvstin Covrbe', au Palais, en la Gallerie/ des
Merciers, à la Palme./ M. DC. LI./ Avec Privilege
dv Roy. 8 *prel. leaves;* *the 4th blank, and* 307 *pp.*
Map at page 1. *Calf.* 4*to.* (10*s.* 6*d.* 2339)

RELIGIOUS INTELLIGENCE and Seasonable
Advice from Abroad : Concerning Lay-Preaching
and Exhortation. Collection I. [II. III. IV.]
from the Connecticut Evangelical Magazine, No.
1ft, 2d & 3d. and Mr. Edwards President of
Princeton College, New Jersey, his thoughts on
Religion, &c. *Edinburgh :* T. Ross and Sons,
1801-2. 4 *Parts.* No. I. *Title and* 62 *pp.* No. II.
60 *pp.* No. III. *viii and pp.* 3—55. No. IV. 1802.
Title and 58 *pp.* 12*mo.* (6*s.* 6*d.* 2340)

REMARKS On Several Acts of Parliament Relating more efpecially to the Colonies abroad ; As
alfo on diverfe Acts of Assemblies there : Together with A Comparifon of the Practice of the
Courts of Law in fome of the Plantations, with
thofe of Westminster Hall : And a modeft Apology for the former, fo far as they materially differ
from the latter. Wherein is likewife contain'd, A
Difcourfe concerning the 4½ per Cent. Duty paid
in Barbados, and the Leeward Iflands. *London,*
T. Cooper. 1742. 3 *prel. leaves, signed* 'T. M.' *and*
125 *pp.* *Half morocco.* 8*vo.* (4*s.* 6*d.* 2341)

REMARKS on the French Memorials concerning
the Limits of Acadia ; Printed at the Royal Printing-houfe at Paris, and diftributed by the French

Minifters at all the Foreign Courts of Europe. With two Maps, Exhibiting the Limits: One according to the Syftem of the French, as inferted in the faid Memorials; The other conformable to the English Rights, as fupported by the Authority of Treaties, continual Grants of the French Kings, and exprefs paffages of the beft French Authors. To which is added, An Answer to the Summary Discussion, &c. *London:* T. Jefferys, MDCCLVI. *Title; explanation of maps,* 1 *leaf.* *Text* 110 *pp.* 2 *copperplate maps.* *Half mor.* 8vo.   (10s. 6d.   2342)

REMARKS upon a Letter Publifhed in the London Chronicle, or Univerfal Evening Poft, N°. 115. Containing an Enquiry into the Causes of the Failure of the late Expedition againft Cape Breton. In a Letter to a Member of Parliament. *London;* M. Cooper. MDCCLVII. 30 *pp.* *Half morocco.*
8vo.   (5s. 6d.   2343)

REMARKS on the Letter address'd to Two Great Men. In a Letter to the Author of that Piece. *London:* R. and J. Dodsley, [1759?] *Title and pp.* 5—64. *Half morocco.* 8vo.   (4s. 6d.   2344)

REMARKS on the Review of the Controversy between Great Britain and her Colonies. In which The Errors of its Author are expofed, and The Claims of the Coloneies vindicated, Upon the Evidence of Hiftorical Facts and authentic Records. To which is fubjoined, A Proposal for terminating the prefent unhappy Dispute with the Colonies; Recovering their Commerce; Reconciliating their Affection; Securing their Rights; And eftablifhing their Dependence on a juft and permanent Basis. Humbly fubmitted to the Confideration of the British Legislature. *London:* T. Becket and P. A. De Hondt, MDCCLXIX. *Half-title, title and* 126 *pp.* *Half morocco.* 8vo.   (7s. 6d.   2345)

REMARKS on the New Essay of the Pensylvanian Farmer; and on the Resolves and In*tructions Prefixed to that Essay; By the Author of the Right of the Britifh Legiflature vindicated. *London,* T. Becket. MDCCLXXV. *Title and* 62 *pp.* *Half morocco.* 8vo.   (4s. 6d.   2346)

REMARKS on the Patriot. Including some Hints respecting the Americans: With an Address to the Electors of Great Britain. *London :* Richardson and Urquhart. 1775. *Title and 46 pp. Half morocco. 8vo.* (4s. 6d. 2347)

REMARKS on the Principal Acts of the Thirteenth Parliament of Great Britain. By the Author of Letters concerning the Prefent State of Poland. Vol. I. [*all published*] Containing Remarks on the Acts relating to the Colonies. With a Plan of Reconciliation. *London,* Payne. MDCCLXXV. *xvi pp.* 'Contents' 4, *and 500 pp. 8vo.* (10s. 6d. 2348)

REMARKS on the Rescript of the Court of Madrid, and on the Manifesto of the Court of Versailles. In a Letter to the People of Great Britain. To which is added an Appendix, Containing the Rescript, the Manifesto, and a Memorial of Dr. Franklyn to the Court of Versailles. *London :* T. Cadell, MDCCLXXIX. *3 prel. leaves and 91 pp. Half morocco. 8vo.* (7s. 6d. 2349)

REMARKS on the Review of Inchiquin's Letters, published in the Quarterly Review ; addressed to the Right Honorable George Canning, Esquire. By an Inhabitant of New-England. *Boston :* Published by Samuel T. Armstrong, No. 50, Cornhill. 1815. *176 pp. 8vo.* (3s. 6d. 2350)

REMEMBRANCER (THE), or Impartial Repository of Public Events. *London :* J. Almon, [*and* J. Debrett]. MDCCLXXV. *to* 1783. *Fifteen Volumes.* Vol. I. *260 pp. With 2 maps of Boston.* Vol. II. Part I. for the Year 1776. *Title and pp. 5—371. Index ii—iv.* Vol. III. Part II. For the Year 1776. *Title and 356 pp.* Vol. IV. Part III. For the Year 1776. *Title and 350 pp. Index, 6 pp. Without the two maps at pp.* 261, 290. Vol. V. For the Year 1777. *Portrait of Franklin, Title and 314 pp. Index* 8 *pp.* Vol. VI. For the Year 1778. *Title and 374 pp. Index 7 pp.* Vol. VII. For the Year 1778, and Beginning of 1779. *Title and 400 pp. Index 6 pp.* Vol. VIII. For the Year 1779. *Title and 386 pp. Index 4 pp. Catalogue of Books, etc.* 8 *pp.* Vol. IX. For the Year 1780. *Title and 384 pp. Index 6 pp.* Vol. X. For the Year 1780. *Part II. iv and 380 pp. Catalogue of Books, etc.* 8 *pp.* Vol. XI. For the Year 1781. *Part I. 2 prel. leaves, and 375 pp.* Vol. XII. For the Year 1781. *Part II.*

Title and pp. 3—394 *pp. Index, 2 pp. Catalogue of Books, etc.* 8 *pp.* Vol. XIII. For the Year 1782. Part I. *Title and* 380 *pp. Index 2 pp.* ᵣ Vol. XIV. For the Year 1782. Part II. *2 prel. leaves and 378 pp.* Vol. XVI. For the Year 1783. Part II. *2 prel. leaves and* 380 *pp.* 8*vo.* (10*l.* 10*s.* 2351)

Vol. 15 and 17 are wanting. See No. 599.

RENEY (WILLIAM). A Narrative of the Shipwreck of the Corsair; in the month of January, 1835. On an unknown Reef near the Kingsmill Islands, in the South Pacific Ocean; with a detail of the dreadful Sufferings of the Crew. By William Reney, Chief Mate. London, Longman, 1836. *xvi and* 80 *pp.* 12*mo.* (2*s.* 6*d.* 2352)

REPONSE a la Déclaration du Congrès Américain. Traduite de l'Anglos. *A Londres.* T. Cadell, M,DCC,LXXVII. *Title, v and* 124 *pp. Index* 4 *pp. Old tree calf.* 8*vo.* (5*s.* 6*d.* 2353)

REPRESENTACION/ Politico Legal,/ que haze/ a nuestro Señor Soberano,/ Don Phelipe Quinto,/ (que Dios Guarde)/ Rey Poderoso/ de las Espanas,/ y Emperador Siempre Augusto,/ de las Indias,/ para que se sirva de declarar,/ no tienen los Efpañoles Indianos obice para obte-/ner los empleos Politicos, y Militares de la Ame-/rica; y que deben fer preferidos en todos,/ afsi Ecleſiaſticos, como Se-/culares./ Don Juan Antonio de Ahumada,/ Colegial actual de el Mayor de Santa Maria de/ Todos Santos de Mexico, y Abogado de fu/ Real Audiencia./ *22 Folioed leaves. Unbound. Folio.* (15*s.* 2354)

REPRESENTACION del Ilmo. Sr. Arzobispo de Mejico concerniente a algunos sucesos Anteriores a la Independencia proclamada en Aquella Capital. *Habana:* 1822. Impreso por Campe en la Oficina Liberal. 43 *pp. Half mor.* 4*to.* (3*s.* 6*d.* 2355)

REPRESENTATION (THE) and Memorial of the Council of the Iſland of Jamaica, To the Right Honourable The Lords Commiſſioners for Trade and Plantations. Together with The Addreſſes of the Governour and Council, and Town of Kingſton; and Aſſociation of the Principal Inhabitants. With a Preface, by Mr. Wood. *London:* W. Wilkins. 1716. *Title, viii and* 46 *pp.* 8*vo.* (10*s.* 6*d.* 2356)

REPRESENTATION of the Board of Trade rela-
ting to the Laws made, Manufactures set up, and
Trade carried on, in His Magesty's Plantations in
America. *Whitehall*, January 23, 1733-4. 20 *pp.*
Half morocco. Folio. (10*s.* 6*d.* 2357)

> From this precious document of the Board of Trade we learn
> that several of the Colonies had, for some time previous, levied
> duties upon the importation of Negroes from Africa, (with a
> view probably of ridding themselves of so odious a traffic).
> " We are of opinion," says the Board, " that it would be more
> for the interest of the *English* Merchants that Duties upon
> Negroes should for the future be paid by the Purchaser than by
> the Importer; and His Majesty has, upon our Representation,
> been pleased to send an Instruction to that Effect to all his
> Governours in America."

REPRESENTATION from the Commissioners for
Trade and Plantations, To the Right Honorable
the Lords Spiritual and Temporal, In Parliament
Assembled, In pursuance of their Lordships Addresses to His Majesty of the 1st and 5th of April,
1734. relating to the State of the British Islands
in America, with regard to their Trade, their
Strength, and Fortifications, and to what may be
further necessary for the Encouragement of their
Trade, and Security of those Islands: As likewise
to such Encouragements as may be necessary to
engage the Inhabitants of the British Colonies on
the Continent in America, to apply their Industry
to the Cultivation of Naval Stores of all kinds, and
of such other Products as may be proper for the
Soil of the said Colonies, and do not interfere with
the Trade or Produce of Great Britain. *London:*
John Baskett, 1734. 19 *pp.* 4*to.* (10*s.* 6*d.* 2358)

REPRESENTATION (A) on behalf of the People
called Quakers, to the President and Executive
Council, and the General Assembly of Pennsylvania, &c. *London:* Reprinted by James Phillips,
M.DCC.LXXXII. 15 *pp.* 12*mo.* (4*s.* 6*d.* 2359)

REPRESENTATION (A) on behalf of the People
called Quakers, to the President and Executive
Council, and the General Assembly of Pennsylvania, &c. *York:* Reprinted by Walker and Pen-
nington, M.DCC.LXXXII. 12 *pp.* 12*mo.* (4*s.* 6*d.* 2360)

REPUBLIK (Die) der Jesuiten, oder das Umgest-
ürzte Paraguay, welches Eine richtige Erzählung
des Krieges enthält, den diese Geistlichen gegen
die Monarchen Spaniens und Portugals in Amerika
zu führen gewaget. Nach den Sekretariats=Auf-

fätzen der beyderfeitigen Konigl. Commiffarien
und Bevollmächtigten der zweyen Kronen. Auf
befonders ausdrücklichen Befehl des portugiefifchen
Hofes an das Licht geftellt. *Amsterdam,* 1758. 36
pp. Half morocco. 4*to.*   (10*s.* 6*d.*   2361)

RESENDIUS (ANGELO ANDREA). Epitome Rervm
Gestarvm/ in India a Lufitanis, anno fuperiori,
iuxta exem=/plum epiftolæ, quam Nonius Cugna,
dux Indiæ/ max. defignatus, ad regem mifit, ex
vrbe Ca=/nanorio, IIII. Idus Octobris. Anno./
M.D.XXX./ Auctore Angelo Andrea Refendio Lufi-
tano./ *Louanii* apud Seruatium Zaffenum, Anno/
M. D. XXXI. Menfe Iulio. Ad fi=/gnū Regni cœlo-
rum./ 16 *leaves, including title with the reverse
blank; signatures* A *to* D *in fours. Red morocco,
extra, by Mackenzie.* 4*to.*   (2*l.* 12*s.* 6*d.*   2362)

RESOLUTIONS (THE) of the House of Commons,
on the great and constitutional questions between
the Privileges of the House of Commons and the
Prerogative of the Crown; From the 17th of December 1783, to the 10th of March 1784. Including the Mover and Seconder, And the Numbers
in the Divifion on each Motion. Extracted verbatim from the Records of Parliament. *London:*
J. Debrett. M.DCC.LXXXIV. *2 prel. leaves and* 51 *pp.
Half morocco.* 8*vo.*   (4*s.* 6*d.*   2363)

REVIEW (A) of All that hath pafs'd between the
Courts of Great Britain and Spain, Relating to
Our Trade and Navigation From the Year 1721,
to the Prefent Covention; With fome Particular
Observations Upon it. *London:* H. Goreham 1739.
Half-title, title, and text 60 *pp. Half morocco.*
8*vo.*   (4*s.* 6*d.*   2364)

REVIEW (A) of The Rector Detected or the
Colonel Reconnoitred. Part the First. *Williams-
burg,* Printed by Jofeph Royle, MDCCLXIV. 29 *pp.
Half morocco.* 4*to.*   (10*s.* 6*d.*   2365)

REVIEW (A) of the Government and Grievances
of the Province of Quebec, since the Conquest of
it by the British Arms. To which is added An
Appendix, containing extracts from Authentic
Papers. *London:* J. Stockdale M,DCC,LXXXVIII.
Half-title, title, and text 111 *pp. Half morocco.*
8*vo.*   (5*s.* 6*d.*   2366)

REYNOLDS (Theophilus). Cursory Observations,
addressed to the Planters and Others, interested in
the West India Trade; in which a more profitable
mode of Territorial Appropriation is pointed out,
and illustrated by example. By Theophilus Reynolds, L.L.D. *Liverpool,* F. B. Wright, 1808. 15
pp. 8vo. (3s. 6d. 2367)

RIBERA (Diego de). Concentos/ Fvnebres,/ Me-
tricos/ Lamentos, qve explican,/ Demoſtraciones
publicas, de reconcidos afeĉtos, en/ los Fvnerales
devidos al Illuſtriſſimo,/ Reverendiſſimo, y Exce-
lentiſſimo Señor Maeſtro/ D. Fr. Payo Enriquez/
de Ribera,/ Digniſſimo Arçobiſpo, que fue de eſta
Ciudad de/ Mexico, Virrey, y Capitan General en
ella, que/ deſcanza en Paz./ Escribelos/ Con memorias de ſu empeñado agradecimiento,/ el Br. D.
Diego de Ribera, Presbytero, y/ los dedica por la
razon de juſtos titulos,/ Al/ Excelentissimo Señor
Conde de Paredes/ Marques de la Laguna, Virrey,
y Capitan General,/ de eſta Nueva-/Eſpaña, y Preſidente de la Real/ Audiencia, y Chancilleria./
¶ Con Licencia/ En *Mexico,* por la Viuda de Bernardo Calderon, año de 1684./ *22 unnumbered
leaves. 4to.* (1l. 1s. 2368)

RIBAS (Andres Perez de). Historia/ de los Trivm-
phos de Nuestra/ Santa Fee entre Gentes las mas
Barbaras,/ y fieras del nueuo Orbe:/ conſeguidos
por los Soldados, de la/ Milicia de la Compañia de
Ieſvs en las Miſsiones/ de la Prouincia de Nueua-/
Eſpaña./ Refierense assi mismo las coſtvmbres,/
ritos, y ſuperſticiones que vſauan eſtas Gentes:/ ſus
pueſtos, y temples:/ las vitorias que de algunas
dellas alcaçaron con las armas los Ca-/tolicos Eſpañoles, quando les obligaron à tomarlas: y las
dichoſas/ muertes de veinte Religioſos de la Compañia, que en va-/rios pueſtos, y a manos de varias
Naciones,/ dieron ſus vidas, por la predica-/cion
del ſanto Euan-/gelio./ Dedicada a la mvy Catolica
Mageſtad/ del Rey N. S. Felipe Qvarto./ Escrita
por el Padre Andres Perez de Ribas,/ Prouincial
en la Nueua Eſpaña, natural de Cordoua./ Año
1645./ Con Privilegio./ En *Madrid.* Por Alöſo
de Paredez, júto a los Eſtudios de la Cõpañia./—
(History of the triumphs of our holy faith among
the most barbarous and savage nations of the new

world; obtained by the soldiers of the army of the
Company of Jesus, in the Missions of the Province
of New Spain. Likewise are reported the customs,
rites and superstitions which those nations practised ; their places and temples ; the victories which
were obtained over some of them by the arms of
the Spanish Catholics, when they obliged them to
take them ; and the happy deaths of twenty priests
of the Company, who in various places, and by the
hands of various nations gave up their lives for the
preaching of the holy Gospel. Dedicated to the
most Catholic Majesty of the King our Lord Philip
the fourth. Written by the Father Andrew Perez
de Ribas, Provincial in New Spain, native of Cordova. In the year 1645. With privilege. Madrid,
by Alonzo de Paredes, near the Hall of the Company.) 16 *prel. leaves and text* 756 *pp. Vellum.*
Folio.   (4*l.* 4*s.*   2369)

RICHSHOFFER (Ambrosius). Ambrofij Richfz-
hoffers,/ Brafzilianifch ʒ und Weſt Indianifche/
Reiſze Befchreibung/ Straſzburg/ Beÿ Joſzias
Städeln, Aᵒ. 1677./ *2 prel. leaves; viz. Portrait of
Richſhoffer, and Engraved Title : Text pp.* 3—182.
Sonnets, 4 *pp. Errata* 1 *page. Copperplate maps
and plates at pp.* 49, 57, 58, *and* 129. *Boards.*
Small 8vo.   (12*s.* 6*d.*   2370)

RIGHT (The) of the British Legislature To Tax
the American Colonies Vindicated ; and the Means
of Asserting that Right proposed. *London :* T.
Becket, MDCCLXXIV. *Title and* 50 *pp. Half morocco.*
8vo.   (4*s.* 6*d.*   2371)

RIGHTS (The) of Great Britain Asserted against
the Claims of America : Being an Answer to the
Declaration of the General Congress. [By James
Macpherson, Translator of Ossian.] The Second
Edition. *London :* T. Cadell, MDCCLXXVI. *Title and*
92 *pp.* ' Appendix ' *a folded sheet at page* 80. *Half
morocco. 8vo.*   (5*s.* 6*d.*   2372)

RIGHTS (The) of Great Britain Asserted against
the Claims of America : Being an Answer to the
Declaration of the General Congress. The Third
Edition, with Additions. *London :* T. Cadell,
MDCCLXXVI. *Title and* 96 *pp. Half morocco.*
8vo.   (4*s.* 6*d.*   2373)

RIGHTS (The) of Great Britain Asserted against the Claims of America: Being an Answer to the Declaration of the General Congress. The Fourth Edition, with Additions. *London:* T. Cadell, MDCCLXXVI. *2 prel. leaves and* 103 *pp.* 'Appendix' *at page* 77, *a folded sheet.* 12*mo.* (4s. 6d. 2374)

RIGHTS (The) of Great-Britain Asserted against the Claims of America: Being an Answer to the Declaration of the General Congress. The Sixth Edition, with Additions. *Edinburgh:* Printed for Charles Elliot. M,DCC,LXXVI. *2 prel. leaves and* 98 *pp.* 'Appendix' *at page* 92, *a folded sheet.* 12*mo.* (4s. 6d. 2375)

RIGHTS (The) of Great Britain Asserted against the Claims of America: Being an Answer to the Declaration of the General Congress. The Ninth Edition. To which is now added, a Further Refutation of Dr. Price's State of the National Debt. *London:* T. Cadell, MDCCLXXVI. *2 prel. leaves and* 131 *pp.* 'Appendix' *a folded sheet at page* 99. *Half morocco.* 8*vo.* (4s. 6d. 2376)

RIGHTS (The) of Great Britain Asserted against the Claims of America: Being an Answer to the Declaration of the General Congress. The Tenth Edition. To which is now added, a Further Refutation of Dr. Price's State of the National Debt. *London:* T. Cadell, MDCCLXXVI. *2 prel. leaves and* 131 *pp.* 'Appendix' *a folded sheet at page* 99. *Half morocco.* 8*vo.* (4s. 6d. 2377)

RIO (Antonio del). Description of the Ruins of an Ancient City, discovered near Palenque, in the Kingdom of Guatemala, in Spanish America; translated from the Original Manuscript Report of Captain Don Antonio Del Rio: Followed by Teatro Critico Americano; or, a critical investigation and research into The History of the Americans, by Doctor Paul Felix Cabrera, of the City of New Guatemala. *London:* Henry Berthoud, 1822. *xiii pp.* 'Teatro Critico' 1 *page. Text* 128 *pp.* 17 *plates.* 4*to.* (10s. 6d. 2378)

ROBERTS (George). The Four Years Voyages of Capt. George Roberts; being a Series of Uncommon Events, Which befell him In a Voyage to the Iflands of the Canaries, Cape de Verde, and

Barbadoes, from whence he was bound to the Coaſt of Guiney. The Manner of his being taken by Three Pyrate Ships, commanded by Low, Ruſ-fell, and Spriggs, who, after having plundered him, and detained him 10 Days, put him aboard his own Sloop, without Provisions, Water, &c. and with only two Boys, one of Eighteen, and the other of Eight Years of Age. The Hardships he endur'd for above 20 Days, 'till he arriv'd at the Iſland of St. Nicholas, from whence he was blown off to Sea (before he could get any Suſtenance) without his Boat and biggeſt Boy, whom he had ſent aſhore; and after Four Days of Difficulty and Diſtreſs, was Shipwreck'd on the Unfrequented Iſland of St. John, where after he had remained near two Years, he built a Veſſel to bring himſelf off. With a particular and curious Deſcription and Draught of the Cape de Verd Iſlands; their Roads, Anchoring Places, Nature and Production of the Soils; The Kindneſs and Hoſpitality of the Natives to Strangers, their Religion, Manners, Cuſtoms, and Superſtitions, &c. Together with Obſervations on the Minerals, Mineral Waters, Metals, and Salts, and of Nitre with which ſome of theſe Iſlands abound. Written by Himſelf, And interſpers'd with many Pleaſant and Profitable Remarks, very inſtructive for all thoſe who uſe this Trade, or who may have the Misfortune to meet with any of the like Diſtreſſes either by Pyracy or Shipwreck. Adorn'd with ſeveral Copper Plates. *London:* A. Bettesworth, and J. Osborn, 1726. *3 prel. leaves and 458 pp. 4 Plates and Draught of all the Cape de Verd Iſlands. Old calf. 8vo.* (8s. 6d. 2379)

ROBERTS (WILLIAM). An Account of the First Discovery of Florida. With a Particular Detail of the ſeveral Expeditions and Descents made on that Coaſt. Collected from the beſt Authorities By William Roberts. Illuſtrated by a general Map, and ſome particular Plans, together with a geogra-phical Deſcription of that Country, By T. Jefferys, Geographer to His Majesty./ *London:* T. Jefferys, MDCCLXIII. *viii pp. Contents 2 and 102 pp. 7 Maps and Plans. 4to.* (8s. 6d. 2380)

ROBINSON (JOHN). Eſſayes;/ or,/ Observations/ Divine and/ Morall./ Collected ovt of/ holy Scriptures, Ancient and/ Moderne Writers, both

di-/vine and humane./ As alfo, out of the great
volume/ of mens manners : Tending to the/ furtherance of knowledge and vertue./ By Iohn
Robinson./ The fecond Edition, with two Tables,
the one of/ the Authours quoted ; The other of the
mat-/ters contained in the Obfervations./ *London,*/
Printed by I. D. for I. Bellamie, at the/ three
golden Lyons in Cornhill neere/ the Royall Exchange. 1638./ *16 prel. leaves and 566 pp. Old
calf. 12mo.*   (2l. 12s. 6d. 2381)

ROBINSON (John). A/ Ivstification/ of/ Separa-
tion/ from the Church of England./ Againft Mr
Richard Bernard his invective,/ intitvled ;/ *The
Separatists schifme.*/ By John Robinson./ Printed
in the yeere 1639./ *382 pp. followed by 3 leaves of
Table. Fine copy in old calf. 4to.* (5l. 5s. 2382)

ROBINSON (John). A/ Ivst and Necessary/
Apologie/ of certain/ Christians,/ No leffe con-
tumeliously then com-/monly called Brovvnists,/
or Barrovvists./ By Mr. Iohn Robin-/son, Paftor
of the English/ Church at Leyden./ Publifhed firft
in Latin in his and/ the Churches name over which
he/ was fet : After tranflated into En-/glifh by
himfelf, and now republifhed for/ the fpeciall and
common good of/ our own countrymen./ [*Leyden?*]
Printed in the yeer of our Lord,/ m,dc,xliiii./ *72
pp. including the Title. Red morocco extra, by Bedford. 24mo.*   (5l. 5s. 2383)

ROBINSON (Matthew). Peace the best Policy or
Reflections upon the Appearance of a Foreign
War, the present state of Affairs at Home and the
Commission for Granting Pardons in America. In
a Letter to a Friend by Matt. Robinson M.? *Lon-
don:* J. Almon, mdcclxxvii. *Title and 112 pp.
Half morocco. 8vo.*   (4s. 6d. 2384)

ROBINSON (William). Several/ Epistles/ Given
forth by Two of the/ Lords Faithful Servants,/
Whom he fent to/ New-England,/ to/ Bear Wit-
nefs to his Everlafting Truth./ And were there
(by the Priefts, Rulers, and Profeffors)/ after cruel
and long Imprifonment, and inhumane/ Whippings
and Banifhment, put to death ; for/ no other Caufe,
but for keeping the/ Commandments of God, and/
Teftimony of Jefus./ William Robinfon./ William

Leddra./ Here is alfo prefixed W. R. his Teftimony of his Call to/ that Service, for obedience unto which, he under-/went the wrath of Men, but hath obtained/ Everlafting Peace and Reft with God. *London*, Printed in the Year, 1669. 11 *pp.* 4*to.* (1*l.* 1*s.* 2385)

ROBSON (JOSEPH). An Account of six years residence in Hudson's-Bay, From 1733 to 1736, and 1744 to 1747. By Joseph Robson, Late Surveyor and Supervifor of the Buildings to the Hudfon's-bay Company. Containing a Variety of Facts, Observations, and Discoveries, tending to fhew, I. The vaft Importance of the Countries about Hudson's-Bay to Great Britain, on Account of the extenfive Improvements that may be made there in many beneficial Articles of Commerce, particularly in the Furs and in the Whale and Seal Fisheries. And, II. The interefted Views of the Hudfon's-bay Company; and the abfolute Neceffity of laying open the Trade, and making it the Object of National Encouragement, as the only Method of keeping it out of the Hands of the French. To which is added an Appendix; containing, I. A fhort Hiftory of the Difcovery of Hudfon's-bay; and of the Proceedings of the Englifh there fince the Grant of the Hudfon's-bay Charter: Together with Remarks upon the Papers and Evidence produced by that Company before the Committee of the Honourable Houfe of Commons, in the Year 1749. II. An Eftimate of the Expence of building the Stone Fort, called Prince of Wales's-fort, at the entrance of Churchill-river. III. The Soundings of Nelfon-river. IV. A Survey of the Courfe of Nelson-river. V. A Survey of Seal and Gillam's Iflands. And, VI. A Journal of the Winds and Tides at Churchill-river, for Part of the Years 1746 and 1747. The Whole illuftrated, By a Draught of Nelson and Hayes's Rivers; a Draught of Churchill-river; and Plans of York-Fort, and Prince of Wales's Fort. *London*: J. Payne. MDCCLII. *Title, vi and* 84 *pp.* 'Appendix' 95 *pp.* 3 *Maps. Old calf.* 8*vo.* (7*s.* 6*d.* 2386)

ROCHEFORT (CESAR DE). [*Engraved title*] Histoire/ Naturelle et Morale/ des/ Iles Antilles de/ l'Amerique./ A Rotterdam,/ Chez Arnout Leers.

Marchant Librair. 1658./ [*Printed title*] Histoire/
Naturelle et Morale/ des/ Iles Antilles/ de l'Ame-
rique./ Enrichie de plufieurs belles figures des
Raretez les plus/ confiderables qui y font d'écrites./
Avec vn Vocabulaire Caraïbe./ A *Roterdam,*/ Chez
Arnould Leers,/ M.DC.LVIII :/ *First Edition.* 8 *prel.*
leaves; viz. Two titles, ' Epistre.' *Signed* ' L. D. P.'
4 *pp* ; ' Preface,' 6 *pp* ; ' Avertissement,' 2 *pp* ;
Text 527 *pp* ; ' Table,' 12 *pp.* *Fine copy.* *Vellum.*
4to. (1*l.* 10*s.* 6*d.* 2387)

ROCHEFORT (Cesar de). [*Engraved title*] His-
toire/ Natvrelle et Morale/ Des/ Iles Antilles de/
l'Amerique/ [*Printed title*] Histoire/ Naturelle et
Morale/ des/ Iles Antilles/ de l'Amerique./ En-
riche d'un grand nombre de belles Figures en taille
douce,/ des Places & des Raretez les plus confiderables,/ qui y font décrites./ Avec un Vocabulaire
Caraïbe./ Seconde Edition./ Reveuë & augmentée
de plufieurs Defcriptions, & de quelques/ éclair-
ciffemens, qu'on defiroit en la precedente./ A
Roterdam,/ Chez Arnout Leers,/ M.DC.LXV./ 18
prel. leaves; viz. Two titles ; ' Epistre,' 11 *pp.* *Signed*
' De Rochefort' ; ' Preface,' 5 *pp* ; ' Avertissement,' 4 *pp* ; ' Copies Lettres,' 12 *pp* ; *Text* 583
pp ; ' Table,' 13 *pp* : *Copperplates at pp.* 53, 332,
412. *Vellum. 4to.* (1*l.* 1*s.* 2388)

ROCHEFORT (Cesar de). Le Tableau/ de/ L'Isle
de Tabago,/ ou de la/ Nouvelle Oüalchre,/ L'une
des Ifles Antilles de/ l'Amerique,/ Dependante de
la fouveraineté des Hauts &/ Puiffans Seigneurs
les Eftats Generaus/ des Provinces Unies des
Pais-bas./ A *Leyde*/ Chez Jean Le Carpentier/
cIↃIↃCLXV./ 8 *prel. leaves and* 144 *pp. Vellum.*
8vo. (15*s.* 2389)

ROCHEFORT (Cesar de). Relation/ de L'Isle/
de Tabago,/ ou de la/ Novvelle Oüalcre./ l'vne
des Isles Antilles/ de l'Ameriqve./ Par le Sieur
de Rochefort./ A *Paris,*/ Chez Lovys Billaine,
au fecond/ Pilier de la Grand' Sale du Palais.
M. DC. LXVI./ Auec Permiffion./ 8 *prel. leaves and*
128 *pp. Old calf.* 12*mo.* (10*s.* 6*d.* 2390)

ROCHEFORT (Cesar de). Histoire/ Natvrelle/
des/ Iles Antilles/ de l'Ameriqve :/ Par Mr. De
Rochfort./ A *Lyon,*/ Chez Christofle Fovrmy,/ rüe

Merciere, à la Bibliotheque./ M.DC.LXVII./ *Two
volumes.* Tomè Premier, 32 *prel. leaves, the la st
blank, and* 566 *pp. Copperplates at pp.* 13, 29 5.
Tome Second, 3 *prel. leaves and* 680 *pp. Copperplate at page* 115. *Old calf.* 12*mo.* (12*s.* 6*d.* 2391)

ROCHEFORT (CESAR DE). Hiſtoriſche/ Beſchrei-
bung/ Der/ Antillen Inſeln in/ America gelegen/
In ſich begreiffend deroſelben/ Gelegenheit, darinnen befindli=/chen natürlichen Sachen, ſampt
deren/ Einwohner Sitten und Gebräuchen mit/
45. Kupfferſtücken gezieret./ von/ dem Herrn de
Rochefort,/ zum zweyten mahl in Franzöſi=/ ſcher
Sprach an den Tag ge=/geben,/ nunmehr aber/ in
die Teutſche überſetzet./ *Frankfurt,*/ In Verlegung
Wilhelm Serlins, Buchdru=/ckers und Buchhand-
lers. 1668. *Two Volumes.* (Buch I.) 11 *prel.
leaves, including frontispiece, and* 430 *pp.* ' Innhalt.'
11 *pp. Copperplates at pp.* 29, 104, 105, 106, 107,
109, 111, 118, 119, 123, 124, 126, 138, 141, 142,
143, 148, 149, 153, 156, 162, 166 (2), 180, 182,
189, 192, 195, 205, 215, 233, 264, 271, 301, 307(2),
311, 321, 335, 353. (Buch II.) 6 *prel. leaves,* 33
and 514 *pp.* 12*mo.* (7*s.* 6*d.* 2392)

ROCHEFORT (CESAR DE). [*Engraved title*] His-
toire/ Naturelle et Morale/ Des/ Iles Antilles de/
l'Amerique/ Derniere Edition reveuë et/ augmentée./ [*Printed title*] Histoire/ Naturelle et
Morale/ des/ Iles Antilles/ de l'Amerique,/ Enrichie d'un grand nombre de belles Figures en
taille douce, qui/ repreſentent au naturel les Places,
& les Raretez les plus/ conſiderables qui y ſont
décrites./ Avec un Vocabulaire Caraïbe./ Derniere Edition./ Reveuë & augmentée par l'Autheur
d'un Recit de l'Eſtat preſent des/ celebres Colonies
de la Virginie, de Marie-Land, de la Caroline, du/
nouveau Duché d' York, de Penn-Sylvania, & de la
nouvelle An-/gleterre, ſituées dans l'Amerique
ſeptentrionale, & qui rele-/vent de la Couronne du
Roy de la grand' Bretagne./ Tiré fidelement des
memoires des habitans des mêmes Colonies,/ en
faveur de ceus, qui auroyent le deſſein de s'y/
transporter pour s'y établie./ A *Rotterdam,*/ Chez
Reinier Leers,/ M.DC.LXXXI./ 18 *prel. leaves, including the engraved and printed titles. Text* 583 *pp ;
Table,* 13 *pp. Second title,* ' Recit/ de l'Estat/ Pre-

sent des/ Celebres Colonies,' *etc.* 48 *pp.* *Large*
folding plates at pp. 53, 332, *and* 412. *Fine copy in*
old red morocco. 4*to.*   (1*l.* 1*s.*   2393)

ROCHEFOUCAULD-LIANCOURT (Duc de la).
Voyage dans les Etats-Unis d'Amérique, fait en
1795, 1796 et 1797.   Par La Rochefoucauld-Liancourt.   *A Paris* Du Pont, Buisson, Charles Pon-
gens, L'an VII de la République.   (1799) *Eight*
Volumes.   Tome Premier.   *xxiv and* 365 *pp.*   *Map*
at page 1.   Tome Second.   *Half-title, title, iv and* 349
pp.   Tome Troisième.   *Half-title, title, iv and* 384 *pp.*
Tome Quatrième.   *Half-title, title, iii and* 349 *pp.*
Map at page 1.   Tome Cinquième.   *Half-title, title,*
iv and 400 *pp.*   Tome Sixième.   *Half-title, title, iii*
and 336 *pp.*   'Tableau,' *etc. at page* 266, *a folded*
sheet.   Tome Septième.   *Half-title, title, iv and* 366.
Map at page 155.   Tome Huitième.   *Half-title, title,*
and 244 *pp ; folded sheets at page* 172, *numbered*
I—VI.   *Calf extra.*   8*vo.*   (1*l.* 1*s.*   2394)

RODRIGUES DE MELLO (Joseph).   Josehpi
Rodrigues de Mello Lusitani Portuensis de Rus-
ticis Brasiliæ Rebus Carminum Libri IV. Accedit
Prudentii Amaralii Brasiliensis de Sacchari Opificio
Carmen.   *Romæ* MDCCLXXXI.   Ex Typographia Fra-
truⁿ Puccinelliorum.   *viii and* 206 *pp.*   4 *copper-*
plates at the end.   *Vellum.*   8*vo.*   (12*s.* 6*d.*   2395)

RODRIGUEZ (Antonio).   Relacion/ de las Fiestas/
qve ala Immacv-/lada Concepcion dela Virgen
N. Señora ſe hizieron en la Real Ciudad de Lima
en/ el Perù, y principalmente delas q hizo la Con/
gregacion dela Expeⁿacion del Parto/ en la Cō-
pañia de Ieſus año 1617./   Dirigida al Excelen-
tissimo/ Señor Principe de Eſquilache Virrey deſtos
Reynos./   Por el Bachiller Antonio Rodrigvez/ de
Leon Profeſſor delos derechos Pontificio y Ceſareo./
¶ Con licencia impreſſo en *Lima* por Franciſco del
Canto./   Acoſta de Iuan Fernandez Higuera mercader.   Año 1618./   *2 prel. leaves ; viz. Title, the*
reverse blank, 'Erratas,' *and* 'Tassa:' 1 *page ;*
'Aprobacion,' 1 *page ; Text* 80 *folioed leaves.*
4*to.*   (1*l.* 11*s.* 6*d.*   2396)

RODRIGUEZ (Manuel).   Señor./   [*Begins*] Manuel
Rodriguez de la Compañia de Iſevs, Procurador/
general por las Provincias de Indias, dize : *etc.*

[*Ending*] liberal Mano, y Catolico zelo de V.
Mageſtad. 4 *unnumbered pages. Half morocco.*
Folio. (1*l.* 1*s.* 2397)

RODRIGUEZ LAMEGO (Manuel). ✢/ Assi-
ento/ y Capitvlacion qve/ se tomo con Manvel
Rodrigvez/ Lamego, ſobre la renta y prouiſion
general de eſclauos/ negros que ſe nauegan a las
Indias por tiempo/ de ocho años, y precio de ciento
y veinte mil/ du cados cada año./ Año de 1623./
17 *folioed leaves. Half mor. Folio.* (1*l.* 1*s.* 2398)

ROEBUCK (John). An Enquiry, whether The
Guilt of the Present Civil War in America, ought
to be imputed to Great Britain or America. By
John Roebuck, M. D., F. R. S. A new Edition.
London: John Donaldson, MDCCLXXVI. *Title and*
69 *pp. Half morocco.* 8*vo.* (4*s.* 6*d.* 2399)

ROGERS (Abraham). Abraham Rogers/ Offne
Thür/ zu dem verborgenen/ heydenthum :/ Oder,/
Warhaftige Vorweiſung deſz/ Lebens, und der
Sitten, ſamt der Religion,/ und dem Gottesdienſt
der Bramines, auf der/ Cuſt Chormandel, und
denen herumliz/genden Ländern :/ Mit kurtzen
Anmerkungen,/ Aus dem Niederländiſchen über-
ſetzt./ Samt/ Chriſtoph Arnolds/ Auserleſenen
Zugaben,/ Von den Aſiatiſchen, Africaniſchen, und
Ame-/ricaniſchen Rëligions=ſachen, ſo in XL / Capital verfaſſt./ Alles/ Mit einem nothwendigen/
Regiſter./ *Nürnberg,*/ In Verlegung, Johann Andreas Endters, und/ Wolffgang deſz Jüng-Seel.
Erben./ M.DC.LXIII./ 8 *prel. leaves, including the*
engraved and printed titles; Text 998 pp. followed
by 19 leaves of Register and one page of errata. Nu-
merous plates. Vellum. 8*vo.* (15*s.* 2400)

ROGERS (Robert). A Concise Account of North
America: Containing A Deſcription of the ſeveral
British Colonies on that Continent, including the
Iſlands of Newfoundland, Cape Breton, &c. As
to Their Situation, Extent, Climate, Soil, Produce,
Riſe, Government, Religion, Preſent Boundaries,
and the Number of Inhabitants ſuppoſed to be in
each. Also of The Interior, or Weſterly Parts of
the Country, upon the Rivers St. Laurence, the
Mississipi, Christino, and the Great Lakes. To
which is ſubjoined, An Account of the ſeveral

Nations and Tribes of Indians refiding in thofe
Parts, as to their Cuftoms, Manners, Government,
Numbers, &c. Containing many Ufeful and En-
tertaining Facts, never before treated of. By Major
Robert Rogers. *London:* Printed for the Author,
MDCCLXV. *viii and* 264 *pp.* 8*vo.*   (9*s.* 2401)

ROGERS (ROBERT). Journals of Major Robert
Rogers: Containing An Account of the feveral
Excurfions he made under the Generals who commanded upon the Continent of North America,
during the late War. From which may be collected
The moft material Circumftances of every Campaign
upon that Continent, from the Commencement to
the Conclufion of the War. To which is added An
Hiftorical Account of the Expedition againft the
Ohio Indians in the Year 1764, under the com-
mand of Henry Bouquet, Efq; Colonel of Foot,
and now Brigadier General in America, including
his Tranfactions with the Indians, relative to the
Delivery of the Prifoners, and the Preliminaries of
Peace. With an Introductory Account of the
Proceeding Campaign, and Battle at Bufhy-Run.
Dublin: R. Acheson, M,DCC,LX,IX. *x and* 218 *pp.*
'An Hiftorical Account of the Expedition againft
the Ohio Indians, in the year MDCCLXIV,'/ *etc. xx
and* 99 *pp. Old calf.* 12*mo.*   (10*s.* 6*d.* 2402)

ROGERS (WOODES). A Cruising Voyage round the
World: Firft to the South Seas, thence to the
East-Indies, and homewards by the Cape of Good
Hope. Begun in 1708, and finifh'd in 1711. Containing a Journal of all the Remarkable Tranf-
actions; particularly, Of the Taking of Puna and
Guiaquil, of the Acapulco Ship, and other Prizes;
An Account of Alexander Selkirk's living alone
four Years and four Months in an Ifland; and A
brief Defcription of feveral Countries in our Courfe
noted for Trade, efpecially in the South-Sea. With
Maps of all the Coaft, from the beft Spanifh Manu-
fcript Draughts. And an Introduction relating to
the South-Sea Trade. By Captain Woodes Rogers,
Commander in Chief on this Expedition, with the
Ships Duke and Dutchefs of Briftol. *London:* A.
Bell and B. Lintot, M.DCC.XII. *xxii and* 428 *pp.*
'Appendix,' 56 *pp.* 'Index," 14 *pp.* 4 *maps. Old
calf.* 8*vo.*   (10*s.* 6*d.* 2403)

ROGERS (Woodes). A Cruising Voyage round
the World: Firſt to the South-Sea, thence to the
East-Indies, and homewards by the Cape of Good
Hope. Begun in 1708, and finiſh'd in 1711. *etc.*
The Second Edition, Corrected. *London,* Andrew
Bell and Bernard Lintot, M.DCC.XVIII. *xix and* 428
pp; ' Appendix,' 57 *pp; Index,* 7 *pp. Maps at page*
1 *of Text, and pp.* 1, 10, 33, *and* 51, *of Appendix.*
Old calf. 8vo. (10s. 6d. 2404)

ROGERS (Woodes). A Cruising Voyage round
the World: *etc.* The Second Edition, Corrected.
London : Bernard Lintot, M.DCC.XXVI. [*The same*
as Second Edition, of 1718, *except a new title, and*
having in addition two plates at pp. 62 *and* 101, *repre-*
senting the Aligator and Crocodile, drawn from life
in London, 1739. *Old calf.* 8vo. (10s. 6d. 2405)

ROLLE (Denys). To the Right Honourable the
Lords of His Majesty's Moſt Honourable Privy
Council. The Humble Petition of Denys Rolle,
Eſq ; ſetting forth the Hardſhips, Inconveniencies,
and Grievances, which have attended him in his
Attempts to make a Settlement in Eaſt Florida,
humbly praying ſuch Relief, as in their Lordſhips
Wiſdom ſhall ſeem meet. [*London* 17—] 85 *pp.*
Plan at page 72. ' Grants by the Governor of
South Carolina,' *a folded sheet.* ' Copies of his
Excellency Governor Grant's Letters, and alſo
Copies of the rough Drafts from which Mr. Rolle's
Letters to the Governor were wrote, containing
the full Import of the ſame.' 47 *pp. Half morocco.*
8vo. (1l. 1s. 2406)

ROLT (Richard). A New and Accurate History of
South-America : Containing A particular Account
of ſome Accidents leading to the Diſcovery of the
New World ; of the Diſcovery made by Columbus,
and other Adventures ; of the ſeveral Attempts
made to find out a North East and North-Weſt
Paſſage ; and what Parts of America are ſubject
to the different European Powers. With A full
Deſcription of the Spanish Provinces of Chili,
Paraguay, Peru, and Terra Firma. Of Guiana ;
particularly of Surinam belonging to the Dutch,
and of Cayenne belonging to the French ; of Brazil
ſubject to the Crown of Portugal ; of that Part of

Paraguay poffeffed by the Jesuits, where thy have eftablifhed a New Monarchy; and of the various Nations of Indians throughout this extenfive Territory : As alfo of all the moft remarkable Iflands adjacent to its Coafts. Including the Geographical, Natural, Political, and Commercial Hiftory of every Province : With the Religion, Manners and Cuftoms of the Inhabitants. With Dissertations on the Britifh, Spanifh, Portuguefe, French, Dutch, and Indian Settlements. By Mr. Rolt. *London :* T. Gardner, m.dcc.lvi. *8 prel. leaves and 576 pp. With map of South-America by Eman Bowen. 8vo.* (7s. 6d. 2407)

ROMERO DE MELLA (Nicolas). Por/ Don Nicolas Romero/ de Mella, Contador de tributos, y azo-/gues de la Nueua Efpaña./ En/ El pleyto que trata con el feñor Fifcal./ Sobre/ La reftitucion del dicho oficio; y en fatisfacion de los cargos que le hi-/zo el feñor Licenciado Don Pedro de Galuez, del Confejo de fu/ Mageftad, en el Supremo de las Indias, el año de 53./ En la vifita de los Miniftros, y Oficiales/ Reales del Reyno de/ Mexico./ [1655] *26 folioed leaves. Half mor. Folio.* (1l. 1s. 2408)

ROSS (John). An Explanation of Captain Sabine's remarks on the late Voyage of discovery to Baffin's Bay. By Captain John Ross, R. N. *London :* John Murray, 1819. *Half-title, title, and 54 pp. 8vo.* (2s. 6d. 2409)

ROSS (Robert). A Sermon, Preached at New Town, December 8th, 1773. On Church Government and Difcipline. By Robert Ross, A. M. Paftor of the Church of Chrift in Stratfield. With A Preface and an Appendix, Containing Some Remarks on the Rev. Mr. David Judson's Reply to faid Sermon. *New-Haven.* Printed by Thomas and Samuel Green. [1773.] *58 pp. Unbound. 8vo.* (4s. 6d. 2410)

ROTHERAM (John). An Essay on Faith, and its connection with Good Works. By John Rotheram, M. A. Rector of Ryton in the County of Durham, and Chaplain to the Lord Bishop of Durham. Third Edition. London, Printed : *New-York,* Reprinted and Soldby J. Parker, at the New-Printing-Office, in Beaver-Street. m.dcc.lxvii. *viii and 126 pp. 8vo.* (5s. 6d. 2411)

ROUSSIGNAC (Jacques de). The Earth twice
ſhaken wonderfully :/ Or, an/ Analogical Diſcourſe
of Earthquakes,/ its Natural Cauſes, Kinds, and
Manifold Effects ;/ occaſioned/ By the laſt of theſe,
which happened on the/ Eighth Day of September
1692. at Two of the Clock/ in the Afternoon./
Divided into/ Philoſophical Theorems, pick'd out
of many/ Famous Modern, and Ancient Treatiſes,/
Tranſlated into Engliſh ;/ With Reference to that
unuſual One, that happened in/ Queen Elizabeth's
Reign, on the ſame Day, 8th. of September 1601./
at the ſame Hour, which was ſenſibly felt throughout all Europe,/ and ſome part of Aſia in the ſame
Moment, as much as it is found out./ A dorned,/
With an Account of many ſtupendous and won-
derful/ Events in Germany, Italy, and other King-
doms./ Wherein/ Some Obſervations are made
upon the Circumſtances, wherein/ theſe Two Earth-
quakes agree, and in others wherein they differ./
By J.[acques] D.[e] R.[ouſſignac ?] French Mi-
niſter./ *London :* Printed for the Author, at Sion's
Colledge, near/ Cripplegate ; and to be Sold at
Mr. Cockrel, Bookſeller, at the Sign/ of the Three
Legs in the Poultry, and at Mr. Vaillant, French
Book-/ſeller, in the Strand, over-againſt the French
Savoy's Church, 169¾./ *4 prel. leaves and 47 pp.*
4to. (7s. 6d. 2412)

ROWLANDSON (Mary). A true/ History/ of
the/ Captivity & Reſtoration/ of/ Mrs. Mary Row-
landson,/ A Miniſter's Wife in New-England./
Wherein is ſet forth, The Cruel and Inhumane/
Uſage ſhe underwent amongſt the Heathens, for/
Eleven Weeks time : And her Deliverance from/
them./ Written by her own Hand, for her Private
Uſe : And now made/ Publick at the earneſt
Deſire of ſome Friends, for the Benefit/ of the
Afflicted./ Whereunto is annexed,/ A Sermon of
the Poſſibility of God's Forſaking a Peo-/ple that
have been near and dear to him./ Preached by
Mr. Joſeph Rowlandſon, Husband to the ſaid Mrs.
Rowlandſon :/ It being his laſt Sermon./ Printed
firſt at New-England : And Re-printed at *London,*
and ſold/ by Joſeph Poole, at the Blue Bowl in the
Long-Walk, by Chriſts-/Church Hoſpital./ 1682./
3 prel. leaves and 36 pp. 4to. (1l. 11s. 6d. 2413)

RUIZ DE LEON (FRANCISCO). Hernandia, triumphos de la Fe, y gloria de las Armas Españolas. Poema Heroyco. Conquista de Mexico, cabeza del imperio Septentrional de la Nueva-España. Proezas de Hernan-Cortes, Catholicos Blasones Militares, y grandez as del Nuevo Mundo. Lo cantaba Don Francisco Ruiz de Leon, hijo de la Nueva-España, y reverente lo consagra a la Soberana, Catholica Magestad de su Rey, y Señor Natural Don Fernando Sexto, en la real Catholica Magestad de la Reyna Nuestra Señora Doña Maria Barbara, (que Dios guarde) y a las dos Magestades, Por Mano del excellentissimo Señor Duque de Alva, &c. Con Privilegio. *En Madrid :* Viuda de Manuel Fernandez, 1755. 10 *prel. leaves and* 383 *pp. Vellum. 4to.* (1*l.* 11*s.* 6*d.* 2414)

RULES for the St. Andrew's Society in Philadelphia. *Philadelphia :* Printed by B. Franklin, and D. Hall. MDCCLI. 16 *pp. 8vo.* (1*l.* 1*s.* 2415)

RULING (THE) & Ordaining Power of Congregational Bishops, or Presbyters, Defended. Being Remarks on fome Part of Mr. P. Barclay's Persuasive, lately diftributed in New-England. By an Impartial Hand. In a Letter to a Friend. *Boston :* Printed for Samuel Gerrifh and Sold at his Shop near the Brick Meeting-Houfe in Cornhill, 1724. *Title and* 45 *pp. 8vo.* (12*s.* 6*d.* 2416)

RUMSEY (JAMES). A Short Treatise on the application of Steam, whereby is clearly shewn, from actual experiments, that Steam may be applied to propel Boats or Vessels of any burthen againft rapid currents with great velocity. The fame Principles are alfo introduced with Effect, by a Machine of a fimple and cheap Conftruction, for the Purpofe of raising Water fufficient for the working of Grist-Mills, Saw-Mills, &c. And for watering Meadows and other purposes of Agriculture. By James Rumsey, Of Berkeley County, Virgina. *Philadelphia,* Printed by Joseph James : Chesnut-Street. M,DCC,LXXXVIII. 26 *pp. Uncut.* 8*vo.* (10*s.* 6*d.* 2417)

RUSSELL (WILLIAM). The History of America from its Discovery by Columbus to the conclusion of the late War. With an Appendix, containing

an account of the rise and progress of the present
unhappy contest between Great Britain and her
Colonies. By William Russell, Esq. of Gray's-
Inn. *London*: Fielding and Walker, MDCCLXXVIII.
Two Volumes. Volume I. *iv and 596 pp. 28 maps
and plates.* Volume II. 630 *pp.* 'Directions for
placing the Maps and Cuts.' *2 pp. 23 maps and
plates. 4to.* (15s. 2418)

RUTHERFURD (SAMUEL). A/ Survey/ of the/
Survey of that Summe/ of Church-Difcipline/
Penned by Mr. Thomas Hooker,/ Late Paftor of
the Church at Hartford upon/ Connecticot in New
England./ Wherein/ The Way of the Churches of
N. England/ is now re-examined; Arguments in
favour/ thereof winnowed; The Principles of that/
Way difcuffed; and the Reafons of moft/ feeming
ftrength and nerves, removed./ By Samuel Ruther-
furd, Profeffor of Divinity in/ the Univerfity of S.
Andrews in Scotland./ *London,*/ Printed by J. G.
for Andr. Crook, at the Green Dragon/ in St
Pauls Church-yard. M. DC. LVIII./ *4 prel. leaves and
521 pp. Old calf. 4to.* (2*l.* 12*s.* 6*d.* 2419)

ABINE (Edward). Remarks on the Account of The late Voyage of Discovery to Baffin's Bay, published By Captain J. Ross, R. N. By Captain Edward Sabine, Royal Artillery. *London :* Richard and Arthur Taylor, 1819. *40 pp. Unbound. 8vo.* (*See No. 2409*). (*3s. 6d.* 2420)

SACK (Albert von). A Narrative of a Voyage to Surinam; of a Residence there during 1805, 1806, and 1807; and of the Author's return to Europe by the Way of North America. By Baron Albert von Sack, Chamberlain to his Prussian Majesty. *London :* G. and W. Nicol, 1810. *7 prel. leaves, including engraved title; and 282 pp. Frontispiece. Sketch at page 1. Plate at page 101. Half calf. 4to.* (*7s. 6d.* 2421)

SACKVILLE (*Lord George*). The Trial Of the Right Honourable Lord George Sackville, At A Court Martial Held at the Horfe-Guards, February 29, 1760, for An Enquiry into his Conduct, Being charged with Difobedience of Orders, While he commanded the Britifh Horfe in Germany. Together with His Lordfhip's Defence. *London :* W. Owen, [1760.] *viii and 342 pp. Wanting pp. 319-20. Half morocco. 8vo.* (*7s. 6d.* 2422)

SAGAN/ Landnama/ vm pyrftu bygging Iflands af/ Nordmonnum./ Symbolum Regium./ Pieta=/ te &/ Iusti=/tia./ Skalhollte,/ Dryckt af Hendr: Krufe/ A MDCLXXXVIII. *5 prel. leaves and 182 pp. 'Registvr' etc. 10 leaves. Half morocco. 4to.* (*2l. 2s.* 2423)

Chronicle of the first Colonisation of Iceland, by the Norwegians. (Northmen).

SAGARD (Gabriel). [*Engraved title*] Le Grand/ Voyage Dv Pays/ des Hurons, Situé en L'A=/ merique uers la mer douce/ ez dernieres confins de/ la nouuelle France/ Ou il est traicte de tout/ ce qui est du paÿs et du/ gouuernement des Sauuages/ Auec un Dictionnaire/ de la Langue huronne/ Par Fr. Gabriel Sagard/ Recollect de S^r. Francois/ de la prouince S^r. Denis./ A Paris Chez Denys/ Moreau rue S^r. Jacques à/ La Salamandre 1632/. [*Printed title*] Le Grand Voyages/ dv Pays des Hvrons,/ fitué, en l'Amerique vers la Mer/ douce, és derniers confins/ de la nouuelle France,/ dite Canada./ Où il eft amplement traité de tout ce qui eft du pays, des/ mœurs & du naturel des Sauuages, de leur gouuernement/ & façons de faire, tant dedans leurs pays, qu'allans en voya-/ges : De leur foy & croyance ; De leurs confeils & guerres, & de quel genre de tourmens ils font mourir leurs prifonniers./ Comme ils fe marient, & efleuent leurs enfans : De leurs Me-/decins, & des remedes dont ils vfent à leurs maladies : De/ leurs dances & chanfons : De la chaffe, de la pefche, & des oyfeaux & animaux terreftres & aquatiques qu'ils ont. Des/ richeffes du pays : Comme ils cultiuent les terres, & accom-/modent leur Meneftre. De leur deüil, pleurs & lamenta-/tions, & comme ils enfeueliffent & enterrent leurs morts./ Auec vn Dictionaire de la langue Huronne, pour la com-/modi-/te de ceux qui ont à voyager dans le pays, & n'ont/ l'intelligence d'icelle langue./ Par F. Gabriel Sagard Theodat, Recollet de/ S. François, de la Prouince de S. Denys en France./ A *Paris*, Chez Denys Moreav, ruë S. Iacques, à/ la Salamandre d'Argent./ M.DC.XXXII./ Auec Priuilege du Roy./ *12 prel. leaves and 380 pp ; followed by 2 blank leaves.* ‘ Dictionaire de la Langve’ *etc.* 12 *pp ; and* ‘ Les Mots Francois tournez en Huron,’ *66 unpaged leaves;* ‘ Table des choses,’ *etc.* 14 *pp. Imperfect, wanting pp.* 150—173. *Old calf.* 8*vo.* (3*l.* 3*s.* 2424)

SAGITTARIUS'S Letters and Political Specula-tions. Extracted From the Public Ledger. Hum-bly Inscribed To the very Loyal and truly Pious Doctor Samuel Cooper, Paftor of the Congrega-tional Church in Brattle Street. *Boston :* Printed : By Order of the Select Men and fold at Donation

Hall, for the Benefit of the diftreffed Patriots.
MDCCLXXV. *Title and* 127 *pp. Calf extra, by Bedford.* 8vo. (15s. 2425)

SAINT DOMINGO. Betrachtungen über den gegenwärtigen zuftand der franzöfifchen Colonie zu San Domingo. Aus dem Franzöfifchen überfetzt und mit einigen Anmerkungen verfehen. *Leipzig,* bey Johann Friedrich Junius. 1779. *Two Volumes.* Erfter Theil, 8 *prel. leaves and text* 310 *pp.* Zweyter Theil, 2 *prel. leaves and text* 332 *pp. Half calf.* 8vo. (7s. 6d. 2426)

SAINT DOMINGO. History of the Island of St. Domingo, from its firft Discovery by Columbus to the present period. *London:* Printed for Archibald Constable and Co. Edinburgh: 1818. *xiv and* 446 *pp.* 8vo. (6s. 6d. 2427)

SAINT DOMINGO. Histoire de l'Ile de Saint-Domingue, depuis l'Epoque de sa dècouverte par Christophe Colomb Jusqu'a l'Année 1818. Publiée sur des documents authentiques, et suivie de Pièces justificatives, Telles que la Correspondance de Toussaint-Louverture avec Buonaparte; le Cérémonial de la Cour d'Haïty; la Constitution de ce royaume; l'Almanach royal d'Haïty; la Correspondance du comte de Limonade, et le Manifeste du roi Christophe. *A Paris,* Delaunay, 1819. *Half-title, title, ii pp. and text* 390 *pp. Half-calf.* 8vo. (5s. 6d. 2428)

SAINT JOHN (J. HECTOR). Letters from an American Farmer; describing certain Provincial Situations, Manners, and Customs, not generally known; and conveying some idea of the late and present interior circumstances of the British Colonies in North America. Written for the Information of a Friend in England, by J. Hector St. John, a Farmer in Pennsylvania. *London,* Thomas Davies, MDCCLXXXII. 8 *prel. leaves and* 318 *pp. With* 2 *maps. Half calf.* 8vo. (5s. 6d. 2429)

SALLE (MONSIEUR DE LA). An/ Account/ of/ Monfieur de la Salle's/ laft/ Expedition and Discoveries/ in/ North America./ Prefented to the French King,/ And Publifhed by the/ Chevalier Tonti, Governor of Fort St. Lo-/uis, in the Province of the Iflinois./ Made Englifh from the

Paris Original./ Also/ The Adventures of the
Sieur de/ Montavban, Captain of the French/
Buccaneers on the Coaſt of Guinea, in the/ Year
1695./ *London,/* Printed for J. Tonſon at the
Judge's Head, and S. Buckly/ at the Dolphin in
Fleet-ſtreet, and R. Knaplock, at the/ Angel and
Crown in St. Paul's Church-Yard. 1698./ *Title
and* 211 *pp.* ' A/ Relation/ of a/ Voyage/ Made by
the/ Sieur de Montauban,'/ *etc.* 44 *pp. Half calf.*
8vo.   (15s.   2430)

SARATE (Augustine). See ZARATE (Augus-
TINE).

SARMIENTO DE GAMBOA (Pedro). Viage al
estrecho de Magallanes Por el Capitan Pedro Sarmiento de Gambóa En los años de 1579. y 1580.
Y Noticia de la Expedicion Que despues hizo para
poblarle. En *Madrid :* 1768. *lxxxiv and* 402 *pp.*
3 *Plates.* ' Declaration que De órden del Virréi
del Perú D. Francisco de Borja,/' *etc. Title and
xxxiii pp. Old calf. 4to.*   (18s.   2431)

SCHEDÆ/ Ara Prests/ Froda/ Vm Island./ Pren-
tadar i *Skalhollte* af Hendrick Kruſe./ Anno 1688./
On the reverse of the title ; ' Ad Leĉtorem.' *etc. Text*
14 *pp.* ' Regiſtur' *etc ;* 4 *leaves. Half morocco.*
4to.   (1l. 11s. 6d.   2432)

SCHMIDEL (Huldericus).   Vera hiſtoria,/ Ad-
mirandæ cvivs-/ dam nauigationis, quam Hul-/
dericus Schmidel, Straubingenſis, ab Anno 1534./
uſque ad annum 1554. in Americam vel nouum/
Mundum, iuxta Braſiliam & Rio della Plata, con-
fecit ·Quid/ per hoſce annos 19. ſuſtinuerit, quam
varias & quam mirandas/ regiones at homines
viderit. Ab ipſo Schmidelio Germanice,/ deſcripta :
Nunc vero, emendatis & correĉtis Vrbium, Regio-/
num & Fluminum, nominibus, Adieĉta etiam tab-
ula/ Geographica, figuris & alijs notationi-/bus
quibuſdam in hanc for-/mam reduĉta./ *Noribergæ,/*
Impenſis Levini Hulſij. 1599./ *Title the reverse blank,
and* 101 *pp. Portrait of the Author. Copperplate
etchings at pp.* 6, 11, 12, 13, 15, 17, 18, 21, 25, 26,
32, 37, 40, 63, 69, 79, 97. *With the Map. Unbound.*
4to.   (3l. 3s.   2433)

SCHMIDT (Ulrich). Warhafftige Be=/ſchriebunge
aller/ vnd mancherley ſorgfeltigen Schif=/farten,

auch viler vnbekanten erfundnen Landtfchafften,
Infu=/len, Königreichen, vnd Stedten, von derfel-
bigē gelegenheyt, wefen, gebreuchen,/ fitten, Religion, Künft vnd handtierung. Item von allerley
gewächfz,/ Metallen, Specereyen, vnd anderer
dinge mehr, fo von jhnen in vnfere/ Land geführt
vnd gebracht werden./ Auch von mancherley
gefahr, ftreitt vnd fcharmützeln, fo fich zwifchen
jnen vnd/ den vnfern, beyde zu Waffer vnd Lande,
wunderbarlich zugetragen. Item von/ erfchreck-
licher, feltzamer Natur vnd Eygenfchafft der
Leuthfreffer, Dergleichen vorhin in keinen/ Chronicken oder Hiftorien befchrieben, mit fchönen
Concordantzen vnd einem vol=/kommen Regifter,
zur fürderung des gemeinen nutzes/ zufamen ge-
tragen./ Durch Vlrich Schmidt von Straubingen,
vnd andern mehr, fodafelbft/ in eigener Perfon ge-
genwertig gewefen, vnd folches erfaren./ Getruckt
zu *Franckfurt am Mayn*, Anno 1567/. *6 prel. leaves;
viz. Title reverse blank*, ' Den Ehrneften, Fürfichti=/
gen, Erfamen vnd weifen Herrn, Stetmeiftern vnd/
Rath der löblichen Reichfzftadt Schwäbifchen
Hall,/ meinen infondern günftigen lie=/ben Herren.'/ *8 pp.* 1 *blank leaf. Text*, 110 *folioed leaves.*
' Warhafftige vnd liebliche Be=/fchreibung eticher
fürnemen Indianifchen Landt=/fchafften vnd Infulen, die vormals in keiner Chronicken gedacht,/'
etc. 59 *folioed leaves; and Colophon leaf, the reverse
blank. Blue morocco extra. Folio.* (4*l.* 4*s.* 2434)

SCHOEPF (Io. DAVIDIS). D. Io. Davidis Schœpf/
Seren. Marggrav. Brand. Onold. et Cvlmb. Med.
Avl. et Milit. Coll. Med. Membr. Materia Medica
Americana potissimvm Regni Vegetabilis. *Erlangae*
Svmtibvs Io. Iac. Palmii. MDCCLXXXVII. *xviii and*
170 *pp. Old calf. 8vo.* (7*s.* 6*d.* 2435)

SCHOMBURGK (ROBERT H.). A Description of
British Guiana, Geographical and Statistical: Exhibiting its resources and Capabilities, together
with the present and future condition and prospects
of the Colony. By Robert H. Schomburgk, Esq.
London: Simpkin, Marfhall and Co. 1840. 2
prel. leaves and text 155 *pp. With map. Cloth.
8vo.* (3*s.* 6*d.* 2436)

SCHONER (JOANNES). Ioannis Scho-/neri Caro-

lostadii Opvscv-/lvm Geographicvm ex Diver-
sorvm Li/bris ac cartis fumma cura & diligentia
colle=/ctum, accomodatum ad recenter ela=/boratum
ab eodem globum de=/fcriptionis terrenæ. [*Basel*
1533.] 21 *unpaged leaves including title. On the
reverse of the title is a woodcut of the Globe. Half
morocco. 4to.* (1*l.* 1*s.* 2437)

SCHOUTEN (Gulielmus Cornelius). Iovrnal/
ov Relation/ exacte dv voyage de Gvill. Schovten,/
dans les Indes : Par vn nouueau/ deftroit, & par
les grandes Mers/ Auftrales qu'il à defcouuert,
vers/ le Pole Antartique./   Enfemble des Nov-/
uelles Terres auparauant incognuës,/ Ifles, Fruicts,
Peuples, & Animaux/ eftranges, qu'il a trouué en
fon chemin :/ Et des rares obferuations qu'il y à
fait/ touchant la declinaifon de l'Aymant./   A
Paris./   Chez M. Gobert, au Palais en la gallerie/
des prifonniers : Et les Cartes, chez M. Tauernier,
Graueur du Roy, de/meurant au pont Marchand./
M. DC. XVIII./   *7 prel. leaves and 232 pp.   Maps and
plates at pp. 9, 57, 73, 103, 113, 137, 153 and 169.
Calf extra by Bedford. 8vo.*   (2*l.* 2*s.*   2438)

SCHOUTEN (Gulielmus Cornelius). Iovrnal/ ov
Relation/ exacte dv Voyage/ de Gvill. Schovten,/
dans les Indes : Par vn nouueau/ deftroir, & par
les grandes Mers/ Auftrales qu'il à defcouuert,
vers/ le Pole Antartique./   Enfemble des Nov-/
uelles Terres auparauant incognuës,/ Ifles, Fruicts,
Peuples, & Animaux/ eftranges, qu'il a trouué en
fon chemin :/   Et des rares obferuations qu'il y à
fait/ touchant la declinaifon de l'Aymant./   A
Paris,/ Chez M. Gobert, au Palais en la gallerie/
des prifonniers : Et les Cartes, chez M./ Tauernier,
Graueur du Roy, de-/meurant au pont Marchand./
M.DC.XIX./   *7 prel. leaves and 232 pp.   Without the
maps and plates. 8vo.*   (1*l.* 11*s.* 6*d.*   2439)

SCHOUTEN (Gulielmus Cornelius). Jovrnal/
Ou/ Description/ dv merveillevx Voyage de/
Gvillavme Schovten, Hollandois natif de/ Hoorn,
fait es années 1615. 1616. & 1617./   Comme (en
circum-navigeant le Globe ter-/restre) il a def-
couvert vers le Zud du deftroit de Magellan vn/
nouveau paffage, jufques à la grande Mer de Zud./
Enfemble,/ Des avantures admirables qui luy font

advenues en/ defcouvrant du plufieurs Ifles, &
peuples eftranges./ A *Amstredam,*/ Chez Ian
Ianffon, Libraire, demeurant fur l'Eau,/ a la Carte
Marine. 1619. 4 *prel. leaves* ; *viz. Title with copperplate engraving of ships in full sail, the reverse blank ;*
' Preface. Au lecteur debonnaire.' *5 pp* ; ' Sur
l'amirable navigation de Gvillavme Schovten, Natif
de Hoorn.' 1 *page. Copperplate engraving of the
Globe with 6 portraits and 2 ships: Text* 80 *pp.
With copperplate engravings at pp.* 14, 24, 41, 45,
49, 51. 4*to.*
(2*l.* 2*s.* 2440)

SCHOUTEN (GULIELMUS CORNELIUS). Diarivm/
vel/ Defcriptio laboriofiffimi, & Moleftiffimi/ Jtin-
eris, facti à/ Gvilielmo Cornelii/ Schovtenio, Hor-
nano./ Annis 1615. 1616. & 1617./ Cum à parte
Auftrali freti Magellanici, novum ductum, aut/
fretum, in Magnum Mare Auftrale detexit, totum q/
Orbem terrarum circumnavigavit./ Quas Infulas,
& regiones, & populos viderit,/ & quæ pericula
fubierit./ *Amsterdami*, Apud Petrum Kærium. A°.
1619./ 4 *prel. leaves, and* 71 *pp. 6 maps and plates.*
4*to.*
(2*l.* 2*s.* 2441)

SEABURY (SAMUEL). The nature and extent of
the Apostolical Commission. A Sermon, preached
at the Consecration of the Right Reverend Dr.
Samuel Seabury, Bishop of the Episcopal Church
in Connecticut. By a Bishop of the Episcopal
Church in Scotland. *London:* John, Francis, and
Charles Rivington, MDCCLXXXV. 32 *pp. Unbound.*
4*to.*
(3*s.* 6*d.* 2442)

SEASONABLE Advice, to The Members of the
Britifh Parliament, concerning Conciliatory Measures with America ; and an Act of Perpetual
Insolvency, for Relief of Debtors: With Some
Strictures on the reciprocal Duties of Sovereigns,
and Senators. *London:* J. Bew, M,DCC,LXXV. *viii
and* 38 *pp. Half morocco.* 8*vo.* (5*s.* 6*d.* 2444)

SECKER (THOMAS). A Letter To the Right Honourable Horatio Walpole, Efq ; Written Jan. 9,
1750-1, By the Right Reverend Thomas Secker,
LL.D. Lord Bishop of Oxford: Concerning Bishops in America. *London:* J. and F. Rivington,
MDCCLXIX. 2 *prel. leaves and* 28 *pp. Unbound.*
8*vo.*
(4*s.* 6*d.* 2445)

SELKIRK (*Earl of*). A Sketch of the British Fur Trade in North America; with Observations relative to the North-West Company of Montreal. By the Earl of Selkirk. Second Edition. *London:* James Ridgway. 1816. *3 prel. leaves and 130 pp. Half calf. 8vo.* (3s. 6d. 2446)

SELLER (John). America. *A small Atlas in 28 copperplate engravings. Calf extra by F. Bedford. 12mo.* (18s. 2447)

SENTIMENTS (The) of a Foreigner, on the Disputes of Great-Britain with America. Translated from the French. *Philadelphia:* Printed by James Humphreys, Junior; in Front-Street. M,DCC,LXXV. *27 pp. Half morocco. 8vo.* (4s. 6d. 2448)

SEPP (Antony). R. R. P. P. Antonij Sepp,/ und Antonij Böhm,/ Der Societät Jesu Prieſtern,/ Neu=vermehrte/ Reiſs=Beſchrei=/bung,/ Wie ſelbe aufs Hiſpanien in Para=/quariam kommen./ Und Kurtzer Bericht der denck=/wurdigſten Sachen, ſelbiger Land=/ſchafft, Völckern, und Arbeitung der/ P. P. Miſſionariorum./ Gezogen,/ Auſs denen R. P. Sepp, Soc. Jesu mit/ eigner Hand geſchriebenen Brieffen,/ Von Steph. Ign. Sepp von Seppenb,/ und Rech: Prieſtern, J. U. C. als leib=/lichen Brudern./ Drilte und verbeſſerte Edition,/ Mit Erlaubnuſz der Obern./ *Passau,* Druckts und verlegts Georg Adam Höller, 1698./ *336 pp. Old calf. 12mo.* (10s. 6d. 2449)

SEPULVEDÆ (Joannis Genesii) Cordubensis Opera, Cum Edita, Tum Inedita, Accurante Regia Historiæ Academia. *Matriti.* Ex Typographia Regia de la Gazeta. Anno M.DCC.LXXX. *Four Volumes. Volumen Primum. 8 prel. leaves, cxliv pp, 24 pp, 4 leaves, xlvi pp, Portrait of Charles 5th. and 468 pp. 'Monitum ad Lectorem' 2 pp. Volumen Secundum. 3 prel. leaves, lxvi and 544 pp. 'Index' 75 leaves. Volumen Tertium. 3 prel. leaves, xxviii and 244 pp. 'Index' 9 leaves, half-title, Summarium 7 leaves, 134 pp. 'Index' 7 leaves, half-title and 399 pp. Index 11 pp. Volumen Quartum. 3 prel. leaves, and 591 pp. Index 21 pp. Old calf. 4to.* (3l. 3s. 2450)

SERGEANT (John). The Cauſes and Danger of Delusions in the Affairs of Religion Conſider'd and caution'd againſt, With particular Reference to the Temper of the preſent Times. In a Sermon Preach'd at Springfield, April 4. 1743. In the Audience of the aſſociated Paſtors of the County of Hampſhire. By John Sergeant, M. A. Paſtor of the Church of Chriſt in Stockbridge. Publiſh'd at the Deſire of the Hearers. *Boston*, Printed for S. Eliot in Cornhil. 1743. *36 pp. Half morocco. 8vo.* (7s. 6d. 2451)

SERGEANT (John). A Letter From the Revᵈ. Mr. Sergeant Of Stockbridge, to Dr. Colman Of Boston ; Containing Mr. Sergeant's Propoſal of a more effectual method for the Education of Indian Children ; to raiſe 'em if poſſible into a civil and induſtrious People; by introducing the Engliſh Language among them ; and thereby inſtilling into their Minds and Hearts, with a more laſting Impreſſion, the Principles of Virtue and Piety. Made publick by Dr. Colman at the Deſire of Mr. Sergeant, with ſome general Account of what the Rev. Mr. Isaac Hollis of - - - - has already done for the Sons of this Indian Tribe of Houſſatannoc, now erected into a Townſhip by the General Court, and called Stockbridge. *Boston*, Printed by Rogers and Fowle, for D. Henchman in Cornhill. 1743. *16 pp. Half morocco. 8vo.* (10s. 6d. 2452)

SERIOUS ADDRESS (A) To thoſe Who unneceſſarily frequent the Tavern, and Often ſpend the Evening in Publick Houſes. By ſeveral Miniſters. To which is added, A private Letter on the Subject, by the late Rev. Dr. Increaſe Mather. *Boston*, N. E. Printed for S. Gerriſh, at the lower end of Cornhill. 1726. *Title, iv, and 30 pp. Unbound. 8vo.* (7s. 6d. 2453)

SEVERAL Conferences Between ſome of the principal People amongſt the Quakers in Pennsylvania, and the Deputies from the Six Indian Nations, In Alliance with Britain; In Order to reclaim their Brethren the Delaware Indians from their Defection, and put a Stop to their Barbarities and Hoſtilities. To which is prefix'd (As introductory to the ſaid Conferences) Two Addreſſes from the ſaid Quakers; one to the Lieutenant-Governor, and the other to the General-Aſſembly of the Pro-

vince of Pennſylvania; as alſo the Lieutenant-
Governor's Declaration of War againſt the ſaid
Delaware Indians, and their Adherents. *Newcastle
upon Tyne:* I. Thompson and Company. MDCCLVI.
28 *pp.* 8*vo.*   (10*s.* 6*d.* 2454)

SEWALL (JOSEPH). The Holy Spirit Convincing
the World of Sin, of Righteouſneſs, and of Judgment, conſidered in Four Sermons: The two former
delivered at the Tueſday - Evening Lecture in
Brattle-Street, January 20th & March 3: The
other at the Old-South-Church in Boston, April 17
& 26, 1741. By Joſeph Sewall, D.D. *Boston:*
Printed by J. Draper, for D. Hehchman in Cornhil.
1741. *Title; vi and* 134 *pp.* 12*mo.* (10*s.* 6*d.* 2455)

SEWALL (SAMUEL). Phænomena quædam/ Apoc-
alyptica/ Ad Aſpectum Novi Orbis configurata./
Or, ſome few Lines towards a deſcription of the
New/ Heaven/ As It makes to thoſe who ſtand upon
the/ New Earth/ By Samuel Sewall ſometime
Fellow of Harvard Colledge at/ Cambridge in
New-England./ *Massachvset;*/ Boston, Printed by
Bartholomew Green, and John Allen,/ And are to
be ſold by Richard Wilkins, 1697./ 4 *prel. leaves;
viz. Title the reverse blank*, 'To the Honorable, Sir
William Aſhvrst Knight, Governour; and the
Company For the Propagation of the Gospel to
the Indians in New-England, and places adjacent,
in America.' 2 *pp;* 'To the Honorable William
Stoughton Eſq. Lieut. Governour and Commander
in Chief, in and over His Majeſties Province of
the Maſſachuſets Bay in New England.' 3 *pp;*
'Pſalm 139. 7--10.' 1 *page. Text* 60 *pp. Morocco
by Bedford.* 4*to.*   (7*l.* 7*s.* 2456)

SEWEL (WILLIAM). The History of the Rise,
Increase, and Progress, Of the Christian People
called Quakers: Intermixed with several Remarkable Occurrences. Written Originally in Low-
Dutch, and alſo Tranſlated into English, By William Sewel. The Third Edition, Corrected. *Philadelphia:* Printed and Sold by Samuel Keimer in
Second Street. MDCCXXVIII. 6 *prel. leaves and* 694
pp. 'Index' 16 *pp. Calf extra. Imperfect, wanting
2 leaves of the Index. Folio.*   (2*l.* 2*s.* 2457)

SEWEL (WILLIAM). The History of the Rise,

Increase and Progress, of the Christian People called Quakers; with several Remarkable Occurrences intermixed. Written originally in Low-Dutch, and alſo tranſlated into English, By William Sewel. The Third Edition, corrected. *Burlington,* New-Jersey: Printed and Sold by Isaac Collins, M.DCC.LXXIV. *xii and* 812 *pp.* 'Index' 16 *pp. Old calf. Folio.*   (2*l.* 2*s.* 2458)

SEYBERT (ADAM). Statistical Annals: Embracing Views of the Population, Commerce, Navigation, Fisheries, Public Lands, Post-Office Establishment, Revenues, Mint, Military and Naval Establishments, Expenditures, Public Debt and Sinking Fund, of the United States of America: Founded on Official Documents: Commencing on the Fourth of March Seventeen Hundred and Eighty-nine and ending on the Twentieth of April Eighteen Hundred and Eighteen. By Adam Seybert, M. D. A Member of the House of Representatives of the United States, from the State of Pennsylvania; Member of the American Philosophical Society; Honorary Member of the Philosophical and Literary Society of New-York; Fellow of the Royal Society of Gœttingen, &c. *Philadelphia:* Thomas Dobson & Son, 1818. *xxviii and* 803 *pp. Boards.* 4*to.*   (15*s.* 2459)

SEYFRIED (JOH. HEINRICH). Poliologia,/ Das iſt:/ Accurate/ Beſchreibung/ Aller vornehmſten in der ganzen Welt/ befindlichen/ Städten, Schlöſſern und Ve=/ſtungen/ So wol was ihre Erbauung, Fortifi=/cation, Religion, Herrſchafft und Regie=/rungs=Form, als auch Die von ihrem Urſprung an,/ bis auf gegenwärtige Zeit ſich ereignete kriegs=und/ Friedens, Freud und Leid betreffende Beg=/benheiten betrifft./ In zweyen abſonderlichen Theilen/ dergeſtalt vorgeſtellet,/ Daſz im erſten die berühmteſten Orte in ganz/ Europa, im andern aber die in Aſia, Africa und/ America befindliche, ausführlich nach dem Alphabet/ abgehandelt werden,/ Und zwar alles und jedes mit ſonderbarem Fleiſz/ zu eines jedem Leſers nutzlicher Ergötzung zuſamm/getragen, und nun zum an=dernmal verbeſſert her=/ausgeben durch/ Joh. Heinrich Seyfried, Hochfürſtl. Durchl./ zu Pfalz Sulzbach Hof=kammer=Rath./ *Nürnberg,/*

Verlegts Johann Leonhard Buggel, 1695./ *Two Volumes.* Theil I. 14 *prel. leaves with folding map of the world; Text,* 480 *pp ; and one blank leaf.* Theil II. 13 *prel. leaves and one blank leaf ; Text, pp.* 3—357. *Blue morocco extra gilt, by Hayday.* 8vo.　　　　　　　　　　　　　(1*l.* 1*s.*　2460)

SHARP (BARTHOLOMEW). The/ Voyages/ and/ Adventures/ of/ Capt. Barth. Sharp/ And others, in the/ South Sea :/ Being/ a Journal of the fame./ Also/ Capt. Van Horn with his Buccanieres fur-/ prizing of la Vera Cruz./ To which is added/ The true Relation of Sir Henry Morgan/ his Expedition againft the Spaniards in the/ Weft-Indies, and his taking Panama./ Together with/ The Prefident of Panama's Account of the fame/ Expedition : Tranflated out of Spanifh./ And Col. Beefton's adjuftment of the Peace be-/tween the Spaniards and Englifh in the Weft Indies./ Publifhed by P. A. Esq ;./ *London*/ Printed by B. W. for R. H. and S. T. and are to be fold/ by Walter Davis in Amen-Corner. MDCLXXXIV./ 12 *prel. leaves and* 172 *pp. Calf.* 8vo.　　　　(15*s.*　2461)

SHARP (GRANVILLE). Extract from a Representation of the Injustice and Dangerous Tendency of tolerating Slavery ; or Admitting the leaft Claim of private Property in the Perfons of Men in England. By Granville Sharp. First printed in London. MDCCLXIX. *Title, and pp.* 147—198. *Index,* 6 *pp. Half morocco.* 8vo.　　(4*s.* 6*d.*　2462)

SHARP (GRANVILLE). A General Plan for laying out Towns and Townships on the New-Acquired Lands in the East Indies, America, or elsewhere ; In order to promote Cultivation, and raise the Value of all the adjoining Land, at the Price of giving gratis the Town-Lots, and, in some Cases (as in new Colonies), also the small Out-Lots, to the first Settlers and their Heirs so long as they possess no other Land ; and on equitable Conditions. First Printed in 1794. Second Edition 1804. 24 *pp. With plan.* 8vo.　　　　(4*s.* 6*d.*　2463)

SHARP (JOHN). A Sermon Preached at Trinity-Church in New-York, in America, Auguft 13, 1706, At the Funeral Of the Right Honourable Katherine Lady Cornbury, Baronefs Clifton of

Leighton Bromſwold, &c. Heireſs to the moſt noble Charles Duke of Richmond and Lenox, Wife to his Excellency Edward Lord Viſcount Cornbury, Her Majeſty's Captain General, and Governor in Chief of the Provinces of New-York, New-Jerſey, and Territories depending thereon in America, &c. By John Sharp, A. M. Chaplain to the Queen's Forces in the Province of New York. *London :* Printed by H. Hills, [1708.] 16 *pp. Half morocco.* 8*vo.* (7*s.* 6*d.* 2464)

SHARP (John). A Sermon Preached at Trinity-Church in New-York, in America, Auguſt 13. 1706. At the Funeral Of the Right Honourable Katherine Lady Cornbury, Baroneſs Clifton of Leighton Bromſwold, &c. Heireſs to the moſt Noble Charles Duke of Richmond and Lenox, and Wife to his Excellency Edward Lord Viſcount .Cornbury, Her Majeſty's Captain General, and Governor in chief of the Provinces of New-York, New-Jerſey, and Territories depending thereon in America, &c. By John Sharp, A. M. Chaplain to the Queen's Forces in the Province of New-York. *London :* J. Morphew, 1708. 16 *pp. Unbound.* 8*vo.* (7*s.* 6*d.* 2465)

SHEBBEARE (J.) An Answer to the Queries, contained in A Letter to Dr. Shebbeare, Printed in the Public Ledger, Auguſt 10. Together with Animadversions on Two Speeches In Defence of the Printers of A Paper, ſubſcribed a South Briton. The First pronounced by The Right Hon. Thomas Townsend, in the Houſe of Commons, And printed in the London Packet of February 18. The Second by The Right Learned Counſellor Lee, in Guild-hall, And printed in the Public Ledger of Auguſt 12. In the Examination of which a Compariſon naturally ariſes between the public and private Virtues of Their Preſent Majeſties, and thoſe of King William and Queen Mary. The Merits, alſo of Roman Catholics, and of Diſſenters from the Church of England, reſpecting Allegiance and Liberty, and their Claims to National Protection, are fairly ſtated, from their paſt and preſent Tranſactions. By J. Shebbeare, M.D. *London :* S. Hooper, *Title and text* 179 *pp. Half morocco.* 8*vo.* (4*s.* 6*d.* 2466)

SHEBBEARE (J.) An Essay on the Origin, Progrefs and Eftablifhment of National Society; in which The Principles of Government, the Definitions of phyfical, moral, civil, and religious Liberty, contained in Dr. Price's Obfervations, &c. are fairly examined and fully refuted : Together with A Juftification of the Legiflature, in reducing America to Obedience by Force. To which is added An Appendix on the Excellent and admirable in Mr. Burke's fecond printed Speech of the 22d of March, 1775. By J. Shebbeare, M.D. *London:* J. Bew, M.DCC.LXXVI. *Title and 212 pp. Half morocco. 8vo.* (4s. 6d. 2467)

SHEBBEARE (J.) An Essay on the Origin, Progrefs and Eftablifhment of National Society; in which The Principles of Government, the Definitions of phyfical, moral, civil and religious Liberty, contained in Dr. Price's Obfervations, &c. are fairly examined and fully refuted : Together with A Juftification of the Legiflature, in reducing America to Obedience by Force. To which is added an Appendix on the Excellent and admirable in Mr. Burke's fecond printed Speech of the 22d of March, 1775. By J. Shebbeare, M.D. Second Edition. *London:* J. Bew, MDCCLXXVI. *Title and 212 pp. 8vo.* (4s. 6d. 2468)

SHEFFIELD (John *Lord*). Observations on the Commerce of the American States. By John Lord Sheffield. A New Edition, much enlarged. With an Appendix, Containing Tables of the Imports and Exports of Great Britain to and from all Parts. Alfo, the Exports of America, &c. With Remarks on thofe Tables, and on the late Proclamations, &c. *London:* J. Debrett, MDCCLXXXIV. *8 prel. leaves and 288 pp. Tables numbered* I *to* XI. 'The Tonage' *etc.* 1 *page. 8vo.* (6s. 6d. 2469)

SHEFFIELD (John *Lord*). Observations on the Commerce of the American States. By John Lord Sheffield. With an Appendix ; Containing Tables of the Imports and Exports of Great Britain to and frcm all Parts, from 1700 to 1783. Alfo the Exports of America, &c. With Remarks on thofe Tables, on the Trade and Navigation of Great Britain, and on the late Proclamations, &c. The Sixth Edition, enlarged. With a Complete Index to the whole. *London:* J. Debrett, M,DCC,LXXXIV. *2 prel. leaves;* 'Introduction' *xlvii pp;* 'Errata' *1 page, Text* 345 *pp. Tables numbered* I *to* XVI. 'The Tonage' 1 *page;* 'Contents' 4 *pp;* 'Index' 17 *pp;* 'Errata' 1 *page. 8vo.*   (7s. 6d.   2470)

SHELVOCKE (GEORGE). A Voyage round the World By the Way of the Great South Sea, Perform'd in the Years 1719, 20, 21, 22, in the Speedwell, of London, of 24 Guns and 100 Men, (under His Majesty's Commiſſion to cruize on the Spaniards in the late War with the Spaniſh Crown) till ſhe was caſt away on the Iſland of Juan Fernandes, in May 1720; and afterwards continu'd in the Recovery, the Jesus Maria and Sacra Familia, &c. By Capt. George Shelvocke, Commander of the Speedwell, Recovery, &c. in this Expedition. *London:* J. Senex, MDCCXXVI. 4 *prel. leaves;* 'Preface' *xxxii pp;* 'Contents' 4 *pp; Text* 468 *pp. Copperplate map: and plates at pp.* 106, 253, *and* 404 (2). *Old calf. 8vo.*   (10s. 6d.   2471)

SHEPARD (THOMAS). The/ Sincere/ Convert/ Diſcovering/ the Paucity/ of true Believers;/ And the great Difficultie of/ Saving Converſion./ By Tho. Shepheard, ſometimes/ of Immanuel Colledge in Cambridge./ *London,/* Printed by T. P. and M. S. and are/ to be ſold by John Sweeting, at the Angel/ in Popes-head Alley, 1643./ 9 *prel. leaves and* 266 *pp. Old morocco. 8vo.*   (15s.   2472)

SHEPARD (THOMAS). The/ Sound Beleever./ Or,/ A Treatise/ of/ Evangelicall Converſion./ Diſcovering/ The work of Chriſts Spirit, in/ reconciling of a ſinner to God./ By Tho: Shepard, ſometimes/ of Emmanuel Colledge in Cambridge,/ Now Preacher of Gods Word/ in New England./ *London,/* Printed for R. Dawlman 1645./ 3 *prel. leaves and* 352 *pp. Old morocco. 8vo.*   (15s.   2473)

SHEPARD (THOMAS). Theses Sabbaticæ./ Or,/ The Doɔtrine/ of the/ Sabbath :/ Wherein/ The Sabbaths [1. Morality./ II. Change./ III. Beginning./ IV. Sanɔtification./] are clearly/ diſcuſſed./ Which were firſt handled more largely in/ ſundry Sermons in Cambridge in New-England/ in opening of the fourth Commandment./ In unfolding whereof many Scriptures are cleared, divers

Cafes of Con-/fcience refolved, and the Morall Law
as a rule of life to a Believer,/ occafionally and
diftinctly handled./ By Thomas Shepard, Paftor
of the Church of/ Chrift at Cambridge in New-
England./ *London*, Printed by T. R. and E. M.
for John Rothwell at Sun and/ Fountaine in Pauls
Church-yard. 1649./ *Four Parts.* Part I. 10 *prel.
leaves and* 152 *pp.* Second Part. 32 *pp.* Third *and*
Fourth Part. 50 *pp. Old calf. 4to.* (1*l.* 1*s.* 2474)

SHEPARD (Thomas). Certain/ Select Cases/ Refolved./ Specially, tending to the right/ ordering
of the heart, that/ we may comfortably walk/ with
God in our general/ and particular Callings./ By
Thomas Shephard,/ Sometimes of Emanuel-Col-
ledge/ in Cambridge, Now Preacher of/ Gods
Word in New-/England./ *London*, Printed by
W. H. for John Rothwell, at the Sun/ and Fountain in Pauls Church-yard, near/ the little North-
door. 1650./ 4 *prel. leaves and* 87 *pp. Old calf.*
8*vo.*   (10*s.* 6*d.* 2475)

SHEPARD (Thomas). Subjection/ to/ Chrift/ in
all his/ Ordinances,/ and Appointments,/ The beft
means to preferve our/ Liberty./ Together with
. a/ Treatise/ Of Ineffectual Hearing the Word ;/
How we may know whether we have heard/ the
fame effectually : And by what means it may/ become effectual unto us./ With fome remarkable
Paffages of his life./ By Tho. Shephard, late
Paftor of the Church/ of Chrift in Cambridge in
New-England./ Now published by Mr. Jonathan
Michell/ Paftor of the faid Church in New-England./ *London*, Printed for John Rothwell and
are to be fold by/ Tho. Brewfter, at the three
Bibles, in Pauls Church-/yard neer the Weft end
1652./ 8 *prel. leaves and* 195 *pp.   Table* 11 *pp.
Old calf. 8vo.*   (15*s.* 2476)

SHEPARD (Thomas). The/ Sound Beleever./ A/
Treatise/ of/ Evangelicall Converfion./ Discover-
ing/ The work of Chrifts Spirit, in/ reconciling of
a Sinner to God./ By Thomas Shepard,/ fometimes of Emmanuel Coledge in Cam-/bridge, now
Preacher of Gods Word in/ New-England./ *London*,/ Printed for Andrew Crooke at the/ Green-
Dragon in Pauls-church-yard,/ M.DC.LIII./ *Title,*

3 prel. pp; and Text 317 pp. Table 3 pp. Calf.
8vo. (12s. 6d. 2477)

SHEPARD (THOMAS). Subjection to Christ,/ in
all his/ Ordinances/ and/ Appointments,/ The best
means to preserve our Liberty./ Together with a/
Treatise/ of/ Ineffectual hearing the Word ;/ How
we may know whether we/ have heard the same
effectually :/ And by what means it may become/
effectual unto us./ With some remarkable passages
of his life/ By Tho. Shephard late Pastor of the
Church/ of Christ in Cambridge in New-England./
Now published by Mr. Jonathan Michel,/ Pastor
of the said Church in New-England./ *London,*
Printed for Tho. Brewster, at the three Bibles in
Pauls Church-yard. 1654./ *6 prel. leaves and* 195
pp. 'Table' 11 *pp. Calf. Small 8vo.* (15s. 2478)

SHEPARD (THOMAS). The/ Sincere Convert :/
Discovering/ The small number of true/ Beleevers,/
And the great difficulty of Saving/ Conversion./
Wherein is excellently and plainly opened/ these
choice and Divine Principles ;/ Viz. [1. That there
is a God, and this God is most glorious./ 2. That
God made man in a blessed estate./ 3. Man's misery
by his Fall./ 4. Christ the only Redeemer by price./
5. That few are saved, and that with difficulty./
6. That mans perdition is of himself./ Whereto is
now added the Saints Jewell,/ shewing how to
apply the Promises; And/ the Souls Invitation
unto Jesus Christ./ By Tho. Sheppard, sometimes
of Emanuel/ Colledge in Cambridge./ Corrected
and much amended by the Author./ *London,*
Printed by E. Cotes, for John Sweeting,/ at the
Angel in Popes-head Alley, 1655./ *8 prel. leaves*
and 247 *pp. Calf. 8vo.* (10s. 6d. 2479)

SHEPARD (THOMAS). Theses Sabbaticæ./ Or,/
The Doctrine/ of the/ Sabbath./ Wherein/ The/
Sabbaths/ [I. Morality,/ II. Change,/ III. Beginning,/ IV. Sanctification,] are clear-/ly discus-/sed./
Which were first handled more largely/ in sundry
Sermons in Cambridg in New-Eng-/land, in opening of the fourth Commandment./ In unfolding
whereof many Scriptures are cleared, di-/vers Cases
of Conscience resolved, and the Moral/ Law as a
rule of Life to a Believer, occasional-/ly and dis-

tinctly handled./ By Thomas Shepard, Paftor of the Church of/ Christ at Cambridge in New-England./ *London*, Printed by S. G. for John Rothwel at the Foun-/tain and Bear in Goldfmiths row in Cheap-fide./ 1655./ 14 *prel. leaves and* 320 *pp. followed by* 3 *prel. leaves and* 32 *pp. with* 2 *prel. leaves,* 1 *and* 17 *pp. Old calf.* 8*vo.* (10s. 6d. 2480)

SHEPARD (Thomas). The/ Parable/ of the/ Ten Virgins/ opened & applied :/ Being the Sub-ftance of divers/ Sermons/ on Matth. 25. 1,—13./ Wherein, the Difference between the Sincere Chriftian and/ the moft Refined Hypocrite, the Nature and Characters of Saving/ and of Common Grace, the Dangers and Difeafes incident to/ moft flourifhing Churches or Chriftians, and other Spi-ritual/ Truths of greateft importance, are clearly/ difcovered, and practically Improved./ By/ Thomas Shepard/ late Worthy and Faithfull Paftor of the Church of Chrift at/ Cambridge in New-England./ Now Publifhed from the Authors own Notes, at the defires of/ many, for the common Benefit of the Lords people,/ By/ Jonathan Mitchell Minifter at Cambridge,/ Tho : Shepard, Son to the Reverend Author,/ now Minifter at Charles-Town in New-England./ *London,*/ Printed by J. H. for John Rothwell, at the Fountain in Goldfmiths-Row in Cheap-fide,/ and Samuel Thomfon at the Bifhop's Head in Pauls Church-yard. 1660./ *Two Parts.* Part I. 4 *prel. leaves and* 240 *pp.* Part II. 203 *pp. Table.* 5 *pp. Old calf. Folio.* (18s. 2481)

SHEPARD (Thomas). The/ Sincere Convert,/ Discovering/ The fmall number of true/ Beleevers,/ And the great difficulty of Saving/ Converfion./ Wherein is excellently and plainly opened/ thefe choice and Divine Principles :/ Viz. [1. That there is a God, and this God is moft glorious./ 2. That God made man in a bleffed eftate./ 3. Mans mifery by his fall./ 4. Chrift the only Redeemer by Price./ 5. That few are faved, and that with difficulty./ 6. That mans perdition is of himfelf./ Whereto is now added the Saints Jewel, fhewing/ how to apply the promife ; And the Souls Invi-/tation unto Jefus Chrift./ By Tho. Shepherd, fometimes of Emanuel/ Colledge in Cambridge./ Corrected and much amended by the Author./ *London,*

Printed by Tho: Mabb, for Robert Horne,/·at the Angel in Popes-head-alley. 1664./ 8 *prel. leaves and* 216 *pp. Half calf.* 8*vo.* (10s. 6d. 2482)

SHEPARD (THOMAS). The/ Sincere Convert :/ Difcovering the fmall number of/ True Believers,/ And the great difficulty of/ faving Converfion./ Wherein are excellently and plainly opened thefe/ choice and Divine Principles :/ Viz. 1. That there is a God, and this God is moft glorious./ 2. That God made Man in a bleffed eftate./ 3. Mans mifery by his Fall./ 4. Chrift the onely Redeemer by price./ 5. That few are faved, and that with difficulty./ 6. That Mans perdition is of himself./ Whereto is now added/ The Saint's Jewel, fhewing how to/ apply the Promifes ; and/ The Soul's In-vitation unto/ Jefus Chrift./ By Tho. Sheppard, fometimes of Emanuel/ College in Cambridge./ Corrected and much amended by the Author./ *London,*/ Printed by J. Flefher for Robert Horne at Grefham-college, in/ the first Court in Bifhopf-gate-ftreet. 1667./ 8 *prel. leaves and* 237 *pp. Old calf.* 8*vo.* (10s. 6d. 2483)

SHEPARD (THOMAS). The/ Sincere Convert :/ Difcovering the fmall number of/ True Believers,/ And the great difficulty of/ Saving Converfion./ Wherein are excellently and plainly opened thefe/ choice and Divine Principles :/ Viz. 1. That there is a God, and this God is moft glorious./ 2. That God made Man in a bleffed eftate./ 3. Man's mifery by his Fall./ 4. Chrift the onely Redeemer by price./ 5. That few are faved, and that with difficulty./ 6. That Man's perdition is of himfelf./ Whereto is now added/ The Saint's Jewel, fhewing how to/ apply the Promifes ; and/ The Soul's Invitation unto/ Jefus Chrift./ By Tho. Sheppard, fometimes of Emanuel/ Colledge in Cambridge./ *London,*/ Printed by E. Flefher for Robert Horn at the South En-/trance of the Royal Exchange. 1672./ 8 *prel. leaves and* 223 *pp. Calf.* 8*vo.* (10s. 6d. 2484)

SHEPARD (THOMAS). The/ Parable/ of the/ Ten Virgins/ Opened & Applied :/ Being the Sub-ftance of divers/ Sermons/ on Matth. 25. 1,---13./ Wherein, the Difference between the Sincere Chriftian and/ the moft Refined Hypocrite, the

Nature & Characters of Saving/ and of Common Grace, the Dangers and Diseases incident to/ most flourishing Churches or Christians, and other Spiritual/ Truths of greatest importance, are clearly/ discovered, and practically Improved,/ By/ Thomas Shepard/ Late Worthy and Faithful Pastor of the Church of Christ at/ Cambridge in New-England./ Now published from the Authors own Notes, at the desires of/ many, for the common Benefit of the Lords people,/ By/ Jonathan Mitchell Minister at Cambridge./ Tho. Shepard, Son to the Reverend Author,/ now Minister at Charles-Town. in New-England./ Re-printed, and carefully Corrected in the Year,/ 1695./ *Two Parts.* Part I. *4 prel. leaves and 232 pp.* Part II. *190 pp. Table, 5 pp. Old calf. Folio.* (18s. 2485)

SHEPARD (THOMAS). The Sound Believer. A Treatise of Evangelicall Conversion. Discovering The Work of Christ's Spirit, in reconciling of a Sinner to God. By Tho. Shepherd, sometimes of Emanuel Colledge in Cambridge, Now Preacher of God's Word in New-England. *Aberdeen,* Printed by James Nicol, 1730. *325 pp. Table 3 pp. 12mo.* (15s. 2486)

[SHERMAN (ROGER).] A Sermon, of a new kind, Never preached, nor ever will be; Containing a Collection of Doctrines, Belonging to the Hopkintonian Scheme of Orthodoxy; Or the Marrow of the most Modern Divinity. And an Address to the Unregenerate, agreeable to the Doctrines. *New-Haven;* Printed and Sold by T. and S. Green. *28 pp. Half mor. 12mo.* (10s. 6d. 2487)

SHIPLEY (JONATHAN). A Sermon Preached before the Incorporated Society for the Propagation of the Gospel in Foreign Parts; at their Anniversary Meeting in the Parish Church of St. Maryle-Bow, On Friday February 19, 1773. By the Right Reverend Jonathan Lord Bishop of St. Asaph. London Printed: *Boston,* New-England, Re-Printed: And to be Sold by Thomas and John Fleet, at the Heart and Crown in Cornhill, 1773. *17 pp. Half morocco. 8vo.* (4s. 6d. 2488)

SHIRLEY (WILLIAM). A Letter from William Shirley, Esq; Governor of Massachuset's Bay, To

his Grace the Duke of Newcaſtle: With A Journal
of the Siege of Louisbourg, and other Operations
of the Forces, during the Expedition againſt the
French Settlements on Cape Breton; Drawn up
at the Deſire of the Council and Houſe of Repreſentatives of the Province of Maſſachuſet's Bay;
approved and atteſted by Sir William Pepperrell,
and the other Principal Officers who commanded
in the ſaid Expedition. Publiſhed by Authority.
London: E. Owen. 1746. 32 *pp. Half morocco.*
8vo.   (7s. 6d. 2489)

SHIRLEY (WILLIAM). A Letter from William
Shirley, Eſq; Governor of Maſſachuſetts-Bay, To
His Grace the Duke of Newcaſtle: With A Journal
of the Siege of Louiſbourg, and other Operations
of the Forces, during the Expedition againſt the
French Settlements on Cape-Breton; drawn up
at the Deſire of the Council and Houſe of Repreſentatives of the Province of Maſſachuſetts-Bay;
approved and atteſted by Sir William Pepperrell,
and the other Principal Officers who commanded
in the ſaid Expedition. Publiſhed by Authority.
London: Printed 1746. *Boston:* Re-printed by
Rogers and Fowle, for Joshua Blanchard, at the
Bible and Crown in Dock-Square. 1746. 16 *pp.*
8vo.   (10s. 6d. 2490)

SHIRLEY (WILLIAM). The Conduct of Major
Gen. Shirley, Late General and Commander in
Chief of His Majesty's Forces in North America.
Briefly stated. *London:* R. and J. Dodsley, 1758.
viii and 131 *pp. Half mor. 8vo.* (10s. 6d. 2491)

SHORT/ (A) Account/ of the/ Manifeſt Hand of
God/ That hath Fallen upon Several/ Marſhals and
their Deputies/ Who have made Great Spoil and
Havock of the/ Goods of the People of God called/
Quakers,/ in the/ Iſland of Barbadoes,/ For their
Testimony againſt Going or Sending/ to the Militia./ With a Remarkable Account of some others
of the Perſe-/cutors of the ſame People in the ſame
Iſland. Together/ with an Abſtract of their Sufferings./ *London,* Printed and Sold by T. Sowle,
near the/ Meeting-houſe in White-hart-court in
Gracious-street. 1696./ 23 *pp.* 'An Abstract' *etc.*
a folded sheet. 4to.   (1l. 1s. 2492)

SHORT (A) Account of the Interest and Conduct of the Jamaica Planters. In an Address to the Merchants, Traders, and Liverymen of the City of London. *London:* M. Cooper, MDCCLIV. *Title and* 21 *pp.* 8vo. (4s. 6d. 2493)

SHORT (A) History of the Conduct of the Present Ministry, With Regard to the American Stamp Act. *London:* J. Almon, 1766. 21 *pp. Half morocco.* 8vo. (4s. 6d. 2494)

SHORT (A) History of the Conduct of the present Ministry, With Regard to the American Stamp Act. The Second Edition. *London:* J. Almon, 1766. 21 *pp. Half morocco.* 8vo. (4s. 6d. 2495)

SHORT (A) Account Of that Part of Africa Inhabited by the Negroes. With Refpect to the Fertility of the Country, the good Difpofition of many of the Natives, and the Manner by which the Slave Trade is carried on. Extracted from divers Authors, in order to fhew the Iniquity of that Trade, and the Falfity of the Arguments ufually advanced in its Vindication. With Quotations from the Writings of feveral Perfons of Note, viz. George Wallis, Francis Hutcheson, and James Foster, and a large Extract from a Pamphlet, lately publifhed in London, on the Subject of the Slave Trade. The Third Edition. Philadelphia: Printed *London:* Reprinted by W. Baker and J. W. Galabin, MDCCLXVIII. 80 *pp.* 8vo. (7s. 6d. 2496)

SHORT Address to the Government, the Merchants, Manufacturers, and the Colonists in America, and the Sugar Islands, On the prefent State of Affairs. By a Member of Parliament. *London,* G. Robinson, MDCCLXXV. *Title and* 40 *pp. Half morocco.* 8vo. (5s. 6d. 2497)

SHORT (A) History of the Opposition during the Laft Seffion of Parliament. The Third Edition. *London:* T. Cadell, MDCCLXXIX. 58 *pp. Unbound.* 8vo. (4s. 6d. 2498)

SHORT (A) History of the Oppofition during the Laft Seffion of Parliament. The Third Edition. *London:* T. Cadell, MDCCLXXIX. *vi and* 58 *pp. Half morocco.* (4s. 6d. 2499)

SHOWER (JOHN). Practical Reflections on the Earthquakes That have happened in Europe and

America, But chiefly in the. Islands of Jamaica,
England, Sicily, Malta, &c. With a Particular
and Hiftorical Account of them, and divers other
Earthquakes. By John Shower. The Second
Edition. *London:* Cook, James, and Kingman,
Mdccl. *Title, viii, and* 98 *pp.* 8*vo.* (4*s.* 6*d.* 2500)

SIGFRID (Isaac). Theological Theses, Containing
the chief Heads of the Christian Doctrine, Deduced
from Axioms; Compofed and publickly defended
in Prefence and under the Direction of the very
reverend and moft judicious John Henry Ringier,
V. D. M. And Profeffor of controverfial Divinity
in the Academy At Bern. By Isaac Sigfrid, of
Zoffingen in Bern, and Daniel Wyttenbach, of
Bern, In Order to obtain the Honour of the S.
Ministry. 1747. (Tranflated from Latin.) To which
is added a Difcourse by Gerrit Lydekker. A.B.
New-York. Printed and Sold by Samuel Brown
at the Foot of Botbaker's-Hill, between the New-
Dutch Church and Fly-Market. 1766. 6 *prel.*
leaves and 55 *pp.* ' A Discourse' *etc. Title and* 113 *pp.*
' Advertifement.' 4 *pp.* 8*vo.* (10*s.* 6*d.* 2501)

SIGNS (The) of the Times consider'd : Or, The high
Probability, that the prefent Appearances in New-
England, and the Weft of Scotland, are a Prelude
of the Glorious Things promifed to the Church in
the latter Ages. *Edinburgh,* T. Lumisden and J.
Robertson; md.cc.xlii. 3 *prel. leaves; Text, pp.*
5—34. 8*vo.* (5*s.* 6*d.* 2502)

SILLERY (Madame). A Selection from the Annals of Virtue, of Madame Sillery: Containing
the Moft important and Interefting Anecdotes from
the Histories of Spain, Portugal, China, Japan,
and America: With fome Account of the Manners,
Customs, Arts and Sciences of France. Translated
from the French By Elizabeth Mary James. *Bath.*
S. Hazard, m.dcc.xciv. 4 *prel. leaves and text* 255
pp. ' Subscribers.' *and* ' Errata.' 8 *pp.* *Old calf.*
8*vo.* (7*s.* 6*d.* 2503)

SIMON (Pedro). ✤/ Primera Parte/ De las Noticias hiftoriales/ de las Conquiftas de tier/ra firme
en las Indias/ Occidentales./ Compvesto por el
Padre/ Fray Pedro Simon Prouincial/ de la Sera-
fico Orden de San Fran=/cisco, del Nueuo Reyno
de Granada/ en las Indias, Lector Jubilado en

Sa=/cra Theologia, y qualificador del San^{to}/ Officio, hijo de la Prouincia de Car/thagena en Caſtilla,/ Natural de/ la Parrilla Obiſpado de/ Cuenca./ Dirigido/ A nvestro invic=/tiſſimo y maior Monarca/ del Antiguo y nuebo Mun/do Philippo quarto en ſu/ Real y supremo Conſejo/ de las Indias./ [*Colophon*] Con Privilegio,/ Del Rey nueſtro Señor, en *Cuenca* por/ Domingo de la Iglesia, Año./ de 1627./ *7 prel. leaves including engraved title, text* 671 *pp ; Table* 11 *leaves ; Table de Vocablos* 9 *leaves.* 2 *of the* 7 *prel. leaves are wanting. Vellum. Folio.* (2*l.* 2504)

SIMONDE DE SISMONDI (J. C. L.) De l'Intérêt de la France a l'égard de la Traite des Négres, par J. C. L. Simonde de Sismondi. A *Genève,* J. J. Paschoud, et a *Paris,* 1814. 59 *pp.* 8*vo.* (2*s.* 6*d.* 2505)

SIVERS (Henrich). Bericht/ Von/ Gröhnland,/ Gezogen aus zwo Chroniken: Einer alten Ihs=/ländiſchen, und einer neuen Däniſchen; übergeſand/ in Frantzöſiſcher Sprahche/ An/ Herren von der Mote den Wayer von einem/ unbenandten Meiſter, und gedruckt zu/ Pariſs bey Auguſtin kürbe in s./ Anno 1647./ Jetzo aber Deutſch gegäben, und, um deſto färtiger ihn/ zu gebrauchen, unterſchihdlich eingeteihlet/ Von/ Henrich Sivers./ *Hamburg./* In Verlägung Johan Naumans und Jurgen Wolfs./ Gedruckt im Jahr Chriſti/ 1674./ 3 *prel. leaves and* 70 *pp. with* 2 *seq. pp. Copperplate map of Greenland, engraved by J. Wichman. Half Russia.* 4*to.* (15*s.* 2506)

SLADE (William). Vermont State Papers ; being a Collection of Records and Documents, connected with the Assumption and Establishment of Government by the People of Vermont; together with the Journal of the Council of Safety, the First Constitution, the Early Journals of the General Assembly, and the Laws from the Year 1779 to 1786, inclusive. To which are added the Proceedings of the First and Second Councils of Censors. Compiled and Published by William Slade, Jun : Secretary of State. *Middlebury :* J. W. Copeland, Printer. 1823. *xx and pp.* 9—568. *Calf extra by Bedford.* 8*vo.* (15*s.* 2507)

SMALLEY (John). The Consistency of the Sinner's Inability to comply with the Gospel; with his inexcusable Guilt in not complying with it, illustrated and confirmed: In two Discourses, On John vi[th], 44th. By John Smalley, A. M. Paftor of a Church in Farmington. *Hartford:* Printed by Green & Watson, near the Great Bridge. M,DCC,LXIX. 71 *pp.* 8*vo.* (4*s.* 6*d.* 2508)

SMITH (Aaron). The Atrocities of the Pirates; being a Faithful Narrative of the Unparalleled Sufferings enduded by the Author during his Captivity among the Pirates of the Island of Cuba; with an account of the excesses and barbarities of those Inhuman Freebooters. By Aaron Smith, (Who was himself afterwards tried at the Old Bailey as a Pirate, and acquitted.) *London:* G. and W. B. Whittaker, 1824. *xi pp. and text* 214 *pp. Boards.* 12*mo.* (4*s.* 6*d.* 2509)

SMITH (John). A Map of Virginia./ VVith a Descripti-/on of the Covntrey, the/ Commodities, People, Govern-/ment and Religion./ VVritten by Captaine Smith, fometimes Go-/vernour of the Countrey./ Wherevnto is annexed the/ proceedings of thofe Colonies, fince their firft/ departure from England, with the difcourfes,/ Orations, and relations of the Salvages,/ and the accidents that befell/ them in all their Iournies/ and difcoveries./ Taken faithfvlly as they/ were written out of the writings of/ Doctor Rvssell. Richard Wiffin./ Tho. Stvdley. Will. Phetti Place./ Anas Todkill. Nathaniel Povvell./ Ieffra Abot. Richard Pots./ And the relations of divers other diligent obfervers there/ prefent then, and now many of them in England./ By VV[illiam]. S[trackey]. At *Ox-ford,*/ Printed by Jofeph Barnes. 1612./ 4 *prel. leaves and* 39 *pp; Second title and* ' To the Reader ' 2 *leaves, and* 110 *pp. Map of Virginia. Fine copy in blue morocco by Bedford.* 4*to.* (12*l.* 12*s.* 2510)

SMITH (John). The/ Generall Historie/ of/ Virginia, New-England, and the Summer/ Ifles: with the names of the Adventurers,/ Planters, and Governours from their/ firft beginning An°: 1584. to this/ prefent 1624./ With the Procedings of those Severall Colonies/ and the Accidents that

befell them in all their/ Journyes and Difcoveries./
Alfo the Maps and Defcriptions of all thofe/
Countryes, their Commodities, people,/ Govern-
ment, Cuftomes, and Religion/ yet knowne./
Divided into sixe Bookes./ By Captaine Iohn
Smith fometymes Governour/ in thofe Countryes
& Admirall./ of New England./ *London.*/ Printed
by I. D. and/ I. H. for Michael/ Sparkes./ 1624./
Engraved title and 6 prel. leaves. Text pp. 1 *to* 96
and 105 *to* 248; *and Errata. With the* 4 *maps com-
plete. Folio.*   (10*l.* 10*s.* 2511)

SMITH (John). A Sea Grammar,/ With/ the
Plaine Exposition/ of Smiths Accidence for young/
Sea-men, enlarged./ Diuided into fifteene Chapters: What they are you/ may partly conceive by
the Contents. Written by Captaine Iohn Smith,
fometimes/ Governour of Virginia, and Admirall
of/ New-England./ *London,*/ Printed by Iohn
Haviland,/ 1627./ *6 prel. leaves and text* 86 *pp.*
4*to.*   (3*l.* 3*s.* 2512)

SMITH (John). The/ True Travels,/ Adventvres,/
and/ Observations/ of/ Captaine Iohn Smith,/ In
Europe, Afia, Affrica, and America, from Anno/
Domini 1593. to 1629./ His Accidents and Sea-
fights in the Straights; his Service/ and Stratagems
of warre in Hungaria, Tranfilvania, Wallachia,
and/ Moldavia, againft the Turks, and Tartars;
his three fingle combats/ betwixt the Chriftian
Armie and the Turkes./ After how he was taken
prifoner by the Turks, fold for a Slave, fent into/
Tartaria; his defcription of the Tartars, their
ftrange manners and cuftomes of/ Religions, Diets,
Buildings, Warres, Feafts, Ceremonies, and/ Living; how hee flew the Bafhaw of Nalbrits in
Cambia,/ and efcaped from the Turkes and Tartars./ Together with a continuation of his generall
Hiftory of Virginia,/ Summer-Iles, New England,
and their proceedings, fince 1624. to this/ prefent
1629; as alfo of the new Plantations of the great/
River of the Amazons, the Iles of S^t. Chriftopher,
Mevis,/ and Barbados in the Weft Indies./ All
written by actuall Authours whofe names/ you
shall finde along the Hiftory./ *London,*/ Printed
by J. H. for Thomas Slater, and are to bee/ fold
at the Blew Bible in Greene Arbour./ 1630./ 6

prel. leaves and 60 *pp. wanting the large copperplate
engraving in six compartments. Cloth.*
Folio. (1*l.* 11*s.* 6*d.* 2513)

SMITH (John). Advertisements/ For the unexpe-
rienced Planters of/ New-England, or any where./
Or,/ The Path-way to experience to erect a/ Plantation./ With the yearely proceedings of this
Country in Fishing/ and Planting, since the yeare
1614. to the yeare 1630./ and their present estate./
Also how to prevent the greatest inconveniences,
by their/ proceedings in Virginia, and other Plantations,/ by approved examples./ With the Countries Armes, a description of the Coast,/ Harbours,
Habitations, Land-markes, Latitude and/ Longitude: with the Map, allowed by our Royall/ King
Charles./ By Captaine Iohn Smith, sometimes
Governour of Virginia, and Admirall of New-
England./ *London,*/ Printed by Iohn Haviland,
and are to be sold by/ Robert Milbovrne, at the
Grey-hound/ in Pauls Church-yard. 1631./ 4
prel. leaves and 40 *pp. Map.* 4*to.* (5*l.* 5*s.* 2514)

SMITH (John). The/ Generall Historie/ of/
Virginia, New=England, and the Summer/ Isles:
with the names of the Adventurers,/ Planters,
and Governours from their/ first beginning An°:
1584. to this/ present 1626./ With the Procedings
of those Severall Colonies/ and the Accidents that
befell them in all their/ Journyes and Discoveries./
Also the Maps and Descriptions of all those/ Countryes, their Commodities, people,/ Government,
Customes, and Religion/ yet knowne./ Divided
into sixe Bookes./ By Captaine Iohn Smith some-
tymes Governour/ in those Countryes & Admirall/
of New England./ *London./* Printed by I. D.
and/ I. H. for Edward/ Blackmore/ Anno 1632./
*Engraved frontispiece, and in every other respect the
same as the first Edition of* 1624, *with the* 4 *maps.*
Folio. (10*l.* 10*s.* 2515)

SMITH (John). Reisen, Entdeckungen und Un-
ternehmungen des Schifs=Capitain Johann Schmidt
oder John Smith; welche den wahren Ursprung
derer Englischen Colonien in Nord=Amerika be-
wirkt haben, und ihn deutlich vor Augen stellen:
Erdstentheils aus desselben ligenen Schriften bes-

2   z z

chrieben von Carl Friedrich Scheibler, Paſtor zu
Hansfelde, Zartzig und Schwend in Preuſſiſch
Pommern. *Berlin,* bei Siegismund Friedrich Heſſe.
1782. *232 pp. and 1 leaf of Errata. Half calf.*
8vo. (10s. 6d. 2516)

SMITH (John). The Trve Travels, Adventvres
and Observations of Captaine Iohn Smith, in
Europe, Asia, Africke, and America: Beginning
about the yeere 1593, and continued to this present
1629. From the London Edition of 1629. *Rich-*
mond: Republished at the Franklin Press. William W. Gray, Printer. 1819. *Two Volumes.*
Vol. I. *7 prel. leaves and 247 pp. Portrait of Smith,*
plates at pp. 14, 113, map at 149. Vol. II. *Fron-*
tispiece; xi and 282 pp. Calf. 8vo. (18s. 2517)

SMITH (John). An Authentic Copy of the Minutes
of Evidence on the Trial of John Smith, a Missionary, in Demerara; Held at the Colony House,
in George Town, Demerara, on Monday, the 13th
Day of October, 1823, and 27 following Days; on
a Charge of exciting the Negroes to Rebellion;
copied verbatim, From a Report as Ordered to be
printed, by the House of Commons, 22d of March,
1824. With an Appendix, including The Affidavit
of Mrs. Jane Smith, the Petition presented to the
House of Commons, from the Directors of the
London Missionary Society, Letters of Mr. John
Smith. And other interesting Documents. *Lon-*
don: Samuel Burton, 1824. *179 pp. Boards.*
8vo. (4s. 6d. 2518)

SMITH (Joshua Hett). An Authentic Narrative
of the causes which led to the death of Major
Andrè, Adjutant-General of his Majesty's Forces
in North America. By Joshua Hett Smith, Esq.
Counsellor at Law, late Member of the Convention
of the State of New York. To which is added a
Monody on the death of Major Andrè. By Miss
Seward. *London:* Mathews and Leigh, 1808. *vii*
and 358 pp. Portrait, map, and plate. Half calf.
8vo. (7s. 6d. 2519)

SMITH (Joshua Toulmin). The Discovery of
America by the Northmen in the Tenth Century.
By Joshua Toulmin Smith, Author of " Progress
of Philosophy among the Ancients; " " Compara-

tive view of ancient History, with explanation of
Chronological Eras;" etc. With Two Maps.
London: Charles Tilt, 1839. *xii and* 344 *pp.* 2
maps and 2 plates. 8vo.   (4s. 6d.   2520)

SMITH (SAMUEL). The History of the Colony of
Nova-Cæsaria, or New-Jersey: Containing, an Account of its First Settlement, Progressive Improvements, the Original and present Constitution, and
other events, to the Year 1721. With some particulars since; and a short view of its present state.
By Samuel Smith. *Burlington, in New-Jersey:*
Printed and Sold by James Parker: Sold also by
David Hall, in Philadelphia. M,DCC,LXV. *x and* 574
pp. Fine copy. Old calf. 8vo.   (2l. 2s.   2521)

SMITH (WILLIAM). A New Voyage to Guinea:
Describing The Customs, Manners, Soil, Climate,
Habits, Buildings, Education, Manual Arts, Agri-
culture, Trade, Employments, Languages, Ranks
of Diſtinction, Habitations, Diverſions, Marriages,
and whatever elſe is memorable among the Inhabit-
ants.   Likewise, An Account of their Animals,
Minerals, &c. With great Variety of entertaining
Incidents, worthy of Obſervation, that happen'd
during the Author's Travels in that large Country.
Illuſtrated with Cutts, engrav'd from Drawings
taken from the Life. With an Alphabetical Index.
By William Smith, Eſq; Appointed by the Royal
African Company to ſurvey their Settlements,
make Diſcoveries, &c. *London:* John Nourse,
MDDCXLIV. [1744] *iv and* 276 *pp. Index* 8 *pp.*
Frontispiece and plates at pp. 8, 147, 148, 151. *Tree*
calf. 8vo.   (7s. 6d.   2522)

SMITH (WILLIAM). A Natural History of Nevis,
And the reſt of the Engliſh Leeward Charibee Iſlands in America. With many other Obſervations
on Nature and Art; Particularly, An Introduction
to The Art of Decyphering. In Eleven Letters
from the Rev^d Mr. Smith, ſometime Rector of St.
John's at Nevis, and now Rector of St. Mary's in
Bedford; to the Rev^d Mr. Mason, B.D. Wood-
wardian Profeſſor, and Fellow of Trinity-College,
in Cambridge. *Cambridge:* J. Benthan, MDCCXLV.
3 *prel. leaves (with errata) and* 318 *pp.* 'Index' 9
pp. Old calf. 8vo.   (5s. 6d.   2523)

SMITH (WILLIAM). Histoire de la Nouvelle-York, depuis la Découverte de cette Province jusqu'a notre Siécle, Dans laquelle on rapporte les démêlés qu'elle a eus avec les Canadiens & les Indiens; les Guerres qu'elle a foutenues contre ces Peuples; les Traités & les Alliances qu'elle a faits avec eux, &c. On y a joint Une Defcription Géographique du Pays, & une Hiftoire Abrégée de fes Habitans, de leur Religion, de leur Gouvernement Civil & Eccléfiaftique, &c. Par William Smith. Traduite de l'Anglois par M. E*** A *Londres*. M.DCC. LXVII. *xvi and* 415 *pp. old calf.* 8vo.   (8s. 6d. 2524)

SMITH (WILLIAM). A Sermon On the Present Situation of American Affairs. Preached in Christ-Church. June 23, 1775, At the Requeft of the Officers of the Third Battalion of the City of Philadelphia, and Diftrict of Southwark. By William Smith, D.D. Provost of the College in that City. Philadelphia Printed: *London* Re-printed, Edward and Charles Dilly. M.DCC.LXXV. *2 prel. leaves, iv and* 32 *pp.* 8vo.   (3s. 6d. 2525)

SMITH (WILLIAM). The History of the Province of New-York, from the first discovery. To which is annexed A Defcription of the Country, an Account of the Inhabitants, their Trade, Religious and Political State, and the Conftitution of the Courts of Juftice in that Colony. By William Smith, A.M. *London:* J. Almon, MDCCLXXVI. *viii and* 334 *pp. Calf extra by Bedford.* 8vo. (15s. 2526)

SMITH (WILLIAM). Eulogium on Benjamin Franklin, LL.D. President of the American Philosophical Society, &c. &c. Delivered March 1, 1791, in Philadelphia, before both Houses of Congress, and the American Philosophical Society, &c. By William Smith, D.D. One of the Vice-Prefidents of the faid Society, and Provoft of the College and Academy of Philadelphia. *London:* T. Cadell, MDCCXCII. *Half-title, title, and 39 pp.* 8vo.   (4s. 6d. 2527)

SMYTH (J. F. D.) A Tour in the United States of America: Containing An Account of the Present Situation of that Country; The Population, Agriculture, Commerce, Customs and Manners of the Inhabitants; Anecdotes of feveral Members of the Congress, and General Officers in the American

Army; and Many other very fingular and interefting Occurrences. With A Defcription of the Indian Nations, the general Face of the Country, Mountains, Forefts, Rivers, and the moft beautiful, grand, and picturefque Views through-out that vaft Continent. Likewise Improvements in Husbandry that may be adopted with great Advantage in Europe. By J. F. D. Smyth, Esq. *London*, G. Robinson, MDCCLXXXIV. *Two Volumes.* Vol. I. 12 *prel. leaves, and* 400 *pp.* Vol. II. 6 *prel. leaves and* 456 *pp.* 8*vo.* (8*s.* 6*d.* 2528)

SNOWDEN (RICHARD). The American Revolution: Written in Scriptural, or, Ancient Historical Style. By Richard Snowden. *Baltimore:* Printed by W. Pechin, No. 10, Second-street. [ ] 360 *pp.* 'The Columbiad; or a Poem on the American War, in Thirteen Cantoes. By Richard Snowden. *Baltimore:* Printed by W. Pechin, No. 10, Second-street.' 44 *pp. Old calf. Small* 8*vo.* (10*s.* 6*d.* 2529)

SOBER Remarks on a Book lately Reprinted at Bofton, Entituled, A Modeft Proof Of the Order and Government fettled by Christ and his Apoftles in the Church. In a Letter to a Friend. The Second Edition. *Boston* in N. E. Printed for Samuel Gerrifh, and Sold at his Shop near the Brick Meeting-Houfe in Cornhill. 1724. 4 *prel. leaves and* 126 *pp.* 8*vo.* (15*s.* 2530)

SOLIS Y RIBADENEYRA (ANTONIO DE). Historia/ de la Conqvista/ de Mexico,/ Poblacion, y Progrefsos/ de la America Septentrional,/ conocida por el nombre/ de/ Nveva Efpaña./ Efcriviala/ Don Antonio de Solis,/ Secretario de fu Mageftad, y su Chronifta/ mayor de las Indias./ Y/ la pone a los pies del/ Rey Nvestro Señor,/ por mano del/ Excelentissimo Señor/ Conde de Oropefa./ En *Madrid.*/ En la Imprenta de Bernardo de Villa-Diego, Impreffor de fu Mageftad./ Año M.DC. LXXXIV./ *First Edition.* 17 *prel. leaves including the engraved title containing the portrait of the Author. Text* 548 *pp.* 'Indice' 15 *pp. old calf. Large Paper. Folio.* (1*l.* 5*s.* 2531)

SOLIS Y RIBADENEYRA (ANTONIO DE). Historia/ de la Conqvista/ de Mexico,/ Poblacion, y Progressos/ de la America Septentrional,/ conocida por el nombre/ de Nveva España./ Escriviala/ Don Antonio de Solis,/ Secretario de sv Magestad, y sv Chronista/ mayor de las Indias,/ Dedicase al Illvstrissimo Señor/ Don Gvillen de Rocafvll/ y Rocaberti, por la gracia de Dios vizconde/ de Rocaberti, Conde de Peralada, y de Albatera, &c./ Año 1691./ *Barcelona.*/ En la Imprenta de Ioseph Llopis, Impreffor de Libros; y à fu cofta./ Vendefe en fu Cafa, en la calle de Santo Domingo./ 10 *prel. leaves and text* 548 *pp.* 'Indice' 15 *pp. Old calf. Folio.*　　　(15s. 2532)

SOLIS Y RIBADENEYRA (Antonio de). Histoire/ De la Conquête du/ Mexique,/ Ou de la Nouvelle/ Espagne./ Par Fernand Cortez./ Traduite de l'Efpagnol de Don/ Antonio de Solis,/ par l'Auteur du Triumvirat./ A la *Haye*,/ Chez Adrian Moetjens,/ Marchand Libraire prés la Cour, à la/ Libraire Françoife./ M.DC.XCII./ *Two Volumes.* Tom. I. 18 *prel. leaves and* 412 *pp.* 'Table.' 15 *pp. Copperplates at pp.* 1, 35, 44, 184, 341, 342, 344, 345, 350, 365, 409. Tome II. 6 *prel. leaves and* 378 *pp.* 'Table' 15 *pp. Copperplates at pp.* 176, 336, 371. *12mo.*　　　(10s. 6d. 2533)

SOLIS Y RIBADENEYRA (Antonio de). Histoire de la Conquête du Mexique, ou de la Nouvelle Espagne, par Fernand Cortez, Traduite de l'Efpagnol de Dom Antoine de Solis, par l'Auteur du Triumvirat. *A Paris*, Par la Compagnie des Libraires. M.DCC.IV. *Two Volumes.* Tome I. 18 *prel. leaves and* 412 *pp.* 'Table' 20 *pp. Copperplate Map and plates at pp.* 1, 35, 44, 184, 341, 345, 346, 348, 365, 408. Tome II. 6 *prel. leaves and* 380 (379) *pp.* 'Table' 15 *pp. Plates at pp.* 177, 243, 336, 372. *Old calf. Small 8vo.*　　　(7s. 6d. 2534)

SOLIS Y RIBADENEYRA (Antonio de). Historia de la Conqvista de Mexico, Poblacion, y Progressos de la America Septentrional, conocida por el Nombre de Nueva España, escriviala Don Antonio de Solis, Secretario de fu Mageftad, y fu Choronifta mayor de las Indias. Dedicada al Excelentissimo Señor Don Joseph de Solis Val-Derrabano Pacheo Giron Guzman y Luzon, Cavallero del Abito de Santiago, Conde de Montellano, Adelantado de la Provincia de Yucatan, Governador del Confejo Real de Caftilla, &c. Con Privilegio:

En *Madrid*: Antonio Gonçalez de Reyes. 1704.
12 *prel. leaves and text* 352 *pp.* 'Indice,' 15 *pp.*
Folio. (15s. 2535)

SOLIS Y RIBADENEYRA (Antonio de). Histoire de la Conqueste du Mexique, ou de la Nouvelle Espagne, par Fernand Cortez, Traduite de
l'Efpagnol de Dom Antoine de Solis, par l'Auteur
du Triumvirat. Quatrie'me Edition, À *Paris*, Par
la Compagnie des Libraires. MDCCXIV. *Two Vo-*
lumes. Tome I. 17 *prel. leaves and text* 537 *pp. Table*
19 *pp. Map and plates at pp.* 1, 43, 243, 412, 435,
447, 452, 454, 476. 534. Tome II. 7 *prel. leaves*
and text 494 *pp. Table* 15 *pp.* ' Privilege du Roy.'
3 *pp. Plates at pp.* 229, 435, 485. *Old calf.*
Small 8vo. (7s. 6d. 2536)

SOLIS Y RIBADENEYRA (Antonio de). The
History of the Conqueſt of Mexico by the Spaniards.
Done into English from the Original Spanish of
Don Antonio de Solis, Secretary and Hiſtorio-
grapher to His Catholick Majeſty. By Thomas
Townsend, Eſq; *London*: T. Woodward, M.DCC.
XXIV. *Portrait of Cortes.* 9 *prel. leaves, Text, Books*
1 *and* 2, 163 *pp. Plate and Map at pp.* 1 *and* 31.
Books 3 *and* 4, 252 *pp. Plates at pp.* 50, 69, 70,
72. *Book* 5, 152 *pp. Plates at pp.* 124 *and* 146. *Old*
calf. Folio. (10s. 6d. 2537)

SOLIS Y RIBADENEYRA (Antonio de). The
History of the Conqueſt of Mexico by the Spaniards.
Done into English from the Original Spanish of
Don Antonio de Solis, Secretary and Hiſtorio-
grapher to His Catholick Majeſty. By Thomas
Townsend, Eſq; Illuſtrated with Copper Plates.
Dublin: S. Powell, MDCCXXVII. *Two Volumes.*
Vol. I. 18 *prel. leaves and pp.* 25-455. *Plates at pp.*
383, 396, 417, 422. Vol. II. *Title and pp.* 457-970.
With map. Old calf. 12*mo.* (7s. 6d. 2538)

SOLIS Y RIBADENEYRA (Antonio de). Histoire de la Conqueste du Mexique ou de la Nouvelle Espagne, par Fernand Cortez, Traduite de
l'Efpagnol de Dom Antoine de Solis, par l'Auteur
du Triumvirat. Cinquième Edition. À *Paris*, Par
la Compagnie des Libraires. M.DCC.XXX. *Two Vo-*
lumes. Tome I. 16 *prel. leaves and* 606 *pp. Table*
and Privilege 26 *pp. Map and Plates at pp.* 1, 49,

62, 274, 466, 504, 505, 511, 514, 528. Tome II.
6 *prel. leaves and* 560 *pp. Table* 22 *pp. Plates at pp.*
261, 494, 549. *Old calf. Small* 8*vo.* (7*s.* 6*d.* 2539)

SOLIS Y RIBADENEYRA (ANTONIO DE). The
History of the Conquest of Mexico by the Span-
iards. Tranflated into English from the Original
Spanish of Don Antonio de Solis, Secretary and
Historiographer To His Catholick Majesty, By
Thomas Townsend, Efq; Late Lieutenant Colonel
in Brig. Gen. Newton's Regiment. The whole
Tranflation Revised and Corrected By Nathanael
Hooke, Efq; Tranflator of The Travels of Cyrus,
and The Life of the Archbishop of Cambray. *Lon-
don:* T. Woodward, and H. Lintot, MDCCXXXVIII.
Two Volumes. Vol. I. 3 *prel. leaves, x and* 479 *pp.
Portrait of Cortes: Plates at pp.* 1, 52, 359, 393, 4,
398. Vol. II. *xii and* 475 *pp. Plates at pp.* 430,
465. *Old calf.* 8*vo.* (7*s.* 6*d.* 2540)

SOLIS Y RIBADENEYRA (ANTONIO DE). *Another copy, the same as above, Printed for* 'John Osborn.' (7*s.* 6*d.* 2541)

SOLIS Y RIBADENEYRA (ANTONIO DE). The
History of the Conquest of Mexico by the Span-
iards. Tranflated from the Original Spanish of Don
Antonio de Solis, Secretary and Hiftoriographer to
His Catholick Majefty, By Thomas Townsend,
Efq; The whole Tranflation Revifed and Corrected
By Nathanael Hooke, Efq; Author of The Roman
History, &c. The Third Edition. *London:* H.
Lintot; J. Whiston and B. White. MDCCLIII. *Two
Volumes.* Vol. I. *xvi and* 384 *pp. Portrait of
Cortes and Plates at pp.* 1, 17, 290, 318, 321. Vol.
II. *x and* 386 *pp. Plates at pp.* 317 *and* 377. *Boards.*
8*vo.* (7*s.* 6*d.* 2542)

SOLIS Y RIBADENEYRA (ANTONIO DE). Histoire de la Conquête du Mexique, ou de la Nouvelle Espagne. Par Fernand Cortez, Traduite de
l'Efpagnol de Dom Antoine de Solis, par l'Auteur
du Triumvirat. Sixième Edition. A *Paris,* M. DCC.
LIX. *Two Volumes.* Tome I. *xxxi and* 606 *pp.
Table and Privilege* 26 *pp. Map and plates at pp.* 1,
49, 274, 504, 5, 511, 514, 529. Tome II. 6 *prel.
leaves and* 560 *pp. Table* 22 *pp. Plates at pp.* 261,
494, 549. *Old calf. Small* 8*vo.* (7*s.* 6*d.* 2543)

SOLIS Y RIBADENEYRA (Antonio de). Historia de la Conquista de Mexico, Poblacion, y Progressos de la America Septentrional, conocida por
el nombre de Nueva España. Escrivala Don Antonio de Solis y Rivadeneyra, Secretario de fu
Mageſtad, y fu Chroniſta Mayor de las Indias. En
Madrid, Juan de San Martin. 1763. 12 *prel. leaves
and* 476 *pp. Vellum. 4to.* (10s. 6d. 2544)

SOLIS Y RIBADENEYRA (Antonio de). Historia de la Conquista de Mexico, Poblacion, y Progressos de la America Septentrional, conocida por
el nombre de Nueva España. Escriviala Don Antonio de Solis y Rivadeneyra, Secretario de su
Magestad, y su Chronista Mayor de las Indias.
En *Madrid*; Don Antonio Mayoral. 1768. 12 *prel.
leaves and* 549 *pp. Vellum. 4to.* (10s. 6d. 2545)

SOLIS Y RIBADENEYRA (Antonio de). Historia de la Conquista de Mexico, Poblacion, y Pro-
gresos de la America Septentrional, conocida por
el Nombre de Nueva España. Escribiala Don Antonio de Solis y Ribadeneyra, Secretario de su
Magestad, y su Cronista Mayor de las Indias.
Dividida en dos Tomos, e Ilustrada con Laminas
finas. Con las licentias Necesarias. *Barcelona*:
Por Thomas Piferrer. 1771. *Two Volumes.* Tomo
I. 12 *prel. leaves and* 479 *pp. Map and plates at pp.*
1, 48, 390, 395, 397, 464. Tomo II. 6 *prel. leaves and*
488 *pp. Plates at pp.* 199, 264. *8vo.* (10s. 6d. 2546)

SOLIS Y RIBADENEYRA (Antonio de). Historia de la Conquista de Mexico, poblacion y pro-
gresos de la America Septentrional, conocida por
el nombre de Nueva España. Escribiala D. Antonio de Solis y Rivadeneyra, Secretario de su
Magestad, y su Chronista Mayor de las Indias. En
Madrid, D. Antonio Fernandez. 1790. 10 *prel.
leaves and* 549 *pp. Old calf. 4to.* (10s. 6d. 2547)

SOLIS Y RIBADENEYRA (Antonio de). Historia de la Conquista de Mexico, Poblacion, y Pro-
gresos de la América Septentrional, conocida por
el Nombre de Nueva-España. Escribiala Don Antonio de Solis, Secretario de su Magestad, y
Cronista mayor de las Indias. Dividida en Tres
Tomos. *Madrid*: MDCCXCI. Don Placido Barco

Lopez. *Three Volumes.* Tomo I. 16 *prel. leaves
and* 357 *pp. Indice* 9 *pp.* Tomo II. *2 prel. leaves
and* 500 *pp.* Tomo III. *2 prel. leaves and* 364 *pp.
Small 8vo.* (10s. 6d. 2548)

SOLORZANO PEREIRA (Juan de). [*Engraved
title*] Politica Indiana/ de/ el D^or. D. Jvan de Solor-
zano/ Pereira Cavallero del Orden de/ Santiago, del
Confejo del Rey/ N. S^r. elos Supremos de Cas/tilla
y de la/ Indias/ Dirigida/ Al Rey Nvestro S^r,/ en
fu Real y Supremo Confejo/ de las Indias/ por
mano del Exmo./ S^r. Conde de Castrillo/ Prefidente
delmefmo/ Confejo &c./ Con Privilegio en Madrid en la Officina/ de Diego diaz de la Carrera/
An'o de 1647./ [*Printed title*] Politica Indiana./
Sacada en Lengva Castellana de/ los dos tomos del
derecho, i govierno mvnicipal/ de las Indias Occidentales qve mas copiosamente/ escribio en la
Latina./ El Dotor Don Ivan de Solorzano Pe-
reira/ caballero del orden de Santiago, del/ Confejo
del Rey Nueftro Señor en los Supremos/ de Caftilla,
i de las Indias./ Por el Mesmo Avtor,/ Dividida
en feis Libros./ En los qvales con gran distincion,
i estvdio/ fe trata, i refuelve todo lo tocante al Defcubrimiento, Defcripcion, Adqui-/ficion, i Reten-
cion de las mefmas Indias, i fu govierno particular,
afsi cerca/ las Perfonas de los Indios, i fus Servicios,
Tributos, Diezmos, i Encomien-/das, como de lo
Efpiritual, i Eclefiaftico, cerca de fu Dotrina, Pat-
ronazgo/ Real, Iglefias, Prelados, Prebendados,
Curas Seculares, i Regulares, Inqui-/fidores, Comif-
farios de Cruzada, i de las Religiones. I en lo
Temporal, cerca/ de todos los Magiftrados feculares,
Virreyes, Prefidentes, Audiencias,/ Confejo Supremo, i Iunta de Guerra dellas, con infercion, i/
declaracion de las muchas cedulas Reales que/ para
efto fe han defpachado./ Añadidas/ mvchas cosas,
que no estan en los tomos/ Latinos, i en particular
todo el Libro Sexto, que en diez i fiete Capitulos
trata de/ la Hazienda Real de las Indias, Regalias,
Derechos, i Miembros de que fe/ compone, i del
modo en que fe adminiftra; i de los Oficiales/
Reales, Tribunales de Cuentas, i Cafa de la/ Contratacion de Sevilla./ Obra de svmo trabaio, i de
igval importancia,/ i utilidad, no folo para los de las
Provincias de las Indias, fino de las de Efpa-/ña, i

otras Naciones, de qualquier Profeſsion que ſean,
por la gran va-/riedad de coſas que comprehende,
adornada de todas/ letras, i eſcrita con el metodo,
claridad,/ i lenguaje que por ella/ parecerà./ Con
dos Indices muy diſtintos, i copioſos, uno de los
Libros, i Capitulos en que ſe/ divide : i otro de las
coſas notables que contiene./ Con Privilegio,/ En
Madrid. Por Diego Diaz de la Carrera./ Año M.DC.
XLVIII./ *24 prel. leaves ; viz. Engraved and printed
titles* 2 *leaves* ; ' Cenſvra del Señor *etc.* Licencias '
etc. 2 *leaves* ; ' Al Rei Nᵗᵒ Sᵒʳ Don Felipe IV.' *etc.*
7 *leaves* ; ' Al Excelentissimo Señor Don Garcia de
Haro i Avellaneda,' *etc.* 3 *leaves* ; *copperplate engraved portrait,* 1 *leaf* ; ' Al Retrato del Autor deſte
libro.' *etc.* 1 *leaf* ; ' Al Lector.' 3 *leaves* ; ' Indice
de los Libros,' *etc.* 5 *leaves* : *Text* 1040 *pp.* ' Indice mvy Copioso ' *etc.* 52 *leaves. Vellum. Fine
copy. Folio.*   (1*l.* 1*s.* 2549)

SOLORZANO PEREIRA (JUAN DE). D. D. Io-
annis/ de Solorzano/ Pereira,/ I.V.D. ex eqvestri
Militia/ D. Iacobi, et in supremis Castellæ,/ &
Indiarum Conſiliis Senatoris;/ de Indiarum Ivre ;/
sive/ de jvsta Indiarum Occidentalium/ Inquiſi-
tione, Acquiſitione, & Retentione./ Cui acceſſit
alia ejusdem avthoris/ Diſputatio de Parricidii
Crimine./ Cum duplici Indice, primo Librorum
& Capitum ; altero Rerum notabilium abſolu-
tiſſimo./ Editio nouiſſima ab innumeris, quibus
priores deformatæ erant mendis emaculata./ *Lugduni,*/ Sumptibus Lavrentii Anisson./ M.DC.LXXII./
Cvm Svperiorvm Permissu./ *Two Volumes.* Tomvs
Primvs. 12 *prel. leaves and* 438 *pp. Indexes* 44 *leaves ;
followed by* 64 *pp. of text, and* 8 *leaves of Index.*
Tomvs Secvndvs. 6 *prel. leaves, and* 858 *pp. Index*
71 *leaves. Folio.*   (10*s.* 6*d.* 2550)

SOME Account of the North-America Indians;
their Genius, Charaĉters, Cuſtoms, and Diſpoſi-
tions, towards the French and Engliſh Nations.
To which are added, Indian Miscellanies, viz. 1.
The Speech of a Creek-Indian againſt the immoderate Uſe of Spirituous Liquors; delivered in a
National Aſſembly of the Creeks, upon the breaking
out of the late War. 2. A Letter from Yariza, an
Indian Maid of the Royal Line of the Mohawks,
to the principal Ladies of New-York. 3. Indian

Songs of Peace. 4. An American Fable. Collected by a learned and ingenious Gentleman in
the Province of Penfylvania. *London:* R. Griffiths,
[1754] 68 *pp. Half mor.* 8*vo.* (10*s.* 6*d.* 2551)

SOME Remarks on a Pamphlet, call'd, Reflections,
on the Conftitution and Management of the Trade
to Africa, Demonstrating the Author's abufive
Afperfions therein contained, to be ill-Grounded,
the Matters of Fact wrong Reprefented, and the
late Management of that Trade fet in a True Light.
With An Account, of the Needful Charge of the
Britifh Settlements in Africa; in what manner
they may be beft Maintain'd, and the Trade carry'd
on to the Benefit of this Nation, and our Plantations in America. [*London*] Printed in the Year,
MDCCIX. 32 *pp. Half mor.* 8*vo.* (4*s.* 6*d.* 2552)

SOME Considerations on the Consequences Of the
French Settling Colonies on the Mississippi, With
refpect to the Trade and Safety of the English
Plantations in America and the Weft-Indies. From
a Gentleman of America, to his Friend in London.
London: J. Roberts, 1720. *Half-title, title, and* 60
pp. With map. Half mor. 8*vo.* (7*s.* 6*d.* 2553)

SOME Observations on the Affiento Trade, As it
has been Exercifed by the South-Sea Company ;
proving the Damage Which will accrue thereby to
the Britifh Commerce and Plantations in America,
And particularly to Jamaica. To which is annexed
A Sketch of the Advantages of that Ifland to Great
Britain, by its annual Produce, and by its Situation
for Trade or War. Addreffed to His Grace the
Duke of Newcastle, One of his Majefty's Principal
Secretaries of State. By a Perfon who refided
feveral Years at Jamaica. *London:* H. Whitridge,
MDCCXXVIII. *iv and text* 38 *pp. Half morocco.*
8*vo.* (5*s.* 6*d.* 2554)

SOME Observations on Extracts taken out of the
Report from the Lords-Commiffioners for Trade
and Plantations. [*London*, 1730] 4 *pp. folded and
bound in calf. Folio.* (8*s.* 6*d.* 2555)

SOME Considerations Humbly offer'd upon the Bill
Now depending in the Houfe of Lords, Relating
to the Trade between the Northern Colonies and

the Sugar-Iflands. In a Letter to a Noble Peer. [*London*], MDCCXXXII. 19 *pp. Half morocco.*
8*vo.* (4*s.* 6*d.* 2556)

SOME Fruits of Solitude, in Reflections and Maxims, Relating to the Conduct of Human Life. In Two Parts. The Eight Edition. *Newport*, Rhode-Ifland : Printed by James Franklin, at the Town-School-Houfe, 1749. 6 *prel. leaves and* 158 *pp. Table* 7 *pp.* 'More Fruits of Solitude: Being The Second Part of Reflections and Maxims, Relating to the Conduct of Human Life. *Newport*, Rhode Ifland : Printed by James Franklin, at the Town School-Houfe, 1749.' 3 *prel. leaves: imperfect, wanting all after page* 106. 12*mo.* (10*s.* 6*d.* 2557)

SOME Observations on the Bill, Intitled, "An Act for granting to His Majefty an Excife upon Wines, and Spirits diftilled, fold by Retail or confumed within this Province, and upon Limes, Lemons, and Oranges." *Boston :* Printed in the Year, 1754. *Title and text* 12 *pp. Half morocco.*
Small 8*vo.* (2*l.* 2*s.* 2558)

SOME Hints to People in Power, on the Prefent Melancholy Situation of our Colonies in North America. *London :* J. Hinxman MDCCLXIII. *Half morocco.* 48 *pp.* 8*vo.* (5*s.* 6*d.* 2559)

SOME Thoughts on the Method Of Improving and Securing the Advantages which accrue to Great-Britain from the Northern Colonies. *London :* J. Wilkie, MDCCLXV. 23 *pp. Half morocco.*
8*vo.* (4*s.* 6*d.* 2560)

SOME Important Observations, Occafioned by, and adapted to, The Publick Fast, Ordered by Authority, December 18th, A.D. 1765. On Account of the Peculiar Circumstances of the prefent Day. Now humbly offered to the Publick, By the Author. *Newport :* Printed and fold by Samuel Hall. 1766. *Half-title, title, and pp.* 3—61. *Half mor.*
4*to.* (10*s.* 6*d.* 2561)

SOME Candid Suggestions towards Accommodation of Differences with America. Offered to Con-sideration of the Public. *London :* T. Cadell, MDCCLXXV. 33 *pp. Half mor.* 8*vo.* (4*s.* 6*d.* 2562)

SOME Reasons for approving of the Dean of Glou-

cester's Plan, of separating from the Colonies;
with a Proposal for a further Improvement. *London:* N. Conant, M.DCC.LXXV. 32 *pp. Half morocco.* 8*vo.*   (4*s.* 6*d.* 2563)

SOME Seasonable Observations and Remarks upon
The State of our Controversy with Great Britain;
And on the Proceedings of the Continental Congress : Whereby many interefting Facts are related,
and Methods propofed for our fafety and an Accommodation. By a Moderate Whig. *America:*
Printed and fold in the Year MDCCLXXV. 14 *pp.*
Half morocco. 8*vo.*   (7*s.* 6*d.* 2564)

SOME Transactions between the Indians and Friends
in Pennsylvania, In 1791 & 1792. *London:* James
Phillips, MDCCXCII. 14 *pp. Half morocco.*
8*vo.*   (3*s.* 6*d.* 2565)

SOME Considerations on this question; Whether
the British Government acted wisely in granting
to Canada her present constitution ? With an Appendix ; containing Documents, &c. By a British
Settler. *Montreal:* Printed and Sold by J. Brown/
No. 20, St. François Xavier Street. 1810. 26 *pp.*
Half morocco. 8*vo.*   (4*s.* 6*d.* 2566)

SOME Account of the conduct of the Religious
Society of Friends towards the Indian Tribes in
the Settlement of the Côlonies of East and West
Jersey and Pennsylvania: with a brief narrative
of their labours for the Civilization and Christian
Instruction of the Indians, from the time of their
settlement in America, to the year 1843. Published
by the Aborigines Committee of The Meeting for
Sufferings. *London:* Edward Marsh, 1844. 2
prel. leaves and text 247 *pp. With two coloured maps.*
8*vo.*   (4*s.* 6*d.* 2567)

SOMER-ISLANDS. A True/ Relation/ of the/
Illegal Proceedings/ of the/ Somer-Islands-Company/ in their/ Courts at London./ And the like
done by their Governour/ Sir John Heydon, Knight,
and his Council, in the/ Somer-Islands./ In all
Humility prefented to the Honourable Knights,/
Citizens and Burgeffes Affembled in Parliament./
Craving from them to be Relieved from the following/ Oppressions./ *London:* Printed in the

Year 1678./ *Title, the reverse blank;* 'Contents' *on*
A 2, 1 *page, the reverse blank ; Text pp.* 1 *to* 12 *; Con-*
tents 1 *page, the recto blank; continuation of text*
(A 2) *pp.* 13 *to* 26. *Calf extra by Bedford.*
4*to.*   (2*l.* 2*s.*   2568)

SÓTO (Fernando de). A/ Relation/ of the/ Invafion
and Conqueft/ of/ Florida/ by the/ Spaniards Under
the Command of/ Fernando de Soto./ Written
in Portuguefe by a Gentleman/ of the Town of
Elvas./ Now Englished./ To which is Subjoyned
Two Journeys of the/ prefent Emperour of China
into Tartary/ in the Years 1682, and 1683./ With
fome Difcoveries made by the Spaniards in/ the
Ifland of California, in the Year 1683./ *London :*
Printed for John Lawrence, at the Angel in the
Poultry/ over againft the Compter. 1686./ *7 prel.*
leaves and 272 *pp. Calf.* 8*vo.*   (1*l.* 1*s.*   2570)

SOTWEED REDIVIVUS: Or the Planters Look-
ing-Glafs. In Burlefque Verfe. Calculated for
the Meridian of Maryland. By E. C. Gent. *An-*
napolis : Printed by William Parks, for the Author.
M.DCC.XXX. *viii and text* 28 *pp. Half morocco.*
4*to.*   (15*s.*   2571)

SOULES (François). Histoire des Troubles de
L'Amérique Anglaise, Ecrite fur les Mémoires les
plus authentiques ; Dédiée a sa Majesté Très-
Chrétienne ; Par François Soulés. Avec des Cartes.
A *Paris,* Buisson, 1787. *Three Volumes.* Tome
Premier. 4 *prel. leaves and* 379 *pp.* Tome Second.
Half-title, title, and 365 *pp.* Tome Troisième. *Half-*
title, title, and 420 *pp.* 8*vo.*   (10*s.* 6*d.*   2572)

SOUSA COUTINHO (Francisco de). Propositie/
Ghedaen/ Ter Vergaderinge van hare Hoogh
Mog. d'Hee-/ren Staten Generael der Vereenigde
Neder-/landen, In's Graven-Hage den 16 Au-/
gufti, 1647./ Door den Heer/ Francisco de Sousa
Coutinho,/ Raedt van fijn Coninckl. Majeft. van/
Portvgal : Sijnen Gouverneur ende Capiteyn
Ghenerael van de/ Vlaemfche Eylanden./ Geno
emt/ Met den felven Tijtel van den Staet van
Brafil./ Ende/ Ambaffadeur by Hare Hoogh
Moogende./ Gedruckt, Anno 1647./ *4 leaves.*
Calf by Hayday. 4*to.*   (10*s.* 6*d.*   2573)

SOUTH CAROLINA. A True State of the Cafe between the Inhabitants of South Carolina, and the Lords Proprietors of that Province; containing an Account of the Grievances under which they labour. 4 *pp. Folio.*   (7s. 6d. 2574)

SOUTH CAROLINA. A New and Accurate Account of the Provinces of South-Carolina and Georgia: With many curious and ufeful Obfervations on the Trade, Navigation and Plantations of Great-Britain, compared with her moft powerful maritime Neighbours in antient and modern Times. *London*, J. Worrall, 1732. *Half-title, title, and* 76 *pp. Half morocco. 8vo.*   (10s. 6d. 2575)

SOUTH CAROLINA. A New and Accurate Account of the Provinces of South-Carolina and Georgia: With many curious and ufeful Obfervations on the Trade, Navigation and Plantations of Great-Britain, compared with her moft powerful maritime Neighbours in antient and modern Times. *London:* J. Worrall, 1733. *Half-title, title, and* 76 *pp. 8vo.*   (10s. 6d. 2576)

SOUTH CAROLINA. An Historical Account of the Rise and Progress Of the Colonies of South Carolina and Georgia. In Two Volumes. Alexander Donaldson, *London.* M. DCC. LXXIX. *Two Volumes.* Vol. I. *xiv and* 347 *pp.* Vol. II. *ix and* 329 *pp. Calf. 8vo.*   (16s. 6d. 2577)

SOUTHERNE (THOMAS). Oroonoko:/ A/ Tragedy/ As it is Acted at the/ Theatre=Royal,/ By His Majesty's Servants./ Written by Tho. Southerne./ *London:/* Printed for H. Playford in the Temple= Change. B. Tooke/ at the Middle=Temple=Gate. And S. Buckley at the/ Dolphin againft St. Dunftan's Church in Fleetftreet./ MDCXCVI./ 4 *prel. leaves and* 84 *pp.* ' Epiloge.' 2 *pp. Half morocco.* 4to.   (7s. 6d. 2578)

SPAFFORD (HORATIO GATES). A Gazetteer of the State of New-York; carefully written from original and authentic materials arranged on a new plan, In Three Parts: Comprising, First—A comprehensive geographical and statistical view of the whole state, conveniently disposed under separate heads: Second—An ample general view of each county, in alphabetical order, with topo-

graphical and statistical tables, showing the civil
and political divisions, population, post-offices,
&c: Third — A very full and minute topographical description of each town or township, city,
borough, village, &c. &c. In the whole state,
Alphabetically arranged; as also its lakes, rivers,
creeks, with every other subject of topographical
detail; forming a complete Gazetteer or Geographical Dictionary of the State of New York. With
an accurate Map of the State. By Horatio Gates
Spafford, A.M. Author of a Geography of the
United States, a Member of the New-York Historical Society, and a Corresponding Secretary of
the Society of Arts. *Albany:* Printed and published by H. C. Southwick, No. 94, State-Street.
1813. *334 pp. Appendix, ii pp. 8vo.* (4s. 6d. 2579)

SPANIARDS/ (The)/ Cruelty and Treachery to
the/ English/ In the time of/ Peace and War,/
Discovered,/ Being the Council of a Perfon of/
Honour to King James, then upon Treaty/ of
Peace with them, for to infift upon a/ Free Trade
in the Weft-Indies/ With fome Expedients for the
fub-/jecting of the Spaniard in America, to/ the
Obedience of England./ Now tendred to the Confideration of His Highnefs/ The Lord Protector,
and his Council./ *London.*/ Printed by J. M. for
Lodowick Lloyd and are to be fold at his/ Shop,
at the Sign of the Caftle in Cornhil, 1656./ *2 prel.
leaves, viz. Title and Dedication, signed ‘ D. K.’
Text 56 pp. Half morocco. 4to.* (1l. 1s. 2580)

SPANISH AMERICA. Observations on the present state of Spanish America, and on the most
effectual method of terminating the present com-
motions there. By a Spaniard, a Lover of his
Country. Translated from the Spanish. *London:*
R. Wilks, 1817. *Title, and text 45 pp. Half morocco. 8vo.* (3s. 6d. 2581)

SPANISH EMPIRE (The) in America. Containing, A fuccinct Relation of the Difcovery and
Settlement of its feveral Colonies; a View of their
refpective Situations, Extent, Commodities, Trade,
&c. And A full and clear Account of the Commerce with Old Spain by the Galleons, Flota, &c.
Also of the Contraband Trade with the English,

Dutch, French, Danes, and Portuguefe. With
An exact Defcription of Paraguay. By an English
Merchant. *London:* M. Cooper. 1747. 6 *prel.
leaves and 330 pp. Old calf.* 8*vo.* (10s. 6d. 2582)

SPARKS (JARED). The Library of American Biography. Conducted By Jared Sparks. *Boston:*
Hilliard, Gray, and Co. London : Richard James
Kennett. 1834—9. *Ten Volumes, original Editions.*
12*mo.*   (1*l.* 11s. 6d. 2583)

SPECIMEN (A) of Naked Truth, from a British
Sailor, A fincere Wellwifher, to the Honour, and
Profperity of the prefent Royal Family, and his
Country. *London:* W. Webb, MDCCXLVI. 30 *pp.
Half morocco.* 8*vo.*   (4s. 6d. 2584)

SPEECH (THE) of a Creek-Indian, against the
Immoderate Use of Spirituous Liquors. Delivered
In a National Affembly of the Creeks upon the
breaking out of the late War. To which are
added, 1. A Letter from Yariza, an Indian Maid
of the Royal Line of the Mohawks, to the principal
Ladies of New York. 2. Indian Songs of Peace.
3. An American Fable. Together with Some Remarks upon the Characters and Genius of the
Indians, and upon their Cuftoms and Ceremonies
at making War and Peace. *London:* R. Griffiths,
M.DCC.LIV. 68 *pp.* 8*vo.* (*See* 2551) (7s. 6d. 2585)

SPEECH (THE) of Mr. P------ And feveral
others, In a certain auguft Affembly On a late important Debate : With an Introduction of the
Matters preceding it. [*London*] Printed in the
Year —66. [1766] *Title and pp.* 5—34. *Unbound.*
8*vo.*   (4s. 6d. 2586)

SPEECH (A) intended to have been spoken on the
Bill for altering the Charters of the Colony of
Massachusett's Bay. [By Dr. Shipley Bishop of
St. Asaph.] *London:* T. Cadell, MDCCLXXIV. *vii
and 36 pp. Half morocco.* 8*vo.*   (4s. 6d. 2587)

SPEECH (A) intended to have been spoken on the
Bill for altering the Charters of the Colony of
Massachusett's Bay. The Second Edition. *London:* T. Cadell, MDCCLXXIV. *vii and 36 pp. Half
morocco.* 8*vo.*   (3s. 6d. 2588)

SPEECH (A) intended to have been spoken on the

Bill for altering the Charters of the Colony of Massachusett's-Bay. The Fourth Edition. *London*: T. Cadell, M DCC LXXIV. *vii and 36 pp. Half morocco. 8vo.*   (3s. 6d.   2589)

SPEECH (A) intended to have been spoken on the Bill for altering the Charters of the Colony of Massachusett's Bay. The Sixth Edition. London, Printed. *Boston*: Reprinted, and Sold by Edes and Gill, in Queen-Street. M.DCC.LXXIV. *24 pp. Half morocco. 8vo.*   (4s. 6d.   2590)

SPEECH (A) never intended to be Spoken, in answer to a Speech intended to have been Spoken on the Bill for altering the Charter of the Colony of Massachusett's Bay. Dedicated to the Right Reverend The Lord Bishop of St. A——. *London*: J. Knox, MDCCLXXIV. *iv and 34 pp. Errata 1 page. Half morocco. 8vo.*   (4s. 6d.   2591)

SPEECH (A) never intended to be Spoken, in answer to a Speech intended to have been Spoken on the Bill for altering the Charter of the Colony of Massachusett's Bay. Dedicated to the Right Reverend The Lord Bishop of St. A——. *London*: J. Knox, MDCCLXXIV. *iv and 35 pp. Half morocco. 8vo.*   (4s. 6d.   2591*)

SPEECH (THE) of a Scots Weaver: Dedicated to Richard Glover, Efq. *London*: W. Nicoll, MDCCLXXIV. *65 pp. At the end of the Dedication signed* 'Thermopilæ.' *Half morocco. 8vo.*   (4s. 6d.   2592)

SPEECH (A) intended to have been delivered in the House of Commons in Support of the Petition from the General Congress at Philadelphia. By the Author of an Appeal to the Justice and Interests of Great-Britain. *London*: M.DCC.LXXV. *Half-title, title, and 67 pp. Half mor. 8vo.* (4s. 6d.   2593)

SPEECH (A) on some Political Topics, The substance of which Was intended to have been Delivered in the House of Commons, On Monday the 14th of December, 1778, When the Estimates of the Army were agreed to in the Committee of Supply. *London*: T. Cadell, MDCCLXXIX. *4 prel. leaves and 71 pp. Half mor. 8vo.* (4s. 6d.   2594)

SPEILBERGEN (JORIS VAN). Ooft ende Weft-In-

difche/ Spieghel/ Waer in Befchreven werden de
twee laetfte Na=/vigatien, ghedaen inde Jaeren
1614.1615.1616.1617. ende 1618. De/ eene door den
vermaerden Zee-Helt loris van Speilberger door
de/ Strate van Magallanes, ende foo rondtom den
gantfchen Aerdt-/Cloot, met alle de Batallien foo
te Water als te Lande ghefchiet./ Hier fyn mede
by ghevoecht tvvee Hiftorien, de eene vande Oost
ende de andere vande West-/Indien, met het ghetal
der Schepen, Forten, Soldaten ende Gefchut./ De
andere ghedaen by lacob le Maire, de welcke in't
Zuyden/ de Straet Magellanes, een nieuwe Straet
ontdeckt heeft, met de Befchrijvinghe/ aller Landen, Volcken ende Natien. Alles verciert met
fchoone Caerten ende figueren hier toe dienftelijck./
't Amstelredam./ By Jan Janffz, Boeckvercooper
op't Water inde Pas-Caert./ Ao. M. DC. XXI./ 4
prel. leaves and pp. 9-192. *Copperplates numbered* 2-
18, *and* 20-25. *Vellum. Oblong* 4to. (*2l. 2s.* 2595)

SPENCER (THOMAS). A True and Faithful/ Re-
lation/ of the/ Proceedings/ of the/ Forces of Their
Majesties/ K. William and Q. Mary,/ In their Ex-
pedition againft the French,/ in the/ Caribby If-
lands/ in the/ West-Indies :/ Under the Conduct of
His Excellency Chriftopher/ Codrington, Captain
General and Comman-/der in Chief of the faid
Forces,/ In the Years 1689. and 1690./ Written
by Thomas Spencer, Jun. Secretary to/ the Honourable Sir Timothy Thornhil Baronet, to whofe
Re-/giment he was Mufter-Mafter, and fupplied
the Place of/ Commiffary./ *London,* Printed for
Robert Clavel at the Peacock, at the Weft-/End of
St. Paul's Church-yard, 1691./ *Reverse of title
blank; Dedication to Admiral Edward Russell,* 2
pages. Text 12 *pp. in very close type. Fine copy.*
4to. (*1l.* 11s. *6d.* 2596)

SPITILLI (GASPAR). Brevis et/ Compendiosa
Nar-/ratio Missionvm Qva-/rvndam Orientis et/
Occidentis./ Excerpta ex quibufdam litteris a
PP. Petro/ Martinez Prouinciali Indiæ Orientalis,
P./ Ioanne de Atienza Prouinciali Peruanæ, P.
Pietro Diaz Prouinciali Mexcicanæ Pro-/uincia-
rum, datis anno 1590 & 1591. Ad/ Reueren. P.
Generalem. Societatis Iesv./ Et collecta per P.

Gafparum Spitilli/ eiufdem Societatis./ *Antverpiæ./*
Excudebat Martinus Nutius ad infigne dua-/rum
Cyconiarum. Anno 1593./ 52 *pp. Calf extra by*
Riviere. 12*mo.* (15*s.* 2597)

SPIZELIUS (THEOPHILUS). Theophili Spizelii/
Elevatio/ Relationis/ Montezinianæ/ de Repertis
in America/ Tribubus Israeliticis ;/ et Discussio/
Argumentorum./ Pro Origine Gentium Ameri-/
canarum Israelitica/ A/ Menaſſe Ben Israel/ in
מקוה ישראל Seu Spe/ Israelis/ Conquisitorum/. Cum
celeberrimi viri/ Johannis Buxtorfii/ de Judaico
isto conatu ad/ Theophilum Spizelium/ Epistola./
Basileæ./ Apud Joannem König, 1661./ 12 *prêl.*
leaves and text 128 *pp. Calf extra by Riviere.*
Small 8vo. (18*s.* 2598)

SPOTORNO (GIAMBATTISTA). Della Origine e
della Patria di Cristoforo Colombo libri tre di
Don Giambattista Spotorno Barnabita, *Genova*
1819. Andrea Frugoni, 247 *pp: Uncut. Half mor.*
8vo. (10*s.* 6*d.* 2599)

SPRENGEL (MATTHIAS CHRISTIAN). Briefe über
Portugal, nebſt einem Anhang über Braſilien. Aus
dem Franzöſiſchen. Mit Anmerkungen herausgegeben von Matthias Chriſt. Sprengel, Profeſſor
der Geſchichte in · Halle. *Leipzig*, in der Weygandfchen Buchhandlung, 1782. 6 *prel. leaves and*
290 *pp. half calf. Small 8vo.* (4*s.* 6*d.* 2600)

STADEN (HANS). Warhaftig/ Hiſtoria vnd beſchreibung eyner Landt=/fchafft der Wilden, Nacke-
ten, Grimmigen Menſchfreſſer/ Leuthen, in der
Newenwelt America gelegen, vor vnd nach/ Chriſti
geburt im Land zü Heſſen vnbekant, bifz vff diſe
ij./ nechſt vergangene jar, Da ſie Hans Staden von
Hom=/berg aufz Heſſen durch ſein eygne erfarung
erkant,/ vnd yetzo durch den truck en tag gibt./
Dedicirt dem Durchlenchtigen Hochgebornen
herrn,/ H. Philipſen Landtgraff zü Heſſen, Graff
zü Catzen/ elnbogen, Dietz, Ziegenhain vnd Nidda,
ſeinem G. H./ Mit eyner vorrede D. Joh. Dryandri, genant Eychman,/ Ordinarij Profeſſoris Medici zü Marpurgk./ Inhalt des Büchlins volget
nach den Vorreden./ Getruckt zü *Marpurg*, im jar
ʍ. D. LVII./ [*Colophon*] Zü Marpurg im Kleeblatt,

bei/ Andres Kolben, vff Faſtnacht. 1557./ *8 prel.
leaves; viz. Title the reverse blank,* 'Dem Durchleuchtigen vnd Hoch=/gebornen Fürſten vnd Herrn,
Herrn Philipſen/ Landtgrauen zü Heſſen, Grauen
zü/ Catzenelnbogen, Diez, Ziegenhain/ vnd Nidda,
ⲅc. Meinem/ gnedigen Fürſten/ vnd Herrn,'/ *2 pp.*
'Dem Wolgebornen hern H. Philipſen/ Graff zü
Naſſaw vnd Sarprück ⲅc. meinem in Gne=/digen
Hern. Wünſcht D. Dryander viel heyls/ mit erbie-
tunge ſeiner Dienſte./ *10 pp.* 'Inhalt des büchs'/
1 page. 'Was hilfft' *etc. underneath a large woodcut of a Ship in full sail;* 'Die Landtſchafft mit den
genanten hauingen,' *etc. a folded woodcut map of*
'Amerika ooer Praſilien.' *Text in 81 leaves, signatures* a *to* t *in fours,* v *in five; many woodcuts with
the text. Fine copy. Vellum.* 4to. (8l. 8s. 2601)

STADEN (Hans). Varhaftige./ be=/ſchreibung
eyner Landſchaffe der wilden/ nacketen/ grimmigen
menſchenfreſſer leuthen, in der newen/ welt Ame-
rica gelegen. Vor vnd nach Chriſti geburt imland/
zü Heſſen vnbekant, biſz vff! diſe zwey negſt vergangene jar,/ Daſie Hans Staden von Homberg
aufz Heſſen durch ſein/ eygne erfarung erkant, vnd
ytzt durch den truck an tag gibt. Vnd zum andern
mal fleiſſig corrigirt vnd gebeſſert./ Dedicirt dem
Durchleuchtigen hochgebornen fürſten/ H. Philipſen Landtgraue zü Heſſen, Graff zü Catzen=/elu-
bogen, Dietz, Ziegenhain vn̄ Nidda, ſeinem G. H./
Miteyner verrede D. Ioh. Dryandri, genant Eychman,/ Ordinarij Profeſſoris Medici zü Marpurg./
Inhalt des büchlins volget nach den vorreden./
[*Colophon*] Getruckt zü *Marpurg* im/ Heſſen land,
bei Andres Colben,/ Vff Mariæ Geburts tag,/ Anno
M. D. LVII. *Very poor copy.* 4to. (2l. 2s. 2602)

STAMLER (John). Dialogvs. Iohannis Stamler.
Avgvstn./ De Diversarvm Gencivm Sectis/ et
Mvndi Religionibvs./ Regiſtrũ operis reſpice in
fine./ [*Colophon*] Impreſſum *Auguste:* per Erthar-
dum oglin. & Jeorgiũ Nadler Cura/ correctõne et
diligentia venerabilis domini Wolfgangi Aittinger/
pſpiteri Auguſteñ. ac bonarum Artium zc. Ma-
giſtri Collonienſs/ Anno noſtre ſalutis. 1. 50. &. 8.
die. 22. menſis May. zc./ *2 prel. leaves; viz. Title
engraved both sides,* 'Reverendo. in. Christo. Patri.

et . Domino.' *etc.* 1 *page;* ' ⁋ Germani . Freidancer .
et . Trviecrart . ad . Lectorem' *etc.* 1 *page. Text
XXXII folioed leaves;* ' Registrvm.' 3 *pp. Calf by
Hayday. Folio.* (1*l.* 11*s.* 6*d.* 2603)

STANHOPE (GEORGE). The early Converſion of
Iſlanders, a wiſe Expedient for propagating Chriſ-
tianity. A Sermon, Preached before the Incorporated Society for the Propagation of the Goſpel
in Foreign Parts; at their Anniversary Meeting in
the Pariſh-Church of St. Mary-le-Bow; On Friday
the 19th of Feb. 1713-14. By George Stanhope,
D.D. Dean of Canterbury, and Chaplain in Ordinary to Her Majesty. *London:* J. Downing, 1714.
39 *pp. With 2 Plans at pp. 36 and 37. Half mor.
8vo.* (4*s.* 6*d.* 2604)

STATE (THE) of the Sugar-Trade; shewing the
Dangerous Consequences that Muſt attend any additional Duty thereon. *London:* E. Say, 1747.
24 *pp. Half mor. 4to.* (4*s.* 6*d.* 2605)

STATE of the Britiſh and French Colonies in North
America, With Reſpeċt to Number of People,
Forces, Forts, Indians, Trade and other Advantages. In which are conſidered, I. The defenceleſs
Condition of our Plantations, and to what Cauſes
owing. II. Pernicious Tendency of the French
Encroachments, and the fitteſt Methods of fruſtrat-
ing them. III. What it was occaſioned their preſent Invaſion, and the Claims on which they ground
their Proceedings. With a Proper Expedient propoſed for preventing future Diſputes. In Two
Letters to a Friend. *London:* A Millar, MDCCLV.
Title and 150 *pp. 8vo.* (10*s.* 6*d.* 2606)

STATE (A) of the Claim of His Majeſty's Bermuda
Subjeċts to the Right of Gathering Salt at Turks
Iſlands, Referred to by the Governor, Council, and
Aſſembly of Bermuda, in their Memorial of the 7th
Day of May, 1790, to the Right Honourable Wil-
liam Wyndham Grenville, His Majeſty's Secretary
of State for the American Department. *London:*
Printed in the Year 1790. *Title and* 26 *pp. half
morocco. 4to.* (7*s.* 6*d.* 2607)

STEARNS (SAMUEL). The American Oracle. Comprehending An Account of Recent Discoveries in

the Arts and Sciences, with a variety of Religious, Political, Physical, and Philosophical subjects, Neceffary to be known in all Families, for the Promotion of their prefent Felicity and future Happiness. By the Honourable Samuel Stearns, LL.D. and Doctor of Physic; Astronomer to his Majesty's Province of Quebec, and New Brunswic; also to the Commonwealth of Massachusetts, and the State of Vermont, in America. *London:* J. Lackington, 1791. *viii and text 627 pp. Index xviii pp. Bound. 8vo.* (7s. 6d. 2608)

STEDMAN (C.) The History of the Origin, Progress, and Termination of the American War. By C. Stedman, who served under Sir W. Howe, Sir H. Clinton, and the Marquis Cornwallis. In Two Volumes. *London:* Printed for the Author; 1794. *Two Volumes.* Vol. I. *xv and 399 pp. 7 Plates at pp.* 127, 195, 210, 214, 352, 362, 377. Vol. II. *xv and 449 pp.* 'Index.' *13 pp. 8 Plates at pp.* 132, 185, 210, 329, 342, 358, 400, 412. *Old calf.* 4to. (1l. 11s. 6d. 2609)

STEPHEN (JAMES). The Speech of James Stephen, Esq. In the Debate in the House of Commons, March 6, 1809, on Mr. Whitbread's Motion relative to the late overtures of the American Government: With supplementary remarks on the recent Order in Council. *London:* J. Butterworth, and J. Hatchard, 1809. *iv and 126 pp. Half morocco. 8vo.* (4s. 6d. 2610)

STEPHENS (WILLIAM). The Castle-Builders; or, the History of William Stephens, of the Ifle of Wight, Efq; lately deceafed. A Political Novel, Never before publifhed in any Language. *London:* Printed for the Author. MDCCLIX. *xv and 198 pp.* 'Contents.' *pp. ix, and x. 8vo.* (10s. 6d. 2611)

STEPHENSON (MARMADUKE). A Call/ from/ Death to Life,/ and/ Out of the Dark wayes and Worfhips of the World where/ the Seed is held in Bondage under the Merchants of/ Babylon, Written by Marmaduke Stephenson ;/ Who (together with another dear Servant of the Lord called/ William Robinson) hath (fince the Writing hereof) fuffer-/ed Death, for bearing Witneffe to the fame

Truth,/ amongft the Profeffors of Boftons Jurifdic-
tion/ in New England./ With a True Copy of Two
Letters, which they Writ to the Lords/ People a
little before their Death./ And alfo the True Copy
of a Letter as it came to our hands, from/ a Friend
in New England, which gives a brief Relation of
the/ manner of their Martyrdom, with fome of the
Words which they/ expreft at the time of their fuf-
fering./ *London*, Printed for Thomas Simmons, at
the Sign of the/ Bull and Mouth near Alderfgate.
1660./ *32 pp. half mor.* 4*to.* (1*l.* 11*s.* 6*d.* 2612)

STEUART (ADAM). Some/ Observations/ and/
Annotations/ Upon the/ Apologetical Narration,/
Humbly fubmitted to the Honour-/able Houses of
Parliament;/ The moft Reverend and Learned/
Divines/ of the/ Assembly,/ And all the Proteftant
Churches here/ in this Ifland, and abroad./ *Lon-
don*,/ Printed for Chriftopher Meredith, and are to
be fold in/ Pauls Church-yard at the fign of the
Crane. 1643./ *4 prel. leaves, signed* ' A. S.' *and* 71
pp. half mor. 4*to.*   (7*s.* 6*d.* 2613)

STEUART (ADAM). An/ Answer/ to a/ Libell/
Intituled,/ A Coole Conference/ Betweene the
cleered/ Reformation/ and the/ Apologetical Narration,/ Brought together by a Wel-willer to both ;/
Wherein are cleerely refuted what ever he bringeth
a-/gainft the Reformation cleared, moft humbly
fub-/mitted to the judgement of the Honorable
Houfes/ of Parliament, the moft Learned and Re-/
verend Divines of the Affembly,/ and all the Re-
formed/ Churches./ By Adam Stevart./ Imprinted
at *London*, 1644./ *3 prel. leaves and 62 pp. half mor.*
4*to.*   (7*s.* 6*d.* 2614)

STEVENS (JOHN). A New Collection of Voyages
and Travels, Into feveral Parts of the World, none
of them ever before Printed in Englifh. Containing, 1. The Defcription, &c. of the Molucco and
Philippine Iflands, by L. de Argenfola. 2. A new
Account of Carolina, by Mr. Lawfon. 3. The
Travels of P. de Cieza, in Peru. 4. The Travels
of the Jefuits in Ethiopia. 5. The Captivity of the
Sieur Mouette in Fez and Morocco. 6. The Travels
of P. Teixeira from India to the Low-Countries by
Land. 7. A Voyage to Madagafcar by the Sieur

Cauche. In Two Volumes, Illuſtrated with ſeveral Maps and Cuts. *London,* J. Knapton, 1711. *Two Volumes.* Vol. I. 6 *prel. leaves including the collective title,* 'Molucco and Philippine Iſlands, &c.' 260 *pp. Index.* 8 *pp.* 'A New Voyage to Carolina;' *etc.* 3 *prel. leaves and* 258 *pp. Lately publiſh'd etc.* 1 *page. With map and* 2 *plates.* Vol. II. 5 *prel. leaves including collective title* 'Travels of P. de Cieza, &c.' 244 *pp. The contents and Index* 11 *pp.* 'The Travels of the Jesuits in Ethiopia:' *etc.* 2 *prel. leaves and* 264 *pp. The contents and Index* 16 *pp.* 'The Travels of the Sieur Mouette,' *etc.* 115 *pp. The contents and Index* 5 *pp.* 'The Travels of Peter Teixeira,' *etc.* 81 *pp. The contents and Index* 6 *pp.* 'A Voyage to Madagascar, *etc.* By Francis Cauche,' 77 *pp. Index.* 3 *pp. With* 2 *maps and plate. Large Paper, calf extra, gilt edges by F. Bedford.* 4*to.* (10*l.* 10*s.* 2615)

STIGLIANI (Tomaso). Del/ Mondo/ Nvovo/ del Cavalier/ Tomaſo Stigliani./ Venti Primi Canti./ Co i sommarii dell' istesso/ Autore dietro à ciaſchedun d' eſſi, e/ con vna lettera del medeſimo in fine,/ la qual diſcorre ſopra d' alcuni riceuu-/ti auuerti-mēti intorno à tutta l' opera./ Con Priuilegio del Sereniſſimo di P. P./ In *Piacenza* por Aleſſandro Bazacchi. 1617./ 700 *pp.* 'Gli Errori dell Stampa' *etc.* 6 *pp.* 12*mo.* (2*l.* 2*s.* 2616)

STILES (Ezra). A Discourse on the Christian Union: The Subſtance of which was delivered before The Reverend Convention of the Congregational Clergy In the Colony of Rhode-Island; Aſſembled at Bristol April 23. 1760. By Ezra Stiles, A.M. Pastor of the ſecond Congregational Church in Newport. *Boston:* N. E. Printed and ſold by Edes and Gill. MDCCLXI. 139 *pp. Half morocco.* 8*vo.* (4*s.* 6*d.* 2617)

STILES (Ezra). The United States elevated to Glory and Honor. A Sermon, Preached before His Excellency Jonathan Trumbull, Esq. L.L.D. Governor and Commander in Chief, And the Honorable The General Assembly of The State of Connecticut, Convened at Hartford, At the Anniverſary Election, May 8th, 1783. By Ezra Stiles,

D.D. President of Yale-College. *New-Haven:* Printed by Thomas & Samuel Green. M,DCC, LXXXIII. *96 pp. half mor. 8vo. (4s. 6d.* 2618)

STILES (EZRA). A History of three of the Judges of King Charles I. Major-General Whalley, Major-General Goffe, and Colonel Dixwell: Who, at the Restoration, 1660, Fled to America; and were secreted and concealed, in Massachusetts and Connecticut, for near thirty years. With an Account of Mr. Theophilus Whale, of Narraganfett, Suppofed to have been alfo one of the Judges. By President Stiles. *Hartford:* Printed by Elisha Babcock. 1794. *357 pp. Errata, and Advertisement 1 page. Portrait of Stiles facing Title, 8 plates at pp. 129, 77, 80, 114, 126, 136, 202, 345, numbered I to IX. Calf extra by Bedford. 8vo.* (1l. 1s. 2619)

STITH (WILLIAM). The History of the Firft Discovery and Settlement of Virginia: Being An Essay towards a General History of this Colony. By William Stith, A. M. Rector of Henrico Parifh, and one of the Governors of William and Mary College. *Williamsburg:* Printed by William Parks, M,DCC,XLVII. *viii and 331 pp.* 'An Appendix to the Firft Part of the History of Virginia,' *etc. v and 34 pp. Old calf. 8vo.* (1l. 11s. 6d. 2620)

STITH (WILLIAM). The History of the Firft Discovery and Settlement of Virginia. By William Stith, A.M. Prefident of the College of William and Mary in Virginia. Virginia, Printed: *London,* Reprinted for S. Birt in Ave-Mary-Lane. M.DCC. LIII. *viii and 331 pp.* 'An Appendix to the First Part of the History of Virginia,' *etc. v and 34 pp. Old calf. 8vo.* (1l. 11s. 6d. 2621)

STODDARD (SOLOMON). Gospel Order/ Revived,/ Being an Anfwer to a Book lately fet forth by the Reverend Mr. Increafe Mather, Prefident/ of Harvard Colledge, &c./ Entituled,/ The Order of the Gofpel, &c./ Dedicated to the Churches of Chrift in New-England./ By fundry Minifters of the Gofpel in New-England./ Printed in the Year 1700./ *6 prel. leaves; viz.* 'Advertifement.' *facing title; title,* 'The Epiftle Dedicatory, To the Churches of Chrift in N. England.' *8 pp. Text*

40 *pp.* *Fine copy in morocco by Francis Bedford.*
4to.   (4*l.* 4*s.* 2622)

> The Advertisement facing the title is as follows : " The *Reader* is
> defired to take Notice that the Prefs | in *Boston* is fo much under
> the aw of the Reverend | Author, whom we anfwer, and his
> Friends that we | could not obtain of the Printer there to print
> the fol-| lowing Sheets, which is the only true Reafon why we |
> have fent the Copy fo far for its Impreffion and where | it printed
> with fome Difficulty."

STODDARD (SOLOMON). The/ Doctrine/ of/ Inftituted Churches/ Explained and Proved/ from
the/ Word/ of/ God./ By Solomon Stoddard, A.M.
Minifter of the Gofpel in/ Northampton, New-
England./ *London :* Printed for Ralph Smith, at
the Bible under the Piazza of the Royal/ Exchange
in Cornhil. 1700./ *Title and* 34 *pp. morocco by
Bedford.* 4to.   (2*l.* 12*s.* 6*d.* 2623)

STODDARD (SOLOMON). The/ Way for a People/
To Live Long in the Land that/ God/ Hath given
them./ A Sermon/ Preached before His Excel-
lency,/ The Governour, the Honoured/ Council and
Affembly of the Province/ of the Maffachufetts-
Bay in New-England,/ on the 26. of May 1703.
At the Election/ of Her Majefties Council
By Solomon Stoddard,   / And Paftor of
Northampton./ *Boston :/* Printed by Bartholomew
Green and John Allen, for B   / and are to be
Sold at his Shop under the Weft End of the/ Town
Houfe. 1703./ *Title and* 25 *pp. morocco by Bedford.*
4to.   (2*l.* 2*s.* 2624)

STODDARD (SOLOMON). An Answer/ to some/
Cafes of Confcience/ Refpecting the Country./ By
Solomon Stoddard, A.M. Paftor in Northampton./
[*Colophon*] *Boston* in New-England :/ Printed by
B. Green : Sold by Samuel Gerrifh, at his Shop
near the/ Brick Meeting-Houfe in Corn Hill. June
25th. 1722./ 15 *pp. morocco extra by Bedford.*
4to.   (2*l.* 2*s.* 2625)

STORIES of popular Voyages and Travels ; with
illustrations. Containing abridged Narratives of
recent Travels of some of the most popular writers
on South America. With a preliminary sketch of
the Geography, History, and Productions of that
Country. New Edition. *London :* Whittaker,
Treacher, and Co., MDCCXXX. *Half-title, title, iv*

and 259 *pp. With Engraved title, map and* 3 *Plates.*
12*mo.* (2*s.* 6*d.* 2626)

STORK (Dr.) An Extract from the Account of
East Florida, Publiſhed by Dr. Stork, who reſided
a conſiderable Time in Auguſtine, the Metropolis
of that Province. With the obſervations of Denys
Rolle, who formed a Settlement on St. John's river,
in the ſame Province. With his Proposals to Such
Perſons as may be inclined to ſettle thereon. *London :* Printed in the year MDCCLXVI. *Title and* 39
pp. half mor. 8*vo.* (7*s.* 6*d.* 2627)

STORK (WILLIAM). A Description of East-Florida,
with a Journal, kept by John Bartram of Philadelphia, Botanist to his Majesty for The Floridas ;
upon A Journey from St. Augustine up the River
St. John's, as far as the Lakes. With Explanatory
Botanical Notes. Illuſtrated with an accurate
Map of East-Florida, and two Plans ; one of St.
Augustine, and the other of the Bay of Espiritu
Santo. The Third Edition, much enlarged and improved. *London :* W. Nicoll, MDCCLXIX. 2 *prel.
leaves, viii and* 40 *pp.* ' A Journal,' *etc. Title, xii and*
36 *pp. Map and* 2 *Plans.* 4*to.* (8*s.* 6*d.* 2628)

STORY (THOMAS). A Determination of the Case of
Mr. Thomas Story, and Mr. James Hoskins, Relating to an Affair of the Pennſylvania Company,
&c. *London :* J. Roberts, 1724. 11 *pp. Unbound.*
4*to.* (15*s.* 2629)

STOUGHTON (WILLIAM). An/ Assertion/ for/
True and Christian/ Church-Policie :/ Wherein/
Certain Politike Objections made against/ the
Planting of Pastors and Elders in/ every Congre-
gation are suffici=/ently answered. &c./ By/ Wil-
liam Stoughton/ Fellow of New Coll. Oxon./ and
Magistrate of the Colony of Mas=/sachusets, New
Eng./ *London :/* Printed in the Yeare, 1642./ 5
prel. leaves and 178 *pp. The Title Written. Calf.*
4*to.* (1*l.* 1*s.* 2630)

SUAREZ DE FIGUEROA (CHRISTOVAL). Hechos/
de Don Garcia/ Hvrtado de Mendoça,/ [Quatro]
Marques de Cañete./ A Don Ivan Andres/ Hur-
tado de Mendoça/ su hijo Marques de Cañete,/
Señor de las Villas de Argete/ y su partido, Mon-

tero mayor/ del Rey ñro señor, Guarda/ mayor de
la ciudad/ de Cuenca, ett³./ Por el Doctor Chris-
toval/ Suarez de Figueroa./ En *Madrid*, en la
Imprenta Real./ Año 1616./ *Engraved title*, 8 *prel.
leaves and* 324 *pp. old calf.* 4to. (*2l. 12s. 6d.* 2631)

Mendoza, the 4th Marquis di Canete, was Captain General of
Chile, and afterwards Viceroy of Peru.

SUCCINCT Account of the Treaties and Negociations between Great Britain and the United States
of America, relating to the Boundary between the
British possessions of Lower Canada and New
Brunswick, in North America, and the United
States of America. [*London.*] 206 *pp. Contents* 1
page. Map of North America. 8*vo.* (7*s. 6d.* 2632)

Privately printed, and having the autograph of the Earl of
Anglesey.

SUCCINCT (A) View of the Origin of our Colonies,
with Their Civil State, Founded by Queen Elizabeth, Corroborated by Succeeding Princes, and
Confirmed by Acts of Parliament; whereby The
Nature of the Empire eftablifhed in America, And
the Errors of various Hypotheses formed thereupon, may be clearly understood with Obfervations
on the Commercial, Beneficial and Perpetual Union
of the Colonies with this Kingdom. Being An
Extract from an Essay lately publifhed, Entitled
The Freedom of Speech and Writing, &c. *London:*
MDCCLXVI. *Title and* 46 *pp.* 8*vo.* (7*s. 6d.* 2633)

SUMMARY (A) View of the Rights of British
America, Set forth in fome Resolutions intended
for The Inspection of the prefent Delegates of the
People of Virginia, now in Convention. By a
Native, and Member of the Houfe of Burgeffes.
Williamsburg, Printed. *London*, Re-printed for
G. Kearsly, 1774. *2 prel. leaves, viz. Title and
Preface; Dedication* ' To the King' *pp. v—xvi,
Signed* 'Tribunus.' *Text pp.* 5—44. *Half morocco.*
8*vo.* (4*s. 6d.* 2634)

SUMMARY (A) Account of the present flourishing
State of the Island of Tobago, with a Plan of the
Island. *London:* S. Hooper, MDCCLXXVII. *iv and
pp.* 7—80. 8*vo.* (4*s. 6d.* 2635)

SUMMERSETT (JAMES, *a Negro*). The Original

Report of the celebrated Case of James Summersett which decided that American Slaves on reaching English ground are Free. *Manuscript. 132 pp. 4to.* (1*l.* 11*s.* 6*d.* 2635*)

SUPREMACY (The) of the British Legislature over the Colonies candidly discussed. *London: J. Johnson,* MDCCLXXV. *2 prel. leaves and 38 pp. Half morocco. 8vo.* (4*s.* 6*d.* 2636)

SUTCLIFF (Robert). Travels in some parts of North America, in the years 1804, 1805, & 1806, by Robert Sutcliff. *York: C. Peacock,* 1811. *xi and 293 pp. With 6 plates. Calf. 12mo.* (5*s.* 2637)

SYMMES (Thomas). Utile Dulci. Or, A Joco-Serious Dialogue, Concerning Regular Singing: Calculated for a Particular Town, (where it was publickly had, On Friday Oct. 12. 1722.) but may ferve fome other places in the fame Climate. By Thomas Symmes, Philomuficus. *Boston:* Printed by B. Green, for Samuel Gerrifh, near the Brick Meeting Houfe in Cornhill. 1723. *Title, ii and 59 pp. Half morocco. Small 8vo.* (15*s.* 2638)

AILFER (PATRICK). A True and Historical Narrative Of the Colony of Georgia In America, From the firſt Settlement thereof until this preſent Period: Containing The moſt authentick Faĉts, Matters and Tranſaĉtions therein; together with His Majeſty's Charter, Repreſentations of the People, Letters, &c. And a Dedication to his Excellency General Oglethorpe. By Pat. Tailfer, M.D. Hugh Anderson, M.A. Da. Douglas, and others, Land-holders in Georgia, at preſent in Charles-Town in South-Carolina. *Charles-Town,* South-Carolina: Printed by P. Timothy, for the Authors, M.DCC.XLI. *xviii and* 118 *pp. Half-mor.* 8vo.   (7s. 6d.   2639)

TALBOT (EDWARD ALLEN). Five Years Residence in the Canadas: Including a Tour through Part of the United States of America, in the Year 1823. By Edward Allen Talbot, Esq., of the Talbot Settlement, Upper Canada. In Two Volumes. *London:* Longman, 1824. *Two Volumes.* Vol. I. *xvi and* 419 *pp.* 1 *plate.* Vol. II. 400 *pp.* 1 *plate. Boards.* 8vo.   (7s. 6d.   2640)

TAMAIO DE VARGAS (THOMAS). Restavracion/ de la Civdad del Salvador,/ i baìa de Todos-Sanctos,/ en la Provincia del Brasil./ Por las Armas de/ Don Philippe ⅳ. el Grande,/ Rei Catholico/ De las Eſpañas i Indias, &c./ A Sv Mageſtad/ Don Thomas Tamaio de Vargas/ ſu Chroniſta./ Año 1628./ Con Privilegio./ En *Madrid:* Por la vivda de Alonso Martin./ 8 *prel. leaves, the eighth blank, and* 178 *folioed leaves.* 'Svmma de lo Particvlar' *etc.* 8 *pp. Vellum.* 4to.   (2l. 2s.   2641)

TAXATION no Tyranny; an Answer to the Resolutions and Address of the American Congress.
[By Dr. Samuel Johnson.] *London,* Cadell,
MDCCLXXV. *Half-title, title, and* 91 *pp. Half mor.*
8vo.   (4s. 6d. 2642)

TAXATION no Tyranny; an Answer to the Reso-
lutions and Address of the American Congress.
The Third Edition. *London:* T. Cadell, MDCCLXXV.
Half-title, title, and 91 *pp.* 8vo.   (4s. 6d. 2643)

TAXATION. The Pamphlet, entitled, "Taxation
no Tyranny," candidly considered, and it's arguments, and pernicious doctrines, Exposed and
Refuted. *London:* W. Davis, [1775.] *Half-title,
title, and text* 132 *pp. Calf extra by F. Bedford.*
8vo.   (2l. 2s. 2644)
With many manuscript additions and corrections in the handwriting of Burke.

TAXATION. An Answer to a Pamphlet, entitled
Taxation no Tyranny. Addressed to the Author,
and to Persons in Power. *London:* J. Almon,
MDCCLXXV. 63 *pp.* 8vo.   (4s. 6d. 2645)

TAXATION, Tyranny. Addressed to Samuel Johnson, L.L.D. *London:* J. Bew, M.DCC.LXXV. *Title
and* 80 *pp. Half morocco.* 8vo.   (4s. 6d. 2646)

TEMPLEMAN (THOMAS). A New Survey of the
Globe: Or, an Accurate Mensuration of all the
Empires, Kingdoms, Countries, States, principal
Provinces, Counties, & Islands in the World.
The Area is given in Square Miles, by which the
Extent, Magnitude, and true Proportion, that one
Country bears to another, are exactly known.
The Diſtant and Separate Territories, of every
Prince, and State, are collected together, and ſo
regularly plac'd. that at one View, their whole
Dominions may be seen. The chief City, or Town,
of every Kingdom, Province, and Island, the Lon-
gitude, Latitude, & nearest Distance from London
in British Miles. The Protestant Kingdoms and
States, distinguish'd from thoſe of the Roman
Catholicks; a Compariſon between the greatneſs
and extent of their ſeveral Dominions, the difference ballanc'd and demonſtrated. Also the Antient
Perſian and Roman Empires, compar'd with the
present Ruſsian, Turkish and other great Empires:

And what Proportion the Known and Habitable
Earth bears to ye Seas and unknown Parts. A
Collection of all the Noted Sea-Ports in the World,
ſhewing in what Country they are, & to whom
Subject, with their Longitude, Latitude, and diſ-
tance from the Port of London, by Sea; Alſo the
Settlements & Factories, belonging to the Eng-
liſh, Dutch, French, Portugueſe, Spaniards, &c.
in the East and West-Indies, Africa, and other
Parts. With Notes Explanatory & Political,
wherein the Number of People in all ye principal
Countries and Cities of Europe are severally cal-
culated from the Number of Houses or Bills of
Mortality. By Thomas Templeman of S^t. Edmunds-
Bury, Suffolk. Engraved by T. Cole in Great
Kirby Street Hatton Garden *London.* [1776?]
Engraved title, 'To the Honble James Reynolds,
Eſq;' *etc.* 1 *page, Introduction, List of Subscribers
and Table x pp. Plates numbered* 1 *to* 35. *Old calf.
Oblong* 4to. (15s. 2647)

TENNENT (GILBERT). The Neceſſity of holding
faſt the Truth repreſented in Three Sermons on
Rev. iii. 3. Preached at New-York, April 1742.
With an Appendix, Relating to Errors lately
vented by ſome Moravians in thoſe Parts. To
which are added, A Sermon on the Prieſtly-Office
of Chriſt, And another, On the Virtue of Charity.
Together with A Sermon of a Dutch Divine on
taking the little Foxes; faithfully tranſlated. By
Gilbert Tennent, M.A. Miniſter of the Goſpel at
New-Brunſwick, in New-Jerſey. *Boston:* Printed
and Sold by S. Kneeland and T. Green in Queen-
Street, over againſt the Priſon. MDCCXLIII. *Title,
vi and* 110 *pp.* 'Two Sermons' *etc. Title and* 37
pp. 'A Sermon By Abraham Hellenbrock,' *etc.
Title and* 31 *pp.* 8vo. (10s. 6d. 2648)

TENNENT (GILBERT). Sermons on Important
Subjects; adapted To the Perilous State of the
British Nation, lately preached in Philadelphia.
By Gilbert Tennent, A.M. Miniſter of the Gospel.
Philadelphia: Printed by James Chattin, at the
Neweſt-Printing-Office, on the South Side of the
Jerſey-Market. 1758. *xxxvii pp. one blank leaf,
and text* 425 *pp. Calf extra by F. Bedford.*
8vo. (15s. 2649)

TERNAUX-COMPANS (Henri). Notice sur la
Colonie de la Nouvelle Suède. Par H. Ternaux-
Compans. *Paris.* Arthur Bertrand, 1843. *Half-
title, title, text 29 pp. and map. Half morocco.*
8*vo.*   (5s. 2650)

TESTIMONY (The) of the People called Quakers,
given forth by a Meeting of the Reprefentatives of
faid People, in Pennsylvania and New-Jersey,
held at Philadelphia the twenty-fourth Day of the
firft Month, 1775. *Signed* ' James Pemberton.'
Single sheet. Folio.   (2s. 6d. 2651)

THACHER (Peter). A Sermon, preached to the
Society in Brattle Street, Boſton, November 14,
1790. And occasioned by the Death of The Hon.
James Bowdoin, Efq. L.L.D. F.R.S. Lately Governor of the Commonwealth of Massachusetts.
By Peter Thacher, A.M. Pastor of the Church in
Brattle Street. Printed at *Boston,* by I. Thomas
and E. T. Andrews, Faust's Statue, N°. 45, Newbury Street. MDCCXCI. *27 pp. Half morocco.*
4*to.*   (4s. 6d. 2652)

THATCHER (B. B.) Indian Biography or an
Historical Account of those individuals who have
been distinguished among the North American
Natives as Orators, Warriors, Statesmen, and
other remarkable Characters. By B. B. Thatcher,
Esq. In Two Volumes. *New-York:* J. & J. Harper,
1832. *Two Volumes.* Vol. I. *Title and pp.* 5—324.
With plate, and Portrait of Red Jacket. Vol. II.
Title and pp. 5—320. 12*mo.*   (5s. 2653)

THEVENOT (Melchisadec). Recueil/ de Voy-
ages/ de Mʳ/ Thevenot./ Dedié au Roy./ A
Paris,/ Chez Estienne Michallet/ ruë S. Jaques à
l' Image S. Paul./ M.DC.LXXXI./ Avec Privilege
du Roy./ *Title, on the reverse* ' Suite du Recueil.'
and 16 *pp. Map at page* 10. ' Découverte de quelques pays et Nations de l'Amerique Septentrionale.'
43 *pp. with* ' Carte, *etc.* 1673.' ' Voyage d'un Am-
bassadevr que le Tzaar de Moscovie envoya par
Terre a la Chine l' Année 1653. 18 *pp.* ' Explication des Lettres de la Figure ſuivante.' 2 *pp. with
map.* ' Discours sur l'Art de la Navigation,' *etc.*
32 *pp.* ' Histoire Naturelle de l'Ephemere.' 20 *pp.*
' Table' *etc. engraved figures* 13 *pp. with* 2 *folded*

plates. ' Histoire Naturelle du Cancellus, ou Bernard l'Hermite, Reprefentée par Figures.' 8 *pp.*
with plate. ' Le Cabinet de Mr. Svvammerdam,
Docteur en Medecine,' *etc.* 16 *pp.* *Old calf.*
8*vo.* (5*l.* 5*s.* 2654)

This little volume is particularly valued on account of its containing Father Marquette's Relation of his voyage down the Mississippi River in 1673, with the map of his route, &c.

THEVET (ANDREW). Historia/ dell' India Ame-
rica/ detta Altramente/ Francia Antartica,/ di M.
Andrea Tevet ;/ Tradotta di Francese in/ Lingva
Italiana, da/ M. Givseppe Horologgi./ Con Privilegio./ In *Vinegia* Appresso Gabriel/ Giolito
de' Ferrari/ MDLXI./ 16 *prel. leaves ; viz. Title, reverse blank,* ' All' Illvstriss. et Eccellentissimo Signore, Il Signor Paolo Giordano Orsino, Givseppe
Horologgi.' 14 *pp.* ' Tavola ' 16 *pp.* *Text* 363 *pp.*
' Registro ' 1 *page, followed by one leaf with Printer's
device. Vellum. Small 8vo.* (2*l.* 2*s.* 2655)

THEVET (ANDREW). ¶ The Nevv/found vvorlde,
or/ Antarctike, wherin is contai-/ned wōderful and
ftrange/ things, as well of humaine crea=/tures, as
Beaftes, Fifhes, Foules, and Ser-/pents, Trees,
Plants, Mines of/ Golde and Siluer : garnished
with/ many learned aucthorities,/ trauailed and
written in the French/ tong, by that excellent
learned/ man, mafter Andrevve/ Thevet./ And
now nevvly tranflated into Englifhe,/ wherein is
reformed the errours of/ the auncient Cofmo-/gra-
phers./ ¶ Imprinted at *London,*/ by Henrie Bynneman, for/ Thomas Hacket./ And are to be fold
at his fhop in Poules Church/ yard, at the figne of
the Key./ [*Colophon*] ' ¶ Imprinted at London, in
Knight-/rider ftrete, by Henry Bynneman, for/
Thomas Hacket./ 1568./ 8 *prel. leaves ; viz. Title
in a broad type metal border, the reverse blank,* ' ¶ To
the right honorable Sir Henrie Sidney, Knight of
the moft Noble order of the Garter, Lorde Prefident
of Wales, and Marches of the fame, Lord Deputie
Generall of the Queenes Maiefties Realme of Ireland, Your humble Orator Thomas Hacket wifheth
the fauoure of God, long and happy life, encreafe of
honor, continuall health and felicitie.' 4 *pp.* ' ¶ An
Admonition to the Reader.' 1 *page.* ' In prayfe of
the Author.' 1 *page.* ' ¶ To my Lord the Right

reuerend Cardinall of Sens, keper of the great
feales of France : Andrew Theuet wifheth peace
and felicitie.' 8 pp. *Text* 138 *folioed leaves.* ' ¶ The
Table of the Chapters of this prefent Boke.' 4 *vp.
Fine copy.* 4*to.*   (10*l.* 10*s.* 2656)

THEY Run and We Run Written on the late Engagement between Admiral Keppel & the Duc de
Chartres July 27th. 1778 off Ushant. *A song, with
music. Single sheet, half mor. Folio.* (3*s.* 6*d.* 2657)

THOM (ADAM). The Claims to the Oregon Territory considered. By Adam Thom, Esq., Recorder
of Rupert's Land. *London* : Smith, Elder and Co.,
1844. *iv and* 44 *pp.* 8*vo.*   (2*s.* 6*d.* 2658)

THOMAS (DALBY). An/ Hiftorical Account/ of
the/ Rife and Growth of the/ Weft-India/ Colonies,/ And of the Great Advantages they/ are to
England, in refpect/ to Trade/. Licenced According to Order/. *London,*/ Printed for Jo Hindmarfh
at the Golden-Ball, over/. againft the Royal-Exchange. 1690./ 3 *prel. leaves and* 53 *pp. Half calf.*
4*to.*   (1*l.* 11*s.* 6*d.* 2659)

THOMAS (GABRIEL). An Hiftorical and Geographical Account/ of the/ Province and Country/
of/ Pensilvania ;/ and of/ Weft-New-Jerfey/ in/
America./ The Richnefs of the Soil, the Sweetnefs
of the Situation,/ the Wholefomenefs of the Air,
the Navigable Rivers, and/ others, the prodigious
Encreafe of Corn, the flourifhing/ Condition of the
City of Philadelphia, with the ftately/ Buildings,
and other Improvements there. The ftrange/
Creatures, as Birds, Beafts, Fifhes, and Fowls,
with the/ feveral forts of Minerals, Purging Waters,
and Stones,/ lately difcovered. The Natives,
Aborigines,/ their Lan-/guage, Religion, Laws,
and Cuftoms ; The firft Planters,/ the Dutch,
Sweeds, and Englifh, with the number of/ its In-
habitants; As alfo a Touch upon George Keith's/
New Religion, in his fecond Change fince he left
the/ Quakers./ With a Map of both Countries./
By Gabriel Thomas,/ who refided there about
Fifteen Years./ *London,* Printed for, and Sold by
A. Baldwin, at/ the Oxon Arms in Warwick-Lane,
1698./ 4 *prel. leaves followed by map and* ' Hiftory

of Penſilvania,' 55 *pp.* 'History of New-Jersey,'
6 *prel. leaves and* 34 *pp.* 8*vo.* (1*l.* 11*s.* 6*d.* 2660)

THOMAS (Pascoe). A True and Impartial Journal
of a Voyage to the South - Seas, and Round the
Globe, In His Majeſty's Ship the Centurion, Under
the Command of Commodore George Anſon.
Wherein All the material Incidents during the
ſaid Voyage, from its Commencement in the Year
1740 to its Concluſion in 1744, are fully and faithfully related, having been Committed to Paper at
the Time they happen'd. Together with ſome
hiſtorical Accounts of Chili, Peru, Mexico, and the
Empire of China; Exact Deſcriptions of ſuch
Places of Note as were touch'd at. And Variety
of occaſional Remarks. To which is added, A
large and General Table of Longitudes and Latitudes, aſcertain'd from accurate obſervations, or
(where thoſe are wanting) from the beſt printed
Books and Manuſcripts taken from the Spaniards
in this Expedition: Alſo the Variations of the
Compaſs throughout the Voyage, and the Soundings and Depths of Water along the different
Coaſts: And laſtly, several curious Observations
on a Comet ſeen in the South Seas, on the Coaſt of
Mexico. By Pascoe Thomas, Teacher of the Mathematicks on board the Centurion. *London,* S.
Birt. MDCCXLV. 8 *prel. leaves and* 347 *pp. Appendix* 39 *pp. Old calf.* 8*vo.* (10*s.* 6*d.* 2661)

THOMPSON (Thomas). An Account of Two
Missionary Voyages By the Appointment of the
Society for the Propagation of the Goſpel in
Foreign Parts. The one to New Jersey in North
America, the other from America to the Coaſt of
Guiney. By Thomas Thompson, A.M. Vicar of
Reculver in Kent. *London:* Benj. Dod, MDCCLVIII.
2 *prel. leaves and* 87 *pp.* 8*vo.* (10*s.* 6*d.* 2662)

THOROWGOOD (Thomas). Ievvs in America,/
or,/ Probabilities/ That the Americans are of/ that
Race./ With the removall of ſome/ contrary rea-
ſonings, and earneſt de/ſires for effectuall endeavours to make them Chriſtian./ Propoſed by Tho:
Thorovvgood, B.D. one of the/ Aſſembly of Divines./ *London,* Printed by W. H. for Tho. Slater,
and are be to ſold/ at his ſhop at the ſigne of the

Angel in Duck lane, 1650./ 20 *prel. leaves; viz.
Title, the reverse blank,* ' To the Honovrable Knights
and Gentlemen that have refidence in, and relation
to the County of Norfolk, Peace, from the God of
Peace.' 14 *pp.* 'The Preface to the Reader.' 8 *pp.*
' An Epiftolicall Difcourfe Of Mr. Iohn Dvry, To
Mr. Thorowgood.' 16 *pp. Text* 139 *pp. Half mo-
rocco.* 4*to.* (4*l.* 4*s.* 2663)

THOROWGOOD (THOMAS). Jews/ in/ America,/
or/ Probabilities, that thofe Indians are/ Judaical,
made more probable by fome Ad-/ditionals to the
former Conjectures./ An Accurate Discourse is
premifed of/ Mr. John Elliot, (who firft preached
the Gofpel/ to the Native in their own Language)
touching/ their Origination, and his Vindication of
the/ Planters./ Tho. Thorowgood S. T. B. Nor-
folciencis./ *London,*/ Printed for Henry Brome at
the Gun in Ivie-lane. 1660./ 5 *prel. leaves; viz.
Title, reverse blank,* ' To the King's Most Excellent
Majesty.' 8 *pp;* ' To the Noble Knights, Ladies,
and Gentlemen of Norfolk,' *etc.* 33 *pp.* ' Jevves in
America. Summe of the firft Treatife.' 2 *pp; half-
title,* ' Jewes in America.' ' The learned Conjectures of Reverend Mr. John Eliot touching the
Americans,' *etc.* 28 *pp.* ' Chap. I. A short Difcourfe,
concerning the New World, or America." 67 *pp.*
4*to.* (4*l.* 4*s.* 2664)

THOUGHTS on Trade in General, our West-Indian
in Particular, our Continental Colonies, Canada,
Guadaloupe, and the preliminary Articles of Peace.
Addressed to the Community. *London :* John
Wilkie, MDCCLXIII. 86 *pp; dated* ' December 1762.'
and signed ' Ignotus.' *half mor.* 8*vo.* (4*s.* 6*d.* 2665)

THOUGHTS on the Origin and Nature of Government Occafioned by The late Difputes between
Great Britain and her American Colonies. Written
in the Year 1766. *London :* T. Becket and P. A.
de Hondt, MDCCLXIX. 64 *pp. Half morocco.*
8*vo.* (4*s.* 6*d.* 2666)

THOUGHTS on the Cause of the present Discontents. The Fourth Edition. *London,* J. Dodsley,
MDCCLXX. *Title and* 118 *pp. Half morocco.*
8*vo.* (5*s.* 6*d.* 2667)

THOUGHTS on the Late Transactions respecting Falkland's Iflands. [By Dr. Samuel Johnson.] *London :* T. Cadell, MDCCLXXI. *Title and 75 pp. Half morocco. 8vo.* (4s. 6d. 2668)

THOUGHTS on the Late Transactions respecting Falkland's Iflands. The Second Edition. *London :* T. Cadell, MDCCLXXI. *Half-title, title, and 75 pp. Half morocco. 8vo.* (4s. 6d. 2669)

THOUGHTS on the Late Transactions respecting Falkland's Iflands. London : Printed, *New-York :* Re-printed, by H. Gaine, at his Book-Store and Printing-Office, at the Bible and Crown, in Hanover-Square. M, DCC, LXXI. 48 pp. *Half morocco. 8vo.* (7s. 6d. 2670)

THOUGHTS on the Act For making more Effectual Provifion for the Government of the Province of Quebec. *London :* T. Becket, MDCCLXXIV. *Title and pp. 5-39. Half morocco. 8vo.* (5s. 6d. 2671)

THOUGHTS upon the Political Situation of the United States of America, in which that of Massachusetts Is more particularly confidered. With some Observations on the Constitution for a Federal Government. Addressed to the People of the Union. By a Native of Boston. Printed at Worcester, Massachusetts, by Isaiah Thomas. MDCCLXXXVIII. 209 pp. (7s. 6d. 2672)

THOUGHTS On Civilization, And the gradual Abolition of Slavery in Africa and the Weft Indies. Printed for J. Sewell, No. 32, Cornhill. [*London,* 1790 ?] 12 pp. *Half mor. 8vo.* (3s. 6d. 2673)

THOUGHTS on the Canada Bill, now depending in Parliament. *London :* J. Debrett, M.DCC.XCI. *Half-title, title, and 50 pp. half mor. 8vo.* (4s. 6d. 2674)

THREE Letters to a Member of Parliament, On the Subject of the Present Dispute with our American Colonies. *London,* T. Lowndes, MDCCLXXV. *Title and 74 pp. Half mor. 8vo.* (4s. 6d. 2675)

THROOP (BENJAMIN). Religion and Loyalty, the Duty and Glory of a People ; Illustrated in a Sermon. From 1 Peter 2. 17. Preached before the General Assembly of the Colony of Connecticut, at Hartford, On the Day of the Anniverfary Election, May 11th, 1753. By Benjamin Throop, A.M. Paftor of a Church in Norwich. *New-London*: Printed by Timothy Green, Printer to the Governor and Company, MDCCLVIII. *Title and pp. 5-37. 12mo.*   (7s. 6d. 2676)

THUMB (THOMAS). The Monster of Monsters: A true and faithful Narrative of a moft remarkable Phænomenon lately feen in this Metropolis; to the great Surprize and Terror of His Majesty's good Subjects: Humbly Dedicated to all the Virtuofi of New-England. By Thomas Thumb, Efq. [*Boston*], Printed in July 1754. 24 pp. *Red morocco gilt. 12mo.*   (2l. 2s. 2677)

THYSIUS (ANTONIUS). Antonii Thysii JC./ His-toria Navalis,/ Sive/ Celeberrimorvm/ Præliorum,/ quæ/ Mari ab antiquiffimis temporibus ufque ad Pacem Hi-/fpanicum Batavi, Fœderatiq; Belgæ, utplurimum victores/ gefferunt, luculenta defcrip-tio./ *Lugduni Batavorum,/* Ex Officina Joannis Maire, cIɔ Iɔclvii./ *4 prel. leaves, 305 pp. and 7 pp. of Index. Calf extra. 4to.*   (1l. 1s. 2678)

TITFORD (W. J.) Sketches towards a Hortus Botanicus Americanus; or, Coloured Plates (with a Catalogue and concise and familiar description of many species) of New and Valuable Plants of the West Indies and North and South America. Also of several others, Natives of Africa and the East Indies: Arranged after the Linnæan System. With a concise and comprehensive Glossary of terms, prefixed, and a general Index. By W. J. Titford, M.D. Corresponding Member of the So-ciety for the Encouragement of Arts, &c. *London*: Printed for the Author, by C. Stower, Hackney: 1811. *15 prel. leaves including colored Frontispiece, and pp. 4-137. 17 colored plates; Text to plates 30 pp. English Index, 4 pp. Addenda, iv pp. List of Subscribers, 4 pp. 4to.*   (10s. 6d. 2679)

TJASSENS (JOHAN). Zee-Politie,/ Der/ Vereenigde Nederlanden,/ Vertoont in een Tafel,/ Ende in twee Boecken befchreven,/ door/ Johan Tjassens,/ Waer achter gevoecht zijn eenige Saecken tot on-/derrechtnge, en Kenniffe, tot de Politie die-nende. In *'sGraven-Hage,/* By Johan Vely Boeck-verkooper, A°. 1669.*/ 24 prel. leaves and 391 pp. Large paper. Vellum. 4to.* (2l. 2s. 2680)

TOUCH STONE (A) for the Clergy. To which is added, a Poem, wrote By a Clergyman in Virginia, In a Storm of Wind and Rain. Printed in the Year 1771. *16 pp. 8vo.* (4s. 6d. 2681)

TRACTS (SELECT) relating to Colonies. Consisting of I. An Effay on Plantations. By Sir Francis Bacon Lord Chancellor of England. II. Some Paffages taken out of the Hiftory of Florence, &c. III. A Treatife. By John De Witt Penfioner of Holland. IV. The Benefit of Plantations of Colonies. By William Penn. V. A Difcourfe concerning Plantations. By Sir Josiah Child. *London,* J. Roberts. *4 prel. leaves and 40 pp. Unbound. 8vo.* (7s. 6d. 2682)

TRATADO de Amistad, Límites y Navegacion concluido entre el Rey Nuestro Señor y los Estados Unidos de América : Firmado en San Lorenzo el Real à 27 de Octubre de 1795. *Madrid,* 1796. *Title and 54 pp. In double columns, in Spanish and English,* 'Modelo del Pasaporte' (2). *Half morocco. 4to.* (7s. 6d. 2683)

TRAVELLER'S DIRECTORY (THE), and Emigrant's Guide ; containing general descriptions of different routes through the States of New-York, Ohio, Indiana, Illinois, and the Territory of Michigan, with short descriptions of the Climate, Soil, Productions, Prospects, &c. *Buffalo :* Steele & Faxon. 1832. *82 pp. Contents 2 pp. Boards. 12mo.* (2s. 6d. 2684)

TRAVELLER'S GUIDE (THE) to America ; comprehending a concise and accurate description of the Western States of Alabama Mississippi, Louisiana, Tennessee, Kentucky, Michigan, Indiana, Missouri, and the Territory of Illinois, with necessary instructions and advice to Settlers and Emigrants, also, an Account of Upper and Lower Canada, With much useful Information concerning the State of the Country, Soil, Provisions, &c. and Two Letters from Mr. Emmett, Containing interesting and valuable remarks on the State of Society, pointing out those Trades and qualifications which prove most advantageous in the United

States. *Cork:* John Bolster, Patrick Street. 1818.
71 *pp. 12mo.* (4*s.* 6*d.* 2685)

TRAVELS (The) Of feveral Learned Miſſioners of
the Society of Jesus, into Divers Parts of the
Archipelago, India, China, and America. Containing a general Defcription of the moſt remar-
able Towns; with a particular Account of the
Cuſtoms, Manners and Religion of thoſe feveral
Nations, the whole interfpers'd with Philoſophical
Obſervations and other curious Remarks. Tranflated from the French Original publiſh'd at Paris
in the Year 1713. *London:* R. Goſling, MDCCXIV.
8 *prel. leaves and* 336 *pp. Index, Books Printed, etc.*
16 *pp.* 2 *plates at pp.* 176 *and* 215. *Old calf.*
8*vo.* (7*s.* 6*d.* 2686)

TRAVELS in North America. *Dublin:* Printed by
Brett Smith, Mary-Street. 1824. 180 *pp. including Frontispiece and Title; woodcuts on pp.* 93, 123,
140, 145. *12mo.* (2*s.* 6*d.* 2687)

TREATIES/ (Several)/ of/ Peace and Commerce/
Concluded between the late/ King/ Of Bleſſed Memory Deceaſed,/ and other/ Princes and States;/
with/ Additional Notes in the Margin, Referring/
to the feveral Articles in each Treaty, and a Table./
Reprinted and Publiſhed by His Majeſties/ Efpecial
Command./ *London/* Printed by His Majeſties
Printers, and fold by/ Edward Poole at the Sign
of the Ship over a-/gainſt the Royal Exchange.
1686./ 2 *prel. leaves; viz. Title, reverse blank,* 'Table
of the Treaties.' 1 *page. Text* 269 *pp. Half morocco.*
4*to.* (10*s.* 6*d.* 2688)

TREATIES. A General Collection of Treatys Declarations of War, Manifeſtos, and other Publick
Papers, Relating to Peace and War, Among the
Potentates of Europe, from 1648 to the preſent
Time. Particularly The Treaty of Munſter 1648.
The Pyrenean Treaty, with the French King's and
the Infanta's Renunciation of the Spaniſh Dominions, 1659. The Sale of Dunkirk 1662. The
Peace betwixt England and France, and England
and Holland in 1667. The Treaty of Aix-la-Cha-
pelle. The Triple League 1668. Treatys of Commerce between England, France, Spain and Holland. Treaty of Nimeguen 1678. Defenſive Alliance

betwixt England and Holland 1678./ Declarations
of War by the Allys againſt France 1688, 1689 and
1702. The firſt Grand Alliance 1689. The ſeparate
Peace betwixt France and Savoy 1696. Treaty of
Reſwick 1697. Treatys of Partition 1698, &c.
The ſecond Grand Alliance. Treaty for ſecuring
the Hanover Succeſſion. Uſurpations of France
ſince the Treaty of Munſter. The Right of the
Crown of England to Hudſon's-Bay. With many
others, to be ſeen in the Contents. To which is
prefix'd, An Hiſtorical Account of the French
King's Breach of the moſt Solemn Treatys. *London:* J. Darby 1710. 44 *and* 448 *pp. Old calf.*
8*vo.*   (7*s.* 6*d.* 2689)

TREATIES. A General Collection of Treatys, De-
clarations of War, Manifeſtos, and other Publick
Papers, relating to Peace and War. In Four
Volumes. *etc.* The Second Edition. *London:* J. J.
and P. Knapton, *etc.* M.DCC.XXXII. *Four Volumes.*
Vol. I. 32 *and* 448 *pp.* Vol. II. *xxii, Errata i, and*
560 *pp.* 'The Contraƈt of Marriage of the moſt
Chriſtian King with the moſt Serene Infanta, eldeſt
Daughter of the Catholick King. The 7th of No-
vember, 1659.' 23 *pp.* Vol. III. *xxxix and* 492 *pp.*
Vol. IV. 4 *prel. leaves and* 458 [490] *pp.* 'Cata-
logue' *etc.* 13 *pp. Old calf.* 8*vo.* (1*l.* 1*s.* 2690)

TREATISE (A) on the Cotton Trade: In twelve
Letters. Addreſſed to the Levant Company, Weſt-
India Planters, and Merchants. By Experience.
Printed for the Author, *London;* [17—]. *Half-
title, title, iii to vi and* 63 *pp.* 12*mo.* (3*s.* 6*d.* 2691)

TREATY/ Of Peace,/ Good Correſpondence & Neu-
trality/ in/ America,/ Between the moſt Serene
and Mighty Prince/ James II./ By the Grace of
God,/ King of Great Britain, France and Ireland,/
Defender of the Faith, &c./ And the moſt Serene
and Mighty Prince/ Lewis XIV./ The Moſt
Chriſtian King:/ Concluded the $\frac{6}{16}$th Day of Novemb. 1686./ Publiſhed by His Majeſties Command./ *In the Savoy:* Printed by Thomas Newcomb, One of/ His Majeſties Printers. MDCLXXXVI./
20 *pp. Half morocco.* 4*to.* (7*s.* 6*d.* 2692)

TREATY (The) Held with the Indians of the Six
Nations at Philadelphia, in July 1742. To which

is Prefix'd An Account of the firft Confederacy of
the Six Nations, their prefent Tributaries, De-
pendents, and Allies. *London:* Re-printed. T.
Sowle Raylton and Luke Hinde, [1743?] *xii and*
38 *pp. Half morocco.* 8*vo.*   (10*s.* 6*d.* 2693)

TREATY of Amity, Commerce, and Navigation,
between His Britannic Majesty and the United
States of America; by their President, with the
advice and consent of the Senate, Nov. 19, 1794.
London: J. Debrett, 1795. 25 *pp. Half morocco.*
8*vo.*   (2*s.* 6*d.* 2694)

TROTT (NICHOLAS). The Laws of the Britifh Plantations in America, Relating to the Church and
the Clergy, Religion and Learning. Collected in
One Volume. By Nicholas Trott, LL.D. Chief
Juftice of the Province of South-Carolina. *London:* B. Cowse. MDCCXXI. 13 *prel. leaves and* 435
pp. Large paper. Calf. Folio. (1*l.* 11*s.* 6*d.* 2695)

TRVE (THE)/ Relation/ of that vvor-/thy Sea Fight,
which/ two of the Eaft India Shipps, had/ with 4
Portingals, of great force and bur-/then, in the
Perfian Gulph./ With the Lamentable/ Death of
Captaine Andrew/ Shilling./ With/ other Memorable Ac-/cidents, in that/ Voiage./ Printed this
2. of Iuly./ *London.*/ Printed by I. D. for Nathaniel Newbery and William/ Sheffard, and are
to be fold in Popes-head Alley./ 1622./ *Title,
and* 22 *pp.* 4*to.*   (2*l.* 2*s.* 2696)

TRUE (A) State Of the Prefent difference between
the Royal African Company, and the Separate
Traders: Shewing The Irregularities and Impofitions of the Joint-Stock Managers; the Ufeleinefs
of their Forts; the Expence they are at in the
Maintenance of the fame; the Charge of fupporting
them in a Condition of Defence; the vaft Sums
they have receiv'd by the Ten per Cent. Duty in
order thereunto, and what has been mifapply'd to
their own private Ufes; the Advantages and Reafonablenefs of an Open Trade to Africa; and,
laftly, the Danger of an Exclufive Trade, not only
to the Traders of South and North Britain, but, to
our American Plantations. Written by a True
Lover of his Country, and humbly fubmitted to

the Wife Confideration of Both Houfes of Parliament. *London :* Printed in the Year 1710. *40 pp.
With plan at page* 5. *4to.* (10s. 6d. 2697)

TRUE (A) Account of the Aloe Americana or
Africana, Which is now in Bloffom in Mr.
Cowell's Garden at Hoxton ; Which is upwards
of Twenty Foot high, and has already put forth
Thirty Branches for Flowers, all upon one Stem,
Twelve whereof are already fairly Opened and
Blown out. As also Of Two other Exotick Plants,
call'd, the Cereus, or Torch-Thiftle, Which have
likewife put forth their Bloffoms in Mr. Cowell's
faid Garden. The like whereof has never been
feen in England before. *London :* T. Warner,
1729. *4 prel. leaves and text* 44 *pp. With copperplate of the Torch-Thistle at page* 40. *Half morocco.
8vo.* (7s. 6d. 2698)

TRUE (A) State of the Case Between the Britifh
Northern-Colonies and the Sugar Iflands In Ame-
rica, Impartially Confidered, With Refpect to the
Bill now depending in the Right Honourable the
Houfe of Lords, Relating to the Sugar Trade.
M.DCC.XXXII. *Title and text* 46 *pp. Half morocco.
4to.* (10s. 6d. 2699)

TRUE (A) and Particular Relation Of the Dreadful
Earthquake Which happen'd At Lima, the Capital
of Peru, and the neighbouring Port of Callao, On
the 28th of October, 1746. With an Account likewife of every Thing material that paffed there
afterwards to the end of November following.
Publifhed at Lima by Command of the Viceroy,
And Tranflated from the Original Spanifh, By a
Gentleman who refided many Years in thofe
Countries. To which is added, A Description of
Callao and Lima before their Deftruction ; and of
the Kingdom of Peru in general, with its Inhabitants ; fetting forth their Manners, Cuftoms, Religion, Government, Commerce, &c. Interfperfed
with Paffages of Natural Hiftory and phyfiological
Difquifitions ; particularly an Enquiry into the
Cause of Earthquakes. The Whole illuftrated with
a Map of the Country about Lima, Plans of the
Road and Town of Callao, another of Lima; and
feveral Cuts of the Natives, drawn on the Spot

by the Tranflator. The Second Edition. *London :*
T. Osborne, MDCCXLVIII. *xxiii and text* 341 *pp.*
Map of Lima, and plates numbered 1 to IX. Old calf.
8vo. (7s. 6d. 2700)

TRVE (The) Sentiments of America : Contained in
a Collection of Letters sent from the Hovse of
Representatives of the Province of Massachvsetts
Bay to several Persons of High Rank in this
Kingdom. Together with certain Papers relating
to a svpposed Libel on the Governor of that Pro-
vince and a Dissertation on the Canon and the
Fevdal Law. *London,* I. Almon, 1768. *Title,*
' The following refolution ' *etc.* 1 *page : Text pp.*
5-158. *Half morocco. 8vo.* (7s. 6d. 2701)

TRUE (The) Conftitutional Means For putting an
End to the Disputes between Great-Britain and
her American Colonies. *London,* T. Becket and
P. A. De Hondt, MDCCLXIX. *Title and* 38 *pp.*
Half morocco. 8vo. (4s. 6d. 2702)

TRUTH Triumphant or a Defence of the Church of
England, against The Second Solemn League and
Covenant, published under the Title of the Glorious
Combination &c. With Addresses to the Members
of the Dutch Churches, and To all Friends of Re-
ligion, Liberty, and Peace. *New-York,* MDCCLXIX.
Title, Preface, and text 64 *pp. Half morocco.*
4to. (1l. 1s. 2702*)

TRUMBULL (John). Autobiography, Reminis-
cences and Letters of John Trumbull, from 1756.
to 1841. *New-York & London :* Wiley and Putnam.
New-Haven : B. L. Hamlen. 1841. *xvi and* 439
pp. With 23 *plates. 8vo.* (7s. 6d. 2703)

TRYON (Thomas). Tryon's Letters, Domeftick
and Foreign, To feveral Perfons of Quality : Occafionally diftributed in Subjects, Viz. Philofophical,
Theological, and Moral. By Tho. Tryon. Author
of the Way to Health, Long Life, and Happinefs.
London : Geo. Conyers, and Eliz. Harris, 1700.
Title and 240 *pp. 8vo.* (10s. 6d. 2704)

TRYON (Thomas). Tryon's Letters upon Several
Occafions. viz. 1. Of Hearing. 2. Of Smelling. 3.
Of Tafting. 4. Of Seeing. 5. Of Feeling. 6. Of
the Making of Coal-Fires. 7. Of the Making of

Bricks, Tyles, &c. 8. Of Religion. 9. Of Dropfies.
10. Of various Opinions in Religion. 11. Of the
Humanity of Chrift. 12. Of an Afflicted Mind.
13. Of Faith, Hope and Charity. 14. Of God's
Permiffion for Killing and Eating of Beafts. 15.
Of a Soldier's Life. 16. Of the Fountain of Dark-
ness. 17. Of the Fountain of Love and Light. 18.
Of Cleannefs. 19. Of Flefh-Broaths, &c. 20. Of
the Right and Left Hands. 21. Of Corpulency of
the Body. 22. Of Fevers. 23. Of Education. 24.
Of Smells. 25. Of Predeftination. 26. Of Death.
27. Of Judicial Astrology. 28. Of Perpetual Mo-
tion. 29. Of Mufick. 30. Of Languages. 31. Of
Times for Eating. 32. To a Planter of Sugar. 33.
To a Gentleman in Barbadoes. 34. To a Planter,
about the Manufactury of Cotton. 35. Of the
Making of Sugar. 36. Of the Burial of Birds. 37.
Of Fermentation. By Tho. Tryon. Author of the
Way to Health, Long Life, and Happinefs. *London:* Geo. Conyers, and Eliz. Harris, 1700. 7
prel. leaves and 240 *pp.* 8*vo.* (7*s.* 6*d.* 2705)

TUCKER (GEORGE). The Life of Thomas Jefferson,
Third President of the United States ; with parts
of his Correspondence never before Published,
and notices of his Opinions on Questions of Civil
Government, National Policy, and Constitutional
Law. By George Tucker, Professor of Moral
Philosophy in the University of Virginia. In Two
Volumes. *London:* Charles Knight, MDCCCXXXVII.
Two Volumes. Vol. I. *xxii and* 612 *pp. Portrait of
Jefferson.* Vol. II. *x and* 587 *pp. Cloth boards.*
8*vo.* (10*s.* 6*d.* 2706)

TUCKER (JOHN). A Sermon Preached at Cam-
bridge, before his Excellency Thomas Hutchinson,
Efq ; Governor: His Honor Andrew Oliver, Efq ;
Lieutenant-Governor, The Honorable His Ma-
jesty's Council, And the Honorable House of Re-
presentatives, of the Province of the Maffachufetts-
Bay in New-England, May 29th. 1771. Being
the Anniverfary for the Election of His Majesty's
Council for faid Province. By John Tucker, A.M.
Paftor of the Firft Church in Newbury. *Boston:*
New-England: Printed by Richard Draper,
Printed to His Excellency the Governor, and the
Honorable His Majefty's Council. MDCCLXXI. 63
pp. Half morocco. 8*ro.* (7*s.* 6*d.* 2707)

TUCKER (Josiah). An Humble Address and earnest Appeal to those respectable personages in Great-Britain and Ireland, who, by their great and permanent interest in Landed property, their liberal education, elevated rank and enlarged views, are the ablest to judge, and the fittest to decide, whether a connection with, or a separation from the Continental Colonies of America, be most for the national advantage, and the lasting benefit of their Kingdoms. By Josiah Tucker, D.D. Dean of Glocester. *Glocester:* R. Raikes, m.dcc.lxxv. 93 pp. 'An Account' *etc. folded sheet at page* 49. *Half morocco.* 8vo. (4s. 6d. 2708)

TUCKER (Josiah). An Humble Address and earnest appeal to those respectable personages in Great-Britain and Ireland, who, by their great and permanent Interest in Landed property, their liberal education, elevated rank, and enlarged views are the ablest to judge, and the fittest to decide, whether a connection with, or a separation from the Continental Colonies of America, be most for the national advantage, and the lasting benefit of these Kingdoms. Second Edition, Corrected. By Josiah Tucker, D.D. Dean of Glocester. *Glocester:* R. Raikes; m.dcc.lxxv. 93 pp. ' An Account' *etc. folded sheet at page* 49. *Half morocco.* 8vo. (4s. 6d. 2709)

TUCKER (Josiah). A Letter to Edmund Burke, Efq; Member of Parliament for the City of Bristol, and Agent for the Colony of New York, &c. in answer to his Printed Speech, said to be spoken in the House of Commons on the Twenty-Second of March, 1775. By Josiah Tucker, D.D. Dean of Glocester. *Glocester:* R. Raikes; m.dcc.lxxv. 58 pp. *Half morocco.* 8vo. (4s. 6d. 2710)

TUCKER (Josiah). A Series of Answers to certain popular Objections against separating from the Rebellious Colonies, and discarding them entirely : being the concluding Tract of the Dean of Glocester, on the Subject of American Affairs. *Glocester;* R. Raikes; M,dcc,lxxvi. 108 pp. *Contents* 5 pp. *Half morocco.* 8vo. (4s. 6d. 2711)

TUCKER (Josiah). Cui Bono? or, an Inquiry, what benefits can arise either to the English or the

Americans, the French, Spaniards, or Dutch, from the greatest Victories, or Successes in the present War, being a series of Letters addressed to Monsieur Necker, late controller General of the Finance of France. Third Edition, with an additional preface. With a plan for a general pacification. By Josiah Tucker, D.D. Dean of Glocester. *London :* T. Cadell, M.DCC.LXXXII. *Title and pp. v-xxv. Text pp.* 3-141. *Half mor. 8vo.* (7s. 6d. 2712)

TUCKER (Josiah). Four Letters on important National Subjects, addressed to the Right Honourable the Earl of Shelburne, His Majesty's First Lord Commissioner of the Treasury. By Josiah Tucker, D.D. Dean of Glocester. *Glocester :* R. Raikes. M DCC.LXXXIII. *vii and* 119 *pp.* 'At a Meeting, *etc.* January 24th, 1783. Resolved, That the following Letter, *etc.* be Printed,' *etc.* 23 *pp. Half morocco. 8vo.* (4s. 6d. 2713)

TUDOR (William). The Life of James Otis, of Massachusetts : Containing also, Notices of some contemporary Characters and events from the year 1760 to 1775. By William Tudor. *Boston :* Wells and Lilly. 1823. *xx and* 508 *pp. With portrait of Otis. Half morocco. 8vo.* (7s. 6d. 2714)

TUMULTIBUS (De) Americanis de que Eorum conciliatoribus meditatio Senilis. *Oxonii :* E Typographeo Clarendoniano. J. Fletcher, and D. Prince ; B. White, Londini. M DCC LXXVI. *2 prel. leaves and 36 pp. Half mor. 8vo.* (4s. 6d. 2715)

TUTCHIN (Mr.). The/ Earth-quake/ of/ Jaimaca,/ Defcrib'd in a/ Pindarick Poem./ By Mr.Tutchin./ *London,*/ Printed, and are to be fold by R. Baldwin, near the/ Oxford-Arms in Warwick-Lane, 1692./ *8 pp. Half morocco. Folio.* (7s. 6d. 2716)

TVVO/ Famovs/ Sea-Fights./ Lately made,/ Betwixt the Fleetes of the King of/ Spaine, and the Fleetes of the/ Hollanders./ The one, in the Weft-Indyes :/ The other,/ The Eight of this prefent moneth of/ February, betwixt Callis and/ Gravelin./ In the former, the Hollander fuffered./ In the latter, the Spaniard loft./ Two Relations not vnfit for thefe Times to animate/ Noble Spirits to attempt and accomplifh/ brave Actions./ *London,*/ Printed

for Nath : Bvtter and Nic : Bovrne,/ with Priviledge. 1639./ *16 unnumbered pages. Half morocco.*
4to. (1*l.* 11*s.* 6*d.* 2717)

TWO Papers On the Subject of Taxing the British
Colonies in America. The First entitled, " Some
" Remarks on the moſt rational and effeƈtual
" Means that can be uſed in the preſent Conjunc-
" ture for the future Security and Preſervation of
" the Trade of Great-Britain, by proteƈting and
" advancing her Settlements on the North Conti-
" nent of America." The other, " A Proposal for
" eſtabliſhing by Aƈt of Parliament the Duties
" upon Stampt Paper and Parchment in all the
" Britiſh American Colonies." *London :* J. Almon,
1767. *22 pp. Half morocco. 8vo.* (7*s.* 6*d.* 2718)

CHTERITZ (Heinrich von). Kurtze/ Reiſe Beſchreibung/ Hr. Heinrich von Uchteritz,/ Lieutenants, Erbſaſſen auff Modelwitz/ in Meiſſen, ꝛc./ Worinnen vermeldet, was er auf derſelben für Unglück und/ Glück gehabt, ſonderlich wie er gefangen nach Weſt-Indien geführet,/ zur Sclaverey verkaufft, und auff der/ Inſel Barbados/ Durch den namen ſeines Herrn Vettern Johann Chriſtoff von Uchteritz,/ uff Medewitz und Spansdorff Erbgeſeſſen, Cammer-Junckern auff/ Gottorff, wunderlich errettet und erlöſet worden./ *Weiſ-jenfels* bey Johann Chriſtian Wohlfarten, Im Jahr 1705./ 32 *pp.* 4*to.* (1*l.* 1*s.* 2719)

ULLOA (Antonio de). Noticias Americanas: Entretenimientos Phisicos - Historicos, sobre La América, Meridional, y la Septentrional Oriental. Comparacion General De los Territorios, Climas, y Produciones en las tres especies, Vegetales, Animales, y Minerales: Con Relacion Particular De las Petrificaciones de Cuerpos Marinos de los Indios naturales de aquellos Paises, sus costumbres, y usos: De las Antiguedades: Discurso sobre la Lengua, y sobre el modo en que pasaron los primeros Pobladores. Su Autor Don Antonio de Ulloa, Comendador de Ocaña, en el Orden - de Santiago, Gefe de Esquadra de la Real Armada, de la Real Sociedad de Londres, y de las Reales Academias de las Ciencias de Stockolmo, Berlín, &c. En *Madrid:* Don Francisco Manuel de Mena, mdcclxxii. 12 *prel. leaves and* 407 *pp.* 'Erratas,' 1 *page. Vellum.* 4*to.* (15*s.* 2720)

ULTIMAS noticias del Reino de Nueva-España.
[*Colophon*] *Habana.*—1821. Diaz de Castro.   8
pp. Half morocco. 4to.   (2s. 6d.   2721)

UMFREVILLE (Edward). The Present State of
Hudson's Bay. Containing a full description of
that Settlement, and the adjacent Country; and
likewise of the Fur Trade, with hints for its improvement, &c. &c. To which are added, Remarks
and Observations made in the Inland parts, during
a residence of near Four Years; a specimen of
Five Indian Languages; and a Journal of a Journey from Montreal to New-York. By Edward
Umfreville; Eleven Years in the service of the
Hudson's. Bay Company, and Four Years in the
Canada Fur Trade. *London:* Charles Stalker,
mdccxc. *Half-title, title, vii and* 230 *pp.* ' An Account' *etc. at page* 82. ' Plan of a Buffalo Pound,'
at page 160. ' A Specimen of sundry Indian Languages,' *etc. at page* 202. 8vo.   (7s. 6d.   2722)

USSELYNX (William). Argonavtica Gvstavi-
ana;/ Das ist:/ Nothwendige Nach Richt/ Von
der Yewen Seefahrt vnd/ Kauffhandlung;/ So
von dem Weilandt Allerdurchleuchtigsten, Grosz-
mäch=/tigsten vnd Siegreichesten Fürsten vnnd
Herrn, Herrn Gvstavo/ Adolpho Magno, der
Schweden, Gothen vnd Wenden König Grosz=/
Fürsten in Finnlandt, Hertzogen zu Ehesten vnd
Carelen, Herrn zu Inger=/manlandt, ꝛc. Allerg-
lorwürdigsten Seeligsten Andenckens,/ durch an
richtung einer/ General Handel=Compagnie,/ So-
cietet oder Gesellschafft,/ In dero Reich vnd
Landen, zu derselben sonderbahrem Auff=/nehmen
vnd Flor, aufz hohem Verstandt vnd Rath, vor
wenig Jahren/ zu stifften angefangen :/ Anietzo
aber der Teutschen Evangelischen Nation, inson-
der=/heit den jenigen welche sich in S. K. M.
Freundschafft, devotion, oder Ver=/bündnusz be-
geben, vnd sich dieses grossen Vortheils, bey so
stattlicher Gelegenheit, gebrauchen/ wollen, zu
vnermeszlichem Nutz vnd Frommen, ufz König-
licher Mildigkeit, zuneigung vnd Gnade,/ mitgetheilet worden : vnd mit dem förderlichsten, ver-
mittels gnädiger verleihung desz/ Allerhöchsten,
fortgesetzet vnd völlig zu Werck gerichtet/ werden

foll./ Daraufz denn ein jedweder claren, gründ-
lichen, vnd zu feinem Behuff fatfamen Bericht vnd
Wiffenfchafft diefes Hochwichtigen Wercks ein-
nehmen, vnd wie daffelbe nicht al=/lein an fich
felbft fondern auch diefes orths, Chriftlich, hoch-
rühmlich, Rechtmäffig vnd hocnützlich,/ auch
practicierlich vnd ohne groffe difficulteten fey, zur
gnüge verftehen kan,/ Dabey auch zugleich ver-
nünfftig erachten vnnd ermeffen mag : Ob jhme
vnd den feinigen, wefz/ Standes oder Condition er
jmmer feyn möchte, diefes hiemit jhme angewiefe-
nen vorhabens, zwifchen diefem vnd dem, ge=/liebts
Gott, nächft kommenden Newen Jahrs Tage, durch
einfchreibung feines Namens vnd einer gewiffen
Poft/ Geldes, es fey fo viel es wolle, fich theilhafftig
zu machen rathfam vnd thunlich/ erfunden werden
möchte./ Was aber für allerhandt vnterfchiedene
Schrifften, diefe Sache betreffendt,/ allhier beyfa-
men vorhanden; folches wird die nächftfolgende
Seite zeigen./ Gedruckt zu *Franckfurt am Mayn*,
bey Cafpar Rödteln,/ Im Jahr Chrifti 1633. Menfe
Junio./ Mit der Cron Schweden Freyheit./ 10
prel. leaves; viz. Title, on the reverse 'Verzeichnufz
derer Sachen vnd Schrifften,' *etc.* 'Der Königlichen May. vnd Reiche Schwe=/den Rath,' *etc.* 3
pp. 'Kurtzer Extract' *etc.* 2 *pp.* 'Ne pagina va-
caret;' *etc.* 1 *page.* 'Oct Roy Vnd Privilegivm,'
etc. 8 *pp.* 'Ampliatio Oder Erweiterung Defz Privilegii,' *etc.* 4 *pp.* 'Formular/ Defz/ Manifest/
Vnd/ Vergleich=oder Contract=brief=/fes,' *etc.* 56
pp. 'Mercvrivs Germaniæ,' *etc.* 51 *pp. Bound.*
Folio.   (10*l.* 10*s.* 2723)

UTENHOVE (Jan). Commenta=/riolvs/ Paralle-
los,/ sive/ Libellvs Affertorius (quo Principum
im-/primis duorum, Hifpaniarum fcilicet/ & Indiarum Regis auguftiffimi,/ Regis Philippi inquã
Secundi, & Turcici/ Magni Imperatoris Mahu-
metis Tertij/ Vires, opes, prouinciæ, atque forma
eas/ bene adminiftrandi & regendi tempore/ belli
atque pacis explicantur, armaq;, &/ arcana dete-
guntur infinita) nunc/ primùm ex Iohannis Boteri
Itali libris/ ideoma verfus in Latinum ex Italo/
fermone, nullius antea excufus typis./ *Coloniæ
Agrippinæ,*/ Apud Lambertum Andreæ. Anno
м. D. XCVII./ *26 leaves, the 16th and the last blank.*

'Typis Orbis Terrarvm' *on the reverse of 3rd, and
recto of the 4th leaves.* 'Tvrcici Imperii Descriptio'
*on the reverse of the 17th and recto of the 18th leaves.
Half morocco. 4to.*   (1*l.* 1*s.*   2724)

ALDES (Antonio). Derrotero de las Costas de España en el Océano Atlántico, y de las Islas Azores ó Terceras para inteligencia y uso de las Cartas Esféricas Presentadas al Rey Nuestro señor por el Exc^{mo}. Sr. Boylio Fr. Don Antonio Valdés, Teniente General de la Real Armada, del Consejo de Estado, Secretario de Estado, y del Despacho Universal de Marina. Y Construidas de Órden de S. M. Por el Brigadier de la Real Armada Don Vicente Tofiño de San Miguel, Director de las Academias de Guardias Marinas, de la Real de la Historia, correspondiente de la de las Ciencias de Paris, Socio de la de Lisboa, Socio Literato de la Sociedad Bascongada, y de mérito de la de los Amigos del Pais de Palma. De Orden Superior. *Madrid.* Por la Viuda de Ibarra, Hijos y Compañia. Año MDCCLXXXIX. *Title, xviii and 247 pp. Large paper. Calf. 8vo.* (15s. 2725)

VALLE (Alonso del). Memorial y Carta en que/ el Padre Alonso del Valle Procvrador/ general de la Prouincia de Chile, repreſenta a N. muy Reuerendo Padre/ Mucio Vitileſqui, Prepoſito general de la Compañia de Ieſvs, la ne-/ceſsidad que ſus miſsiones tienen de ſujetos para los glorio-/ſos empleos de ſus Apoſtolicos/ miniſterios./ *[At the end] Seuilla* y Março 12. de 1642./ *10 unnumbered leaves. Folio.* (1l. 11s. 6d. 2726)

VALLETTE (Elie). The Deputy Commissary's Guide Within the Province of Maryland together With plain and sufficient directions for Testators to form, and Executors to perform their Wills and Testaments; for administrators to compleat their Administrations, and for every Person any way

concerned in deceased Person's Estates, to proceed
therein with Safety to themselves and others. by
Elie Vallette. Register of the Prerogative.—*Annapolis.* Printed by Ann C——, MDCC—. *Engraved
title, iv and 248 pp. Index 9 pp. Contents of the Appendix 2 pp.* 'Table of Descent.' *at page* 106. *Title-
page mutilated. 8vo.*   (15s. 2727)

VANDER DONCK (ADRIAEN). Beschryvinge/
Van/ Nieuvv-Nederlant,/ (Gelijck het tegenwoor-
digh in Staet is) Begrijpende de Nature, Aert,
gelegentheyt en vruchtbaerheyt/ van het selve
Landt; mitsgaders de proffijtelijcke ende gewenste
toevallen, die/ aldaer tot onderhondt der Menschen,
(soo uyt haer selven als van buyten inge-/bracht)
gevonden worden. Als mede de maniere en onge-
meyne Eygenschap-/pen vande Wilden ofte Natu-
rellen vanden Lande. Ende een by sonder verhael/
vanden wonderlijcken Aert ende het Weesen der
Bevers./ Daer noch by-gevoeght is/ Een Discours
over de gelentheyt van Nieuw-Nederlandt,/ tusschen
een Nederlandts Patriot, ende een Nieuw Neder-
lander./ Beschreven door/ Adriaen vander Donck,
Beyder Rechten Doctoor, die tegenwoordigh/ noch
in Nieuw-Nederlandt is./ En hier achter by ge-
voeght/ Het voordeeligh Reglement vande Ed :
Hoog. Achtbare/ Heeren de Heeren Burgermeesteren deser Stede,/ betreffende de saken van Nieuw
Nederlandt./ Den tweeden Druck./ Met een per-
tinent Kaertje van 'tzelve Landt verçiert,/ en van
veel druck-fouten gesuyvert./ *'t Aemsteldam,* By
Evert Nieuwenhof, Boeck-verkooper, woonende
op/ 't Ruslandt, in 't Schrijf-boeck, Anno 1656./
Met Privilegie voor 15 Jaren./ *4 prel. leaves ; viz.
Title, on the reverse* 'Extract uyt Privilege.' *etc.
Four woodcuts of coats of arms,* 'Opdracht, Aen De
Hoogloffelijcke, Wel-wijze en voor zienige Heeren,'
etc. Signed 'E. Nieuwenhof.' *2 pp.* 'Mitsgaders,
Aen de Erentfeste, Wijse ende seer Waerdige
Heeren,' *etc. 2 pp.* 'Aan de Leeser.' *1 page,* 'Op
de Voorstanders en de Beschrijvinge.' *etc. 1 page.
Map,* 'Nova Belgica sive Nieuw Nederlandt.'
Text 100 *pp.* 'Register,' *4 pp.* 'Conditien,/ Die
door de Heeren Burgermeesteren der Stade/ Am-
sterdam ; volgens 't gemaecte Accoort met de
West-Indische/ Compagnie, ende d'Approbatie van

hare Hog: Mog: de Heeren/ Staten General der Vereenighde Nederlanden, daer/ op gevolght, gepresenteert werden aen alle de gene, die/ als Coloniers na Nieuw-Nederlandt willen vertrecken;/ welcke haer sullen hebben te addresseren aen de E. E. Hee-/ren Coenraed Burgh, Raedt ende Ond-Schepen, Henrick Roeters, Opper-Commissaris van de Wisselbanck, Eduart/ Man, Isaac van Beeck, Hector Pietersz. ende Ioan Tayspil, als/ Commissarisen ende Directeurs, hier toe by de Heeren/ Burgermeesteren vernoemt, &c./ t' *Amsterdam*,/ Met consent vande Ed. Hoog. Achtbare Heeren, de Heeren Borgermeesteren,/ By Evert Nieuwenhoff Boeckverkooper opt Ruslandt/ in 't Iaer. 1656./ *Title, reverse blank, text* 5 *pp.* 'Lyste.' 1 *page. Fine copy in blue mor. extra, by Bedford.* 4*to.* (16*l.* 2728)

VARENIUS (BERNHARDUS). Geographia/ Generalis,/ In qua affectiones generales/ Telluris explicantur/ Autore/ Bernh: Varenio/ Med: D./ *Amstelodami.*/ Ex Officina Elzeviriana. 1671./ *Engraved title*, 19 *prel. leaves and* 784 *pp. Folded sheets at pp.* 8 (2), 66, 126, 172. *Vellum.* 12*mo.* (10*s.* 6*d.* 2729)

VARGAS (MANUEL DE). ✠/ Relacion de los Milagros qve/ Dios nuestro señor ha obrado por vna Imagẽ del glorioso P. S. Frã/ cisco de Borja en el nueuo Reyno de Granada, sacada de los proces/sos originales de la informacion, y aprouaciõ que dellos hizo el Ilus/trissimo señor D. Iulian de Cortazar Arçobispo de Santa Fè,/ Por el P. Manuel de Vargas de la Compañia de Iesus./ [*Colophon*] Con licencia del Ordinario, En *Madrid* por Andres de Para,/ Año de 1629./ 2 *leaves. Folio.* (1*l.* 1*s.* 2730)

VAUGHAN (SAMUEL). A Refutation of a False Aspersion first thrown out upon Samuel Vaughan, Esq. In the Public Ledger of the Twenty-third of August 1769, And since that Time industriously Propagated, with an intent to Injure Him in the Eye of the Public. *London:* E. and C. Dilly, MDCCLXIX. 2 *prel. leaves and* 26 *pp. Half morocco.* 8*vo.* (3*s.* 6*d.* 2731)

VAZQUEZ DE MEDINA (JUAN). Por/ Ivan Vazqvez de/ Medina, vezíno de la Ciudad de Me-/ xico, y Tesorero de la Casa de/ la moneda de ella./

En el Pleyto/ con/ D. Iuan Francifco Centeno, y
D. Iuan/ Ánfaldo de Vera./ Sobre/ la confirmacion
del dicho oficio./ [1662.] *24 folioed leaves.*
Folio.   (12*s.* 6*d.* 2732)

VEITIA LINAGE (Joseph de). Norte/ de la con-
tratacion/ de las Indias/ Occidentales./ Dirigido
Al Exc^{mo}. Señor/ D. Gaspar/ de Bracamonte/ y
Gvzman,/ Conde de Peñaranda, Gentilhombre de
la Camara del Rey/ Nueftro Señor, de fus Confejos
de Eftado, y Guerra,/ y de la Iunta del Govierno
Vniverfal/ deftos Reynos./ Y/ Presidente antes
del Consejo Svpremo/ de las Indias, ya del de
Italia./ Por/ D. Ioseph de Veitia Linage,/ Caval-
lero de la Orden de Santiago, Señor de la Cafa de
Veitia,/ del Confejo de fu Mageftad, fu Teforero,
Juez Oficial de la Real/ Audiencia de la Cafa de la
Contratacion/ de las Indias./ Con Privilegio :/ En
Sevilla, Por Iuan Francifco de Blas, Impreffor
mayor de dicha Ciudad. Año 1672./ 16 *prel.*
leaves; Libro Primero 299 *pp. Libro Segvndo* 264
pp. Indice 70 *pp; and Colophon leaf. Fine copy.*
Folio.   (1*l.* 11*s.* 6*d.* 2734)

VELASQUEZ DE CARDENAS, Y LEON (Car-
los Celedonio). Breve Practica, y Regimen del
Confessonario de Indios, en Mexicano, y Castel-
lano ; para instruccion del Confessor Principiante,
Habilitacion, y examen del Penitente, que dispone
Para los Seminaristas El Br. D. Carlos Celedonio
Velasquez de Cardenas, y Leon, Colegial Real del
Pontificio, y Real Colegio Seminario, y fu Vice-
Rector, Cathedratico dos vezes de Philofophia, de
Mayores, Rhetorica, y Letras Humanas, Exami-
nador Synodal de efte Arzobifpado, Cura del Par-
tido de S. Miguel Xaltocan, y Juez Eclefiaftico de
él, y fus anexos Quantitlan, y Tultitlan. De Zum-
pahuacan, Capuluac, y ahora de la Concepcion de
Otumba, Cura por S. M. y Juez Eclefiaftico por el
Ilmò. Sr. Dr. Don Manuel Jofeph Rubio, y Salinas,
de la Santa Sede Apoftolica, del Confejo de S. M.
Digniffimo Arzobifpo de Mexico.   Y la Dedica al
Eminentiffimo Señor San Carlos Borromeo, Cardenal de Santa Praxede, Vigilantiffimo Arzobifpo
de Milan. Con las Licencias Necessarias. 12 *prel.*
leaves and 54 *pp. Small* 8*vo.*   (4*l.* 4*s.* 2735)

VENEGAS (MIGUEL). Noticia de la California, y de su Conquista temporal, y espiritual hasta el tiempo presente. Sacada de la Historia Manuscrita, formada en Mexico año de 1739. por el Padre Miguel Venegas, de la Compañia de Jesus; y de otras Noticias, y Relaciones antiguas, y modernas. Añadida de algunos Mapas particulares, y uno general de America Septentrional, Afsia Oriental, y Mar del Sùr intermedio, formados fobre las Memorias mas recientes, y exactas, que je publican juntamente. Dedicada al Rey N^tro. Señor por la Provincia de Nueva-Efpaña, de la Compañia de Jefus. En *Madrid:* Viuda de Manuel Fernandez, M.D.CCLVII. *Three Volumes.* Tomo Primero, 12 *prel. leaves and* 240 *pp. with map at page* 1. Tomo Segundo, 4 *prel. leaves and* 564 *pp.* Tomo Tercero, 4 *prel. leaves and* 436 *pp. with maps at pp.* 194, 236, *and* 436. *Old calf extra.* 4*to.* (3*l.* 3*s.* 2736)

VENEGAS (MIGUEL). A Natural and Civil History of California: Containing An accurate Defcription of that Country, Its Soil, Mountains, Harbours, Lakes, Rivers, and Seas ; its Animals, Vegetables, Minerals, and famous Fifhery for Pearls. The Customs of the Inhabitants, Their Religion, Government, and Manner of Living, before their Converfion to the Chriftian Religion by the miffionary Jesuits. Together with Accounts of the feveral Voyages and Attempts made for fettling California and taking actual Surveys of that Country, its Gulf, and Coaft of the South Sea. Illuftrated with Copper Plates and an Accurate Map of the Country and the adjacent Seas. Tranflated from the original Spanifh of Miguel Venegas, a Mexican Jefuit, publifhed at Madrid 1758. In Two Volumes. *London,* James Rivington, 1759. *Two Volumes.* Vol. 1. 10 *prel. leaves and* 455 *pp. Frontispiece, map at page* 13, *and plate at page* 36. Vol. II. 4 *prel. leaves and* 387 *pp. Frontispiece and plate at p.* 141. *Fine copy, calf.* 8*vo.* (1*l.* 1*s.* 2737)

VERNON (ADMIRAL). A New Ballad On the Taking of Porto-Bello, By Admiral Vernon. *London:* R. Dodsley, 1740. 7 *pp. Folio.* (7*s.* 6*d.* 2738)

VERNON (ADMIRAL). The Genuine Speech Of the Truly Honourable Adm-------l V-------- N,

to the Sea-Officers, at a Council of War, Just
before The Attack of C--------- A. As communicated by a Perſon of Honour then preſent, in
a Letter to his Friend. *London:* T. Cooper,
M,DCC,XLI. *Half-title, title, and* 19 *pp. Unbound.*
8vo. (4s. 6d. 2739)

VERY (A) short and candid Appeal to Free Born
Britons. By An American. *London:* Printed for
the Author, MDCCLXXIV. *Title and* 28 *pp. Signed,*
'A Carolinian.' *Half morocco.* 8vo. (4s. 6d. 2740)

VESPUCCI (AMERIGO). Alberic⁹ veſpucci⁹ lau-
rẽtio/ petri franciſci de medicis Salutem plurimã
dicit/ Felix/ Jehan lambert/ [*Paris* 1505] *Title
with woodcut figures, the reverse blank; text in* 9 *unnumbered pages, signature* a. *Fine copy in brown
morocco extra, by Bedford.* 4to. (21l. 2741)

VESPUCCI (AMERIGO). De ora antarctica/ per regem Portugallie/ pridem inuenta./ [*Colophon*] Impreſſum *Argentine* per Mathiam hupfuff. M.vᶜ.v./
6 *leaves, with woodcut of figures and ships on the title,
signature* A. *Fine copy with rough leaves, in brown
morocco extra, by Bedford.* 4to. (21l. 2742)

VESPUCCI (AMERIGO). Cum Privilegio/ ✣ Paeſi
Nouamente retrouati. Et Nouo Mondo oa A
berico veſputio Fiorentino intitulato. [*Colophon*]
❡ Stampato in *Vicentia* cũ la impenſa de Mgro/
Henrico Vicentino: & diligente cura & indu/ ſtria
de Zãmaria ſuo ſiol nel. M.ccccvii. a/ di. iii. de
Nouembre. Cum gratia &/ priuilegio p ãni. x.
como nella/ ſua Bolla appare: che p/ ſõa del Do-
minio Ve/ neto nõ ardiſca ĩ/ primerlo./ *Title, reverse blank;* 'Tabula Cõmunis.' 9 *pp;* Montalboddo
Fracan. al ſuo amiciſſimo Ioãnimaria/ Anzolello
Vicentino. S.'/ 1 *page. Text in* 120 *leaves, Primo
Libro to Libro Sexto, signatures* a *to* D *in fours, the
last leaf blank. Two leaves in facsimile, viz. Title
and last leaf of the Table. morocco.* 4to. (21l. 2743)

VESPUCCI (AMERIGO). Cosmographiæ/ Intro-
dvctio/ cvm qvibvs/dam Geome/triæ/ ac/ Astro-
no/miæ principiis ad/ eam rem necessariis/ Inſuper
quattuor Americi/ Veſpucij nauigationes./ Vni-
uerſalis Coſmographiæ deſcriptio tam/ in ſolido
qzplano, eis etiam inſeris/ quæ Ptholomeo ignota
a nu/peris reperta ſunt./ Disthycon' Cum deus

aftra regat, & terræ climata Cæfar Nec tellus, nec eis fydera maius habent./ *20 unnumbered leaves, signatures* A, B *in* 6, *and* C *and* D *in four leaves; on the reverse of the title, commencing* ' Divo Maximiliano Cæsari sem/per Avgvsto Gymnasivm/ vosagense' *etc. ending on the last leaf* ' Hactenus exequuti capita *etc.* Finis introductionis.' *the reverse blank. Wanting a folded sheet in signature* C, *counted as two leaves, with a woodcut of the globe, on the reverse, commencing* ' Propofitum eft hoc libello quandam Cosmographie introductionē fcribere : quam nos tam '/ *ending* ' fignauimus fed hæc iam miffa facientes.'/ ' Qvattvor Americi/ Vespvtii Navi/gationes/' *etc.* [*Colophon*] Finitū. iiij. kl. Septē/bris Anno fupra fef/quimillefimū. vij./ [*Guatier Lud, St Dié*] *32 unnumbered leaves, signatures* A (a) *to* f, *the reverse of the last leaf blank. Unbound.* 4*to.*   (10*l.* 10*s.* 2744)

VESPUCCI (AMERIGO). Cosmographæ Introdv=/ ctio, cvm qvibvs/dam Geome/triæ/ ac/ Astrono/ miæ principiis ad/ eam rem necessariis./ Infuper quatuor Americi Ve=/fpucij nauigationes./ Vniuerfalis Cofmographie defcriptio/ tam in folido qz plano, eis etiam/ infertis que Ptholomeo/ ignota a nuperis/ reperta funt./ Distichon./ Cum deus aftra regat, & terræ climata Cæfar/ Nec tellus nec eis fydera maius habent./ *18 unnumbered leaves* [1*st, 2*nd, 5*th, and 6th, are of the first Edition, May* 7*th,* 1507 ?] *the remainder are of the edition as above. On the reverse of the title* ' Maximiliano Cæsari Avgvsto/ Philesivs Vogesigena.' 4*to.* (8*l.* 8*s.* 2745)

VESPUCCI (AMERIGO). Cofmographie intro/ductio : cum quibufdam Geome=/trie ac Aftronomie princi/pijs ad eam rem/ neccffarijs./ Infuper quattuor Americi Ve/fpucij nauigationes./ Vniuerfalis Cofmographie defcriptio/ tam in folido qz plano, eis etiam/ infertis que Ptholomeo/ ignota, a nuperis/ reperta funt./ Cum deus aftra regat, et terre climata Cefar/ Nec tellus, nec eis fydera maius babent./ [*Colophon*] Preffit apud *Argentora*,/ cos hoc opus Ingeniofus vir Joannes/ grüniger. Anno poft natu fal=/uatorē fupra fefquimil=/lefimū Nono./ Joanne Adelpho Mulicho Argentineñ Caftigatore./ 32 *leaves, the reverse of the last leaf blank. Signatures* A *to* F. A, B, D, *and* E, *in fours,* C *in six,* F *in eight leaves. Fine copy. Unbound.* 4*to.* (10*l.* 10*s.* 2746)

VESPUCCI (Amerigo). Paeſi nouamente ritrouati per/ la Nauigatione di Spagna in Calicut. Et da Alber/tutio Veſputio Fiorentino intitulato Mon/do Nouo: Ncuamente Impreſſa./ [*Colophon*] ❡ Stampata in *Venetia* per Zorzi de Ruſconi milla-/neſe: Nel. M.ccccc.xyii. a di. xyiii. Agoſto./ *124 unnumbered leaves, with woodcut of the City of Venice on the title; the reverse of the last leaf blank; signatures* A *in four,* b *to* q *in eights. Blue morocco extra.* 8vo.   (31*l.* 10s.   2747)

VESPUCCI (Amerigo). Paeſi nouamente retrouati. & Nouo Mŏdo da Alberico Veſputio Flo=/rētino intitulato./ [*Colophon*] ❡ Stampato in *Milano* con la impenſa de Io. Iacobo & fratelli da/ Lignano: & diligente cura & induſtria de Ioanne Angelo ſcinzen/ zeler: nel. M.cccccxix. a di. v. de Mazo./ *Title with woodcut of figures and ships, on the reverse,* 'Tabvla;' '❡ Montalboddo Fracan,' *etc.* 7 *pp. Text in 79 leaves, Libro Primo to Libro Sexto, signatures* a *to* u *in fours, the last leaf blank. Vellum.* 4to.   (21*l.*   2748)

VESPUCCI (Amerigo). Vita di Amerigo Vespucci. *pp.* 25—35. *With portrait of* 'Americ. Vespuccius.' *Half morocco.* 4to.   (7*s.* 6*d.*   2749)

VETANCURT (Augustin de). Arte/ de lengva/ Mexicana, /✛ dispvesto ✛/ Por orden, y mandato de N. Rᵐᵒ P./ Fr. Francisco Treviño, Predica-/dor Theologo, Padre de la ſanta Provincia de Burgos, y Comiſſario/ General de todas las de la Nueva-Eſpaña, y por el Reverendo,/ y Venerable Diffini-torio de la Provincia del Santo Evangelio./ Dedi-cado al Bienventvrado/ S. Antonio de Padva./ Por el P. Fr. Auguſtin de Vetancurt hijo de/ la dicha Provincia del Santo Evangelio, Predicador jubilado, ex/ lector de Theologia, y Preceptor de la lengua Mexicana, Vicario/ de la Capilla de S. Joseph de los Naturales en el Convento/ de N. P. S. Francisco de Mexico./ Con licencia, *Mexico* por Franciſco Rodriguez Lupercio. 1673./ 6 *prel. leaves; viz. Title, the reverse blank;* 'Approbabion del R. P. Fray Damian de la Serna,' *etc.* 2 *pp;* 'Parecer del Doctor, y Maestro Don Antonio de la Torre, y Arellano,' *etc.* 1 *page;* 'Licencia del Ordinario,' 1 *page;* 'Censvra del Doctor, y Maestro

Don Ygnacio de Hoyos, Santillana,' *etc.* 1 *page;*
Patente de N. M. R. P. Provincial.' 1 *page;* ' Al
Lector.' 1 *page;* ' Dedicatoria,' 3 *pp:* Te*x*t 49 *folioed
leaves, for* 50; *2 folios* 14. ' Instrvccion Breve
Para/ adminiſtrar los Santos Sacramẽtos/ de la
Confeſſion, Uiatico, Matrimonio, y Vela-/ciones en
la la lengua Mexicana.' 13 *pp;* 'Catecismo Mexi-
cano.' 3 *pp. 4to.* (5*l.* 5*s.* 2750)

VETANCURT (Augustin de). Teatro/ Mexicano/
Descripcion Breve/ de los Svcessos Exemplares,/
Historicos,/ Politicos,/ Militares, y Religioſos del
nuevo mundo/ Occidental de las Indias,/ Dedicado/
Al Eſpoſo de la que es del miſmo Dios Eſpoſa,/ Padre
putativo del Hijo, que es Hijo del miſmo/ Dios
Christo, Dios, y hombre verdadero./ Al que con el
ſudor de ſu reſtro ſustentó al que/ todo lo ſuſtenta :
Al que fue Angel de Guarda de/ la Ciudad de Dios
milagro de ſu Omnipotencia,/ y abiſmo de la gracia./
Maria Señora Nvestra./ Al glorioso Patriarca de la
casa de Dios Señor S. Joseph./ Dispvesto/ Por el
R. P. Fr. Avgvstin de Vetancvrt, Mexicano, hijo
de la miſma Provincia, Difinidor actual, Ex-Lector/
de Theologia, Predicador Jubilado General, y ſu
Chroniſta/ Apoſtolico, Vicario, y Cura Miniſtro, por
ſu Mageſtad, de/ la Igleſia Parrochial de S. Joseph
de los Naturales/ de Mexico./ Con Licencia de los
Svperiores./ En *Mexico* por Doña Maria de Benavides Viuda de Iuan de Ribera, Año de/ 1698./ 6
prel. leaves. Parts 1 *and* 2, 66 *pp. and* 168 *pp; Indice* 2 *pp;* ' Tratado de la Ciudad de Mexico,' *etc.*
56 *pp. Followed by the title to the Second Volume :*
' Chronica/ de la/ Provincia del Santo Evangelio/
de Mexico./ Quarta parte del Teatro Mexicano
de los/ fucceſſos Religioſos./ Compuesta/ por el
Reverendo Padre/ Fray Auguſtin de Vetancur,
Mexicano, hijo de la miſma/ Provincia, Definidos
actual, Ex-Lector de Theologia,/ Predicador Iubi-
lado General, y ſu Chroniſta Appostolico,/ Vicario
y Cura Miniſtro, por ſu Mageſtad,/ de la Igleſia
Parrochial de San Ioseph/ de los Naturales de
Mexico./ *etc.* Con licencia de los Svperiores./ En
Mexico, por Doña Maria de Benavides Viuda de
Iuan de Ribera. Año de/ 1697./ 6 *prel. leaves and*
138 *pp;* ' Menologio Franciscano de los varones
masseñalados, que con ſus vadas exemplares,' *etc.*
1 *page, the reverse blank, and* 156 *pp. Two volumes.*
Vellum. Folio. (6*l.* 16*s.* 6*d.* 2751)

VIAGE, y svcesso de los Cara-/uelones, Galeoncetes
de la guarda de Cartagena de las/ Indias, y su costa.
Y la grandiosa victoria que han tenido cōtra los
Cossarios Piratas en aquel Mar,/ este año 1621.
los quales en el hazian grandes robos, y por esto
cessauan las contrataciones,/ con gran daño de las
costas y vezinos de tierra firme./ [*Colophon:*] Con
licencia, Impressa en *Madrid*, por la viuda de Cosme
Delgado. Año de mil/ y seyscientos y veinte y
vno./ *2 leaves. Half mor. Folio.* (1*l.* 1*s* 2752)

VIAGGIO (IL)/ fatto da gli Spa/gnivoli a/ torno a'l/
Mondo./ Con Gratia per Anni. XIIII./ MDXXXVI./
4 prel. leaves; viz. Title, the reverse blank, ' A'l Let-
tore.' *4 pp. and a half ; Text 47 unnumbered leaves ;*
'Capitolo. VI.' *1 page, the reverse blank. Signatures*
A *to* M *in fours. Half mor.* 4*to.* (10*l.* 10*s.* 2753)

VIAUD (PIERRE). The Shipwreck and Adventures
of Monsieur Pierre Viaud, A Native of Bourdeaux,
and Captain of a Ship. Translated from the French,
By Mrs. Griffith. *London*, T. Davies, MDCCLXXI.
xii and 276 *pp. Frontispiece.* 8*vo.* (4*s.* 6*d.* 2754)

VEITIA LINAGE (JOSEPH DE). The/ Rule/ Establish'd in Spain,/ for the/ Trade/ in the/ West Indies./ Being a proper Scheme for Direct-/ing the
Trade to the/ South Sea,/ Now by Act of Parliament to be/ Establish'd in Great Britain./ Translated from the Spanish by Captain/ John Stevens./
To which are Added,/ Two Compleat Lists : One,
of the Goods Transported/ out of Europe to the
Spanish West Indies; the other, of/ Commodities
brought from these Parts into Europe./ *London,*
Printed for Samuel Crouch, at the corner of/
Popes-Head Alley in Cornhill./ [1700?] *13 prel.
leaves, and text* 367 *pp. Index* 9 *pp. Old calf.*
8*vo.* (15*s.* 2755)

IEW (A) of the Depredations and Ravages Committed by the Spaniards on the British Trade and
Navigation. Most humbly offer'd to the Consideration of the Parliament of Great Britain. *London :*
W. Hinchliffe, 1731. *Title, ix and* 44 *pp. Half
morccco.* 8*vo.* (5*s.* 6*d.* 2756)

VIEW (A) of the Controversy between Great-Britain and her Colonies : Including a Mode of Determining their present Disputes, Finally and Effec-

tually; and of preventing All Future Contentions.
In a Letter to the Author of a full Vindication of
The Meafures of the Congrefs, from the Calumnies
of their Enemies. By A. W. Farmer. Author of
Free Thoughts, &c. *New-York*: Printed by James
Rivington, M,DCC,LXXIV. 37 *pp. Half morocco.*
8vo. (7s. 6d. 2757)

VIEW (A) of the Controversy between Great-Britain and her Colonies: Including a Mode of Determining their Prefent Difputes, Finally and Effectually; and of preventing all future contentions.
In a Letter to the Author of A Full Vindication of
the Meafures of the Congrefs, from the Calumnies
of their Enemies. By A. W. Farmer, Author of
Free Thoughts, &c. New-York, Printed: *London*
Reprinted Richardson and Urquhart, 1775. *Half-
title, title and 90 pp. 8vo.* (7s. 6d. 2758)

VIEW (A) of the History of Great-Britain, during
the Administration of Lord North, to the Second
Session of the Fifteenth Parliament. In Two
Parts. With Statements of the Public Expenditure
in that Period. *London:* G. Wilkie, MDCCLXXXII.
Title, ii and 412 pp. 8vo. (8s. 6d. 2759)

The First Part was published in the preceding year, under the
title of the History of Lord North's Administration.

VIEW (A) of the State of Parties in the United
States of America; being an Attempt to Account
for the present Ascendancy of the French, or De-
mocratic Party, in that Country; in two Letters
to a Friend. By a Gentleman who has recently
visited the United States. *Edinburgh:* John Ballantyne and Co. 1812. 110 *pp. 8vo.* (2s. 6d. 2760)

VIEWS of Society and Manners in America; in a
series of letters from that country to a friend in
England, during the years 1818, 1819, and 1820.
By an Englishwoman. *London:* Longman, 1821.
x and 523 pp. Half calf. 8vo. (6s. 2761)

VILBAO (LUIS DE). Sermon de la Fe/ en el Solene/
y General Avto, qve/ fu Tribunal Santo celebrò
en la/ Ciûdad de Lima./ El Domingo tercero de
Aduiento, que fue dia de Santo/ To Ǝ as Apoftol, à
21. de Diziembre, de 1625. años./ Por el Padre
Maeftro Fray Luis de Vilbao, de la Sagra/ da Orden
de Predicadores, Calificador del Santo Ofi-/cio, y

Catredatico proprietario de Prima de Teo-/logia en
la Real Vniuerfidad de los Reyes./ Al Excelen-
tiffimo Señor D. Diego Ferdinandez de Cordoua
Marques/ de Guadalcazar, Virrey, y Capitan General deflos Reynos/ del Piru, &c./ Año de 1626./
Impreffo en *Lima;* Con licencia de fu Excelencia./
Title and folioed leaves 2 *to* 18. *Calf extra by Bedford.* 4*to.*   (1*l.* 11*s.* 6*d.* 2762)

VILLAGOMEZ (PEDRO DE). Discvrso/ Ivridico/
sobre/ Que pertenece a la Dignidad Arçobifpal, ò/
Epifcopal, el nombrar, y remover los Colecto-/res
delas Iglefias Catedrales de las Indias,/ fin depen-
dencia del Real Pa-/tronazgo./ Por/ El llvstrissimo
Señor Don/ Pedro de Villagomez, Arçobifpo de la
Santa/ Iglefia Metropolitana de la ciudad de los
Re-/yes, del Confejo de fu/ Mageftad./ Capitvlo I./
Relacion del cafo, motivos, intento, y diuifion/ de
efte difcurfo./ [*End*] Annuat Deus per Chriftum
Dominum no-/ftrum, Amen. *Lima* y Diziembre 10.
de 1653./ Pedro Arçobifpo de Lima./ 60 *folioed
leaves.* 4*to.*   (1*l.* 11*s.* 6*d.* 2763)

VILLAGRA (GASPAR DE). Historia/ de la Nveva/
Mexico, del Capitan/ Gaspar de Villagra./ Dirigida al Rey D. Felipe/ nueftro feñor Tercero defte
nombre./ Año 1610./ Con privilegio./ En *Alcala*,
por Luys Martinez Grande./ A cofta de Baptifta
Lopez mercador de libros./ [*Colophon.*] Impreffo
en Alcala de/ Henares, por Luys/ Martinez Gräde./
Año. 1610./ 24 *prel. leaves including portrait of
author: Text* 287 *folioed leaves, and Colophon one
leaf. Blue morocco extra by Bedford. Very fine copy.
Small* 8*vo.*   4*l.* 14*s.* 6*d.* 2764)

VILLE (JEAN BAPTISTE DE). Histoire des Plantes
de l'Europe, et des plus Usite'es qui viennent
d'Afie, d'Afrique, & d'Amerique. Où l'on voit
leurs Figures, leurs noms, en quel temps elles
fleuriffent, & le lieu où elles croiffent. Avec un
Abrégé de leurs qualitez, & de leurs Vertus fpeci-
fiques. Divifée en deux Tomes, & rangée fuivant
l'ordre du Pinax de Gafpard Baubin. *A Lyon*,
Chez Nicolas De Ville, MDCCVII. *Two Volumes.*
Tome Premier. 24 *prel. leaves and* 442 *pp.* Tome II.
Title and pp. 445—866. *Table* 80 *pp. Old calf.*
12*mo.*   (10*s.* 6*d.* 2765)

VINCENT (Thomas). An Explicatory Catechifm:
Or, an Explanation of the Assemblies Shorter
Catechifm. Wherein all the Anfwers in the Affemblies Catechifm are taken abroad in Under-Quef-
tions and Anfwers, the Truth explain'd and proved
by Reafon and Scripture feveral Cafes of Confcience
refolv'd fome chief Controverfies in Religion ftated,
with Arguments againft divers Errors. Ufeful to
be read in private Families, after Examination in
the Catechism itfelf, for the more clear and thorough
underftanding of what is therein Learn'd. By
Thomas Vincent, fometimes Minifter of Maudlin
Milk-ftreet in London. *Boston* in New-England:
Printed for D. Henchman, over againft the Brick-
Meeting Houfe in Cornhill, John Phillips, at the
Stationers-Arms, and T. Hincock, at the Bible and
Three Crowns near the Town-Dock. 1729. *Title,
viii and* 315 *pp.* 12*mo.* (10s. 6d. 2766)

VINDICATION (A) of The Proceedings of The
Eastern Association In Fairfield County; and of
The Council that cenfured Mr. White, And difmiffed
him from his Paftoral Relation to The First Church
in Danbury: In a Letter To The Reverend Mr.
Joseph Bellamy, In which the whole Procefs is
fairly reprefented, contrary to the falfe Reprefentations and abufive Reflections contained in a
Pamphlet called A Brief Narrative of their Proceedings. By the Committee Of the First Society
in Danbury. *New-Haven:* Printed by B. Mecom.
1764. 78 *pp.* 8*vo.* (7s. 6d. 2767)

VIRGINIA. The/ New Life/ of Virginea:/ Declaring the/ former svccesse and pre-/fent eftate of
that plantation, being the fecond/ part of Noua
Britannia./ Publifhed by the authoritie of his
Maiefties/ Counfell of Virginea./ *London,/* Imprinted by Felix Kynston for William Welby,
dwelling at the/ figne of the Swan in Pauls Church-
yard. 1612./ *Title (facsimile) with woodcut, portrait,
and coat of arms, the reverse blank;* 'To the Right/
Worshipful and/ Worthie Knight Sir/ Thomas
Smith of London, Gouernour of the/ Mofcouia and
Eaft Indie Companies, one of/ his Maiefties Counfell for Virginea,/ and Treafurer for the Colony :/
Peace and health in Chrift./ 4 *pp. Signed* 'R. I.'
Text, 'The New Life of Virginea.' *in* 24 *unnumbered leaves.* 4*to.* (5l. 5s. 2768)

VIRGINIA. A Perfect Defcription of/ Virginia :/ Being,/ A full and true Relation of the prefent State/ of the Plantation, their Health, Peace, and Plenty : the number/ of people, with their abundance of Cattell, Fowl, Fifh, &c. with feverall/ forts of rich and good Commodities, which may there be had, either/ Naturally, or by Art and Labour. Which we are fain to/ procure from Spain, France, Denmark, Swedeland, Germany,/ Poland, yea, from the Eaft-Indies. There/ having been nothing related of the/ true eftate of this Planta-/tion thefe 25 years./ Being fent from Virginia, at the requeft of a Gentleman of worthy note, who defired to know the true State of Virginia as it now ftands./ Also,/ A Narration of the Countrey, within a few/ dayes journey of Virginia, Weft and by South, where people come/ to trade : being related to the Governour, Sir William Berckley,/ who is to go himfelfe to difcover it with 30 horfe, and 50 foot,/ and other things needfull for his enterprize./ With the manner how the Emperor Nichotawance/ came to Sir William Berckley, attended with five petty Kings,/ to doe Homage, and bring Tribute to King Charles. With his folemne Proteftation, that the Sun and Moon fhould lofe/ their Lights, before he (or his people in that Country), fhould prove difloyall, but ever to keepe Faith/ and Allegiance to King Charles./ *London*, Prind for Richard Wodenoth, at the Star under Peters/ Church in Cornhill. 1649./ *2 prel. leaves; viz. 1st. on verso the royal arms: 2nd. Title, reverse blank; text 19 pp. Morocco extra by Bedford, fine copy.* 4to. (10*l.* 10s. 2769)

VIRGINIA. The Case of the Planters of Tobacco in Virginia, As reprefented by Themselves; figned by the Prefident of the Council, and Speaker of the Houfe of Burgeffes. To which is added, a Vindication Of the faid Reprefentation. *London:* J. Roberts, 1733. *64 pp. Half mor.* 8vo. (7s. 6d. 2770)

VIRGINIAN. The American Wanderer, through Various Parts of Europe, in a series of Letters to a Lady, (Interfperfed with a Variety of interesting Anecdotes,) By a Virginian. *Dublin*, B. Smith, MDCCLXXXIII. *xxiii & 288 pp.* 12mo. (7s. 6d. 2771)

VOLNEY (C. F.) View of the Climate and Soil
of the United States of America: To which are
annexed some Accounts of Florida, The French
Colony of the Scioto, certain Canadian Colonies,
and the Savages or Natives: Tranflated from the
French of C. F. Volney, Member of the Conserva-
tive Senate, and the French National Institute,
and Honorary Member of the American Philosophical Society at Philadelphia, the Asiatic Society
at Calcutta, the Atheneums of Avignon, Alençon,
&c. With Maps and Plates. *London:* J. Johnson,
1804. *xxiv pp. Table of Contents, pp. iii vi. Text* 504
pp. Plates at pp. 59, 99. *Two maps at the end.*
8vo. (*6s. 6d.* 2772)

VOYAGE dans la Haute Pensylvanie et dans l'Etat
de New York, Par un Membre adoptif de la nation
Onéida. Traduit et publié par l'auteur des Lettres
d'un Cultivateur Américain. De L'emprimerie de
Crapelet. A *Paris* Au IX—1801. *Three Volumes.*
Tome Premier. *xxxii pp. including Frontispiece; Text*
427 *pp. Plates at pp.* 115, 119, 253. *Map at the end.*
Tomo Second. *xiv and* 434 *pp. Plates at pp.* 131,
182, 192. *Map at the end.* Tome Troisieme. *xii*
and 410 *pp.* 'Indication' *etc. folded sheet at page*
166, *folded sheet at page* 173. *Plates at pp.* 197, 199.
'Tableau' *etc. at pp.* 252, 253. *Half calf.*
8vo. (*12s. 6d.* 2773)

VOYAGES. An Historical Account of all the Voyages round the World, performed by English
Navigators; including those lately undertaken By
Order of his Present Majesty. The whole Faith-
fully Extracted from the Journals of the Voyagers.
Drake, undertaken in 1577-80. Cavendish, 1586-
88. Cowley, 1683-86. Dampier, 1689-96. Cooke,
1708-11. Rogers, 1708-11. Clipperton and Shel-
vocke, 1719-22. Anson, undertaken in 1740-44.
Byron, 1764-66. Wallis, 1766-68. Carteret, 1766-
69, and Cook, 1768-71. Together with that of
Sydney Parkinson, Draftfman to Joseph Banks,
Efq; who circumnavigated the Globe with Capt.
Cook, in his Majefty's Ship the Endeavour. And
The Voyage of Monf. Bougainville round the
World, Performed by Order of the French King.
Illuftrated with Maps, Charts, and Hiftorical
Prints. In Four Volumes. To which is added,

An Appendix. Containing the Journal of a Voyage to the North Pole, by the Hon. Commodore Phipps, and Captain Lutwidge. *London:* F. Newbery, MDCCLXXIV. *Four Volumes.* Volume the First. *Title, l prel. pp. List of Subscribers, 5 pp. Directions to the Bookbinder for placing the plates, 1 page ; Text 480 pp ; 1 map and 15 plates.* Volume the Second. *Title and 440 pp. 8 plates.* Volume the Third. MDCCLXXIII. *viii and 470 pp. 4 Charts and 15 Plates,* 1 *wanting at page* 327. Volume the Fourth. MDCCLXXIII. *Title and 364 pp. The Bookseller's Advertisement, 2 pp;* 'Supplement, containing the Journal of a Voyage,' *etc. Title and 118 pp. 5 plates, map, and chart. Half calf. 8vo.* (1*l.* 1*s.* 2774)

VOYAGES. A new Collection of Voyages, Discoveries and Travels : Containing Whatever is worthy of Notice, in Europe, Asia, Africa and America : In respect to The Situation and Extent of Empires, Kingdoms, and Provinces; their Climates, Soil, Produce, &c. With the Manners and Customs of the several Inhabitants ; their Government, Religion, Arts, Sciences, Manufactures, and Commerce. The whole consisting of such English and Foreign Authors as are in most Esteem ; including the Descriptions and Remarks of some late celebrated Travellers, not to be found in any other Collection. Illustrated with a Variety of accurate Maps, Plans, and elegant engravings. In Seven Volumes. *London:* J. Knox, MDCCLXVII. *Seven Volumes.* Vol. I. 8 *prel. leaves and* 515 *pp.* Vol. II. 2 *prel. leaves and* 496 *pp.* Vol. III. 2 *prel. leaves and* 520 *pp.* Vol. IV. 2 *prel. leaves and* 464 *pp.* Vol. V. 2 *prel. leaves and* 472 *pp.* Vol. VI. 2 *prel. leaves and* 543 *pp.* Vol. VII. 2 *prel. leaves and* 528 *pp. Old calf. 8vo.* (1*l.* 10*s.* 2775)

There is in the first Volume a list of 49 maps and plates.

VOYAGES. Interesting Account of the Early Voyages, made by the Portuguese Spaniards, &c. To Africa, East and West-Indies. The Discovery of Numerous Islands; with Particulars of the Lives of those Eminent Navigators. Including the Life and Voyages of Columbus. To which is prefixed the Life of that Great Circumnavigator Captain Cook, with particulars of his Death. Extracted from Dr. Kipps's. *London:* Printed for the Proprietors, M,DCC,XC. *12 prel. leaves and pp.* 7-276. *Plates and maps at pp.* 7, 8, 17, 25, 32, 40, 48. *Old calf.* 4to. (10s. 6d. 2776)

VOYAGES. A General Collection of Voyages and Discoveries, made by the Portuguese and the Spaniards during the Fifteenth and Sixteenth Centuries. Containing the interesting and entertaining Voyages of the Celebrated Gonzalez and Vaz, Gonzalez Zarco, Lanzerota, Diogo Gill, Cada Mosto, Pedro di Sintra, Diogo d'Azambuza Bartholomew Diac, Vasco de Gama, Voyages to the Canary Islands, Voyages of Columbus, Nino and Guierra, Ojeda and Vespusius Cortereal, Alvarez Cabral, Francis Almeed, Albuquerque, Andrea Corsali, Voyage to St. Thomas, Voyage of de Solis, Pinzon, &c. Voyage of John Ponce, Grijalva, Nicuessa, Cortes, Ojeda and Ocampo, Magellan. With other Voyages, to the East-Indies, the West-Indies, Round the World, &c. Adorned with Copper-Plates, Maps, &c. *London:* W. Richardson, MDCCLXXXIX. *5 prel. leaves and pp.* 7-518. *Plates and maps.* 4to. (12s. 6d. 2777)

VUE de la Colonie Espagnole du Mississipi, ou des Provinces de Louisiane et Floride Occidentale, en l'Année 1802. Par un observateur résident sur les lieux : Ouvrage accompagné de deux cartes dressées avec soin, et artistement gravées et enluminées. B . . . . . . - Duvallon, Editeur. *Paris.* 1803. *xx and* 318 *pp. Table Abrégée* 5 *pp. Avis au Relieur,* & *Errata et Additions.* 4 *pp. With 2 colored maps. Half calf.* 8vo. (5s. 6d. 2778)

ADSWORTH (Benjamin). An
Effay, for the Charitable Spreading
of the Gospel into Dark Ignorant
Places: Being a Sermon (now fome-
thing Inlarged) Preach'd at the
Lecture in Bofton, Octob. 16. 1718.
By Benjamin Wadfworth, A.M.
Paftor of a Church of Chrift in Bofton, N.E.
Boston: Printed by B. Green, for Benj. Eliot, at
his Shop. 1718. *Title and 36 pp. Unbound.*
12mo.   (10s. 6d. 2779)

WADSWORTH (Benjamin). The Gospel not
Oppofed, but by the Devil and Mens Lufts. A
Lecture Sermon Preach'd at Bofton, Jan. 8. 1718,
19. From Mat. x. 34. By Benjamin Wadfworth,
A.M. Paftor of a Church of Chrift in Bofton, N.E.
Boston, N.E. Printed by B. Green, for Benj.
Eliot, at his Shop. 1719. *Title, and 46 pp. Unbound.*
12mo.   (10s. 6d. 2780)

WADSWORTH (Benjamin). Vicious Courfes,
Procuring Poverty. Defcrib'd and Condemn'd.
A Lecture Sermon, Preach'd at Bofton, Feb. 19.
1718, 19. By Benjamin Wadfworth, A.M. Paftor
of a Church of Chrift in Bofton, N.E. *Boston*,
Printed by John Allen, for Benjamin Eliot, at his
Shop in King ftreet, 1719. *Title and 32 pp. Unbound.*
12mo.   (10s. 6d. 2781)

WAFER (Lionel). A New/ Voyage/ and/ De-
scription/ of the/ Ifthmus of America,/ Giving an
Account of the/ Author's Abode there,/ The Form
and Make of the Country,/ the Coafts, Hills, Rivers, &c. Woods,/ Soil, Weather, &c. Trees,
Fruit, Beafts,/ Birds, Fifh, &c./ The Indian In-

habitants, their Features,/ Complexion, &c. their
Manners, Cu-/ftoms, Employments, Marriages,
Feasts,/ Hunting, Computation, Language, &c./
With Remarkable Occurrences in the South/ Sea,
and elfewhere./ By Lionel Wafer. Illuftrated
with feveral Copper=Plates./ *London :* Printed
for James Knapton, at the Crown in/ St. Paul's
Church-yard, 1699./ 4 *prel. leaves and* 224 *pp.
Index* 14 *pp. Books, etc.* 2 *pp. Map at page* 1, *plates
at pp.* 28, 103, 141. *Old calf.* 8*vo.* (18*s.* 2782)

WAFER (Lionel). A New Voyage and Description
of the Isthmus of America. Giving An Account
of the Author's Abode there, The Form and Make
of the Country, the Coafts, Hills, Rivers, &c.
Woods, Soil, Weather, &c. Trees, Fruit, Beasts,
Birds, Fish, &c. The Indian Inhabitants their
Features, Complxion, &c their Manners, Cuftoms,
Employments, Marriages, Feafts, Hunting, Com-
putation, Language, &c. With Remarkable Oc-
currences in the South-Sea and elfewhere. By
Lionel Wafer. The Second Edition To which are
added, The Natural Hiftory of thofe Parts, By a
Fellow of the Royal Society: And Davis's Expe-
dition to the Gold Mines in 1702. Illuftrated with
feveral Copper-Plates. *London,* Printed for James
Knapton, At the Crown in St. Pauls Church-Yard.
MDCCIV. 8 *prel. leaves and* 283 *pp : Index.* 12 *pp :
Map and* 3 *plates. Old calf.* 8*vo.* (15*s.* 2783)

WAGHENAER (L. J.) The Mariners Mirrovr/
Wherein may playnly be feen the courfes, heights,
dif=/tances, depths, foundings, flouds and ebs,
rifings of/ lands, rocks, fands and fhoalds, with the
marks for th'en=/trings of the Harbouroughs, Havens and Ports of the greateft part of Europe :
their feueral traficks and commodities : Together
w.th the Rules and inftrumĕts/ of Navigation./
Firft made & fet fourth in diuers exact Sea-Charts,
by that famous/ Nauigator Lvke Wagenar of En-
chuifen And now fitted with necefsarie/ additions
for the ufe of Englifhmen by/ Anthony Ashley./
.Herein alfo may be underftood the exploits lately
atchiued by the right/ Honorable the L. Admiral
of Englãd with her Ma.ties Nauie; and fome/ former feruices don by that worthy Knight/ Sr. Fra :
Drake./ [*London,* 1588.] 24 *leaves of preliminary*

matter, including engraved title. Copperplate maps (1) *to* (22) *with description printed on each map.* 'The Second Part/ of the Mariners Mirrovr/ contein-ing in diuers perfect plots & sea Charts boeth the Northern and Eastern/ Navigation :/ viz. From the Streights between Douer and Callis, the/ coasts of England, Scotland, Norway, Emden, Yut=/land ct. with all the founds of Denmark & the Baltick/ sea unto Wiburgh and the Narue/ With their par-ticular descriptions/ trafiks and commodities./ *En-graved title and copperplate maps* I *to* XXIII, *with description printed on each map. And* 12 *copperplate maps of the various engagements between the English and Spanish Fleets, the last being a map of* ' Anglia ' *Without descriptions and unnumbered. Unbound. Folio.* (3*l.* 13*s.* 6*d.* 2784)

WALKER (Hovenden). A Journal : Or full Ac-count Of the late Expedition to Canada. With an Appendix Containing Commiffions, Orders, In-ftructions, Letters, Memorials, Courts - Martial, Councils of War, &c. relating thereto. By Sir Hovenden Walker, Kᵗ. London : Printed for D. Browne at the Black-Swan, W. Mears at the Lamb, without Temple Bar, and G. Strahan at the Golden Ball againft the Exchange in Cornhill, 1720. *2 prel. leaves and text* 304 *pp. Old calf.* 8*vo.* (1*l.* 1*s.* 2785)

WALKER (James). Letters on the West Indies. By James Walker. *London :* Rest Fenner, 1818. *xvi and* 268 *pp.* 8*vo.* (4*s.* 6*d.* 2786)

WALLACE (Edward J.) The Oregon Question determined by the Rules of International Law. By Edward J. Wallace, M. A., Barrister-at-Law, Bombay. *London :* A. Maxwell & Son, 1846. 39 *pp.* 8*vo.* (2*s.* 6*d.* 2787)

WALLER (William). An/ Efsay/ on the/ Value of the Mines,/ late of Sir Carbery Price./ By William Waller, Gent./ Steward of the said Mines./ ˙Writ for the private Satisfaction of/ all the Partners./ *London :/* Printed in the Year, mdcxcviii./ 12 *prel. leaves, and* 55 *pp. With two folding sheets, one a woodcut plan of Potosi. Old red morocco, fine copy.* 8*vo.* (12*s.* 6*d.* 2788)

WALTER (Thomas). Flora Carolina, secundum

Systema Vegetabilium Perillustris Linnæi digesta; Characteres essentiales Naturalesve et diferentias veras exhibens; cum emendationibus numerosis: Descriptionum antea evulgatarum: Adumbrationes stirpium plus mille continens: Necnon, generibus novis non paucis, speciebus plurimis novisq. Ornata. Auctore Thomas Walter, Agriola. *Londini:* J. Fraser: M,DCC,LXXXVIII. *viii and* 263 *pp. Plate facing title.* 8*vo.* (7*s.* 6*d.* 2789)

WANSEY (HENRY). The Journal of an Excursion to the United States of North America, in the Summer of 1794. Embellished with The Profile of General Washington, and an Aqua-tinta View of the State House, at Philadelphia. By Henry Wansey, F.A.S. A Wiltshire clothier. *Saliſbury:* J. Easton; 1796. *xiii pp. half-title and* 290 *pp: Index,* 12 *pp: Errata,* 1 *page. Profile facing title, and plate at page* 131. 8*vo.* (6*s.* 6*d.* 2790)

WARD (NATHANIEL). The/ Simple Cobler/ Of/ Aggavvam in America./ Willing/ To help'mend his Native Country, la-/mentably tattered, both in the upper-Leather/ and fole, with all the honeſt ſtiches he can take./ And as willing never to bee paid for his work,/ by Old Engliſh wonted pay./ It is his Trade to patch all the year long, gratis./ Therefore I pray Gentlemen keep your purſes./ By Theodore de la Guard./ *London,/* Printed by John Dever & Robert Ibbitſon, for Stephen Bow-tell, at the/ ſigne of the Bible in Popes Head-Alley, 1647./ 2 *prel. leaves; viz. Title, the reverse blank;* ' To the Reader.' 1 *page; Text,* 80 *pp. Fine large and clear copy, with rough leaves. Morocco by Bedford.* (5*l.* 5*s. Others* 3*l.* 3*s. and* 2*l.* 2*s.* 2791)

WARD (NATHANIEL). *Another copy, very fine, in calf extra by Bedford, having on the title-page the autograph of White Kennet.* (5*l.* 5*s.* 2792)

WARDEN (D. B.) A Chorographical and Statistical Description of the District of Columbia, the seat of the General Government of the United States, with an engraved plan of the District, and view of the Capitol. *Paris:* printed and sold by Smith, Rue Montmorency. 1816. *vii and* 212 *pp. Index,* 2 *pp. Plan at page* 1. *Plate at page* 34. *Calf.* 8*vo.* (12*s.* 6*d.* 2793)

WARREN (George). An Impartial/ Description/ of/ Surinam/ upon/ The Continent of Guiana/ in/ America./ With a Hiftory of feveral ftrange Beafts, Birds,/ Fifhes, Serpents, Infeéts, and Cuftoms of/ that Colony, &c./ Worthy the Perufal of all, from the experience of/ George Warren Gent./ *London*, Printed by William Godbid for Nathaniel Brooke/ at the Angel in Grefham-Colledge, in the fecond yard/ from Bifhopfgate-ftreet. 1667./ 2 *prel. leaves; viz. Title the reverse blank.* 'To the Reader.' 2 *pp. Text,* 28 *pp.* 4*to.* (1*l.* 11*s.* 6*d.* 2794)

WASHINGTON. The Campaigns of the British Army at Washington and New Orleans, in the Years 1814-1815. By the Author of the Subaltern. Fourth Edition, corrected and revised. *London:* John Murray, MDCCCXXXVI. *iv and* 389 *pp. Cloth. Uncut.* 12*mo.* (3*s.* 6*d.* 2795)

WASHINGTON (George). The Journal of Major George Wafhington, sent by the Hon. Robert Dinwiddie, Efq; His Majefty's Lieutenant-Governor, and Commander in Chief of Virginia, to the Commandant of the French Forces on Ohio. To which are added, the Governor's Letter: and a translation of the French Officer's Anfwer. With a New Map of the Country as far as the Mississippi. Williamsburgh Printed, *London*, Reprinted for T. Jefferys, MDCCLIV. 32 *pp. With the map. Half morocco.* 8*vo.* (1*l.* 1*s.* 2796)

WASHINGTON (George). Letters from General Washington, To feveral of his Friends in the Year 1776. In which are set forth A fairer and fuller View of American Politics, Than ever yet transpired, Or the Public could be made acquainted with through any other Channel. *London :* J. Bew, M.DCC.LXXVII. *Title, and* 73 *pp. Half morocco.* 8*vo.* (10*s.* 6*d.* 2797)

WASHINGTON (George). A Poetical Epistle to his Excellency George Washington, Esq. Commander in Chief of the Armies of the United States of America, from An Inhabitant of the State of Maryland. To which is annexed, A Short Sketch of General Washington's Life and Charater. Annapolis Printed 1779: *London:* Reprinted for C. Dilly, MDCCLXXX. 24 *pp. Unbound.* 4*to.* (10*s.* 6*d.* 2798)

WASHINGTON (GEORGE). A Message of the
President of the United States to Congress relative
to France and Great-Britain. Delivered December
5, 1793. With the Papers therein referred to.
To which are added the French originals. Pub-
lished by order of the House of Representatives.
Philadelphia: Printed by Childs and Swaine.
M,DCC,XCIII. 103 *pp. half mor. 8vo.* (10s. 6d. 2799)

WASHINGTON (GEORGE). Official Letters to the
Honorable American Congress, Written during
the War between the United Colonies and Great
Britain, by his Excellency, George Washington,
Commander in Chief of the Continental Forces,
now President of the United States. Copied by
Special Permiſſion from the Original Papers pre-
served in the Office of the Secretary of State,
Philadelphia. *London:* Cadell Junior and Davies,
1795. *Two Volumeſs.* Vol. I. *viii and* 364 *pp.*
Vol. II. *Half-title, title, and* 384 *pp. Uncut.*
8vo.   (10s. 6d. 2800)

WASHINGTON (GEORGE). Memory of Washington: Comprising a sketch of his Life and Character; and the National Testimonials of Respect.
Also, a collection of Eulogies and Orations. With
a copious Appendix. *Newport.* R. I. Printed by
Oliver Farnsworth. 1800. 246 *pp. Subscribers'
Names,* 6 *pp. Portrait of G. Washington. Calf.*
12mo.   (10s. 6d. 2801)

WASHINGTON (GEORGE). Letters from his Excellency General Washington, to Arthur Young,
Esq. F.R.S. Containing an Account of his Husbandry, with a Map of his Farm; his Opinions on
various Questions in Agriculture; and many particulars of the Rural Economy of the United
States. *London:* B. M'Millan, 1801. *vi and* 172
pp. With the map. 8vo.   (7s. 6d. 2802)

WATERTON (CHARLES). Wanderings in South
America, the North-West of the United States,
and the Antilles, in the years 1812, 1816, 1820,
and 1824. With original instructions for the perfect preservation of Birds, &c. for Cabinets of
Natural History. By Charles Waterton, Esq.
London: J. Mawman, 1825. *vii and* 326 *pp. Plate
facing title. Large paper. 4to.* (7s. 6d. 2803)

WATTS (Isaac). A Guide to Prayer. Or, A Free and Rational Account of the Gift, Grace and Spirit of Prayer, With plain Directions how every Chriftian may attain them. By I. Watts, D.D. The Eighth Edition Corrected. *Boston:* Printed by J. Draper, for D. Henchman in Cornhil. Mdcc.xxxix. *Title, x and 228 pp. Table 4 pp. 12mo.* (1l. 1s. 2804)

WEBB (John). The Young-Mans Duty, Explained and Preffed upon Him. In A Sermon From Eccles. xii. 1. Preached to a Society of Young Men, On a Lords-Day Evening: And now Publifhed at their Requeft. By John Webb, A.M. and Paftor of a Church of Chrift in Bofton. Recommended by the Reverend, Increase Mather, D.D. *Boston:* Printed by S. Kneeland, for D. Henchman, at the Corner Shop over againft the Brick Meeting-Houfe. 1718. *Title, ii pp. and wanting all after page 32. Small 8vo.* (8s. 6d. 2805)

WEBSTER (Pelatiah). Political Essays on the Nature and Operation of Money, Public Finances, and other Subjects: Publifhed during the American War, and continued up to the prefent Year, 1791. By Pelatiah Webster, A.M. *Philadelphia:* Printed and sold by Joseph Crukshank, No. 91, High-Street. m dcc xci. *viii and 504 pp. Half calf. 8vo.* (8s. 6d. 2806)

WELCH-COBLER. The honeft/ Welch-Cobler,/ for her do fcorne to call her/felfe the fimple Welch-Cobler:/ Although her thinkes in all her/ Confciences, if her had as many as would ftand/ betweene Paules and Sharing-Croffe that her have/ not fo much wit as her Prother Cobler of A-/merica, yet her thinke her may have as much/ knavery; and though her have not fo much Creek,/ which her holds to be Heathenifh; nor Hebrew,/ which her holds to be Shewifh Language; nor/ Latine, which is the Language of Rome, yet her/ fhall endever her felfe to teliver her felfe in as/ cood Tialect as her can for her hart plood, for the/ petter underftanding of all her friends and kind-/red, whether Comro or Sifs, wherein her fhall/ find variety of counfells, profitable inftructions, feafonable cautions, to prevent tangers that may come/ upon all her countrymen here; Her alfo fhall find fome/ truth, little honefty, fome wit, and a creat teale of

2   3 E

kna-/verie./ By Shinkin ap Shone, ap Griffith, ap
Gearard, ap Shiles, ap/ Shofeph, ap Lewis, ap
Laurence, ap Richard, ap Tho-/mas, ap Sheffre,
ap Sheames, ap Taffie, ap Harie,/ All Shentleman
in Wales./ [*London*] Printed by M. Shinkin,
Printer to S. Taffie, and/ are to be fold at the Signe
of the Goat on the/ Welch Mountaine. 1647./ 8
pp. 4to. (1*l.* 1*s.* 2807)

WELD (Isaac). Travels through the States of
North America, and the Provinces of Upper and
Lower Canada, during the Years 1795, 1796, and
1797. By Isaac Weld Junior. Illustrated and
embellished with Sixteen Plates. *London:* John
Stockdale, 1799. *xxiv and* 464 *pp. Books, etc.* 8 *pp.*
' *Erratum.' pasted at the bottom of the list of plates.*
With the 16 *plates. Half calf. 4to.* (10*s.* 6*d.* 2808)

WELD (Isaac). Travels through the States of
North America, and the Provinces of Upper and
Lower Canada, during the Years 1795, 1796, and
1797. ▪ By Isaac Weld, Junior. Third Edition.
Illustrated and embellished with sixteen plates.
In Two Volumes. *London:* John Stockdale, 1800.
Two Volumes. Vol. I. *xx and* 427 *pp.* 2 *maps and*
9 *plates.* Vol. II. *viii and* 376 *pp.* 5 *plates. Half*
calf. 8vo. (7*s.* 6*d.* 2809)

WELD (Isaac). Travels through the States of
North America, and the Provinces of Upper and
Lower Canada, during the Years 1795, 1796, and
1797. By Isaac Weld, Jun. Fourth Edition.
Illustrated and Embellished with Sixteen Plates.
In two Volumes. *London:* John Stockdale, 1807.
Two Volumes. Vol. I. *xx and* 427 *pp.* 2 *maps and*
9 *plates.* Vol. II. *viii and* 376 *pp.* 5 *plates. Half*
calf. 8vo. (7*s.* 6*d.* 2810)

WELDE (T.) A/ Short Story/ of the/ Rife, reign,
and ruine of the Antinomians,/ Familifts & Libertines, that infected the Churches/ of/ New-England :/ And how they were confuted by the
Affembly of Mi-/nifters there : As alfo of the
Magiftrates proceedings/ in Court againft them./
Together with Gods ftrange and remarkable judge-/
ments from Heaven upon fome of the chief fomenters
of/ thefe Opinions ; And the lamentable death of
M⁵. Hutchifon./ Very fit for thefe times ; here

being the fame errours amongft/ us, and acted by the fame fpirit./ Publifhed at the inftant requeft of fundry, by one that was an eye/ and eare-witneffe of the carriage of matters there./ *London,/* Printed for Ralph Smith at the figne of the Bible in Corn-hill/ neare the Royall Exchange. 1644./ 10 *prel. leaves; viz. Title in a metal type border, the reverse blank;* 'To the Reader.' *Signed* 'T. W.' 1 *page.* 'The Preface.' *Signed* 'T. Welde.' 16 *pp: Text* 66 *pp. Calf extra by Bedford.* 4*to.* (2*l.* 12*s.* 6*d.* 2811)

WEMMS (WILLIAM). The Trial of William Wemms, James Hartegan, William M'Cauley, Hugh White, Mathew Killroy, William Warren, John Carrol, and Hugh Montgomery, Soldiers in his Majefty's 29th Regiment of Foot, For the Murder of Crifpus Attucks, Samuel Gray, Samuel Maverick, James Caldwell, and Patrick Carr, On Monday Evening, the 5th of March, 1770, at the Superior Court of Judicature, Court of Affize, and general Goal Delivery, held at Boston. The 27th Day of November, 1770, by Adjournment. Before the Hon. Benjamin Lynde, John Cushing, Peter Oliver, and Edmund Trowbridge, Esquires, Justices of faid Court. Publifhed by Permiffion of the Court. Taken in Short Hand by John Hodgson. *Boston:* Printed by J. Fleeming, and fold at his Printing-Office, nearly oppofite the White-horfe Tavern in Newbury-ftreet. M,DCC,LXX. 217 *pp. Calf extra by Bedford.* 8*vo.* (18*s.* 2812)

WESLEY (JOHN). An Old Fox Tarr'd and Feathered. Occasioned by what is called Mr. John Wesley's Calm Addrefs to our American Colonies. By an Hanoverian. A Calm Addrefs to our American Colonies. *London:* Printed for the Author; [1775.] 16 *pp. Half mor.* 8*vo.* (4*s.* 6*d.* 2813)

WESLEY (JOHN). A Calm Address to our American Colonies. By John Wesley, M.A. *London,* R. Hawes, [1775.] 23 *pp. Half morocco.* 12*mo.* (4*s.* 6*d.* 2814)

WESLEY (JOHN). A Calm Address to our American Colonies. By John Wesley, M.A. *London:* R. Hawes, MDCCLXXV. 23 *pp. Half morocco.* 12*mo.* (3*s.* 6*d.* 2815)

WESLEY (JOHN). A Calm Address to our Ame-

rican Colonies. By John Wesley, M.A. A New
Edition, Corrected, and Enlarged. *London,* Robert
Hawes, [1776.] 22 *pp.* 12*mo.*   (4*s.* 6*d.* 2816)

WESLEY (John). A Calm Addrefs to the Inhabitants of England. By John Wesley. *London:* J.
Fry and Co. M.DCC.LXXVII. 21 *pp. Half morocco.*
12*mo.*   (3*s.* 6*d.* 2817)

WESLEY (John). Some Observations on Liberty:
Occafioned by a late Tract. By John Wesley,
M.A. *London,* R. Hawes, 1776. 36 *pp. Half mo-
rocco.* 12*mo.*   (3*s.* 6*d.* 2818)

WEST (John). The Substance of a Journal during
a residence at the Red River Colony British North
America: And frequent excursions among the
North West American Indians, in the years 1820,
1821, 1822, 1823. Second Edition, enlarged with
a Journal of a Mission to the Indians of New
Brunswick, and Nova Scotia, and the Mohawks
on the Ouse or Grand River, Upper Canada.
1825-1826. By John West, A.M. Late Chaplain
to the Hon. The Hudson's Bay Company. L. B.
Seeley and Son, *London.* MDCCCXXVII. *xvi and* 326
pp. With 4 *plates. Cloth.* 8*vo.*   (5*s.* 2819)

WEST INDIA COMPANY. Nader Prolongatie
van het Octroy voor de Westindische Compagnie.
en van de eerfte prolongatie van dien, voor den
tyd van nog dertig jaaren. Gearrefteert den 8
Augufty 1730. In 's *Gravenhage,* By Jacobus
Scheltus, Anno 1730. 20 *pp. Calf, by Hayday.*
4*to.*   (10*s.* 6*d.* 2820)

WEST-INDIES. Weft-vnnd Oft Indifcher/ Luft-
gart:/ Das ift,/ Eygentliche Erzehlung,/ Wann
vnd von wem die Newe Welt erfunden,/ befägelt,
vnd eingenommen worden, vnd was fich Denck-/
würdiges darbey zugetragen./ Neben Befchreibung aller deren Landfchafften,/ Infeln, Völcker,
Thieren, Früchten, Gewächfen, fo/ beydes in
Weft=vnd Oft Indien zu finden./ Wie auch Ver-
faffung der fürnembften Schiffahrten fo/ nicht allein
dahin, fonderen auch vmb die gantze Welt von den
Spa=/nieren, Engelländeren, Holländeren, &c. ver-
richter/ worden./ Aufz glaubwürdigen Schrifften
zufamen gezogen./ Gedruckt zu *Cöllen,*/ Bey
Wilhelm Lützenkirchen,/ Anno MDCXVIII./ 4

prel. leaves; viz. Title, the reverse blank. ' Dem
Hochwürdigen in Gott Vatter vnnd Herren, Herren
Hugoni,' *etc.* 4 *pp, signed* ' Gaſpar Ens L. Wilhelm
Lutzenkirchen.' ' An den Günſtigen Leſer.' 2 *pp :*
Text, 436 *pp.* ' Des Oſt Indiſchen Luſtgar=/tens/
Erſter Theil :/' 236 *pp. Vellum.* 4*to.* (2*l.* 2*s.* 2821)

WEST INDIES. [*Printed title*] West-Indische/
Spieghel,/ '*t Amstelredam,* By Broer Ianſz. ende
Iacob Pieterſz. Wachter, Boeck-/vercooper op
den Dam, inde Wachter. Anno 1624./ [*Engraved
title*] Weſt-Indiſche/ Spieghel,/ Waer inne men
fien kan,/ Alle de Eylanden, Provintien, Lant-
ſchappen, het/ Machtige Ryck van Mexico, en
'*t Gout/ en Silver-rycke Landt van Peru./ 'Tſampt/
De Courſen, Havenen, Klippen,/ Koopmanschap-
pen, etc. ſoo wel inde Noort als in/ de Zuyt-zee.
Als mede hoe die vande/ Spanjaerden eerſt ge in-
vadeert ſyn./ Door/ Athanasium Inga,/ Peruaen,
van Cuſco./ 4 *prel. leaves; viz. Engraved and printed
titles,* ' Toe eyghen-Brief.' 4 *pp :* *Text* 435 *pp.*
' Regiſter des Boecks :' 7 *pp.* 2 *maps,* '*t Noorder
deel van West Indien' *and* '*t Zuyder deel van
West-Indien.' *Vellum.* 4*to.* (1*l.* 11*s.* 6*d.* 2822)

WETMORE (James). A Vindication of The Pro-
feſſors of the Church of England in Connecticut.
Againſt The Invectives contained in a Sermon
preached at Stanford by Mr. Noah Hobart, Dec.
31. 1746. In a Letter to a Friend. By James
Wetmore, A.M. Rector of the Pariſh of Rye, and
Miſſionary from the venerable Society for the Propagation of the Goſpel in foreign Parts. *Boston :*
N. E. Printed and Sold by Rogers and Fowle in
Queen-ſtreet. MDCCXLVII. 45 *pp. Half morocco.*
8*vo.* (10*s.* 6*d.* 2823)

WHAT think ye of the Congress now ? Or, an Enquiry, how far the Americans Are bound to abide
by, and execute, the Decisions of the late Continental Congress. With a Plan, By Samuel Galloway, Eſq ; for a Proposed Union between Great-
Britain and the Colonies. To which is added, An
Alarm to the Legislature of the Province of New-
York. Occaſioned by the preſent Political Disturbances. Addreſſed to the Representatives in
General Assembly convened. New York, Printed
by J. Rivington : *London,* Reprinted for Richard-

son Urquhart, 1775. *Title and 90 pp. Half mo-*
rocco. 8vo.   (7s. 6d. 2824)

WHEATLEY (PHILLIS). Poems on various sub-
jects, religious and moral. By Phillis Wheatley,
Negro Servant to Mr. John Wheatley, of Boston,
in New England. *London:* Printed for A. Bell,
Bookſeller, Aldgate; and ſold by Meſſrs. Cox and
Berry, King Street, Boston. MDCCLXXIII. 124 *pp.*
Contents, 3 *pp. With frontispiece portrait. Calf.*
8vo.   (10s. 6d. 2825)

WHEELOCK (ELEAZAR). A plain and faithful
Narrative of the Original Deſign, Riſe, Progreſs
and preſent State of the Indian Charity-School At
Lebanon, in Connecticut. By Eleazar Wheelock,
A.M. Pastor of a Church in Lebanon. *Boston:*
Printed by Richard and Samuel Draper, in New-
bury-ſtreet. M.DCC.LXIII. 55 *pp. Half morocco.*
8vo.   (7s. 6d. 2826)

WHEELOCK (ELEAZAR). A Brief Narrative of
the Indian Charity-School, In Lebanon in Connecticut, New England. Founded and Carried on
by That faithful Servant of God The Rev. Mr.
Eleazar Wheelock. *London:* J. and W. Oliver,
MDCCLXVI. 48 *pp. Half mor. 8vo.* (5s. 6d. 2827)

WHITAKER (NATHANAEL). Two Sermons: On
the Doctrine of Reconciliation. Together with
an Appendix, in answer to a Dialogue wrote to
discredit the main Truths contained in these Discourses, By the Reverend William Hart, Of Say-
brook, in Connecticut. By Nathanael Whitaker,
D.D. Miniſter of the Goſpel in Salem, in Massachusetts-Bay. *Salem,* New-England: Printed by
Samuel Hall, in the main Street. MDCCLXX. 168
pp. 8vo.   (6s. 6d. 2828)

WHITBOURNE (RICHARD). A/ Discovrse/ and
Discovery/ of Nevv-fovnd-land, with/ many reaſons to prooue how worthy and be-/neficiall a
Plantation may there be made,/ after a far better
manner than/ now it is./ Together with the Lay-/
ing open of certaine enor-/mities and abuſes committed by ſome that trade/ to that Countrey, and
the meanes laide/ downe for reformation/ thereof./
Written by Captaine Richard Whitbourne of/ Ex-
mouth, in the County of Deuon, and pub-/liſhed

by Authority./ Imprinted at *London* by *Felix Kyngston*, for/ William Barret. 1620./ 9 *prel. leaves* ; *viz. Title,* on the reverse *the royal arms* ; ' To the High/ and Mightie Prince,/ Iames, By the Grace of/ God, King of Great Brittaine, France/ and Ireland, Defender of the/ Faith, &c.'/ (A 3) 4 *pp* ; *signed* ' Richard Whitbovrne.' ' To his Maiefties good/ Subiects.' (B) 4 *pp* : *signed* ' R. W.'. ' The Preface be-/ing an Indvction to/ the follow- ing Difcourfe.'/ (B 3) 8 *pp. in italics* ; *Text,* (D) 69 *pp. followed by one blank page* ; ' A conclufion to the Reader, containing/ a particular Defcription, and relation/ of fome things omitted in the for-/mer Difcourfe.'/ 4 *pp. Fine copy, in calf extra, by Bed- ford.* 4*to.* (4*l.* 4*s.* 2829)

WHITBOURNE (RICHARD). A/ Discovrse/ And Discovery/ of Nevv-found-land, with/ many rea- fons to prooue how worthy and bene-/ficiall a Plantation may there be made, after a far/ better manner than now it is./ Together with the laying/ open of certaine enormities/ and abufes committed by fome that trade to that/ Countrey, and the meanes laid downe for/ reformation thereof./ Written by Captaine Richard Whitbourne of/ Ex- mouth, in the County of Deuon, and pub-/lifhed by Authority./ As alfo, an Inuitation : and like- wife certaine Letters fent/ from that Countrey ; which are printed in the/ latter part of this Booke./ Imprinted at *London* by Felix Kingfton./ 1622./ 11 *prel. leaves* ; *viz. Title,* on the reverse *the royal arms* ; ' At Theobalds, the 12. of Aprill 1622.' 1 *page* ; ' After our very hearty Commendations to your good Lordfhips,' *etc.* 1 *page* ; ' The names of fome, who haue vndertaken to/ helpe and aduance his Maiefties Plantation in/ the New-found-land. viz.' 2 *pp* ; *signed* ' R. W.' ' To the High/ and Mightie Prince,/ Iames, by the Grace of/ God, King of great Brittaine, France/ and Ireland, De- fender of the/ Faith, &c./ 4 *pp* ; *signed* ' Richard Whitbovrne.' ' To his Maiefties good/ Subiects.'/ 4 *pp* ; *signed* ' R. W.' ' The Preface,/ being an indvc-/tion to the following/ Difcourfe / 8 *pp* : *Text* 107 *pp.* ' A Conclufion to the former Difcourfe,' *etc.* 5 *pp* ; *signed* ' R. W.' ' A Letter from Captaine Edward Wynne, Go-/uernour of the Colony at Ferryland, within the/ Prouince of Aualon, in

Newfound-land, vnto/ the Right Honorable Sir
George Calvert/ Knight, his Maiefties Principall
Secre-/tary. Iuly 1622,/ *and 3 other Letters, pp.*
1 *to* 15. (*pp.* 35, 70, *and* 71, *are paged* 3, 100, *and*
101.) *Calf extra, by Bedford.* 4*to.* (4*l.* 4*s.* 2830)

WHITBOURNE (Richard). A/ Difcovrfe/ and
Discovery/ of nevv - fovnd - land, with/ many
reafons to prooue how worthy and bene-/ficial a
Plantation may there be made, after a/ better
manner than it was./ Together with the laying/
open of certain enormities/ and abufes committed
by fome that trade to that/ Countrey, and the
meanes laid downe for/ reformation thereof./
Written by Captaine Richard Whitbourne of/ Ex-
mouth, in the County of Deuon, and pub-/lifhed
by Authority./ As alfo a louing Inuitation and
likewife the copies of certaine/ Letters fent from
that Countrey; which are printed in/ the latter
part of this Booke. Imprinted at *London* by Felix
Kingston. 1623./ *9 prel. leaves; viz. Title, on the
reverse the royal arms, and* ' Moft humbly,' *etc.* ' At
Theobalds, the 12. of Aprill 1622.' 1 *page,* 'After
our very hearty Commendations to your good Lordfhips,' *etc.* 1 *page;* [' The names of fome, who haue
vndertaken to helpe and aduance his Maiefties
Plantation in the New-found-land. viz.' *2 pp.
signed* ' R. W.' *wanting.*] 'To the High/ and
Mightie Prince,/ Iames, by the Grace of God,/
King of great Brittaine, France and Ireland,/ Defender of the Faith, &c.'/ *2 pp.* ' To his Maiefties
good Subieĉts.' *3 pp;* ' The Preface,' *7 pp. Text,*
97 *pp;* ' A Conclufion to the former Difcourfe,' *etc.*
4 *pp.* ' A Letter from Captaine Edward Wynne,'
etc. and 3 other Letters, pp. 1 *to* 15. 4*to.* (3*l.* 2831)

WHITEFIELD (George). A Journal of a Voyage
from London to Savannah in Georgia. In Two
Parts. Part I. From London to Gibraltar. Part II.
From Gibraltar to Savannah. By George Whitefield A.B. of Pembroke College, Oxford. [With a
fhort Preface, fhewing the Reafons of its Publication. *London*, James Hutton, 1738.] *Title, iv and*
58 *pp. Title-page mutilated. Half morocco.*
8*vo.* (4*s.* 6*d.* 2832)

WHITEFIELD (George). A Journal of a Voyage
from London to Savannah in Georgia. In Two

Parts. Part I. From London to Gibralter. Part II.
From Gibralter to Savannah. By George Whitefield, A.B. of Pembroke-College, Oxford. With a
fhort Preface, fhewing the Reafon of its Publication. The Fifth Edition. *London,* James Hutton,
MDCCXXXIX. *55 pp. 8vo.* (4s. 6d. 2833)

WHITEFIELD (GEORGE). A Continuation Of the
Reverend Mr. Whitefield's Journal, From his
Arrival at Savannah, To his Return to London.
London, James Hutton, M.DCC.XXXIX. *2 prel. leaves
and 38 pp.* 'Advertifement.' 1 *page. Half morocco.
8vo.* (5s. 6d. 2834)

WHITEFIELD (GEORGE). A Continuation Of the
Reverend Mr. Whitefield's Journal From his Arrival at Savannah, To his Return to London. The
Second Edition. *London:* W. Strahan, MDCCXXXIX.
2 prel. leaves and 38 pp. 8vo. (5s. 6d. 2835)

WHITEFIELD (GEORGE). [*First title*] The Rev.
Mr. Whitefield's Answer to the Bishop of London's
last Pastoral Letters. The Second Edition. With
the Supplement. [*Second title*] The Rev. Mr.
Whitefield's Answer to the Bishop of London's last
Pastoral Letter. *London:* W. Strahan, MDCCXXXIX.
Text, pp. 3-28. 'A Supplement to The Rev. Mr.
Whitefield's Answer,' *etc. 8pp. 8vo.* (2s. 6d. 2836)

WHITEFIELD (GEORGE). The heinous Sin of
Drunkenness A Sermon Preached on Board the
Whitaker. By George Whitefield, A.B. of Pem-
broke College, Oxford. *London:* C. Whitefield,
MDCCXXXIX. *Wanting all after page 20. Unbound.
8vo.* (2s. 6d. 2837)

WHITEFIELD (GEORGE). Thankfulnefs for Mercies received a neceffary Duty A Farewel Sermon
Preached on Board the Whitaker, At Anchor near
Savannah in Georgia, On Sunday May the 17th,
1738. By George Whitefield, A.B. of Pembroke College, Oxford. *London:* C. Whitefield,
MDCCXXXIX. *Title and pp.* 3-24. *8vo.* (2s. 6d. 2838)

WHITEFIELD (GEORGE). A Continuation Of the
Reverend Mr. Whitefield's Journal, From his
Embarking after the Embargo, To his Arrival at
Savannah in Georgia. *London:* W. Strahan 1740.
88 pp. 8vo. (5s. 6d. 2839)

WHITEFIELD (GEORGE). An Account of Money
Received and Difburfed for the Orphan-House in

Georgia. By George Whitefield, A. B. Late of
Pembroke-College, Oxford. To which is prefixed
A Plan of the Building. *London:* W. Strahan
for T. Cooper, 1741. *Title and 45 pp. With the Plan.*
8vo.   (7s. 6d. 2840)

WHITEFIELD (George). A Letter To the Reverend Mr. John Wesley: In Answer to his Sermon, entituled, Free-Grace. By George Whitefield, A. B. Late of Pembroke-College, Oxford.
London: W. Strahan for T. Cooper, 1741. *31 pp.*
8vo.   (2s. 6d. 2841)

WHITEFIELD (George). A Continuation of the
Account of the Orphan-House in Georgia. From
January 174⁰/₁, to June 1742. To which are alfo
fubjoin'd, Some Extracts from an Account of a
Work of a like Nature, carried on by the late
Profeffor Franck in Glaucha near Hall in Saxony.
By George Whitefield, A. B. Late of Pembroke-
College in Oxford. *Edinburgh,* T. Lumisden and
J. Robertson; M.DCC.XLII. *85 pp. Unbound.*
12mo.   (4s. 6d. 2842)

WHITEFIELD (George). A Continuation Of the
Reverend Mr. Whitefield's Journal, From a few
Days after his Return to Georgia To his Arrival
at Falmouth, on the 11th of March, 1741. Con-
taining An Account of the Work of God at Georgia,
Rhode-Ifland, New-England, New-York, Penn-
fylvania and South-Carolina. The Seventh Journal.
The second Edition. *London:* W. Strahan;
MDCCXLIV. *88 pp. Half mor.* 8vo. (5s. 6d. 2843)

WHITEFIELD (George). A Short Account of
God's Dealings With the Reverend Mr. George
Whitefield, A. B. late of Pembroke-College, Oxford, from His Infancy to the Time of his entring
into Holy Orders. Written by Himself, on board
the Elizabeth, Captaine Stephenfon, bound from
London to Philadelphia and fent over by him to
be publifhed for the Benefit of the Orphan Houfe
in Georgia. The Second Edition. *London:* W.
Strahan, MDCCXLIV. *46 pp. Half morocco.*
12mo.   (4s. 6d. 2844)

WHITEFIELD (George). Britain's Mercies, and
Britain's Duty; Reprefented in a Sermon Preach'd
at the New-Building in Philadelphia, On Sunday

Auguſt 24, 1746. Occaſioned by the Suppreſſion of the late Unnatural Rebellion. By George White-field, A. B. Late of Pembroke - College, Oxon. The Second Edition. *Boston :* Printed and Sold by S. Kneeland and T. Green in Queen-Street. 1746. *Title and pp. 5-22. 8vo.*   (2s. 6d. 2845)

WHITEFIELD (GEORGE). Britain's Mercies, and Britain's Duty. Represented in a Sermon Preach'd at Philadelphia, On Sunday Auguſt 24, 1746. And occaſioned by the Suppression Of the late Unnatural Rebellion. By George Whitefield, A. B. Late of Pembroke College, Oxon. Philadelphia Printed : *London* Re-printed, For J. Robinson, 1746. *24 pp. Half morocco. 8vo.* (2s. 6d. 2846)

WHITEFIELD (GEORGE). The Two First Parts of his Life, with his Journals, Reviſed, corrected, and abridged, By George Whitefield, A. B. Chaplain to the Right Hon. the Counteſs of Huntingdon. *London :* W. Strahan, MDCCLVI. *3 prel. leaves and 446 pp. Old calf. 12mo.*   (7s. 6d. 2847)

WHITELOCKE (JOHN). Trial of Lieutenant General John Whitelocke, Commander in Chief of the Expedition against Buenos Ayres. By Court-Martial, held in Chelsea College, On Thursday, the 28th January, 1808, and succeeding days. *London :* Samuel Tipper, 1808. *Half-title, title, and 214 pp. 1 blank leaf.* ' Appendix,' *12 pp. Plan of the march, etc. 8vo.*   (4s. 6d. 2848)

WHITNEY (PETER). The History of the County of Worcester, in the Commonwealth of Massachusetts : With a Particular Account of every Town from its first Settlement to the preſent Time ; Including its Ecclesiastical State, together with a Geographical Description of the same. To which is prefixed, a Map of the County, at Large, from actual Survey. By Peter Whitney, A. M. Miniſter of the Goſpel in Northborough, in ſaid County. Printed at *Worcester,* Massachusetts, by Isaiah Thomas, Sold by him in Worcester, by ſaid Thomas and Andrews, in Boston, and by ſaid Thomas and Carlisle, in Walpole, Newhampſhire. MDCCXCIII. *339 pp. With the map. Calf. 8vo.* (12s. 6d. 2849)

WHOLSOME Severity reconciled with/ Christian Liberty./ Or,/ The true Reſolution of a preſent

Con-/troverfie concerning Liberty of/ Conscience./
Here you have the Queſtion ſtated, the middle/
way betwixt Popiſh Tyrannie and Schiſmatizing/
Liberty approved, and alſo confirmed from/ Scripture, and the teſtimonies of Divines,/ yea of whole
Churches :/ The chiefe Arguments and Exceptions
uſed in The/ Bloudy Tenent, The Compaſſionate
Samaritane,/ M. S. to A. S. &c. examined./ Eight
Diſtinctions added for qualifying and/ clearing the
whole matter./ And in concluſion a Paraenetick to
the five Apo-/logiſts for chooſing Accommodation
rather/ then Toleration./ Imprimatur. Ia. Cranford. Decemb. 16. 1644./ *London*,/ Printed for
Chriſtopher Meredith, and are to be ſold/ at the
Signe of the Crane in Pauls Churchyard. 1645./
4 *prel. leaves and* 40 *pp. half mor. 4to.* (1*l*. 1*s*. 2850)

WIGGLESWORTH (Edward). The Bleſſedneſs
of the Dead who die in the Lord. A Sermon
Preached at the Publick Lecture, Tueſday, April
6. 1731. In the Hall of Harvard=College, In
Cambridge, N. E. Upon the News of the Death of
Thomas Hollis, Eſq ; of London, The moſt bountiful Benefactor to that Society. By Edward
Wigglesworth, D. D. And Hollis-Profeſſor of Divinity. Publiſhed at the Deſire of the Preſident
and Fellows of Harvard-College. *Boston* in New-
England : Printed for S. Gerriſh, at the lower End
of Cornhil. 1731. *Title, iv and* 23 *pp. Unbound.*
8*vo*.   (4*s*. 6*d*.   2851)

WIGGLESWORTH (Edward). A Letter To the
Reverend Mr. George Whitefield, By Way of
Reply To his Anſwer to the College Teſtimony
againſt him and his Conduct. By Edward Wig-
gleſworth, D. D. Profeſſor of Divinity in ſaid College. To which is added, The Reverend Preſident's
Answer To the Things charg'd upon Him by the
ſaid Mr. Whitefield, as Inconſiſtences. *Boston*,
N. E. Printed and ſold by T. Fleet, at the Heart
and Crown in Cornhill. 1745. 61 *pp.* ' Postcript.'
2 *pp.* 'The Reverend Preſident's Answer,' 5 *pp.
signed* ' Edward Holyoke.' 4*to*. (7*s*. 6*d*.   2852)

WIGGLESWORTH (Edward). Calculations on
American Population, with A Table for eſtimating
the annual Increaſe of Inhabitants in the Britiſh
Colonies : The Manner of its Conſtruction Ex-

plained; and Its Ufe Illuftrated. By Edward
Wigglesworth, M.A. Hollis Profeffor of Divinity
at Cambridge. *Boston:* Printed and Sold by John
Boyle in Marlboro' Street. MDCCLXXV. 24 *pp.*
Half morocco. 8vo. (7s. 6d. 2853)

WILBERFORCE (SAMUEL). A History of the
Protestant Episcopal Church in America. By
Samuel Wilberforce, M.A. Chaplain to H. R. H.
Prince Albert, and Archdeacon of Surrey. *London:* James Burns, 1844. *xvi and* 456 *pp.* *Map
and table.* *Cloth, uncut.* 12mo. (3s. 6d. 2854)

WILCOCKE (SAMUEL HULL). History of the Viceroyalty of Buenos Ayres; containing the most
accurate details relative to the Topography, History, Commerce, Population, Government, &c.
&c. Of that Valuable Colony. By Samuel Hull
Wilcocke. Illustrated with plates. *London:* Sherwood, Neely, and Jones, [1806]. 2 *prel. leaves and*
576 *pp.* *Map facing title, chart and plates at pp.* 58,
172, 336, 415, 418, 457. 8vo. (7s. 6d. 2855)

WILKES (CHARLES). Narrative of the United
States' Exploring Expedition, during the Years
1838, 1839, 1840, 1841, 1842. By Charles Wilkes,
U. S. N. Commander of the Expedition, Member
of the American Philosophical Society, &c. Condensed and Abridged. *London:* Whittaker and
Co., [1845.] 4 *prel. leaves and* 372 *pp.* *Half calf.*
8vo. (5s. 2856)

WILKINSON (JAMES). Burr's Conspiracy exposed; and General Wilkinson vindicated against
the slanders of his Enemies on that important
occasion. 1811. *Title, Advertisement* 1 *page, Introduction, pp.* 3-18. *Text, pp.* 3-99. *Appendix* 136
pp. *Half calf.* 8vo. (7s. 6d. 2857)

WILKINSON (JAMES). Memoirs of My own
Times. By General James Wilkinson. In Three
Volumes. *Philadelphia:* Printed by Abraham
Small. 1816. *Two Volumes.* Vol. I. *xv and* 855 *pp.*
7 *Returns* A *to* G. 'Appendix,' 42 *pp.* 'Errata,'
2 *pp. facsimile letters at pp.* 282, 283. Vol. II. *Title
and* 578 *pp.* 'Appendix.' 260 *pp.* [*Vol.* 3 *wanting*]
Half calf. 8vo. (1l. 1s. 2858)

WILLARD (SAMUEL). A/ Sermon/ Preached upon
Ezek. 22. 30, 31./ Occafioned by the Death of the/

much honoured/ John Leveret Efq ;/ Governour
of the Colony of the/ Mattachufets. N. E./ By S.
W. Teacher of the South Church/ in Bofton./
Boston ;/ Printed by John Fofter, in the Year
1679./ *Title in a type metal border, the reverse blank,
and text,* 13 *pp. Fine copy, in morocco, by Bedford.*
4*to.* (3*l.* 3*s.* 2859)

WILLARD (SAMUEL). The Duty of a People that
have Renewed/ their Covenant with God./ Opened
and Urged in/ A Sermon/ Preached to the fecond
Church in Bofton in/ New-England, March 17.
16$\frac{79}{80}$. after/ that Church had explicitly and moft/
folemnly renewed the Ingagement/ of themfelves
to God, and one to another./ By Samvel VVillard,
Teacher of a Church in/ Bofton in New-England./
Boston, Printed by John Fofter. 1680. *Title, reverse blank, and* 13 *pp. Fine copy in morocco, by
Bedford.* 4*to.* (3*l.* 3*s.* 2860)

WILLARD (SAMUEL). Ne Sutor ultra Crepidam./
Or brief/ Animadversions/ Upon the New-Eng-
land/ Anabaptifts/ late fallacious/ Narrative ;/
Wherein the Notorious Miftakes/ and Falfhoods
by them Publifhed, are detected./ By Samuel
Willard, Teacher of a Church in Bofton in New-
England. *Boston* in New-England,/ Printed by
S. Green upon Affignment of S. Sewall. And are
to be Sold/ by Sam. Philips, at the Weft end of
the Exchange : 1681./ 4 *prel. leaves; viz. Title, re-
verse blank,* ' To the Reader.' 5 *pp. signed* ' Increase
Mather.' *Text* 27 *pp. Fine copy in morocco, by
Bedford.* 4*to.* (4*l.* 4*s.* 2861)

WILLARD (SAMUEL). The Movrners/ Cordial/
Againft Exceffive/ Sorrovv/ Difcovering what
grounds of Hope/ Gods People have concerning
their/ dead/ Friends/ By Samuel Willard, Teacher
of a/ Church in Bofton./ *Bofton,* Printed by Benjamin Harris, and/ John Allen. 1691./ Very
Suitable to be given at Funerals./ 4 *and* 138 *pp.*
16*mo.* (1*l.* 1*s.* 2862)

WILLARD (SAMUEL). Love's/ Pedigree./ Or/ A
Difcourfe fhewing the Grace of/ Love in a Believer
to be of/ A Divine Original/ Delivered in a/ Ser-
mon/ Preached at the Lecture in Boston,/ Febr.
29. $\frac{1699}{1700}$./ By S. Willard, Teacher of a Church

there./ *Boston,* in N. E. Printed by B. Green, and/ J. Allen. Sold by Benjamin Eliot, at his Shop/ under the Weſt End of the Town Houſe. 1700./ *Title & pp.* 3-28. 16*mo.* (10*s.* 6*d.* 2863)

WILLARD (SAMUEL). The Peril/ of the/ Times Diſplayed./ Or,/ The Danger of Mens taking up/ with a/ Form of Godlineſs,/ But Denying the Power of it./ Being/ The Subſtance of ſeveral Sermons/ Preached :/ By Samuel Willard,/ Teacher of a Church in Boſton. N. E. *Boſton,* Printed by B. Green, & J. Allen,/ Sold by Benjamin Eliot. 1700./ 168 *pp.* 12*mo.* (1*l.* 1*s.* 2864)

WILLARD (SAMUEL). A Compleat Body of Divinity in Two Hundred and Fifty Expository Lectures on the Aſſembly's Shorter Catechiſm wherein The Doctrines of The Christian Religion are unfolded, their Truth confirm'd, their Excellence diſplay'd, their Uſefulneſs improv'd; contrary Errors & Vices refuted & expos'd, Objeſtions anſwer'd, Controverſies ſettled, Caſes of Conſcience reſolv'd; and a great Light thereby reflected on the preſent Age. By the Reverend & Learned Samuel Willard, M. A. Late Paſtor of the South Church in Boſton, and Vice-Preſident of Harvard College in Cambridge, in New-England. Prefac'd by the Paſtors of the ſame Church. *Boston* in New-England: Printed by B. Green and S. Kneeland for B. Eliot and D. Henchman, and Sold at their Shops. MDCCXXVI. *Title, iv, 6, and* 914 *pp. A Catalogue, etc.* 1 *page. Folio.* (3*l.* 3*s.* 2865)

WILLIAMS (DANIEL). Man made Righteous/ by/ Chriſt's Obedience./ Being two/ Sermons/ at/ Pinners-Hall./ With Enlargements, &c./ Alſo ſome/ Remarks/ on/ Mr. Mather's Poſtſcript, &c./ By Daniel Williams./ *London*/ Printed for J. Dunton at the Raven/ in the Poultry, 1694./ 6 *prel. leaves and* 238 *pp. Old calf.* 8*vo.* (7*s.* 6*d.* 2866)

WILLIAMS (EDWARD). Virginia:/ More eſpecially the South part thereof,/ Richly and truly valued: viz./ The fertile Carolana, and no leſſe excellent Iſle of Roa-/noak, of Latitude from 31. to 37. Degr. relating the/ meanes of rayſing infinite profits to the Adventu-/rers and Planters./ The ſecond Edition, with Addition of/ The Discovery

of Silkworms,/ with their benefit./ And Implanting
of Mulbury Trees./ Also/ The Dreſſing of Vines,
for the rich Trade of ma-/king Wines in Virginia./
Together with/ The making of the Saw-mill, very
uſefull in Virginia,/ for cutting of Timber and
Clapbord to build with-/all, and its Converſion to
many as profitable Uſes./ By E. W. Gent./ *London,*/ Printed by T. H. for John Stephenſon, at the
Signe of/ the Sun below Ludgate. 1650./ *6 prel.
leaves ; viz. Title, the reverse blank,* ' To the worthy
Gentlemen, Adventurers and Plan-/ters in Virginia.'/ *2 pp ;* ' To the Supreme Authority of this
Nation, The/ Parliament of England.'/ *8 pp; signed*
' Ed. Williams.' *Text,* 47 *pp.* ' The Table.' 8 *pp.*
' Virginias/ Diſcovery of/ Silke-Wormes,/ with
their benefit./ And/ The Implanting of Mulberry
Trees./ Alſo/ The dreſſing and keeping of Vines,
for the rich Trade/ of making Wines there./ Together with/ The making of the Saw-mill, very
uſefull in Virginia,/ for cutting of Timber and
Clapboard, to build with-/all, and its converſion to
other as profitable Uſes./ *London,*/ Printed by T.
H. for John Stephenſon, at the ſigne of/ the Sun,
below Ludgate. 1650./ *4 prel. leaves ; viz. one blank
leaf ; Title, reverse blank;* ' To all the Virginia
Merchants, Adventures, and Planters.' *4 pp. signed*
' Ed. Williams.' *Text,* 78 *pp. 2 maps, one with and one
without the portrait of Drake.* 4to. (15*l.* 15*s.* 2867)

WILLIAMS (GRIFFITH). An Account Of the Island
of Newfoundland, With the Nature of its Trade,
And Method of carrying on the Fishery. With
Reasons for the great Decreaſe of that moſt valuable
Branch of Trade. By Capt. Griffith Williams, Of
the Royal Regiment of Artillery, who reſided in
the Iſland Fourteen Years when a Lieutenant, and
now has a Command there. To which is annexed,
A Plan To exclude the French from that Trade.
Propoſed to the Adminiſtration in the Year 1761,
By Capt. Cole. [*London*], Printed for Capt. Thomas
Cole, M.DCC.LXV, *Half-title, title, and* 35 *pp. Half
morocco.* 8*vo.*   (4*s.* 6*d.*   2868)

WILLIAMS (JOHN). An Enquiry into the Truth
of the Tradition, concerning the Diſcovery of
America, By Prince Madog ab Owen Gwynedd,
about the year, 1170. By John Williams, L.L.D.

London: J. Brown, M.DCCXCI. *viii and* 82 *pp.*
'Appendix.' 3 *pp.* 8*vo.* (10*s.* 6*d.* 2869)

WILLIAMS (JOHN). Farther Observations, on
the Difcovery of America, by Prince Madog ab
Gwynedd, about the year, 1170. Containing the
account given by General Bowles, the Creek or
Cherokee Indian, lately in London, and by feveral
others, of a Wellh Tribe or Tribes of Indians, now
living in the Weftern parts of North America.
By John Williams, L.L.D. *London:* J. Brown,
M.DCCXCII. *ix and* 51 *pp.* 8*vo.* (7*s.* 6*d.* 2870)

WILLIAMS (JONATHAN). Thermometrical Navigation. Being A Series of Experiments and Observations, tending to Prove, that by ascertaining The
Relative Heat of the Sea-Water from time to time,
The Paffage of a Ship through the Gulph Stream,
and from deep water into soundings, May be discovered in Time to avoid Danger, although (owing
to tempestuous weather,) it may be impossible To
heave the Lead or obferve the Heavenly Bodies.
Extracted from the American Philosophical Transactions. Vol. 2 & 3. With Additions and Improvements. *Philadelphia:* Printed and Sold by
R. Aitken, No. 22, Market Street. 1799. *xii and*
98 *pp.* 'Postcript,' 4 *pp. With map.* Old calf.
8*vo.* (7*s.* 6*d.* 2871)

WILLIAMS (ROGER). The/ Blovdy Tenent,/ of
Persecution, for caufe of/ Conscience, difcuffed,
in/ A Conference betweene/ Trvth and Peace./
VVho,/ In all tender Affection, prefent to the
High/ Court of Parliament, (as the Refult of/
their Difcourfe) thefe, (amongft other/ Paffages)
of higheft confideration./ [*London*] Printed in the
Year 1644./ 12 *prel. leaves; viz. Title, the reverse
blank;* 'Firft, That the blood of fo many hundred
thoufand fouls of Proteftants and Papifts,' *etc.* 4
pp; 'To the Right Honorable, both Houfes of the
High Court of Parliament.' 4 *pp;* 'To every
Courteous Reader.' 3 *pp;* 'A Table of the principall Contents of the Booke.' 10 *pp: Text* 247 *pp.*
Red morocco by F. Bedford. 4*to.* (7*l.* 7*s.* 2872)

WILLIAMS (ROGER). The/ Bloody Tenent/ yet/
·More Bloody:/ by/ Mr. Cottons endevour to

2   3 F

wash it white in the/ Blood of the Lambe ;/ Of
whofe precious Blood, fpilt in the/ Blood of his
Servants; and/ Of the blood of Millions fpilt in
former and/ later Wars for Confcience fake,/ that/
Moft Bloody Tenent of Perfecution for caufe of/
Confcience, upon a fecond Tryal, is found now
more/ apparently and more notorioufly guilty./
In this Rejoynder to Mr. Cotton, are principally/
I. The Name of Perfecution,/ II. The Power of
the Civill Sword/ in Spirituals/] Examined/ III.
The Parliaments permiffion of/ Diffenting Con-
fciences/] Juftified./ Alfo (as a Teftimony to M^r.
Clarks Narrative) is added/ a Letter to Mr En-
dicot Governor of the Maffachufets in N. E./ By
R. Williams of Providence in New-England./
London, Printed for Giles Calvert, and are to be
fold at/ the black-fpread-Eagle at the Weft-end of
Pauls, 1652./ *20 prel. leaves; viz. Title in a type
metal border, the reverse blank;* ' To the Moft Honorable the Parliament of the Common-wealth of
England.' *signed* ' Roger Williams,' 18 *pp;* 'To
the feveral Refpective General Courts, efpecially
that of the Maffachufets in N. England.' *signed*
' Roger Williams.' 7 *pp;* ' To the Merciful and
Compafsi-nate Reader.' *signed* ' Roger Williams.'
12 *pp: Text* 320 *pp.* ' The Principal Contents.' 16
pp. Old calf. 4*to.*   (7*l.* 7*s.*   2873)

WILLIAMS (ROGER). The Bloudy Tenant of
Presecution for Cause of Conscience Discused :
And Mr. Cotton's Letter examined and answered.
By Roger Williams. Edited for The Hanserd
Knollys Society, by Edward Bean Underhill.
London: J. Haddon, 1848. *xlvi pp. Title and* 440
pp. ' Second Annual Report,' *etc.* 8 *pp. Cloth.*
8*vo.*   (7*s.* 6*d.*   2874)

WILLIAMS (ROGER). To the King's Moft Excellent Majesty./ The Humble Petition of Roger
Williams of London, Mariner, Your Majefty's
moft Loyal and Dutiful Subject./ [*London.* 1680?]
Single sheet. Half morocco. Folio. (7*s.* 6*d.*   2875)

WILLIAMS (SAMUEL). The Natural and Civil
History of Vermont. By Samuel Williams, LL.D.
Member of the Meteorological Society in Germany
of the Philosophical Society in Philadelphia and
of the Academy of Arts and Sciences in Maffa-

chusetts. Publiſhed according to Act of Congress. Printed at *Walpole,* Newhampshire, by Isaiah Thomas and David Carlisle, Jun. Sold at their Bookstore, in Walpole, and by ſaid Thomas, at his Bookstore, in Worceſter. MDCCXCIV. *xvi and* 416 *pp. Map of Vermont. Calf. 8vo.* (7s. 6d. 2876)

WILLSON (MARCIUS). American History: Comprising Historical Sketches of the Indian Tribes; a description of American Antiquities, with an inquiry into their origin and the origin of the Indian Tribes; History of the United States, with appendices shewing its connection with European History: History of the present British Provinces; History of Mexico; and History of Texas, brought down to the time of its admission into the American Union. By Marcius Wilson, Author of School History of the United States, comprehensive Chart of American History etc. *New York:* Mark H. Newman & Co. No. 199 Broadway. 1847. 672 *pp. Cloth. 8vo.* (8s. 6d. 2878)

WILMORE (JOHN). The/ Case/ of/ John Wilmore/ Truly and Impartially Related:/ Or, a/ Looking= Glaſs/ for all/ Merchants and Planters/ That are Concerned in the/ American Plantations./ *London,*/ Printed for Edw. Powell at the White Swan in/ Little Brittain, MDCLXXXII./ *Title and* 17 *pp; signed* 'John Wilmer.' *Folio.* (1l. 1s. 2879)

WILMOT (JOHN EARDLEY -). Historical View of the Commission for enquiring into the Losses, Services, and Claims, of the American Loyalists, at the close of the War between Great Britain and her Colonies, in 1783: With an Account of the Compensation granted to them by Parliament in 1785 and 1788. By John Eardley-Wilmot, Esq. *London,* J. Nichols, 1815. *viii and* 204 *pp. With plate of the* 'Reception of the American Loyalists by Great Britain, in the year 1783.' *Half calf. 8vo.* (7s. 6d. 2880)

WILSON (H.) The Shipwreck of the Antelope Eaſt-India Packet, H. Wilson, Eſq. Commander, on the Pelew Islands, ſituate in the Weſt Part of the Pacific Ocean; In August 1783. Containing the subsequent Adventures of the Crew with a ſingular Race of People hitherto unknown to Europeans. With Interefting Particulars of Lee Boo, Second Son of the Pelew King, To the Time of his Death, at Capt. Wilson's Houfe at Rotherhithe. By One of the Unfortunate Officers. *London:* D. Brewman, MDCCLXXXVIII. *viii and* 134 *pp. With plate.* 8*vo.* (4*s.* 6*d.* 2881)

WILSON (James). Commentaries on the Constitution of the United States of America. With that Constitution prefixed, in which are unfolded, the Principles of Free Government, and the Superior Advantages of Republicanism demonstrated By James Wilson, LL.D. Profeffor of Laws in the College and University of the Commonwealth of Pennfylvania, one of the Affociate Judges of the Supreme Court of the United States, and appointed by the Legiflature of Pennfylvania to form a Digeft of the Laws of that State; and By Thomas M'Kean, LL.D. Chief Juftice of the Commonwealth of Pennfylvania. The whole extracted from Debates, publifhed in Philadelphia, By T. Lloyd. *London:* J. Debrett, 1792. 4 *prel. leaves and pp.* 4-147. *Index, 2 pp. Errata, 1 page.* 8*vo.* (7*s.* 6*d.* 2882)

WILSON (Thomas). The Knowledge and Practice of Christianity Made Easy To the Meaneft Capacities: Or, an Essay towards an Instruction for the Indians; Which will likewife be of Ufe To all fuch who are called Christians, but have not well confidered the Meaning of the Religion they profefs: Or, who profess to know God, but in Works do deny Him. In Twenty Dialogues. Together with Directions and Prayers, for The Heathen World, Missionaries, Catechumens, Private Persons, Families, Of Parents for their Children, For Sundays, &c. The Twelfth Edition. By the Right Reverend Father in God, Thomas, Lord Bifhop of Sodor and Man. *London:* John Rivington M,DCC,LXXVI. 4 *prel. leaves, xxiv and* 280 *pp. Calf.* 12*mo.* (7*s.* 6*d.* 2883)

WILSON (Thomas W.) An Authentic Narrative of the Piratical Descents upon Cuba made By hordes from the United States, headed by Narciso Lopez, a native of South America; to which are added some interesting letters and declarations from the prisoners, with a list of their names, &c. By Thomas W. Wilson. *Havana* September 1851. 44 *pp.* 4*to.* (2*s.* 6*d.* 2884)

WINCHESTER (ELHANAN). The Gospel of Christ
No Caufe of Shame: Demonftrated in two Difcourfes on the Subject. By Elhanan Winchester.
Philadelphia: Printed by B. Towne. 1783. 140
pp. 8vo. (4s. 6d. 2885)

WINCHESTER (ELHANAN). An Oration on the
Discovery of America. Delivered in London,
October the 12th, 1792, being Three Hundred
Years from the day on which Columbus landed in
the New World. By Elhanan Winchester. *London:* Printed for the Author, MDCCXCII. 32 *pp.*
8vo. (2s. 6d. 2886)

WINCHESTER (ELHANAN). An Oration on the
Discovery of America. Delivered in London,
October the 12th, 1792, being Three Hundred
Years from the day on which Columbus landed in
the New World. The Second Edition, with an
Appendix, containing among other Things a description of the City of Washington, in the District
of Columbia; illustrated with an accurate engraving. By Elhanan Winchester. *London:* Printed
for the Author, [1792.] 77 *pp. Schedule, a folded
sheet; A List of the Publications of the Author, etc.
2 pp. With the Plan of Washington. Half morocco.*
8vo. (5s. 6d. 2887)

WINSLOW (EDWARD). New-Englands/ Sala-
mander,/ discovered/ By an irreligious and fcorne-
full/ Pamphlet, called New-Englands Jonas/ caft
up at London, &c. Owned by Major Iohn/ Childe,
but not probable to be written by him./ Or,/ A
fatisfactory anfwer to many afperfi-/ons caft upon
New-England therein./ Wherein our government
there is fhewed to/ bee legall and not Arbitrary,
being as neere the Law/ of England as our condition will permit./ Together/ With a briefe Reply
to what is written in an-/fwer to certaine paffages
in a late Booke called/ Hypocrifie unmasked./ By
Edw. Winflow./ *London:* Printed by Ric. Cotes,
for John Bellamy, and are to bee/ fold at his fhop
at the figne of the three Golden Lions in/ Cornehill
neare the Royall Exchange, 1647./ *Title in a narrow type metal border, the reverse blank: Text 29 pp.
Fine large copy, with rough leaves. Red morocco
extra, by Bedford. 4to.* (21l. 2888)

WINTERBOTHAM (W.) An Historical Geographical Commercial, and Philosophical View of the American United States, and of the European Settlements in America and the West-Indies. by W. Winterbotham. In Four Volumes. *London:* J. Ridgway, 1795. *Four Volumes.* Vol. I. 9 *prel. leaves, and* 591 *pp. Portrait of Washington,* 2 *maps and* 1 *plate.* Vol. II. 2 *prel. leaves, and* 493 *pp. Portrait of Penn,* 2 *maps and* 1 *plate.* Vol. III. 2 *prel. leaves, and* 525 *pp. Portrait of Franklin,* 2 *maps and* 6 *plates.* Vol. IV. 2 *prel. leaves, and* 415 *pp.* 'Appendix,' 54*pp.* 'Index,' 9 *pp.* 'Directions to the Binder,' 2 *pp. Portrait of Winterbotham, maps, tables, and plates. Calf.* 8*vo.* (18*s.* 2889)

WINTHROP (JOHN). A Journal Of the Transactions and Occurrences in the ſettlement of Maſſachuſetts and the other New-England Colonies, from the year 1630 to 1644: Written by John Winthrop, Eſq. Firſt Governor of Maſſachuſetts: And now firſt publiſhed from a correct copy of the original Manuſcript. *Hartford:* Printed By Elisha Babcock. M,DCC,XC. 3 *prel. leaves and* 364 *pp; Contents,* 4 *pp. Calf.* (15*s.* 2890)

WIRT (WILLIAM). Sketches of the Life and Character of Patrick Henry. By William Wirt, of Richmond, Virginia. Second Edition, Corrected by the Author. *Philadelphia:* James Webster, 1818. *xv and* 427 *pp.* 'Appendix,' *xii. With portrait of Patrick Henry. Calf.* 8*vo.* (7*s.* 6*d.* 2891)

WISDOM (THE), and Policy of the French in the Construction of their Great Offices, So as beſt to anſwer the Purpoſes of extending their Trade and Commerce, and enlarging their Foreign Settlements. With Some Observations in relation to the Disputes now ſubſiſting between the English and French Colonies in America. *London:* R. Baldwin, MDCCLV. *Title, text and* 133 *pp. Half morocco.* 8*vo.* (7*s.* 6*d.* 2892)

WITHERSPOON (John). An Address to the Natives of Scotland residing in America. Being an Appendix to a Sermon preached at Princeton on a General Fast. By John Witherspoon, D. D. Prefident of the College at New Jersey. *London:* Fielding and Walker, m,dcc,lxxviii. *iv and 24 pp. Half morocco. 8vo.* (2s. 6d. 2893)

WITHERSPOON (John). The Dominion of Providence over the Passions of Men. A Sermon, preached at Princeton, May 17, 1775, being the General Fast Appointed by the Congress through the United Colonies. By John Witherspoon, D.D. Prefident of the College of New Jersey. Philadelphia printed; *London* reprinted, For Fielding and Walker, m,dcc,lxxviii. *iv and 44 pp. Half morocco. 8vo.* (2s. 6d. 2894)

WITHERSPOON (John). Christian Magnanimity: A Sermon, Preached at Princeton, September, 1775—the Sabbath preceding the Annual Commencement; And again with Additions, September 23. 1787. To which is added, an Address to the Senior Class Who were to receive the Degree of Bachelor of Arts. By John Witherspoon, D.D. L.L.D. Prefident of the College of New-Jerfey. *Princeton:* Printed by James Tod. m.dcc.lxxxvii. *iv and 44 pp. 8vo.* (2s. 6d. 2895)

WITHERSPOON (John). A Sermon on the Religious Education of Children. Preached, in the Old Presbyterian Church in New-York, to a very numerous Audience, on the Evening of the second Sabbath in May. By the Rev. John Witherspoon, D.D. President of Princeton College. *Elizabeth-Town:* Printed by Shepard Kollock, m,dcc,lxxxix. *24 pp. 8vo.* (2s. 6d. 2896)

WOLCOTT (Roger). Poetical/ Meditations,/ being the/ Improvement/ of some/ Vacant Hours,/ By Roger Wolcott, Efq;/ With a/ Preface/ By the Reverend/ Mr. Bulkley of Colchefter./ New London:/ Printed and Sold by T. Green,/ 1725./ *Half-title*,' Mr. Wolcott's/ Poetical Meditations.'/ *Title, reverse blank;* 'The Preface,' *lvi pp. signed* 'John Bulkley,' *and dated* 'Colchefter, December 24./ 1724./' 'To the Reverend/ Mr. Timothy Edwards./ *ii pp. signed* 'R. W.' *and dated* 'Windfor, January

4th./ 1722,3.'/ *Text,* 'Some Improvement of vacant Hours,/ By Roger Wolcott, Efq ;'/ *18 pages, containing six minor poems on religious subjects. Then comes* ' A Brief Account/ of the/ Agency/ Of the Honourable/ John Winthrop, Efq ;/ in the Court of/ King Charles the Second,/ Anno Dom. 1662./ When he Obtained for the Colony of Con-/necticut His Majefty's Gracious Charter.'/ *pages 19 to 78,* ' Finis.' *Then follows* ' Errata,' *one page ;* ' Advertisement' *3 pages, signed* ' Joseph Dewey,' *and dated* ' Colchefter/ 1725./' *Red morocco extra by Bedford.* 8*vo.*   (7*l.* 17*s.* 6*d.*   2899)

It has been stated that Mr. Dewey, a maker of woollen cloth, in Colchester, Connecticut, was at the expense of printing this book, on the condition of inserting his advertisement at the end. Indeed the worthy clothier intimates as much in his advertisement: " having been fomething at Charge in promoting the Publifhing the fore-going Meditations, do here take the Liberty to Advertife my Country-People of fome Rules which ought to be obferved, in doing their part, that fo the Clothiers might be affifted in the better performance of what is expected of them, that the Cloth which is made among us may both Wear and Laft, better, than it can poffibly do, Except thefe following Directions are Obferved by us." Then follow his seven Rules.

The interest of this book centres in the historical poem upon Winthrop's obtaining of Charles II. the Charter of Connecticut. After the Restoration, the " Sages of Connecticut" sent Winthrop their Governor to England to present an address, and

" To ask the King for CHARTER Liberties."

Soon after, it was announced to Charles who " was in his Council sat," that
" An Agent from Connecticut doth wait,
    With an Addrefs before your Palace Gate."

Winthrop admitted, discharges himself in homespun numbers, redolent rather of truth than poetry, filling some sixty pages, in which he recounts the national, civil, political, and military history of the Colony from the earliest time till " great Safacus and his Kingdom fell," lingering long about that beautiful river, that

" Calmly on a gentle wave doth move ;
As if 'twere drawn to Thetis house by love.
The Waters Fresh and Sweet, & he that fwims
In it, Recruits and Cures his Surfeit Limbs.
The Fifherman the Fry with Pleafure gets,
With Seins, Pots, Angles, and his Tramel-nets.
In it swim Salmon, Sturgion, Carp and Eels,
Above fly Cranes, Geefe, Duck, Herons and Teals ;
And Swans which take fuch Pleafure as they fly,
They sing their Hymns oft long before they Dy."

After reciting the exploits of Capt. John Mason, the Pequot War, and the fall of Sasacus, the Agent concludes :—

" And we Your Supplyants before the Throne,
Beg leave to hope while all your Favours Taft,
Connecticut will not be overpaft."

" Great CHARLES who gave attention all the while,
Looking on Winthrop with a Royal Smile,
Until that of his Fathers woes he fpeaks,
Which drew the Chriftal Rivers down his Cheeks.

But feeing Winthrop his Addrefs had clos'd,
The King his Mind and Countenance Compos'd,
And with as bright an Air of Majesty,
As Phœbus fhews when he Serenes the Sky, }
Made this Refolve upon the Agency,

Be it so then, and WE OUR SELF *Decree*
CONNECTICUT *shall be a* COLONY:
*Enfranchis'd with such Ample Liberties
As Thou,* Their Friend, *shalt best for them Devise;
And farther know Our Royal Pleasure thus,
And so it is Determened by* US;
Chief in the Patent WINTHROP *Thou shalt stand,
And Valiant* Mason *next at thy right Hand.
And for Chief Senators and Patentees,
Take Men of Wealth and known Abilities;
Men of Estates and Men of Influence,
Friends to their Country and to* US *Their Prince.*

*And may the People of that Happy Place
Whom thou hast so Endeared to My Grace;
Till times last Exit, through Succeeding Ages,
Be Blest with Happy English Privileges.
And that they may be so, bear thou from hence
To them these Premonitions from their Prince.*

*First, Let all Officers in Civil Trust
Always Espouse their Countrys Interest.
Let Law and Right be Precious in their Eyes,
And hear the Poor Mans Cause when e're he Crys.
Preserve Religion Pure and Understand,
That is the Firmest Pillar of the Land:
Let it be kept in Credit in the Court
And never fail for want of due Support.*

*And let the Sacred Order of the Gown,
With Zeal apply the Business that's their own.
So Peace may Spring from th' Earth & Righteousness,
Look down from Heaven, Truth and Judgment Kiss.*

*Then, Let the Freemen of your Corporation,
Always beware of the Insinuation,
Of those which always Brood Complaint and Fear,
Such Plagues are Dangerous to Infect the Air:
Such Men are Over-Laden with Compassion
Having Mens Freedom in such Admiration:
That every Act of Order or Restraint
They'll Represent as matter of Complaint.
And this is no New Doctrine, 'tis a Rule
Was taught in Satans first Erected School.
It serv'd his turn with wonderful Success,
And ever since has been his Master-piece.
'Tis true the sleight by which that field was won,
Was argued from man's benefit alone.
But these outdo him in that way of Evil,
And will sometimes for God's sake play the Devil.*

*And Lastly, Let Your New English Multitude,
Remember well a bond of* Gratitude
*Will Lye on them and their Posterity
Do bear in mind their* Freedom *came by* Thee."

WOLLASTON (WILLIAM). The Religion of Nature delineated. *London:* Samuel Palmer, 1726.
219 *pp. Index* 11 *pp. Calf extra, by F. Bedford.*
4to. (1*l.* 11*s.* 6*d.* 2900)

This is the Book which Franklin mentions in his Autobiography
as having worked upon, while a press-man with Samuel Palmer,
in London.

WOOD (WILLIAM). Nevv/ Englands/ Prospect./
A true, lively, and experimen-/tall defcription of
that part of America,/ commonly called Nevv-
England :/ difcovering the ftate of that Coun-/trie,
both as it ftands to our new-come/ Englifh Planters:
and to the old/ Native Inhabitants./ Laying downe
that which may both enrich the/ knowledge of
the mind-travelling Reader,/ or benefit the future
Voyager./ By William Wood./ Printed at *London*
by Tho. Cotes, for Iohn Bellamie, and are to be
fold/ at his fhop, at the three Golden Lyons in
Corne-hill, neere the/ Royall Exchange. 1634./
4 *prel. leaves; viz. Title, the reverse blank,* 'To the
Right Worship-/full, my much honored Friend,/
Sir William Armyne,/ Knight and Baronet.'/ 2 *pp.
signed* 'W. W.' 'To the Reader,' 2 *pp. signed*
'W. W.' 'To the Author, his fingular good/
Friend, M*r*. William Wood.'/ 1 *page, signed* 'S. W.'
'The Table' *and* 'Errata,' 1 *page. Text,* 98 *pp.*
'Becaufe many have defired to heare fome of the
Na-/tives Language, I have here inferted a fmall
Nomen-/clator,' *etc.* 5 *pp. With map of* 'The South
part of Nevv-England, as it is Planted this yeare,
1634.' 4*to.* (5*l.* 5*s.* 2901)

WOOD (WILLIAM). Nevv/ Englands/ Prospect./
A true, lively, and experimen-/tall defcription of
that part of America,/ commonly called Nevv-
England :/ difcovering the ftate of that Coun-/trie,
both as it ftands to our new-come/ Englifh Planters;
and to the old/ Native Inhabitants./ Laying downe
that which may both enrich the/ knowledge of
the mind-travelling Reader,/ or benefit the future
Voyager./ By William Wood./ Printed at *London*
by Tho. Cotes for Iohn Bellamie, and are to be
fold/ at his fhop, at the three Golden Lyons in
Corne-hill, neere the/ Royall Exchange. 1635./
4 *prel. leaves; viz. Title, the reverse blank,* 'To the
Right Worfhipfull,/ my much honoured friend,
Sir/ William Armyne, Knight/ and Baronet,'/ 2 *pp.
signed* 'W. W. 'To the Reader,' 2 *pp. signed*
'W. W.' 'To the Author, his fingular good
Friend, M*r*. William Wood,' 1 *page, signed* 'S. W.'
'The Table,' 1 *page. Text* 83 *pp.* 'Becaufe many
have defired to heare fome of the Na-/tives Lan-
guage,' *etc.* 5 *pp. With map of* 'The South part of

Nevv-England, as it is Planted this yeare, 1635.'
Old calf. *4to.* (*4l. 14s. 6d.* 2902)

WOOD (WILLIAM). New/ Englands/ Prospect./
A true, lively, and experimentall/ defcription of
that part of America com-/monly called New-
England: dif-/covering the ftate of that Country,
both as/ it ftands to our new-come Englifh Plan-/
ters; and to the old Native/ Inhabitants./ Laying
down that which may both en-/rich the knowledge
of the mind-travelling/ Reader, or benefit the future
Voyager./ By William Wood/ *London,*/ Printed
by Iohn Dawfon, and are to be fold by Iohn Bel-
lamy/ at his fhop, at the three Golden Lyons in
Corne-/hill, neere the Royall Exchange,/ 1639./
4 prel. leaves; viz. Title, the reverse blank, 'To the
Right Worfhipfull, my/ much honoured friend,
Sir William/ Armyne, Knight and Baronet,'/ *2 pp.
signed* 'W. W.' 'To the Reader,' *2 pp. signed*
'W. W.' 'To the Author, his fingular good
Friend M^r. William Wood,' *1 page, signed* 'S. W.'
'The Table,' *1 page. Text,* 83 *pp.* 'Becaufe many
have defired to heare fome of the Natives lan-
guage,' *etc. 5 pp. With map of* 'The South part of
New-England, as it is Planted this yeare 1639.'/
Brown morocco extra. 4to. (*4l. 14s. 6d.* 2903)

WOOD (WILLIAM). William Wood; - - - - - Appel-
lant. David Polhill, Efq; and others, on Behalf
of themfelves, and other, the Proprietors of Gold
and Silver Mines in Jamaica Refpondents. The
Appellant's Case. To be Heard at the Bar of the
House of Lords, on [Wednesday] the [Fourth]
Day of [February] Day of [February] 1746.
[*London.* 1746.] *3 pp. Folio.* (*4s. 6d.* 2904)

WOOLMAN (JOHN). Considerations on keeping
Negroes; Recommended to the Professors of
Christianity, of every Denomination. Part Second.
By John Woolman. *Philadelphia:* Printed by B.
Franklin, and D. Hall. 1762. *52 pp. Unbound.
8vo.* (*10s. 6d.* 2905)

WOOLMAN (JOHN). A Journal of the Life, Gospel
Labours, and Christian Experiences of that Faithful
Minister of Jesus Christ, John Woolman, Late of
Mount-Holly, in the Province of New-Jersey,
North-America. To which are added, His Works,

containing his laſt Epiſtle and other Writings.
Dublin : R. M. Jackson, 1794. *xv and* 464 *pp. Calf.*
8*vo.* (7*s.* 6*d.* 2906)

WORD (A) of Comfort to a Melancholy Country.
Or the Bank of Credit Erected in the Maſſachuſetts-
Bay, Fairly Defended by a Diſcovery of the Great
Benefit, accruing by it to the Whole Province ;
With a Remedy for Recovering a Civil State when
Sinking under Deſperation by a Defeat on their
Bank of Credit. By Amicus Patriæ. *Boston :*
Printed in the Year, 1721. 2 *prel. leaves and* 58 *pp.*
16*mo.* (1*l.* 1*s.* 2907)

WORSLEY (Israel). A View of the American
Indians, their General Character, Customs, Language, Public Festivals, Religious Rites, and Traditions : Shewing them to be the Descendants of
The Ten Tribes of Israel. The Language of Pro-
phecy concerning them, and the course by which
they travelled from Media into America. By Israel
Worsley. *London :* June, MDCCCXXVIII. Printed
for the Author. *Half-title, title, xii and* 185 *pp.*
12*mo.* (3*s.* 6*d.* 2908)

WRIGHT (Edward). Certain Errors/ in/ Navigation./ Detected and Corrected/ By Edw. Wright./
With many Additions that were not/ in the former
Editions./ *London./* Printed by joſeph Moxon./
and ſold at his Shop at the Atlas on Corn-hill.
1657./ *Engraved title,* 12 *prel. leaves, and* 224 *pp ;*
' The Division of the whole Art of Navigation.'
110 *pp :* ' Made and ſold by Joſeph Moxon,' *etc.*
1 *page ;* ' The Haven-finding Art,' *etc.* 20 *pp. Diagrams at pp.* 38, 57, 65, 148. *Platt for sailing to the
Azores, on copper, at page* 91, 2*d. Part. Calf.*
4*to.* (1*l.* 11*s.* 6*d.* 2909)

WRIGHT (John). The American Negotiator, or
the Various Currencies of the British Colonies in
America ; As well the Islands, as the Continent.
The Currencies of Nova Scotia, Canada, New
England, New York, East Jersey, Pensylvania,
West Jersey, Maryland, Virginia, North Carolina,
South Carolina, Georgia, &c. And of the Islands
of Barbadoes, Jamaica, St. Christopher's, Antigua,
Nevis, Montserrat, &c. Reduced into Engliſh
Money, By a Series of Tables ſuited to the ſeveral

Exchanges between the Colonies and Britain, adapted to all the Variations that from Time to Time have, or may happen. With Tables reducing the current money of the Kingdom of Ireland into Sterling, and the contrary, at all the Variations of Exchange. Also, a Chain of Tables for the inter-changeable Reduction of the Currencies of the Colonies into each other. And many other ufeful Tables relating to the Trade in America. By J. Wright, Accomptant. The Third Edition. *London:* J. Smith, MDCCLXV. *lxxx and 326 pp. Old calf. 8vo.* (6s. 6d. 2910)

WYETH (JOSEPH). Remarks/ on/ Dr. Bray's Me-morial, &c./ With Brief Obfervations/ On fome Paffages in the Acts of his Vifitation/ in/ Mary-land,/ And on his/ Circular Letter to the Clergy there ;/ Subfequent to the faid Vifitation./ By Jofeph Wyeth./ *London,* Printed and Sold by T. Sowle, in White-Hart-/Court in Gracious-ftreet, 1701./ 51 *pp. 4to.* (10s. 6d. 2911)

WYNKELMANN (HANS JUST). [*Engraved title*] Hans Just/ Winkelmans/ Americanifcher/ Neuer Welt/ Befchreibung/ Gedruckt zu Oldenburg/ 1664./ [*Printed title*] Der/ Americanifchen/ Neuen Welt/ Befchreibung,/ Darinnen deren Erfindung, Lager, Natur, Eigenfchaft,/ Sitten, Barbarey, und unerhörte Graufamkeit der Einwohner, Thier, Vögel,/ Fifchen und anderer; Beneben einer wun-derbaren Schifffart und Reife Be=/fchreibung nach Brafilien Hans von Staden, bürtig aus Homburg in Heffen ;/ Was er vor felzame wunderbare Länder und wilde Leute gefehen ; Was er in=/nerhalb acht Jahren ausgeftanden, und wie der högfte Gott ihn aus fo Vielfal=/tiger grofer Gefahr errettet habe &c. Mit vielen nachdenklichen Fragen/ und noth-wendigen Figuren ausgezieret und zu=/fammen getragen/ Durch Hanf Juft Wynkelmann./ Ged-ruckt zu *Oldenburg* bey Henrich = Conrad Zim-mern,/ Im Jahr Chrifti 1664./ 8 *prel. leaves; viz. Engraved and printed titles,* ' Dem Hochwürdigen, Durchleuchtigen, Hoch=/gebornen Fürften und Herrn,'/ 1 *page* ; ' Als Alexander,' *etc.* 4 *pp;* ' And den mit Stand und Verftand/ Hochgeneigten Lefer./ 5 *pp* ; ' Ordnungs=Regifter der Capiteln,' 2 *pp* ; *Folded sheet, a portrait of the Author; Text 228 pp* ;

Portrait of the Author, 1 *page;* ' Register,' 11 *pp.*
Oblong 4*to.* (2*l.* 12*s.* 6*d.* 2912)

WYNNE. A General History of the British Empire
in America. Containing, An Historical, Political,
and Comercial View of the English Settlements;
including all the Countries in North-America, and
the West-Indies, ceded by the Peace of Paris. In
Two Volumes. By Mr. Wynne. *London,* W.
Richardson and L. Urquhart, MDCCLXX. *Two Vo-*
lumes. Vol. I. *Title; Contents vi pp; Introduction,*
pp. iii-viii; text 520 *pp. With map.* Vol. II. *Title,*
vi and 546 *pp. Half calf.* 8*vo.* (12*s.* 6*d.* 2912*)

WYTFLIET (CORNELIUS). Descriptionis/ Ptole-
maicæ/ Avgmentvm./ Siue/ Occidentis Notitia/
Breui commentario/ illustrata/ Studio et opera/
Cornely Wytfliet/ Louaniensis./ *Lovanii*/ Tijpis
Iohannis Bogardi/ Anno Domini M.D.xcvii./ *En-*
graved title, 3 *prel. leaves,* 19 *maps; followed by*
Text 191 *pp; List of maps,* 1 *page. First Edition.*
Pigskin. Folio. (1*l.* 11*s.* 6*d.* 2913)

WYTFLIET (CORNELIUS). Descriptionis/ Ptole-
maicæ/ Avgmentvm./ siue/ Occidentis Notitia/
Breui commentario/ illustrata, et hac ſe⸗/cunda
editione magna/ sui parte aucta/ Cornelio Wytfliet
Louanienſi/ auctore./ *Lovanii*/ Tijpis Gerardi Ri-
uij/ Anno Domini. cɔ. ɔ. xcıιx./ *Engraved title,*
3 *prel. leaves and* 19 *maps; followed by Text,* 191 *pp.*
List of Maps, 1 *page. Folio.* (1*l.* 11*s.* 6*d.* 2914)

IMENEZ (Francisco). Las Historias del Origen de los Indios de esta Provincia de Guatemala, traducidas de la lengua Quiché al Castellano para mas comodidad de los Ministros del S. Evangelio. Por el R. P. F. Francisco Ximenez, cura Doctrinero por el Real Patronato del Pueblo de S. Thomas Chuila. Exactamente segun el texto Español del Manuscrito original que se halla en la Biblioteca de la Universidad de Guatemala, Publicado por la Primera vez, y aumentado con una introduccion y anotaciones por el Dr. C. Scherzer. A expensas de la Imperial Academia de las Ciencias. *Londres*: Trübner & Co. 1857. *xvi and 216 pp. Unbound.* 8vo. (8s. 6d. 2915)

ALE-COLLEGE subject to the General Assembly. *New-Haven:* Printed by Thomas and Samuel Green. M,DCC,LXXXIV. 44 *pp.* 8*vo.* (7*s.* 6*d.* 2916)

YONGE (F.) A View of the Trade of South-Carolina, with Proposals Humbly Offer'd for Improving the same. [*London.* 1722.] *Privately printed.* 16 *pp.* Half *mor.* 8*vo.* (7*s.* 6*d.* 2917)

ARATE (Augustin). Le Histoire/ Del Sig. Agostino/ di Zarate/ Contatore et Consigliero/ del l'Imperatore Carlo V./ Dello Scoprimento et Conqvista del Perv,/ nelle quali fi ha piena & particolar relatione delle cofe fucceffe, in quelle bande,/ dal principio fino alla pacificatione delle Prouincie, fi in quel che tocca/ allo fcoprimento, come al fucceffo delle guerre ciuili occorfe/ fra gli Spagnuoli & Capitani, che lo conquiftarono./ Nvovamente di Lingva Castigliana Tradotte/ Dal. S. Alfonso Vlloa./ Con Privilegio./ In *Vinegia* appresso Gabriel/ Giolito de' Ferrari./ MDLXIII. 8 *prel. leaves*; *viz. Title, the reverse blank*; 'All' Illvstriss. Signore il S. Gvido Brandolino Conte di Valdemarini,' *etc.* 3 *pp*; 'Tavola,' 11 *pp*; *Text* 294 *pp*; *in Italics. Vellum. 4to.*   (3*l*. 3*s*.   2918)

ZARATE (Augustin). [*First title*] The/ Difcoverie and Conqvest/ of the Prouinces of Perv, and/ the Nauigation in the South/ Sea, along that Coaft./ And alfo of the ritche Mines/ of Potosi./ [*Woodcut of*] · The · Riche · Mines · of · Potossi ·/ ¶ Imprinted at London by Richard Ihones. Febru. 6. 1581./ *The reverse blank.* [*Second title*] ❧ The ftrange and/ delectable Hiftory of the/ difcouerie and Conqueft of the/ Prouinces of Peru, in the/ South Sea./ And of the notable things which/ there are found : and alfo of the bloudie/ ciuill vvarres vvhich there hap=/pened for gouernment./ Written in foure bookes, by/ Auguftine Sarate, Auditor for/ the Emperour his Maieftie in the/ fame prouinces and firme land./ And alfo of the ritche/ Mines of Potofi./ Tranflated out of the Spanish/ tongue, by T. Nicholas./ Imprinted at *London* by Richard/ Ihones, dwelling ouer againft the/ Fawlcon, by Holburne bridge. 1581./ *Within*

2   3 G

a woodcut border of figures, the reverse blank. ' 🖝 To
the Right Ho-/nourable, Maifter Thomas Wilson,/
Doctor of the Ciuill Lawe, and one/ of the principall Secretaries, to the/ Queenes moft excellent
Maieftie.'/ *6 pp. signed* 'Thomas Nicholas,' *in
Roman type.* 'To the Reader,' *6 pp. in black letter :
Text, black letter, in* 89 *leaves,* 1 *to* 12, *and* 89, *not
folioed ; folios* 16, 17, 28 *and* 19, *for* 17, 18, 19 *and*
20 ; *with woodcuts on the reverse of folios* 16, 20, 46,
58, 85. 'The difcovery of the ritche Mynes of/
Potofi & how captaine Carauajell toke into his
power,'/ *woodcut the same as on the first title,* 3 *pp.*
'The Table of the Chapters,' 3 *pp. Red morocco
extra, by Bedford.* 4*to.*   (10*l.* 10*s.* 2919)

ZARATE (Augustin de). Histoire/ de la/ Dé-
couverte/ et de la/ Conquete/ du/ Perou./ Traduite
de l'Efpagnol/ D'Augustin de Zarate,/ Par S.D.C./
A *Amsterdam,*/ Chez J. Louis de Lorme, Libraire
fur/ le Rockin, à la Liberté./ M.DCC./ *Two Volumes.*
Tome Premier. 19 *prel. leaves, and* 307 *pp. Frontispiece, plates and map at pp.* 4, 8, 12, 16, 34, 36,
54, 114, 130, 149, 153, 290. Tome Second. 3 *prel.
leaves, and* 408 *pp. Old calf.* 12*mo.* (10*s.* 6*d.* 2920)

ZARATE (Augustin de). Histoire de la Découverte et de la Conquete du Perou. Traduite de
l'Efpagnol D'Augustin de Zarate, Par S. D. C.
A *Paris*, Par la Compagnie des Libraires. MDCCXVI.
Two Volumes. Tome Premier. 20 *prel. leaves and*
360 *pp. Frontispiece, plates and map, at pp.* 5, 10,
15, 20, 29, 41, 43, 64, 133, 155, 176, 177, 185, 340.
Tome Second. 4 *prel. leaves and* 479 *pp. Fine copy.
Old calf.* 12*mo.*   (10*s.* 6*d.* 2921)

ZARATE (Augustin de). Histoire de la Découverte et de la Conquête du Perou. Traduite de
l'Efpagnol D'Augustin de Zarate, Par S. D. C.
A *Paris*, Rue S. Jacques, Chez Michel Guignard,
près la Fontaine S. Severin, à l'Image S. Jean,
M.DCCXVI. *Two Volumes.* Tome Premier. 20 *prel.
leaves, and* 360 *pp. Frontispiece.* Tome Second. 4
prel. leaves and 479 *pp.* 12*mo.*   (10*s.* 6*d.* 2922)

ZARATE (Augustin de). Histoire de la Découverte et de la Conquête du Perou. Traduite de
l'Espagnol D'Agustin de Zarate, Par S. D. C.
A *Paris*, Par la Compagnie des Libraires. M. DCC.

XLII. *Two Volumes.* Tome Premier. 20 *prel. leaves and* 360 *pp. Frontispiece, plates and map at pp.* 5, 10, 15, 20, 29, 41, 43, 64, 133, 155, 176, 177, 185, 340. Tome Second. 4 *prel. leaves and* 479 *pp. Old calf.* 12*mo.* (10*s.* 6*d.* 2923)

ZARATE (Augustin de). Histoire de la Découverte et de la Conquête du Perou, Traduite de l'Espagnol D'Augustin de Zarate, Par S. D. C. A *Paris,* Par la Compagnie des Libraires. m. dcc. lxxiv. *Two Volumes.* Tome Premier. *xl and* 360 *pp. Frontispiece, plates and map at pp.* 5, 10, 15, 20, 29, 41, 43, 64, 133, 155, 176, 177, 185, 340. Tome Second. *viii and* 479 *pp.* 12*mo.* (10*s.* 6*d.* 2924)

ZENGER (John Peter). The Tryal of John Peter Zenger of New-York, Printer, Who was lately Try'd and Acquitted for Printing and Publishing a Libel againſt the Government. With the Pleadings and Arguments on both Sides. *London :* J. Wilford, 1738. *Title and 32 pp. Half morocco.* 4*to.* (7*s.* 6*d.* 2925)

ZENGER (John Peter). The Tryal of John Peter Zenger, of New-York, Printer, Who was lately Try'd and Acquitted for Printing and Publishing a Libel againſt the Government. With the Pleadings and Arguments on both Sides. The Second Edition. *London :* Printed for J. Wilford, 1738. *Title and* 32 *pp. Half morocco.* 4*to.* (7*s.* 6*d.* 2926)

ZENGER (John Peter). The Tryal of John Peter Zenger, of New-York, Printer, Who was lately Try'd and Acquitted for Printing and Pubilshing a Libel againſt the Government. With the Pleadings and Arguments on both Sides. The Fourth Edition. *London,* J. Wilford, 1738. *Title and* 32 *pp.* 4*to.* (7*s.* 6*d.* 2927)

ZENGER (John Peter). The Case and Tryal of John Peter Zenger, of New-York, Printer, Who was lately tryed and acquitted for Printing and Publishing a Libel againſt the Government. With The Pleadings and Arguments on both Sides. *London :* J. Wilford, 1750. 60 *pp. Half morocco.* 8*vo.* (5*s.* 6*d.* 2928)

ZENGER (John Peter). The Trial of John Peter Zenger, Of New-York, Printer: Who was charged

with having printed and publifhed a Libel againſt
the Government; and acquitted. With a Narrative
of his case. To which is now added, being never
printed before, the Trial of Mr. William Owen,
Bookseller, near Temple - Bar, Who was alfo
Charged with the Publication of a Libel againſt
the Government; of which he was honourably
acquitted by a Jury of Free-born Englifhmen,
Citizens of London. *London:* J. Almon, MDCCLXV.
59 pp. Half morocco. 8vo. (*4s. 6d.* 2929)

ZENO (CATERINO). De i Commentarii del/ Viaggio
in Perfia di M. Caterino Zeno il K./ & delle guerre
fatte nell' Imperio Perfiano,/ dal tempo di Vſſun-
caſſano in quà./ Libri Dve./ Et dello fcopri-
mento/ dell' Ifole Frislanda, Eslanda, Engroue-
landa, Efto/tilanda, & Icaria, fatto fotto il Polo
Artico, da/ due fratelli zeni, M. Nicolò il K. e M.
Antonio./ Libro Vno./ Con vn difegno particolare
di/ tutte le dette parte di tramontana de lor fco-
perte./ Con gratia, et Privilegio./ In *Venetia*/
Per Francefco Marcolini. MDLVIII./ *Title, the reverse blank;* 'Al Reverendiſſimo/ Monſignor M./
Daniel Barbaro/ Eletto Patriarcha/ D'Aqvilegia./
Francefco Marcolini. Vmilſeruo.'/ *2 pp.* 'Proemio
de l'Avtore/ ne i dve Libri de' com-/mentarii del
Viaggio in/ Perfia & delle guerre Perfiane/ di M.
Caterino Zeno il/ Cavalliere,'/ *6 pp.* 'Errori,' 1
*page. Text commencing on the reverse of folio 5, and
ending on folio 58; on the reverse, the Printer's device. With* 'Carta da Navegar de Nicolo et Antonio Zeni Fvrono in Tramontana Lano. M.CCC.
LXXX.' *Russia. 8vo.* (*10l.* 10s. 2930)

ZENO (CATERINO). *Another copy, wanting the map.
8vo.* (*2l.* 12s. 6d. 2931)

ZIMMERMANN (E. A. W. DE). Essai de Com-
paraison entre La France et Les Etats-Unis de
L'Amérique Septentrionale, par rapport à leur sol,
à leur climat, à leurs productions, à leurs habitans,
à leur constitution, et à leur formation progressive.
Par Mr. E. A. W. de Zimmermann, Conseiller de
Cour et Professeur à Brunsvic, de l'Académie de
Petersbourg; Goettingen; Bologne; de la Société
Linn. de Londres, etc. Traduit de l'Allemand et
Enrichi de Développemens et de Notes par l'Au-
teur même. Tome I. à *Leipzig,* Chez Reinicke et

Hinrichs./ 1797. *viii and* 494 *pp. List, and Division, etc.* 4 *pp. Old calf.* 8*vo.* (4*s.* 6*d.* 2932)

ZISNEROS (JOSEPH DE). Discvrso/ qve en el insigne/ Avto de la Fe, celebrado en/ esta Real cuidad de Lima, aueinte y tres de/ Enero de 1639. años :/ Predico el M. R. P. F. Ioseph de Zisne-/ros, Calificador de la suprema, y general Inquisicion, Padre de la S. Pro-/uincia de la Concepcion, y Comissario general en todos estos Reynos/ del Pirù, y Tierrafirme, del Orden de N. P. S. Francisco./ Dirigido/ al Exmo Señor Don Lvis Geronymo de/ Cabrera y Bobadilla, Conde de Chincon, Virrey, Gouerna/dor, y Capitan General de los Reynos del Pirú, y Tierrasir-/ma, Gentilhõbre de la Camara de su Magestad, y de su Ilaue/dorada, de los Consejos de gnerra, y estado, Comẽdador/ del campo de Critana, del ordẽ de Santiago./ Impresso en *Lima* por Geronymo de Contreras, año 1639./ [*Colophon.*] Con licencia./ Impresso/ en Lima por/ Geronymo de/ Contreras, Im-/pressor de libros, fron-/tero de la Cruz de gradas,/ Año de 1639./ 5 *prel. leaves, viz. Title in a metal type border, and woodcut of arms, the reverse blank;* 'Aprobacion del M. R. P. M. F. Iuan de Ribera Prouincial,' *etc.* 3 *pp. signed* 'Fr. Iuan de Ribera.' 'Dedicatoria,' 4 *pp. signed* 'Fr. Ioseph de Zisneros Comissario general.' *Text in* 15 *folioed leaves. Calf extra.* 4*to.* (1*l.* 11*s.* 6*d.* 2933)

ZURLA (PLACIDO). Il Mappa Mondo di Fra Mauro Camaldolese Descritto ed Illustrato da D. Placido Zurla dello stess' ordine *Venezia* 1806. 164 *pp. With* 2 *plates. Large Paper.* 4*to.* (1*l.* 1*s.* 2934)

𝕷𝖆𝖚𝖘 𝕯𝖊𝖔.